Programming Language
Pragmatics

About the Author

Michael L. Scott is a professor of computer science at the University of Rochester, where he chaired the Computer Science Department from 1996 to 1999. He received his Ph.D. in computer sciences in 1985 from the University of Wisconsin-Madison, where he was a member of the Crystal and Charlotte research groups. His research interests lie in parallel and distributed computing, including operating systems, languages, architecture, and tools. He is the designer of the Lynx distributed programming language and a co-designer of the Charlotte and Psyche parallel operating systems, the Bridge parallel file system, and the Cashmere distributed shared memory system. His MCS mutual exclusion lock, co-designed with John Mellor-Crummey of Rice University, appears in a wide variety of commercial and academic systems.

Dr. Scott is a member of the Institute of Electrical and Electronics Engineers, the Association for Computing Machinery, the Union of Concerned Scientists, and Computer Professionals for Social Responsibility. He has served on a wide variety of program committees and grant review panels, and has been a principal or co-investigator on grants from the NSF, ONR, DARPA, NASA, the Department of Defense, the Ford Foundation, and Digital Equipment Corporation (now Compaq). He has contributed to the GRE advanced exam in computer science, and is the author of more than fifty refereed publications. He received a Bell Labs Doctoral Scholarship in 1983 and an IBM Faculty Development Award in 1986.

Programming Language Pragmatics

Michael L. Scott
University of Rochester

M K ®

MORGAN KAUFMANN PUBLISHERS

AN IMPRINT OF ACADEMIC PRESS
A Harcourt Science and Technology Company
SAN FRANCISCO   SAN DIEGO   NEW YORK   BOSTON
LONDON   SYDNEY   TOKYO

Senior Editor: Denise E. M. Penrose
Director of Production and Manufacturing: Yonie Overton
Production Editor: Edward Wade
Editorial Coordinator: Meghan Keeffe
Cover Design: Ross Carron Design
Text Design: Rebecca Evans and Associates
Composition: Babel Press, Ed Sznyter
Technical Illustration: Cherie Plumlee
Copyeditor: Donna King, Progressive Publishing Alternatives
Proofreader: Christine Sabooni
Indexer: Ty Koontz
Printer: Courier Corporation

ENGINEER
QA
76.7
.S38
2000

Designations used by companies to distinguish their products are often claimed as trademarks or registered trademarks. In all instances where Morgan Kaufmann Publishers is aware of a claim, the product names appear in initial capital or all capital letters. Readers, however, should contact the appropriate companies for more complete information regarding trademarks and registration.

Morgan Kaufmann Publishers
340 Pine Street, Sixth Floor, San Francisco, CA 94104-3205, USA
http://www.mkp.com

ACADEMIC PRESS
A Harcourt Science and Technology Company
525 B Street, Suite 1900, San Diego, CA 92101-4495, USA
http://www.academicpress.com

Academic Press
Harcourt Place, 32 Jamestown Road, London, NW1 7BY, United Kingdom
http://www.academicpress.com

Advice, Praise, and Errors: Any correspondence related to this publication or intended for the author should be addressed to the Editorial and Sales Office of Morgan Kaufmann Publishers, Dept. PLP APE or sent electronically to *plp@mkp.com*. Information regarding error sightings is encouraged; electronic mail can be sent to *plpbugs@mkp.com*. Please check the errata page at *www.mkp.com/plp* to see if the bug has already been reported.

Library of Congress Cataloging-in-Publication Data

Scott, Michael Lee
    Programming language pragmatics / Michael L. Scott.
        p.   cm.
    Includes bibliographical references and index.
    ISBN 1-55860-442-1 (hardback) – ISBN 1-55860-578-9 (paperback)
    1. Programming languages (Electronic computers) I. Title.
    QA76.7.S38 2000
    005.13–dc21
                                                              99-047125
                                                              CIP

This book is printed on acid-free paper.

To my three Irish roses

Contents

* Indicates advanced or optional material that may be skipped in the interest of time.

Preface

A course in computer programming provides the typical student's first exposure to the field of computer science. Most of the students in such a course will have had previous exposure to computers, in the form of games and other personal computer applications, but it is not until they write their own programs that they begin to appreciate how these applications work. After gaining a certain level of facility as programmers (presumably with the help of a good course in data structures and algorithms), the natural next step is to wonder how programming languages work. This book provides an explanation.

In the conventional "systems" curriculum, the material beyond data structures (and possibly computer organization) is compartmentalized by subarea, with courses in programming languages, compilers, computer architecture, operating systems, database management systems, and possibly software engineering, graphics, or user interface systems. One problem with this approach is that many of the most interesting things in computer science occur at the *boundaries* between these subareas. The RISC revolution, for example, has forged an intimate alliance between computer architecture and compiler construction. The advent of microkernels has blurred the boundary between the operating system kernel and the language run-time library. The spread of Java-based systems has similarly blurred the boundary between the compiler and the run-time library. Aggressive memory systems for supercomputers are redefining the relative roles of the operating system, the compiler, and the hardware. And programming language design has always been heavily influenced by implementation issues. Increasingly both educators and researchers are recognizing the need to focus on these interactions.

Another problem with the compartmentalized curriculum is that it offers more courses than the typical undergraduate can afford to take. A student who wants to gain a solid background in theory, artificial intelligence, numerical methods, or various allied fields cannot afford to take five upper-level courses in systems. Rather than give the student an in-depth look at two or three relatively narrow subareas, I believe it makes sense to provide an integrated look at the most fundamental material *across* subareas.

At its core, *Programming Language Pragmatics* is a book about how programming languages work. It is in some sense a mixture of traditional texts in programming languages and compilers, with just enough assembly-level architecture to accommodate the student who has not yet had a course in computer organization. It is not a language survey text: rather than enumerate the details of many different languages, it focuses on concepts that underlie all of the languages the student is likely to encounter, illustrating those concepts with examples from various languages. It is also not a compiler construction text: rather than explain how to build a compiler (a task few programmers will ever need to tackle in its entirety, though they may use front-end techniques in other tools), it explains how a compiler works, what it does to a source program, and why. Language design and implementation are thus explored together, with an emphasis on the ways in which they interact. When discussing iteration (Section 6.5.1), we can see how semantic issues (what is the scope of an index variable? what happens if the body of a loop tries to modify the index or loop bounds?) have interacted with pragmatic issues (how many branch instructions must we execute in each iteration of the loop? how do we avoid arithmetic overflow when updating the index?) to shape the evolution of loop constructs. When discussing object-oriented programming, we can see how the tension between semantic elegance and implementation speed has shaped the design of languages such as Smalltalk, Eiffel, C++, and Java.

In the typical undergraduate curriculum, this book is intended for the programming languages course. It has a bit less survey-style detail than certain other texts, but it covers the same breadth of languages and concepts, and includes much more information on implementation issues. Students with a strong interest in language design should be encouraged to take additional courses in such areas as formal semantics, type theory, or object-oriented design. Similarly, students with a strong interest in language implementation should take a subsequent course in compiler construction. With this book as background, the compiler course will be able to devote much more time than is usually possible to code generation and optimization, where most of the interesting work these days is taking place.

At the University of Rochester, the material in this book has been used for over a decade to teach a course entitled "Software Systems." The course draws a mixture of mid- to upper-level undergraduates and first-year graduate students. The book should also be of value to professional programmers and other practitioners who simply wish to gain a better understanding of what's going on "under the hood" in their favorite programming language. By integrating the discussion of syntactic, semantic, and pragmatic (implementation) issues, the book attempts to provide a more complete and balanced treatment of language design than is possible in most texts. The hope is that students will come to understand why language features were designed the way they were, and that as programmers they will be able to choose an appropriate language for a given application, learn new languages easily, and make clear and efficient use of any given language.

In most chapters the concluding section returns to the theme of design and implementation, highlighting interactions between the two that appeared in preceding sections. In addition, Appendix B contains a summary list of interactions, with references to the sections in which they are discussed. These interactions are grouped into several categories, including language features that most designers now believe were mistakes, at least in part because of implementation difficulties; potentially useful features omitted from some languages because of concern that they might be too difficult or slow to implement; and language features introduced at least in part to facilitate efficient or elegant implementations.

Some chapters (2, 4, 5, 9, and 13) have a heavier emphasis than others on implementation issues. These can be reordered to a certain extent with respect to the more design-oriented chapters, but it is important that Chapter 5 or its equivalent be covered before Chapters 6, 7, or 8. Many readers will already be familiar with some or all of the material in Chapter 5, most likely from a course on computer organization. In this case the chapter can easily be skipped. Be warned, however, that later chapters assume an understanding of the assembly-level architecture of modern (i.e., RISC) microprocessors. Some readers may also be familiar with some of the material in Chapter 2, perhaps from a course on automata theory. Much of this chapter can then be read quickly, pausing perhaps to dwell on such practical issues as recovery from syntax errors.

For self-study, or for a full-year course, I recommend working through the book from start to finish. In the one-semester course at Rochester, we also cover most of the book, but at a somewhat shallower level. The lectures focus on the instructor's choice of material from the following chapters and sections: 1, 2.1 through 2.2.3, 3, 4, 6, 7, 8, 9.1 through 9.3, and 10 through 12. Students are asked to read all of this material except for those sections marked with an asterisk. They are also asked to skim Chapter 5; most have already taken a course in computer organization.

For a more traditional programming languages course, one would leave out Section 2.2 and Chapters 4, 5, and 9, and deemphasize the implementation-oriented material in the remaining chapters, devoting the extra time to more careful examination of semantic issues and to alternative programming paradigms (e.g., the foundational material in Chapter 11). For a school on the quarter system, one appealing option is to offer an introductory one-quarter course and two optional follow-on courses. The introductory quarter might cover these chapters and sections: 1, 2.1 through 2.2.3, 3, 6, 7, and 8.1 through 8.4. A language-oriented follow-on quarter might cover Sections 8.5 through 8.6, Chapters 10 through 12, and possibly supplementary material on formal semantics, type systems, or other related topics. A compiler-oriented follow-on quarter might cover Sections 2.2.4 through 2.3, and Chapters 4, 5 (if necessary), 9, and 13, and possibly supplementary material on automatic code generation, aggressive code improvement, programming tools, and so on. One possible objection to this organization is that it leaves object orientation and functional and logic programming out of the introductory quarter. An alternative would be to start with a broader and more exclusively design-oriented view, moving Sections 1.4 through 1.6 and 2.2.1 through 2.2.3 into the compiler-oriented quarter, deemphasizing the implementation-oriented material in Chapters 6 through 8, and adding Sections 10.1 through 10.4, 10.6, and the nonfoundational material in Chapter 11.

I assume that the typical reader already has significant experience with at least one high-level imperative programming language. Exactly which language it is shouldn't matter. Examples are drawn from a wide variety of languages, but always with enough comments and other discussion that readers not familiar with the language should be able to understand them easily. Algorithms, when needed, are presented in an informal pseudocode that should be self-explanatory. `Real programming language code is set in this font (Computer Modern)`. Pseudocode is set in this font (UniversLight).

Each of the chapters ends with review questions and a set of more challenging exercises. Particularly valuable are those exercises that direct students toward languages or techniques that they are unlikely to have encountered elsewhere, or to encounter elsewhere soon. I recommend programming assignments in C++ or Java; Scheme, ML, or Haskell; and Prolog. An assignment in exception handling is also a good idea; it may be written in Ada, C++, Java, ML, or Modula-3. If concurrency is covered, an assignment should be given in SR, Java, Ada, or Modula-3, depending on local interest. Sources for language implementations are noted in Appendix A.

In addition to these smaller projects (or in place of them if desired), instructors may wish to have students work on a language implementation. Since building even the smallest compiler from scratch is a full-semester job, students at Rochester have been given the source for a working compiler and asked to make modifications. For many, this is their first experience reading, understanding, and modifying a large existing program—a valuable exercise in and of itself. The Rochester PL/0 compiler translates a simple language due to Wirth [Wir76, pp. 307–347] into MIPS I assembly language, widely considered the "friendliest" of the commercial RISC instruction sets. An excellent MIPS interpreter ("SPIM") is available from the Computer Science Department at the University of Wisconsin (*www.cs.wisc.edu/~larus/spim.html*). Source for the compiler itself is available from Rochester (*ftp://ftp.cs.rochester.edu/pub/packages/plzero/*). It is written in C++, with carefully separated phases and extensive documentation.

About the Cover

The triangular icon on the cover is meant to symbolize the syntactic, semantic, and pragmatic facets of programming language design, each of which finds meaning in the context of the other two. This book aims to pay equal attention to all three facets; it takes its name from the one that tends to receive the least attention in other language texts.

Acknowledgments

Many people have contributed to this book. My thanks to the many reviewers who contributed comments and suggestions, including Greg Andrews, John Boyland, Preston Briggs, Jim Larus, Steve Muchnick, David Notkin, Ron Olsson, Constantine Polychronopoulos, and others who remain anonymous. I have done my best to address their concerns; the errors that remain are entirely my own. My thanks also to the students of CSC 2/454 (formerly 2/452) who served as guinea pigs for early versions of the book, and whose feedback served to improve it greatly. Thanks in particular to Donna Byron and Brandon Sanders for their extensive comments, to Scott Ventura for the web browser example of Section 12.2.3, and to Angkul Kongmunvattana for helping me understand the difference between useful and distracting cross-references.

I am of course indebted to the hard-working staff of Morgan Kaufmann Publishers, and to Denise Penrose, Mike Morgan, Edward Wade, and Meghan Keeffe in particular. The University of Rochester and its Computer Science Department provided a stimulating and supportive academic home while I was working on the book. Sarada George and Dianne Reiman Cass spent days chasing bibliographic references. Finally, my thanks to my family for 5 long years of patience.

The original manuscript for this book was composed on an Apple Powerbook Duo computer using Marc Parmet's port of the `emacs` text editor and Andrew Trevorrow's OzTEX version of TEX. Diagrams were drawn with Adobe Illustrator.

Introduction

The first electronic computers were monstrous contraptions, filling several rooms, consuming as much electricity as a good-size factory, and costing millions of 1940s dollars (but with the computing power of a modern hand-held calculator). The programmers who used these machines believed that the computer's time was more valuable than theirs. They programmed in machine language. Machine language is the sequence of bits that directly controls a processor, causing it to add, compare, move data from one place to another, and so forth at appropriate times. Specifying programs at this level of detail is an enormously tedious task. The following program calculates the greatest common divisor (GCD) of two integers, using Euclid's algorithm. It is written in machine language, expressed here as hexadecimal (base 16) numbers, for the MIPS R4000 processor.

```
27bdffd0 afbf0014 0c1002a8 00000000 0c1002a8 afa2001c 8fa4001c
00401825 10820008 0064082a 10200003 00000000 10000002 00832023
00641823 1483fffa 0064082a 0c1002b2 00000000 8fbf0014 27bd0020
03e00008 00001025
```

As people began to write larger programs, it quickly became apparent that a less error-prone notation was required. Assembly languages were invented to allow operations to be expressed with mnemonic abbreviations. Our GCD program looks like this in MIPS assembly language:

```
        addiu  sp,sp,-32
        sw     ra,20(sp)          b      C
        jal    getint             subu   a0,a0,v1
        nop                 B:     subu   v1,v1,a0
        jal    getint       C:     bne    a0,v1,A
        sw     v0,28(sp)           slt    at,v1,a0
        lw     a0,28(sp)    D:     jal    putint
        move   v1,v0               nop
        beq    a0,v0,D             lw     ra,20(sp)
        slt    at,v1,a0            addiu  sp,sp,32
A:      beq    at,zero,B           jr     ra
        nop                        move   v0,zero
```

Assembly languages were originally designed with a one-to-one correspondence between mnemonics and machine language instructions, as shown in this example.[1] Translating from mnemonics to machine language became the job of a systems program known as an *assembler*. Assemblers were eventually augmented with elaborate "macro expansion" facilities to permit programmers to define parameterized abbreviations for common sequences of instructions. The correspondence between assembly language and machine language remained obvious and explicit, however. Programming continued to be a machine-centered enterprise: each different kind of computer had to be programmed in its own assembly language, and programmers thought in terms of the instructions that the machine would actually execute.

As computers evolved, and as competing designs developed, it became increasingly frustrating to have to rewrite programs for every new machine. It also became increasingly difficult for human beings to keep track of the wealth of detail in large assembly language programs. People began to wish for a machine-independent language, particularly one in which numerical computations (the most common type of program in those days) could be expressed in something more closely resembling mathematical formulae. These wishes led in the mid-1950s to the development of the original dialect of Fortran, the first arguably high-level programming language. Other high-level languages soon followed, notably Lisp and Algol.

Translating from a high-level language to assembly or machine language is the job of a systems program known as a *compiler*. Compilers are substantially more complicated than assemblers because the one-to-one correspondence between source and target operations no longer exists when the source is a high-level language. Fortran was slow to catch on at first, because human programmers, with some effort, could almost always write assembly language programs that would run faster than what a compiler could produce. Over time, however, the performance gap has narrowed, and eventually reversed. Increases in hardware complexity (due to pipelining, multiple function units, etc.) and continuing improvements in compiler technology have led to a situation in which a state-of-the-art compiler will usually generate better code than a human being will. Even in cases in which human beings can do better, increases in computer speed and program size have made it increasingly important to economize on programmer effort, not only in the original construction of programs, but in subsequent program *maintenance*—enhancement and correction. Labor costs now heavily outweigh the cost of computing hardware.

---

[1] Each of the 23 lines of assembly code in the example is encoded in the corresponding 32 bits of the machine language. Note for example that the two `sw` (store word) instructions begin with the same 11 bits (`afa` or `afb`). Those bits encode the operation (`sw`) and the base register (`sp`).

The Art of Language Design

Today there are thousands of high-level programming languages, and new ones continue to emerge. Human beings use assembly language only for special-purpose applications. In a typical undergraduate class, it is not uncommon to find users of scores of different languages. Why are there so many? There are several possible answers:

Evolution. Computer science is a young discipline; we're constantly finding better ways to do things. The late 1960s and early 1970s saw a revolution in "structured programming," in which the goto-based control flow of languages such as Fortran, Cobol, and Basic[2] gave way to while loops, case statements, and similar higher-level constructs. In the late 1980s the nested block structure of languages such as Algol, Pascal, and Ada began to give way to the object-oriented structure of Smalltalk, C++, Eiffel, and the like.

Special Purposes. Many languages were designed for a specific problem domain. The various Lisp dialects are good for manipulating symbolic data and complex data structures. Snobol and Icon are good for manipulating character strings. C is good for low-level systems programming. Prolog is good for reasoning about logical relationships among data. Each of these languages can be used successfully for a wider range of tasks, but the emphasis is clearly on the specialty.

Personal Preference. Different people like different things. Much of the parochialism of programming is simply a matter of taste. Some people love the terseness of C; some hate it. Some people find it natural to think recursively; others prefer iteration. Some people like to work with pointers; others prefer the implicit dereferencing of Lisp, Clu, and ML. The strength and variety of personal preference make it unlikely that anyone will ever develop a universally acceptable programming language.

Of course, some languages are more successful than others. Of the many that have been designed, only a few dozen are widely used. What makes a language successful? Again there are several answers:

Expressive Power. One commonly hears arguments that one language is more "powerful" than another, though in a technical sense they are all equivalent—each can be used, if awkwardly, to write anything written in the others. Still, language features clearly have a huge impact on the programmer's ability to write

---

2 The name of each of these languages is sometimes written entirely in uppercase letters and sometimes in mixed case. For consistency's sake, I adopt the convention in this book of using mixed case for languages whose names are pronounced as words (e.g., Fortran, Cobol, Basic), and uppercase for those pronounced as a series of letters (e.g., APL, PL/I, ML).

clear, concise, and maintainable code, especially for very large systems. There is no comparison, for example, between early versions of Basic on the one hand, and Common Lisp or Ada on the other. The factors that contribute to expressive power—abstraction facilities in particular—are a major focus of this book.

Ease of Use for the Novice. While it is easy to pick on Basic, one cannot deny its success. Part of that success is due to its very low "learning curve." Logo is popular among elementary-level educators for a similar reason: even a 5-year-old can learn it. Pascal was taught for many years in introductory programming language courses because, at least in comparison to other "serious" languages, it is compact and easy to learn. Java currently seems poised to play a similar role in the future.

Ease of Implementation. In addition to its low learning curve, Basic is successful because it could be implemented easily on tiny machines, with limited resources. Forth has a small but dedicated following for similar reasons. Arguably the single most important factor in the success of Pascal was that its designer, Niklaus Wirth, developed a simple, portable implementation of the language, and shipped it free to universities all over the world (see the bullet at the bottom of page 12). The Java designers have taken similar steps to make their language available for free to almost anyone who wants it.

Excellent Compilers. Fortran owes much of its success to extremely good compilers. In part this is a matter of historical accident. Fortran has been around longer than anything else, and companies have invested huge amounts of time and money in making compilers that generate very fast code. It is also a matter of language design, however: Fortran dialects prior to Fortran 90 lack recursion and pointers, features that greatly complicate the task of generating fast code (at least for programs that can be written in a reasonable fashion without them!). In a similar vein, some languages (e.g., Common Lisp) are successful in part because they have compilers and supporting tools that do an unusually good job of helping the programmer manage very large projects.

Economics, Patronage, and Inertia. Finally, there are factors other than technical merit that greatly influence success. The backing of a powerful sponsor is one. Cobol and PL/I, at least to first approximation, owe their life to IBM. Ada owes its life to the United States Department of Defense: it contains a wealth of excellent features and ideas, but the sheer complexity of implementation would likely have killed it if not for the DoD backing. Some languages remain widely used long after "better" alternatives are available because of a huge base of installed software and programmer expertise, which would cost too much to replace.

Clearly no one factor determines whether a language is "good." As we study programming languages, we shall need to consider issues from several points of view. In particular, we shall need to consider the viewpoints of both the programmer and the language implementor. Sometimes these points of view will

declarative		
	functional	Lisp/Scheme, ML, Haskell
	dataflow	Id, Val
	logic, constraint-based	Prolog, VisiCalc
imperative		
	von Neumann	Fortran, Pascal, Basic, C, ...
	object-oriented	Smalltalk, Eiffel, C++, Java

Figure 1.1 Classification of Programming Languages. Note that the categories are fuzzy, and open to debate. In particular, it is possible for a functional language to be object-oriented, and many authors do not consider functional programming to be declarative.

be in harmony, as in the desire for execution speed. Often, however, there will be conflicts and tradeoffs, as the conceptual appeal of a feature is balanced against the cost of its implementation. The tradeoff becomes particularly thorny when the implementation imposes costs not only on programs that use the feature, but also on programs that do not.

In the early days of computing the implementor's viewpoint was predominant. Programming languages evolved as a means of telling a computer what to do. For programmers, however, a language is more aptly defined as a means of expressing algorithms. Just as natural languages constrain exposition and discourse, so programming languages constrain what can and cannot be expressed, and have both profound and subtle influence over what the programmer can *think*. Donald Knuth (a pioneer in computer algorithms and typesetting) has suggested that programming be regarded as the art of telling another human being what one wants the computer to do [Knu84]. This definition perhaps strikes the best sort of compromise. It acknowledges that both conceptual clarity and implementation efficiency are fundamental concerns. This book attempts to capture this spirit of compromise, by simultaneously considering the conceptual and implementation aspects of each of the topics it covers.

1.2 The Programming Language Spectrum

The many existing languages can be classified into families based on their model of computation. Figure 1.1 shows a common set of families. The top-level division distinguishes between the *declarative* languages, in which the focus is on *what* the computer is to do, and the *imperative* languages, in which the focus is on *how* the computer should do it. Declarative languages are in some sense "higher level"; they are more in tune with the programmer's point of view, and less with the implementor's point of view. Imperative languages predominate, however, mainly for performance reasons. There is a tension in the design of declarative languages between the desire to get away from "irrelevant" implementation details, and the need to remain close enough to the details to at least control the outline of an algorithm. The design of efficient algorithms, after all, is what much of computer science is about. It is not yet clear to what extent, and in what problem domains, we can expect compilers to discover good algorithms for problems stated at a very high level. In any domain in which the compiler cannot find a good algorithm, the programmer needs to be able to specify one explicitly.

Within the declarative and imperative families, there are several important subclasses.

- *Functional* languages employ a computational model based on the recursive definition of functions. They take their inspiration from the *lambda calculus*, a formal computational model developed by Alonzo Church in the 1930s. In essence, a program is considered a function from inputs to outputs, defined in terms of simpler functions through a process of refinement. Languages in this category include Lisp, ML, and Haskell.

- *Dataflow* languages model computation as the flow of information (*tokens*) among primitive functional *nodes*. They provide an inherently parallel model: nodes are triggered by the arrival of input tokens, and can operate concurrently. Id and Val are examples of dataflow languages. Sisal, a descendant of Val, is more often described as a functional language.

- *Logic* or *constraint-based* languages take their inspiration from propositional logic. They model computation as an attempt to find values that satisfy certain specified relationships, using goal-directed search through a list of logical rules. Prolog is the best-known logic language. The term can also be applied to the programmable aspects of spreadsheet systems such as VisiCalc, Excel, or Lotus 1-2-3.

- The *von Neumann* languages are the most familiar and successful. They include Fortran, Pascal, Basic, C, and all of the others in which the basic means of computation is the modification of variables.[3] Von Neumann languages are sometimes described as computing via *side effects*. Whereas functional languages are based on expressions that have values, von Neumann languages are based on statements (assignments in particular) that influence subsequent computation by changing the value of memory.

- *Object-oriented* languages are comparatively recent, though their roots can be traced to Simula 67. Most are closely related to the von Neumann languages, but have a much more structured and distributed model of both memory and computation. Rather than picture computation as the operation of a monolithic processor on a monolithic memory, object-oriented languages picture

---

3 John von Neumann (1903–1957) was a mathematician and computer pioneer who helped to develop the concept of *stored program* computing, which underlies most computer hardware. In a stored program computer, both programs and data are represented as bits in memory, which the processor repeatedly fetches, interprets, and updates.

it as interactions among semi-independent *objects*, each of which has both its own internal state and executable functions to manage that state. Smalltalk is the purest of the object-oriented languages; C++ is the most widely used. It is also possible to devise object-oriented functional languages (the best known of these is the CLOS [Kee89] extension to Common Lisp), but they tend to have a strong imperative flavor.

One might suspect that concurrent languages also form a separate class (and indeed this book devotes a chapter to the subject), but the distinction between concurrent and sequential execution is mostly orthogonal to the classifications above. Most concurrent programs are currently written using special library packages or compilers in conjunction with a sequential language such as Fortran or C. A few widely used languages, including Java, Ada, and Modula-3, have explicitly concurrent features. Researchers are investigating concurrency in each of the language classes mentioned here.

It should be emphasized that the distinctions among language classes are not clear-cut. The division between the von Neumann and object-oriented languages, for example, is often very fuzzy, and most of the functional and logic languages include some imperative features. The descriptions above are meant to capture the general flavor of the classes, without providing formal definitions.

Imperative languages—von Neumann and object-oriented—receive the bulk of the attention in this book. Many issues cut across family lines, however, and the interested reader will discover much that is applicable to alternative computational models in most of the chapters of the book. Chapter 11 is devoted exclusively to functional and logic languages.

1.3 Why Study Programming Languages?

Programming languages are central to computer science, and to the typical computer science curriculum. Like most car owners, students who have become familiar with one or more high-level languages are generally curious to learn about other languages, and to know what is going on "under the hood." Learning about languages is interesting. It's also practical.

For one thing, a good understanding of language design and implementation can help one choose the most appropriate language for any given task. Most languages are better for some things than for others. No one would be likely to use APL for symbolic computing or string processing, but other choices are not nearly so clear-cut. Should one choose C, C++, or Modula-3 for systems programming? Fortran or Ada for scientific computations? Ada or Modula-2 for embedded systems? Visual Basic or Java for the next generation of word processor? This book should help equip you to make such decisions.

Similarly, this book should make it easier to learn new languages. Many languages are closely related. Java is easier to learn if you already know C++. Modula-2 is easier to learn if you already know Pascal. More important, there are basic concepts that underlie all programming languages. Most of these concepts are the subject of chapters in this book: types, control (iteration, selection, recursion, nondeterminacy, concurrency), abstraction, and naming. Thinking in terms of these concepts makes it easier to assimilate the syntax (form) and semantics (meaning) of new languages, compared to picking them up in a vacuum. The situation is analogous to what happens in natural languages: a good knowledge of grammatical forms makes it easier to learn a foreign language.

Whatever language you learn, understanding the decisions that went into its design and implementation will help you use it better. This book should help you

Understand obscure features. The typical C++ programmer rarely uses unions, multiple inheritance, variable numbers of arguments, or the .* operator. (If you don't know what these are, don't worry!) Just as it simplifies the assimilation of new languages, an understanding of basic concepts makes it easier to understand these features when you look up the details in the manual.

Choose among alternative ways to express things, based on a knowledge of implementation costs. In Pascal, for example, programmers need to avoid using value parameters for very large types, because of copying costs. In Algol 60, they need to avoid call-by-name parameters. With certain (poor) compilers, they need to adopt special programming idioms to get the fastest code: pointers for array traversal in C; with statements to factor out common address calculations in Pascal; x*x instead of x**2 in Basic. In any language, they need to be able to evaluate the tradeoffs among alternative implementations of abstractions—for example between computation and table lookup for functions like bit set cardinality, which can be implemented either way.

Make good use of debuggers, assemblers, linkers, and related tools. In general, the high-level language programmer should not need to bother with implementation details. There are times, however, when an understanding of those details proves extremely useful. The tenacious bug or unusual system-building problem is sometimes a lot easier to handle if one is willing to peek at the bits.

Simulate useful features in languages that lack them. Certain very useful features are missing in older languages, but can be emulated by following a deliberate (if unenforced) programming style. In older dialects of Fortran, for example, programmers familiar with modern control constructs can use comments and self-discipline to write well-structured code. Similarly, in languages with poor abstraction facilities, comments and naming conventions can help imitate modular structure, and the extremely useful *iterators* of Clu and Icon (which we will study in Section 6.5.3) can be imitated with functions and static variables. In Fortran 77 and other languages that lack recursion, an iterative program can be derived via mechanical hand transformations, starting with recursive pseudocode. In languages without named constants or enumeration types, variables that are initialized once and never changed thereafter can make code much more readable and easy to maintain.

Finally, this book should help prepare you for further study in language design or implementation, should you be so inclined. It will also equip you to understand the interactions of languages with operating systems and architectures, should those areas draw your interest.

Most programmers will never design or implement a full-scale programming language, but the skills required to do so are useful on a smaller scale as well. Many systems programs and applications have a language-like flavor to them:

- command interpreters (Unix shells [`sh`, `csh`, `ksh`], IBM's JCL)
- report-generating systems (RPG, Awk)
- programmable editors (`emacs`)
- programmable applications (HyperCard, VisiCalc)
- configuration files and command-line options (lots of examples)

Knowing about "real" languages will make it easier to use these language-like relatives, and to design things like them.

⅂.4 Compilation and Interpretation

At the highest level of abstraction, the compilation and execution of a program in a high-level language look something like this:

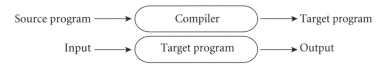

The compiler *translates* the high-level source program into an equivalent target program (typically in machine language), and then goes away. At some arbitrary later time, the user tells the operating system to run the target program. The compiler is the locus of control during compilation; the target program is the locus of control during its own execution. The compiler is itself a machine language program, presumably created by compiling some other high-level program. When written to a file in a format understood by the operating system, machine language is commonly known as *object code*.

An alternative style of implementation for high-level languages is known as *interpretation*.

Unlike a compiler, an interpreter stays around for the execution of the application. In fact, the interpreter is the locus of control during that execution. In effect, the interpreter implements a virtual machine whose "machine language" is the high-level programming language. The interpreter reads statements in that language more or less one at a time, executing them as it goes along.

In general, interpretation leads to greater flexibility and better diagnostics (error messages) than does compilation. Because the source code is being executed directly, the interpreter can include an excellent source-level debugger. It can also cope with languages in which fundamental characteristics of the program, such as the sizes and types of variables, or even which names refer to which variables, can depend on the input data. Some language features are almost impossible to implement without interpretation: in Lisp and Prolog, for example, a program can write new pieces of itself and execute them on the fly. Delaying decisions about program implementation until run time is known as *late binding*; we will discuss it at greater length in Section 3.1.

Compilation, by contrast, generally leads to better performance. In general, a decision made at compile time is a decision that does not need to be made at run time. For example, if the compiler can guarantee that variable x will always lie at location 49378, it can generate machine language instructions that access this location whenever the source program refers to x. By contrast, an interpreter may need to look x up in a table every time it is accessed, in order to find its location. Since the (final version of a) program is compiled only once, but generally executed many times, the savings can be substantial, particularly if the interpreter is doing unnecessary work in every iteration of a loop.

While the conceptual difference between compilation and interpretation is clear, most language implementations include a mixture of both. They typically look like this:

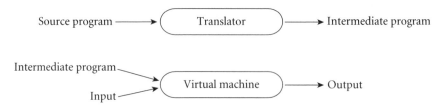

We generally say that a language is "interpreted" when the initial translator is simple. If the translator is complicated, we say that the language is "compiled." The distinction can be confusing because "simple" and "complicated" are subjective terms, and because it is possible for a compiler (complicated translator) to produce code that is then executed by a complicated virtual machine (interpreter). In this latter case, we still say that the language is compiled if the translator analyzes it thoroughly (rather than effecting some "mechanical" transformation), and if the intermediate program does not bear a strong resemblance to the source. These two characteristics—thorough analysis and nontrivial transformation—are the hallmarks of compilation.

In practice one sees a broad spectrum of implementation strategies. For example:

- Most interpreted languages employ an initial translator (a *preprocessor*) that removes comments and white space, and groups characters together into *tokens* such as keywords, identifiers, numbers, and symbols. The translator may also expand abbreviations in the style of a macro assembler. Finally, it may identify higher-level syntactic structures, such as loops and subroutines. The goal is to produce an intermediate form that mirrors the structure of the source, but can be interpreted more efficiently.

  In some very early implementations of Basic, the manual actually suggested removing comments from a program in order to improve its performance. These implementations were pure interpreters; they would reread (and then ignore) the comments every time they executed a given part of the program. They had no initial translator.

- The typical Fortran implementation comes close to pure compilation. The compiler translates Fortran source into machine language. Usually, however, it counts on the existence of a *library* of subroutines that are not part of the original program. Examples include mathematical functions (`sin`, `cos`, `log`, etc.) and I/O. The compiler relies on a separate program, known as a *linker*, to merge the appropriate library routines into the final program:

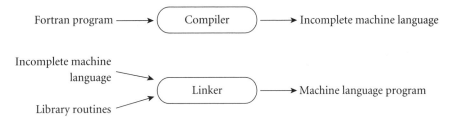

In some sense, one may think of the library routines as extensions to the hardware instruction set. The compiler can then be thought of as generating code for a virtual machine that includes the capabilities of both the hardware and the library.

In a more literal sense, one can find interpretation in the Fortran routines for formatted output. Fortran permits the use of `format` statements that control the alignment of output in columns, the number of significant digits and type of scientific notation for floating-point numbers, inclusion/suppression of leading zeros, and so on. Programs can compute their own formats on the fly. The output library routines include a format interpreter. A similar interpreter can be found in the `printf` routine of C and its descendants.

- Many compilers generate assembly language instead of machine language. This convention facilitates debugging, since assembly language is easier for people to read, and isolates the compiler from changes in the format of machine language files that may be mandated by new releases of the operating system (only the assembler must be changed, and it is shared by many compilers).

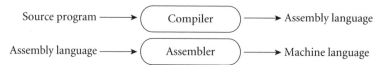

■ Compilers for C (and for many other languages running under Unix) begin with a preprocessor that removes comments and expands macros. The preprocessor can also be instructed to delete portions of the code itself, providing a *conditional compilation* facility that allows several versions of a program to be built from the same source.

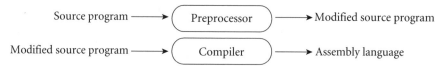

■ C++ implementations based on the early AT&T compiler actually generate an intermediate program in C, instead of in assembly language.

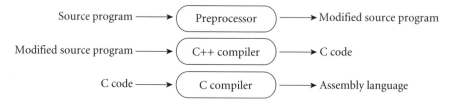

The C++ compiler is indeed a true compiler. It performs a complete analysis of the syntax and semantics of the C++ source program, and with very few exceptions generates all of the error messages that a programmer will see prior to running the program. In fact, programmers are generally unaware that the C compiler is being used behind the scenes. The C++ compiler does not invoke the C compiler unless it has generated C code that should pass through the second round of compilation without producing any error messages.

Occasionally one will hear the C++ compiler referred to as a preprocessor, presumably because it generates high-level output that is in turn compiled. I consider this a misuse of the term: compilers attempt to "understand" their source; preprocessors do not. Preprocessors perform transformations based on simple pattern matching, and may well produce output that will generate error messages when run through a subsequent stage of translation.

■ Many early Pascal compilers were built around a set of tools distributed by Niklaus Wirth. These included

– a Pascal compiler, written in Pascal, that would generate output in *P-code*, a simple stack-based language

– the same compiler, already translated into P-code

– a P-code interpreter, written in Pascal

To get a local implementation of Pascal, the user of the tool set needed only to translate the P-code interpreter (by hand) into some locally available language. This translation was not a difficult task; the interpreter was small. By running the P-code version of the compiler on top of the P-code interpreter, one could then compile arbitrary Pascal programs into P-code, which could in turn be run on the interpreter. To get a faster implementation, one could modify the Pascal version of the Pascal compiler to generate a locally available variety of assembly or machine language, instead of generating P-code (a somewhat more difficult task). This compiler could then be "run through itself" in a process known as *bootstrapping*, a term derived from the intentionally ridiculous notion of lifting oneself off the ground by pulling on one's bootstraps.

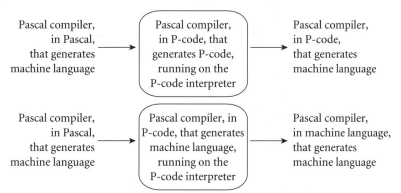

At this point, the P-code interpreter and the P-code version of the Pascal compiler could simply be thrown away. More often, however, programmers would choose to keep these tools around. The P-code version of a program tends to be significantly smaller than its machine language counterpart. On a circa 1970 machine, the savings in memory and disk requirements could really be important. Moreover, as noted near the beginning of this section, an interpreter will often provide better run-time diagnostics than will the output of a compiler. Finally, an interpreter allows a program to be rerun immediately after modification, without waiting for recompilation—a feature that can be particularly valuable during program development. Many of the best programming environments for Pascal, C, and other imperative languages still include both a compiler and an interpreter.

One will sometimes find compilers for languages (e.g., Lisp, Prolog, Smalltalk, etc.) that permit a lot of late binding, and are traditionally interpreted. These compilers generally work in conjunction with an interpreter. The compiler does its best to figure things out at compile time. When it can't, it generates code that will invoke the interpreter at run time.

- In some cases a programming system may deliberately delay compilation until the last possible moment. One example occurs in implementations of Lisp or Prolog that invoke the compiler on the fly, to translate newly created source into machine language. Another example occurs in implementations of Java. The Java language definition defines a machine-independent intermediate form known as *byte code*. Byte code is the standard format for distribution of Java programs; it allows programs to be transferred easily over the Internet, and then run on any platform. The first Java implementations were based on byte-code interpreters, but more recent (faster) implementations employ a *just-in-time* compiler that translates byte code into machine language immediately before each execution of the program.

- On many machines (particularly those designed before the mid-1980s), the assembly-level instruction set is not actually implemented in hardware, but in fact runs on an interpreter. The interpreter is written in low-level instructions called *microcode* (or *firmware*), which is stored in read-only memory and executed by the hardware. We will consider microcode and microprogramming further in Section 5.5.

As some of these examples make clear, a compiler does not necessarily translate from a high-level language into machine language. It is becoming increasingly common for compilers, especially prototypes, to generate C as output. A little farther afield, text formatters such as TEX and `troff` are actually compilers, translating high-level document descriptions into commands for a laser printer or phototypesetter. (Many laser printers themselves incorporate interpreters for the Postscript page-description language.) Query language processors for database systems are also compilers, translating languages such as SQL into primitive operations on files. There are even compilers that translate logic-level circuit specifications into photographic masks for computer chips. Though the focus in this book is on imperative programming languages, the term "compilation" applies whenever we translate automatically from one nontrivial language to another, with full analysis of the meaning of the input.

1.5 Programming Environments

Compilers and interpreters do not exist in isolation. Programmers are assisted in their work by a host of other tools. Assemblers, debuggers, preprocessors, and linkers were mentioned earlier. Editors are familiar to every programmer. They may be assisted by cross-referencing facilities that allow the programmer to find the point at which an object is defined, given a point at which it is used. Pretty printers help enforce formatting conventions. Style checkers enforce syntactic or semantic conventions that may be tighter than those enforced by the compiler (see Exercise 1.6). Configuration management tools help keep track of dependences among the (many versions of) separately compiled modules in a large software system. Perusal tools exist not only for text but also for intermediate languages that may be stored in binary. Profilers and other performance analysis tools often work in conjunction with debuggers to help identify the pieces of a program that consume the bulk of its computation time.

In Unix, as in most other relatively old environments, programming tools are generally executed individually, at the explicit request of the user. If a running program terminates abnormally with a "bus error" (invalid address) message, the user may choose to invoke a debugger to examine the "core" file dumped by the operating system. He or she may then attempt to identify the program bug by setting breakpoints, enabling tracing, and so on, and running the program again under the control of the debugger. Once the bug is found, the user will invoke the editor to make an appropriate change. He or she will then recompile the modified program, possibly with the help of a configuration manager.

There is a trend toward the development of more *integrated* environments, in which the various tools function in a less disjointed fashion. When an invalid address error occurs in an integrated environment, a new window is likely to appear on the user's screen, with the line of source code at which the error occurred highlighted. Breakpoints and tracing can then be set in this window without explicitly invoking a debugger. Changes to the source can be made without explicitly invoking an editor. The editor may also incorporate knowledge of the language syntax, providing templates for all the standard control structures, and checking syntax as it is typed in. If the user asks to rerun the program after making changes, a new version may be built without explicitly invoking the compiler or configuration manager.

Integrated environments have been developed for a variety of languages and systems. They are fundamental to Smalltalk—it is nearly impossible to separate the language from its window-based environment—and are widely used with Common Lisp. They are also common on personal computers; examples include the Visual Studio environment from Microsoft, and the CodeWarrior tools from Metrowerks. Several less ambitious environments are commercially available for Unix C programmers, and much of the appearance of integration can be achieved within sophisticated editors such as `emacs`.

1.6 An Overview of Compilation

Compilers are among the most well-studied types of computer programs. In a typical compiler, compilation proceeds through a series of well-defined *phases*, shown in Figure 1.2. Each phase discovers information of use to later phases, or transforms the program into a form that is more useful to the subsequent phase.

The first few phases (up through semantic analysis) serve to figure out the meaning of the source program. They are sometimes called the *front end* of the

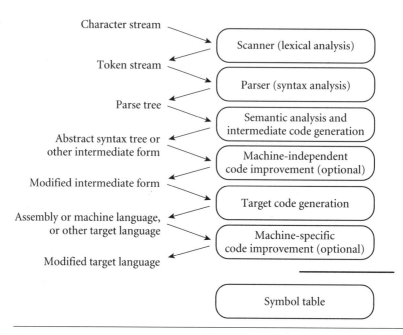

Character stream

Scanner (lexical analysis)

Token stream

Parser (syntax analysis)

Parse tree

Semantic analysis and
intermediate code generation

Abstract syntax tree or
other intermediate form

Machine-independent
code improvement (optional)

Modified intermediate form

Target code generation

Assembly or machine language,
or other target language

Machine-specific
code improvement (optional)

Modified target language

Symbol table

Figure 1.2 Phases of compilation. Phases are listed on the right and the forms in which information is passed between phases are listed on the left. The symbol table serves throughout compilation as a repository for information about identifiers.

compiler. The last few phases serve to construct an equivalent target program. They are sometimes called the *back end* of the compiler. Many compiler phases can be created automatically from a formal description of the source and/or target languages.

One will sometimes hear compilation described as a series of *passes*. A pass is a phase or set of phases that is serialized with respect to the rest of compilation: it does not start until previous phases have completed, and it finishes before any subsequent phases start. If desired, a pass may be written as a separate program, reading its input from a file and writing its output to a file. Compilers are commonly divided into passes so that the front end may be shared by compilers for more than one machine (target language), and so that the back end may be shared by compilers for more than one source language. Prior to the dramatic increases in memory sizes of the mid to late 1980s, compilers were also sometimes divided into passes to minimize memory usage: as each pass completed, the next could reuse its code space.

1.6.1 Lexical and Syntax Analysis

Consider the greatest common divisor (GCD) program introduced at the beginning of this chapter. Written in Pascal, the program might look like this:

```
program gcd (input, output);
var i, j : integer;
begin
    read (i, j);
    while i <> j do
        if i > j then i := i - j
        else j := j - i;
    writeln (i)
end.
```

Scanning and parsing serve to recognize the structure of the program, without regard to its meaning. The scanner reads characters ('p', 'r', 'o', 'g', 'r', 'a', 'm', ' ', 'g', 'c', 'd', etc.) and groups them into *tokens*, which are the smallest meaningful units of the program. In our example, the tokens are

program	gcd	(	input	,	output	)	;
var	i	,	j	:	integer	;	begin
read	(	i	,	j	)	;	while
i	<>	j	do	if	i	>	j
then	i	:=	i	-	j	else	j
:=	j	-	i	;	writeln	(	i
)	end	.					

Scanning is also known as *lexical analysis*. The principal purpose of the scanner is to simplify the task of the parser, by reducing the size of the input (there are many more characters than tokens) and by removing extraneous characters. The scanner also typically removes comments, produces a listing if desired, and tags tokens with line and column numbers, to make it easier to generate good diagnostics in later phases. One could design a parser to take characters instead of tokens as input—dispensing with the scanner—but the result would be awkward and slow.

Parsing organizes tokens into a *parse tree* that represents higher-level constructs in terms of their constituents. The ways in which these constituents combine are defined by a set of potentially recursive rules known as a *context-free grammar*. For example, we know that a Pascal program consists of the keyword program, followed by an identifier (the program name), a parenthesized list of files, a semicolon, a series of definitions, and the main begin ... end block, terminated by a period:

program → PROGRAM *identifier* (*identifier more_identifiers*) ; *block* .

where

block → *labels constants types variables subroutines* BEGIN *statement*
        more_statements END

and

more_identifiers → , *identifier more_identifiers*

or

more_identifiers → ϵ

Here ϵ represents the empty string; it indicates that *more_identifiers* can simply be deleted.

A context-free grammar is said to define the *syntax* of the language; parsing is therefore known as *syntactic analysis*. There are many possible grammars for Pascal (an infinite number, in fact); the fragment shown above is based loosely on the "circles-and-arrows" syntax diagrams found in the original Pascal text [JW91]. A full parse tree for our GCD program (based on a full grammar not shown here) appears in Figure 1.3. Much of the complexity of this figure stems from (1) the use of such artificial "constructs" as *more_statements* and *more_expressions* to represent lists of arbitrary length, and (2) the use of the equally artificial *term*, *factor*, and so on, to capture precedence and associativity in arithmetic expressions. Grammars and parse trees will be covered in more detail in Chapter 2.

In the process of scanning and parsing, the compiler checks to see that all of the program's tokens are well-formed, and that the sequence of tokens conforms to the syntax defined by the context-free grammar. Any malformed tokens (e.g., `123abc` or `$@foo` in Pascal) should cause the scanner to produce an error message. Any syntactically invalid token sequence (e.g., `A := B C D` in Pascal) should lead to an error message from the parser.

1.6.2 Semantic Analysis and Intermediate Code Generation

Semantic analysis is the discovery of *meaning* in a program. The semantic analysis phase of compilation recognizes when multiple occurrences of the same identifier are meant to refer to the same program entity, and ensures that the uses are consistent. In most languages the semantic analyzer tracks the *types* of both identifiers and expressions, both to verify consistent usage and to guide the generation of code in later phases.

To assist in its work, the semantic analyzer typically builds and maintains a *symbol table* data structure that maps each identifier to the information known about it. Among other things, this information includes the identifier's type, internal structure (if any), and scope (the portion of the program in which it is valid).

Using the symbol table, the semantic analyzer enforces a large variety of rules that are not captured by the hierarchical structure of the context-free grammar and the parse tree. For example, it checks to make sure that

▪ Every identifier is declared before it is used.

▪ No identifier is used in an inappropriate context (calling an integer as a subroutine, adding a string to an integer, referencing a field of the wrong type of record, etc.).

- Subroutine calls provide the correct number and types of arguments.
- Labels on the arms of a `case` statement are distinct constants.
- Every function contains at least one statement that specifies a return value.

In many compilers, the work of the semantic analyzer takes the form of *semantic action routines*, invoked by the parser when it realizes that it has reached a particular point within a production.

Of course, not all semantic rules can be checked at compile time. Those that can are referred to as the *static semantics* of the language. Those that must be checked at run time are referred to as the *dynamic semantics* of the language. Examples of rules that must often be checked at run time include

- Variables are never used in an expression unless they have been given a value.
- Pointers are never dereferenced unless they refer to a valid object.
- Array subscript expressions lie within the bounds of the array.
- Every function specifies a value before returning.

When it cannot enforce rules statically, a compiler will often produce code to perform appropriate checks at run time, aborting the program or generating an *exception* if one of the checks then fails. (Exceptions will be discussed in Section 8.5.) Some rules, unfortunately, may be unacceptably expensive or impossible to enforce, and the language implementation may simply fail to check them. The reference manual for Ada has a formal notion of rules that need not necessarily be enforced: a program that breaks such a rule is said to be *erroneous*.

A parse tree is sometimes known as a *concrete syntax tree*, because it demonstrates, completely and concretely, how a particular sequence of tokens can be derived under the rules of the context-free grammar. Once we know that a token sequence is valid, however, much of the information in the parse tree is irrelevant to further phases of compilation. In the process of checking static semantic rules, the semantic analyzer typically transforms the parse tree into an *abstract syntax tree* (otherwise known as an *AST*, or simply a *syntax tree*) by removing most of the "artificial" nodes in the tree's interior. The semantic analyzer also *annotates* the remaining nodes with useful information, such as pointers from identifiers to their symbol table entries. The annotations attached to a particular node are known as its *attributes*. A syntax tree for our GCD program is shown in Figure 1.4.

In many compilers, the annotated syntax tree constitutes the intermediate form that is passed from the front end to the back end. In other compilers, semantic analysis ends with a traversal of the tree that generates some other intermediate form. Often this alternative form resembles assembly language for an extremely simple idealized machine. In a suite of related compilers, the front ends for several languages and the back ends for several machines would share a common intermediate form.

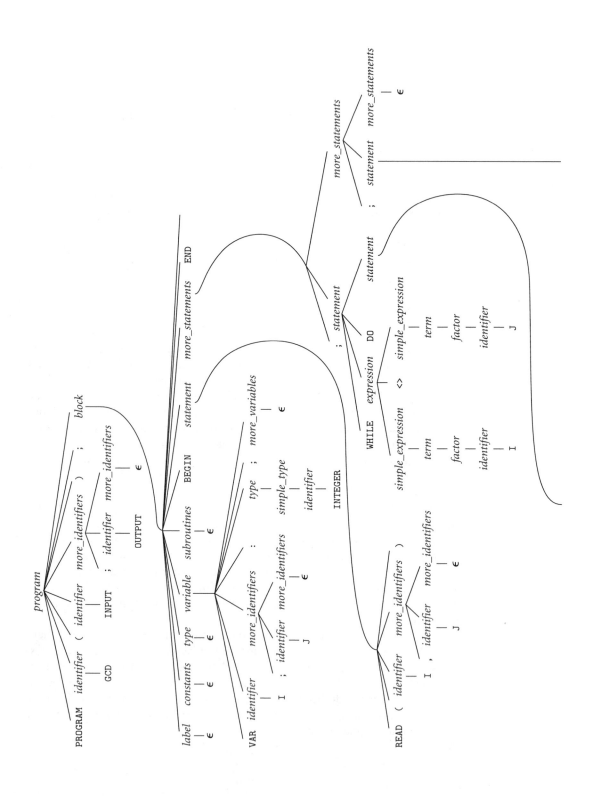

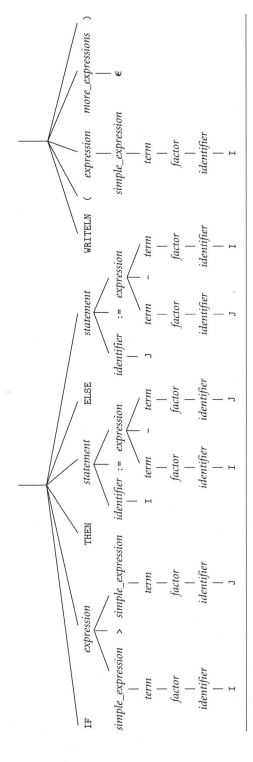

Figure 1.3 Parse tree for the GCD program. The symbol ∈ represents the empty string.

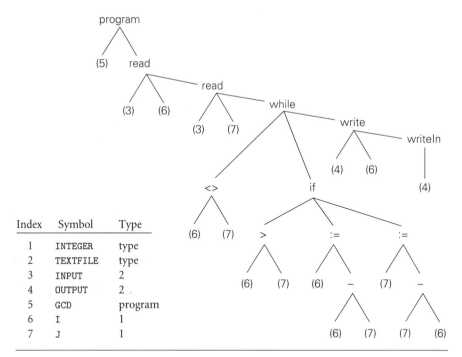

Index	Symbol	Type
1	INTEGER	type
2	TEXTFILE	type
3	INPUT	2
4	OUTPUT	2
5	GCD	program
6	I	1
7	J	1

Figure 1.4 Syntax tree and symbol table for the GCD program.

1.6.3 Target Code Generation

The code generation phase of a compiler translates the intermediate form into the target language. Given the information contained in the syntax tree, generating correct code is usually not a difficult task (generating *good* code is harder, as we shall see in Section 1.6.4). To generate assembly or machine language, the code generator traverses the symbol table to assign locations to variables, and then traverses the syntax tree, generating loads and stores for variable references, interspersed with appropriate arithmetic operations, tests, and branches. Naive code for our GCD example appears in Figure 1.5, in MIPS assembly language. It was generated automatically by a simple pedagogical compiler.

The assembly language mnemonics may appear a bit cryptic, but the comments on each line (not generated by the compiler!) should make the correspondence between Figures 1.4 and 1.5 generally apparent. A few hints: sp, ra, at, a0, v0, and t0–t9 are registers (special storage locations, limited in number, that can be accessed very quickly). 28(sp) refers to the memory location 28 bytes beyond the location whose address is in register sp. jal is a subroutine call ("jump and link"); the first argument is passed in register a0, and the return value comes back in register v0. Nop is a "no-op"; it does no useful work, but delays the program for one time cycle, allowing a two-cycle load or branch

```
        addiu   sp,sp,-32       # reserve room for local variables
        sw      ra,20(sp)       # save return address
        jal     getint          # read
        nop
        sw      v0,28(sp)       # store i
        jal     getint          # read
        nop
        sw      v0,24(sp)       # store j
        lw      t6,28(sp)       # load i
        lw      t7,24(sp)       # load j
        nop
        beq     t6,t7,D         # branch if i = j
        nop
A:      lw      t8,28(sp)       # load i
        lw      t9,24(sp)       # load j
        nop
        slt     at,t9,t8        # determine whether j < i
        beq     at,zero,B       # branch if not
        nop
        lw      t0,28(sp)       # load i
        lw      t1,24(sp)       # load j
        nop
        subu    t2,t0,t1        # t2 := i - j
        sw      t2,28(sp)       # store i
        b       C
        nop
B:      lw      t3,24(sp)       # load j
        lw      t4,28(sp)       # load i
        nop
        subu    t5,t3,t4        # t5 := j - i
        sw      t5,24(sp)       # store j
C:      lw      t6,28(sp)       # load i
        lw      t7,24(sp)       # load j
        nop
        bne     t6,t7,A         # branch if i <> j
        nop
D:      lw      a0,28(sp)       # load i
        jal     putint          # writeln
        nop
        move    v0,zero         # exit status for program
        b       E               # branch to E
        nop
        b       E               # branch to E
        nop
E:      lw      ra,20(sp)       # retrieve return address
        addiu   sp,sp,32        # deallocate space for local variables
        jr      ra              # return to operating system
        nop
```

Figure 1.5 Naive MIPS assembly language for the GCD program.

instruction to complete (branch and load delays were a common feature in early RISC machines; we will consider them in Section 5.6.1). Arithmetic operations generally operate on the second and third arguments, and put their result in the first.

Often a code generator will save the symbol table for later use by a symbolic debugger, for example by including it as comments or some other nonexecutable part of the target code.

1.6.4 Code Improvement

Code improvement is often referred to as *optimization*, though it seldom makes anything optimal in any absolute sense. It is an optional phase of compilation whose goal is to transform a program into a new version that computes the same result more efficiently—more quickly or using less memory, or both.

Some improvements are machine independent. These can be performed as transformations on the intermediate form. Other improvements require an understanding of the target machine (or of whatever will execute the program in the target language). These must be performed as transformations on the target program. Thus code improvement often appears as two additional phases of compilation, one immediately after semantic analysis and intermediate code generation, the other immediately after target code generation.

Applying a good code improver to the code in Figure 1.5 produces the code shown on page 1. Comparing the two programs, we can see that the improved version is quite a lot shorter. Conspicuously absent are most of the loads and stores. The machine-independent code improver is able to verify that i and j can be kept in registers throughout the execution of the main loop (this would not have been the case if, for example, the loop contained a call to a subroutine that might reuse those registers, or that might try to modify i or j). The machine-specific code improver is then able to assign i and j to actual registers of the target machine. In our example the machine-specific improver is also able to *schedule* (reorder) instructions to eliminate several of the no-ops. Careful examination of the instructions following the loads and branches will reveal that they can be executed safely even when the load or branch has not yet completed. For modern microprocessor architectures, particularly those with so-called *superscalar* RISC instruction sets (ones in which separate functional units can execute multiple instructions simultaneously), compilers can usually generate better code than can human assembly language programmers.

1.7 Summary and Concluding Remarks

In this chapter we introduced the study of programming language design and implementation. We considered why there are so many languages, what makes them successful or unsuccessful, how they may be categorized for study, and what benefits the reader is likely to gain from that study. We noted that language design and language implementation are intimately related to one another. Obviously an implementation must conform to the rules of the langauge. At the same time, a language designer must consider how easy or difficult it will be to implement various features, and what sort of performance is likely to result for programs that use those features.

Language implementations are commonly differentiated into those based on interpretation and those based on compilation. We noted, however, that the difference between these approaches is fuzzy, and that most implementations include a bit of each. As a general rule, we say that a language is compiled if execution is preceded by a translation step that (1) fully analyzes both the structure (syntax) and meaning (semantics) of the program, and (2) produces an equivalent program in a significantly different form. The bulk of the implementation material in this book pertains to compilation.

Compilers are generally structured as a series of *phases*. The first few phases—scanning, parsing, and semantic analysis—serve to analyze the source program. Collectively these phases are known as the compiler's *front end*. The final few phases—intermediate code generation, code improvement, and target code generation—are known as the *back end*. They serve to build a target program—preferably a fast one—whose semantics match those of the source.

Chapters 3, 6, 7, 8, and 10 form the core of the rest of this book. They cover fundamental issues of language design, both from the point of view of the programmer and from the point of view of the language implementor. To support the discussion of implementations, Chapters 2 and 4 describe compiler front ends in more detail than has been possible in this introduction. Chapter 5 provides an overview of assembly-level architecture. Chapters 9 and 13 discuss compiler back ends, including assemblers and linkers. Additional language paradigms are covered in Chapters 11 and 12. Appendix A lists the principal programming languages mentioned in the text, together with a geneological chart and bibliographic references. Appendix B highlights some of the many connections between language design and language implementation.

1.8 Review Questions

1.1 What is the difference between machine language and assembly language?

1.2 In what way(s) are high-level languages an improvement on assembly language? In what circumstances does it still make sense to program in assembler?

1.3 On modern machines, do assembly language programmers still tend to write better code than a good compiler produces? Why or why not?

1.4 Why are there so many programming languages?

1.5 What makes a programming language successful?

1.6 Name three languages in each of the following categories: von Neumann, functional, object-oriented. Name two logic languages. Name two widely used concurrent languages.

1.7 What distinguishes declarative languages from imperative languages?

1.8 What organization spearheaded the development of Ada?

1.9 What is generally considered the first high-level programming language?

1.10 What was the first functional language?

1.11 Name two languages in which a program can write new pieces of itself "on-the-fly."

1.12 Explain the distinction between interpretation and compilation. What are the comparative advantages and disadvantages of the two approaches?

1.13 What is the difference between a compiler and a preprocessor?

1.14 What was the intermediate form employed by the original AT&T C++ compiler?

1.15 What is P-code?

1.16 What is bootstrapping?

1.17 What is a just-in-time compiler?

1.18 Briefly describe three "unconventional" compilers—compilers whose purpose is not to prepare a high-level program for execution on a microprocessor.

1.19 Describe six kinds of tools that commonly support the work of a compiler within a larger programming environment.

1.20 List the principal phases of compilation, and describe the work performed by each.

1.21 Describe the form in which a program is passed from the scanner to the parser; from the parser to the semantic analyzer; from the semantic analyzer to the intermediate code generator.

1.22 What distinguishes the front end of the compiler from the back end?

1.23 What is the difference between a phase and a pass of compilation? Under what circumstances does it make sense for a compiler to have multiple passes?

1.24 What is the purpose of the compiler's symbol table?

1.25 What is the difference between static and dynamic semantics?

1.9 Exercises

1.1 Errors in a computer program can be classified according to when they are detected and, if they are detected at compile time, what part of the compiler detects them. Using your favorite imperative language, give an example of

(a) a lexical error, detected by the scanner

(b) a syntax error, detected by the parser

(c) a static semantic error, detected by semantic analysis

(d) a dynamic semantic error, detected by code generated by the compiler

(e) an error that the compiler can neither catch nor easily generate code to catch (this should be a violation of the language definition, not just a program bug)

1.2 Algol family languages are typically compiled, while Lisp family languages, in which many issues cannot be settled until run time, are typically interpreted. Is interpretation simply what one "has to do" when compilation is infeasible, or are there actually some *advantages* to interpreting a language, even when a compiler is available?

1.3 If you have access to a Unix system, run your favorite compiler with the −v command-line flag. It should respond by printing messages describing the various subprograms it invokes (some compilers use a different letter for this option; check the man page). You are likely to see at least four or five subprograms: a preprocessor, two passes of the compiler itself, probably an assembler, and the linker. If possible, run these programs yourself, individually. Examine their input and output files with a text editor or, for binary files, a binary listing program such as od or nm.

1.4 The gcd program on page 17 might also be written

```
program gcd (input, output);
var i, j : integer;
begin
    read (i, j);
    while i <> j do
        if i > j then i := i mod j
        else j := j mod i;
    writeln (i)
end.
```

Does this program compute the same result? If not, can you fix it? Under what circumstances would you expect one or the other to be faster?

1.5 The Unix make utility allows the programmer to specify *dependences* among the separately compiled pieces of a program. If file *A* depends on file *B* and file *B* is modified, make deduces that *A* must be recompiled, in case any of the changes to *B* would affect the code produced for *A*. How accurate is this sort of dependence management? Under what circumstances will it lead to unnecessary work? Under what circumstances will it fail to recompile something that needs to be recompiled?

1.6 C has a reputation for being a relatively "unsafe" high-level language. In particular, it allows the programmer to mix operands of different sizes and types in many more ways than do its "safer" cousins. The Unix lint utility can be used to search for potentially unsafe constructs in C programs. In effect, many of the rules that are enforced by the compiler in other languages are optional in C, and are enforced (if desired) by a separate program. What do you think of this approach? Is it a good idea? Why or why not?

1.7 Get together with a classmate whose principal programming experience is with a language in a different category of Figure 1.1. (If your experience is mostly in C, for example, you might search out someone with experience in Lisp.) Compare notes. What are the easiest and most difficult aspects of programming, in each of your experiences? Pick some simple problem (e.g., sorting, or identification of connected components in a graph) and solve it using each of your favorite languages. Which solution is more elegant (do the two of you agree)? Which is faster? Why?

1.8 For the language with which you are most familiar, list three things you wish had been differently designed. Why do you think they were designed the way they were? How would you fix them if you had the chance to do it over? Would there be any negative consequences, for example in terms of compiler compilexity or program execution speed?

1.9 Write a program that commits a dynamic semantic error (e.g., division by zero, access off the end of an array, dereference of a `nil` pointer). What happens when you run this program? Does the compiler give you options to control what happens? Devise an experiment to evaluate the cost of run-time semantic checks. If possible, try this exercise with more than one language or compiler.

1.10 In your favorite implementation of C or Pascal, what is the limit on the size of integers? What happens in the event of arithmetic overflow? What are the implications of size limits on the portability of programs from one machine/compiler to another? How do the answers to these questions differ for Java? For Scheme? (You may need to find a manual.)

1.11 Why is it difficult to tell whether a program is correct? How do you go about finding bugs in your code? What kinds of bugs are revealed by testing? What kinds of bugs are not? (For more formal notions of program correctness, see the bibliographic notes at the end of Chapter 4.)

1.10 Bibliographic Notes

The compiler-oriented chapters of this book attempt to convey a sense of what the compiler does, rather than explaining how to build one. A much greater level of detail can be found in other texts. The ones by Aho, Sethi, and Ullman [ASU86] and Fischer and LeBlanc [FL88] have for years been the standards in the field. More up-to-date coverage can be found in the recent text by Appel [App97]. High-quality texts on programming language design include those of Louden [Lou93], Sebesta [Seb99], and Sethi [Set96].

Some of the best information on the history of programming languages can be found in the proceedings of conferences sponsored by the Association for Computing Machinery in 1978 and 1993 [Wex78, Ass93]. Another excellent reference is Horowitz's 1987 text [Hor87]. A broader range of historical material can be found in the quarterly *IEEE Annals of the History of Computing*. Given the importance of personal taste in programming language design, it is inevitable that some language comparisons should be marked by strongly worded opinions. Examples include the writings of Dijkstra [Dij82], Hoare [Hoa81], Kernighan [Ker81], and Wirth [Wir85a].

Most personal computer software development now takes place in integrated programming environments. Influential precursors to these environments include the Genera Common Lisp environment from Symbolics Corp. [WMWM87] and the Smalltalk [Gol84], Interlisp [TM81], and Cedar [SZBH86] environments at the Xerox Palo Alto Research Center.

Programming Language Syntax

Unlike natural languages such as English or Chinese, computer languages must be precise. Both their form (syntax) and meaning (semantics) must be specified without ambiguity, so that both programmers and computers can tell what a program is supposed to do. To provide the needed degree of precision, language designers and implementers use formal syntactic and semantic notation. To facilitate the discussion of language features in later chapters, we will cover this notation first, in the current chapter and in Chapter 4.

To introduce the notions of syntax and semantics, it is useful perhaps to think about numbers. Consider first the Arabic numerals with which we represent numbers. These numerals are composed of digits, which we can enumerate as follows ('|' means "or"):

$digit \rightarrow$ 0 | 1 | 2 | 3 | 4 | 5 | 6 | 7 | 8 | 9

Digits are the syntactic building blocks for numbers. In the usual notation, we say that a natural number is represented by an arbitrary-length (nonempty) string of digits, beginning with a nonzero digit:

$non\_zero\_digit \rightarrow$ 1 | 2 | 3 | 4 | 5 | 6 | 7 | 8 | 9
$natural\_number \rightarrow non\_zero\_digit\ digit\ *$

Here the "Kleene[1] star" meta-symbol (*) is used to indicate zero or more repetitions of the symbol to its left.

Of course, digits are only symbols: ink blobs on paper or pixels on a screen. They carry no meaning in and of themselves. We add semantics to digits when we say that they represent the natural numbers from zero to nine, as defined by mathematicians. Alternatively, we could say that they represent colors, or

---

[1] Stephen Kleene (1909–1994), a mathematician at the University of Wisconsin, was responsible for much of the early development of the theory of computation, including much of the material in Section 2.3.

the days of the week in a decimal calendar. These would constitute alternative semantics for the same syntax. In a similar fashion, we define the semantics of natural numbers by associating a base-10, place-value interpretation with each string of digits. Similar syntax rules and semantic interpretations can be devised for rational numbers, (limited-precision) real numbers, arithmetic, assignments, control flow, declarations, and indeed all of programming languages.

Distinguishing between syntax and semantics is useful for at least two reasons. First, different programming languages often provide features with very similar semantics but very different syntax. It is generally much easier to learn a new language if one is able to identify the common (and presumably familiar) ideas beneath the unfamiliar syntax. Second, there are some very efficient and elegant algorithms that a compiler or interpreter can use to discover the syntactic structure (but not the semantics!) of a computer program, and these algorithms can be used to drive the rest of the compilation or interpretation process.

Semantic analysis is the subject of Chapter 4. In the current chapter we focus on syntax: how we specify the structural rules of a programming language, and how a compiler identifies the structure of a given input program. These two tasks—specifying syntax rules and figuring out how (and whether) a given program was built according to those rules—are distinct. The first is of interest mainly to programmers, who want to write valid programs. The second is of interest mainly to compilers, which need to analyze those programs. The first task relies on *regular expressions* and *context-free grammars*, which specify how to generate valid programs. The second task relies on *scanners* and *parsers*, which recognize program structure. We address the first of these tasks in Section 2.1, the second in Section 2.2. In Section 2.3 we take a deeper look at the formal theory underlying scanning and parsing. Possibly nowhere else in computer science is the connection between theory and practice so clear and so compelling.

2.1 Specifying Syntax: Regular Expressions and Context-Free Grammars

Formal specification of syntax requires a set of rules. How complicated (expressive) the syntax can be depends on the kinds of rules we are allowed to use. It turns out that what we intuitively think of as tokens can be formally specified using just three kinds of rules: concatenation, alternation (choice among a finite set of alternatives), and so-called "Kleene closure" (repetition an arbitrary number of times). Specifying most of the rest of what we intuitively think of as syntax requires one additional kind of rule: recursion (creation of a construct from simpler instances of the same construct). Any set of strings that can be defined in terms of the first three rules is called a *regular set*, or sometimes a *regular language*. Regular sets are generated by *regular expressions* and recognized by scanners. Any set of strings that can be defined if we add recursion is called a *context-free language* (CFL). Context-free languages are generated by *context-free grammars* (CFGs) and recognized by parsers.(Terminology can be confusing here. The meaning of the word "language" varies greatly, depending on whether we're talking about "formal" languages [e.g., regular or context-free], or programming languages. A formal language is just a set of strings, with no accompanying semantics.)

2.1.1 Tokens and Regular Expressions

Tokens are the basic building blocks of programs. They include keywords, identifiers, numbers, punctuation marks, and other symbols. Pascal, for example, has 64 kinds of tokens, including 21 symbols (+, -, ;, :=, .., etc.), 35 keywords (`begin`, `end`, `div`, `record`, `while`, etc.), integer literals (e.g., `137`), real (floating-point) literals (e.g., `6.022e23`), character/string literals (e.g., `'snerk'`), identifiers (`MyVariable`, `YourType`, `maxint`, `readln`, etc., 39 of which are predefined), and two different kinds of comments.

Upper- and lowercase letters in identifiers and keywords are considered distinct in some languages (e.g., Modula-2/3 and C/C++/Java), and identical in others (e.g., Ada, Common Lisp, Fortran 90, and Pascal). Thus `foo`, `Foo`, and `FOO` all represent the same identifier in Ada, but different identifiers in C. Modula-2 and Modula-3 require keywords and predefined (built-in) identifiers to be written in uppercase; C, C++, and Java require them to be written in lowercase. A few languages (notably Modula-3 and Standard Pascal) allow only letters and digits in identifiers. Most (including many actual implementations of Pascal) allow underscores. A few (notably Lisp) allow a variety of additional characters. For the sake of clarity and consistency across languages, we will allow underscores in the Pascal examples in this book.

Some language implementations impose limits on the maximum length of identifiers, but most avoid such unnecessary restrictions. Most modern languages are also more-or-less *free format*, meaning that a program is simply a sequence of tokens: what matters is their order with respect to one another, not their physical position within a printed line or page. "White space" (blanks, tabs, carriage returns, and line and page feed characters) between tokens is usually ignored, except to the extent that it is needed to separate one token from the next. There are a few exceptions to these rules. Some language implementations limit the maximum length of a line, to allow the compiler to store the current line in a fixed-length buffer. Dialects of Fortran prior to Fortran 90 use a *fixed format*, with 72 characters (the width of an IBM punch card) per line, and with different columns within the line reserved for different purposes. Line breaks serve to separate statements in several other languages, Haskell, Occam, and SR. Haskell and Occam also give special significance to indentation. The body of a loop, for example, consists of precisely those subsequent lines that are indented farther than the header of the loop.

To specify tokens, we use the notation of regular expressions. A regular expression is one of the following:

1. a character

2. the empty string, denoted ϵ

3. two regular expressions next to each other, meaning any string generated by the first one followed by (concatenated with) any string generated by the second one

4. two regular expressions separated by a vertical bar (|), meaning any string generated by the first one *or* any string generated by the second one

5. a regular expression followed by a Kleene star, meaning the concatenation of zero or more strings generated by the expression in front of the star

Parentheses are used to avoid ambiguity about where the various subexpressions start and end.[2]

Returning to the example of Pascal, numeric literals can be generated by the following regular expressions:

$digit \rightarrow$ 0 | 1 | 2 | 3 | 4 | 5 | 6 | 7 | 8 | 9

$unsigned\_integer \rightarrow digit\ digit\ ^*$

$unsigned\_number \rightarrow unsigned\_integer$ ((. $unsigned\_integer$) | ϵ)
$$((e (+ | - | \epsilon) unsigned\_integer) | \epsilon)$$

To generate a valid string, we scan the regular expression from left to right, choosing among alternatives at each vertical bar, and choosing a number of repetitions at each Kleene star. Within each repetition we may make different choices at vertical bars, generating different substrings. Note that while we have allowed later definitions to build on earlier ones, nothing is ever defined in terms of itself. Such recursive definitions are the distinguishing characteristic of context-free grammars, described in the following section.

2.1.2 Context-Free Grammars

Regular expressions work well for defining tokens. They are unable, however, to specify *nested* constructs, which are central to programming languages. Consider for example the structure of an arithmetic expression.

$expression \rightarrow$ identifier | number | - $expression$ | ($expression$)
 | $expression\ operator\ expression$
$operator \rightarrow$ + | - | * | /

---

2 Some authors use λ to represent the empty string. Some use a period (.), rather than juxtaposition, to indicate concatenation. Some use a plus sign (+), rather than a vertical bar, to indicate alternation.

Here the ability to define a construct in terms of itself is crucial. Among other things, it allows us to ensure that left and right parentheses are matched, something that cannot be accomplished with regular expressions (see Section 2.3.3 for more details).

Each of the rules in a context-free grammar is known as a *production*. The symbols on the left-hand sides of the productions are known as *variables*, or *nonterminals*. There may be any number of productions with the same left-hand side. Symbols that are to make up the strings derived from the grammar are known as *terminals* (shown here in `Computer Modern` font). They cannot appear on the left-hand side of any production. In a programming language, the terminals of the context-free grammar are the language's tokens. One of the nonterminals, usually the one on the left-hand side of the first production, is called the *start symbol*. It names the construct defined by the overall grammar.

The notation for context-free grammars is sometimes called Backus-Naur Form (BNF), in honor of John Backus and Peter Naur, who devised it for the definition of the Algol-60 programming language [NBB+63]. Strictly speaking, the vertical bar, Kleene star, and meta-level parentheses of regular expressions are not allowed in BNF, but they do not change the expressive power of the notation, and are commonly included for convenience. Sometimes one sees a "Kleene plus" ($^+$) as well; it indicates one or more instances of the symbol or group of symbols in front of it.[3] When augmented with these extra operators, the notation is often called extended BNF (EBNF). The construct

$$operator \rightarrow + \mid - \mid * \mid /$$

for example, is simply shorthand for

$$operator \rightarrow +$$
$$operator \rightarrow -$$
$$operator \rightarrow *$$
$$operator \rightarrow /$$

which is also sometimes written

$$operator \rightarrow +$$
$$\rightarrow -$$
$$\rightarrow *$$
$$\rightarrow /$$

---

3 Some authors use square brackets ([ ]) to indicate one or more instances of the symbols inside, and curly braces ({ }) to indicate zero or more instances of the symbols inside. Some other authors use square brackets to indicate zero or one instances of the symbols inside—that is, to indicate that those symbols are optional.

In a similar vein,

identifier_list → identifier (, identifier)*

can be rewritten as

identifier_list → identifier
identifier_list → *identifier_list* , identifier

Many tokens, such as identifier and number above, have many possible spellings (i.e., may be represented by many possible strings of characters). The parser is oblivious to these; it does not distinguish one identifier from another. The semantic analyzer does distinguish them, however, so the scanner must save the spelling of each "interesting" token for later use.

2.1.3 Derivations and Parse Trees

A context-free grammar shows us how to generate syntactically valid strings of terminals: Begin with the start symbol. Choose a production with the start symbol on the left-hand side; replace the start symbol with the right-hand side of that production. Now choose a nonterminal S in the resulting string, choose a production P with S on its left-hand side, and replace S with the right-hand side of P. Repeat this process until no nonterminals remain.

As an example, we can use our grammar for expressions to generate the string "slope * x + intercept":

expression ⇒ *expression operator* <u>*expression*</u>
         ⇒ *expression* <u>*operator*</u> identifier
         ⇒ <u>*expression*</u> + identifier
         ⇒ *expression operator* <u>*expression*</u> + identifier
         ⇒ *expression* <u>*operator*</u> identifier + identifier
         ⇒ <u>*expression*</u> * identifier + identifier
         ⇒ identifier * identifier + identifier
          (slope)   (x)   (intercept)

The ⇒ meta-symbol indicates that the right-hand side was obtained by using a production to replace some nonterminal in the left-hand side. At each line we have underlined the symbol S that is replaced in the following line. A series of replacement operations that shows how to derive a string of terminals from the start symbol is called a *derivation*. Each string of symbols along the way is called a *sentential form*. The final sentential form, consisting of only terminals, is called the *yield* of the derivation. We sometimes elide the intermediate

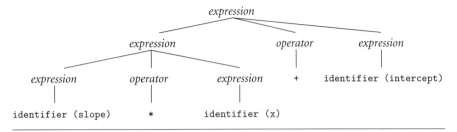

Figure 2.1 **Parse tree for** slope * x + intercept.

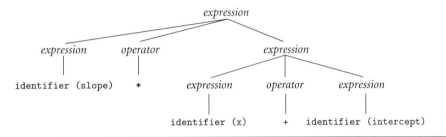

Figure 2.2 **Alternative (less desirable) parse tree for** slope * x + intercept. The fact that more than one tree exists implies that our grammar is ambiguous.

steps and write *expression* ⇒* slope * x + intercept, where the meta-symbol ⇒* means "yields after zero or more replacements." In this particular derivation, we have chosen at each step to replace the right-most nonterminal with the right-hand side of some production. This replacement strategy leads to a *right-most* derivation, also called a *canonical* derivation. There are many other possible derivations, including *left-most* and options in-between. Most parsers are designed to find a particular derivation (usually the left-most or right-most).

We saw in Chapter 1 that we can represent a derivation graphically as a *parse tree*. The root of the parse tree is the start symbol of the grammar. The leaves of the tree are its yield. Each internal node, together with its children, represents the use of a production.

A parse tree for our example expression appears in Figure 2.1. This tree is not unique. At the second level of the tree, we could have chosen to turn the operator into a * instead of a +, and to further expand the expression on the right, rather than the one on the left (see Figure 2.2). The fact that some strings are the yield of more than one parse tree tells us that our grammar is *ambiguous*. Ambiguity turns out to be a problem when trying to build a parser: it requires some extra mechanism to drive a choice between equally acceptable alternatives.

A moment's reflection will reveal that there are infinitely many context-free grammars for any given context-free language. Some of these grammars are much more useful than others. In this text we will avoid the use of ambiguous

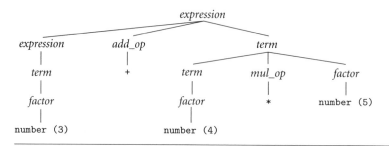

Figure 2.3 Parse tree for 3 + 4 * 5, with precedence.

grammars (though most parser generators allow them, by means of *disambiguating* rules). We will also avoid the use of so-called *useless* symbols: nonterminals that cannot generate any string of terminals, or terminals that cannot appear in the yield of any derivation.

When designing the grammar for a programming language, we generally try to find one that reflects the internal structure of programs in a way that is useful to the rest of the compiler. (We shall see in Section 2.2.5 that we also try to find one that can be parsed efficiently, which can be a bit of a challenge.) One place in which structure is particularly important is in arithmetic expressions, where we can use productions to capture the *associativity* and *precedence* of the various operators. Associativity tells us that the operators in most languages group left-to-right, so that 10 − 4 − 3 means (10 − 4) − 3 rather than 10 − (4 − 3). Precedence tells us that multiplication and division in most languages group more tightly than addition and subtraction, so that 3 + 4 * 5 means 3 + (4 * 5) rather than (3 + 4) * 5. (These rules are not universal; we will consider them again in Section 6.1.1.) Here is a better version of our expression grammar:

1. *expression* → *term* | *expression add_op term*
2. *term* → *factor* | *term mult_op factor*
3. *factor* → identifier | number | − *factor* | (*expression*)
4. *add_op* → + | −
5. *mult_op* → * | /

This grammar is unambiguous. It captures precedence in the way *factor*, *term*, and *expression* build on one another, with different operators appearing at each level. It captures associativity in the second halves of lines 1 and 2, which build sub*expression*s and sub*term*s to the left of the operator, rather than to the right. In Figure 2.3, we can see how building the notion of precedence into the grammar makes it clear that multiplication groups more tightly than addition in 3 + 4 * 5, even without parentheses. In Figure 2.4, we can see that subtraction groups more tightly to the left, so that 10 − 4 − 3 would evaluate to 3, rather than to 9.

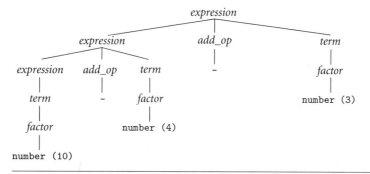

Figure 2.4 Parse tree for 10 – 4 – 3, with left associativity.

2.2 Recognizing Syntax: Scanners and Parsers

Together, the scanner and parser for a programming language are responsible for discovering the syntactic structure of a given program. This process of discovery, or *syntax analysis*, is a necessary first step toward translating the program into an equivalent program in the target language. (It's also the first step toward interpreting the program directly. In general, we will focus on compilation, rather than interpretation, for the remainder of the book. Most of what we shall discuss either has an obvious application to interpretation, or is obviously irrelevant to it.)

The parser is the heart of a typical compiler. It calls the scanner to obtain the tokens of the input program, assembles the tokens together into a parse tree, and passes the tree (perhaps one subroutine at a time) to the later phases of the compiler, which perform semantic analysis and code generation and improvement. In effect, the parser is "in charge" of the entire compilation process; this style of compilation is sometimes referred to as *syntax-directed translation*.

By grouping input characters into tokens, the scanner dramatically reduces the number of individual items that must be inspected by the more computationally intensive parsing algorithm. In addition, the scanner typically removes comments (so the parser doesn't have to worry about them appearing throughout the context-free grammar), produces an annotated source listing if desired, and tags tokens with line and column numbers, to make it easier to generate high-quality error messages in later phases. Since scanners normally deal only with nonrecursive constructs, nested comments require special treatment. Some languages disallow them. Others require the language implementor to augment the scanner with special-purpose comment-handling code.

Both scanning and parsing benefit from a rich and well-studied theoretical foundation. In theoretical parlance, a scanner is a *deterministic finite automaton* (DFA) that recognizes the tokens of a programming language. A parser is a deterministic *push-down automaton* (PDA) that recognizes the language's context-free syntax. It turns out that one can generate scanners and parsers automatically from regular expressions and CFGs. This task is performed by tools such as Unix's `lex` and `yacc`.[4] The theory behind scanning and parsing is discussed in more detail in Section 2.3.

2.2.1 Scanning

Suppose for a moment that we are writing a scanner for Pascal. We might sketch the process as follows:

```
we skip any initial white space (spaces, tabs, and newlines)
we read the next character
if it is a ( we look at the next character
    if that is a * we have a comment;
        we skip forward through the terminating *)
    otherwise we return a left parenthesis and reuse the look-ahead
if it is one of the one-character tokens ([ ] , ; = + − etc.)
    we return that token
if it is a . we look at the next character
    if that is a . we return .. 5
    otherwise we return . and reuse the look-ahead
if it is a < we look at the next character
    if that is a = we return <=
    otherwise we return < and reuse the look-ahead
etc.
if it is a letter we keep reading letters and digits
        and maybe underscores until we can't anymore;
    then we check to see if it is a keyword
        if so we return the keyword
        otherwise we return an identifier
    in either case we reuse the character beyond the end of the token
if it is a digit we keep reading until we find a nondigit
    if that is not a . we return an integer and reuse the nondigit
    otherwise we keep looking for a real number
        if the character after the . is not a digit we return
        an integer and reuse the . and the look-ahead
etc.
```

---

4 At many sites, `lex` and `yacc` have been superseded by the GNU `flex` and `bison` tools. These independently developed, noncommercial alternatives are available without charge from the Free Software Foundation at *www.fsf.org/software*. They provide a superset of the functionality of `lex` and `yacc`.

5 The double-dot `..` token is used to specify ranges in Pascal (e.g., `type day = 1..31`).

After announcing a token the scanner returns to the parser. When invoked again it repeats the algorithm from the beginning, using the next available characters of input (including any look-ahead that was peeked at but not consumed the last time). As a rule, we accept the longest possible token in each invocation of the scanner. Thus `foobar` is always `foobar` and never `f` or `foo` or `foob`. More to the point, `3.14159` is a real number and never `3`, `.`, and `14159`. White space (blanks, tabs, carriage returns, comments) is generally ignored, except to the extent that it separates tokens (e.g., `foo bar` is different from `foobar`).

It is not difficult to flesh out the algorithm above by hand, to produce code in some programming language. This ad hoc style of scanner is often used in production compilers; the code is fast and compact. In some cases, however, it makes sense to build a scanner in a more structured way, as an explicit representation of a finite automaton. We can again write the code by hand (this option basically amounts to a highly stylized ad hoc scanner), or we can use a *scanner generator* to build it automatically from a set of regular expressions. Because regular expressions are significantly easier to write and modify than is an ad hoc scanner, automatically generated scanners are often used during language or compiler development, or when ease of implementation is more important that the last little bit of run-time performance. In effect, regular expressions constitute a declarative programming language for a limited problem domain: namely that of scanning.

Figure 2.5 shows part of an automaton for a Pascal scanner. The automaton starts in a distinguished initial state. It then moves from state to state based on the next available character of input. When it reaches one of a designated set of final states it recognizes the token associated with that state. The "longest possible token" rule means that the scanner returns to the parser only when the next character cannot be used to continue the current token.

We can build a scanner that explicitly captures the "circles-and-arrows" structure of a finite automaton in either of two main ways. One embeds the automaton in the control flow of the program using gotos or nested case (switch) statements; the other, described later in this section, uses a table and a driver. The nested case statement approach appears in Figure 2.6. The outer case statement covers the states of the finite automaton. The inner case statements cover the transitions out of each state. Most of the inner clauses simply set a new state. Some return from the scanner with the current token.

Two aspects of the code in Figure 2.6 do not strictly follow the form of a finite automaton. One is the handling of keywords. The other is the need to peek ahead in order to distinguish between the dot in the middle of a real number and a double dot that follows an integer.

Keywords in most languages (including Pascal) look just like identifiers, but are reserved for a special purpose (some authors use the term reserved word

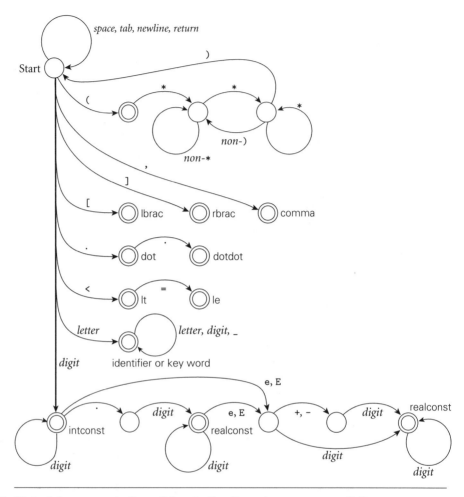

Figure 2.5 Pictorial representation of (part of) a Pascal scanner as a finite automaton. Scanning for each token begins in the state marked "Start." The states in which a token is recognized are double-circled.

instead of keyword[6]). It is possible to write a finite automaton that distinguishes between keywords and identifiers, but it requires a lot of states. To begin with, there must be a separate state, reachable from the initial state, for each letter that might begin a keyword. For each of these, there must then be a state for

---

6 Keywords (reserved words) are not the same as predefined identifiers. Predefined identifers can be redefined to have a different meaning; keywords cannot. The scanner does not distinguish between predefined and other identifiers. It does distinguish between identifiers and keywords. In Pascal, keywords include `begin`, `div`, `record`, and `while`. Predefined identifiers include `integer`, `writeln`, `true`, and `ord`.

```
state := start
loop
    case state of
        start :
            erase text of current token
            case input_char of
            ' ', '\t', '\n', '\r' : no_op
            '[' : state := got_lbrac
            ']' : state := got_rbrac
            ',' : state := got_comma
            . . .
            '(' : state := saw_lparen
            '.' : state := saw_dot
            '<' : state := saw_lthan
            . . .
            'a'..'z', 'A'..'Z' :
                state := in_ident
            '0'..'9' : state := in_int
            . . .
            else error
        . . .
        saw_lparen: case input_char of
            '*' : state := in_comment
            else return lparen
        in_comment: case input_char of
            '*' : state := leaving_comment
            else no_op
        leaving_comment: case input_char of
            ')' : state := start
            else state := in_comment
        . . .
        saw_dot : case input_char of
            '.' : state := got_dotdot
            else return dot
        . . .
        saw_lthan : case input_char of
            '=' : state := got_le
            else return lt
        . . .
```

Figure 2.6 Outline of a Pascal scanner written as an explicit finite automaton, in the form of nested case **statements in a loop** *(continued).*

```
in_ident : case input_char of
    'a'..'z', 'A'..'Z', '0'..'9', '_' : no_op
    else
        look up accumulated token in keyword table
        if found, return keyword
        else return identifier
...
in_int : case input_char of
    '0'..'9' : no_op
    '.' :
        peek at character beyond input_char;
            if '0'..'9', state := saw_real_dot
            else
                unread peeked-at character
                return intconst
    'a'..'z', 'A'..'Z', '_' : error
    else return intconst
...
saw_real_dot : ...

...
got_lbrac : return lbrac
got_rbrac : return rbrac
got_comma : return comma
got_dotdot : return dotdot
got_le : return le
...
append input_char to text of current token
read new input_char
```

Figure 2.6 (continued)

---

each possible second character of a keyword (e.g., to distinguish between file, for, and from). It is a nuisance (and a likely source of errors) to enumerate these states by hand. Likewise, while it is easy to write a regular expression that represents a keyword (b e g i n | e n d | w h i l e | ...), it is not at all easy to write an expression that represents a (nonkeyword) identifier (Exercise 2.5). Most scanners, both hand-written and automatically generated, therefore treat keywords as "exceptions" to the rule for identifiers. Before returning an identifier to the parser, the scanner looks it up in a hash table or trie to make sure it isn't really a keyword, as shown.

Whenever one legitimate token is a prefix of another, the "longest possible token" rule says that we should continue scanning. If some of the intermediate strings are not valid tokens, however, we can't tell whether a longer token is possible without looking more than one character ahead. This problem arises in Pascal in only one case, sometimes known as the "dot-dot problem." If the scanner has seen a 3 and has a dot coming up in the input, it needs to peek at the character beyond the dot in order to distinguish between 3.14 (a single token designating a real number), 3..5 (three tokens designating a range), and 3.foo (three tokens that the scanner should accept, even though the parser will object to seeing them in that order).

In messier languages, a scanner may need to look an arbitrary distance ahead. In Fortran IV, for example, DO 5 I = 1,25 is the header of a loop (it executes the statements up to the one labeled 5 for values of I from 1 to 25), while DO 5 I = 1.25 is an assignment statement that places the value 1.25 into the variable DO5I. Spaces are ignored in (pre-'90) Fortran input, even in the middle of variable names. Moreover, variables need not be declared, and the terminator for a DO loop is simply a label, which the parser can ignore. After seeing DO, the scanner cannot tell whether the 5 is part of the current token until it reaches the comma or dot. It has been widely (but apparently incorrectly) claimed that NASA's Mariner 1 space probe was lost due to accidental replacement of a comma with a dot in a case similar to this one in flight control software.[7] Dialects of Fortran starting with Fortran 77 allow (in fact encourage) the use of alternative syntax for loop headers, in which an extra comma makes misinterpretation less likely: DO 5,I = 1,25.

In Pascal, the dot-dot problem can be handled as a special case, as shown in Figure 2.6. In languages requiring larger amounts of look-ahead, the scanner can take a more general approach. In any case of ambiguity, it assumes that a longer token will be possible, but remembers that a shorter token could have been recognized at some point in the past. It also buffers all characters read beyond the end of the shorter token. If the optimistic assumption leads the scanner into an error state, it "unreads" the buffered characters so that they will be seen again later, and returns the shorter token. Unfortunately, the lexical structure of Fortran is so complex that even this more general technique may not suffice. Some of the problems, and a possible solution, are discussed in an article by Dyadkin [Dya95].

Figure 2.6 uses control flow—a loop and nested case statements—to represent a finite automaton. An alternative approach represents the automaton as a data structure: a two-dimensional table. A driver program uses the current state and input character to index into the table (see Figure 2.7). Each entry in the table specifies whether to move to a new state (and if so, which one), return a token (and if so, which one), or announce an error.

---

7 In actuality, the faulty software for Mariner 1 appears to have stemmed from a missing "bar" punctuation mark (indicating an average) in hand-written notes from which the software was derived [Cer89, pp. 202–203]. The Fortran DO loop error does appear to have occurred in at least one piece of NASA software, but no serious harm resulted [Web89].

```
state = 1..number_of_states
action_rec = record
      action : (move, recognize, error)
      new_state : state
      token_found : token

scan_tab : array [char, state] of action_rec
keyword_tab : set of record
      k_image : string
      k_token : token
—— these two tables are created by a scanner generator tool

tok : token
image : string
cur_state : state
cur_char : char

cur_state := start_state
image := null
repeat
      loop
          read cur_char
          case scan_tab[cur_char, cur_state].action
              move:
                    cur_state := scan_tab[cur_char, cur_state].new_state
              recognize:
                    tok := scan_tab[cur_char, cur_state].token_found
                    exit inner loop
              error:
                    —— print error message and recover; probably start over
          append cur_char to image
      —— end inner loop
until tok not in [white_space, comment]
look image up in keyword_tab and replace tok with appropriate keyword if found
return (tok, image)
```

Figure 2.7 Outline of the driver for a table-driven scanner.

As a general rule, hand-written scanners tend to use nested case statements, while most (but not all [BC93]) automatically generated scanners use tables. Tables are hard to create by hand, but easier than code to create from within a program. Unix's `lex`/`flex` tool produces C language output containing tables and a customized driver. Some other scanner generators produce tables for use with a hand-written driver, which can be written in any language.

As in a hand-written scanner, the table-driven code of Figure 2.7 looks tokens up in a table of keywords immediately before returning. Unlike the hand-written scanner, the table-driven code requires a special mechanism to cope with comments and with "white space"—spaces, tabs, and newlines. These character sequences are not meaningful to the parser, and would in fact be very difficult to represent in a grammar (Exercise 2.14). To avoid returning them, the scanner driver repeats its main loop until it finds a "useful" token.

Lexical Errors

The code in Figure 2.7 deals explicitly with errors in scanning: *lexical errors*. In some cases the next character of input may be neither an acceptable continuation of the current token nor the start of another token. In such cases the scanner must print an error message and perform some sort of recovery so that compilation can continue, if only to look for additional errors. Fortunately, lexical errors are relatively rare—most character sequences do correspond to token sequences—and relatively easy to handle. The most common approach is simply to (1) throw away the current, invalid token, (2) skip forward until a character is found that can legitimately begin a new token, (3) restart the scanning algorithm, and (4) count on the error-recovery mechanism of the parser to cope with any cases in which the resulting sequence of tokens is not syntactically valid.

Of course the need for error recovery is not unique to table-driven scanners; any scanner must cope with errors. We did not show the code to do so in the ad hoc scanner at the beginning of this section, nor in Figure 2.6, but it would have to be there in practice. The code in Figure 2.7 also shows that the scanner must return both the kind of token found and its character-string image (spelling); again this requirement applies to all types of scanners. For some tokens the character-string image is redundant: all semicolons look the same, after all, as do all `while` keywords. For other tokens, however (e.g., identifiers, character strings, and numeric constants), the image is needed for semantic analysis. It is also useful for error messages: "undeclared identifier" is not as nice as "`foo` has not been declared."

Significant Comments

Many language implementations provide for certain *significant comments*, or *pragmas*. These are generally comments in the sense that they do not affect the meaning (semantics) of the program, but they do affect the compilation process. Pragmas are usually handled by the scanner because, like comments, they can occur anywhere in the source program and would therefore be a nuisance if passed on to the parser. Ada is unusual in that its pragmas are an official part of the language. They may appear only in specific places in the grammar, and are therefore best handled by the parser or semantic analysis phases of compilation. Some pragmas instruct the compiler to alter its behavior in specific ways:

- Turn source listing on or off.

- Turn various kinds of run-time checks (e.g., pointer or subscript checking) on or off.

- Turn certain code improvements on or off (e.g., on in inner loops to improve performance; off otherwise to improve compilation speed).

- Turn performance profiling on or off.

Other pragmas provide the compiler with hints about the source program that may allow it to do a better job:

- Variable x is very heavily used (it may be a good idea to keep it in a register).

- Subroutine F is a pure function: its only effect on the rest of the program is the value it returns.

- Subroutine S is not (indirectly) recursive (its storage may be statically allocated).

- Variable names x and y are never aliases for the same location.

- 32 bits of precision (instead of 64) suffice for floating-point variable x.

2.2.2 Top-Down and Bottom-Up Parsing

As noted above, a context-free grammar (CFG) is a *generator* for a CF language. A parser is a language *recognizer*. It can be shown that for any CFG we can create a parser that runs in $O(n^3)$ time, where n is the length of the input program.[8] There are two well-known parsing algorithms that achieve this bound: Earley's algorithm [Ear70], and the Cocke-Younger-Kasami (CYK) algorithm [Kas65, You67]. Cubic time is much too slow for parsing sizable programs, but fortunately not all grammars take that long. There are large classes of grammars for which we can build parsers that run in linear time. The two most important of these classes are called LL and LR.

LL stands for "Left-to-right, Left-most derivation." LR stands for "Left-to-right, Right-most derivation." In both classes the input is read left-to-right. An LL parser discovers a left-most derivation; an LR parser discovers a right-most derivation. We will cover LL parsers first. They are generally considered to be simpler and easier to understand. They can be written by hand or generated automatically from an appropriate grammar by a parser-generating tool. The class of LR grammars is larger, and some people find the structure of the grammars more intuitive, especially in the part of the grammar that deals with arithmetic expressions. LR parsers are almost always constructed by a parser-generating

---

8 In general, an algorithm is said to run in time $O(f(n))$, where n is the length of the input, if its running time $t(n)$ is proportional to $f(n)$ in the worst case. More precisely, we say $t(n) = O(f(n)) \iff \exists c, m[n > m \longrightarrow t(n) < cf(n)]$.

tool. Both classes of parsers are used in production compilers, though LR parsers are more common.

LL parsers are also called "top-down," or "predictive" parsers. They construct a parse tree from the root down, predicting at each step which production will be used to expand the current node, based on the next available token of input. LR parsers are also called "bottom-up" parsers. They construct a parse tree from the leaves up, recognizing when a collection of leaves or other nodes can be joined together as the children of a single parent. We can illustrate the difference between top-down and bottom-up parsing by means of a simple example. Consider the following grammar for a comma-separated list of identifiers, terminated by a semicolon:

id_list → id *id_list_tail*

id_list_tail → , id *id_list_tail*

id_list_tail → ;

These are the productions that would normally be used for an identifier list in a top-down parser. They can also be parsed bottom-up (most top-down grammars can be). In practice they would not be used in a bottom-up parser, for reasons that will become clear in a moment, but the ability to handle them either way makes them good for this example.

Progressive stages in the top-down and bottom-up construction of a parse tree for the string A, B, C; appear in Figure 2.8. The top-down parser begins by predicting that the root of the tree (*id_list*) will be replaced by id *id_list_tail*. It then matches the id against a token obtained from the scanner. (If the scanner produced something different, the parser would announce a syntax error.) The parser then moves down into the first (in this case only) nonterminal child and predicts that *id_list_tail* will be replaced by , *id id_list_tail*. To make this prediction it needs to peek at the upcoming token (a comma), which allows it to choose between the two possible expansions for *id_list_tail*. It then matches the comma and the id and moves down into the next *id_list_tail*. In a similar, recursive fashion, the top-down parser works down the tree, left-to-right, predicting and expanding nodes and tracing out a left-most derivation of the fringe of the tree.

The bottom-up parser, by contrast, begins by noting that the left-most leaf of the tree is an id. The next leaf is a comma and the one after that is another id. The parser continues in this fashion, shifting new leaves from the scanner into a forest of partially completed parse tree fragments, until it realizes that some of those fragments constitute a complete right-hand side. In this grammar, that doesn't occur until the parser has seen the semicolon—the right-hand side of *id_list_tail* → ;. With this right-hand side in hand, the parser reduces the semicolon to an *id_list_tail*. It then reduces , id *id_list_tail* into another *id_list_tail*. After doing this one more time it is able to reduce id *id_list_tail* into the root of the parse tree, *id_list*.

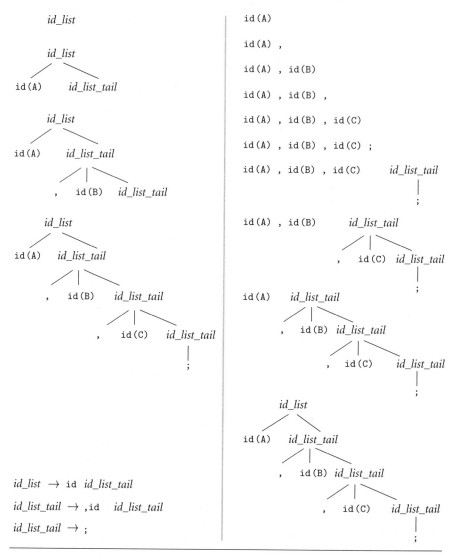

Figure 2.8 **Top-down (left) and bottom-up parsing (right).**

At no point does the bottom-up parser predict what it will see next. Rather, it shifts tokens into its forest until it recognizes a right-hand side, which it then reduces to a left-hand side. Because of this behavior, bottom-up parsers are sometimes called shift-reduce parsers. Looking up the figure, from bottom to top, we can see that the shift-reduce parser traces out a right-most (canonical) derivation, in reverse.

There are several important subclasses of LR parsers, including SLR, LALR, and "full LR." SLR and LALR are important for their ease of implementation, full LR for its generality. LL parsers can also be grouped into SLL and "full LL" subclasses. We will cover the differences among them only briefly here; for further information see any of the standard compiler-construction or parsing theory textbooks [ASU86, AU72, FL88, App97].

One commonly sees LL or LR (or whatever) written with a number in parentheses after it: LL(2) or LALR(1), for example. This number indicates how many tokens of look-ahead are required in order to parse. Almost all real compilers use just one token of look-ahead. In the remainder of this section we will look at LL(1) grammars and hand-written parsers in more detail. In Sections 2.2.5 and 2.2.6 we will consider automatically generated LL(1) and LR(1) (actually SLR(1)) parsers.

The problem with our example grammar, for the purposes of bottom-up parsing, is that it forces the compiler to shift all the tokens of an *id_list* into its forest before it can reduce any of them. In a very large program we might run out of space. Sometimes there is nothing that can be done to avoid a lot of shifting. In this case, however, we can use an alternative grammar that allows the parser to reduce prefixes of the *id_list* into nonterminals as it goes along:

id_list → *id_list_prefix* ;
id_list_prefix → *id_list_prefix* , id
           → id

This grammar cannot be parsed top-down, because when we see an id on the input and we're expecting an *id_list_prefix*, we have no way to tell which of the two possible productions we should predict (more on this dilemma in Section 2.2.5). As shown in Figure 2.9, however, the grammar works well bottom-up.

2.2.3 Recursive Descent

To illustrate top-down (predictive) parsing, let us consider the grammar for a simple "calculator" language, shown in Figure 2.10. The calculator allows values to be read into (numeric) variables, which may then be used in expressions. Expressions in turn can be written to the output. Control flow is strictly linear. The end-marker ($$) pseudo-token is produced by the scanner at the end of the input. This token allows the parser to terminate cleanly once it has seen the entire program. As in regular expressions, we use the symbol ϵ to denote the empty string. A production with ϵ on the right-hand side is sometimes called an *epsilon production*.

It may be helpful to compare the *expr* portion of Figure 2.10 to the expression grammar on page 38. Most people find that previous, LR grammar to be significantly more intuitive. It suffers, however, from a problem similar to that of the *id_list* grammar at the end of the previous section: if we see an identifier on the input when expecting an *expression*, we have no way to tell which of the two

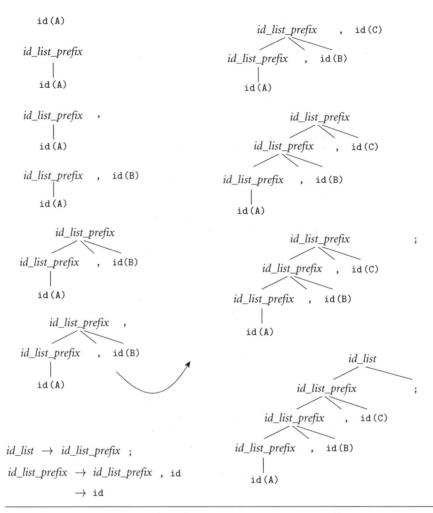

Figure 2.9 Bottom-up parse of A, B, C; **using a grammar that allows lists to be collapsed incrementally.**

possible productions to predict. The grammar of Figure 2.10 avoids this problem by merging the common prefixes of right-hand sides into a single production, and by using new symbols (*term_tail* and *factor_tail*) to generate additional operators and operands as required. The transformation has the unfortunate side effect of placing the operands of a given operator in separate right-hand sides. In effect, we have sacrificed grammatical elegance in order to be able to parse predictively.

So how do we parse a string with our calculator grammar? We saw the basic idea in Figure 2.8. We start at the top of the tree and predict needed productions on the basis of the current left-most nonterminal in the tree and the current input *program* → *stmt_list* $$

stmt_list → *stmt stmt_list* | ϵ

stmt → id := *expr* | read id | write *expr*

expr → *term term_tail*

term_tail → *add_op term term_tail* | ϵ

term → *factor factor_tail*

factor_tail → *mult_op factor factor_tail* | ϵ

factor → (*expr*) | id | literal

add_op → + | -

mult_op → * | /

Figure 2.10 LL(1) grammar for a simple calculator language.

token. We can formalize this process in one of two ways. The first, described in the remainder of this section, is to build a *recursive descent parser* by hand. The second, described in Section 2.2.5, is to use a parser generator to build an *LL parse table* which is then read by a driver program. These two options are reminiscent of the nested case statements and table-driven approaches to building a scanner that we saw in Section 2.2.1. Recursive descent parsers are most often used when the language to be parsed is relatively simple, or when a parser-generator tool is not available.

A recursive descent parser has a subroutine for every nonterminal in the grammar. It also has a mechanism to inspect the next token available from the scanner and a routine (call it match) to consume this token and in the process verify that it is the one that was expected (as specified by an argument). If the token is not the one expected, match announces a syntax error and triggers a recovery mechanism (to be discussed in Section 2.2.4). The outline of a recursive descent parser for our calculator language appears in Figure 2.11.

Suppose now that we are to parse a simple program to read two numbers and print their sum and average:

```
read A
read B
sum := A + B
write sum
write sum / 2
```

The parse tree for this program appears in Figure 2.12. The parser begins by calling the subroutine program. After noting that the initial token is a **read**, program calls stmt_list and then attempts to match the end-of-file pseudo-token. (In the parse tree, the root, *program*, has two children, *stmt_list* and $$.) Procedure stmt_list again notes that the upcoming token is a **read**. This observation allows it to determine that the current node (*stmt_list*) generates *stmt stmt_list* (rather than ϵ). It therefore calls stmt and stmt_list before returning. Contin-

```
procedure match (expected)
    if input_token = expected
        consume input_token
    else error

—— this is the start routine:
procedure program
    case input_token of
        id, read, write, $$ :
            stmt_list
            match ($$)
        otherwise error

procedure stmt_list
    case input_token of
        id, read, write : stmt; stmt_list
        $$ : skip        —— epsilon production
        otherwise error

procedure stmt
    case input_token of
        id : match (id); match (:=); expr
        read : match (read); match (id)
        write : match (write); expr
        otherwise error

procedure expr
    case input_token of
        id, literal, ( : term; term_tail
        otherwise error

procedure term_tail
    case input_token of
        +, − : add_op; term; term_tail
        ), id, read, write, $$ :
            skip        —— epsilon production
        otherwise error

procedure term
    case input_token of
        id, literal, ( : factor; factor_tail
        otherwise error
```

Figure 2.11 Outline of a recursive descent parser for the calculator language. Execution begins in procedure program. The recursive calls trace out a traversal of the parse tree. Not shown is code to save this tree (or some similar structure) for use by later phases of the compiler *(continued)*.

```
procedure factor_tail
    case input_token of
        *, / : mult_op; factor; factor_tail
        +, -, ), id, read, write, $$ :
            skip        -- epsilon production
        otherwise error

procedure factor
    case input_token of
        id : match (id)
        literal : match (literal)
        ( : match ((); expr; match ())
        otherwise error

procedure add_op
    case input_token of
        + : match (+)
        - : match (-)
        otherwise error

procedure mult_op
    case input_token of
        * : match (*)
        / : match (/)
        otherwise error
```

Figure 2.11 *(continued)*

uing in this fashion, the execution path of the parser traces out a left-to-right depth-first traversal of the parse tree. Because the *stmt_list* nonterminal appears in the right-hand side of a *stmt_list* production, the stmt_list subroutine must call itself—hence the name of the parsing technique.

Without additional code (not shown in Figure 2.12), the parser merely verifies that the program is syntactically correct (i.e., that none of the otherwise error clauses in the **case** statements are executed and that match always sees what it expects to see). To be of use to the rest of the compiler—which must produce an equivalent target program in some other language—the parser must save the parse tree or some other representation of program fragments as an explicit data structure. To save the parse tree itself, we can allocate and link together records to represent the children of a node immediately before executing the recursive subroutines and match invocations that represent those children. We shall need to pass each recursive routine an argument that points to the record that is to be expanded (i.e., whose children are to be discovered). Procedure match will also need to save information about certain tokens (e.g., character-string

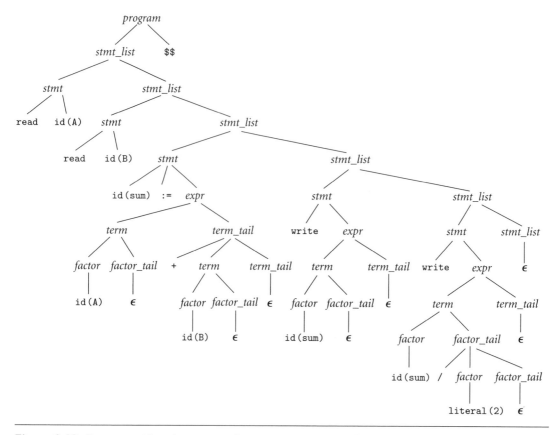

Figure 2.12 Parse tree for the sum-and-average program using the grammar of Figure 2.10.

representations of identifiers and literals) in the leaves of the tree.

As we saw in Chapter 1, the parse tree contains a great deal of irrelevant detail that need not be saved for the rest of the compiler. It is therefore rare for a parser to construct a full parse tree explicitly. More often it produces an abstract syntax tree or some other more terse representation. In a recursive descent compiler, a syntax tree can be created by allocating and linking together records in only a subset of the recursive calls.

Perhaps the trickiest part of writing a recursive descent parser is figuring out which tokens should label the arms of the case statements. Each arm represents one production: one possible expansion of the symbol for which the subroutine was named. The tokens that label a given arm are those that *predict* the production. A token X may predict a production for either of two reasons: (1) the right-hand side of the production, when recursively expanded, may yield a string beginning with X, or (2) the right-hand side may yield nothing (i.e., it is ϵ, or a string of nonterminals that may recursively yield ϵ), and X may begin the yield of what comes *next*. In Section 2.2.5 we will formalize the notion of prediction using sets called FIRST and FOLLOW. Informally, FIRST(*foo*) is the set of all tokens that could be the start of a *foo*, plus ϵ if *foo* $\Rightarrow^*$ ϵ, while FOLLOW(*foo*) is the set of all tokens that could come after a *foo* in some valid program, plus ϵ if *foo* can be the final token in the program.

2.2.4* Syntax Errors

Suppose we are parsing a Pascal program and see the following code fragment in a context where a statement is expected:

```
A := (B,C + D);
```

We will detect a syntax error immediately after the B, when the comma appears from the scanner. At this point the simplest thing to do is just to print an error message and halt. This naive approach is generally not acceptable, however: it would mean that every run of the compiler reveals no more than one syntax error. Since most programs, at least at first, contain numerous such errors, we really need to find as many as possible now (we'd also like to continue looking for semantic errors). To do so, we must modify the state of the parser and/or the input stream so that the upcoming token(s) are acceptable. We shall probably want to turn off code generation, disabling the back end of the compiler: since the input is not a valid program, the code will not be of use, and there's no point in spending time creating it.

Panic Mode

In general, the term *syntax error recovery* is applied to any technique that allows the compiler to continue looking for errors later in the program. One simple approach is known as *panic mode*. It defines a small set of "safe symbols" that delimit clean points in the input. When an error occurs, a panic mode recovery algorithm deletes input tokens until it finds a safe symbol, then backs the parser out to a context in which that symbol might appear. In the earlier example, a recursive descent parser with panic mode recovery might delete input tokens until it finds the semicolon, return from all subroutines called from within stmt, and restart the body of stmt itself.

Unfortunately, panic mode tends to be a bit drastic. By limiting itself to a static set of "safe" symbols at which to resume parsing, it admits the possibility of deleting a significant amount of input while looking for such a symbol. Worse, if some of the deleted tokens are "starter" symbols that begin large-scale constructs in the language (e.g., begin, procedure, while), we shall almost surely see spurious cascading errors when we reach the end of the construct. Consider the following fragment of code in Modula-2:

```
IF a b THEN x;
ELSE y;
END;
```

When it discovers the error at b in the first line, a panic mode recovery algorithm is likely to skip forward to the semicolon, thereby missing the THEN. When the parser finds the ELSE on line 2 it will produce a spurious error message. When it finds the END on line 3 it will think it has reached the end of the enclosing structure (e.g., the whole subroutine), and will probably generate additional cascading errors on subsequent lines. Panic mode tends to work acceptably only in relatively "unstructured" languages, such as Basic and Fortran, which don't have many "starter" symbols.

Phrase-Level Recovery

We can improve the quality of recovery by employing different sets of "safe" symbols in different contexts. Parsers that incorporate this improvement are said to implement *phrase-level recovery*. When it discovers an error in an expression, for example, a phrase-level recovery algorithm can delete input tokens until it reaches something that is likely to follow an expression. This more local recovery is better than always backing out to the end of the current statement, because it gives us the opportunity to examine the parts of the statement that follow the erroneous expression.

Niklaus Wirth, the inventor of Pascal, published an elegant implementation of phrase-level recovery for recursive descent parsers in 1976 [Wir76, Sec. 5.9]. The simplest version of his algorithm depends on the FIRST and FOLLOW sets defined at the end of Section 2.2.3. If the parsing routine for nonterminal foo discovers an error at the beginning of its code, it deletes incoming tokens until it finds a member of FIRST(*foo*), in which case it proceeds, or a member of FOLLOW(*foo*), in which case it returns:

```
procedure foo
    if (input_token ∉ FIRST(foo)) and (ε ∉ FIRST(foo))
        announce_error              −− print message for the user
        repeat
            delete_token
        until input_token ∈ (FIRST(foo) ∪ FOLLOW(foo) ∪ {$$})
    case input_token of
        . . . : . . .
        . . . : . . .                −− valid starting tokens
        . . . : . . .
        otherwise return             −− error or foo → ε
```

To complete the algorithm, the match routine must be altered so that it will insert an expected token when something else appears:

```
procedure match (expected)
    if input_token = expected
        consume input_token
    else
        announce_error
```

Finally, to simplify the code, the common prefix of the various nonterminal subroutines can be moved into an error-checking subroutine:

```
procedure check_for_error (first_set, follow_set)
    if (input_token ∉ first_set) and (ε ∉ first_set)
        announce_error
        repeat
            delete_token
        until input_token ∈ first_set ∪ follow_set ∪ {$$}
```

Context-Sensitive Look-Ahead

Though simple, the recovery algorithm just described has an unfortunate tendency, when *foo* → *ε*, to predict one or more epsilon productions when it should really announce an error right away. This weakness is known as the *immediate error detection* problem. It stems from the fact that FOLLOW(*foo*) is context-independent: it contains all tokens that may follow *foo* somewhere in some valid program, but not necessarily in the current context in the current program.

As an example, consider the following incorrect code in our calculator language:

```
Y := (A * X X*X) + (B * X*X) + (C * X)
```

To a human being, it is pretty clear that the programmer forgot a * in the x^3 term of a polynomial. The recovery algorithm isn't so smart. It will see an identifier (X) coming up on the input when it is inside the following routines:

```
program
stmt_list
stmt
expr
term
factor
expr
term
factor_tail
factor_tail
```

Since an `id` can follow an *expr* in some programs (e.g., A := B   C := D), the two factor_tails, the term, and the inner expr will all return uneventfully. At that point, however, factor will call match, expecting to see a right parenthesis. Seeing an `id` instead, match will announce an error and insert the parenthesis. Afterwards there will be a host of cascading errors, as the input is transformed into

```
Y := (A * X)
X := X
B := X*X
C := X
```

To avoid inappropriate epsilon predictions, Wirth introduces the notion of context-specific FOLLOW sets, passed into each nonterminal subroutine as an explicit parameter. In our example, we would pass `id` as part of the FOLLOW set for the initial, outer expr, which is called as part of the production *stmt* → id := *expr*, but *not* into the second, inner expr, which is called as part of the production *factor* → (*expr*). The nested calls to term and factor_tail will end up being called with a FOLLOW set whose only member is a right parenthesis. When the inner call to factor_tail discovers that `id` is not in FIRST(*factor_tail*), it will delete tokens up to the right parenthesis before returning. The net result is a single error message, and a transformation of the input into

```
Y := (A * X) + (B * X*X) + (C * X)
```

That's still not the "right" interpretation, but it's a lot better than it was.

The final version of Wirth's phrase-level recovery employs one additional heuristic: to avoid cascading errors it refrains from deleting members of a statically defined set of "starter" symbols (e.g., `begin`, `procedure`, `(` etc.). These are the symbols that tend to require matching tokens later in the program. If we see a starter symbol while deleting input, we give up on the attempt to delete the rest of the erroneous construct. We simply return, even though we know that the starter symbol will not be acceptable to the calling routine. With context-specific FOLLOW sets and starter symbols, phrase-level recovery looks like this:

```
procedure check_for_error (first_set, follow_set)
    if input_token ∉ first_set
        announce_error
        repeat
            delete_token
        until input_token ∈ first_set ∪ follow_set ∪ starter_set ∪ {$$}

procedure expr (follow_set)
    check_for_error (FIRST(expr), follow_set)
    case input_token of
        . . . : . . .
        . . . : . . .                    valid starting tokens
        . . . : . . .
        otherwise return
```

Exception-Based Recovery

An attractive alternative to Wirth's technique relies on the exception-handling mechanisms available in many modern languages, including Ada, Modula-3, C++, Java, and ML. Rather than implement recovery for every nonterminal in the language (a somewhat tedious task), the exception-based approach identifies a small set of contexts to which we back out in the event of an error. For example, we might choose to back out to the nearest expression or statement. In the limit, if we choose a single place to "back out to," we have an implementation of panic mode recovery.

We will consider this style of error recovery in more detail when we cover the subject of exception handling in Section 8.5.3. The basic idea is to attach an exception handler (a special syntactic construct) to the blocks of code in which we want to implement recovery. Then when we detect an error (possibly nested many procedure calls deep), we *raise* a syntax error exception ("`raise`" is a built-in command in languages with exceptions). The language implementation then unwinds the stack to the most recent context in which we have an exception handler, which it executes in place of the remainder of the block to which the handler is attached. For phrase-level (or panic mode) recovery, the handler can delete input tokens until it sees one with which it can recommence parsing. If it sees a starter symbol that it doesn't want to delete, it can *reraise* the exception, popping us out to the next handler back on the chain of procedure calls.

Error Productions

As a general rule, it is desirable for an error recovery technique to be as language-independent as possible. Even in a recursive descent parser, which is hand-written for a particular language, it is nice to be able to encapsulate error recovery in the check_for_error and match subroutines. Sometimes, however, one can obtain much better repairs by being highly language specific. Most languages have a few unintuitive rules that programmers tend to violate in predictable ways. In Pascal, for example, semicolons are used to separate statements, but many programmers think of them as *terminating* statements instead. Most of the time the difference is unimportant, since a statement is allowed to be empty. In the following, for example,

```
begin
    x := (-b + sqrt(b*b -4*a*c)) / (2*a);
    writeln (x);
end;
```

the compiler parses the `begin...end` block as a sequence of three statements, the third of which is empty. In the following, however,

```
if d <> 0 then
    a := n/d;
else
    a := n;
end;
```

the compiler must complain, since the `then` part of an `if...then...else` construct must consist of a single statement in Pascal. A Pascal semicolon is never allowed immediately before an `else`, but programmers put them there all the time. Rather than try to tune a general recovery or repair algorithm to deal correctly with this problem, most Pascal compiler writers modify the grammar: they include an extra production that allows the semicolon, but causes the semantic analyzer to print a warning message, telling the user that the semicolon shouldn't be there. Similar error productions are used in C compilers to cope with "anachronisms" that have crept into the language as it evolved. Syntax that was valid only in early versions of C is still accepted by the parser, but evokes a warning message.

2.2.5 Table-Driven Top-Down Parsing

Table-driven LL parsing mirrors the structure of a recursive descent parser. Instead of using its procedure call chain to trace out a tree traversal, the parser maintains a stack containing a list of the symbols it expects to see in the future. These are precisely the nodes of the parse tree that have not yet been visited, but are part of the right-hand side of some production that has been predicted.

The driver iterates around a loop in which it performs the following actions. If there is a terminal at top-of-stack, the parser attempts to match the terminal against an incoming token from the scanner. If the token does not match, the parser announces a syntax error and initiates an error-recovery procedure in order to get itself back into a state in which it can continue looking for further errors. (We will return to error recovery below.) If there is a nonterminal at top-of-stack, the parser uses that nonterminal together with the next available input token to index into a two-dimensional table that tells it which production to predict (or whether to announce a syntax error and initiate recovery).

Initially, the parse stack contains the start symbol of the grammar (in our case, *program*). When it predicts a production, the parser pops the left-hand-side symbol off the stack and pushes the right-hand-side symbols in reverse order, so the first symbol of the right-hand side is at the top. It also pops a terminal off the stack whenever it matches it against a token from the scanner. Figure 2.13 shows a trace over time of the contents of the stack of an LL(1) parser as it reads the sum-and-average program.

Predict Sets

As we noted at the end of Section 2.2.3, predict sets are defined in terms of simpler sets called FIRST and FOLLOW, where FIRST(*foo*) is the set of all tokens that could be the start of a *foo*, plus ϵ if *foo* $\Rightarrow^*$ ϵ, and FOLLOW(*foo*) is the set of all tokens that could come after a *foo* in some valid program, plus ϵ if *foo* can be the final token in the program. If we extend the domain of FIRST in the obvious

Parse stack	Input stream	Comment
program	read A read B ...	initial stack contents
stmt_list $$	read A read B ...	predict program → stmt_list $$
stmt stmt_list $$	read A read B ...	predict stmt_list → stmt stmt_list
read id stmt_list $$	read A read B ...	predict stmt → read id
id stmt_list $$	A read B ...	match read
stmt_list $$	read B sum := ...	match id
stmt stmt_list $$	read B sum := ...	predict stmt_list → stmt stmt_list
read id stmt_list $$	read B sum := ...	predict stmt → read id
id stmt_list $$	B sum := ...	match read
stmt_list $$	sum := A + B ...	match id
stmt stmt_list $$	sum := A + B ...	predict stmt_list → stmt stmt_list
id := expr stmt_list $$	sum := A + B ...	predict stmt → id := expr
:= expr stmt_list $$	:= A + B ...	match id
expr stmt_list $$	A + B ...	match :=
term term_tail stmt_list $$	A + B ...	predict expr → term term_tail
factor factor_tail term_tail stmt_list $$	A + B ...	predict term → factor factor_tail
id factor_tail term_tail stmt_list $$	A + B ...	predict factor → id
factor_tail term_tail stmt_list $$	+ B write sum ...	match id
term_tail stmt_list $$	+ B write sum ...	predict factor_tail → ε
add_op term term_tail stmt_list $$	+ B write sum ...	predict term_tail → add_op term term_tail
+ term term_tail stmt_list $$	+ B write sum ...	predict add_op → +
term term_tail stmt_list $$	B write sum ...	match +
factor factor_tail term_tail stmt_list $$	B write sum ...	predict term → factor factor_tail
id factor_tail term_tail stmt_list $$	B write sum ...	predict factor → id
factor_tail term_tail stmt_list $$	write sum ...	match id
term_tail stmt_list $$	write sum write ...	predict factor_tail → ε
stmt_list $$	write sum write ...	predict term_tail → ε
stmt stmt_list $$	write sum write ...	predict stmt_list → stmt stmt_list
write expr stmt_list $$	write sum write ...	predict stmt → write expr
expr stmt_list $$	sum write sum / 2	match write
term term_tail stmt_list $$	sum write sum / 2	predict expr → term term_tail
factor factor_tail term_tail stmt_list $$	sum write sum / 2	predict term → factor factor_tail
id factor_tail term_tail stmt_list $$	sum write sum / 2	predict factor → id
factor_tail term_tail stmt_list $$	sum write sum / 2	match id
term_tail stmt_list $$	write sum / 2	predict factor_tail → ε
stmt_list $$	write sum / 2	predict term_tail → ε
stmt stmt_list $$	write sum / 2	predict stmt_list → stmt stmt_list
write expr stmt_list $$	write sum / 2	predict stmt → write expr
expr stmt_list $$	sum / 2	match write
term term_tail stmt_list $$	sum / 2	predict expr → term term_tail
factor factor_tail term_tail stmt_list $$	sum / 2	predict term → factor factor_tail
id factor_tail term_tail stmt_list $$	sum / 2	predict factor → id
factor_tail term_tail stmt_list $$	/ 2	match id
mult_op factor factor_tail term_tail stmt_list $$	/ 2	predict factor_tail → mult_op factor factor_tail
/ factor factor_tail term_tail stmt_list $$	/ 2	predict mult_op → /
factor factor_tail term_tail stmt_list $$	2	match /
literal factor_tail term_tail stmt_list $$	2	predict factor → literal
factor_tail term_tail stmt_list $$		match literal
term_tail stmt_list $$		predict factor_tail → ε
stmt_list $$		predict term_tail → ε
$$		predict stmt_list → ε

Figure 2.13 Trace of a table-driven LL(1) parse of the sum-and-average program.

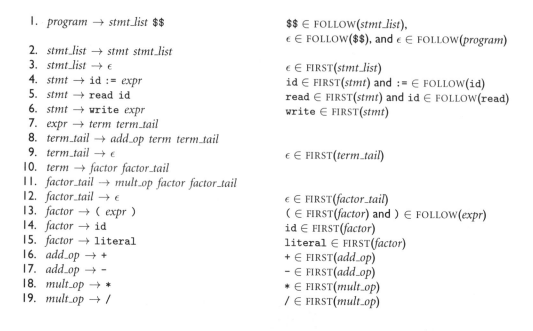

1. *program* → *stmt_list* $$ $$ ∈ FOLLOW(*stmt_list*),

     ε ∈ FOLLOW($$), and ε ∈ FOLLOW(*program*)

2. *stmt_list* → *stmt stmt_list*
3. *stmt_list* → ε   ε ∈ FIRST(*stmt_list*)
4. *stmt* → id := *expr*   id ∈ FIRST(*stmt*) and := ∈ FOLLOW(id)
5. *stmt* → read id   read ∈ FIRST(*stmt*) and id ∈ FOLLOW(read)
6. *stmt* → write *expr*   write ∈ FIRST(*stmt*)
7. *expr* → *term term_tail*
8. *term_tail* → *add_op term term_tail*
9. *term_tail* → ε   ε ∈ FIRST(*term_tail*)
10. *term* → *factor factor_tail*
11. *factor_tail* → *mult_op factor factor_tail*
12. *factor_tail* → ε   ε ∈ FIRST(*factor_tail*)
13. *factor* → (*expr*)   (∈ FIRST(*factor*) and) ∈ FOLLOW(*expr*)
14. *factor* → id   id ∈ FIRST(*factor*)
15. *factor* → literal   literal ∈ FIRST(*factor*)
16. *add_op* → +   + ∈ FIRST(*add_op*)
17. *add_op* → -   - ∈ FIRST(*add_op*)
18. *mult_op* → *   * ∈ FIRST(*mult_op*)
19. *mult_op* → /   / ∈ FIRST(*mult_op*)

Figure 2.14 "Obvious" facts about the LL(1) calculator grammar.

way to include *strings* of symbols, we then say that the predict set of a production $A → β$ is FIRST($β$) (except for ε), plus FOLLOW($β$) if $β ⇒^* ε$.

We can illustrate the algorithm to construct these sets using our calculator grammar (Figure 2.10). We begin with "obvious" facts about the grammar and build on them inductively. If we recast the grammar in plain BNF (no EBNF '|' constructs), then it has 19 productions. The "obvious" facts arise from adjacent pairs of symbols in right-hand sides. In the first production, we can see that $$ ∈ FOLLOW(*stmt_list*). In the fourth (*stmt* → id := *expr*), id ∈ FIRST(*stmt*) and := ∈ FOLLOW(id). In the fifth and sixth productions (*stmt* → read id | write *expr*), {read, write} ⊂ FIRST(*stmt*), and id ∈ FOLLOW(read). The complete set of "obvious" facts appears in Figure 2.14.

From the "obvious" facts we can deduce a larger set of facts during a second pass over the grammar. For example, in the second production (*stmt_list* → *stmt stmt_list*) we can deduce that {id, read, write} ⊂ FIRST(*stmt_list*), because we already know that {id, read, write} ⊂ FIRST(*stmt*), and a *stmt_list* can begin with a *stmt*. Similarly, in the first production, we can deduce that $$ ∈ FIRST(*program*), because we already know that ε ∈ FIRST(*stmt_list*).

In the eleventh production (*factor_tail* → *mult_op factor factor_tail*), we can deduce that {(, id, literal} ⊂ FOLLOW(*mult_op*), because we already know that {(, id, literal} ⊂ FIRST(*factor*), and *factor* follows *mult_op* in the right-hand side. In the seventh production (*expr* → *term term_tail*), we can deduce that) ∈ FOLLOW(*term_tail*), because we already know that) ∈ FOLLOW(*expr*), and a *term_tail* can be the last part of an *expr*. In this same production, we can also deduce that) ∈ FOLLOW(*term*), because the *term_tail* can generate ε (ε ∈ FIRST(*term_tail*)), allowing a *term* to be the last part of an *expr*.

There is more that we can learn from our second pass through the grammar, but the examples above cover all the different kinds of cases. To complete our calculation of PREDICT sets, we continue with additional passes over the grammar until we don't learn any more (i.e., we don't add anything to any of the FIRST and FOLLOW sets). We then construct the PREDICT sets. Stated a bit more formally,

$$\text{FIRST}(\alpha) \equiv \{a : \alpha \Rightarrow^* a\,\beta\} \cup (\text{ if } \alpha \Rightarrow^* \epsilon \text{ then } \{\epsilon\} \text{ else } \varnothing)$$

$$\text{FOLLOW}(A) \equiv \{a : S \Rightarrow^+ \alpha\,A\,a\,\beta\} \cup (\text{ if } S \Rightarrow^* \alpha\,A \text{ then } \{\epsilon\} \text{ else } \varnothing)$$

$$\text{PREDICT}(A \to \alpha) \equiv (\text{FIRST}(\alpha) \smallsetminus \{\epsilon\}) \cup \\ (\text{ if } \alpha \Rightarrow^* \epsilon \text{ then } \text{FOLLOW}(A) \text{ else } \varnothing)$$

Following conventional notation, we use uppercase Roman letters near the beginning of the alphabet to represent nonterminals, uppercase Roman letters near the end of the alphabet to represent arbitrary grammar symbols (terminals or nonterminals), lowercase Roman letters near the beginning of the alphabet to represent terminals (tokens), lowercase Roman letters near the end of the alphabet to represent token strings, and lowercase Greek letters to represent strings of arbitrary symbols.

The algorithm to compute FIRST, FOLLOW, and PREDICT sets appears in Figure 2.15. Note that FIRST sets for strings of length greater than one are calculated on demand; they are not stored explicitly. The algorithm is guaranteed to terminate (i.e., converge on a solution), because the sizes of the sets are bounded by the number of nonterminals in the grammar. The complete FIRST, FOLLOW, and PREDICT sets for symbols in our calculator language appear in Figure 2.16. The parse table appears in Figure 2.17.

If in the process of calculating PREDICT sets we find that some token belongs to the PREDICT set of more than one production with the same left-hand side, then the grammar is not LL(1), because we will not be able to choose which of the productions to employ when the left-hand side is at the top of the parse stack (or we are in the left-hand side's subroutine in a recursive descent parser) and we see the token coming up in the input. This sort of ambiguity is known as a *predict-predict conflict*; it can arise either because the same token can begin more than one right-hand side, or because it can begin one right-hand side and can also appear after the left-hand side in some valid program, and one possible right-hand side can generate ε. In the next section we will explore the sorts of grammatical idioms that cause a grammar not to be LL(1).

It is possible to extend the definitions of FIRST and FOLLOW sets to deal with k tokens of look-ahead, instead of only one. If we do this, however, we encounter a

First sets for all symbols:
    for all terminals a, FIRST(a) := $\{a\}$
    for all nonterminals X, FIRST(X) := $\varnothing$
    for all productions $X \rightarrow \epsilon$, add ϵ to FIRST(X)
    repeat
        <outer> for all productions $X \rightarrow Y_1\ Y_2\ \ldots Y_k$,
            <inner> for i in $1 \ldots k$
                add (FIRST(Y_i) $\setminus \{\epsilon\}$) to FIRST(X)
                if $\epsilon \notin$ FIRST(Y_i) (yet)
                    continue outer loop
            add ϵ to FIRST(X)
    until no further progress

First set subroutine for string $X_1\ X_2 \ldots X_n$, similar to the inner loop above:
    return_value := $\varnothing$
    for i in $1 \ldots n$
        add (FIRST(X_i) $\setminus \{\epsilon\}$) to return_value
        if $\epsilon \notin$ FIRST(X_i)
            return
    add ϵ to return_value

Follow sets for all symbols:
    FOLLOW($\$\$$) := $\{\epsilon\}$
    FOLLOW(S) := $\{\epsilon\}$, where S is the start symbol
    for all other symbols X, FOLLOW(X) := $\varnothing$
    repeat
        for all productions $A \rightarrow \alpha\ B\ \beta$,
            add (FIRST(β) $\setminus \{\epsilon\}$) to FOLLOW(B)
        for all productions $A \rightarrow \alpha\ B$
            or $A \rightarrow \alpha\ B\ \beta$, where $\epsilon \in$ FIRST(β),
            add FOLLOW(A) to FOLLOW(B)
    until no further progress

Predict sets for all productions:
    for all productions $A \rightarrow \alpha$
        PREDICT($A \rightarrow \alpha$) := (FIRST(α) $\setminus \{\epsilon\}$)
            $\cup$ (if $\alpha \Rightarrow^* \epsilon$ then FOLLOW(A) else $\varnothing$)

Figure 2.15 Algorithm to calculate FIRST, FOLLOW, **and** PREDICT **sets for an LL(1) grammar.**
We assume that the grammar contains an end-marker ($\$\$$), so that $\epsilon \notin$ FOLLOW(S).

FIRST

program {id, read, write, $$}
stmt_list {id, read, write, ϵ}
stmt {id, read, write}
expr {(, id, literal}
term_tail {+, -, ϵ}
term {(, id, literal}
factor_tail {*, /, ϵ}
factor {(, id, literal}
add_op {+, -}
mult_op {*, /}

Also note that FIRST(a) = {a} $\forall$ tokens a.

FOLLOW

id {+, -, *, /,), :=, id, read, write, $$}
literal {+, -, *, /,), id, read, write, $$}
read {id}
write {(, id, literal}
({(, id, literal}
) {+, -, *, /,), id, read, write, $$}
:= {(, id, literal}
+ {(, id, literal}
- {(, id, literal}
* {(, id, literal}
/ {(, id, literal}
$$ {ϵ}
program {ϵ}
stmt_list {$$}
stmt {id, read, write, $$}

expr {), id, read, write, $$}
term_tail {), id, read, write, $$}
term {+, -,), id, read, write, $$}
factor_tail {+, -,), id, read, write, $$}
factor {+, -, *, /,), id, read, write, $$}
add_op {(, id, literal}
mult_op {(, id, literal}

PREDICT

program $\rightarrow$ *stmt_list* $$ {id, read, write, $$}
stmt_list $\rightarrow$ *stmt stmt_list* {id, read, write}
stmt_list $\rightarrow$ ϵ {$$}
stmt $\rightarrow$ id := *expr* {id}
stmt $\rightarrow$ read id {read}
stmt $\rightarrow$ write *expr* {write}
expr $\rightarrow$ *term term_tail* {(, id, literal}
term_tail $\rightarrow$ *add_op term term_tail* {+, -}
term_tail $\rightarrow$ ϵ {), id, read, write, $$}
term $\rightarrow$ *factor factor_tail* {(, id, literal}
factor_tail $\rightarrow$ *mult_op factor factor_tail* {*, /}
factor_tail $\rightarrow$ ϵ {+, -,), id, read, write, $$}
factor $\rightarrow$ (*expr*) {(}
factor $\rightarrow$ id {id}
factor $\rightarrow$ literal {literal}
add_op $\rightarrow$ + {+}
add_op $\rightarrow$ - {-}
mult_op $\rightarrow$ * {*}
mult_op $\rightarrow$ / {/}

Figure 2.16 FIRST, FOLLOW, **and** PREDICT **sets for the calculator language.**

more serious version of the immediate error detection problem described in Section 2.2.4. There we saw that the use of context-independent FOLLOW sets could cause us to overlook a syntax error until after we had needlessly predicted one or more epsilon productions. Context-specific FOLLOW sets solved the problem, but did not change the set of *valid* programs that could be parsed with one token of look-ahead. If we define LL(k) to be the set of all grammars that can be parsed predictively using the top-of-stack symbol and k tokens of look-ahead, then it turns out that for $k > 1$ we must adopt a context-specific notion of FOLLOW sets in order to parse correctly. Our previous parsing algorithm—the one based on context-independent FOLLOW sets—is really SLL, rather than true LL. For $k = 1$, the two algorithms can parse the same set of grammars. For $k > 1$, LL is strictly more powerful.

Top-of-stack nonterminal	Current input token											
	id	literal	read	write	:=	(	)	+	–	*	/	$$
program	1	–	1	1	–	–	–	–	–	–	–	1
stmt_list	2	–	2	2	–	–	–	–	–	–	–	3
stmt	4	–	5	6	–	–	–	–	–	–	–	–
expr	7	7	–	–	–	7	–	–	–	–	–	–
term_tail	9	–	9	9	–	–	9	8	8	–	–	9
term	10	10	–	–	–	10	–	–	–	–	–	–
factor_tail	12	–	12	12	–	–	12	12	12	11	11	12
factor	14	15	–	–	–	13	–	–	–	–	–	–
add_op	–	–	–	–	–	–	–	16	17	–	–	–
mult_op	–	–	–	–	–	–	–	–	–	18	19	–

Figure 2.17 LL(1) parse table for the calculator language. Table entries indicate the production to predict (as numbered in Figure 2.14). A dash indicates an error. When the top-of-stack symbol is a terminal, the appropriate action is always to match it against an incoming token from the scanner.

Writing an LL(1) Grammar

When working with a top-down parser generator, one has to acquire a certain facility in writing and modifying LL(1) grammars. The two most common obstacles to "LL(1)-ness" are *left recursion* and *common prefixes*.

Left recursion occurs when the first symbol on the right-hand side of a production is the same as the symbol on the left-hand side. Here again is the grammar from page 51, which cannot be parsed top-down:

id_list → *id_list_prefix* ;
id_list_prefix → *id_list_prefix* , id
           → id

The problem is in the second and third productions; with *id_list_prefix* at top-of-stack and an id on the input, a predictive parser cannot tell which of the productions it should use. (Recall that left recursion is *desirable* in bottom-up grammars, because it allows recursive constructs to be discovered incrementally, as in Figure 2.9.)

Common prefixes occur when two different productions with the same left-hand side begin with the same symbol or symbols. Here is an example that commonly appears in Algol-family languages:

stmt → id := *expr*
      → id (*argument_list*)   –– procedure call

Clearly id is in the FIRST set of both right-hand sides, and therefore in the PREDICT set of both productions.

Both left recursion and common prefixes can be removed from a grammar mechanically. The general case is a little tricky (see Exercise 2.16), because the prediction problem may be an indirect one (e.g., $S \to A \; \alpha$ and $A \to S \; \beta$, or $S \to A \; \alpha$, $S \to B \; \beta$, $A \Rightarrow^* a \; \gamma$, and $B \Rightarrow^* a \; \delta$). We can see the general idea in the examples above, however. Our left-recursive definition of *id_list* can be replaced by the right-recursive variant we saw on page 49:

id_list $\to$ id *id_list_tail*

id_list_tail $\to$, id *id_list_tail*

id_list_tail $\to$;

Our common-prefix definition of *stmt* can be made LL(1) by a technique called *left factoring*:

stmt $\to$ id *stmt_list_tail*

stmt_list_tail $\to$:= *expr* | (*argument_list*)

Of course, simply eliminating left recursion and common prefixes is *not* guaranteed to make a grammar LL(1). There are infinitely many non-LL *languages*—languages for which no LL grammar exists—and the mechanical transformations to eliminate left recursion and common prefixes work on their grammars just fine. Fortunately, the few non-LL languages that arise in practice can generally be handled by augmenting the parsing algorithm with one or two simple heuristics.

The best known example arises in Pascal, in which the else part of an if statement is optional. The natural grammar fragment

stmt $\to$ if *condition* *then_clause* *else_clause* | *other_stmt*

then_clause $\to$ then *stmt*

else_clause $\to$ else *stmt* | ϵ

is ambiguous; it allows the else in if C_1 then if C_2 then S_1 else S_2 to be paired with either then. The less natural grammar fragment

stmt $\to$ *balanced_stmt* | *unbalanced_stmt*

balanced_stmt $\to$ if *condition* then *balanced_stmt* else *balanced_stmt*
               | *other_stmt*

unbalanced_stmt $\to$ if *condition* then *stmt*
                 | if *condition* then *balanced_stmt* else *unbalanced_stmt*

can be parsed bottom-up but not top-down (there is *no* pure top-down grammar for Pascal else statements). A *balanced_stmt* is one with the same number of thens and elses. An *unbalanced_stmt* has more thens.

The usual approach, whether parsing top-down or bottom-up, is to use the ambiguous grammar together with a "disambiguating rule," which says that in the case of a conflict between two possible productions, the one to use is the one that occurs first, textually, in the grammar. In the ambiguous fragment above, the fact that *else_clause* → else *stmt* comes before *else_clause* → ε ends up pairing the else with the nearest then, as desired.

Better yet, a language designer can avoid this sort of problem by choosing different syntax. The ambiguity of the *dangling else* problem in Pascal leads to problems not only in parsing, but in writing and maintaining correct programs. Most Pascal programmers have at one time or another written a program like this one:

```
if P <> nil then
    if P^.val = goal then
        foundIt := true
else
    endOfList := true
```

Indentation notwithstanding, the Pascal manual states that an else clause matches the closest unmatched then, in this case the inner one, which is clearly not what the programmer intended. To get the desired effect, the Pascal programmer must write

```
if P <> nil then begin
    if P^.val = goal then
        foundIt := true
end
else
    endOfList := true
```

Many other Algol-family languages (including Modula, Modula-2, and Oberon, all more recent inventions of Pascal's designer, Niklaus Wirth) require explicit *end markers* on all structured statements. The grammar fragment for if statements in Modula-2 looks something like this:

stmt → IF *condition then_clause else_clause* END | *other_stmt*

then_clause → THEN *stmt_list*

else_clause → ELSE *stmt_list* | ε

The addition of the END eliminates the ambiguity. Modula-2 uses END to terminate all its structured statements. Ada and Fortran 77 end an if with end if (and a while with end while, etc.). Algol 68 creates its terminators by spelling the initial keyword backwards (if...fi, case...esac, do...od, etc.).

One problem with end markers is that they tend to bunch up. In Pascal one can write

```
if A = B then ...
else if A = C then ...
else if A = D then ...
else if A = E then ...
else ...
```

With end markers this becomes

```
if A = B then ...
else if A = C then ...
else if A = D then ...
else if A = E then ...
else ...
end end end end
```

To avoid this awkwardness, languages with end markers generally provide an `elsif` keyword (sometimes spelled `elif`):

```
if A = B then ...
elsif A = C then ...
elsif A = D then ...
elsif A = E then ...
else ...
end
```

With `elsif` clauses added, the Modula-2 grammar fragment for `if` statements looks like this:

stmt → IF *condition then_clause elsif_clauses else_clause* END | *other_stmt*

then_clause → THEN *stmt_list*

elsif_clauses → ELSIF *condition then_clause elsif_clauses* | ϵ

else_clause → ELSE *stmt_list* | ϵ

Locally Least-Cost Error Recovery*

Given the similarity to recursive descent parsing, it is straightforward to implement phrase-level recovery in a table-driven top-down parser. Whenever we encounter an error entry in the parse table, we simply delete input tokens until we find a member of a statically defined set of starter symbols (including $$), or a member of the FIRST or FOLLOW set of the nonterminal at the top of the parse stack.[9] If we find a member of the FIRST set, we continue the main loop of the driver. If we find a member of the FOLLOW set or the starter set, we pop the nonterminal off the parse stack first. If we encounter an error in match, rather than in the parse table, we simply pop the token off the parse stack.

But we can do better than this! Since we have the entire parse stack easily accessible (it was hidden in the control flow and procedure calling sequence of recursive descent), we can enumerate all possible combinations of insertions and

---

9 This description uses global FOLLOW sets. If we want to use context-specific look-aheads instead, we can peek farther down in the stack. A token is an acceptable context-specific look-ahead if it is in the FIRST set of the second symbol A from the top in the stack or, if it would cause us to predict $A \rightarrow \epsilon$, the FIRST set of the third symbol B from the top or, if it would cause us to predict $B \rightarrow \epsilon$, the FIRST set of the fourth symbol from the top, and so on.

deletions that would allow us to continue parsing. Given appropriate metrics, we can then evaluate the alternatives to pick the one that is in some sense "best."

Because perfect error recovery (actually error *repair*) would require that we read the programmer's mind, any practical technique to evaluate alternative "corrections" must rely on heuristics. For the sake of simplicity, most compilers limit themselves to heuristics that (1) require no semantic information, (2) do not require that we "back up" the parser or the input stream (i.e., to some state prior to the one in which the error was detected), and (3) do not change the spelling of tokens or the boundaries between them. A particularly elegant algorithm that conforms to these limits was published by Fischer, Milton, and Quiring in 1980 [FMQ80, FL88]. As originally described, the algorithm was limited to languages in which programs could always be corrected by inserting appropriate tokens into the input stream, without ever requiring deletions. It is relatively easy, however, to extend the algorithm to encompass deletions and substitutions. We consider the insert-only algorithm first; the version with deletions employs it as a subroutine. We do not consider substitutions here.[10]

The FMQ error-repair algorithm requires the compiler writer to assign an insertion cost $C(t)$ and a deletion cost $D(t)$ to every token t. (Since we cannot change where the input ends, we have $C(\$\$) = D(\$\$) = \infty$.) This assignment of costs is the only language-dependent component of FMQ; given these costs the algorithm is entirely automatic. In any given error situation, it chooses the least cost combination of insertions and deletions that allows the parser to consume one more token of real input. The state of the parser is never changed; only the input is modified (rather than pop a stack symbol, the repair algorithm pushes its yield onto the input stream).

As in phrase-level recovery in a recursive descent parser, the FMQ algorithm needs to address the immediate error detection problem. There are several ways we could do this. One would be to use a full LL parser. Another would be to inspect the stack when predicting an epsilon production, to see if what lies underneath will allow us to accept the incoming token. The first option significantly increases the size and complexity of the parser. The second option leads to a non-linear-time parsing algorithm. Fortunately, there is a third option. We can save all changes to the stack (and calls to the semantic analyzer's action routines) in a temporary buffer until the match routine accepts another real token of input. If we discover an error before we accept a real token, we undo the stack changes and throw away the buffered calls to action routines. Then we can pretend we recognized the error when a full LL parser would have.

---

10 A substitution can always be effected as a deletion/insertion pair, but we might want ideally to give it special consideration. For example, we probably want to be cautious about deleting a left square bracket or inserting a left parenthesis, since both of these symbols must be matched by something later in the input, at which point we are likely to see cascading errors. But substituting a left parenthesis for a left square bracket is in some sense more plausible, especially given the differences in array subscript syntax in different programming languages.

```
function find_insertion (a : token) : string
      -- assume that the parse stack consists of symbols X_n,...X_2, X_1,
      -- with X_n at top-of-stack
      ins := ??
      prefix := ε
      for i in n..1
            if C(prefix) ≥ C(ins)
                  -- no better insertion is possible
                  return ins
            if C(prefix . E(X_i, a)) < C(ins)
                  -- better insertion found
                  ins := prefix . E(X_i, a)
            prefix := prefix . S(X_i)
      return ins
```

Figure 2.18 Outline of a function to find a least-cost insertion that will allow the parser to accept the input token a**.** The dot character (.) is used here for string concatenation.

We now consider the task of repairing with only insertions. We begin by extending the notion of insertion costs to strings in the obvious way: if $w = a_1a_2...a_n$, we have $C(w) = \sum_{i=1}^{n} C(a_i)$. Using the cost function C, we then build a pair of tables S and E. The S table is one-dimensional, and is indexed by grammar symbol. For any symbol X, $S(X)$ is a least-cost string of terminals derivable from X. That is,

$$S(X) = w \iff X \Rightarrow^* w \text{ and } \forall x \text{ such that } X \Rightarrow^* x, \ C(w) \leq C(x)$$

Clearly $S(a) = a \ \forall$ tokens a.

The E table is two-dimensional, and is indexed by symbol/token pairs. For any symbol X and token a, $E(X, a)$ is the lowest-cost prefix of a in X; that is, the lowest cost token string w such that $X \Rightarrow^* wax$. If X cannot yield a string containing a, then $E(X, a)$ is defined to be a special symbol ?? whose insertion cost is ∞. If $X = a$, or if $X \Rightarrow^* ax$, then $E(X, a) = \epsilon$, where $C(\epsilon) = 0$.

To find a least-cost insertion that will repair a given error, we execute the function find_insertion, shown in Figure 2.18. The function begins by considering the least-cost insertion that will allow it to derive the input token from the symbol at the top of the stack (there may be none). It then considers the possibility of "deleting" that top-of-stack symbol (by inserting its least-cost yield into the input stream) and deriving the input token from the second symbol on the stack. It continues in this fashion, considering ways to derive the input token from ever deeper symbols on the stack, until the cost of inserting the yields of the symbols above exceeds the cost of the cheapest repair found so far. If it reaches the bottom of the stack without finding a finite-cost repair, then the error cannot be repaired by insertions alone.

```
function find_repair : string, int
        -- assume that the parse stack consists of symbols Xₙ,...X₂, X₁,
        -- with Xₙ at top-of-stack,
        -- and that the input stream consists of tokens a₁, a₂, a₃, ...
        i := 0      -- number of tokens we're considering deleting
        best_ins := ??
        best_del := 0
        loop
                cur_ins := find_insertion (aᵢ₊₁)
                if C(cur_ins) + D(a₁...aᵢ) < C(best_ins) + D(a₁...a_best_del)
                        -- better repair found
                        best_ins := cur_ins
                        best_del := i
                i +:= 1
                if D(a₁...aᵢ) > C(best_ins) + D(a₁...a_best_del)
                        -- no better repair is possible
                        return (best_ins, best_del)
```

Figure 2.19 **Outline of a function to find a least-cost combination of insertions and deletions that will allow the parser to accept one more token of input.**

To produce better-quality repairs, and to handle languages that cannot be repaired with insertions only, we need to consider deletions. As with the insert cost vector C, we extend the deletion cost vector D to strings of tokens in the obvious way. We then embed calls to find_insertion in a second loop, shown in Figure 2.19. This loop repeatedly considers deleting more and more tokens, each time calling find_insertion on the remaining input, until the cost of deleting additional tokens exceeds the cost of the cheapest repair found so far. The search can never fail; it is always possible to find a combination of insertions and deletions that will allow the end-of-file token to be accepted. Since the algorithm may need to consider (and then reject) the option of deleting an arbitrary number of tokens, the scanner must be prepared to peek an arbitrary distance ahead in the input stream and then back up again.

The FMQ algorithm has several desirable properties. It is simple and efficient (given that the grammar is bounded in size, we can prove that the time to choose a repair is bounded by a constant). It can repair an arbitrary input string. Its decisions are locally optimal, in the sense that no cheaper repair can allow the parser to make forward progress. It is table-driven and therefore fully automatic. Finally, it can be tuned to prefer "likely" repairs by modifying the insertion and deletion costs of tokens. Some obvious heuristics include:

- Deletion should usually be more expensive than insertion.

- Common operators (e.g., multiplication) should have lower cost than uncommon operators (e.g., modulo division) in the same place in the grammar.
- Starter symbols (e.g., `begin`, `if`, `(`) should have higher cost than their corresponding final symbols (`end`, `fi`, `)`).
- "Noise" symbols (comma, semicolon, `do`) should have very low cost.

2.2.6 Bottom-Up Parsing

Conceptually, as we saw in Section 2.2.2, a bottom-up parser works by maintaining a forest of partially completed subtrees of the parse tree, which it joins together whenever it recognizes the symbols on the right-hand side of some production used in the right-most derivation of the input string. It creates a new internal node and makes the roots of the joined-together trees the children of that node.

In practice, a bottom-up parser is almost always table-driven. It keeps the roots of its partially completed subtrees on a stack. When it accepts a new token from the scanner, it *shifts* the token into the stack. When it recognizes that the top few symbols on the stack constitute a right-hand side, it *reduces* those symbols to their left-hand side by popping them off the stack and pushing the left-hand side in their place. The role of the stack is the first important difference between top-down and bottom-up parsing: a top-down parser's stack contains a list of what the parser expects to see in the future; a bottom-up parser's stack contains a record of what the parser has already seen in the past.

We also noted earlier that the actions of a bottom-up parser trace out a right-most (canonical) derivation in reverse. The roots of the partial subtrees, left-to-right, together with the remaining input, constitute a sentential form of the right-most derivation. On the right-hand side of Figure 2.8, for example, we have the following series of steps:

stack contents (roots of partial trees)	remaining input
ϵ	A , B , C ;
id (A)	, B , C ;
id (A) ,	B , C ;
id (A) , id (B)	, C ;
id (A) , id (B) ,	C ;
id (A) , id (B) , id (C)	;
id (A) , id (B) , id (C) ;	
id (A) , id (B) , id (C) *id_list_tail*	
id (A) , id (B) *id_list_tail*	
id (A) *id_list_tail*	
id_list	

The last four lines (the ones that don't just shift tokens into the forest) correspond to the right-most derivation:

$program \rightarrow stmt\_list$ **\$\$**

$stmt\_list \rightarrow stmt\_list\ stmt\ |\ stmt$

$stmt \rightarrow$ **id :=** $expr\ |$ **read id** $|$ **write** $expr$

$expr \rightarrow term\ |\ expr\ add\_op\ term$

$term \rightarrow factor\ |\ term\ mult\_op\ factor$

$factor \rightarrow$ **(** $expr$ **)** $|$ **id** $|$ **literal**

$add\_op \rightarrow$ **+** $|$ **-**

$mult\_op \rightarrow$ ***** $|$ **/**

Figure 2.20 LR(1) grammar for the calculator language.

$id\_list \Rightarrow$ **id** id_list_tail

$\Rightarrow$ **id , id** id_list_tail

$\Rightarrow$ **id , id , id** id_list_tail

$\Rightarrow$ **id , id , id ;**

The symbols that need to be joined together at each step of the parse to represent the next step of the backwards derivation are called the *handle* of the sentential form. In the parse trace above, the handles are underlined.

In our *id_list* example, no handles were found until the entire input had been shifted onto the stack. In general this will not be the case. We can obtain a more realistic example by examining an LR version of our calculator language, shown in Figure 2.20. While the LL grammar of Figure 2.10 can be parsed bottom-up, the version in Figure 2.20 is preferable for two reasons. First, it uses a left-recursive production for *stmt_list*. Left recursion allows the parser to collapse long statement lists as it goes along, rather than waiting until the entire list is on the stack and then collapsing it from the end. Second, it uses left-recursive productions for *expr* and *term*. These productions capture left associativity while still keeping an operator and its operands together in the same right-hand side, something we were unable to do in a top-down grammar.

Suppose we are to parse the sum-and-average program from page 53:

```
read A
read B
sum := A + B
write sum
write sum / 2
```

The key to a successful parse will be to figure out when we have reached the end of a right-hand side—that is, when we have a handle at the top of the parse stack. The trick is to keep track of the set of productions we might be "in the middle of" at any particular time, together with an indication of where in those productions we might be.

When we begin execution, the parse stack is empty and we are at the beginning of the production for *program*. (In general, we can assume that there is only one production with the start symbol on the left-hand side; it is easy to modify any grammar to make this the case.) We can represent our location—more specifically, the location represented by the top of the parse stack—with a • in the right-hand side of the production:

program → • *stmt_list* $$

When augmented with a •, a production is called an LR *item*. Since the • in this item is immediately in front of a nonterminal—namely *stmt_list*—we may be about to see the yield of that nonterminal coming up on the input. This possibility implies that we may be at the beginning of some production with *stmt_list* on the left-hand side:

program → • *stmt_list* $$
stmt_list → • *stmt_list stmt*
stmt_list → • *stmt*

And, since *stmt* is a nonterminal, we may also be at the beginning of any production whose left-hand side is *stmt*:

program → • *stmt_list* $$ (State 0)
stmt_list → • *stmt_list stmt*
stmt_list → • *stmt*
stmt → • id := *expr*
stmt → • read id
stmt → • write *expr*

Since all of these last productions begin with a terminal, no additional items need to be added to our list. The original item (*program* → • *stmt_list* $$) is called the *basis* of the list. The additional items are its *closure*. The list represents the initial state of the parser. As we shift and reduce, the set of items will change, always indicating which productions *may* be the right one to use next in the derivation of the input string. If we reach a state in which some item has the • at the end of the right-hand side, we can reduce by that production. Otherwise, as in the current situation, we must shift. Note that if we need to shift, but the incoming token cannot follow the • in any item of the current state, then a syntax error has occurred. We will consider error recovery in more detail in Section 2.2.6.

Our upcoming token is a read. Once we shift it onto the stack, we know we are in the following state:

stmt → read • id   (State 1)

This state has a single basis item and an empty closure—the • precedes a terminal. After shifting the A, we have

stmt → read id • (State 1′)

We now know that read id is the handle, and we must reduce. The reduction pops two symbols off the parse stack and pushes a *stmt* in their place, but what should the new state be? We can see the answer if we imagine moving back in time to the point at which we shifted the read—the first symbol of the right-hand side. At that time we were in the state labeled "State 0" above, and the upcoming tokens on the input (though we didn't look at them at the time) were read id. We have now consumed these tokens, and we know that they constituted a *stmt*. By pushing a *stmt* onto the stack, we have in essence replaced read id with *stmt* on the input stream, and have then "shifted" the nonterminal, rather than its yield, into the stack. Since one of the items in State 0 was

stmt_list → • *stmt*

we now have

stmt_list → *stmt* • (State 0′)

Again we must reduce. We remove the *stmt* from the stack and push a *stmt_list* in its place. Again we can see this as "shifting" a *stmt_list* when in State 0. Since two of the items in State 0 have a *stmt_list* after the •, we don't know (without looking ahead) which of the productions will be the next to be used in the derivation, but we don't have to know. The key advantage of bottom-up parsing over top-down parsing is that we don't need to predict ahead of time which production we shall be expanding.

Our new state is as follows:

program → *stmt_list* • $$ (State 2)

stmt_list → *stmt_list* • *stmt*

stmt → • id := *expr*

stmt → • read id

stmt → • write *expr*

The first two productions are the basis; the others are the closure. Since no item has a • at the end, we shift the next token, which happens again to be a read, taking us back to State 1. Shifting the B takes us to State 1′ again, at which point we reduce. This time however, we go back to State 2 rather than State 0 before shifting the left-hand side *stmt*. Why? Because we were in State 2 when we began to read the right-hand side.

The Characteristic Finite State Machine and LR Parsing Variants

An LR-family parser keeps track of the states it has traversed by pushing them into the parse stack, along with the grammar symbols. The parser actually pays no attention to the symbols; it only inspects the states. The symbols are important for semantic analysis—they hold the pointers to parse-tree fragments—but they are useless to the parser itself.

We can think of the "shift" rules of an LR-family parser as the transition function of a finite automaton, much like the automata we used to model scanners. Each state of the automaton corresponds to a list of items that indicate where the parser might be at some specific point in the parse. The transition for input symbol X (which may be either a terminal or a nonterminal) moves to a state whose basis consists of items in which the • has been moved across an X in the right-hand side, plus whatever items need to be added as closure. The lists are constructed by a bottom-up parser generator in order to build the automaton, but are not needed during parsing.

It turns out that the simpler members of the LR family of parsers—LR(0), SLR(1), and LALR(1)—all use the same automaton, called the *characteristic finite-state machine*, or CFSM. Full LR parsers use a machine with (for most grammars) a much larger number of states. The differences between the algorithms lie in how they deal with states that contain a *shift-reduce conflict*—one item with the • in the middle (suggesting the need for a shift) and another with the • at the end (suggesting the need for a reduction). An LR(0) parser works only when there are no such states. It can be proven that with the addition of an end-marker (i.e., $$), any language that can be deterministically parsed bottom-up has an LR(0) grammar. Unfortunately, the LR(0) grammars for real programming languages tend to be prohibitively large and unintuitive.

SLR (simple LR) parsers peek at upcoming input and use FOLLOW sets to resolve conflicts. An SLR parser will call for a reduction via $A \rightarrow \alpha$ only if the upcoming token(s) are in FOLLOW(α). It will still see a conflict, however, if the tokens are also in the FIRST set of any of the symbols that follow a • in other items of the state. LALR (look-ahead LR) parsers improve on SLR by using local (state-specific) look-ahead instead of global FOLLOW sets, much as full LL uses local look-ahead to improve on SLL.

Conflicts can still arise in an LALR parser when the same set of items can occur on two different paths through the CFSM. Both paths will end up in the same state, at which point state-specific look-ahead can no longer distinguish between them. A full LR parser duplicates states in order to keep paths disjoint when their local look-aheads are different.

LALR parsers are the most common bottom-up parsers in practice. They are the same size and speed as SLR parsers, but are able to resolve more conflicts. Full LR parsers for real programming languages tend to be very large. Several researchers have developed techniques to reduce the size of full-LR tables, but LALR works sufficiently well in practice that the extra complexity of full LR is usually not required. `Yacc/bison` produces C code for an LALR parser.

Bottom-Up Parsing Tables

Like a table-driven LL(1) parser, an SLR(1), LALR(1), or LR(1) parser executes a loop in which it repeatedly inspects a two-dimensional table to find out what action to take. However, instead of using the current input token and top-of-stack nonterminal to index into the table, an LR-family parser uses the current input token and the current parser state (which can be found at the top of the stack). "Shift" table entries indicate the state that should be pushed. "Reduce" table entries indicate the number of states that should be popped and the nonterminal that should be pushed back onto the input stream, to be shifted by the state uncovered by the pops. There is always one popped state for every symbol on the right-hand side of the reducing production. The state to be pushed next can be found by indexing into the table using the uncovered state and the newly recognized nonterminal.

The CFSM for our bottom-up version of the calculator grammar appears in Figure 2.21. States 6, 7, 9, and 13 contain potential shift-reduce conflicts, but all of these can be resolved with global FOLLOW sets. SLR parsing therefore suffices. In State 6, for example, FIRST(*add_op*) ∩ FOLLOW(*stmt*) = ∅. In addition to shift and reduce rules, we allow the parse table as an optimization to contain rules of the form "shift and then reduce." This optimization serves to eliminate trivial states such as 0′ and 1′ (page 78), in which there is only a single item, with the • at the end. A complete trace of the actions of an SLR(1) parser on the sum-and-average program appears in Figure 2.22.

Handling Epsilon Productions

The careful reader may have noticed that the grammar of Figure 2.20, in addition to using left-recursive rules for *stmt_list*, *expr* and *term*, differs from the grammar of Figure 2.10 in one other way: it defines a *stmt_list* to be a sequence of one or more *stmt*s, rather than zero or more. (This means, of course, that it defines a different language.) To capture the same language as Figure 2.10, the productions

program → *stmt_list* \$\$

stmt_list → *stmt_list* *stmt* | *stmt*

in Figure 2.20 would need to be replaced with

program → *stmt_list* \$\$

stmt_list → *stmt_list* *stmt* | ϵ

Note that it does in general make sense to have an empty statement list. In the calculator language it simply permits an empty program, which is admittedly silly. In real languages, however, it allows the body of a structured statement to be empty, which can be very useful. One frequently wants one arm of a case or multiway if...then...else statement to be empty, and an empty while loop

	State	Transitions
0.	$program \rightarrow \bullet\ stmt\_list$ **$$**	on *stmt_list* shift and goto 2
	$stmt\_list \rightarrow \bullet\ stmt\_list\ stmt$	
	$stmt\_list \rightarrow \bullet\ stmt$	on *stmt* shift and reduce (pop 1 state, push *stmt_list* on input)
	$stmt \rightarrow \bullet$ **id** $:=\ expr$	on **id** shift and goto 3
	$stmt \rightarrow \bullet$ **read id**	on **read** shift and goto 1
	$stmt \rightarrow \bullet$ **write** $expr$	on **write** shift and goto 4
1.	$stmt \rightarrow$ **read** $\bullet$ **id**	on **id** shift and reduce (pop 2 states, push *stmt* on input)
2.	$program \rightarrow stmt\_list\ \bullet$ **$$**	on **$$** shift and reduce (pop 2 states, push *program* on input)
	$stmt\_list \rightarrow stmt\_list\ \bullet\ stmt$	on *stmt* shift and reduce (pop 2 states, push *stmt_list* on input)
	$stmt \rightarrow \bullet$ **id** $:=\ expr$	on **id** shift and goto 3
	$stmt \rightarrow \bullet$ **read id**	on **read** shift and goto 1
	$stmt \rightarrow \bullet$ **write** $expr$	on **write** shift and goto 4
3.	$stmt \rightarrow$ **id** $\bullet\ :=\ expr$	on **:=** shift and goto 5
4.	$stmt \rightarrow$ **write** $\bullet\ expr$	on *expr* shift and goto 6
	$expr \rightarrow \bullet\ term$	on *term* shift and goto 7
	$expr \rightarrow \bullet\ expr\ add\_op\ term$	
	$term \rightarrow \bullet\ factor$	on *factor* shift and reduce (pop 1 state, push *term* on input)
	$term \rightarrow \bullet\ term\ mult\_op\ factor$	
	$factor \rightarrow \bullet$ **(** $expr$ **)**	on **(** shift and goto 8
	$factor \rightarrow \bullet$ **id**	on **id** shift and reduce (pop 1 state, push *factor* on input)
	$factor \rightarrow \bullet$ **literal**	on **literal** shift and reduce (pop 1 state, push *factor* on input)
5.	$stmt \rightarrow$ **id** $:=\ \bullet\ expr$	on *expr* shift and goto 9
	$expr \rightarrow \bullet\ term$	on *term* shift and goto 7
	$expr \rightarrow \bullet\ expr\ add\_op\ term$	
	$term \rightarrow \bullet\ factor$	on *factor* shift and reduce (pop 1 state, push *term* on input)
	$term \rightarrow \bullet\ term\ mult\_op\ factor$	
	$factor \rightarrow \bullet$ **(** $expr$ **)**	on **(** shift and goto 8
	$factor \rightarrow \bullet$ **id**	on **id** shift and reduce (pop 1 state, push *factor* on input)
	$factor \rightarrow \bullet$ **literal**	on **literal** shift and reduce (pop 1 state, push *factor* on input)
6.	$stmt \rightarrow$ **write** $expr\ \bullet$	on FOLLOW(*stmt*) = {**id**, **read**, **write**, **$$**} reduce
	$stmt \rightarrow expr\ \bullet\ add\_op\ term$	(pop 2 states, push *stmt* on input)
		on *add_op* shift and goto 10
	$add\_op \rightarrow \bullet$ **+**	on **+** shift and reduce (pop 1 state, push *add_op* on input)
	$add\_op \rightarrow \bullet$ **−**	on **−** shift and reduce (pop 1 state, push *add_op* on input)

Figure 2.21 CFSM for the calculator grammar (Figure 2.20). Basis and closure items in each state are separated by a horizontal rule. Trivial reduce-only states have been eliminated by use of "shift and reduce" transitions *(continued)*.

	State	Transitions
7.	$expr \rightarrow term \bullet$ $term \rightarrow term \bullet mult\_op\ factor$ ——————————— $mult\_op \rightarrow \bullet *$ $mult\_op \rightarrow \bullet /$	on FOLLOW$(expr) = \{$id, read, write, $\$\$$,), +, -$\}$ reduce (pop 1 state, push $expr$ on input) on $mult\_op$ shift and goto 11 on $*$ shift and reduce (pop 1 state, push $mult\_op$ on input) on $/$ shift and reduce (pop 1 state, push $mult\_op$ on input)
8.	$factor \rightarrow (\bullet expr)$ ——————————— $expr \rightarrow \bullet term$ $expr \rightarrow \bullet expr\ add\_op\ term$ $term \rightarrow \bullet factor$ $term \rightarrow \bullet term\ mult\_op\ factor$ $factor \rightarrow \bullet (expr)$ $factor \rightarrow \bullet$ id $factor \rightarrow \bullet$ literal	on $expr$ shift and goto 12 on $term$ shift and goto 7 on $factor$ shift and reduce (pop 1 state, push $term$ on input) on $($ shift and goto 8 on id shift and reduce (pop 1 state, push $factor$ on input) on literal shift and reduce (pop 1 state, push $factor$ on input)
9.	$stmt \rightarrow$ id := $expr \bullet$ $expr \rightarrow expr \bullet add\_op\ term$ ——————————— $add\_op \rightarrow \bullet +$ $add\_op \rightarrow \bullet -$	on FOLLOW$(stmt) = \{$id, read, write, $\$\$\}$ reduce (pop 3 states, push $stmt$ on input) on add_op shift and goto 10 on $+$ shift and reduce (pop 1 state, push add_op on input) on $-$ shift and reduce (pop 1 state, push add_op on input)
10.	$expr \rightarrow expr\ add\_op \bullet term$ ——————————— $term \rightarrow \bullet factor$ $term \rightarrow \bullet term\ mult\_op\ factor$ $factor \rightarrow \bullet (expr)$ $factor \rightarrow \bullet$ id $factor \rightarrow \bullet$ literal	on $term$ shift and goto 13 on $factor$ shift and reduce (pop 1 state, push $term$ on input) on $($ shift and goto 8 on id shift and reduce (pop 1 state, push $factor$ on input) on literal shift and reduce (pop 1 state, push $factor$ on input)
11.	$term \rightarrow term\ mult\_op \bullet factor$ ——————————— $factor \rightarrow \bullet (expr)$ $factor \rightarrow \bullet$ id $factor \rightarrow \bullet$ literal	on $factor$ shift and reduce (pop 3 states, push $term$ on input) on $($ shift and goto 8 on id shift and reduce (pop 1 state, push $factor$ on input) on literal shift and reduce (pop 1 state, push $factor$ on input)
12.	$factor \rightarrow (expr \bullet)$ $expr \rightarrow expr \bullet add\_op\ term$ ——————————— $add\_op \rightarrow \bullet +$ $add\_op \rightarrow \bullet -$	on $)$ shift and reduce (pop 3 states, push $factor$ on input) on add_op shift and goto 10 on $+$ shift and reduce (pop 1 state, push add_op on input) on $-$ shift and reduce (pop 1 state, push add_op on input)
13.	$expr \rightarrow expr\ add\_op\ term \bullet$ $term \rightarrow term \bullet mult\_op\ factor$ ——————————— $mult\_op \rightarrow \bullet *$ $mult\_op \rightarrow \bullet /$	on FOLLOW$(expr) = \{$id, read, write, $\$\$$,), +, -$\}$ reduce (pop 3 states, push $expr$ on input) on $mult\_op$ shift and goto 11 on $*$ shift and reduce (pop 1 state, push $mult\_op$ on input) on $/$ shift and reduce (pop 1 state, push $mult\_op$ on input)

Figure 2.21 (continued)

Parse stack	Input stream	Comment
0	read A read B . . .	
0 read 1	A read B . . .	shift read
0	*stmt* read B . . .	shift id(A) & reduce by *stmt* → read id
0	*stmt_list* read B . . .	shift *stmt* & reduce by *stmt_list* → *stmt*
0 *stmt_list* 2	read B sum . . .	shift *stmt_list*
0 *stmt_list* 2 read 1	B sum := . . .	shift read
0 *stmt_list* 2	*stmt* sum := . . .	shift id(B) & reduce by *stmt* → read id
0	*stmt_list* sum := . . .	shift *stmt* & reduce by *stmt_list* → *stmt_list* *stmt*
0 *stmt_list* 2	sum := A . . .	shift *stmt_list*
0 *stmt_list* 2 id 3	:= A + . . .	shift id(sum)
0 *stmt_list* 2 id 3 := 5	A + B . . .	shift :=
0 *stmt_list* 2 id 3 := 5	*factor* + B . . .	shift id(A) & reduce by *factor* → id
0 *stmt_list* 2 id 3 := 5	*term* + B . . .	shift *factor* & reduce by *term* → *factor*
0 *stmt_list* 2 id 3 := 5 *term* 7	+ B write . . .	shift *term*
0 *stmt_list* 2 id 3 := 5	*expr* + B write . . .	reduce by *expr* → *term*
0 *stmt_list* 2 id 3 := 5 *expr* 9	+ B write . . .	shift *expr*
0 *stmt_list* 2 id 3 := 5 *expr* 9	*add_op* B write . . .	shift + & reduce by *add_op* → +
0 *stmt_list* 2 id 3 := 5 *expr* 9 *add_op* 10	B write sum . . .	shift *add_op*
0 *stmt_list* 2 id 3 := 5 *expr* 9 *add_op* 10	*factor* write sum . . .	shift id(B) & reduce by *factor* → id
0 *stmt_list* 2 id 3 := 5 *expr* 9 *add_op* 10	*term* write sum . . .	shift *factor* & reduce by *term* → *factor*
0 *stmt_list* 2 id 3 := 5 *expr* 9 *add_op* 10 *term* 13	write sum . . .	shift *term*
0 *stmt_list* 2 id 3 := 5	*expr* write sum . . .	reduce by *expr* → *expr* *add_op* *term*
0 *stmt_list* 2 id 3 := 5 *expr* 9	write sum . . .	shift *expr*
0 *stmt_list* 2	*stmt* write sum . . .	reduce by *stmt* → id := *expr*
0	*stmt_list* write sum . . .	shift *stmt* & reduce by *stmt_list* → *stmt*
0 *stmt_list* 2	write sum . . .	shift *stmt_list*
0 *stmt_list* 2 write 4	sum write sum . . .	shift write
0 *stmt_list* 2 write 4	*factor* write sum . . .	shift id(sum) & reduce by *factor* → id
0 *stmt_list* 2 write 4	*term* write sum . . .	shift *factor* & reduce by *term* → *factor*
0 *stmt_list* 2 write 4 *term* 7	write sum . . .	shift *term*
0 *stmt_list* 2 write 4	*expr* write sum . . .	reduce by *expr* → *term*
0 *stmt_list* 2 write 4 *expr* 6	write sum . . .	shift *expr*
0 *stmt_list* 2	*stmt* write sum . . .	reduce by *stmt* → write *expr*
0	*stmt_list* write sum . . .	shift *stmt* & reduce by *stmt_list* → *stmt_list* *stmt*
0 *stmt_list* 2	write sum / . . .	shift *stmt_list*
0 *stmt_list* 2 write 4	sum / 2 . . .	shift write
0 *stmt_list* 2 write 4	*factor* / 2 . . .	shift id(sum) & reduce by *factor* → id
0 *stmt_list* 2 write 4	*term* / 2 . . .	shift *factor* & reduce by *term* → *factor*
0 *stmt_list* 2 write 4 *term* 7	/ 2 $$	shift *term*
0 *stmt_list* 2 write 4 *term* 7	*mult_op* 2 $$	shift / & reduce by *mult_op* → /
0 *stmt_list* 2 write 4 *term* 7 *mult_op* 11	2 $$	shift *mult_op*
0 *stmt_list* 2 write 4 *term* 7 *mult_op* 11	*factor* $$	shift literal(2) & reduce by *factor* → literal
0 *stmt_list* 2 write 4	*term* $$	shift *factor* & reduce by *term* → *term* *mult_op* *factor*
0 *stmt_list* 2 write 4 *term* 7	$$	shift *term*
0 *stmt_list* 2 write 4	*expr* $$	reduce by *expr* → *term*
0 *stmt_list* 2 write 4 *expr* 6	$$	shift *expr*
0 *stmt_list* 2	*stmt* $$	reduce by *stmt* → write *expr*
0	*stmt_list* $$	shift *stmt* & reduce by *stmt_list* → *stmt_list* *stmt*
0 *stmt_list* 2	$$	shift *stmt_list*
0	*program*	shift $$ & reduce by *program* → *stmt_list* $$
[done]		

Figure 2.22   Trace of a table-driven SLR(1) parse of the sum-and-average program. States in the parse stack are shown in boldface type. Symbols in the parse stack are for clarity only; they are not needed by the parsing algorithm. Parsing begins with the initial state of the CFSM (State 0) in the stack. It ends when we reduce by *program* → *stmt_list* $$, uncovering State 0 again and pushing *program* onto the input stream.

allows a parallel program (or the operating system) to wait for a signal from another process or an I/O device.

If we look at the CFSM for the calculator language, we discover that State 0 is the only state that needs to be changed in order to allow empty statement lists. The item

$$stmt\_list \rightarrow \ . \ stmt$$

becomes

$$stmt\_list \rightarrow \ . \ \epsilon$$

which is equivalent to

$$stmt\_list \rightarrow \epsilon \ .$$

or simply

$$stmt\_list \rightarrow \ .$$

The entire state is then

$program \ \rightarrow \ . \ stmt_list \ $$	on $stmt\_list$ shift and goto 2

$stmt\_list \ \rightarrow \ . \ stmt\_list \ stmt$	
$stmt\_list \ \rightarrow \ .$	on $$ reduce (pop 0 states, push $stmt\_list$ on input)
$stmt \ \rightarrow \ . \ $id := $expr$	on id shift and goto 3
$stmt \ \rightarrow \ . \ $read id	on read shift and goto 1
$stmt \ \rightarrow \ . \ $write $expr$	on write shift and goto 4

The look-ahead for item

$$stmt\_list \rightarrow \ .$$

is FOLLOW(*stmt_list*), which is the end-marker, $$. Since $$ does not appear in the look-aheads for any other item in this state, our grammar is still SLR(1). It is worth noting that epsilon productions prevent a grammar from being LR(0), since one can never tell whether to "recognize" ϵ without peeking ahead. An LR(0) grammar never has epsilon productions.

Phrase-Level Error Recovery

Locally least-cost repair is possible in bottom-up parsers, but it isn't as easy as it is in top-down parsers. The advantage of a top-down parser is that the content of the parse stack unambiguously identifies the context of an error, and specifies the constructs expected in the future. The stack of a bottom-up parser, by contrast, describes a set of possible contexts, and says nothing explicit about the future.

In practice, most bottom-up parsers tend to rely on panic-mode or phrase-level recovery. The intuition is that when an error occurs, the top few states on the parse stack represent the shifted prefix of an erroneous construct. Recovery consists of popping these states off the stack, deleting the remainder of the construct from the incoming token stream, and then restarting the parser, possibly after shifting a fictitious nonterminal to represent the erroneous construct.

Unix's `yacc/bison` provides a typical example of bottom-up phrase-level recovery. In addition to the usual tokens of the language, `yacc/bison` allows the compiler writer to include a special token, `error`, anywhere in the right-hand sides of grammar productions. When the parser built from the grammar detects a syntax error, it

1. Calls the function `yyerror`, which the compiler writer must provide. Normally, `yyerror` simply prints a message (e.g., "parse error"), which `yacc/bison` passes as an argument

2. Pops states off the parse stack until it finds a state in which it can shift the `error` token (if there is no such state, the parser terminates)

3. Inserts and then shifts the `error` token

4. Deletes tokens from the input stream until it finds a valid look-ahead for the new (post `error`) context

5. Temporarily disables reporting of further errors

6. Resumes parsing

If there are any semantic action routines associated with the production containing the `error` token, these are executed in the normal fashion. They can do such things as print additional error messages, modify the symbol table, patch up semantic processing, prompt the user for additional input in an interactive tool (`yacc/bison` can be used to build things other than batch-mode compilers), or disable code generation. The rationale for disabling further syntax errors is to make sure that we have really found an acceptable context in which to resume parsing before risking cascading errors. `Yacc/bison` automatically re-enables the reporting of errors after successfully shifting three real tokens of input. A semantic action routine can re-enable error messages sooner if desired by calling the built-in routine `yyerrorok`.

For our example calculator language, we can imagine building a `yacc/bison` parser using the bottom-up grammar of Figure 2.20. For panic mode recovery, we might want to back out to the nearest statement:

stmt → `error`
      `{printf ("parsing resumed at end of current statement\n");}`

The semantic routine written in curly braces would be executed when the parser recognizes *stmt* → error.[11] Parsing would resume at the next token that can follow a statement—in our calculator language, at the next id, read, write, or $$. A weakness of the calculator language, from the point of view of error recovery, is that the current, erroneous statement may well contain additional ids. If we resume parsing at one of these, we are likely to see another error right away. We could avoid the error by disabling error messages until several real tokens have been shifted. In a language in which every statement ends with a semicolon, we could have more safely written:

stmt → error ;
        {printf ("parsing resumed at end of current statement\n");}

In both of these examples we have placed the error symbol at the beginning of a right-hand side, but there is no rule that says it must be so. We might decide, for example, that we will abandon the current statement whenever we see an error, unless the error happens inside a parenthesized expression, in which case we will attempt to resume parsing after the closing parenthesis. We could then add the following production:

factor → (error)
        {printf ("parsing resumed at end of
                parenthesized expression\n");}

In the CFSM of Figure 2.21, it would then be possible in State 8 to shift error, delete some tokens, shift), recognize *factor*, and continue parsing the surrounding expression. Of course, if the erroneous expression contains nested parentheses, the parser may not skip all of it, and a cascading error may still occur.

Because yacc/bison creates LALR parsers, it automatically employs context-specific look-ahead, and does not usually suffer from the immediate error detection problem. (A full LR parser would do slightly better.) In an SLR parser, a good error recovery algorithm needs to employ the same trick we used in the SLL case. Specifically, we buffer all stack changes and calls to semantic action routines until the shift routine accepts a real token of input. If we discover an error before we accept a real token, we undo the stack changes and throw away the buffered calls to semantic routines. Then we can pretend we recognized the error when a full LR parser would have.

---

[11] The syntax shown here is not the same as that accepted by yacc/bison, but is used for the sake of consistency with earlier material.

2.3* Theoretical Foundations

Our understanding of the relative roles and computational power of scanners, parsers, regular expressions, and context-free grammars is based on the formalisms of *automata theory*. In automata theory, a *formal language* is a set of strings of symbols drawn from a finite *alphabet*. A formal language can be specified either by a set of rules (such as regular expressions or a context-free grammar) that generate the language, or by a *formal machine* that *accepts* (*recognizes*) the language. A formal machine takes strings of symbols as input and outputs either "yes" or "no." A machine is said to accept a language if it says "yes" to all and only those strings that are in the language. Alternatively, a language can be defined as the set of strings for which a particular machine says "yes."

Formal languages can be grouped into a series of successively larger classes known as the *Chomsky hierarchy*.[12] Most of the classes can be characterized in two ways: by the types of rules that can be used to generate the set of strings, or by the type of formal machine that is capable of recognizing the language. As we have seen, *regular languages* are defined by using concatenation, alternation, and Kleene closure, and are recognized by a scanner. *Context-free languages* are a proper superset of the regular languages. They are defined by using concatenation, alternation, and recursion (which subsumes Kleene closure), and are recognized by a parser. A scanner is a concrete realization of a *finite automaton*, a type of formal machine. A parser is a concrete realization of a *push-down automaton*. Just as context-free grammars add recursion to regular expressions, push-down automata add a stack to the memory of a finite automaton. There are additional levels in the Chomsky hierarchy, but they are less directly applicable to compiler construction, and are not covered here.

It can be proven, constructively, that regular expressions and finite automata are equivalent: one can construct a finite automaton that accepts the language defined by a given regular expression, and vice versa. Similarly, it is possible to construct a push-down automaton that accepts the language defined by a given context-free grammar, and vice versa. The grammar-to-automaton constructions are in fact performed by scanner and parser generators such as `lex` and `yacc`. Of course, a real scanner does not accept just one token; it is called in a loop so that it keeps accepting tokens repeatedly. This detail is accommodated by having the scanner accept the alternation of all the tokens in the language, and by having it continue to consume characters until no longer token can be constructed.

At each level of the Chomsky hierarchy, machines can be either *deterministic* or *nondeterministic*. A deterministic automaton always performs the same operation in a given situation. A nondeterministic automaton can perform any

---

12 Noam Chomsky (1928–), a linguist and social philosopher at the Massachusetts Institute of Technology, developed much of the early theory of formal languages.

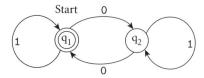

Figure 2.23 **DFA for the language consisting of all strings of zeros and ones in which the number of zeros is even.**

of a *set* of operations. A nondeterministic machine is said to accept a string if there exists a choice of operation in each situation that will eventually lead to the machine saying "yes." It turns out that nondeterministic and deterministic finite automata are equally powerful: for any NFA there is a DFA that accepts the same language. The same is not true of push-down automata: there are context-free languages that are accepted by an NPDA but not by any DPDA. Fortunately, DPDAs suffice in practice to accept the syntax of real programming languages. Practical scanners and parsers are always deterministic.

2.3.1 Finite Automata

Precisely defined, a deterministic finite automaton (DFA) M consists of (1) a finite set Q of *states*, (2) a finite alphabet Σ of input symbols, (3) a distinguished *initial* state $q_1 \in Q$, (4) a set of distinguished *final* states $F \subseteq Q$, and (5) a *transition function* $\delta : Q \times \Sigma \to Q$ that chooses a new state for M based on the current state and the current input symbol. M begins in state q_1. One by one it consumes its input symbols, using δ to move from state to state. When the final symbol has been consumed, M is interpreted as saying "yes" if it is in a state in F; otherwise it is interpreted as saying "no." We can extend δ to take strings, rather than symbols, as inputs, allowing us to say that M accepts string x if $\delta(q_1, x) \in F$. We can then define $L(M)$, the language accepted by M, to be the set $\{x \mid \delta(q_1, x) \in F\}$. In a nondeterministic finite automaton (NFA), the transition function, δ, is multivalued: the automaton can move to any of a *set* of possible states from a given state on a given input. In addition, it may move from one state to another "spontaneously"; such transitions are said to take input symbol ϵ.

We can illustrate these definitions with an example. Consider the circles-and-arrows automaton of Figure 2.23. This simple two-state machine accepts all strings of zeros and ones in which the number of zeros is even. $\Sigma = \{0, 1\}$ is the machine's input alphabet. $Q = \{q_1, q_2\}$ is the set of states; q_1 is the initial state; $F = \{q_1\}$ is the set of final states. The transition function can be represented by a set of triples $\delta = \{(q_1, 0, q_2), (q_1, 1, q_1), (q_2, 0, q_1), (q_2, 1, q_2)\}$. In each triple (q_i, a, q_j), $\delta(q_i, \mathsf{a}) = q_j$.

To show that regular expressions, NFAs, and DFAs are of equivalent expressive power, it suffices to provide an algorithm for transforming one into the other.

Specifically, (1) for any DFA we can build an equivalent regular expression, (2) for any regular expression we can build an equivalent NFA, and (3) for any NFA we can build an equivalent DFA. A scanner generator employs constructions (2) and (3), followed by a fourth construction that minimizes the number of states in the DFA. We will illustrate all four constructions here, using the even-number-of-zeros language as an example. A more formal and general treatment can be found in any automata theory text [HU79, Sip97].

We begin with the transformations performed by a scanner generator. The first of these converts a regular expression to an NFA. It employs three subconstructions, illustrated in parts (b)–(d) of Figure 2.24, to build larger NFAs to represent the concatenation, alternation, or Kleene closure of the regular expressions represented by smaller NFAs. Each step preserves three invariants: there are no transitions into the initial state, there is a single final state, and there are no transitions out of the final state. These invariants allow smaller machines to be joined into larger machines without any ambiguity about where to create the connections, and without creating any unexpected paths. The bottom part of the figure shows the result of applying these constructions to a regular expression—(1*01*0)*1*—that happens to be equivalent to our example DFA. In this particular example alternation is not required.

Because the definition of acceptance by an NFA requires that we "guess" the right transition to take at each machine step (or explore all possible transitions concurrently), NFAs are not well suited to building a scanner. We can use a "set of subsets" construction to transform the NFA into a DFA. The key idea is for the state of the DFA after reading a given input to represent the *set* of states that the NFA might have reached on the same input. We illustrate the construction (Figure 2.25) using the NFA from our running example. Initially, before it accepts any input, our NFA may be in State 1, or it may make epsilon transitions to States 2, 3, 5, 11, 12, or 14. We thus create an initial State *A* for our DFA to represent this set. On an input of 1, our NFA may move from State 3 to State 4, or from State 12 to State 13. It has no other transitions on this input from any of the states in *A*. From States 4 and 13, however, the NFA may make epsilon transitions to any of States 3, 5, 12, or 14. We therefore create DFA State *B* as shown. On a 0, our NFA may move from State 5 to State 6, from which it may reach States 7 and 9 by epsilon transitions. We therefore create DFA State *C* as shown, with a transition from *A* to *C* on 0. Careful inspection reveals that a 1 will leave the DFA in State *B*, while a 0 will move it from *B* to *C*. Continuing in this fashion, we end up creating three additional states. Each state that "contains" the final state (State 14) of the NFA is marked as a final state of the DFA.

In our example, the DFA ends up being smaller than the NFA, but this is only because our regular language is so simple. In theory, the number of states in the DFA may be exponential in the number of states in the NFA, but this extreme is also uncommon in practice. For the scanner of a programming language, the DFA tends to be larger than the NFA, but not outlandishly so.

Starting from a regular expression we have now constructed an equivalent DFA. Though this DFA has five states, we know (from Figure 2.23) that a two-

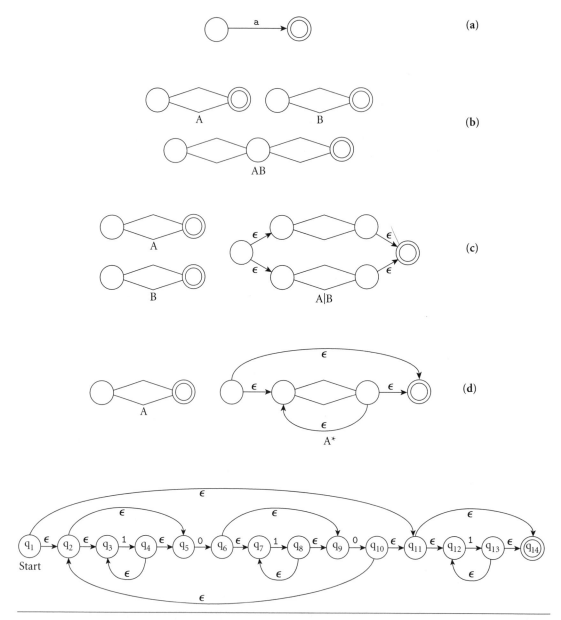

Figure 2.24 Construction of an NFA equivalent to a given regular expression. Part (a) shows the base case: the automaton for the single letter a. Parts (b), (c), and (d), respectively, show the constructions for concatenation, alternation, and Kleene closure. At the bottom is the NFA created by these constructions for the regular expression (1*01*0)* 1*.

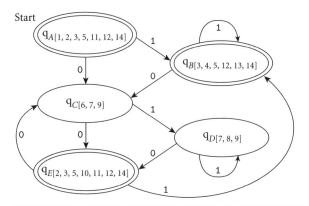

Figure 2.25 A DFA equivalent to the NFA at the bottom of Figure 2.24. Each state of the DFA represents the *set* of states that the NFA could be in after seeing the same input.

state machine exists. The final step of a scanner generator is typically to construct the *minimal* equivalent DFA. The construction works inductively. Initially we place the states of the (not necessarily minimal) DFA into two equivalence classes: final states and nonfinal states. We then repeatedly search for an equivalence class C and an input symbol a such that when given a as input, the states in C make transitions to states in $k > 1$ different equivalence classes. We then partition C into k classes in such a way that all states in a given new class would move to a member of the same old class on a. When we are unable to find a class to partition in this fashion we are done. In our example, the original placement puts States A, B, and E in one class (final states) and C and D in another. In all cases, a 1 leaves us in the current class, while a 0 takes us to the other class. Consequently, no class requires partitioning, and we are left with the two-state DFA of Figure 2.23.

To complete our proof that regular expressions, NFAs, and DFAs have equal expressive power, we must now show how to derive a regular expression that will generate the strings accepted by a given DFA. This transformation employs a dynamic programming algorithm, building solutions to successively more complicated subproblems from a table of solutions to simpler subproblems. Each subproblem requires us to find a regular expression r_{ij}^k that characterizes all strings that will cause the machine to move from state q_i to state q_j without going through any state with a subscript larger than k. Initially, let $\{a_1, a_2, \ldots, a_m\}$ be the set of all symbols $a \in \Sigma$ such that $\delta(q_i, a) = q_j$. Then if $i = j$ we have

$$r_{ij}^0 = a_1 \mid a_2 \mid \ldots \mid a_m \mid \epsilon \text{ (or just } \epsilon \text{ if the set of as is empty)}$$

If $i \neq j$, then

$$r_{ij}^0 = a_1 \mid a_2 \mid \ldots \mid a_m \text{ (or the empty regular expression if the set of as is empty)}$$

In our tiny example DFA, $r_{11}^0 = r_{22}^0 = 1 \mid \epsilon$, and $r_{12}^0 = r_{21}^0 = 0$.

We now work inductively on k. At each step, we let $r_{ij}^k = r_{ij}^{k-1} \mid r_{ik}^{k-1} r_{kk}^{k-1*} r_{kj}^{k-1}$. If any of the constituent regular expressions is empty, we omit its term of the outermost alternation. At the end, our overall answer is $r_{1f_1}^n \mid r_{1f_2}^n \mid \ldots \mid r_{1f_t}^n$, where $n = |Q|$ is the total number of states and $F = \{q_{f_1}, q_{f_2}, \ldots, q_{f_t}\}$ is the set of final states. In the first inductive step in our example,

$$r_{11}^1 = (\, 1 \mid \epsilon \,) \mid (\, 1 \mid \epsilon \,) (\, 1 \mid \epsilon \,)^* (\, 1 \mid \epsilon \,)$$
$$r_{12}^1 = 0 \mid (\, 1 \mid \epsilon \,) (\, 1 \mid \epsilon \,)^* 0$$
$$r_{22}^1 = (\, 1 \mid \epsilon \,) \mid 0 (\, 1 \mid \epsilon \,)^* 0$$
$$r_{21}^1 = 0 \mid 0 (\, 1 \mid \epsilon \,)^* (\, 1 \mid \epsilon \,)$$

In the second and final inductive step,

$$r_{11}^2 = (\, (\, 1 \mid \epsilon \,) \mid (\, 1 \mid \epsilon \,) (\, 1 \mid \epsilon \,)^* (\, 1 \mid \epsilon \,) \,) \mid$$
$$(\, 0 \mid (\, 1 \mid \epsilon \,) (\, 1 \mid \epsilon \,)^* 0 \,)$$
$$(\, (\, 1 \mid \epsilon \,) \mid 0 (\, 1 \mid \epsilon \,)^* 0 \,)^*$$
$$(\, 0 \mid 0 (\, 1 \mid \epsilon \,)^* (\, 1 \mid \epsilon \,) \,)$$

Since F has a single member (q_1), this expression is our final answer. Obviously it isn't in a minimal form, but it is correct.

2.3.2 Push-Down Automata

A deterministic push-down automaton (DPDA) N consists of (1) Q, (2) Σ, (3) q_1, and (4) F, as in a DFA, plus (6) a finite alphabet Γ of stack symbols, (7) a distinguished initial stack symbol $Z_1 \in \Gamma$, and (5′) a transition function $\delta : Q \times \Gamma \times \{\Sigma \cup \{\epsilon\}\} \rightarrow Q \times \Gamma^*$, where Γ^* is the set of strings of zero or more symbols from Γ. N begins in state q_1, with symbol Z_1 in an otherwise empty stack. It repeatedly examines the current state q and top-of-stack symbol Z. If $\delta(q, \epsilon, Z)$ is defined, N moves to state r and replaces Z with α in the stack, where $(r, \alpha) = \delta(q, \epsilon, Z)$. In this case N does not consume its input symbol. If $\delta(q, \epsilon, Z)$ is undefined, N examines and consumes the current input symbol a. It then moves to state s and replaces Z with β, where $(s, \beta) = \delta(q, \text{a}, Z)$. N is interpreted as accepting a string of input symbols x if and only if it consumes the symbols and ends in a state in F.

As with finite automata, a nondeterministic push-down automaton (NPDA) is distinguished by a multivalued transition function: an NPDA can choose any of a set of new states and stack symbol replacements when faced with a given state, input, and top-of-stack symbol. If $\delta(q, \epsilon, Z)$ is nonempty, N can also choose a new state and stack symbol replacement without inspecting or consuming its current input symbol. While we have seen that nondeterministic and deterministic finite automata are equally powerful, this correspondence does not carry over to push-down automata: there are context-free languages that are accepted by an NPDA but not by any DPDA.

The proof that CFGs and NPDAs are equivalent in expressive power is more complex than the corresponding proof for regular expressions and finite automata. The proof is also of limited practical importance for compiler construction; we do not present it here. While it is possible to create an NPDA for any CFL, that NPDA may in some cases require exponential time to recognize strings in the language. (The $O(n^3)$ algorithms mentioned in Section 2.2.2 do not take the form of PDAs.) Practical programming languages can all be expressed with LL or LR grammars, which can be parsed with a (deterministic) PDA in linear time.

An LL(1) PDA is very simple. Because it makes decisions solely on the basis of the current input token and top-of-stack symbol, its state diagram is trivial. All but one of the transitions is a self-loop from the initial state to itself. A final transition moves from the initial state to a second, final state when it sees $$ on the input and the stack. The state diagram for an LR family parser is substantially more interesting: it's the characteristic finite-state machine (CFSM). A little study reveals that if we define every state to be accepting, then the CFSM, without its stack, is a DFA that recognizes the grammar's *viable prefixes*. These are all the strings of grammar symbols that can begin a sentential form in the canonical (right-most) derivation of some string in the language, and that do not extend beyond the end of the handle. The algorithms to construct LL(1) and SLR(1) PDAs from suitable grammars were given in Sections 2.2.5 and 2.2.6.

2.3.3 Grammar and Language Classes

As we noted in Section 2.1.2, a scanner is incapable of recognizing arbitrarily nested constructs. The key to the proof is to realize that we cannot count an arbitrary number of left-bracketing symbols with a finite number of states. Consider, for example, the problem of accepting the language $0^n 1^n$. Suppose there is a DFA M that accepts this language. Suppose further that M has m states. Now suppose we feed M a string of $m + 1$ zeros. By the *pigeonhole principle* (you can't distribute m objects among $p < m$ pigeonholes without putting at least two objects in some pigeonhole), M must enter some state q_i twice while scanning this string. Without loss of generality, let us assume it does so after seeing j zeros and again after seeing k zeros, for $j \neq k$. Since we know that M accepts the string $0^j 1^j$ and the string $0^k 1^k$, and since it is in precisely the same state after reading 0^j and 0^k, we can deduce that M must also accept the strings $0^j 1^k$ and $0^k 1^j$. Since these strings are not in the language, we have a contradiction: M cannot exist.

Within the family of context-free languages, one can prove similar theorems about the constructs that can and cannot be recognized using various parsing algorithms. Containment relationships among the classes of grammars accepted by popular linear-time algorithms appear in Figure 2.26.

Grammars can be found in every region of the figure. Examples appear in Figure 2.27. Proofs that they lie in the regions claimed are deferred to Exercise 2.28.

For any context-free grammar G and parsing algorithm P, we say that G is a P grammar (e.g., an LL(1) grammar) if it can be parsed using that algorithm. By extension, for any context-free *language L*, we say that L is a P language if there exists a P grammar for L (this may not be the grammar we were given). Containment relationships among the classes of languages accepted by the popular parsing algorithms appear in Figure 2.28. Again, languages can be found in every region; examples appear in Figure 2.29. Proofs are deferred to Exercise 2.29. Note that every context-free language that can be parsed deterministically has an SLR(1) grammar. Moreover, any language that can be parsed deterministically and in which no valid string can be extended to create another valid string (this is called the *prefix property*) has an LR(0) grammar. If we restrict our attention to languages with an explicit $$ marker at end-of-file, then they all have the prefix property, and therefore LR(0) grammars.

The relationships among language classes are not as rich as the relationships among grammar classes. Most real programming languages can be parsed by any of the popular parsing algorithms, though the grammars are not always pretty, and special-purpose "hacks" may sometimes be required when a language is almost, but not quite, in a given class. The principal advantage of the more powerful parsing algorithms (e.g., full LR) is that they can parse a wider variety of grammars for a given language. In practice this flexibility makes it easier for the compiler writer to find a grammar that is intuitive and readable, and that facilitates the creation of semantic action routines.

2.4 Summary and Concluding Remarks

In this chapter we have introduced the formalisms of regular expressions and context-free grammars, and the algorithms that underlie scanning and parsing in practical compilers. We also discussed syntax error recovery, and presented a quick overview of relevant parts of automata theory. Regular expressions and context-free grammars are language *generators*: they specify how to construct valid strings of characters or tokens. Scanners and parsers are language *recognizers*: they indicate whether a given string is valid. The principal job of the scanner is to reduce the quantity of information that must be processed by the parser, by grouping characters together into tokens, and by removing comments and white space. Scanner and parser generators automatically translate regular expressions and context-free grammars into scanners and parsers.

Practical parsers for programming languages (parsers that run in linear time) fall into two principal groups: top-down (also called LL or predictive) and bottom-up (also called LR or shift-reduce). A top-down parser constructs a parse tree starting from the root and proceeding in a left-to-right depth-first

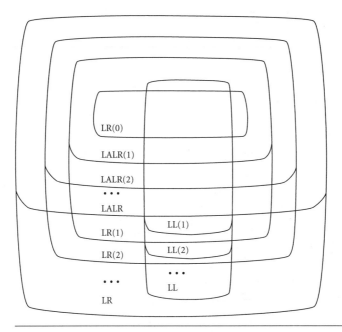

Figure 2.26 Containment relationships among popular grammar classes. In addition to the containments shown, SLL(k) is just inside LL(k), but has the same relationship to everything else, and SLR(k) is just inside LALR(k), but has the same relationship to everything else.

LL(2) but not SLL:
$S \rightarrow$ a A a $\mid$ b A b a
$A \rightarrow$ b $\mid \epsilon$

SLL(k) but not LL($k - 1$):
$S \rightarrow$ a^{k-1} b $\mid$ a^k

LR(0) but not LL:
$S \rightarrow A$ b
$A \rightarrow A$ a $\mid$ a

SLL(1) but not LALR:
$S \rightarrow A$ a $\mid B$ b $\mid$ c C
$C \rightarrow A$ b $\mid B$ a
$A \rightarrow D$
$B \rightarrow D$
$D \rightarrow \epsilon$

SLL(k) and SLR(k) but not LR($k - 1$):
$S \rightarrow A$ a^{k-1} b $\mid B$ a^{k-1} c
$A \rightarrow \epsilon$
$B \rightarrow \epsilon$

LALR(1) but not SLR:
$S \rightarrow$ b A b $\mid A$ c $\mid$ a b
$A \rightarrow$ a

LR(1) but not LALR:
$S \rightarrow$ a C a $\mid$ b C b $\mid$ a D b $\mid$ b D a
$C \rightarrow$ c
$D \rightarrow$ c

Unambiguous but not LR:
$S \rightarrow$ a S a $\mid \epsilon$

Figure 2.27 Examples of grammars in various regions of Figure 2.26.

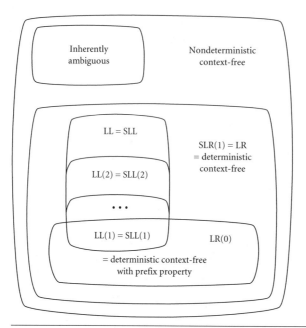

Figure 2.28 Containment relationships among popular language classes.

Non-deterministic language:
$$\{a^n b^n c : n \geq 1\} \cup \{a^n b^{2n} d : n \geq 1\}$$

Inherently ambiguous language:
$$\{a^i b^j c^k : i = j \text{ or } j = k; \ i, j, k \geq 1\}$$

Language with LL(k) grammar but no LL($k-1$) grammar:
$$\{a^n (\,b\,|\,c\,|\,b^k d\,)^n : n \geq 1\}$$

Language with LR(0) grammar but no LL grammar:
$$\{a^n b^n : n \geq 1\} \cup \{a^n c^n : n \geq 1\}$$

Figure 2.29 Examples of languages in various regions of Figure 2.28.

traversal. A bottom-up parser constructs a parse tree starting from the leaves, again working left-to-right, and combining partial trees together when it recognizes the children of an internal node. The stack of a top-down parser contains a prediction of what will be seen in the future; the stack of a bottom-up parser contains a record of what has been seen in the past.

Top-down parsers tend to be simple, both in the parsing of valid strings and in the recovery from errors in invalid strings. Bottom-up parsers are more powerful, and in some cases lend themselves to more intuitively structured grammars, though they suffer from the inability to embed action routines at arbitrary points in a right-hand side (we will discuss this point in more detail in Section 4.5.1). Both varieties of parser are used in real compilers, though bottom-up parsers are more common. Top-down parsers tend to be smaller in terms of code and data size, but modern machines provide ample memory for either.

Both scanners and parsers can be built by hand if an automatic tool is not available. Hand-built scanners are simple enough to be relatively common. Hand-built parsers are generally limited to top-down recursive descent, and are generally used only for comparatively simple languages (e.g., Pascal but not Ada). Automatic generation of the scanner and parser has the advantage of increased reliability, reduced development time, and easy modification and enhancement.

Various features of language design can have a major impact on the complexity of syntax analysis. In many cases, features that make it difficult for a compiler to scan or parse also make it difficult for a human being to write correct, maintainable code. We have seen two examples in this chapter. In the first, the lexical structure of Fortran permits radically different constructs to differ in lexically trivial ways, requiring large amounts of scanner look-ahead, and making it easy for the programmer to introduce bugs. (A much smaller instance of lexical complexity occurs in the "dot-dot problem" of Pascal.) In the second example, the structure of Pascal's `if...then...else` statement makes it difficult or impossible to parse the language without ambiguity-resolving heuristics. It also makes it easy to write code whose semantics do not match the programmer's intent. This interplay between language design, implementation, and use will be a recurring theme throughout the remainder of the book.

2.5 Review Questions

2.1 What is the difference between syntax and semantics?

2.2 What is a Kleene star?

2.3 What are the three basic operations that can be used to build complex regular expressions from simpler regular expressions?

2.4 What additional operation (beyond the three of regular expressions) is provided in context-free grammars?

2.5 What is Backus-Naur form? When and why was it devised?

2.6 Name a language in which indentation affects program syntax.

2.7 When discussing context-free languages, what is a *derivation*? What is a sentential form?

2.8 What is the difference between a right-most derivation and a left-most derivation? Which one of them is also called *canonical*?

2.9 What does it mean for a context-free grammar to be *ambiguous*?

2.10 Why must a scanner save the text of tokens?

2.11 What is a pragma?

2.12 Why must a scanner sometimes "peek" at upcoming characters?

2.13 What are associativity and precedence?

2.14 Summarize the difference between LL and LR parsing. Which one of them is also called "bottom-up"? "Top-down"? Which one is also called "predictive"? "Shift-reduce"? What do "LL" and "LR" stand for?

2.15 What kind of parser (top-down or bottom-up) is most common in production compilers?

2.16 What kind of parser is produced by `yacc/bison`?

2.17 What are the advantages of an automatically generated scanner, in comparison to a hand-written one? Why do most commercial compilers use a hand-written scanner anyway? Why don't they use a hand-written parser?

2.18 What are FIRST and FOLLOW sets? What are they used for?

2.19 Describe two situations in which context-specific FOLLOW sets may be useful.

2.20 Describe two common idioms in context-free grammars that cannot be parsed top-down.

2.21 What is the "dangling `else`" problem? How is it avoided in modern languages?

2.22 Explain the significance of the characteristic finite state machine in LR parsing.

2.23 What is the significance of the dot (•) in an LR item?

2.24 What distinguishes the *basis* from the *closure* of an LR state?

2.25 What is the *handle* of a right sentential form?

2.26* What is *panic mode*? What is its principal weakness?

2.27* What are *cascading errors*?

2.28* Why might a parser that incorporates a high-quality general-purpose error recovery algorithm still benefit from error productions?

2.29 What formal machine captures the behavior of a scanner? A parser?

2.30 State three ways in which a real scanner differs from the formal machine.

2.31* How many states does a top-down parser have?

2.32* Is every LL(1) grammar also LR(1)? Is it LALR(1)?

2.33* Does every LR language have an SLR(1) grammar?

2.6 Exercises

2.1 Some languages (e.g., C) distinguish between upper- and lowercase letters in identifiers. Others (e.g., Ada) do not. Which convention do you prefer? Why?

2.2 What do you think of Occam and Haskell's use of indentation to delimit control constructs (Section 2.1.1)? Would you expect this convention to make program construction and maintenance easier or harder? Why?

2.3 Write regular expressions to capture

(a) Strings in C. These are delimited by double quotes ("), and may not contain newline characters. They may contain a double quote if it is preceded by a single backslash. You may find it helpful to introduce short-hand notation to represent any character that is *not* a member of a small specified set.

(b) Comments in Pascal. These are delimited by (* and *), as shown in Figure 2.5.

(c) Floating-point constants in Ada. These are the same as in Pascal (see the definition of *unsigned_number* on page 34), except that (1) an underscore is permitted between digits, and (2) an alternative numeric base may be specified by surrounding the nonexponent part of the number with pound signs, preceded by a base in decimal (e.g. 16#6.a7#e+2). In this latter case, the letters a..f (both upper and lower case) are permitted as digits. Use of these letters in an inappropriate (e.g., decimal) number is an error, but need not be caught by the scanner.

2.4 Show (as "circles-and-arrows" diagrams) the finite automata for parts (a) and (c) of Exercise 2.3.

2.5 Build a regular expression that captures all sequences of letters other than `file`, `for`, and `from`. For notational convenience, you may assume the existence of a *not* operator that takes a set of letters as argument and matches any *other* letter. Comment on the practicality of constructing a regular expression for all sequences of letters other than the keywords of a large programming language.

2.6 Consider the following grammar:

$$G \rightarrow S \ \$\$$$
$$S \rightarrow A \ M$$
$$M \rightarrow S \mid \epsilon$$
$$A \rightarrow \text{a} \ E \mid \text{b} \ A \ A$$
$$E \rightarrow \text{a} \ B \mid \text{b} \ A \mid \epsilon$$
$$B \rightarrow \text{b} \ E \mid \text{a} \ B \ B$$

(a) Describe in English the language that the grammar generates. (b) Show a parse tree for the string a b a a. (c) Is the grammar LL(1)? If so, show the parse table; if not, identify a prediction conflict.

2.7 Many tools that are capable of searching for patterns in ASCII text, including editors, web search engines, and the Unix `grep`, `sed`, `awk`, and perl utilities, use some variant of regular expressions to specify the target of a search. Learn the details of one or more of these variants. Prove or disprove that they are equal in expressive power to the basic regular expressions introduced in Section 2.1.1.

2.8 Build an ad hoc scanner for the calculator language. As output, have it print a list, in order, of the input tokens.

2.9 Build a nested-case-statements finite automaton that converts all letters in its input to lower case, except within Pascal-style comments and strings. A Pascal comment is delimited by { and }, or by (* and *). Comments do not nest. A Pascal string is delimited by single quotes (' ... '). A quote character can be placed in a string by doubling it ('Madam, I''m Adam.'). This upper-to-lower mapping can be useful if feeding a program written in standard Pascal (which ignores case) to a compiler that considers upper- and lowercase letters to be distinct.

2.10 Rebuild the automaton of the previous question using lex/flex.

2.11 Give an example of a grammar that captures right associativity for an exponentiation operator (e.g. ** in Fortran).

2.12 Give an example of a grammar that captures all the levels of precedence for arithmetic expressions in C.

2.13 Write top-down and bottom-up grammars for the language consisting of all well-formed regular expressions. Arrange for all operators to be left-associative. Give Kleene closure the highest precedence and alternation the lowest precedence.

2.14 Suppose that the expression grammar on page 38 were to be used in conjunction with a scanner that did *not* remove comments from the input, but rather returned them as tokens. How would the grammar need to be modified to allow comments to appear at arbitrary places in the input?

2.15 Build a complete recursive descent parser for the calculator language. As output, have it print a trace of its matches and predictions.

2.16 Flesh out the details of an algorithm to eliminate left recursion and common prefixes in an arbitrary context-free grammar.

2.17 In some languages an assignment can appear in any context in which an expression is expected: the value of the expression is the right-hand side of the assignment, which is placed into the left-hand side as a side effect. Consider the following grammar fragment for such a language. Explain why it is not LL(1), and discuss what might be done to make it so.

$expr \rightarrow$ id := $expr$

$expr \rightarrow term\ term\_tail$

$term\_tail \rightarrow$ + $term\ term\_tail\ |\ \epsilon$

$term \rightarrow factor\ factor\_tail$

$factor\_tail \rightarrow$ * $factor\ factor\_tail\ |\ \epsilon$

$factor \rightarrow$ ($expr$) $|$ id

2.18 Construct a trace over time of the forest of partial parse trees manipulated by a bottom-up parser for the string "A, B, C" using the grammar on page 51 (the one that is able to collapse prefixes of the *id_list* as it goes along).

2.19 Construct the CFSM for the *id_list* grammar found on page 49 and verify that it can be parsed bottom-up with *zero* tokens of look-ahead.

2.20 Modify the grammar in Exercise 2.19 to allow an *id_list* to be empty. Is the grammar still LR(0)?

2.21 Consider the following grammar for a declaration list:

decl_list → *decl_list decl* ; | *decl* ;

decl → id : *type*

type → int | real | char

      → array const .. const of *type*

      → record *decl_list* end

Construct the CFSM for this grammar. Use it to trace out a parse (as in Figure 2.22) for the following input program:

```
foo : record
        a : char
        b : array 1..2 of real
     end
```

2.22 The dangling else problem of Pascal is not shared by Algol 60. To avoid ambiguity regarding which then is matched by an else, Algol 60 prohibits if statements immediately inside a then clause. The Pascal fragment

```
if C1 then if C2 then S1 else S2
```

must be written as either

```
if C1 then begin if C2 then S1 end else S2
```

or

```
if C1 then begin if C2 then S1 else S2 end
```

in Algol 60. Show how to write a grammar for conditional statements that enforces this rule. (Hint: you will want to distinguish in your grammar between conditional statements and nonconditional statements; some contexts will accept either, some only the latter.)

2.23 Find a manual for yacc/bison, or consult a compiler textbook [ASU86] to learn about *operator precedence parsing*. Explain how it could be used to simplify the grammar of Exercise 2.12.

2.24 Use `lex/flex` and `yacc/bison` to construct a parser for the calculator language. Have it output a trace of its shifts and reductions.

2.25* Experiment with syntax errors in your favorite compiler. Feed the compiler deliberate errors and comment on the quality of the recovery or repair. How often does it do the "right thing"? How often does it generate cascading errors? Speculate as to what sort of recovery or repair algorithm it might be using.

2.26* Give an example of an erroneous program fragment in which consideration of semantic information (e.g., types) might help one make a good choice between two plausible "corrections" of the input.

2.27* Give an example of an erroneous program fragment in which the "best" correction would require one to "back up" the parser (i.e., to undo recent predictions/matches or shifts/reductions).

2.28* Prove that the grammars in Figure 2.27 lie in the regions claimed.

2.29* Prove that the languages in Figure 2.29 lie in the regions claimed.

2.30* Prove that regular expressions and *left-linear grammars* are equally powerful. A left linear grammar is a context-free grammar in which every right-hand side contains at most one nonterminal, and then only at the left-most end.

2.7 Bibliographic Notes

Our coverage of scanning and parsing in this chapter has of necessity been brief. Considerably more detail can be found in texts on parsing theory [AU72] and compiler construction [ASU86, FL88, App97]. Many compilers of the early 1960s employed recursive descent parsers. Lewis and Stearns [LS68] and Rosenkrantz and Stearns [RS70] published early formal studies of LL grammars and parsing. The original formulation of LR parsing is due to Knuth [Knu65]. Bottom-up parsing became practical with DeRemer's discovery of the SLR and LALR algorithms [DeR69, DeR71]. W. L. Johnson et al. [JPAR68] describe an early scanner generator. The Unix `lex` tool is due to Lesk [Les75]. `Yacc` is due to S. C. Johnson [Joh75].

Further details on formal language theory can be found in a variety of textbooks, including the classic work by Hopcroft and Ullman [HU79] and the more recent work of Sipser [Sip97]. Kleene [Kle56] and Rabin and Scott [RS59] proved the equivalence of regular expressions and finite automata. The proof that finite automata are unable to recognize nested constructs is based on a theorem known as the *pumping lemma*, due to Bar-Hillel, Perles, and Shamir [BHPS61]. Context-free grammars were first explored by Chomsky [Cho56] in the context of natural language. Independently, Backus and Naur developed BNF for the syntactic description of Algol 60 [NBB$^+$63]. Ginsburg and Rice [GR62] recognized the equivalence of the two notations. Chomsky [Cho62] and Evey [Eve63] demonstrated the equivalence of context-free grammars and push-down automata.

Fischer and LeBlanc's text [FL88] contains an excellent survey of error recovery and repair techniques, with references to other work. The phrase-level recovery mechanism for recursive descent parsers described in Section 2.2.4 is due to Wirth [Wir76, Sec. 5.9]. The locally least-cost recovery mechanism for table-driven LL parsers described in Section 2.2.5 is due to Fischer, Milton, and Quiring [FMQ80]. Dion published a locally least-cost bottom-up repair algorithm in 1978 [Dio78]. It is quite complex, and requires very large precomputed tables. More recently, McKenzie, Yeatman, and De Vere have shown how to effect the same repairs without the precomputed tables, at a higher but still acceptable cost in time [MYD95].

Names, Scopes, and Bindings

"High-level" programming languages take their name from the relatively high level, or degree of abstraction, of the features they provide, relative to those of the assembly languages that they were originally designed to replace. The adjective "abstract," in this context, refers to the degree to which language features are separated from the details of any particular computer architecture. The early development of languages such as Fortran, Algol, and Lisp was driven by a pair of complementary goals: machine independence and ease of programming. By abstracting the language away from the hardware, designers not only made it possible to write programs that would run well on a wide variety of machines, but also made the programs easier for human beings to understand.

Machine independence is a fairly simple concept. Basically it says that a programming language should not rely on the features of any particular instruction set for its efficient implementation. Machine dependences still become a problem from time to time (as of this writing, for example, standards committees for C are wrestling with the issue of how best to accommodate new machines with 64-bit arithmetic), but with a few noteworthy exceptions (Java comes to mind) it has probably been 30 years since the desire for greater machine independence has really driven language design. Ease of programming, on the other hand, is a much more elusive and compelling goal. It affects every aspect of language design, and has historically been less a matter of science than of aesthetics and trial and error.

This chapter is the first of five to address core issues in language design. The others are Chapters 6, 7, 8, and 10. In Chapter 6 we will look at control-flow constructs, which allow the programmer to specify the order in which operations are to occur. In contrast to the jump-based control flow of assembly languages, high-level control flow relies heavily on the lexical nesting of constructs. In Chapter 7 we will look at types, which allow the programmer to organize program data and the operations on them. In Chapters 8 and 10 we will look at subroutines and classes. In the current chapter we will look at *names*.

A name is a mnemonic character string used to represent something else. Names in most languages are identifiers (alpha-numeric tokens), though certain other symbols, such as + or :=, can also be names. Names allow us to refer to variables, constants, operations, types, and so on using symbolic identifiers rather than low-level concepts like addresses. Names are also essential in the context of a second meaning of the word *abstraction*. In this second meaning, abstraction is a process by which the programmer associates a name with a potentially complicated program fragment, which can then be thought of in terms of its purpose or function, rather than in terms of how that function is achieved. By hiding irrelevant details, abstraction reduces conceptual complexity, making it possible for the programmer to focus on a manageable subset of the program text at any particular time. Subroutines are *control abstractions*: they allow the programmer to hide arbitrarily complicated code behind a simple interface. Classes are *data abstractions*: they allow the programmer to hide data representation details behind a (comparatively) simple set of operations.

We will look at several major issues related to names. Section 3.1 introduces the notion of *binding time*, which refers not only to the binding of a name to the thing it represents, but also in general to the notion of resolving any design decision in a language implementation. Section 3.2 outlines the various mechanisms used to allocate and deallocate storage space for objects, and distinguishes between the lifetime of an object and the lifetime of a binding of a name to that object.[1] Section 3.3 notes that most name-to-object bindings are usable only within a limited region of a given high-level program, and examines the *scope* rules that define this region. The complete set of bindings in effect at a given point in a program is known as the current *referencing environment*. Section 3.4 expands on the notion of scope rules by considering the ways in which a referencing environment may be bound to a subroutine that is passed as a parameter, returned from a function, or stored in a variable. Section 3.5 discusses overloading, which allows a name to refer to more than one object in a given scope, depending on the context of the reference. The discussion touches on several related topics, including coercion, polymorphism, generic subroutines, and aliases. Finally, Section 3.6 discusses pitfalls related to naming in programming language design.

3.1 The Notion of Binding Time

A *binding* is an association between two things, such as a name and the thing it names. *Binding time* is the time at which a binding is created or, more generally, the time at which any implementation decision is made (we can think of this

---

[1] For want of a better term, we will use the term "object" throughout Chapters 3–8 to refer to anything that might have a name: variables, constants, types, subroutines, modules, and others. In many modern languages, including Smalltalk, Eiffel, C++, Java, Modula-3, and Ada 95, "object" has a more formal meaning, which we will consider in Chapter 10.

as binding an answer to a question). There are many different times at which decisions may be bound:

Language design time: In most languages, the control flow constructs, the set of fundamental (primitive) types, the available *constructors* for creating complex types, and many other aspects of language semantics are chosen when the language is designed.

Language implementation time: Most language manuals leave a variety of issues to the discretion of the language implementor. Typical examples include the precision (number of bits) of the fundamental types, the coupling of I/O to the operating system's notion of files, the organization and maximum sizes of stack and heap, and the handling of run-time exceptions such as arithmetic overflow.

Program writing time: Programmers, of course, choose algorithms, data structures, and names.

Compile time: Compilers choose the mapping of high-level constructs to machine code, including the layout of statically defined data in memory.

Link time: Since most compilers support *separate compilation*—compiling different modules of a program at different times—and depend on the availability of a library of standard subroutines, a program is usually not complete until the various modules are joined together by a linker. The linker chooses the overall layout of the modules with respect to one another, and resolves intermodule references. When a name in one module refers to an object in another module, the binding between the two is not finalized until link time.

Load time: Load time refers to the point at which the operating system loads the program into memory so that it can run. In primitive operating systems, the choice of machine addresses for objects within the program is not finalized until load time. Most modern operating systems distinguish between virtual and physical addresses. Virtual addresses are chosen at link time; physical addresses can actually change at run time. The processor's memory management hardware translates virtual addresses into physical addresses during each individual instruction at run time.

Run time: Run time is actually a very broad term that covers the entire span from the beginning to the end of execution. Bindings of values to variables occur at run time, as do a host of other decisions that vary from language to language. Run time subsumes program start-up time, module entry time, elaboration time (the point at which a declaration is first "seen"), subroutine call time, block entry time, and statement execution time.

The terms *static* and *dynamic* are generally used to refer to things bound before run time and at run time, respectively. Clearly "static" is a coarse term. So is "dynamic."

It is difficult to overemphasize the importance of binding times in the design and implementation of programming languages. In general, early binding times are associated with greater efficiency. Later binding times are associated with greater flexibility. Compiler-based language implementations tend to be more efficient than interpreter-based implementations because they make earlier decisions. For example, a compiler analyzes the syntax and semantics of global variable declarations once, before the program ever runs. It decides on a layout for those variables in memory, and generates efficient code to access them wherever they appear in the program. A pure interpreter, by contrast, must analyze the declarations every time the program begins execution. In the worst case, an interpreter may reanalyze the local declarations within a subroutine each time that subroutine is called. If a call appears in a deeply nested loop, the savings achieved by a compiler that is able to analyze the declarations only once may be very large. As we shall see in the following section, a compiler will not usually be able to predict the address of a local variable at compile time, since space for the variable will be allocated dynamically on a stack, but it can arrange for the variable to appear at a fixed offset from the location pointed to by a certain register at run time.

Some languages are difficult to compile because their definitions require certain fundamental decisions to be postponed until run time, generally in order to increase the flexibility or expressiveness of the language. Smalltalk, for example, delays all type checking until run time. All operations in Smalltalk are cast in the form of "messages" to "objects." A message is acceptable if and only if the object provides a handler for it. References to objects of arbitrary types (classes) can then be assigned into arbitrary named variables, as long as the program never ends up sending a message to an object that is not prepared to handle it. This form of *polymorphism*—allowing a variable name to refer to objects of multiple types—allows the Smalltalk programmer to write very general-purpose code, which will correctly manipulate objects whose types had yet to be fully defined at the time the code was written. We will mention polymorphism again in Section 3.5, and discuss it further in Chapters 7 and 10.

3.2 Object Lifetime and Storage Management

In any discussion of names and bindings, it is important to distinguish between names and the objects to which they refer, and to identify several key events:

- The creation of objects
- The creation of bindings
- References to variables, subroutines, types, and so on, all of which use bindings
- The deactivation and reactivation of bindings that may be temporarily unusable

■ The destruction of bindings

■ The destruction of objects

The period of time between the creation and the destruction of a name-to-object binding is called the binding's *lifetime*. Similarly, the time between the creation and destruction of an object is the object's lifetime. These lifetimes need not necessarily coincide. In particular, an object may retain its value and the potential to be accessed even when a given name can no longer be used to access it. When a variable is passed to a subroutine by *reference*, for example (as it typically is in Fortran or with var parameters in Pascal), the binding between the parameter name and the variable that was passed has a lifetime shorter than that of the variable itself. It is also possible, though generally a sign of a program bug, for a name-to-object binding to have a lifetime *longer* than that of the object. This can happen, for example, if an object created via the Pascal new operator is passed as a var parameter and then deallocated (dispose-ed) before the subroutine returns. A binding to an object that is no longer live is called a *dangling reference*. Dangling references will be discussed further in Sections 3.4 and 7.7.2.

Object lifetimes generally correspond to one of three principal *storage allocation* mechanisms, used to manage the object's space:

1. *Static* objects are given an absolute address that is retained throughout the program's execution.

2. *Stack* objects are allocated in last-in, first-out order, usually in conjunction with subroutine calls and returns.

3. *Heap* objects may be allocated and deallocated at arbitrary times. They require a more general (and expensive) storage management algorithm.

Global variables are the obvious example of static objects, but not the only one. The instructions that constitute a program's machine-language translation can also be thought of as statically allocated objects. In addition, we will see examples in Section 3.3.1 of variables that are local to a single subroutine, but retain their values from one invocation to the next; their space is statically allocated. Numeric and string-valued constant literals are also statically allocated, for statements such as A := B/14.7 or writeln ('hello, world'). (Small constants are often stored within the instruction itself; larger ones are assigned a separate location.) Finally, most compilers produce a variety of tables that are used by run-time support routines, e.g., for debugging, dynamic type checking, garbage collection, exception handling, and other purposes; these are also statically allocated. Statically allocated objects whose value should not change during program execution (e.g., instructions, constants, and certain run-time tables) are often allocated in protected, read-only memory, so that any inadvertent attempt to write to them will cause a processor interrupt, allowing the operating system to announce a run-time error.

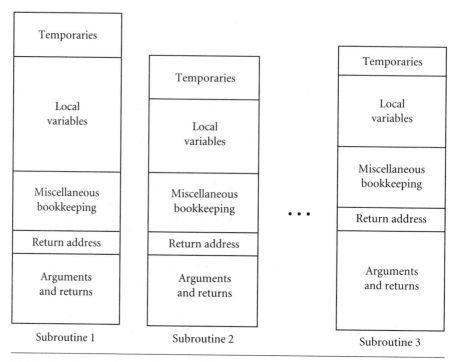

Figure 3.1 **Static allocation of space for subroutines in a language or program without recursion.**

Logically speaking, local variables are created when their subroutine is called, and destroyed when it returns. If the subroutine is called repeatedly, each invocation is said to create and destroy a separate *instance* of each local variable. It is not always the case, however, that a language implementation must perform work at run time corresponding to these create and destroy operations. Recursion was not originally supported in Fortran (it was added in Fortran 90), largely because of the expense of stack manipulation on the IBM 704. Without recursion, there can never be more than one invocation of a subroutine active at any given time. A compiler may therefore choose to use static allocation for local variables, effectively arranging for the variables of different invocations to share the same locations, and thereby avoiding any run-time overhead for creation and destruction (Figure 3.1).

In many languages a constant is required to have a value that can be determined at compile time. Usually the expression that specifies the constant's value is permitted to include only literal (*manifest*) constants and built-in functions and arithmetic operators. These sorts of *compile-time constants* can always be allocated statically, even if they are local to a recursive subroutine: multiple instances can share the same location. In other languages (e.g., C and Ada), constants are simply variables that cannot be changed after elaboration time. Their values, though unchanging, can depend on other values that are not known until run time. These *elaboration-time constants*, when local to a recursive subroutine, must be allocated on the stack.

Along with local variables and elaboration-time constants, the compiler typically stores a variety of other information associated with the subroutine, including:

Arguments and return values. Modern compilers keep these in registers whenever possible, but sometimes space in memory is needed.

Temporaries. These are usually intermediate values produced in complex calculations. Again, a good compiler will keep them in registers whenever possible.

Bookkeeping information. This may include the subroutine's return address (also called the *dynamic link*), saved registers, debugging information, and various other values that we will study later.

3.2.1 Stack-Based Allocation

If a language permits recursion, static allocation of local variables is no longer an option, since the number of instances of a variable that may need to exist at the same time is conceptually unbounded. Fortunately, the natural nesting of subroutine calls makes it easy to allocate space for locals on a stack. A simplified picture of a typical stack appears in Figure 3.2. Each instance of a subroutine at run time has its own *frame* (also called an *activation record*) on the stack, containing arguments and return values, local variables, temporaries, and bookkeeping information. Arguments and return values lie at the bottom of the frame, where they are easily accessible to the caller. The organization of the remaining information is implementation-dependent: it varies from one language and compiler to another.

Maintenance of the stack is the responsibility of the subroutine *calling sequence*—the code executed by the caller immediately before and after the call—and of the *prologue* (code executed at the beginning) and *epilogue* (code executed at the end) of the subroutine itself. Sometimes the term "calling sequence" is used to refer to the combined operations of the caller, the prologue, and the epilogue. We will study calling sequences in more detail in Section 8.2.

While the location of a stack frame cannot be predicted at compile time (the compiler cannot in general tell what other frames may already be on the stack), the offsets of objects *within* a frame usually *can* be statically determined. Moreover, the compiler can arrange (in the calling sequence or prologue) for a particular register, known as the *frame pointer* to always point to a known location within the frame of the current subroutine. Code that needs to access a particular object within the frame (e.g., a local variable) can then find the object's address by adding its predetermined offset to the value in the frame pointer. As we will see in Section 5.4.1, almost every processor provides an *addressing mode* that allows this addition to be specified implicitly as part of an ordinary `load`

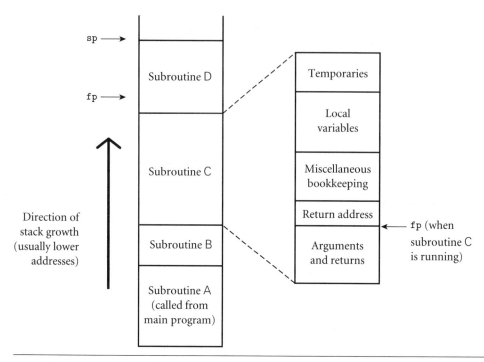

Figure 3.2 Stack-based allocation of space for subroutines. We assume here that subroutine A has been called by the main program, and that it then calls subroutine B. Subroutine B subsequently calls C, which in turn calls D. At any given time, the stack pointer (sp) register points to the first unused location on the stack, and the frame pointer (fp) register points to a known location within the frame (activation record) of the current subroutine. The relative order of fields within a frame may vary from machine to machine and compiler to compiler.

or `store` instruction. The stack grows "downward" toward lower addresses in most language implementations. Some machines provide special `push` and `pop` instructions that assume this direction of growth. Arguments and returns typically have positive offsets from the frame pointer; local variables, temporaries, and bookkeeping information typically have negative offsets.

Even in a language without recursion, it can be advantageous to use a stack for local variables, rather than allocating them statically. In most programs the pattern of potential calls among subroutines does not permit all of those subroutines to be active at the same time. As a result, the total space needed for local variables of currently active subroutines is seldom as large as the total space across *all* subroutines, active or not. A stack may therefore require substantially less memory at run time than would be required for static allocation.

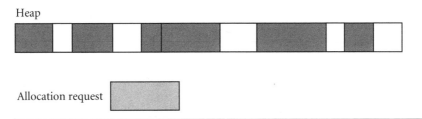

Figure 3.3 External fragmentation. The shaded blocks are in use; the clear blocks are free. While there is more than enough total free space remaining to satisfy an allocation request of the illustrated size, no single remaining block is large enough.

3.2.2 Heap-Based Allocation

A *heap* is a region of storage in which subblocks can be allocated and deallocated at arbitrary times.[2] Heaps are required for the dynamically allocated pieces of linked data structures, and for dynamically resized objects such as fully general character strings, lists, and sets, whose size may change as a result of an assignment statement or other update operation.

There are many possible strategies to manage space in a heap. We review the major alternatives here; details can be found in any data-structures textbook. The principal concerns are speed and space, and as usual there are tradeoffs between them. Space concerns can be further subdivided into issues of internal and external *fragmentation*. Internal fragmentation occurs when a storage-management algorithm allocates a block that is larger than required to hold a given object; the extra space is then unused. External fragmentation occurs when the blocks that have been assigned to active objects are scattered through the heap in such a way that the remaining, unused space is composed of multiple blocks: there may be quite a lot of free space, but no one piece of it may be large enough to satisfy some future request (see Figure 3.3).

Many storage-management algorithms maintain a single linked list—the *free list*—of heap blocks not currently in use. Initially the list consists of a single block comprising the entire heap. At each allocation request the algorithm searches the list for a block of appropriate size. With a *first fit* algorithm we select the first block on the list that is large enough to satisfy the request. With a *best fit* algorithm we search the entire list to find the smallest block that is large enough to satisfy the request. In either case, if the chosen block is significantly larger than required, then we divide it in two and return the unneeded portion to the free list as a smaller block. (If the unneeded portion is below some minimum threshold in size, we may leave it in the allocated block as internal fragmentation.) When a

---

2 Unfortunately, the term "heap" is also used for a common tree-based implementation of a priority queue. These two uses of the term have nothing to do with one another.

block is deallocated and returned to the free list, we check to see whether either or both of the physically adjacent blocks are free; if so, we coalesce them.

Intuitively, one would expect a best fit algorithm to do a better job of reserving large blocks for large requests. At the same time, it has higher allocation cost than a first fit algorithm, because it must always search the entire list, and it tends to result in a larger number of very small "left-over" blocks. Which approach—first fit or best fit—results in lower external fragmentation depends on the distribution of size requests.

In any algorithm that maintains a single free list, the cost of allocation is linear in the number of free blocks. To reduce this cost to a constant, some storage management algorithms maintain separate free lists for blocks of different sizes. Each request is rounded up to the next standard size (at the cost of internal fragmentation) and allocated from the appropriate list. In effect, the heap is divided into "pools," one for each standard size. The division may be static or dynamic. Two common mechanisms for dynamic pool adjustment are known as the *buddy system* and the *Fibonacci heap*. In the buddy system, the standard block sizes are powers of two. If a block of size 2^k is needed, but none is available, a block of size 2^{k+1} is split in two. One of the halves is used to satisfy the request; the other is placed on the kth free list. When a block is deallocated, it is coalesced with its "buddy"—the other half of the split that created it—if that buddy is free. Fibonacci heaps are similar, but use Fibonacci numbers for the standard sizes, instead of powers of two. The algorithm is slightly more complex, but leads to slightly lower internal fragmentation, because the Fibonacci sequence grows more slowly than 2^n.

The problem with external fragmentation is that the ability of the heap to satisfy requests may degrade over time. Multiple free lists may help, by clustering small blocks in relatively close physical proximity, but they do not eliminate the problem. It is always possible to devise a sequence of requests that cannot be satisfied, even though the total space required is less than the size of the heap. If size pools are statically allocated, one need only exceed the maximum number of requests of a given size. If pools are dynamically readjusted, one can "checkerboard" the heap by allocating a large number of small blocks and then deallocating every other one, in order of physical address, leaving an alternating pattern of small free and allocated blocks. To eliminate external fragmentation, we must be prepared to *compact* the heap, by moving already-allocated blocks. This task is complicated by the need to find and update all outstanding references to a block that is being moved. We will discuss compaction further in Sections 7.7.2 and 7.7.3.

3.2.3 Garbage Collection

Allocation of heap-based objects is always triggered by some specific operation in a program: appending to the end of a list, assigning a long value into a previously short string, and so on. Deallocation is also explicit in some languages (e.g.,

Pascal and C). As we shall see in Section 7.7, however, many languages specify that objects are to be deallocated implicitly when it is no longer possible to reach them from any program variable. The run-time library for such a language must then provide a *garbage collection* mechanism to identify and reclaim unreachable objects. Most functional languages require garbage collection, as do many more recent imperative languages, including Ada, Modula-3, and Java.

The traditional arguments in favor of explicit deallocation are implementation simplicity and execution speed. Even naive implementations of automatic garbage collection add significant complexity to the implementation of a language with a rich type system, and even the most sophisticated garbage collector can consume nontrivial amounts of time in certain programs. If the programmer can correctly identify the end of an object's lifetime, without too much run-time bookkeeping, the result is likely to be faster execution.

The argument in favor of automatic garbage collection, however, is compelling: manual deallocation errors are among the most common and costly bugs in real-world programs. If an object is deallocated too soon, the program may follow a *dangling reference*, accessing memory now used by another object. If an object is *not* deallocated at the end of its lifetime, then the program may "leak memory," eventually running out of heap space. Deallocation errors are notoriously difficult to identify and fix. Over time, both language designers and programmers have increasingly come to consider automatic garbage collection an essential language feature. Garbage-collection algorithms have improved, reducing their run-time overhead; language implementations have become more complex in general, reducing the marginal complexity of automatic collection; and leading-edge applications have become larger and more complex, making the benefits of automatic collection ever more appealing.

3.3 Scope Rules

The textual region of the program in which a binding is active is its *scope*. In most modern languages, the scope of a binding is determined statically, that is, at compile time. In C, for example, we introduce a new scope upon entry to a subroutine. We create bindings for local objects and deactivate bindings for global objects that are "hidden" by local objects of the same name. On subroutine exit, we destroy bindings for local variables and reactivate bindings for any global objects that were hidden. These manipulations of bindings may at first glance appear to be run-time operations, but they do not require the execution of any code: the portions of the program in which a binding is active are completely determined at compile time. We can look at a C program and know which names refer to which objects at which points in the program based on purely textual rules. For this reason, C is said to be *statically scoped* (some authors say *lexically scoped*[3]). Other languages, including APL, Snobol, and early dialects of Lisp, are *dynamically scoped*: their bindings depend on the flow of execution at run time. We will examine static and dynamic scope in more detail in Sections 3.3.1 and 3.3.2.

In addition to talking about the "scope of a binding," we sometimes use the word scope as a noun all by itself, without a specific binding in mind. Informally, a scope is a program region of maximal size in which no bindings change (or at least none are destroyed). Algol 68 and Ada use the term *elaboration* to refer to the process by which declarations become active when control first enters a scope. Elaboration entails the creation of bindings. In many languages, it also entails the allocation of stack space for local objects, and possibly the assignment of initial values. In Ada it can entail a host of other things, including the execution of error-checking or heap-space-allocating code, the propagation of exceptions, and the creation of concurrently executing *tasks* (to be discussed in Chapter 12).

At any given point in a program's execution, the set of active bindings is called the current *referencing environment*. The set is principally determined by static or dynamic *scope rules*. We shall see that a referencing environment generally corresponds to a sequence of scopes that can be examined (in order) to find the current binding for a given name.

In some cases, referencing environments also depend on what are (in a confusing use of terminology) called *binding rules*. Specifically, when a reference to a subroutine *S* is stored in a variable, passed as a parameter to another subroutine, or returned as a function value, one needs to determine when the referencing environment for *S* is chosen: that is, when the binding between the reference to *S* and the referencing environment of *S* is made. The two principal options are *deep binding*, in which the choice is made when the reference is first created, and *shallow binding*, in which the choice is made when the reference is finally used. We will examine these options in more detail in Section 3.4.

3.3.1 Static Scope

In a language with static (lexical) scoping, the bindings between names and objects can be determined at compile time by examining the text of the program, without consideration of the flow of control at run time. Typically, the "current" binding for a given name is the one encountered most recently in a top-to-bottom scan of the program, though as we shall see there are many variants on this basic theme.

---

3 *Lexical scope* is actually a better term than *static scope*, because scope rules based on nesting can be enforced at run time instead of compile time if desired. In fact, in Common Lisp and Scheme it is possible to pass the unevaluated text of a subroutine declaration into some other subroutine as a parameter, and then use the text to create a lexically nested declaration at run time.

The simplest static scope rule is probably that of early versions of Basic, in which there was only a single, global scope. In fact, there were only a few hundred possible names, each of which consisted of a letter optionally followed by a digit. There were no explicit declarations; variables were declared implicitly by virtue of being used.

Scope rules are somewhat more complex in Fortran, though not much so.[4] Fortran distinguishes between global and local variables. The scope of a local variable is limited to the subroutine in which it appears; it is not visible elsewhere. Variable declarations are optional. If a variable is not declared, it is assumed to be local to the current subroutine and to be of type `integer` if its name begins with the letters I–N, or `real` otherwise. (Different conventions for implicit declarations can be specified by the programmer. In Fortran 90, the programmer can also turn off implicit declarations, so that use of an undeclared variable becomes a compile-time error.)

Global variables in Fortran may be partitioned into `common` blocks, which are then "imported" by subroutines. `Common` blocks are designed to support separate compilation: they allow a subroutine to import only a subset of the global environment. Unfortunately, Fortran requires each subroutine to declare the names and types of the variables in each of the common blocks it uses, and there is no standard mechanism to ensure that the declarations in different subroutines are the same. In fact, Fortran explicitly allows the declarations to be different. A programmer who knows the data layout rules employed by the compiler can use a completely different set of names and types in one subroutine to refer to the data defined in another subroutine. The underlying bits will be shared, but the effect of this sharing is highly implementation-dependent. A similar effect can be achieved through the (mis)use of `equivalence` statements, which allow the programmer to specify that a set of variables share the same location(s). `Equivalence` statements are a precursor of the variant records and unions of languages such as Pascal and C. Their intended purpose is to save space in programs in which only one of the `equivalence`-ed variables is in use at any one time.

Semantically, the lifetime of a local Fortran variable (both the object itself and the name-to-object binding) encompasses a single execution of the variable's subroutine. Programmers can override this rule by using an explicit `save` statement. A `save`-ed variable has a lifetime that encompasses the entire execution of the program. Instead of a logically separate object for every invocation of the subroutine, the `save` statement arranges for a single object that retains its value from one invocation of the subroutine to the next. (The name-to-variable binding, of course, is inactive when the subroutine is not executing, because the name is out of scope.)

---

4 Fortran and C have evolved considerably over the years. Unless otherwise noted, comments here apply to the Fortran 77 dialect [Ame78a], and to ANSI Standard C [Ame90, Gar89]. Comments on Ada refer to both Ada 83 [Ame83] and Ada 95 [Int95b] unless otherwise noted.

In practice, it is common for all local variables in Fortran to behave as if they were `save`-ed, because language implementations frequently employ the static allocation strategy described in the previous section. It is dangerous practice to depend on this implementation artifact, however, because it is not guaranteed by the language definition. In a Fortran compiler that uses a stack to save space, or that exploits knowledge of the patterns of calls among subroutines to overlap statically allocated space (see Exercise 3.10), non-`save`-ed variables may *not* retain their values from one invocation to the next.

Nested Subroutines

The ability to nest subroutines inside each other, introduced in Algol 60, is a feature of many modern languages, including Pascal and Ada. Just as the local variables of a Fortran subroutine are not visible to other subroutines, any constants, types, variables, or subroutines declared within a subroutine are not visible outside that subroutine in Algol-family languages. More formally, Algol-style nesting gives rise to the *closest nested scope rule* for resolving bindings from names to objects: a name that is introduced in a declaration is known in the scope in which it is declared, and in each internally nested scope, unless it is *hidden* by another declaration of the same name in one or more nested scopes. To find the object referenced by a given use of a name, we look for a declaration with that name in the current, innermost scope. If there is one, it defines the active binding for the name. Otherwise, we look for a declaration in the immediately surrounding scope. We continue outward, examining successively surrounding scopes, until we reach the outer nesting level of the program, where global objects are declared. If no declaration is found at any level, then the program is in error.

Many languages provide a collection of *built-in*, or *predefined objects*, such as I/O routines, trigonometric functions, and in some cases types such as `integer` and `char`. It is common to consider these to be declared in an extra, invisible, outermost scope, which surrounds the scope in which global objects are declared. The search for bindings described in the previous paragraph terminates at this extra, outermost scope, if it exists, rather than at the scope in which global objects are declared. This outermost scope convention makes it possible for a programmer to define a global object whose name is the same as that of some predefined object (whose "declaration" is thereby hidden, making it unusable).

An example of nested scopes appears in Figure 3.4.[5] In this example, procedure P2 is called only by P1, and need not be visible outside. It is therefore declared inside P1, limiting its scope (its region of visibility) to the portion of the program shown here. In a similar fashion, P4 is visible only within P1, P3 is visible only within P2, and F1 is visible only within P4. Under the standard

---

5 This code is not contrived; it was extracted from an implementation of the FMQ error repair algorithm described in Section 2.2.5.

```
procedure P1 (A1 : T1);
var X : real;
    ...
    procedure P2 (A2 : T2);
        ...
        procedure P3 (A3 : T3);
        ...
        begin
            ...         (* body of P3 *)
        end;
        ...
    begin
        ...             (* body of P2 *)
    end;
    ...
    procedure P4 (A4 : T4);
        ...
        function F1 (A5 : T5) : T6;
        var X : integer;
        ...
        begin
            ...         (* body of F1 *)
        end;
        ...
    begin
        ...             (* body of P4 *)
    end;
    ...
begin
    ...                 (* body of P1 *)
end
```

Figure 3.4 Example of nested subroutines in Pascal.

rules for nested scopes, F1 could call P2 and P4 could call F1, but P2 could not call F1.

Though they are hidden from the rest of the program, nested subroutines are able to access the parameters and local variables (and other local objects) of the surrounding scope(s). In our example, P3 can name (and modify) A1, X, and A2, in addition to A3. Because P1 and F1 both declare local variables named X, the inner declaration hides the outer one within a portion of its scope. Uses of X in F1 refer to the inner X; uses of X in other regions of the code shown here refer to the outer X.

We have already seen that the compiler can arrange for a frame pointer register to point to the frame of the currently running subroutine at run time. Target code can use this register to access local objects. But what about objects in lexically surrounding scopes? To find these we need a way to find the frames corresponding to those scopes at run time. Since a deeply nested subroutine may

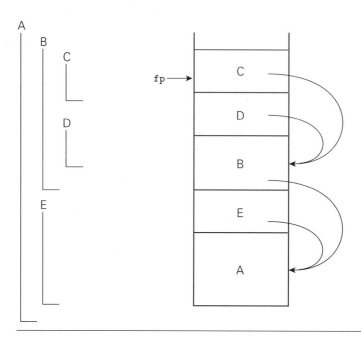

Figure 3.5 Static chains. Subroutines A, B, C, D, and E are nested as shown on the left. If the sequence of nested calls at run time is A, E, B, D, and C, then the static links in the stack will look as shown on the right. The code for subroutine C can find local objects at known offsets from the frame pointer. It can find local objects of the surrounding scope, B, by dereferencing its static chain once and then applying an offset. It can find local objects in B's surrounding scope, A, by dereferencing its static chain twice and then applying an offset.

call a routine in an outer scope, it is *not* the case that the lexically surrounding scope corresponds to the caller's scope at run time. At the same time, we can be sure that there *is* some frame for the surrounding scope somewhere below in the stack, since the current subroutine could not have been called unless it was visible, and it could not have been visible unless the surrounding scope was active.

The simplest way in which to find the frames of surrounding scopes is to maintain a *static link* in each frame that points to the "parent" frame: the frame of the most recent invocation of the lexically surrounding subroutine. If a subroutine is declared at the outermost nesting level of the program, then its frame will have a nil static link at run time. If a subroutine is nested *k* levels deep, then its frame's static link, and those of its parent, grandparent, and so on, will form a *static chain* of length *k* at run time. To find a variable or parameter declared in a scope *j* lexical nesting levels outward, target code at run time can dereference the static chain *j* times, and then add the appropriate offset. Static chains are illustrated in Figure 3.5. We will discuss the code required to maintain them in Section 8.2.

A name-to-object binding that is hidden by a nested declaration of the same name is said to have a *hole* in its scope. In most languages the object whose name is hidden is inaccessible in the nested scope (unless it has more than one name; see below). Some languages allow the programmer to access the outer meaning of a name by applying a *qualifier* or *scope resolution operator*. In Ada, for example, a name may be prefixed by the name of the scope in which it is declared, using syntax that resembles the specification of fields in a record. `My_proc.X`, for example, refers to the declaration of `X` in subroutine `My_proc`, regardless of whether some other `X` has been declared in a lexically closer scope. In C++, which does not allow subroutines to nest, `::X` refers to a global declaration of `X`, regardless of whether the current subroutine also has an `X`.[6]

In many languages, including Algol, C, and Ada (but not Pascal), local variables can be declared not only at the beginning of any subroutine, but also at the top of any `begin...end` ({...}) block. Declarations in these nested blocks hide outer declarations with the same name, just as declarations at the beginnings of subroutines do. Variables declared in nested blocks can be very useful, as for example in the following C code:

```
{
    int temp = a;
    a = b;
    b = temp;
}
```

Keeping the declaration of `temp` lexically adjacent to the code that uses it makes the program easier to read, and eliminates any possibility that this code will interfere with another variable named `temp`. In some languages, including Algol 68, C++, and Java, declarations may appear not only at the tops of blocks, but wherever a statement may appear. The scope of the declaration then extends to the end of the current innermost block. No run-time work is needed to allocate or deallocate space for variables declared in nested blocks; their space can be included in the total space for local variables allocated in the subroutine prologue and deallocated in the epilogue. Exercise 3.9 considers how to minimize the total space required.

Some languages, particularly those that are intended for interactive use, permit the programmer to redeclare an object: to create a new binding for a given name in a given scope. Interactive programmers commonly use redeclarations to fix bugs. In most interactive languages, the new meaning of the name replaces the old in all contexts. In ML, however, the old meaning of the name may remain accessible to functions that were elaborated before the name was redeclared. This design choice in ML can sometimes be counterintuitive. It probably reflects the fact that ML is usually compiled, bit by bit on the fly, rather than interpreted. A

---

6 The C++ `::` operator is also used to name members (fields) of a base class that are hidden by members of a derived class; we will consider this use in Section 10.2.2.

language such as Scheme, which is lexically scoped but usually interpreted, stores the binding for a name in a known location. A program accesses the meaning of the name indirectly through that location: if the meaning of the name changes, all accesses to the name will use the new meaning. In ML, previously elaborated functions have already been compiled into a form (often machine code) that accesses the meaning of the name directly.

Modules

A major challenge—perhaps *the* major challenge—in the construction of any large body of software is how to divide the effort among programmers in such a way that work can proceed on multiple fronts simultaneously. This modularization of effort depends critically on the notion of *information hiding*, which makes objects and algorithms invisible, whenever possible, to portions of the system that do not need them. Properly modularized code reduces the "cognitive load" on the programmer by minimizing the amount of information required to understand any given portion of the system. In a well-designed program the interfaces between modules are as "narrow" (i.e., simple) as possible, and any design decision that is likely to change is hidden inside a single module. This latter point is crucial, since maintenance (bug fixes and enhancement) consumes many more programmer years than does initial construction for most commercial software.

In addition to reducing cognitive load, information hiding has several more pedestrian benefits. First, it reduces the risk of name conflicts: with fewer visible names, there is less chance that a newly introduced name will be the same as one already in use. Second, it safeguards the integrity of data abstractions: any attempt to access objects outside of the subroutine(s) to which they belong will cause the compiler to issue an "undefined symbol" error message. Third, it helps to compartmentalize run-time errors: if a variable takes on an unexpected value, we can generally be sure that the code that modified it is in the variable's scope.

Unfortunately, the information hiding provided by nested subroutines is limited to objects whose lifetime is the same as that of the subroutine in which they are hidden. When control returns from a subroutine, its local variables will no longer be live: their values will be discarded. We have seen a partial solution to this problem in the form of the `save` statement in Fortran. A similar directive exists in several other languages: the own variables of Algol and the `static` variables of C, for example, retain their values from one invocation of a subroutine to the next. As an example of the use of static variables, consider the code in Figure 3.6. The subroutine `gen_new_name` can be used to generate a series of distinct character-string names. A compiler could use these in its assembly language output. Labels, for example, might be named L1, L2, L3, and so on; subroutines could be named S1, S2, S3, and so on.

Static variables allow a subroutine such as `gen_new_name` to have "memory"—to retain information from one invocation to the next—while protecting that memory from accidental access or modification by other parts of the program.

```
/*
    Place into *s a new name beginning with the letter l and
    continuing with the ascii representation of an integer guaranteed
    to be distinct in each separate call.  s is assumed to point to
    space large enough to hold any such name; for the short ints used
    here, seven characters suffice.  l is assumed to be an upper or
    lower-case letter.  sprintf 'prints' formatted output to a string.
*/
void gen_new_name (char *s, char l) {
    static short int name_nums[52];
        /* C guarantees that static local variables are initialized
        to zeros */
    int index = (l >= 'a' && l <= 'z') ? l-'a' : 26 + l-'A';
    name_nums[index]++;
    sprintf (s, "%c%d\0", l, name_nums[index]);
}
```

Figure 3.6 C code to illustrate the use of static variables.

Put another way, static variables allow programmers to build single-subroutine abstractions. Unfortunately, they do not allow the construction of abstractions whose interface needs to consist of more than one subroutine. Suppose, for example, that we wish to construct a *stack* abstraction. We should like to hide the representation of the stack—its internal structure—from the rest of the program, so that it can be accessed only through its push and pop routines. We can achieve this goal in many languages through use of a *module* construct.

A module allows a collection of objects—subroutines, variables, types, etc.—to be encapsulated in such a way that (1) objects inside are visible to each other, but (2) objects on the inside are not visible on the outside unless explicitly *exported*, and (3) (in many languages) objects outside are not visible on the inside unless explicitly *imported*. Modules can be found in Clu (which calls them *clusters*), Modula (1, 2, and 3), Turing, Ada (which calls them *packages*), Standard C++ (which calls them *namespaces*), and many other modern languages. They can also be emulated to some degree through use of the separate compilation facilities of C; we will discuss this possibility in Section 3.6 below. As an example of the use of modules, consider the stack abstraction shown in Figure 3.7. This stack can be embedded anywhere a subroutine might appear in a Modula-2 program.

Bindings to variables declared in a module are inactive outside the module, not destroyed. In our stack example, s and top have the same lifetime they would have had if not enclosed in the module. If stack is declared at the program's outermost nesting level, then s and top retain their values throughout the execution of the program, though they are visible only to the code inside push and pop. If stack is declared inside some subroutine sub, then s and top have the same lifetime as the local variables of sub. If stack is declared inside some other module mod, then s and top have the same lifetime as they would

```
CONST stack_size = ...
TYPE element = ...
...
MODULE stack;
IMPORT element, stack_size;
EXPORT push, pop;
TYPE
    stack_index = [1..stack_size];
VAR
    s   : ARRAY stack_index OF element;
    top : stack_index;           (* first unused slot *)

PROCEDURE error; ...

PROCEDURE push (elem : element);
BEGIN
    IF top = stack_size THEN
        error;
    ELSE
        s[top] := elem;
        top := top + 1;
    END;
END push;

PROCEDURE pop () : element;   (* A Modula-2 function is just a *)
BEGIN                        (* procedure with a return type. *)
    IF top = 1 THEN
        error;
    ELSE
        top := top - 1;
        RETURN s[top];
    END;
END pop;
                                   VAR x, y : element;
BEGIN                              ...
    top := 1;                      push (x);
END stack;                         ...
                                   y := pop;
```

Figure 3.7 Stack abstraction in Modula-2.

have had if not enclosed in either module. Type stack_index, which is also declared inside stack, is likewise visible only inside push and pop. The issue of lifetime is not relevant for types or constants, since they have no mutable state.

Our stack abstraction has two imports: the type (element) and maximum number (stack_size) of elements to be placed in the stack. Element and stack_size must be declared in a surrounding scope; the compiler will complain if they are not. With one exception, element and stack_size are the *only* names from surrounding scopes that will be visible inside `stack`. The exception is that predefined (*pervasive*) names, such as `integer` and `arctan`, are visible without being imported. Our stack also has two exports: `push` and `pop`. These are the only names inside of `stack` that will be visible in the surrounding scope.

Most module-based languages allow the programmer to specify that certain exported names are usable only in restricted ways. Variables may be exported read-only, for example, or types may be exported *opaquely*, meaning that variables of that type may be declared, passed as arguments to the module's subroutines, and possibly compared or assigned to one another, but not manipulated in any other way. To facilitate separate compilation, many module-based languages (Modula-2 among them) also allow a module to be divided into a declaration part (or *header*) and an implementation part (or *body*). Code that uses the exports of a given module can then be compiled as soon as the header exists; it is not dependent on the body. As a practical matter, many languages allow the header of a module to be subdivided into a "public" part, which specifies the interface to the rest of the program, and a "private" part, which is not visible outside the module, but is needed by the compiler, for example to determine the storage requirements of opaque types. Restricted exports, separate compilation, and public and private portions of headers will be discussed in more detail in Section 10.2.

Modules into which names must be explicitly imported are said to be *closed scopes*. By extension, scopes that do not require imports are said to be *open scopes*. Modules are closed in Modula (1, 2, and 3) but open in Ada. Nested subroutines are open scopes in most Algol family languages. Important exceptions are Euclid, in which both module and subroutine scopes are closed, Turing and Modula (1), in which subroutines are optionally closed, and Clu, which outlaws the use of nonlocal variables entirely. A subroutine in Euclid must explicitly import any nonpervasive name that it uses from a surrounding scope. A subroutine in Turing or Modula can also import names explicitly; if it does so then no other nonlocal names are visible. Import lists serve to document the program: the use of names from surrounding scopes is really part of the interface between a subroutine and the rest of the program. Requiring explicit imports forces the programmer to document this interface more precisely than is required in other languages. Outlawing nonlocal variables serves a similar purpose in Clu, though nonlocal constants and subroutines can still be named, without explicit import.

In addition to making programs easier to understand and maintain, import lists help a Euclid or Turing compiler to enforce language rules that prohibit the creation of *aliases*. An alias is an extra name for something that already has a name in the current scope. We have already seen aliases in the form of Fortran `common` blocks and `equivalence` statements. We have also noted that they arise in the variant records and unions of languages such as Pascal and C, and they arise naturally in programs that make use of pointer-based data structures. Another way to create aliases in many languages is to pass a variable by reference to a subroutine that also accesses that variable directly (consider variable `sum` in Figure 3.8). As a general rule, aliases tend to make programs more confusing than

```
double sum, sum_of_squares;
...
void accumulate (double& x)      // x passed by reference
{
    sum += x;
    sum_of_squares += x * x;
}
...
accumulate (sum);
```

Figure 3.8 Example of a potentially problematic alias in C++. Procedure accumulate probably does not do what the programmer intended when sum is passed as a parameter.

---

they otherwise would be. They also make it much more difficult for a compiler to perform important code improvements, as we will see in Section 13.3. Because it knows the names of all variables imported into a subroutine, a Euclid or Turing compiler is able to generate an error message when the programmer attempts to pass one of these as a reference parameter.

If a Turing subroutine does not contain an import list, the compiler creates an implicit list that includes precisely those external objects accessed by the subroutine. As in Euclid, items in the import list (whether explicit or implicit) may not be passed to the subroutine by reference. Modula has no similar rule; its import lists are simply for documentation and information hiding.

Module Types and Classes

Modules facilitate the construction of abstractions by allowing data to be made private to the subroutines that use them. As defined in Modula-2, Turing, or Ada 83, however, modules are most naturally suited to creating only a single instance of a given abstraction. The code in Figure 3.7, for example, does not lend itself to applications that require several stacks. For such an application, the programmer must either replicate the code (giving the new copy another name), or adopt an alternative organization in which the module becomes a "manager" for instances of a stack *type*, which is then exported (see Figure 3.9). This latter organization requires additional subroutines to create/initialize and possibly destroy stack instances, and it requires that every subroutine (push, pop, create) take an extra parameter, to specify the stack in question. Clu addresses this problem by automatically making *every* module ("cluster") the manager for a type. In fact, the only variables that may appear in a cluster (other than static variables in subroutines) are the representation of that type.

An alternative solution to the multiple instance problem can be found in Simula, Euclid, and (in a slightly different sense) ML, which treat modules as *types*, rather than simple encapsulation constructs. Given a module type, the programmer can declare an arbitrary number of similar module objects. The skeleton of a Euclid stack appears in Figure 3.10. As in the (single) Modula-2 stack of

```
CONST stack_size = ...
TYPE element = ...
...
MODULE stack_manager;
IMPORT element, stack_size;
EXPORT stack, init_stack, push, pop;
TYPE
    stack_index = [1..stack_size];
    STACK = RECORD
        s : ARRAY stack_index OF element;
        top : stack_index;              (* first unused slot *)
    END;

PROCEDURE init_stack (VAR stk : stack);
BEGIN
    stk.top := 1;
END init_stack;

PROCEDURE push (VAR stk : stack; elem : element);
BEGIN
    IF stk.top = stack_size THEN
        error;
    ELSE
        stk.s[stk.top] := elem;
        stk.top := stk.top + 1;
    END;
END push;

PROCEDURE pop (VAR stk : stack) : element;
BEGIN                                        var A, B : stack;
    IF stk.top = 1 THEN                      var x, y : element;
        error;                               ...
    ELSE                                     init_stack (A);
        stk.top := stk.top - 1;              init_stack (B);
        return stk.s[stk.top];               ...
    END;                                     push (A, x);
END pop;                                     ...
                                             y := pop (B);
END stack;
```

Figure 3.9 Manager module for stacks in Modula-2.

Figure 3.7, Euclid allows the programmer to provide initialization code that is executed whenever a new stack is created. Euclid also allows the programmer to specify finalization code that will be executed at the end of a module's lifetime. This feature is not needed for an array-based stack, but would be useful if elements were allocated from a heap, and needed to be reclaimed.

The difference between the module-as-manager and module-as-type approaches to abstraction is reflected in the lower right of Figures 3.9 and 3.10.

```
const stack_size := ...
type element : ...
...
type stack = module
     imports (element, stack_size)
     exports (push, pop)
type
     stack_index = 1..stack_size
var
     s   : array stack_index of element
     top : stack_index

procedure push (elem : element) = ...
function pop returns element = ...
...
initially
     top := 1
end stack
```

```
var A, B : stack
var x, y : element
...
A.push (x)
...
y := B.pop
```

Figure 3.10 Module type for stacks in Euclid. Unlike the code in Figure 3.7, the code here can be used to create an arbitrary number of stacks.

With module types, the programmer can think of the module's subroutines as "belonging" to the stack in question (`A.push (x)`), rather than as outside entities to which the stack can be passed as an argument (`push (A, x)`). Conceptually, there is a separate pair of `push` and `pop` operations for every stack. In practice, of course, it would be highly wasteful to create multiple copies of the code. As we shall see in Chapter 10, all stacks share a single pair of `push` and `pop` operations, and the compiler arranges for a pointer to the relevant stack to be passed to the operation as an extra, hidden parameter. The implementation turns out to be very similar to the implementation of Figure 3.9, but the programmer need not think of it that way.[7]

As an extension of the module-as-type approach to data abstraction, many languages now provide a *class* construct for *object-oriented programming*. To first approximation, classes can be thought of as module types that have been augmented with an *inheritance* mechanism. Inheritance allows new classes to be defined as extensions or refinements of existing classes. Inheritance facilitates a programming style in which all or most operations are thought of as belonging to objects, and in which new objects can inherit most of their operations from existing objects, without the need to rewrite code. Classes have their roots in Simula-67, and are the central innovation of object-oriented languages such as Smalltalk, Eiffel, C++, and Java. Inheritance mechanisms can also be found

---

7 It is interesting to note that Turing, which was derived from Euclid, reverts to Modula-2 style modules, in order to avoid implementation complexity [HMRC88, p. 9].

in several languages that are not usually considered object-oriented, including Modula-3, Ada 95, and Oberon. We will examine inheritance and its impact on scope rules in Chapter 10.

Module types and classes (ignoring issues related to inheritance) require only simple changes to the scope rules defined for modules in the previous section. Every instance A of a module type or class (e.g., every stack) has a separate copy of the module or class's variables. These variables are then visible when executing one of A's operations. They may also be indirectly visible to the operations of some other instance B if A is passed as a parameter to one of those operations. This rule makes it possible in most object-oriented languages to construct binary (or more-ary) operations that can manipulate the variables of more than one instance of a class. In C++, for example, we could create an operation that determines which of two stacks contains a larger number of elements:

```
class stack {
    ...
    bool deeper (stack other) {      // function declaration
        return (top > other.top);
    }
    ...
}
...
if (A.deeper(B)) ...
```

Within the `deeper` operation of stack A, `top` refers to `A.top`. Because `deeper` is an operation of class `stack`, however, it is able to refer not only to the variables of A (which it can access directly by name), but also to the variables of any *other* stack that is passed to it as an argument. Because these variables belong to a different stack, `deeper` must name that stack explicitly, for example as in `other.top`. In a module-as-manager style program, of course, module subroutines would access all instance variables via parameters.

3.3.2 Dynamic Scope

In a language with dynamic scoping, the bindings between names and objects depend on the flow of control at run time, and in particular on the order in which subroutines are called. In comparison to the static scope rules discussed in the previous section, dynamic scope rules are generally quite simple: the "current" binding for a given name is the one encountered most recently *during execution*, and not yet destroyed by returning from its scope.

Languages with dynamic scoping include APL [Ive62], Snobol [GPP71], and early dialects of Lisp [MAE+65, Moo78, TM81] and Perl.[8] Because the flow of

---

8 Scheme and Common Lisp are statically scoped, though the latter allows the programmer to specify dynamic scoping for individual variables. Lexical scope was added to Perl in version 5. The programmer now chooses static or dynamic scoping explicitly in each variable declaration.

```
1.  a : integer              -- global declaration

2.  procedure first
3.      a := 1

4.  procedure second
5.      a : integer          -- local declaration
6.      first ()

7.  a := 2
8.  if read_integer () > 0
9.      second ()
10. else
11.     first ()
12. write_integer (a)
```

Figure 3.11 Static versus dynamic scope. Program output depends on both scope rules and, in the case of dynamic scope, a value read at run time.

control cannot in general be predicted in advance, the bindings between names and objects in a language with dynamic scope cannot in general be determined by a compiler. As a result, many semantic rules in a language with dynamic scope become a matter of dynamic semantics rather than static semantics. Type checking in expressions and argument checking in subroutine calls, for example, must in general be deferred until run time. To accommodate all these checks, languages with dynamic scoping tend to be interpreted, rather than compiled.

As an example of dynamic scope, consider the program in Figure 3.11. If static scoping is in effect, then this program prints a 1. If dynamic scoping is in effect, then the program prints either a 1 or a 2, depending on the value read at line 8 at run time. Why the difference? At issue is whether the assignment to the variable a at line 3 refers to the global variable declared at line 1 or to the local variable declared at line 5. Static scope rules require that the reference resolve to the closest lexically enclosing declaration, namely the global a. Procedure first changes a to 1, and line 12 prints this value.

Dynamic scope rules, on the other hand, require that we choose the most recent, active binding for a at run time. We create a binding for a when we enter the main program. We create another when and if we enter procedure second. When we execute the assignment statement at line 3, the a to which we are referring will depend on whether we entered first through second or directly from the main program. If we entered through second, then we will assign the value 1 to second's local a. If we entered from the main program, we will assign the value 1 to the global a. In either case, the write at line 12 will refer to the global a, since second's local a will be destroyed, along with its binding, when control returns to the main program.

```
max_score : integer        -- maximum possible score

function scaled_score (raw_score : integer) : real
    return raw_score / max_score * 100
. . .
procedure foo
    max_score : real := 0        -- highest percentage seen so far
    . . .
    foreach student in class
        student.percent := scaled_score (student.points)
        if student.percent > max_score
            max_score := student.percent
```

Figure 3.12 The problem with dynamic scoping. Procedure scaled_score probably does not do what the programmer intended when dynamic scope rules allow procedure foo to change the meaning of max_score.

It is not entirely clear whether the use of dynamic scoping in Lisp and other early interpreted languages was deliberate or accidental. One reason to think that it may have been deliberate is that it makes it very easy for an interpreter to look up the meaning of a name: all that is required is a stack of declarations (we will examine this stack more closely in Section 3.3.4). Unfortunately, this simple implementation has a very high run-time cost, and experience indicates that dynamic scoping makes programs harder to understand. The modern consensus seems to be that dynamic scoping is usually a bad idea (see Exercises 3.14 and 3.15 for two exceptions).

With dynamic scoping in effect, no program fragment that makes use of non-local names is guaranteed a predictable referencing environment. In Figure 3.12, for example, the declaration of a local variable in procedure foo accidentally redefines a global variable used by function scaled_score, which is then called from foo. Since the global max_score is an integer, while the local max_score is a floating-point number, dynamic semantic checks in at least some languages will result in a type clash message at run time. If the local max_score had been an integer, no error would have been detected, but the program would almost certainly have produced incorrect results. This sort of error can be very hard to find.

The principal argument in *favor* of dynamic scoping is that it facilitates the customization of subroutines. Suppose, for example, that we have a library routine print_integer that is capable of printing its argument in any of several bases (decimal, binary, hexadecimal, etc.). Suppose further that we want the routine to use decimal notation most of the time, and to use other bases only in a few special cases; we do not want to have to specify a base explicitly on each individual call. We can achieve this result with dynamic scoping by having print_ integer obtain its base from a nonlocal variable print_base. We can establish the default behavior by declaring a variable print_base and setting its value to 10 in a scope encountered early in execution. Then, any time we want to change the base temporarily, we can write:

```
begin        -- nested block
    print_base : integer := 16      -- use hexadecimal
    print_integer (n)
```

The problem with this argument is that there are usually other ways to achieve the same effect, without dynamic scoping. One option would be to have print_integer use decimal notation in all cases, and create a another routine, print_integer_with_base, that takes a second argument. In a language such as Ada or C++, one could make the base an optional (default) parameter of a single print_integer routine, or use overloading to give the same name to both routines. (We will consider default parameters in Section 8.3.2; overloading is discussed in Section 3.5.)

Unfortunately, using two different routines for printing (or one routine with two calling sequences) requires that the caller know what is going on. In our example, alternative routines work fine if the calls are all made in the scope in which the local print_base variable would have been declared. If that scope calls subroutines that in turn call print_integer, however, we cannot in general arrange for the called routines to use the alternative interface. A second alternative to dynamic scoping solves this problem: we can create a static variable, either global or encapsulated with print_integer inside an appropriate module, that controls the base. To change the print base temporarily, we can then write:

```
begin        -- nested block
    print_base_save : integer := print_base
    print_base := 16       -- use hexadecimal
    print_integer (n)
    print_base := print_base_save
```

The possibility that we may forget to restore the original value, of course, is a potential source of bugs. With dynamic scoping the value is restored automatically.

3.3.3 Symbol Tables

To keep track of the names in a statically scoped program, a compiler relies on a data abstraction called a *symbol table*. At the most basic level, the symbol table is a dictionary: it maps names to the information the compiler knows about them. The most basic operations, which we will call insert and lookup, serve to place a new mapping (a name-to-object binding) into the table and to retrieve (nondestructively) the information held in the mapping for a given name. Static scope rules in most languages impose additional complexity by requiring that the referencing environment be different in different parts of the program. It is tempting to try to accommodate these rules simply by adding a remove operation. As the semantic analysis phase of the compiler scans the code from beginning to end, it could insert new mappings at the beginning of each scope and remove them at the end. Unfortunately, several factors make this straightforward approach impractical:

- The ability of inner declarations to hide outer ones in most languages with nested scopes means that the symbol table has to be able to contain an arbitrary number of mappings for a given name. The lookup operation must return the innermost mapping, and outer mappings must become visible again at end of scope.

- Records (structures) in Algol-family languages have some of the properties of scopes, but do not share their nicely nested structure. When it sees a record declaration, the semantic analyzer must remember the names of the record's fields (recursively, if records are nested). At the end of the declaration, the field names must become invisible. Later, however, whenever a variable of the record type appears in the program text (as in my_rec.field_name), the record fields must suddenly become visible again for the part of the reference after the dot. In Pascal and other languages with with statements, field names must become visible in a multi-statement context.

- Names are sometimes used before they are declared, even in Algol-family languages. Both Algol 60 and Algol 68, for example, permit *forward references* to labels. Pascal avoids these by requiring labels to be declared at the beginning of their scope, but still permits forward references in pointer declarations:

```
type
    company = record
        CEO : ^person;        (* forward reference *)
        ...
    end;
    person = record
        employer : ^company;
        ...
    end;
```

- Pascal and other languages also allow *forward declarations* of subroutines in order to support mutual recursion:

```
procedure Q (A, B : integer); forward;
procedure P (A, B : integer);
begin
    ...
    Q (3, 4);
    ...
end;
```

```
procedure Q;          (* parameters are not repeated in Pascal *)
begin
   ...
   P (4, 5);
   ...
end;
```

When it sees the forward declaration in this code, the semantic analyzer must remember Q's parameters, so it can make them visible later, in the body of Q, but must make them invisible in the meantime. This operation is similar to remembering the field names of records.

▪ While it may be desirable to forget names at the end of their scope, and even to reclaim the space they occupy in the symbol table, information about them may need to be saved for use by a *symbolic debugger*. The debugger is a tool that allows the user to manipulate a running program: starting it, stopping it, and reading and writing its data. In order to parse high-level commands from the user (e.g., to print the value of `my_firm^.revenues[1999]`), the debugger must have access to the compiler's symbol table. To make it available at run time, the compiler typically saves the table in a hidden portion of the final machine-language program.

Most variations on static scoping can be handled by augmenting a basic dictionary-style symbol table with additional enter_scope and leave_scope operations to keep track of visibility. Nothing is ever deleted from the table; the entire structure is retained throughout compilation, and then saved for the debugger. A symbol table with visibility can be implemented in several different ways; the approach described here is due to LeBlanc and Cook [CL83].

Each scope, as it is encountered, is assigned a serial number. The outermost scope (the one that contains the predefined identifiers), is given number 0. The scope containing programmer-declared global names is given number 1. Additional scopes are given successive numbers as they are encountered. All serial numbers are distinct; they do not represent the level of lexical nesting, except in as much as nested subroutines naturally end up with numbers higher than those of surrounding scopes.

All names, regardless of scope, are entered into a single large hash table, keyed by name. Each entry in the table then contains the symbol name, its category (variable, constant, type, procedure, field name, parameter, etc.) scope number, type (a pointer to another symbol table entry), and additional, category-specific fields.

In addition to the hash table, the symbol table has a *scope stack* that indicates, in order, the scopes that comprise the current referencing environment. As the semantic analyzer scans the program, it pushes and pops this stack whenever it enters or leaves a scope, respectively. Entries in the scope stack contain the scope number, an indication of whether the scope is closed, and in some cases further information.

```
procedure lookup (name)
    pervasive := best := nil
    apply hash function to name to find appropriate chain
    foreach entry e on chain
        if e.name = name        -- not something else with same hash value
            if e.scope = 0
                pervasive := e
            else
                foreach scope s on scope stack, top first
                    if s.scope = e.scope
                        best := e        -- closer instance
                    elsif best <> nil and then s.scope = best.scope
                        exit inner loop        -- won't find better
                    if s.closed
                        exit inner loop        -- can't see farther
    if best <> nil
        while best is an import or export entry
            best := best.real_entry
        return best
    elsif pervasive <> nil
        return pervasive
    else
        return nil      -- name not found
```

Figure 3.13 LeBlanc-Cook symbol table lookup **operation.**

To look up a name in the table, we scan down the appropriate hash chain looking for entries that match the name we are trying to find. For each matching entry, we scan down the scope stack to see if the scope of that entry is visible. We look no deeper in the stack than the top-most closed scope. Imports and exports are made visible outside their normal scope by creating additional entries in the table; these extra entries contain pointers to the real entries. We don't have to examine the scope stack at all for entries with scope number 0: they are pervasive. Pseudocode for the lookup algorithm appears in Figure 3.13.

The lower right portion of Figure 3.14 contains the skeleton of a Modula-2 program. The remainder of the figure shows the configuration of the symbol table for the referencing environment of the with statement in procedure P2. The scope stack contains four entries representing, respectively, the with statement, procedure P2, module M, and the global scope. The scope for the with statement indicates the specific record variable to which names (fields) in this scope belong. The outermost, pervasive scope is not explicitly represented.

All of the entries for a given name appear on the same hash chain, since the table is keyed on name. In this example, A2, F2, and T have also ended up on a

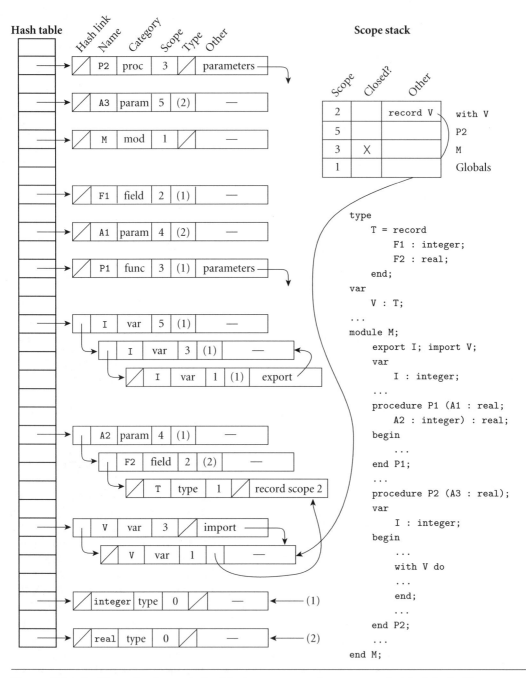

Figure 3.14 LeBlanc-Cook symbol table for an example program in Modula-2. The scope stack represents the referencing environment of the with statement in procedure P2. For the sake of clarity, the many pointers from type fields to the symbol table entries for integer and real are shown as parenthesized (1)s and (2)s, rather than as arrows.

single chain, due to hash collisions. Variables V and I (M's I) have extra entries, to make them visible across the boundary of closed scope M. When we are inside P2, a lookup operation on I will find P2's I; neither of the entries for M's I will be visible. The entry for type T indicates the scope number to be pushed onto the scope stack during with statements. The entry for each subroutine contains the head pointer of a list that links together the subroutine's parameters, for use in analyzing calls (additional links of these chains are not shown). During code generation, many symbol table entries would contain additional fields, for information such as size and run-time address.

3.3.4 Association Lists and Central Reference Tables

In a language with dynamic scoping, an interpreter (or the output of a compiler) must perform operations at run-time that correspond to the insert, lookup, enter_scope and leave_scope symbol table operations in the implementation of a statically scoped language. In principle, any organization used for a symbol table in a compiler could be used to track name-to-object bindings in an interpreter, and vice versa. In practice, implementations of dynamic scoping tend to adopt one of two specific organizations: an *association list* or a *central reference table*. Association lists are simple and elegant, but can be very inefficient. Central reference tables resemble a simplified LeBlanc-Cook symbol table, without the separate scope stack; they require more work at scope entry and exit than do association lists, but they make *lookup* operations fast. Pictorial representations of the two competing approaches appear in Figure 3.15.

An association list (or *A-list* for short) is simply a list of name/value pairs. A-lists are widely used for dictionary abstractions in Lisp; they are supported by a rich set of built-in functions in most Lisp dialects. It is therefore natural for Lisp interpreters to use an A-list to keep track of name-value bindings, and even to make this list explicitly visible to the running program. Since bindings are created when entering a scope, and destroyed when leaving or returning from a scope, the A-list functions as a stack. When execution enters a scope at run time, the interpreter pushes bindings for names declared in that scope onto the front of the A-list. When execution finally leaves a scope, these bindings are removed. To look up the meaning of a name in an expression, the interpreter searches from the front of the list until it finds an appropriate binding (or reaches the end of the list, in which case an error has occurred). Each entry in the list contains whatever information is needed to perform semantic checks (e.g., type checking, which we will consider in Section 7.2) and to find variables and other objects that occupy memory locations. In Figure 3.15, the first (top) entry on the A-list represents the I in procedure P. The second entry represents the J in procedure Q.

The problem with using an association list to represent a program's referencing environment is that it can take a long time to find a particular entry in the list, particularly if it represents an object declared in a scope encountered early

Referencing environment A-list

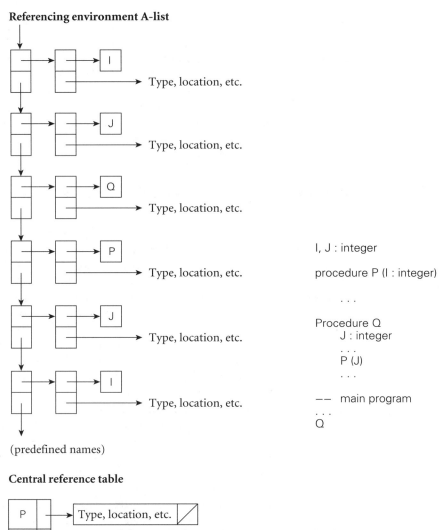

I, J : integer

procedure P (I : integer)

. . .

Procedure Q
  J : integer
  . . .
  P (J)
  . . .

−− main program
. . .
Q

(predefined names)

Central reference table

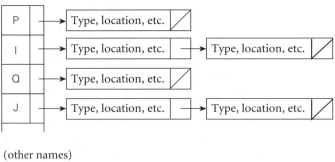

(other names)

Figure 3.15 Implementation of dynamic scoping using an association list (top left) or central reference table (bottom). Both structures show the referencing environment that will be in effect for the code on the right after the main program calls Q and it in turn calls P.

in the program's execution, and now buried deep in the list. A central reference table is designed to address this problem. It contains a list (stack) of entries for each distinct name in the program, with the most recent occurrence of each at the beginning of the list. Looking up a name is now easy: the current meaning is found at the beginning of the list in the appropriate slot in the table. If the program is compiled and the set of names is known at compile time, then each name can have a statically assigned slot in the table, which the compiled code can refer to directly. If the program is not compiled, or the set of names is not statically known, then a hash function will need to be used at run time to find the appropriate slot.

When control enters a new scope at run time, entries must be pushed onto the beginning of every list in the central reference table whose name is (re)declared in that scope. When control leaves a scope for the final time, these entries must be popped. The work involved is somewhat more expensive than pushing and popping an A-list, but not dramatically more so, and lookup operations are now much faster. In contrast to the symbol table of a compiler for a language with static scoping, entries in the central reference table for a given scope do not need to be saved when the scope completes execution; the space can be reclaimed.

Within the Lisp community, implementation of dynamic scoping via an association list is sometimes called *deep binding*, because the lookup operation may need to look arbitrarily deep in the list. Implementation via a central reference table is sometimes called *shallow binding*, because it finds the current association at the head of a given reference chain. Unfortunately, the terms "deep and shallow binding" are also more widely used for a completely different purpose, discussed in the following section. To avoid potential confusion, some authors use "deep and shallow access" [Seb99] or "deep and shallow search" [Fin96] for the implementations of dynamic scoping.

3.4 The Binding of Referencing Environments

We have seen in the previous section how scope rules determine the referencing environment of a given statement in a program. Static scope rules specify that the referencing environment depends on the lexical nesting of program blocks in which names are declared. Dynamic scope rules specify that the referencing environment depends on the order in which declarations are encountered at run time. An additional issue that we have not yet considered arises in languages that allow one to create a *reference* to a subroutine, for example by passing it as a parameter. When are scope rules applied to such a subroutine: when the reference is first created, or when the routine is finally called? The question is particularly important for languages with dynamic scoping, though we shall see that it matters even in languages with static scoping. As an example of the former, consider the program fragment shown in Figure 3.16. (As in Figure 3.11, we use an Algol-like syntax, even though Algol-family languages are usually statically scoped.)

```
type person = record
    . . .
    age : integer
    . . .
threshold : integer
people : database

function older_than (p : person) : boolean
    return p.age ≥ threshold

procedure print_person (p : person)
    -- Call appropriate I/O routines to print record on standard output.
    -- Make use of nonlocal variable line_length to format data in columns.
    . . .

procedure print_selected_records (db : database
        predicate, print_routine : procedure)
    line_length : integer

    if device_type (stdout) = terminal
        line_length := 80
    else      -- Standard output is a file or printer.
        line_length := 132
    foreach record r in db
        -- Iterating over these may actually be
        -- a lot more complicated than a 'for' loop.
        if predicate (r)
            print_routine (r)

-- main program
. . .
threshold := 35
print_selected_records (people, older_than, print_person)
```

Figure 3.16 Program to illustrate the importance of binding rules. One might argue that deep binding is appropriate for the environment of function older_than (for access to threshold), while shallow binding is appropriate for the environment of procedure print_person (for access to line_length).

Procedure print_selected_records in our example is assumed to be a general-purpose routine that knows how to traverse the records in a database, regardless of whether they represent people, sprockets, or salads. It takes as parameters a database, a predicate to make print/don't print decisions, and a subroutine that knows how to format the data in the records of this particular database. In Section 3.3.2 we hypothesized a print_integer library routine that would print in any of several bases, depending on the value of a nonlocal variable print_base.

Here we have hypothesized in a similar fashion that print_person uses the value of nonlocal variable line_length to calculate the number and width of columns in its output. In a language with dynamic scope, it is natural for procedure print_selected_records to declare and initialize this variable locally, knowing that code inside print_routine will pick it up if needed. For this coding technique to work, the referencing environment of print_routine must not be created until the routine is actually called by print_selected_records. This late binding of the referencing environment of a subroutine that has been passed as a parameter is known as *shallow binding*. It is usually the default in languages with dynamic scoping.

For function older_than, by contrast, shallow binding may not work well. If, for example, procedure print_selected_records happens to have a local variable named threshold, then the variable set by the main program to influence the behavior of older_than will not be visible when the function is finally called, and the predicate will be unlikely to work correctly. In such a situation, the code that originally passes the function as a parameter has a particular referencing environment (the current one) in mind; it does not want the routine to be called in any other environment. It therefore makes sense to bind the environment at the time the routine is first passed as a parameter, and then restore that environment when the routine is finally called. This early binding of the referencing environment is known as *deep binding*. The need for deep binding is sometimes referred to as the *funarg problem* in Lisp.

3.4.1 Subroutine Closures

Deep binding is implemented by creating an explicit representation of a referencing environment (generally the one in which the subroutine would execute if called at the present time) and bundling it together with a reference to the subroutine. The bundle as a whole is referred to as a *closure*. Usually the subroutine itself can be represented in the closure by a pointer to its code. If an association list is used to represent the referencing environment of a program with dynamic scoping, then the referencing environment in a closure can be represented by a top-of-stack (beginning of A-list) pointer. When a subroutine is called through a closure, the main pointer to the referencing environment A-list is temporarily replaced by the saved pointer, making any bindings created since the closure was created temporarily invisible. New bindings created *within* the subroutine are pushed using the temporary pointer. Because the A-list is represented by pointers (rather than an array), the effect is to have two lists—one representing the temporary referencing environment resulting from use of the closure and the other the main referencing environment that will be restored when the subroutine returns—that share their older entries.

If a central reference table is used to represent the referencing environment of a program with dynamic scoping, then the creation of a closure is more complicated. In the general case, it may be necessary to copy the entire main array of the central table and the first entry on each of its lists. Space and time overhead may be reduced if the compiler or interpreter is able to determine that only some of the program's names will be used by the subroutine in the closure (or by things that the subroutine may call). In this case, the environment can be saved by copying the first entries of the lists for only the "interesting" names. When the subroutine is called through the closure, these entries can then be pushed onto the beginnings of the appropriate lists in the central reference table.

Deep binding is often available as an option in languages with dynamic scope. In early dialects of Lisp, for example, the built-in primitive `function` takes a function as its argument and returns a closure whose referencing environment is the one in which the function would execute if called at the present time. This closure can then be passed as a parameter to another function. If and when it is eventually called, it will execute in the saved environment. (Closures work slightly differently from "bare" functions in most Lisp dialects: they must be called by passing them to the built-in primitives `funcall` or `apply`.)

Deep binding is generally the default in languages with static (lexical) scoping. At first glance, one might be tempted to think that the binding time of referencing environments would not matter in languages with static scoping. After all, the meaning of a statically scoped name depends on its lexical nesting, not on the flow of execution, and this nesting is the same whether it is captured at the time a subroutine is passed as a parameter or at the time the subroutine is called. The catch is that a running program may have more than one *instance* of an object that is declared within a recursive subroutine. A closure in a language with static scoping captures the current instance of every object, at the time the closure is created. When the closure's subroutine is called, it will find these captured instances, even if newer instances have subsequently been created by recursive calls.

One could imagine combining static scoping with shallow binding [VF82], but the combination does not seem to make much sense, and does not appear to have been adopted in any language. Figure 3.17 contains a Pascal program that illustrates the impact of binding rules in the presence of static scoping. This program prints a 1. With shallow binding it would print a 2.

It should be noted that binding rules matter with static scoping only when accessing objects that are neither local nor global. If an object is local to the currently executing subroutine, then it does not matter whether the subroutine was called directly or through a closure; in either case local objects will have been created when the subroutine started running. If an object is global, there will never be more than one instance, since the main body of the program is not recursive. Binding rules are therefore irrelevant in languages such as C, which has no nested subroutines, or Modula-2, which allows only outermost subroutines to be passed as parameters. (They are also irrelevant in languages such as PL/I and Ada 83, which do not permit subroutines to be passed as parameters at all.)

Suppose then that we have a language with static scoping in which nested subroutines can be passed as parameters, with deep binding. To represent a closure for subroutine *S*, we can simply save a pointer to *S*'s code together with the static link that *S* would use if it were called right now, in the current environment. When *S* is finally called, we temporarily restore the saved static link, rather than

```
program binding_example (input, output);

procedure A (I : integer; procedure P);

    procedure B;
    begin
        writeln (I);
    end;

begin (* A *)
    if I > 1 then
        P
    else
        A (2, B);
end;

procedure C; begin end;

begin (* main *)
    A (1, C);
end.
```

Figure 3.17 Deep binding in Pascal. When B is called via formal parameter P, two instances of I exist. Because the closure for P was created in the initial invocation of A, it uses that invocation's instance of I, and prints a 1.

creating a new one. When *S* follows its static chain to access a nonlocal object, it will find the object instance that was current at the time the closure was created.

3.4.2 First- and Second-Class Subroutines

In general, a value in a programming language is said to have *first-class* status if it can be passed as a parameter, returned from a subroutine, or assigned into a variable. Simple types such as integers and characters are first-class values in most programming languages. By contrast, a "second-class" value can be passed as a parameter, but not returned from a subroutine or assigned into a variable, and a "third-class" value cannot even be passed as a parameter. As we will see in Section 8.3.1, labels are third-class values in most programming languages, but second-class values in Algol. Subroutines are second-class values in most imperative languages, but third-class values in Ada 83. They are first-class values in all functional programming languages and, with certain restrictions, in some imperative languages as well, including Modula-2, Modula-3, Ada 95, C, and C++.[9]

---

9 Some authors would say that first-class status requires the ability to create new values at run time. Under this definition, subroutines are first-class values in functional languages such as Lisp, ML, and Haskell, but not in Modula-2, Modula-3, Ada 95, C, or C++.

So far in this section we have considered the ramifications of second-class subroutines. First-class subroutines in a language with nested scopes introduce an additional level of complexity: they raise the possibility that a reference to a subroutine may outlive the execution of the scope in which that routine was declared. If local objects are destroyed (and their space reclaimed) at the end of each scope's execution, then the referencing environment captured in a long-lived closure might become full of dangling references. To avoid this problem, most functional languages specify that local objects have *unlimited extent*: their lifetimes continue indefinitely. Their space can be reclaimed only when the garbage collection system is able to prove that they will never be used again. Local objects (other than `own`/`static` variables) in Algol-family languages have *limited extent*: they are destroyed at the end of their scope's execution. Space for local objects with limited extent can be allocated on a stack. Space for local objects with unlimited extent must generally be allocated on a heap.

Given the desire to maintain stack-based allocation for the local variables of subroutines, imperative languages with first-class subroutines must generally adopt alternative mechanisms to avoid the dangling reference problem for closures. C and C++, of course, do not have nested scopes. Modula-2 allows references to be created only to outermost subroutines (outermost routines are first-class values; nested routines are third-class values). Modula-3 allows nested subroutines to be passed as parameters, but only outermost routines to be returned or stored in variables (outermost routines are first-class values; nested routines are second-class values). Ada 95 allows a nested routine to be returned, but only if the scope in which it was declared is at least as wide as that of the declared return type. This containment rule, while more conservative than strictly necessary, makes it impossible to propagate a subroutine reference to a portion of the program in which the routine's referencing environment is not active.

3.5 Overloading and Related Concepts

So far in our discussion of naming and scopes we have assumed that every name must refer to a distinct object in every scope. This is not necessarily the case. A name that can refer to more than one object in a given scope is said to be *overloaded*. (Contrast this notion to that of aliases, in which two or more names refer to a single object in a given scope.) Semantic rules for overloading require that the specific context of each individual use of the name contain sufficient clues to deduce which meaning (binding) is intended.

Most programming languages provide at least a limited form of overloading. In C, for example, the plus sign (+) is used to name two different functions: integer and floating-point addition. Most programmers don't worry about the distinction between these two functions—both are based on the same mathematical concept, after all—but they take arguments of different types and perform very different operations on the underlying bits. Ada also supports overloading in the context of enumeration constants. In Figure 3.18, for example, the con-

```
declare
    type month is (jan, feb, mar, apr, may, jun, jul, aug, sep, oct, nov, dec);
    type print_base is (dec, bin, oct, hex);
    mo : month;
    pb : print_base;
begin
    mo := dec;        -- the month dec
    pb := oct;        -- the print_base oct
    print (oct);      -- error!  insufficient context to decide
```

Figure 3.18 Overloading of enumeration constants in Ada.

stants oct and dec refer either to months or to numeric bases, depending on the context in which they appear.

Within the symbol table of a compiler, overloading must be handled by arranging for the *lookup* routine to return a *list* of possible meanings for the requested name. The semantic analyzer must then choose from among the elements of the list based on context. When the context is not sufficient to decide, as in the call to print in Figure 3.18, then the semantic analyzer must announce an error. Most languages that allow overloaded enumeration constants allow the programmer to provide appropriate context explicitly. In Ada, for example, one can say

```
print (month'(oct));
```

In Modula-3, *every* use of an enumeration constant must be prefixed with a type name, even when there is no chance of ambiguity:

```
mo := month.dec;
pb := print_base.oct;
```

In C, C++, and standard Pascal, one cannot overload enumeration constants at all; every constant visible in a given scope must be distinct.

Both Ada and C++ have elaborate facilities for overloading subroutine names. (Most of the C++ facilities carry over to Java.) A given name may refer to an arbitrary number of subroutines in the same scope, so long as the subroutines differ in the number or types of their arguments. C++ examples appear in Figure 3.19.[10]

Ada, C++, and Fortran 90 also allow the built-in arithmetic operators (+, -, *, etc.) to be overloaded with user-defined functions. Ada and C++ do this by defining alternative *prefix* forms of each operator, and defining the usual infix forms to be abbreviations (or "syntactic sugar") for the prefix forms. In Ada, A + B is short for "+"(A, B). If "+" is overloaded, it must be possible to determine

---

[10] C++ actually provides more elegant ways to handle both I/O and user-defined types such as complex. We will examine these in Section 7.9 and Chapter 10.

```
struct complex {
    double real, imaginary;
};
enum base {dec, bin, oct, hex};

int i;
complex x;

void print_num (int n) ...
void print_num (int n, base b) ...
void print_num (complex c) ...

print_num (i);      // uses the first function above
print_num (i, hex); // uses the second function above
print_num (x);      // uses the third function above
```

Figure 3.19   Simple example of overloading in C++. In each case the compiler can tell which function is intended by the number and types of arguments.

the intended meaning from the types of A and B. In C++, A + B is short for A.operator+(B), where A is a member of a class (module type) that defines an operator+ function. The class-based style of abbreviation in C++ resembles a similar facility in Clu. Since the abbreviation expands to an unambiguous name (i.e., A's operator+; not any other), one might be tempted to say that no "real" overloading is involved, and this is in fact the case in Clu. In C++, however, there may be more than one definition of A.operator+, allowing the second argument to be of several types.

It is worth distinguishing overloading from several closely related concepts, including coercion, polymorphism, and generics. All three of these subjects will be treated in more detail in later chapters: coercion in Section 7.2.3, polymorphism in Chapters 7 and 10, and generics in Section 8.4. We describe them only briefly here.

Coercion is a process in which the compiler automatically converts an object of one type into an object of another type when it is used in a context in which the second type is expected. Where in Ada one might write

```
function abs (n : integer) return integer is ...
function abs (x : real) return real is ...
```

in Fortran one could get by with the single function

```
real function abs (x)
real x
...
```

If the Fortran function is called in a context that expects an integer (e.g., i = abs (j)), the compiler will automatically convert the argument (j) to a floating-point number, call `abs`, and then convert the result back to an integer.[11] While both overloading and coercion can be used to achieve the same effect in this example (i.e., to allow the programmer to take the absolute value of both integers and reals), the two mechanisms are really very different, and address different sets of problems. In this specific example, the Ada code defines two separate functions; the compiler chooses between them based on the type of the argument. The Fortran code defines a single function; the compiler coerces integers into reals and reals into integers (via truncation) to make that function work in different contexts. As we shall see in Section 7.2.3, coercion is somewhat controversial. Pascal provides a limited number of coercions. Fortran and C provide more. C++ provides an extremely rich set, and allows the programmer to define more. Ada as a matter of principle coerces nothing but explicit constants, subranges, and in certain cases arrays.

Sometimes problems that can be solved with overloaded subroutine names can also be solved by writing a subroutine with *polymorphic* parameters, which can represent objects of more than one type. Where a compiler with coercion rules is able in certain cases to automatically convert an actual parameter (i.e., an argument in a subroutine call) into a formal parameter (the one named in the subroutine header) of a different type, polymorphic parameters are able to represent *unconverted* arguments of several types. Those types must either have some characteristics in common (and the subroutine must not depend on any other characteristics), or else the arguments must be self-descriptive in a way that allows the subroutine to customize its behavior appropriately. Polymorphism is fundamental to many functional and object-oriented languages, including Lisp/Scheme, ML, Smalltalk, and (to a more limited extent) C++ and Java. An absolute value function with a polymorphic parameter, for example, can be written to accept an argument of any type that in turn supports comparison to zero and negation. As a more realistic example, it is trivial in Lisp to write a function that counts the number of elements in a linked list, regardless of the types of the elements themselves. All that is required is that the argument type provide a "successor" operation and a test for a null successor. Even Modula-2 and the ISO/ANSI standard for Pascal provide a (very) limited form of polymorphism via so-called *conformant array* parameters, whose bounds are not specified in the subroutine header but may be determined at run time by calling a built-in function.

Subroutines with polymorphic parameters (also called, more simply, polymorphic subroutines) are sometimes confused with *generic subroutines*. A generic subroutine or module is a *template* that can be used to create multiple *concrete* subroutines or modules that differ in minor ways. In some sense, the local stack module of Figure 3.7 is a primitive sort of generic module. Because it imports

---

11 In fact, most Fortran implementations provide built-in functions for both real (`abs`) and integer (`iabs`) absolute value. Calling the integer version is much more efficient than calling the real version with an integer argument, because it operates on the integer directly, and avoids the overhead of the conversions.

```
generic
    type item is private;
    with function "<"(x, y : item) return Boolean;
function min (x, y : item) return item;

function min (x, y : item) return item is
begin
    if x < y then return x;
    else return y;
    end if;
end min;

function string_min is new min (string, "<");
function date_min is new min (date, date_precedes);
```

Figure 3.20 Use of a generic subroutine in Ada.

the `element` type and `stack_size` constant, it can be inserted (with a text editor) into any context in which these names are declared, and will produce a "customized" stack for that context when compiled. Early versions of C++ formalized this mechanism with a *template* facility implemented with preprocessor macros. Later versions of C++ have made templates a fully supported language feature. Generic subroutines and modules are also supported in Clu, Ada, and Modula-3.

A simple example in Ada appears in Figure 3.20. The initial (bodyless) declaration of `min` is preceded by a `generic` clause specifying that two things are required in order to create a concrete instance of a minimum function: an `item` type, and a corresponding comparison routine. This declaration is followed by the actual code for `min` (the initial declaration is comparable to a `forward` declaration in Pascal). Given appropriate declarations of `string` and `date` types (not shown), we can create functions to return the lesser of pairs of objects of these types as shown in the last two lines. The `"<"` operation mentioned in the definition of `string_min` is presumably overloaded; the compiler resolves the overloading by finding the version of `"<"` that takes arguments of type `item`, where `item` is already known to be `string`.

Where a polymorphic subroutine is a single object capable of accepting arguments of multiple types, a generic subroutine allows the programmer to create *multiple* objects that accept arguments of different types. If desired, Ada allows the resulting objects to share a single, overloaded name. C++ requires them to do so. Clu does not define new names at all, but rather includes the "generic parameters" in every instance of the name (e.g., `min[date](my_date)`).[12] In

---

[12] This method of naming concrete instances is not as awkward as it might first appear, since the generic mechanism in Clu is most often used for generic *clusters*. Since a Clu cluster is a module *type*, the only place its name appears is in the declaration of an instance of the type; the instance itself is then free of the generic parameter names.

the underlying implementation, a polymorphic subroutine is usually a single body of code, while the concrete instances of a generic subroutine usually use separate (similar but different) copies of the code. In most implementations, the instantiation of generic subroutines and modules occurs at compile time.

3.6 Naming-Related Pitfalls in Language Design

We saw in Chapter 2 how the `do` loop syntax and white space rules of Fortran can make a program difficult for a compiler to scan, or for a human being to understand. We also saw how the syntax of Pascal `if...then...else` statements complicates parsing, and can lead to programming errors. In this section we consider several other potential pitfalls in language design, in this case related to naming.

3.6.1 Scope Rules

We have seen how the redeclaration of a name in an inner scope creates a hole in the scope of the outer object. If the outer object is a subroutine, that routine becomes inaccessible in the hole (unless the language provides a scope resolution operator, as mentioned in Section 3.3.1). In particular, a recursive subroutine cannot declare a local object with the same name as the subroutine itself. This is presumably expected, and acceptable, behavior. It has an extra dimension in Pascal, however, which uses "assignment" to the name of the function to specify a return value:

```
function foo : integer;
...
type foo = ...
...
begin (* foo *)
    ...
    foo := 10;          (* static semantic error! *)
```

Pascal scope rules imply that the function name `foo` can be hidden by the nested type declaration, making it impossible to return a value from the function. Because every function must return a value, most Pascal compilers will issue an error message at the type declaration, rather than at the assignment. Specification of return values by "assignment" to the function name can also be awkward in functions that compute their values incrementally, as we shall see in Section 8.3.3. Most Algol-family languages since Pascal provide an alternative mechanism for returning a value from a function, either via a `return` *value* statement (which is still awkward for incremental computations) or by giving the return value its own, first-class name.

Pascal also specifies that the scope of a declaration is the entire block in which it is declared, including the space between the beginning of the block and the declaration (but excluding any holes in the scope, of course). In addition, every identifier that is not predefined must be declared before it is used. These rules can have some strange consequences when declarations refer to each other:

```
const missing = -1;
...
procedure foo;
const
    null = missing;        (* static semantic error! *)
    ...
    missing = 0;
```

Pascal rules say that the second declaration of `missing` covers all of `foo`, so the declaration of `null` refers to `missing` before it is declared. The semantic analyzer should therefore issue an error message at the declaration of `null`. This message may be confusing to the programmer. It also complicates compilation, because the semantic analyzer cannot simply scan the declarations top-to-bottom: it cannot determine the validity of the declaration of `null` until it has seen the later declaration of `missing`. To avoid the complication, some Pascal compilers will (incorrectly) accept the code above, giving `null` the value −1.

The problem gets worse:

```
procedure foo;
    ...
end; (* foo *)
...
procedure A;
    ...
    procedure B;
    begin
        ...
        foo;            (* static semantic error! *)
        ...
    end; (* inner *)
    ...
    procedure foo;
```

Here the reference to `foo` (within procedure `inner`) and the declaration of `foo` are widely separated. Again, the semantic analyzer must scan the entire scope of `A` before it knows whether the call is semantically valid. The intentions of the programmer are unclear. Pascal rules say that the error is a call to (the second) `foo` before it has been declared. It is quite possible, however, that the programmer meant to call the first `foo`, in which case the error message may be rather confusing. These sorts of "reference before declaration" errors are avoided in most Pascal successors (and in some dialects of Pascal itself) by specifying that the scope of an identifier is not the entire block in which it is declared (excluding holes), but rather the portion of that block from the declaration to the end (again excluding holes). If our program fragments had been written in Ada, for example, no semantic errors would be reported. The declaration of `null` would refer to the first (outer) declaration of `missing`; the call to `foo` would refer to the first (outer) procedure. As we saw in Section 3.3.1, ML extends this convention to say that the scope of an identifier extends from its declaration either to the end of the block or to the point at which the name is redeclared.

The question of exactly where the scope of a declaration begins is complicated by the need to define recursive types and mutually recursive subroutines. In Pascal, pointer types are an exception to the rule that names must be declared before they are used:

```
type
    Alink = ^A;
    A = record
        next : Alink;
        data : ...
```

Here the declaration of `Alink` is allowed to contain a *forward reference* to `A`. A similar exception occurs in the scope rules of Modula-2. Unfortunately, exceptional cases make programs harder for both humans and compilers to understand. C, C++, and Ada address the recursive structure problem by prohibiting forward references, but permitting *incomplete* type declarations. In Ada one would say

```
type A;
type Alink is access A;
type A is record
        next : Alink;
        data : ...
```

Interestingly, as we saw in Section 3.3.3, Pascal provides a similar form of incomplete specification for mutually recursive subroutines; it does not permit forward references to a subroutine without a forward declaration. Modula-3 adopts a different solution: it specifies, as in Pascal, that the scope of a name spans the entire block in which it is declared (except for holes), but it abandons the requirement that names be declared before they are used. Java and C++ take a mixed approach: variables must be declared before they are used, but types (classes) need not; their scope extends over the entire module (package) in which they are declared. In a similar vein, members of a Java or C++ class are visible throughout the code of the member functions of the class, regardless of the order in which the members are declared.

3.6.2* Separate Compilation

Since most large programs are constructed and tested incrementally, and since the compilation of a very large program can be a multihour operation, any language designed to support large programs must provide a separate compilation facility. Because they are designed for encapsulation and provide a narrow interface, modules are the natural choice for the "compilation units" of many programming languages. The separate module headers and bodies of Modula-3 and Ada, for example, are explicitly intended for separate compilation, and reflect experience gained with more primitive facilities in other languages.

The initial version of C was designed at Bell Laboratories in the late 1960s. It has evolved considerably over the past 25–30 years, but prior to the C9X standard (under development as of this writing [Int98a]) its scope rules and separate compilation facilities remained largely unchanged. The principal rules for 1990 ANSI Standard C can be summarized as follows (certain details and special cases are omitted):

- If a name is declared inside a *block* (any construct, including a function body or compound statement, that is delimited by {...}), then its scope extends from its declaration to the end of the block (except for holes), unless it is a statement label, in which case its scope is the entire function in which it appears. If a name is declared outside any function, then its scope extends from the declaration to the end of the file in which it appears.

- If the declaration of a variable contains the keyword `extern`, or if it appears outside of any block and does not contain the keyword `static`, then the variable is *linked* with any other declaration of the same external variable in any file of the program. In other words, files in the same program that contain matching external variable declarations actually share the same variable.

- If the declaration of a function does not contain the keyword `static`, then it is linked to any other (nonstatic) declaration of the same function in any file of the program. (A function declaration may consist of just the header; see below.)

- An object (variable or function) that is externally linked must have a *definition* in exactly one file of a program. A variable is defined when it is given an initial value, or is declared outside any block without the `extern` keyword. A function is defined when its body (code) is given.

Many implementations of C relax the final rule to permit zero or one definitions of an externally linked variable. In these implementations, the linker (the program that knits separately compiled files together into a program) creates an implicit definition for any variables that need one.

The "linkage" rules of ANSI C provide a way of associating names in one file with names in another file. The rules are most easily understood in terms of their implementation. Most language-independent linkers are designed to deal with *symbols*: character-string names for locations in a machine-language program. The linker's job is to assign every symbol a location in the final program, and to embed the address of the symbol in every machine-language instruction that makes a reference to it. To do this job, the linker needs to know which symbols can be used to resolve unbound references in other files, and which are local to a given file. C's rules suffice to provide this information. For the programmer, however, there is no formal notion of *interface*, and no mechanism to make a name visible in some, but not all files. Moreover, nothing ensures that the declarations of an external object found in different files will be compatible: it is entirely possible, for example, to declare an external variable as a multifield record in one file and as a floating-point number in another. The compiler is not required to catch such errors, and the resulting bugs can be very difficult to find.

Fortunately, C programmers have developed conventions on the use of external declarations that tend to minimize errors in practice. These conventions rely on the *file inclusion* facility of a macro preprocessor. The programmer creates files in pairs that correspond roughly to the interface and the implementation of a module. The name of an interface file ends with .h; the name of the corresponding implementation file ends with .c. Every object *defined* in the .c file is *declared* in the .h file. At the beginning of the .c file, the programmer inserts a directive that is treated as a special form of comment by the compiler, but that causes the preprocessor to include a verbatim copy of the corresponding .h file. This inclusion operation has the effect of placing "forward" declarations of all the module's objects at the beginning of its implementation file. Any inconsistencies with definitions later in the file will result in error messages from the compiler. The programmer also instructs the preprocessor at the top of each .c file to include a copy of the .h files for all of the modules on which the .c file depends. As long as the preprocessor includes identical copies of a given .h file in all the .c files that use its module, no inconsistent declarations will occur. Of course, all global names must be distinct, since there is no mechanism for scoping beyond the level of an individual file. Many programmers therefore embed a module's name in the name of each of its external objects (e.g., scanner_nextSym). Unfortunately, it is easy to forget to recompile one or more .c files when a .h file is changed, and this can lead to very subtle bugs. Tools such as Unix's make utility help minimize such errors by keeping track of the dependences among modules.

The separate compilation facilities of Java address many of C's problems. Specifically, Java introduces a formal notion of module, called a *package*. Every *compilation unit*, which may be a file or (in some implementations) a record in a database, belongs to exactly one package, but a package may consist of many compilation units, each of which begins with an indication of the package to which it belongs:

```
package foo;
public class foo_type_1 { ...
```

Unless explicitly declared as public, a class in Java is visible in all and only those compilation units that belong to the same package.

A compilation unit in Java that needs to use classes from another package can access them either by using *fully qualified* names, or by *importing* them explicitly:

```
foo.foo_type_1 my_first_obj;
```

or

```
import foo.foo_type_1;
...
foo_type_1 my_first_obj;
```

or

```
import foo.*;           // import everything from foo
...
foo_type_1 my_first_obj;
```

Exactly which packages are available for import depends on the conventions of the host system on which Java is installed. Programming conventions based on Internet addresses encourage programmers to create package names that are unique, worldwide.

Standard C++ provides a more sophisticated notion of *namespace* that generalizes the scoping mechanisms already provided for classes and functions, breaks the tie between module and compilation unit, and centralizes the declarations of names exported from a module into a clearly identifiable interface. Any collection of names can be declared inside a `namespace`:

```
namespace foo {
    class foo_type_1;       // declaration
    ...
}
```

Actual definitions of the objects within `foo` can then appear in any file:

```
class foo::foo_type_1 { ...    // full definition
```

Definitions of objects declared in different namespaces can appear in the same file if desired.

As in Java, a C++ programmer can access the objects in a namespace using fully qualified names, object-by-object import, or namespace-at-a-time import:

```
foo.foo_type_1 my_first_obj;
```

or

```
using foo.foo_type_1;
...
foo_type_1 my_first_obj;
```

or

```
using namespace foo;    // import everything from foo
...
foo_type_1 my_first_obj;
```

The C9X version of C is likely to have facilities reminiscent of C++.

In Modula and Ada, the programmer can create a hierarchy of modules within a single compilation unit by means of lexical nesting (module C, for example, may be declared inside of module B, which in turn is declared inside of module A). In a similar vein, the Java or Ada 95 programmer can create a hierarchy of separately compiled modules by means of *multipart names*:

```
package A.B;
class B_type_1 { ...        // Java

package A.B is ...          -- Ada 95
```

In these examples package `A.B` is said to be a *child* of package `A`. In Ada 95 the child behaves roughly as though it had been nested inside of the parent, so that all the names in the parent are automatically visible (nested packages are open scopes in Ada). In Java, by contrast, multipart names work by convention only: there is no special relationship between packages `A` and `A.B`. If `A.B` needs to refer to names in `A`, then `A` must export them and `A.B` must import them. Child packages in Ada 95 are reminiscent of derived classes in C++, except that they support a module-as-manager style of abstraction, rather than a module-as-type style. We will consider the Ada 95 facilities further in Section 10.2.3.

3.7 Summary and Concluding Remarks

This chapter has addressed the subject of names, and the *binding* of names to objects (in a broad sense of the word). We began with a general discussion of the notion of *binding time*: the time at which a name is associated with a particular object or, more generally, the time at which an answer is associated with any open question in language or program design or implementation. We defined the notion of *lifetime* for both objects and name-to-object bindings, and noted that they need not be the same. We then introduced the three principal storage allocation mechanisms—static, stack, and heap—used to manage space for objects.

In Section 3.3 we described how the binding of names to objects is governed by *scope rules*. In some languages, scope rules are dynamic: the meaning of a name is found in the most recently entered scope that contains a declaration and that has not yet been exited. In most modern languages, however, scope rules are static, or *lexical*: the meaning of a name is found in the closest lexically surrounding scope that contains a declaration. We found that lexical scope rules vary in important but sometimes subtle ways from one language to another. We considered what sorts of scopes are allowed to nest, whether scopes are *open* or *closed*, and whether the scope of a name encompasses the entire block in which it is declared, or only the portion after the declaration.

In Section 3.3.1 we saw how static links allow code in a language with static scoping to locate the local objects of surrounding scopes at run time. In Sections 3.3.3 and 3.3.4 we saw how symbol tables (for static scoping) and association lists and reference tables (for dynamic scoping) are used to keep track of name-to-object bindings. We then considered the question of when to bind a referencing environment to a subroutine that is passed as a parameter, returned from a function, or stored in a variable. Near the end of the chapter, we revisited the question of whether a name must be declared before it is used, and how the answer affects the declaration of mutually recursive types and subroutines.

Some of the more complicated aspects of lexical scoping illustrate the evolution of language support for data abstraction, a subject to which we will return in Chapter 10. We began by describing the `own` or `static` variables of languages such as Algol 60 and C, which allow a variable that is local to a subroutine to retain its value from one invocation to the next. We then noted that simple modules can be seen as a way of making long-lived objects local to a group of subroutines, in such a way that they are not visible to other parts of the program. At the next level of complexity, we noted that some languages treat modules as types, allowing the programmer to create an arbitrary number of instances of the abstraction defined by a module. We contrasted this module-as-abstraction style of programming with the module-as-manager approach. Finally, we noted that object-oriented languages extend the module-as-abstraction approach by providing an inheritance mechanism that allows new abstractions (classes) to be defined as extensions or refinements of existing classes.

In Section 3.5 we examined several ways in which bindings relate to one another. Aliases arise when two or more names in a given scope are bound to the same object. Overloading arises when one name is bound to multiple objects. We noted that some of the effects of overloading can sometimes arise through very different mechanisms: coercion, polymorphism, and generic subroutines.

Among the topics considered in this chapter, we saw several examples of useful features (recursion, static scoping, forward references, first-class subroutines, unlimited extent) that have been omitted from certain languages because of concern for their implementation complexity or run-time cost. We also saw one example of a feature (the private part of a module specification) introduced expressly to facilitate a language's implementation. In several additional aspects of language design (late v. early binding, static v. dynamic scope, support for coercions and conversions, toleration of pointers and other aliases), we saw that implementation issues play a major role.

We ended the chapter with a series of examples that illustrate some of the thornier aspects of naming and scope rule design. Even in very successful and popular languages, subtle implications of the rules can make programs surprisingly difficult to understand or to compile. As we saw with the lexical and syntactic issues discussed in Chapter 2, rules that are difficult to implement in a compiler are often difficult for human beings to understand as well. In future chapters we will see several further examples of features that are both confusing and hard to compile. Of course, semantic utility and ease of implementation do not always go together. Many easy-to-compile features (`goto` statements, for example) are of questionable value at best. We will also see several examples of highly useful and (conceptually) simple features, such as garbage collection (Section 7.7.3) and unification (Sections 7.2.5 and 11.3.1), whose implementations are quite complex.

3.8 Review Questions

3.1   What is *binding time*?

3.2   Explain the distinction between decisions that are bound statically and those that are bound dynamically.

3.3   What is the advantage of binding things as early as possible? What is the advantage of delaying bindings?

3.4   Explain the distinction between the *lifetime* of a name-to-object binding and its *visibility*.

3.5   What is a *dangling reference*?

3.6   What determines whether an object is allocated statically, on the stack, or in the heap?

3.7   List the objects and information commonly found in a stack frame.

3.8   What is a *frame pointer*? What is it used for?

3.9   What is a *static chain*? What is it used for?

3.10   What is a *calling sequence*?

3.11   What is *elaboration*?

3.12   What are internal and external *fragmentation*?

3.13   What is *garbage collection*?

3.14   What do we mean by the *scope* of a name-to-object binding?

3.15   Describe the difference between static and dynamic scope.

3.16   What is a *referencing environment*?

3.17   Describe the difference between deep and shallow *binding* of referencing environments.

3.18   Explain the distinction between limited and unlimited *extent* of objects in a local scope.

3.19   Explain the distinction between "modules as managers" and "modules as types."

3.20   What does it mean for a scope to be *closed*?

3.21   What are *aliases*? Why are they considered a problem in language design and implementation?

3.22   Why does the use of dynamic scoping imply the need for run-time type checking?

3.23   Give an argument in favor of dynamic scoping.

3.24   What are *forward references*? Why are they prohibited or restricted in many programming languages?

3.25   Explain the purpose of a compiler's symbol table.

3.26   Describe the *association list* and *central reference table* data structures used to implement dynamic scoping.

3.27 What is a *closure*? What is it used for? How is it implemented?

3.28 Explain the difference between *overloading, coercion, generics,* and *polymorphism*.

3.9 Exercises

3.1 Indicate the binding time (e.g., when the language is designed, when the program is linked, when the program begins execution, etc.) for each of the following decisions in your favorite programming language and implementation. Explain any answers you think are open to interpretation.

- The number of built-in functions (`abs, cosine,` etc.)
- The variable declaration that corresponds to a particular variable reference (use)
- The maximum length allowed for a constant (literal) character string
- The referencing environment for a subroutine that is passed as a parameter
- The address of a particular library routine
- The total amount of space occupied by program code and data

3.2 In Fortran 77, local variables are typically allocated statically. In Algol and its descendants (e.g., Pascal and Ada), they are typically allocated in the stack. In Lisp they are typically allocated at least partially in the heap. What accounts for these differences? Give an example of a program in Pascal or Ada that would not work correctly if local variables were allocated statically. Give an example of a program in Scheme or Common Lisp that would not work correctly if local variables were allocated on the stack.

3.3 Give two examples in which it might make sense to delay the binding of an implementation decision, even though sufficient information exists to bind it early.

3.4 Experiment with naming rules in your favorite programming language. Read the manual, and write and compile some test programs. Does the language use lexical or dynamic scope? Can scopes nest? Are they open or closed? Does the scope of a name encompass the entire block in which it is declared, or only the portion after the declaration? How does one declare mutually recursive types or subroutines? Can subroutines be passed as parameters, returned from functions, or stored in variables? If so, when are referencing environments bound?

3.5 Many languages distinguish between the *declaration* of an object and its *definition*. We saw an example in C in Section 3.6.2. In the general sense of the term, a declaration introduces a name, binds it to a scope, and possibly provides other limited information, allowing the name to be used in some restricted way. A definition provides complete information. A declaration may be used without a definition for two main purposes: to hide information, or to delay a binding. Give an example that illustrates each of these purposes in some language with which you are familiar. (For hints, see Section 7.1.1.)

3.6 Give three concrete examples drawn from programming languages with which you are familiar in which a variable is live but not in scope.

3.7 List the keywords (reserved words) of one or more programming languages. List the predefined identifiers. (Recall that every keyword is a separate token. An identifier cannot have the same spelling as a keyword.) What criteria do you think were used to decide which names should be keywords and which should be predefined identifiers? Do you agree with the choices? Why or why not?

3.8 Modula-2 provides no way to divide the header of a module into a public part and a private part: everything in the header is visible to the users of the module. Is this a major shortcoming? Are there disadvantages to the public/private division (e.g., as in Ada)? (For hints, see Section 10.2.)

3.9 Consider the following fragment of code in C:

```
{   int a, b, c;
    . . .
    {   int d, e;
        . . .
        {   int f;
            . . .
        }
        . . .
    }
    . . .
    {   int g, h, i;
        . . .
    }
    . . .
}
```

Assume that each integer variable occupies four bytes. How much total space is required for the variables in this code? Describe an algorithm that a compiler could use to assign stack frame offsets to the variables of arbitrary nested blocks, in a way that minimizes the total space required.

3.10 Consider the design of a Fortran 77 compiler that uses static allocation for the local variables of subroutines. Expanding on the solution to the previous question, describe an algorithm to minimize the total space required for these variables. You may find it helpful to construct a *call graph* data structure in which each node represents a subroutine and each directed arc indicates that the subroutine at the tail may call the subroutine at the head.

3.11 Consider the following pseudocode:

```
x : integer      -- global

procedure set_x (n : integer)
    x := n

procedure print_x
    write_integer (x)

procedure first
    set_x (1)
    print_x

procedure second
    x : integer
    set_x (2)
    print_x

set_x (0)
first ()
print_x
second ()
print_x
```

What does this program print if the language uses static scoping? What does it print with dynamic scoping? Why?

3.12 For the program of the previous question, assume dynamic scope and an association list representation of the referencing environment. Trace the changes made to the association list over the course of the program's execution.

3.13 Consider the programming idiom illustrated in the print_base_save example at the end of Section 3.3.2. One of the reviewers for this book suggests that we think of this idiom as a way of implementing a central reference table for dynamic scope. Explain what is meant by this suggestion.

3.14 We learned in Section 3.3.2 that modern languages have generally abandoned dynamic scoping. One place they can still be found is in the so-called *environment variables* of the Unix programming environment. If you are not familiar with them, read the manual page for your favorite shell (command interpreter—sh, csh, etc.) to learn how these behave. Explain why the usual alternatives to dynamic scoping (default parameters and static variables) are not appropriate in this case.

3.15 If you are familiar with the exception-handling mechanism of Ada, Modula-3, C++, Java, or ML, consider how this mechanism relates to the issue of scoping. Conventionally, a **raise** or **throw** statement is thought of as referring to an exception, which it passes as a parameter to a handler-finding library routine. In each of the languages mentioned, the exception itself must be declared in some surrounding scope, and is subject to the usual static scope rules. Describe an alternative point of view, in which the `raise` or `throw` is actually a reference to a *handler*, to which it transfers control directly. Assuming this point of view, what are the scope rules for handlers? Are these rules consistent with the rest of the language? Explain. (For further information on exceptions, see Section 8.5.)

3.16 Assuming a LeBlanc-Cook style symbol table, explain how the compiler finds the symbol table information (e.g., the type) of a complicated reference such as `my_firm^.revenues[1999]`.

3.17 Consider the following pseudocode:

```
x : integer      -- global

procedure set_x (n : integer)
    x := n

procedure print_x
    write_integer (x)

procedure foo (S, P : function; n : integer)
    x : integer
    if n in {1, 3}
        set_x (n)
    else
        S (n)
    if n in {1, 2}
        print_x
    else
        P

set_x (0); foo (set_x, print_x, 1); print_x
set_x (0); foo (set_x, print_x, 2); print_x
set_x (0); foo (set_x, print_x, 3); print_x
set_x (0); foo (set_x, print_x, 4); print_x
```

Assume that the language uses dynamic scoping. What does the program print if the language uses shallow binding? What does it print with deep binding? Why?

3.18 Compare the mechanisms for overloading of enumeration names in Ada and Modula-3 (Section 3.5). One might argue that the (historically more recent) Modula-3 approach moves responsibility from the compiler to the programmer: it requires even an unambiguous use of an enumeration constant to be annotated with its type. Why do you think this approach was chosen by the language designers? Do you agree with the choice? Why or why not?

3.19 Write a program in C++ or Ada that creates at least two concrete types or subroutines from the same template/generic. Compile your code to assembly language and look at the result. Describe the mapping from source to target code.

3.20 Do you think coercion is a good idea? Why or why not?

3.21 Give three examples of features that are *not* provided in some language with which you are familiar, but that are common in other languages. Why do you think these features are missing? Would they complicate the implementation of the language? If so, would the complication (in your judgment) be justified?

3.22* Create a C program in which a variable is exported from one file and imported by another, but the declarations in the files disagree with respect to type. You should be able to arrange for the program to compile and link successfully, but behave incorrectly. Try the same thing in Ada, Modula-3, or C++. What happens?

3.10 Bibliographic Notes

This chapter has traced the evolution of naming and scoping mechanisms through many different languages, including Fortran (several versions), Basic, Algol 60 and 68, Pascal, Simula, C and C++, Euclid, Turing, Modula (1, 2, and 3), Ada (83 and 95), Oberon, Eiffel, and Java. Bibliographic references for all of these can be found in Appendix A.

Both modules and objects trace their roots to Simula, which was developed by Dahl, Nygaard, Myhrhaug, and others at the Norwegian Computing Centre in the mid-1960s. (Simula I was implemented in 1964; descriptions in this book pertain to Simula 67.) The encapsulation mechanisms of Simula were refined in the 1970s by the developers of Clu, Modula, Euclid, and related languages. Other Simula innovations—inheritance and dynamic method binding in particular—provided the inspiration for Smalltalk, the original and arguably purest of the object-oriented languages. Modern object-oriented languages, including Eiffel, C++, Java, CLOS, Modula-3, and Ada 95, represent to a large extent a reintegration of the evolutionary lines of encapsulation on the one hand and inheritance and dynamic method binding on the other.

The notion of information hiding originates in Parnas's classic paper "On the Criteria to be Used in Decomposing Systems into Modules" [Par72]. Comparative discussions of naming, scoping, and abstraction mechanisms can be found, among other places, in Liskov et al.'s discussion of Clu [LSAS77], Liskov and Guttag's text [LG86, Chap. 4], the Ada Rationale [IBFW91, Chaps. 9–12], Harbison's text on Modula-3 [Har92, Chaps. 8–9], Wirth's early work on modules [Wir80], and his later discussion of Modula and Oberon [Wir88a]. Further information on object-oriented languages can be found in Chapter 10.

For a detailed discussion of overloading and polymorphism, see the survey by Cardelli and Wegner [CW85]. Cailliau [Cai82] provides a lighthearted discussion of many of the scoping pitfalls noted in Section 3.6.1. Abelson and Sussman [AS96, p. 11n] attribute the term "syntactic sugar" to Peter Landin.

Semantic Analysis 4

In Chapter 2 we considered the topic of programming language syntax. In the current chapter we turn to the topic of semantics. Informally, syntax concerns the *form* of a valid program, while semantics concerns its *meaning*. It is conventional to say that the syntax of a language is precisely that portion of the language definition that can be described conveniently by a context-free grammar, while the semantics is that portion of the definition that cannot. This convention is useful in practice, though it does not always agree with intuition. When we require, for example, that the number of arguments contained in a call to a subroutine match the number of formal parameters in the subroutine definition, it is tempting to say that this requirement is a matter of syntax. After all, we can count arguments without knowing what they mean. Unfortunately, we cannot count them with context-free rules, or in the presence of separate compilation. Similarly, while it is possible to write a context-free grammar in which every function must contain at least one `return` statement, the required complexity makes this strategy very unattractive. In general, any rule that requires the compiler to compare things that are separated by long distances, or to count things that are not properly nested, ends up being a matter of semantics.

Semantic rules are further divided into *static* and *dynamic* semantics, though again the line between the two is somewhat fuzzy. The compiler enforces static semantic rules at compile time. It generates code to enforce dynamic semantic rules at run time. Certain errors, such as division by zero, or attempting to index into an array with an out-of-bounds subscript, cannot usually be caught at compile time, since they are likely to occur only for certain input values. In special cases, a compiler may be able to tell that a certain error will always or never occur, regardless of run-time input. In these cases, the compiler can generate an error message at compile time, or refrain from generating code to perform the check at run time, as appropriate. Basic results from computability theory, however, tell us that no algorithm can make these predictions correctly for arbitrary programs: there will inevitably be cases in which an error will always occur, but the compiler cannot tell, and must delay the error message until run time; there will also be cases in which an error can never occur, but the compiler cannot tell, and must incur the cost of unnecessary run-time checks.

Both semantic analysis and intermediate code generation can be described in terms of annotation, or "decoration" of a parse tree or syntax tree. The annotations themselves are known as *attributes*. Numerous examples of static and dynamic semantic rules will appear in subsequent chapters. In this current chapter we focus primarily on the mechanisms a compiler uses to enforce the static rules. We will consider intermediate code generation in Chapter 9.

In Section 4.1 we consider the role of the semantic analyzer in more detail, considering both the rules it needs to enforce and its relationship to other phases of compilation. Most of the rest of the chapter is then devoted to the subject of *attribute grammars*. Attribute grammars provide a formal framework for the decoration of a tree. This framework is a useful conceptual tool even in compilers that do not build a parse tree or syntax tree as an explicit data structure. We introduce the notion of an attribute grammar in Section 4.2. We then consider various ways in which such grammars can be applied in practice. Section 4.3 discusses the issue of *attribute flow*, which constrains the order(s) in which nodes of a tree can be decorated. In practice, most compilers require decoration of the parse tree (or the evaluation of attributes that would reside in a parse tree if there were one) to occur in the process of an LL or LR parse. Section 4.4 presents *action routines* as an ad hoc mechanism for such on-the-fly evaluation. In Section 4.5 we consider the management of space for parse tree attributes.

One particularly common compiler organization uses action routines during parsing solely for the purpose of constructing a syntax tree, which is then decorated during a separate traversal (and can be formalized with a separate attribute grammar). We consider the decoration of syntax trees in Section 4.6.

4.1 The Role of the Semantic Analyzer

Programming languages vary dramatically in their choice of semantic rules. In Section 3.5, for example, we saw a range of approaches to coercion, from languages like Fortran and C, which allow operands of many types to be intermixed in expressions, to languages like Ada, which do not. Languages also vary in the extent to which they require their implementations to perform dynamic checks. At one extreme, C requires no checks at all, beyond those that come "free" with the hardware (e.g., division by zero, or attempted access to memory outside the bounds of the program). At the other extreme, Java takes great pains to check as many rules as possible, in part to ensure that an untrusted program cannot do anything to damage the memory or files of the machine on which it runs.

In the typical compiler, the interface between semantic analysis and intermediate code generation defines the boundary between the *front end* and the *back end*. The exact division of labor varies a bit from compiler to compiler: it can be hard to say exactly where analysis (figuring out what the program means) ends and synthesis (expressing that meaning in some new form) begins. Many compilers actually carry a program through more than one intermediate form.

In one common organization, described in more detail in Chapter 9, the semantic analyzer creates an annotated syntax tree, which the intermediate code generator then translates into a linear form reminiscent of the assembly language for some idealized machine. After machine-independent code improvement, this linear form is then translated into yet another form, patterned more closely on the assembly language of the target machine. That form may then undergo machine-specific code improvement.

Compilers also vary in the extent to which semantic analysis and intermediate code generation are interleaved with parsing. With fully separated phases, the parser passes a full parse tree on to the semantic analyzer, which converts it to a syntax tree, fills in the symbol table, performs semantic checks, and passes it on to the code generator. With fully interleaved phases, there may be no need to build either the parse tree or the syntax tree in its entirety: the parser can call semantic check and code generation routines "on-the-fly" as it parses each expression, statement, or subroutine of the source. We will focus on an organization in which construction of the syntax tree is interleaved with parsing (and the parse tree is not built), but semantic analysis occurs during a separate traversal of the syntax tree.

Many compilers that implement dynamic checks provide the option of disabling them if desired. It is customary in some organizations to enable dynamic checks during program development and testing, and then disable them for production use, to increase execution speed. The wisdom of this practice is questionable: Tony Hoare, one of the key figures in programming language design,[1] has likened the programmer who disables semantic checks to a sailing enthusiast who wears a life jacket when training on dry land, but removes it when going to sea [Hoa89, p. 198]. Errors may be less likely in production use than they are in testing, but the consequences of an undetected error are significantly worse. Moreover, with the increasing use of multi-issue, superscalar processors (to be described in Section 5.5), it is often possible for dynamic checks to execute in instruction slots that would otherwise go unused, making them virtually free. On the other hand some dynamic checks (e.g., for use of uninitialized variables) are sufficiently expensive that they are rarely implemented.

A few programming languages (e.g., Euclid and Eiffel) allow the programmer to specify logical *assertions*, *invariants*, *preconditions*, and *postconditions* that must be verified by dynamic semantic checks. An assertion is a statement that a specified condition is expected to be true when execution reaches a certain point in the code. In Euclid, for example, one can write

```
assert denominator not= 0
```

---

[1] Among other things, Hoare invented the quicksort algorithm and the `case` statement, contributed to the design of Algol W, and was one of the leaders in the development of axiomatic semantics. In the area of concurrent programming, he refined and formalized the *monitor* construct (to be described in Section 12.3.3), and designed the CSP programming model and notation. He received the ACM Turing Award in 1980.

An invariant is a condition that is expected to be true at all "clean points" of a given body of code. In Eiffel, for example, the programmer can specify an invariant on the data inside a class: the invariant is expected to be true at the beginning and end of all of the class's subroutines. Similar invariants for loops are expected to be true before and after every iteration. Pre- and postconditions are expected to be true at the beginning and end of subroutines, respectively.

Assertions, of course, could be used to cover the other three sorts of checks, but not as clearly or succinctly. Invariants, preconditions, and postconditions are a prominent part of the header of the code to which they apply, and can cover a potentially large number of places where an assertion would otherwise be required. Euclid and Eiffel implementations allow the programmer to disable assertions and related constructs when desired, to eliminate their run-time cost.

4.2   Attribute Grammars

In Chapter 2 we learned how to use a context-free grammar to specify the syntax of a programming language. Here, for example, is an LR (bottom-up) grammar for arithmetic expressions composed of constants, with precedence and associativity:

$$E \rightarrow E + T$$
$$E \rightarrow E - T$$
$$E \rightarrow T$$
$$T \rightarrow T * F$$
$$T \rightarrow T / F$$
$$T \rightarrow F$$
$$F \rightarrow - F$$
$$F \rightarrow (E)$$
$$F \rightarrow \texttt{const}$$

This grammar will generate all properly formed constant expressions over the basic arithmetic operators, but it says nothing about their meaning. To tie these expressions to mathematical concepts (as opposed to, say, floor tile patterns or dance steps), we need additional notation. The most common is based on *attributes*. In our expression grammar, we can associate a val attribute with each E, T, F, and $\texttt{const}$ in the grammar. The intent is that for any symbol S, S.val will be the meaning, as an arithmetic value, of the token string derived from S. We assume that the val of a $\texttt{const}$ is provided to us by the scanner. We must then invent a set of rules for each production, to specify how the vals of different symbols are related. The resulting *attribute grammar* is shown in Figure 4.1.

In this simple grammar, every production has a single rule. We will see more complicated grammars later, in which productions can have several rules. The

1. $E_1 \rightarrow E_2 + T$
    ▷ E_1.val := sum (E_2.val, T.val)

2. $E_1 \rightarrow E_2 - T$
    ▷ E_1.val := difference (E_2.val, T.val)

3. $E \rightarrow T$
    ▷ E.val := T.val

4. $T_1 \rightarrow T_2 * F$
    ▷ T_1.val := product (T_2.val, F.val)

5. $T_1 \rightarrow T_2 / F$
    ▷ T_1.val := quotient (T_2.val, F.val)

6. $T \rightarrow F$
    ▷ T.val := F.val

7. $F_1 \rightarrow - F_2$
    ▷ F_1.val := additive_inverse (F_2.val)

8. $F \rightarrow (E)$
    ▷ F.val := E.val

9. $F \rightarrow$ const
    ▷ F.val := const.val

Figure 4.1 A simple attribute grammar for constant expressions, using the standard arithmetic operations.

rules come in two forms. Those in productions 3, 6, 8, and 9 are known as *copy rules*; they specify that one attribute should be a copy of another. The other rules invoke *semantic functions* (sum, quotient, additive_inverse, etc.). In this example, the semantic functions are all familiar arithmetic operations. In general, they can be arbitrarily complex functions specified by the language designer. Each semantic function takes an arbitrary number of arguments (each of which must be an attribute of a symbol in the current production: no constants, global variables, etc.), and each computes a single result, which must likewise be assigned into an attribute of a symbol in the current production. When more than one symbol of a production has the same name, subscripts are used to distinguish them. These subscripts are solely for the benefit of the semantic functions; they are not part of the context-free grammar itself.

In a strict definition of attribute grammars, copy rules and semantic function calls are the only two kinds of permissible rules. In practice, it is common to allow rules to consist of small fragments of code in some well-defined notation (e.g., the language in which a compiler is being written), so that simple semantic functions can be written out "in-line." These code fragments are not allowed to refer to any variables or attributes outside the current production (we will relax this restriction when we discuss action routines in Section 4.4 below). In our examples we use a ▷ symbol to introduce each code fragment corresponding to a single semantic function.

The fact that semantic functions must be written in some already-existing notation stems from the fact that attribute grammars do not really specify the meaning of a program; rather, they provide a way of associating a program with something else that presumably has meaning. Neither the notation for semantic functions nor the types of the attributes themselves (i.e., the domain of values passed to and returned from semantic functions) is intrinsic to the attribute grammar notion. In the example above, we have used an attribute grammar to associate numeric values with the symbols in our grammar, using semantic functions drawn from ordinary arithmetic. In the code generation phase of a compiler, we might associate fragments of target machine code with our symbols, using semantic functions written in some existing programming language. If we were interested in defining the meaning of a programming language in a machine-independent way, our attributes might be domain theory *denotations* (these are the basis of *denotational semantics*). If we were interested in proving theorems about the behavior of programs in our language, our attributes might be logical inference rules (this is the basis of *axiomatic semantics*).[2] These more formal concepts are beyond the scope of this text (but see the Bibliographic Notes at the end of the chapter). We will use attribute grammars primarily as a framework for building a syntax tree, checking semantic rules, and (in Chapter 9) generating code.

4.3 Attribute Flow

Just as a context-free grammar does not specify how it should be parsed, an attribute grammar does not specify the order in which attribute rules should be evaluated. But just as different classes of context-free grammars are amenable to different parsing algorithms, so too are different classes of attribute grammars amenable to different evaluation orders. The process of evaluating attributes is called *annotation* or *decoration* of the parse tree. Figure 4.2 shows an annotated parse tree for the expression (1 + 3) * 2, using the attribute grammar of Figure 4.1. Once annotation is complete, the value of the overall expression can be found in the val attribute of the root of the tree.

The attribute grammar shown in Figure 4.1 is very simple. Each symbol has at most one attribute (the punctuation marks have none). Moreover, they are all so-called *synthesized attributes*: their values are calculated (synthesized) only in

---

2 It's actually stretching things a bit to discuss axiomatic semantics in the context of attribute grammars. Axiomatic semantics is intended not so much to define the meaning of programs as to permit one to prove that a given program satisfies some desired property (e.g. computes some desired function).

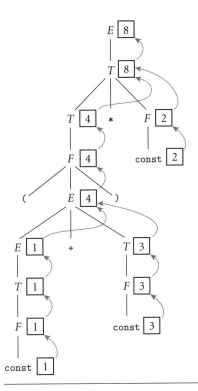

Figure 4.2 **Annotation of a parse tree for** (1 + 3) * 2. The val attributes of symbols are shown in boxes. Curving arrows represent the attribute flow, which is strictly upward in this case.

productions in which their symbol appears on the left-hand side. Tokens (terminals) often have intrinsic properties (e.g., the character-string representation of an identifier or the value of a numeric constant); in a compiler these are synthesized attributes initialized by the scanner. An attribute grammar in which all attributes are synthesized is said to be *S-attributed*. The arguments to semantic functions in an S-attributed grammar are always attributes of symbols on the right-hand side of the current production, and the return value is always placed into an attribute of the left-hand side of the production.

In general, we can imagine (and will in fact have need of) attributes whose values are calculated when their symbol is on the right-hand side of the current production. Such attributes are said to be *inherited*. They allow contextual information to flow into a symbol from above or from the side, so that the rules of that production can be enforced in different ways in different contexts. Symbol table information is commonly passed from symbol to symbol by means of inherited attributes. Inherited attributes of the root of the parse tree can be used to represent the surrounding environment (characteristics of the target machine, command-line arguments to the compiler, etc.).

1. $E \rightarrow T \; TT$
   ▷ TT.st := T.val   ▷ E.val := TT.val

2. $TT_1 \rightarrow + \; T \; TT_2$
   ▷ TT_2.st := TT_1.st + T.val   ▷ TT_1.val := TT_2.val

3. $TT_1 \rightarrow - \; T \; TT_2$
   ▷ TT_2.st := TT_1.st − T.val   ▷ TT_1.val := TT_2.val

4. $TT \rightarrow \epsilon$
   ▷ TT.val := TT.st

5. $T \rightarrow F \; FT$
   ▷ FT.st := F.val   ▷ T.val := FT.val

6. $FT_1 \rightarrow * \; F \; FT_2$
   ▷ FT_2.st := FT_1.st × F.val   ▷ FT_1.val := FT_2.val

7. $FT_1 \rightarrow / \; F \; FT_2$
   ▷ FT_2.st := FT_1.st ÷ F.val   ▷ FT_1.val := FT_2.val

8. $FT \rightarrow \epsilon$
   ▷ FT.val := FT.st

9. $F_1 \rightarrow - \; F_2$
   ▷ F_1.val := $-$ F_2.val

10. $F \rightarrow (\; E \;)$
    ▷ F.val := E.val

11. $F \rightarrow$ const
    ▷ F.val := const.val

Figure 4.3 An attribute grammar for constant expressions based on an LL(1) CFG.

The pattern in which information moves from one attribute to another is known as *attribute flow*. In an S-attributed attribute grammar, attribute flow is strictly bottom-up. Grammars to perform semantic analysis for practical languages generally require some non-S-attributed flow. The need tends to be particularly great in attribute grammars whose underlying context-free grammar is intended for top-down parsing. In the example we have seen so far (Figure 4.1), the underlying CFG is SLR(1). To produce an equivalent attribute grammar based on an LL(1) CFG, we must employ inherited attributes, as shown in Figure 4.3. Attribute flow for a parse of $(1 + 3) * 2$ appears in Figure 4.4. The relative complexity of the attribute flow arises from the fact that the left and right operands of a given operator are not together in the same production. To capture the left associativity of the arithmetic operators, the value of the left operand of each operator must be carried into the TT and FT productions by the st (subtotal) attribute.

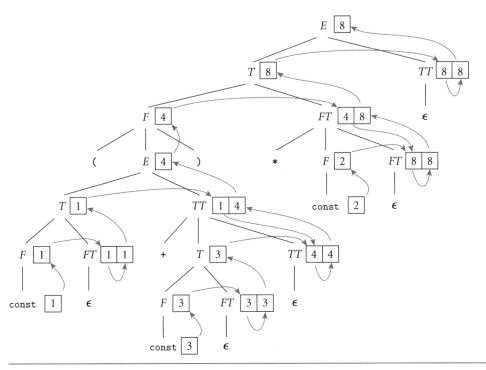

Figure 4.4 Annotation of a top-down parse tree for $(1 + 3) * 2$**, using the attribute grammar of Figure 4.3.** Curving arrows again represent attribute flow, which is no longer bottom-up, but is still left-to-right.

An attribute grammar does not explicitly specify when the various semantic functions are to be invoked, or even in what order. In particular, the order of the rules in each production is immaterial; attribute flow may require them to execute in any order. If in Figure 4.3 we were to reverse the order in which the rules appear in productions 1, 2, 3, 5, 6, and/or 7 (listing the rule for symbol.val first), it would be a purely cosmetic change; the grammar would not be altered.

Because their flow is strictly bottom-up, the attribute rules of Figure 4.1 can be evaluated by visiting the nodes of the parse tree in exactly the same order that they are generated by the parser. In fact, they can be evaluated on-the-fly during parsing, by interleaving parsing and semantic analysis (attribute evaluation). The attribute grammar of Figure 4.3 is a good bit messier than that of Figure 4.1, but it is still *L-attributed*: its attributes can be evaluated by visiting the nodes of the parse tree in a single left-to-right, depth-first traversal (the same order in which they are visited by a top-down parser). If we say that an attribute A.s *depends on* an attribute B.t if B.t is ever passed to a semantic function that returns a value for A.s, then we can define L-attributed grammars more formally with the following two rules: (1) each synthesized attribute of a left-hand side symbol depends only on that symbol's own inherited attributes or on attributes (synthesized or inherited) of the production's right-hand side symbols; and (2) each inherited attribute of a right-hand side symbol depends only on inherited attributes of the left-hand side symbol or on attributes (synthesized or inherited) of symbols to its left in the right-hand side.

S-attributed attribute grammars are the most general class of attribute grammars that can be evaluated on-the-fly during an LR parse. L-attributed grammars are a proper superset of S-attributed grammars. They are the most general class of attribute grammars that can be evaluated on-the-fly during an LL parse.

A compiler that interleaves semantic analysis and code generation with parsing is said to be a *one-pass compiler.*[3] It is unclear whether interleaving semantic analysis with parsing makes a compiler simpler or more complex; it's mainly a matter of taste. If intermediate code generation is interleaved with parsing, one need not build a syntax tree at all (unless of course the syntax tree *is* the intermediate code). Moreover, it is often possible to write the intermediate code to an output file on-the-fly, rather than accumulating it in the attributes of the root of the parse tree. The resulting space savings were important for previous generations of computers, which had very small main memories.

On the other hand, semantic analysis is easier to perform during a separate traversal of a syntax tree, because that tree reflects the program's semantic structure better than the parse tree does, especially with a top-down parser, and because one has the option of traversing the tree in an order other than that chosen by the parser. If we choose not to interleave parsing and semantic analysis, we still need to add attribute rules to the context-free grammar, but they serve only to create the syntax tree—not to enforce semantic rules or generate code. Figures 4.5 and 4.6 contain bottom-up and top-down attribute grammars, respectively, to build a syntax tree for constant expressions. The attributes in these grammars hold neither numeric values nor target code fragments; instead they point to nodes of the syntax tree. Function make_leaf returns a pointer to a newly allocated syntax tree node containing the value of a constant. Functions make_un_op and make_bin_op return pointers to newly allocated syntax tree nodes containing a unary or binary operator, respectively, and pointers to the supplied operand(s). Figures 4.7 and 4.8 show stages in the annotation of parse trees for (1 + 3) * 2, using the grammars of Figures 4.5 and 4.6, respectively.

An attribute grammar is *well-defined* if its rules determine a unique set of values for the attributes of every possible parse tree. An attribute grammar is *noncircular* if no attribute ever depends (transitively) on itself. (A grammar can be circular and still be well-defined if attributes are guaranteed to converge to a unique value.) An algorithm that invokes the attribute rules of a parse tree in an

---

3 Most authors use the term *one-pass* only for compilers that translate all the way from source to target code in a single pass. Some authors insist only that intermediate code be generated in a single pass, and permit additional pass(es) to translate intermediate code to target code.

$E_1 \rightarrow E_2 + T$
  ▷ E_1.ptr := make_bin_op ("+", E_2.ptr, T.ptr)

$E_1 \rightarrow E_2 - T$
  ▷ E_1.ptr := make_bin_op ("−", E_2.ptr, T.ptr)

$E \rightarrow T$
  ▷ E.ptr := T.ptr

$T_1 \rightarrow T_2 * F$
  ▷ T_1.ptr := make_bin_op ("×", T_2.ptr, F.ptr)

$T_1 \rightarrow T_2 / F$
  ▷ T_1.ptr := make_bin_op ("÷", T_2.ptr, F.ptr)

$T \rightarrow F$
  ▷ T.ptr := F.ptr

$F_1 \rightarrow - F_2$
  ▷ F_1.ptr := make_un_op ("$^+/_-$", F_2.ptr)

$F \rightarrow (E)$
  ▷ F.ptr := E.ptr

$F \rightarrow$ const
  ▷ F.ptr := make_leaf (const.val)

Figure 4.5 Bottom-up attribute grammar to construct a syntax tree.

order that respects its attribute flow is called a *translation scheme.* If we inter-leave semantic analysis (and possibly intermediate code generation) with parsing, then a bottom-up parser must in the general case use an S-attributed translation scheme; a top-down parser must use an L-attributed translation scheme. (Depending on the structure of the grammar, it is often possible for a bottom-up parser to accommodate some non-S-attributed attribute flow; we will consider this possibility in Section 4.5.1.) If we choose to separate parsing and semantic analysis into separate passes, then the code that builds the parse tree or syntax tree must still use an S-attributed or L-attributed translation scheme (as appropriate), but the semantic analyzer can use a more powerful scheme if desired. There are certain tasks, such as the generation of code for "short-circuit" Boolean expressions (to be discussed in Sections 6.1.4 and 6.4.1) that are easiest to accomplish with a non-L-attributed scheme.

$E \rightarrow T\ TT$
  ▷ TT.st := T.ptr
  ▷ E.ptr := TT.ptr

$TT_1 \rightarrow +\ T\ TT_2$
  ▷ TT_2.st := make_bin_op ("+", TT_1.st, T.ptr)
  ▷ TT_1.ptr := TT_2.ptr

$TT_1 \rightarrow -\ T\ TT_2$
  ▷ TT_2.st := make_bin_op ("$-$", TT_1.st, T.ptr)
  ▷ TT_1.ptr := TT_2.ptr

$TT \rightarrow \epsilon$
  ▷ TT.ptr := TT.st

$T \rightarrow F\ FT$
  ▷ FT.st := F.ptr
  ▷ T.ptr := FT.ptr

$FT_1 \rightarrow *\ F\ FT_2$
  ▷ FT_2.st := make_bin_op ("$\times$", FT_1.st, F.ptr)
  ▷ FT_1.ptr := FT_2.ptr

$FT_1 \rightarrow /\ F\ FT_2$
  ▷ FT_2.st := make_bin_op ("$\div$", FT_1.st, F.ptr)
  ▷ FT_1.ptr := FT_2.ptr

$FT \rightarrow \epsilon$
  ▷ FT.ptr := FT.st

$F_1 \rightarrow -\ F_2$
  ▷ F_1.ptr := make_un_op ("$^+/_-$", F_2.ptr)

$F \rightarrow (\ E\ )$
  ▷ F.ptr := E.ptr

$F \rightarrow \texttt{const}$
  ▷ F.ptr := make_leaf (const.val)

Figure 4.6 Top-down attribute grammar to construct a syntax tree.

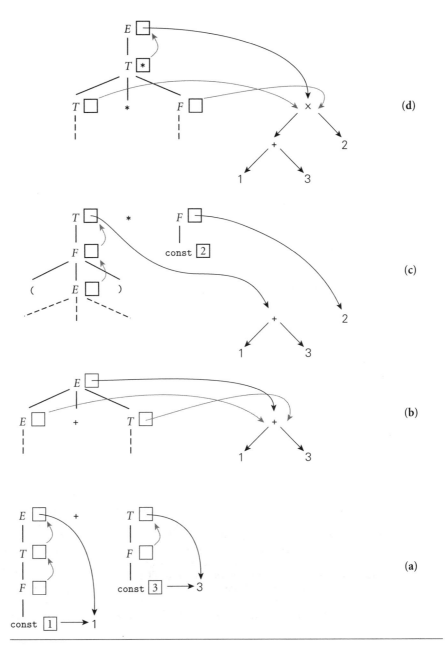

Figure 4.7 Construction of a syntax tree via annotation of a bottom-up parse tree, using the grammar of Figure 4.5. In diagram (a), the values of the constants 1 and 3 have been placed in new syntax tree leaves. Pointers to these leaves propagate up into the attributes of E and T. In (b), the pointers to these leaves become child pointers of a new internal + node. In (c) the pointer to this node propagates up into the attributes of T, and a new leaf is created for 2. Finally, in (d), the pointers from T and F become child pointers of a new internal × node, and a pointer to this node propagates up into the attributes of E.

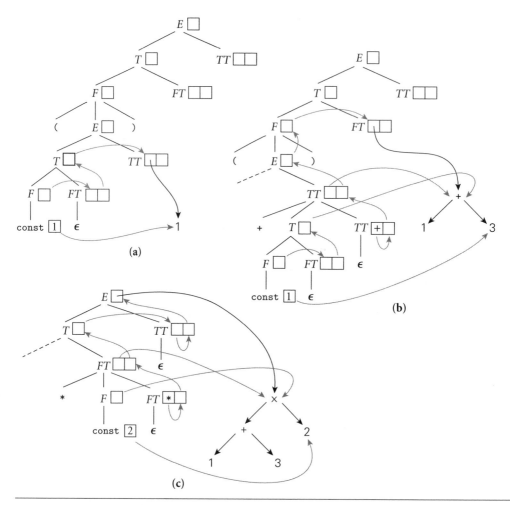

Figure 4.8 Construction of a syntax tree via annotation of a top-down parse tree, using the grammar of Figure 4.6. In the top diagram, (a), the value of the constant 1 has been placed in a new syntax tree leaf. A pointer to this leaf then propagates to the st attribute of TT. In (b), a second leaf has been created to hold the constant 3. Pointers to the two leaves then become child pointers of a new internal + node, a pointer to which propagates from the st attribute of the bottom-most TT, where it was created, all the way up and over to the st attribute of the top-most FT. In (c), a third leaf has been created for the constant 2. Pointers to this leaf and to the + node then become the children of a new × node, a pointer to which propagates from the st of the lower FT, where it was created, all the way to the root of the tree.

4.4 Action Routines

Just as there are automatic tools that will construct a parser for a given context-free grammar, there are automatic tools that will construct a semantic analyzer (attribute evaluator) for a given attribute grammar. Attribute evaluator generators are heavily used in syntax-based editors [TR81], incremental compilers [SDB84], and programming language research. Most production compilers, however, use an ad hoc, hand-written translation scheme, interleaving parsing with at least the initial construction of a syntax tree, and possibly all of semantic analysis and intermediate code generation. Because they are able to evaluate the attributes of each production as it is parsed, they do not need to build the full parse tree.

An ad hoc translation scheme that is interleaved with parsing takes the form of a set of *action routines*. An action routine is a semantic function that the programmer (grammar writer) instructs the compiler to execute at a particular point in the parse. Most parser generators allow the programmer to specify action routines. In an LL parser generator, an action routine can appear anywhere within a right-hand side. A routine at the beginning of a right-hand side will be called as soon as the parser predicts the production. A routine embedded in the middle of a right-hand side will be called as soon as the parser has matched (the yield of) the symbol to the left. The implementation mechanism is simple: when it predicts a production, the parser pushes *all* of the right-hand side onto the stack: terminals (to be matched), nonterminals (to drive future predictions), and pointers to action routines. When it finds a pointer to an action routine at the top of the parse stack, the parser simply calls it.

To make this process more concrete, consider again our LL(1) grammar for constant expressions. Action routines to build a syntax tree while parsing this grammar appear in Figure 4.9. The only difference between this grammar and the one in Figure 4.6 is that the action routines (delimited here with curly braces) are embedded among the symbols of the right-hand sides; the work performed is the same. The ease with which the attribute grammar can be transformed into the grammar with action routines is due to the fact that the attribute grammar is L-attributed. If it required more complicated flow, we would not be able to cast it in the form of action routines.

In an LR parser generator, one cannot in general embed action routines at arbitrary places in a right-hand side, since the parser does not in general know what production it is in until it has seen all or most of the yield. LR parser generators therefore permit action routines only after the point at which the production being parsed can be identified unambiguously. If the attribute flow of the action routines is strictly bottom-up (as it is in an S-attributed attribute grammar), then execution at the end of right-hand sides is all that is needed. The attribute grammars of Figures 4.1 and 4.5, in fact, are essentially identical to the action routine versions. If the action routines are responsible for a significant part of semantic analysis, however (as opposed to simply building a syntax tree),

$E \rightarrow T \{ \text{T.st} := \text{T.ptr} \} \ TT \{ \text{E.ptr} := \text{TT.ptr} \}$

$TT_1 \rightarrow + T \{ TT_2.\text{st} := \text{make\_bin\_op} ("+", TT_1.\text{st}, \text{T.ptr}) \} \ TT_2 \{ TT_1.\text{ptr} := TT_2.\text{ptr} \}$

$TT_1 \rightarrow - T \{ TT_2.\text{st} := \text{make\_bin\_op} ("-", TT_1.\text{st}, \text{T.ptr}) \} \ TT_2 \{ TT_1.\text{ptr} := TT_2.\text{ptr} \}$

$TT \rightarrow \epsilon \{ \text{TT.ptr} := \text{TT.st} \}$

$T \rightarrow F \{ \text{F.st} := \text{F.ptr} \} \ FT \{ \text{T.ptr} := \text{FT.ptr} \}$

$FT_1 \rightarrow * F \{ FT_2.\text{st} := \text{make\_bin\_op} ("\times", FT_1.\text{st}, \text{F.ptr}) \} \ FT_2 \{ FT_1.\text{ptr} := FT_2.\text{ptr} \}$

$FT_1 \rightarrow / F \{ FT_2.\text{st} := \text{make\_bin\_op} ("\div", FT_1.\text{st}, \text{F.ptr}) \} \ FT_2 \{ FT_1.\text{ptr} := FT_2.\text{ptr} \}$

$FT \rightarrow \epsilon \{ \text{FT.ptr} := \text{FT.st} \}$

$F_1 \rightarrow - F_2 \{ F_1.\text{ptr} := \text{make\_un\_op} ("^+/_-", F_2.\text{ptr}) \}$

$F \rightarrow (E) \{ \text{F.ptr} := \text{E.ptr} \}$

$F \rightarrow \textbf{const} \{ \text{F.ptr} := \text{make\_leaf} (\text{const.ptr}) \}$

Figure 4.9 **LL(1) grammar with action routines to build a syntax tree.**

then they will often need contextual information in order to do their job. To obtain and use this information in an LR parse, they will need some (necessarily limited) access to inherited attributes or to information outside the current production. We will consider this issue further in Section 4.5.1.

Any attribute evaluation method requires space to hold the attributes of the grammar symbols. If we are building an explicit parse tree, then the obvious approach is to store attributes in the nodes of the tree themselves. If we are not building a parse tree then we need to find a way to keep track of the attributes for the symbols we have seen (or predicted) but not yet finished parsing. The details differ in bottom-up and top-down parsers; they are discussed in Section 4.5. In both families of parsers, it is common for some of the contextual information for action routines to be kept in global variables. The symbol table in particular is usually global. We can be sure that the table will always represent the current referencing environment, because we control the order in which action routines (including those that modify the environment at the beginnings and ends of scopes) are executed. In a pure attribute grammar we should need to pass symbol table information into and out of productions through inherited and synthesized attributes.

4.5* Space Management for Attributes

As noted in Section 4.4, a compiler that does not build an explicit parse tree requires some other mechanism to allocate, deallocate, and refer to storage space for attributes. For a bottom-up parser with an S-attributed grammar, the obvious approach is to maintain an *attribute stack* that directly mirrors the parse stack: next to every state number on the parse stack is an attribute record for the symbol we shifted when we entered that state. Entries in the attribute stack

1. (
2. (1
3. (F_1
4. (T_1
5. (E_1
6. (E_1 +
7. (E_1 + 3
8. (E_1 + F_3
9. (E_1 + T_3
10. (E_4
11. (E_4)
12. F_4
13. T_4
14. T_4 *
15. T_4 * 2
16. T_4 * F_2
17. T_8
18. E_8

Figure 4.10 Parse/attribute stack trace for $(1 + 3) * 2$, **using the grammar of Figure 4.1.** Subscripts represent val attributes; they are not meant to distinguish among instances of a symbol.

are pushed and popped automatically by the parser driver; space management is not an issue for the writer of action routines. Complications arise if we try to achieve the effect of inherited attributes, but these can be accommodated within the basic attribute-stack framework.

For a top-down parser with an L-attributed grammar, we have two principal options. The first option is automatic, but more complex than for bottom-up grammars. It still uses an attribute stack, but one that does not mirror the parse stack. The second option has lower space overhead, and saves time by "short-cutting" copy rules, but requires action routines to allocate and de-allocate space for attributes explicitly.

4.5.1 Bottom-Up Evaluation

Figure 4.10 shows a trace of the parse and attribute stack for $(1 + 3) * 2$, using the attribute grammar of Figure 4.1. For the sake of clarity, we show a single, combined stack for the parser and attribute evaluator, and we omit the CFSM state numbers.

It is easy to evaluate the attributes of symbols in this grammar, because the grammar is S-attributed. In an automatically generated parser, such as those produced by yacc/bison, the attribute rules associated with the productions of the grammar in Figure 4.1 would constitute action routines, to be executed when their productions are recognized. For yacc/bison, they would be written in C, with "pseudostructs" to name the attribute records of the symbols in each production. Attributes of the left-hand side symbol would be accessed as fields of the pseudostruct $$. Attributes of right-hand side symbols would be accessed as fields of the pseudostructs $1, $2, etc. To get from line 9 to line 10, for example, in the trace of Figure 4.10, we would use an action routine version of the first rule of the grammar in Figure 4.1: $$.val = $1.val + $3.val.

When a bottom-up action routine is executed, the attribute records for symbols on the right-hand side of the production can be found in the top few entries of the attribute stack. The attribute record for the symbol on the left-hand side of the production (i.e., $$) will not yet lie in the stack: it is the task of the action routine to initialize this record. After the action routine completes, the parser pops the right-hand side records off the attribute stack and replaces them with $$. In yacc/bison, if no action routine is specified for a given production, the default action is to "copy" $1 into $$. Since $$ will occupy the same location, once pushed, that $1 occupied before being popped, this "copy" can be effected without doing any work.

Inherited attributes

Unfortunately, it is not always easy to write an S-attributed grammar. A simple example in which inherited attributes are desirable arises in C or Fortran-style variable declarations, in which a type name precedes the list of variable names:

dec → *type id_list*

id_list → id

id_list → *id_list* , id

Let us assume that *type* has a synthesized attribute tp that contains a pointer to the symbol table entry for the type in question. Ideally, we should like to pass this attribute into *id_list* as an inherited attribute, so that we may enter each newly declared identifier into the symbol table, complete with type indication, as it is encountered. When we recognize the production *id_list* → id, we know that the top record on the attribute stack will be the one for id. But we know more than this: the next record down must be the one for *type*. To find the type of the new entry to be placed in the symbol table, we may safely inspect this "buried" record. Though it does not belong to a symbol of the current production, we can count on its presence because there is no other way to reach the *id_list* → id production.

Now what about the id in *id_list* → *id_list* , id? This time the top three records on the attribute stack will be for the right-hand symbols id, , , and *id_list*. Immediately below them, however, we can still count on finding the entry for *type*, waiting for the *id_list* to be completed so that *dec* can be recognized. Using nonpositive indices for pseudostructs below the current production, we can write action routines as follows:

$dec \rightarrow type\ id\_list$

$id\_list \rightarrow$ `id` { declare_id ($1.name, $0.tp) }

$id\_list \rightarrow id\_list$ `, id` { declare_id ($3.name, $0.tp) }

Records deeper in the attribute stack could be accessed as $–1, $–2, etc.

While *id_list* appears in two places in this grammar fragment, both occurrences are guaranteed to lie above a *type* record in the attribute stack, the first because it lies next to *type* in a right-hand side; the second by induction, because it is the beginning of the yield of the first. There are grammars, however, in which a symbol that needs inherited attributes occurs in productions in which the underlying symbols are not the same. We can still handle inherited attributes in such cases, but only by modifying the underlying context-free grammar. An example can be found in languages such as Perl, in which the meaning of an expression (and of the identifiers and operators within it) depends on the *context* in which that expression appears. Some Perl contexts expect arrays. Others expect numbers, strings, or Booleans. To correctly analyze an expression, we must pass the expectations of the context into the expression subtree as inherited attributes. Here is a grammar fragment that captures the problem:

$stmt \rightarrow$ `id := ` *expr*

$\quad \rightarrow \ldots$

$\quad \rightarrow$ `if` *expr* `then` *stmt*

$expr \rightarrow \ldots$

Within the production for *expr*, the parser doesn't know whether the surrounding context is an assignment or the condition of an `if` statement. If it is a condition, then the expected type of the expression is Boolean. If it is an assignment, then the expected type is that of the identifier on the assignment's left-hand side. This identifier can be found two records below the current production in the attribute stack. To allow these cases to be treated uniformly, we can add *semantic hook*, or "marker" symbols to the grammar. Semantic hooks generate ϵ, and thus do not alter the language defined by the grammar; their only purpose is to hold inherited attributes.

$stmt \rightarrow$ `id := ` A *expr*

$\quad \rightarrow \ldots$

$\quad \rightarrow$ `if` B *expr* `then` *stmt*

$A \rightarrow \epsilon$ { $$.tp := $–1.tp }

$B \rightarrow \epsilon$ { $$.tp := Boolean }

$expr \rightarrow \ldots$ { if $0.tp = Boolean then ... }

Since the epsilon production for a semantic hook can provide an action routine, it is tempting to think of semantic hooks as a general technique to insert action routines in the middle of bottom-up productions. Unfortunately this is not the case: semantic hooks can be used only in places where the parser can be sure that it is in a given production. Placing a semantic hook anywhere else will break the "LR-ness" of the grammar, causing the parser generator to reject the modified grammar. Consider the following example:

1. *stmt* → *l_val* := *expr*
2.   → id *args*
3. *l_val* → id *quals*
4. *quals* → *quals* . id
5.   → *quals* (*expr_list*)
6.   → ε
7. *args* → (*expr_list*)
8.   → ε

An *l-value* in this grammar is a "qualified" identifier: an identifier followed by optional array subscript and record field qualifiers.[4] We have assumed that the language follows the notation of Fortran and Ada, in which parentheses delimit both procedure call arguments and array subscripts. In the case of procedure calls, it would be natural to want an action routine to pass the symbol-table index of the subroutine into the argument list as an inherited attribute, so that it can be used to check the number and types of arguments:

stmt → id *A* *args*
A → ε { \$\$.proc_index := lookup (\$0.name) }

If we try this, however, we will run into trouble, because the procedure call

```
foo (1, 2, 3);
```

and the array element assignment

```
foo (1, 2, 3) := 4;
```

begin with the same sequence of tokens. Until it sees the token after the closing parenthesis, the parser cannot tell whether it is working on production 1 or

---

4 In general, an l-value in a programming language is anything to which a value can be assigned (i.e., anything that can appear on the left-hand side of an assignment). From a low-level point of view, this is basically an address. An r-value is anything that can appear on the right-hand side of an assignment. From a low-level point of view, this is a value that can be stored at an address. We will discuss l-values and r-values further in Section 6.1.2.

production 2. The presence of *A* in production 2 will therefore lead to a shift-reduce conflict; after seeing an `id`, the parser will not know whether to recognize *A* or shift (.

In general, the right-hand side of a production in a context-free grammar is said to consist of the *left corner* and the *trailing part*. In the left corner we cannot be sure which production we are parsing; in the trailing part the production is uniquely determined. In an LL(1) grammar, the left corner is always empty. In an LR(1) grammar, it can consist of up to the entire right-hand side. Semantic hooks can safely be inserted in the trailing part of a production, but not in the left corner. `Yacc/bison` recognizes this fact explicitly by allowing action routines to be embedded in right-hand sides. It automatically converts the production

$$S \rightarrow \alpha \ \{ \text{your code here} \} \ \beta$$

to

$$S \rightarrow \alpha \ A \ \beta$$
$$A \rightarrow \epsilon \ \{ \text{your code here} \}$$

for some new, distinct symbol *A*. If the action routine is not in the trailing part, the resulting grammar will not be LALR(1), and `yacc/bison` will produce an error message.

In our procedure call and array subscript example, we cannot place a semantic hook before the *args* of production 2 because this location is in the left corner. If we wish to look up a procedure name in the symbol table before we parse the arguments, we will need to combine the productions for statements that can begin with an identifier, in a manner reminiscent of the *left factoring* discussed in Section 2.2.5:

$$stmt \rightarrow \text{id} \ A \ quals \ assign\_opt$$
$$A \rightarrow \epsilon \ \{ \$\$.\text{id\_index} := \text{lookup} \ (\$0.\text{name}) \}$$
$$quals \rightarrow quals \ . \ \text{id}$$
$$\rightarrow quals \ (\ expr\_list \ )$$
$$\rightarrow \epsilon$$
$$assign\_opt \rightarrow := \ expr$$
$$\rightarrow \epsilon$$

This change eliminates the shift-reduce conflict, but at the expense of combining the entire grammar subtrees for procedure call arguments and array subscripts. To use the modified grammar we will have to write action routines for *quals* that work for both kinds of constructs, and this can be a major nuisance. Users of LR-family parser generators often find that there is a tension between the desire for grammar clarity and parsability on the one hand, and the need for semantic hooks to set inherited attributes on the other.

4.5.2 **Top-Down Evaluation**

Top-down parsers, as discussed in Chapter 2, come in two principal varieties: hand-written recursive descent, and automatically generated table-driven. Attribute management in recursive descent parsers is almost trivial: inherited attributes of symbol *foo* take the form of parameters passed into the parsing routine named foo; synthesized attributes are the return parameters. These synthesized attributes can then be passed as inherited attributes to symbols later in the current production, or returned as synthesized attributes of the current left-hand side.

Attribute space management for automatically generated top-down parsers is somewhat more complex. Because they allow action routines at arbitrary locations in a right-hand side, top-down parsers avoid the need to modify the grammar in order to insert semantic hooks. (Of course, because they must have empty left corners, top-down grammars can be harder to write in the first place.) Because the parse stack describes the future, instead of the past, we cannot employ an attribute stack that simply mirrors the parse stack. Our two principal options are to equip the parser with a (more complicated) algorithm for automatic space management, or to require action routines to manage that space explicitly.

Automatic Management

Automatic management of attribute space for top-down parsing is more complicated than it is for bottom-up parsing. It is also more space-intensive. We can still use an attribute stack, but it has to contain all of the symbols in all of the productions between the root of the (hypothetical) parse tree and the current point in the parse. All of the right-hand side symbols of a given production are adjacent in the stack; the left-hand side is buried in the right-hand side of a deeper (closer to the root) production.

We can observe the operation of a top-down attribute stack in Figure 4.12. The left-hand column of this figure shows the parse stack. The right-hand column shows the attribute stack. Three global pointers index into the attribute stack. One (shown as an "arrow-boxed" L in the figure) identifies the record in the attribute stack that holds the attributes of the left-hand side symbol of current production. The second (shown as an arrow-boxed R in the figure) identifies the first symbol on the right-hand side of the production. L and R allow the action routines to find the attributes of the symbols of the current production. The third pointer (shown as an arrow-boxed N in the figure) identifies the first symbol within the right-hand side that has not yet been completely parsed. It allows the parser to update L correctly when a production is predicted.

At any given time, the attribute stack contains all symbols of all productions on the path between the root of the parse tree and the symbol currently at the top of the parse stack. Figure 4.13 identifies these symbols graphically at the point in

$E \rightarrow T \ \{ \ \text{TT.st} := \text{T.val} \ \}^{\mathbf{1}} \ TT \ \{ \ \text{E.val} := \text{TT.val} \ \}^{\mathbf{2}}$

$TT_1 \rightarrow + \ T \ \{ \ TT_2.\text{st} := TT_1.\text{st} + \text{T.val} \ \}^{\mathbf{3}} \ TT_2 \ \{ \ TT_1.\text{val} := TT_2.\text{val} \ \}^{\mathbf{4}}$

$TT_1 \rightarrow - \ T \ \{ \ TT_2.\text{st} := TT_1.\text{st} - \text{T.val} \ \}^{\mathbf{5}} \ TT_2 \ \{ \ TT_1.\text{val} := TT_2.\text{val} \ \}^{\mathbf{6}}$

$TT \rightarrow \epsilon \ \{ \ \text{TT.val} := \text{TT.st} \ \}^{\mathbf{7}}$

$T \rightarrow F \ \{ \ \text{FT.st} := \text{F.val} \ \}^{\mathbf{8}} \ FT \ \{ \ \text{T.val} := \text{FT.val} \ \}^{\mathbf{9}}$

$FT_1 \rightarrow * \ F \ \{ \ FT_2.\text{st} := FT_1.\text{st} \times \text{F.val} \ \}^{\mathbf{10}} \ FT_2 \ \{ \ FT_1.\text{val} := FT_2.\text{val} \ \}^{\mathbf{11}}$

$FT_1 \rightarrow / \ F \ \{ \ FT_2.\text{st} := FT_1.\text{st} \div \text{F.val} \ \}^{\mathbf{12}} \ FT_2 \ \{ \ FT_1.\text{val} := FT_2.\text{val} \ \}^{\mathbf{13}}$

$FT \rightarrow \epsilon \ \{ \ \text{FT.val} := \text{FT.st} \ \}^{\mathbf{14}}$

$F_1 \rightarrow - \ F_2 \ \{ \ F_1.\text{val} := - \ F_2.\text{val} \ \}^{\mathbf{15}}$

$F \rightarrow (\ E \ ) \ \{ \ \text{F.val} := \text{E.val} \ \}^{\mathbf{16}}$

$F \rightarrow \texttt{const} \ \{ \ \text{F.val} := \text{C.val} \ \}^{\mathbf{17}}$

Figure 4.11 **LL(1) grammar for constant expressions, with action routines.** The bold-face superscripts are for reference in Figure 4.12.

Figure 4.12 immediately above the 8 elided lines. Symbols to the left in the parse tree have already been reclaimed; those to the right have yet to be allocated.

At start-up, the attribute stack contains a record for the goal symbol, pointed at by N. When we push the right-hand side of a predicted production onto the parse stack, we add an "end-of-production" marker, represented by a colon in the figure. At the same time, we push records for the right-hand-side symbols onto the attribute stack. (These are *added* to the attribute stack; they do not replace the left-hand side.) Prior to pushing these entries, we save the current L and R pointers in another stack (not shown). We then set L to the old N, and make R and N point to the newly pushed right-hand side.

When we see an action symbol at the top of the parse stack (shown in the figure as a small bold number), we pop it and execute the corresponding action routine. When we match a terminal at the top of the parse stack, we pop it and move N forward one record in the attribute stack. When we see an end-of-production marker at the top of the parse stack, we pop it, set N to the attribute record following the one currently pointed at by L, pop everything from R forward off of the attribute stack, and restore the most recently saved values of L and R.

It should be emphasized that while the trace is long and tedious, its complexity is completely hidden from the writer of action routines. Once the space management routines are integrated with the driver for a top-down parser generator, all the compiler writer sees is the grammar of Figure 4.11. In comparing Figures 4.10 and 4.12, it should also be noted that reduction and execution of a production's action routine are shown as a single step in the LR trace; they are shown separately in the LL trace, making that trace appear more complex than it really is.

parse stack	attribute stack
E $	$\boxed{N}\,E_?$
T 1 TT 2 : $	$\boxed{L}\,E_?\,\boxed{R}\,\boxed{N}\,T_?\,TT_{?,?}$
F 8 FT 9 : 1 TT 2 : $	$E_?\,\boxed{L}\,T_?\,TT_{?,?}\,\boxed{R}\,\boxed{N}\,F_?\,FT_{?,?}$
(E) 16 : 8 FT 9 : 1 TT 2 : $	$E_?\,T_?\,TT_{?,?}\,\boxed{L}\,F_?\,FT_{?,?}\,\boxed{R}\,\boxed{N}\,(\,E_?\,)$
E) 16 : 8 FT 9 : 1 TT 2 : $	$E_?\,T_?\,TT_{?,?}\,\boxed{L}\,F_?\,FT_{?,?}\,\boxed{R}\,(\,\boxed{N}\,E_?\,)$
T 1 TT 2 :) 16 : 8 FT 9 : 1 TT 2 : $	$E_?\,T_?\,TT_{?,?}\,F_?\,FT_{?,?}\,(\,\boxed{L}\,E_?\,)\,\boxed{R}\,\boxed{N}\,T_?\,TT_{?,?}$
F 8 FT 9 : 1 TT 2 :) 16 : 8 FT 9 : 1 TT 2 : $	$E_?\,T_?\,TT_{?,?}\,F_?\,FT_{?,?}\,(\,E_?\,)\,\boxed{L}\,T_?\,TT_{?,?}\,\boxed{R}\,\boxed{N}\,F_?\,FT_{?,?}$
C 17 : 8 FT 9 : 1 TT 2 :) 16 : 8 FT 9 : 1 TT 2 : $	$E_?\,T_?\,TT_{?,?}\,F_?\,FT_{?,?}\,(\,E_?\,)\,T_?\,TT_{?,?}\,\boxed{L}\,F_?\,FT_{?,?}\,\boxed{R}\,\boxed{N}\,C_1$
17 : 8 FT 9 : 1 TT 2 :) 16 : 8 FT 9 : 1 TT 2 : $	$E_?\,T_?\,TT_{?,?}\,F_?\,FT_{?,?}\,(\,E_?\,)\,T_?\,TT_{?,?}\,\boxed{L}\,F_?\,FT_{?,?}\,\boxed{R}\,C_1\,\boxed{N}$
: 8 FT 9 : 1 TT 2 :) 16 : 8 FT 9 : 1 TT 2 : $	$E_?\,T_?\,TT_{?,?}\,F_?\,FT_{?,?}\,(\,E_?\,)\,T_?\,TT_{?,?}\,\boxed{L}\,F_1\,FT_{?,?}\,\boxed{R}\,C_1\,\boxed{N}$
8 FT 9 : 1 TT 2 :) 16 : 8 FT 9 : 1 TT 2 : $	$E_?\,T_?\,TT_{?,?}\,F_?\,FT_{?,?}\,(\,E_?\,)\,\boxed{L}\,T_?\,TT_{?,?}\,\boxed{R}\,F_1\,\boxed{N}\,FT_{?,?}$
FT 9 : 1 TT 2 :) 16 : 8 FT 9 : 1 TT 2 : $	$E_?\,T_?\,TT_{?,?}\,F_?\,FT_{?,?}\,(\,E_?\,)\,\boxed{L}\,T_?\,TT_{?,?}\,\boxed{R}\,F_1\,\boxed{N}\,FT_{1,?}$
14 : 9 : 1 TT 2 :) 16 : 8 FT 9 : 1 TT 2 : $	$E_?\,T_?\,TT_{?,?}\,F_?\,FT_{?,?}\,(\,E_?\,)\,T_?\,TT_{?,?}\,F_1\,\boxed{L}\,FT_{1,?}\,\boxed{R}\,\boxed{N}$
: 9 : 1 TT 2 :) 16 : 8 FT 9 : 1 TT 2 : $	$E_?\,T_?\,TT_{?,?}\,F_?\,FT_{?,?}\,(\,E_?\,)\,T_?\,TT_{?,?}\,F_1\,\boxed{L}\,FT_{1,1}\,\boxed{R}\,\boxed{N}$
9 : 1 TT 2 :) 16 : 8 FT 9 : 1 TT 2 : $	$E_?\,T_?\,TT_{?,?}\,F_?\,FT_{?,?}\,(\,E_?\,)\,\boxed{L}\,T_?\,TT_{?,?}\,\boxed{R}\,F_1\,FT_{1,1}\,\boxed{N}$
: 1 TT 2 :) 16 : 8 FT 9 : 1 TT 2 : $	$E_?\,T_?\,TT_{?,?}\,F_?\,FT_{?,?}\,(\,E_?\,)\,\boxed{L}\,T_1\,TT_{?,?}\,\boxed{R}\,F_1\,FT_{1,1}\,\boxed{N}$
1 TT 2 :) 16 : 8 FT 9 : 1 TT 2 : $	$E_?\,T_?\,TT_{?,?}\,F_?\,FT_{?,?}\,(\,\boxed{L}\,E_?\,)\,\boxed{R}\,T_1\,\boxed{N}\,TT_{?,?}$
TT 2 :) 16 : 8 FT 9 : 1 TT 2 : $	$E_?\,T_?\,TT_{?,?}\,F_?\,FT_{?,?}\,(\,\boxed{L}\,E_?\,)\,\boxed{R}\,T_1\,\boxed{N}\,TT_{1,?}$
+ T 3 TT 4 : 2 :) 16 : 8 FT 9 : 1 TT 2 : $	$E_?\,T_?\,TT_{?,?}\,F_?\,FT_{?,?}\,(\,E_?\,)\,T_1\,\boxed{L}\,TT_{1,?}\,\boxed{R}\,\boxed{N}\,+\,T_?\,TT_{?,?}$
T 3 TT 4 : 2 :) 16 : 8 FT 9 : 1 TT 2 : $	$E_?\,T_?\,TT_{?,?}\,F_?\,FT_{?,?}\,(\,E_?\,)\,T_1\,\boxed{L}\,TT_{1,?}\,\boxed{R}\,+\,\boxed{N}\,T_?\,TT_{?,?}$
F 8 FT 9 : 3 TT 4 : 2 :) 16 : 8 FT 9 : 1 TT 2 : $	$E_?\,T_?\,TT_{?,?}\,F_?\,FT_{?,?}\,(\,E_?\,)\,T_1\,TT_{1,?}\,+\,\boxed{L}\,T_?\,TT_{?,?}\,\boxed{R}\,\boxed{N}\,F_?\,FT_{?,?}$
C 17 : 8 FT 9 : 3 TT 4 : 2 :) 16 : 8 FT 9 : 1 TT 2 : $	$E_?\,T_?\,TT_{?,?}\,F_?\,FT_{?,?}\,(\,E_?\,)\,T_1\,TT_{1,?}\,+\,T_?\,TT_{?,?}\,\boxed{L}\,F_?\,FT_{?,?}\,\boxed{R}\,\boxed{N}\,C_3$
⟨ eight lines omitted ⟩	
3 TT 4 : 2 :) 16 : 8 FT 9 : 1 TT 2 : $	$E_?\,T_?\,TT_{?,?}\,F_?\,FT_{?,?}\,(\,E_?\,)\,T_1\,\boxed{L}\,TT_{1,?}\,\boxed{R}\,+\,T_3\,\boxed{N}\,TT_{?,?}$
TT 4 : 2 :) 16 : 8 FT 9 : 1 TT 2 : $	$E_?\,T_?\,TT_{?,?}\,F_?\,FT_{?,?}\,(\,E_?\,)\,T_1\,\boxed{L}\,TT_{1,?}\,\boxed{R}\,+\,T_3\,\boxed{N}\,TT_{4,?}$
7 : 4 : 2 :) 16 : 8 FT 9 : 1 TT 2 : $	$E_?\,T_?\,TT_{?,?}\,F_?\,FT_{?,?}\,(\,E_?\,)\,T_1\,TT_{1,?}\,+\,T_3\,\boxed{L}\,TT_{4,?}\,\boxed{R}\,\boxed{N}$
: 4 : 2 :) 16 : 8 FT 9 : 1 TT 2 : $	$E_?\,T_?\,TT_{?,?}\,F_?\,FT_{?,?}\,(\,E_?\,)\,T_1\,TT_{1,?}\,+\,T_3\,\boxed{L}\,TT_{4,4}\,\boxed{R}\,\boxed{N}$
4 : 2 :) 16 : 8 FT 9 : 1 TT 2 : $	$E_?\,T_?\,TT_{?,?}\,F_?\,FT_{?,?}\,(\,E_?\,)\,T_1\,\boxed{L}\,TT_{1,?}\,\boxed{R}\,+\,T_3\,TT_{4,4}\,\boxed{N}$
: 2 :) 16 : 8 FT 9 : 1 TT 2 : $	$E_?\,T_?\,TT_{?,?}\,F_?\,FT_{?,?}\,(\,E_?\,)\,T_1\,\boxed{L}\,TT_{1,4}\,\boxed{R}\,+\,T_3\,TT_{4,4}\,\boxed{N}$
2 :) 16 : 8 FT 9 : 1 TT 2 : $	$E_?\,T_?\,TT_{?,?}\,F_?\,FT_{?,?}\,(\,\boxed{L}\,E_?\,)\,\boxed{R}\,T_1\,TT_{1,4}$
:) 16 : 8 FT 9 : 1 TT 2 : $	$E_?\,T_?\,TT_{?,?}\,F_?\,FT_{?,?}\,(\,\boxed{L}\,E_4\,)\,\boxed{R}\,T_1\,TT_{1,4}$
) 16 : 8 FT 9 : 1 TT 2 : $	$E_?\,T_?\,TT_{?,?}\,\boxed{L}\,F_?\,FT_{?,?}\,\boxed{R}\,(\,E_4\,\boxed{N}\,)$
16 : 8 FT 9 : 1 TT 2 : $	$E_?\,T_?\,TT_{?,?}\,\boxed{L}\,F_?\,FT_{?,?}\,\boxed{R}\,(\,E_4\,)\,\boxed{N}$
: 8 FT 9 : 1 TT 2 : $	$E_?\,T_?\,TT_{?,?}\,\boxed{L}\,F_4\,FT_{?,?}\,\boxed{R}\,(\,E_4\,)\,\boxed{N}$
8 FT 9 : 1 TT 2 : $	$E_?\,\boxed{L}\,T_?\,TT_{?,?}\,\boxed{R}\,F_4\,\boxed{N}\,FT_{?,?}$
FT 9 : 1 TT 2 : $	$E_?\,\boxed{L}\,T_?\,TT_{?,?}\,\boxed{R}\,F_4\,\boxed{N}\,FT_{4,?}$
* F 10 FT 11 : 9 : 1 TT 2 : $	$E_?\,T_?\,TT_{?,?}\,F_4\,\boxed{L}\,FT_{4,?}\,\boxed{R}\,\boxed{N}\,*\,F_?\,FT_{?,?}$
F 10 FT 11 : 9 : 1 TT 2 : $	$E_?\,T_?\,TT_{?,?}\,F_4\,\boxed{L}\,FT_{4,?}\,\boxed{R}\,*\,\boxed{N}\,F_?\,FT_{?,?}$
C 17 : 10 FT 11 : 9 : 1 TT 2 : $	$E_?\,T_?\,TT_{?,?}\,F_4\,FT_{4,?}\,*\,\boxed{L}\,F_?\,FT_{?,?}\,\boxed{R}\,\boxed{N}\,C_2$
17 : 10 FT 11 : 9 : 1 TT 2 : $	$E_?\,T_?\,TT_{?,?}\,F_4\,FT_{4,?}\,*\,\boxed{L}\,F_?\,FT_{?,?}\,\boxed{R}\,C_2\,\boxed{N}$
: 10 FT 11 : 9 : 1 TT 2 : $	$E_?\,T_?\,TT_{?,?}\,F_4\,FT_{4,?}\,*\,\boxed{L}\,F_2\,FT_{?,?}\,\boxed{R}\,C_2\,\boxed{N}$
10 FT 11 : 9 : 1 TT 2 : $	$E_?\,T_?\,TT_{?,?}\,F_?\,\boxed{L}\,FT_{4,?}\,\boxed{R}\,*\,F_2\,\boxed{N}\,FT_{?,?}$
FT 11 : 9 : 1 TT 2 : $	$E_?\,T_?\,TT_{?,?}\,F_?\,\boxed{L}\,FT_{4,?}\,\boxed{R}\,*\,F_2\,\boxed{N}\,FT_{8,?}$
⟨ six lines omitted ⟩	
1 TT 2 : $	$\boxed{L}\,E_?\,\boxed{R}\,T_8\,\boxed{N}\,TT_{?,?}$
TT 2 : $	$\boxed{L}\,E_?\,\boxed{R}\,T_8\,\boxed{N}\,TT_{8,?}$
7 : 2 : $	$E_?\,T_8\,\boxed{L}\,TT_{8,?}\,\boxed{R}\,\boxed{N}$
: 2 : $	$E_?\,T_8\,\boxed{L}\,TT_{8,8}\,\boxed{R}\,\boxed{N}$
2 : $	$\boxed{L}\,E_?\,\boxed{R}\,T_8\,TT_{8,8}\,\boxed{N}$
: $	$\boxed{L}\,E_8\,\boxed{R}\,T_8\,TT_{8,8}\,\boxed{N}$
$	$E_8\,\boxed{N}$

Figure 4.12 Trace of the parse stack (left) and attribute stack (right) for $(1 + 3) * 2$**, using the grammar (and action routine numbers) of Figure 4.11.** Subscripts in the attribute stack indicate the values of attributes. For symbols with two attributes, st comes first.

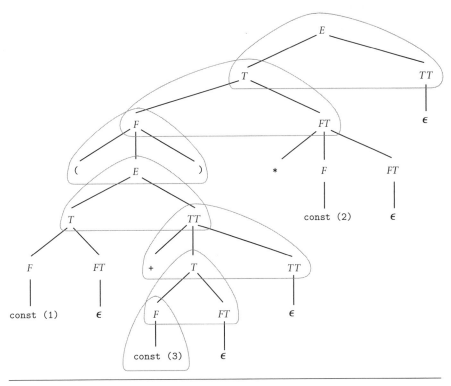

Figure 4.13 **Productions with symbols currently in the attribute stack during a parse of** (1 + 3) * 2 **(using the grammar of Figure 4.11), at the point where we are about to parse the** 3. In Figure 4.12 this point corresponds to the line immediately above the 8 elided lines.

Ad Hoc Management

One drawback of automatic space management for top-down grammars is the frequency with which the compiler writer must specify copy routines. Of the 17 action routines in Figure 4.9 or 4.11, 12 simply move information from one place to another. The time required to execute these routines can be minimized by copying pointers, rather than large records, but compiler writers may still consider the copies a nuisance.

An alternative is to manage space explicitly within the action routines, pushing and popping an ad hoc *semantic stack* only when information is generated or consumed. Using this technique, we can replace the action routines of Figure 4.9 with the simpler version shown in Figure 4.14. Variable cur_tok is assumed to contain the synthesized attributes of the most recently matched token. The semantic stack contains pointers to syntax tree nodes. The push_leaf routine creates a node for a specified constant and pushes a pointer to it onto the semantic stack. The un_op routine pops the top pointer off the stack, makes it the child of a newly created node for the specified unary operator, and pushes a pointer

$$E \rightarrow T \; TT$$
$$TT \rightarrow + \; T \; \{ \; \text{bin\_op} \; ("+") \; \} \; TT$$
$$TT \rightarrow - \; T \; \{ \; \text{bin\_op} \; ("-") \; \} \; TT$$
$$TT \rightarrow \epsilon$$
$$T \rightarrow F \; FT$$
$$FT \rightarrow * \; F \; \{ \; \text{bin\_op} \; ("\times") \; \} \; FT$$
$$FT \rightarrow / \; F \; \{ \; \text{bin\_op} \; ("\div") \; \} \; FT$$
$$FT \rightarrow \epsilon$$
$$F \rightarrow - \; F \; \{ \; \text{un\_op} \; ("^{+}/_{-}") \; \}$$
$$F \rightarrow (\; E \;)$$
$$F \rightarrow \text{const} \; \{ \; \text{push\_leaf} \; (\text{cur\_tok.val}) \; \}$$

Figure 4.14 Ad hoc management of attribute space in an LL(1) grammar to build a syntax tree.

to that node back on the stack. The bin_op routine pops the top *two* pointers off the semantic stack and pushes a pointer to a newly created node for the specified binary operator. When the parse of E is completed, a pointer to a syntax tree describing its yield will be found in the top-most record on the semantic stack. The advantage of ad hoc space management is clearly the smaller number of rules and the elimination of the inherited attributes used to represent left context. The disadvantage is that the compiler writer must be aware of what is in the semantic stack at all times, and must remember to push and pop it when appropriate.

One further advantage of an ad hoc semantic stack is that it allows action routines to push or pop an arbitrary number of records. With automatic space management, the number of records that can be seen by any one routine is limited by the number of symbols in the current production. The difference is particularly important in the case of productions that generate lists. In Section 4.5.1 we saw an SLR(1) grammar for declarations in the style of C and Fortran, in which the type name precedes the list of identifiers. Here is an LL(1) grammar fragment for a language in the style of Pascal and Ada, in which the variables precede the type:

$$dec \rightarrow id\_list : type$$
$$id\_list \rightarrow \text{id} \; id\_list\_tail$$
$$id\_list\_tail \rightarrow , \; id\_list$$
$$\rightarrow \epsilon$$

Without resorting to non-L-attributed flow (see Exercise 4.12), we cannot pass the declared type into *id_list* as an inherited attribute. Instead, we must save up the list of identifiers and enter them into the symbol table *en masse* when the type is finally encountered. With automatic management of space for attributes, the action routines would look something like this:

$dec \rightarrow id\_list$: $type$ { declare_vars (id_list.chain, type.tp) }

$id\_list \rightarrow$ id id_list_tail { id_list.chain := append (id.name, id_list_tail.chain) }

$id\_list\_tail \rightarrow$, id_list { id_list_tail.chain := id_list.chain }

$\rightarrow \epsilon$ { id_list_tail.chain := nil }

With ad hoc management of space, we can if desired eliminate the linked list:

$dec \rightarrow$ { push (marker) }
    id_list : $type$
    { pop (tp)
      pop (name)
      while name <> marker
          declare_var (name, tp)
          pop (name) }

$id\_list \rightarrow$ id { push (cur_tok.name) } id_list_tail

$id\_list\_tail \rightarrow$, id_list

$\rightarrow \epsilon$

Neither automatic nor ad hoc management of attribute space in top-down parsers is clearly superior to the other. The ad hoc approach eliminates the need for many copy rules and inherited attributes, and is consequently somewhat more time- and space-efficient. It also allows lists to be embedded in the semantic stack. On the other hand, it requires that the programmer who writes the action routines be continually aware of what is in the stack and why, in order to push and pop it appropriately. In the final analysis, the choice is mainly a matter of taste.

4.6 Annotating a Syntax Tree

In our discussion so far we have used attribute grammars solely to decorate parse trees. As we mentioned in the chapter introduction, attribute grammars can also be used to decorate syntax trees. If our compiler uses action routines simply to build a syntax tree, then the bulk of semantic analysis and intermediate code generation will use the syntax tree as base.

Figure 4.15 contains a bottom-up CFG for a calculator language with types and declarations. The grammar differs from that of Figure 2.20 (page 76) in three ways: (1) we allow declarations to be intermixed with statements, (2) we differentiate between integer and real constants (presumably the latter contain a decimal point), and (3) we require explicit conversions between integer and real operands. The intended semantics of our language requires that every identifier be declared before it is used, and that types not be mixed in operations.

Extrapolating from the example in Figure 4.5, it is easy to add semantic functions or action routines to the grammar of Figure 4.15 to construct a syntax tree

$program \rightarrow stmt\_list$ **\$\$**

$stmt\_list \rightarrow stmt\_list\ decl\ |\ stmt\_list\ stmt\ |\ \epsilon$

$decl \rightarrow$ **int id** $|$ **real id**

$stmt \rightarrow$ **id** $:=\ expr\ |$ **read id** $|$ **write** $expr$

$expr \rightarrow term\ |\ expr\ add\_op\ term$

$term \rightarrow factor\ |\ term\ mult\_op\ factor$

$factor \rightarrow (\ expr\ )\ |$ **id** $|$ **int_const** $|$ **real_const** $|$ **float** $(\ expr\ )\ |$ **trunc** $(\ expr\ )$

$add\_op \rightarrow$ **+** $|$ **-**

$mult\_op \rightarrow$ ***** $|$ **/**

Figure 4.15 Context-free grammar for a calculator language with types and declarations. The intent is that every identifier be declared before use, and that types not be mixed in computations.

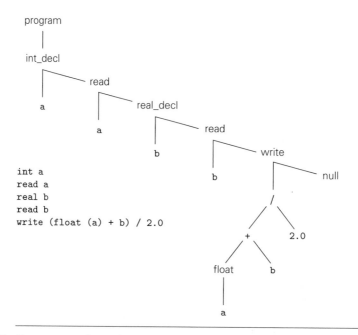

Figure 4.16 Syntax tree for a simple calculator program.

for the calculator language (Exercise 4.16). The obvious structure for such a tree would represent expressions as we did in Figure 4.7, and would represent a program as a linked list of declarations and statements. As a concrete example, Figure 4.16 contains the syntax tree for a simple program to print the average of an integer and a real.

Much as a context-free grammar describes the possible structure of parse trees for a given programming language, we can use a *tree grammar* to represent the possible structure of syntax trees. As in a CFG, each production of a tree grammar represents a possible relationship between a parent and its children in the tree. The parent is the symbol on the left-hand side of the production; the children are the symbols on the right-hand side. The productions used in Figure 4.16 might look something like this:

program → *item*

int_decl : item → *id item*

read : item → *id item*

real_decl : item → *id item*

write : item → *expr item*

null : item → ε

'/' : expr → *expr expr*

'+' : expr → *expr expr*

float : expr → *expr*

id : expr → ε

real_const : expr → ε

Here the notation *A : B* on the left-hand side of a production means that *A* is one kind of *B*, and may appear wherever a *B* is expected on a right-hand side.

Tree grammars and context-free grammars differ in important ways. A context-free grammar is meant to define (generate) a language composed of strings of tokens, where each string is the fringe (yield) of a parse tree. Parsing is the process of finding a tree that has a given yield. A tree grammar, as we use it here, is meant to define (or generate) the trees themselves. We have no need for a notion of parsing: we can easily inspect a tree and determine whether (and how) it can be generated by the grammar. Our purpose in introducing tree grammars is to provide a framework for the decoration of syntax trees. Semantic rules attached to the productions of a tree grammar can be used to define the attribute flow of a syntax tree in exactly the same way that semantic rules attached to the productions of a context-free grammar are used to define the attribute flow of a parse tree. We will use a tree grammar in the remainder of this section to perform static semantic checking. In Chapter 9 we will show how additional semantic rules can be used to generate intermediate code.

Figure 4.17 contains a complete tree attribute grammar for our calculator language with types. Once decorated, the *program* node at the root of the syntax tree will contain a list, in a synthesized attribute, of all static semantic errors in the program. (The list will be empty if the program is free of such errors.) Each *item* or *expr* node has an inherited attribute symtab that contains a list, with types, of all identifiers declared to the left in the tree. Each *item* node also has an inherited attribute errors_in that lists all static semantic errors found to its left *program* → *item*

    ▷ item.symtab := nil

    ▷ program.errors := item.errors_out

    ▷ item.errors_in := nil

int_decl : *item$_1$* → *id item$_2$*

    ▷ declare_name (id, item$_1$, item$_2$, int)

    ▷ item$_1$.errors_out := item$_2$.errors_out

real_decl : *item$_1$* → *id item$_2$*

    ▷ declare_name (id, item$_1$, item$_2$, real)

    ▷ item$_1$.errors_out := item$_2$.errors_out

read : *item$_1$* → *id item$_2$*

    ▷ item$_2$.symtab := item$_1$.symtab

    ▷ if <id.name, ?> ∈ item$_1$.symtab

        item$_2$.errors_in := item$_1$.errors_in

      else

        item$_2$.errors_in := item$_1$.errors_in + [id.name "undefined at" id.location]

    ▷ item$_1$.errors_out := item$_2$.errors_out

write : *item$_1$* → *expr item$_2$*

    ▷ expr.symtab := item$_1$.symtab

    ▷ item$_2$.symtab := item$_1$.symtab

    ▷ item$_2$.errors_in := item$_1$.errors_in + expr.errors

    ▷ item$_1$.errors_out := item$_2$.errors_out

':=' : *item$_1$* → *id expr item$_2$*

    ▷ expr.symtab := item$_1$.symtab

    ▷ item$_2$.symtab := item$_1$.symtab

    ▷ if <id.name, A> ∈ item$_1$.symtab   −− for some type A

        if A <> error and expr.type <> error and A <> expr.type

            item$_2$.errors_in := item$_1$.errors_in + ["type clash at" item$_1$.location]

        else

            item$_2$.errors_in := item$_1$.errors_in

      else

        item$_2$.errors_in := item$_1$.errors_in + [id.name "undefined at" id.location]

    ▷ item$_1$.errors_out := item$_2$.errors_out

null : *item* → ε

    ▷ item.errors_out := item.errors_in

Figure 4.17 Attribute grammar to decorate an abstract syntax tree for the calculator language with types. We use square brackets to delimit error messages and pointed brackets to delimit symbol table entries. Juxtaposition indicates concatenation within error messages; the '+' and '−' operators indicate insertion and removal in lists. We assume that every node has been initialized by the scanner or by action routines in the parser to contain an indication of the location (line and column) at which the corresponding construct appears in the source (see Exercise 4.17). The '?' symbol is used as a "wild card"; it matches any type *(continued)*.

$id : expr \rightarrow \epsilon$
    ▷ if <id.name, A> $\in$ expr.symtab   -- for some type A
        expr.errors := nil
        expr.type := A
    else
        expr.errors := [id.name "undefined at" id.location]
        expr.type := error

$int\_const : expr \rightarrow \epsilon$
    ▷ expr.type := int

$real\_const : expr \rightarrow \epsilon$
    ▷ expr.type := real

$`+' : expr_1 \rightarrow expr_2\ expr_3$
    ▷ $expr_2$.symtab := $expr_1$.symtab
    ▷ $expr_3$.symtab := $expr_1$.symtab
    ▷ check_types ($expr_1$, $expr_2$, $expr_3$)

$`-' : expr_1 \rightarrow expr_2\ expr_3$
    ▷ $expr_2$.symtab := $expr_1$.symtab
    ▷ $expr_3$.symtab := $expr_1$.symtab
    ▷ check_types ($expr_1$, $expr_2$, $expr_3$)

$`\times' : expr_1 \rightarrow expr_2\ expr_3$
    ▷ $expr_2$.symtab := $expr_1$.symtab
    ▷ $expr_3$.symtab := $expr_1$.symtab
    ▷ check_types ($expr_1$, $expr_2$, $expr_3$)

$`\div' : expr_1 \rightarrow expr_2\ expr_3$
    ▷ $expr_2$.symtab := $expr_1$.symtab
    ▷ $expr_3$.symtab := $expr_1$.symtab
    ▷ check_types ($expr_1$, $expr_2$, $expr_3$)

$float : expr_1 \rightarrow expr_2$
    ▷ $expr_2$.symtab := $expr_1$.symtab
    ▷ convert_type ($expr_2$, $expr_1$, int, real, "float of non-int")

$trunc : expr_1 \rightarrow expr_2$
    ▷ $expr_2$.symtab := $expr_1$.symtab
    ▷ convert_type ($expr_2$, $expr_1$, real, int, "trunc of non-real")

Figure 4.17 *(continued on next page)*

```
macro declare_name (id, cur_item, next_item : syntax_tree_node; t : type)
    if <id.name, ?> ∈ cur_item.symtab
        next_item.errors_in := cur_item.errors_in + ["redefinition of" id.name "at" cur_item.location]
        next_item.symtab := cur_item.symtab − <id.name, ?> + <id.name, error>
    else
        next_item.errors_in := cur_item.errors_in
        next_item.symtab := cur_item.symtab + <id.name, t>
macro check_types (result, operand1, operand2)
    if operand1.type = error or operand2.type = error
        result.type := error
        result.errors := operand1.errors + operand2.errors
    else if operand1.type <> operand2.type
        result.type := error
        result.errors := operand1.errors + operand2.errors + ["type clash at" result.location]
    else
        result.type := operand1.type
        result.errors := operand1.errors + operand2.errors
macro convert_type (old_expr, new_expr : syntax_tree_node; from_t, to_t : type; msg : string)
    if old_expr.type = from_t or old_expr.type = error
        new_expr.errors := old_expr.errors
        new_expr.type := to_t
    else
        new_expr.errors := old_expr.errors + [msg "at" old_expr.location]
        new_expr.type := error
```

Figure 4.17 *(continued)*

in the tree, and a synthesized attribute errors_out to propagate the final error list back to the root. Each *expr* node has one synthesized attribute that indicates its type and another that contains a list of any static semantic errors found inside.

Our handling of semantic errors illustrates a common technique. In order to continue looking for other errors we must provide values for any attributes that would have been set in the absence of an error. To avoid cascading error messages, we choose values for those attributes that will pass quietly through subsequent checks. In our specific example we employ a pseudo-type called error, which we associate with any symbol table entry or expression for which we have already generated a message.

In our example grammar we accumulate error messages into a synthesized attribute of the root of the syntax tree. In an ad hoc attribute evaluator we might be tempted to print these messages on the fly as the errors are discovered. In practice, however, particularly in a multipass compiler, it makes sense to buffer the messages, so they can be interleaved with messages produced by other phases of the compiler, and printed in program order at the end of compilation.

Though it takes a bit of checking to verify the fact, our attribute grammar is noncircular and well-defined. No attribute is ever assigned a value more than once. (The helper routines in Figure 4.17 should be thought of as macros, rather than semantic functions. For the sake of brevity we have passed them entire tree nodes as arguments. Under a strict formulation of attribute grammars each would be replaced by two separate semantic functions. Each of those functions would take only attributes as arguments, and would assign its result into a single attribute.)

One could convert our attribute grammar into executable code using an automatic attribute evaluator generator. Alternatively, one could create an ad hoc evaluator in the form of mutually recursive subroutines (Exercise 4.15). In the latter case attribute flow would be explicit in the calling sequence of the routines. We could then choose if desired to keep the symbol table in global variables, rather than passing it from node to node through attributes. Most compilers employ the ad hoc approach.

4.7 Summary and Concluding Remarks

This chapter has discussed the task of semantic analysis. We reviewed the sorts of language rules that can be classified as syntax, static semantics, and dynamic semantics, and discussed the issue of whether to generate code for dynamic semantic checks. We also considered the role that the semantic analyzer plays in a typical compiler. We noted that both the enforcement of static semantic rules and the generation of intermediate code can be cast in terms of decoration, or *annotation*, of a parse tree or syntax tree. We then presented attribute grammars as a formal framework for this annotation process.

An attribute grammar associates *attributes* with each symbol in a context-free grammar or tree grammar, and *attribute rules* with each production. *Synthesized* attributes are calculated only in productions in which their symbol appears on the left-hand side. The synthesized attributes of tokens are initialized by the scanner. *Inherited* attributes are calculated in productions in which their symbol appears within the right-hand side; they allow calculations internal to a symbol to depend on the context in which the symbol appears. Inherited attributes of the start symbol (goal) can represent the external environment of the compiler. Strictly speaking, attribute grammars allow only *copy rules* (assignments of one attribute to another) and simple calls to *semantic functions*, but we usually relax this restriction to allow more-or-less arbitrary code fragments in some existing programming language.

Just as context-free grammars can be categorized according to the parsing algorithm(s) that can use them, attribute grammars can be categorized according to the complexity of their pattern of *attribute flow*. S-attributed grammars, in which all attributes are synthesized, can naturally be evaluated in a single bottom-up pass over a parse tree, in precisely the order the tree is discovered by an LR-family parser. L-attributed grammars, in which all attribute flow is depth-first left-to-right, can be evaluated in precisely the order that the parse tree is predicted and matched by an LL-family parser. Attribute grammars with more complex patterns of attribute flow are not commonly used in production compilers, but are valuable for syntax-based editors, incremental compilers, and various other tools.

While it is possible to construct automatic tools to analyze attribute flow and annotate parse trees, most compilers rely on *action routines*, which the compiler writer embeds in the right-hand sides of productions to evaluate attribute rules at specific points in a parse. In an LL-family parser, action routines can be embedded at arbitrary points in a production's right-hand side. In an LR-family parser, action routines must follow the production's *left corner*. Space for attributes in a bottom-up compiler is naturally allocated in parallel with the parse stack. Inherited attributes must be "faked" by accessing the synthesized attributes of symbols known to lie below the current production in the stack. Space for attributes in a top-down compiler can be allocated automatically, or managed explicitly by the writer of action routines. The automatic approach has the advantage of regularity, and is easier to maintain; the ad hoc approach is slightly faster and more flexible.

In a *one-pass* compiler, which interleaves scanning, parsing, semantic analysis, and code generation in a single traversal of its input, semantic functions or action routines are responsible for all of semantic analysis and code generation. More commonly, action routines simply build a syntax tree, which is then annotated during separate traversal(s) in subsequent pass(es).

In subsequent chapters (6–8 and 10 in particular) we will consider a wide variety of programming language constructs. Rather than present the actual attribute grammars required to implement these constructs, we will describe their semantics informally, and give examples of the target code. We will return to attribute grammars in Chapter 9, when we consider the generation of intermediate code in more detail.

4.8 Review Questions

4.1   What determines whether a language rule is a matter of syntax or of static semantics?

4.2   Why is it impossible to detect certain program errors at compile time, even though they can be detected at run time?

4.3   What is an *attribute grammar*?

4.4   What are programming *assertions*? What is their purpose?

4.5   What is the difference between *synthesized* and *inherited* attributes?

4.6   Give two examples of information that is typically passed through inherited attributes.

4.7 What is *attribute flow*?

4.8 What is a *one-pass* compiler?

4.9 What does it mean for an attribute grammar to be *S-attributed*? *L-attributed*? What is the significance of these grammar classes?

4.10 What is the difference between a semantic function and an action routine?

4.11 Some compilers perform all semantic checks and intermediate code generation in action routines. Others use action routines to build a syntax tree and then perform semantic checks and intermediate code generation in separate traversals of the syntax tree. Discuss the tradeoffs between these two strategies.

4.12* Explain how to manage space for synthesized attributes in a bottom-up parser.

4.13* Explain how to manage space for inherited attributes in a bottom-up parser.

4.14* Define *left corner* and *trailing part*.

4.15* Under what circumstances can an action routine be embedded in the right-hand side of a production in a bottom-up parser? Equivalently, under what circumstances can a marker symbol be embedded in a right-hand side without rendering the grammar non-LR?

4.16* Summarize the tradeoffs between automatic and ad hoc management of space for attributes in a top-down parser.

4.17* At any given point in a top-down parse, which symbols will have attribute records in an automatically managed attribute stack?

4.18 Describe the similarities and differences between context-free grammars and tree grammars.

4.19 How can a semantic analyzer avoid the generation of cascading error messages?

4.9 Exercises

4.1 Explain how to write a context-free-grammar in which every function must contain at least one `return` statement.

4.2 Give two examples of reasonable semantic rules that *cannot* be checked at reasonable cost, either statically or by compiler-generated code at run time.

4.3 Suppose that we want to translate constant expressions into the postfix, or "reverse Polish" notation of logician Jan Łukasiewicz. Postfix notation does not require parentheses. It appears in stack-based languages such as Postscript, Forth, and the P-code and Java byte code intermediate forms mentioned in Section 1.4. It also serves as the input language of certain Hewlett-Packard (HP) brand calculators. When given a number, an HP calculator pushes it onto an internal stack. When given an operator, it pops the top two numbers, applies the operator, and pushes the result. The display shows the value at the top of the stack. To compute 2 * (5 – 3) / 4 one would enter 2 5 3 – * 4 /.

Using the underlying CFG of Figure 4.1, write an attribute grammar that will associate with the root of the parse tree a sequence of calculator button pushes, seq, that will compute the arithmetic value of the tokens derived from that symbol. You may assume the existence of a function buttons (c) that returns a sequence of button pushes (ending with ENTER on an HP calculator) for the constant c. You may also assume the existence of a concatenation function for sequences of button pushes.

4.4   Repeat the previous exercise using the underlying CFG of Figure 4.3.

4.5   Consider the following grammar for reverse Polish arithmetic expressions:

$$E \rightarrow E \; E \; op \mid \texttt{id}$$
$$op \rightarrow + \mid - \mid * \mid /$$

Assuming that each id has a synthesized attribute name of type string, and that each E and op has an attribute val of type string, write an attribute grammar that arranges for the val attribute of the root of the parse tree to contain a translation of the expression into conventional infix notation. For example, if the leaves of the tree, left to right, were "A A B – * C /", then the val field of the root would be "((A * (A – B)) / C)". As an extra challenge, write a version of your attribute grammar that exploits the usual arithmetic precedence and associativity rules to use as few parentheses as possible.

4.6   A CFG-based attribute evaluator capable of handling non-L-attributed attribute flow needs to take a parse tree as input. Explain how to build a parse tree automatically during a top-down or bottom-up parse (i.e., without explicit action routines).

4.7   Write an LL(1) grammar with action routines and automatic attribute space management that generates the reverse Polish translation described in Exercise 4.3.

4.8   (a) Write a context-free grammar for polynomials in *x*. Add semantic functions to produce an attribute grammar that will accumulate the polynomial's derivative (as a string) in a synthesized attribute of the root of the parse tree.

   (b) Replace your semantic functions with action routines that can be evaluated during parsing.

4.9   (a) Write a context-free grammar for `case` or `switch` statements in the style of Pascal or C. Add semantic functions to ensure that the same label does not appear on two different arms of the construct.

   (b) Replace your semantic functions with action routines that can be evaluated during parsing.

4.10 Write an algorithm to determine whether the rules of an arbitrary attribute grammar are noncircular. (Your algorithm will require exponential time in the worst case [JOR75].)

4.11* Repeat Exercise 4.7 using ad hoc attribute space management. Instead of accumulating the translation into a data structure, however, write it to a file on the fly.

4.12* Rewrite the grammar for declarations at the end of Section 4.5.2 (page 191), without the requirement that your attribute flow be L-attributed. Try to make the grammar as simple and elegant as possible (you shouldn't need to accumulate lists of identifiers).

4.13* Fill in the missing lines in Figure 4.12.

4.14* One problem with automatic space management for attributes in a top-down parser occurs in lists and sequences. Consider for example the following grammar:

$block \rightarrow$ **begin** $stmt\_list$ **end**

$stmt\_list \rightarrow stmt\ stmt\_list\_tail$

$stmt\_list\_tail \rightarrow$; $stmt\_list\ |\ \epsilon$

$stmt \rightarrow \ldots$

After predicting the final statement of an n-statement block, the attribute stack will contain the following (linebreaks and indentation are for clarity only):

```
block begin stmt_list end
      stmt stmt_list_tail ; stmt_list
      stmt stmt_list_tail ; stmt_list
      stmt stmt_list_tail ; stmt_list
      { n times }
```

If the attribute stack is of finite size, it is guaranteed to overflow for some long but valid block of straight-line code. The problem is especially unfortunate since, with the exception of the accumulated output code, none of the repeated symbols in the attribute stack contains any useful attributes once its substructure has been parsed.

Suggest a technique to "squeeze out" useless symbols in the attribute stack, dynamically. Ideally, your technique should be amenable to automatic implementation, so it does not constitute a burden on the compiler writer.

Also, suppose you are using a compiler with a top-down parser that employs an automatically managed attribute stack, but does not squeeze out useless symbols. What can you do if your program causes the compiler to run out of stack space? How can you modify your program to "get around" the problem?

4.15 Rewrite the attribute grammar of Figure 4.17 in the form of an ad hoc tree traversal consisting of mutually recursive subroutines in your favorite programming language. Keep the symbol table in a global variable, rather than passing it through arguments.

4.16 Write an attribute grammar based on the CFG of Figure 4.15 that will build a syntax tree with the structure described in Figure 4.17.

4.17 Augment the attribute grammar of Figure 4.5, Figure 4.6, or Exercise 4.16 to initialize a synthesized attribute in every syntax tree node that indicates the location (line and column) at which the corresponding construct appears in the source program. You may assume that the scanner initializes the location of every token.

4.18 Modify the CFG and attribute grammar of Figures 4.15 and 4.17 to permit mixed integer and real expressions, without the need for `float` and `trunc`. You will want to add an annotation to any node that must be coerced to the opposite type, so that the code generator will know to generate code to do so. Be sure to think carefully about your coercion rules. In the expression `my_int + my_real`, for example, how will you know whether to coerce the integer to be a real, or to coerce the real to be an integer?

4.19 Explain the need for the $A : B$ notation on the left-hand sides of productions in a tree grammar. Why isn't similar notation required for context-free grammars?

4.10 Bibliographic Notes

Much of the early theory of attribute grammars was developed by Knuth [Knu68]. Lewis, Rosenkrantz, and Stearns [LRS74] introduced the notion of an L-attributed grammar. Watt [Wat77] showed how to use marker symbols to emulate inherited attributes in a bottom-up parser. Jazayeri, Ogden, and Rounds [JOR75] showed that exponential time may be required in the worst case to decorate a parse tree with arbitrary attribute flow. Articles by Courcelle [Cou84] and Engelfriet [Eng84] survey the theory and practice of attribute evaluation. The best-known language-based editor (based on attribute grammars) is the Cornell Program Synthesizer, due to Titelbaum and Reps [TR81]. Magpie [SDB84] is an incremental compiler. Action routines to implement many language features can be found in the texts of Fischer and LeBlanc [FL88] or Appel [App97]. Further notes on attribute grammars can be found in Aho, Sethi, and Ullman's text [ASU86, pp. 340–342].

Marcotty, Ledgard, and Bochmann [MLB76] provide a survey of formal notations for programming language semantics. The seminal paper on axiomatic semantics is by Hoare [Hoa69]. An excellent book on the subject is Gries's *The Science of Programming* [Gri81]. The seminal paper on denotational semantics is by Scott and Strachey [SS71]. Texts on the subject include those of Stoy [Sto77] and Gordon [Gor79].

Assembly-Level Computer Architecture

As described in Chapter 1, a compiler is simply a translator. It translates programs written in one language into programs written in another language. This second language can be almost anything—some other high-level language, phototype-setting commands, VLSI (chip) layouts—but most of the time it's the machine language for some available computer.

Just as there are many different programming languages, there are many different machine languages, though the latter tend to display considerably less diversity than the former. Each machine language corresponds to a different *processor architecture*. Formally, an architecture is the interface between the hardware and the software: the language generated by a compiler, or by a programmer writing for the bare machine. The *implementation* of the processor is a concrete realization of the architecture, generally in hardware.[1] This chapter provides a brief introduction to those aspects of processor architecture and implementation of particular importance to compiler writers. For readers who have seen the material before, the chapter may be skimmed as a review.

To generate correct code, it suffices for a compiler writer to understand the target architecture. To generate *fast* code, it is generally necessary to understand the implementation as well, because it is the implementation that determines the relative speeds of alternative translations of a given language construct.

Processor implementations change over time, as people invent better ways of doing things, and as technological advances (e.g., increases in the number of transistors that will fit on one chip) make things feasible that were not feasible before. Processor architectures also change, for at least two reasons. Some technological advances can be exploited only by changing the hardware/software

---

1 In microprogrammed machines, which we will consider in Section 5.5, the implementation may actually be an interpreter, running on some simpler underlying hardware.

interface, for example by increasing the number of bits that can be added or multiplied in a single instruction. In addition, experience with compilers and applications often suggests that certain new instructions would make programs simpler or faster. Occasionally, technological and intellectual trends converge to produce a revolutionary change in both architecture and implementation. We will discuss three such changes in Section 5.5: the development of microprogramming in the early 1960s, the development of the microprocessor in the early 1970s, and the development of RISC machines in the early 1980s.

Most of the discussion in this chapter, and indeed in the rest of the book, will assume that we are compiling for a modern RISC machine. Roughly speaking, a RISC machine is one that sacrifices richness in the instruction set in order to increase the number of instructions that can be executed per second. Where appropriate, we will devote a limited amount of attention to earlier, CISC machines. The most popular processor architecture in the world—the Intel x86, used in the IBM PC and clones—is still a CISC design, but most other manufacturers have switched to RISC.

We begin our discussion in Section 5.1 with a high-level overview of the architecture of a simple computer workstation. In the following three sections we consider the hierarchical organization of memory, the types (formats) of data found in memory, and the instructions used to manipulate them. The coverage is necessarily somewhat cursory and high-level; much more detail can be found in books on computer architecture (e.g., in Chapter 2 of Hennessy and Patterson's outstanding text [HP96]).

We review the evolution of RISC machines in Section 5.5, with particular emphasis on the interplay between architecture and compilation. We illustrate the differences between CISC and RISC machines using the Motorola 680x0 and MIPS instruction sets as examples. Finally, in Section 5.6, we consider some of the issues that make compiling for modern processors a challenging task.

5.1 Workstation Macro-Architecture

Most modern computers consist of a collection of *devices* that talk to each other over internal communication lines—typically one or more *buses* (Figure 5.1). From the point of view of language implementation, the most important device is the *processor*; the second most important is main memory. Other devices include disks, keyboards, screens, networks, robotic sensors/effectors, serial ports, and so on.

Almost all modern computers use the von Neumann *stored program model* of computing: a program is simply a collection of bits in memory that the processor *interprets* as instructions, rather than as integers, floating point numbers, or some other sort of data. All a processor does is repeatedly

1. Fetch an instruction from memory

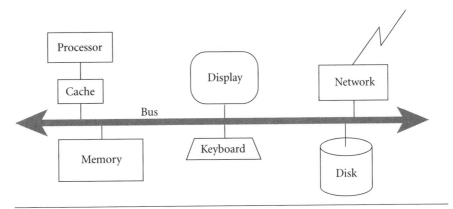

Figure 5.1 Architecture of a generic computer workstation.

2. Decode the instruction: figure out what it says to do

3. Fetch any needed operands from registers or from memory

4. Execute the operation

5. Store any result(s) back into registers or memory

This set of operations is referred to as the *fetch–execute cycle*. The processor runs this cycle continually, regardless of the meaning of the instructions. One can point a processor's instruction fetch logic at a long string of floating-point numbers and it will blithely begin to execute them: it will do *something*, though that something probably won't make much sense. If the processor attempts to execute a bit pattern that has no interpretation as an instruction, or if an instruction attempts to do something invalid (e.g., access a protected region of memory, or perform some other "privileged" operation), then the hardware will generate an *interrupt*, but the processor still will not stop. The interrupt will cause the processor to jump to a predetermined location in the operating system, where it will continue to fetch and execute instructions. (The code in the operating system will presumably print some sort of error message and then terminate the offending program.) When it has nothing else to do, the operating system will enter an infinite loop. The loop will terminate when some device other than the processor—the clock, for example, or a disk or keyboard—generates an interrupt.

The typical processor consists of a collection of *functional units*, one or more for each of the tasks enumerated above (instruction fetch, instruction decode, operand fetch, arithmetic execution, and write-back), plus additional units to hold register contents and control the flow of information from one place to another. One could imagine an implementation in which all of the work for a particular instruction is completed before work on the next instruction begins, and in fact this is how many computers used to be constructed. The problem with this organization is that most of the functional units are idle most of the time.

TIME $\longrightarrow$

inst. 1	fetch inst.	decode inst.	execute op.	access memory	store result		
inst. 2		fetch inst.	decode inst.	execute op.	access memory	store result	
inst. 3			fetch inst.	decode inst.	execute op.	access memory	store result
inst. 4				fetch inst.	decode inst.	execute op.	access memory	store result
...							

Figure 5.2 Execution of a simple pipelined processor. Each instruction takes five clock cycles to complete, but absent any stalls due to inter-instruction conflicts or dependences, one instruction completes on every cycle.

Beginning with the early supercomputers of the 1960s, processor implementations have increasingly moved toward a *pipelined* organization, in which the functional units work like the stations on an assembly line, with several consecutive instructions passing through different pipeline stages simultaneously.

A simple example pipeline for a RISC machine is shown in Figure 5.2. The first pipeline stage fetches an instruction from memory. The second stage decodes the instruction and retrieves its operands (if any) from registers. The third stage performs an arithmetic/logical operation or, in the case of a load or store instruction, calculates a memory address. The fourth stage accesses memory (for load and store instructions), or updates the program counter (for branches). Finally the fifth stage puts results (if any) back into registers. Typical modern machines are significantly more aggressive. Their pipelines may be 10 or more stages deep, and there may be several pipelines operating in parallel. A multiple-pipeline machine is said to be *superscalar*; in principle it can start a new instruction in every pipe in every cycle.

Pipelining can dramatically improve processor performance, but it is not a panacea. In particular, a pipeline will *stall* if the same functional unit is needed in two different instructions simultaneously, or if an earlier instruction has not yet produced a result by the time it is needed in a later instruction, or if the outcome of a conditional branch is not known by the time the next instruction needs to be fetched. A simple example of a stall in our example machine appears in Figure 5.3. Here we have assumed that the first instruction requires more work to execute than can be completed in one cycle. While it occupies the execute pipeline stage, the next three instructions are forced to wait (the pipeline cannot advance), and no instruction is started in cycle 4.

We shall see in Section 5.6 that many stalls can be avoided by adding a little extra hardware and then choosing carefully among the various ways of translating a given construct into target code. An important example occurs in the

TIME ⟶

fetch inst.	decode inst.	execute op.	⟶	access memory	store result			
	fetch inst.	decode inst.	[ ]	execute op.	access memory	store result		
		fetch inst.	[ ]	decode inst.	execute op.	access memory	store result	
			[ ]	fetch inst.	decode inst.	execute op.	access memory	store result
				fetch inst.	decode inst.	execute op.	access memory	store result

Figure 5.3 Simple example of a pipeline stall. When the first instruction requires an extra cycle to execute, later instructions must wait. No instruction starts in cycle 4.

case of floating-point arithmetic, which is typically much slower than integer arithmetic. Rather than stall the entire pipeline when executing a floating-point instruction, we can build a separate functional unit for floating-point math, and arrange for it to operate on a separate set of floating-point registers. In effect, this strategy leads to a *pair* of pipelines—one for integers and one for floating-point—that share their first few stages. The integer branch of the pipeline can continue to execute while the floating-point unit is busy, so long as subsequent instructions do not require the floating-point result. The need to reorder, or *schedule*, instructions so that those that conflict with or depend on one another are separated in time is one of the principal reasons why compiling for modern processors is hard.

5.2 The Memory Hierarchy

Memory on most machines consists of a numbered sequence of eight-bit bytes. It is not uncommon for modern workstations to contain hundreds of megabytes of memory—much too much to fit on the same chip as the processor. Because memory is off-chip (in fact, on the other side of the bus), getting at it is much slower that getting at things on-chip. Most computers therefore employ a *memory hierarchy*, in which things that are used more often are kept close at hand. A typical memory hierarchy, with access times and capacities, is shown in Figure 5.4.

Only three of the levels of the memory hierarchy—registers, memory, and devices—are a visible part of the hardware/software interface. Compilers manage registers explicitly, loading them from memory when needed and storing them back to memory when done, or when the registers are needed for something else. Devices are generally accessed only by the operating system. To read a file, send

	typical access time	typical capacity
registers	2–5ns	64–512 bytes
primary cache	4–10ns	8K–256K bytes
secondary cache	20–100ns	512K–4M bytes
main memory	50ns–1μs	8M–4G bytes
disk	5–15ms	500M–1T bytes
tape	1–50s	effectively unlimited

Figure 5.4 **The memory hierarchy.** Access times and capacities are approximate, based on 1999 technology. Registers must be accessed within a single pipeline stage. Primary cache typically responds in one or two clock cycles; secondary cache in more like 10 cycles. Main memory on a supercomputer can be as fast as secondary cache; on a workstation it is typically much slower. Disk and tape times are constrained by the movement of physical parts.

a message, or perform some other device-specific function, a user-level program must transfer control into the operating system.

Registers are special locations that can hold (a very small amount of) data that can be accessed very quickly. A typical RISC machine has a few (often two) sets of registers that are used to hold integer and floating-point operands. It also has several special-purpose registers, including the *program counter* (PC) and the *processor status register*. The program counter holds the address of the next instruction to be executed. It is usually incremented automatically during the fetch–execute cycle; branches work by changing it explicitly. The processor status register contains a variety of bits of importance to the operating system (privilege level, interrupt priority level, trap enable bits) and, on some machines, a few bits of importance to the compiler writer. Principal among these are *condition codes*, which indicate whether the most recent arithmetic or logical operation resulted in a zero, a negative value, and/or arithmetic overflow. (We will consider condition codes in more detail in Section 5.4.)

Caches serve to improve the apparent response time of memory by keeping recently accessed memory locations (and locations adjacent to them) in special, high-speed memory. Primary caches are typically located on the same chip as the processor; secondary caches are typically larger, and may be located either on or off the chip. Caches are managed entirely in hardware on most machines. A memory access that finds its data in the cache is said to be a *cache hit*. An access that does not find its data in the cache is said to be a *cache miss*. On a miss, the hardware automatically loads a *line* of the cache with a contiguous region of memory containing the requested location. (Cache lines vary from as few as 8 to as many as 256 bytes in length.) Assuming that the cache was already full, the load will displace some other line, which is written back to memory if it has been modified.

Because registers are available in every instruction, while memory, even when successfully cached, can lead to pipeline stalls, good compilers expend a great deal of effort trying to make sure that the data they need most often are in registers, and trying to minimize the amount of time spent moving data back and forth between registers and memory. We will consider algorithms for register management in Section 5.6.2.

While a compiler could theoretically exploit knowledge of the hardware's cache management strategy in order to improve performance, current compilers are able to do this only to a limited extent. For the most part, compilers assume that every memory access will hit in the cache, and that the important goal is to make sure that the pipeline can continue to operate during the one–two cycles that it takes the cache to respond. The assumption is generally a good one, since most machines achieve a cache hit rate of well over 90% (often over 99%).

A final characteristic of memory that is important to the compiler is known as data *alignment*. Most machines are able to manipulate operands of several sizes, typically one, two, four, and eight bytes. Terminology varies, but it is common to refer to these as byte, half-word, word (or sometimes long-word), and double-word operands, respectively. Most recent architectures require *n*-byte operands to appear in memory at addresses that are evenly divisible by *n*. Integers, for example, which typically occupy four bytes, must appear at a location whose address is evenly divisible by four. This restriction occurs for two reasons. First, buses are designed in such a way that data are delivered to the processor over bit-parallel, aligned communication paths. Loading an integer from an odd address would require that the bits be shifted, adding logic (and time) to the load path. Second, there are usually not enough bits in an instruction to specify both an operation (e.g., load) and a full address. As we will see in Section 5.4.1, it is typical to specify an address in terms of an *offset* from some *base location* specified by a register. Requiring that integers be word-aligned allows the offset to be specified in words, rather than in bytes, quadrupling the amount of memory that can be accessed using offsets from a given base register.

5.3 Data Representation

Data in the memory of most computers are untyped: bits are simply bits. *Operations* are typed, in the sense that different operations *interpret* the bits in memory in different ways. Typical *data formats* include

1. Instructions
2. Addresses
3. Binary integers (various lengths)
4. Floating-point numbers (various lengths)
5. Characters
6. (Occasionally) binary-coded decimal numbers

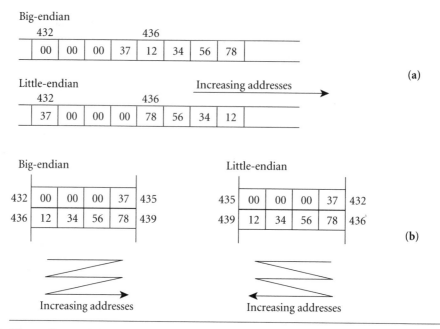

Figure 5.5 **Big-endian and little-endian byte orderings.** Two four-byte quantities, the numbers 37_{16} and $12\,34\,56\,78_{16}$, stored at addresses 432 and 436, respectively (a). The same situation, with memory visualized as a byte-addressable array of words (b).

Integers typically come in half-word, word, and (recently) double-word lengths. Floating-point numbers typically come in word and double-word lengths, commonly referred to as *single* and *double precision*. Some machines store the least-significant byte of a multi-word datum at the address of the datum itself, with bytes of increasing numeric significance at higher-numbered addresses. Other machines store the bytes the opposite order. The first option is called *little-endian*; the second is called *big-endian*. In either case, an n-byte datum stored at address t occupies bytes t through $t + n - 1$. The advantage of a little-endian organization is that it is tolerant of variations in operand size. If the value 37 is stored as a word and then a byte is read from the same location, the value 37 will be returned. On a big-endian machine, the value 0 will be returned (the upper eight bits of the number 37, when stored in 32 bits). The problem with the little-endian approach is that it seems to scramble the bytes of integers, when read from left to right (see Figure 5.5a). Little-endian-ness makes a bit more sense if one thinks of memory as a (byte-addressable) array of words (Figure 5.5b). Among CISC machines, the Intel x86 and the Digital VAX are little-endian. The IBM 360/370 and the Motorola 680x0 are big-endian. Most of the first-generation RISC machines were big-endian; most of the current RISC machines can run in either mode.

Support for characters varies widely. Most CISC machines will perform arbitrary arithmetic and logical operations on one-byte quantities. Many CISC machines also provide instructions that perform operations on strings of characters, such as copying, comparing, or searching. Most RISC machines will load and store bytes from or to memory, but operate only on longer quantities in registers. Early versions of the Compaq Alpha processor would not load or store bytes, but had instructions to move individual bytes among words already loaded into registers.

The binary-coded decimal (BCD) data format devotes one *nibble* (four bits—half a byte) to each decimal digit. Machines that support BCD can perform arithmetic directly on the BCD representation of a number, without converting it to and from binary form. This capability is particularly useful in business and financial applications, which treat their data as both numbers and character strings (converting a string of ASCII digits to or from BCD is much easier than converting it to or from binary). BCD format can be found on many (though by no means all) CISC machines, and on at least one RISC machine: the IBM PowerPC.

5.3.1 Integer Arithmetic

Binary integers are almost universally represented in two related formats: straightforward binary place-value for unsigned numbers, and *two's complement* for signed numbers. An n-bit unsigned integer has a value in the range $0 .. 2^n - 1$, inclusive. An n-bit two's complement integer has a value in the range $-2^{n-1} .. 2^{n-1} - 1$, inclusive. Most instruction sets provide two forms of most of the arithmetic operators: one for unsigned numbers and one for signed numbers. Even for languages in which integers are always signed, unsigned arithmetic is important for the manipulation of addresses (e.g., pointers).

The smallest two's complement value (-2^{n-1}) is represented by a one followed by $n-1$ zeros. Successive values are obtained by adding one, using ordinary place-value addition. Though several other representations for signed integers are possible, two's complement has several desirable properties:

1. Non-negative numbers have the same representation as they do in unsigned format.

2. The most significant bit of every negative number is one; the most significant bit of every nonnegative number is zero.

3. A single addition algorithm works for all combinations of negative and non-negative numbers.

The addition algorithm for unsigned binary numbers is the obvious binary analogue of the familiar right-to-left addition of decimal numbers. The addition algorithm for two's complement numbers is the same, except for the mechanism used to detect *overflow*. Overflow occurs when the result of an arithmetic operation exceeds the range of numbers representable in the given format. For unsigned integers, overflow occurs when there is a carry out of the most significant place. For two's complement numbers, overflow occurs when the carry into the most significant place differs from the carry out of the most significant place. For example, with four-bit two's complement numbers, 1100 + 0110 (−4 + 6) does not overflow, because the carries into and out of the left-most place are both one. However both 0101 + 0100 (5 + 4) and 1011 + 1100 (−5 + −4) cause overflow; in the first case the carries in and out are one and zero, respectively; in the second case they are zero and one, respectively. Different machines handle overflow in different ways. Some generate a trap (an interrupt) on overflow. Some set a bit that can be tested in software. Some provide two add instructions, one for each option. Some provide a single add that can be made to do either, depending on the value of a bit in a special register.

The additive inverse of a two's complement number is obtained by flipping all the bits, adding one, and discarding any overflow. Subtraction can be implemented almost trivially using an adder, by flipping the bits of the subtrahend, providing a one as the "carry" into the least-significant place, and "adding" as usual. Multiplication and division of signed numbers are a bit trickier than addition and subtraction, but still more or less straightforward.

5.3.2 Floating-Point Arithmetic

A floating-point number consists of a *mantissa* or *significand*, *sig*, an *exponent*, *exp*, and (usually) a sign bit, *s*. The value of a floating-point number is then $-1^s \times sig \times 2^{exp}$. Prior to the mid-1980s, floating-point formats and semantics tended to vary greatly across brands and even models of computers. Different manufacturers made different choices regarding the number of bits in each field, their order, and their internal representation. They also made different choices regarding the behavior of arithmetic operators with respect to rounding, underflow, overflow, invalid operations, and the representation of extremely small quantities. With the completion in 1985 of IEEE standard number 754, however, the situation has changed dramatically. Most processors developed in subsequent years conform to the formats and semantics of this standard.

The IEEE standard defines two sizes of floating-point numbers. Single precision numbers have a sign bit, eight bits of exponent, and 23 bits of significand. They are capable of representing numbers whose magnitudes vary from roughly 10^{-38} to 10^{38}. Double precision numbers have 11 bits of exponent and 52 bits of significand. They represent numbers whose magnitudes vary from roughly 10^{-308} to 10^{308}. The exponent is *biased* by subtracting the most negative possible value from it, so that it may be represented by an unsigned number.

Most values in the IEEE standard are *normalized* in such a way that the number of bits in the significand is really one more than the number explicitly represented: in the value 1.*something* × 2^{exp}, the one is superfluous, and is omitted

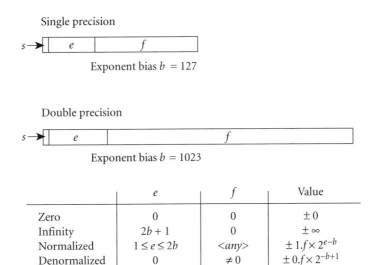

Single precision

Exponent bias $b = 127$

Double precision

Exponent bias $b = 1023$

	e	f	Value
Zero	0	0	± 0
Infinity	$2b + 1$	0	$\pm \infty$
Normalized	$1 \le e \le 2b$	$<any>$	$\pm 1.f \times 2^{e-b}$
Denormalized	0	$\ne 0$	$\pm 0.f \times 2^{-b+1}$
NaN	$2b + 1$	$\ne 0$	NaN

Figure 5.6   The IEEE 754 floating-point standard. For normalized numbers, the exponent is $e - 127$ or $e - 1023$, depending on precision. The significand is $1 + f \times 2^{-23}$ or $1 + f \times 2^{-52}$, again depending on precision. Field f is called the *fractional part*, or *fraction*. Bit patterns in which e is all ones (255 for single precision, 2047 for double precision) are reserved for infinities and NaNs. Bit patterns in which e is zero but f is not are used for denormal (gradual underflow) numbers.

in the representation. Exceptions to this rule occur near zero: very small numbers can be represented (with reduced precision) as $0.something \times 2^{min+1}$, where *min* is the smallest (largest negative) exponent available in the format. Many older floating point standards disallow such *denormal numbers*, leading to a *gap* between zero and the smallest representable positive number that is larger than the gap between the two smallest representable positive numbers. Because it includes denormals, the IEEE standard is said to provide for *gradual underflow*. Denormal numbers are represented with a zero in the exponent field (denoting a maximally negative exponent) together with a nonzero fraction.

The conventions of the IEEE 754 standard are summarized in Figure 5.6. In addition to single- and double-precision formats, the standard also provides for vendor-defined "extended" single- and double-precision numbers (not shown here). These extended formats are required to have at least 32 and 64 significant bits (31 and 63 explicit) in the significand, respectively.

Floating-point arithmetic is sufficiently complicated that entire books have been written about it. Some of the characteristics of the IEEE standard of particular interest to compiler writers include:

- The bit patterns used to represent nonnegative floating-point numbers are ordered in the same way as integers. As a result, an ordinary integer comparison operation can be used to determine which of two numbers is larger.

- Zero is represented by a bit pattern consisting entirely of zeros. There is also (confusingly) a "negative zero," consisting of a sign bit of one and zeros in all other positions.

- Two bit patterns are reserved to represent positive and negative infinity. These values behave in predictable ways. For example, any positive number divided by zero yields positive infinity. Similarly, the arctangent of positive infinity is $\pi/2$.

- Certain other bit patterns are reserved for special "not-a-number" (NaN) values. These values are generated by nonsensical operations, such as square root of a negative number, addition of positive and negative infinity, or division of zero by zero. Almost any operation on an NaN produces another NaN. As a result, many algorithms can dispense with internal error checks: they can follow the steps that make sense in the absence of errors, and then check the final result to make sure it's not an NaN. Some NaNs, not normally generated by arithmetic operations, can be set by the compiler explicitly to represent uninitialized variables or other special situations; these *signaling NaNs* produce an interrupt if used.

An excellent introduction to both integer and floating-point arithmetic, together with suggestions for further reading, can be found in David Goldberg's appendix to Patterson and Hennessy's architecture text [HP96, app. A].

5.4 Instruction Set Architecture

Machine language instructions can generally be grouped into four main categories:

1. *Data movement.* Load and store instructions copy data back and forth between registers and memory. Move instructions copy data between registers. Additional instructions may swap the contents of registers, or the bytes within a register. Some CISC machines provide instructions to copy arbitrary-length byte strings from one memory location to another, or to push or pop a stack in memory, automatically updating the register used as the top-of-stack pointer.

2. *Computation.* Many instructions compute arithmetic or logical operations: add, subtract, multiply, divide, negate, and, or, xor, not, shift, and so on. Architectures vary greatly in how to specify operands (see below). CISC machines often provide a richer set of operations than do RISC machines. The Digital VAX, for example, provided an instruction to compute the value of an arbitrary polynomial at a given point.

3. *Control Transfer.* While the terminology is not universal, most authors use jump for an unconditional transfer of control, and branch for a conditional

transfer. (On some machines, `jump` is used for a transfer to an absolute address, while `branch` is used for a transfer forward or backward a certain distance from the current location.) Subroutine `call` instructions save the old address for use in a `return`. On a RISC machine, `call` is sometimes called `jump and link` (`jal`). On a CISC machine, the instruction may do a lot of extra work, such as saving registers, creating stack space for local variables, setting up a frame pointer register, and so on. The `return` instruction may undo some of these operations; on a RISC machine an ordinary `jump` instruction serves as a `return`.

4. *Special Operations.* Special instructions manipulate portions of the processor state that are normally hidden from user programs. The only one generally of interest to compiler writers is `trap`, which generates an interrupt in order to transfer control into the operating system. On most machines all other special operations can be executed only when the processor is running in a special "privileged" mode. Interrupts move the processor to privileged mode at the same time that they transfer control to the operating system. The operating system can return control to the user program (and to unprivileged mode) by executing a `return from exception` (`rte`) instruction.

Within each instruction, the operation to be performed is encoded in a bit field called the *opcode*.

On a RISC machine, computational instructions operate on values held in registers: a `load` instruction must be used to bring a value from memory into a register before it can be used as an operand. CISC machines usually allow all or most computational instructions to access operands directly in memory. RISC machines are therefore said to provide a *load-store* or *register-register* architecture; CISC machines are said to provide a *register-memory* architecture. Some early (1950s and 1960s) machines provided a memory-memory architecture in which all operands were accessed directly in memory; there were no registers.

For binary operations, instructions on RISC machines generally specify three registers: two sources and a destination. Some CISC machines (e.g., the VAX) also provide three-address instructions. Others (e.g., the x86 and the 680x0) provide only two-address instructions; one of the operands is always overwritten by the result. Two-address instructions are more compact, but three-address instructions allow both operands to be reused in subsequent operations. This reuse is crucial on RISC machines: it minimizes the number of artificial restrictions on the ordering of instructions, allowing the compiler to perform more extensive instruction scheduling.

5.4.1 Addressing Modes

One can imagine many different ways in which a computational instruction might specify the location of its operands. These correspond to various *addressing modes*:

register: The operand is in a register.

immediate: The operand is a constant contained in the instruction itself.

absolute: The operand is in a memory location whose address is a constant contained in the instruction itself. Some global variables are accessed using absolute addressing.

register indirect: The operand is in a memory location whose address is in a register. Register indirect mode is the normal way to access data whose address has just been computed, or to which we have a pointer.

displacement: The operand is in a memory location a constant distance away from the location whose address is in a register. Displacement addressing with respect to the frame pointer is the usual way to access local variables.

indexed: The operand is in a memory location whose address is the sum of the values in two registers. Indexed addressing is useful for arrays: one register (the *base*) contains the address of the array; the second (the *index*) contains the offset of the desired element.

scaled: As in indexed addressing, the address of the operand is computed from values in a pair of registers. The value in the index register, however, is multiplied by the size of the operand in bytes (inferred from the opcode) before adding it to the value in the base register. Some machines provide an addressing mode that combines displacement and indexed or displacement and scaled addressing.

memory indirect: The *address of* the operand is in a memory location whose address is in a register. Memory indirect addressing is used when a register holds the address of a pointer.

auto-increment/decrement: Some machines can update the contents of a register as a side effect of using it in an address computation. Most commonly this occurs in register indirect addressing. The side effect is to add or subtract the size of the operand (inferred from the opcode) from the contents of the indirect register. On the Hewlett-Packard PA-RISC, the result of the sum in displacement or indexed addressing can be used to update the value of the base register. Auto-increment/decrement addressing is useful for stepping through arrays.

Other modes are of course possible; these are the most common ones. CISC machines tend to provide many addressing modes; RISC machines provide comparatively few. More specifically, RISC machines support only register and immediate addressing modes for computational instructions. Most support only displacement and indexed modes for load and store instructions (by specifying a displacement of zero, of course, one can obtain the effect of register indirect addressing).

5.4.2 Conditional Branches

Conditional branches are generally controlled in one of two ways. On most CISC machines they use *condition codes*. As mentioned in Section 5.2, condition codes are usually implemented as a set of bits in a special *processor status register*. All or most of the arithmetic and logical instructions update the condition codes as a side effect. The exact number of bits varies from machine to machine, but three is a common number: one each to indicate whether the operation resulted in a zero value, a negative value, and/or an overflow or carry. To implement the following test, for example,

```
A := B + C
if A = 0 then
     body
```

a compiler for the 680x0 might generate

```
        movl    B, d0    ; move long-word B into register d0
        addl    C, d0    ; add
        movl    d0, A    ; and store
        bne     L1       ; branch if result not equal to zero
        body
L1:
```

For cases in which the value that is to control the branch has not just been computed or moved, most machines provide `compare` and `test` instructions. Again on the 680x0:

```
                     movl    A, d0
if A < B then        cmpl    d0, B    ; compare long integers
     body            bge     L1       ; branch if A >= B
                     body
              L1:
```

```
                     tstl    C        ; test long integer
if C > 0 then        ble     L1       ; branch if C <= 0
     body            body
              L1:
```

Unfortunately, traditional condition codes make it difficult to implement some very important performance enhancements. Specifically, the fact that they are set by almost every instruction tends to preclude implementations in which unrelated instructions can complete in parallel, or even out of order—in effect, there are no independent instructions. There are several possible ways to address this problem; the handling of conditional branches is one of the areas in which extant RISC machines vary most from one another. The Sparc architecture makes setting condition codes optional. The PowerPC architecture provides eight separate sets of condition codes; compare and branch instructions specify the set to use. The MIPS, PA-RISC, and Alpha architectures have no condition codes (at least not for integer operations); instead they provide various combination instructions that compare registers against zero or each other, and branch depending on the outcome.

5.5 The Evolution of Processor Architecture

As technology advances, there are occasionally times when it becomes feasible to design machines in a very different way.

During the 1950s and the early 1960s, the instruction set of a typical computer was implemented by soldering together large numbers of discrete components (transistors, capacitors, etc.) that performed the required operations. To build a faster computer, one generally designed new, more powerful instructions, which required extra hardware. This strategy had the unfortunate effect of requiring assembly language programmers (or compiler writers, though there weren't many of them back then) to learn a new language every time a new and better computer came along.

A fundamental breakthrough occurred in the early 1960s, when IBM hit upon the idea of *microprogramming*. Microprogramming allowed a company to provide the *same* instruction set across a whole line of computers, from inexpensive slow machines to expensive fast machines. The basic idea was to build a "micro-engine" in hardware that executed an interpreter program in "firmware." The interpreter in turn implemented the "machine language" of the computer—in this case, the IBM 360 instruction set. More expensive machines had fancier micro-engines, with more direct support for the instructions seen by the assembly-level programmer. The top-of-the-line machines had everything in hardware. In effect, the architecture of the machine became an abstract interface behind which hardware designers could hide implementation details, much as the interfaces of modules in modern programming languages allow software designers to limit the information available to users of an abstraction.

In addition to allowing the introduction of computer families, microprogramming made it comparatively easy for architects to extend the instruction set. Numerous studies were published in which researchers identified some series of instructions that commonly occurred in sequence (e.g., the instructions that jump to a subroutine and update bookkeeping information in the stack), and then introduced a new instruction to perform the same function as the sequence. The new instruction was usually faster than the sequence it replaced, and almost always shorter (and code size was more important then than now).

A second breakthrough occurred in the mid-1970s, when very large scale integration (VLSI) chip technology reached the point at which a simple microprogrammed processor (one whose instructions manipulated eight-bit quantities) could be implemented entirely on one inexpensive chip. The chip boundary is important because it takes much more time and power to drive signals across macroscopic output pins than it does across intrachip connections, and because the number of pins on a chip is limited by packaging issues. With an entire processor on one chip, it became feasible to build a personal computer.

By the early 1980s, several factors converged to make a third breakthrough possible. First, VLSI technology reached the point at which a 32-bit processor with a sufficiently simple instruction set could be implemented on a single chip, *without* microprogramming. Second, improvements in processor speed were beginning to outstrip improvements in memory speed, increasing the relative penalty for accessing memory, and thereby increasing the pressure to keep things in registers. Third, compiler technology had advanced to the point at which compilers could often match (and sometimes exceed) the quality of code produced by the best assembly language programmers. Taken together, these factors suggested a *reduced instruction set computer* (RISC) architecture with a fast, all-hardware implementation, a comparatively low-level instruction set, a large number of registers, and an optimizing compiler.

The advent of RISC machines ran counter to the trend in microprocessor design, but was to a large extent consistent with established trends for supercomputers. Supercomputer instruction sets had always been relatively simple and low-level, in order to facilitate pipelining. Among other things, effective pipelining depends on having most instructions take the same, constant number of cycles to execute, and on minimizing dependences that would prevent a later instruction from starting execution before its predecessors have finished. A major problem with the trend toward more complex instruction sets was that it made it difficult to design high-performance implementations. Instructions on the VAX, for example, can vary in length from one to more than 50 bytes, and in execution time from one to thousands of cycles. Both of these factors tend to lead to pipeline stalls. Variable length instructions make it difficult to even find the next instruction until the current one has been studied extensively. Variable execution time makes it difficult to keep all the pipeline stages busy. The original VAX (the 11/780) was shipped in 1978, but it wasn't until 1985 that Digital was able to ship a successfully pipelined version, the 8600.[2]

A common misconception is that small instruction sets are the distinguishing characteristic of RISC machines. A somewhat better characterization is that RISC machines are machines in which a new instruction can usually be started in every pipeline on every cycle, and in which all possible mechanisms have been exploited to minimize the cycle time (i.e., to maximize the clock rate). Put another way, total execution time on any machine can be expressed as the number of instructions executed times the cycle time times the average number of cycles per instruction. The CISC philosophy is to minimize execution time by reducing the number of instructions. The RISC philosophy is to minimize execution time

---

2 An alternative approach, to maintain microprogramming but pipeline the microengine, was adopted by the 8800 and, more recently, by Intel's Pentium Pro.

by reducing the length of the cycle and the number of (nonoverlapped) cycles per instruction.

We have already seen how pipelining allows us (in the absence of conflicts and dependences) to start a new instruction in every pipeline on every cycle. Cycle time is then determined by how long it takes to perform the most complex subtask that may be required in any pipeline stage for any instruction. If we add a new instruction to a nonpipelined machine, the time required to execute that instruction is (to first approximation) independent of the time required to execute all other instructions, since instructions are executed one at a time. If we add a new instruction to a pipelined machine, however, and that instruction requires more time in, say, the integer execution stage than do existing instructions, then we will be forced to slow down the clock, thereby slowing not only the new instruction, but *every* instruction on the machine. This interdependence among instructions motivates the architect to design an instruction set in which almost everything requires the same small amount of work.

When one sees a computer advertised as, say, 300 MHz, that means it executes 300 million cycles per second, but the number has at best only a very rough correspondence to performance. Even on a RISC machine, one cannot assume that cycles per second equals instructions per second. Conflicts and dependences among instructions will periodically force the pipeline to stall. At the same time, most recent processor implementations have more than one pipeline running in parallel. In the absence of dependences, these *superscalar* processors can start *more* than one instruction per cycle. Things are particularly confusing on a CISC machine. The complexity of a CISC instruction set will generally mean fewer instructions executed per second, but each instruction on the average will do more work than it does on a RISC machine. On both classes of machines, the performance achieved in practice will depend critically on the mix of instructions produced by the compiler. Given two machines with identical clock rates but different processors and compilers, the only sure way to tell which will run faster is to run them, on the specific set of applications for which they will be used in practice.

5.5.1 Two Example Architectures: The 680x0 and MIPS

We can illustrate the differences between CISC and RISC machines by examining a representative pair of architectures: the Motorola 680x0 and the MIPS. While the Intel x86 is the most widely used CISC design (in fact, the most widely used processor architecture of any kind), it does not make a very good example. The original model, the 8086, was announced in 1978. Major changes introduced by the 8087, 80286, and 80386, while technically backward compatible, were often out of keeping with the philosophy of the earlier generations. The result is a machine with an enormous number of nonorthogonal features and special cases. The Motorola 68000, introduced in 1979 as a noncompatible successor to the earlier 6800, has also been extended several times, but in a much more consistent fashion. Its features reflect the same basic philosophy as the less idiosyncratic parts of the x86, but are substantially easier to explain. The 680x0 was the processor of choice for engineering workstations in the 1980s, and was adopted by Apple for the original Macintosh. It has since been replaced for these purposes by various RISC machines, but remains popular in embedded (device-control) applications. All models of the 680x0 are microprogrammed.

In comparison to CISC machines, RISC machines display comparatively little variation among competing architectures. The MIPS architecture, begun as a commercial spin-off of research at Stanford University, is one of the simplest of the major commercial alternatives. It too has evolved, through four generations as of 1999, but with one exception—a jump to 64-bit integer operands and addresses in 1991—the changes have been relatively minor. MIPS processors were used by Digital Equipment Corp. for a few years prior to the development of the Alpha architecture, and by Silicon Graphics, Inc. throughout the 1990s (SGI plans to switch to Intel processors around the turn of the century). MIPS-based tools are widely used in academia. All models of the MIPS are implemented entirely in hardware; they are not microprogrammed.

Memory Access and Addressing Modes

Like all RISC machines, the MIPS has a load/store architecture. Its memory access instructions provide only register indirect and displacement addressing modes (some RISC machines provide more), plus absolute addressing for locations in the first 64K of memory. On the 680x0, by contrast, most instructions can obtain one (but not both) of their operands from memory. Twelve different addressing modes are available for these references, with three additional modes to specify the targets of branches. MIPS instructions are three-address. 680x0 instructions are two-address: the result of a computation overwrites one of the operands, which may be in either a register or memory.

Registers

The 680x0 has 16 32-bit integer registers, plus the program counter and condition codes. The integer registers are divided into two groups, for *data* and *addresses*. The various addressing modes require that base and index values be in address registers. Most of the arithmetic and logical instructions require that operands be in data registers. Limiting the registers available for various purposes allows a register name to be encoded in only three bits. Address register a7 is reserved for the stack pointer. It is treated specially by instructions to call and return from subroutines, and to allocate and deallocate activation records. Multiply and divide instructions have the option of specifying an arbitrary *pair* of registers (rather than a single register) for a 64-bit product or a quotient/remainder pair.

Floating-point support for the 680x0 is provided by an optional coprocessor, the 68881 or 68882. The coprocessor provides a set of seven 80-bit extended precision floating-point data registers, a second set of condition codes, and two control and status registers that alter the behavior of floating-point arithmetic, or provide additional information about the outcome of recent operations. The separate set of condition codes is required because the coprocessor executes concurrently with the main processor. Branches based on the outcome of integer operations use the regular condition codes; branches based on the outcome of floating-point operations use the floating-point condition codes. Both the 6888x and the MIPS implement the IEEE 754 floating-point standard.

The MIPS has a total of 64 registers, 32 integer and 32 floating-point, plus the program counter, a pair of special registers, called LO and HI, used by multiply and divide instructions, a floating-point control and status register analogous to the ones on the 6888x, and an eight-bit floating-point condition code register. The segregation of integer and floating-point registers economizes on encoding space: the opcode indicates whether an operation takes integer or floating-point operands, and then five bits suffice to specify an operand register, instead of six. In addition, as on the 680x0, the separate register sets allow separate integer and floating-point pipelines to operate concurrently without interference, except when an instruction attempts to copy a value between the two register sets. In early generations of the MIPS, integer registers were 32 bits long; in more recent generations they are 64. Double-precision (64-bit) floating-point has always been available, but in early generations it required that the floating-point registers be grouped together in pairs. Branches based on the outcome of floating-point operations use the floating-point condition codes. Other branches employ combination instructions that test or compare values in registers and branch based on the outcome; there are no integer condition codes.

Integer register r0 on the MIPS always contains a zero. This design trick allows several simplifications in instruction encoding. Where the 680x0 provides a clear (clr) instruction, for example, the MIPS achieves the same effect by copying from r0 to the desired location. Similarly, absolute addressing (in the low 64K of memory) is really just 16-bit displacement addressing with respect to register r0. The only other nonorthogonal characteristic of the register set lies in the handling of return addresses: the jump and link (jal—call) instruction places its return address in register r31.

Integer multiply instructions on the MIPS write their results to registers LO and HI (with n-bit operands, the result of a multiply may require $2n$ bits). Divides always generate both a quotient and a remainder, in LO and HI respectively. Special move instructions copy from LO and/or HI to/from integer registers.

The register sets of the two machines are illustrated pictorially in Figure 5.7. The most striking difference between the two is the sheer number of registers on the RISC machine—nearly three times as many as on the CISC machine. The integer registers are also wider on the MIPS, but this is a simple artifact of time: the 68000 was one of the first machines to make the jump from 16- to 32-bit registers, in 1979. The MIPS when first introduced had 32-bit integer registers as well.

Beyond the special treatment given some registers in hardware, the designers of both the 680x0 and the MIPS recommend additional conventions to be

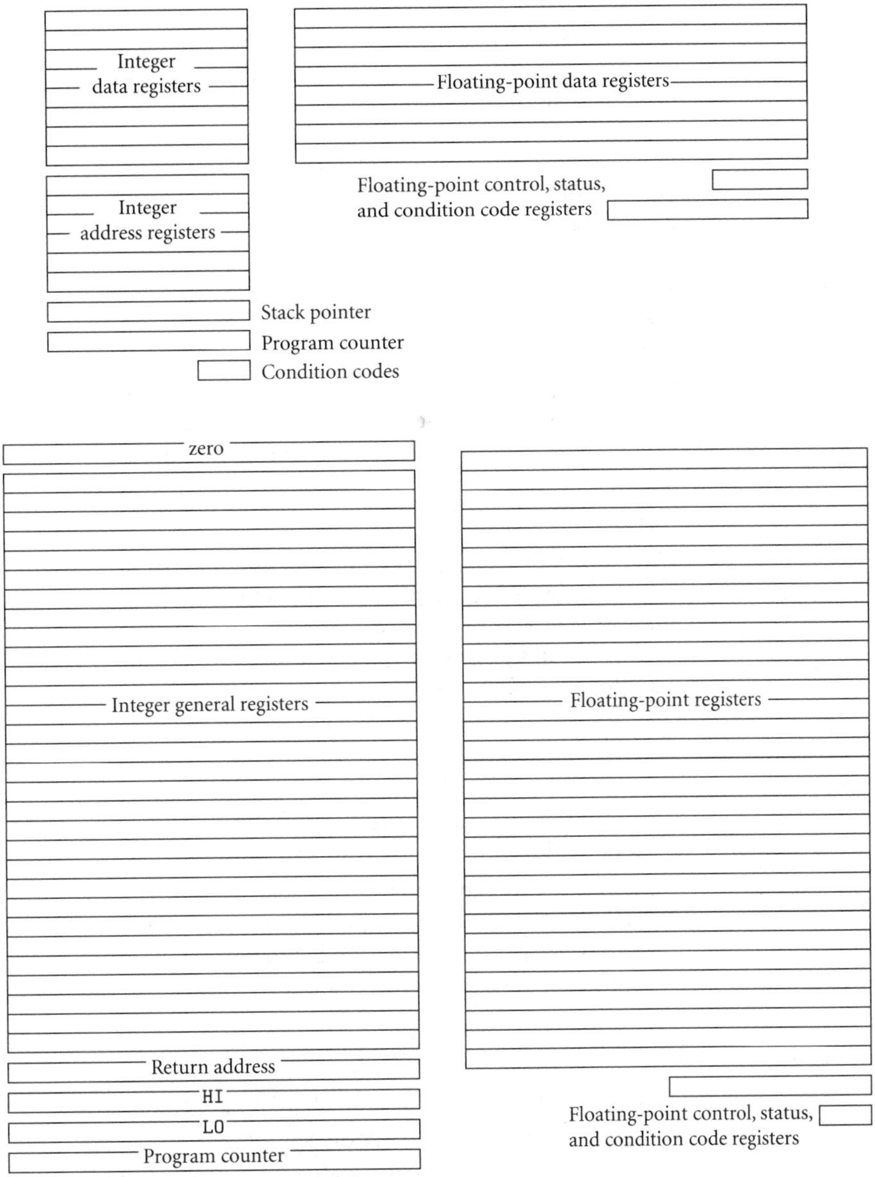

Integer
data registers

Floating-point data registers

Integer
address registers

Floating-point control, status,
and condition code registers

Stack pointer
Program counter
Condition codes

zero

Integer general registers

Floating-point registers

Return address
HI
LO
Program counter

Floating-point control, status,
and condition code registers

Figure 5.7 Register sets of the Motorola 680x0 (top, with 6888x floating-point processor included) and MIPS IV (bottom). In both cases, only those registers of interest to the user-level programmer are shown. Both architectures provide many additional registers of use to the operating system.

enforced by software. On the 680x0, register a6 is generally used for a frame pointer, and function values are returned in register d0 (or in the pair d0:d1 in the case of 64-bit return values). On the MIPS, the conventions are much more elaborate. Register r1 is reserved for use as a temporary in common two or three-instruction sequences. Registers r2 and r3 are used for expression evaluation and function returns. Registers r4..r7 are used for subroutine parameters. Registers r8..r15, r24, and r25 are used for values that the callee need not save across subroutine calls (and that must therefore be saved by the caller if desired). Registers r16..r23 are used for values that the callee must save and restore. (Calling sequences will be discussed in more detail in Section 5.6.2.) Registers r26 and r27 are reserved for use by the operating system kernel; from the point of view of a user program their values can change spontaneously. Register r28 is used as a base for displacement addressing of global variables. Registers r29 and r30 are used for the stack pointer and frame pointer, respectively.

Instructions

While it can be difficult to count the instructions in a given instruction set (the 680x0 can branch on any of 14 different combinations of the condition codes; does this mean it has 14 conditional branch instructions, or one with 14 variants?), it is still clear that the 680x0 has more, and more complex, instructions than does the MIPS. Some of the features of the 680x0 not found in the MIPS include:

- Binary-coded decimal arithmetic.
- Bit field operations. These provide a fast and concise alternative to various combinations of ands, ors, and shifts.
- Miscellaneous "combination" instructions. These perform the same task as some multi-instruction sequence, but require less code space and presumably run faster. Examples include byte and register swaps, array bounds checks, subroutine calls and returns, stack operations, and loop control.

On the other hand, the MIPS provides:

- "Building-block" instructions that allow a 32-bit quantity to be loaded into a register with a two-instruction sequence.
- Separate 32- and 64-bit versions of most of the arithmetic, logical, and memory-access (load/store) instructions.
- Nullifying branches (to be discussed in Section 5.6.1).
- Conditional traps. These are in some sense a generalization of the array bounds-checking instructions of the 680x0; they provide a fast way to drop into the operating system on a dynamic semantic error.

More important than any difference in the number or types of instructions, however, is the difference in how those instructions are encoded. Like most CISC

```
      f1 := 0
      goto L2
L1:   f2 := *r1           −− load
      f1 := f1 + f2
      r1 := r1 + 8         −− floating-point numbers are 8 bytes long
      r2 := r2 − 1
L2:   if r2 > 0 goto L1
```

Figure 5.8 Example of pseudo-assembler notation. The code shown sums the elements of a floating-point vector of length n. At the beginning, register r1 is assumed to point to the vector and register r2 is assumed to contain n. At the end, register f1 contains the sum.

machines, the 680x0 places a heavy premium on minimizing code size (and thus the need for memory at run time), at the expense of comparatively difficult instruction decoding. Instructions range from 2 to 22 bytes in length. The first word (2 bytes) always specifies the opcode and the number of additional words. Depending on the instruction and the addressing modes of operands, the additional words may contain constants, addresses, offsets, bit field specifications, or any of several other special types of data.

Like most RISC machines, the MIPS employs fixed-length, 32-bit instructions with relatively simple encodings. The first six bits specify the opcode. The remaining bits contain (1) a 26-bit jump displacement, (2) a pair of register specifiers and a 16-bit constant, or (3) three register specifiers and 11 additional bits, some of which are used by special-purpose instructions.

Many of the register-register operations contain unused bits, and operations that might be specified with, say, 48 bits on the 680x0 require two full instructions (64 bits) on the MIPS.

5.5.2 Pseudoassembler Notation

At various times throughout the remainder of this book, we will need to consider sequences of machine instructions corresponding to some high-level language construct. Rather than present these sequences in the assembly language of some particular processor architecture, we will (in most cases) rely on a simple notation designed to represent a generic RISC machine. A simple example of this notation appears in Figure 5.8.

The notation is meant to be as self-explanatory as possible. Unless otherwise noted, each line of code corresponds to a single instruction. There are no control-flow constructs other than gotos and subroutine calls. A statement may be preceded by a label (a name followed by a colon), in order to serve as the target of a goto or call. As in Ada, comments begin with −− and run through end-of-line.

Unless otherwise noted, we will assume an unlimited number of registers. These come in two classes, one for integer values and addresses, the other for (double-precision) floating-point values. The integer registers are named r1, r2, ... The floating-point registers are named f1, f2, ... In addition, four integer registers have special names:

sp: The stack pointer. Points by convention at the first unused word on the program's main stack.

fp: The frame pointer. Points by convention at the activation record (stack frame) of the current subroutine.

gp: The globals pointer. Points by convention at the program's global variables.

ra: The return address. This is the only register treated specially by the hardware: the call instruction places its return address in ra:

```
    call foo
    ...

foo: ...
    goto *ra          -- return from subroutine
```

Load and store instructions look like simple assignments. They can use either of two addressing modes: register indirect and displacement. Register indirect addressing was used for the load in Figure 5.8. Displacement addressing allows a small constant to be added to (or subtracted from) the base address contained in a register:

```
r1 := *(fp−12)     -- load from 12 bytes into activation record
r2 := *(gp+132)   -- load from 132 bytes into global variables
```

Most assembly languages use separate load and store instructions for different sizes of operands. Unless otherwise noted, we will assume that a load or store of an integer register moves four bytes, while a load or store of a floating-point register moves eight bytes. In some cases we will simplify the notation by using a "pointer to record" notation, or even just a name:

```
r1 := r2→field     -- load
my_var := r3       -- store
```

If my_var is a local variable, then the second instruction is shorthand for displacement addressing at an appropriate offset from the stack or frame pointer; if my_var is a global variable, then the offset is with respect to the globals pointer.

Register–register moves also look like simple assignments. Arithmetic and logical operations look like an assignment whose left-hand side is a register and whose right-hand side is an operator applied to registers:

```
r1 := r2 ^ r3        -- exclusive or
r1 := -r1            -- negation
```

We will borrow the set of operators from C; it has a nice rich set (see Figure 6.1, page 253).

For control flow we will assume that the hardware can perform a comparison and branch in a single instruction, where the comparison tests the contents of a register against a small constant, or the contents of another register. Unless otherwise noted, we will ignore the issue of load and branch delays. In particular, we will assume (unless otherwise noted) that there are no architecturally visible load or branch delay slots. (The subject of delays will be addressed in Section 5.6.1).

5.6 Compiling for Modern Processors

Programming a RISC machine by hand, in assembly language, is a tedious undertaking. Only loads and stores can access memory, and then only with limited addressing modes. Moreover the limited space available in fixed-size instructions means that a nonintuitive two-instruction sequence is required to load a 32-bit constant or to jump to an absolute address. In some sense, complexity that used to be hidden in the microcode of CISC machines has been exported to the compiler.

Fortunately, most of the code for modern processors is generated by compilers, which don't get bored or make careless mistakes, and can easily deal with comparatively primitive instructions. In fact, when compiling for recent implementations of the Pentium architecture, compilers generally limit themselves to a small, RISC-like subset of the instruction set, which the processor can pipeline effectively. Old programs that make use of more complex instructions still run, but not as fast; they don't take full advantage of the hardware.

The real difficulty in compiling for modern processors lies not in the need to use primitive instructions, but in the need to keep the pipeline full and to make effective use of registers. A user who trades in a 486-based PC for one with a Pentium II will typically find that while old programs do run faster on the new machine, the speed improvement is seldom as dramatic as the difference in clock rates would lead one to expect. Improvements will generally be much better if one is able to obtain new program versions that have been compiled with the newer processor in mind.

5.6.1 Keeping the Pipeline Full

Four main problems may cause a pipelined processor to stall:

1. A load instruction may miss in the cache.

2. Two concurrently executing instructions may *conflict*, in the sense that they need to use the same functional unit at the same time.

3. An instruction may need data that has not yet been produced by an earlier but still executing instruction.

4. Until the outcome (and target) of a branch instruction are determined, the processor does not know the location from which to fetch subsequent instructions.

Problem (1) is usually addressed by building larger or more highly associative caches; most current compilers simply assume that every load will hit in the cache, and accept the resulting stalls when the assumption is incorrect. Problem (2) can also be solved, albeit at some expense, by building extra hardware. Most processors, for example, have two connections to memory (cache), so that the memory access stage of the pipeline can load or store a value at the same time that the instruction fetch stage of the pipeline is loading a later instruction. The situation shown in Figure 5.3, in which the execute stage of the pipeline needs more than one cycle for certain instructions, can be avoided by moving slower operations to a separate functional unit in a separate branch of the pipeline. This approach is commonly taken for floating-point arithmetic. To avoid conflicts in the writeback (store results) stage of the pipeline, the floating-point unit employs a separate set of registers and a separate write-back unit. Because integer multiplication and division are significantly more time-consuming than other arithmetic operations, they cannot generally be handled by the standard integer execute unit. Some RISC machines provide separate functional units for these operations; others perform them in the floating-point unit.

Problem (2) also arises in superscalar processors, which do not generally duplicate all of the execution logic. A two-way superscalar processor, for example, might provide two copies of the functional units for instruction fetch, instruction decode, integer execute, and writeback, but only one unit each for floating-point operations and memory access. To keep the pipelines full we must choose an order for instructions that not only computes the correct result, but also avoids consecutive floating-point instructions and consecutive loads and stores. Many superscalar processors incorporate special hardware that will reorder instructions on-the-fly to eliminate conflicts, so long as it can guarantee that the new order will compute the same results. This technique is known as *out-of-order* execution. On other machines the compiler must choose a good instruction order statically.

Problem (3) above can sometimes be addressed in hardware, for example by "forwarding" the output of the execute stage of one instruction directly into the execute stage of the following instruction, without going through the registers. This technique does not help, however, if a result has not yet been produced by the time that it is needed. In our simple example pipeline, a stall may still occur if a load instruction is followed by an instruction that needs the loaded value, since the memory access stage of the first instruction will occupy the same time slot as the execute stage of the second (Figure 5.9). A stall may also occur when

TIME ⟶

r1 := X (load)	fetch inst.	decode inst.	execute op.	access memory	store result	
r3 := r1 + r2		fetch inst.	decode inst.	[ ]	execute op.	access memory	store result
			fetch inst.	[ ]	decode inst.	execute op.	access memory	...
				[ ]	fetch inst.	decode inst.	execute op.	...
					fetch inst.	decode inst.	...

Figure 5.9 Load penalty pipeline stall. When the second instruction attempts to use r1, it must wait until the end of the first instruction's memory access stage, incurring a one-cycle penalty. No instruction starts in cycle 4.

the result of a slow-to-complete floating-point operation is needed too soon by another instruction, or when there is a data dependence among concurrently executing instructions on a superscalar processor.

The general technique of reordering instructions at compile time so as to maximize processor performance is known as *instruction scheduling*. On a machine that executes instructions in the order provided by the compiler, the goal of instruction scheduling is to identify a valid order that will minimize pipeline stalls. To achieve this goal the compiler requires a detailed model of the processor. On a machine that is capable of out-of-order instruction execution, the goal of instruction scheduling is simply to maximize *instruction-level parallelism* (ILP): the degree to which unrelated instructions lie near one another in the instruction stream. A compiler for such a machine may be able to make do with a less detailed processor model. At the same time, it may need to ensure a higher degree of ILP, since out-of-order execution tends to be found on machines with several pipelines.

Problem (4) has a large potential performance penalty: as illustrated in Figure 5.10, a naive implementation of our example pipeline would stall the processor for three cycles on every branch, in order to allow the new PC to be computed. Hardware tricks can reduce this to a single cycle, but a longer pipeline would lengthen it again, and there is no way to eliminate it entirely. The most effective solution in practice is for the hardware to *predict* the outcome of the branch, based on past behavior, and to execute speculatively down the predicted path. Assuming that it takes care to avoid any irreversible operations, the processor will then suffer stalls only in the case of an incorrect prediction. Again, the compiler can help, either by identifying instructions that can be executed regardless of the direction of the branch, or by predicting the outcome of certain branches statically.

TIME ⟶

fetch inst.	decode inst.	execute op.	update PC	store result				
	fetch inst.	[ ]	[ ]	fetch inst.	decode inst.	execute op.	access memory	store result
				fetch inst.	decode inst.	execute op.	...	
					fetch inst.	decode inst.	...	

Figure 5.10 Branch penalty pipeline stall. When the first instruction is found to be a branch (at the end of the decode stage), a naive implementation would abandon the second instruction and wait until the PC is determined at the end of the memory access/update PC stage, thereby incurring a three-cycle penalty.

Of the various instructions that can cause a pipeline stall, loads and branches are by far the most common, and it is to these that we devote our attention for the remainder of this section.

Loads

In our simple example pipeline, a load instruction uses the execute stage of the pipeline to perform the address arithmetic required for displacement or indexed addressing. The memory access stage is then used to read data from the cache. If a cache miss occurs, the pipeline will stall while data is read from memory. Cache misses need to be rare, since memory can take scores of cycles to respond. Even with a cache hit, however, data will not be available until the end of the memory access stage. The number of cycles that must elapse before a subsequent instruction can use the result of a cache-hit load is known as the *load delay*. Our example pipeline has a one-cycle load delay. If the instruction immediately after a load attempts to use the loaded value, a one-cycle *load penalty* (stall) will occur (Figure 5.9). Longer pipelines can have load delays of two or even three cycles.

To avoid load penalties (in the absence of out-of-order execution), the compiler must schedule one or more unrelated instructions into the *delay slot*(s) between a load and a subsequent use. In the following code, for example, our simple pipeline will incur a one-cycle penalty between the second and third instructions:

```
r2 := r1 + r2
r3 := A            -- load
r3 := r3 + r2
```

If we swap the first two instructions, then the penalty goes away:

```
r3 := A              -- load
r2 := r1 + r2
r3 := r3 + r2
```

The second instruction gives the first instruction time enough to retrieve A before it is needed in the third instruction.

To maintain program correctness, an instruction-scheduling algorithm must respect all *dependences* among instructions. These dependences come in three varieties:

1. *flow* dependence (also called *true* or *read-write* dependence): a later instruction uses a value produced by an earlier instruction.
2. *anti*-dependence (also called *read-write* dependence): a later instruction overwrites a value read by an earlier instruction.
3. *output* dependence (also called *write-write* dependence): a later instruction overwrites a value written by a previous instruction.

Anti-dependences and output dependences can always be eliminated by *renaming* registers. In the following, for example, anti-dependences prevent us from moving either the instruction before the load or the one after the add into the delay slot of the load:

```
r3 := r1 + 3         -- immovable ⚹
r1 := A              -- load
r2 := r1 + r2
r1 := 3              -- immovable ⚹
```

If we use a different register as the target of the load, however, then either instruction can be moved:

```
r3 := r1 + 3         -- movable ↓
r5 := A              -- load
r2 := r5 + r2
r1 := 3              -- movable ↑
```

The need to rename registers in order to move instructions can increase the number of registers needed by a given stretch of code. To maximize opportunities for out-of-order execution, an increasing number of superscalar processor implementations perform register renaming dynamically in hardware. These processors possess more physical registers than are visible in the instruction set. As instructions are considered for execution, any that use the same architectural register for independent purposes are given separate physical copies on which to do their work. If a processor does not perform hardware register renaming, then the compiler must balance the desire to eliminate pipeline stalls against the desire to minimize the demand for registers (so that they can be used for other purposes).

In order to detect the flow dependence between a load of a register and its subsequent use, a processor must include so-called *interlock* hardware. To minimize chip area, several of the very early RISC processors provided this hardware only in the case of cache misses. The result was an architecturally visible *delayed load* instruction, in which the value of the loaded register was undefined in the immediately subsequent instruction slot. Filling the delay slot of a delayed load with an unrelated instruction was a matter of correctness, not just of performance. If a compiler was unable to find a suitable "real" instruction, it had to fill the delay slot with a *no-op* (nop)—an instruction that has no effect. More recent RISC machines have abandoned delayed loads; their implementations are fully interlocked. Within processor families old binaries continue to work correctly; the (nop) instructions are simply redundant.

Branches

Successful pipelining depends on knowing the address of the next instruction before the current instruction has completed, or has even been fully decoded. With fixed-size instructions a processor can infer this address for straight-line code, but not for the code that follows a branch.[3] As we saw in Figure 5.10, a naive implementation of our simple pipeline would incur a three-cycle penalty on every branch. To reduce this penalty in hardware, we can move most of the work of a branch into the decode stage of the pipeline. Doing so requires an extra adder (the normal one is likely to be in use for the execute stage of another instruction), which computes the target of the branch in parallel with logic to determine if the branch should be taken. At the very end of the stage, the outcome of the test is used to select from among the two possible PC values, both of which have already been computed. A significant amount of extra hardware is required, but since branches constitute something like 15% of all instructions in typical programs,[4] the expenditure seems justified: it yields a performance improvement on the order of 20%.

But even a one-cycle branch delay incurs a serious cost. By removing it we could hope to recoup an additional 13% improvement. Deeper pipelines exacerbate the problem: even with branch computations pushed forward as far as possible, one can easily end up with a two or three cycle branch delay.

Several early RISC machines adopted a *delayed branch* strategy similar to the delayed loads described above. In these machines the instruction immediately after the branch is executed regardless of the outcome of the branch. If the

---

3 In this context, branches include not only the control flow for conditionals and loops, but also subroutine calls and returns.

4 This is a very rough number. For the SPEC benchmarks, Hennessy and Patterson report percentages varying from 4 to 26 [HP96, p. 165].

branch is not taken, all occurs as one would normally expect. If the branch is taken, however, the order of instructions is: the branch itself, the instruction after the branch, and then the instruction at the target of the branch.

Because control may go either of two directions at a branch, finding an instruction to fill a delayed branch slot is slightly trickier than finding one to fill a delayed load slot. The few instructions immediately before the branch are the most obvious candidates for moving, provided that they do not contribute to the calculation that controls the branch, and that we don't have to move them past the target of some other branch:

```
B := r2          -- movable ↓
r1 := r2 * r3    -- immovable ⚹
if r1 > 0 goto L1
nop
```

(This code sequence assumes that branches are delayed. Unless otherwise noted, we will assume throughout the remainder of the book that they are not.)

To address the problem of unfillable branch delay slots, some more recent RISC machines provide *nullifying* conditional branch instructions. A nullifying branch includes a bit that indicates the direction that the compiler "expects" the branch to go. The hardware executes the instruction in the delay slot only if the branch goes the expected direction. While the branch instruction is making its way down the pipeline, the hardware begins to execute the next instruction. Ideally, by the time it must begin the instruction after that, it will know the outcome of the branch. If the outcome matches the prediction, then the pipeline will proceed without stalling. If the outcome does not match the prediction, then the (not yet completed) instruction in the delay slot will be abandoned, incurring a one-cycle penalty.

Unfortunately, as architects have moved to more aggressive, deeply pipelined processor implementations, multi-cycle branch delays have become the norm, and architecturally visible delay slots no longer suffice to hide them. A few processors have been designed with an architecturally visible branch delay of more than one cycle, but this is not generally considered a viable strategy: it is simply too difficult to find enough instructions to schedule into the slots. Several processors retain one-slot delayed branches (sometimes with optional nullification) for the sake of backward compatibility, and as a means of reducing, but not eliminating, branch penalties. With or without delayed branches, many processors also employ elaborate hardware mechanisms to predict the outcome *and targets* of branches early, so that the pipeline can continue anyway. When a prediction turns out to be incorrect, of course, the hardware must ensure that none of the incorrectly fetched instructions have visible effects. Even when hardware is able to predict the outcome of branches, it can be useful for the compiler to do so also, in order to schedule instructions to minimize load delays in the most likely cross-branch code paths. We will return to the topic of instruction scheduling in Section 13.6.

5.6.2 **Register Allocation**

The load/store architecture of RISC machines explicitly acknowledges that moving data between registers and memory is expensive. A store instruction costs a minimum of one cycle—more if several stores are executed in succession and the memory system can't keep up. A load instruction costs a minimum of one or two cycles (depending on whether the delay slot can be filled), and can cost scores of cycles in the event of a cache miss. These same costs are present on many CISC machines (certainly on those that are pipelined and have caches), even if they don't stand out as prominently in a casual perusal of assembly code. In order to minimize the use of loads and stores, a good compiler must keep things in registers whenever possible. We saw an example in Chapter 1: the most striking difference between the "optimized" code on page 1 and the naive code of Figure 1.5 (page 23) is the absence in the former of most of the loads and stores. As improvements in processor speed continue to outstrip improvements in memory speed, the cost in cycles of a cache miss continues to increase, making good register usage increasingly important.

Register allocation is typically a two-stage process. In the first stage the compiler identifies the portions of the abstract syntax tree that represent *basic blocks*: straight-line sequences of code with no branches in or out. Within each basic block it assigns a "virtual register" to each loaded or computed value. In effect, this assignment amounts to generating code under the assumption that the target machine has an unbounded number of registers. In the second stage, the compiler maps virtual registers of an entire subroutine onto the physical, hardware registers of the machine, using the same physical register when possible to hold different virtual registers at different times, and *spilling* virtual registers to memory when there aren't enough physical registers to go around.

We will examine this two-stage process in more detail in Section 13.8. For now, we illustrate the ideas with a simple example. Suppose we are compiling a function that computes the dot product of two n-element floating-point vectors:

```
dp := 0
for i in 1..n do
    dp +:= A[i] × B[i]
```

After some simple code improvements and the assignment of virtual registers, the assembly language for this function on a RISC machine is likely to look something like the code in Figure 5.11. This code uses three integer virtual registers and four floating-point virtual registers. For each of these we can compute the range over which the value in the register is useful, or *live*. This range extends from the point at which the value is defined to the last point at which the value is used. For register f3, for example, the range is only one instruction long, from the assignment at line 7 to the use at line 8. For register r3, the range is the union of two subranges, one that extends from the assignment at line 3 to the use (and

```
 1.        r1 := &A              -- pointer to A[1]
 2.        r2 := &B              -- pointer to B[1]
 3.        r3 := n               -- count of elements yet to go
 4.        f1 := 0               -- accumulated dot product (floating-point)
 5.        goto L2
 6.  L1:  f2 := *r1             -- A[i] (floating-point)
 7.        f3 := *r2             -- B[i] (floating-point)
 8.        f4 := f2 × f3
 9.        f1 := f1 + f4
10.        r1 := r1 + 8          -- 8 bytes per double-word
11.        r2 := r2 + 8
12.        r3 := r3 - 1
13.  L2:  if r3 <> 0 goto L1
14.        . . .                 -- return value in f1
```

Figure 5.11 RISC assembly code for a vector dot product.

redefinition) at line 12, and another that extends from this redefinition around the loop to the same spot again.

Once we have calculated live ranges for all virtual registers we can create a mapping onto the physical registers of the machine. We can use a single physical register for two virtual registers only if their live ranges do not overlap. If the number of physical registers required is larger than the number available on the machine (after reserving a few for special values such as the stack pointer), then at various points in the code we will have to write (*spill*) some of the virtual registers to memory in order to make room for the others. If the number of physical registers required is less than the number available, so much the better: it will reduce the amount of work required for subroutine calls.

In our example program, the live ranges for virtual registers f2 and f4 are disjoint, as are the ranges for f3 and f4. We can therefore use a single physical register to hold both f4 and (one of) f2 or f3. All other virtual registers will need to be mapped to separate physical registers. In all, we will need three physical integer registers and three physical floating-point registers.

Interaction with Instruction Scheduling

From the point of view of execution speed, the code in Figure 5.11 has at least two problems. First, of the eight instructions in the loop, fully half are devoted to bookkeeping: updating the pointers, decrementing the loop count, and testing the terminating condition. Second, when run on a pipelined machine, the code will experience a very high number of stalls.

We noted in Section 5.6.1 that floating-point instructions commonly employ a separate, longer pipeline. Because they take more cycles to complete, there can be

```
 1.       r1 := &A              -- pointer to A[1]
 2.       r2 := &B              -- pointer to B[1]
 3.       r3 := n               -- count of elements yet to go
 4.       f1 := 0               -- accumulated dot product (floating-point)
 5.       goto L2
 6.  L1:  f2 := *r1             -- A[i] (floating-point)
 7.       f3 := *r2             -- B[i] (floating-point)
 8.       r1 := r1 + 8
 9.       f4 := f2 × f3
10.       r2 := r2 + 8
11.       r3 := r3 − 1
12.       f1 := f1 + f4
13.  L2:  if r3 <> 0 goto L1
14.       . . .                 -- return value in f1
```

Figure 5.12 The dot product with instruction scheduling. With a four-cycle multiply delay, the add at line 12 will still stall for two cycles while waiting for the result of the multiply at line 9 to appear in register f4.

a significant delay before their results are available for use in other instructions. Suppose that floating-point add and multiply instructions must be followed by two and four cycles, respectively, of unrelated computation (these are modest figures; real machines often have longer delays). Also suppose that the result of a load is not available for the usual one-cycle delay. To keep things from getting too complicated, suppose that the hardware successfully predicts the outcome and target of the branch at the bottom of the loop, so that no additional delay occurs there. In the code in Figure 5.11, the pipeline will stall for one cycle before the multiply at line 8 (a load delay) and for four cycles before the add at line 9 (a multiply delay). Added to the eight instructions, this implies a total of 13 cycles per loop iteration (i.e., per vector element). By rescheduling the instructions in the loop (Figure 5.12) we can reduce this total to 10 cycles per vector element. In this case the number of physical registers required—three integer and three floating-point—remains the same. In general, however, we will find that instruction scheduling has a tendency to overlap the live ranges of virtual registers whose ranges were previously disjoint, leading to an increase in the number of physical registers required.

An example of this tension between register allocation and instruction scheduling appears if we attempt to improve further the performance of our dot product function. To reduce the per-element loop overhead, we can apply a common code improvement technique known as *loop unrolling*. (We will discuss this technique in more detail in Section 13.7.) We replicate the code in the body of the loop m times, and then iterate over the expanded body $\lfloor n/m \rfloor$ times. To make sure in the general case that the overall effect remains the same, we must

```
 1.        r1 := &A                    -- pointer to A[1]
 2.        r2 := &B                    -- pointer to B[1]
 3.        r3 := n                     -- count of elements yet to go
 4.        f1 := 0                     -- accumulated dot product (floating-point)
 5.        goto L2
 6.  L1:   f2 := *r1                   -- A[i]
 7.        f3 := *r2                   -- B[i]
 8.        f4 := f2 × f3
 9.        f1 := f1 + f4
10.        f5 := *(r1+8)               -- A[i+1]
11.        f6 := *(r2+8)               -- B[i+1]
12.        f7 := f5 × f6
13.        f1 := f1 + f7
14.        r1 := r1 + 16               -- 8 bytes per double-word,
15.        r2 := r2 + 16               -- 2 double-words per iteration
16.        r3 := r3 - 2
17.  L2:   if r3 <> 0 goto L1
18.        . . .                       -- return value in f1
```

Figure 5.13 Dot product code, unrolled twice.

precede or follow the unrolled loop with a copy of the original loop that iterates
n mod m times. Though it obviously increases code size, loop unrolling reduces
the number of tests, branches, and related bookkeeping by a factor of m. It also
increases opportunities for instruction scheduling within the body of the loop.

If we assume for simplicity that n is evenly divisible by two, and we unroll our
loop twice ($m = 2$), we obtain the code in Figure 5.13. As before, we have used
a separate virtual register for each loaded or computed value. Because there is
more computation in the unrolled loop than there was in the original version,
we now require seven floating-point virtual registers instead of only four. Note
that we update r1, r2, and r3 only once in each iteration of the unrolled loop.
The loads at lines 10 and 11 must therefore use displacement addressing instead
of register indirect.

If we calculate live ranges for the virtual registers in our unrolled loop, we
discover that a single physical register can cover virtual registers f2, f4, f5, and
f7, and that another can cover f3 and f6, allowing us to get by with only three
physical floating-point registers. This result is not surprising: we already knew
that we could make do with three in the original version of the loop.

But what of instruction scheduling? In the (unscheduled) code in Figure 5.13,
the pipeline will stall for one cycle before the multiply instructions at lines 8
and 12 (load delays) and for four cycles before the add instructions at lines 9
and 13 (multiply delays). These stalls contribute to an overall time of 22 cycles
per (double) iteration, or 11 cycles per vector element. If we schedule instruc-

```
 1.        r1 := &A              -- pointer to A[1]
 2.        r2 := &B              -- pointer to B[1]
 3.        r3 := n               -- count of elements yet to go
 4.        f1 := 0               -- accumulated dot product (floating-point)
 5.        goto L2
 6.  L1: f2 := *r1               -- A[i]
 7.       f3 := *r2              -- B[i]
 8.       f5 := *(r1+8)          -- A[i+1]
 9.       f4 := f2 × f3
10.       f6 := *(r2+8)          -- B[i+1]
11.       r1 := r1 + 16
12.       f7 := f5 × f6
13.       r2 := r2 + 16
14.       f1 := f1 + f4
15.       r3 := r3 − 2
16.       f1 := f1 + f7
17.  L2: if r3 <> 0 goto L1
18.       . . .                  -- return value in f1
```

Figure 5.14 Dot product code, unrolled twice and scheduled. Here the only instruction that will stall is the add at line 16: its argument f1 is not available until three cycles after the add at line 14.

tions carefully (Figure 5.14) we can eliminate 9 of the 10 stalls, for an overall time of 13 cycles per (double) iteration, or 6.5 cycles per vector element, a 35% improvement over the scheduled version of the original loop (Figure 5.12). Unfortunately, the intermingling of instructions from the unrolled iterations has caused the live ranges of the virtual registers to overlap more than before. Where once we could cover virtual registers f2, f3, f4, f5, f6, and f7 with only two physical registers, now we require three. (Under certain circumstances, it may be possible to eliminate the remaining stalls in both the original and unrolled versions of the loop, by scheduling instructions across the branch at the bottom of the loop. We explore this possibility in Exercise 5.15. In Section 13.7 we will consider a technique known as *software pipelining*, which does an even better job of facilitating instruction scheduling.)

The Impact of Subroutine Calls

The register allocation scheme outlined above depends implicitly on the compiler being able to see all of the code that will be executed over a given span of time (e.g., an invocation of a subroutine). But what if that code includes calls to other subroutines? If a subroutine were called from only one place in the program, we could allocate registers (and schedule instructions) across both the caller and the callee, effectively treating them as a single unit. Most of the time, however, a subroutine is called from many different places in a program, and the code improvements that we should like to make in the context of one caller will be different from the ones that we should like to make in the context of a different caller. For small, simple subroutines, the compiler may actually choose to expand a copy of the code at each call site, despite the resulting increase in code size. This *inlining* of subroutines can be an important form of code improvement, particularly for object-oriented languages, which tend to have very large numbers of very simple subroutines.

When inlining is not an option, most compilers treat each subroutine as an independent unit. When a body of code for which we are attempting to perform register allocation makes a call to a subroutine, there are several issues to consider:

- Parameters must generally be passed. Ideally, we should like to pass them in registers.
- Any registers that the callee will use internally, but which contain useful values in the caller, must be spilled to memory and then reread when the callee returns.
- Any variables that the callee might load from memory, but which have been kept in a register in the caller, must be written back to memory before the call, so that the callee will see the current value.
- Any variables to which the callee might store a value in memory, but which have been kept in a register in the caller, must be reread from memory when the callee returns, so that the caller will see the current value.

If the caller does not know exactly what the callee might do (this is often the case—the callee might not have been compiled yet), then the compiler must make conservative assumptions. In particular, it must assume that the callee reads and writes *every* variable visible in its scope. The caller must write any such variable back to memory prior to the call, if its current value is (only) in a register. If it needs the value of such a variable after the call, it must reread it from memory. In a language such as C, in which pointer arithmetic can allow a callee to access any location in memory, the compiler must assume that a not-yet-compiled callee will access every variable in the program.

With perfect knowledge of both the caller and the callee, the compiler could arrange across subroutine calls to save and restore precisely those registers that are both in use in the caller and needed (for internal purposes) in the callee. Without this knowledge, we can choose either for the caller to save and restore the registers it is using, before and after the call, or for the callee to save and restore the registers it needs internally, at the top and bottom of the subroutine. In practice it is conventional to choose the latter alternative for at least some static subset of the register set, for two reasons. First, while a subroutine may be called from many locations, there is only one copy of the subroutine itself. Saving and restoring registers in the callee, rather than the caller, can save substantially on

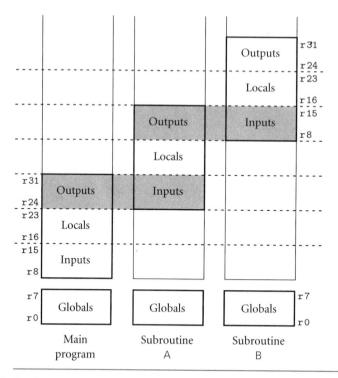

Figure 5.15 Register windows. When the main program calls subroutine A, and again when A calls B, register names r0–r7 continue to refer to the same locations, but register names r8–r31 are changed to refer to a new, overlapping window. High-numbered registers in the caller share locations with low-numbered registers in the callee.

code size. Second, because many subroutines (particularly those that are called most frequently) are very small and simple, the set of registers used in the callee tends, on average, to be smaller than the set in use in the caller. We will look at subroutine *calling sequences* in more detail in Chapter 8.

As an alternative to saving and restoring registers on subroutine calls and returns, the original Berkeley RISC machines [PD80, Pat85] incorporated a hardware mechanism known as *register windows*. The basic idea is to provide a very large set of physical registers, most of which are organized as a collection of overlapping windows (Figure 5.15). A few register names (r0–r7 in the figure) always refer to the same locations, but the rest (r8–r31 in the figure) are interpreted relative to the currently active window. On a subroutine call, the hardware moves to a different window. To facilitate the passing of parameters, the old and new windows overlap: the top few registers in the caller's window (r24–r31 in the figure) are the same as the bottom few registers in the callee's window (r8–r15 in the figure). On a machine with register windows, the compiler places values of use only within the current subroutine in the middle part of the window. It moves values to the upper part of the window to pass them to a subroutine, within which they are read from the lower part of the window.

Since the number of physical windows is fixed, a long chain of subroutine calls can cause the hardware to run off the end of the register set, resulting in a "window overflow" interrupt that drops the processor into the operating system. The interrupt handler then treats the set of available windows as a circular buffer. It copies the contents of one or more windows to memory and then resumes execution. Later, a "window underflow" interrupt will occur when control attempts to return into a window whose contents have been written to memory. Again the operating system recovers, by restoring the saved registers and resuming execution. In practice, eight windows appear to suffice to make overflow and underflow relatively rare on typical programs.

Register windows have been used in several RISC processors, but only one of these, the Sparc, is commercially significant today. The advantage of windows, of course, is that they reduce the amount of memory traffic on subroutine calls. At the same time, the very large register set occupies chip area that other processors can use for other purposes (caches, more aggressive pipelines, more or faster functional units, etc.). More significantly, register windows significantly increase the amount of state associated with the currently running program. When the operating system decides to give the processor to a different application for a while (something that most systems do several times per second), it must save all of this state to memory or arrange for the processor to trap back into the OS if the new process attempts to access an unsaved window. Worse, while register windows nicely capture the referencing environment of a single thread of control, they do not work well for languages that need more than one referencing environment. Several language features to be considered in future chapters, including continuations (Section 6.2), iterators (Section 6.5.3), and coroutines (Section 8.6), are very hard to implement on a machine with register windows. It is questionable whether the cost of these complications outweighs the advantage of avoiding memory traffic on subroutine calls, particularly when most of that traffic consists of cache hits.

An attractive alternative to register windows is to perform register allocation across subroutine calls. Code improvement techniques that consider the entire body of a subroutine (as opposed to just one basic block) are often referred to as "global optimizations." The term is somewhat confusing, not only because the techniques are seldom truly optimizations (they don't produce the *best* code, just reasonably good) but also because "global" does *not* refer to the program as a whole. To further reduce the impact of subroutine calls, not only for register allocation but also for instruction scheduling and for several other important forms of code improvement, much of the recent research in compiler technology has been aimed at "truly global" techniques, known as *interprocedural optimizations*. Since programmers are generally unwilling to give up separate compilation (recompiling hundreds of thousands of lines of code is a very time-consuming operation), a practical interprocedural code improver must do much of its work at link time. One of the (many) challenges to be overcome is to develop a division of labor and an intermediate representation that allow the compiler to do as much work as possible during (separate) compilation, but leave enough of the details undecided that the link-time code improver is able to do its job.

5.7 Summary and Concluding Remarks

Computer architecture has a major impact on the sort of code that a compiler must generate, and the sorts of code improvements it must effect in order to obtain acceptable performance. Since the early 1980s, the trend in processor design has been to equip the compiler with more and more knowledge of the low-level details of processor implementation, so that the generated code can use the implementation to its fullest. This trend has blurred the traditional dividing line between processor architecture and implementation: while a compiler can generate correct code based on an understanding of the architecture alone, it cannot generate fast code unless it understands the implementation as well. In effect, timing issues that were once hidden in the microcode of microprogrammed processors (and which made microprogramming an extremely difficult and arcane craft) have now been exported into the compiler.

In the first several sections of this chapter we surveyed the macroarchitecture of a typical workstation-class computer, the organization of memory and the representation of data (including integer and floating-point arithmetic), the variety of typical assembly language instructions, and the evolution of modern RISC machines. As examples we compared the Motorola 680x0 and the MIPS. We also introduced a simple notation to be used for assembly language examples in later chapters. In the final major section we discussed why compiling for modern machines is hard. The principal tasks include *instruction scheduling*, for load and branch delays and for multiple functional units, and *register allocation*, to minimize memory traffic. We noted that there is often a tension between these tasks, and that both are made more difficult by frequent subroutine calls.

As of 1999 there are five principal commercial RISC architectures: Alpha (Digital/Compaq), MIPS (SGI, NEC), PA-RISC (Hewlett-Packard), PowerPC (IBM, Motorola, Apple), and Sparc (Sun, Texas Instruments, Fujitsu). In addition the x86 CISC architecture (Intel, AMD, Cyrix) continues to evolve, with the more recent Pentium implementations providing performance only slightly below that of RISC machines of comparable cost, and with 64-bit Merced processors scheduled to become available around the time this text is published.

As processor and compiler technology continue to evolve, it is likely that processor implementations will continue to become more complex, and that compilers will take on additional tasks in order to harness that complexity. What is not clear at this point is the form that processor complexity will take. While traditional CISC machines are definitely giving way to RISC machines, both of the basic design philosophies are still very much alive [SW94]. The "CISC-ish" philosophy says that newly available resources (e.g., increases in chip area) should be used to implement functions that must currently be performed in software, such as vector operations, decimal arithmetic, or new modes of addressing; the "RISC-ish" philosophy says that resources should be used to improve the speed of existing functions, for example by increasing cache size, employing faster but larger functional units, or deepening the pipeline and decreasing the cycle time.

Where the first-generation RISC machines from different vendors differed from one another only in minor details, the more recent generations are beginning to diverge, with the Alpha and MIPS taking the more RISC-ish approach, the PA-RISC and PowerPC taking the more CISC-ish approach, and the Sparc somewhere in the middle. It is not yet clear which approach will prove to be the most effective over the course of the next few years. For both approaches, however, it is clear that processor and compiler technology will continue to develop together.

5.8 Review Questions

5.1   What is the world's most popular instruction set architecture?

5.2   What is the difference between big-endian and little-endian addressing?

5.3   What is the purpose of a cache?

5.4   Why do many machines have more than one *level* of cache?

5.5   How many processor cycles does it typically take to access primary (on-chip) cache? How many cycles does it typically take to access main memory?

5.6   What is data *alignment*? Why do many processors insist upon it?

5.7   List four common formats (interpretations) for bits in memory.

5.8   Explain how to compute the additive inverse (negative) of a two's complement number.

5.9   Explain how to detect overflow in two's complement addition.

5.10   What is IEEE standard number 754? Why is it important?

5.11   What is a floating-point NaN?

5.12   What are the tradeoffs between two-address and three-address instruction formats?

5.13   What is microprogramming? What breakthroughs did its invention make possible?

5.14   What is pipelining?

5.15   List the four principal causes of pipeline stalls.

5.16   Summarize the difference between the CISC and RISC philosophies in instruction set design.

5.17   Why do RISC machines allow only load and store instructions to access memory?

5.18   Name three CISC architectures. Name three RISC architectures.

5.19   What three research groups share the credit for inventing RISC? (See Bibliographic Notes at the end of this chapter.)

5.20   What are condition codes? Why do some architectures not provide them? What do they provide instead?

5.21   Describe at least five different addressing modes. Which of these are commonly supported on RISC machines?

5.22   How can the designer of a pipelined machine cope with instructions (e.g., floating-point arithmetic) that take much longer than others to compute?

5.23   List at least three "complex" instructions provided by the 680x0 instruction set but not provided by the MIPS instruction set.

5.24   What is a *delayed load* instruction?

5.25   What is a *nullifying branch* instruction?

5.26   What is a pipeline *interlock*?

5.27   What is *instruction scheduling*? Why is it important on modern machines?

5.28   What is *branch prediction*? Why is it important?

5.29   Describe the interaction between instruction scheduling and register allocation.

5.30   What is the *live range* of a register?

5.31   What is *loop unrolling*? What benefits does it provide? What is its cost?

5.32   What are *register windows*? Which commercial instruction set includes them? What are their advantages and disadvantages?

5.33   What is *subroutine inlining*? What benefits does it provide? When is it possible? What is its cost?

5.34   Summarize the impact of subroutine calls on register allocation.

5.9 Exercises

5.1   What is the largest positive number in 32-bit two's complement arithmetic? What is the smallest (largest magnitude) negative number? Why are these numbers not the additive inverse of each other?

5.2   Prove that a two's complement addition operation overflows (produces a result that cannot be specified in the available number of bits) if and only if the carry into most significant place differs from the carry out of most significant place, as described in Section 5.3.1.

5.3   What is the single-precision IEEE floating-point number closest to 6.022×10^{23}?

5.4   Occasionally one sees a C program in which a double-precision floating-point number is used as an integer counter. Why might a programmer choose to do this?

5.5   Consider sending a message containing a string of integers over the Internet. What problems may occur if the sending and receiving machines have different "endian-ness"? How might you solve these problems?

5.6   Why do you think RISC machines standardized on 32-bit instructions? Why not some smaller or larger length? Why not variable lengths?

5.7 Consider a machine with three condition codes, N, Z, and O. N indicates whether the most recent arithmetic operation produced a negative result. Z indicates whether it produced a zero result. O indicates whether it produced a result that cannot be represented in the available precision for the numbers being manipulated (i.e., outside the range $0..2^n$ for unsigned arithmetic, $-2^{n-1}..2^{n-1}-1$ for signed arithmetic). Suppose we wish to branch on condition A op B, where A and B are unsigned binary numbers, for op $\in \{<, \leq, =, \neq, >, \geq\}$. Suppose we subtract B from A, using two's complement arithmetic. For each of the six conditions, indicate the logical combination of condition-code bits that should be used to trigger the branch. Repeat the exercise on the assumption that A and B are signed, two's complement numbers.

5.8 Write algorithms to convert binary-coded decimal numbers to binary, and vice versa. Try writing the routines in assembly language for your favorite machine (if your machine has special instructions for this purpose, pretend you're not allowed to use them). How many cycles are required for the conversion?

5.9 We indicated in Section 5.5 that if one adds a new instruction to a non-pipelined, microcoded machine, the time required to execute that instruction is (to first approximation) independent of the time required to execute all other instructions. Why is it not strictly independent? What factors could cause overall execution to become slower when a new instruction is introduced?

5.10 Is microprogramming an idea that has outlived its usefulness, or are there application domains for which it still makes sense to build a microprogrammed machine? Defend your answer.

5.11 Suppose that loads constitute 25% of the typical instruction mix on a certain machine. Suppose further that 15% of these loads miss in the on-chip (primary) cache, with a penalty of 40 cycles to reach main memory. What is the contribution of cache misses to the average number of cycles per instruction? You may assume that instruction fetches always hit in the cache. Now suppose that we add an off-chip (secondary) cache that can satisfy 90% of the misses from the primary cache, at a penalty of only 10 cycles. What is the effect on cycles per instruction?

5.12 With the development of deeper, more complex pipelines, delayed loads and branches have become significantly less appealing as features of a RISC instruction set. Why is it that designers have been able to eliminate delayed loads in more recent machines, but have had to retain delayed branches?

5.13 Show the live ranges for the virtual registers in Figure 5.14. Which virtual registers can share a single physical register?

5.14 Some processors, including the PowerPC and recent members of the x86 family, require one or more cycles to elapse between a condition-determining instruction and a branch instruction that uses that condition. What options does a scheduler have for filling such delays?

5.15 Consider the code in Figures 5.12 and 5.14. Though a significant amount of instruction scheduling has been performed, some pipeline stalls will still occur when executing these loops. Specifically, if we assume a one-cycle load delay, a two-cycle floating-point add delay, and a four-cycle floating-point multiply delay, there will be a two-cycle stall before line 12 in Figure 5.12, and a one-cycle stall before line 16 in Figure 5.14. To eliminate these stalls, we might consider copying instructions from the head of the loop (i.e., the loads at label L1) into the stalling delays at the bottom of the loop, and then moving label L1 to a later instruction. Show the resulting code. Also, discuss the circumstances under which this transformation might be a good or bad idea. (Hint: when is it safe and/or efficient to access "elements" beyond the end of an array?)

5.16 Branch prediction can be performed statically (in the compiler) or dynamically (in hardware). In the static approach, the compiler guesses which way the branch will usually go, encodes this guess in the instruction, and schedules instructions for the expected path. In the dynamic approach, the hardware keeps track of the outcome of recent branches, notices branches that recur (because they are in loops), and predicts that they will go the same way they did the last time. Discuss the tradeoffs between these two approaches. What are their comparative advantages and disadvantages?

5.17 Consider a machine with a three-cycle penalty for incorrectly predicted branches and a zero-cycle penalty for correctly predicted branches. Suppose that in a typical program 20% of the instructions are conditional branches, which the compiler or hardware manages to predict correctly 75% of the time. What is the impact of incorrect predictions on the average number of cycles per instruction? Suppose the accuracy of branch prediction can be increased to 90%. What is the impact on cycles per instruction?

Suppose that the number of cycles per instruction would be 1.5 with perfect branch prediction. What is the percentage slowdown caused by mispredicted branches? Now suppose that we have a superscalar processor on which the number of cycles per instruction would be 0.6 with perfect branch prediction. Now what is the percentage slowdown caused by mispredicted branches? What do your answers tell you about the importance of branch prediction on superscalar machines?

5.18 If you have access to both CISC and RISC machines, compile a few programs for both machines and compare the size of the target code. Can you generalize about the "space penalty" of RISC code?

5.19 If you have access to computers of more than one type, compile a few programs on each machine and time their execution. (If possible, use the same compiler [e.g., gcc] and options on each machine.) Discuss the factors that may contribute to different run times. How closely do the ratios of run times mirror the ratios of clock rates? Why don't they mirror them exactly?

5.20 Translate the high-level pseudocode for vector dot product (p. 234) into your favorite programming language, and run it through your favorite compiler. Examine the resulting assembly language. Experiment with different levels of optimization (code improvement). Discuss the quality of the code produced.

5.21 Try to write a code fragment in your favorite programming language that requires so many registers that your favorite compiler is forced to spill some registers to memory (compile with a high level of optimization). How complex does your code have to be?

5.22 If you have access to a compiler that generates code for a machine with architecturally visible load delays, run some programs through it and evaluate the degree of success it has in filling delay slots (an unfilled slot will contain a nop instruction). What percentage of slots is filled? Suppose the machine had interlocked loads. How much space could be saved in typical executable programs if the nops were eliminated?

5.23 Experiment with small subroutines in C++ to see how much time can be saved by expanding them inline.

5.10 Bibliographic Notes

The standard reference in computer architecture is the graduate-level text by Patterson and Hennessy [HP96]. Much of the same material, in somewhat more accessible form, can be found in the undergraduate computer organization text by the same authors [PH98]. Competing texts include those of Tanenbaum [Tan99] and Stallings [Sta00].

The "RISC revolution" of the early 1980s was spearheaded by three separate research groups. The first to start (though last to publish [Rad82]) was the 801 group at IBM's T. J. Watson Research Center, led by John Cocke. IBM's Power and PowerPC architectures, though not direct descendants of the 801, take significant inspiration from it. The second group (and the one that coined the term "RISC") was led by David Patterson [PD80, Pat85] at UC Berkeley. The commercial Sparc architecture is a direct descendant of the Berkeley RISC II design. The third group was led by John Hennessy at Stanford [HJBG81]. The commercial MIPS architecture is a direct descendant of the Stanford design.

Much of the history of pre-1980 processor design can be found in the text by Siewiorek, Bell, and Newell [SBN82]. This classic work contains verbatim reprints of many important original papers. In the context of RISC processor design, Smith and Weiss [SW94] contrast the more "RISCy" and "CISCy" design philosophies in their comparison of implementations of the PowerPC and Alpha architectures. Appendix C of Hennessy and Patterson's architecture text summarizes the similarities and differences among the PA-RISC, PowerPC, MIPS, and Sparc. Appendix D describes the x86. Current manuals for all the popular commercial processors are available from their manufacturers.

An excellent treatment of computer arithmetic can be found in Goldberg's appendix to the Hennessy and Patterson architecture text [Gol96]. The IEEE 754 floating-point standard was printed in *ACM SIGPLAN Notices* in 1985 [IEE87]. Muchnick's advanced compilers text [Muc97] is an excellent source for information on instruction scheduling, register allocation, subroutine optimization, and other aspects of compiling for modern machines.

Control Flow

Having considered the mechanisms that a compiler uses to enforce semantic rules (Chapter 4) and the characteristics of the target machines for which compilers must generate code (Chapter 5), we now return to core issues in language design. Specifically, we turn in this chapter to the issue of *control flow* or *ordering* in program execution. Ordering is fundamental to most (though not all) models of computing. It determines what should be done first, what second, and so forth, to accomplish some desired task. We can organize the language mechanisms used to specify ordering into seven principal categories:

1. *sequencing:* Statements are to be executed (or expressions evaluated) in a certain specified order—usually the order in which they appear in the program text.

2. *selection:* Depending on some run-time condition, a *choice* is to be made among two or more statements or expressions. Selection is also sometimes referred to as *alternation*.

3. *iteration:* A given fragment of code is to be executed repeatedly, either a certain number of times, or until a certain run-time condition is true.

4. *procedural abstraction:* A potentially complex collection of control constructs (a *subroutine*) is encapsulated in a way that allows it to be treated as a single unit, often subject to parameterization.

5. *recursion:* An expression is defined in terms of (simpler versions of) itself, either directly or indirectly; the computational model requires a stack on which to save information about partially evaluated instances of the expression. Recursion is usually defined by means of self-referential subroutines.

6. *concurrency:* Two or more program fragments are to be executed/evaluated "at the same time," either in parallel on separate processors, or interleaved on a single processor in a way that achieves the same effect.

7. *nondeterminacy:* The ordering or choice among statements or expressions is deliberately left unspecified, implying that any alternative will lead to correct

results. Some languages require the choice to be random, or fair, in some formal sense of the word.

Though the syntactic and semantic details vary from language to language, these seven principal categories cover all of the control-flow constructs and mechanisms found in most programming languages. A programmer who thinks in terms of these categories, rather than the syntax of some particular language, will find it easy to learn new languages, evaluate the tradeoffs among languages, and design and reason about algorithms in a language-independent way.

Subroutines are the subject of Chapter 8. Concurrency is the subject of Chapter 12. The bulk of this chapter (Sections 6.3 through 6.7) is devoted to a study of the five remaining categories. We begin in Section 6.1 by examing expression evaluation. We consider the syntactic form of expressions, the precedence and associativity of operators, the order of evaluation of operands, and the semantics of the assignment statement. In Section 6.2 we consider the difference between *structured* and *unstructured* (goto-based) control flow.

It should be noted that the relative importance of different categories of control flow varies significantly among the different classes of programming languages. Sequencing, for example, is central to imperative (von Neumann and object-oriented) languages, but plays a relatively minor role in functional languages, which emphasize the evaluation of expressions, deemphasizing or eliminating statements (e.g., assignments) that affect program output in any way other than through the return of a value. Similarly, functional languages make heavy use of recursion, while imperative languages tend to emphasize iteration. Logic languages tend to deemphasize or hide the issue of control flow entirely: the programmer simply specifies a set of inference rules; the language implementation must find an order in which to apply those rules that will allow it to deduce values that satisfy some desired property.

6.1 Expression Evaluation

An expression generally consists of either a simple object (e.g., a literal constant, or a named variable or constant) or an *operator* or function applied to a collection of operands or arguments, each of which in turn is an expression. It is conventional to use the term *operator* for built-in functions that use special, simple syntax, and to use the term *operand* for the argument of an operator. In Algol-family languages, function calls consist of a function name followed by a parenthesized, comma-separated list of arguments, as in

```
my_func (A, B, C)
```

Algol-family operators are simpler: they typically take only one or two arguments, and dispense with the parentheses and commas:

```
a + b
- c
```

As we saw in Section 3.5, some languages define the operators as *syntactic sugar* for more "normal" looking functions. In Ada, for example, a + b is short for "+"(a, b); in C++, a + b is short for a.operator+(b).

In general, a language may specify that function calls (operator invocations) employ prefix, infix, or postfix, notation. These terms indicate, respectively, whether the function name appears before, among, or after its several arguments. Most imperative languages use infix notation for binary operators and prefix notation for unary operators and other functions (with parentheses around the arguments). Lisp uses prefix notation for all functions, but places the function name *inside* the parentheses, in what is known as *Cambridge Polish*[1] notation:

```
(* (+ 1 3) 2)              ; that would be (1 + 3) * 2 in infix
(append a b c my_list)     ; this is a comment
```

Smalltalk uses infix notation for all functions (which it calls messages), including those defined by the user. The following sends a "displayOn: at:" message to graphical object myBox, with arguments myScreen and 100@50 (a pixel location). It corresponds to what other languages would call the invocation of the "displayOn: at:" function with arguments myBox, myScreen, and 100@50.

```
myBox displayOn: myScreen at: 100@50
```

This sort of multiword infix notation occurs occasionally in Algol-family languages as well.[2] In Algol one can say

```
a = if b <> 0 then a/b else 0;
```

Here "if...then...else" is a three-operand infix operator. The equivalent operator in C is written "...?...:...":

```
a = b != 0 ? a/b : 0;
```

Postfix notation is used for most functions in Postscript, Forth, the input language of certain hand-held calculators, and the intermediate code of some compilers. Postfix appears in a few places in other languages as well. Examples include the pointer deferencing operator (^) of Pascal and the post-increment and decrement operators (++ and --) of C, C++, and Java.

6.1.1 Precedence and Associativity

Most languages provide a rich set of built-in arithmetic and logical operators. When written in infix notation, without parentheses, these operators lead to

---

[1] Prefix notation was popularized by Polish logicians of the early 20th century; Lisp-like parenthesized syntax was first employed (for noncomputational purposes) by philosopher W. V. Quine of Harvard University (Cambridge, MA).

[2] Most authors use the term "infix" only for binary operators. Multiword operators may be called "mixfix," or left unnamed.

ambiguity as to what is an operand of what. In Fortran, for example, which uses `**` for exponentiation, how should we parse `a + b * c**d**e/f`? Should this group as

```
((((a + b) * c)**d)**e)/f
```

or

```
a + (((b * c)**d)**(e/f))
```

or

```
a + ((b * (c**(d**e)))/f)
```

or yet some other option? (In Fortran, the answer is the last of the options shown.) In any given language, the choice among alternative evaluation orders depends on the *precedence* and *associativity* of operators, concepts we introduced in Section 2.1.3. Issues of precedence and associativity do not arise in prefix or postfix notation.

Precedence rules specify that certain operators, in the absence of parentheses, group "more tightly" than other operators. Associativity rules specify that sequences of operators of equal precedence group to the right or to the left. In most languages multiplication and division group more tightly than addition and subtraction. Other levels of precedence vary widely from one language to another. Figure 6.1 shows the levels of precedence for several well-known languages.

The precedence structure of C (and of its descendants, C++ and Java) is substantially richer than that of most other languages. It is, in fact, richer than shown in Figure 6.1, because several additional constructs, including type casts, function calls, array subscripting, and record field selection, are classified as operators in C. It is probably fair to say that most C programmers do not remember all of their language's precedence levels. The intent of the language designers was presumably to ensure that "the right thing" will usually happen when parentheses are not used to force a particular evaluation order. Rather than count on this, however, the wise programmer will consult the manual or add parentheses.

It is also probably fair to say that the relatively flat precedence hierarchy of Pascal is a mistake. In particular, novice Pascal programmers frequently write conditions such as

```
if A < B and C < D then (* ouch *)
```

Unless A, B, C, and D are all of type Boolean, which is unlikely, this code will result in a static semantic error, since the rules of precedence cause it to group as A < (B and C) < D. (And even if all four operands are of type Boolean, the result is almost sure to be something other than what the programmer intended.) Most languages avoid this problem by giving arithmetic operators higher precedence than relational (comparison) operators, which in turn have higher precedence than the logical operators. Notable exceptions include APL and Smalltalk, in

Fortran	Pascal	C	Ada
		++, -- (post-inc., dec.)	
**	not	++, -- (pre-inc., dec.), +, - (unary), & (address of), * (contents of), ! (logical not), ~ (bit-wise not)	abs (absolute value), not, **
*, /	*, /, div, mod, and	* (binary), /, % (modulo division)	*, /, mod, rem
+, -	+, - (unary and binary), or	+, - (binary)	+, - (unary)
		<<, >> (left and right bit shift)	+, - (binary), & (concatenation)
.eq., .ne., .lt., .le., .gt., .ge. (comparisons)		<, >, <=, >= (inequality tests)	=, /= , <=, >, >= (comparisons)
.not.		==, != (equality tests)	
		& (bit-wise and)	
		^ (bit-wise exclusive or)	
		| (bit-wise inclusive or)	
.and.		&& (logical and)	and, or, xor (logical operators)
.or.		|| (logical or)	
.eqv., .neqv. (logical comparisons)		?: (if…then…else)	
		=, +=, -=, *=, /=, %=, >>=, <<=, &=, ^=, |= (assignment)	
		, (sequencing)	

Figure 6.1 Operator precedence levels in Fortran, Pascal, C, and Ada. The operators at the top of the figure group most tightly.

which all operators are of equal precedence; parentheses *must* be used to specify grouping.

Associativity rules are somewhat more uniform across languages, but still display some variety. The basic arithmetic operators almost always associate left-to-right, so 9 - 3 - 2 is 4 and not 8. In Fortran, as in Mathematics, the exponentiation operator (**) associates right-to-left, so 4**3**2 is 262144 and not 4096. In Ada, exponentiation does not associate: one must write either (4**3)**2 or 4**(3**2); the language syntax does not allow the unparenthesized form. In languages that allow assignments inside expressions (an option we will consider more in Section 6.1.2), assignment associates right-to-left. Thus in C, a = b = a + c assigns a + c into b and then assigns the same value into a.

Because the rules for precedence and associativity vary so much from one language to another, a programmer who works in several languages is wise to make liberal use of parentheses.

6.1.2 **Assignments**

In a purely functional language, expressions are the building blocks of programs, and computation consists entirely of expression evaluation. The effect of any individual expression on the overall computation is limited to the value that expression provides to its surrounding context. Complex computations employ recursion to generate a potentially unbounded number of values, expressions, and contexts.

In an imperative language, by contrast, computation typically consists of an ordered series of changes to the values of variables in memory. Assignments provide the principal means by which to make the changes. Each assignment takes a pair of arguments: a value and a reference to a variable into which the value should be placed.

In general, a programming language construct is said to have a *side effect* if it influences subsequent computation (and ultimately program output) in any way other than by returning a value for use in the surrounding context. Purely functional languages have no side effects. As a result, the value of an expression in such a language depends only on the referencing environment in which the expression is evaluated, *not* on the time at which the evaluation occurs. If an expression yields a certain value at one point in time, it is guaranteed to yield the same value at any point in time. In fancier terms, expressions in a purely functional language are said to be *referentially transparent*.

By contrast, imperative programming is sometimes described as "computing by means of side effects." While the evaluation of an assignment may sometimes yield a value, what we really care about is the fact that it changes the value of a variable, thereby affecting the result of any later computation in which the variable appears.

Many (though not all) imperative languages distinguish between *expressions*, which always produce a value, and may or may not have side effects, and *statements*, which are executed *solely* for their side effects, and return no useful value.

What Is a Variable?

On the surface, assignment appears to be a very straightforward operation. Below the surface, however, there are some subtle but important differences in the semantics of assignment in different imperative languages. These differences are often invisible, because they do not affect the behavior of simple programs. They have a major impact, however, on programs that use pointers, and will be explored in further detail in Section 7.7. We provide an introduction to the issues here.

Consider the following assignments in C:

```
d = a;
a = b + c;
```

In the first statement, the right-hand side of the assignment refers to the *value* of a. In the second statement, the left-hand side refers to the *location* of a. Both interpretations are possible because a variable in C (and in Pascal, Ada, and many other languages) is a named container for a value. We sometimes say that Pascal and its relatives use a *value model* of variables. Because of their use on the left-hand side of assignment statements, expressions that denote locations are referred to as *l-values*. Expressions that denote values (possibly the value stored in a location) are referred to as *r-values*. Under a value model of variables, a given expression can be either an l-value or an r-value, depending on the context in which it appears.

Of course, not all expressions can be l-values, because not all values have a location, and not all names are variables. In Pascal, for example, it makes no sense to say 2 + 3 := a, or even a := 2 + 3, if a is the name of a constant. By the same token, not all l-values are simple names; both l-values and r-values can be complicated expressions. In C, for example, one may write

```
(f(a)+3)->b[c]  =  2;
```

In this expression f(a) returns a pointer to some element of an array of structures (records). The assignment places the value 2 into the c-th element of field b of the third structure after the one to which f's return value points. In C++ it is even possible for a function to return a "reference" to a structure, rather than a pointer to it, allowing one to write g(a).b[c] = 2. We will consider references further in Section 8.3.1.

Several languages make the distinction between l-values and r-values more explicit by employing a *reference model* of variables. In Clu, for example, a variable is not a named container for a value; rather, it is a named *reference to* a value. The following fragment of code is syntactically valid in both Pascal and Clu:

```
b  :=  2;
c  :=  b;
a  :=  b  +  c;
```

A Pascal programmer might describe this code by saying: "We put the value 2 in b and then copy it into c. We then read these values, add them together, and place the resulting 4 in a." The Clu programmer would say: "We let b refer to 2 and then let c refer to it also. We then pass these references to the + operator, and let a refer to the result, namely 4."

These two ways of thinking are illustrated in Figure 6.2. With a value model of variables, as in Pascal, any integer variable can contain the value 2. With a reference model of variables, as in Clu, there is (at least conceptually) only *one* 2—a sort of Platonic Ideal—to which any variable can refer. The practical effect is the same in this example, because integers are *immutable*: the value of 2 never changes, so we can't tell the difference between two copies of the number 2 and two references to "the" number 2. As we shall see in Section 7.7.1, most compilers for languages with a reference model will actually use multiple copies of immutable objects for the sake of efficiency.

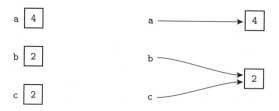

Figure 6.2 The value (left) and reference (right) models of variables. Under the reference model, it becomes important to distinguish between variables that refer to the same object and variables that refer to different objects whose values happen (at the moment) to be equal.

In a language that uses the reference model, every variable is an l-value. When it appears in a context that expects an r-value, it must be *dereferenced* to obtain the value to which it refers. In most languages with a reference model (including Clu), the dereference is implicit and automatic. In ML, the programmer must use an explicit dereference operator, denoted with a prefix exclamation point. We will discuss the ML type system further in Section 7.7.1.

The difference between the value and reference models of variables becomes particularly important (specifically, it can affect program output and behavior) if the values to which variables refer can change "in place," as they do in many programs with linked data structures, or if it is possible for variables to refer to different objects that happen to have the "same" value. In this latter case it becomes important to distinguish between variables that refer to the same object and variables that refer to different objects whose values happen (at the moment) to be equal. (Lisp, as we shall see in Sections 7.10 and 11.2.1, provides more than one notion of equality, to accommodate this distinction.) We will discuss the value and reference models of variables further in Section 7.7. Languages that employ (some variant of) the reference model include Algol 68, Clu, Lisp/Scheme, ML, Haskell, and Smalltalk. Java uses a value model for built-in types and a reference model for user-defined types (classes).

Orthogonality

One of the principal design goals of Algol 68 was to make the various features of the language as *orthogonal* as possible. Orthogonality means that features can be used in any combination, that the combinations all make sense, and that the meaning of a given feature is *consistent*, regardless of the other features with which it is combined. The name is meant to draw an explicit analogy to orthogonal vectors in linear algebra: none of the vectors in an orthogonal set depends on (or can be expressed in terms of) the others, and all are needed in order to describe the vector space as a whole.

Algol 68 was one of the first languages to make orthogonality a principal design goal, and in fact few languages since have given the goal such weight. Among other things, Algol 68 is said to be *expression-oriented*: it has no separate notion of statement. Arbitrary expressions can appear in contexts that would call for a statement in a language such as Pascal, and constructs that are considered to be statements in other languages can appear within expressions. The following, for example, is valid in Algol 68:

```
begin
    a := if b < c then d else e;
    a := begin f(b); g(c) end;
    g(d);
    2 + 3
end
```

Here the value of the if...then...else construct is either the value of its then part or the value of its else part, depending on the value of the condition. The value of the "statement list" on the right-hand side of the second assignment is the value of its final "statement," namely the return value of g(c). There is no need to distinguish between procedures and functions, because every subroutine call returns a value. The value returned by g(d) is discarded in the code above. Finally, the value of the code fragment as a whole is 5, the sum of 2 and 3.

C takes an approach intermediate between Pascal and Algol 68. It distinguishes between statements and expressions, but allows any expression to appear in a context that expects a statement, and provides special expression forms for selection and sequencing. Algol 60 defines if...then...else as both a statement and an expression.

Both Algol 68 and C allow assignments within expressions. The value of an assignment is simply the value of its right-hand side. Unfortunately, where most of the descendants of Algol 60 uses the := token to represent assignment, C follows Fortran in simply using =. It uses == to represent a test for equality (Fortran uses .eq.). Moreover, C lacks a separate Boolean type. In any context that would require a Boolean value in other languages, C accepts an integer (or anything that can be coerced to be an integer). It interprets zero as false; any other value is true. As a result, both of the following constructs are valid—common—in C:

```
if (a == b) {
    /* do the following if a equals b */

if (a = b) {
    /* assign b into a and then do
        the following if the result is nonzero */
```

Programmers who are accustomed to Pascal or some other language in which = is the equality test frequently write the second form above when the first is what is intended. This sort of bug can be very hard to find. Though it provides a separate bool type, C++ shares the problem of C, because it provides automatic coercions from numeric, pointer, and enumeration types. Java eliminates the problem by introducing a separate boolean type, and by disallowing integers in Boolean contexts. The assignment operator is still =, and the equality test is still

==, but the statement if (a = b) ... will generate a compile-time type clash error unless a and b are booleans, which is generally unlikely.

Initialization

Because they already provide a construct (the assignment statement) to specify the value of a variable, imperative languages do not always provide a means of specifying an initial value for a variable in its declaration. There are at least two reasons, however, why such initial values may be useful:

1. In the case of statically allocated variables (as discussed in Section 3.2), an initial value that is specified in the context of the declaration can be placed into memory by the compiler. If the initial value is set by an assignment statement instead, it will generally incur execution cost at run time.

2. One of the most common programming errors is to use a variable in an expression before giving it a value. One of the easiest ways to prevent such errors (or at least ensure that erroneous behavior is repeatable) is to give every variable a value when it is first declared.

Some languages (e.g., Pascal) have no initialization facility at all; all variables must be given values by explicit assignment statements. To avoid the expense of run-time initialization of statically allocated variables, many Pascal implementations provide initialization as a language extension, generally in the form of a := *expr* immediately after the name in the declaration. Unfortunately, the extension is usually nonorthogonal, in the sense that it only works for variables of simple, built-in types. A more complete and orthogonal approach to initialization requires a notation for *aggregates*: compile-time constant values of user-defined composite types. Aggregates can be found in several languages, including C, Ada, Fortran 90, and ML; we will discuss them further in Section 7.1.2. It should be emphasized that initialization saves time only for variables that are statically allocated. Variables allocated in the stack or heap at run time must be initialized at run time.[3] It is also worth noting that the problem of using an uninitialized variable occurs not only after elaboration, but also as a result of any operation that destroys a variable's value without providing a new one. Two of the most common such operations are explicit deallocation of an object referenced through a pointer and modification of the *tag* of a variant record. We will consider these operations further in Sections 7.7 and 7.3.4, respectively.

If a variable is not given an initial value explicitly in its declaration, the language may specify a default value. In C, for example, uninitialized, statically allocated variables are guaranteed to be represented in memory by a string of

---

3 For variables that are accessed indirectly (e.g., in languages that employ a reference model of variables), a compiler can often reduce the cost of initializing a stack or heap variable by placing the initial value in static memory, and only creating the pointer to it at elaboration time.

zero bits. For integers, floating-point numbers, and characters (which are basically just one-byte integers in C), the result is numerically zero. For character strings, the result is an empty (zero-length) string. The designers of C chose not to incur the run-time cost of automatically zero-filling uninitialized variables that are allocated in the stack or heap. The programmer can specify an initial value if desired; the effect is the same as if an assignment had been placed at the beginning of the code for the variable's scope.

C++ allows the programmer to define types for which initialization of dynamically allocated variables occurs automatically, even when no initial value is specified in the declaration. C++ also distinguishes carefully between initialization and assignment. Initialization is interpreted as a call to a *constructor* function for the variable's type, with the initial value as an argument. In the absence of coercion, assignment is interpreted as a call to the type's assignment operator or, if none has been defined, as a simple bit-wise copy of the value on the assignment's right-hand side. The distinction between initialization and assignment is particularly important for user-defined abstract data types that perform their own storage management. A typical example occurs in variable-length character strings. An assignment to such a string must generally deallocate the space consumed by the old value of the string before allocating space for the new value. An initialization of the string must simply allocate space.

Java requires that a value be "definitely assigned" to a variable before that variable is used in any expression. The language definition includes a precise definition of "definitely assigned," based on the control flow of the program. Roughly speaking, every possible control path to an expression must assign a value to every variable in that expression. The C++ distinction between initialization and assignment does not apply in Java, because Java uses a reference model for variables of user-defined object types, and because it provides for automatic storage reclamation. Assignment of user-defined types in Java is never a bit-wise copy. We will return to these issues again in Chapter 10 when we consider the object-oriented features of C++ and Java in more detail.

Instead of giving every uninitialized variable a default value, a language or implementation can choose to define the use of an uninitialized variable as a dynamic semantic error, and can catch these errors at run time. The advantage of the semantic checks is that they will often identify a program bug that is masked or made more subtle by the presence of a default value. With appropriate hardware support, uninitialized variable checks can even be as cheap as default values, at least for certain types. In particular, a compiler that relies on the IEEE standard for floating-point arithmetic can fill uninitialized floating-point numbers with a *signaling NaN* value, as discussed in Section 5.3.2. Any attempt to use such a value in a computation will result in a hardware interrupt, which the language implementation may catch (with a little help from the operating system), and use to trigger a semantic error message.

For most types on most machines, unfortunately, the costs of catching all uses of an uninitialized variable at run time are considerably higher. If every possible bit pattern of the variable's representation in memory designates some legitimate value (and this is often the case), then extra space must be allocated somewhere to hold an initialized/uninitialized flag. This flag must be set to "uninitialized" at elaboration time and to "initialized" at assignment time. It must also be checked (by extra code) at every use, or at least at every use that the code improver is unable to prove is redundant. Dynamic semantic checks for uninitialized variables are common in interpreted languages, which already incur significant overhead on every variable access. Because of their cost, however, the checks are usually not performed in languages that are compiled.

As in the case of any potential error that depends on the flow of control at run time, it is provably impossible for the compiler to catch all uses of uninitialized variables. It *is* possible to catch them, however, under certain restricted programming models, which eliminate the dependence on run-time control flow. A trivial example occurs with "straight-line" code, in which the order in which statements will be executed at run time is data-independent. A second occurs in the notion of definite assignment in Java. A third can be found in the *typestate* system of the Hermes programming language, described in the Bibliographic Notes at the end of this chapter.

Combination Assignment Operators

Because they rely so heavily on side effects, imperative programs must frequently *update* a variable. It is thus common to see statements such as

```
a := a + 1;
```

or, worse

```
b.c[3].d := b.c[3].d * e;
```

in Pascal. Such statements are not only cumbersome to write and read (the reader must scan both sides of the assignment carefully to see if they really are the same), they also result in redundant address calculations (or at least extra work to eliminate the redundancy in the code improvement phase of compilation). If the address calculation has a side effect, then we may need to write a pair of statements instead. Consider the following code in Pascal:

```
procedure update (A : int_array;
                  function index_fn (n : integer) : integer);
var i, j : integer;
begin
    (* calculate i *)
    ...
    j := index_fn (i);
    A[j] := A[j] + 1;
```

Here we cannot safely write

```
A[index_fn(i)] := A[index_fn(i)] + 1;
```

We have to introduce the temporary variable j because we don't know whether index_fn has a side effect or not. If it is being used, for example, to keep a log of elements that have been updated, then we will want to make sure that update calls it only once.

To eliminate the clutter and compile- or run-time cost of redundant address calculations, and to avoid the issue of repeated side effects, many languages, beginning with Algol 68, and including C and several nonstandard dialects of Pascal, provide so-called *assignment operators* to update a variable. Using assignment operators, the statements at the beginning of this section can be written as follows:

```
a +:= 1;
b.c[3].d *:= e;
```

In addition to being aesthetically cleaner, the assignment operator form guarantees that the address calculation is performed only once. In C, of course, there is no colon in the operator:

```
a += 1;
b.c[3].d *= e;
```

As shown in Figure 6.1, C provides 10 different assignment operators, one for each of its binary arithmetic and logical operators. C also provides prefix and postfix increment and decrement operations. These are handy in code that uses an index or a pointer to traverse an array:

```
A[--i] = b;
*p++ = *q++;
```

When prefixed to an expression, the ++ or -- operator increments or decrements its operand *before* providing a value to the surrounding context. In its postfix form, ++ or -- updates its operand *after* providing a value. In the example just shown, if i is 3 and p and q point to the initial elements of a pair of arrays, then b will be assigned into the second element of A (not the third), and the second assignment will copy the initial elements of the arrays (not the second elements). The prefix forms of ++ and -- are syntactic sugar for += and -=. We could have written

```
A[i -= 1] = b;
```

above. The postfix forms are not syntactic sugar. To obtain an effect similar to the second statement above we would need an auxiliary variable and a lot of extra notation:

```
*(t = p, p += 1, t) = *(t = q, q += 1, t);
```

Both the assignment operators (+=, -=) and the increment and decrement operators (++, --) do "the right thing" when applied to pointers in C. If p points to an object that occupies *n* bytes in memory (counting any bytes required for alignment, as discussed in Section 5.2), then p += 3 points $3n$ bytes higher in memory.

We have already seen that the right associativity of assignment (in languages that allow assignment in expressions) allows one to write things like a = b = c. In some languages, including Clu, ML, and Perl, it is also possible to write

```
a, b := c, d;
```

Here the comma in the right-hand side is *not* the sequencing operator of C. Rather, it serves to define a expression, or *tuple*, consisting of multiple r-values. The comma operator on the left-hand side produces a tuple of l-values. The effect of the assignment is to copy c into a and d into b.[4] While we could just as easily have written

```
a := c; b := d;
```

the multiway (tuple) assignment allows us to write things like

```
a, b := b, a;
```

which would otherwise require auxiliary variables. Moreover, the availability of multiway assignment in Clu and Perl allows functions to return tuples, as well as single values:

```
a, b, c := foo (d, e, f);
```

This notation eliminates the asymmetry (nonorthogonality) of functions in most programming languages, which allow an arbitrary number of arguments, but only a single return. ML generalizes the idea of multiway assignment into a powerful *pattern-matching* mechanism; we will examine this mechanism in more detail in Section 7.2.5.

6.1.3 Ordering Within Expressions

While precedence and associativity rules define the order in which binary infix operators are applied within an expression, they do not specify the order in which the operands of a given operator are evaluated. For example, in the expression

```
a - f(b) - c * d
```

we know from associativity that f(b) will be subtracted from a before performing the second subtraction, and we know from precedence that the right operand of that second subtraction will be the result of c * d, rather than merely c,

---

4 The syntax shown here is for Clu. Perl follows C in using = for assignment. ML requires parentheses around each tuple.

but without additional information we do not know whether `a - f(b)` will be evaluated before or after `c * d`. Similarly, in a subroutine call with multiple arguments

```
f (a, g(b), c)
```

we do not know the order in which the arguments will be evaluated.

There are two main reasons why the order can be important:

1. *Side effects:* If `f(b)` may modify `d`, then the value of `a - f(b) - c * d` will depend on whether the first subtraction or the multiplication is performed first. Similarly, if `g(b)` may modify `a` and/or `c`, then the values passed to `f (a, g(b), c)` will depend on the order in which the arguments are evaluated.

2. *Code improvement:* The order of evaluation of subexpressions has an impact on both register allocation and instruction scheduling. In the expression `a * b + f(c)`, it is probably desirable to call `f` before evaluating `a * b`, because the product, if calculated first, would need to be saved during the call to `f`, and `f` might want to use all the registers in which it might easily be saved. In a similar vein, consider the sequence

```
a := B[i];
c := a * 2 + d * 3;
```

   Here it is probably desirable to evaluate `d * 3` before evaluating `a * 2`, because the previous statement, `a := B[i]`, will need to load a value from memory. Because loads are slow, if the processor attempts to use the value of `a` in the next instruction (or even the next few instructions on many machines), it will have to wait. If it does something unrelated instead (i.e., evaluate `d * 3`), then the load can proceed in parallel with other computation.

Because of the importance of code improvement, most language manuals say that the order of evaluation of operands and arguments is undefined. (Java is unusual in this regard: it requires left-to-right evaluation.) In the absence of an enforced order, the compiler can choose whatever order results in faster code. Some language implementations (e.g., for dialects of Fortran) go even further and allow the compiler to *rearrange* expressions involving operators whose mathematical abstractions are commutative, associative, and/or distributive, in order to generate faster code. Consider the following Fortran fragment:

```
a = b + c
d = c + e + b
```

Some compilers will rearrange this as

```
a = b + c
d = b + c + e
```

They can then recognize the *common subexpression* in the first and second statements, and generate code equivalent to

```
a = b + c
d = a + e
```

Similarly,

```
a = b/c/d
e = f/d/c
```

may be rearranged as

```
t = c * d
a = b/t
e = f/t
```

Unfortunately, while mathematical arithmetic obeys a variety of commutative, associative, and distributive laws, computer arithmetic is not as predictable. The problem is that numbers in a computer are of limited precision. With 32-bit arithmetic, the expression b − c + d can be evaluated safely left-to-right if a, b, and c are all integers between two billion and three billion (2^{32} is a little less than 4.3 billion). If the compiler attempts to reorganize this expression as b + d − c, however (e.g., in order to delay its use of c), then arithmetic overflow will occur.

Many languages, including Pascal and most of its descendants, provide dynamic semantic checks to detect arithmetic overflow. In some implementations these checks can be disabled to eliminate their run-time overhead. Other languages, including C and its descendants, provide no such checks. In C and C++, the effect of arithmetic overflow is implementation-dependent. In Java, it is well defined: the language definition specifies the size of all numeric types, and requires two's complement integer and IEEE floating-point arithmetic. In Common Lisp, there is no a priori limit on the size of numbers; space is allocated to hold extra-large values on demand.

Even in the absence of overflow, the limited precision of floating-point arithmetic can cause different arrangements of the "same" expression to produce significantly different results, invisibly. Single-precision IEEE floating-point numbers devote one bit to the sign, eight bits to the exponent (power of two), and 23 bits to the mantissa. Under this representation, a + b is guaranteed to result in a loss of information if $|\log_2(a/b)| > 23$. Thus if b = −c, then a + b + c will appear to be zero, instead of a, if the magnitude of a is small, while the magnitude of b and c is large. In a similar vein, a number like 0.1 cannot be represented precisely, because its binary representation is a "repeating decimal": 0.0001001001.... For certain values of x, (0.1 + x) * 10.0 and 1.0 + (x * 10.0) can differ by as much as 25%, even when 0.1 and x are of the same magnitude.

To limit such surprises, most compilers (if they rearrange expressions at all) guarantee not to violate the ordering imposed by parentheses. The programmer can therefore use parentheses to prevent the application of arithmetic "identities" when desired. No similar guarantee exists with respect to the order of evaluation of operands and arguments. It is therefore unwise to write expressions in which a side effect of evaluating one operand or argument can affect the value of another. As we shall see in Section 6.3, some languages, notably Euclid and Turing, outlaw such side effects.

6.1.4 Short-Circuit Evaluation

Boolean expressions provide a special and important opportunity for code improvement and increased readability. Consider the expression (a < b) and (b < c). If a is greater than b, there is really no point in checking to see whether b is less than c; we know the overall expression must be false. Similarly, in the expression (a > b) or (b > c), if a is indeed greater than b there is no point in checking to see whether b is greater than c; we know the overall expression must be true. A compiler that performs *short-circuit evaluation* of Boolean expressions will generate code that skips the second half of both of these computations when the overall value can be determined from the first half. Short-circuit evaluation can save significant amounts of time in certain situations:

```
if (very_unlikely_condition && very_expensive_function()) ...
```

But time is not the only consideration, or even the most important. Short-circuiting changes the *semantics* of Boolean expressions. In C, for example, one can use the following code to search for an element in a list:

```
p = my_list;
while (p && p->key != val)
    p = p->next;
```

C short-circuits its && and || operators, and uses zero for both nil and false, so p->key will be accessed if and only if p is non-nil. The syntactically similar code in Pascal does not work, because Pascal does not short-circuit and and or:

```
p := my_list;
while (p <> nil) and (p^.key <> val) do      (* ouch! *)
    p := p^.next;
```

Here both of the <> relations will be evaluated before and-ing their results together. At the end of an unsuccessful search, p will be nil, and the attempt to access p^.key will be a run-time (dynamic semantic) error, which the compiler may or may not have generated code to catch. To avoid this situation, the Pascal programmer must introduce an auxiliary Boolean variable and an extra level of nesting:

```
1.  function tally (word : string) : integer;
2.     (* Look up word in hash table.  If found, increment tally; If not
3.         found, enter with a tally of 1.  In either case, return tally. *)
       ...
4.  function misspelled (word : string) : Boolean;
5.     (* Check to see if word is mis-spelled and return appropriate
6.         indication.  If yes, increment global count of mis-spellings. *)
       ...
7.  while not eof (doc_file) do begin
8.     w := get_word (doc_file);
9.     if (tally (w) = 10) and misspelled (w) then
10.        writeln (w)
11. end;
12. writeln (total_misspellings);
```

Figure 6.3 Pascal code that counts on the evaluation of Boolean operands.

```
p := my_list;
still_searching := true;
while still_searching do
    if p = nil then
        still_searching := false
    else if p^.key = val then
        still_searching := false
    else
        p := p^.next;
```

Short-circuit evaluation can also be used to avoid out-of-bound subscripts:

```
const MAX = 10;
int A[MAX];                    /* indices from 0 to 9 */
...
if (i >= 0 && i < A_MAX && A[i] > foo) ...
```

division by zero:

```
if (d <> 0 && n/d > threshold) ...
```

and various other errors. It is not necessarily as attractive for situations in which a Boolean subexpression can cause a side effect. Suppose we wish to print a list of all misspelled words that appear 10 or more times in a given document, together with a count of the total number of misspellings. Pascal code for this task appears in Figure 6.3. Here the if statement at line 9 tests the conjunction of two subexpressions, both of which have important side effects. If short-circuit evaluation is used, the program will not compute the right result. The code can be rewritten to eliminate the need for non-short-circuit evaluation, but one might argue that the result is more awkward than the version shown.

So now we have seen situations in which short-circuiting is highly desirable, and others in which at least some programmers would find it undesirable. A few languages, among them Clu, Ada, and C, provide both regular *and* short-circuit Boolean operators. (Similar flexibility can be achieved with `if...then...else` in an expression-oriented language such as Algol 68; see Exercise 6.10.) In Clu, the regular Boolean operators are `and` and `or`; the short-circuit operators are `cand` and `cor` (for *conditional* `and` and `or`):

```
if d ~= 0 cand n/d > threshold then ...
```

In Ada, the regular operators are also `and` and `or`; the short-circuit operators are the two-word operators `and then` and `or else`:

```
found_it := p /= null and then p.key = val;
```

(Clu and Ada use `~=` and `/=`, respectively, for "not equal.") C's logical `&&` and `||` operators short-circuit; the bit-wise `&` and `|` operators can be used as non-short-circuiting alternatives when their arguments are logical (zero or one) values.

When used to determine the flow of control in a selection or iteration construct, short-circuit Boolean expressions do not really have to calculate a Boolean value; they simply have to ensure that control takes the proper path in any given situation. We will look more closely at the generation of code for short-circuit expressions in Section 6.4.1.

6.2 Structured and Unstructured Flow

Control flow in assembly languages is achieved by means of conditional and unconditional jumps (branches). Early versions of Fortran mimic the low-level approach by relying heavily on `goto` statements for most nonprocedural control flow:

```
    if A .lt. B goto 10
    ...
10:
```

The `10:` on the bottom line is a *statement label*. `Goto` statements also feature prominently in other early imperative languages. In Cobol and PL/I, for example, they provide the only means of writing logically controlled (`while`-style) loops. Algol 60 and its successors provide a wealth of non-`goto`-based constructs, but until recently most Algol-family languages still provided `goto` as an option.

Throughout the late 1960s and much of the 1970s, language designers debated hotly about the merits and evils of `goto`s. It seems fair to say the detractors won. Ada allows `goto`s only in very limited contexts. Modula (1, 2, and 3), Clu, Eiffel, and Java do not allow them at all. Fortran 90 and C++ allow them primarily for compatibility with their predecessor languages. Java has no `goto`, though it reserves the token as a keyword, to make it easier for a Java compiler to produce good error messages when a programmer uses a C++ `goto` by mistake.

The abandonment of `gotos` was part of a larger "revolution" in software engineering known as *structured programming*. Structured programming was the "hot trend" of the 1970s, in much the same way that object-oriented programming has become the trend of the 1990s. Structured programming emphasizes top-down design (i.e., progressive refinement), modularization of code, structured types (records, sets, pointers, multi-dimensional arrays), descriptive variable and constant names, and extensive commenting conventions. The developers of structured programming were able to demonstrate that within a subroutine, almost any well-designed imperative algorithm can be elegantly expressed with only sequencing, selection, and iteration. Instead of labels, structured languages rely on the boundaries of lexically nested constructs as the targets of branching control.

Many of the structured control-flow constructs familiar to modern programmers were pioneered by Algol 60. These include the `if...then...else` construct and both enumeration (`for`) and logically (`while`) controlled loops. The `case` statement was introduced by Wirth and Hoare in Algol W [WH66] as an alternative to the more unstructured computed `goto` and `switch` constructs of Fortran and Algol 60, respectively. `Case` statements were adopted in limited form by Algol 68, and more completely by Pascal, Modula, C, Ada, and a host of modern languages. Once the principal structured constructs had been defined, most of the controversy surrounding `gotos` revolved around a small number of special cases, each of which was eventually addressed in structured ways:

Mid-loop exit and continue: A common use of `gotos` in Pascal is to break out of the middle of a loop:

```
    while true do begin
        readln (line);
        if all_blanks (line) then goto 100;
        consume_line (line)
    end;
100:
```

Less commonly, one also sees a label *inside* the end of a loop, to serve as the target of a `goto` that terminates a given iteration early. As we shall see in Section 6.5.4, mid-loop exits are supported by special "one-and-a half" loop constructs in languages such as Modula, C, and Ada. C, Fortran 90, and a few other languages also provide a `continue` (C) or `cycle` (Fortran 90) statement to skip the remainder of the current loop iteration.

Early returns from subroutines: `Gotos` are used fairly often in Pascal to terminate the current subroutine:

```
    procedure consume_line (var line: string);
        ...
```

```
      begin
          ...
              if line[i] = '%' then goto 100;
                  (* rest of line is a comment *)
          ...
  100:
      end;
```

At a minimum, this `goto` statement avoids putting the remainder of the procedure in an `else` clause. If the terminating condition is discovered within a deeply nested `if...then...else`, it may avoid introducing an auxiliary variable that must be tested repeatedly in the remainder of the procedure (`if not comment_line then ...`).

The obvious alternative to this use of `goto` is to provide an explicit `return` statement. Algol 60 does not have one, and neither does Pascal, but Fortran always has, and most modern Algol descendants have adopted it.

Errors and other exceptions: In many programs, particularly those that must cope with unexpected inputs, a deeply nested construct or, worse, a deeply nested subroutine, may discover that it is not only unable to proceed with its usual function, but lacks the contextual information required to recover in any graceful way. The only recourse in such a situation is to "back out" of the nested context to some point in the program that is able to recover. Conditions that require a program to "back out" are called *exceptions*. We saw an example in Section 2.2.4, where we considered phrase-level recovery from syntax errors in a recursive-descent parser.

The most straightforward, but generally least satisfactory way to cope with exceptions is to use auxiliary Boolean variables within a subroutine (`if still_ok then ...`) and to return status values from calls:

```
my_proc (args, status);
if status = ok then ...
```

Some of the clumsiness of this approach can be resolved by using `goto` statements to branch out of a nested context. Pascal actually allows a `goto` to branch to a label *outside* the current subroutine, and promises to appropriately repair the run-time stack of subroutine call information in such a situation. This repair operation is known as *unwinding*. It requires not only that we deallocate the stack frames of any subroutines from which we have escaped, but also that we perform any bookkeeping operations, such as restoration of register contents, that would have been performed when returning from those routines. Algol 60 goes so far as to allow labels to be passed as parameters, so that a nested subroutine can perform a `goto` to a caller-defined location. PL/I allows labels to be stored in variables.

Unfortunately, nonlocal `goto`s are difficult to implement correctly, and even more difficult to understand. They are a nightmare for program maintenance. An increasing number of languages, including Clu, Ada, C++, Common Lisp,

Haskell, Java, ML, and Modula-3, provide a structured *exception handling* mechanism that regularizes both the implementation and the semantics. We will discuss exception handling in more detail in Section 8.5.

The notion of nonlocal `goto`s that unwind the stack can be generalized by defining what are known as *continuations*. In low-level terms, a continuation consists of a code address and a referencing environment to be restored when jumping to that address. In higher-level terms, a continuation is an abstraction that captures a *context* in which execution might continue. All nonlocal jumps can be explained in terms of continuations: they capture not only `goto`s out of a nested subroutine but also subroutine calls and returns themselves, as well as several subjects to be discussed in future chapters, including exception handling, call-by-name parameters (Section 8.3.1), iterators (Section 6.5.3), and coroutines (Section 8.6). Continuations are fundamental to denotational semantics. They also appear as first-class values in certain languages (notably Scheme), effectively allowing the available set of control flow constructs to be extended under programmer control. First-class continuations are an extremely powerful facility. They can be very useful if used in well-structured ways (i.e., by defining new control-flow constructs); they also allow the undisciplined programmer to construct completely inscrutable programs. The implementation of continuations in Scheme is surprisingly straightforward. Rather than attempt to "clean up" the old referencing environment when jumping through a continuation, Scheme simply activates the new environment and relies on a general *garbage collection* facility to clean up the old one when it is no longer accessible. We will consider garbage collection in Section 7.7.3.

6.3 Sequencing

Like assignment, sequencing is central to imperative programming. It is the principal means of controlling the order in which side effects (e.g., assignments) occur: when one statement follows another in the program text, the first statement executes before the second. In most imperative languages, lists of statements can be enclosed with `begin...end` or `{...}` delimiters and then used in any context in which a single statement is expected. Such a delimited list is usually called a *compound statement*. A compound statement preceded by a set of declarations (as in the body of a Pascal subroutine) is usually called a *block*.

In languages such as Algol 68 and C, which blur or eliminate the distinction between statements and expressions, the value of a statement (expression) list is the value of its final element. In Common Lisp, the programmer can also choose to return the value of the first or second element. Of course, sequencing is a useless operation unless the subexpressions that do not play a part in the return value have side effects. The various sequencing constructs in Lisp are used only in program fragments that do not conform to a purely functional programming model.

Even in imperative languages, there is debate as to the value of certain kinds of side effects. In Euclid and Turing, for example, functions (that is, subroutines that return values, and that therefore can appear within expressions) are not permitted to have side effects. Among other things, side-effect-freedom ensures that a Euclid or Turing function, like its counterpart in mathematics, is always *idempotent*: if called repeatedly with the same set of arguments, it will always return the same value, and the number of consecutive calls (after the first) will not affect the results of subsequent execution. In addition, side-effect-freedom for functions means that the value of a subexpression will never depend on whether that subexpression is evaluated before or after calling a function in some other subexpression. These properties make it easier for a programmer or theorem-proving system to reason about program behavior. They also simplify code improvement, for example by permitting the safe rearrangement of expressions.

Unfortunately, there are some situations in which side effects in functions are highly desirable. We saw one example in the gen_new_name function of Figure 3.6 (page 123). Another arises in the typical interface to a pseudo-random number generator:

```
procedure srand (seed : integer)
    −− Initialize internal tables.
    −− The pseudo-random generator will return a different
    −− sequence of values for each different value of seed.

function rand () : integer
    −− No arguments; returns a new "random" number.
```

Obviously rand needs to have a side effect, so that it will return a different value each time it is called. One could always recast it as a procedure with a reference parameter:

```
procedure rand (var n : integer)
```

but most programmers would find this less appealing. Ada strikes a compromise: it allows side effects in functions in the form of changes to static or global variables, but does not allow a function to modify its parameters.

6.4 Selection

Selection statements in most imperative languages employ some variant of the if...then...else notation introduced in Algol 60:

```
if condition then statement
else if condition then statement
else if condition then statement
```

```
. . .
```
`else` *statement*

As we saw in Section 2.2.5, languages differ in the details of the syntax. In Algol 60 and Pascal both the `then` clause and the `else` clause are defined to contain a single statement (this can of course be a `begin...end` compound statement). To avoid grammatical ambiguity, Algol 60 requires that the statement after the `then` begin with something other than `if` (`begin` is fine). Pascal eliminates this restriction in favor of a "disambiguating rule" that associates an `else` with the closest unmatched `then`. Algol 68, Fortran 77, and more modern languages avoid the ambiguity by allowing a statement *list* to follow either `then` or `else`, with a terminating keyword at the end of the construct. To keep terminators from piling up at the end of nested `if` statements, most languages with terminators provide a special `elsif` or `elif` keyword. In Modula-2, one writes

```
IF a = b THEN ...
ELSIF a = c THEN ...
ELSIF a = d THEN ...
ELSE ...
END
```

In Lisp, the equivalent construct is

```
(cond
    ((= A B)
        (...))
    ((= A C)
        (...))
    ((= A D)
        (...))
    (T
        (...)))
```

Here `cond` takes as arguments a sequence of pairs. In each pair the first element is a condition; the second is an expression to be returned as the value of the overall construct if the condition evaluates to T (T means "true" in most Lisp dialects).

6.4.1 Short-Circuited Conditions

While the condition in an `if...then...else` statement is a Boolean expression, there is usually no need for evaluation of that expression to result in a Boolean value in a register. Most machines provide conditional branch instructions that capture simple comparisons. Put another way, the purpose of the Boolean expression in a selection statement is not to compute a value to be stored, but to cause control to branch to various locations. This observation allows us to generate particularly efficient code (called *jump code*) for expressions that are amenable to the short-circuit evaluation of Section 6.1.4. Jump code is applicable not only to selection statements such as `if...then...else`, but to logically controlled loops as well; we will consider the latter in Section 6.5.4.

In the usual process of code generation, either via an attribute grammar or via ad hoc syntax tree decoration, a synthesized attribute of the root of an expression subtree acquires the name of a register into which the value of the expression will be computed at run time. The surrounding context then uses this register name when generating code that uses the expression. In jump code, *inherited* attributes of the root inform it of the addresses to which control should branch if the expression is true or false respectively. Jump code can be generated quite elegantly by an attribute grammar, particularly one that is *not* L-attributed (see Exercise 6.9).

Suppose, for example, that we are generating code for the following source:

```
if ((A > B) and (C > D)) or (E <> F) then
        then_clause
else
        else_clause
```

In Pascal, which does not use short-circuit evaluation, the output code would look something like this:

```
        r1 := A              -- load
        r2 := B
        r1 := r1 > r2
        r2 := C
        r3 := D
        r2 := r2 > r3
        r1 := r1 & r2
        r2 := E
        r3 := F
        r2 := r2 <> r3
        r1 := r1 | r2
        if r1 = 0 goto L2
L1:     then_clause          -- (label not actually used)
        goto L3
L2:     else_clause
L3:
```

The root of the subtree for ((A > B) and (C > D)) or (E <> F) would name r1 as the register containing the expression value. In jump code, by contrast, the inherited attributes of the condition's root would indicate that control should "fall through" to L1 if the condition is true, or branch to L2 if the condition is false. Output code would then look something like this:

```
        r1 := A
        r2 := B
        if r1 <= r2 goto L4
        r1 := C
        r2 := D
        if r1 > r2 goto L1
L4:  r1 := E
        r2 := F
        if r1 = r2 goto L2
L1:  then_clause
        goto L3
L2:  else_clause
L3:
```

Here the value of the Boolean condition is never explicitly placed into a register. Rather it is implicit in the flow of control. Moreover for most values of A, B, C, D, and E, the execution path through the jump code is shorter and therefore faster (assuming good branch prediction) than the straight-line code that calculates the value of every subexpression. If the value of a short-circuited expression is needed explicitly, it can of course be generated, while still using jump code for efficiency. The Ada fragment

```
found_it := p /= null and then p.key = val;
```

is equivalent to

```
if p /= null and then p.key = val then
    found_it := true;
else
    found_it := false;
end if;
```

and can be translated as

```
        r1 := p
        if r1 = 0 goto L1
        r2 := r1→key
        if r2 <> val goto L1
        r1 := 1
        goto L2
L1:  r1 := 0
L2:  found_it := r1
```

The astute reader will notice that the first goto L1 can be replaced by goto L2, since r1 already contains a zero in this case. The code improvement phase of the compiler will notice this also, and make the change. It is easier to fix this sort of thing in the code improver than it is to generate the better version of the code in the first place. The code improver has to be able to recognize jumps to redundant instructions for other reasons anyway; there is no point in building special cases into the short-circuit evaluation routines. There will be other "obvious" opportunities for code improvement in future examples; we will not comment on them individually.

6.4.2 Case/Switch Statements

The `case` statements of Algol W and its descendants provide alternative syntax for a special case of nested `if...then...else`. When each condition compares the same integer expression to a different compile-time constant, then the following code (written here in Modula-2)

```
i := ...   (* potentially complicated expression *)
IF i = 1 THEN
    clause_A
ELSIF i IN 2, 7 THEN
    clause_B
ELSIF i IN 3..5 THEN
    clause_C
ELSIF (i = 10) THEN
    clause_D
ELSE
    clause_E
END
```

can be rewritten as

```
CASE ...   (* potentially complicated expression *) of
    1:       clause_A
|   2, 7:    clause_B
|   3..5:    clause_C
|   10:      clause_D
    ELSE     clause_E
END
```

The elided code fragments (*clause_A*, *clause_B*, etc.) after the colons and the ELSE are called the *arms* of the CASE statement. The lists of constants in front of the colons are CASE statement *labels*. The constants in the label lists must be disjoint, and must be of a type compatible with the tested expression. Most languages allow this type to be anything whose values are discrete: integers, characters, enumerations, and subranges of the same.

The CASE statement version of the code above is certainly less verbose than the IF...THEN...ELSE version, but syntactic elegance is not the principal motivation for providing a CASE statement in a programming language. The principal motivation is to facilitate the generation of efficient target code. The IF... THEN... ELSE statement is most naturally translated as follows:

```
     r1 := ...              -- calculate tested expression
     if r1 <> 1 goto L1
     clause_A
     goto L6
L1:  if r1 = 2 goto L2
     if r1 <> 7 goto L3
L2:  clause_B
     goto L6
L3:  if r1 < 3 goto L4
     if r1 > 5 goto L4
     clause_C
     goto L6
L4:  if r1 <> 10 goto L5
     clause_D
     goto L6
L5:  clause_E
L6:
```

Rather than test its expression sequentially against a series of possible values, the case statement is meant to *compute* an address to which it jumps in a single instruction. The general form of the target code generated from a case statement appears in Figure 6.4. The code at label L6 can take any of several forms. The most common of these simply indexes into an array:

```
T:   &L1               -- tested expression = 1
     &L2
     &L3
     &L3
     &L3
     &L5
     &L2
     &L5
     &L5
     &L4               -- tested expression = 10
L6:  r1 := ...         -- calculate tested expression
     if r1 < 1 goto L5
     if r1 > 10 goto L5    -- L5 is the "else" arm
     r1 -:= 1
     r2 := T[r1]
     goto *r2
L7:
```

```
        goto L6            -- jump to code to compute address
L1:  clause_A
        goto L7
L2:  clause_B
        goto L7
L3:  clause_C
        . . .
L4:  clause_D
        goto L7
L5:  clause_E
        goto L7

L6:  r1 := . . .           -- computed target of branch
        goto *r1
L7:
```

Figure 6.4 General form of target code generated for a five-arm case **statement.** One could eliminate the initial goto L6 and the final goto L7 by computing the target of the branch at the top of the generated code, but it may be cumbersome to do so, particularly in a one-pass compiler. The form shown adds only a single jump to the control flow in most cases, and allows the code for all of the arms of the case statement to be generated as encountered, before the code to determine the target of the branch can be deduced.

Here the "code" at label T is actually a table of addresses, known as a *jump table*. It contains one entry for each integer between the lowest and highest values, inclusive, found among the **case** statement labels. The code at L6 checks to make sure that the tested expression is within the bounds of the array (if not, we should execute the **else** arm of the **case** statement). It then fetches the corresponding entry from the table and branches to it.

A linear jump table is fast. It is also space-efficient when the overall set of **case** statement labels is dense and does not contain large ranges. It can consume an extraordinarily large amount of space, however, if the set of labels is nondense, or includes large value ranges. Alternative methods to compute the address to which to branch include sequential testing, hashing, and binary search. Sequential testing (as in an **if...then...else** statement) is the method of choice if the total number of **case** statement labels is small. It runs in time $O(n)$, where n is the number of labels. A hash table is attractive if the range of label values is large, but has many missing values and no large ranges. With an appropriate hash function it will run in time $O(1)$. Unfortunately, a hash table requires a separate entry for each possible value of the tested expression, making it unsuitable for statements with large value ranges. Binary search can accommodate ranges easily. It runs in time $O(\log n)$, with a relatively low constant factor.

To generate good code for all possible `case` statements, a compiler needs to be prepared to use a variety of lookup strategies. During compilation it can generate code for the various arms of the case statement as it finds them, while simultaneously building up an internal data structure to describe the label set. Once it has seen all the arms, it can decide which form of target code to generate. For the sake of simplicity, most compilers employ only some of the possible implementations. Many use binary search in lieu of hashing. Some generate only indexed jump tables; others only that plus sequential testing. Users of less sophisticated compilers may need to restructure their `case` statements if the generated code turns out to be unexpectedly large or slow.

As with `if...then...else` statements, the syntactic details of `case` statements vary from language to language. Pascal and C do not allow ranges in their label lists, presumably to save the compiler from the need to use binary search. In keeping with the style of its other structured statements, Pascal defines each arm of a `case` statement to contain a single statement; `begin...end` delimiters are required to bracket statement lists. Modula, Ada, Fortran 90, and many other languages expect arms to contain statement lists by default.

Standard Pascal does not include a default clause: all values on which to take action must appear explicitly in label lists. It is a dynamic semantic error for the expression to evaluate to a value that does not appear. Most Pascal compilers permit the programmer to add a default clause, labeled either `else` or `otherwise`, as a language extension. Modula provides for an optional `else` clause in the language definition. If one does not appear in a given `case` statement, then it is a dynamic semantic error for the tested expression to evaluate to a missing value. Ada requires arm labels to cover *all* possible values in the domain of the type of the tested expression. If the type of tested expression has a very large number of values, then this coverage must be accomplished using ranges or an `others` clause. In some languages, notably C and Fortran 90, it is *not* an error for the tested expression to evaluate to a missing value. Rather, the entire construct has no effect when the value is missing.

C's syntax for `case` (`switch`) statements (retained by C++ and Java) is unusual in other respects:

```
switch (...  /* tested expression */) {
    case 1:  clause_A
             break;
    case 2:
    case 7:  clause_B
             break;
    case 3:
    case 4:
    case 5:  clause_C
             break;
    case 10: clause_D
             break;
    default: clause_E
             break;
}
```

Here each possible value for the tested expression must have its own label within the `switch`; ranges are not allowed. In fact, lists of labels are not allowed, but the effect of lists can be achieved by allowing a label (such as 2, 3, and 4 above) to have an *empty* arm that simply "falls through" into the code for the subsequent label. Because of the provision for fall-through, an explicit `break` statement must be used to get out of the `switch` at the end of an arm, rather than falling through into the next. There are rare circumstances in which the ability to fall through is convenient:

```
letter_case = lower;
switch (c) {
    ...
    case 'A' :
        letter_case = upper;
        /* FALL THROUGH! */
    case 'a' :
        ...
        break;
    ...
}
```

Most of the time, however, the need to insert a `break` at the end of each arm—and the compiler's willingness to accept arms without breaks, silently—is a recipe for unexpected and difficult-to-diagnose bugs.

Historically, `case` statements are a descendant of the computed `goto` statement of Fortran and the `switch` construct of Algol 60. In early versions of Fortran, one can specify multiway branching based on an integer value as follows:

```
goto (15, 100, 150, 200), I
```

If `I` is one, control jumps to the statement labeled 15. If `I` is two, control jumps to the statement labeled 100. If `I` is outside the range 1..4, the statement has no effect. Any integer-valued expression could be used in place of `I`. Computed `goto`s are still allowed in Fortran 90, but are identified by the language manual as a "deprecated" feature, retained to facilitate compilation of old programs.

In Algol 60, a `switch` is essentially an array of labels:

```
switch S := L15, L100, L150, L200;
...
goto S[I];
```

Algol 68 eliminates the `goto`s by, in essence, indexing into an array of statements, but the syntax is rather cumbersome.

6.5 Iteration

Iteration and recursion are the two mechanisms that allow a computer to perform the same set of operations repeatedly. Without at least one of these mechanisms, the running time of a program (and hence the amount of work it can do and the amount of space it can use) is a linear function of the size of the program text, and the computational power of the language is no greater than that of a finite automaton. In a very real sense, it is iteration and recursion that make computers useful. In this section we focus on iteration. Recursion is the subject of Section 6.6.

Programmers in imperative languages tend to use iteration more than they use recursion (recursion is more common in functional languages). In most languages, iteration takes the form of *loops*. Like the statements in a sequence, the iterations of a loop are generally executed for their side effects: their modifications of variables. Loops come in two principal varieties; these differ in the mechanisms used to determine how many times they iterate. An *enumeration-controlled* loop is executed once for every value in a given finite set. The number of iterations is therefore known before the first iteration begins. A *logically controlled* loop is executed until some Boolean condition (which must necessarily depend on values altered in the loop) changes value. The two forms of loops share a single construct in Algol 60. They are distinct in most later languages.

6.5.1 Enumeration-Controlled Loops

Enumeration-controlled loops are as old as Fortran. The Fortran syntax and semantics have evolved considerably over time. In Fortran I, II, and IV a loop looks something like this:

```
      do 10 i = 1, 10, 2
         ...
  10: continue
```

The number after the do is a label that must appear on some statement later in the current subroutine; the statement it labels is the last one in the *body* of the loop: the code that is to be executed multiple times. Continue is a "no-op": a statement that has no effect. Using a continue for the final statement of the loop makes it easier to modify code later: additional "real" statements can be added to the bottom of the loop without moving the label.[5]

The variable name after the label is the *index* of the loop. The comma-separated values after the equals sign indicate the initial value of the index, the

---

5 The continue statement of C probably takes its name from this typical use of the no-op in Fortran, but its semantics are very different: the C continue starts the next iteration of the loop even when the current one has not finished.

maximum value it is permitted to take, and the amount by which it is to increase in each iteration (this is called the *step size*). A bit more precisely, the loop above is equivalent to

```
        i = 1
   10:     ...
        i = i + 2
        if i <= 10 goto 10
```

Index variable i in this example will take on the values 1, 3, 5, 7, and 9 in successive loop iterations. Compilers can translate this loop into very simple, fast code for most machines.

In practice, unfortunately, this early form of loop proved to have several problems. Some of these problems were comparatively minor. The loop bounds and step size (1, 10, and 2 in our example) were required to be positive integer constants or variables: no expressions were allowed. Fortran 77 removed this restriction, allowing arbitrary positive and negative integer and real expressions. Also, as we saw in Section 2.2.1 (page 45), trivial lexical errors can cause a Fortran IV compiler to misinterpret the code as an ordinary sequence of statements beginning with an assignment. Fortran 77 makes such misinterpretation less likely by allowing an extra comma after the label in the do loop header. Fortran 90 takes back the ability to use real numbers for loop bounds and step sizes. The problem with reals is that limited precision can cause comparisons (e.g., between the index and the upper bound) to produce unexpected or even implementation-dependent results when the values are close to one another.

The more serious problems with the Fortran IV do loop are a bit more subtle:

- If statements in the body of the loop (or in subroutines called from the body of the loop) change the value of i, then the loop may execute a different number of times than one would assume based on the bounds in its header. If the effect is accidental, the bug is hard to find. If the effect is intentional, the code is hard to read.

- Goto statements may jump into or out of the loop. Code that jumps out and (optionally) back in again is expressly allowed (if difficult to understand). On the other hand, code that simply jumps in, without properly initializing i, almost certainly represents a programming error, but will not be caught by the compiler.

- If control leaves a do loop via a goto, the value of i is the one most recently assigned. If the loop terminates normally, however, the value of i is implementation-dependent. From the example above, one might expect the value to be the first one outside the loop bounds: $L + (\lfloor (U - L)/S \rfloor + 1) \times S$, where L, U, and S are the lower and upper bounds of the loop and the step size, respectively. Unfortunately, if the upper bound is close to the largest value that can be represented given the precision of integers on the target machine, then the increment at the bottom of the final iteration of the loop may cause arithmetic overflow. On most machines this overflow will result in an apparently negative value, which will prevent the loop from terminating correctly. On some it will cause a run-time exception that requires the intervention of the operating system in order to continue execution. To ensure correct termination and/or avoid the cost of an exception, a compiler must generate more complex (and slower) code when it is unable to rule out overflow at compile time. In this event, the index may contain its final value (not the "next" value) after normal termination of the loop.

▪ Because the test against the upper bound appears at the bottom of the loop, the body will always be executed at least once, even if the "low" bound is larger than the "high" bound.

These problems are important in a larger context than merely Fortran IV. They must be addressed in the design of enumeration-controlled loops in any language. Consider the arguably more friendly syntax of Modula-2:

```
FOR i := first TO last BY step DO
    ...
END
```

where `first`, `last`, and `step` can be arbitrarily complex expressions of an integer, enumeration, or subrange type. Based on the above discussion, one might ask

1. Can `i`, `first`, and/or `last` be modified in the loop? If so, what is the effect on control?

2. What happens if `first` is larger than `last` (or smaller, in the case of a negative `step`)?

3. What is the value of `i` when the loop is finished?

4. Can control jump into the loop from outside?

Changes to loop indices or bounds

Most languages, including Algol 68, Pascal, Ada, Fortran 77 and 90, and Modula-3, prohibit changes to the loop index within the body of an enumeration-controlled loop. They also guarantee to evaluate the bounds of the loop exactly once, before the first iteration, so any changes to variables on which those bounds depend will not have any effect on the number of iterations executed. Modula-2 is vague; the manual says that the index "should not be changed" by the body of the loop [Wir85b, Sec. 9.8]. ISO Pascal goes to considerable lengths to prohibit modification. Paraphrasing slightly, it says [Int90, Sec. 6.8.3.9] that the index variable must be declared in the closest enclosing block, and that neither the body of the `for` statement itself, nor any statement contained in a subroutine local to the block can "threaten" the index variable. A statement is said to threaten a variable if it

- assigns to it.
- passes it to a subroutine by reference.
- reads it from a file.
- is a structured statement containing a simpler statement that threatens it.

The prohibition against threats in local subroutines is made because a local variable will be accessible to those subroutines, and one of them, if called from within the loop, might change the value of the variable even if it is not passed to it by reference.

Empty Bounds

Modern languages refrain from executing an enumeration-controlled loop if the bounds are empty. In other words, they test the terminating condition *before* the first iteration. The initial test requires a few extra instructions, but leads to much more intuitive behavior. The loop

```
for i := first to last by step do
    ...
end
```

can be translated as

```
        r1 := first
        r2 := step
        r3 := last
L1: if r1 > r3 goto L2
        ...                    -- loop body; use r1 for i
        r1 := r1 + r2
        goto L1
L2:
```

A slightly better if less straightforward translation is

```
        r1 := first
        r2 := step
        r3 := last
        goto L2
L1: ...                        -- loop body; use r1 for i
        r1 := r1 + r2
L2: if r1 <= r3 goto L1
```

The advantage of this second version is that each iteration of the loop contains a single conditional branch, rather than a conditional branch at the top and an unconditional branch at the bottom. (We will consider yet another version in Exercise 13.5.)

The translations shown above work only if $\text{first} + (\lfloor(\text{last}-\text{first})/\text{step}\rfloor + 1) \times \text{step}$ does not exceed the largest representable integer. If the compiler cannot verify this property at compile time, then it will have to generate more cautious code (to be discussed in more detail later in this section).

The astute reader may also have noticed that the code shown here implicitly assumes that `step` is positive. If `step` is negative, the test for termination must "go the other direction." If `step` is not a compile-time constant, then the compiler cannot tell which form of test to use. Some languages, including Pascal and Ada, require the programmer to predict the sign of the step. In Pascal, one must say

```
for i := 10 downto 1 do ...
```

In Ada, one must say

```
for i in reverse 1..10 do ...
```

Modula-2 and Modula-3 do not require special syntax for "backward" loops, but insist that `step` be a compile-time constant, so the compiler can tell the difference (Modula (1) has no `for` loop). In Fortran 77 and Fortran 90, which have neither a special "backward" syntax nor a requirement for compile-time constant steps, the compiler can use an "iteration count" variable to control the loop:

```
        r1 := first
        r2 := step
        r3 := max(⌊(last − first + step)/step⌋, 0)        –– iteration count
                –– NB: this calculation may require several instructions.
                –– It is guaranteed to result in a value within the
                –– precision of the machine, but we have to be careful
                –– to avoid overflow during its calculation.
        if r3 <= 0 goto L2
L1: ...                          –– loop body; use r1 for i
        r1 := r1 + r2
        r3 := r3 − 1
        if r3 > 0 goto L1
        i := r1
L2:
```

The use of the iteration count avoids the need to test the sign of `step` within the loop. It also avoids problems with overflow when testing the terminating condition (assuming that we have been suitably careful in calculating the iteration count). Some processors, including the PowerPC, PA-RISC, and most CISC machines, can decrement the iteration count, test it against zero, and conditionally branch, all in a single instruction. In simple cases, the code improvement phase of the compiler may be able to use a technique known as *induction variable elimination* to eliminate the need to maintain both r1 and r3.

Access to the Index Outside the Loop

Several languages, including Fortran IV and Pascal, leave the value of the loop index undefined after termination of the loop. Others, such as Fortran 77 and Algol 60, guarantee that the value is the one "most recently assigned." For "normal" termination of the loop, this is the first value that exceeds the upper bound. It is not clear what happens if this value exceeds the largest value representable on the machine (or the smallest value in the case of a negative step size). A similar question arises in Pascal, in which the type of an index can be a subrange or enumeration. In this case the first value "after" the upper bound can often be invalid:

```
var c : 'a'..'z';
...
for c := 'a' to 'z' do begin
    ...
end;
(* what comes after 'z'? *)
```

Examples such as this illustrate the rationale for leaving the final value of the index undefined in Pascal. The alternative—defining the value to be the last one that was valid—would force the compiler to generate slower code for every loop, with two branches in each iteration, instead of one:

```
        r1 := 'a'
        r2 := 'z'
        if r1 > r2 goto L3      -- Code improver may remove this test,
                                -- since 'a' and 'z' are constants.
L1:     ...                     -- loop body; use r1 for i
        if r1 = r2 goto L2
        r1 := r1 + 1
        -- NB: Pascal step size is always 1 (or −1 if downto)
        goto L1
L2:     i := r1
L3:
```

Note that the compiler must generate this sort of code in any event (or use an iteration count) if arithmetic overflow may interfere with testing the terminating condition.

Several languages, including Algol W, Algol 68, Ada, Modula-3, and the new international standard for C++ avoid the issue of the value held by the index outside the loop by making the index a local variable *of* the loop. The header of the loop is considered to contain a *declaration* of the index. Its type is inferred from the bounds of the loop, and its scope is the loop's body. Because the index is not visible outside the loop, its value is not an issue. Since it is not visible even to local subroutines, much of the concept of "threatening" in Pascal becomes unnecessary. Finally, there is no chance that a value held in the index variable before the loop, and needed after, will inadvertently be destroyed. (Of course, the programmer must not give the index the same name as any variable that must be accessed within the loop, but this is a strictly local issue: it has no ramifications outside the loop.)

Jumps

Algol 60, Fortran 77, and most of their successors place restrictions on the use of the `goto` statement that prevent it from entering a loop from outside. `Goto`s can be used to *exit* a loop prematurely, but this is a comparatively clean operation; questions of uninitialized indices and bounds do not arise. As we shall see below, many languages provide an `exit` statement as a semistructured alternative to a loop-escaping `goto`.

6.5.2 Combination Loops

Algol 60, as mentioned above, provides a single loop construct that subsumes the properties of more modern enumeration- and logically controlled loops. The general form is given by

for_stmt → `for` *id* `:=` *for_list* `do` *stmt*

for_list → *enumerator* (`,` *enumerator*)*

enumerator → *expr*

          → *expr* `step` *expr* `until` *expr*

          → *expr* `while` *condition*

Here the index variable takes on values specified by a sequence of enumerators, each of which can be a single value, a range of values similar to that of modern enumeration-controlled loops, or an expression with a terminating condition. Each expression in the current enumerator is reevaluated at the top of the loop. This reevaluation is what makes the `while` form of enumerator useful: its condition typically depends on the current value of the index variable. All of the following are equivalent:

```
for i := 1, 3, 5, 7, 9 do ...
for i := 1 step 2 until 10 do ...
for i := 1, i + 2 while i < 10 do ...
```

In practice the generality of the Algol 60 `for` loop turns out to be overkill. The repeated reevaluation of bounds, in particular, can lead to loops that are very hard to understand. Some of the power of the Algol 60 loop is retained in a cleaner form in the `for` loop of C.

C's `for` loop is, strictly speaking, logically controlled. Any enumeration-controlled loop, however, can be rewritten in a logically controlled form (this is of course what the compiler does when it translates into assembler), and C's `for` loop is deliberately designed to facilitate writing the logically controlled equivalent of a Pascal or Algol-style `for` loop. Our Modula-2 example

```
FOR i := first TO last BY step DO
    ...
END
```

would usually be written in C as

```
for (i = first; i <= last; i += step) {
    ...
}
```

C defines this to be precisely equivalent to

```
i = first;
while (i <= last) {
    ...
    i += step;
}
```

This definition means that it is the programmer's responsibility to worry about the effect of overflow on testing of the terminating condition. It also means that both the index and any variables contained in the terminating condition can be modified by the body of the loop, or by subroutines it calls, and these changes *will* affect the loop control. This, too, is the programmer's responsibility.

Any of the three substatements in the `for` loop header can be null (the condition is considered true if missing). Alternatively, a substatement can consist of a sequence of comma-separated expressions. The advantage of the C `for` loop over its `while` loop equivalent is compactness and clarity. In particular, all of the code affecting the flow of control is localized within the header. In the `while` loop, one must read both the top and the bottom of the loop to know what is going on.

6.5.3* Iterators

In all of the examples we have seen so far (with the possible exception of code in Algol 60 or C), a `for` loop is used to iterate over the elements of an arithmetic sequence. In general, however, we may wish to iterate over the elements of any well-defined set. Clu, which emphasizes data abstraction, allows any set-like abstract data type to provide an *iterator* that enumerates its items. The Clu `for` loop is then designed to incorporate a call to an iterator. The Modula-2 fragment

```
FOR i := first TO last BY step DO
    ...
END
```

would be written as follows in Clu:

```
from_to_by = iter (from, to, by : int) yields (int)
    i : int := from
    if by > 0 then
        while i <= to do
            yield i
            i +:= by
        end
    else
        while i >= to do
            yield i
            i +:= by
        end
    end
end from_to_by
```

Figure 6.5 Possible implementation of the `from_to_by` **iterator in Clu.** This code may not work correctly if either the comparisons or increment result in arithmetic overflow.

```
for i in from_to_by (first, last, step) do
    ...
end
```

Here `from_to_by` is a built-in iterator that produces the integers from `first` to `first` + $\lfloor$`last` − `first`/`step`$\rfloor$ × `step` in increments of `step`.

Clu programmers can write their own iterators for arbitrary abstract types. A binary tree abstraction, for example, might provide `pre_order`, `in_order`, and `post_order` iterators to enumerate its elements according to the various canonical traversals. A possible implementation of the `from_to_by` iterator appears in Figure 6.5. It uses the `yield` statement to return control to the calling `for` loop. On the next iteration of the loop it continues execution where it last left off. When it terminates, the loop terminates also.

Each `for` loop in Clu calls only a single iterator, but `for` loops can be nested, and iterators can be recursive. Raphael Finkel [Fin96, p. 41] presents a particularly elegant algorithm that uses iterators to enumerate all structurally distinct binary trees with a given total number of nodes. A Clu version of this algorithm appears in Figure 6.6.

Generators in Icon

Iterators are also found in Icon, which calls them *generators*. Like Clu, Icon uses iterators for enumeration-controlled iteration. Our canonical `for` loop example would be written as follows in Icon:

```
every i := first to last by step do {
    ...
}
```

```
bin_tree = cluster is ..., tree_gen, print, ...        % export list
    node = record [left, right : bin_tree]
    rep = variant [some : node, empty : null]
    ...
    tree_gen = iter (k : int) yields (cvt)
        if k = 0 then yield rep$make_empty(nil)
            % just the empty tree
        else
            for i : int in from_to (1, k) do
                for l : bin_tree in tree_gen (i-1) do
                    for r : bin_tree in tree_gen (k-i) do
                        yield rep$make_some(node${l, r})
                    end
                end
            end
        end
    end tree_gen
...
end bin_tree
...
for t : bin_tree in bin_tree$tree_gen (n) do
    bin_tree$print (t)
end
```

Figure 6.6 Clu iterator to enumerate all binary trees of n **nodes.** In this (simplistic) example we have assumed that tree nodes contain no data other than their left and right child pointers. Within the bin_tree cluster, the rep (representation) declaration indicates that a binary tree is either a node or empty. The tree_gen iterator is defined recursively. For all possible partitions of $n-1$ nodes among the left and right subtrees, it yields all structurally distinct trees with that partition. The cvt (convert) in the header of tree_gen indicates that the return value is a bin_tree whose internal structure (rep) should be visible to the code of tree_gen itself, but not to the caller.

Here ...to...by... is a built-in infix generator. Because Icon is intended largely for string manipulation, most of its built-in generators operate on strings. Find (substr, str) generates the positions (indices) within string str at which an occurrence of the substring substr can be found. Upto (chars, str) generates the positions within string str at which any character in chars appears. (The initial argument to find is a string, delimited by double quote marks; the initial argument to upto is a cset [character set], delimited by single quote marks.) The prefix operator ! generates all elements of its operand, which can be a string, list, record, file, or table.

In comparison to Clu, the generators of Icon are more deeply embedded in the semantics of the language. For example, a generator can be used in any context that expects an expression. The larger context is then capable of generating multiple results. The following code will print all positions in s that follow a blank:

```
every i := 1 + upto (' ', s) do {
    write (i)
}
```

This can even be written as

```
every write (1 + upto (' ', s))
```

Generators in Icon are used not only for iteration, but also for *goal-directed search*, implemented via *backtracking*. Where most languages use Boolean expressions to control selection and logically controlled loops, Icon uses a more general notion of *success* and *failure*. A conditional statement such as

```
if 2 < 3 then {
    ...
}
```

is said to execute not because the condition 2 < 3 is true, but because the *comparison* 2 < 3 *succeeds*. The distinction is important for generators, which are capable of producing results repeatedly until one of them causes the surrounding context to succeed (or until no more results can be produced). For example, in

```
if (i := find ("abc", s)) > 6 then {
    ...
}
```

the body of the `if` statement will be executed only if the string `"abc"` appears beyond the sixth position in `s`. Because `find` generates its results in order, `i` will represent the first such position (if any). The execution model is as follows: `find` is capable of generating all positions at which `"abc"` occurs in `s`. Suppose the first such occurrence is at position 2. Then `i` is assigned the value 2, but the comparison 2 > 6 fails. Because there is a generator inside the failed expression, Icon will resume that generator and reevaluate the expression for the next generated value. It will continue this reevaluation process until the comparison succeeds, or until the generator runs out of values, in which case it (the generator) fails, the overall expression fails definitively, and the body of the `if` is skipped.

If a failed expression contains more than one generator, all possible values will be explored systematically. The body of the following `if`, for example, will be executed if an only if an `x` appears at the same position in both `s` and `t`, with `i` denoting the first such matching position:

```
if (i := find ("x", s)) = find ("x", t) then {
    ...
}
```

If there is no matching position, then i will be set to the position of the final x in s, but the body of the loop will be skipped. If the programmer wishes to avoid changing i in the case where the overall test fails, then the *reversible assignment* operator, <- can be used instead of :=. When Icon backtracks past a reversible assignment, it restores the original value.

Any user-defined subroutine in Icon can be a generator if it uses the suspend *expr* statement instead of return *expr*. Suspend is Icon's equivalent of yield. If the expression following suspend contains an invocation of a generator, then the subroutine will suspend repeatedly, once for each generated value.

Enumerating without Iterators

Iterators pose some special implementation problems. In the normal flow of control among subroutines, space for local variables, arguments, and bookkeeping information can naturally be allocated on a stack. With an iterator, however, control may jump back and forth to the point of call many times. Because state must be maintained for both contexts concurrently, straightforward stack-based allocation no longer suffices. We will consider alternative implementations in Section 8.6.3.

In a language without iterators, one can often achieve a similar effect through programming conventions, albeit with considerably less elegance. Suppose, for example, that we have defined a binary tree data structure in C, and wish to be able to iterate over its nodes using pre-order (depth-first) traversal. Code to accomplish this task appears in Figure 6.7. It consists of a data structure tree_iter, four interface subroutines (ti_create, ti_done, ti_val, and ti_next), and one auxilliary subroutine (ti_push). The data structure encapsulates all the information that would be held in the local variables, parameters, and program counter of an iterator, if we had a real one. The subroutines create a tree_iter, test to see if it is done, generate the next node if it is not done, and finally destroy it. While it would be possible to define our iterator recursively (calls to tree_iter_next would allocate subiterators dynamically), it is more convenient in this case to adopt an iterative traversal algorithm, with an explicit stack of nodes that have yet to be explored. Given the definitions in Figure 6.7, we can then write

```
tree_node *my_tree;
tree_iter ti;
...
for (ti_create (my_tree, &ti); !ti_done (ti); ti_next (&ti)) {
    tree_node *n = ti_val (ti);
    ...
}
ti_delete (&ti);
```

```c
typedef struct tree_node {
    data val;
    struct tree_node *left, *right;
} tree_node;

/* a tree_iter contains a list-based stack of
   tree_nodes (subtrees) that have yet to be visited */

typedef struct list_node {
    tree_node *tn;
    struct list_node *next;
} list_node;

typedef list_node *tree_iter;

void ti_push (tree_node *n, tree_iter *tp) {
    if (n) {
        list_node *t = *tp;
        *tp = (tree_iter) malloc (sizeof (list_node));
        (*tp)->tn = n;   (*tp)->next = t;
    }
}

void ti_create (tree_node *root, tree_iter *tp) {
    *tp = 0;
    ti_push (root, tp);
}

int ti_done (tree_iter ti) {return (ti == 0);}

tree_node *ti_val (tree_iter ti) {
    assert (ti != 0);
    return ti->tn;
}

void ti_next (tree_iter *tp) {
    tree_node *n = ti_val (*tp);
    tree_iter t = (*tp)->next;
    free (*tp);
    *tp = t;
    ti_push (n->right, tp);   ti_push (n->left, tp);
}

void ti_delete (tree_iter *tp) {
    while (*tp != 0) {
        tree_iter t = (*tp)->next;
        free (*tp);
        *tp = t;
    }
}
```

Figure 6.7 Code to iterate in pre-order over the nodes of a binary tree in C.

Euclid facilitates the emulation of iterators by defining the semantics of `for` loops in terms of the interface to a *generator* module. A generator is an ordinary user-defined module that exports variables named `value` and `stop`, and a procedure named `Next`. These exports serve the same purposes as the `ti_val`, `ti_done`, and `ti_next` subroutines in our C example. The effect of the `ti_create` and `ti_done` routines is subsumed by the normal initialization and finalization sections of the module. The main loop of our example would be written as follows in Euclid:

```
for n in TreeIterModule loop
    ...
end loop
```

This code is equivalent to

```
begin
    var ti : TreeIterModule       {initialization code executes here}
    loop
        exit when ti.stop
        n := ti.value
        ...
        ti.Next
    end loop                      {finalization code executes here}
end
```

but is substantially easier to read. Like the ad hoc routines of our C example, a Euclid generator module must keep track of its state in variables: there is no Clu-style `yield` statement. The advantage of Euclid generators over ad hoc conventions in C is that the programmer does not have to call any interface routines explicitly: initialization and finalization of the generator takes the place of creation and deletion calls; the special form of `for` statement takes the place of the other calls.

In C++, a binary tree would most likely be defined as a specialized *container*: an object that holds references to other objects (in this case the nodes of the tree). The standard interface to a container includes the iterator functions `begin` and `end`. The first of these initializes an iterator to refer to the first object in the container; the second returns a reference to a final pseudo-object that can be used to test for completion:

```
// definition of tree and tree_iter types not shown here
for (tree_iter n = my_tree.begin (); n != my_tree.end (); ++n) {
    ... // make use of data n->val
}
```

This code relies for its correct operation on several special features of C++, including automatically invoked *constructor* and *destructor* functions for a `tree_iter` object, and overloading of the comparison (`!=`), increment (`++`), and dereference (`->`) operators. Java provides similar functionality (without the operator overloading) in the form of objects that support a standard `Enumeration` interface:

```
Enumeration e = my_tree.elements ();
while (e.hasMoreElements ()) {
    tree_node n = (tree_node) e.nextElement ();
    ... // make use of data n.val
}
```

6.5.4 Logically Controlled Loops

In comparison to enumeration-controlled loops, logically controlled loops have many fewer semantic subtleties. The only real question to be answered is where within the body of the loop the terminating condition is tested. By far the most common approach is to test the condition before each iteration. The familiar while loop syntax to do this was introduced in Algol-W and retained in Pascal:

while *condition* do *statement*

As with selection statements, most Pascal successors use an explicit terminating keyword, so that the body of the loop can be a statement list.

Neither (pre-90) Fortran nor Algol 60 really provides a while loop construct; their loops were designed to be controlled by enumeration. To obtain the effect of a while loop in Fortran 77, one must resort to gotos:

```
10:  if negated_condition goto 20
      . . .
      goto 10
20:
```

In Algol 60 one must introduce a spurious "index" variable:

for i := *irrelevant_expression* while *condition* do *statement*

Post-test Loops

Occasionally it is handy to be able to test the terminating condition at the bottom of a loop. Pascal introduced special syntax for this case, which was retained in Modula but dropped in Ada. A *post-test loop* allows us, for example, to write

```
repeat
    readln (line)
until line[1] = '$';
```

instead of

```
readln (line);
while line[1] <> '$' do
    readln (line);
```

The difference between these constructs is particularly important when the body of the loop is longer. Note that the body of a post-test loop is always executed at least once.

C provides a post-test loop whose condition works "the other direction" (i.e., "while" instead of "until"):

```
do {
    line = read_line (stdin);
} while line[0] != '$';
```

Midtest Loops

Finally, as we saw in Section 6.2, it is sometimes appropriate to test the terminating condition in the middle of a loop. This "midtest" can be accomplished with an `if` and a `goto` in most languages, but a more structured alternative is preferable. Modula (1) introduced a *midtest*, or *one-and-a-half loop* that allows a terminating condition to be tested as many times as desired within the loop:

```
loop
        statement_list
when condition exit
        statement_list
when condition exit
        ...
end
```

Using this notation, The Pascal construct

```
    while true do begin
        readln (line);
        if all_blanks (line) then goto 100;
        consume_line (line)
    end;
 100:
```

can be written as follows in Modula (1):

```
LOOP
    line := ReadLine;
WHEN AllBlanks (line) EXIT;
    ConsumeLine (line)
END;
```

The `WHEN` clause here is syntactically part of the `LOOP` construct. The syntax ensures that an `EXIT` can occur only within a `LOOP`, but it has the unfortunate side-effect of preventing an exit from within a nested construct. Modula-2 abandoned the `WHEN` clause in favor of a simpler `EXIT` statement, which is typically placed inside an `IF` statement:

```
LOOP
    line := ReadLine;
    IF AllBlanks (line) THEN EXIT END;
    ConsumeLine (line)
END;
```

Because EXIT is no longer part of the LOOP construct syntax, the semantic analysis phase of compilation must ensure that EXITs appear only inside LOOPs. There may still be an arbitrary number of them inside a given LOOP. Modula-3 allows an EXIT to leave a WHILE, REPEAT, or FOR loop, as well as a plain LOOP.

The C break statement, which we have already seen in the context of switch statements, can be used in a similar manner:

```
for (;;) {
    line = read_line (stdin);
    if (all_blanks (line)) break;
    consume_line (line);
}
```

Here the missing condition in the for loop header is assumed to always be true; for some reason, C programmers have traditionally considered this syntax to be be stylistically preferable to the equivalent while (1).

The exit statement of Euclid and Ada has a slightly different form:

```
loop
    get_line (line, length);
        -- out parameter length indicates number of characters read
        -- into out parameter line
    exit when all_blanks (line, length);
    consume_line (line, length);
end loop;
```

As in Modula-2, exit can appear anywhere inside a loop, not just at the outermost nesting level. As in Modula-3, it can also be used to leave a while or for loop. An extra advantage of the Ada exit is that it allows an optional specification of the loop that is to be terminated. Specifying a loop name allows control to escape from a multi-level loop:

```
outer: loop
    get_line (line, length);
    for i in 1..length loop
        exit outer when line(i) = '$';
        consume_char (line(i));
    end loop;
end loop outer;
```

Java extends the C/C++ break statement in a similar fashion: Java loops can be labeled as in Ada, and the break statement takes an optional loop name as parameter.

6.6 Recursion

Unlike the control-flow mechanisms discussed so far, recursion requires no special syntax. In any language that provides subroutines (particularly functions), all that is required is to permit functions to call themselves, or to call other functions that then call them back in turn. Most programmers learn in a data structures class that recursion and (logically controlled) iteration provide equally powerful means of computing functions: any iterative algorithm can be rewritten, automatically, as a recursive algorithm, and vice versa. We will compare iteration and recursion in more detail in the first subsection below. In the following subsection we will consider the possibility of passing *unevaluated* expressions into a function. While usually inadvisable, due to implementation cost, this technique will sometimes allow us to write elegant code for functions that are only defined on a subset of the possible inputs, or that explore logically infinite data structures.

6.6.1 Iteration and Recursion

As we noted in Section 3.2, Fortran 77 and certain other languages do not permit recursion. A few functional languages do not permit iteration. Most modern languages, however, provide both mechanisms. Iteration is in some sense the more "natural" of the two in imperative languages, because it is based on the repeated modification of variables. Recursion is the more natural of the two in functional languages, because it does *not* change variables. In the final analysis, which to use in which circumstance is mainly a matter of taste. To compute a sum,

$$\sum_{1 \le i \le 10} f(i)$$

it seems natural to use iteration. In C one would say:

```
typedef int (*int_func) (int);
int summation (int_func f, int low, int high) {
    /* assume low <= high */
    int total = 0;
    int i;
    for (i = low; i <= high; i++) {
        total += f(i);
    }
    return total;
}
```

To compute a value defined by a recurrence,

$$\gcd(a, b) \equiv \begin{cases} a & \text{if } a = b \\ \gcd(a-b, b) & \text{if } a > b \\ \gcd(a, b-a) & \text{if } b > a \end{cases}$$

(positive integers, a, b)

recursion may seem more natural:

```
int gcd (int a, int b) {
    /* assume a, b > 0 */
    if (a == b) return a;
    else if (a > b) return gcd (a-b, b);
    else return gcd (a, b-a);
}
```

In both these cases, the choice could go the other way:

```
typedef int (*int_func) (int);
int summation (int_func f, int low, int high) {
    /* assume low <= high */
    if (low == high) return f (low);
    else return f (low) + summation (f, low+1, high);
}

int gcd (int a, int b) {
/* assume a, b > 0 */
    while (a != b) {
        if (a > b) a = a-b;
        else b = b-a;
    }
    return a;
}
```

It is often argued that iteration is more efficient than recursion. It is more accurate to say that *naive implementation* of iteration is usually more efficient than naive implementation of recursion. In the examples above, the iterative implementations of summation and greatest divisors will be more efficient than the recursive implementations if the latter make real subroutine calls that allocate space on a run-time stack for local variables and bookkeeping information. An "optimizing" compiler, however, particularly one designed for a functional language, will often be able to generate excellent code for recursive functions. It is particularly likely to do so for *tail-recursive* functions such as gcd above. A tail-recursive function is one in which additional computation never follows a recursive call: the return value is simply whatever the recursive call returns. For such functions, dynamically allocated stack space is unnecessary: the compiler can *reuse* the space belonging to the current iteration when it makes the recursive call. In effect, a good compiler will recast the recursive gcd function above as:

```
int gcd (int a, int b) {
    /* assume a, b > 0 */
start:
    if (a == b) return a;
    else if (a > b) {
        a = a-b; goto start;
    } else {
        b = b-a; goto start;
    }
}
```

Even for functions that are not tail-recursive, automatic, often simple transformations can produce tail-recursive code. The general case of the transformation employs conversion to what is known as *continuation-passing style* [FWH92, Chaps. 8–9]. In effect, a recursive function can always avoid doing any work after returning from a recursive call by passing that work into the recursive call, in the form of a continuation.

Some specific transformations (not based on continuation-passing) are often employed by skilled users of functional languages. Consider, for example, the recursive summation function above, written here in Scheme:

```
(define summation (lambda (f low high)
    (if (= low high)
        (f low)                                    ; then part
        (+ (f low) (summation f (+ low 1) high))))) ; else part
```

Note that Scheme, like all Lisp dialects, uses Cambridge Polish notation for expressions. The `lambda` keyword plays roughly the same role as the `function` keyword in Pascal. As recursive calls return, our code calculates the sum from "right to left": from `high` down to `low`. If the programmer (or compiler) recognizes that addition is associative, we can rewrite the code in a tail-recursive form:

```
(define summation (lambda (f low high subtotal)
    (if (= low high)
        (+ subtotal (f low))
        (summation f (+ low 1) high (+ subtotal (f low))))))
```

Here the `subtotal` parameter accumulates the sum from left to right, passing it into the recursive calls. Because it is tail recursive, this function can be translated into machine code that does not allocate stack space for recursive calls. Of course, the programmer won't want to pass an explicit `subtotal` parameter to the initial call, so we hide it (the parameter) in an auxiliary, "helper" function:

```
(define summation (lambda (f low high)
  (letrec ((sum-helper (lambda (low subtotal)
            (let ((new_subtotal (+ subtotal (f low))))
              (if (= low high)
                  new_subtotal
                  (sum-helper (+ low 1) new_subtotal))))))
    (sum-helper low 0))))
```

The `let` construct in Scheme serves to introduce a nested scope in which local names (e.g., `new_subtotal`) can be defined. The `letrec` construct permits the definition of recursive functions (e.g., `sum-helper`).

Detractors of functional programming sometimes argue, incorrectly, that recursion leads to *algorithmically inferior* programs. Fibonacci numbers, for example, are defined by the mathematical recurrence

$$F_n \atop \text{(nonnegative integer } n) \equiv \begin{cases} 1 & \text{if } n = 0 \text{ or } n = 1 \\ F_{n-1} + F_{n-2} & \text{otherwise} \end{cases}$$

The naive way to implement this recurrence in Scheme is

```scheme
(define fib (lambda (n)
    (cond ((= n 0) 1)
          ((= n 1) 1)
          (#t (+ (fib (- n 1)) (fib (- n 2)))))))
          ; #t means 'true' in Scheme
```

Unfortunately, this algorithm takes exponential time, when linear time is possible. In C, one might write

```c
int fib (int n) {
    int f1 = 1; int f2 = 1;
    int i;
    for (i = 2; i <= n; i++) {
        int temp = f1 + f2;
        f1 = f2; f2 = temp;
    }
    return f2;
}
```

One can write this iterative algorithm in Scheme: Scheme includes (nonfunctional) iterative features. It is probably better, however, to draw inspiration from the tail-recursive version of the summation example above, and write the following $O(n)$ recursive function:

```scheme
(define fib (lambda (n)
    (letrec ((fib-helper (lambda (f1 f2 i)
                (if (= i n)
                    f2
                    (fib-helper f2 (+ f1 f2) (+ i 1))))))
        (fib-helper 0 1 0))))
```

For a programmer accustomed to writing in a functional style, this code is perfectly natural. One might argue that it isn't "really" recursive; it simply casts an iterative algorithm in a tail recursive form, and this argument has some merit. Despite the algorithmic similarity, however, there is an important difference between the iterative algorithm in C and the tail-recursive algorithm in Scheme: the latter has no side effects. Each recursive call of the `fib-helper` function creates a new scope, containing new variables. The language implementation may be able to reuse the space occupied by previous instances of the same scope, but it guarantees that this optimization will never introduce bugs.

We have already noted that many primarily functional languages, including Common Lisp, Scheme, and ML, provide certain nonfunctional features, including iterative constructs that are executed for their side effects. It is also possible to define an iterative construct as syntactic sugar for tail recursion, by arranging for successive iterations of a loop to introduce new scopes. The only tricky part is to make values from a previous iteration available in the next, when all local names have been reused for different variables. The dataflow language Val [McG82]

```
function fib (n : integer returns integer)
for initial
    f1 := 0;
    f2 := 1;
    i := 0;
while i < n repeat
    i := old i + 1;
    f1 := old f2;
    f2 := old f1 + old f2;
returns value of f2
end for
end function
```

Figure 6.8 Fibonacci function in Sisal. Each iteration of the `while` loop defines a new scope, with new variables named `i`, `f1`, and `f2`. The previous instances of these variables are available in each iteration as `old i`, `old f1`, and `old f2`. The entire `for` construct is an *expression*; it can appear in any context in which a value is expected.

and its successor, Sisal, provide this capability through a special keyword, `old`. Figure 6.8 contains side-effect-free iterative code for our Fibonacci function in Sisal. We will mention Sisal again in Sections 11.2.5 and 12.3.4.

6.6.2 Applicative- and Normal-Order Evaluation

Throughout the discussion so far we have assumed implicitly that arguments are evaluated before passing them to a subroutine. This need not be the case. It is possible to pass a representation of the *unevaluated* arguments to the subroutine instead, and to evaluate them only when (if) the value is actually needed. The former option (evaluating before the call) is known as *applicative-order evaluation*; the latter (evaluating only when the value is actually needed) is known as *normal-order evaluation*. Normal-order evaluation is what naturally occurs with macros. It also occurs with *call-by-name* parameters (to be discussed in Section 8.3.1), and occasionally in functional languages (to be discussed in Section 11.2.2).

Historically, C has relied heavily on macros for small, nonrecursive "functions" that need to execute quickly. To determine whether one integer divides another evenly, the C programmer might write:

```
#define DIVIDES(n,a) (!((n) % (a)))
/* true (nonzero) iff n has no remainder modulo a */
```

In every location in which the programmer uses `DIVIDES`, the compiler (actually a preprocessor that runs before the compiler) will substitute the right-hand side of the macro definition, textually, with parameters substituted as appropriate: `DIVIDES (x, y + z)` $\Rightarrow$ `(!((x) % (y + z)))`.

Macros suffer from several limitations. In the code above, for example, the parentheses around `a` and `n` in the right-hand side of the definition are essential. Without them, `DIVIDES (x, y + z)` would be replaced by `(!(x % y + z))`, which is the same as `(!((x % y) + z))`, according to the rules of precedence. More importantly, in a definition such as

```
#define MAX(a,b) ((a) > (b) ? (a) : (b))
```

the expression `MAX (x++, y++)` may behave unexpectedly, since the increment side effects will happen more than once. In general, normal-order evaluation is safe only if arguments cause no side effects when evaluated. Because macros are purely textual abbreviations, they cannot be incorporated naturally into high-level naming and scope rules. Given the following definition, for example,

```
#define SWAP(a,b) {int t = (a); (a) = (b); (b) = t;}
```

problems will arise if the programmer writes `SWAP (x, t)`.

All of these problems can be avoided in C by using real functions instead of macros. In most C implementations, however, the macros are much more efficient. They avoid the overhead of the subroutine call mechanism (including register saves and restores), and the code they generate can be integrated into any code improvements that the compiler is able to effect in the code surrounding the call. In C++, and in some C implementations, the programmer can obtain the best of both worlds by prefacing a function definition with a special `inline` keyword. This keyword instructs the compiler to expand the definition of the function at the point of call, if possible. The resulting code is then generally as efficient as a macro, but has the semantics of a function call.

Algol 60 uses normal-order evaluation by default (applicative order is also available). This choice was presumably made to mimic the behavior of macros. Most programmers in those days wrote mainly in assembler, and were accustomed to macro facilities. Because the parameter-passing mechanisms of Algol 60 are part of the language, rather than textual abbreviations, problems such as misinterpreted precedence or naming conflicts do not arise. Side effects, however, are still very much an issue. We will discuss Algol 60 parameters in more detail in Section 8.3.1.

From the points of view of clarity and efficiency, applicative-order evaluation is generally preferable to normal-order evaluation. It is therefore natural for it to be employed in most languages. In some circumstances, however, normal-order evaluation can actually lead to faster code, or to code that works when applicative-order evaluation would lead to a run-time error. In both cases, what matters is that normal-order evaluation will sometimes not evaluate an argument at all, if its value is never actually needed. Scheme provides for optional normal-order evaluation in the form of built-in functions called `delay` and `force`.[6] These functions actually provide an implementation of *lazy evaluation*. In the absence of side effects, lazy evaluation has the same semantics as normal-order evaluation, but the implementation keeps track of which expressions have already been evaluated, so it can reuse their values if they are needed more than

---

6 Actually, `delay` is a *special form*, rather than a function. Its argument is passed to it unevaluated.

once in a given referencing environment. A delayed expression is sometimes called a *promise*. The mechanism used to keep track of which promises have already been evaluated is sometimes called *memoization*. Because applicative-order evaluation is the default in Scheme, the programmer must use special syntax not only to pass an unevaluated argument, but also to use it. In Algol 60, subroutine headers indicate which arguments are to be passed which way; neither the point of call nor uses of parameters within subroutines need to distinguish between them. Lazy evaluation is used in all cases in the functional languages Miranda and Haskell.

A common use of lazy evaluation is to create so-called *infinite* or *lazy data structures* that are "fleshed out" on demand. The following example, adapted from the Scheme manual [KCR98, p. 28], creates a "list" of all the natural numbers:

```
(define naturals
  (letrec ((next (lambda (n) (cons n (delay (next (+ n 1))))))))
    (next 1)))
(define head car)
(define tail (lambda (stream) (force (cdr stream))))
```

Here cons can be thought of, roughly, as a concatenation operator. Car returns the head of a list; cdr returns everything but the head. Given these definitions, we can access as many natural numbers as we want:

```
(head naturals)                  ⇒ 1
(head (tail naturals))           ⇒ 2
(head (tail (tail naturals)))    ⇒ 3
```

The list will occupy only as much space as we have actually explored. More elaborate lazy data structures (e.g., trees) can be valuable in combinatorial search problems, in which a clever algorithm may explore only the "interesting" parts of a potentially enormous search space.

6.7* Nondeterminacy

The final category of control flow to be considered in this chapter is nondeterminacy. A nondeterministic construct is one in which the choice between alternatives (i.e., between control paths) is deliberately unspecified. We have already seen examples of nondeterminacy in the evaluation of expressions (Section 6.1.3): in most languages, operator or subroutine arguments may be evaluated in any order. In Algol 68, this lack of ordering is explicitly defined as an example of nondeterminacy, which the language designers call *collateral* execution. Several other built-in constructs are nondeterministic in Algol 68, and an explicit *collateral statement* allows the programmer to specify nondeterminacy in the evaluation of arbitrary expressions when desired.

Dijkstra [Dij75] has advocated the use of nondeterminacy for selection and logically controlled loops. His *guarded command* notation has been adopted by several languages. One of these is SR, which we will study in more detail in Chapter 12. Imagine for a moment that we are writing a function to return the maximum of two integers. In C, we would probably employ a code fragment something like this:

```
if (a > b) max = a;
else max = b;
```

Of course, we could also write

```
if (a >= b) max = a;
else max = b;
```

These fragments differ in their behavior when a = b: the first sets max = b; the second sets max = a. As a practical matter the difference is irrelevant, since a and b are equal, but it is in some sense aesthetically unpleasant to have to make an arbitrary choice between the two. More important, the arbitrariness of the choice makes it more difficult to reason about the code formally, or to prove it is correct. In a language with guarded commands (the example here is in SR), one could write:

```
if a >= b -> max := a
[] b >= a -> max := b
fi
```

The general form of this construct is

```
if  condition -> stmt_list
[]  condition -> stmt_list
[]  condition -> stmt_list
...
fi
```

Each of the conditions in this construct is known as a *guard*. The guard and its following statement, together, are called a *guarded command*. When control reaches an `if` statement in a language with guarded commands, a nondeterministic choice is made among the guards that evaluate to true, and the statement list following the chosen guard is executed. In SR, the final condition may optionally be `else`. If none of the conditions evaluates to true, the statement list following the `else`, if any, is executed. If there is no `else`, the `if` statement as a whole has no effect. (In Dijkstra's original proposal, there was no `else` guard option, and it was a dynamic semantic error for none of the guards to be true.) Interestingly, SR provides no separate `case` construct: the SR compiler detects when the conditions of an `if` statement test the same expression against a nonoverlapping set of compile-time constants, and generates table-lookup code as appropriate.

SR uses guarded commands for several purposes in addition to selection. Its logically controlled looping construct (again patterned on Dijkstra's proposal) looks very much like the `if` statement:

```
process client:
    loop
        toss coin
        if heads, send read request to server
                  wait for response
        if tails,  send write request to server
                  wait for response

process server:
    loop
            receive read request
            reply with data
        OR
            receive write request
            update data and reply
```

Figure 6.9 Example of a concurrent program that requires nondeterminacy. The server must be able to accept either a read or a write request, whichever is available at the moment. If it insists on receiving them in any particular order, deadlock may result.

```
do condition -> stmt_list
[] condition -> stmt_list
[] condition -> stmt_list
...
od
```

For each iteration of the loop, a nondeterministic choice is made among the guards that evaluate to true, and the statement list following the chosen one is executed. The loop terminates when none of the guards is true (there is no else guard option for loops). Using this notation, we can write Euclid's greatest common divisor algorithm as follows:

```
do a > b -> a := a - b
[] b > a -> b := b - a
od
gcd := a
```

While nondeterministic constructs have a certain appeal from an aesthetic and formal semantics point of view, their most compelling advantages arise in concurrent programs, for which they can affect correctness. Imagine, for example, that we are writing a simple dictionary program to support computer-aided design on a network of personal computers. The dictionary keeps a mapping from part names to their specifications. A dictionary server process handles requests from clients on other workstations on the network. Each request may be either a read (return me the current specification for part X) or a write (define part Y as follows).[7] Clients send requests at unpredictable times. As a result, the server cannot tell at any given time whether it should try to receive a read or a write request. If it makes the wrong choice the entire system may deadlock (see Figure 6.9).

Most message-based concurrent languages provide at least one nondeterministic construct that can be used to specify communication with any of several possible communication partners. In SR, one could write our dictionary server as follows:

```
# declarations of request types:
op read_data (n : name) returns val : description
op write_data (n : name; val : description)

# local subroutines:
proc lookup ...          # find info in dictionary
proc update ...          # change info in dictionary

# code for server:
process server
    do true ->           # "forever" loop
        in read_data (n) returns val -> val := lookup (n)
        [] write_data (n, val) -> update (n, val)
        ni
    od
end
```

Here `in` is a nondeterministic construct whose guards can contain communication statements. The guard `write_data (n, val)` will evaluate to true if and only if some client is attempting to send a request containing a new specification for a part. We shall see in Section 12.4.3 that more elaborate guards can allow a server to constrain the types of requests that it is willing to receive at a given point in time, or even to "peek" inside a message to see if it is acceptable. If none of the guards of an `in` statement is true, the server waits until one is.

What happens if two or more guards evaluate to true? How does the language implementation choose among them? We have glossed over this issue so far. The most naive implementation would treat a guarded command construct like a conventional `if...then...else`:

---

7 This is of course an oversimplified example. Among other things, any real system of this sort would need a mechanism to lock parts in the dictionary, so that no two clients would ever end up designing new specifications for the same part concurrently.

```
server:
    loop
        if read_data request available
            . . .
        elsif write_data request available
            . . .
        else wait until some request is available
```

The problem with this implementation is that it always favors one type of request over another; if read_data requests are always available, write_data requests will never be received. A slightly more sophisticated implementation would maintain a circular list of the guards in each set of guarded commands. Each time it encounters the construct in which these commands appear, it would check guards beginning with the one after the one that succeeded last time. This technique works well in many cases, but can fail consistently in others. In the following, for example, the guard of the first in statement combines a communication test with a Boolean condition:

```
process silly
var count : int := 0
    do true ->
        in A() st count % 2 = 1 -> ...
        [] B() -> ...
        [] C() -> ...
        ni
        count++
    od
```

This example is somewhat contrived, but illustrates the problem. The st ("such that") clause in the first guard indicates that it can be chosen only on odd iterations of the loop. Now imagine that A, B, and C requests are always available. If we always check guards starting with the one after the one that succeeded last time (beginning at first with the initial guard), then B will be chosen in the first iteration (because count mod 2 $\neq$ 1), C will be chosen in the second iteration (when count = 2), B will be chosen again in the third iteration (because again count mod 2 $\neq$ 1), and so forth. A will never be chosen.

Ideally, what we would like in a nondeterministic construct is a guarantee of *fairness*. This turns out to be trickier than one might expect: there are several plausible ways that "fair" might be defined. Certainly we would like to guarantee that no guard that is always true is always skipped. Probably, we would like to guarantee that no guard that is true infinitely often (in a hypothetical infinite sequence of iterations) is always skipped. Better, we might ask that any guard that is true infinitely often be chosen infinitely often. This stronger notion of fairness will obtain if the choice among true guards is genuinely random. Unfortunately, good pseudo-random number generators are expensive enough that we probably don't want to use them to choose among guards. As a result, most implementations of guarded commands are not provably fair. Many simply employ the circular list technique. Others use somewhat "more random" heuristics. Some machines, for example, provide a fast-running clock register that can be read efficiently in user-level code. A reasonable "random" choice of the guard to evaluate first can be made by interpreting this clock as an integer, and computing its remainder modulo the number of guards.

One final issue has to do with side effects. Guarded command constructs make a nondeterministic choice among the guards that evaluate to true. They do *not*, however, guarantee that all guards will be evaluated before the choice is made; the implementation is free to ignore the rest of the guards once it has chosen one that is true. A program may therefore produce unexpected or even unpredictable results if any of the guards have side effects. This problem is the programmer's responsibility in SR. An alternative would have been to prohibit side effects and have the compiler verify their absence.

6.8 Summary and Concluding Remarks

In this chapter we introduced the principal forms of control flow found in programming languages: sequencing, selection, iteration, recursion, concurrency, and nondeterminacy. Sequencing specifies that certain operations are to occur in order, one after the other. Selection expresses a choice among two or more control-flow alternatives. Iteration and recursion are the two ways to execute operations repeatedly. Recursion defines an operation in terms of simpler instances of itself; iteration repeats an operation for its side effect(s). Sequencing and iteration are fundamental to imperative (especially von Neumann) programming. Recursion is fundamental to functional programming. Nondeterminacy allows the programmer to leave certain aspects of control flow deliberately unspecified. We touched on concurrency only briefly; it will be the subject of Chapter 12.

Our survey of control-flow mechanisms was preceded by a discussion of expression evaluation. We considered the distinction between l-values and r-values, and between the value model of variables, in which a variable is a named container for data, and the reference model of variables, in which a variable is a reference to a data object. We considered issues of precedence, associativity, and ordering within expressions. We examined short-circuit Boolean evaluation and its implementation via jump code, both as a semantic issue that affects the correctness of expressions whose subparts are not always well defined, and as an implementation issue that affects the time required to evaluate complex Boolean expressions.

In our survey we encountered many examples of control-flow constructs whose syntax and semantics have evolved considerably over time. Particularly noteworthy has been the phasing out of `goto`-based control flow and the emergence of a consensus on structured alternatives. While convenience and readability are difficult to quantify, most programmers would agree that the control flow constructs of a language such as Ada are a dramatic improvement over those of, say, Fortran IV. Examples of features in Ada that are specifically designed to rectify control-flow problems in earlier languages include explicit terminators (end if, end loop, etc.) for structured constructs; elsif clauses; label ranges and others clauses in case statements; implicit declaration of for loop indices as read-only local variables; explicit return statements; multi-level loop exit statements; and exceptions.

The evolution of constructs has been driven by many goals, including ease of programming, semantic elegance, ease of implementation, and run-time efficiency. In some cases these goals have proven complementary. We have seen for example that short-circuit evaluation leads both to faster code and (in many cases) to cleaner semantics. In a similar vein, the introduction of a new local scope for the index variable of an enumeration-controlled loop avoids both the semantic problem of the value of the index after the loop and (to some extent) the implementation problem of potential overflow.

In other cases improvements in language semantics have been considered worth a small cost in run-time efficiency. We saw this in the addition of a pretest to the Fortran do loop and in the introduction of midtest loops (which almost always require at least two branch instructions). Iterators provide another example: like many forms of abstraction, they add a modest amount of run-time cost in many cases (e.g., in comparison to explicitly embedding the implementation of the enumerated set in the control flow of the loop), but with a large pay-back in modularity, clarity, and opportunities for code reuse. Sisal's developers would argue that even if Fortran does enjoy a performance edge in some cases, functional programming provides a more important benefit: facilitating the construction of correct, maintainable code. The developers of Java would argue that for many applications the portability and safety provided by extensive semantic checking, standard-format numeric types, and so on are far more important than speed.

Certainly the ability of Sisal to compete with Fortran at all is due to advances in compiler technology, and to advances in automatic code improvement in particular. We have seen several other examples of cases in which compiler improvements have made it possible for language designers to incorporate features once considered too expensive. Fortran 90's elimination of restrictions on bounds and step size/direction for do loops requires that the compiler be prepared to generate code employing an iteration count. Label ranges in Ada case statements require that the compiler be prepared to generate code employing binary search. In-line functions in C++ eliminate the need to choose between the inefficiency of tiny functions and the messy semantics of macros. Exceptions (as we shall see in Section 8.5.4) can be implemented in such as way that they incur no cost in the common case (when they do not occur), but the implementation is quite tricky.

Some implementation techniques (e.g., rearranging expressions to uncover common subexpressions, or avoiding the evaluation of guards in a nondeterministic construct once an acceptable choice has been found) are sufficiently important to justify a modest burden on the programmer (e.g., adding parentheses where necessary to avoid overflow or ensure numeric stability, or ensuring that expressions in guards are side-effect-free). Other semantically useful mechanisms (e.g., lazy evaluation, continuations, or truly random nondeterminacy) are usually considered complex or expensive enough to be worthwhile only in special circumstances (if at all).

In comparatively primitive languages, we can often obtain some of the benefits of missing features through programming conventions. In early dialects of Fortran, for example, we can limit the use of gotos to patterns that mimic the control flow of more modern languages. In languages without short-circuit evaluation, we can write nested selection statements. In languages without iterators, we can write sets of subroutines that provide equivalent functionality.

6.9 Review Questions

6.1 Name seven major categories of control-flow mechanisms.

6.2 What distinguishes *operators* from other sorts of functions?

6.3 Explain the difference between *prefix*, *infix*, and *postfix* notation. What is *Cambridge Polish* notation? Name two programming languages that use postfix notation.

6.4 Why don't issues of associativity and precedence arise in Postscript or Forth?

6.5 What does it mean for an expression to be *referentially transparent*?

6.6 What is the difference between a *value* model of variables and a *reference* model of variables? Why is the distinction important?

6.7 What is an *l-value*? An *r-value*?

6.8 Why is the distinction between *mutable* and *immutable* values important in the implementation of a language with a reference model of variables?

6.9 Define *orthogonality* in the context of programming language design.

6.10 What does it mean for a language to be *expression-oriented*?

6.11 Given the ability to assign a value into a variable, why is it useful to be able to specify an *initial* value?

6.12 What are *aggregates*? Why are they useful?

6.13 Explain the notion of *definite assignment* in Java.

6.14 Why is it generally expensive to catch all uses of uninitialized variables at run time?

6.15 What are the advantages of updating a variable with an *assignment operator*, rather than with a regular assignment in which the variable appears on both the left- and right-hand sides?

6.16 Why do most languages leave unspecified the order in which the arguments of an operator or function are evaluated?

6.17 What is *short-circuit* Boolean evaluation? Why is it useful? How is it implemented?

6.18 Describe three common uses of the `goto` statement, and show how to avoid them using structured control-flow alternatiaves.

6.19 Why is sequencing a comparatively unimportant form of control flow in Lisp?

6.20 What does it mean for a function to be *idempotent*?

6.21 Explain why it may sometimes be useful for a function to have side effects.

6.22 Why do imperative languages commonly provide a `case` statement in addition to `if...then...else`?

6.23 Describe three different search strategies that might be employed in the implementation of a `case` statement, and the circumstances in which each would be desirable.

6.24 Describe three subtleties in the implementation of enumeration-controlled loops.

6.25 Why do most languages not allow the bounds or increment of an enumeration-controlled loop to be floating-point numbers?

6.26 Explain the value of the *iterators* (*generators*) of Clu, Icon, and Euclid. Show how they can be simulated in other imperative languages. Explain the notions of *success* and *failure* in Icon.

6.27 Give an example in which a *midtest* loop results in more elegant code than does a pretest or post-test loop.

6.28 What is a *tail recursive* function? Why is tail recursion important?

6.29 Explain the difference between *applicative* and *normal order* evaluation of expressions. Under what circumstances is each desirable?

6.30 Give examples of some of the common pitfalls associated with the use of macros.

6.31 What is *lazy evaluation*? What are *promises*? What is *memoization*?

6.32 Give two reasons why a programmer might sometimes want control flow to be *nondeterministic*.

6.33 Give three alternative definitions of *fairness* in the context of nondeterminacy.

6.10 Exercises

6.1 We noted in Section 6.1.1 that most binary arithmetic operators are left-associative in most programming languages. At the same time, we noted in Section 6.1.3 that most compilers are free to evaluate the operands of a binary operator in either order. Are these statements contradictory? Why or why not?

6.2 Translate the following expression into postfix and prefix notation:

$$[-b + \text{sqrt}(4 \times a \times c)]/(2 \times a)$$

Do you need a special symbol for unary negation?

6.3 In Lisp, most of the arithmetic operators are defined to take two or more arguments, rather than strictly two. Thus (* 2 3 4 5) evaluates to 120, and (- 16 9 4) evaluates to 3. Show that parentheses are necessary to disambiguate arithmetic expressions in Lisp (in other words, give an example of an expression whose meaning is unclear when parentheses are removed).

In Section 6.1.1 we claimed that issues of precedence and associativity do not arise with prefix or postfix notation. Reword this claim to make explicit the hidden assumption.

6.4 Using your favorite language and compiler, investigate the order of evaluation of subroutine parameters. Are they usually evaluated left-to-right or right-to-left? Are they ever evaluated in the other order? (Can you be sure?) Write a program in which the order makes a difference in the results of the computation.

6.5 Consider the different approaches to arithmetic overflow adopted by Pascal, C, Java, and Common Lisp, as described in Section 6.1.3. Speculate as to the differences in language design goals that might have caused the designers to adopt the approaches they did.

6.6 Languages that employ a reference model of variables also tend to employ automatic garbage collection. Is this more than a coincidence? Explain.

6.7 In Section 6.1.2 we noted that C uses = for assignment and == for equality testing. The language designers state "Since assignment is about twice as frequent as equality testing in typical C programs, it's appropriate that the operator be half as long." [KR78, p. 17]. What do you think of this rationale?

6.8 Consider a language implementation that wishes to catch every use of an uninitialized variable. In Section 6.1.2 we noted that for types in which every possible bit pattern represents a valid value, extra space must be used to hold an initialized/uninitialized flag. Dynamic checks in such a system can be expensive, largely because of the address calculations needed to access the flags. We can reduce the cost in the common case by having the compiler generate code to automatically initialize every variable with a distinguished *sentinel* value. If at some point we find that a variable's value is different from the sentinel, then that variable must have been initialized. If its value *is* the sentinel, we must double-check the flag. Describe a plausible allocation strategy for initialization flags, and show the assembly language sequences that would be required for dynamic checks, with and without the use of sentinels.

6.9 Write an attribute grammar, based on the following context-free grammar, that accumulates jump code for Boolean expressions (with short-circuiting) into a synthesized attribute of *condition*, and then uses this attribute to generate code for `if` statements.

stmt → `if` *condition* `then` *stmt* `else` *stmt*

     → *other_stmt*

condition → *c_term* | *condition* `or` *c_term*

c_term → *relation* | *c_term* `and` *relation*

relation → *c_fact* | *c_fact comparator c_fact*

c_fact → `identifier` | `not` *c_fact* | `(` *condition* `)`

comparator → `<` | `<=` | `=` | `<>` | `>` | `>=`

(Hint: your task will be easier if you do *not* attempt to make the grammar L-attributed. For further details see Fischer and LeBlanc's compiler book [FL88, Sec. 14.1.4].)

6.10 Neither Algol 60 nor Algol 68 employs short-circuit evaluation for Boolean expressions. In both languages, however, an `if...then...else` construct can be used as an expression. Show how to use `if...then...else` to achieve the effect of short-circuit evaluation.

6.11 Consider the following expression in C: `a/b > 0 && b/a > 0`. What will be the result of evaluating this expression when `a` is zero? What will be the result when `b` is zero? Would it make sense to try to design a language in which this expression is guaranteed to evaluate to `false` when either `a` or `b` (but not both) is zero? Explain your answer.

6.12 As noted in Section 6.4.2, languages vary in how they handle the situation in which the tested expression in a `case` statement does not appear among the labels on the arms. C and Fortran 90 say the statement has no effect. Pascal and Modula say it results in a dynamic semantic error. Ada says that the labels must *cover* all possible values for the type of the expression, so the question of a missing value can never arise at run time. What are the tradeoffs among these alternatives? Which do you prefer? Why?

6.13 In an expression-oriented language such as Algol 68 or Lisp, a `while` loop (a `do` loop in Lisp) has a value as an expression. How do you think this value should be determined? (How is it determined in Algol 68 and Lisp?) Is the value a useless artifact of expression orientation, or are there reasonable programs in which it might actually be used? What do you think should happen if the condition on the loop is such that the body is never executed?

6.14 Recall the "blank line" example from page 296, here written in Modula-2:

```
LOOP
    line := ReadLine;
    IF AllBlanks (line) THEN EXIT END;
    ConsumeLine (line)
END;
```

Show how you might accomplish the same task using a `while` or `repeat` loop, if midtest loops were not available. (Hint: one alternative duplicates part of the code; another introduces a Boolean flag variable.) How do these alternatives compare to the midtest version?

6.15 Give an example of a midtest loop that cannot easily be written as a `while` or `repeat` loop (i.e., without duplicating code, introducing one or more Boolean flags, or embedding code with side effects into a condition).

6.16 Rubin [Rub87] used the following example (rewritten here in C) to argue in favor of a `goto` statement:

```c
int first_zero_row = -1;        /* none */
int i, j;
for (i = 0; i < n; i++) {
    for (j = 0; j < n; j++) {
        if (A[i][j]) goto next;
    }
    first_zero_row = i;
    break;
next: ;
}
```

The intent of the code is to find the first all-zero row, if any, of an $n \times n$ matrix. Do you find the example convincing? Is there a good structured alternative in C? In any language?

6.17 Bentley [Ben86, chap. 4] provides the following informal description of binary search:

> We are to determine whether the sorted array `X[1..N]` contains the element `T`.... Binary search solves the problem by keeping track of a range within the array in which `T` must be if it is anywhere in the array. Initially, the range is the entire array. The range is shrunk by comparing its middle element to `T` and discarding half the range. The process continues until `T` is discovered in the array or until the range in which it must lie is known to be empty.

Write code for binary search in your favorite imperative programming language. What loop construct(s) did you find to be most useful? NB: when he asked more than a hundred professional programmers to solve this problem, Bentley found that only about 10% got it right the first time, without testing.

6.18 A *loop invariant* is a condition that is guaranteed to be true at a given point within the body of a loop on every iteration. Loop invariants play a major role in *axiomatic semantics*, a formal reasoning system used to prove properties of programs. In a less formal way, programmers who identify (and write down!) the invariants for their loops are more likely to write correct code. Show the loop invariant(s) for your solution to the preceding exercise. (Hint: you will find the distinction between $<$ and $\leq$ [or between $>$ and $\geq$] to be crucial.)

6.19 If you have taken a course in automata theory or recursive function theory, explain why `while` loops are strictly more powerful than `for` loops. (If you haven't had such a course, skip this question!) Note that we're referring here to Pascal-style `for` loops, not C-style.

6.20 Show how to calculate the number of iterations of a general Fortran 90-style `do` loop. Your code should be written in an assembler-like notation, and should be guaranteed to work for all valid bounds and step sizes. Be careful of overflow! (Hint: While the bounds and step size of the loop can be either positive or negative, you can safely use an unsigned integer for the iteration count.)

6.21 Extend the Clu `bin_tree` cluster of Figure 6.6 to contain a value of type `data` in each node, in addition to left and right child pointers. Then write iterators that will enumerate the data values of a tree according to preorder, in-order, and postorder traversal:

```
pre_order = iter (t : cvt) yields data ...
in_order = iter (t : cvt) yields data ...
post_order = iter (t : cvt) yields data ...
```

Within each iterator you will want to use a `tagcase` statement to do different things depending on whether the root node has children:

```
tagcase t
    tag empty :
        ...
    tag some (n : node) :
        ...     % code here can refer to n.right and n.left
end
```

6.22 Rewrite the algorithm of Figure 6.6 in some language that does not have iterators. How difficult was your task? If you have access to a Scheme implementation, try writing a version that uses continuations to build the equivalent of iterators.

6.23 If you are familiar with standard C++, write a `bin_tree` container class that supports the `begin` and `end` iterator functions, as mentioned at the end of section 6.5.3. You will probably need to consult a reference on the C++ standard library [Str97, sections 3.7 and 19.2].

6.24 Write a tail-recursive function in Scheme or ML to compute n factorial ($n! = \prod_{1 \le i \le n} i = 1 \times 2 \times \cdots \times n$). (Hint: You will probably want to define a "helper" function, as discussed in Section 6.6.1.)

6.25 Rewrite the algorithm in Figure 6.7 to traverse the tree in inorder and/or postorder.

6.26 Give an example in C in which an inline subroutine may be significantly faster than a functionally equivalent macro. Give another example in which the macro is likely to be faster. (Hint: Think about applicative versus normal-order evaluation of arguments.)

6.27 Explain why the following guarded commands in SR are *not* equivalent:

```
if a < b -> c := a        if a < b -> c := a
[] b < c -> c := b        [] b < c -> c := b
[] else -> c := d         [] true -> c := d
fi                        fi
```

6.11 Bibliographic Notes

Many of the issues discussed in this chapter feature prominently in papers on the history of programming languages. Pointers to several such papers can be found in the bibliographic notes for Chapter 1. Fifteen papers comparing Ada, C, and Pascal can be found in the collection edited by Feuer and Gehani [FG84]. References for individual languages can be found in Appendix A.

Niklaus Wirth has been responsible for a series of influential languages over a 30-year period, including Pascal [Wir71], its predecessor Algol W [WH66], and the successors Modula [Wir77b], Modula-2 [Wir85b], and Oberon [Wir88b]. The `case` statement of Algol W is due to Hoare [Hoa81]. Guarded commands are due to Dijkstra [Dij75].

Debate over the supposed merits or evils of the `goto` statement dates from at least the early 1960s, but became a good bit more heated in the wake of a 1968 article by Dijkstra ("Goto Statement Considered Harmful" [Dij68b]). The structured programming movement of the 1970s took its name from the text of Dahl, Dijkstra, and Hoare [DDH72]. A dissenting letter by Rubin in 1987 ("'GOTO Considered Harmful' Considered Harmful"; exercise 6.16) [Rub87] elicited a flurry of responses.

What has been called the "reference model of variables" in this chapter is called the "object model" in Clu; Liskov and Guttag describe it in Sections 2.3 and 2.4.2 of their text on abstraction and specification [LG86]. Clu iterators are described in an article by Liskov et al. [LSAS77], and in Chapter 6 of the book by Liskov and Guttag [LG86]. Icon generators are discussed in Chapters 11 and 14 of the text by Griswold and Griswold [GG97]. The tree-enumeration algorithm of Section 6.5.3 was originally presented (without iterators) by Solomon and Finkel [SF80].

Several texts discuss the use of invariants (Exercise 6.18) as a tool for writing correct programs. Particularly noteworthy are the works of Dijkstra [Dij76] and Gries [Gri81]. Kernighan and Plauger provide a more informal discussion of the art of writing good programs [KP78].

The *typestate* mechanism mentioned in Section 6.1.2 appears in the Hermes programming language, designed by Robert Strom and his associates at IBM's T. J. Watson Research Center [SBG$^+$91]. Every variable in Hermes has a *typestate* at every point in its scope. The typestate determines the set of operations that are permissible on the variable at that point. Moreover every type (both built-in and user-defined) has a *typestate DAG*. In this DAG typestate *A* is an ancestor of typestate B if every operation that is valid for a variable in typestate A is also valid for that variable when in typestate B. Straight-line code changes typestate in obvious ways. For example, assigning into a previously uninitialized variable moves it to the "initialized" typestate. Doing a `delete` on a pointer moves it to the "uninitialized" typestate. When code paths merge (e.g. at the bottom of an `if...then...else`), the typestate of a variable at the next statement is the closest common ancestor of the previous typestates. Simple types have simple typestate DAGs, but the DAGs for complicated types can be quite elaborate.

The Blizzard [SFL+94] and Shasta [SG96] systems for software distributed shared memory (S-DSM) make use of sentinels (Exercise 6.8). We will discuss S-DSM in Section 12.2.1.

Michaelson [Mic89, chap. 8] provides an accessible formal treatment of applicative-order, normal-order, and lazy evaluation. Friedman, Wand, and Haynes provide an excellent discussion of continuation-passing style [FWH92, chaps. 8–9].

Data Types

Most programming languages include a notion of *type* for expressions and/or objects.[1] Types serve two principal purposes:

1. Types provide implicit context for many operations, so that the programmer does not have to specify that context explicitly. In Pascal, for instance, the expression a + b will use integer addition if a and b are of `integer` type; it will use floating-point addition if a and b are of `real` type. Similarly, the operation new p, where p is a pointer, will allocate a block of storage from the heap that is the right size to hold an object of the type pointed to by p; the programmer does not have to specify (or even know) this size. In C++ and Java, the operation `new my_type ()` not only allocates (and returns a pointer to) a block of storage sized for an object of type `my_type`; it also automatically calls any user-defined initialization (*constructor*) function that has been associated with that type.

2. Types limit the set of operations that may be performed in a semantically valid program. They prevent the programmer from adding a character and a record, for example, or from taking the arctangent of a set, or passing a file as a parameter to a subroutine that expects an integer. While no type system can promise to catch every nonsensical operation that a programmer might put into a program by mistake, good type systems catch enough mistakes to be highly valuable in practice.

The first section of this chapter looks more closely at the meaning and purpose of types, and presents some basic definitions. The second section addresses questions of *type equivalence* and *type compatibility*: when can we say that two types are the same, and when can we use a value of a given type in a given context? The remaining sections consider syntactic, semantic, and pragmatic issues

---

[1] Recall that unless otherwise noted we are using the term "object" informally to refer to anything that might have a name. Object-oriented languages, which we will study in Chapter 10, assign a different, more formal, meaning to the term.

for some of the most important varieties of types: records, arrays, strings, sets, pointers, and files. The section on pointers includes a more detailed discussion of the naming issues (what is a variable?) introduced in Section 6.1.2, and of the heap management issues introduced in Section 3.2. The section on files includes a discussion of input and output.

7.1 Type Systems

In Section 5.3 we noted that computer hardware is capable of interpreting bits in memory in several different ways. The various functional units of a processor may interpret bits as, among other things, instructions, addresses, characters, and integer and floating-point numbers of various lengths. The bits themselves, however, are untyped; the hardware on most machines makes no attempt to keep track of which interpretations correspond to which locations in memory. Assembly languages reflect this lack of typing: operations of any kind can be applied to values in arbitrary locations. High-level languages, on the other hand, almost always associate values and types, to provide the contextual information and error-checking alluded to above.

Informally, a *type system* consists of (1) a mechanism for defining types and associating them with certain language constructs, and (2) a set of rules for *type equivalence*, *type compatibility*, and *type inference*. The constructs that must have types are precisely those that have values, or that can refer to objects that have values. These constructs include named constants, variables, record fields, parameters, and sometimes subroutines; explicit (manifest) constants (e.g., 17, 3.14, "foo"); and more complicated expressions containing these. Type equivalence rules determine when the types of two values are the same. Type compatibility rules determine when a value of a given type can be used in a given context. Type inference rules define the type of an expression based on the types of its constituent parts or (sometimes) the surrounding context.

The distinction between the type of an expression (e.g., a name) and the type of the object to which it refers is important in a language with polymorphic variables or parameters, since a given name may refer to objects of different types at different times. In a language without polymorphism, the distinction doesn't matter.

Subroutines are considered to have types in some languages, but not in others. Subroutines need to have types if they are first- or second-class values (i.e., if they can be passed as parameters, returned by functions, or stored in variables). In each of these cases there is a construct in the language whose value is a dynamically determined subroutine; type information allows the language to limit the set of acceptable values to those that provide a particular subroutine interface (i.e., particular numbers and types of parameters). In a statically scoped language that never creates references to subroutines dynamically (one in which subroutines are always third-class values), the compiler can always identify the subroutine to which a name refers, and can ensure that the routine is called correctly without necessarily employing a formal notion of subroutine types.

Type checking is the process of ensuring that a program obeys the language's type compatibility rules. A violation of the rules is known as a *type clash*. A language is said to be *strongly typed* if it prohibits, in a way that the language implementation can enforce, the application of any operation to any object that is not intended to support that operation. A language is said to be *statically typed* if it is strongly typed and type checking can be performed at compile time. In the strictest sense of the term, few languages are statically typed. In practice, the term is often applied to languages in which most type checking can be performed at compile time, and the rest can be performed at run time.

A few examples: Ada is strongly typed, and for the most part statically typed (certain type constraints must be checked at run time). A Pascal implementation can also do most of its type checking at compile time, though the language is not quite strongly typed: untagged variant records (to be discussed in Section 7.3) are its only loophole. ANSI C is significantly more strongly typed than its predecessor dialects, but still significantly less strongly typed than Pascal. Its loopholes include unions, subroutines with variable numbers of parameters, and the interoperability of pointers and arrays (to be discussed in Section 7.7.1). Implementations of C rarely check anything at run time. A few high-level languages (e.g., Bliss [WRH71]) are completely untyped, like assembly languages.

Dynamic (run-time) type checking is a form of late binding, and tends to be found in languages that delay other issues until run time as well. Lisp, Scheme, and Smalltalk, for example, are dynamically typed. Operations in Smalltalk check at run time to see if the types of their operands are acceptable.[2] Operations in Lisp and Scheme may either check their operands at run time, or simply assume that they are acceptable (thereby forgoing type checking).

Languages with dynamic scoping are generally dynamically typed (or not typed at all): if the compiler can't identify the object to which a name refers, it usually can't determine the type of the object either. Polymorphism may imply the need for run-time type checking, but need not necessarily. Lisp, Scheme, and Smalltalk are dynamically typed because they allow arbitrary variables to refer to arbitrary objects, and to be passed to arbitrary operations. On the other hand, several object-oriented languages other than Smalltalk (Eiffel is one example) are polymorphic but statically typed (or very nearly so): they allow a variable X of type T to refer to an object of any type derived from T. (We will discuss derived types further in Chapter 10.) Since derived types are required to support all of the operations of the base type, the compiler can be sure that any operation acceptable for an object of type T will be acceptable for any object referred to by X.

---

2 Under the Smalltalk programming model, one performs an operation by sending a *message* to an *object*. The object (a technical term in Smalltalk) is thought of as an active entity that examines the message to see if it is one that it is prepared to accept. Type errors manifest themselves as unexpected messages.

In a more ambitious vein, ML, Miranda, and Haskell provide a richly polymorphic type system in which the compiler infers for every object and expression a (possibly unique) type that captures precisely those properties that the object or expression must have to be used in the context(s) in which it appears. With rare exceptions, the programmer does not specify the types of objects explicitly. The task of the compiler is to determine whether there exists a consistent assignment of types to objects in the program that guarantees, statically, that no operation will ever be applied to a value of an inappropriate type at run time. This job can be formalized as the problem of *unification*; we will discuss it further in Section 7.2.5.

7.1.1 The Definition of Types

Some early high-level languages (e.g., Fortran 77, Algol 60, and Basic) provide a small, built-in, and nonextensible set of types. As we saw in Section 3.3.1, Fortran does not require variables to be declared; it incorporates default rules to determine the type of undefined variables based on the spelling of their names (Basic has similar rules). As noted in the previous section, a few languages (e.g., Bliss) dispense with types, while others keep track of them automatically at compile time (as in ML, Miranda, or Haskell) or at run time (as in Lisp/Scheme or Smalltalk). In most languages, however, users must explicitly declare the type of every object, together with the characteristics of every type that is not built-in.

Many languages distinguish between the *declaration* of a type or other object and its *definition*. A declaration introduces a name and indicates (usually implicitly, by virtue of where it appears) the scope in which that name will be visible. A definition describes the type or object to which the name is bound. Usually a single syntactic construct serves both purposes (declaration and definition). In some cases, however, it is useful to be able to declare a name without defining the thing that it names. The principal examples are forward declarations of types and subroutines (Section 3.3.3), and the declaration of opaque types and other aspects of the interface of a data abstraction (Section 3.3.1 and Chapter 10). The definition of a constant must include the constant's value. In many languages, the definition of a variable can also include an initial value (Section 6.1.2).

There are at least three ways to think about types, which we may call the *denotational*, *constructive*, and *abstraction-based* points of view. From the denotational point of view, a type is simply a set of values. A value has a given type if it belongs to the set; an object has a given type if its value is guaranteed to be in the set. From the constructive point of view, a type is either one of a small collection of *built-in* types (integer, character, Boolean, real, etc.; also called *primitive* or *predefined* types), or a *composite* type created by applying a type *constructor* (`record`, `array`, `set`, etc.) to one or more simpler types. (This use of the term "constructor" is unrelated to the initialization functions of C++ and Java. It also differs in a more subtle way from the use of the term in ML.) From the abstraction-based point of view, a type is an *interface* consisting of a set of operations with well-defined and mutually consistent semantics. For most programmers (and language designers), types usually reflect a mixture of these viewpoints.

In denotational semantics (one of the leading ways to formalize the meaning of programs), a set of values is known as a *domain*. Types are domains. The meaning of an expression in denotational semantics is a value from the domain that represents the expression's type. (Domains are in some sense a generalization of types. The meaning of any language construct is a value from a domain. The meaning of an assignment statement, for example, is a value from a domain whose elements are functions. Each function maps a *store*—a mapping from names to values that represents the current contents of memory—to another store, which represents the contents of memory after the assignment.) One of the nice things about the denotational view of types is that it allows us in many cases to describe user-defined composite types (records, arrays, etc.) in terms of mathematical operations on sets. We will allude to these operations again in Section 7.1.2.

Because it is based on mathematical objects, the denotational view of types usually ignores implementation issues such as limited precision and word length. This limitation is less serious than it might at first appear: errors such as arithmetic overflow are usually implemented outside of the type system of a language anyway: they result in a run-time error, but this error is not called a type clash.

When a programmer defines an enumerated type (e.g., hue = (red, green, blue)), he or she certainly thinks of this type as a set of values. For most other varieties of user-defined type, however, one typically does not think in terms of sets of values. Rather, one usually thinks in terms of the way the type is built from simpler types, or in terms of its meaning or purpose. These ways of thinking reflect the constructive and abstraction-based points of view. The constructive point of view was pioneered by Algol W and Algol 68, and is characteristic of most languages designed in the 1970s and 1980s. The abstraction-based point of view was pioneered by Simula-67 and Smalltalk, and is characteristic of modern object-oriented languages. It can also be adopted as a matter of programming discipline in non-object-oriented languages. We will discuss the abstraction-based point of view in more detail in Chapter 10. The remainder of this chapter focuses on the constructive point of view.

7.1.2 The Classification of Types

The terminology for types varies some from one language to another. This section includes definitions for the most common terms. Most languages provide built-in types similar to those supported in hardware by most processors: integers, characters, Booleans, and real (floating-point) numbers.

Booleans (sometimes called *logicals*) are typically implemented as one-byte quantities, with 1 representing true and 0 representing false. C is unusual in its lack of a Boolean type: where most languages would expect a Boolean value,

C expects an integer; zero means `false`, anything else means `true`. As noted in Section 6.5.3, Icon replaces Booleans with a more general notion of *success* and *failure*.

Characters have traditionally been implemented as one-byte quantities as well, typically (but not always) using the ASCII encoding. More recent languages (e.g., Java) use a two-byte representation that can accommodate the *Unicode* character set. Unicode is an international standard designed to capture the characters of a wide variety of languages. Its first 128 characters (`\u0000` through `\u007f`) are identical to ASCII. Standard C++ provides both regular and "wide" characters, though it does not specify the correspondence between characters and bit patterns. Wide characters have sufficient precision to accommodate Unicode.

A few languages (e.g., C and Fortran) distinguish between different lengths of integers and real numbers; most do not, and leave the choice of precision to the implementation. Unfortunately, differences in precision across language implementations lead to a lack of portability: programs that run correctly on one system may produce run-time errors or erroneous results on another. Java is unusual in that it provides several lengths of numeric types, but specifies the precision of each.

A few languages (e.g., C and Modula-2) provide both signed and unsigned integers (Modula-2 calls unsigned integers *cardinals*). A few languages (e.g., Fortran, Common Lisp, and Scheme) provide a built-in complex type, usually implemented as a pair of floating-point numbers that represent the real and imaginary Cartesian coordinates. Other languages (e.g. C++) support complex numbers in a standard library. A few languages (e.g., Scheme and Common Lisp) provide a built-in rational type, usually implemented as a pair of integers that represent the numerator and denominator. Common Lisp and most dialects of Scheme support integers (and rationals) of arbitrary precision; the implementation uses multiple words of memory where appropriate.

Ada supports *fixed point* types, which are represented internally by integers, but have an implied decimal point at a programmer-specified position among the digits. Fixed-point numbers provide a compact representation of nonintegral values (e.g., dollars and cents) within a restricted range. For example, 32-bit hardware integers can represent fixed-point numbers with two digits to the right of the decimal point in the range of roughly negative one billion to positive one billion. Double-precision (64-bit) numbers would be required to capture the same range in floating-point, since single-precision IEEE floating-point numbers have only 23 bits of significand (Section 5.3.2). Other languages, notably Cobol and PL/I, provide a *decimal* type for fixed-point representation of integers in binary-coded decimal format (Section 5.3). Addition and subtraction of fixed-point numbers (with the same number of decimal places) can use ordinary integer operations. Multiplication and division are slightly more complicated, as are operations on values with different numbers of digits to the right of the decimal point (see Exercise 7.3). As noted in Section 5.3, some processor architectures provide special instructions for calculations on decimal integers.

Integers, Booleans, and characters are all examples of *discrete* types (also called *ordinal* types): the domains to which they correspond are countable, and have a well-defined notion of predecessor and successor for each element other than the first and the last. (In most implementations the number of possible integers is finite, but this is usually not reflected in the type system.) Two varieties of user-defined types, enumerations and subranges, are also discrete. Discrete, rational, real, and complex types together constitute the *scalar* types. Scalar types are also sometimes called *simple* types.

Enumeration Types

Enumerations were introduced by Wirth in the design of Pascal. They facilitate the creation of readable programs, and allow the compiler to catch certain kinds of programming errors. An enumeration type consists of a set of named elements. In Pascal, one can write:

```
type weekday = (sun, mon, tue, wed, thu, fri, sat);
```

The values of an enumeration type are ordered, so comparisons are generally valid (mon < tue), and there is usually a mechanism to determine the predecessor or successor of an enumeration value (in Pascal, tomorrow := succ (today)). The ordered nature of enumerations facilitates the writing of enumeration-controlled loops:

```
for today := mon to fri do begin ...
```

It also allows enumerations to be used to index arrays:

```
var daily_attendance : array [weekday] of integer;
```

An alternative to enumerations, of course, is simply to declare a collection of constants:

```
const sun = 0; mon = 1; tue = 2; wed = 3; thu = 4; fri = 5; sat = 6;
```

In C, the difference between the two approaches is purely syntactic:

```
enum weekday {sun, mon, tue, wed, thu, fri, sat};
```

is essentially equivalent to

```
typedef int weekday;
const weekday sun = 0, mon = 1, tue = 2,
              wed = 3, thu = 4, fri = 5, sat = 6;
```

In Pascal and most of its descendants, however, the difference between an enumeration and a set of integer constants is much more significant: the enumeration is a full-fledged type, incompatible with integers. Using an integer or an enumeration value in a context expecting the other will result in a type clash error at compile time.

Values of an enumeration type are typically represented by small integers, usually a consecutive range of small integers starting at zero. In many languages these *ordinal values* are semantically significant, because built-in functions can be used to convert an enumeration value to its ordinal value, and sometimes vice versa. In Pascal, the built-in function `ord` takes an argument of any enumeration type (including `char` and `Boolean`, which are considered built-in enumerations) and returns the argument's ordinal value. The built-in function `chr` takes an argument i of type integer and returns the character whose ordinal value is i (or generates a run-time error if there is no such character). In Ada, `weekday'pos(mon) = 1` and `weekday'val(1) = mon`.

Ada and ANSI C allow the programmer to specify the ordinal values of enumeration types, if the default assignment is undesirable. In C, one could write

```
enum mips_special_regs {gp = 28, fp = 30, sp = 29, ra = 31};
```

(The intuition behind these values is explained in Section 5.5.1, page 224.) In Ada this declaration would be written

```
type mips_special_regs is (gp, sp, fp, ra);      -- must be sorted
for mips_special_regs use (gp => 28, sp => 29, fp => 30, ra => 31);
```

As noted in Section 3.5, Pascal and C do not allow the same element name to be used in more than one enumeration type in the same scope. Ada does allow this; the name is overloaded. It must be possible whenever the name is used to infer the desired type from context.

Subrange Types

Like enumerations, subranges were first introduced in Pascal, and are found in most subsequent Algol-family languages. A subrange is type whose values comprise a contiguous subset of the values of some discrete *base* type (also called the *parent* type). In Pascal and most of its descendants, one can declare subranges of integers, characters, enumerations, and even other subranges. In Pascal, subranges look like this:

```
type test_score = 0..100;
     workday = mon..fri;
```

In Ada one would write

```
type test_score is new integer range 0..100;
subtype workday is weekday range mon..fri;
```

The `range...` portion of the definition in Ada is called a type *constraint*. In this example `test_score` is a *derived* type, incompatible with integers. The `workday` type, on the other hand, is a *constrained subtype*; `workday`s and `weekday`s can be more or less freely intermixed. The distinction between derived types and subtypes is a valuable feature of Ada; we will discuss it further in Section 7.2.1.

One could of course use integers to represent test scores, or a `weekday` to represent a `workday`. Using an explicit subrange has several advantages. For one thing, it helps to document the program. A comment could also serve as documentation, but comments have a bad habit of growing out of date as programs change, or of being omitted in the first place. Because the compiler analyzes a subrange declaration, it knows the expected range of subrange values, and can generate code to perform dynamic semantic checks to ensure that no subrange variable is ever assigned an invalid value. These checks can be valuable debugging tools. In addition, since the compiler knows the number of values in the subrange, it can sometimes use fewer bits to represent subrange values than it would need to use to represent arbitrary integers. In the example above, `test_score` values can be stored in a single byte.

Most implementations employ the same bit patterns for integers and subranges, so subranges whose values are large require large storage locations, even if the number of distinct values is small. The following type, for example,

```
type water_temperature = 273..373;  (* degrees Kelvin *)
```

would be stored in at least two bytes. While there are only 101 distinct values in the type, the largest (373) is too large to fit in a single byte in its natural encoding. (An unsigned byte can hold values in the range $0..255$; a signed byte can hold values in the range $-128..127$.)

Composite Types

Nonscalar types are usually called *composite*, or *constructed* types. They are generally created by applying a *type constructor* to one or more simpler types. Common composite types include records (structures), variant records (unions), arrays, sets, pointers, lists, and files. All but pointers and lists are easily described in terms of mathematical set operations (pointers and lists can be described mathematically as well, but the description is less intuitive).

Records were introduced by Cobol, and have been supported by most languages since the 1960s. A record consists of collection of *fields*, each of which belongs to a (potentially different) simpler type. Records are akin to mathematical *tuples*; a record type corresponds to the Cartesian product of the types of the fields.

Variant records differ from "normal" records in that only one of a variant record's fields (or collections of fields) is valid at any given time. A variant record type is the *union* of its field types, rather than their Cartesian product.

Arrays are the most commonly used composite types. An array can be thought of as a function that maps members of an *index* type to members of a *component* type. Arrays of characters are often referred to as *strings*, and are often supported by special-purpose operations not available for other arrays.

Sets, like enumerations and subranges, were introduced by Pascal. A set type is the mathematical powerset of its base type, which must usually be discrete. A variable of a set type contains a collection of distinct elements of the base type.

Pointers are l-values. A pointer value is a *reference* to an object of the pointer's base type. Pointers are often but not always implemented as addresses. They are most often used to implement *recursive* data types. A type T is recursive if an object of type T may contain one or more references to other objects of type T.

Lists, like arrays, contain a sequence of elements, but there is no notion of mapping or indexing. Rather, a list is defined recursively as a pair consisting of a head element and a reference to a sublist. While the length of an array must be specified at elaboration time in most (though not all) languages, lists are always of variable length. To find a given element of a list, a program must examine all previous elements, recursively or iteratively, starting at the head. Because of their recursive definition, lists are fundamental to programming in most functional languages.

Files are intended to represent data on mass-storage devices, outside the memory in which other program objects reside. Like arrays, most files can be conceptualized as a function that maps members of an index type (generally integer) to members of a component type. Unlike arrays, files usually have a notion of *current position*, which allows the index to be implied implicitly in consecutive operations. Files often display idiosyncrasies inherited from physical input/output devices. In particular, the elements of some files must be accessed in sequential order.

We will examine composite types in more detail in Sections 7.3 through 7.9.

Orthogonality

In Section 6.1.2 we discussed the importance of orthogonality in the design of expressions, statements, and control-flow constructs. Orthogonality is equally important in the design of type systems. Languages vary greatly in the degree of orthogonality they display. A language with a high degree of orthogonality tends to be easier to understand, to use, and to reason about in a formal way. We have noted that languages such as Algol 68 and C enhance orthogonality by eliminating (or at least blurring) the distinction between statements and expressions. To characterize a statement that is executed for its side effect(s), and that has no useful values, some languages provide an "empty" type. In C and Algol, for example, a subroutine that is meant to be used as a procedure is generally declared with a "return" type of void. In ML, the empty type is called unit. If the programmer wishes to call a subroutine that does return a value, but the value is not needed in this particular case (all that matters is the side effect[s]), then the return value in C can be *cast* to void (casts will be discussed in Section 7.2.2):

```
foo_index = insert_in_symbol_table (foo);
...
(void) insert_in_symbol_table (bar);    /* don't care where it went */
    /* cast is optional; implied if omitted */
```

In a language (e.g., Pascal) without an empty type, the latter of these two calls
would need to use a dummy variable:

```
var dummy : symbol_table_index;
...
dummy := insert_in_symbol_table (bar);
```

The type system of Pascal is more orthogonal than that of (pre-Fortran 90)
Fortran. Among other things, it allows arrays to be constructed from any discrete
index type and any component type; pre-Fortran 90 arrays are always indexed by
integers and have scalar components. At the same time, Pascal displays several
nonorthogonal wrinkles. As we shall see in Section 7.3, it requires that variant
fields of a record follow all other fields. It limits function return values to scalar
and pointer types. It requires the bounds of each array to be specified at compile
time except when the array is a formal parameter of a subroutine. Perhaps most
important, while it allows subroutines to be passed as parameters, it does not
provide true subroutine types: a subroutine cannot be returned by a function or
stored in a variable. By contrast, the type system of ML, which we will examine
in Section 7.2.5, is almost completely orthogonal.

One particularly useful aspect of type orthogonality is the ability to specify
literal values of arbitrary composite types. Several languages provide this capability, but many others do not. Pascal and Modula provide notation for literal
character strings and sets, but not for arrays, records, or recursive data structures. The lack of notation for most user-defined composite types means that
many Pascal and Modula programs must devote time in every program run to
initializing data structures full of compile-time constants.

Composite values in Ada are specified using *aggregates*:

```
type person is record
        name : string (1..10);
        age : integer;
     end record;
p, q : person;
A, B : array (1..10) of integer;
...
p := ("Jane Doe  ", 37);
q := (age => 36, name => "John Doe  ");
A := (1, 0, 3, 0, 3, 0, 3, 0, 0, 0);
B := (1 => 1, 3 | 5 | 7 => 3, others => 0);
```

Here the aggregates assigned into p and A are *positional*; the aggregates assigned
into q and B name their elements explicitly. The aggregate for B uses a shorthand
notation to assign the same value (3) into array elements 3, 5, and 7, and to assign a 0 into all unnamed fields. Several languages, including C, Fortran 90, Lisp,

and ML, provide similar capabilities. In C, explicit composite values are called *initializers*; they can be used only in declarations, not in arbitrary statements. ML provides a very general facility for composite expressions, based on the use of *constructors* (to be discussed in Section 7.2.5).

7.2 Type Checking

In most statically typed languages, every definition of an object (constant, variable, subroutine, etc.) must specify the object's type. Moreover, many of the contexts in which an object might appear are also typed, in the sense that the rules of the language constrain the types that an object in that context may validly possess. In the subsections below we will consider the topics of *type equivalence*, *type compatibility*, and *type inference*. Of the three, type compatibility is the one of most concern to programmers. It determines when an object of a certain type can be used in a certain context. At a minimum, the object can be used if its type and the type expected by the context are equivalent (i.e., the same). In many languages, however, compatibility is a looser relationship than equivalence: objects and contexts are often compatible even when their types are different. Our discussion of type compatibility will touch on the subjects of type *conversion* (also called *casting*), which changes a value of one type into a value of another, type *coercion*, which performs a conversion automatically in certain contexts, and *nonconverting* type casts, which are sometimes used in systems programming to interpret the bits of a value of one type as if they represented a value of some other type.

Whenever an expression is constructed from simpler subexpressions, the question arises: given the types of the subexpressions (and possibly the type expected by the surrounding context), what is the type of the expression as a whole? This question is answered by type inference. Type inference is often trivial: the sum of two integers is still an integer, for example. In other cases (e.g., when dealing with sets) it is a good bit trickier. Type inference plays a particularly important role in ML, Miranda, and Haskell, in which all type information is inferred.

7.2.1 Type Equivalence

In a language in which the user can define new types, there are two principal ways of defining type equivalence. *Structural equivalence* is based on the content of definitions: roughly speaking, two types are the same if they consist of the same components, put together in the same way. *Name equivalence* is based on the lexical occurrence of type definitions: roughly speaking, each definition introduces a new type. Structural equivalence is used in Algol-68, Modula-3, and (with various wrinkles) C and ML. It was also used in many early implementations of Pascal. Name equivalence is the more popular approach in recent languages. It is used in Java, in standard Pascal, and in most Pascal descendants, including Ada.

The exact definition of structural equivalence varies from one language to another. It requires that one decide which potential differences between types are important, and which may be considered unimportant. Most people would probably agree that the format of a declaration should not matter: in a Pascal-like language with structural equivalence,

```
type foo = record a, b : integer end;
```

should be considered the same as

```
type foo = record
    a, b : integer
end;
```

These definitions should probably also be considered the same as

```
type foo = record
    a : integer;
    b : integer
end;
```

But what about

```
type foo = record
    b : integer;
    a : integer
end;
```

Should the reversal of the order of the fields change the type? Here the answer is not as clear: ML says no; most languages say yes.

In a similar vein, the definition of structural equivalence should probably "factor out" different representations of constants: again in a Pascal-like notation,

```
type str = array [1..10] of char;
```

should be considered the same as

```
type str = array [1..2*5] of char;
```

On the other hand, these should probably be considered different from

```
type str = array [0..9] of char;
```

Here the length of the array has not changed, but the index values are different.

To determine if two types are structurally equivalent, a compiler can expand their definitions by replacing any embedded type names with their respective definitions, recursively, until nothing is left but a long string of type constructors, field names, and built-in types. If these expanded strings are the same, then the types are equivalent, and conversely. Recursive and pointer-based types complicate matters, since their expansion does not terminate, but the problem is not insurmountable; we consider a solution in Exercise 7.21.

Structural equivalence is a straightforward but somewhat low-level, implementation-oriented way of thinking about types. Its principal problem is an inability to distinguish between types that the programmer may think of as distinct, but which happen by coincidence to have the same internal structure:

```
1.  type student = record
2.      name, address : string
3.      age : integer

4.  type school = record
5.      name, address : string
6.      age : integer

7.  x : student;
8.  y : school;
9.  . . .
10. x := y;            -- is this an error?
```

Most programmers would probably want to be informed if they accidentally assigned a value of type school into a variable of type student, but a compiler whose type checking is based on structural equivalence will blithely accept such an assignment.

Name equivalence is based on the assumption that if the programmer takes the effort to write two type definitions, then those definitions are probably meant to represent different types. In the example above, variables x and y will be considered to have different types under name equivalence: x uses the type declared at line 1; y uses the type declared at line 4.

One subtlety that arises in the use of name equivalence has to do with alias types. When the definition of a type consists simply of the name of another type, should the two be considered different or the same? Consider the following module in Modula-2:

```
TYPE stack_element = INTEGER;
MODULE stack;
IMPORT stack_element;
EXPORT push, pop;
    ...
PROCEDURE push (elem : stack_element);
    ...
PROCEDURE pop () : stack_element;
    ...
```

Here the stack module is meant to serve as an abstraction that allows the programmer, via textual inclusion, to create a stack of any desired type (in this case integer). If aliased types are not considered equivalent, then the stack is no longer reusable; it cannot be used for objects whose type has a name of the programmer's choosing.

Unfortunately, there are other times, even in Modula-2, when aliased types should probably not be the same:

```
TYPE celsius_temp = REAL;
     fahrenheit_temp = REAL;
VAR  c : celsius_temp;
     f : fahrenheit_temp;
...
f := c;                    (* this should probably be an error *)
```

A language in which aliased types are considered distinct is said to have *strict name equivalence*. A language in which aliased types are considered equivalent is said to have *loose name equivalence*. Most Pascal-family languages (including Modula-2) use loose name equivalence. Ada achieves the best of both worlds by allowing the programmer to indicate whether an alias represents a *derived* type or a *subtype*. A subtype is compatible with its base (parent) type; a derived type is incompatible. (Subtypes of the same base type are also compatible with each other.) Our examples above would be written:

```
subtype stack_element is integer;
...
type celsius_temp is new integer;
type fahrenheit_temp is new integer;
```

Modula-3, which relies on structural type equivalence, achieves some of the effect of derived types through use of a *branding* mechanism. A BRANDED type is distinct from all other types, regardless of structure. Branding is permitted only for pointers and abstract objects (in the object-oriented sense of the word). Its principal purpose is not to distinguish among types such as celsius_temp and fahrenheit_temp above, but rather to prevent the programmer from using structural equivalence, deliberately or accidentally, to look inside an abstraction that is supposed to be opaque.

One way to think about the difference between strict and loose name equivalence is to remember the distinction between declarations and definitions. Under strict name equivalence, a declaration type A = B is considered a definition. Under loose name equivalence it is merely a declaration; A shares the definition of B.

Consider the following example:

1. type cell   = −− whatever
2. type alink   = pointer to cell
3. type blink   = alink
4. p, q : pointer to cell
5. r   : alink
6. s   : blink
7. t   : pointer to cell
8. u   : alink

Here the declaration at line 3 is an alias; it defines blink to be "the same as" alink. Under strict name equivalence, line 3 is both a declaration and a definition, and blink is a new type, distinct from alink. Under loose name equivalence, line 3 is just a declaration; it uses the definition at line 2.

Under strict name equivalence, p and q have the same type, because they both use the *anonymous* (unnamed) type definition on the right-hand side of line 5, and r and u have the same type, because they both use the definition at line 2. Under loose name equivalence, r, s, and u all have the same type, as do p and q. Under structural equivalence, all six of the variables shown have the same type, namely pointer to whatever cell is.

Both structural and name equivalence can be tricky to implement in the presence of separate compilation. We will return to this issue in Section 9.6.

7.2.2 Type Conversion and Casts

In a language with static typing, there are many contexts in which values of a specific type are expected. In the statement

a := *expression*

we expect the right-hand side to have the same type as a. In the expression

a + b

the overloaded + symbol designates either integer or floating-point addition; we therefore expect either that a and b will both be integers, or that they will both be reals. In a call to a subroutine,

foo (arg1, arg2, . . . , argN)

we expect the types of the arguments to match those of the formal parameters, as declared in the subroutine's header.

Suppose for the moment that we require in each of these cases that the types (expected and provided) be exactly the same. Then if the programmer wishes to use a value of one type in a context that expects another, he or she will need to specify an explicit *type conversion* (also sometimes called a type *cast*). Depending on the types involved, the conversion may or may not require code to be executed at run time. There are three principal cases:

1. The types would be considered structurally equivalent, but the language uses name equivalence. In this case the types employ the same low-level representation, and have the same set of values. The conversion is therefore a purely conceptual operation; no code will need to be executed at run time.

2. The types have different sets of values, but the intersecting values are represented in the same way. One type may be a subrange of the other, for example, or one may consist of two's complement signed integers, while the other is unsigned. If the provided type has some values that the expected type does not, then code must be executed at run time to ensure that the current value is among those that are valid in the expected type. If the check fails, then a dynamic semantic error results. If the check succeeds, then the underlying representation of the value can be used, unchanged. Some language implementations may allow the check to be disabled, resulting in faster but potentially unsafe code.

3. The types have different low-level representations, but we can nonetheless define some sort of correspondence among their values. A 32-bit integer, for example, can be converted to a double-precision IEEE floating-point number with no loss of precision. Most processors provide a machine instruction to effect this conversion. A floating-point number can be converted to an integer by rounding or truncating, but fractional digits will be lost, and the conversion will overflow for many exponent values. Again, most processors provide a machine instruction to effect this conversion. Conversions between different lengths of integers can be effected by discarding or sign-extending high-order bytes.

We can illustrate these options with the following examples of type conversions in Ada:

```
n : integer;          -- assume 32 bits
r : real;             -- assume IEEE double-precision
t : test_score;       -- as above
c : celsius_temp;     -- as above
...
t := test_score (n);  -- run-time semantic check required
n := integer (t);     -- no check req.; every test_score is an int
r := real (n);        -- requires run-time conversion
n := integer (r);     -- requires run-time conversion and check
n := integer (c);     -- no run-time code required
c := celsius_temp (n); -- no run-time code required
```

In each of these last six lines, the name of a type is used as a pseudo-function that performs a type conversion. The first conversion requires a run-time check to ensure that the value of n is within the bounds of a test_score. The second conversion requires no code, since every possible value of t is acceptable for n. The third and fourth conversions require code to change the low-level representation of values. The fourth conversion also requires a semantic check. It is generally understood that converting from a floating-point value to an integer results in the loss of fractional digits; this loss is not an error. If the conversion results in integer overflow, however, an error needs to result. The final two conversions require no run-time code; the integer and celsius_temp types (at least as we have defined them) have the same sets of values and the same underlying representation. A purist might say that celsius_temp should be defined as `new integer range -273..integer'last`, in which case a run-time semantic check would be required on the final conversion.

Occasionally, particularly in systems programs, one needs to change the type of a value *without* changing the underlying implementation; in other words, to interpret the bits of a value of one type as if they were another type. One common example occurs in memory allocation algorithms, which use a large array of characters or integers to represent a heap, but then reinterpret portions of that array as pointers and integers (for bookkeeping purposes), or as various user-allocated data structures. Another common example occurs in high-performance numeric software, which may need to reinterpret a floating-point number as an integer or a record, in order to extract the exponent, significand, and sign fields. These fields can be used to implement special-purpose algorithms for square root, trigonometric functions, and so on.

A change of type that does not alter the underlying bits is called a *nonconverting type cast*. It should not be confused with use of the term *cast* for conversions in languages such as C. In Ada, nonconverting casts can be effected using instances of a built-in generic subroutine called `unchecked_conversion`:

```
-- assume 'float' has been declared to match IEEE single-precision
function cast_float_to_int is
    new unchecked_conversion (float, integer);
function cast_int_to_float is
    new unchecked_conversion (integer, float);
...
f := cast_int_to_float (n);
n := cast_float_to_int (f);
```

A type conversion in C (i.e., what C calls a type cast) is specified by using the name of the desired type, in parentheses, as a prefix operator:

```
r = (float) n;   /* generates code for run-time conversion */
n = (int) r;     /* also run-time conversion, with no overflow check */
```

C and its descendants do not perform run-time checks for arithmetic overflow on any operation.

A nonconverting type cast can often be achieved in C by taking the address of an object, converting the type of the resulting pointer, and then dereferencing:

```
r = *((float *) &n);
```

This arcane bit of hackery works because pointers to integers and pointers to floating-point values have the same representation in C: namely, an address. The ampersand operator (`&`) means "address of," or "pointer to." The parenthesized (`float *`) is the type name for "pointer to float" (float is a built-in floating-point type). The prefix `*` operator is a pointer dereference. The cast produces no run-time code; it merely causes the compiler to interpret the bits of n as if it were a `float`. The reinterpretation will work as expected if and only if (1) n is an object that has an address (rather than being, say, a constant or a built-up arithmetic expression; unfortunately the trick does not work for these); and (2) int and float types occupy the same number of bytes. This second condition is often but not always true in C: it is common for int to correspond to 32-bit integers and for float to correspond to single-precision IEEE floating-point. If n does not have an address then the compiler will announce a static semantic error. If int and float do not occupy the same number of bytes, then the effect of the cast may depend on a variety of factors, including the relative size of the objects, the alignment and "endian-ness" of memory (Section 5.3), and the choices the compiler has made regarding what to place in adjacent locations in memory. In some languages (including C), the effect of a nonconverting cast can also be achieved with unions or variant records (see Exercise 7.8).

Standard C++ inherits the casting mechanism of C, but also provides a family of semantically cleaner alternatives. Specifically, static_cast performs a type conversion, reinterpret_cast performs a nonconverting type cast, and dynamic_cast allows programs that manipulate pointers of polymorphic types to perform assignments whose validity cannot be guaranteed statically, but can be checked at run time (more on this in Chapter 10).

Any nonconverting type cast constitutes a dangerous subversion of the language's type system. In a language with a weak type system such conversions can be difficult to find. In a language with a strong type system, the use of explicit nonconverting type casts at least labels the dangerous points in the code, facilitating debugging if problems arise.

7.2.3 Type Compatibility and Coercion

Most languages do not require equivalence of types in every context. Instead, they merely say that a value's type must be compatible with that of the context in which it appears. In an assignment statement, the type of the right-hand side must be compatible with that of the left-hand side. The types of the operands of + must either both be compatible with the built-in integer type, or both be compatible with the built-in floating-point type. In a subroutine call, the types of any arguments passed into the subroutine must be compatible with the types of the corresponding formal parameters, and the types of any formal parameters passed back to the caller must be compatible with the types of the corresponding arguments.

The definition of type compatibility varies greatly from language to language. Ada takes a relatively restrictive approach: an Ada type S is compatible with an expected type T if and only if (1) S and T are equivalent, (2) one is a subtype of the other (or both are subtypes of the same base type), or (3) both are arrays, with the same numbers and types of elements in each dimension. Pascal is only slightly more lenient: in addition to allowing the intermixing of base and subrange types, it allows an integer to be used in a context where a real is expected.

Whenever a language allows a value of one type to be used in a context that expects another, the language implementation must perform an automatic, implicit conversion to the expected type. This conversion is called a *type coercion*. Just as with the explicit conversions discussed in the previous section, a coercion may require run-time code to perform a dynamic semantic check, or to convert between low-level representations. Ada coercions sometimes need the former, though never the latter:

```
d : weekday;           -- as above
k : workday;           -- as above
type calendar_column is new weekday;
c : calendar_column;
...
k := d;     -- run-time check required
d := k;     -- no check required; every workday is a weekday
c := d;     -- static semantic error;
            -- weekdays and calendar_columns are not compatible
```

To perform this third assignment in Ada we would have to use an explicit conversion:

```
c := calendar_column (d);
```

Coercions are a controversial subject in language design. Because they allow types to be mixed without an explicit indication of intent on the part of the programmer, they represent a significant weakening of type security. Fortran and C, which have relatively weak type systems, perform quite a bit of coercion. They allow values of most numeric types to be intermixed in expressions, and will coerce types back and forth "as necessary." Here are some examples in C:

```
short int s;
unsigned long int l;
char c;     /* may be signed or unsigned -- implementation-dependent */
float f;    /* usually IEEE single-precision */
double d;   /* usually IEEE double-precision */
...
s = l;  /* l's low-order bits are interpreted as a signed number. */
l = s;  /* s is sign-extended to the longer length, then
            its bits are interpreted as an unsigned number. */
s = c;  /* c is either sign-extended or zero-extended to s's length;
            the result is then interpreted as a signed number. */
f = l;  /* l is converted to floating-point. Since f has fewer
            significant bits, some precision may be lost. */
d = f;  /* f is converted to the longer format; no precision lost. */
f = d;  /* d is converted to the shorter format; precision may be lost.
            If d's value cannot be represented in single-precision, the
            result is undefined, but NOT a dynamic semantic error. */
```

Fortran 90 allows arrays and records to be intermixed if their types have the same shape. Two arrays have the same shape if they have the same number of dimensions, each dimension has the same size, and the individual elements have the same shape. These rules are roughly equivalent to the compatibility rules for arrays in Ada, but Fortran 90 allows arrays to be used in many more contexts. Specifically, it allows its full set of arithmetic operations to be applied, element-by-element, to array-valued operands.

Two Fortran 90 records have the same shape if they have the same number of fields, and corresponding fields, in order, have the same shape. Field *names* do not matter, nor do the actual high and low bounds of array dimensions. C does not allow records (structures) to be intermixed unless they are structurally equivalent, with identical field names. C provides no operations that take an entire array as an operand. C does, however, allow arrays and *pointers* to be intermixed in many cases; we will discuss this unusual form of type compatibility further in Section 7.7.1.

Most modern languages reflect a trend toward static typing and away from type coercion. Some language designers have argued, however, that coercions are a natural way in which to support abstraction and program extensibility, by making it easier to use new types in conjunction with existing ones. C++ in particular provides an extremely rich, *programmer-extensible* set of coercion rules. When defining a new type (a *class* in C++), the programmer can define coercion operations to convert values of the new type to and from existing types. These rules interact in complicated ways with the rules for resolving overloading (Section 3.5); they add significant flexibility to the language, but are one of the most difficult C++ features to understand and use correctly.

We have noted (in Section 3.5) that overloading and coercion (as well as polymorphism and generics) can sometimes be used to similar effect. It is worth repeating some of the distinctions here. An overloaded name can refer to more than one object; the ambiguity must be resolved by context. In the expression a + b, for example, + may refer to either the integer or the floating-point addition operation. In a language without coercion, a and b must either both be integer or both be real; the compiler chooses the appropriate interpretation of + depending on their type. In a language with coercion, + refers to the floating-point addition operation if either a or b is real; otherwise it refers to the integer addition operation. If only one of a and b is real, the other is coerced to match. One could imagine a language in which + was not overloaded, but rather referred to floating-point addition in all cases. Coercion could still allow + to take integer arguments, but they would always be converted to real. The problem with this approach is that conversions from integer to floating-point format take a nonnegligible amount of time, especially on machines without hardware conversion instructions, and floating-point addition is significantly more expensive than integer addition.

In most languages literal (manifest) constants (e.g., numbers, character strings, the empty set [[ ]] or the null pointer [nil]) can be intermixed in expressions with values of many types. One might say that constants are overloaded: nil for example might be thought of as referring to the null pointer value for whatever type is needed in the surrounding context. More commonly, however, constants are simply treated as a special case in the language's type-checking rules. Internally, the compiler considers a constant to have one of a small number of built-in "constant types" (int const, real const, string, nil), which it then coerces to some more appropriate type as necessary, even if coercions are not supported elsewhere in the language. Ada formalizes this notion of "constant type" for numeric quantities: an integer constant (one without a decimal point) is said to have type `universal_integer`; a floating-point constant (one with an embedded decimal point and/or an exponent) is said to have type `universal_real`. The `universal_integer` type is compatible with any type derived from `integer`; `universal_real` is compatible with any type derived from `real`.

For systems programming, or to facilitate the writing of general-purpose *container* objects (lists, stacks, queues, sets, etc.) that hold references to other objects, several languages provide a "generic reference" type. In C and C++, this type is called `void *`. In Clu it is called `any`; in Modula-2, `address`; in Modula-3, `refany`; in Java, `Object`. Arbitrary l-values can be assigned into an object of generic reference type, with no concern about type safety: because the type of the object referred to by a generic reference is unknown, the compiler will not allow any operations to be performed on that object. Assignments back into objects of a particular reference type (e.g., a pointer to a programmer-specified record type) are a bit trickier, if type safety is to be maintained. We would not want a generic reference to a floating-point number, for example, to be assigned into a variable that is supposed to hold a reference to an integer, because subsequent operations on the "integer" would interpret the bits of the object incorrectly. In object-oriented languages, the question of how to ensure the validity of a generic to specific assignment generalizes to the question of how to ensure the validity of any assignment in which the type of the object on left-hand side supports operations that the object on the right-hand side may not.

One way to ensure the safety of generic to specific assignments (or, in general, less specific to more specific assignments) is to make objects self-descriptive: that is, to include in the representation of each object an indication of its type. This approach is common in object-oriented languages: it is taken in Java, Eiffel, Modula-3, and Standard C++. (Smalltalk objects are self-descriptive, but Smalltalk variables are not typed.) Type tags in objects can consume a nontrivial amount of space, but allow the implementation to prevent the assignment of an object of one type into a variable of another. In Java, a generic to specific assignment requires a type cast, but will generate an exception if the generic reference does not refer to an object of the casted type. In Eiffel, the equivalent operation uses a special assignment operator (`?=` instead of `:=`); in C++ it uses a `dynamic_cast` operation. Java programmers frequently create container classes that hold objects of the generic reference class `Object`. When an object is removed from a container, it must be assigned (with a type cast) into a variable of an appropriate class before anything interesting can be done with it:

```
import java.util.*;     // library containing Stack container class
...
Stack my_stack = new Stack();
String s = "Hi, Mom";
foo f = new foo ();     // f is of user-defined class type foo
```

```
...
my_stack.push (s);
my_stack.push (f);         // we can push any kind of object on a stack
...
s = (String) my_stack.pop();
    // type cast is required, and will generate an exception at run
    // time if element at top-of-stack is not a string
```

In a language without type tags, the assignment of a generic reference into an object of a specific reference type cannot be checked, because objects are not self-descriptive: there is no way to identify their type at run time. The programmer must therefore resort to an (unchecked) type conversion. C++ minimizes the overhead of type tags by permitting dynamic_cast operations only on objects of polymorphic types. A thorough explanation of this restriction requires an understanding of virtual member functions and their implementation, something we defer to Sections 10.4.1 and 10.4.2.

7.2.4 Type Inference

We have seen how type checking ensures that the components of an expression (e.g., the arguments of a binary operator) have appropriate types. But what determines the type of the overall expression? In most cases, the answer is easy. The result of a binary operator usually has the same type as the operands. The result of a function call has the type declared in the function's header. The result of an assignment (in languages in which assignments are expressions) has the same type as the left-hand side. In a few cases, however, the answer is not obvious. In particular, operations on subranges and on composite objects do not necessarily preserve the types of the operands. We examine these cases in the two subsections below. In the following section we consider a more elaborate form of type inference found in ML, Miranda, and Haskell.

Subranges

For simple arithmetic operators, the principal type system subtlety arises when one or more operands have subrange types (what Ada calls subtypes with range constraints). Given the following Pascal definitions, for example,

```
type Atype = 0..20;
     Btype = 10..20;
var  a : Atype;
     b : Btype;
```

what is the type of a + b? Certainly it is neither Atype nor Btype, since the possible values range from 10 to 40. One could imagine it being a new anonymous subrange type with 10 and 40 as bounds. The usual answer in Pascal and its descendants is to say that the result of any arithmetic operation on a subrange is of the subrange's base type, in this case integer.

In Ada, the type of an arithmetic expression assumes special significance in the header of a `for` loop (Section 6.5.1), because it determines the type of the index variable. For the sake of uniformity, Ada says that the index of a `for` loop always has the base type of the loop bounds, whether they are built-up expressions or simple variables or constants.

If the result of an arithmetic operation is assigned into a variable of a subrange type, then a dynamic semantic check may be required. To avoid the expense of some unnecessary checks, a compiler may keep track at compile time of the largest and smallest possible values of each expression, in essence computing the anonymous `10..40` type. Appropriate bounds for the result of an arithmetic operator can always be calculated from the values for the operands. In addition, for example,

```
result.min := operand1.min + operand2.min
result.max := operand1.max + operand2.max
```

For subtraction,

```
result.min := operand1.min − operand2.max
result.max := operand1.max − operand2.min
```

The rules for other operators are analogous. When an expression is assigned to a subrange variable, or passed as a subrange parameter, the compiler can decide on the need for checks based on the bounds of the expected type and on the minimum and maximum values maintained for the expression. If the minimum possible value of the expression is smaller than the lower bound of the expected type, or if the maximum possible value of the expression is larger than the upper bound of the expected type, a run-time check is required. At the same time, if the minimum possible value of the expression is larger than the upper bound of the expected type, or the maximum possible value of the expression is smaller than the lower bound of the expected type, then the compiler can issue a semantic error message at compile time.

It should be noted that this bounds-tracking technique will not eliminate all unnecessary checks. In the following Ada code, for example, a compiler that aimed to do a perfect job of predicting the need for dynamic semantic checks would need to predict the possible return values of a programmer-specified function:

```
a : integer range 0..20;
b : integer range 10..20;
function foo (i : integer) return integer is ...
...
a := b - foo (10);    -- does this require a dynamic semantic check?
```

If `foo (10)` is guaranteed to lie between 0 and 10, then no dynamic check is required; the assignment is sure to be ok. If `foo (10)` is guaranteed to be greater than 20 or less than -10, then again no check is required; an error can be announced at compile time. Unfortunately, the value of foo may depend on values read at run time. Even if it does not, basic results in complexity theory imply that no compiler will be able to predict the behavior of all user-specified functions. Because of these limitations, the compiler must inevitably generate some unnecessary run-time checks; straightforward tracking of the minimum and maximum values for expressions is only a heuristic that allows us to eliminate some unnecessary checks in practice. More sophisticated techniques can be used to eliminate many checks in loops; we will consider these in Section 13.5.2.

Composite Types

Most built-in operators in most languages take operands of built-in types. Some operators, however, can be applied to values of composite types, including aggregates. Type inference becomes an issue when an operation on composites yields a result of a different type than the operands.

Character strings provide a simple example. In Pascal, the literal string 'abc' has type array [1..3] of char. In Ada, the analogous string (denoted "abc") is considered to have an incompletely specified type that is compatible with any three-element array of characters. In the Ada expression "abc" & "defg", "abc" is a three-character array, "defg" is a four-character array, and the result is a seven-character array formed by concatenating the two. For all three, the size of the array is known but the bounds and the index type are not; they must be inferred from context. The seven-character result of the concatenation could be assigned into an array of type array (1..7) of character or into an array of type array (weekday) of character, or into any other seven-element character array.

Operations on composite values also occur when manipulating sets in Pascal and Modula. As with string concatenation, operations on sets do not necessarily produce a result of the same type as the operands. Consider the following example in Pascal:

```
var  A : set of 1..10;
     B : set of 10..20;
     C : set of 1..15;
     i : 1..30;
...
C := A + B * [1..5, i];
```

Pascal provides three operations on sets: union (+), intersection (*), and difference (-). Set operands are said to have compatible types if their elements have the same base type T. The result of a set operation is then of type set of T. In the example above, A, B, and the constructed set [1..5, i] all have the same base type, namely integer. The type of the right-hand side of the assignment is therefore set of integer. When an expression is assigned to a set variable, or passed as a set parameter, a dynamic semantic check may be required. In the example, the assignment will require a check to ensure that none of the possible values between 16 and 20 actually occur in the set.

As with subranges, a compiler can avoid the need for checks in certain cases by keeping track of the minimum and maximum possible members of the set expression. Because a set may have many members, some of which may be known at compile time, it can be useful to track not only the largest and smallest values that may be in a set, but also the values that are known to be in the set (see Exercise 7.7).

In Section 7.2.3 we noted that Fortran 90 allows all of its built-in arithmetic operations to be applied to arrays. The result of an array operation has the same shape as the operands. Each of its elements is the result of applying the operation to the corresponding elements of the operand arrays. Since shape is preserved, type inference is not an issue.

7.2.5* The ML Type System

The most sophisticated form of type inference occurs in certain functional languages, notably ML, Miranda, and Haskell. Programmers have the option of declaring the types of objects in these languages, in which case the compiler behaves much like that of a more traditional statically typed language. As we noted near the beginning of Section 7.1, however, programmers may also choose not to declare certain types, in which case the compiler will infer them, based on the known types of manifest constants, the explicitly declared types of any objects that have them, and the syntactic structure of the program. Here is an ML version of the tail-recursive Fibonacci function introduced in Section 6.6.1:

```
1.  fun fib (n) =
2.      let fun fib_helper (f1, f2, i) =
3.          if i = n then f2
4.          else fib_helper (f2, f1+f2, i+1)
5.      in
6.          fib_helper (0, 1, 0)
7.      end;
```

The `let` construct introduces a nested scope: function `fib_helper` is nested inside `fib`. The body of `fib` is the expression `fib_helper (0, 1, 0)`. The body of `fib_helper` is an `if...then...else` expression; it evaluates to either `f2` or to `fib_helper (f2, f1+f2, i+1)`, depending on whether the third argument to `fib_helper` is `n` or not.

Given this function definition, an ML compiler will reason roughly as follows: Parameter `i` of `fib_helper` must have type `int`, because it is added to 1 at line 4. Similarly, parameter `n` of `fib` must have type `int`, because it is compared to `i` at line 3. In the specific call to `fib_helper` at line 6, the types of all three arguments are `int`, so in this context at least, the types of `f1` and `f2` are `int`. Moreover the type of `i` is consistent with the earlier inference, namely `int`, and the types of the arguments to the recursive call at line 4 are similarly consistent. Since fib_helper returns f2 at line 3, the result of the call at line 6 will be an int. Since fib immediately returns this result as its own result, the return type of fib is int.

Because ML is a functional language, every construct in ML is an expression. The ML type system infers a type for every object and every expression. Because functions are first-class values, they too have types. The type of fib above is int -> int; that is, a function from integers to integers. The type of fib_helper is int * int * int -> int; that is, a function from integer triples to integers. In denotational terms, int * int * int is a three-way Cartesian product.

Type correctness in ML amounts to what we might call type *consistency*: a program is type correct if the type checking algorithm can reason out a unique type for every expression, with no contradictions and no ambiguous occurrences of overloaded symbols such as +. If the programmer uses an object inconsistently, the compiler will complain. In a program containing the following expressions,

```
fun circum (r) = r * 2.0 * 3.14159;
...
circum (7)
```

the compiler will infer that circum's parameter is of type real, and will then complain when we attempt to pass an integer argument.

Though usually compiled instead of interpreted, ML is intended for interactive use. The programmer interacts with the ML system "on-line," giving it input a line at a time. The system compiles this input incrementally, binding machine language fragments to function names, and producing any appropriate compile-time error messages. This style of interaction blurs the traditional distinction between interpretation and compilation, but has more of the flavor of the latter. The language implementation remains active during program execution, but it does not actively manage the execution of program fragments: it *transfers* control to them and waits for them to return.

In comparison to languages in which programmers must declare all types explicitly, ML's type inference system has the advantage of brevity and convenience for interactive use. More important, it provides a powerful form of polymorphism more or less for free. While all uses of objects in an ML program must be consistent, they do not have to be completely specified.

```
fun compare (x, p, q) =
    if x = p then
        if x = q then "both"
        else "first"
    else
        if x = q then "second"
        else "neither";
```

The equality test (=) is a built-in polymorphic function of type 'a * 'a -> bool; that is, a function that takes a pair of arguments of the same type and produces a

Boolean result. The token 'a is called a *type variable*; it stands for any type. Every instance of 'a in a given call to = must represent the same type, but instances of 'a in different calls can be different. Starting with the type of =, an ML compiler can reason that the type of compare is 'a * 'a * 'a -> string. Thus compare is polymorphic; it does not depend on the types of x, p, and q, so long as they are all the same. The key point to observe is that the programmer did not have to do anything special to make compare polymorphic: polymorphism is a natural consequence of ML-style type inference.

An ML compiler verifies type consistency with respect to a well-defined set of constraints. Specifically,

- All occurrences of the same identifier (subject to scope rules) must have the same type.
- In an if...then...else expression, the condition must be of type bool, and the then and else clauses must have the same type.
- A programmer-defined function has type 'a -> 'b, where 'a is the type of the function's parameter, and 'b is the type of its result. As we shall see shortly, all functions have a single parameter. One obtains the *appearance* of multiple parameters by passing a *tuple* as argument.
- When a function is applied (called), the type of the argument that is passed must be the same as the type of the parameter in the function's definition. The type of the application (call) is the same as the type of the result in the function's definition.

In any case where two types *A* and *B* must be "the same," the ML compiler must *unify* what it knows about *A* and *B* to produce a (potentially more detailed) description of their common type. For example, if the compiler has determined that E1 is an expression of type 'a * int (that is, a two-element tuple whose second element is known to be an integer), and that E2 is an expression of type string * 'b, then in the expression if x then E1 else E2, it can infer that 'a is string and 'b is int. Thus x is of type bool, and E1 and E2 are of type string * int. Unification is a powerful technique. In addition to its role in type inference, it is central to the computational model of Prolog and other logic languages. We will consider this role in Section 11.3. In the general case the cost of unifying the types of two expressions can be exponential [Mai90], but the pathological cases tend not to arise in practice.

As in most functional languages, ML programmers tend to make heavy use of lists. In languages such as Lisp and Scheme, which are dynamically typed, lists may contain objects of arbitrary types. In ML, all elements of a given list must have the same type, but—and this is important—functions that manipulate lists without performing operations on their members can take any kind of list as argument:

```
fun append (l1, l2) =
    if l1 = nil then l2
    else hd (l1) :: append (tl (l1), l2);
```

```
fun member (x, 1) =
    if 1 = nil then false
    else if x = hd (1) then true
    else member (x, tl (1));
```

Here `append` is of type `'a list * 'a list -> 'a list`; `member` is of type `'a * 'a list -> bool`. The reserved word `nil` represents the empty list. The built-in `::` constructor is analogous to `cons` in Lisp. It takes an element and a list and tacks the former onto the beginning of the latter; its type is `'a * 'a list -> 'a list`. The `hd` and `tl` functions are analogous to `car` and `cdr` in Lisp. They return the head and the remainder, respectively, of a list created by `::`.

Lists are most often written in ML using "square bracket" notation. The token `[]` is the same as `nil`. `[A, B, C]` is the same as `A :: B :: C :: nil`. Only "proper" lists—those that end with `nil`—can be represented with square brackets. The `append` function defined above is actually provided in ML as a built-in infix constructor, `@`. The expression `[a, b, c] @ [d, e, f, g]` evaluates to `[a, b, c, d, e, f, g]`.

Since ML lists are homogeneous (all elements have the same type), one might wonder about the type of `nil`. To allow it to take on the type of any list, `nil` is defined not as an object, but as a built-in polymorphic function of type `unit -> 'a list`. The built-in type `unit` is simply a placeholder, analogous to `void` in C. A function that takes no arguments is said to have a parameter of type `unit`. A function that is executed only for its side effects (ML is not purely functional) is said to return a result of type `unit`.

We have already seen that the equality test (`=`) is a built-in polymorphic operator. The same is not true of ordering tests (`<`, `<=`, `>=`, `>`) or arithmetic operators (`+`, `-`, `*`). The equality test can be defined as a polymorphic function because it accepts arguments of *any* type. The relations and arithmetic operators work only on certain types. To avoid limiting them to a single type of argument (e.g., integers), ML defines them as overloaded names for a collection of built-in functions, each of which operates on objects of a different type (integers, floating-point numbers, strings, etc.). The programmer can define additional such functions for new types.

Unfortunately, overloading sometimes interferes with type inference: there may not be enough information in an otherwise valid program to resolve which function is named by an overloaded operator:

```
fun square (x) = x * x;    (* error *)
```

In this function the compiler will not be able to tell whether `*` refers to integer or floating-point multiplication, and will issue an error message. The programmer can eliminate the ambiguity by declaring a type explicitly: writing

```
fun square (x : int) = x * x;
```

In addition to allowing the resolution of overloaded symbols, explicit type declarations serve as "verified documentation" in ML programs. ML programmers often declare types for variables even when they aren't required, because the declarations make a program easier to read and understand. Readability could also be enhanced by comments, of course, but programmer-specified types have a very important advantage: the compiler understands their meaning, and ensures that all uses of an object are consistent with its declared type.

In our discussion so far, we have been "glossing over" another key feature of ML and its types: namely, pattern matching. One of the simplest forms of pattern matching occurs in functions of more than one parameter. Strictly speaking, such functions do not exist. Every function in ML takes a *single* argument, but this argument may be a *tuple*. A tuple resembles a record in an Algol-family language, except that its members are identified by position, rather than by name. As an example, the function `compare` defined above takes a three-element tuple as argument. All of the following are valid:

```
compare (1, 2, 3);
let val t = ("larry", "moe", "curly") in compare (t) end;
let val d = (2, 3) in
    let val (a, b) = d in
        compare (1, a, b)
    end
end;
```

Here pattern matching occurs not only between the parameters and arguments of the call to `compare`, but also between the left- and right-hand sides of the `val` construct. (The reserved word `val` serves to declare a name. The construct `fun inc (n) = n+1;` is syntactic sugar for `val inc = (fn n => n+1);`.)

As a somewhat more plausible example, we can define a highly useful function that reverses a two-element tuple:

```
fun swap (a, b) = (b, a);
```

Since ML is (mostly) functional, swap is not intended to exchange the value of objects; rather, it takes a two-element tuple as argument, and produces the symmetrical two-element tuple as a result. Pattern matching in ML works not only for tuples, but for any built-in or user-defined *constructor* of composite values. Constructors include the parentheses used for tuples, the square brackets used for lists, several of the built-in operators (`::`, `@`, etc.), and user-defined constructors of `datatypes` (see below). Literal constants are even considered to be constructors, so the tuple `t` can be matched against the pattern `(1, x)`: the match will succeed only if `t`'s first element is 1.

In a call such as `compare (t)` or `swap (2, 3)`, an ML implementation can tell at compile time that the pattern match will succeed: it knows all necessary information about the structure of the value being matched against the pattern. In other cases, the implementation can tell that a match is doomed to fail, generally because the types of the pattern and the value cannot be unified. The more interesting cases are those in which the pattern and the value have the same type (i.e., could be unified), but the success of the match cannot be determined until run time. If l is of type int list, for example, then an attempt to "deconstruct" l into its head and tail may or may not succeed, depending on l's value:

```
let val head :: rest = l in ...
```

If l is nil, the attempted match will produce an *exception* at run time (we will consider exceptions further in Section 8.5).

We have seen how pattern matching works in function calls and val constructs. It is also supported by a case expression. Using case, the append function above could have been written as follows:

```
fun append (l1, l2) =
    case l1 of
        nil => l2
     | h :: t => h :: append (t, l2);
```

Here the code generated for the case expression will pattern-match l1 first against nil and then against h :: t. The case expression evaluates to the subexpression following the => in the first arm whose pattern matches. The compiler will issue a warning message at compile time if the patterns of the arms are not exhaustive, or if the pattern in a later arm is completely covered by one in an earlier arm (implying that the latter will never be chosen). A useless arm is probably an error, but harmless, in the sense that it will never result in a dynamic semantic error message. Nonexhaustive cases may be intentional, if the programmer can predict that the pattern will always work at run time. Our append function would have generated such a warning if written as follows:

```
fun append (l1, l2) =
    if l1 = nil then l2
    else let val h::t = l1 in h :: append (t, l2) end;
```

Here the compiler is unlikely to realize that the let construct in the else clause will only be elaborated if l1 is nonempty. (This example looks easy enough to figure out, but the general case is uncomputable, and most compilers won't contain special code to recognize easy cases.)

When the body of a function consists entirely of a case expression, it can also be written as a simple series of alternatives:

```
fun append (nil, l2) = l2
  | append (h::t, l2) = h :: append (t, l2);
```

Pattern matching features prominently in other languages as well, particularly those (such as Snobol, Icon, and Perl) that place a heavy emphasis on strings. ML-style pattern matching differs from that of string-oriented languages in its integration with static typing and type inference. Snobol, Icon, and Perl are all dynamically typed.

By casting "multiargument" functions in terms of tuples, ML eliminates the asymmetry between the arguments and return values of functions in many other languages. As shown by swap above, a function can return a tuple just as easily as it can take a tuple argument. Pattern matching allows the elements of the tuple to be extracted by the caller:

```
let val (a, b) = swap (c, d) in ...
```

Here a will have the value given by d; b will have the value given by c.

In addition to lists and tuples, ML provides built-in constructors for records, together with a datatype mechanism that allows the programmer to introduce other kinds of composite types. A record is a composite object in which the elements have names, but no particular order (the language implementation must chose an order for its internal representation, but this order is not visible to the programmer). Records are specified using a "curly brace" constructor: {name => "Abraham Lincoln", elected => 1860}. (The same value can be denoted {elected => 1860, name => "Abraham Lincoln"}.)

ML's datatype mechanism introduces a type name and a collection of constructors for that type. In the simplest case, the constructors are all functions of zero arguments, and the type is essentially an enumeration:

```
datatype weekday = sun | mon | tue | wed | thu | fri | sat;
```

In more complicated examples, the constructors have arguments, and the type is essentially a union (variant record):

```
datatype yearday = mmdd of int * int | ddd of int;
```

This code defines mmdd as a constructor that takes a pair of integers as argument, and ddd as a constructor that takes a single integer as argument. The intent is to allow days of the year to be specified either as (month, day) pairs or as integers in the range 1..366. In a non–leap year, the Fourth of July could be represented either as mmdd (7, 4) or as ddd (188), though the equality test mmdd (7, 4) = ddd (188) would fail unless we made yearday an *abstract* type (similar to the Euclid module types of Section 3.3.1), with its own, special, equality operation.

ML's datatypes can even be used to define recursive types, without the need for pointers. The canonical ML example is a binary tree:

```
datatype int_tree = empty | node of int * int_tree * int_tree;
```

By introducing an explicit type variable in the definition, we can even create a generic tree whose elements are of any homogeneous type:

```
datatype 'a tree = empty | node of 'a * 'a tree * 'a tree;
```

Given this definition, the tree

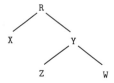

can be written `node ('R', node ('X', empty, empty), node ('Y', node ('Z', empty, empty), node ('W', empty, empty)))`. Recursive types also appear in Lisp, Clu, Java, and other languages with a reference model of variables; we will discuss them further in Section 7.7.

Because of its use of type inference, ML generally provides the effect of structural type equivalence. Definitions of `datatypes` can be used to obtain the effect of name equivalence when desired:

```
datatype celsius_temp = ct of int;
datatype fahrenheit_temp = ft of int;
```

A value of type `celsius_temp` can then be obtained by using the `ct` constructor:

```
val freezing = ct (0);
```

Unfortunately, `celsius_temp` does not automatically inherit the arithmetic operators and relations of `int`: unless the programmer defines these operators explicitly, the expression `ct (0) < ct (20)` will generate an error message along the lines of "operator not defined for type."

7.3   Records (Structures) and Variants (Unions)

As we have seen, record types allow related data of heterogeneous types to be stored and manipulated together. Some languages (notably Algol 68, C, C++, and Common Lisp) use the term *structure* (declared with the keyword `struct`) instead of *record*. Fortran 90 simply calls its records "types": they are the only form of programmer-defined type other than arrays, which have their own special syntax. Structures in C++ are defined as a special form of *class* (one in which members are globally visible by default). Java has no distinguished notion of `struct`; its programmers use classes in all cases.

7.3.1   Syntax and Operations

In Pascal, a simple record might be defined as follows:

```
type two_chars = packed array [1..2] of char;
    (* a 'packed' array of char is compatible with a quoted string *)
type element = record
    name : two_chars;
    atomic_number : integer;
    atomic_weight : real;
    metallic : Boolean
end;
```

In C, the corresponding declaration would be

```
struct element {
    char name[2];
    int atomic_number;
    double atomic_weight;
    char metallic;              /* C has no Boolean type */
};
```

Each of the record components is known as a *field*. To refer to a given field of a record, most languages use "dot" notation. In Pascal:

```
var copper : element;
const AN = 6.022e23;      (* Avogadro's number *)
...
copper.name := 'Cu';
atoms := mass / copper.atomic_weight * AN;
```

The C notation is similar to that of Pascal; in Fortran 90 one would say `copper%name` and `copper%atomic_weight`. Cobol and Algol 68 reverse the order of the field and record names: `name of copper` and `atomic_weight of copper`. ML's notation is also "reversed," but uses a prefix #: `#name copper` and `#atomic_weight copper`. (Fields of an ML record can also be extracted using patterns.) In Common Lisp, one would say `(element-name copper)` and `(element-atomic_weight copper)`.

Most languages allow record definitions to be nested. Again in Pascal:

```
type short_string = packed array [1..30] of char;
type ore = record
    name : short_string;
    element_yielded : record
        name : two_chars;
        atomic_number : integer;
        atomic_weight : real;
        metallic : Boolean
    end
end;
```

Alternatively, one could say

```
type ore = record
    name : short_string;
    element_yielded : element
end;
```

In Fortran 90 and Common Lisp, only the second alternative is permitted: record fields can have record types, but the declarations cannot be lexically nested. Naming for nested records is straightforward: `malachite.element_yielded .atomic_number` in Pascal or C; `atomic_number of element_yielded of malachite` in Cobol; `#atomic_number #element_yielded malachite` in ML; `(element-atomic_number (ore-element_yielded malachite))` in Common Lisp.

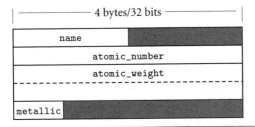

Figure 7.1 Likely layout in memory for objects of type element **on a 32-bit machine.**
Alignment restrictions lead to the shaded "holes."

As noted in Section 7.2.1, ML differs from most languages in specifying that the order of record fields is insignificant. The ML record value {name = "Cu", atomic_number = 29, atomic_weight = 63.546, metallic = true} is the same as the value {atomic_number = 29, name = "Cu", atomic_weight = 63.546, metallic = true} (they will test true for equality). ML tuples are defined as abbreviations for records whose field names are small integers. The values ("Cu", 29), {1 = "Cu", 2 = 29}, and {2 = 29, 1 = "Cu"} will all test true for equality.

7.3.2 Memory Layout and Its Impact

Much of the reason why the order of fields is important has to do with implementation. The fields of a record are usually stored in adjacent locations in memory. In its symbol table, the compiler keeps track of the offset of each field within each record type. When it needs to access a field, the compiler typically generates a load or store instruction with displacement addressing. For a local object, the base register is the frame pointer; for a global object, the base register is the globals pointer. In either case, the displacement is the sum of the record's offset from the register and the field's offset within the record.

A likely layout for our element type on a 32-bit machine appears in Figure 7.1. Because the name field is only two characters long, it occupies two bytes in memory. Since atomic_number is an integer, and must (on most machines) be longword-aligned, there is a two-byte "hole" between the end of name and the beginning of atomic_number. Similarly, since Boolean variables (in most language implementations) occupy a single byte, there are three bytes of empty space between the end of the metallic field and the next aligned location. In an array of elements, most compilers would devote 20 bytes to every member of the array.

Pascal allows the programmer to specify that a record type (or an array, set, or file type) should be packed:

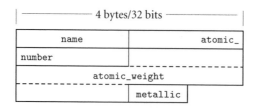

Figure 7.2 Likely memory layout for packed element **records.** The atomic_number and atomic_weight fields are nonaligned, and can only be read or written (on most machines) via multi-instruction sequences.

```
type element = packed record
    name : two_chars;
    atomic_number : integer;
    atomic_weight : real;
    metallic : Boolean
end;
```

The keyword packed indicates that the compiler should optimize for space instead of speed. In most implementations a compiler will implement a packed record without holes, by simply "pushing the fields together." To access a nonaligned field, however, it will have to issue a multi-instruction sequence that retrieves the pieces of the field from memory and then reassembles them in a register. A likely packed layout for our element type (again for a 32-bit machine) appears in Figure 7.2. It is 15 bytes in length. An array of packed element records would probably devote 16 bytes to each member of the array; i.e., it would align each element. A packed array of packed records would probably devote only 15 bytes to each; only every fourth element would be aligned. Ada and Modula-3 provide more elaborate packing mechanisms, which allow the programmer to specify precisely how many bits are to be devoted to each field.

Most languages allow a value to be assigned to an entire record in a single operation:

```
my_element := copper;
```

Ada also allows records to be compared for equality (if my_element = copper then . . .), but most other languages (including Pascal, Modula, C, and C++) do not, though C++ allows the programmer to define equality tests for individual record types. For small records, both copies and comparisons can be performed in-line on a field-by field basis. For longer records, we can save significantly on code space by deferring to a library routine. A block_copy routine can take source address, destination address, and length as arguments, but the analogous block_compare routine would fail on records with different (garbage) data in the holes. One solution is to arrange for all holes to contain some predictable value (e.g., zero), but this requires code at every elaboration point. Another is to have the compiler generate a customized field-by-field comparison routine

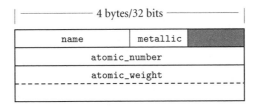

Figure 7.3 Rearranging record fields to minimize holes. By sorting fields according to the size of their alignment constraint, a compiler can minimize the space devoted to holes, while keeping the fields aligned.

for every record type. Different routines would be called to compare records of different types. Languages such as Pascal and C avoid the whole issue by simply outlawing full-record comparisons.

In addition to complicating comparisons, holes in records waste space. Packing eliminates holes, but at potentially heavy cost in access time. A compromise, adopted by some compilers, is to sort a record's fields according to the size of their alignment constraints. All byte-aligned fields come first, followed by any half-word aligned fields, word-aligned fields, and (if the hardware requires) double-word-aligned fields. For our `element` type, the resulting rearrangement is shown in Figure 7.3. In most cases, reordering of fields is purely an implementation issue: the programmer need not be aware of it, so long as all instances of a record type are reordered in the same way. The exception occurs in systems programs, which sometimes "look inside" the implementation of a data type with the expectation that it will be mapped to memory in a particular way. A kernel programmer, for example, may count on a particular layout strategy in order to define a record that mimics the organization of memory-mapped control registers for a particular Ethernet device. C and C++, which are designed in large part for systems programs, guarantee that the fields of a `struct` will be allocated in the order declared. The first field is guaranteed to have the coarsest alignment required by the hardware for any type (generally a four- or eight-byte boundary). Subsequent fields have the natural alignment for their type. To accommodate systems programs, Ada and C++ allow the programmer to specify nonstandard alignment for the fields of specific record types.

7.3.3* `With` **Statements**

In programs with complicated data structures, manipulating the fields of a deeply nested record can be awkward:

```
ruby.chemical_composition.elements[1].name := 'Al';
ruby.chemical_composition.elements[1].atomic_number := 13;
ruby.chemical_composition.elements[1].atomic_weight := 26.98154;
ruby.chemical_composition.elements[1].metallic := true;
```

Pascal provides a `with` statement to simplify such constructions:

```
with ruby.chemical_composition.elements[1] do begin
    name := 'Al';
    atomic_number := 13;
    atomic_weight := 26.98154;
    metallic := true
end;
```

The `with` statement introduces a nested scope in which the fields of the named record become visible as if they were ordinary variables. The record is said to be *opened*. As shown in Figure 3.14 (page 136), a `with` statement can be implemented within the compiler by pushing an entry that represents the record type onto the symbol table scope stack.

Pascal `with` statements are a formalization of the *elliptical references* of Cobol and PL/I, a language feature that permits portions of a fully qualified name to be omitted if no ambiguity results. In our example above, `name of elements(1) of chemical_composition of ruby` could probably be abbreviated `name of elements(1) of ruby`, since `ruby` is unlikely to have a field named `elements` within anything other than its `chemical_composition` field. The rest of the reference is required, however, if there is another record of the same type as `ruby` in the current scope, and if the `elements` array within that type contains more than a single element.

Elliptical references can be difficult to read, since they rely implicitly on the uniqueness of field names. A `with` statement specifies the elided information more explicitly, making misunderstandings less likely. The `with` statements of Pascal still suffer from problems however:

1. There is no easy way to manipulate fields of two records of the same type simultaneously (e.g., to copy some of the fields of one into corresponding fields of the other). A `with` statement can be used to open one of the records, but not the other.

2. Naming conflicts arise if any of the fields of an opened record have the same name as local objects. Since the `with` statement is a nested scope, the local objects become temporarily inaccessible.

3. In a long `with` statement, or in nested `with` statements that open records of different types, the correspondence between field names and the records to which they belong can become unclear.

Modula-3 addresses these problems by redefining the `with` statement in a more general form. Rather than opening a record, a Modula-3 WITH statement introduces one or more aliases for complicated expressions. Recasting the example above in the style of Modula-3, one would write:

```
WITH e = ruby.chemical_composition.elements[1] DO
    e.name := "Al";
    e.atomic_number := 13;
    e.atomic_weight := 26.98154;
    e.metallic := true;
END;
```

Here e is an alias for `ruby.chemical_composition.elements[1]`. The fields of the record are not *directly* visible, but they can be accessed easily, simply by prepending 'e.' to their names. To access more than one record at a time, one can write

```
WITH e = whatever, f = whatever DO
    e.field1 := f.field1;
    e.field3 := f.field3;
    e.field7 := f.field7;
END;
```

Modula-3 WITH statements can even be used to create aliases for objects other than records, e.g., to test and then use a complicated expression without writing it out twice:

```
WITH d = complicated_expression DO
    IF d <> 0 THEN val := n/d ELSE val := 0 END;
END;
```

A similar effect, of course, can be achieved in C without a special construct:

```
{
    my_struct *e = whatever;
    my_struct *f = whatever;
    e->field1 = f->field1;
    e->field3 = f->field3;
    e->field7 = f->field7;
}
```

```
{
    double d = complicated_expression
    val = (d ? n/d : 0);
}
```

This code depends on the ability of the C programmer to declare variables in nested blocks and to create pointers to nonheap objects. Pascal does not permit nested declarations; neither Pascal nor Modula-3 permit the nonheap pointers. Reference types in C++, which we will introduce in Section 8.3.1, can be used in place of pointers in the C example above to produce an even closer approximation of the Modula-3 WITH statement.

Both Pascal and Modula-3 with statements are implemented in a target program by creating a hidden pointer to the opened or aliased record. All uses of the record inside the with statement access fields efficiently via offsets from the hidden pointer. Equivalent efficiency can usually be achieved without the with statement, but only if the complier implements global common subexpression analysis, a nontrivial form of code improvement that we defer to Section 13.4.

7.3.4 **Variant Records**

A variant record provides two or more alternative fields or collections of fields, only one of which is valid at any given time. In Pascal, we might augment our element type as follows:

```
type long_string = packed array [1..200] of char;
type string_ptr = ^long_string;
type element = record
    name : two_chars;
    atomic_number : integer;
    atomic_weight : real;
    metallic : Boolean;
    case naturally_occurring : Boolean of
      true : (
        source : string_ptr;
            (* textual description of principal commercial source *)
        prevalence : real;
            (* percentage, by weight, of Earth's crust *)
    );
      false : (
        lifetime : real;
            (* half-life in seconds of the most stable known isotope *)
    )
end;
```

Here the `naturally_occurring` field of the record is known as its *tag*, or *discriminant*. A `true` tag indicates that the element has at least one naturally occurring stable isotope; in this case the record contains two additional fields—source and prevalence—that describe how the element may be obtained and how commonly it occurs. A `false` tag indicates that the element results only from atomic collisions or the decay of heavier elements; in this case, the record contains an additional field—lifetime—that indicates how long atoms so created tend to survive before undergoing radioactive decay. Each of the parenthesized field lists (one containing `source` and `prevalence`, the other containing `lifetime`) is known as a *variant*. Either the first or the second variant may be useful, but never both at once. From an implementation point of view, these nonoverlapping uses mean that the variants may share space (see Figure 7.4).

Variant records have their roots in the `equivalence` statement of Fortran I and in the `union` types of Algol 68. The Fortran syntax looks like this:

```
integer i
real r
logical b
equivalence (i, r, b)
```

The `equivalence` statement informs the compiler that i, r, and b will never be used at the same time, and should share the same space in memory.

Pascal's principal contribution to union types (retained by Modula and Ada) was to integrate them with records. This was an important contribution, be-

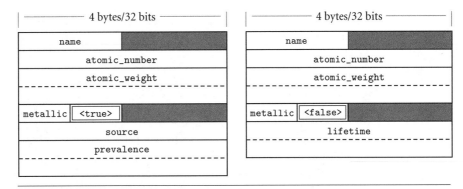

Figure 7.4 Likely memory layouts for `element` **variants.** The value of the `naturally_occurring` field (shown here with a double border) determines which of the interpretations of the remaining space is valid. Type `string_ptr` is assumed to be represented by a (four-byte) pointer to dynamically allocated storage.

cause the need for alternative types seldom arises anywhere else. In our running example, we use the same field-name syntax to access both the `atomic_weight` and `lifetime` fields of an `element`, despite the fact that the former is present in every `element`, while the latter is present only in those that are not naturally occurring. Without the integration of records and unions, the notation is less convenient. Here is an example in C:

```
struct element {
    char name[2];
    int atomic_number;
    double atomic_weight;
    char metallic;
    char naturally_occurring;
    union {
        struct {
            char *source;
            double prevalence;
        } natural_info;
        double lifetime;
    } extra_fields;
} copper;
```

Because the `union` is not a part of the `struct`, we have to introduce two extra levels of naming. The third field is still `copper.atomic_weight`, but the `source` field must be accessed as `copper.extra_fields.natural_info.source`. A similar situation occurs in ML, in which `datatypes` can be used for unions, but the notation is not integrated with records (Exercise 7.14).

Safety

One of the principal problems with `equivalence` statements is that they provide no built-in means of determining which of the `equivalence`-ed objects is currently valid: the program must keep track. Mistakes in which the programmer writes to one object and then reads from the other are relatively common:

```
r = 3.0
...
print '(I10)', i
```

Here the `print` statement, which attempts to output i as a 10-digit integer, will (in most implementations) take its bits from the floating-point representation of 3.0: almost certainly a mistake, but one that the language implementation will not catch.

Fortran `equivalence` statements introduce an extreme case of aliases: not only are there two names for the "same thing" (in this case the same block of storage), but the types associated with those names are different. To address this potential source of bugs, the Algol 68 designers required that the language implementation track `union`-ed types at run time:

```
union (int, real, bool) uirb
    # uirb can be an integer, a floating-point number, or a Boolean #
...
uirb := 1        # uirb is now an integer #
...
uirb := 3.14     # uirb is now a floating-point number #
```

To use the value stored inside a union, the programmer must employ a special form of `case` statement (called a *conformity clause* in Algol 68) that determines which type is currently valid:

```
case uirb in
    (int i) : print (i),
    (real r) : print (r),
    (bool b) : print (b)
esac
```

The labels on the arms of the `case` statement provide names for the "deunified" values. A similar `tagcase` construct can be found in Clu.

To enforce correct usage of union types in Algol 68, the language implementation must maintain a hidden variable for every union object that indicates which type is currently valid. When an object of a union type is assigned a value, the hidden variable is also set, to indicate the type of the value just assigned. When execution encounters a conformity clause, the hidden field is inspected to determine which arm to execute.

In effect, the tag field of a Pascal variant record is an explicit representation of the hidden variable required in an Algol 68 union. Our integer/floating-point/Boolean example could be written as follows in Pascal:

```
type tag = (is_int, is_real, is_bool);
var uirb : record
    case which : tag of
        is_int : (i : integer);
        is_real : (r : real);
        is_bool : (b : Boolean)
end;
```

Unfortunately, while the hidden tag of an Algol 68 union can only be changed implicitly, by assigning a value of a different type to the union as a whole, the tag of a Pascal variant record can be changed by an ordinary assignment statement. The compiler can generate code to verify that a field in variant *v* is never accessed unless the value of the tag indicates that *v* is currently valid, but this is not enough to guarantee type safety. It can catch errors of the form

```
uirb.which := is_real;
uirb.r := 3.0;
...
writeln (uirb.i);   (* dynamic semantic error *)
```

but it cannot catch the following:

```
uirb.which := is_real;
uirb.r := 3.0;
uirb.which := is_int;
...                  (* no intervening assignment to i *)
writeln (uirb.i);   (* ouch! *)
```

Any Pascal implementation will accept this code, but the output is likely to be erroneous, just as it was in Fortran.

Semantically speaking, changing the tag of a Pascal variant record should make the remaining fields of the variant *uninitialized*. It is possible, by adding hidden fields, to flag them as such and generate a semantic error message on any subsequent access, but the code to do so is expensive [FL80], and outlaws programs which, while arguably erroneous, are permitted by the language definition (see Exercise 7.11).

The situation in Pascal is actually worse than our example so far might imply. Additional insecurity stems from the fact that Pascal's tag fields are *optional*. We could eliminate the which field of our uirb record:

```
var uirb : record
    case tag of
        is_int : (i : integer);
        is_real : (r : real);
        is_bool : (b : Boolean)
end;
...
uirb.r := 3.0;
...                  (* no intervening assignment to i *)
writeln (uirb.i);   (* ouch! *)
```

Now the language implementation is not required to devote any space to either an explicit or hidden tag, but even the limited form of checking (make sure the tag has an appropriate value when a field of a variant is accessed) is no longer possible (but see Exercise 7.12). Variant records with tags (explicit or hidden) are known as *discriminated unions*. Variant records without tags are known as *nondiscriminated unions*.

The degree of type safety provided is arguably the most important dimension of variation among the variant records and union types of modern languages. Though designed after Algol 68 (and borrowing its union terminology), the union types of C are semantically closer to Fortran's equivalence statements. Their fields share space, but nothing prevents the programmer from using them in inappropriate ways. By contrast, the variant records of Ada are syntactically similar to those of Pascal, but are as type-safe as the unions of Algol 68. Concerned at the lack of type safety in Pascal and Modula-2, and reluctant to introduce the complexity of Ada's rules, the designers of Modula-3 chose to eliminate variant records from the language entirely. They note [Har92, p. 110] that much of the same effect can be obtained via object types and subtypes. The designers of Java, likewise, dropped the unions of C and C++.

Variants in Ada*

Ada variant records must always have a tag (called the *discriminant* in Ada). Moreover, the tag can never be changed without simultaneously assigning values to all of the fields of the corresponding variant. The assignment can occur either via whole-record assignment (e.g., A := B, where A and B are variant records), or via assignment of an aggregate (e.g., A := {which => is_real, r => pi};). In addition to appearing as a field within the record, the discriminant of a variant record in Ada must also appear in the header of the record's declaration:

```
type element (naturally_occurring : Boolean := true) is record
    name : string (1..2);
    atomic_number : integer;
    atomic_weight : real;
    metallic : Boolean;
    case naturally_occurring is
        when true =>
            source : string_ptr;
            prevalence : real;
        when false =>
            lifetime : real;
    end case;
end record;
```

Here we have not only declared the discriminant of the record in its header, we have also specified a default value for it. A declaration of a variable of type element has the option of accepting this default value:

```
copper : element;
```

or overriding it:

```
plutonium : element (false);
neptunium : element (naturally_occurring => false);
    -- alternative syntax
```

If the type declaration for `element` did not specify a default value for `naturally_occurring`, then all variables of type `element` would have to provide a value. These rules guarantee that the tag field of a variant record is never uninitialized.

An Ada record variable whose declaration specifies a value for the discriminant is said to be *constrained*. Its tag field can never be changed by a subsequent assignment. This immutability means that the compiler can allocate just enough space to hold the specified variant; this space may in some cases be significantly smaller than would be required for other variants. A variable whose declaration does not provide an initial value for the discriminant is said to be *unconstrained*. Its tag can be changed (via whole-record assignment), so the space it occupies must be large enough to hold any possible variant. An Ada subtype definition can also constrain the discriminant(s) of its parent type:

```
subtype natural_element is element (true);
```

Variables of type `natural_element` will all be constrained; their `naturally_occurring` field cannot be changed. Because `natural_element` is a subtype, rather than a derived type, values of type `element` and `natural_element` are compatible with each other, though a run-time semantic check will usually be required to assign the former into the latter.

To facilitate space-saving in constrained variant records, Ada requires that all variant parts of a record appear at the end. This rule ensures that every field has a constant offset from the beginning of the record, with no holes (in any variant) other than those required for alignment. When a constrained variant record is elaborated, the Ada run-time system need only allocate sufficient space to hold the specified variant, which is never allowed to change. Pascal has a similar rule, designed for a similar purpose. When a variant record is allocated from the heap in Pascal (via the built-in `new` operator), the programmer has the option of specifying `case` labels for the variant portions of the record. A record so allocated is never allowed to change to a different variant, so the implementation can allocate precisely the right amount of space.

Modula-2, which does not provide `new` as a built-in operation, eliminates the ordering restriction on variants. All variables of a variant record type must be large enough to hold any variant. The usual implementation assigns a fixed offset to every field, with holes following small internal variants as necessary (see Figure 7.5 and Exercise 7.13).

```
TYPE element = RECORD
    name : ARRAY [1..2] OF CHAR;
    metallic : BOOLEAN;
    CASE naturally_occurring : BOOLEAN OF
        TRUE :
            source : string_ptr;
            prevalence : REAL;
      | FALSE :
            lifetime : REAL;
    END;
    atomic_number : INTEGER;
    atomic_weight : REAL;
END;
```

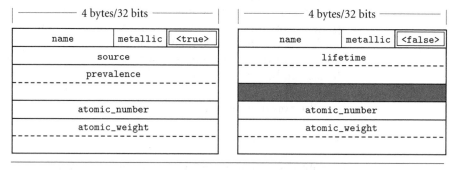

Figure 7.5 Likely memory layout for a variant record in Modula-2. Here the variant portion of the record is not required to lie at the end. Every field has a fixed offset from the beginning of the record, with internal holes as necessary following small-size variants.

Ada uses record discriminants not only for variant tags, but in general for any value that affects the size of a record. Here is an example that uses a discriminant to specify the length of an array:

```
type element_array is array (integer range <>) of element;
type alloy (num_components : integer) is record
    name : string (1..30);
    components : element_array (1..num_components);
    tensile_strength : real;
end record;
```

The <> notation in the initial definition of element_array indicates that the bounds are not statically known. We will have more to say about dynamic arrays in Section 7.4.2. As with discriminants used for variant tags, the programmer must either specify a default value for the discriminant in the type declaration (we did not do so above), or else every declaration of a variable of the type must specify a value for the discriminant (in which case the variable is constrained, and the discriminant cannot be changed).

7.4 Arrays

Arrays are the most common and important composite data types. They have been a fundamental part of almost every high-level language, beginning with Fortran I. Unlike records, which group related fields of disparate types, arrays are usually homogeneous. Semantically, they can be thought of as a mapping from an *index type* to a *component* or *element type*. Some languages (e.g., Fortran) require that the index type be `integer`; many languages allow it to be any discrete type. A few languages (e.g., Awk and Perl) allow nondiscrete index types. The resulting *associative* arrays must generally be implemented with hash tables, rather than with the (much more efficient) contiguous allocation described below (Section 7.4.3). Associative arrays in C++ are known as `maps`; they are supported by a standard library template. For the purposes of this chapter, we will assume that array indices are discrete. Some languages (e.g., Fortran 77) require that the element type of an array be scalar. Most (including Fortran 90) allow any element type.

7.4.1 Syntax and Operations

Most languages refer to an element of an array by appending a subscript—delimited by parentheses or square brackets—to the name of the array. In Fortran and Ada, one says `A(3)`; in Pascal and C, one says `A[3]`. Since parentheses are generally used to delimit the arguments to a subroutine call, square bracket subscript notation has the advantage of distinguishing between the two. The difference in notation makes a program easier to compile and, arguably, easier to read. Fortran's use of parentheses for arrays stems from the absence of square bracket characters on IBM keypunch machines, which at one time were widely used to enter Fortran programs. Ada's use of parentheses represents a deliberate decision on the part of the language designers to embrace notational ambiguity for functions and arrays. If we think of an array as a mapping from the index type to the element type, it makes perfectly good sense to use the same notation used for functions. In some cases, a programmer may even choose to change from an array to a function-based implementation of a mapping, or vice versa (Figure 7.6).

Declarations

In some languages one declares an array by appending subscript notation to the syntax that would be used to declare a scalar. In C:

```
char upper[26];
```

In Fortran:

```
character, dimension (1:26) :: upper
character(26) upper      ! shorthand notation
```

```
subtype lc_letter is character range 'a'..'z';
upper : array (lc_letter) of character :=
    ('A', 'B', 'C', 'D', 'E', 'F',
     'G', 'H', 'I', 'J', 'K', 'L',
     'M', 'N', 'O', 'P', 'Q', 'R',
     'S', 'T', 'U', 'V', 'W', 'X',
     'Y', 'Z');


----------------

subtype lc_letter is character range 'a'..'z';
function upper (l : lc_letter) return character is
    uc_offset : constant integer :=
        character'pos ('A') - character'pos ('a');
begin
    return character'val (character'pos (l) + uc_offset);
end upper;
```

Figure 7.6 The similarity of functions and arrays in Ada. Here we show two ways of implementing a mapping from lower- to uppercase letters. In either case, upper('a') is 'A'.

In C, the lower bound of an index range is always zero: the indices of an n-element array are $0..n-1$. In Fortran, the lower bound of the index range is one by default. Fortran 90 allows a different lower bound to be specified if desired (using the notation shown in the first of the two declarations above).

In other languages, arrays are declared with an **array** constructor. In Pascal:

```
var upper : array ['a'..'z'] of char;
```

In Ada:

```
upper : array (character range 'a'..'z') of character;
```

Most languages make it easy to declare multidimensional arrays:

```
matrix : array (1..10, 1..10) of real;     -- Ada

real, dimension (10,10) :: matrix          ! Fortran
```

In some languages (e.g., Pascal, Ada, and Modula-3), one can also declare a multidimensional array by using the **array** constructor more than once in the same declaration. In Modula-3,

```
VAR matrix : ARRAY [1..10], [1..10] OF REAL;
```

is syntactic sugar for

```
VAR matrix : ARRAY [1..10] OF ARRAY [1..10] OF REAL;
```

and `matrix[3, 4]` is syntactic sugar for `matrix[3][4]`. Similar equivalences hold in Pascal.

In Ada, by contrast,

```
matrix : array (1..10, 1..10) of real;
```

is not the same as

```
matrix : array (1..10) of array (1..10) of real;
```

The former is a two-dimensional array, while the latter is an array of one-dimensional arrays. With the former declaration, we can access individual real numbers as `matrix(3, 4)`; with the latter we must say `matrix(3)(4)`. The two-dimensional array is arguably more elegant, but the array of arrays supports additional operations: it allows us to name the rows of `matrix` individually (`matrix(3)` is a 10-element, single-dimensional array), and it allows us to take *slices*, as discussed in the following section.

In C, one must also declare an array of arrays, and use two-subscript notation, but C's integration of pointers and arrays (to be discussed in Section 7.7.1) means that slices are not supported.

```
double matrix [10][10];
```

Given this definition, `matrix[3][4]` denotes an individual element of the array, but `matrix[3]` denotes a *reference*, either to the third row of the array or to the first element of that row, depending on context.

Slices and Array Operations

A *slice* or *section* is a rectangular portion of an array. Fortran 90 provides extensive facilities for slicing. Figure 7.7 illustrates some of the possibilities, using the declaration of `matrix` shown above. In Ada, only one-dimensional arrays may be sliced; a slice is simply a contiguous range of elements.

In most languages, the only operations permitted on an array are selection of an element (which can then be used for whatever operations are valid on its type), and assignment. A few languages (e.g., Ada and Fortran 90) allow arrays to be compared for equality. Ada allows one-dimensional arrays whose elements are discrete to be compared for *lexicographic ordering*: A < B if the first element of A that is not equal to the corresponding element of B is less than that corresponding element. Ada also allows the built-in logical operators (`or`, `and`, `xor`) to be applied to Boolean arrays.

Fortran 90 has a very rich set of *array operations*: built-in operations that take entire arrays as arguments. Because Fortran uses structural type equivalence, the operands of an array operator need only have the same element type and shape. In particular, slices of the same shape can be intermixed in array operations, even if the arrays from which they were sliced have very different shapes. Any of the built-in arithmetic operators will take arrays as operands; the result is an array,

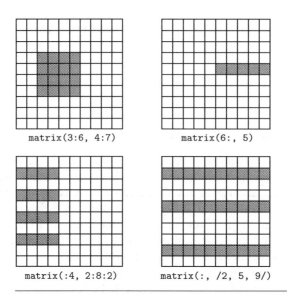

matrix(3:6, 4:7)   matrix(6:, 5)

matrix(:4, 2:8:2)   matrix(:, /2, 5, 9/)

Figure 7.7 Array slices (sections) in Fortran 90. Much like the values in the header of an enumeration-controlled loop (Section 6.5.1), $a : b : c$ in a subscript indicates positions $a, a + c, a + 2c, \ldots$ through b. If a or b is omitted, the corresponding bound of the array is assumed. If c is omitted, 1 is assumed. It is even possible to use negative values of c in order to select positions in reverse order. The slashes in the second subscript of the lower right example delimit an explicit list of positions.

of the same shape as the operands, whose elements are the result of applying the operator to corresponding elements. As a simple example, A + B is an array each of whose elements is the sum of the corresponding elements of A and B. Fortran 90 also provides a huge collection of *intrinsic*, or built-in functions. More than 60 of these (including logic and bit manipulation, trigonometry, logs and exponents, type conversion, and string manipulation) are defined on scalars, but will also perform their operation element-wise if passed arrays as arguments. The function tan (A), for example, returns an array consisting of the tangents of the elements of A. Many additional intrinsic functions are defined solely on arrays. These include searching and summarization, transposition, and reshaping and subscript permutation.

An equally rich set of array operations can be found in APL, an array manipulation language developed by Iverson and others in the early to mid-1960s. APL was designed primarily as a terse mathematical notation for array manipulations. It employs an enormous character set that makes it difficult to use with conventional keyboards. Its variables are all arrays, and many of the special characters denote array operations. APL implementations are designed for interpreted, interactive use. They are best suited to "quick and dirty" solution of mathematical problems. The combination of very powerful operators with very terse notation makes APL programs notoriously difficult to read and understand.

7.4.2 **Dimensions, Bounds, and Allocation**

In all of the examples in the previous section, the number of dimensions and bounds of each array (what Fortran calls its *shape*) were specified in the declaration. This need not be the case. And even when the shape of an array is specified, it may depend in some languages on values that are not known at compile time. The time at which the shape of an array is bound has a major impact on how storage for the array is managed. At least five cases arise:

global lifetime, static shape — If the shape of an array is known at compile time, and if the array can exist throughout the execution of the program, then the compiler can allocate space for the array in static global memory.

local lifetime, static shape — If the shape of the array is known at compile time, but the array should not exist throughout the execution of the program (generally because it is a local variable of a potentially recursive subroutine), then space can be allocated in the subroutine's stack frame at run time.

local lifetime, shape bound at elaboration time — In some languages (e.g., Ada), the shape of an array may not be known until elaboration time. In this case it is still possible to place the space for the array in the stack frame of its subroutine, but an extra level of indirection is required (see Figure 7.8). In order to ensure that every local object can be found using a known offset from the frame pointer, we divide the stack frame into a *fixed-size part* and a *variable-size part*. An object whose size is statically known goes in the fixed-size part. An object whose size is not known until elaboration time goes in the variable-size part, and a pointer to it goes in the fixed-size part. (We shall see in Section 7.4.3 that the pointer must be augmented with a descriptor, or *dope vector*, that specifies any bounds that were not known at compile time.) If the elaboration of the array is buried in a nested block, the compiler delays allocating space (i.e., changing the stack pointer) until the block is entered. It still allocates space for the pointer among the local variables when the subroutine itself is entered.

arbitrary lifetime, shape bound at elaboration time — In Java, every array variable is a reference to an object in the object-oriented sense of the word. The declaration int[] A does not allocate space; it simply creates a reference. To make the reference refer to something, the programmer must either explicitly allocate a new object from the heap (A = new int[size]) or assign a reference from another array (A = B), which already holds a reference to an object in the heap. In either case, the size of an array, once allocated, never changes.

arbitrary lifetime, dynamic shape — If the size of an array can change as the result of executable statements, then allocation in the stack frame will not suffice, because the space at both ends of an array might be in use for something else when the array needs to grow. To allow the size to change, an array must generally be allocated from the heap. (A pointer to the array still resides in the fixed-size

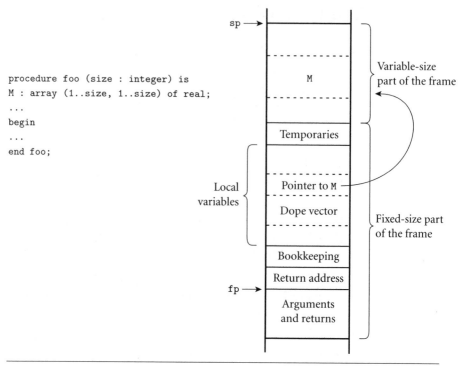

```
procedure foo (size : integer) is
M : array (1..size, 1..size) of real;
...
begin
...
end foo;
```

Figure 7.8 **Allocation in Ada of local arrays whose shape is bound at elaboration time.** Here M is a square two-dimensional array whose width is determined by a parameter passed to foo at run time. The compiler arranges for a pointer to M to reside at a static offset from the frame pointer. M cannot be placed among the other local variables because it would prevent those higher in the frame from having static offsets. Additional variable-size arrays are easily accommodated. The purpose of the *dope vector* field is explained in Section 7.4.3.

portion of the stack frame.) In most cases, increasing the size will require that we allocate a larger block, copy any data that is to be retained from the old block to the new, and then deallocate the old.

Arrays of static shape are heavily used by many kinds of programs. Arrays whose shape is not known until elaboration time are also very common, particularly in numerical software. Many scientific programs rely on numerical libraries for linear algebra and the manipulation of systems of equations. Since different programs use arrays of different shapes, the subroutines in these libraries need to be able to take arguments whose size is not known at compile time.

Early versions of Pascal required the shape of all arrays to be specified statically. Standard Pascal relaxes this requirement by providing for *conformant array* parameters to subroutines:

```
procedure DotProduct (A, B : array [lower..upper : integer] of real);
var i : integer;
    rtn : real;
begin
    rtn := 0;
    for i := lower to upper do rtn := rtn + A[i] * B[i];
    DotProduct := rtn
end;
```

Here `lower` and `upper` are initialized at the time of call, providing `DotProduct` with the information it needs to understand the shape of A and B. Conformant arrays can be passed either by value or by reference. C also supports dynamic-size array parameters, as a natural consequence of its merger of arrays and pointers (to be discussed in Section 7.7.1). C arrays are always passed by reference.

Pascal does not allow a local variable to be an array of dynamic shape. Ada does. Among other things, local arrays can be declared to match the shape of dynamic-size array parameters, facilitating the implementation of algorithms that require "scratch space." Figure 7.9 contains an Ada example. The program shown plays Conway's game of Life [Gar70]. (Life is a *cellular automaton* meant to model biological populations.) The main routine allocates a local array the same size as the game board, which it uses to calculate successive generations. Note that much more efficient algorithms exist; we present this one because it is brief and clear.

The `<>` notation in the definition of `lifeboard` indicates that the bounds of the array are not statically known. Ada actually defines an array type to *have* no bounds. The type of any array with bounds is a *constrained subtype* of an array type with the same number of dimensions but unknown bounds. Bounds of a dynamic array can be obtained at run-time through use of the *array attributes* `'first` and `'last`. `A'first(1)` is the low bound of A's first dimension; `A'last(2)` is the upper bound of its second dimension. The expression `A'range` is short for `A'first..A'last`.

Several languages, including Snobol, Icon, and Perl, allow strings—arrays of characters—to change size after elaboration time. Java provides a similar capability (with a similar implementation), but describes the semantics differently: string variables in Java are references to immutable string objects:

```
String s = "short";
...
s = s + " but sweet";   // + is the concatenation operator
```

Here the declaration `String s` introduces a string variable, which we initialize with a reference to the constant string `"short"`. In the subsequent assignment, `+` creates a new string containing the concatenation of the old `s` and the constant `"suffix"`; `s` is then set to refer to this new string, rather than the old. A Java string, by the way, is *not* the same as an array of characters: strings are immutable, but elements of an array can be changed in place.

Dynamically resizable arrays (other than strings) appear in APL, Perl, and Common Lisp. They are also supported by the `vector` classes of the C++ and

```
type presence is integer range 0..1;
type lifeboard is array (integer range <>, integer range <>) of presence;
    -- cell is 1 if occupied; 0 otherwise
    -- border row around the edge is permanently empty
unexpected : exception;
procedure life (B : in out lifeboard;
                  generations : in integer) is
T : lifeboard (B'range(1), B'range(2));
    -- mimic the bounds of B
begin
    for i in 1..generations loop
        T := B;    -- copy board, including empty borders
        for i in B'first(1)+1..B'last(1)-1 loop
            for j in B'first(2)+1..B'last(2)-1 loop
                case T(i-1, j-1) + T(i-1, j) + T(i-1, j+1)
                        + T(i, j-1) + T(i, j+1)
                        + T(i+1, j-1) + T(i+1, j) + T(i+1, j+1) is
                    when 0 | 1 => B(i, j) := 0;
                        -- die of loneliness
                    when 2 => B(i, j) := T(i, j);
                        -- no-op; survive if present
                    when 3 => B(i, j) := 1;
                        -- reproduce
                    when 4..8 => B(i, j) := 0;
                        -- die of overcrowding
                    when others =>
                        raise unexpected;
                end case;
            end loop;
        end loop;
    end loop;
end life;
```

Figure 7.9 Dynamic local arrays in Ada.

Java standard libraries. Fortran 90 allows specification of the bounds of an array to be delayed until after elaboration, but it does not allow those bounds to change once they have been defined:

```
real, dimension(:,:), allocatable :: mat
    ! mat is two-dimensional, but with unspecified bounds
...
allocate (mat (a:b, 0:m-1))
    ! first dimension has bounds a..b; second has bounds 0..m-1
...
deallocate (mat)
    ! implementation is now free to reclaim mat's space
```

A similar effect can be obtained in some languages through the use of pointers (see Exercise 7.17).

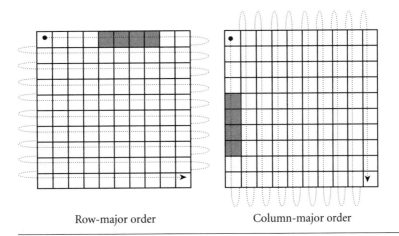

Row-major order   Column-major order

Figure 7.10 Row- and column-major memory layout for two-dimensional arrays. In row-major order, the elements of a row are contiguous in memory; in column-major order, the elements of a column are contiguous. The second cache line of each array is shown, on the assumption that each element is an eight-byte floating-point number, that cache lines are 32 bytes long (a common size), and that the array begins at a cache line boundary.

7.4.3 Memory Layout

Arrays in most language implementations are stored in contiguous locations in memory. In a one-dimensional array, the second element of the array is stored immediately after the first (subject to alignment constrains); the third is stored immediately after the second, and so forth. For arrays of records, it is common for each subsequent element to be aligned at an address appropriate for any type; small holes between consecutive records may result. On some machines, an implementation may even place holes between elements of built-in types. Some languages (e.g., Pascal) allow the programmer to specify that an array be packed. A packed array generally has no holes between elements, but access to its elements may be slow. A packed array of records may have holes *within* the records, unless they too are packed.

For multidimensional arrays, it still makes sense to put the first element of the array in the array's first memory location. But which element comes next? There are two reasonable answers, called *row-major* and *column-major* order. In row-major order, consecutive locations in memory hold elements that differ by one in the final subscript (except at the ends of rows). A[2, 4], for example, is followed by A[2, 5]. In column-major order, consecutive locations hold elements that differ by one in the *initial* subscript: A[2, 4] is followed by A[3, 4]. These options are illustrated for two-dimensional arrays in Figure 7.10. The layouts for three or more dimensions are analogous. Fortran uses column-major order;

most other languages use row-major order.[3] The advantage of row-major order is that it makes it easy to define a multidimensional array as an array of subarrays, as described in Section 7.4.1. With column-major order, the elements of the subarray would not be contiguous in memory.

The difference between row- and column-major layout can be important for programs that use nested loops to access all the elements of a large, multidimensional array. On modern machines the speed of such loops is often limited by memory system performance, which depends heavily on the effectiveness of caching (Section 5.2). Figure 7.10 shows the orientation of cache lines for row- and column-major layout of arrays. If a small array is accessed frequently, all or most of its elements are likely to remain in the cache, and the orientation of cache lines will not matter. For a large array, however, many of the accesses that occur during a full-array traversal are likely to result in cache misses, because the corresponding lines have been evicted from the cache (to make room for other things) since the last traversal. If array elements are accessed in order of consecutive addresses, then each miss will bring into the cache not only the desired element, but the next several elements as well. If elements are accessed *across* cache lines instead (i.e., along the rows of a Fortran array, or the columns of an array in most other languages), then there is a good chance that almost every access will result in a cache miss, dramatically reducing the performance of the code.

Some languages employ an alternative to contiguous allocation for some arrays. Rather than require the rows of an array to be adjacent, they allow them to lie anywhere in memory, and create an auxiliary array of pointers to the rows. If the array has more than two dimensions, it may be allocated as an array of pointers to arrays of pointers to .... This *row-pointer* memory layout requires more space in most cases, but has two potential advantages. First, it sometimes allows individual elements of the array to be accessed more quickly, especially on CISC machines with slow multiplication instructions (see the section on address calculations below). Second, it allows the rows to have different lengths, without devoting space to holes at the ends of the rows; the lack of holes may sometimes offset the increased space for pointers. C and C++ provide both contiguous and row-pointer organizations for multidimensional arrays. Technically speaking, the contiguous layout is a true multidimensional array, while the row-pointer layout is an array of pointers to arrays. Java uses the row-pointer layout for all arrays.

By far the most common use of the row-pointer layout in C is to represent arrays of strings. A typical example appears in Figure 7.11. In this example (representing the days of the week), the row-pointer memory layout consumes

---

3 Correspondence with Frances Allen, an IBM Fellow and Fortran pioneer, suggests that column-major order was orginally adopted in order to accommodate idiosyncrasies of the console debugger and instruction set of the IBM model 704 computer, on which the language was first implemented.

```
char days[][10] = {                      char *days[] = {
    "Sunday", "Monday", "Tuesday",           "Sunday", "Monday", "Tuesday",
    "Wednesday", "Thursday",                 "Wednesday", "Thursday",
    "Friday", "Saturday"                     "Friday", "Saturday"
};                                       };
...                                      ...
days[2][3] == 's';  /* in Tuesday */     days[2][3] == 's';  /* in Tuesday */
```

Figure 7.11 Row pointers v. contiguous array allocation in C. The declaration on the left is a true two-dimensional array. The slashed boxes are NUL bytes; the shaded areas are holes. The declaration on the right is an array of pointers to arrays of characters. In both cases, we have omitted bounds in the declaration that can be deduced from the size of the initializer (aggregate). Both data structures permit individual characters to be accessed using double subscripts, but the memory layout (and corresponding address arithmetic) is quite different.

57 bytes for the characters themselves (including a NUL byte at the end of each string), plus 28 bytes for pointers (assuming a 32-bit architecture), for a total of 85 bytes. The contiguous layout alternative devotes ten bytes to each day (room enough for Wednesday and its NUL byte), for a total of 70 bytes. The additional space required for the row-pointer organization comes to 21 percent. In other cases, row pointers may actually save space. A Pascal compiler written in C, for example, would probably use row pointers to store the character-string representations of the 35 Pascal keywords. This data structure would use $35 \times 4 = 140$ bytes for the pointers, plus 180 bytes for the keywords, for a total of 320 bytes. Since the longest keyword (procedure) requires 10 bytes (including space for the NUL), a contiguous two-dimensional array would consume $35 \times 10 = 350$ bytes. In this case, row pointers *save* a little over 9%.

Address Calculations

For the usual contiguous layout of arrays, calculating the address of a particular element is somewhat complicated, but straightforward. Suppose a compiler is given the following declaration for a three-dimensional array:

A : array $[L_1 .. U_1]$ of array $[L_2 .. U_2]$ of array $[L_3 .. U_3]$ of elem_type;

Let us define constants for the sizes of the three dimensions:

$$S_3 = \text{size of elem\_type}$$
$$S_2 = (U_3 - L_3 + 1) \times S_3$$
$$S_1 = (U_2 - L_2 + 1) \times S_2$$

Here the size of a row (S_2) is the size of an individual element (S_3) times the number of elements in a row (assuming row-major layout). The size of a plane (S_1) is the size of a row (S_2) times the number of rows in a plane. The address of A[i, j, k] is then

$$\text{address of A}$$
$$+(i - L_1) \times S_1$$
$$+(j - L_2) \times S_2$$
$$+(k - L_3) \times S_3$$

As written, this computation involves five multiplications and 10 additions/subtractions. We could compute the entire expression at run time, but in most cases a little rearrangement reveals that much of the computation can be performed at compile time. In particular, if the bounds of the array are known at compile time, then S_1, S_2, and S_3 are compile-time constants, and the subtractions of lower bounds can be distributed out of the parentheses:

$$(i \times S_1) + (j \times S_2) + (k \times S_3) + \text{address of A}$$
$$-[(L_1 \times S_1) + (L_2 \times S_2) + (L_3 \times S_3)]$$

The bracketed expression in this formula is a compile-time constant (assuming the bounds of A are statically known). If A is a global variable, then the address of A is statically known as well, and can be incorporated in the bracketed expression. If A is a local variable of a subroutine (with static shape), then the address of A can be decomposed into a static offset (included in the bracketed expression) plus the contents of the frame pointer at run time. We can think of the address of A plus the bracketed expression as calculating the location of an imaginary array whose [i, j, k]th element coincides with that of A, but whose lower bound in each dimension is zero. This imaginary array is illustrated in Figure 7.12.

If A's elements are integers, and are allocated contiguously in memory, then the instruction sequence to load A[i, j, k] into a register looks something like this:

```
    -- assume i is in r1, j is in r2, and k is in r3
1.  r4 := r1 × S₁
2.  r5 := r2 × S₂
3.  r6 := &A − L₁ × S₁ − L₂ × S₂ − L₃ × 4   -- one or two instructions
4.  r6 := r6 + r4
5.  r6 := r6 + r5
6.  r7 := *r6[r3]                            -- load
```

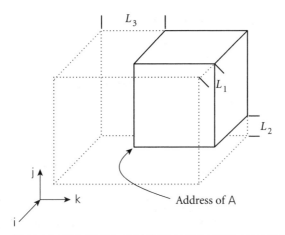

Figure 7.12 Virtual location of an array with nonzero lower bounds. By computing the constant portions of an array index at compile time, we effectively index into an array whose starting address is offset in memory, but whose lower bounds are all zero.

We have assumed that the hardware provides an indexed addressing mode, and that it scales its indexing by the size of the quantity loaded (in this case a four-byte integer).

If i, j, and/or k is known at compile time, then additional portions of the calculation of the address of A[i, j, k] will move from the dynamic to the static part of the formula shown above. If all of the subscripts are known, then the entire address can be calculated statically. Conversely, if any of the bounds of the array are not known at compile time, then portions of the calculation will move from the static to the dynamic part of the formula. For example, if L_1 is not known until run time, but k is known to be 3 at compile time, then the calculation becomes

$$(i \times S_1) + (j \times S_2) - (L_1 \times S_1) + \text{address of } \mathbf{A} - [(L_2 \times S_2) + (L_3 \times S_3) - (3 \times S_3)]$$

Again, the bracketed part can be computed at compile time. If lower bounds are always restricted to zero, as they are in C, then they never contribute to run-time cost.

In all our examples, we have ignored the issue of dynamic semantic checks for out-of-bound subscripts. We explore the code for these in Exercise 7.19. In Section 13.5.2 we will consider code improvement techniques that can be used to eliminate many checks statically, particularly in enumeration-controlled loops.

The notion of "static part" and "dynamic part" of an address computation generalizes to more than just arrays. Suppose, for example, that V is a messy local array of records containing a nested, two-dimensional array in field M. The address of V[i].M[3, j] could be calculated as

$$i \times S_1^V$$
$$-L_1^V \times S_1^V$$
$$+\textbf{M's offset as a field}$$
$$+(3 - L_1^M) \times S_1^M$$
$$+j \times S_2^M$$
$$-L_2^M \times S_2^M$$
$$+\textbf{fp}$$
$$+\text{offset of } \textbf{V} \text{ in frame}$$

Here the calculations on the left must be performed at run time; the calculations on the right can be performed at compile time. (The notation for bounds and size places the name of the variable in a superscript and the dimension in a subscript: L_2^M is the lower bound of the second dimension of M.)

Address calculation for arrays that use row pointers is comparatively straight-forward. Using our three-dimensional array A as an example, the expression A[i, j, k] is equivalent to (*(*A[i])[j])[k] or, in more Pascal-like notation, A[i]^[j]^[k]. The instruction sequence to load A[i, j, k] into a register looks something like this:

```
        —— assume i is in r1, j is in r2, and k is in r3
    1.  r4 := &A              —— one or two instructions
    2.  r4 := *r4[r1]
    3.  r4 := *r4[r2]
    4.  r7 := r4[r3]
```

Assuming that the loads at lines 2 and 3 hit in the cache, this code will be comparable in cost to the instruction sequence for contiguous allocation shown above (given load delays). If the intermediate loads miss in the cache, it will be slower. On a 1970s CISC machine, the balance would probably tip in favor of the row-pointer code: multiplies would be slower, and memory accesses faster. In any event (contiguous or row-pointer allocation, old or new machine), important code improvements will often be possible when several array references use the same subscript expression, or when array references are embedded in loops.

Dope Vectors

For every array, a compiler maintains dimension, bounds and size information in the symbol table. For every record, it maintains the offset of every field. When the bounds and size of array dimensions are statically known, the compiler can look them up in the symbol table in order to compute the address of elements of the array. When the bounds and size are not statically known, the compiler must arrange for them to be available when the compiled program needs to compute an address at run time. The usual mechanism employs a *run-time descriptor*, or *dope vector* for the array.[4] Typically, a dope vector for an array of dynamic shape will contain the lower bound of each dimension and the size of every dimension except the last (which will always be statically known). If the language implementation performs dynamic semantic checks for out-of-bounds subscripts in array references, then the dope vector will need to contain upper bounds as well. Given upper and lower bounds, the size information is redundant, but it is usually included anyway, to avoid computing it repeatedly at run time.

If some of the dimension bounds or sizes for an array are known at compile time, then they may be omitted from the dope vector. One might imagine, then, that the size of a dope vector would depend on the number of statically unknown quantities. More commonly, it depends only on the number of dimensions: the modest loss in space is offset by the comparative simplicity of always being able to find a given bound or size at the same offset within the dope vector for any array of the appropriate number of dimensions.

The dope vector for an array of dynamic shape is generally placed next to the pointer to the array in the fixed-size part of the stack frame. The contents of the dope vector are initialized at elaboration time, or whenever the array changes shape. If one fully dynamic array is assigned into a second, and the two are of different shapes and sizes, then run-time code will not only need to deallocate the old heap space of the target array, allocate new space, and copy the data into it, it will also need to copy information from the dope vector of the source array into the dope vector of the target.

In some languages a record may contain an array of dynamic shape. In order to arrange for every field to have a static offset from the beginning of the record, a compiler can treat the record much like the fixed-size portion of the stack frame, with a pointer to the array at a fixed offset in the record, and the data in the variable-size part of the current stack frame. The problem with this approach is that it abandons contiguous allocation for records. Among other things, a block copy routine can no longer be used to assign one record into another. An arguably preferable approach is to abandon fixed field offsets and create dope vectors for dynamic-size records, just as we do for dynamic-size arrays. The dope vector for a record lists the offsets of the record's fields. All of the actual data then goes in the variable-size part of the stack frame or the heap (depending on whether sizes are known at elaboration time).

7.5 Strings

In many languages, a string is simply an array of characters. In other languages, strings have special status, with operations that are not available for arrays of

---

4 The name "dope vector" presumably derives from the notion of "having the dope on (something)," a colloquial expression that originated in horse racing: advance knowledge that a horse has been drugged ("doped") is of significant, if unethical, use in placing bets.

other sorts. In particular, several languages that do not in general allow arrays to change size dynamically, do provide this flexibility for strings. The rationale is twofold. First, manipulation of variable-length strings is fundamental to a huge number of computer applications, and in some sense "deserves" special treatment. Second, the fact that strings are one-dimensional, have one-byte elements, and never contain references to anything else makes dynamic-size strings easier to implement than general dynamic arrays.

Almost all programming languages allow literal strings to be specified as a sequence of characters, usually enclosed in single or double quote marks. Some languages (e.g., C) distinguish between literal characters (usually delimited with single quotes) and literal strings (usually delimited with double quotes). Other languages (e.g., Pascal) make no distinction: a character is just a string of length one. Most languages also provide *escape sequences* that allow nonprinting characters and quote marks to appear inside of strings. In Pascal, for example, a quote mark is included in a string by doubling it: `'ab''cde'` is a six-character string whose third character is a quote mark. In C, any character can be represented by following a backslash with the numeric value of the character in ASCII, expressed as a three-digit octal (base eight) number: `"ab\006cde"` is a six-character string whose third character is a form-feed (control-F) character. Many of the most common control characters have special abbreviations in C, many of which have been adopted by other languages as well. For example, \n is a line feed; \t is a tab; \r is a carriage return; \\ is a backslash. Java retains the shorthand notation for common control characters (\n, etc), but uses a different notation for numeric escapes: \uxxxx, where xxxx is the four-digit hexadecimal representation of a two-byte (16-bit) Unicode character.

The set of operations provided for strings is strongly tied to the implementation envisioned by the language designer(s). Specifically, some languages require that the length of a string-valued variable be bound no later than elaboration time, allowing the variable to be implemented as a contiguous array of characters in the current stack frame. Languages in this category include C, Pascal, and Ada. Other languages allow the length of a string-valued variable to change over its lifetime, requiring that the variable be implemented as a block or chain of blocks in the heap. Languages in this category include Lisp, Icon, ML, and Java.

In Pascal, a string is a packed array of characters with a lower bound of one. In addition to the usual array operations (subscripting and assignment), Pascal allows its relational operators (=, <>, <, <=, >, >=) to be applied to strings. For the final four of these (the *ordering* operators), the comparison is made on the basis of *lexicographic* (dictionary) order according to the underlying character set (usually ASCII). As noted in Section 7.4.1, Ada supports lexicographic comparisons for any one-dimensional array type whose elements are discrete. As noted in Section 7.2.4, it also supports concatenation on these types. It is important to note that while concatenation produces a string that is longer than its arguments, that string can only be used in a context that *expects* a longer string; it cannot, for example, be assigned back into the same variable that was used for one of the arguments. C provides no special features for strings other than the ability to create a pointer to a string literal. Because of C's unification of arrays and pointers, even assignment of strings is not supported. Given the declaration `char *s` (or, equivalently, `char s[]`), the statement `s = "abc"` makes `s` point to the constant `"abc"` in static storage. If `s` is declared as an array, rather than a pointer (`char s[3]`), then the statement will trigger an error message from the compiler. To assign one array into another in C, the program must copy the elements individually.

Languages that allow strings of dynamic size generally assume that the implementation will allocate strings from the heap. In ML, `string` is one of the five built-in types, and an expression of type `string` can be of any length. ML provides built-in operators to concatenate strings and to determine the length of a string. The ability to write string-valued functions makes it easy to define additional operators. Most Lisp dialects provide similar capabilities. Java and C++ provide strings as predefined classes of object (in the formal, object-oriented sense), and include a variety of string-manipulation functions. As noted in the previous section, a Java string variable is a *reference* to a string. Assigning a new value to a string variable makes it refer to a different object. Concatenation and other string operators implicitly create new objects. The space used by objects that are no longer reachable from any variable is recollected automatically.

More powerful capabilities are found in languages such as Snobol, Icon, and Perl, which were expressly designed for the manipulation of strings. As we saw in Section 6.5.3, mechanisms for searching for patterns within strings are a key part of Icon's distinctive generator-based control flow. Icon has dozens of built-in string operators, to concatenate strings, extract random or specific substrings or characters, return the size of a string, compare for lexicographic ordering, and so on. Icon also provides a wealth of built-in string-valued functions (e.g., to embed a shorter string in a longer one, reverse a string, or trim characters off the end), and a rich set of generators for searching. The string facilities of Perl are comparable to those of Icon, though Perl's generator (iterator) mechanism is a less fundamental part of the language.

7.6 Sets

A programming language set is an unordered collection of an arbitrary number of distinct values of a common type. Sets were introduced by Pascal, and are found in many more recent languages as well. They are a useful form of composite type for many applications. Pascal supports sets of any discrete type, and provides union, intersection, and difference operations:

```
var A, B, C : set of char;
    D, E : set of weekday;
...
A := B + C;    (* union; C := {x | x is in B or x is in C} *)
A := B * C;    (* intersection; C := {x | x is in B and x is in C} *)
A := B - C;    (* difference; C := {x | x is in B and x is not in C} *)
```

The type from which elements of a set are drawn is known as the *base* or *universe* type. Icon supports sets of characters (called *csets*), but not sets of any other base type. As we saw in Section 6.5.3, csets play an important role in Icon's search facilities. Ada does not provide a set constructor for types, but its generic facility can be used to define a set package (module) with functionality comparable to the sets of Pascal [IBFW91, pp. 242–244].

There are many ways to implement sets, including arrays, hash tables, and various forms of trees. The most common implementation employs a bit vector whose length (in bits) is the number of distinct values of the base type. A set of characters, for example (in a language that uses ASCII) would be 128 bits—16 bytes—in length. A one in the kth position in the bit vector indicates that the kth element of the base type is a member of the set; a zero indicates that it is not. Operations on bit-vector sets can make use of fast logical instructions on most machines. Union is bit-wise or; intersection is bit-wise and; difference is bit-wise not, followed by bit-wise and.

Unfortunately, bit vectors do not work well for large base types: a set of integers, represented as a bit vector, would consume some 500 megabytes on a 32-bit machine. With 64-bit integers, a bit-vector set would consume more memory than is currently contained on all the computers in the world. Because of this problem, many languages (including early versions of Pascal, but not the ISO standard) limit sets to base types of fewer than some fixed number of members. Both 128 and 256 are common limits; they suffice to cover characters. A few languages (e.g., early versions of Modula-2) limit base types to the number of elements that can be represented by a one-word bit vector, but there is really no excuse for such a severe restriction. A language that permits sets with very large base types must employ an alternative implementation (e.g., a hash table). It will still be expensive to represent sets with enormous numbers of elements, but reasonably easy to represent sets with a modest number of elements drawn from a very large universe.

7.7 Pointers and Recursive Types

A recursive type is one whose objects may contain one or more references to other objects of the type. Most recursive types are records, since they need to contain something in addition to the reference, implying the existence of heterogeneous fields. Recursive types are used to build a wide variety of "linked" data structures, including lists and trees.

In languages such as Lisp, ML, Clu, or Java, which use a reference model of variables, it is easy for a record of type foo to include a reference to another record of type foo: every variable (and hence every record field) *is* a reference anyway. In languages such as C, Pascal, or Ada, which use a value model of variables, recursive types require the notion of a *pointer*: a variable (or field) whose value is a reference to some object. Pointers were first introduced in PL/I.

In some languages (e.g., Pascal, Ada 83, and Modula-3), pointers are restricted to point only to objects in the heap. The only way to create a new pointer value (without using variant records or casts to by-pass the type system) is to call a built-in function that allocates a new object in the heap and returns a pointer to it. In other languages (e.g., PL/I, Algol 68, C, C++, and Ada 95), one can create a pointer to a nonheap object by using an "address of" operator. We will examine pointer operations and the ramifications of the reference and value models in more detail in the first subsection.

It is common for programmers (and even textbook writers) to equate pointers with addresses, but this is a mistake. A pointer is a high-level concept: a reference to an object. An address is a low-level concept: the location of a word in memory. Pointers are often implemented as addresses, but not always. On a machine with a *segmented* memory architecture, a pointer may consist of a segment id and an offset within the segment. In a language that attempts to catch uses of dangling references, a pointer may contain both an address and an access key.

In any language that permits new objects to be allocated from the heap, the question arises: how and when is storage reclaimed for objects that are no longer needed? In short-lived programs it may be acceptable simply to leave the storage unused, but in most cases unused space must be reclaimed, to make room for other things. A program that fails to reclaim the space for objects that are no longer needed is said to "leak memory." If such a program runs for an extended period of time, it may run out of space and crash.

Many languages, including C, C++, Pascal, and Modula-2, require the programmer to reclaim space explicitly. Other languages, including Lisp, ML, Modula-3, Ada, and Java, require the language implementation to reclaim unused objects automatically. Explicit storage reclamation simplifies the language implementation, but raises the possibility that the programmer will forget to reclaim objects that are no longer live (thereby leaking memory), or will accidentally reclaim objects that are still in use (thereby creating *dangling references*). Automatic storage reclamation (otherwise known as *garbage collection*) dramatically simplifies the programmer's task, but raises the question of how the language implementation is to distinguish garbage from active objects. We will discuss these issues further in Sections 7.7.2 and 7.7.3.

7.7.1 Syntax and Operations

Operations on pointers include allocation and deallocation of objects in the heap, dereferencing of pointers to access the objects to which they point, and assignment of one pointer into another. The behavior of these operations depends heavily on whether the language is functional or imperative, and on whether it employs a reference or value model for variables/names.

Functional languages generally employ a reference model for names (a purely functional language has no variables or assignments). Objects in a functional language tend to be allocated automatically as needed, with a structure determined by the language implementation. Most implementations of Lisp, for example, build lists out of two-pointer blocks called cons cells. Lisp's imperative features allow the programmer to modify cons cells explicitly, but this ability must be used with care: because of the reference model, a cons cell is commonly part of the object to which more than one variable refers; a change made through one variable will often change other variables as well.

Variables in an imperative language may use either a value or a reference model, or some combination of the two. The value model, in which a variable is a container for a value, will be familiar to most readers. In C, Pascal, or Ada, which employ a value model, the assignment A := B puts the value of B into A. If we want B to refer to an object, and we want A := B to make A refer to the object to which B refers, then A and B must be pointers.

In Clu and Smalltalk, which employ a reference model, the assignment A := B always makes A refer to the same object to which B refers. A straightforward implementation would represent every variable as an address, but this would lead to very inefficient code for built-in types. A better and more common approach is to use addresses for variables that refer to *mutable* objects such as tree nodes, whose value can change, but to use actual values for variables that refer to *immutable* objects such as integers, real numbers, and characters. In other words, while every variable is semantically a reference, it does not matter whether a reference to the number 3 is implemented as the address of a 3 in memory or as the value 3 itself: since the value of "*the* 3" never changes, the two are indistinguishable.

Java charts an intermediate course, in which the usual implementation of the reference model is made explicit in the language semantics. Variables of built-in Java types (integers, floating-point numbers, characters, and Booleans) employ a value model; variables of user-defined types (strings, arrays, and other objects in the object-oriented sense of the word) employ a reference model. The assignment A := B in Java places the value of B into A if A and B are of built-in type; it makes A refer to the object to which B refers if A and B are of user-defined type.

Reference Model

In Section 7.2.5, we saw that ML datatypes can be used to declare recursive types:

```
datatype chr_tree = empty | node of string * chr_tree * chr_tree;
```

The node constructor of a chr_tree builds tuples containing a reference to a string (ML does not have a separate character type) and two references to chr_trees.

It is natural in ML to include a chr_tree within a chr_tree because every variable is a reference. The tree node ('R', node ('X', empty, empty), node ('Y', node ('Z', empty, empty), node ('W', empty, empty))) (page 350) would most likely be represented in memory as shown in Figure 7.13.

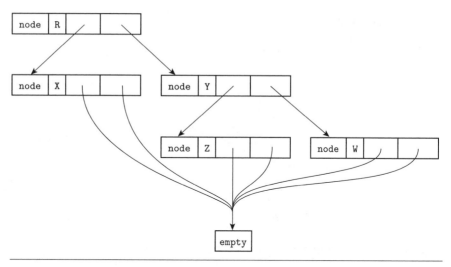

Figure 7.13 Implementation of a tree in ML.

Each individual rectangle in this figure represents a block of storage allocated from the heap. In effect, the tree is a tuple (record) tagged to indicate that it is a node. This tuple in turn refers to two other tuples that are also tagged as nodes. At the fringe of the tree are tuples that are tagged as empty; these contain no further references. Because all empty tuples are the same, the implementation is free to use just one, and to have every reference point to it.

In Lisp, which uses a reference model of variables but is not statically typed, our tree could be specified textually as '(#\R (#\X () ()) (#\Y (#\Z () ()) (#\W () ()))), and would be represented in memory as shown in Figure 7.14. The parentheses in Lisp denote a *list*, which in Lisp consists of two references: one to the head of the list and one to the remainder of the list (which is itself a list). The prefix #\ notation serves the same purpose as surrounding quotes in other languages. As we noted in Section 7.7.1, a Lisp list is almost always represented in memory by a cons cell containing two pointers. A binary tree can be represented as a three-element (three cons cell) list. The first cell represents the root; the second and third cells represent the left and right subtrees. Each heap block is tagged to indicate whether it is a cons cell or an *atom*. An atom is anything other than a cons cell; that is, an object of a built-in type (integer, real, character, string, etc.), or a user-defined structure (record) or array. The uniformity of Lisp lists (everything is a cons cell or an atom) makes it easy to write polymorphic functions, though without the static type checking of ML.

If one programs in a purely functional style in ML or in Lisp, the data structures created with recursive types turn out to be acyclic. New objects refer to old ones, but old ones never change, and thus never point to new ones. Circular structures can be defined only by using the imperative features of the languages. In ML, these features include an explicit notion of pointer, discussed briefly in

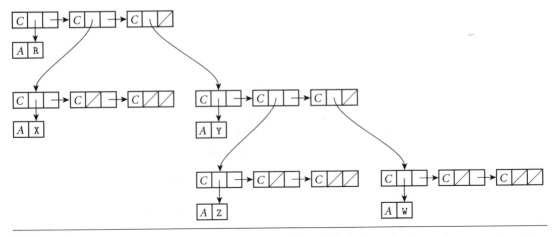

Figure 7.14 Implementation of a tree in Lisp. A diagonal slash through a box indicates a `nil` pointer. The *C* and *A* tags serve to distinguish the two kinds of memory blocks: cons cells and blocks containing atoms.

the "value model" section below.

Even when writing in a functional style, one often finds a need for *types* that are *mutually recursive*. In a compiler, for example, it is likely that symbol table records and syntax tree nodes will need to refer to each other. A syntax tree node that represents a subroutine call will need to refer to the symbol table record that represents the subroutine. The symbol table record, for its part, will need to refer to the syntax tree node at the root of the subtree that represents the subroutine's code. If types are declared one at a time, and if names must be declared before they can be used, then whichever mutually recursive type is declared first will be unable to refer to the other. ML addresses this problem by allowing types to be declared together in a group:

```
datatype sym_tab_rec = variable of ...
    | type of ...
    | ...
    | subroutine of {code => syn_tree_node, ...}
and syn_tree_node = expression of ...
    | loop of ...
    | ...
    | subr_call of {subr => sym_tab_rec, ...};
```

Mutually recursive types of this sort are trivial in Lisp, since it is dynamically typed. (Common Lisp includes a notion of structures, but field types are not declared. In simpler Lisp dialects programmers use nested lists in which fields are merely positional conventions.)

Value Model

In Pascal, our tree data type would be declared as follows:

```
type chr_tree_ptr = ^chr_tree;
    chr_tree = record
        left, right : chr_tree_ptr;
        val : char
    end;
```

The Ada declaration is similar:

```
type chr_tree;
type chr_tree_ptr is access chr_tree;
type chr_tree is record
    left, right : chr_tree_ptr;
    val : character;
end record;
```

In C, the equivalent declaration[5] is

```
struct chr_tree {
    struct chr_tree *left, *right;
    char val;
};
```

As mentioned in Sections 3.3.3 and 3.6.1, Pascal permits forward references in the declaration of pointer types, to support recursive types. Ada and C use incomplete type declarations instead.

No aggregate syntax is available for linked data structures in Pascal, Ada, or C; a tree must be constructed node by node. To allocate a new node from the heap, the programmer calls a built-in function. In Pascal:

```
new (my_ptr);
```

In Ada:

```
my_ptr := new chr_tree;
```

In C:

```
my_ptr = (struct chr_tree *) malloc (sizeof (struct chr_tree));
```

C's `malloc` is a library function, not a built-in part of the language; hence the need to specify the size of the allocated object, and to cast the return value to the appropriate type. C++ and Java replace `malloc` with a built-in `new`:

```
my_ptr = new chr_tree ( arg_list );
```

---

5 One of the peculiarities of the C type system is that `struct` names are not exactly type names. In this example, the name of the type is the two-word phrase `struct chr_tree`. To obtain a one-word name, one can say `typedef struct chr_tree chr_tree_type`, or even `typedef struct chr_tree chr_tree`: structs and types have separate name spaces, so the same name can be used in each.

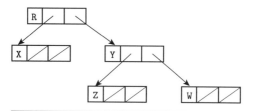

Figure 7.15 Typical implementation of a tree in a language with explicit pointers. As in Figure 7.14, a diagonal slash through a box indicates a `nil` pointer.

In addition to "knowing" the size of the requested type, the C++/Java `new` will automatically call any user-specified *constructor* (initialization) function, passing the specified argument list. In a similar but less flexible vein, Ada's `new` may specify an initial value for the allocated object:

```
my_ptr := new chr_tree'(null, null, 'X');
```

After we have allocated and linked together appropriate nodes in C, Pascal, or Ada, our tree example is likely to be implemented as shown in Figure 7.15. As in Lisp, a leaf is distinguished from an internal node simply by the fact that its two pointer fields are `nil`.

To access the object referred to by a pointer, most languages use an explicit dereferencing operator. In Pascal and Modula this operator takes the form of a postfix "up-arrow":

```
my_ptr^.val := 'X';
```

In C it is a prefix star:

```
(*my_ptr).val = 'X';
```

Because pointers so often refer to records (`struct`s), for which the prefix notation is awkward, C also provides a postfix "right-arrow" operator that plays the role of the "up-arrow dot" combination in Pascal:

```
my_ptr->val = 'X';
```

On the assumption that pointers almost always refer to records, Ada dispenses with dereferencing altogether. The same dot-based syntax can be used to access either a field of the record `foo` or a field of the record *pointed to* by `foo`, depending on the type of `foo`:

```
T : chr_tree;
P : chr_tree_ptr;
...
T.val := 'X';
P.val := 'Y';
```

In those cases in which one actually wants to name the *entire* object referred to by a pointer, Ada provides a special "pseudofield" called `all`:

```
T := P.all;
```

In essence, pointers in Ada are automatically dereferenced when needed. A more ambitious (and unfortunately rather confusing) form of automatic dereferencing can be found in Algol 68.

The imperative features of ML include an assignment statement, but this statement requires that the left-hand side be a pointer: its effect is to make the pointer refer to the object on the right-hand side. To access the object referred to by a pointer, one uses an exclamation point as a prefix dereferencing operator:

```
val p = ref 2;  (* p is a pointer to 2 *)
...
p := 3;         (* p now points to 3 *)
...
let val n = !p in ...
   (* n is simply 3 *)
```

ML thus makes the distinction between l-values and r-values very explicit. Most Algol-family languages blur the distinction by implicitly dereferencing variables on the right-hand side of every assignment statement. Algol 68 and Ada blur the distinction further by dereferencing pointers automatically in certain circumstances.

The imperative features of Lisp do not include a dereferencing operator. Since every object has a self-evident type, and assignment is performed using a small set of built-in operators, there is never any ambiguity as to what is intended. Assignment in Common Lisp employs the setf operator (Scheme uses set!), rather than the more common :=. For example, if foo refers to a list, then (cdr foo) is the right-hand ("rest of list") pointer of foo's cons cell, and the assignment (setf (cdr foo) foo) makes this pointer refer back to foo, creating a one-cons-cell circular list.

Pointers and Arrays in C

Single-dimensional arrays in C are largely interchangeable with pointers. Consider the following declarations:

```
int n;
int *a;        /* pointer to integer */
int b[10];     /* array of 10 integers */
```

Now all of the following are valid:

```
a = b;         /* make a point to (the initial element of) b */
n = a[3];
n = *(a+3);    /* equivalent to previous line */
n = b[3];
n = *(b+3);    /* equivalent to previous line */
```

The third and fifth of these assignments illustrate *pointer arithmetic*: a is coerced to be a pointer to its initial element (the one with index zero). The addition produces a pointer to the element with index 3. The prefix star then dereferences the pointer. For multidimensional arrays with row-pointer layout, a[i][j] is equivalent to (*(a+i))[j] or *(a[i]+j) or *(*(a+i)+j).

In addition to allowing an integer to be added to a pointer, C allows pointers to be subtracted from one another or compared for ordering, provided that they refer to elements of the same array. The comparison p < q, for example, tests to see if p refers to an element closer to the beginning of the array than the one referred to by q. The expression p - q returns the number of array positions that separate the elements to which p and q refer. All arithmetic operations on pointers "scale" their results as appropriate, based on the size of the referenced objects.

Many C programs use pointers instead of subscripts to iterate over the elements of arrays. Before the development of modern optimizing compilers, pointer-based array traversal often resulted in faster code. (With modern compilers, the opposite may be true; certain code improvements are easier for indices than they are for pointers.) Many C programmers would also argue that pointer-based algorithms are more elegant. Certainly the fact that arrays are passed as pointers makes it natural to write subroutines in the pointer style.

Despite the interoperability of pointers and arrays in C, programmers need to be aware that the two are not the same, particularly in the context of variable declarations, which need to allocate space when elaborated. The declaration of a pointer variable allocates space to hold a pointer, while the declaration of an array variable allocates space to hold the whole array. In the case of an array the declaration must specify a size for each dimension. Thus int *a[n], when elaborated, will allocate space for *n* row pointers; int a[n][m] will allocate space for a two-dimensional array with contiguous layout.

To read declarations in C, it is helpful to follow the following rule: start at the name of the variable and work right as far as possible, subject to parentheses; then work left as far as possible; then jump out a level of parentheses and repeat. Thus int *a[n] means that a is an *n*-element array of pointers to integers, while int (*a)[n] means that a is a pointer to an *n*-element array of integers.

In subroutine calls C always passes a pointer to an array, never the full array. When passing a one-dimensional array, the formal parameter may be declared as int a[] or int *a. When passing a two-dimensional array with row-pointer layout, the formal parameter may be declared as int *a[] or int **a. When passing a two-dimensional array with contiguous layout, the formal parameter may be declared as int a[][m] or int (*a)[m]. The size of the first dimension is irrelevant; all that is passed is a pointer, and C performs no dynamic checks to ensure that references are within the bounds of the array.

In all cases, a declaration must allow the compiler (or human reader) to determine the size of the *elements* of an array or, equivalently, the size of the objects referred to by a pointer. Thus neither int a[][] nor int (*a)[] is a valid declaration: neither provides the compiler with the size information it needs to generate code for a + i or a[i]. (An exception: a variable declaration that includes initialization to an aggregate can omit size information if that information can be inferred from the contents of the aggregate.)

The built-in `sizeof` operator returns the size of the entire array when given an array as argument. It returns the size of a pointer when given a pointer as argument. If `a` is an array, `sizeof (a) / sizeof (a[0])` returns the number of elements in the array. In most compilers, `sizeof` generates no code; it can always be evaluated statically.

It is possible but awkward in C to write a subroutine that can manipulate multidimensional arrays whose layout is contiguous, but whose inner dimensions do not have a statically known size. The trick is to pass a pointer to the array, to pass the bounds as additional parameters, and to use pointer arithmetic to perform address calculations explicitly:

```
double determinant (double *M, int rows, int cols) {
    int i, j;
    ...
        val = *(M + (i * cols) + j);     /* M[i][j] */
    ...
}
```

7.7.2 Dangling References

In Section 3.2 we described three *storage classes* for objects: static, stack, and heap. Static objects remain live for the duration of the program. Stack objects are live for the duration of the subroutine in which they are declared. Heap objects have a less well-defined lifetime.

When an object is no longer live, a long-running program needs to reclaim the object's space. Stack objects are reclaimed automatically as part of the subroutine calling sequence. How are heap objects reclaimed? There are two alternatives. Languages such as Pascal, C, and C++ require the programmer to reclaim an object explicitly. In Pascal:

```
dispose (my_ptr);
```

In C:

```
free (my_ptr);
```

In C++:

```
delete my_ptr;
```

C++ provides additional functionality: prior to reclaiming the space, it automatically calls any user-provided *destructor* function for the object. A destructor can reclaim space for subsidiary objects, remove the object from indices or tables, print messages, or perform any other operation appropriate at the end of the object's lifetime.

A *dangling reference* is a live pointer that no longer points to a valid object. In a language such as Algol 68 or C, which allow the programmer to create pointers to stack objects, a dangling reference may be created when a subroutine returns while some pointer in a wider scope still refers to a local object of that subroutine. In a language with explicit reclamation of heap objects, a dangling reference is created whenever the programmer reclaims an object to which pointers still refer. (Note that while the `dispose` and `delete` operators of Pascal and C++ change their pointer argument to `nil`, this does not solve the problem, because *other* pointers may still refer to the same object.) Because a language implementation may reuse the space of reclaimed stack and heap objects, a program that uses a dangling reference may read or write bits in memory that are now part of some other object. It may even modify bits that are now part of the implementation's bookkeeping information, corrupting the structure of the stack or heap.

Algol 68 addresses the problem of dangling references to stack objects by forbidding a pointer from pointing to any object whose lifetime is briefer than that of the pointer itself. Unfortunately, this rule is difficult to enforce. Among other things, since both pointers and objects to which pointers might refer can be passed as arguments to subroutines, dynamic semantic checks are possible only if reference parameters are accompanied by a hidden indication of lifetime. Ada 95 has a more restrictive rule that is easier to enforce: it forbids a pointer from pointing to any object whose lifetime is briefer than that of the pointer's *type*.

Tombstones

Tombstones [Lom75, Lom85] are a mechanism by which a language implementation can catch all dangling references, to objects in both the stack and the heap. The idea is simple: rather than have a pointer refer to an object directly, we introduce an extra level of indirection (see Figure 7.16). When an object is allocated in the heap (or when a pointer is created to an object in the stack), the language run-time system allocates a tombstone. The pointer contains the address of the tombstone; the tombstone contains the address of the object. When the object is reclaimed, the tombstone is modified to contain a value (typically zero) that cannot be a valid address. To avoid special cases in the generated code, tombstones are also created for pointers to static objects.

For heap objects, it is easy to invalidate a tombstone when the program calls the deallocation operation. For stack objects, the language implementation must be able to find all tombstones associated with objects in the current stack frame when returning from a subroutine. One possible solution is to link all stack-object tombstones together in a list, sorted by the address of the stack frame in which the object lies. When a pointer is created to a local object, the tombstone can simply be added to the beginning of the list. When a pointer is created to a parameter, the run-time system must scan down the list and insert in the middle, to keep it sorted. When a subroutine returns, the epilogue portion of the calling sequence invalidates the tombstones at the head of the list, and removes them from the list.

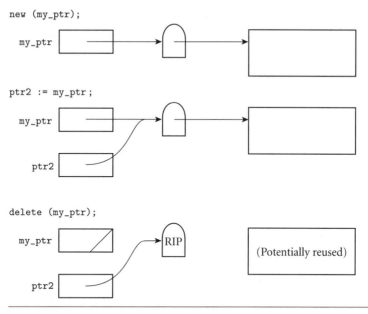

Figure 7.16 Tombstones. A valid pointer refers to a tombstone that in turn refers to an object. A dangling reference refers to an "expired" tombstone.

Tombstones may be allocated from the heap itself or, more commonly, from a separate pool. The latter option avoids fragmentation problems, and makes allocation relatively fast, since the first tombstone on the free list is always the right size.

Tombstones can be expensive, both in time and in space. The time overhead includes (1) creation of tombstones when allocating heap objects or using a "pointer to" operator, (2) checking for validity on every access, and (3) double-indirection. Fortunately, checking for validity can be made essentially free on most machines by arranging for the address in an "invalid" tombstone to lie outside the program's address space. Any attempt to use such an address will result in a hardware interrupt, which the operating system can reflect up into the language run-time system. We can also use our invalid address, in the pointer itself, to represent the constant nil. If the compiler arranges to set every pointer to nil at elaboration time, then the hardware will catch any use of an uninitialized pointer.

The space overhead for tombstones can be significant. The simplest approach is never to reclaim them. Since a tombstone is usually significantly smaller than the object to which it refers, a program will waste less space by leaving a tombstone around forever than it would waste by never reclaiming the associated object. Even so, any long-running program that continually creates and reclaims objects will eventually run out of space for tombstones. A potential solution, which we will consider in Section 7.7.3, is to augment every tombstone with a *reference count*, and reclaim tombstones themselves when the reference count goes to zero.

Tombstones have a valuable side effect. Because of double-indirection, it is easy to change the location of an object in the heap. The run-time system need not locate every pointer that refers to the object; all that is required is to change the address in the tombstone. The principal reason to change heap locations is for *storage compaction*, in which all dynamically allocated blocks are "scooted together" at one end of the heap in order to eliminate external fragmentation. Tombstones are not widely used in language implementations, but the Macintosh operating system uses them internally, for references to system objects such as file and window descriptors.

Locks and Keys

Locks and *keys* [FL80] are an alternative to tombstones. Their disadvantages are that they work only for objects in the heap (or for other objects that have been designed to be referred to by pointers; see Exercise 7.22), and they provide only probabilistic protection from dangling pointers. Their advantage is that they avoid the need to keep tombstones around forever (or to figure out when to reclaim them). Again the idea is simple: Every pointer is a tuple consisting of an address and a key. Every object in the heap begins with a lock. A pointer to an object in the heap is valid only if the key in the pointer matches the lock in the object (see Figure 7.17). When the run-time system allocates a new heap object, it generates a new key value. These can be as simple as serial numbers, but should avoid "common" values such as zero and one. When an object is reclaimed, its lock is changed to some arbitrary value (e.g., zero) so that the keys in any remaining pointers will not match. If the block is subsequently reused for another purpose, we expect it to be very unlikely that the location that used to contain the lock will be restored to its former value by coincidence.

Like tombstones, locks and keys incur significant overhead. They add an extra word of storage to every pointer and to every block in the heap. They increase the cost of copying one pointer into another. Most significantly, they incur the cost of comparing locks and keys on every access (or every provably nonredundant access). It is unclear whether the lock and key check is cheaper or more expensive than the tombstone check. A tombstone check may result in two cache misses (one for the tombstone and one for the object); a lock and key check is unlikely to cause more than one. On the other hand, the lock and key check requires a significantly longer instruction sequence on most machines.

To minimize time and space overhead, most compilers do not by default generate code to check for dangling references. Most Pascal compilers allow the programmer to request dynamic checks, which are usually implemented with locks and keys. In most implementations of C, even optional checks are unavailable.

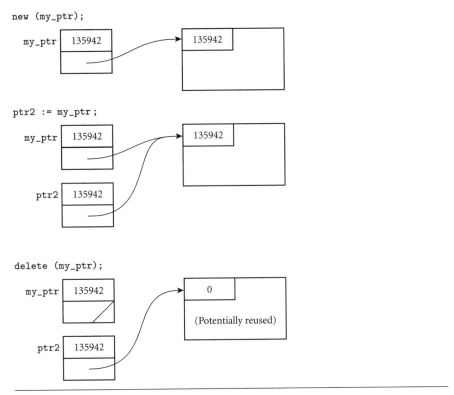

Figure 7.17 Locks and Keys. A valid pointer contains a key that matches the lock on an object in the heap. A dangling reference is unlikely to match.

7.7.3 **Garbage Collection**

Explicit reclamation of heap objects is a serious burden on the programmer and a major source of bugs (memory leaks and dangling references). The code required to keep track of object lifetimes makes programs more difficult to design, implement, and maintain. An attractive alternative is to have the language implementation notice when objects are no longer useful and reclaim them automatically. Automatic reclamation (otherwise known as *garbage collection*) is more-or-less essential for functional languages: delete is a very imperative sort of operation, and the ability to construct and return arbitrary objects from functions means that many objects that would be allocated on the stack in an imperative language must be allocated from the heap in a functional language, to give them unlimited extent.

Over time, automatic garbage collection has become popular for imperative languages as well. It can be found in Clu, Cedar, Ada, Modula-3, and Java, among others. Automatic collection is difficult to implement, but the difficulty pales in comparison to the convenience enjoyed by programmers once the implementation exists. Automatic collection also tends to be slower than manual reclamation, though it eliminates any need to check for dangling references.

Reference Counts

When is an object no longer useful? One possible answer is: when no pointers to it exist.[6] The simplest garbage collection technique simply places a counter in each object that keeps track of the number of pointers that refer to the object. When the object is created, this *reference count* is set to one, to represent the pointer returned by the new operation. When one pointer is assigned into another, the run-time system decrements the reference count of the object formerly referred to by the assignment's left-hand side, and increments the count of the object referred to by the right-hand side. On subroutine return, the calling sequence epilogue must decrement the reference count of any object referred to by a local pointer that is about to be destroyed. When a reference count reaches zero, its object can be reclaimed. Recursively, the run-time system must decrement counts for any objects referred to by pointers within the object being reclaimed, and reclaim those objects if their counts reach zero.

In order for reference counts to work, the language implementation must be able to identify the location of every pointer. When a subroutine returns, it must be able to tell which words in the stack frame represent pointers; when an object in the heap is reclaimed, it must be able to tell which words within the object represent pointers. The standard technique to track this information relies on *type descriptors* generated by the compiler. There is one descriptor for every distinct type in the program. Most descriptors are simply a table that lists the offsets within the type at which pointers can be found, together with the addresses of descriptors for the types of the objects referred to by those pointers. For a tagged variant record (discriminated union) type, the descriptor is a bit more complicated: it must contain a list of values (or ranges) for the tag, together with a table for the corresponding variant. For *untagged* variant records, there is no acceptable solution: reference counts work only if the language is strongly typed (but see the discussion of conservative collection in the next subsection below).

In addition to type descriptors, a compiler that supports reference counts must produce a descriptor for the stack frame of each subroutine. The epilogue code of the subroutine calling sequence begins its work in this descriptor. For each offset listed in the descriptor, it finds the pointer in the frame and if that pointer is non-nil, decrements the reference count of the object to which it refers. If the count reaches zero, it uses the address that accompanied the offset

---

6 Throughout the following discussion we will use the pointer-based terminology of languages with a value model of variables. The techniques apply equally well, however, to languages with a reference model of variables.

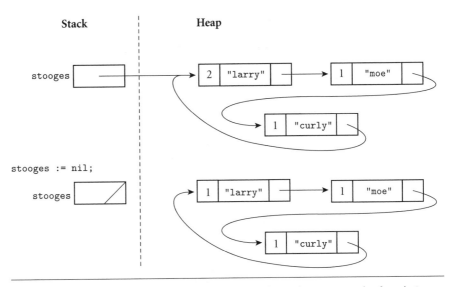

Figure 7.18 Reference counts and circular lists. The list shown here cannot be found via any program variable, but because it is circular, every cell contains a nonzero count.

to find the descriptor for the type of the reclaimed object and then calls itself recursively. When it returns, it reclaims the object's space. To prevent the collector from following garbage addresses, each pointer must be set to `nil` at elaboration time.

Reference counts suffer from the space overhead of an extra, counter field in every heap object. For small objects such as `cons` cells, this overhead may be significant. The ongoing expense of updating reference counts when pointers are changed can also be significant in a program with large amounts of pointer manipulation. The most important problem with reference counts, however, stems from their definition of a "useful object." While it is definitely true that an object is useless if no references to it exist, it may also be useless when references *do* exist.

As shown in Figure 7.18, reference counts may fail to collect circular structures. They work well only for structures that are guaranteed to be noncircular. Many language implementations use reference counts for variable-length strings; strings never contain references to anything else. Most purely functional languages can also use reference counts, since the lack of an assignment statement prevents them from introducing circularity. Finally, reference counts can be used to reclaim tombstones. While it is certainly possible to create a circular structure with tombstones, the fact that the programmer is responsible for explicit deallocation of heap objects implies that reference counts will fail to reclaim tombstones only when the programmer has failed to reclaim the objects to which they refer.

Mark-and-Sweep Collection

A better definition of a "useless" object is one that cannot be reached by following a chain of valid pointers starting from outside the heap. According to this definition, the blocks in the bottom half of Figure 7.18 are useless, even though their reference counts are nonzero. The standard mechanism to identify useless blocks, under this more accurate definition, is known as *mark-and-sweep garbage collection*. The simplest form of mark-and-sweep collection proceeds in three steps. We run these steps when the amount of free space remaining in the heap falls below some minimum threshold.

1. The collector walks through the heap, tentatively marking every block as "useless."

2. Beginning with all pointers outside the heap, the collector recursively explores all linked data structures in the program, marking each newly discovered block as "useful." (When it encounters a block that is already marked as "useful," the collector knows it has reached the block over some previous path, and returns without recursing.)

3. The collector again walks through the heap, moving every block that is still marked "useless" to the free list.

Several potential problems with this algorithm are immediately apparent. First, both the initial and final walks through the heap require that the collector be able to tell where every "in-use" block begins and ends. In a language with variable-size heap blocks, every block must begin with an indication of its size, and of whether it is currently free. Second, the collector must be able in Step 2 to find the pointers contained within each block. The standard solution is to place a pointer to a type descriptor near the beginning of each block.

The space overhead for bookkeeping information in heap blocks is not as large as it might first appear. If every type descriptor contains an indication of size, then a heap block that includes the address of its type descriptor need not include its size as a separate field (though the extra indirection required to find the size in the descriptor makes walking the heap more expensive). Moreover, since a type descriptor must be word-aligned on most machines, the two low-order bits of its address are guaranteed to be zero. If we are willing to mask these bits out before using the address, we can use them to store the "free" and "useful" flags.

The exploration step (Step 2) of mark-and-sweep collection is naturally recursive. The obvious implementation needs a stack whose maximum depth is proportional to the longest chain through the heap. In practice, the space for this stack may not be available: after all, we run garbage collection when we're about to run out of space![7] An alternative implementation of the exploration

---

7   In many language implementations, the stack and heap grow toward each other from opposite ends of memory; if the heap is full, the stack can't grow. In a system with virtual memory the distance between the two may theoretically be enormous, but the space that backs them up on disk is still limited, and shared between them.

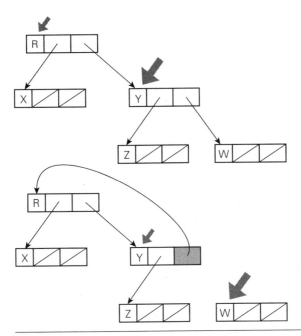

Figure 7.19 Heap exploration via pointer reversal. The block currently under examination is indicated by the large grey arrow. The previous block is indicated by the small grey arrow. As the garbage collector moves from one block to the next, it changes the pointer it follows to refer back to the previous block. When it returns to a block it restores the pointer. Each reversed pointer must be marked, to distinguish it from other, forward pointers in the same block. We assume in this figure that the root node R is outside the heap, so none of its pointers are reversed.

step uses a technique first suggested by Schorr and Waite [SW67] to embed the equivalent of the stack in already-existing fields in heap blocks. More specifically, as the collector explores the path to a given block, it *reverses* the pointers it follows, so that each points *back* to the previous block instead of forward to the next. This pointer-reversal technique is illustrated in Figure 7.19. As it explores, the collector keeps track of the current block and the block from whence it came (the two grey arrows in the figure).

When it returns from block W to block Y, the collector uses the reversed pointer in Y to restore its notion of previous block (R in our example). It then flips the reversed pointer back to W and updates its notion of current block to Y. If the block to which it has returned contains additional pointers, the collector proceeds forward again; otherwise it returns across the previous reversed pointer and tries again. At most one pointer in every block will be reversed at any given time. This pointer must be marked, probably by means of another bookkeeping field at the beginning of each block. (We could mark the pointer by setting one of its low-order bits, but the cost in time would probably be prohibitive: we'd have to search the block on every visit.)

In a language with variable-size heap blocks, the garbage collector can reduce external fragmentation by performing storage compaction, as noted in the discussion of tombstones above. Compaction with tombstones is easier, because there is only a single pointer to each object. Many garbage collectors employ a technique known as *stop-and-copy* that achieves compaction while simultaneously eliminating Steps 1 and 3 in the standard mark and sweep algorithm. Specifically, they divide the heap into two regions of equal size. All allocation happens in the first half. When this half is (nearly) full, the collector begins its exploration of reachable data structures. Each reachable block is copied into the second half of the heap, with no external fragmentation. The old version of the block, in the first half of the heap, is overwritten with a "useful" flag and a pointer to the new location. Any other pointer that refers to the same block (and is found later in the exploration) is set to point to the new location. When it finishes its exploration, all useful objects have been moved (and compacted) into the second half of the heap, and nothing in the first half is needed anymore. The collector can therefore swap its notion of first and second halves, and the program can continue. Obviously, this algorithm suffers from the fact that only half of the heap can be used at any given time, but in a system with virtual memory it is only the virtual space that is underutilized; each "half" of the heap can occupy most of physical memory as needed. Moreover, by eliminating Steps 1 and 3 of standard mark and sweep, stop and copy incurs overhead proportional to the number of nongarbage blocks, rather than the total number of blocks.

In comparison to reference counts, mark-and-sweep collection has lower overhead during normal operation; it incurs cost only when space runs low and the collector is invoked. The space overheads of the two approaches are comparable (type descriptor addresses in every block, plus a reference count or reversed pointer indication). Unfortunately, because it delays its work until space runs low, mark-and-sweep collection tends to suffer from the "stop-the-world" phenomenon: for interactive applications, execution occurs in bursts, with awkward pauses for garbage collection in-between. Worse, the cost of collection is highest when it is needed most: when the number of heap blocks to traverse is very large.

To reduce the cost of collection, some garbage collectors employ a "generational" technique, in which garbage is collected only among recently allocated objects. Any heap block that survives some small number of collections (often one) is assumed to be permanent. As with the compacting collector described above, the heap is divided into halves, but these halves are never reversed. Garbage collection occurs in the first half. Objects that survive one or more collections are moved into the second half, where they are never considered for collection again. This approach works well in practice, trading accuracy for a significant reduction in run-time cost. The risk is that a pathological program that uses dynamically allocated objects for a long time, but not forever, may fill the "permanent" half of its heap with garbage. The burstiness of collection can also be addressed by performing garbage collection incrementally, interleaving it with normal execution or running it in parallel on a multiprocessor. Efficient, effective garbage collection techniques remain an active area of research.

Language implementors have traditionally assumed that automatic storage reclamation is possible only in languages that are strongly typed: both reference counts and mark-and-sweep collection require that we be able to find the pointers within an object. If we are willing to admit the possibility that some garbage will go unclaimed (as we already do with generational collection) it turns out that we can implement mark-and-sweep collection without being able to find pointers [BW88]. The key is to observe that the number of blocks in the heap is much smaller than the number of possible bit patterns in an address. The odds that a word in memory that is not a pointer into the heap will happen to contain a bit pattern that looks like such a pointer are relatively small. If we assume, conservatively, that everything that seems to point to a heap block is in fact a valid pointer, then we can proceed with mark-and-sweep collection. When space runs low, the collector (as usual) tentatively marks all blocks in the heap as useless. It then scans all word-aligned quantities in the stack and in global storage. If any of these "pointers" contains the address of a block in the heap, the collector marks that block as useful. Recursively, the collector then scans all word-aligned quantities in the block, and marks as useful any other blocks whose addresses are found therein. Finally (as usual), the collector reclaims any blocks that are still marked useless. The algorithm is completely safe (in the sense that it never reclaims useful blocks) so long as the programmer never "hides" a pointer. In C, for example, the collector is unlikely to function correctly if the programmer casts a pointer to `int` and then `xors` it with a constant, with the expectation of restoring and using the pointer at a later time. In addition to sometimes leaving garbage unclaimed, conservative collection suffers from the inability to perform compaction: the collector can never be sure which "pointers" should be changed.

7.8 Lists

A list is defined recursively as either the empty list or a pair consisting of an object (which may be either a list or an atom) and another (shorter) list. Lists are ideally suited to programming in functional and logic languages, which do most of their work via recursion and higher-order functions (to be described in Section 11.2.3). In Lisp, in fact, a program *is* a list, and can extend itself at run time by constructing a list and executing it (this capability will be examined further in Section 11.2.1; it depends heavily on the fact that Lisp delays almost all semantic checking until run time).

Lists can also be used in imperative programs. Clu provides a built-in type constructor for lists, and a list class is easy to write in Java. In any language with records and pointers, the programmer can build lists by hand. Since many of the standard list operations tend to generate garbage, lists work best in a language with automatic garbage collection.

We have already discussed certain aspects of lists in ML (Section 7.2.5) and Lisp (Section 7.7.1). As we noted in those sections, lists in ML are homogeneous:

every element of the list must have the same type. Lisp lists, by contrast, are heterogeneous: any object may be placed in a list, so long as it is never used in an inconsistent fashion.[8] The different approaches to type in ML and in Lisp lead to different implementations. An ML list is usually a chain of blocks, each of which contains an element and a pointer to the next block. A Lisp list is a chain of `cons` cells, each of which contains *two* pointers, one to the element and one to the next `cons` cell (see Figures 7.13 and 7.14). In both semantics (homogeneity vs. heterogeneity) and implementation (chained blocks v. `cons` cells), Clu resembles ML, while Prolog (to be discussed in Section 11.3.1) resembles Lisp.

Both ML and Lisp provide convenient notation for lists. An ML list is enclosed in square brackets, with elements separated by commas: `[a, b, c, d]`. A Lisp list is enclosed in parentheses, with elements separated by white space: `(a b c d)`. In both cases, the notation represents a *proper* list: one whose innermost pair consists of the final element and the empty list. In Lisp, it is also possible to construct an *improper* list, whose final pair contains two elements. (Strictly speaking, such a list does not conform to the standard recursive definition.) Lisp systems provide a more general, but cumbersome *dotted* list notation that captures both proper and improper lists. A dotted list is either an atom (possibly `nil`) or a pair consisting of two dotted lists separated by a period and enclosed in parentheses. The dotted list `(a . (b . (c . (d . nil))))` is the same as `(a b c d)`. The list `(a . (b . (c . d)))` is improper; its final `cons` cell contains a pointer to `d` in the second position, where a pointer to a list is normally required.

Both ML and Lisp provide a wealth of built-in polymorphic functions to manipulate arbitrary lists. Because programs are lists in Lisp, Lisp must distinguish between lists that are to evaluated and lists that are to be left "as is," as structures. To prevent a literal list from being evaluated, the Lisp programmer may quote it: `(quote (a b c d))`, abbreviated `'(a b c d)`. To evaluate an internal list (e.g., one returned by a function), the programmer may pass it to the built-in function `eval`. In ML, programs are not lists, so a literal list is always a structural aggregate.

The most fundamental operations on lists are those that construct them from their components or extract their components from them. In Lisp:

```
(cons 'a '(b))        ⇒  (a b)
(car '(a b))          ⇒  a
(car nil)             ⇒  ??
(cdr '(a b c))        ⇒  (b c)
(cdr '(a))            ⇒  nil
(cdr nil)             ⇒  ??
(append '(a b) '(c d)) ⇒  (a b c d)
```

---

8 Recall that objects are self-descriptive in Lisp. The only type checking occurs when a function "deliberately" inspects an argument to see whether it is a list or an atom of some particular type.

Here we have used $\Rightarrow$ to mean "evaluates to." The names of the functions `car` and `cdr` are historical accidents: they derive from the names of certain registers on the machine on which Lisp was first implemented. The latter function is pronounced "coulder." The `car` and `cdr` of the empty list (`nil`) are defined to be `nil` in Common Lisp; in Scheme they result in a dynamic semantic error. In ML the equivalent operations are written as follows:

```
a :: [b]        ⇒  [a, b]
hd [a, b]       ⇒  a
hd []           ⇒  run-time exception
tl [a, b, c]    ⇒  [b, c]
tl [a]          ⇒  nil
tl []           ⇒  run-time exception
[a, b] @ [c, d] ⇒  [a, b, c, d]
```

Run-time exceptions may be *caught* by the program if desired; further details will appear in Section 8.5.

Both ML and Lisp provide many additional list functions, including ones that test a list to see if it is empty; return the length of a list; return the nth element of a list, or a list consisting of all but the first n elements; reverse the order of the elements of a list; search a list for elements matching some predicate; or apply a function to every element of a list, returning the results as a list.

Miranda and Haskell provide lists that resemble those of ML, but with an important additional mechanism, known as *list comprehensions*. A common form of list comprehension comprises an expression, an enumerator, and one or more filters. The following, for example, denotes a list of the squares of all odd numbers less than 100:

```
[i*i | i <- [1..100]; i mod 2 = 1]
```

Here the vertical bar means "such that"; the left arrow is roughly equivalent to "is a member of." We could of course write an equivalent expression with a collection of appropriate functions. The brevity of the list comprehension syntax, however, can sometimes lead to remarkably elegant programs (see, for example, Exercise 7.25).

7.9* Files and Input/Output

Input/output (I/O) facilities allow a program to communicate with the outside world. In discussing this communication, it can be helpful to distinguish between *interactive* I/O and I/O with files. Interactive I/O generally implies communication with a human user, who works in parallel with the running program, and whose input to the program may depend on earlier output from the program (e.g., prompts). Files generally refer to off-line storage implemented by the operating system. Files may be further categorized into those that are *temporary* and those that are *persistent*. Temporary files exist for the duration of a single program run; their purpose is to store information that is too large to fit in the memory available to the program. Persistent files allow a program to read data that existed before the program began running, and to write data that will continue to exist after the program has ended.

Persistent files are the principal mechanism by which programs that run at different times communicate with each other. A few language proposals (e.g., Argus [LS83] and χ [SH92]) allow ordinary variables to persist from one invocation of a program to the next, and a few experimental operating systems (e.g., Opal [CLFL94] and Hemlock [GSB+93]) provide persistence for variables outside the language proper. In addition, some language-specific programming environments, such as those for Smalltalk and Common Lisp, provide a notion of *workspace* that includes persistent named variables. These examples, however, are more the exception than the rule. For the most part, data that needs to outlive a particular program invocation needs to reside in files.

I/O is one of the most difficult aspects of a language to design, and one of the ones that displays the least commonality from one language to the next. The problem is that both interactive and file-based I/O tends to be intimately tied to the capabilities of the host operating system. In the first two subsections below we consider interactive and file-based I/O. We then focus on the common case of I/O on *text files*. A text file is stored as readable characters, which may be converted to and from other types by I/O operations.

7.9.1 Interactive I/O

On a modern machine, interactive I/O usually occurs through a graphical user interface (GUI: "gooey") system, with a mouse, a keyboard, and a bit-mapped screen that in turn support windows, menus, scrollbars, buttons, sliders, and so on. GUI characteristics vary significantly among, say, Microsoft Windows, the Macintosh, and Unix's X; the differences are one of the principal reasons it is so difficult to port applications across platforms.

Within a single platform, the facilities of a GUI system usually take the form of library routines (to create or resize a window, print text, draw a polygon, and so on). Input events (mouse move, button push, keystroke) may be placed in a queue that is accessible to the program, or tied to *event handler* subroutines that are called by the operating system when the event occurs. Because the handler is triggered from outside, its activities must be *synchronized* with those of the main program; we will discuss synchronization further in Section 12.3.

A few programming languages—notably Smalltalk and Java—attempt to incorporate a standard set of GUI mechanisms into the language. The Smalltalk design team was part of the original group at Xerox's Palo Alto Research Center (PARC) that invented mouse-and-window based interfaces in the early 1970s. Unfortunately, while the Smalltalk GUI is successful within the confines of the language, it tends not to integrate well with the "look and feel" of the host system on which it runs. In a similar vein, Java's facilities for windows, menus, and other components currently have a "least common denominator" look to them as well. Smalltalk's GUI is a fundamental part of the language; Java's takes the form of a standard set of library routines. The Java routines and their interface are likely to evolve over time.

The "parallel execution" of the program and the human user that characterizes interactive systems is difficult to capture in a functional programming model. A functional program that operates in a "batch" mode (taking its input from a file and writing its output to a file) can be modeled as a function from input to output. A program that interacts with the user, however, requires a very concrete notion of program ordering, because later input may depend on earlier output. If both input and output take the form of an ordered sequence of tokens, then interactive I/O can be modeled using lazy data structures, in a manner reminiscent of the "infinite" lists of Section 6.6.2. How to handle more general (e.g. GUI) I/O in a functional program remains an open problem. We will consider these issues again in Sections 11.2.2 and 11.2.5.

7.9.2 File-Based I/O

Files, like interactive I/O, can be incorporated directly into the language, or provided via library routines. In the latter case, it is still a good idea for the language designers to suggest a standard library interface, to promote portability of programs across platforms. The lack of such a standard in Algol 60 is widely credited with impeding the language's widespread use. One of the principal reasons to incorporate I/O into the language proper is to make use of special syntax. In particular, several languages, notably Fortran and Pascal, provide built-in I/O facilities in order to obtain "subroutines" that take a variable number of parameters, some of which may be optional.

Depending on the needs of the programmer and the capabilities of the host operating system, data in files may be represented in binary form, much as it is in memory, or as *text*. In a binary file, the number 1066_{10} would represented by the 32-bit value 10000101010_2. In a text file, it would probably be represented by the ASCII string "1066". Temporary files are usually kept in binary form for the sake of speed and convenience. Persistent files are commonly kept in both forms. Text files are more easily ported across systems: issues of word size, byte order, alignment, floating-point format, and so on do not arise. Text files also have the advantage of human readability: they can be manipulated by text editors and related tools. Unfortunately, text files tend to be large, particularly when used to hold numeric data. A double-precision floating-point number occupies only eight bytes in binary form, but can require as many as 24 characters in decimal notation (not counting any surrounding white space). Text files also incur the cost of binary to ASCII conversion on output, and ASCII to binary conversion on input. Mechanisms to control these conversion operations tend to be the most complicated part of I/O; we discuss them in the following section.

When I/O is built into a language, files are usually declared using a built-in type constructor, as they are in Pascal:

```
var my_file : file of foo;
```

If I/O is provided by library routines, the library usually provides an opaque type to represent a file. In either case, each file variable is generally bound to an external, operating system–supported file by means of an *open* operation. In C, for example, one says:

```
my_file = open (path_name, flags, mode);
```

The first argument to `open` is a character string that names the file, using the naming conventions of the host operating system. The second argument is a bit vector that indicates whether the file should be readable, writable, or both. This argument also indicates a variety of OS-dependent file properties; on Unix, these include whether the file should be created if it does not exist, whether an `open` of a file that represents a communication line should wait until a connection is established (as opposed to letting the OS make the connection in the background), and whether subsequent writes of a real file should be forced through to persistent storage before returning (as opposed to being buffered in the OS). For files that are created as part of the `open` call, the `mode` parameter indicates access rights. When a program is done with a file, it can break the association between the file variable and the external object by using a *close* operation:

```
close (my_file);
```

In response to a call to `close`, the operating system may perform certain "finalizing" operations, such as unlocking an exclusive file (so that it may be used by other programs), rewinding a tape drive, or forcing the contents of buffers out to disk.

Most files, both binary and text, are stored as a linear sequence of characters, words, or records. Every open file then has a notion of *current position*: an implicit reference to some element of the sequence. Each `read` or `write` operation implicitly advances this reference by one position, so that successive operations access successive elements, automatically. In a *sequential* file, this automatic advance is the only way to change the current position. Sequential files usually correspond to media such as printers and tapes, in which the current position has a physical representation (how many pages we've printed; how much tape is on each spool) that is difficult to change.

In other, *random-access* files, the programmer can change the current position to an arbitrary value by issuing a *seek* operation. In a few programming languages (e.g., Cobol and PL/I), random-access files (also called *direct* files) have no notion of current position. Rather, they are *indexed* on some key, and every `read` or `write` operation must specify a key. A file that can be accessed both sequentially *and* by key is said to be *indexed sequential*.

Random-access files usually correspond to media such as magnetic or optical disks, in which the current position can be changed with relative ease. (Depending on technology, 1990s disks take anywhere from 5 to 200 ms to seek to a new location. Tape drives, by contrast, can take more than a minute. Note that 5 ms is still a very long time—one million cycles on a 200MHz processor—so seeking should never be taken casually, even on a disk.) A few languages—notably Pascal—provide no random-access files, though individual implementations may support random access as a nonstandard language extension.

7.9.3 Text I/O

It is conventional to think of text files as consisting of a sequence of *lines*, each of which in turn consists of characters. In older systems, particularly those designed around the metaphor of punch cards, lines are reflected in the organization of the file itself. A seek operation, for example, may take a line number as argument. More commonly, a text file is simply a sequence of characters. Within this sequence, control (nonprinting) characters indicate the boundaries between lines. Unfortunately, end-of-line conventions are not standardized. In Unix, each line of a text file ends with a *newline* ("control-J") character, ASCII value 10. On the Macintosh, each line ends with a *carriage return* ("control-M") character, ASCII value 13. In MS-DOS, each line ends with a carriage return/line feed pair. Text files are usually sequential.

Despite the muddled conventions for line breaks, text files are much more portable and readable than binary files.[9] Because they do not mirror the structure of internal data, text files require extensive conversions on input and output. Issues to be considered include the base for integer values (and the representation of nondecimal bases); the representation of floating-point values (number of digits, placement of decimal point, notation for exponent); the representation of enumerations and other nonnumeric, nonstring types; and positioning, if any, within columns (right and left justification, zero or white space fill, "floating" dollar signs in Cobol). Some of these issues (e.g., the number of digits in a floating-point number) are influenced by the hardware, but most are dictated by the needs of the application and the preferences of the programmer.

In most languages the programmer can take complete control of input and output formatting by writing it all explicitly, using language or library mechanisms to read and write individual characters only. I/O at such a low level is tedious, however, and most languages also provide more high-level operations.

---

9 We are speaking here, of course, of plain text ASCII files. So-called "rich text" files, consisting of formatted text in particular fonts, sizes, and colors, perhaps with embedded graphics, are another matter entirely. Word processors usually represent rich text with a combination of binary and ASCII data, though ASCII-only standards such as postscript, textual PDF, and RTF can be used to enhance portability.

These operations vary significantly in syntax and in the degree to which they allow the programmer to specify I/O formats. We illustrate the breadth of possibilities with examples from four imperative languages: Fortran, Ada, C, and C++.

Text I/O in Fortran

In Fortran, we could write a character string, an integer, and an array of ten floating-point numbers as follows:

```
character s*20
integer n
real r(10)
...
write (4, '(A20, I10, 10F8.2)'), s, n, r
```

In the `write` statement, the 4 indicates a *unit number*, which identifies a particular output file. The quoted, parenthesized expression is called a *format*; it specifies how the printed variables are to be represented. In this case, we have requested a 20-column ASCII string, a 10-column integer, and 10 eight-column floating-point numbers (with two columns of each reserved for the fractional part of the value). Fortran provides an extremely rich set of these *edit descriptors* for use inside of formats. Cobol and PL/I provide comparable facilities, though with a very different syntax.

Fortran allows a format to be specified indirectly, so it may be used in more than one input or output statement:

```
write (4, 100), s, n, r
...
100 format (A20, I10, 10F8.2)
```

If the programmer does not know, or does not care about, the precise allocation of columns to fields, the format can be omitted:

```
write (4, *), s, n, r
```

In this case, the language run-time system will use default format conventions.

To write to the standard output stream (i.e., the terminal or its surrogate), the programmer can use the `print` statement, which resembles a `write` without a unit number:

```
print*, s, n, r          ! * means default format
```

For input, `read` is used both for standard input and for specific files; in the former case, the unit number is omitted, together with the extra set of parentheses:

```
read 100, s, n, r
...
read*, s, n, r           ! * means default format
```

The star may be omitted in Fortran 90.

In the full form of `read`, `write`, and `print`, additional arguments may be provided in the parenthesized list with the unit number and format. These can be used to specify a variety of additional information, including a label to which to jump on end-of-file; a label to which to jump on other errors; a variable into which to place status codes returned by the operating system; a set of labels (a "namelist") to attach to the output values; and a control code to override the usual automatic advance to the next line of the file. Because there are so many of these optional arguments, most of which are usually omitted, they are usually specified using *named* parameter notation, a notion we defer to Section 8.3.2.

The variety of shorthand versions of `read`, `write`, and `print`, together with the fact that they operate on a variable number of program variables, makes it very difficult to cast them as "ordinary" subroutines. Fortran 90 provides default and keyword parameters (to be described in Section 8.3.2), but Fortran 77 does not, and even in Fortran 90 there is no way to define a subroutine with an *arbitrary* number of parameters.

In Pascal, as in Fortran 77, the parameters of every subroutine are fixed in number and in type. Pascal's `read`, `readln`, `write`, and `writeln` "routines" are therefore built into the language; they are not part of a library. Each takes a variable number of arguments, the first of which may optionally specify a particular file. Unfortunately, Pascal's formatting mechanisms are much less flexible than those of Fortran; programmers are often forced to implement formatting by hand, using `read` and `write` for input and output of individual characters only. In the design of Modula-2, Niklaus Wirth chose to move I/O out of the language proper, and to embed it in a standard library. The designers of Ada took a similar approach. The Modula-2 I/O libraries are relatively primitive: only a modest improvement over character-by-character I/O in Pascal. The Ada libraries are much more extensive, and make heavy use of overloading and default parameters.

Text I/O in Ada

Ada provides a suite of five standard library packages for I/O. The `sequential_IO` and `direct_IO` packages are for binary files. They provide generic file types that can be instantiated for any desired element type. The `IO_exceptions` and `low_level_IO` packages handle error conditions and device control, respectively. The `text_IO` package provides formatted input and output on sequential files of characters.

Using `text_IO`, our original three-variable Fortran output statement would look something like this in Ada:

```
s : array (1..20) of character;
n : integer;
r : array (1..10) of real;
...
```

```
set_output (my_file);
put (n, 10);
put (s);
for i in 1..10 loop put (r(i), 5, 2); end loop;
new_line;
```

In the put of an element of r, the second parameter specifies the number of digits before the decimal point, rather than the width of the entire number (including the decimal point), as it did in Fortran. The put of s will use the string's natural length. If a different length is desired, the programmer will have to write blanks or put a substring explicitly. If precise output positioning is not desired for the integers and real numbers, the extra parameters in their put calls can be omitted; in this case the run-time system will use standard defaults. The programmer can use additional library routines to change these defaults if desired. A call to set_output invokes a similar mechanism: it changes the default notion of output file. There are two overloaded forms of put for every built-in type. One takes a file name as its first argument; the other does not. The last five lines above could have been written:

```
put (my_file, n, 10);
put (my_file, s);
for i in 1..10 loop put (my_file, r(i), 5, 2); end loop;
new_line (my_file);
```

The programmer can of course define additional forms of get and put for arbitrary user-defined types. All of these facilities rely on standard Ada mechanisms; in contrast to Fortran, no support for I/O is built into the language itself.

Text I/O in C

C provides I/O through a library package called stdio; as in Ada, no support for I/O is built into the language itself. Our example output statement would look something like this in C:

```
char s[20];
int n;
double r[10];
...
fprintf (my_file, "%20s%10d", s, n);
for (i = 0; i < 10; i++) fprintf (my_file, "%8.2f");
fprintf (my_file, "\n");
```

The arguments to fprintf are a file, a format string, and a sequence of expressions. The format string has capabilities similar to the formats of Fortran, though the syntax is very different. In general, a format string consists of a sequence of characters with embedded "placeholders," each of which begins with a percent sign. The placeholder %20s indicates a 20-character string; %d indicates an integer in decimal notation; %8.2f indicates an 8-character floating-point number, with two digits to the right of the decimal point. As in Fortran, a single `fprintf` statement can print an arbitrary number of expressions. As in Ada, an explicit `for` loop is needed to print an array. Commonly the format string also contains labeling text and white space:

```
strcpy (s, "four");       /* copy "four" into s */
n = 20;
fprintf (my_file, "%s score and %d years ago\n", s, n);
```

A percent sign can be printed by doubling it:

```
fprintf (my_file, "%d%%\n", 25);       /* prints "25%" */
```

Input in C takes a similar form. The `fscanf` routine takes as argument a file, a format string, and a sequence of pointers to variables. In the common case, every argument after the format is a variable name preceded by a "pointer to" operator:

```
fscanf (my_file, "%s %d %lf", &s, &n, &r[0]);
```

In this call, the `&s` placeholder will match a string of maximal length that does not include white space. If this string is longer than 20 characters (the length of `s`), then `fscanf` will write beyond the end of the storage for the string; no run-time check prevents this. The three-character `%lf` placeholder informs the library routine that the corresponding argument is a `double`; the two-character sequence `%f` would read into a `float`.[10] Accidentally using a placeholder for the wrong size variable is a common error in C; forgetting the ampersand on a trailing argument is another. Both mistakes would be caught by type-safe I/O. Note that we have read a single element of `r`; as with `fprintf`, a `for` loop would be needed to read the whole array.

We have noted above that the I/O routines of Fortran and Pascal are built into the language largely to permit them to take a variable number of arguments. We have also noted that moving I/O into a library in Ada forces us to make a separate call to `put` for every output expression. So how do `fprintf` and `fscanf` work? It turns out that C permits the trailing parameters of a function to be declared as a "variable argument list" (we will discuss these `va_lists` in more detail in Section 8.3.2). Unfortunately, the use of a `va_list` eliminates the possibility of compile-time type checking. Moreover, the lack of run-time type descriptors in C precludes run-time checking as well. If the arguments after the format string in a call to `fprintf` do not correspond in number and type to the placeholders in the format, chaos can result.

To simplify I/O to and from the standard input and output streams, `stdio` provides routines called `printf` and `scanf` that omit the initial arguments of

---

10 C's `doubles` are double-precision IEEE floating-point numbers in most implementations; `floats` are usually single precision.

`fprintf` and `fscanf`. To facilitate the formatting of strings *within* a program, `stdio` also provides routines called `sprintf` and `sscanf`, which replace the initial arguments of `fprintf` and `fscanf` with a pointer to an array of characters. The `sscanf` function "reads" from this array; `sprintf` "writes" to it. Fortran 90 provides similar support for intraprogram formatting through so-called *internal files*.

Text I/O in C++

As a descendant of C, C++ supports the `stdio` library described in the previous subsection. It also supports a new I/O library called `iostream` that exploits the object-oriented features of the language. The `iostream` library is more flexible than `stdio`, provides arguably more elegant syntax (though this is a matter of taste), and is completely type safe.

C++ *streams* use operator overloading to co-opt the `<<` and `>>` symbols normally used for bit-wise shifts. The `iostream` library provides an overloaded version of `<<` and `>>` for each built-in type, and programmers can define versions for new types. To print a character string in C++, one writes

```
my_stream << s;
```

To output a string and an integer we can write

```
my_stream << s << n;
```

This code requires that `my_stream` be an instance of the `ostream` (output stream) class defined in the `iostream` library. The `<<` operator is syntactic sugar for the "operator function" `ostream::operator<<`, as described in Section 3.5. Because `<<` associates left-to-right, the statement above is equivalent to

```
(my_stream.operator<< (s)).operator<< (n);
```

The code works because `ostream::operator<<` returns a reference to its first argument as its result (as we shall see in Section 8.3.1, C++ supports both a value model and a reference model for variables).

As shown so far, output to an `ostream` uses default formatting conventions. To change conventions, one may embed so-called *stream manipulators* in a sequence of `<<` operations. To print n in octal notation (rather than the default decimal), we could write

```
my_stream << oct << n;
```

To control the number of columns occupied by s and n, we could write

```
my_stream << setw (20) << s << setw (10) << n;
```

The `oct` manipulator causes the stream to print all subsequent numeric output in octal. The `setw` manipulator causes it to print its next string or numeric output in a field of a specified minimum width (behavior reverts to the default after a single output).

The `oct` manipulator is declared as a function that takes an `ostream` as a parameter and produces a reference to an `ostream` as its result. Because it is not followed by empty parentheses, the occurrence of `oct` in the output sequence above is *not* a call to `oct`; rather, a reference to `oct` is passed to an overloaded version of `<<` that expects a manipulator function as its right-hand argument. This version of `<<` then calls the function, passing the stream (the left-hand argument of `<<`) as argument.

The `setw` manipulator is even trickier. It is declared as a function that returns a reference to what we might call a "function encapsulator" object. The encapsulator, in turn, contains two things: an integer and a pointer to a function that expects an `ostream` and an integer as argument. The `setw` (20) in the code above can be thought of as an aggregate for an encapsulator containing the number 20 and a pointer to the `setw` manipulator. (More accurately, it's an invocation of a *constructor* function for the encapsulator object. We will discuss constructors in detail in Section 10.3.) The `iostream` library provides an overloaded version of `<<` that expects an encapsulator as its right-hand argument. This version of `<<` calls the function inside the encapsulator, passing it as arguments the stream (the left-hand argument of `<<`) and the integer inside the encapsulator.

The `iostream` library provides a wealth of manipulators to change the formatting behavior of an `ostream`. Because C++ inherits C's handling of pointers and arrays, however, there is no way for an `ostream` to know the length of an array. As a result, our full output example still requires a `for` loop to print the `r` array:

```
char s[20];
int n;
double r[10];
...
my_stream << setw (20) << s << setw (10) << n;
for (i = 0; i < 10; i++)
    my_stream << setiosflags (ios::fixed)
        << setw (8) << setprecision (2) << r[i];
my_stream << "\n":
```

Here the manipulators in the output sequence in the `for` loop specify fixed format (rather than scientific) for floating-point numbers, with a field width of eight, and two digits past the decimal point. The `setiosflags` and `setprecision` manipulators change the default format of the stream; the changes apply to all subsequent output. To avoid calling these manipulators for every member of the array, we could write

```
my_stream.flags (my_stream.flags() | ios::fixed);
my_stream.precision (2);
for (i = 0; i < 10; i++) my_stream << setw (8) << r[i];
```

The `setw` manipulator affects the output width of only a single item. To facilitate the restoration of defaults, the `flags` and `precision` functions return the previous value:

```
int old_flags = my_stream.flags (my_stream.flags() | ios::fixed);
int old_precision = my_stream.precision (2);
for (i = 0; i < 10; i++) my_stream << setw (8) << r[i];
my_stream.flags (old_flags);
my_stream.precision (old_precision);
```

Formatted input in C++ is analogous to formatted output. It uses `istreams` instead of `ostreams`, and the `>>` operator instead of `<<`. It also supports a suite of manipulators comparable to those for output. I/O on the standard input and output streams does not require different functions; the programmer simply begins an input or output sequence with the standard stream name `cin` or `cout`. (In keeping with C tradition, there is also a standard stream `cerr` for error messages.) To support intraprogram formatting of character strings, the `strstream` library provides `istrstream` and `ostrstream` object classes that are derived from `istream` and `ostream`, and that allow a stream variable to be bound to a string instead of to a file.

7.10 Equality Testing and Assignment

For simple, primitive data types such as integers, floating-point numbers, or characters, equality testing and assignment are relatively straightforward operations, with obvious semantics and obvious implementations (bit-wise comparison or copy). For more complicated or abstract data types, however, both semantic and implementation subtleties arise.

Consider for example the problem of comparing two character strings. Should the expression `s = t` determine whether `s` and `t`

- are aliases for one another?
- occupy storage that is bit-wise identical over its full length?
- contain the same sequence of characters?
- would appear the same if printed?

The second of these tests is probably too low-level to be of interest in most programs; it suggests the possibility that a comparison might fail because of garbage in currently unused portions of the space reserved for a string. The other three alternatives may all be of interest in certain circumstances, and may generate different results.

In many cases the definition of equality boils down to the distinction between l-values and r-values: in the presence of references, should expressions be considered equal only if they refer to the same object, or also if the objects to which they refer are in some sense equal? The first option (refer to the same object) is known as a *shallow* comparison. The second (refer to equal objects) is called a *deep* comparison. For complicated data structures (e.g., lists or graphs) a deep comparison may require recursive traversal.

In imperative programming languages assignment operations may also be deep or shallow. Under a reference model of variables, a shallow assignment a := b will make a refer to the object to which b refers. A deep assignment will create a copy of the object to which b refers, and make a refer to the copy. Under a value model of variables, a shallow assignment will copy the value of b into a, but if that value is a pointer (or a record containing pointers), then the objects to which the pointer(s) refer will not be copied.

Most programming languages employ both shallow comparisons and shallow assignment. A few (notably the various dialects of Lisp) provide more than one option for comparison. Scheme, for example, has three equality-testing functions:

```
(eq? a b)       ; do a and b refer to the same object?
(eqv? a b)      ; are a and b provably semantically equivalent?
(equal? a b)    ; do a and b have the same recursive structure?
```

The intent behind the eq? predicate is to make the implementation as fast as possible while still producing useful results for many types of operands. The intent behind eqv? is to provide as intuitively appealing a result as possible for as wide a range of types as possible.

The eq? predicate behaves as one would expect for Booleans, symbols (names), and pairs (things built by cons), but can have implementation-defined behavior on numbers, characters, and strings.

```
(eq? #t #t)         ⇒  #t (true)
(eq? 'foo 'foo)     ⇒  #t
(eq? '(a b) '(a b)) ⇒  #f (false); created by separate cons-es
(let ((p '(a b)))
  (eq? p p))        ⇒  #t; created by the same cons
(eq? 2 2)           ⇒  unspecified
(eq? "foo" "foo")   ⇒  unspecified
```

In any particular implementation, numeric, character, and string tests will always work the same way; if (eq? 2 2) returns true, then (eq? 37 37) will return true also. Implementations are free to choose whichever behavior results in the fastest code.

The exact rules that govern the situations in which eqv? is guaranteed to return true or false are quite involved. Among other things, they specify that eqv? should behave as one might expect for numbers, characters, and nonempty strings, and that two objects will never test true for eqv? if there are any circumstances under which they would behave differently. (Conversely, however, eqv? is allowed to return false for certain objects—functions, for example—that would behave identically in all circumstances.) The eqv? predicate is "less discriminating" than eq?, in the sense that eqv? will never return `false` when eq? returns `true`.

For structures (lists), eqv? returns `false` if its arguments refer to different root cons cells. In many programs this is not the desired behavior. The equal? predicate recursively traverses two lists to see if their internal structure is the same and their leaves are eqv?. The equal? predicate may lead to an infinite loop if the programmer has used the imperative features of Scheme to create a circular list.

Deep assignments are relatively rare. They are used primarily in distributed computing, and in particular for parameter passing in remote procedure call (RPC) systems. These will be discussed in Section 12.4.4.

For user-defined abstractions, no single language-specified mechanism for equality testing or assignment is likely to produce the desired results in all cases. Languages with sophisticated data abstraction mechanisms usually allow the programmer to define the comparison and assignment operators for each new data type—or to specify that equality testing and/or assignment is not allowed.

7.11 Summary and Concluding Remarks

This section concludes the third of our five core chapters on language design (names, control flow, types, subroutines, and classes). In the first two sections we looked at the general issues of type systems and type checking. In the remaining sections we examined the most important composite types: records and variants, arrays and strings, sets, pointers and recursive types, lists, and files. We noted that types serve two principal purposes: they provide implicit context for many operations, freeing the programmer from the need to specify that context explicitly, and they allow the compiler to catch a wide variety of common programming errors. A *type system* consists of a set of built-in types, a mechanism to define new types, and rules for *type equivalence*, *type compatibility*, and *type inference*. Type equivalence determines when two names or values have the same type. Type compatibility determines when a value of one type may be used in a context that "expects" another type. Type inference determines the type of an expression based on the types of its components or (sometimes) the surrounding context. A language is said to be *strongly typed* if it never allows an operation to be applied to an object that does not support it; a language is said to be *statically typed* if it enforces strong typing at compile time.

In our general discussion of types we distinguished between the denotational, constructive, and abstraction-based points of view, which regard types, respectively, in terms of their values, their substructure, and the operations they support. We introduced terminology for the common built-in types and for enumerations, subranges, and the common type *constructors*. We discussed several different approaches to type equivalence, compatibility, and inference, including a detailed examination of the inference rules of ML. We also examined type *conversion*, *coercion*, and *nonconverting casts*. In the area of type equivalence, we contrasted the *structural* and *name*-based approaches, noting that while name equivalence appears to have gained in popularity, structural equivalence retains its advocates.

In our survey of composite types, we spent the most time on records, arrays, recursive types, and files. Key issues for records include the syntax and semantics of variant records, whole-record operations, type safety, and the interaction of each of these with memory layout. Memory layout is also important for arrays, in which it interacts with binding time for shape; static, stack, and heap-based allocation strategies; efficient array traversal in numeric applications; the interoperability of pointers and arrays in C; and the available set of whole-array and *slice*-based operations.

For recursive data types, much depends on the choice between the *value* and *reference models* of variables/names. Recursive types are a natural fall-out of the reference model; with the value model they require the notion of a *pointer*: a variable whose value is a reference. The distinction between values and references is important from an implementation point of view: it would be wasteful to implement built-in types as references, so languages with a reference model generally implement built-in and user-defined types differently. Java reflects this distinction in the language semantics, calling for a value model of built-in types and a reference model for objects of user-defined type classes.

Recursive types are generally used to create linked data structures. In most cases these structures must be allocated from a heap. In some languages, the programmer is responsible for deallocating heap objects that are no longer needed. In other languages, the language run-time system identifies and reclaims such *garbage* automatically. Explicit deallocation is a burden on the programmer, and leads to the problems of *memory leaks* and *dangling references*. The language implementation can't do much to help with memory leaks, but *tombstones* or *locks* and *keys* can be used to catch dangling references. Automatic garbage collection can be expensive, but has proven increasingly popular. Most garbage-collection techniques rely either on *reference counts* or on some form of recursive exploration of currently accessible structures. Techniques in this latter category include *mark-and-sweep*, *stop-and-copy*, and *generational* collection.

Few areas of language design display as much variation as I/O. Our discussion distinguished between *interactive I/O*, which tends to be very platform specific, and *file-based I/O*, which subdivides into *temporary files*, used for voluminous data within a single program run, and *persistent files*, used for off-line storage. Files also subdivide into those that represent their information in a binary form that mimics layout in memory and those that convert to and from character-based *text*. In comparison to binary files, text files generally incur both time and space overhead, but they have the important advantages of portability and human readability.

In our examination of types, we saw many examples of language innovations that have served to improve the clarity and maintainability of programs, often with little or no performance overhead. Examples include the original idea of user-defined types (Algol 68), enumeration and subrange types (Pascal), the integration of records and variants (Pascal), and the distinction between subtypes and derived types in Ada. In Chapter 10 we will examine what many consider the most important innovation of the past thirty years, namely object orientation.

In some cases, the distinctions between languages are less a matter of evolution than of fundamental differences in philosophy. We have already mentioned the choice between the value and reference models of variables/names. In a similar vein, most languages have adopted static typing, but Smalltalk and Lisp work well with dynamic types. Most statically typed languages have adopted name equivalence, but ML and Modula-3 work well with structural equivalence. Most languages have moved away from type coercions, but C++ embraces them: together with operator overloading, they make it possible to define terse, type-safe I/O routines outside the language proper.

As in the previous chapter, we saw several cases in which a language's convenience, orthogonality, or type safety appears to have been compromised in order to simplify the compiler, or to make compiled programs smaller or faster. Examples include the lack of an equality test for records in most languages, the requirement in Pascal and Ada that the variant portion of a record lie at the end, the limitations in many languages on the maximum size of sets, the lack of type checking for I/O in C, and the general lack of dynamic semantic checks in many language implementations. We also saw several examples of language features introduced at least in part for the sake of efficient implementation. These include `packed` types, multilength numeric types, `with` statements, decimal arithmetic, and C-style pointer arithmetic.

At the same time, one can identify a growing willingness on the part of language designers and users to tolerate complexity and cost in language implementation in order to improve semantics. Examples here include the type-safe variant records of Ada; the standard-length numeric types of Java; the variable-length strings and string operators of Icon, Perl, and Java; the late binding of array bounds in Ada; and the wealth of whole-array and slice-based array operations in Fortran 90. One might also include the polymorphic type inference of ML. Certainly one should include the trend toward automatic garbage collection. Once considered too expensive for production-quality imperative languages, garbage collection is now standard not only in such experimental languages as Clu and Cedar, but in Ada, Modula-3, and Java as well.

7.12 Review Questions

7.1 What purpose(s) do types serve in a programming language?

7.2 What is the difference between *type equivalence* and *type compatibility*?

7.3 What is *type inference*?

7.4 What does it mean for a language to be *strongly typed*? *Statically typed*? What prevents, say, C from being strongly typed?

7.5 Name two important programming languages that are strongly but dynamically typed.

7.6 What is a *type clash*?

7.7 Explain the distinction between *declarations* and *definitions*. Give three examples of a declaration that is not a definition.

7.8 Discuss the differences between the *denotational*, *constructive*, and *abstraction-based* views of types.

7.9 What is the difference between *discrete* and *scalar* types?

7.10 Give two examples of languages that lack a Boolean type. What do they use instead?

7.11 In what ways may an enumeration type be preferable to a collection of named constants? In what ways may a subrange type be preferable to its base type? It what ways may a string be preferable to an array of characters?

7.12 What does it mean for a set of language features (e.g., a type system) to be *orthogonal*?

7.13 Discuss the comparative advantages of *structural* and *name* equivalence for types. Name three languages that use each approach. Explain the difference between *strict* and *loose* name equivalence.

7.14 Explain the difference between *type conversion*, *type coercion*, and *nonconverting type casts*.

7.15* Explain how the type inference of ML leads naturally to polymorphism.

7.16* What is *unification*? What is its role in ML?

7.17* Explain the difference between *tuples* and *records* in ML. How does an ML record differ from a record (structure) in Algol-family languages?

7.18 Discuss the significance of "holes" in records. Why do they arise? What problems do they cause? What can be done to minimize these problems?

7.19 What is the purpose of a `with` statement in Pascal or Modula-3? Why doesn't C need such a construct?

7.20 Why is it useful to integrate variants (unions) with records (structs)? Why not leave them as separate mechanisms, as they are in Algol 68 and C?

7.21 Discuss the type safety problems that arise with variant records. How can these problems be addressed?

7.22 What is an array *slice*? For what purposes are slices useful?

7.23 Under what circumstances can an array declared within a subroutine be allocated in the stack? Under what circumstances must it be allocated in the heap?

7.24 Discuss the comparative advantages of *contiguous* and *row-pointer* layout for arrays.

7.25 Explain the difference between *row-major* and *column-major* layout for contiguously allocated arrays. Why does a programmer need to know which layout the compiler uses? Why do most language designers consider row-major layout to be better?

7.26 How much of the work of computing the address of an element of an array can be performed at compile time? How much must be performed at run time?

7.27 What is a *dope vector*? What purpose does it serve?

7.28 Name three languages that provide particularly extensive support for character strings.

7.29 What are the strengths and weaknesses of the bit-vector representation for sets?

7.30 Discuss the tradeoffs between pointers and the recursive types that arise naturally in a language with a reference model of variables.

7.31 Discuss the advantages and disadvantages of the interoperability of pointers and arrays in C.

7.32 What is the difference between a *pointer* and an *address*?

7.33 What are the advantages and disadvantages of allowing pointers to refer to objects that do not lie in the heap?

7.34 What are *dangling references*? How are they created, and why are they a problem? Discuss the comparative advantages of *tombstones* and *locks and keys* as a means of solving the problem.

7.35 What is *garbage*? How is it created, and why is it a problem? Discuss the comparative advantages of *reference counts* and *mark-and-sweep collection* as a means of solving the problem.

7.36 Do dangling references and garbage ever arise in the same programming language? Why or why not?

7.37 Why was automatic garbage collection so slow to be adopted by imperative programming languages?

7.38 Why are lists so heavily used in functional programming languages?

7.39* What are the advantages and disadvantages of building I/O into a programming language, as opposed to providing it through library routines?

7.40* What are the comparative advantages of *text* and *binary* files?

7.41* Summarize the different approaches to text I/O adopted by Fortran, Ada, C, and C++.

7.13 Exercises

7.1 Most modern Algol-family languages use some form of name equivalence for types. Is structural equivalence a bad idea? Why or why not?

7.2 Consider the following declarations:

```
1.  type cell          -- a forward declaration
2.  type cell_ptr = pointer to cell
3.  x : cell
```

4. type cell = record
5.   val : integer
6.   next : cell_ptr
7. y : cell

Should the declaration at line 4 be said to introduce an alias type? Under strict name equivalence, should x and y have the same type? Explain.

7.3   Suppose you are implementing an Ada compiler, and must support arithmetic on 32-bit fixed-point binary numbers with a programmer-specified number of fractional bits. Describe the code you would need to generate to add, subtract, multiply, or divide two fixed-point numbers. You should assume that the hardware provides arithmetic instructions only for integers and IEEE floating point. You may assume that the integer instructions preserve full precision; in particular, integer multiplication produces a 64-bit result. Your description should be general enough to deal with operands and results that have different numbers of fractional bits.

7.4   When Sun Microsystems ported Berkeley Unix from the Digital VAX to the Motorola 680x0, many C programs stopped working, and had to be repaired. In effect, the 680x0 revealed certain classes of program bugs that one could "get away with" on the VAX. One of these classes of bugs occurred in programs that use more than one size of integer (e.g., `short` and `long`), and arose from the fact that the VAX is a little-endian machine, while the 680x0 is big-endian (Section 5.3). Another class of bugs occurred in programs that manipulate both null and empty strings. It arose from the fact that location zero in a process's address space on the VAX always contained a zero, while the same location on the 680x0 is not in the address space, and will generate a bus error if used. For both of these classes of bugs, give examples of program fragments that would work on a VAX but not on a 680x0.

7.5   Ada provides two "remainder" operators, `rem` and `mod` for integer types, defined as follows [Ame83, Sec. 4.5.5]:

> Integer division and remainder are defined by the relation A = (A/B)*B + (A rem B), where (A rem B) has the sign of A and an absolute value less than the absolute value of B. Integer division satisfies the identity (-A)/B = -(A/B) = A/(-B).

> The result of the modulus operation is such that (A mod B) has the sign of B and an absolute value less than the absolute value of B; in addition, for some integer value N, this result must satisfy the relation A = B*N + (A mod B).

Give values of A and B for which A `rem` B and A `mod` B differ. For what purposes would one operation be more useful than the other? Does it make sense to provide both, or is it overkill?

Consider also the % operator of C and the `mod` operator of Pascal. The designers of these languages could have picked semantics resembling those of either Ada's `rem` or its `mod`. Which did they pick? Do you think they made the right choice?

7.6 Some language definitions specify a particular representation for data types in memory, while others specify only the semantic behavior of those types. For languages in the latter class, some implementations guarantee a particular representation, while others reserve the right to choose different representations in different circumstances. Which approach do you prefer? Why?

7.7 Consider the problem of performing range checks on set expressions in Pascal. Given that a set may contain many elements, some of which may be known at compile time, describe the information that a compiler might maintain in order to track both the elements known to belong to the set and the possible range of unknown elements. Then explain how to update this information for the following set operations: union, intersection, and difference. The goal is to determine (1) when subrange checks can be eliminated at run time and (2) when subrange errors can be reported at compile time. Bear in mind that the compiler *cannot* do a perfect job: some unnecessary run-time checks will inevitably be performed, and some operations that must always result in errors will not be caught at compile time. The goal is to do as good a job as possible at reasonable cost.

7.8 Show how variant records can be used in Pascal to interpret the bits of a value of one type as if they represented a value of some other type. Explain why the same technique does not work in Ada. If you have access to an Ada manual, learn how an `unchecked` pragma can be used to get around the Ada rules.

7.9 Are variant records a form of polymorphism? Why or why not?

7.10 Pascal does not permit the tag field of a variant record to be passed to a subroutine by reference (i.e., as a `var` parameter). Why not?

7.11 Explain how to implement dynamic semantic checks to catch references to uninitialized fields of a tagged variant record in Pascal. Changing the value of the tag field should cause all fields of the variant part of the record to become uninitialized. Suppose you want to avoid adding flag fields within the record itself (e.g., to avoid changing the offsets of fields in a systems program). How much harder is your task?

7.12 Explain how to implement dynamic semantic checks to catch references to uninitialized fields of an *untagged* variant record in Pascal. Any assignment to a field of a variant should cause all fields of other variants to become uninitialized. Any assignment that changes the record from one variant to another should also cause all other fields of the new variant to be uninitialized. Again, suppose you want to avoid adding flag fields within the untagged record itself. How much harder is your task?

7.13 We noted in Section 7.3.4 that Pascal and Ada require the variant portions of a record to occur at the end, to save space when a particular record is constrained to have a comparatively small variant part. Could a compiler rearrange fields to achieve the same effect, without the restriction on the declaration order of fields? Why or why not?

7.14* How would you implement the final version of our `element` type in ML? How would you extract the fields of the variant part? Specifically, suppose you have declared a record to represent copper; how would you specify the equivalent of `copper.source`?

7.15 In Section 7.4 we discussed how to differentiate between the constant and variable portions of an array reference, in order to efficiently access the subparts of array and record objects. An alternative approach is to generate naive code and count on the compiler's code improver to find the constant portions, group them together, and calculate them at compile time. Discuss the advantages and disadvantages of each approach.

7.16 Explain how to extend Figure 7.8 to accommodate subroutine arguments that are passed by value, but whose shape is not known until the subroutine is called at run time.

7.17 Explain how to obtain the effect of Fortran 90's `allocate` statement for one-dimensional arrays using pointers in C. You will probably find that your solution does not generalize to multidimensional arrays. Why not? If you are familiar with C++, show how to use its `class` facilities to solve the problem.

7.18 Consider the following Pascal variable declarations:

```
var A : array [1..10, 10..100] of real;
    i : integer;
    x : real;
```

Assume that a real number occupies eight bytes and that `A`, `i`, and `x` are global variables. In something resembling assembly language for a RISC machine, show the code that a reasonable compiler would generate for the following assignment: `x := A[3,i]`. Explain how you arrived at your answer.

7.19 In the examples of Section 7.4.3, show the code that would be required to access `A[i, j, k]` if subscript bounds checking were required.

7.20 Write a library package that might be used by a language implementation to manage sets of elements drawn from a very large base type (e.g., `integer`). You should support membership tests, union, intersection, and difference. Does your package allocate memory from the heap? If so, what would a compiler that assumed the use of your package need to do to make sure that space was reclaimed when no longer needed?

7.21 Pointers and recursive type definitions complicate the algorithm for determining structural equivalence of types. Consider, for example, the following definitions:

```
type A = record
        x : pointer to B
        y : real
type B = record
        x : pointer to A
        y : real
```

The simple definition of structural equivalence given in Section 7.2.1 (expand the subparts recursively until all you have is a string of built-in types and type constructors; then compare them) does not work: we get an infinite expansion (type A = record x : pointer to record x : pointer to record x : pointer to record ...). The obvious reinterpretation is to say two types A and B are equivalent if any sequence of field selections, array subscripts, pointer dereferences, and other operations that takes one down into the structure of A, and that ends at a built-in type, always ends at the same built-in type when used to dive into the structure of B. Under this reinterpretation, A and B above have the same type. Give an algorithm based on this reinterpretation that could be used in a compiler to determine structural equivalence. (Hint: the fastest approach is due to J. Kral [Kr73]. It is based on the algorithm used to find the smallest deterministic finite automaton that accepts a given regular language. This algorithm can be found in any automata theory textbook (e.g., [HU79]).)

7.22 In Ada 83, as in Pascal, pointers (`access` variables) can point only to objects in the heap. Ada 95 allows a new kind of pointer, the `access all` type, to point to other objects as well, provided that those objects have been declared to be `aliased`:

```
type int_ptr is access all Integer;
foo : aliased Integer;
ip : int_ptr;
...
ip := foo'Access;
```

The 'Access attribute is roughly equivalent to C's "address of" (&) operator. How would you implement `access all` types and `aliased` objects? How would your implementation interact with garbage collection, which Ada provides for objects in the heap?

7.23 As noted in Section 7.7.2, Ada 95 forbids an `access all` pointer from referring to any object whose lifetime is briefer than that of the pointer's type. Can this rule be enforced completely at compile time? Why or why not?

7.24 In the discussion of pointers in Section 7.7, we assumed implicitly that every pointer into the heap points to the *beginning* of a dynamically allocated block of storage. In some languages, including Algol 68 and C, pointers may also point to data *inside* a block in the heap. If you were trying to implement dynamic semantic checks for dangling references or, alternatively, automatic garbage collection, how would your task be complicated by the existence of such "internal pointers"?

7.25 Here is a skeleton for the standard quicksort algorithm in Haskell:

```
quicksort [] = []
quicksort (a : l) = quicksort [...] ++ [a] ++ quicksort [...]
```

The ++ operator denotes list concatenation (similar to @ in ML). The : operator is equivalent to ML's : : or Lisp's `cons`. Show how to express the two elided expressions as list comprehensions.

7.26 If you have access to a compiler that provides optional dynamic semantic checks for out-of-bounds array subscripts, use of an inappropriate record variant, and/or dangling or uninitialized pointers, experiment with the cost of these checks. How much do they add to the execution time of programs that make a significant number of checked accesses? Experiment with different levels of optimization (code improvement) to see what effect it has on the overhead of checks.

7.27* Find a Cobol manual and learn about the language's facilities for text I/O. Prepare a written comparison of those facilities to those of the languages described in Section 7.9.3.

7.28* The `readln` and `writeln` procedures of Pascal give special treatment to ends of lines. By contrast, C's `printf` and `scanf` do not; they treat newlines and carriage returns like any other character. What are the comparative advantages of these approaches? Which do you prefer? Why?

7.14 Bibliographic Notes

References to general information on the various programming languages mentioned in this chapter can be found in Appendix A, and in the bibliographic notes for Chapters 1 and 6. Welsh, Sneeringer, and Hoare [WSH77] provide a critique of the original Pascal definition, with a particular emphasis on its type system. Tanenbaum's comparison of Pascal and Algol 68 also focuses largely on types [Tan78]. Cleaveland [Cle86] provides a book-length study of many of the issues in this chapter.

What we have referred to as the denotational model of types originates with Hoare [DDH72]. Denotational formulations of the overall semantics of programming languages are discussed in the bibliographic notes for Chapter 4. A related but distinct body of work uses algebraic techniques to formalize data abstraction; key references include Guttag [Gut77] and Goguen et al. [GTW78].

Mairson [Mai90] proves that the cost of unifying types in ML is $O(2^n)$, where n is the length of the program. Fortunately, the cost is linear in the size of the program's type expressions, so the worst case arises only in programs whose semantics are too complex for a human being to understand anyway. Conway's game of

Life, which appeared in Figure 7.9, was first described by Martin Gardner in his "Mathematical Games" column in *Scientific American* [Gar70]. Hoare [Hoa75] discusses the definition of recursive types under a reference model of variables. Cardelli and Wegner survey issues related to polymorphism, overloading, and abstraction [CW85].

Tombstones are due to Lomet [Lom75, Lom85]. Locks and keys are due to Fischer and LeBlanc [FL80]. The latter also discuss how to check for various other dynamic semantic errors in Pascal, including those that arise with variant records. Constant-space (nonrecursive) mark-and-sweep garbage collection is due to Schorr and Waite [SW67]. Stop-and-copy collection was developed by Fenichel and Yochelson [FY69], based on ideas due to Minsky. Deutsch and Bobrow [DB76] describe an *incremental* garbage collector that avoids the "stop-the-world" phenomenon. Wilson and Johnstone [WJ93] describe a more recent incremental collector. The conservative collector described at the end of Section 7.7.3 is due to Boehm and Weiser [BW88]. Cohen [Coh81] surveys garbage-collection techniques as of 1981; Wilson [Wil9x] provides a more recent view.

Subroutines and Control Abstraction

In the introduction to Chapter 3, we defined *abstraction* as a process by which the programmer can associate a name with a potentially complicated program fragment, which can then be thought of in terms of its purpose or function, rather than in terms of its implementation. We sometimes distinguish between *control abstraction*, in which the principal purpose of the abstraction is to perform a well-defined operation, and *data abstraction*, in which the principal purpose of the abstraction is to represent information.[1] We will consider data abstraction in more detail in Chapter 10.

Subroutines are the principal mechanism for control abstraction in most programming languages. A subroutine performs its operation on behalf of a *caller*, who waits for the subroutine to finish before continuing execution. Most subroutines are parameterized: the caller passes arguments that influence the subroutine's behavior, or provide it with data on which to operate. Arguments are also called *actual parameters*. They are mapped to the subroutine's *formal parameters* at the time a call occurs. A subroutine that returns a value is usually called a *function*. A subroutine that does not return a value is usually called a *procedure*. Most languages require subroutines to be declared before they are used, though a few (including Fortran, C, and Lisp) do not. Declarations allow the compiler to verify that every call to a subroutine is consistent with the declaration; e.g., that it passes the right number and types of arguments.

As noted in Section 3.2.1, the storage consumed by parameters and local variables can in most languages be allocated on a stack. We therefore begin this chapter, in Section 8.1, by reviewing the layout of the stack. We then turn in Section 8.2 to the *calling sequences* that serve to maintain this layout. In the process, we revisit the use of static chains to access nonlocal variables in nested subroutines, and consider an alternative mechanism, known as a *display*, that serves a

---

[1] The distinction between control and data abstraction is somewhat fuzzy, because the latter usually encapsulates not only information, but also the operations that access and modify that information. Put another way, most data abstractions include control abstraction.

similar purpose. We also consider subroutine inlining and the representation of closures. To illustrate some of the possible implementation alternatives, we present a pair of case studies: the GNU `gcc` C compiler for the MIPS instruction set, and the Metrowerks CodeWarrior Pascal compiler for the Motorola 680x0 instruction set.

In Section 8.3 we look more closely at subroutine parameters. We consider parameter-passing *modes*, which determine the operations that a subroutine can apply to its formal parameters and the effects of those operations on the corresponding actual parameters. We also consider conformant arrays, named and default parameters, variable numbers of arguments, and function return mechanisms. Then, in Section 8.5, we consider the handling of exceptional conditions. While exceptions can sometimes be confined to the current subroutine, in the general case they require a mechanism to "pop out of" a nested context without returning, so that recovery can occur in the calling context. After a shorter section on generic subroutines and modules, we turn in Section 8.6 to control abstractions other than subroutines. In particular, we examine the subject of *coroutines*, which allow a program to maintain two or more execution contexts, and to switch back and forth among them. Coroutines can be used to implement iterators (Section 6.5.3), but they have other uses as well, particularly in simulation and in server programs. In Chapter 12 we will use them as the basis for concurrent ("quasiparallel") threads.

8.1 Review of Stack Layout

In Section 3.2.1 we discussed the allocation of space on a subroutine call stack (Figure 3.2, page 112). Each routine, as it is called, is given a new *stack frame*, or *activation record*, at the top of the stack. This frame may contain arguments and/or return values, bookkeeping information (including the return address and saved registers), local variables, and/or temporaries. When a subroutine returns, its frame is popped from the stack.

At any given time, the *stack pointer* register contains the address of the first unused location at the top of the stack. The *frame pointer* register contains an address within the frame. Objects in the frame are accessed via displacement addressing with respect to the frame pointer. If the size of an object (e.g., a local array) is not known at compile time, then the object is placed in a variable-size area at the top of the frame; its address and dope vector are stored in the fixed-size portion of the frame, at a statically known offset from the frame pointer (Figure 7.8, page 370). If there are no variable-size objects, then every object within the frame has a statically known offset from the stack pointer, and the implementation may dispense with the frame pointer, freeing up a register for other use. If the size of an argument is not known at compile time, then the argument may be placed in a variable-size portion of the frame *below* the other arguments, with its address and dope vector at known offsets from the frame

Figure 8.1 Example of subroutine nesting, taken from Figure 3.5.

pointer. Alternatively, the caller may simply pass a temporary address and dope vector, counting on the called routine to copy the argument into the variable-size area at the top of the frame.

In a language with nested subroutines and static scoping (e.g., Pascal, Modula, or Ada), objects that lie in surrounding subroutines, and that are thus neither local nor global can be found by maintaining a *static chain* (Figure 3.5, page 120). Each stack frame contains a reference to the frame of the lexically surrounding subroutine. This reference is called the *static link*. By analogy, the saved value of the frame pointer, which will be restored on subroutine return, is called the *dynamic link*. The dynamic link is a reference to the frame of the caller. The static and dynamic links may or may not be the same, depending on whether the current routine was called by its lexically surrounding routine, or by some other routine nested in that surrounding routine.

Whether or not a subroutine is called directly by the lexically surrounding routine, we can be sure that the surrounding routine is active; there is no other way that the current routine could have been visible, allowing it to be called. Consider for example, the subroutine nesting shown in Figure 8.1. If subroutine D is called directly from B, then clearly B's frame will already be on the stack. How else can D be called? It is not visible in A or E, because it is nested inside of B. A moment's thought makes clear that it is only when control enters B (placing B's frame on the stack) that D comes into view. It can therefore be called by C, or by any other routine (not shown) that is nested inside of C or D, but only because these are also within B.

One disadvantage of static chains is that access to an object in a scope k levels out requires that the static chain be dereferenced k times. If a local object can be loaded into a register with a single (displacement mode) memory access, an object k levels out will require $k + 1$ memory accesses. This number can be reduced to a constant by use of a *display* (see Figure 8.2). A display is simply an embedding of the static chain into an array. The jth element of the display contains a reference to the frame of the most recently active subroutine at lexical nesting level j. The first element of the display is thus a reference to the frame of some subroutine S nested directly inside the main program; the second element

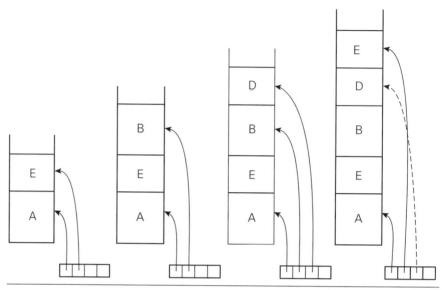

Figure 8.2 Nonlocal access using a display. The stack configurations, from left to right, show the contents of the display for a sequence of subroutine calls, assuming the lexical nesting of Figure 8.1. Display elements above that of the currently executing subroutine are not used.

is a reference to the frame of a routine that is nested inside of S, and so forth, until we reach the currently active routine. If the currently active routine is nested i levels deep, then an object k levels out can be found at a statically known offset from the address stored in element $j = i - k$ of the display.

If the display is stored in memory, then a nonlocal object can be loaded into a register with two memory accesses: one to load the display element into a register, the second to load the object. On a machine with a large number of registers, one might be tempted to reduce the overhead to only one memory access by keeping the entire display in registers, but that would probably be a bad idea: display elements tend to be accessed much less frequently than other things (e.g., local variables) that might be kept in the registers instead. In fact, while displays were popular in the CISC compilers of the 1970s and 1980s, it is no longer clear that they are worth maintaining at all, even in memory.

Most programs don't nest subroutines more than two or three levels deep, so static chains are seldom very long, and variables in surrounding scopes tend not to be accessed very often. If they *are* accessed often, common subexpression optimizations (to be discussed in Chapter 13) are likely to ensure that a pointer to the appropriate frame remains in a register. As shown in the following section, the cost of maintaining a display in the subroutine calling sequence tends to be slightly higher than that of maintaining a static chain, further weakening the argument for displays. Finally, static chains facilitate the creation of closures (Section 3.4). A subroutine that is passed as a parameter, stored in a variable, or returned from a function can be represented as a code address and a static link. If the language implementation uses a display, the straightforward approach is to store the entire display in the closure, and to swap it in and out of the real display whenever the routine in the closure is called. More space-conserving alternatives are possible (see Exercise 8.6), but with higher run-time overhead.

Because the display is a fixed-size array, compilers that use a display to implement access to nonlocal objects generally impose a limit (the size of the display) on the maximum depth to which subroutines may be nested. If this limit is larger than, say, five or six, it is unlikely that any programmer will ever wish for more. Note that the display does not obviate the need for a frame pointer. Because local variables are accessed so often, it is important to have the address of the current frame in a register, where it can be used for displacement-mode addressing. Similarly, on a RISC processor, in which a 32-bit address will not fit in one instruction, it is important to maintain a base register for the most commonly accessed global variables as well.

One final note: some language designers would argue that the development of object-oriented programming (the subject of Chapter 10) has eliminated the need for nested subroutines. Others would even argue that the success of C has shown such routines to be unneeded. Without nested subroutines, of course, the choice between static chains and displays is moot.

8.2 Calling Sequences

In Section 3.2.1 we also mentioned that maintenance of the subroutine call stack is the responsibility of the *calling sequence*—the code executed by the caller immediately before and after a subroutine call—and of the *prologue* (code executed at the beginning) and *epilogue* (code executed at the end) of the subroutine itself. Sometimes the term "calling sequence" is used to refer to the combined operations of the caller, the prologue, and the epilogue.

Tasks that must be accomplished on the way into a subroutine include passing parameters, saving the return address, changing the program counter, changing the stack pointer to allocate space, saving registers (including the frame pointer) that contain important values and that may be overwritten by the callee, changing the frame pointer to refer to the new frame, and executing initialization code for any objects in the new frame that require it. Tasks that must be accomplished on the way out include passing return parameters or function values, executing finalization code for any local objects that require it, deallocating the stack frame (restoring the stack pointer), restoring other saved registers (including the frame pointer), and restoring the program counter. Some of these tasks (e.g., passing parameters) must be performed by the caller, because they differ from call to call. Most of the tasks, however, can be performed either by the caller or the callee. In general, we will save space if the callee does as much work as possible: tasks performed in the callee appear only once in the target program, but tasks performed in the caller appear at every call site, and the typical subroutine is called in more than one place.

Perhaps the trickiest division-of-labor issue pertains to saving registers. As we noted in Section 5.6.2, the ideal approach is to save precisely those registers that are both in use in the caller and needed for other purposes in the callee. Because of separate compilation, however, it is difficult (though not impossible) to determine this intersecting set. A simpler solution is for the caller to save all registers that are in use, or for the callee to save all registers that it will overwrite.

Calling sequence conventions for the MIPS processor, described in the first case study below, strike something of a compromise: registers not reserved for special purposes are divided into two sets of approximately equal size. One set is the caller's responsibility, the other is the callee's responsibility. A callee can assume that there is nothing of value in any of the registers in the caller-saves set; a caller can assume that no callee will destroy the contents of any registers in the callee-saves set. In the interests of code size, the compiler uses the callee-saves registers for local variables and other long-lived values. It uses the caller-saves set for transient values, which are less likely to be needed across calls. The result of these conventions is that the caller-saves registers are seldom saved by either party: the callee knows that they are the caller's responsibility, and the caller knows that they don't contain anything important.

At least part of the work required to maintain the static chain or display must be performed by the caller, rather than the callee, because this work depends on the lexical nesting depth of the caller. Consider first the maintenance of static chains. The standard approach is for the caller to compute the callee's static link and to pass it as an extra, hidden parameter. Two subcases arise:

1. The callee is nested (directly) inside the caller. In this case, the callee's static link should refer to the caller's frame. The caller therefore passes its own frame pointer as the callee's static link.

2. The callee is $k \geq 0$ scopes "outward"—closer to the outer level of lexical nesting. In this case, all scopes that surround the callee also surround the caller (otherwise the callee would not be visible). The caller dereferences its own static link k times and passes the result as the callee's static link.

Displays are slightly more complicated, but not much. Perhaps the most obvious approach would be to maintain the static chain as usual, and simply fill the display at procedure entry and exit, by walking down the chain. In most cases, however, the following (much faster) scheme suffices: when calling a subroutine at lexical nesting level j, the callee saves the current value of the jth display element into the stack, and then replaces that element with a copy of its own (newly created) frame pointer. (Because the callee does all the work, displays may save a little bit on code size, compared to static chains.) Why does this mechanism work? Again, there are two cases:

1. The callee is nested (directly) inside the caller. In this case the caller and the callee share all display elements up to the current level. Putting the callee's frame pointer into the display simply extends the current level by one. It is conceivable that the old value needn't be saved, but in general there is no way to tell. The caller itself might have been called by code that is very deeply nested, and that is counting on the integrity of a very deep display, in which case the old display element *will* be needed. A smart compiler may be able to avoid the save in certain circumstances.

2. The callee is at lexical nesting level j, $k \geq 0$ levels out from the caller. In this case the caller and callee share all display elements up through $j - 1$. The caller's entry at level j is different from the callee's, so the callee must save it before storing its own frame pointer. If the callee in turn calls a routine at level $j + 1$, that routine will change another element of the display, but all old elements will be restored before they are needed again.

If the callee is a *leaf routine*—a subroutine that does not call any other routines[2]—then the display can be left intact; no one will use it before control returns to the caller. If the callee is called through a closure, then the bookkeeping scheme breaks down. A standard technique is to create two "entry points"— starting addresses—for every subroutine. One of these is for "normal" calls, the other for calls through closures. When a closure is created, it contains the address of the alternative entry point. The code at that entry point saves elements 1 through j of the display into the stack (it will have to create a larger-than-normal stack frame in order to do this), and then replaces those elements with values taken from (or calculated from) the closure. The alternative entry then makes a nested call to the main body of the subroutine (it skips the code immediately following the normal entry—the code that creates the normal stack frame and updates the display.) When the subroutine returns, it comes back to the code of the alternative entry, which restores the old value of the display before returning to the actual caller.

In general, maintaining a display is slightly more expensive than maintaining a static chain, though the comparison is not absolute. In the usual case, passing a static link to a called routine requires $k \geq 0$ load instructions in the caller, followed by one store instruction in the callee (to place the static link at the appropriate offset in the stack frame). The store may be skipped in leaf routines, assuming that a register is available to hold the link as long as it is needed. No overhead is required to maintain the static chain when returning from a subroutine. With a display, a nonleaf callee requires two loads and two stores (one each in the prologue and the epilogue) to save and restore display elements.

---

2 A leaf routine is so named because it is a leaf of the subroutine call graph, a data structure mentioned in Exercise 3.10.

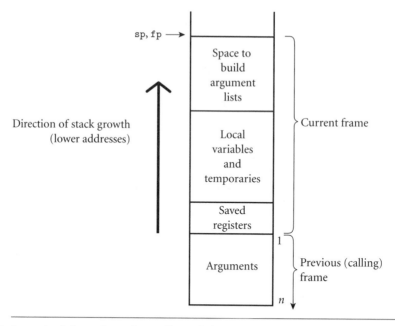

Figure 8.3 **Layout of the subroutine call stack for the GNU MIPS C compiler.**

8.2.1 Case Study: C on the MIPS

Our first case study examines a simple calling sequence (that of C) on a simple machine (the MIPS). An overview of the MIPS can be found in Section 5.5.1. As noted in that section, register r31 (also known as ra) is special-cased by the hardware to receive the return address in jump-and-link (jal) instructions. In addition, register r29 (also known as sp) is reserved by convention for use as the stack pointer, and register r30 (also known as fp) is reserved by convention for the frame pointer, if any. Since the size of every object in the stack is known at compile time in C, a separate frame pointer is not strictly needed, and SGI's C compiler for the MIPS makes do without: it uses displacement-mode offsets from the sp for everything in the current stack frame. The GNU gcc compiler, described here, does use a frame pointer, partly for the sake of uniformity with other architectures and languages (gcc is highly portable), and partly to give it the option of changing the sp during subroutine execution, if desired (see below).[3]

A typical gcc stack frame for the MIPS appears in Figure 8.3. Arguments and locals of the current subroutine are accessed via offsets from the fp. Arguments

---

3 The conventions described here apply to version 2.7.2 of gcc. They have changed in several ways from earlier versions of the compiler, and may well change again.

in the process of being passed to the next routine are assembled at the top of the frame, and are accessed via offsets from the sp. The first four scalar arguments are passed in registers r4–r7 or f12–f15 (depending on type); large or additional arguments are passed on the stack. Space is reserved in the stack for *all* arguments, whether passed in registers or not. In effect, each subroutine begins with some of its arguments already loaded into registers, and with "stale" values in memory. This is a normal state of affairs; optimizing compilers keep values in registers whenever possible. They "spill" values to memory when they run out of registers, or when there is a chance that the value in memory may be accessed directly (e.g., through a pointer, a reference parameter, or the actions of a nested subroutine). The argument build area at the top of the frame is designed to be large enough to hold the largest argument list that may be passed to any called routine. As a result, arguments do not need to be "pushed" in the usual sense of the word: the sp does not change when they are placed into the stack. The relative stability of the sp is in contrast to the typical situation in CISC compilers, as we will see in the second case study below.

In most cases, as shown in Figure 8.3, the sp and fp are the same; they both point to the first unused word on the stack. The exception occurs in programs that use the standard alloca library package to allocate temporary space in the current stack frame, explicitly. Alloca increases the sp (i.e., moves it toward smaller addresses) enough to accommodate the requested space, to which it returns a pointer. Unlike space in the heap, space returned by alloca need not be explicitly freed; it goes away when the current subroutine returns. A frame with dynamically allocated space appears in Figure 8.4.

For languages with nested subroutines (C of course is not among them), MIPS compilers generally use register r2 to pass the static link to a called routine. In all languages, registers r2 and f0 (depending on type) are used to return scalar values from functions. If a return value is a struct, gcc passes a hidden first argument (in r4) whose value is the address into which the return value should be placed. If the return value is to be assigned into a variable (e.g., x = foo ();), the caller can simply pass the address of the variable. If the value is to be passed in turn to another subroutine, the caller can pass the appropriate address within its own argument build area. (Writing the return value into this space will probably destroy the returning function's own arguments, but that's fine: at this point they are no longer needed.) Finally, though one doesn't see this idiom often (and most languages don't support it), C allows the caller to extract a field directly from the return value of a function (e.g., x = foo ().a + y;); in this case the caller must pass the address of a temporary location within the "local variables and temporaries" part of its stack frame.

The calling sequence to maintain the gcc stack is as follows. The caller

1. saves (into the "local variables and temporaries" part of its frame) any caller-saves registers whose values are still needed

2. puts up to four scalar arguments into registers

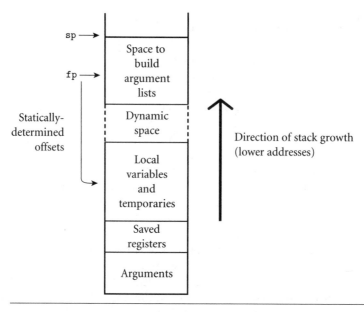

Figure 8.4 A gcc **stack frame on the MIPS with temporary space allocated by** alloca. The difference between the sp and the fp is precisely the size of the dynamic space. Offsets from the fp to local variables and arguments are the same as in Figure 8.3.

3. puts the remaining arguments into the argument build area at the top of the current frame

4. performs a jal instruction, which puts the return address in register ra and jumps to the target address

The caller-saves registers consist of r2–r15, r24, r25, and f0–f19. In a language with nested subroutines, the caller would place the static link into register r2 immediately before performing the jal.

In its prologue, the callee

1. subtracts the frame size (the distance between the first argument and the sp in Figure 8.3) from the sp

2. saves any necessary registers into the beginning of the newly allocated frame, using the sp as the base for displacement-mode addressing

3. copies the sp into the fp

Saved registers include (1) the fp; (2) the ra, if the routine is not a leaf; and (3) any callee-saves temporary registers (r16–r23 and f20–f31) whose values may be changed before returning.

In its epilogue, immediately before returning, the callee

1. places the function return value (if any) into r2, f0, or memory as appropriate

2. copies the `fp` into the `sp`, to deallocate any dynamically allocated space

3. restores saved registers, including the `ra` if necessary, using the `sp` as the base for displacement-mode addressing

4. adds the frame size to the `sp`, to deallocate the frame

5. performs a `j ra` instruction

Finally, if appropriate, the caller moves the return value to wherever it is needed. Caller-saves registers are restored lazily over time, as their values are needed.

Many parts of the calling sequence, prologue, and epilogue can be omitted in common cases, particularly for leaf routines. The simplest leaf routines (e.g., those that compute the standard mathematical functions) don't use the stack at all: they take their arguments in registers, compute entirely in registers, call no other routines, and return their results in registers. Because they do not touch memory (except for instructions, of course), they can be extremely fast, particularly if the processor is good at branch prediction (Section 5.6.1).

To support the use of symbolic debuggers such as `gdb` and `dbx`, compilers generate a variety of assembler pseudo-ops that place information into the object file symbol table. For each subroutine, this information includes the starting and ending addresses of the routine, the size of the stack frame, an indication as to which register (usually `sp` or `fp`) is the base for local objects, an indication as to which register (usually `ra`, if any) holds the return address, and a list of which registers were saved.

8.2.2 Case Study: Pascal on the 680x0

To illustrate the differences between CISC and RISC machines, our second case study considers the Motorola 680x0 (an overview of the processor appears in Section 5.5.1). To illustrate the handling of nested subroutines and closures, we consider a Pascal compiler, namely the Metrowerks CodeWarrior Pascal compiler for the Apple Macintosh.[4] The calling conventions for CISC compilers tend to differ from those of RISC compilers in several important ways. CISC compilers usually

- pass all arguments on the stack, rather than in registers.
- push and pop their arguments, updating the `sp` dynamically, rather than assembling them in a preallocated area.
- dedicate a register to the frame pointer. On the 680x0, the `fp` is register `a6`, by convention.
- rely on relatively complicated special instructions.

---

4 The description here applies to CodeWarrior version 9. Other versions may be different.

The use of the stack to pass arguments reflects the technology of the 1970s, when register sets were significantly smaller and memory access was significantly faster (in comparison to processor speed) than is the case today. To push and pop arguments, CISC machines employ auto-increment and auto-decrement addressing modes, which update the sp as a side effect. Frequent changes in the sp make it difficult (though not impossible) to use it as the base for access to local variables; hence the reliance on a separate fp.

The special instructions for subroutine calls vary significantly from one CISC machine to another. The ones on the 680x0 are relatively simple. The jsr instruction pushes the return address onto the stack, updating the sp. The rts instruction pops the return address off the stack, again updating the sp. The link instruction pushes the fp onto the stack, copies the (updated) sp into the fp, and then allocates space for a stack frame by subtracting a given constant from the sp, all in one instruction. (The fp is not special-cased in hardware; the link instruction takes the name of the register to save and update as an argument.) The unlk instruction reverses the effect of link by copying the fp into the sp and then popping the fp off the stack. In the normal calling sequence (see below), the jsr instruction occurs in the caller, link occurs in the callee's prologue, and unlk and rts occur in the callee's epilogue.

Special instructions allow subroutine calling sequences to be shorter than they would be otherwise, saving on code space. On a microprogrammed machine, they also tend to make calling sequences faster. Even ignoring the overall RISC/CISC argument, however, there is a hazard in building too much generality into the standard subroutine call instructions. On the Digital VAX, for example, the enormously complex calls ("call with arguments in stack") and ret instructions perform many operations that are not needed in the common case. Longer instruction sequences that do less work are actually faster on most VAXen.

Figure 8.5 shows a stack frame for the 680x0. The sp points to the last used location on the stack (not the first unused location, as it did in our MIPS case study). Also in contrast to the MIPS, the arguments are pushed from left to right, so the last one is closest to the fp. There are more "fields" within the frame in this case study, because the compiler passes everything on the stack.

Objects within the area marked "local variables, temporaries, and large copied arguments" in Figure 8.5 are arranged by the compiler in essentially arbitrary order. The handling of arguments and return values depends on their size. Any argument that is four bytes or smaller in size (e.g., a reference or a scalar) is passed directly on the stack, and is aligned at a two-byte boundary. Larger arguments are passed by pushing an address. This address may be either that of some named object (e.g., a local variable of the caller), or that of a temporary location within the caller's frame. The callee then copies from the addressed location into the main body of the new frame. In a similar vein, the caller pushes space to contain a return value of four or fewer bytes; for larger return values, it pushes the address of a temporary location within the main body of its frame.

The calling sequence to maintain the stack is as follows. The caller

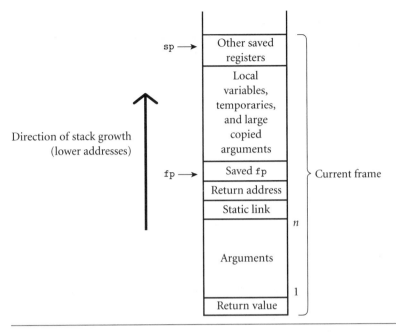

Figure 8.5 Layout of the subroutine call stack for the Metrowerks 680x0 Pascal compiler. The return address and saved `fp` are present in all frames. All other parts of the frame are optional; they are present only if required by the current subroutine.

1. creates space for a small return value, or pushes the address of a large one

2. pushes arguments (or their addresses), left-to-right

3. pushes the static link

4. executes a `jsr` instruction

The first of these steps is skipped if the subroutine is not a function. The second step is skipped if the subroutine has no parameters. The third step is skipped if the subroutine is declared at the outer level of lexical nesting. The `jsr` pushes the return address and jumps to the subroutine.

In its prologue, the callee

1. executes a `link` instruction

2. pushes any registers that need to be saved onto the stack

3. copies any large arguments into the main body of the frame

The `link` instruction decrements the `sp` by enough to accommodate all local variables, large arguments copied from the caller, and temporaries (including large arguments to be passed to further routines). Registers a0, a1, d0, d1, and d2 are never saved; their values are not preserved across subroutine calls (they correspond to the caller-saves registers of the MIPS conventions). Registers a6 and a7 are saved as a matter of course, since they are the fp and sp. Register a5 is used as a base for fast access to global variables; it is never changed. Any of the remaining registers (a2–a4 and d3–d7) that are used by the current subroutine are saved at the top of the frame.

In its epilogue, the callee

1. sets the return value

2. pops any saved registers off the stack

3. executes an unlk instruction

4. pops arguments and the static link off the stack

5. returns

The fourth step is tricky, because the return address is above the static link and arguments (if any) in the stack. If there is no static link and no arguments, nothing needs to be done. If there is a static link but no arguments, or no static link and exactly one word of arguments, then the epilogue executes a move (a7)+ (a7) instruction, which has the effect of popping the second-to-top word out of the stack. If the static link and/or arguments consume more than one word of space, then the epilogue pops the return address into a0 and increments the sp with a separate instruction. In the first two cases, the subroutine returns by using an rts instruction. In the third case, it uses jmp (a0).

The end of the calling sequence would be simpler if the caller removed the arguments, but such a change in responsibility would tend to increase code size, assuming multiple call sites. The caller *is* responsible for removing the return value. For small returns, it uses a pop (move (a7)+, d*n*) instruction. For large returns, the value in the stack is unneeded; it is the address of the return value, which the caller already knows. Rather than "waste" an instruction removing a useless value from the stack, the compiler leaves it alone, allowing the sp to "drift" downward through a series of subroutine calls. It removes accumulated drift explicitly at the bottoms of loops, so stack growth is always bounded. When a subroutine returns, of course, the unlk instruction restores the stack to the state it was in before the call.

Because Pascal allows subroutines to nest, a subroutine that is passed as a parameter must be represented by a closure. In the Metrowerks Pascal compiler, a closure is eight bytes long. The last four bytes are the address of the subroutine's code; the first four bytes are the static link (if any) that should be passed when the subroutine is called. If the subroutine is declared at the outer level of lexical nesting, then the first four bytes are zero. Because the closure is more than four bytes long, it is always passed by pushing its address. Unlike most long arguments, however, the closure is guaranteed to be a temporary, rather than a named object; the callee can be sure that the closure's value will never change, and need not copy it. To call through a closure whose address is in register a0, the compiler generates the following code:

```
; push return value and/or args, if any
move.l  (a0)+, -(a7)    ; push static link
bne     .+4             ; branch over next inst. if link not equal to 0
add.w   #4, a7          ; pop "link"; routine is at outer level
move.l  (a0), a0        ; address of subroutine
jsr     (a0)            ; jump
; pop return value, if any
```

8.2.3 In-Line Expansion

As an alternative to stack-based calling conventions, many language implementations allow certain subroutines to be expanded in-line at the point of call. In-line expansion avoids a variety of overheads, including space allocation, branch delays from the call and return, maintaining the static chain or display, and (often) saving and restoring registers. It also allows the compiler to perform code improvements such as global register allocation and common subexpression elimination across the boundaries between subroutines, something that most compilers can't do otherwise.

In many implementations, the compiler chooses which subroutines to expand in-line and which to compile conventionally. In some languages, the programmer can suggest that particular routines be in-lined. In C++, the keyword inline can be prefixed to a function declaration:

```
inline int max (int a, int b) {return a > b ? a : b;}
```

In Ada, the programmer can request in-line expansion with a *significant comment*, or *pragma*:

```
function max (a, b : integer) return integer is
begin
    if a > b then return a; else return b; end if;
end max;
pragma inline (max);
```

Ada provides a large variety of pragmas. As a rule, they do not affect the semantics of the program; they simply make suggestions to the compiler. In some cases (e.g., the elaborate pragma, which controls the order in which headers for library packages are examined) the compiler is required to follow the suggestion. In other cases (including inline), it is not. The inline keyword in C++ is likewise a suggestion; the compiler can ignore it.

In Section 6.6.2 we noted the similarity between in-line expansion and macros, but argued that the former is semantically preferable. In fact, in-line expansion is semantically neutral: it is purely an implementation technique, with no effect on the meaning of the program. In C, the macro

```
#define MAX(a,b) ((a) > (b) ? (a) : (b))
```

will work incorrectly if passed arguments with side effects: MAX (x++, y++) will increment its larger argument twice. No such problems occur with in-line expansion. Macros also suffer from the inability to perform operations that are not syntactically acceptable in the surrounding context. In C, a macro that "returns" a value must be an expression. Since C is not a completely expression-oriented language like Algol 68, many constructs (e.g., loops) cannot occur within an expression (see Exercise 8.3).

In comparison to real subroutine calls, in-line expansion has the obvious disadvantage of increasing code size, since the entire body of the subroutine appears at every call site. In-line expansion is also not an option in the general case for recursive subroutines. For the occasional case in which a recursive call is possible but unlikely, it may be desirable to generate a true recursive subroutine, but to expand one instance of it in-line at each call site. Consider the following C routine for use in hash-table lookup:

```c
range_t bucket_contents (bucket *b, domain_t x)
{
    if (b->key == x)
        return b->val;
    else if (b->next == 0)
        return ERROR;
    else
        return bucket_contents (b->next, x);
}
```

We can expand this code in-line if we make the nested invocation a true subroutine call. Since most hash chains are only one bucket long, the nested call will usually not occur. The in-line expansion will be faster than a true subroutine call, and smaller than in-line code that handles the general case.

Probably the most important argument for in-line expansion is that it allows programmers to adopt a very modular programming style, with lots of tiny subroutines, without sacrificing performance. This modular programming style is essential for object-oriented languages, as we will see in Chapter 10.

8.3 Parameter Passing

Most subroutines are parameterized: they take arguments that control certain aspects of their behavior, or specify the data on which they are to operate. Parameters are not strictly necessary, in the sense that it is possible to program without them, by "passing" information in global variables (a few languages, including early versions of Basic, require this), but parameters make subroutines much more useful—they increase the level of abstraction—and language designers have developed a wealth of parameter passing mechanisms.

Parameter names that appear in the declaration of a subroutine are known as *formal parameters*. Variables and expressions that are passed to a subroutine in a particular call are known as *actual parameters*. We have been referring to actual parameters as *arguments*. In the first subsection below, we will discuss the most common parameter-passing *modes*, most of which are implemented by passing values, references, or closures. In Section 8.3.2 we will look at additional mechanisms, including conformant array parameters, missing and default parameters, named parameters, and variable-length argument lists. Finally in Section 8.3.3 we will consider mechanisms for returning values from functions.

As we noted in Section 6.1, most languages use a prefix notation for calls to user-defined subroutines, with the subroutine name followed by a parenthesized argument list. Lisp places the function name inside the parentheses, as in (max a b). ML allows the programmer to specify that certain names represent infix operators, which appear between a pair of arguments:

```
infixr 8 tothe;        (* exponentiation *)
fun x tothe 0 = 1.0
  | x tothe n = x * (x tothe (n-1));    (* assume n >= 0 *)
```

The `infixr` declaration indicates that `tothe` will be a right-associative binary infix operator, at precedence level 8 (multiplication and division are at level 7, addition and subtraction at level 6). Fortran 90 also allows the programmer to define new infix operators, but it requires their names to be bracketed with periods (e.g., A .cross. B), and it gives them all the same precedence. Smalltalk uses infix (or "mixfix") notation (without precedence) for all its operations.

The uniformity of Lisp and Smalltalk syntax makes control abstraction particularly effective: user-defined subroutines (functions in Lisp, "messages" in Smalltalk) use the same style of syntax as built-in operations. As an example, consider if...then...else:

```
if a > b then max := a else max := b;        (* Pascal *)

(if (> a b) (setf max a) (setf max b))        ; Lisp

(a > b) ifTrue: [max <- a] ifFalse: [max <- b].    "Smalltalk"
```

In Pascal or C it is clear that if...then...else is a built-in language construct: it does not look like a subroutine call. In Lisp and Smalltalk, on the other hand, the analogous conditional constructs are syntactically indistinguishable from user-defined operations. They are in fact defined in terms of simpler concepts, rather than being built-in, though they require a special mechanism to evaluate their arguments in normal, rather than applicative, order (Section 6.6.2).

8.3.1 Parameter Modes

In our discussion of subroutines so far, we have glossed over the semantic rules that govern parameter passing, and that determine the relationship between actual and formal parameters. Some languages, including C, Fortran, ML, and Lisp, define a single set of rules, which apply to all parameters. Other languages, including Pascal, Modula, and Ada, provide two or more sets of rules, corresponding to different parameter-passing *modes*. As in many aspects of language design, the semantic details are heavily influenced by implementation issues.

Suppose for the moment that x is a global variable in a language with a value model of variables, and that we wish to pass x as a parameter to subroutine p:

```
p (x);
```

From an implementation point of view, we have two principal alternatives: we may provide p with a copy of x's value, or we may provide it with x's address. The two most common parameter-passing modes, called *call by value* and *call by reference*, are designed to reflect these implementations. With value parameters, each actual parameter is assigned into the corresponding formal parameter when a subroutine is called; from then on, the two are independent. With reference parameters, each formal parameter is an *alias* for the corresponding actual parameter; the two refer to the same object, and changes made through one are visible through the other. In most languages (Fortran is an exception; see below) an actual parameter that is to be passed by reference must be an l-value; it cannot be the result of an arithmetic operation, or any other value without an address.

Variations on Value and Reference Parameters

In Pascal, parameters are passed by value by default; they are passed by reference if preceded by the keyword var in their subroutine header's formal parameter list. Parameters in C are always passed by value, though the effect for arrays is unusual: because of the interoperability of arrays and pointers in C (Section 7.7.1), what is passed by value is a pointer; changes to array elements accessed through this pointer are visible to the caller. To allow a called routine to modify a variable other than an array in the caller's scope, the C programmer must pass the address of the variable explicitly:

```
void swap (int *a, int *b) {int t = *a; *a = *b; *b = t;}
...
swap (&v1, &v2);
```

Fortran passes all parameters by reference, but does not require that every actual parameter be an l-value. If a built-up expression appears in an argument list, the compiler creates a temporary variable to hold the value, and passes this variable by reference. A Fortran subroutine that needs to modify the values of its formal parameters without modifying its actual parameters must copy the values into local variables, and modify those instead.

In a language such as Smalltalk, Lisp, ML, or Clu, which use a reference model of variables, an actual parameter is already a reference to an object. Instead of passing the value of the actual parameter or a reference to the actual parameter (neither of which makes sense), these languages provide a single parameter-passing mode in which the actual and formal parameters refer to the same object. Clu calls this mode *call by sharing*. For variables that are implemented as addresses, call by sharing is usually implemented by passing the address. For variables that refer to immutable objects (numbers, characters, etc.) and that are implemented as values, call by sharing is usually implemented by passing the value. In Java, parameters of primitive types are passed by value; object parameters are passed by sharing.

In a language that provides both value and reference parameters (e.g., Pascal or Modula), there are two principal reasons why the programmer might choose one over the other. First, if the called routine is supposed to change the value of an actual parameter, then the programmer must pass the parameter by reference. Conversely, to ensure that the called routine cannot modify the parameter, the programmer can pass the parameter by value. Second, the implementation of value parameters requires copying actuals to formals, a potentially time-consuming operation when arguments are large. Reference parameters can be implemented simply by passing an address. Of course, accessing a parameter that is passed by reference requires an extra level of indirection. If the parameter is used often enough, the cost of this indirection may outweigh the cost of copying the actual parameter.

The potential inefficiency of large value parameters sometimes prompts programmers to pass an argument by reference when passing by value would be semantically more appropriate. Pascal programmers, for example, are commonly taught to use `var` (reference) parameters both for arguments that need to be modified and for arguments that are very large. Unfortunately, the latter justification often leads to buggy code, in which a subroutine modifies an actual parameter that the caller meant to leave unchanged.

To combine the efficiency of reference parameters and the safety of value parameters, Modula-3 provides a READONLY parameter mode. Any formal parameter whose declaration is preceded by READONLY cannot be changed by the called routine: the compiler prevents the programmer from using that formal parameter on the left-hand side of any assignment statement, reading it from a file, or passing it by reference to any other subroutine. Small READONLY parameters are generally implemented by passing a value; larger READONLY parameters are implemented by passing an address. As in Fortran, a Modula-3 compiler will create a temporary variable to hold the value of any built-up expression passed as a large READONLY parameter.

The equivalent of READONLY parameters is also available in ANSI Standard C, which allows any variable or parameter declaration to be preceded by the keyword `const`. Const variables are "elaboration-time constants," as described in Section 3.2. Const parameters are particularly useful when passing addresses:

```
void append_to_log (const huge_record *r) { ...
...
append_to_log (&my_record);
```

Here the keyword `const` applies to the record to which `r` points;[5] the caller must pass the address of its record explicitly, but can be assured that the callee will not change the record's contents.

One traditional problem with parameter modes—and with the `READONLY` mode in particular—is that they tend to confuse the key pragmatic issue (does the implementation pass a value or a reference?) with two semantic issues: is the callee allowed to change the formal parameter and, if so, will the changes be reflected in the actual parameter? C keeps the pragmatic issue separate, by forcing the programmer to pass references explicitly with pointers. Still, its `const` mode serves double duty: is the intent of `const foo *p` to protect the actual parameter from change, or to document the fact that the subroutine thinks of the formal parameter as a constant rather than a variable, or both?

The `READONLY` parameters of Modula-3 share the dual role of `const` parameters in C, but the implementation independence of the Modula-3 version virtually eliminates the need for value parameters: the only real justification left is the relatively minor fact that one can write a value parameter directly, rather than copying to a local variable and then writing that instead. In an attempt to clarify and simplify issues, Ada takes the position that a callee can modify a formal parameter if and only if the changes will affect the actual parameter. Implementation details are then left (mostly) to the compiler.

Parameter Modes in Ada

Ada provides three parameter-passing modes, called `in`, `out`, and `in out`. In parameters pass information from the caller to the callee; they can be read by the callee but not written. Out parameters pass information from the callee to the caller. In Ada 83 they can be written by the callee but not read; in Ada 95 they can be both read and written, but they begin their life uninitialized. In out parameters pass information in both directions; they can be both read and written. Changes to `out` or `in out` parameters always change the actual parameter. For parameters of scalar and access (pointer) types, Ada specifies that all three modes are to be implemented by copying values. For these parameters, then, `in` is call by value, `out` is what some authors call *call by result* (the value of the formal parameter is copied into the actual parameter when the subroutine returns), and `in out` is *call by value/result*, a mode first introduced in Algol-W. For parameters of most constructed types, however, Ada specifically permits an implementation to pass either values or addresses. In most languages, these two different mechanisms would lead to different semantics: changes made to an `in out` parameter that is passed as an address will affect the actual parameter immediately; changes made to an `in out` parameter that is passed as a value will

---

5 Following the usual rules for parsing C declarations (page 390) `r` is a pointer to a `huge_record` whose value is constant. If we wanted `r` to be a constant that points to a `huge_record`, we should need to say `huge_record * const r`.

```
type t is record
    a, b : integer;
end record;
r : t;

procedure foo (s : in out t) is
begin
    r.a := r.a + 1;
    s.a := s.a + 1;
end foo;


...
r.a := 3;
foo (r);
put (r.a);        -- does this print 4 or 5?
```

Figure 8.6 An erroneous Ada program. If parameters are implemented by passing values, then the increment of r.a within foo has no permanent effect: r.a will be overwritten by s.a when foo returns. If parameters are implemented by passing addresses, then the two statements within foo both increment the same object.

not affect the actual parameter until the subroutine returns. One possible way to hide the distinction would be to outlaw the creation of aliases, as Euclid does. Ada takes a simpler tack: a program (e.g., the one in Figure 8.6) that can tell the difference between value and address-based implementations of (nonscalar, nonpointer) in out parameters is said to be erroneous—incorrect, but in a way that the language implementation is not required to check.

The semantics of Ada's parameter modes solve several problems encountered in other languages [IBFW91, Sec. 8.2]. The in mode is appropriate for any parameter not meant to be modified by the called routine; the programmer need not specify (or even worry about) whether it is implemented by passing a value or an address. By allowing the implementation to pass a value, Ada avoids potential problems with alignment (Section 5.2). Large objects are usually aligned at an address appropriate for any built-in type, and may safely be passed by reference. Small objects, however, may not be aligned if they are packed into a record; passing them by value or value/result avoids the need to worry about alignment when accessing the formal parameter. By contrast, Pascal prohibits passing a field of a packed record by reference to avoid this very problem (packed records were described in Section 7.3.2). In a similar vein, when passing a subrange variable by reference, Pascal requires that all possible values of the corresponding formal parameter be valid for the subrange:

```
type small = 1..100;
var  a : 1..10;
     b : 1..1000;
```

```
procedure foo (var n : small);
begin
    n := 100;
    writeln (a);
end;
...
a := 2;
foo (b);    (* ok *)
foo (a);    (* static semantic error *)
```

This restriction is necessary to prevent foo from assigning an out-of-range value into n, and then reading it out of a. Ada has no such restriction: scalars are passed by copying, and range constraints on numeric parameters are checked when the subroutine returns. An Ada program syntactically similar to our Pascal example (with n passed with mode in out) would pass successfully through the compiler, but the second return from foo would result in a dynamic semantic error.

Finally, Ada's semantics for parameter passing allow a single set of modes to be used not only for subroutine parameters, but also for communication among concurrently executing tasks (to be discussed in Chapter 12). When tasks are executing on separate machines, with no memory in common, passing the address of an actual parameter is not a practical option. Most Ada compilers pass large arguments to subroutines as addresses; they pass them to the entry points of tasks by copying.

References in C++

Programmers who switch to C after some experience with Pascal, Modula, or Ada are often frustrated by C's lack of reference parameters. As noted above, one can always arrange to modify an object by passing its address, but then the formal parameter is a pointer, and must be explicitly dereferenced whenever it is used. C++ addresses this problem by introducing an explicit notion of a *reference*. Reference parameters are specified by preceding their name with an ampersand in the header of the function:

```
void swap (int &a, int &b) {int t = a; a = b; b = t;}
```

In the code of this swap routine, a and b are ints, not pointers to ints; no dereferencing is required. Moreover, the caller passes as arguments the variables whose values are to be swapped, rather than passing their addresses.

As in C, a C++ parameter can be declared to be const to ensure that it is not modified. For large types, const reference parameters in C++ provide the same combination of speed and safety found in the READONLY parameters of Modula-3: they can be passed by address, but cannot be changed by the called routine.

References in C++ see their principal use as parameters, but they can appear in other contexts as well. Any variable can be declared to be a reference:

```
int i;
int &j = i;
...
i = 2;
j = 3;
cout << i;              // prints 3
```

Here j is a reference to (an alias for) i. The initializer in the declaration is required; it identifies the object for which j is an alias. Moreover it is not possible later to change the object to which j refers; it will always refer to i.

Any change to i or j can be seen by reading the other. Most C++ compilers implement references with addresses. In this example, i will be assigned a location that contains an integer, while j will be assigned a location that contains the address of i. Despite their different implementation, however, there is no semantic difference between i and j; the exact same operations can be applied to either, with precisely the same results.

While there is seldom any reason to create aliases on purpose in straight-line code, references in C++ are highly useful for at least one purpose other than parameters: namely function returns. Some objects—file buffers, for example—do not support a copy operation, and therefore cannot be passed or returned by value. One can always return a pointer, but just as with subroutine parameters, the subsequent dereferencing operations can be cumbersome. In Section 7.9 we saw how references are used for I/O in C++. The overloaded << and >> operators return a reference to their first argument, which can in turn be passed to subsequent << or >> operations. The syntax

```
cout << a << b << c;
```

is short for

```
((cout.operator<< (a)).operator<< (b)).operator<< (c);
```

Without references, << and >> would have to return a pointer to their stream:

```
((cout.operator<< (a))->operator<< (b))->operator<< (c);
```

or

```
*(*(cout.operator<< (a)).operator<< (b)).operator<< (c);
```

This change would spoil the cascading syntax of the operator form:

```
*(*(cout << a) << b) << c;
```

It should be noted that the ability to return references from functions is not new in C++: Algol 68 provides the same capability. The object-oriented features of C++, and its operator overloading, make reference returns particularly useful.

Closures as Parameters

A closure (a reference to a subroutine, together with its referencing environment) may be passed as a parameter for any of several reasons. The most obvious of these arises when the parameter is declared to be a subroutine. In Standard Pascal, one might write:

```
procedure apply_to_A (function f (n : integer) : integer;
                      var A : array [low..high : integer] of integer);
var i : integer;
begin
    for i := low to high do A[i] := f (A[i]);
end;
```

Early versions of Pascal did not include the full header of the subroutine parameter (e.g., `f`) in the header of the routine (e.g., `apply_to_A`) to which it was being passed. This omission made it difficult or impossible to check at compile time to make sure that the actual and formal parameters expected the same number and types of arguments. The situation in Fortran is similar: Fortran 77 allows a subroutine to be passed as a parameter, but cannot check statically for consistent use. Fortran 90 allows (but does not require) the programmer to specify the parameter's interface.

Modula-2 and -3 (and several other languages) provide first-class subroutine *types*, supporting not only subroutine parameters, but also subroutine variables. In Modula-2 we could write:

```
TYPE int_to_int = PROCEDURE (INTEGER) : INTEGER;
PROCEDURE apply_to_A (f : int_to_int; A : ARRAY OF INTEGER);
VAR i : CARDINAL;    (* unsigned integer *)
BEGIN
    FOR i := 0 TO HIGH(A) DO A[i] := f (A[i]); END;
END apply_to_A;
```

C and C++ support *pointers* to subroutines, both as parameters and as variables:

```
void apply_to_A (int (*f) (int), int A[], int A_size)
{
    int i;
    for (i = 0; i < A_size; i++) A[i] = f (A[i]);
}
```

The syntax `f (n)` is used not only when `f` is the name of a function, but also when `f` is a pointer to a function; the pointer need not be dereferenced explicitly.

Ada 83 does not permit subroutines to be passed as parameters. Some of the same effect can be obtained through generic subroutines (to be discussed in Section 8.4), but not enough; Ada 95 provides first-class pointer-to-subroutine types.

Subroutines are routinely passed as parameters (and returned as results) in functional languages. A list-based version of `apply_to_A` would look something like this in Scheme (for the meanings of `car`, `cdr`, and `cons`, see Section 7.8):

```
(define apply-to-L (lambda (f l)
    (if (null? l) '()
        (cons (f (car l)) (apply-to-L f (cdr l))))))
```

Because Scheme (like Lisp) is not statically typed, there is no need to specify the type of `f`. At run time, a Scheme implementation will announce a dynamic semantic error in `(f (car l))` if `f` is not a function, and in `(null? l)`, `(car l)`, or `(cdr l)` if `l` is not a list.

The code in ML is similar, but the implementation uses inference (Section 7.2.5) to determine the types of `f` and `l` at compile time:

```
fun apply_to_L (f, l) =
    case l of
        nil => nil
    | h :: t => f (h) :: apply_to_L (f, t);
```

The type of `apply_to_L` is `('a -> 'b) * 'a list -> 'b list`.

As described in Section 3.4, referencing environments are required in closures only for nested subroutines. C and C++ get by with subroutine pointers because they have no nested subroutines. Similarly, Modula-2 can implement formal subroutines as mere addresses because it allows only outermost routines to be passed as parameters. Modula-3 is a bit more general: it allows inner subroutines to be passed as parameters (and uses closures to represent them), but though it also allows subroutines to be returned from functions or assigned into variables, it limits these cases to outermost routines, thereby avoiding the need for objects of unlimited extent (again, see Section 3.4).

Call by Name*

Explicit subroutine parameters are not the only language feature that requires a closure to be passed as a parameter. In general, a language implementation must pass a closure whenever the eventual use of the parameter requires computation that depends on the actual parameter or on the context in which it was passed (i.e., for which a compiler cannot generate code that will work for all parameters). An interesting example occurs in the *call by name* parameters of Algol 60 and Simula.

When Algol 60 was defined, most programmers programmed in assembly language (Fortran was only a few years old, and Lisp was even newer). The assembly languages of the day made heavy use of macros, and it was natural for the Algol designers to propose a parameter-passing mechanism that mimicked the behavior of macros.

A call by name parameter is re-evaluated in the caller's referencing environment every time it is used. The effect is as if the called routine had been textually expanded at the point of call, with the actual parameter (which may be a complicated expression) replacing every occurrence of the formal parameter. To avoid the usual problems with macro parameters, the "expansion" is defined to include parentheses around the replaced parameter wherever syntactically valid, and to make "suitable systematic changes" to the names of any formal parameters or local identifiers that share the same name, so that their meanings never conflict [NBB$^+$63, p. 12]. Call by name is the default in Algol 60; call by value is available as an alternative. In Simula call by value is the default; call by name is the alternative.

To implement call by name, Algol 60 implementations pass a hidden subroutine that evaluates the actual parameter in the caller's referencing environment. The hidden routine is usually called a *thunk*.[6] In most cases thunks are trivial. If an actual parameter is a variable name, for example, the thunk simply reads the variable from memory. In some cases, however, a thunk can be elaborate. Perhaps the most famous occurs in what is known as *Jensen's device*, named after Jørn Jensen [Rut67]. The idea is to pass to a subroutine both a built-up expression and one or more of the variables used in the expression. Then by changing the values of the individual variable(s), the called routine can deliberately and systematically change the value of the built-up expression. This device can be used, for example, to write a summation routine:

```
real procedure sum (expr, i, low, high);
    value low, high;
        comment low and high are passed by value;
        comment expr and i are passed by name;
    real expr;
    integer i, low, high;
begin
    real rtn;
    rtn := 0;
    for i := low step 1 until high do
        rtn := rtn + expr;
        comment the value of expr depends on the value of i;
    sum := rtn
end sum
```

Now to evaluate the sum

$$y = \sum_{1 \le x \le 10} 3x^2 - 5x + 2$$

we can simply say

```
y := sum (3*x*x - 5*x + 2, x, 1, 10);
```

In practice, such clever uses of call by name are rather rare, and can be imitated in other languages by use of formal subroutines. At the same time, the cost of calling thunks on every use of a formal parameter proved to be prohibitive, and call by name was dropped in Algol 68.

---

6 In general, a thunk is a procedure of zero arguments used to delay evaluation of an expression. Another example of a thunk can be seen in the `promise` constructor of Exercise 11.10.

	implementation mechanism	permissible operations	change to actual?	alias?
value	value	read, write	no	no
in, const	value or reference	read only	no	maybe
out (Ada)	value or reference	write only	yes	maybe
value/result	value	read, write	yes	no
var, ref	reference	read, write	yes	yes
sharing	value or reference	read, write	yes	yes
in out (Ada)	value or reference	read, write	yes	maybe
name (Algol 60)	closure (thunk)	read, write	yes	yes

Figure 8.7 Parameter passing modes. Column 1 indicates common names for modes. Column 2 indicates implementation via passing of values, references, or closures. Column 3 indicates whether the callee can read or write the formal parameter. Column 4 indicates whether changes to the formal parameter affect the actual parameter. Column 5 indicates whether changes to the formal or actual parameter, during the execution of the subroutine, may be visible through the other.

Label Parameters*

Both Algol 60 and Algol 68 allow a label to be passed as a parameter. If a called routine performs a goto to such a label, control will usually need to escape the local context, unwinding the subroutine call stack. The unwinding operation depends on the location of the label. For each intervening scope, the goto must restore saved registers, deallocate the stack frame, and perform any other operations normally handled by epilogue code. To implement label parameters, Algol implementations pass the address of a hidden subroutine that performs the appropriate operations for the given label.

Label parameters are usually used to handle *exceptional conditions*: conditions that prevent a subroutine from performing its usual operation. Instead of returning, a routine that encounters a problem (invalid input, for example) can perform a goto to a label parameter, on the assumption that the label refers to code that performs some remedial operation, or prints an appropriate error message. In several more recent languages, label parameters have been replaced by more structured exception handling mechanisms, discussed in Section 8.5.

8.3.2 Special-Purpose Parameters

Figure 8.7 contains a summary of the common parameter-passing modes. In this section we examine other aspects of parameter passing.

Conformant Arrays

As we saw in Section 7.4.2, the binding time for array dimensions and bounds varies greatly from language to language, ranging from compile time (Basic and

Pascal) to elaboration time (Ada and Fortran 90) to arbitrary times during execution (APL, Perl, and Common Lisp). In several languages, the rules for parameters are looser than they are for variables. A formal array parameter whose shape is finalized at run time (in a language that usually determines shape at compile time), is called a *conformant*, or *open*, array parameter. An example in Standard Pascal appears on page 371. Further examples, in Pascal, Modula-2, and C, appear around page 450. Because it passes arrays as pointers, C allows actual parameters of different shapes to be passed through the same parameter, but without any run-time checks to ensure that references by the called routine are within the bounds of the actual array.

Default (Optional) Parameters

In Section 3.3.2 we noted that the principal use of dynamic scope is to change the default behavior of a subroutine. We also noted that the same effect can be achieved with *default* parameters. A default parameter is one that need not necessarily be provided by the caller; if it is missing, then a preestablished default value will be used instead.

One common use of default parameters is in I/O library routines (described in Section 7.9.3). In Ada, for example, the put routine for integers has the following declaration in the `text_io` library package:

```
type field is integer range 0..integer'last;
type number_base is integer range 2..16;
default_width : field        := integer'width;
default_base  : number_base := 10;
procedure put (item  : in integer;
               width : in field        := default_width;
               base  : in number_base := default_base);
```

Here the declaration of `default_width` uses the built-in type *attribute* `width` to determine the maximum number of columns required to print an integer in decimal on the current machine (e.g., a 32-bit integer requires no more than 11 columns, including the optional minus sign).

Any formal parameter that is "assigned" a value in its subroutine heading is optional in Ada. In our `text_io` example, the programmer can call put with one, two, or three arguments. No matter how many are provided in a particular call, the code for put can always assume it has all three parameters. The implementation is straightforward: in any call in which actual parameters are missing, the compiler pretends as if the defaults had been provided; it generates a calling sequence that loads those defaults into registers or pushes them onto the stack, as appropriate. On a 32-bit machine, put (37) will print the string "37" in an 11-column field (with nine leading blanks) in base 10 notation. Put (37, 4) will print "37" in a four-column field (two leading blanks), and put (37, 4, 8) will print "45" ($37 = 45_8$) in a four-column field.

Because the `default_width` and `default_base` variables are part of the `text_io` interface, the programmer can change them if desired. When using default values in calls with missing actuals, the compiler loads the defaults from the variables of the package. As noted in Section 7.9.3, there are overloaded instances of put for all the built-in types. In fact, there are two overloaded instances of put for every type, one of which has an additional first parameter that specifies the output file to which to write a value.[7] It should be emphasized that there is nothing special about I/O as far as default parameters are concerned: defaults can be used in any subroutine declaration. In addition to Ada, default parameters appear in C++, Common Lisp, and Fortran 90.

Named Parameters

In all of our discussions so far we have been assuming that parameters are *positional*: the first actual parameter corresponds to the first formal parameter, the second actual to the second formal, and so on. In some languages, including Ada, Modula-3, Fortran 90, and Common Lisp, this need not be the case. These languages allow parameters to be *named*. Named parameters (also called *keyword* parameters) are particularly useful in conjunction with default parameters. In the preceding section, for example, positional notation allows us to write put (37, 4) to print "37" in a four-column field, but it does not allow us to print in octal in a field of default width: any call (with positional notation) that specifies a base must also specify a width, explicitly, because the width parameter comes before the base in put's parameter list. Named parameters provide the Ada programmer with a way around this problem:

```
put (item => 37, base => 8);
```

Because the parameters are named, their order does not matter; we can also write

```
put (base => 8, item => 37);
```

We can even mix the two approaches, using positional notation for the first few parameters, and names for all the rest:

```
put (37, base => 8);
```

In addition to allowing parameters to be specified in arbitrary order, omitting any intermediate default parameters for which special values are not required, named parameter notation has the advantage of documenting the purpose of each parameter. For a subroutine with a very large number of parameters, it can be difficult to remember which is which. Named notation makes the meaning of arguments explicit in the call, as in the following hypothetical example:

---

7 The real situation is actually a bit more complicated: The put routine for integers is nested inside integer_io, a generic package that is in turn inside of text_io. The programmer must *instantiate* a separate version of the integer_io package for each variety (size) of integer type.

```
format_page (columns => 2,
    window_height => 400, window_width => 200,
    header_font => Helvetica, body_font => Times,
    title_font => Times_Bold, header_point_size => 10,
    body_point_size => 11, title_point_size => 13,
    justification => true, hyphenation => false,
    page_num => 3, paragraph_indent => 18,
    background_color => white);
```

Variable Numbers of Arguments

C, C++, and Common Lisp are unusual in that they allow the user to define
subroutines that take a variable number of arguments. We saw examples of such
subroutines in Section 7.9.3: the `printf` and `scanf` functions of the `stdio` I/O
library. In ANSI Standard C, `printf` can be declared as follows:

```
int printf (char *format, ...)
{ ...
```

The ellipsis (. . .) in the function header is a part of the language syntax. It indicates that there are additional parameters following the format, but that their
types and numbers are unspecified. Since C and C++ are statically typed, additional parameters are not type safe. They are type safe in Common Lisp, however,
thanks to dynamic typing.

Within the body of a function with a variable-length argument list, the C
or C++ programmer must use a collection of standard macros to access the
extra arguments. The definition of the macros varies from machine to machine,
depending on how the compiler passes arguments to functions, but the interface
is standardized. In some cases, the "macros" are built into the compiler, which
generates special code for them: they aren't really macros. In `printf`, the macros
would be used as follows:

```
#include <stdarg.h>      /* macros and type definitions */
int printf (char *format, ...)
{
    va_list args;
    va_start (args, format);
    ...
        char cp = va_arg (args, char);
        ...
        double dp = va_arg (args, double);
    ...
    va_end (args);
}
```

Here `args` is defined as an object of type `va_list`, a special (implementation-
dependent) type used to enumerate the elided parameters. The `va_start` macro
takes the last declared parameter (in this case, `format`) as its second argument. It
initializes its first argument (in this case `args`) so that it can be used to enumerate
the rest of the caller's actual parameters. At least one formal parameter must be
declared; they can't all be elided.

Each call to va_arg returns the value of the next elided parameter. Two examples appear above. Each specifies the expected type of the parameter, and assigns the result into a variable of the appropriate type. If the expected type is different from the type of the actual parameter, chaos can result. In printf, the %X placeholders in the format string are used to determine the type: printf contains a large switch statement, with one arm for each possible X. The arm for %c contains a call to va_arg (args, char); the arm for %f contains a call to va_arg (args, double). All C floating-point types are extended to double precision before being passed to a subroutine, so there is no need inside printf to worry about the distinction between floats and doubles. Scanf, on the other hand, must distinguish between pointers to floats and pointers to doubles. The call to va_end allows the implementation to perform any necessary cleanup operations (e.g., deallocation of any heap space used for the va_list, or repair of any changes to the stack frame that might confuse the epilogue code).

Older versions of C use a slightly different set of macros, defined in varargs.h, for variable-length argument lists. The differences between the two sets of macros reflect the introduction of *function prototypes* in ANSI C.[8] In older dialects of C a function header contains only the names of the parameters; the types are declared in a subsequent list, which falls between the header and the body of the function:

```
void my_func (a, b, c)
    int a;
    float b;
    char c;
{   ...
```

The problem with the older syntax (beyond the redundant occurrences of the parameter names) is that "forward" declarations of functions consist of only the header, without the type information. Combined with separate compilation, this lack of information makes it impossible for older versions of C to ensure that actual and formal parameters agree in number and type.

In addition to (different versions of) the va_list, va_start, va_arg, and va_end macros, the varargs package provides placeholders for the parameter lists within and following an old-style function header; these play the role of the ANSI C ellipsis.

8.3.3 Function Returns

Many languages place restrictions on the types of objects that can be returned from a function. In Algol 60 and Fortran, a function must return a scalar value.

---

8 Prototypes were actually introduced in C++, and then adopted back into the parent language. ANSI C accepts the older syntax, as well as the newer, for the sake of backward compatibility. Only the newer is allowed in C++.

In Pascal and early versions of Modula-2, it must return a scalar or a pointer. Most imperative languages are more flexible: Algol 68, Ada, C, and many (nonstandard) implementations of Pascal allow functions to return values of composite type. Modula-3 and Ada 95 allow a function to return a subroutine, implemented as a closure. C has no closures, but allows a function to return a pointer to a subroutine. In functional languages such as Lisp and ML, returning a closure is commonplace.

The syntax by which a function indicates the value to be returned varies greatly. In languages such as Lisp, ML, and Algol 68, which do not distinguish between expressions and statements, the value of a function is simply the value of its body, which is itself an expression.

In several early imperative languages, including Algol 60, Fortran, and Pascal, a function specifies its return value by executing an assignment statement whose left-hand side is the name of the function. As noted in Section 3.6.1, this approach requires an exception to the nested scope rule: the function name must not be hidden from the body of the function by a nested declaration. This inconsistency is eliminated in more recent imperative languages by introducing an explicit `return` statement:

```
return expression
```

In addition to specifying a value, `return` causes the immediate termination of the subroutine. As noted in Section 6.2, this termination avoids the common Pascal idiom of placing a statement label on the last line of a subroutine, and then performing a `goto` to this label. A function that has figured out what to return but doesn't want to return yet can always assign the return value into a temporary variable, and then return it later:

```
    rtn := expression
    ...
return rtn
```

Fortran separates early termination of a subroutine from the specification of return values: it specifies the return value by assigning to the function name, and has a `return` statement that takes no arguments.

Argument-bearing `return` statements and assignment to the function name share one additional shortcoming: they force the programmer to employ a temporary variable in incremental computations. Here is an example in Ada:

```
type int_array is array (integer range <>) of integer;
    -- array of integers with unspecified integer bounds
function A_max (A : int_array) return integer is
rtn : integer;
begin
    rtn := integer'first;
    for i in A'first .. A'last loop
        if A(i) > rtn then rtn := A(i); end if;
    end loop;
    return rtn;
end A_max;
```

Here `rtn` must be declared as a variable so that the function can read it as well as write it. Because `rtn` is a local variable, most compilers will allocate it within the stack frame of `A_max`. The `return` statement must then perform an unnecessary copy to move that variable's value into the return location allocated by the caller.

Some languages eliminate the need for a local variable by allowing the result of a function to have a name in its own right. In SR[9] one can write:

```
procedure A_max (ref A[1:*]: int) returns rtn : int
    rtn := low (int)
    fa i := 1 to ub(A) ->
        if A[i] > rtn -> rtn := A[i] fi
    af
end
```

Here `rtn` can reside throughout its lifetime in the return location allocated by the caller. A similar facility can be found in Eiffel, in which every function contains an implicitly declared object named `Result`. This object can be both read and written, and is returned to the caller when the function returns.

8.4 Generic Subroutines and Modules

Subroutines provide a natural way to perform an operation for a variety of different object values (i.e., parameters). In large programs, the need also often arises to perform an operation for a variety of different object *types*. An operating system, for example, tends to make heavy use of queues, to hold processes, memory descriptors, file buffers, device control blocks, and a host of other objects. The characteristics of the queue data structure are independent of the characteristics of the items placed in the queue. Unfortunately, the standard mechanisms for declaring `enqueue` and `dequeue` subroutines in most languages require that the type of the items be declared, statically. In a language like Pascal or Fortran, this static declaration of item type means that the programmer must create separate copies of `enqueue` and `dequeue` for every type of item, even though the entire text of these copies (other than the type names in the procedure headers) is the same.

Polymorphic subroutines provide a way around the problem, allowing us to declare subroutines whose argument types are incompletely specified. But polymorphism has its drawbacks. As realized in Lisp, it sacrifices compile-time type checking. As realized in ML, it makes the compiler substantially slower and more complicated, and it forces the adoption of a structural view of type equivalence (Section 7.2.1). An alternative, mentioned in Section 3.5, is to provide a *generic*

---

9 The `fa` in SR stands for "for all"; `ub` stands for "upper bound." The `->` symbol is roughly equivalent to `do` and `then` in other languages. All structured statements in SR are terminated by spelling the opening keyword backwards. Semicolons between statements may be omitted if they occur at end-of-line.

```
generic
    type item is private;
        -- can be assigned; other characteristics are hidden
    max_items : in integer := 100;      -- 100 items max by default
package queue is
    procedure enqueue (it : in item);
    function dequeue return item;
private
    subtype index is integer range 1..max_items;
    items : array(index) of item;
    next_free, next_full : index := 1;
end queue;

package body queue is
    procedure enqueue (it : in item) is
    begin
        items(next_free) := it;
        next_free := next_free mod max_items + 1;
    end enqueue;
    function dequeue return item is
        rtn : item := items(next_full);
    begin
        next_full := next_full mod max_items + 1;
        return rtn;
    end dequeue;
end queue;
...
package ready_list is new queue (process);
    -- assume type process has previously been declared
package int_queue is new queue (integer, 50);
    -- only 50 items long, instead of the default 100
```

Figure 8.8 Generic queues in Ada (left) and C++ (right). C++ calls its generics *templates*. Checks for overflow and underflow have been omitted for brevity of presentation *(continued)*.

facility that allows a collection of similar subroutines or modules—with different types in each—to be created from a single copy of the source code. Generic modules are particularly valuable for creating *containers*: data abstractions that hold a collection of objects, but whose operations are generally oblivious to the type of those objects. Examples of containers include lists, stacks, queues, heaps, trees, tables, and relations. Generic subroutines are needed in generic modules, and may also be useful in their own right. A standard example is a sorting routine, which needs to be able to tell when objects are smaller or larger than each other, but does not need to know anything else about them. Languages that provide generics include Clu, Ada, C++ (which calls them *templates*), and Modula-3. A generic "minimum" function in Ada appears in Figure 3.20 (page 148). Ada and C++ examples of a generic queue module appear in Figure 8.8.

Generic subroutines and modules (generic "program units," in Ada termi-

```
template<class item, int max_items = 100>
class queue {
    item items[max_items];
    int next_free;
    int next_full;
public:
    queue () {
        next_free = next_full = 0;       // initialization
    }
    void enqueue (item it) {
        items[next_free] = it;
        next_free = (next_free + 1) % max_items;
    }
    item dequeue () {
        item rtn = items[next_full];
        next_full = (next_full + 1) % max_items;
        return rtn;
    }
};
...
queue<process> ready_list;
queue<int, 50> int_queue;
```

Figure 8.8 *(continued)*

nology) are a purely static mechanism: all the work required to create multiple instances of a queue and to call its enqueue and dequeue routines can be performed at compile time. In Ada, which supports dynamic arrays (Section 7.4.2), the value of max_items may not be known until run time; in C++ it must be a compile-time constant. In the usual case, the compiler creates a *separate copy* of the entire queue abstraction for every instance. If several queues are instantiated with the same set of arguments, then the compiler may share the code of the enqueue and dequeue routines among them. If it is clever, the compiler may even share the code for a queue of integers with the code for a queue of single-precision floating-point numbers, if the two types have the same size, but these sorts of optimizations are not required, and the programmer should not be surprised if they don't occur.

As we noted in Section 3.5, generics have much in common with macros. The designers of Ada describe generic program units as "a restricted form of context-sensitive macro facility" [IBFW91, p. 236]. The designers of C++ describe templates as "a clever kind of macro that obeys the scope, naming, and type rules of C++" [Str91, p. 257]. The difference between macros and generics is much like the difference between macros and in-line subroutines (Sections 6.6.2 and 8.2.3): generics are integrated into the rest of the language, and are understood by the compiler, rather than being tacked on as an afterthought, to be expanded by a preprocessor. In both Ada and C++ (and in Clu and Modula-3), generic parameters are type checked. Arguments to generic subroutines are evaluated exactly once. Names declared inside generic program units obey the normal scoping rules. In Ada, which allows program units to nest, the names of generic actual parameters (e.g., item and max_items in Figure 8.8) are resolved in the referencing environment in which the instance of the generic unit was created, but all other names in the generic unit are resolved in the environment in which the generic unit itself was declared.

In Section 8.3.1 we noted that Ada does not permit subroutines to be passed as parameters, but that some of the same effect can be achieved with generics. We can now elaborate on that statement. Suppose we want to apply a function to every member of an array. This goal is easy to achieve with a generic subroutine:

```
generic
    type item is private;
    type item_array is array (integer range <>) of item;
    with function F (it : in item) return item;
procedure apply_to_array (A : in out item_array);

procedure apply_to_array (A : in out item_array) is
begin
    for i in A'first..A'last loop
        A(i) := F(A(i));
    end loop;
end apply_to_array;
```

Given an array of integers, scores, and a function on integers, foo, we can write:

```
procedure apply_to_ints is new apply_to_array (integer, int_array, foo);
...
apply_to_ints (scores);
```

The limitation of this programming idiom is that the function foo must be statically known. An Ada program cannot choose a function based on some run-time calculation and then use this function as a generic parameter: there is no notation in which to express the concept of a dynamically chosen function.

In Clu, Ada, and Modula-3, a generic program unit must be instantiated explicitly before it can be used. In C++, a generic class must be instantiated, but a generic function need not be. Given the following function template:

```
template<class T>
void sort (T A[], int A_size) { ...
```

and the following objects:

```
int ints[10];
double reals[50];
char *strings[30];
```

we can perform the following function calls without instantiating anything explicitly:

```
sort (ints, 10);
sort (reals, 50);
sort (strings, 30);
```

In each case, the C++ compiler will implicitly instantiate the appropriate version of the `sort` routine. Obviously, `sort` is overloaded. To keep the language manageable, the rules in C++ for resolving overloaded template names (i.e., figuring out which meaning of the name is intended) are significantly more restrictive than the rules for resolving overloaded function names in general. In particular, the compiler will not coerce the arguments to a generic function.

Because a generic program unit is an abstraction, it is important that its interface (the header of its declaration) provide all the information that must be known by a user of the abstraction. Clu and Ada attempt to enforce this rule. Specifically, they require that the operations permitted on a generic parameter type be explicitly declared. In our queue example, the Ada generic clause said

```
type item is private;
```

A `private` type in Ada is one for which the only permissible operations are assignment, testing for equality and inequality, and accessing a few standard attributes (e.g., `size`). To prohibit testing for equality and inequality, the programmer can declare the parameter to be `limited private`. To allow additional operations, the programmer must provide additional information. In simple cases, it may be possible to specify a *type pattern* such as

```
type item is (<>);
```

Here the parentheses indicate that `item` is a discrete type, and will thus support such operations as comparison for ordering (`<`, `>`, etc.) and the attributes `first` and `last`. (As always in Ada, the *box* symbol, `<>`, is a placeholder for missing information: enumeration values, subrange bounds, etc.)

In more complex cases, the Ada programmer can specify the operations of a generic type parameter by means of a trailing `with` clause. We saw examples in the "minimum" example of Figure 3.20 (page 148) and the `apply_to_array` example above. A generic sorting procedure in Ada might look something like this:

```
generic
    type T is private;
    type T_array is array (integer range <>) of T;
    with function "<"(a1, a2 : T) return boolean;
procedure sort (A : in out T_array);
```

Without the `with` clause, procedure `sort` would be unable to compare elements of A for ordering, because type T is private.

In C++ and Modula-3, the code of a generic program unit can (attempt to) perform arbitrary operations on objects of a generic parameter type. If the generic unit is instantiated with a parameter type that does not support that operation, the compiler will announce a static semantic error. Because the header of the generic unit does not necessarily specify which operations will be required, it can be difficult for the programmer to predict whether a particular instantiation will cause an error message. Worse, in some cases the type provided in a generic instantiation may support an operation required by the generic unit's code, but that operation may not do "the right thing." Suppose in our C++ sorting example that the code for the generic `sort` routine makes use of the `<` operator. For `int`s and `double`s, this operator will do what one would expect. For character strings, however, it will compare pointers, to see which referenced character has a lower address. If the programmer is expecting comparison for lexicographic ordering, the results may be surprising!

To avoid unexpected results, C++ and Modula-3 programmers are encouraged to avoid implicit use of the operations of a generic parameter type. There are several ways to make things more explicit in C++ [Str91, pp. 271–277]: the comparison routine can be provided as a member function of class T, an extra argument to the `sort` routine, or an extra generic parameter. To facilitate the first of these options, the programmer may choose to encapsulate the required member functions in a virtual base class from which the type T may inherit via multiple or mix-in inheritance (to be discussed in Section 10.5).

8.5 Exception Handling

Several times in the preceding chapters and sections we have referred to *exception handling* mechanisms. We have delayed discussion of these mechanisms until now because exception handling generally requires the language implementation to "unwind" the subroutine call stack.

An exception can be defined as an unexpected—or at least unusual—condition that arises during program execution. It may be detected automatically by the language implementation, or the program may *raise* it explicitly. The most common exceptions are various sorts of run-time errors. In an I/O library, for example, an input routine may encounter the end of its file before it can read a requested value, or it may find punctuation marks or letters on the input when it is expecting digits. To cope with such errors using mechanisms described so far in this book, the programmer has basically three options, none of which is entirely satisfactory:

1. "Invent" a value that can be used by the caller when a real value could not be returned.
2. Return an explicit "status" value to the caller, who must inspect it after every call. The status may be written into an extra, explicit parameter, stored in a global variable, or encoded as otherwise invalid bit patterns of a function's regular return value.
3. Pass a closure (in languages that support them) for an error-handling routine that the input routine can call when it runs into trouble.

The first of these options is fine in certain cases, but does not work in the general case. Options 2 and 3 tend to clutter up the program, and impose overhead that we should like to avoid in the common case. The tests in option 2 are particularly offensive: they obscure the normal flow of events in the common case. Because they are so tedious and repetitive, they are also a common source of errors; one can easily forget a needed test. Exception-handling mechanisms address these issues by moving error-checking code "out of line," allowing the normal case to be specified simply, and arranging for control to branch to a *handler* when appropriate.

Exception handling was pioneered by PL/I, which includes an executable statement of the form

ON *condition*
    statement

The nested statement (often a GOTO or a BEGIN...END block) is a handler. It is not executed when the ON statement is encountered, but is "remembered" for future reference. It will be executed later if exception *condition* (e.g., OVERFLOW) arises. Because the ON statement is executable, the binding of handlers to exceptions depends on the flow of control at run time.

If a PL/I exception handler is invoked and then "returns" (i.e., does not perform a GOTO to somewhere else in the program), then one of two things will happen. For exceptions that the language designers considered to be fatal, the program itself will terminate. For "recoverable" exceptions, execution will resume at the statement following the one in which the exception occurred. Experience with PL/I indicates that both the dynamic binding of handlers to exceptions and the automatic resumption of code in which an exception occurred are confusing and error-prone.

More recent languages, including Clu, Ada, Modula-3, C++, Java, and ML, all provide exception-handling facilities in which handlers are lexically bound to blocks of code, and in which the execution of the handler *replaces* the yet-to-be-completed portion of the block. As a general rule, if an exception is not handled within the current subroutine, then the subroutine returns abruptly and the exception is raised at the point of call. If the exception is not handled in the calling routine, it continues to propagate back up the dynamic chain. If it is not handled in the program's main routine, then a predefined outermost handler is invoked, and usually terminates the program. In a sense, the dependence of exception handling on the order of subroutine calls might be considered a form of dynamic binding, but it is a much more restricted form than is found in PL/I. Rather than say that a handler in a calling routine has been dynamically bound to an error in a called routine, we prefer to say that the handler is lexically bound to the expression or statement that *calls* the called routine. An exception that is not handled inside a called routine can then be modeled as an "exceptional return"; it causes the calling expression or statement to raise an exception, which is again handled lexically within its subroutine. Exception propagation in Common Lisp can also be described in terms of lexical binding and exceptional returns, but the language manual defines it as a form of dynamic scoping. Common Lisp also differs from most modern languages in the division of labor between the context in which the exception arises and the context in which its propagation ends; we will consider this issue in Exercise 8.17.

In practice, exception handlers tend to be used for three main purposes. First, ideally, a handler will perform some operation that allows the program to recover from the exception and continue execution. For example, in response to an "out of memory" exception in a storage management routine, a handler might request the operating system to allocate additional space to the application, after which it could complete the requested operation. Second, if recovery is not possible, a handler can at least print a helpful error message before the program terminates. Third, when an exception occurs in a given block of code but cannot be handled locally, it is often important to declare a local handler that cleans up any resources allocated in the local block, and then "reraises" the exception, so that it will continue to propagate back to a handler that can (hopefully) recover.

8.5.1 Definition of Exceptions

In many languages, including Clu, Ada, Modula-3, Java, and ML, most dynamic semantic errors result in exceptions, which the program can then catch. The programmer can also define additional, application-specific exceptions. Examples of predefined exceptions include arithmetic overflow, division by zero, end-of-file on input, subscript and subrange errors, and null pointer dereference. The rationale for defining these as exceptions (rather than as fatal errors) is that they may arise in certain valid programs. Some other dynamic errors (e.g., return from a subroutine that has not yet designated a return value) are still fatal in most languages. In C++ and Common Lisp, most exceptions are programmer-defined. (The `signal` library provided by many C and C++ implementations is independent of language-level exceptions; it allows a program to bind handlers dynamically to certain exceptions detected by the operating system.) In Ada, some of the predefined exceptions can be *suppressed* by means of a pragma.

In Ada, `exception` is a built-in type; an exception is simply an object of this type:

```
declare empty_queue : exception;
```

In Modula-3, exceptions are another "kind" of object, akin to constants, types, variables, or subroutines:

```
EXCEPTION empty_queue;
```

In C++ and Java, an exception is an ordinary object, in the object-oriented sense of the word—a value of some class type:

```
class empty_queue { };
```

In ML, `exception` is a constructor, akin to `datatype` (as described in Section 7.2.5).

Most languages allow an exception to be "parameterized," so the code that raises the exception can pass information to the code that handles it. In C++/Java and ML, the "parameters" of an exception are naturally expressed as the fields of the class or constructor:

```
class duplicate_in_set {                 // C++
    item dup;       // element that was inserted twice
};
...
    throw duplicate_in_set (d);

exception duplicate_in_set of item;     (* ML *)
...
    raise duplicate_in_set (d);
```

In Clu and Modula-3, the parameters are included in the exception declaration, much as they are in a subroutine header (the `empty_queue` example above has no parameters). Ada and Common Lisp are unusual in that their exceptions are simply tags: they contain no information other than their name. In Common Lisp, exceptions are not even declared.

The `throw` statement (in C++, Java, and Common Lisp) or `raise` statement (in Ada, Modula-3, and ML) allows the programmer to write code that will raise an exception at run time. A `throw` or `raise` statement is usually embedded in an `if` statement that checks to see if something has gone wrong. PL/I and Clu both use `signal` instead of `throw` or `raise`, and both provide semantics significantly different from those of other exception-handling languages. As noted earlier, PL/I handlers are dynamically bound; exceptions do not propagate back down the dynamic chain. In Clu, `signal` is always an "exceptional `return`": it cannot be handled locally, but rather causes an immediate return from the current subroutine, forcing the caller to recover.

If a subroutine raises an exception but does not catch it internally, it may "return" in an unexpected way. This possibility is an important part of the routine's interface to the rest of the program. Consequently, several languages, including Clu, Modula-3, C++, and Java, include in each subroutine header a list of the exceptions that may propagate out of the routine. This list is mandatory in Modula-3: it is a run-time error if an exception arises that does not appear in the header, but is not caught internally. The list is optional in C++: if it appears, the semantics are the same as in Modula-3; if it is omitted, all exceptions are permitted to propagate. Java adopts an intermediate approach: it segregates its exceptions into "checked" and "unchecked" categories. Checked exceptions must be declared in subroutine headers; unchecked exceptions need not. Unchecked exceptions are typically run-time errors that most programs will want to be fatal (subscript out of bounds, for example)—and that would therefore be a nuisance to declare in every function—but that a highly robust program may want to catch if they occur in library routines.

8.5.2 Exception Propagation

In most languages, including Ada, Clu, Modula-3, C++, and Java, an exception handler is attached to a statement or to a list of statements. In Ada it looks like this:

```
with text_io;   -- import I/O routines (and exceptions)
procedure read_rec ... is
begin
    ...
    begin
        ...
        -- potentially complicated sequence of operations
        -- involving many calls to text_io.get
        ...
    exception
        when end_error => ...
            -- handler to catch any attempt to read past end-of-file
            -- in any of the I/O calls
    end;
    ...
end read_rec;
```

Here we have hypothesized a subroutine to read a record from a file. If the file has been corrupted, it may end in the middle of a record. Rather than check for end-of-file at every read (`get`) operation, we can place the entire series of reads inside a `begin`. . .`end` block that is protected by a single handler.

As written, the handler above will catch only the `end_error` exception, which is declared in package `text_io`. In general, the `exception` part of a `begin`. . . `end` block can have an arbitrary number of handlers, each for a different exception. The syntax of the handlers resembles that of an Ada `case` statement. As in a `case` statement, the final `when` clause can be written to catch all unnamed exceptions:

```
when others => ...
```

Syntax in other languages is similar. In C++:

```
try {
    ...
    // protected block of code
    ...
} catch (end_of_file) {
    ...
} catch (io_error e) {
    // handler for any io_error other than end_of_file
    ...
} catch (...) {
    // handler for any exception not previously named
    // (in this case, the triple-dot ellipsis is a valid C++ token;
    // it does not indicate missing code)
}
```

The handlers attached to a block of code are always examined in order; control is transferred to the first one that *matches* the exception. In Ada, a handler matches if it names the propagating exception, or if it is a "catch-all" others clause. In C++, a handler matches if it names a class from which the exception is derived, or if it is a catch-all. In the example above, let us assume that end_of_file is a subclass of io_error. Then an end_of_file exception, if it arises, will be handled by the first of the three catch clauses. All other I/O errors will be caught by the second catch clause. All non-I/O errors will be caught by the third catch clause. Note that in the second catch clause we have declared a local name, e for the exception object. Within the catch clause, we can refer to the members of e. This mechanism allows the code that raises (throws) the exception to pass information to the handler. The C++ standard library declares exceptions as a hierarchy of classes; programmers are encouraged to use and extend this hierarchy. Java, whose handlers look just like those of C++, provides a similar standard hierarchy.

In an expression-oriented language such as ML or Common Lisp, an exception handler is attached to an expression, rather than to a statement. Since execution of the handler replaces the unfinished portion of the protected code when an exception occurs, a handler attached to an expression must provide a value for the expression. (In a statement-oriented language, the handler—like most statements—is executed for its side effects.) In ML, a handler looks like this:

```
val foo = (f (a) * b) handle Overflow => max_int;
```

Here (f (a) * b) is the protected expression, handle is a keyword, Overflow is a predefined exception (a value built from the exc constructor), and max_int is an expression (in this case a constant) whose value replaces the value of the expression in which the Overflow exception arose. Both the protected expression (here (f (a) * b)) and the handler (here max_int) could in general be arbitrarily complicated, with many nested function calls. Exceptions that arise within a nested call (and are not handled locally) propagate back down the dynamic chain, just as they do in Ada or C++.

In the process of searching for a matching handler, the exception-handling mechanism must "unwind" the run-time stack by reclaiming the stack frames of any subroutines from which the exception escapes. Reclaiming a frame requires not only that its space be popped from the stack, but also that any registers that were saved as part of the calling sequence be restored. (We discuss implementation issues in more detail in Section 8.5.4.)

In C++, an exception that leaves a scope, whether a subroutine or just a nested block, requires the language implementation to call *destructor* functions for any objects declared within that scope. Destructors (to be discussed in more detail in Section 10.3) are often used to deallocate heap space and other resources (e.g., open files). Similar functionality is provided in Common Lisp by an unwind-protect expression, and in Modula-3 and Java by means of try...finally constructs. Code in Modula-3 might look like this:

```
TRY
    myStream := OpenRead (myFileName);        (* protected block *)
    Parse (myStream);
FINALLY                                       (* cleanup code *)
    Close (myStream);
END;
```

A FINALLY clause will be executed whenever control escapes from the corresponding protected block, whether the escape is due to normal completion, an exit from a loop, a return from the current subroutine, or the propagation of an exception. In fact, EXITs and RETURNs in Modula-3 are modeled as exceptions. We have assumed in our example that myStream is not bound to anything at the beginning of the code, and that it is harmless to Close a not-yet-opened stream. If a FINALLY clause is invoked as a result of an exception, the exception is "reraised" automatically at the end of the clause. Several languages, including Clu, Ada, C++, and Java, also allow an ordinary handler to reraise the exception that triggered it, explicitly: the usual syntax is a throw or raise statement without an argument.

If an exception propagates out of the scope in which it was declared, it can no longer be named by a handler, and thus can be caught only by a "catch-all" handler. Modula-3 avoids this problem by requiring all exceptions to be declared at the outermost level of lexical nesting. In most languages, an exception that is declared in a recursive subroutine will be caught by the innermost handler for that exception at run time. In a language with concurrency, one must also consider what will happen if an exception is not handled at the outermost level of a concurrent thread of control. In Modula-3, the entire program terminates abnormally; in Ada and Java, the affected thread terminates quietly.

8.5.3 Example: Phrase-Level Recovery in a Recursive Descent Parser

In Section 2.2.4 we presented a technique for phrase-level recovery from syntax errors in a recursive descent parser. The key idea was this: at the beginning of the subroutine whose job it is to parse a given nonterminal A, we check to see whether the upcoming input token is acceptable. If not, we announce an error and delete tokens until we find one in the FIRST or FOLLOW set of A. A good implementation of this idea requires an extra parameter for every parsing routine (the context-specific FOLLOW set), a call to the error-checking routine in the beginning of every parsing routine, and a globally defined set of "starter" symbols that should not be deleted.

An attractive alternative approach is possible with exceptions. We can avoid the clutter of the extra parameters and the expense of the error-checking calls by declaring a single syntax_error exception and then placing handlers for it at a small number of "clean points" in the parse. In many languages, for example, we could obtain simple, but probably serviceable error recovery by placing one handler around the body of `statement` and another around `declaration`:

```
procedure statement
    try      . . .                        –– code to parse a statement
    except when syntax_error =>
        loop
            if next_token ∈ FIRST(statement)
                statement        –– try again
                return
            elsif next_token ∈ FOLLOW(statement)
                return
            else get_next_token
```

The code for declaration is similar. For better quality repair, we might add handlers around the bodies of expression, aggregate, or other complex constructs. To guarantee that we can always recover from an error, we must ensure that all parts of the grammar lie inside at least one handler. At any point where a syntax error is detected (i.e., when a parsing routine is unable to predict, or when match sees an unexpected input token), we simply raise the syntax_error exception. The exception will propagate back out of an arbitrary number of nested constructs (the number can be very large) until it encounters the innermost protected construct. At that point we will toss the remainder of the phrase and continue with the parse.

8.5.4 Implementation of Exceptions

The most obvious implementation for exceptions maintains a linked-list stack of handlers. When control enters a protected block, the handler for that block is added to the head of the list. When an exception arises, either implicitly or as a result of a `raise` statement, the language run-time system pops the innermost handler off the list and calls it. The handler begins by checking to see if it matches the exception that occurred; if not, it simply reraises it:

```
if exception matches duplicate_in_set
    . . .
else
    reraise exception
```

To implement propagation back down the dynamic chain, each subroutine has an implicit handler that performs the work of the subroutine epilogue code and then reraises the exception. If a protected block of code has handlers for several different exceptions, they are implemented as a single handler containing a multi-arm `if` statement:

if exception matches end_of_file

 ...

elsif exception matches io_error

 ...

else

 ...   -- "catch-all" handler

The problem with this implementation is that it incurs run-time overhead in the common case. Every protected block and every subroutine begins with code to push a handler onto the handler list, and ends with code to pop it back off the list. We can usually do better.

The only real purpose of the handler list is to determine which handler is active. Since blocks of source code tend to translate into contiguous blocks of machine-language instructions, we can capture the correspondence between handlers and protected blocks in the form of a table generated at compile time. Each entry in the table contains two fields: the starting address of a block of code and the address of the corresponding handler. The table is sorted on the first field. When an exception occurs, the language run-time system performs binary search in the table, using the program counter as key, to find the handler for the current block. If that handler reraises the exception, the process repeats: handlers themselves are blocks of code, and can be found in the table. The only subtlety arises in the case of the implicit handlers associated with propagation out of subroutines: such a handler must ensure that the reraise code uses the return address of the subroutine, rather than the current program counter, as the key for table lookup.

The cost of raising an exception is higher in this second implementation, by a factor logarithmic in the number of handlers in the program. But this cost is paid only when an exception actually occurs. On the assumption that exceptions are unusual events, the net impact on performance is clearly beneficial: the cost in the common case is zero. In its pure form the table-based approach requires that the compiler have access to the entire program, or that the linker provide a mechanism to glue subtables together. For a language such as Java, in which code fragments are compiled independently, we can employ a hybrid approach in which the compiler creates a separate table for each subroutine, and each stack frame contains a pointer to the appropriate table.

It is worth noting that exceptions can sometimes be simulated in a language that does not provide them as a built-in. In Section 6.2 we noted that Pascal permits gotos to labels outside the current subroutine, that Algol 60 allows labels to be passed as parameters, and that PL/I allows them to be stored in subroutines. These mechanisms permit the program to escape from a deeply nested context, but in a very unstructured way.

A much more attractive alternative appears in Scheme, which provides a general-purpose function called `call-with-current-continuation`, sometimes abbreviated `call/cc`. This function takes a single argument f, which is itself a function. It calls f, passing as argument a continuation c (a closure) that captures the current program counter and referencing environment. At any point in the future, f can call c to re-establish the saved environment. If nested calls have been made, control pops out of them, as it does with exceptions. More generally, however, c can be saved in variables, returned explicitly by subroutines, or called repeatedly, even after control has returned from f (recall that closures in Scheme have unlimited extent; see Section 3.4). `Call/cc` suffices to build a wide variety of control abstractions, including iterators and coroutines (see below) and the `exits` and `returns` of nonfunctional programs. It even subsumes the notion of returning from a subroutine, though it seldom replaces it in practice.

Intermediate between the anarchy of nonlocal `goto`s and the generality of `call/cc`, most versions of C (including the ANSI standard) provide a pair of library routines entitled `setjmp` and `longjmp`. `Setjmp` takes as argument a buffer into which to capture a representation of the program's current state. This buffer can later be passed to `longjmp` to restore the captured state. `Setjmp` returns C's equivalent of a Boolean value: a 0 or a 1. The 0 indicates "normal" return; the 1 indicates "return" from a `longjmp`. The usual programming idiom looks like this:

```
if (!setjmp (buffer)) {
    /* protected code */
} else {
    /* handler */
}
```

When initially called, `setjmp` returns a 0, and control enters the protected code. If `longjmp (buffer)` is called anywhere within the protected code, or in subroutines called by that code, then `setjmp` will appear to return again, this time with a 1, causing control to enter the handler. Unlike the closure created by `call/cc`, the information captured by `setjmp` has limited extent; once the protected code completes, the behavior of `longjmp (buffer)` is undefined.

`Setjmp` and `longjmp` are usually implemented by saving the current machine registers in the `setjmp` buffer, and by restoring them in `longjmp`. There is no list of handlers; rather than "unwinding" the stack, the implementation simply tosses all the nested frames by restoring old values of the `sp` and `fp`. The problem with this approach is that the register contents at the beginning of the handler do not reflect the effects of the successfully completed portion of the protected code: they were saved before that code began to run. Any changes to variables that have been written through to memory will be visible in the handler, but changes that were being cached in registers will be lost. To address this limitation, C allows the programmer to specify that certain variables are `volatile`. A volatile variable is one whose value in memory can change "spontaneously," for example as the result of activity by an I/O device or a concurrent thread of control. C implementations are required to store volatile variables to memory whenever they are written, and to load them from memory whenever they are read. If a handler needs to see changes to a variable that may be modified by the protected code, then the programmer must include the `volatile` keyword in the variable's declaration.

Because it saves many registers to memory, `setjmp` is quite expensive—more so than entry to a protected block in the "obvious" implementation of exceptions described earlier.

8.6 Coroutines

Given an understanding of the layout of the run-time stack, we can now consider the implementation of more general control abstractions—*coroutines* in particular. Like a continuation, a coroutine is represented by a closure (a code address and a referencing environment), into which we can jump by means of a nonlocal `goto`, in this case a special operation known as `transfer`. The principal difference between the two abstractions is that a continuation is a constant—it does not change once created—while a coroutine changes every time it runs. When we `goto` a continuation, our old program counter is lost, unless we explicitly create a new continuation to hold it. When we `transfer` from one coroutine to another, our old program counter is saved: the coroutine we are leaving is updated to reflect it. Thus, if we perform a `goto` into the same continuation multiple times, each jump will start at precisely the same location, but if we perform a `transfer` into the same coroutine multiple times, each jump will take up where the previous one left off.

In effect, coroutines are execution contexts that exist concurrently, but that execute one at a time, and that transfer control to each other explicitly, by name. Coroutines can be used to implement iterators (Section 6.5.3) and threads (to be discussed in Chapter 12). They are also useful in their own right, particularly for certain kinds of servers, and for discrete event simulation. Threads appear in a variety of languages, including Algol 68, Modula (1), Modula-3, Ada, SR, Occam, and Java. They are also commonly provided (though with somewhat less attractive syntax and semantics) outside the language proper by means of library packages. Coroutines are less common as a programming abstraction. Languages that provide them include Simula and Modula-2. We focus in the following sections on the implementation of coroutines and on their use in iterators (Section 8.6.3) and discrete event simulation (Section 8.6.4).

As a simple example of an application in which coroutines might be useful, imagine that we are writing a "screen-saver" program, which paints a mostly black picture on the screen of an inactive workstation, and which keeps the picture moving, to avoid phosphor "burn-in." Imagine also that our screen-server performs "sanity checks" on the file system in the background, looking for corrupted files. We could write our program as follows:

```
loop
    -- update picture on screen
    -- perform next sanity check
```

The problem with this approach is that successive sanity checks (and to a lesser extent successive screen updates) are likely to depend on each other. On most systems, the file-system checking code has a deeply nested control structure containing many loops. To break it into pieces that can be interleaved with the screen updates, the programmer must follow each check with code that saves the state of the nested computation, and must precede the following check with code that restores that state. A much more attractive approach is to cast the operations as coroutines:[10]

```
us, cfs : coroutine

coroutine update_screen
    -- initialize
    detach
    loop
        . . .
        transfer (cfs)
        . . .

coroutine check_file_system
    -- initialize
    detach
    for all files
        . . .
        transfer (us)
        . . .
            transfer (us)
        . . .
        transfer (us)
        . . .

begin        -- main
    us := new update_screen
    cfs := new check_file_system
    transfer (us)
```

The syntax here is loosely based on that of Simula. When first created, a coroutine performs any necessary initialization operations, and then detaches itself from the main program. The detach operation creates a coroutine object to which control can later be transfered, and returns a reference to this coroutine to the caller. The transfer operation saves the current program counter in

---

10 Threads could also be used in this example, and might in fact serve our needs a bit better. Coroutines suffice because there is a small number of execution contexts (namely two), and because it is easy to identify points at which one should transfer to the other.

the current coroutine object and resumes the coroutine specified as a parameter. The main body of the program plays the role of an initial, default coroutine.

Calls to `transfer` from within the body of check_file_system can occur at arbitrary places, including nested loops and conditionals. A coroutine can also call subroutines, just as the main program can, and calls to `transfer` may appear inside these routines. The context needed to perform the "next" sanity check is captured by the program counter, together with the local variables of check_file_system and any called routines, at the time of the `transfer`.

As in our original screen saver loop, the programmer must specify when to stop checking the file system and update the screen; coroutines make the job simpler by providing a `transfer` operation that eliminates the need to save and restore state explicitly. To decide where to place the calls to `transfer`, we must consider both performance and correctness. For performance, we must avoid doing too much work between calls, so that screen updates aren't too infrequent. For correctness, we must avoid doing a `transfer` in the middle of any check that might be compromised by file access in update_screen. Parallel threads (to be described in Chapter 12) would eliminate the first of these problems by ensuring that the screen updater receives a share of the processor on a regular basis, but would complicate the second problem: we should need to synchronize the two routines explicitly if their references to files could interfere.

8.6.1 Stack Allocation

Because they are concurrent (i.e., simultaneously started but not completed), coroutines cannot share a single stack: their subroutine calls and returns, taken as a whole, do not occur in last-in-first-out order. If each coroutine is declared at the outermost level of lexical nesting (as required in Modula-2), then their stacks are entirely disjoint: the only objects they share are global, and thus statically allocated. Most operating systems make it easy to allocate one stack, and to increase its portion of the virtual address space as necessary during execution. It is usually not easy to allocate an arbitrary number of such stacks; space for coroutines is something of an implementation challenge.

The simplest solution is to give each coroutine a fixed amount of statically allocated stack space. This approach is adopted in Modula-2, which requires the programmer to specify the size and location of the stack when initializing a coroutine. It is a run-time error for the coroutine to need additional space. Some Modula-2 implementations catch the overflow and halt with an error message; others display abnormal behavior. If the coroutine uses less space than it is given, the excess is simply wasted.

If stack frames are allocated from the heap, as they are in most Lisp and Scheme implementations, then the problems of overflow and internal fragmentation are avoided. At the same time, the overhead of each subroutine call is significantly increased. An intermediate option is to allocate the stack in large, fixed-size "chunks." At each call, the subroutine calling sequence checks to see

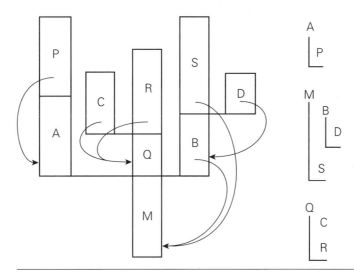

Figure 8.9 A cactus stack. Each branch to the side represents the creation of a coroutine (A, B, C, and D). The static nesting of blocks is shown at right. Static links are shown with arrows. Dynamic links are indicated simply by vertical arrangement: each routine has called the one above it.

whether there is sufficient space in the current chunk to hold the frame of the called routine. If not, another chunk is allocated and the frame is put there instead. At each subroutine return, the epilogue code checks to see whether the current frame is the last one in its chunk. If so, the chunk is returned to a "free chunk" pool.

In any of these implementations, subroutine calls can use the ordinary central stack if the compiler is able to verify that they will not perform a `transfer` before returning [Sco91].

If coroutines can be created at arbitrary levels of lexical nesting (as they can in Simula), then two or more coroutines may be declared in the same non-global scope, and must thus share access to objects in that scope. To implement this sharing, the run-time system must employ a so-called *cactus stack* (see Figure 8.9). Each branch off the stack contains the frames of a separate coroutine. The dynamic chain of a given coroutine ends in the block in which the coroutine began execution. The *static* chain of the coroutine, however, extends down into the remainder of the cactus, through any lexically surrounding blocks. In addition to the coroutines of Simula, cactus stacks are needed for the threads of several parallel languages, including Ada. "Returning" from the main block of a coroutine will generally terminate the program as a whole. Because a coroutine only runs when specified as the target of a `transfer`, there is never any need to terminate it explicitly: if it is running it can transfer to something else, which never transfers back. When a given coroutine is no longer needed, the Modula-2 programmer can simply reuse its stack space. In Simula, the space will be reclaimed via garbage collection when it is no longer accessible.

8.6.2 Transfer

To transfer from one coroutine to another, the run-time system must change the program counter (PC), the stack, and the contents of the processor's registers. These changes are encapsulated in the `transfer` operation: one coroutine calls `transfer`; a different one returns. Because the change happens inside `transfer`, changing the PC from one coroutine to another simply amounts to remembering the right return address: the old coroutine calls `transfer` from one location in the program; the new coroutine returns to a potentially different location. If `transfer` saves its return address in the stack, then the PC will change automatically as a side effect of changing stacks.

So how do we change stacks? The usual approach is simply to change the stack pointer register, and to avoid the use of the frame pointer inside of `transfer` itself. At the beginning of `transfer` we push the return address and all of the other callee-saves registers onto the current stack. We then change the sp, pop the (new) return address and other registers off the new stack, and return:

```
transfer:
        push all registers other than sp (including ra)
        *current_coroutine := sp
        current_coroutine := r1      -- argument passed to transfer
        sp := *r1
        pop all registers other than sp (including ra)
        return
```

The data structure that represents a coroutine or thread is called a *context block*. In a simple coroutine package, the context block contains a single value: the coroutine's sp as of its most recent `transfer`. (A thread package generally places additional information in the context block, such as an indication of priority, or pointers to link the thread onto various scheduling queues. Some coroutine or thread packages choose to save registers in the context block, rather than at the top of the stack; either approach works fine.)

In Modula-2, the coroutine creation routine initializes the coroutine's stack to look like the frame of `transfer`, with a return address and register contents initialized to permit a "return" into the beginning of the coroutine's code. The creation routine sets the sp value in the context block to point into this artificial frame, and returns a pointer to the context block. To begin execution of the coroutine, some existing routine must `transfer` to it.

In Simula (and in the code on p. 475), the coroutine creation routine begins to execute the new coroutine immediately, as if it were a subroutine. After the coroutine completes any application-specific initialization, it performs a `detach` operation. Detach sets up the coroutine stack to look like the frame of `transfer`, with a return address that points to the following statement. It then allows the creation routine to return to its own caller.

In all cases, `transfer` expects a pointer to a context block as argument; by dereferencing the pointer it can find the `sp` of the next coroutine to run. A global (static) variable, called current_coroutine in the code above, contains a pointer to the context block of the currently running coroutine. This pointer allows `transfer` to find the location in which it should save the old `sp`.

8.6.3* Iterators

Given an implementation of coroutines, iterators are almost trivial. Consider the following `for` loop from Section 6.5.3:

```
for i in from_to_by (first, last, step) do
    . . .
end
```

The compiler can translate this as

```
it := new from_to_by (first, last, step, i, done, current_coroutine)
while not done do
    . . .
    transfer (it)
destroy (it)
```

After the loop completes, the implementation can reclaim the space consumed by it.

The definition of `from_to_by` itself is very similar to the code in Figure 6.5:

```
coroutine from_to_by (from, to, by : int;
        ref i : int; ref done : bool; caller : coroutine)
    i := from
    if by > 0 then
        done := from <= to
        detach
        loop
            i +:= by
            done := i <= to
            transfer (caller)    -- yield i
    else
        done := from >= to
        detach
        loop
            i +:= by
            done := i >= to
            transfer (caller)    -- yield i
```

Parameters i and done are passed by reference so that the iterator can modify them in the caller's context. The caller's identity is passed as a final argument so that the iterator can tell which coroutine to resume when it has computed the next loop index. Because the caller is named explicitly, it is easy for iterators to nest, as in Figure 6.6 (page 289).

It is worth noting, however, that while coroutines suffice for the implementation of iterators, they are not *necessary*. A simpler, single-stack implementation is also possible. Because a given iterator (e.g., an instance of from_to_by) is always resumed at the same place in the code (i.e., the top of a given for loop), we can be sure that the subroutine call stack will always contain the same frames whenever the iterator runs. Moreover, since yield statements can appear only in the main body of the iterator (never in nested routines), we can be sure that the stack will always contain the same frames whenever the iterator transfers back to its caller. These two facts imply that we can place the frame of the iterator directly on top of the frame of its caller in a single central stack.

When an iterator is created, its frame is pushed on the stack. When it yields a value, control returns to the for loop, but the iterator's frame is left on the stack. If the body of the loop makes any subroutine calls, the frames for those calls will be allocated beyond the frame of the iterator. Since control must return to the loop before the iterator resumes, we know that such frames will be gone again before the iterator has a chance to see them: if it needs to call subroutines itself, the stack above it will be clear. Likewise, if the iterator calls any subroutines, they will return (popping their frames from the stack) before the for loop runs again. Nested iterators present no special problems (see Exercise 8.19).

8.6.4* Example: Discrete Event Simulation

One of the most important applications of coroutines (and the one for which Simula was designed and named) is *discrete event simulation*. Simulation in general refers to any process in which we create an abstract model of some real-world system, and then experiment with the model in order to infer properties of the real-world system. Simulation is desirable when experimentation with the real world would be complicated, dangerous, expensive, or otherwise impractical. A *discrete event* simulation is one in which the model is naturally expressed in terms of events (typically interactions among various interesting objects) that happen at specific times. In the paragraphs that follow we will consider a traffic simulation, in which events model interactions among automobiles, intersections, and traffic lights. Discrete event simulation is usually not appropriate for the simulation of continuous processes, such as the growth of crystals or the flow of water over a surface, unless these processes are captured at the level of individual particles.

Suppose that we wish to experiment with the flow of traffic in a city. A computerized traffic model, if it captures the real world with sufficient accuracy, will allow us to predict the effects of construction projects, accidents, increased traffic due to new development, or changes to the layout of streets. It is difficult (though certainly not impossible) to write such a simulation in a conventional sequential language. We would probably represent each interesting object (automobile, intersection, street segment, etc.) with a data structure. Our main program would then look something like this:

```
while current_time < end_of_simulation
    calculate next time t at which an interesting interaction will occur
    current_time := t
    update state of objects to reflect the interaction
    record desired statistics
print collected statistics
```

The problem with this approach lies in determining which objects will interact next, and in remembering their state from one interaction to the next. It is in some sense unnatural to represent active objects such as cars with passive data structures, and to make time the active entity in the program. An arguably more attractive approach is to represent each active object with a coroutine, and to let each object keep track of its own state.

If each active object can tell when it will next do something interesting, then we can determine which objects will interact next by keeping the currently inactive coroutines in a priority queue, ordered by the time of their next event. We might begin a one-day traffic simulation by creating a coroutine for each trip to be taken by a car that day, and inserting each coroutine into the priority queue with a "wakeup" time indicating when the trip is to begin:

```
coroutine trip (...)
...
for each trip t
    p := new trip (...)
    schedule (p, t.start_time)
```

Let us assume that we think of street segments as passive, and represent them with data structures. At any given moment, we can model a segment by the number of cars that it is carrying in each direction. This number in turn will affect the speed at which the cars can safely travel. Whenever it awakens, the coroutine representing a trip examines the next street segment over which it needs to travel. Based on the current load on that segment, it calculates how much time it will take to traverse it, and schedules itself to awaken again at an appropriate point in the future:

```
coroutine trip (origin, destination : location)
    plan a route from origin to destination
    detach
    for each segment of the route
        calculate time i to reach the end of the segment
        schedule (current_coroutine, current_time + i)
```

The `schedule` operation is easily built on top of `transfer`:

```
schedule (p : coroutine; t : time)
    —— p may be self or other
    insert (p, t) in priority queue
    if p = current_coroutine      —— self
        extract earliest pair (q, s) from priority queue
        current_time := s
        transfer (q)
```

In some cases, it may be difficult to determine when to reschedule a given object. Suppose, for example, that we wish to more accurately model the effects of traffic signals at intersections. We might represent each traffic signal with a data structure that records the waiting cars in each direction, and a coroutine that lets cars through as the signal changes color:

```
record controlled_intersection =
    EW_cars, NS_cars : queue of trip
    const traversal_time : time
        —— how long it takes one car to get through the intersection
    coroutine signal (EW_duration, NS_duration : time)
        detach
        loop
            change_time := current_time + EW_duration
            while current_time < change_time
                if EW_cars not empty
                    schedule (dequeue (EW_cars), current_time)
                schedule (current_coroutine, current_time + traversal_time)
            change_time := current_time + NS_duration
            while current_time < change_time
                if NS_cars not empty
                    schedule (NS_cars.dequeue(), current_time)
                schedule (current_coroutine, current_time + traversal_time)
```

When it reaches the end of a street segment that is controlled by a traffic signal, a trip need not calculate how long it will take to get through the intersection. Rather, it enters itself into the appropriate queue of waiting cars and "goes to sleep," knowing that the `signal` coroutine will awaken it at some point in the future:

```
coroutine trip (origin, destination : location)
    plan a route from origin to destination
    detach
    for each segment of the route
        calculate time i to reach the end of the segment
```

```
        schedule (current_coroutine, current_time + i)
        if end of segment has a traffic light
            identify appropriate queue Q
            Q.enqueue (current_coroutine)
            sleep()
```

Like `schedule`, `sleep` is easily built on top of `transfer`:

```
sleep ()
    extract earliest pair (q, s) from priority queue
    current_time := s
    transfer (q)
```

The `schedule` operation, in fact, is simply:

```
schedule (p : coroutine; t : time)
    insert (p, t) in priority queue
    if p = current_coroutine
        sleep()
```

Obviously this traffic simulation is too simplistic to capture the behavior of cars in a real city, but it illustrates the basic concepts of discrete event simulation. More sophisticated simulations are used in a wide range of application domains, including all branches of engineering, computational biology, physics and cosmology, and even computer design. Multiprocessor simulations (see reference [VF94], for example) are typically divided into a "front end" that simulates the processors and a "back end" that simulates the memory subsystem. Each coroutine in the front end consists of a machine-language interpreter that captures the behavior of one of the system's microprocessors. Each coroutine in the back end represents a load or a store instruction. Every time a processor performs a load or store, the front end creates a new coroutine in the back end. Data structures in the back end represent various hardware resources, including caches, buses, network links, message routers, and memory modules. The coroutine for a given load or store checks to see if its location is in the local cache. If not, it must traverse the interconnection network between the processor and memory, competing with other coroutines for access to hardware resources, much as cars in our simple example compete for access to street segments and intersections. The behavior of the back end system in turn affects the front end, since a processor must wait for a load to complete before it can use the data, and since the rate at which stores can be injected into the back end is limited by the rate at which they propagate to memory.

8.7 Summary and Concluding Remarks

This chapter has focused on the subject of control abstraction, and on subroutines in particular. Subroutines allow the programmer to encapsulate code behind a narrow interface, which can then be used without regard to its implementation. Control abstraction is crucial for the design and maintenance of any large software system. It is particularly effective from an aesthetic point of view in languages such as Lisp and Smalltalk, which use the same syntax for both built-in and user-defined control constructs.

We began our study of subroutines in Section 8.1 by reviewing the management of the subroutine call stack. We considered the *calling sequences* used to maintain the stack, illustrating issues with two case studies: the GNU `gcc` C compiler for the MIPS instruction set, and the Metrowerks CodeWarrior Pascal compiler for the 680x0. After a brief consideration of in-line expansion, we turned in Section 8.3 to the subject of parameters. We first considered parameter-passing *modes*, all of which are implemented by passing values, references, or closures. We noted that the goals of semantic clarity and implementation speed sometimes conflict: it is usually most efficient to pass a large parameter by reference, but the aliasing that results can lead to program bugs. In Section 8.3.2 we considered special parameter-passing mechanisms, including conformant arrays, default (optional) parameters, named parameters, and variable-length parameter lists. We noted that default and named parameters provide an attractive alternative to the use of dynamic scope. In Section 8.4 we considered the design and implementation of generic subroutines and modules. Generics allow a control abstraction to be parameterized (at compile time) in terms of the types of its parameters, rather than just their values.

In the final two major sections we considered exception-handling mechanisms, which allow a program to "unwind" in a well-structured way from a nested sequence of subroutine calls, and coroutines, which allow a program to maintain two or more execution contexts, and to switch back and forth among them. As examples, we considered the use of exceptions for phrase-level recovery from syntax errors in a recursive descent parser, and the use of coroutines for discrete event simulation. In Chapter 12, we will consider the extension of coroutines to *threads*, which run (or appear to run) in parallel with one another.

In several cases we can discern an evolving consensus about the sorts of control abstractions that a language should provide. The limited parameter-passing modes of languages such as Fortran and Algol 60 have been replaced by more extensive options. The standard positional notation for arguments has been augmented in languages such as Ada and C++ with default and named parameters. Less-structured error-handling mechanisms, such as label parameters, nonlocal `goto`s, and dynamically bound handlers, have been replaced by the more structured exceptions of Ada, C++, Common Lisp, Java, ML, and Modula-3, all of which are lexically scoped within subroutines, and can be implemented at zero cost in the common (no-exception) case. In many cases, implementing these newer features has required that compilers and run-time systems become more complex. Occasionally, as in the case of call-by-name parameters, label parameters, or nonlocal `goto`s, features that were semantically confusing were also difficult to implement, and abandoning them has made compilers simpler. In yet other cases language features that are useful but difficult to implement continue to appear in some languages but not in others. Examples in this category include first-class subroutines, coroutines, iterators, continuations, and local objects with unlimited extent.

8.8 Review Questions

8.1 What is a subroutine *calling sequence*? What does it do? What is meant by the subroutine *prologue* and *epilogue*?

8.2 How do calling sequences typically differ in CISC and RICS compilers?

8.3 Describe how to maintain the *static chain* during a subroutine call.

8.4 What is a *display*? How does it differ from a static chain? How is it maintained during a subroutine call?

8.5 What are the purposes of the *stack pointer* and *frame pointer* registers? Why does a subroutine often need both?

8.6 List the optimizations that can be made to the subroutine calling sequence in the case of a *leaf routine* (one that make no calls itself).

8.7 Why do compilers typically allocate space for arguments in the stack, even when they pass them in registers?

8.8 What is the difference between *actual* and *formal* parameters?

8.9 Describe four common parameter-passing modes. How does a programmer choose which one to use when?

8.10 Explain the rationale for `READONLY` parameters in Modula-3.

8.11 What is *call by name*? What language first provided it? Why isn't it used by the language's descendants?

8.12 What is a *thunk*? What is it used for?

8.13 How does an *in-line subroutine* differ from a *macro*?

8.14 How does a *generic subroutine* differ from a macro?

8.15 What are *named (keyword) parameters*? Why are they useful?

8.16 What is a *conformant (open) array*?

8.17 Give an example in which it is useful to return a reference from a function in C++.

8.18 Describe the algorithm used to identify an appropriate handler when an exception is raised in a language such as Ada or C++.

8.19 Explain why it is useful to define exceptions as classes in C++ and Java.

8.20 Explain how to implement exceptions in a way that incurs no cost in the common case (when exceptions don't arise).

8.21 Summarize the shortcomings of the `setjmp` and `longjmp` library routines of C.

8.22 What is a `volatile` variable in C? Under what circumstances is it useful?

8.23 What was the first high-level programming language to provide coroutines?

8.24 What is the difference between a *coroutine* and a *thread*?

8.25 What is a *cactus stack*?

8.26 Why doesn't the *transfer* library routine need to change the program counter when switching between coroutines?

8.27 Explain how to implement iterators without coroutines.

8.28* What is *discrete event simulation*?

8.9 Exercises

8.1 Describe as many ways as you can in which functions in Algol-family programming languages differ from functions in mathematics.

8.2 Using your favorite language and compiler, write a program that determines the order in which subroutine parameters are evaluated.

8.3 Can you write a macro in C that "returns" the greatest common divisor of a pair of arguments, without calling a subroutine? Why or why not?

8.4 Consider the following (erroneous) program in C:

```
void foo ()
{
    int i;
    printf ("%d ", i++);
}
main ()
{
    int j;
    for (j = 1; j <= 10; j++) foo ();
}
```

Local variable i in subroutine foo is never initialized. On many systems, however, the program will display repeatable behavior, printing 0 1 2 3 4 5 6 7 8 9. Suggest an explanation. Also explain why the behavior on other systems might be different, or nondeterministic.

8.5 The standard calling sequence for the Digital VAX instruction set employs not only a stack pointer (`sp`) and frame pointer (`fp`), but a separate *arguments pointer* (`ap`) as well. Under what circumstances might this separate pointer be useful? In other words, when might it be handy not to have to place arguments at statically known offsets from the `fp`?

8.6 Suppose you wish to minimize the size of closures in a language implementation that uses a display for access to nonlocal objects. Assuming a language such as Pascal or Ada, in which subroutines have limited extent (Section 3.4), explain how an appropriate display for a formal subroutine can be calculated when that routine is finally called, starting with only (1) the value of the frame pointer, saved in the closure at the time that the closure was created, (2) the subroutine return addresses found in the stack at the time the formal subroutine is finally called, and (3) static tables created by the compiler. How costly is your scheme?

8.7 Write (in the language of your choice) a procedure or function that will have four different effects, depending on whether arguments are passed by value, by reference, by value/result, or by name.

8.8 Consider an expression such as a + b that is passed to a subroutine in Fortran. Is there any semantically meaningful difference between passing this expression as a reference to an unnamed temporary (as Fortran does) or passing it by value (as one might, for example, in Pascal)?

8.9 In some implementations of Fortran IV, the following code would print a 3. Can you suggest an explanation? How do you suppose more recent Fortran implementations get around the problem?

```
c  main program
   call foo (2)
   print* 2
   stop
   end
   subroutine foo (x)
       x = x + 1
       return
       end
```

8.10 Suppose you are writing a program in which all parameters must be passed by name. Can you write a subroutine that will swap the values of its actual parameters? Explain. (Hint: consider mutually dependent parameters such as i and A[i].)

8.11 As noted in Section 8.3.1, out parameters in Ada 83 can be written by the callee but not read. In Ada 95 they can be both read and written, but they begin their life uninitialized. Why do you think the designers of Ada 95 made this change? Does it have any drawbacks?

8.12 If you were designing a new imperative language, what set of parameter modes would you pick? Why?

8.13 Does a program run faster when the programmer leaves optional parameters out of a subroutine call? Why or why not?

8.14 Why do you suppose that variable-length argument lists are so seldom supported by high-level programming languages?

8.15 Algol allows labels to be passed as parameters, and allows gotos to these labels. One can imagine using these "nonlocal gotos" to escape from a nested function in response to unexpected conditions, but modern language designers regard label parameters as a bad idea. In what way(s) is the exception handling of Ada, Modula-3, or C++/Java better?

8.16 Find manuals for several languages with exceptions and look up the set of predefined exceptions—those that may be raised automatically by the language implementation. Discuss the differences among the sets defined by different languages. If you were designing an exception-handling facility, what exceptions, if any, would you make predefined? Why?

8.17 In Common Lisp an expression is protected with a `catch` block:

```
(catch 'tag
    expr)
```

Here `tag` is an atom and `expr` is the protected expression. Anywhere within `expr`, the `tag` exception may be raised with a `throw` expression:

```
(throw 'tag val)
```

Here `val` is an expression whose value replaces that of the protected expression `expr` in the `catch` block. Note that unlike all other languages considered in Section 8.5, Common Lisp requires the work of handling the exception (i.e., choosing an alternative value for the protected expression) to occur in the context of the `throw`, at the point where the exception arises, rather than in the context of the `catch`. Show how to build on `catch` and `throw` to obtain more conventional semantics: to defer the work to the context where the exception is caught, rather than where it is raised.

8.18 Show how to implement exceptions in Scheme using `call/cc`.

8.19 Following the code in Figure 6.6, and assuming a single-stack implementation of iterators, trace the contents of the stack during the enumeration of all binary trees with three nodes.

8.20 If you have manuals for Common Lisp, Modula-3, and Java, compare the semantics they provide for `unwind-protect` and `try...finally`. Specifically, what happens if an exception arises within a cleanup clause?

8.21 Use coroutines to build support for iterators in Modula-2. Your code should allow the programmer to create new iterators easily. Try to hide as much of the implementation as possible inside a module. In particular, hide the use of `transfer` inside implementations of routines named `yield` (to be called by an iterator coroutine) and `next` (to be called in the body of a loop). Discuss any weaknesses you encounter in the abstraction facilities of the language.

8.22* One source of inaccuracy in the traffic simulation of Section 8.6.4 has to do with the timing at traffic signals. If a signal is currently green in the EW direction, but the queue of waiting cars is empty, the `signal` coroutine will go to sleep until `current_time + EW_duration`. If a car arrives before the coroutine wakes up again, it will needlessly wait. Discuss how you might remedy this problem.

8.10 Bibliographic Notes

Recursive subroutines became known primarily through McCarthy's work on Lisp [McC60]. Stack-based space management for recursive subroutines developed with compilers for Algol 60 (see for example Randell and Russell [RR64]). (Because of issues of extent, subroutine space in Lisp requires more general, heap-based allocation.) Dijkstra [Dij60] presents an early discussion of the use of displays to access nonlocal data. Hanson [Han81] argues that nested subroutines are unnecessary.

Calling sequences and stack conventions for gcc are partially documented in the texinfo files distributed with the compiler (see *http://www.fsf.org/software*). Metrowerks CodeWarrior also comes with extensive documentation. Several of the details described in this chapter were "reverse engineered" by examining the output of the two compilers.

The Ada language rationale [IBFW91, chap. 8] contains an excellent discussion of parameter-passing modes. Harbison [Har92, secs. 6.2–6.3] describes the Modula-3 modes and compares them to those of other languages. Liskov and Guttag [LG86, p. 25] liken call-by-sharing in Clu to parameter passing in Lisp. Call-by-name parameters have their roots in the lambda calculus of Alonzo Church [Chu41], to be discussed in more detail in Section 11.2.4. Thunks were first described by Ingerman [Ing61]. Fleck [Fle76] discusses the problems involved in trying to write a swap routine with call-by-name parameters (Exercise 8.10).

MacLaren [Mac77] describes exception handling in PL/I. The lexically scoped alternative of Ada, and of several more recent languages, draws heavily on the work of Goodenough [Goo75]. Ada's semantics are described formally by Luckam and Polak [LP80]. Liskov and Snyder [LS79] discuss exception handling in Clu. Friedman, Wand, and Haynes [FWH92, chaps. 8–9] provide an excellent explanation of continuation-passing style in Scheme.

An early description of coroutines appears in the work of Conway [Con63], who uses them to represent the phases of compilation. Birtwistle et al. [BDMN73] provide a tutorial introduction to the use of coroutines for simulation in Simula 67. Cactus stacks date from at least the mid-1960s; they were supported directly in hardware by the Burroughs B6500 and B7500 computers [HD68]. Murer et al. [MOSS96] discuss the implementation of iterators in the Sather programming language (a descendant of Eiffel).

Building a Runnable Program

As noted in Section 1.6, the various phases of compilation are commonly grouped into a *front end* responsible for the analysis of source code and a *back end* responsible for the synthesis of target code. Chapters 2 and 4 discussed the work of the front end, culminating in the construction of a syntax tree. The current chapter turns to the work of the back end, and specifically to code generation, assembly, and linking. We will continue with code improvement in Chapter 13.

In Chapters 6 through 8, we often discussed the code that a compiler would generate to implement various imperative language features. Now we will look at how the compiler produces that code from a syntax tree, and how it combines the output of multiple compilations to produce a runnable program. We begin in Section 9.1 with a more detailed overview of the work of program synthesis than was possible in Chapter 1. We focus in particular on one of several plausible ways of dividing that work into phases. In Section 9.2 we then consider the many possible forms of intermediate code passed between these phases. As examples we present Diana, commonly used by Ada compilers, and RTL, used by the GNU compilers.

In Section 9.3 we discuss the generation of assembly code from an abstract syntax tree, using attribute grammars as a formal framework. In Section 9.4 we discuss the internal organization of binary object files and the layout of programs in memory. Section 9.5 describes assembly. Section 9.6 considers linking.

9.1 Back-End Compiler Structure

As we noted in Chapter 4, there is less uniformity in back-end compiler structure than there is in front-end structure. Even such unconventional compilers as text processors, source-to-source translators, and VLSI layout tools must scan, parse, and analyze the semantics of their input. When it comes to the back end, however, even compilers for the same language on the same machine can have very different internal structure.

As we shall see in Section 9.2 below, different compilers may use different intermediate forms to represent a program internally. Depending on the preferences of the programmers building a compiler, the constraints under which those programmers are working, and the expected user community, compilers may also differ dramatically in the forms of code improvement they perform. A simple compiler, or one designed for speed of compilation rather than speed of target code execution (a "just-in-time" compiler, for example) may not do much improvement at all. A just-in-time or "load-and-go" compiler (one that compiles and then executes a program as a single high-level operation, without writing the target code to a file) may not use a separate linker. In many compilers, much or all of the code generator may be written automatically by a tool (a "code generator generator") that takes a formal description of the target machine as input [GFH82].

9.1.1 An Example

Figure 9.1 illustrates a plausible seven-phase structure for a conventional compiler. The first three phases (scanning, parsing, and semantic analysis) are language-dependent; the last two (target code generation and machine-specific code improvement) are machine-dependent, and the middle two (intermediate code generation and machine-independent code improvement) are (to first approximation) dependent on neither the language nor the machine. The scanner and parser drive a set of action routines that build a syntax tree. The semantic analyzer traverses the tree, performing all static semantic checks and initializing various attributes (mainly symbol table pointers and indications of the need for dynamic checks) of use to the back end.

While certain code improvements can be performed on syntax trees, a less hierarchical representation of the program makes most code improvement easier. Our example compiler therefore includes an explicit phase for intermediate code generation. The code generator begins by grouping the nodes of the tree into *basic blocks*, each of which consists of a maximal-length set of operations that should execute sequentially at run time, with no branches in or out. It then creates a *control flow graph* in which the nodes are basic blocks and the arcs represent interblock control flow. Within each basic block, operations are represented as instructions for an idealized RISC machine with an unlimited number of registers. We will call these *virtual registers*. By allocating a new one for every computed value, the compiler can avoid creating artificial connections between otherwise independent computations too early in the compilation process.

In Section 1.6 we used a simple greatest common divisor (GCD) program to illustrate the phases of compilation. The syntax tree for this program appeared in Figure 1.4; it is reproduced here (in slightly altered form) as Figure 9.2. A corresponding control flow graph appears in Figure 9.3. We will discuss techniques to generate this graph in Section 9.3 and Exercise 9.9. Additional examples of control flow graphs will appear in Chapter 13.

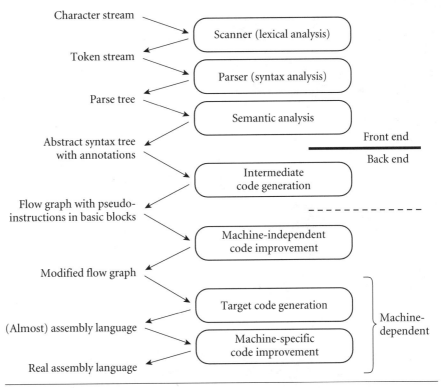

Figure 9.1   **A plausible structure for the compiler back end.** Here we have shown a sharper separation between semantic analysis and intermediate code generation than we considered in Chapter 1 (see Figure 1.2, page 16). Machine-independent code improvement employs an intermediate form that resembles the assembly language for an idealized machine with an unlimited number of registers. Machine-specific code improvement—register allocation and instruction scheduling in particular—employs the assembly language of the target machine. The dashed line shows a common alternative "break point" between the front end and back end of a two-pass compiler.

The second phase of the back end, machine-independent code improvement, performs a variety of transformations on the control flow graph. It modifies the instruction sequence within each basic block to eliminate redundant loads, stores, and arithmetic computations (these are "local" code improvements). It also identifies and removes a variety of redundancies across the boundaries between basic blocks. As an example, an expression whose value is computed immediately before an `if` statement need not be recomputed within the code that follows the `else`. Likewise an expression that appears within the body of a loop need only be evaluated once if its value will not change in subsequent iterations. Some of these "global" code improvements change the number of basic blocks and/or the arcs among them.

Following machine-independent code improvement, the next phase of compi-

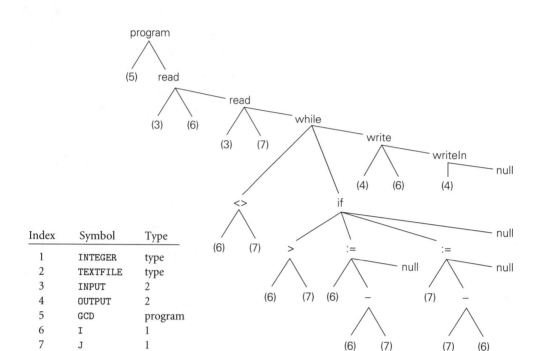

Index	Symbol	Type
1	INTEGER	type
2	TEXTFILE	type
3	INPUT	2
4	OUTPUT	2
5	GCD	program
6	I	1
7	J	1

Figure 9.2 Syntax tree and symbol table for the GCD program. The only difference from Figure 1.4 is the addition of explicit null nodes to terminate statement lists.

lation is target code generation. This phase strings the basic blocks together into a linear program, translating each block into the instruction set of the target machine and generating branch instructions (or "fall-throughs") that correspond to the arcs of the control flow graph. The output of this phase differs from real assembly language primarily in its continued reliance on virtual registers. So long as the pseudoinstructions of the intermediate form are reasonably close to those of the target machine, this phase of compilation, though tedious, is more or less straightforward.

To reduce programmer effort and increase the ease with which a compiler can be ported to a new target machine, target code generators are often generated automatically from a formal description of the machine. Automatically generated code generators all rely on some sort of pattern-matching algorithm to replace sequences of intermediate code instructions with equivalent sequences of target machine instructions. References to several such algorithms can be found in the Bibliographic Notes at the end of this chapter; details are beyond the scope of this book.

The final phase of our example compiler structure consists of register allocation and instruction scheduling, both of which can be thought of as machine-specific code improvement. Register allocation requires that we map the unlimited virtual registers employed in earlier phases onto the bounded set of physical

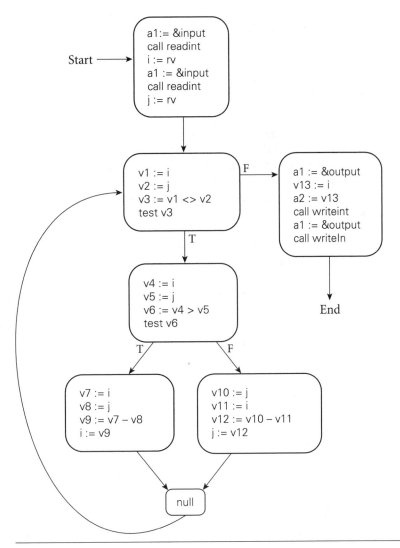

Figure 9.3 Control flow graph for the GCD program. Code within basic blocks is shown in the pseudo-assembly notation of Section 5.5.2, with a different virtual register (here named v1..v13) for every computed value. Registers a1, a2, and rv are used to pass values to and from subroutines.

registers available in the target machine. If there aren't enough physical registers to go around, we may need to generate additional loads and stores to multiplex a given physical register among two or more virtual registers. As described in Section 5.6, instruction scheduling consists of reordering the instructions of each basic block in an attempt to fill the pipeline(s) of the target machine.

9.1.2 **Phases and Passes**

In Section 1.6 we defined a *pass* of compilation as a phase or sequence of phases that is serialized with respect to the rest of compilation: it does not start until previous phases have completed, and it finishes before any subsequent phases start. If desired, a pass may be written as a separate program, reading its input from a file and writing its output to a file. Two-pass compilers are particularly common. They may be divided between the front end and the back end (i.e., between semantic analysis and intermediate code generation) or between intermediate code generation and global code improvement. In the latter case, the first pass is still commonly referred to as the front end and the second pass as the back end.

Like most compilers, our example generates symbolic assembly language as its output (a few compilers, including those written by IBM for the PowerPC, generate binary machine code directly). The assembler (not shown in Figure 9.1) behaves like an extra pass, assigning addresses to fragments of data and code, and translating symbolic operations into their binary encodings. In most cases, the input to the compiler will have consisted of source code for a single compilation unit. After assembly, the output will need to be *linked* to other fragments of the application, and to various pre-existing subroutine libraries. Some of the work of linking may be delayed until load time (immediately prior to program execution) or even until run time (during program execution). We will discuss assembly and linking in Sections 9.5 through 9.7.

9.2 Intermediate Forms

An *intermediate form* (IF) provides the link between the front end and the back end of the compiler, and continues to represent the program during the various back-end phases.

IFs can be classified in terms of their *level*, or degree of machine dependence. High-level IFs are often based on trees or directed acyclic graphs (DAGs) that directly capture the hierarchical structure of modern programming languages. A high-level IF facilitates certain kinds of machine-independent code improvement, incremental program updates (e.g., in a language-based editor), direct interpretation, and other operations based strongly on the structure of the source. Because the permissible structure of a tree can be described formally by a set of productions (as described in Section 4.6), manipulations of tree-based forms can be written as attribute grammars.

Stack-based languages are another common type of high-level IF. We saw two examples of these languages in Section 1.4: the P-code generated by many early Pascal compilers and the byte code used by Java. Stack-based IFs are both simple and compact. Though written in linear form, they closely resemble the result of enumerating tree nodes in post-order. Operations in a stack-based language obtain their operands from, and return their result to, a common implicit stack. For Pascal, the simplicity of P-code interpreters was a major contributing factor to the language's popularity: Pascal was easy to port to a wide variety of machines. For Java, the compactness of byte code helps reduce the time required to send program fragments (*applets*) over low-bandwidth Internet links. Unfortunately, stack-based languages do not lend themselves well to many important code improvements, especially for modern machines. As a result they tend not to be used in most conventional compilers.

The most common medium-level IFs consist of three-address instructions for a simple idealized machine, typically one with an unlimited number of registers. Since the typical instruction specifies two operands, an operator, and a destination, three-address instructions are sometimes called *quadruples*. In older compilers, one may sometimes find an intermediate form consisting of *triples* or *indirect triples* in which destinations are specified implicitly: the index of a triple in the instruction stream serves as the name of the result, and an operand is generally named by specifying the index of the triple that produced it.

Different compilers use different IFs. Many compilers use more than one IF internally, though in the common two-pass organization one of these is distinguished as "the" intermediate form by virtue of being the externally visible link between the front end and the back end. In the example of Section 9.1.1, the syntax trees passed from semantic analysis to intermediate code generation constitute a high-level IF. Control flow graphs containing pseudo-assembly language (passed in and out of machine-independent code improvement) are a medium-level IF. The assembly language of the target machine (initially with virtual registers; later with physical registers) serves as a low-level IF.

Compilers that have back ends for several different target architectures tend to do as much work as possible on a high or medium-level IF, so that the machine-independent parts of the code improver can be shared by different back ends. By contrast, some (but not all) compilers that generate code for a single architecture perform most code improvement on a comparatively low-level IF, closely modeled after the assembly language of the target machine.

In a multilanguage compiler family, an IF that is independent of both source language and target machine allows a software vendor who wishes to sell compilers for n languages on m machines to build just n front ends and m back ends, rather than $n \times m$ integrated compilers. Even in a single-language compiler family, a common, possibly language-dependent IF simplifies the task of porting to a new machine by isolating the code that needs to be changed. In a rich program development environment, there may be a variety of tools in addition to the passes of the compiler that understand and operate on the IF. Examples include editors, assemblers, linkers, debuggers, pretty-printers, and version-management software. In a language system capable of interprocedural (whole-program) code improvement, separately compiled modules and libraries may be compiled only to the IF, rather than the target language, leaving the final stages of compilation to the linker.

To be stored in a file, an IF requires a linear representation. Sequences of quadruples are naturally linear. Tree-based IFs can be linearized via ordered traversal. Structures such as control flow graphs can be linearized by replacing pointers with indices relative to the beginning of the file.

In the following two subsections we will consider a pair of widely used IFs. The first is a high-level tree-based form called Diana [GWEB83], used by most Ada compilers. The second is a medium-level IF called RTL (register transfer language), used by gcc and most of the Free Software Foundation's other GNU compilers (including the Ada 95 Translator, gnat).

9.2.1* Diana

Diana (Descriptive Intermediate Attributed Notation for Ada) is an Ada-specific tree-based IF developed cooperatively by researchers at the University of Karlsruhe in Germany, Carnegie Mellon University, Intermetrics, Softech, and Tartan Laboratories. It incorporates features from two earlier efforts, named TCOL and AIDA.

Diana is very complex (the documentation is 200 pages long), but highly regular, and we can at least give the flavor of it here. It is formally described using a pre-existing notation called IDL [SS89], which stands for Interface Description Language. IDL is widely used for describing abstract data types in a machine- and implementation-independent way. Using IDL-based tools, one can automatically construct routines to translate concrete instances of an abstract data type to and from a standard linear representation written in ASCII. IDL is perfectly suited for Diana. Other uses include multi-database systems, message-passing across distributed networks, and compilation for heterogeneous parallel machines. In addition to providing the interface between the front end and back end of an Ada compiler, Diana frequently serves as the standard representation of fragments of Ada code in a wider program development environment.

Diana structures are defined abstractly as trees, but they are not necessarily represented that way. To guarantee portability across platforms and among the products produced by different vendors, all programs that use Diana must be able to read and write the linear ASCII format. Vendors are allowed (and in fact encouraged) to extend Diana by adding new attributes to the tree nodes, but a tool that produces Diana conforming to the standard must generate all the standard attributes and must never use the standard attributes for nonstandard purposes. Similarly, a tool that consumes Diana conforming to the standard may exploit information in extra attributes if it is provided, but must be capable of functioning correctly when given only the standard attributes.

Ada compilers construct and decorate the nodes of a Diana tree in separate passes. The Diana manual recommends that the construction pass be driven by an attribute grammar. This pass establishes the lexical and syntactic attributes of tree nodes. Lexical attributes include the spelling of identifier names and the location (file name, line and column number) of constructs. Syntactic attributes are the parent–child links of the tree itself.[1] Subsequent traversal(s) of the tree establish the semantic and code-based attributes of tree nodes. Code-based attributes represent low-level properties such as numeric precision that have been specified in the Ada source.

Symbol-table information is represented in Diana as semantic attributes of declarations, rather than as a separate structure. If desired, an *implementation* of Diana can break this information out into a separate structure for convenience, so long as it retains the tree-based abstract interface. Occurrences of names are then linked to their declarations by "cross links" in the tree. A fully attributed Diana structure is therefore in fact a DAG, rather than a tree. The cross links are all among the semantic attributes, so the initial structure (formed of lexical and syntactic attributes) is indeed a tree.

IDL (and thus the Diana definition) employs a tree grammar notation similar to that of Section 4.6. Unlike BNF this notation defines a complete syntax tree, rather than just its fringe (i.e., the yield). To avoid the many "useless" nodes of a typical parse tree, IDL distinguishes between two kinds of symbols, which it calls *classes* and *nodes*. The nodes are the "interesting" symbols—the ones that are in the Diana tree. The classes are the "uninteresting" symbols; they exist to facilitate construction of the grammar. In effect, the distinction between classes and nodes serves the same purpose as the $A : B$ notation in the productions of Section 4.6.

Figure 9.4 contains an IDL example adapted from the Diana manual [GWEB83, p. 26]. The `ExpressionTree` abstraction defined here is much simpler than the corresponding portion of Diana, but it serves to illustrate the IDL notation. An `ExpressionTree` for (1 + 3) * 2 appears in Figure 9.5. Note that the classes (EXP and OPERATOR) do not appear in the tree. Only the nodes (`tree` and `leaf`) appear.

9.2.2* GNU RTL

Many readers will be familiar with the GNU family of compilers, distributed by the Free Software Foundation. These compilers are used very widely in academia, and increasingly in industry as well. GNU compilers are available for C, C++, Objective C, Ada 95, Fortran 77, and Pascal.[2] The C compiler, `gcc`, is the original, and the one most widely used. There are back ends for dozens of processor

---

[1] Terminology here is potentially confusing. We have been using the term "attribute" to refer to annotations appended to the nodes of a parse tree. Diana uses the term for *all* the information stored in the nodes of a syntax tree. This information includes the references to other nodes that define the structure of the tree.

[2] There are unrelated GNU implementations of several other languages as well, including Perl and Smalltalk.

```
Structure ExpressionTree Root EXP is
    -- ExpressionTree is the name of the abstract data type.
    -- EXP is the start symbol (goal) symbol of the grammar.

    Type Source_Position ;
        -- This is a private (implementation-dependent) type.

    EXP  ::= leaf | tree ;
        -- EXP is a class.  By convention, class names are written
        -- in all upper-case letters.  They are defined with "::="
        -- productions.  Their right-hand-sides must be an alternation
        -- of singletons, each of which is either a class or a node.

    tree  => as_op: OPERATOR,  as_left: EXP,  as_right: EXP ;
    tree  => lx_src: Source_Position ;
    leaf  => lx_name: String ; lx_src: Source_Position ;
        -- tree and leaf are nodes.  They are the symbols actually
        -- contained in an ExpressionTree.  Their attributes (including
        -- substructure) are defined by "=>" productions.  Multiple
        -- productions for the same node are NOT alternatives; they
        -- define additional attributes.  Thus, every tree node has four
        -- attributes: as_op, as_left, as_right, and lx_src.  Every leaf
        -- has two attributes: lx_name and lx_src.  By convention,
        -- Diana uses 'lx_' to preface lexical attributes,
        -- 'as_' to preface abstract syntax attributes,
        -- 'sm_' to preface semantic attributes, and
        -- 'cd_' to preface code attributes.

        -- In a more realistic example, leaf would have a sm_dec
        -- attribute that identified its declaration node, where
        -- additional attributes would describe its type, scope, etc.

    OPERATOR  ::=  plus | minus | times | divide ;
    plus => ;  minus => ;  times => ;  divide => ;
        -- OPERATOR is a class consisting of the standard four binary
        -- operators.  The null productions reflect the fact that an
        -- operator's name tells us all we need to know about it.
        -- We could have made the operator of a tree node a private
        -- type, eliminating the need for the null productions and empty
        -- subtree, but this would have pushed operators out of the
        -- machine-independent part of the notation, which is unacceptable.
End
```

Figure 9.4 Example of the IDL notation used to define Diana.

---

architectures, including the Compaq Alpha, HP PA-RISC, IBM PowerPC, Intel x86, Motorola 680x0 and 880x0, SGI MIPS, and Sun Sparc.

Gcc has, in some sense, two IFs. The first is a syntax tree. The second is a list of instruction-like expressions known as Register Transfer Language (RTL). Action routines in the grammar construct the syntax tree. At the end of each statement

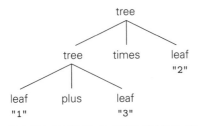

Figure 9.5 **Abstract syntax tree for** (1 + 3) * 2, **using the IDL definition of Figure 9.4.** Every node also has an attribute src of type Source_Position; these are not shown here.

in the source program they translate the syntax tree fragment for that statement into RTL. At the end of each subroutine, they invoke the remaining phases of the compiler to perform code improvement and target code generation. (There can be as many as 20 of these phases, depending on the set of code improvements to be performed.) Once a given subroutine has been compiled, its syntax tree and RTL can be reclaimed (except for any information to be saved for use by the debugger). Both the syntax tree and RTL are meant to be kept in memory across compiler phases, rather than being written to a file. RTL has a human-readable external format, which the compiler can write and (partially) read, but this format is not well suited for automatic manipulation.

The syntax tree constitutes the interface between the front end and the back end of the compiler. The separation is not an entirely clean one, because the syntax tree is somewhat language-dependent, and because the translation from syntax tree to RTL is interleaved with parsing. To construct a front end for a new language, one must extend the definition of the syntax tree to accommodate any features of the language that cannot be represented easily in the existing format, and modify the syntax tree to RTL translation routines to accommodate these extensions. In practice, one is likely to need to make minor modifications to the back end as well. These must be made in such a way that the modified back end continues to work for all the previously compilable languages.

RTL is loosely based on the S-expressions of Lisp. Each RTL expression consists of an operator or expression type and a sequence of operands. In its external form, these are represented by a parenthesized list in which the element immediately inside the left parenthesis is the operator. Internally, RTL expressions are represented by C structs and pointers. This pointer-rich structure constitutes the interface among the compiler's many back-end phases. There are several dozen expression types, including constants, references to values in memory or registers, arithmetic and logical operations, comparisons, bit-field manipulations, type conversions, and stores to memory or registers.

The body of a subroutine consists of a sequence of RTL expressions. Each expression in the sequence is called an insn. Each insn begins with one of six special codes:

```
(insn 8 6 10 (set (reg:SI 2)
        (mem:SI (symbol_ref:SI ("a")))))

(insn 10 8 12 (set (reg:SI 3)
        (mem:SI (symbol_ref:SI ("b")))))

(insn 12 10 14 (set (reg:SI 2)
        (plus:SI (reg:SI 2)
            (reg:SI 3))))

(insn 14 12 15 (set (reg:SI 3)
        (mem:SI (symbol_ref:SI ("c")))))

(insn 15 14 17 (set (reg:SI 2)
        (mult:SI (reg:SI 2)
            (reg:SI 3))))

(insn 17 15 19 (set (mem:SI (symbol_ref:SI ("d")))
        (reg:SI 2)))
```

Figure 9.6 Simplified ASCII version of the RTL for d := (a + b) * c.

insn: an "ordinary" RTL expression.

jump_insn: an expression that may transfer control to a label.

call_insn: an expression that may make a subroutine call.

code_label: a possible target of a jump.

barrier: an indication that the previous insn always jumps away; control will never "fall through" to here.

note: a pure annotation. There are nine different kinds of these, to identify the tops and bottoms of loops, scopes, subroutines, and so on.

The sequence is not always completely linear; insns are sometimes collected into pairs or triples that correspond to target machine instructions with delay slots. Over a dozen different kinds of (non-*note*) annotations can be attached to an individual insn, to identify side effects, specify target machine instructions or registers, keep track of the points at which values are defined and used, automatically increment or decrement registers that are used to iterate over an array, and so on. Insns may also refer to various dynamically allocated structures, including the symbol table.

A simplified insn sequence for the code fragment d := (a + b) * c appears in Figure 9.6. The three leading numbers in each insn represent the insn's unique id and those of its predecessor and successor, respectively. The :SI *mode specifier* on a memory or register reference indicates access to a single (four-byte) integer. Fields for the various insn annotations are not shown.

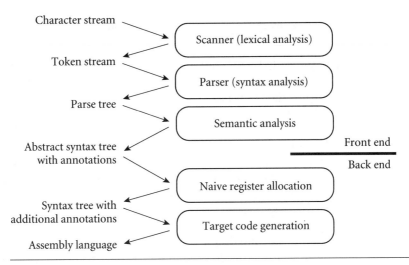

Figure 9.7 A simpler, nonoptimizing compiler structure, assumed in Section 9.3. The target code generation phase closely resembles the intermediate code generation phase of Figure 9.1.

In order to generate target code, the back end matches `insns` against patterns stored in a semi-formal description of the target machine. Both this description and the routines that manipulate the machine-dependent parts of an `insn` are segregated into a relatively small number of separately compiled files. As a result, much of the compiler back end is machine independent, and need not actually be modified when porting to a new machine.

9.3 Code Generation

The back end of Figure 9.1 is too complex to present in any detail in a single chapter. To limit the scope of our discussion, we will content ourselves in this chapter with producing correct but naive code. This choice will allow us to consider a significantly simpler back end. Starting with the structure of Figure 9.1, we drop the machine-independent code improver and then merge intermediate and target code generation into a single phase. This merged phase generates pure, linear assembly language; because we are not performing code improvements that alter the program's control flow, there is no need to represent that flow explicitly in a control flow graph. We also adopt a much simpler register allocation algorithm, which can operate directly on the syntax tree prior to code generation, eliminating the need for virtual registers and the subsequent mapping onto physical registers. Finally, we drop instruction scheduling. The resulting compiler structure appears in Figure 9.7. Its code generation phase closely resembles the intermediate code generation of Figure 9.1.

9.3.1 **An Attribute Grammar Example**

Like semantic analysis, intermediate code generation can be formalized in terms of an attribute grammar, though it is most commonly implemented via hand-written ad hoc traversal of a syntax tree. We present an attribute grammar here for the sake of clarity.

In Figure 1.5 (page 23) we presented naive MIPS assembly language for the GCD program. We will use our attribute grammar example to generate a similar version here, in pseudo-assembly notation. Because this notation is now meant to represent target code, rather than medium or low-level intermediate code, we will assume a fixed, limited register set reminiscent of real machines. We will reserve several registers (a1, a2, sp, rv) for special purposes; others (r1 .. rk) will be available for temporary values and expression evaluation.

Figure 9.8 contains a fragment of our attribute grammar. To save space, we have shown only those productions that actually appear in Figure 9.2. As in Chapter 4, notation such as *while* : *stmt* on the left-hand side of a production indicates that a *while* node in the syntax tree is one of several kinds of *stmt* node; it may serve as the *stmt* in the right-hand side of its parent production. In our attribute grammar fragment, *program*, *expr*, and *stmt* all have a synthesized attribute code that contains a sequence of instructions. *Program* has a synthesized attribute name of type string. *Id* has a synthesized attribute stp that points to the symbol table entry for the identifier. *Expr* has a synthesized attribute reg that indicates the register that will hold the value of the computed expression at run time. *Expr* and *stmt* have an inherited attribute next_free_reg that indicates the next register (in an ordered set of temporaries) that is available for use (i.e., that will hold no useful value at run time) immediately before evaluation of a given expression or statement.

Because we use a symbol table in our example, and because symbol tables lie outside the formal attribute grammar framework, we must augment our attribute grammar with some extra code for storage management. Specifically, prior to evaluating the attribute rules of Figure 9.8, we must traverse the symbol table in order to calculate stack frame offsets for local variables and parameters (none of which occur in the GCD program) and in order to generate assembler directives to allocate space for global variables (of which our program has two). Storage allocation and other assembler directives will be discussed in more detail in Section 9.5.

9.3.2 **Register Allocation**

Evaluation of the rules of the attribute grammar itself consists of two main tasks. In each subtree we first determine the registers that will be used to hold various quantities at run time; then we generate code. Our naive register allocation strategy uses the next_free_reg inherited attribute to manage registers r1 .. rk as

reg_names : array [0..k−1] of register_name := ["r1", "r2", ..., "rk"]
    −− ordered set of temporaries

program → *id stmt*
    ▷ stmt.next_free_reg := 0
    ▷ program.code := ["main:"] + stmt.code + ["goto exit"]
    ▷ program.name := id.stp→name

while : $stmt_1$ → *expr* $stmt_2$ $stmt_3$
    ▷ expr.next_free_reg := $stmt_2$.next_free_reg := $stmt_3$.next_free_reg := $stmt_1$.next_free_reg
    ▷ L1 := new_label (); L2 := new_label ()
      $stmt_1$.code := ["goto" L1] + [L2 ":"] + $stmt_2$.code + [L1 ":"] + expr.code
        + ["if" expr.reg "goto" L2] + $stmt_3$.code

if : $stmt_1$ → *expr* $stmt_2$ $stmt_3$ $stmt_4$
    ▷ expr.next_free_reg := $stmt_2$.next_free_reg := $stmt_3$.next_free_reg := $stmt_4$.next_free_reg :=
        $stmt_1$.next_free_reg
    ▷ L1 := new_label (); L2 := new_label ()
      $stmt_1$.code := expr.code + ["if" expr.reg "goto" L1] + $stmt_3$.code + ["goto" L2]
        + [L1 ":"] + $stmt_2$.code + [L2 ":"] + $stmt_4$.code

assign : $stmt_1$ → *id expr* $stmt_2$
    ▷ expr.next_free_reg := $stmt_2$.next_free_reg := $stmt_1$.next_free_reg
    ▷ $stmt_1$.code := expr.code + [id.stp→name ":=" expr.reg] + $stmt_2$.code

read : $stmt_1$ → id_1 id_2 $stmt_2$
    ▷ $stmt_1$.code := ["a1 := &" id_1.stp→name]   −− file
      + ["call" if id_2.stp→type = int then "readint" else ...]
      + [id_2.stp→name ":= rv"] + $stmt_2$.code

write : $stmt_1$ → *id expr* $stmt_2$
    ▷ expr.next_free_reg := $stmt_2$.next_free_reg := $stmt_1$.next_free_reg
    ▷ $stmt_1$.code := ["a1 := &" id.stp→name]   −− file
      + ["a2 :=" expr.reg]   −− value
      + ["call" if id.stp→type = int then "writeint" else ...] + $stmt_2$.code

writeln : $stmt_1$ → *id* $stmt_2$
    ▷ $stmt_1$.code := ["a1 := &" id.stp→name] + ["call writeln"] + $stmt_2$.code

null : *stmt* → ϵ
    ▷ stmt.code := nil

'<>' : $expr_1$ → $expr_2$ $expr_3$
    ▷ handle_op ($expr_1$, $expr_2$, $expr_3$, "<>")

Figure 9.8 Attribute grammar to generate code from a syntax tree. Square brackets delimit individual target instructions. Juxtaposition indicates concatenation within instructions; the '+' operator indicates concatenation of instruction lists. The handle_op macro is used in three of the attribute rules *(continued)*.

'>' : $expr_1 \rightarrow expr_2\ expr_3$
    ▷ handle_op ($expr_1$, $expr_2$, $expr_3$, ">")

'−' : $expr_1 \rightarrow expr_2\ expr_3$
    ▷ handle_op ($expr_1$, $expr_2$, $expr_3$, "−")

id : $expr \rightarrow \epsilon$
    ▷ expr.reg := reg_names[expr.next_free_reg mod k]
    ▷ expr.code := [expr.reg ":=" expr.stp→name]

macro handle_op (ref result, L_operand, R_operand, op : syntax_tree_node)
    result.reg := L_operand.reg
    L_operand.next_free_reg := result.next_free_reg
    R_operand.next_free_reg := result.next_free_reg + 1
    if R_operand.next_free_reg < k
        spill_code := restore_code := nil
    else
        spill_code := ["*sp :=" reg_name[R_operand.next_free_reg mod k]]
            + ["sp := sp − 4"]
        restore_code := ["sp := sp + 4"]
            + [reg_names[R_operand.next_free_reg mod k] ":= *sp"]
    result.code := L_operand.code + spill_code + R_operand.code
        + [result.reg ":=" L_operand.reg op R_operand.reg] + restore_code

---

Figure 9.8 *(continued)*

an expression evaluation stack. To calculate the value of $(a + b) \times (c − (d / e))$ for example, we would generate the following:

```
r1 := a          -- push a
r2 := b          -- push b
r1 := r1 + r2    -- add
r2 := c          -- push c
r3 := d          -- push d
r4 := e          -- push e
r3 := r3 / r4    -- divide
r2 := r2 − r3    -- subtract
r1 := r1 × r2    -- multiply
```

Allocation of the next register on the "stack" occurs in the production *id : expr* → ϵ, where we use expr.next_free_reg to index into reg_names, the array of temporary register names, and in macro handle_op, where we increment next_free_reg to make this register unavailable during evaluation of the right-hand operand. There is no need to "pop" the "register stack" explicitly; this happens automatically when the attribute evaluator returns to a parent node and uses the parent's (unmodified) next_free_reg attribute. In our example grammar, left-hand operands are the only constructs that tie up a register during the evaluation of anything else. In a more complete grammar, other long-term uses of registers would probably occur in constructs such as for loops (for the step size, index, and bound).

In a particularly complicated fragment of code it is possible to run out of physical registers. In this case we must *spill* one or more registers to memory. Our naive register allocator pushes a register onto the program's subroutine call stack, reuses the register for another purpose, and then pops the saved value back into the register before it is needed again. In effect, physical registers hold the top k elements of an expression evaluation stack of effectively unlimited size.

It should be emphasized that our register allocation algorithm, while correct, makes very poor use of machine resources. We have made no attempt to reorganize expressions to minimize the number of registers used, or to keep commonly used variables in registers over extended periods of time (avoiding loads and stores). If we were generating medium-level intermediate code, instead of target code, we would employ virtual registers, rather than physical ones, and would allocate a new one every time we needed it, never reusing one to hold a different value. Mapping of virtual registers to physical registers would occur much later in the compilation process.

Target code for the GCD program appears in Figure 9.9. The first few lines are generated during symbol table traversal, prior to attribute evaluation. Attribute program.name might be passed to the assembler, to tell it the name of the file into which to place the runnable program. A production-quality compiler would probably also generate assembler directives to embed symbol-table information in the target program. As in Figure 1.5, the quality of our code is very poor. We will investigate techniques to improve it in Chapter 13. In the remaining sections of the current chapter we will consider assembly and linking.

9.4 Address Space Organization

Assemblers, linkers, and loaders typically operate on a pair of related file formats: *relocatable* object code and *executable* object code. Relocatable object code is acceptable as input to a linker; multiple files in this format can be combined to create an executable program. Executable object code is acceptable as input to a loader: it can be brought into memory and run. A relocatable object file includes the following descriptive information:

import table: Identifies instructions that refer to named locations whose addresses are unknown, but are presumed to lie in other files yet to be linked to this one.

```
            -- first few lines generated during symbol table traversal
            .data         -- begin static data
            .word i       -- reserve one word to hold i
            .word j       -- reserve one word to hold j
            .text         -- begin text (code)
            -- remaining lines accumulated into program.code
main:
            a1 := &input  -- "input" and "output" are file control blocks
                          -- located in a library, to be found by the linker
            call readint  -- "readint", "writeint", and "writeln" are library subroutines
            i := rv
            a1 := &input
            call readint
            j := rv
            goto L1
L2: r1 := i               -- body of while loop
            r2 := j
            r1 := r1 > r2
            if r1 goto L3
            r1 := j       -- "else" part
            r2 := i
            r1 := r1 - r2
            j := r1
            goto L4
L3: r1 := i               -- "then" part
            r2 := j
            r1 := r1 - r2
            i := r1
L4:
L1: r1 := i               -- test terminating condition
            r2 := j
            r1 := r1 <> r2
            if r1 goto L2
            a1 := &output
            r1 := i
            a2 := r1
            call writeint
            a1 := &output
            call writeln
            goto exit     -- return to operating system
```

Figure 9.9 Target code for the GCD program, generated from the syntax tree of Figure 9.2, using the attribute grammar of Figure 9.8.

relocation table: Identifies instructions that refer to locations within the current file, but that must be modified at link time to reflect the offset of the current file within the final, executable program.

export table: Lists the names and addresses of locations in the current file that may be referred to in other files.

Imported and exported names are known as *external symbols*.

An executable object file is distinguished by the fact that it contains no references to external symbols. It also defines a starting address for execution. An executable file may or may not be relocatable, depending on whether it contains the tables above.

Internally, an object file is typically divided into several sections, each of which is handled differently by the linker, loader, or operating system. The first section includes the import, export, and relocation tables, together with an indication of how much space will be required by the program for noninitialized static data. Other sections commonly include code (instructions), read-only data (constants, jump tables for `case` statements, etc.), initialized but writable static data, and high-level symbol table information saved by the compiler. The initial descriptive section is used by the linker and loader. The high-level symbol table section is used by debuggers and performance profilers. Neither of these tables is usually brought into memory at run time; neither is needed by the running program.

In its runnable (loaded) form, a program is typically organized into several *segments*. On some machines (e.g., the x86 or PA-RISC), segments are visible to the assembly language programmer, and must be named explicitly in instructions. More commonly on modern machines, segments are simply subsets of the address space that the operating system manages in different ways. Two or three of them—code, constants, and initialized data—correspond to sections of the object file. Code and constants are usually read-only, and are often combined in a single segment; the operating system arranges to receive an interrupt if the program attempts to modify them. (In response to such an interrupt it will most likely print an error message and terminate the program.) Initialized data is writable. At load time, the operating system either reads code, constants, and initialized data from disk, or arranges to read them in at run time, in response to "invalid access" (page fault) interrupts or dynamic linking requests.

In addition to code, constants, and initialized data, the typical running program has two or more additional segments. These include:

uninitialized data: May be allocated at load time or on demand in response to page faults. Usually zero-filled, both to provide repeatable symptoms for programs that erroneously read data they have not yet written, and to enhance security on multiuser systems, by preventing a program from reading the contents of pages written by previous users.

stack: May be allocated in some fixed amount at load time. More commonly, is given a small initial size, and is then extended automatically by the operating system in response to (faulting) accesses beyond the current segment end.

heap: Like stack, may be allocated in some fixed amount at load time. More commonly, is given a small initial size, and is then extended in response to explicit requests (via system call) from heap-management library routines.

files: In many systems, library routines allow a program to *map* a file into memory. The `map` routine interacts with the operating system to create a new segment for the file, and returns the address of the beginning of the segment. The contents of the segment are usually fetched from disk on demand, in response to page faults.

9.5 Assembly

Some compilers translate source files directly into object files acceptable to the linker. More commonly, they generate assembly language that must subsequently be processed by an assembler to create an object file.

In our examples we have consistently employed a symbolic (textual) notation for code. Within a compiler, the representation would not be ASCII text, but it would still be symbolic, most likely consisting of records and linked lists. To translate this symbolic representation into executable code, we must

1. replace opcodes and operands with their machine language encodings
2. replace uses of symbolic names with actual addresses

These are the principal tasks of an assembler.

In the early days of computing, most programmers wrote in assembly language. To simplify the more tedious and repetitive aspects of assembly programming, assemblers often provided extensive macro expansion facilities. With the move to high-level languages, such programmer-centric features have largely disappeared. Most assembly language programs now are written by compilers. At the same time, the evolution of compiler technology and the development of RISC machines have pushed new features into the assembler. In particular, some assemblers now perform some of the machine-specific parts of code improvement, such as instruction scheduling, register allocation, and peephole optimization (to be described in Section 13.2).

When passing assembly language from the compiler to the assembler, it makes sense to use some internal (records and linked lists) representation. At the same time, we must provide a textual front end to accommodate the occasional need for human input:

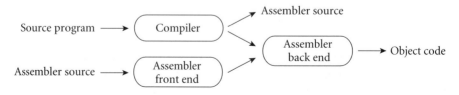

The text-based assembler front end simply translates ASCII source into internal symbolic form. By sharing the assembler back end, the compiler and assembler front end avoid duplication of effort. For debugging purposes, the compiler will generally have an option to dump a textual representation of the code it passes to the assembler.

An alternative organization has the compiler generate object code directly:

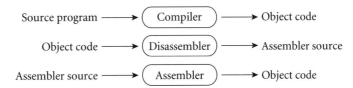

This organization gives the compiler a bit more flexibility: operations normally performed by an assembler (e.g., assignment of addresses to variables) can be performed earlier if desired. Because there is no separate assembly pass, the overall translation to object code may be slightly faster. The stand-alone assembler can be relatively simple. If it is used only for small, special-purpose code fragments, it probably doesn't need to perform instruction scheduling or other machine-specific code improvement. Using a disassembler instead of an assembly language dump from the compiler ensures that what the programmer sees corresponds precisely to what is in the object file. If the compiler uses a fancier assembler as a back end, then program modifications effected by the assembler will not be visible in the assembly language dumped by the compiler.

9.5.1 Emitting Instructions

The most basic task of the assembler is to translate symbolic representations of instructions into binary form. In some assemblers this is an entirely straightforward task, because there is a one-one correspondence between mnemonic operations and instruction op-codes. Many assemblers, however, extend the instruction set in minor ways (often a large number of minor ways) to make the assembly language easier for human beings to read. The MIPS assembler, for example, provides a large number of pseudoinstructions that translate into different real instructions depending on their arguments, or that correspond to multi-instruction sequences. Here are a few examples:

■ Many of the arithmetic/logic instructions come in several variants, depending on whether they take one of their operands from an "immediate" constant field within the instruction, as opposed to taking both from registers. Strictly speaking, these are different instructions; the assembler picks the right one based on the syntax of the operands:

```
add $10, $8, $9      -- r10 := r8 + r9
```

is translated as-is, while

> add $10, $8, 0x12   becomes   addi $10, $8, 0x12

- Some pseudoinstructions actually generate multi-instruction sequences. For example, the pseudoinstruction

```
div $10, $8, $9
```

is meant to divide register 8 by register 9 and put the result in register 10. In actuality, the assembler translates it into the following eleven-instruction sequence:

```
        div $8, $9        -- LO := quotient; HI := remainder
        bne $9, $0, L1    -- branch if divisor not zero
        nop               -- branch delay
        break 0x7         -- trap to operating system
L1: li $1, -1
        bne $9, $1, L2    -- branch if divisor not -1
        lui $1, 0x8000    -- $1 := 0x80000000
        bne $8, $1, L2    -- branch if dividend not minint
        nop               -- branch delay
        break 0x6         -- overflow; trap to OS
L2: mflo $10              -- $10 := quotient
```

In most cases, the hardware integer divide instruction generates an exact quotient and remainder into the special registers LO and HI. The exceptions are division by zero and division of the largest-magnitude negative number (for which two's complement arithmetic has no positive counterpart) by -1. Software must test for these cases; the hardware simply produces invalid results, silently. Assuming the tests succeed, the instruction sequence ends by moving the quotient to the desired target register.

- Because instructions are 32 bits in length, a 32-bit constant cannot be loaded into a register with a single instruction:

> li $14, 0x12345abc   becomes   lui $14, 0x1234
>   ori $14, 0x5abc

The mnemonics li, lui, and ori stand for "load immediate," "load upper immediate," and "or immediate." The lui instruction loads a 16-bit operand into the high-order 16 bits of the target register, and sets the low-order 16 bits to zero.

- The assembler supports a large suite of conditional branch pseudoinstructions, many of which compare a register to a constant or to another register, and branch on the result. The hardware, on the other hand, can only compare a register to zero, or test two registers for equality. Thus

> bge $9, 0x10, foo   becomes   slti $1, $9, 0x10
>   beq $1, $0, foo

The `slti` instruction sets its destination register to one if the source register is less than the immediate operand, or to zero otherwise.

In addition to translating from symbolic to binary instruction representations, most assemblers respond to a variety of *directives*. Examples in the MIPS assembler include:

segment switching: The `.text` directive indicates that subsequent instructions and data should be placed in the code (text) segment. The `.data` directive indicates that subsequent instructions and data should be placed in the initialized data segment. (It is possible, though uncommon, to put instructions in the data segment, or data in the code segment.) The `.space` n directive indicates that n bytes of space should be reserved in the uninitialized data segment. (This latter directive is usually preceded by a label.)

data generation: The `.byte`, `.half`, `.word`, `.float`, and `.double` directives each take a sequence of arguments, which they place in successive locations in the current segment of the output program. They differ in the types of operands. The related `.ascii` directive takes a single character string as argument, which it places in consecutive bytes.

symbol identification: The `.globl` *name* directive indicates that *name* should be entered into the table of exported symbols.

alignment: The `.align` n directive causes the subsequent output to be aligned at an address evenly divisible by 2^n.

In effect, most RISC assemblers implement a virtual machine whose instruction set is "nicer" than that of the real hardware. In addition to pseudoinstructions, the virtual machine typically has nondelayed branches. If desired, the compiler or assembly language programmer can ignore the existence of branch delays. The assembler will move nearby instructions to fill delay slots if possible, or generate `nops` if necessary. (To minimize the number of `nops`, it may still be desirable for the compiler to place independent instructions near the branch, where the assembler will be able to find them.) Note that the task of filling branch delays is substantially easier in the presence of nullifying branches. Assuming that the target of the branch lies within the current file, and is not itself a branch, we can always fill the delay slot with a duplicate of the target instruction, and increment the target address.

Some assemblers go beyond the simple filling of branch delays to provide the final pass of general-purpose instruction scheduling. Though this job can be handled by the compiler, the existence of pseudoinstructions such as the division example above argues strongly for doing it in the assembler. In addition to having two branch delays that might be filled by neighboring instructions, the expanded division sequence can be used as a source of instructions to fill nearby branch, load, or functional unit delays.

9.5.2 Assigning Addresses to Names

Like compilers, assemblers commonly work in several phases. If the input is textual, an initial phase scans and parses the input, and builds an internal representation. In the most common organization there are two additional phases. The first identifies all internal and external (imported) symbols, assigning locations to the internal ones. This phase is complicated by the fact that the length of some instructions (on a CISC machine) or the number of real instructions produced by a pseudoinstruction (on a RISC machine) may depend on the number of significant bits in an address. Given values for symbols, the final phase produces object code.

Within the object file, any symbol mentioned in a `.globl` directive must appear in the table of exported symbols, with an entry that indicates the symbol's address. Any symbol referred to in a directive or an instruction, but not defined in the input program, must appear in the table of imported symbols, with an entry that identifies all places in the code at which such references occur. Finally, any instruction or datum whose value depends on the placement of the current file within a final executable program must be listed in the relocation table.

Traditionally, assemblers for CISC machines distinguished between *absolute* and *relocatable* words in an object file. Absolute words are known at assembly time; they need not be changed by the linker. Examples include constants and register-register instructions. A relocatable word, on the other hand, must be modified by adding to it the address within the final program of the code or data segment of the current object file. A CISC jump instruction, for example, might consist of a one-byte `jmp` opcode followed by a four-byte target address. For a local target, the address bytes in the object file would contain the symbol's offset within the file. The linker would finalize the address by adding the offset of the file's code segment within the final program.

On RISC machines, this single form of relocation no longer suffices. Addresses are encoded into instructions in many different ways, and these encodings must be reflected in the relocation table and the import table. On a MIPS processor, for example, a `j` (jump) instruction has a 26-bit target field. The processor left-shifts this field by two bits and tacks on the high-order four bits of the address of the instruction in the delay slot. To relocate such an instruction, the linker must right-shift and left-truncate the address of the file's code segment, add it into the low-order 26 bits of the instruction, and verify that the target and delay slot instructions share the same top four address bits. In a similar vein, a two-instruction load of a 32-bit quantity (as described on page 512) requires the linker to recalculate the sixteen-bit operands of both instructions.

9.6 Linking

Most language implementations—certainly all that are intended for the construction of large programs—support separate compilation: fragments of the program can be compiled and assembled more-or-less independently. After compilation, these fragments (known as *compilation units*) are "glued together" by a *linker*. In many languages and environments, the programmer explicitly divides the program into modules or files, each of which is separately compiled. More integrated environments may abandon the notion of a file in favor of a database of subroutines, each of which is separately compiled.

The task of a linker is to join together compilation units. A *static linker* does its work prior to program execution, producing an executable object file. A *dynamic linker* (to be described in Section 9.7) does its work after the program has been brought into memory for execution.

Each of the compilation units of a program to be linked must be a relocatable object file. Typically, some of these files will have been produced by compiling fragments of the application being constructed, while others will be general-purpose library packages needed by the application. Since most programs make use of libraries, even a "one-file" application typically needs to be linked.

Linking involves two subtasks: relocation and the resolution of external references. Some authors refer to relocation as *loading*, and call the entire "joining together" process "link-loading." Other authors (including the current one) use "loading" to refer to the process of bringing an executable object file into memory for execution. On very simple machines, or on machines with very simple operating systems, loading entails relocation. More commonly, the operating system uses virtual memory to give every program the impression that it starts at some standard address (e.g., zero). In Section 9.7 we shall see that on many systems loading entails a certain amount of linking.

9.6.1 Relocation and Name Resolution

Each relocatable object file contains the information required for linking: the import, export, and relocation tables. A static linker uses this information in a two-phase process analogous to that described for assemblers in Section 9.5. In the first phase, the linker gathers all of the compilation units together, chooses an order for them in memory, and notes the address at which each will consequently lie. In the second phase, the linker processes each unit, replacing unresolved external references with appropriate addresses, and modifying instructions that need to be relocated to reflect the addresses of their units. These phases are illustrated pictorially in Figure 9.10. Addresses and offsets are assumed to be written in hexadecimal notation, with a page size of 4K (1000_{16}) bytes.

Libraries present a bit of a challenge. Many consist of hundreds of separately compiled program fragments, most of which will not be needed by any particular

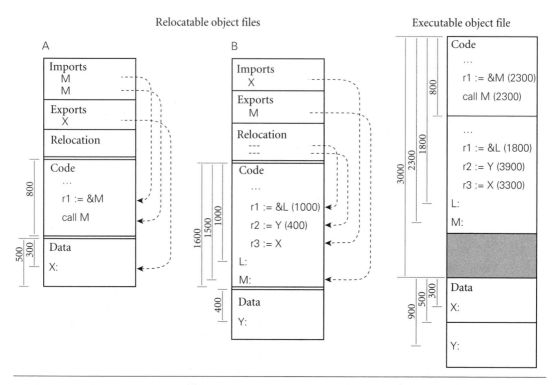

Figure 9.10   Linking relocatable object files A **and** B **to make an executable object file.** A's code section has been placed at offset 0, with B's code section immediately after, at offset 800. To allow the operating system to establish different protections for the code and data segments, A's data section has been placed at the next page boundary (offset 3000), with B's data section immediately after (offset 3500). External references to M and X have been set to use the appropriate addresses. Internal references to L and Y have been updated by adding in the starting addresses of B's code and data sections, respectively.

application. Rather than link the entire library into every application, the linker needs to search the library to identify the fragments that are referenced from the main program. If these refer to additional fragments, then those must be included also, recursively. Many systems support a special library format for relocatable object files. A library in this format may contain an arbitrary number of code and data sections, together with an index that maps symbol names to the sections in which they appear.

9.6.2 Type Checking

Within a compilation unit, the compiler enforces static semantic rules. Across the boundaries between units, it uses module headers to enforce the rules pertaining to external references. In effect, the header for module *M* makes a set of promises regarding M's interface to its users. When compiling the body of M, the compiler ensures that those promises are kept. Imagine what could happen, however, if we compiled the body of M, and then changed the numbers and types of parameters for some of the subroutines in its header file before compiling some user module U. If both compilations succeed, then M and U will have very different notions of how to interpret the parameters passed between them; while they may still link together, chaos is likely to ensue at run time. To prevent this sort of problem, we must ensure whenever M and U are linked together that both were compiled using the same version of M's header.

In most module-based languages, the following technique suffices. When compiling the body of module M we create a dummy symbol whose name uniquely characterizes the contents of M's header. When compiling the body of U we create a reference to the dummy symbol. An attempt to link M and U together will succeed only if they agree on the name of the symbol.

One way to create the symbol name that characterizes M is to use an ASCII representation of the time of the most recent modification of M's header. Because files may be moved across machines, however (e.g., to deliver source files to geographically distributed customers), modification times are problematic: clocks on different machines are often poorly synchronized, and file copy operations often change the modification time. A better candidate is a *checksum* of the header file: essentially the output of a hash function that uses the entire text of the file as key. It is possible in theory for two different but valid files to have the same checksum, but with a good choice of hash function the odds of this error are exceedingly small.

The checksum strategy does require that we know when we're using a module header. Unfortunately, as described in Section 3.6.2, we don't know this in C and C++: headers in these languages are simply a programming convention, supported by the textual inclusion mechanism of the language's preprocessor. Most implementations of C do not enforce consistency of interfaces at link time; instead, programmers rely on configuration management tools (e.g., Unix's make) to recompile files when necessary. Such tools are typically driven by file modification times.

Most implementations of C++ adopt a different approach. The name of each imported or exported symbol in an object file is created by concatenating the corresponding name from the program source with a representation of its type. For an object, the type consists of the class name and a terse encoding of its structure. For a function, it consists of an encoding of the types of the arguments and the return value. For complicated objects or functions of many arguments, the resulting names can be very long. If the linker limits symbols to some too-small maximum length, the type information can be compressed by hashing, at some small loss in security [SF88].

The encoding of type information in symbol names works well in C++, but is too strict for use in C: it would outlaw programming tricks which, while questionable, are permitted by the language definition. Symbol-name encoding is facilitated in C++ by the use of structural equivalence for types. In principle, one could use it in a language with name equivalence, but given that such languages generally have well-structured modules, it is simpler just to use a checksum of the header.

One problem with any technique based on file modification times or checksums is that a trivial change to a header file (modification of a comment, for example, or definition of a new constant not needed by existing users of the interface) can prevent files from linking correctly. A similar problem occurs with configuration management tools: a trivial change may cause the tool to recompile files unnecessarily. A few programming environments address this issue by tracking changes at a granularity smaller than compilation units [Tic86]. Most just live with the need to recompile.

9.7* Dynamic Linking

On a multiuser system, it is common for several instances of a program (an editor or web browser, for example) to be executing simultaneously. It would be highly wasteful to allocate space in memory for a separate, identical copy of the code of such a program for every running instance. Many operating systems therefore keep track of the programs that are running, and set up memory mapping tables so that all instances of the same program share the same read-only copy of the program's code segment. Each instance receives its own writable copy of the data segment. Code segment sharing can save enormous amounts of space. It does not work, however, for instances of programs that are similar but not identical.

Many sets of programs, while not identical, have large amounts of library code in common, for example to manage a graphical user interface. If every application has its own copy of the library, then large amounts of memory may be wasted. Moreover, if programs are statically linked, then much larger amounts of disk space may be wasted on nearly identical copies of the library in separate executable object files.

In the early 1990s, most operating system vendors adopted *dynamic linking*, in order to avoid this waste. Each dynamically linked library resides in its own code and data segments. Every program instance that uses a given library has a private copy of the library's data segment, but shares a single system-wide read-only copy of the library's code segment. These segments may be linked to the remainder of the code when the program is loaded into memory, or they may be linked incrementally on demand, during execution. In addition to saving space, dynamic linking allows a programmer or system administrator to install backward-compatible updates to a library without rebuilding all existing executable object files: the next time it runs, each program will obtain the new version of the library automatically.

To be amenable to dynamic linking, a library must either (1) be located at the same address in every program that uses it, or (2) have no relocatable words in its code segment, so that the content of the segment does not depend on its address. The first approach is straightforward but restrictive: it generally requires that we assign a unique address to every sharable library; otherwise we run the risk that some newly created program will want to use two libraries that have been given overlapping address ranges. In Unix System V R3, which took the unique-address approach, shared libraries could only be installed by the system administrator. This requirement tended to limit the use of dynamic linking to a relatively small number of popular libraries. The second approach, in which a shared library can be linked at any address, allows users to employ dynamic linking whenever they want.

9.7.1 Position-Independent Code

A code segment that contains no relocatable words is said to constitute *position-independent code* (PIC). To generate PIC, the compiler must

1. Use PC-relative addressing, rather than jumps to absolute addresses, for all internal branches.

2. Similarly, avoid absolute references to statically allocated data, by using displacement addressing with respect to some standard base register. If the code and data segments are guaranteed to lie at a known offset from one another, then an entry point to a shared library can compute an appropriate base register value using the PC. Otherwise the caller must set the base register as part of the calling sequence.

3. Use an extra level of indirection for every control transfer out of the PIC segment, and for every load or store of static memory outside the corresponding data segment. The indirection allows the (non-PIC) target address to be kept in the data segment, which is private to each program instance.

Exact details vary among processors, vendors, and operating systems. Conventions for SGI's compilers for the MIPS architecture, under the IRIX 6.2 version of Unix, are illustrated in Figure 9.11. Each shared code segment is accompanied, at a static offset, by a nonshared *linkage table* and, at an arbitrary offset, by a nonshared data segment. The linkage table lists the addresses of all external symbols referenced in the code segment.

As described in Section 8.2.1, any nonleaf subroutine must allocate space in its stack frame to hold the value of the `ra` (return address) register, and must save and restore this register in its prologue and epilogue. Similarly, any subroutine that may call into a dynamically linked shared library must save the `gp` (global pointer) register in the prologue, and restore it after every call into a dynamically linked shared library. At code-generation time, the compiler must know which external symbols lie in such libraries. For a call to one of them, the usual `jal` (jump-and-link) instruction is replaced by a sequence of three instructions. The first of these loads register `t9` from the linkage table, using `gp`-relative addressing.

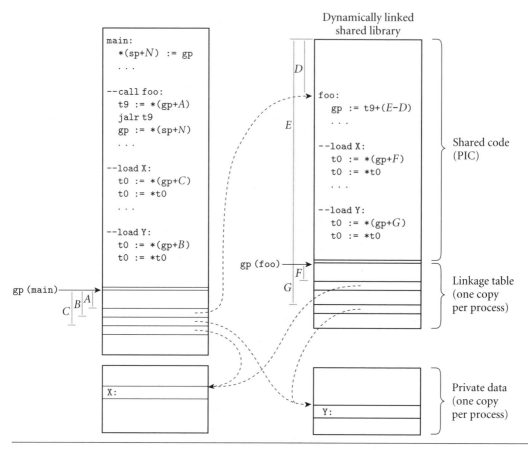

Figure 9.11 A dynamically linked shared library. Because main calls foo, which lies in the library, its prologue and epilogue must save and restore both ra (not shown) and gp. Calls to foo are made indirectly, using an address stored in main's linkage table. Similarly, references to variables X and Y, both of which are globally visible, must employ a level of indirection. In the prologue of foo, gp is set to point to foo's linkage table, using the value in t9. The calling sequence in main restores the old gp when foo returns.

The second is a jalr (jump-and-link-register) instruction, which takes its target address from t9. The third restores the gp. In a similar vein, any load or store of a datum located in a dynamically linked shared library must employ a two-instruction sequence. The first instruction loads the address of the datum from the linkage table using gp-relative addressing. The second loads or stores the datum itself.

The prologue of any subroutine foo that serves as an entry to a dynamically linked shared library must establish a new gp. To do so it takes the value in t9 (i.e., the address of foo) and adds the (statically known) signed difference between foo's offset within the code segment and the distance between the code and the linkage table.

9.7.2 Fully Dynamic (Lazy) Linking

If all or most of the symbols exported by a shared library are referenced by the parent program, then it makes sense to link the library in its entirety at load time. In any given execution of a program, however, there may be references to libraries that are not actually used, because the input data never causes execution to follow the code path(s) on which the references appear. If these "potentially unnecessary" references are numerous, we may avoid a significant amount of work by linking the library *lazily* on demand. Moreover even in a program that uses all its symbols, incremental lazy linking may improve the system's interactive responsiveness by allowing programs to begin execution faster. Finally, a language system that allows the dynamic creation of program components (e.g., as in Common Lisp or Java) must use lazy linking to delay the resolution of external references in compiled components.

The run-time data structures for lazy linking are almost the same as those in Figure 9.11, but they are incrementally created. At load time, the program begins with the main code segment and linkage table, and with all data segments for which addresses need to appear in that linkage table. In our specific example, we would load the data segments of both `main` and `foo`, because the addresses of both `X` (which belongs to `main`) and `Y` (which belongs to `foo`) need to appear in the main linkage table. We would not, however, load the code segment or linkage table of `foo`, despite the fact that the address of `foo` needs to appear in the linkage table. Instead, we would initialize that linkage table entry to refer to a *stub* routine, created by the compiler and included in the main code segment. The code of the stub looks like this:

```
t9 := *(gp+k)      -- lazy linker entry point
t7 := ra
t8 := n            -- index of stub
call *t9           -- overwrites ra
```

The lazy linker itself resides in a (nonlazy) shared library, linked to the program at load time. (Here we have assumed that its address lies at offset k in the linkage table.)

After branching to the lazy linker, control never returns to the stub. Instead, the linker uses the constant n to index into the import table of the program's object file, where it finds the information it needs to identify both the name and the library of the unresolved reference. The linker then loads the library's code segment into memory if it is not already there. At this point it can change ("patch") the linkage table entry through which the stub was called, so that it now points to the library routine. If it needed to load the library's code segment, the linker also creates a copy of the library's linkage table. It initializes all data entries in that table, loading (copies of) the segments to which those entries refer if they (the segments) have not already been loaded as part of an earlier linking operation. For each subroutine entry in the library's linkage table, the linker checks to see whether the relevant code segment has already been loaded. If so, it initializes the entry with the subroutine's address. If not, it initializes it with the address of its stub. Finally, the linker copies `t7` into `ra` and jumps to the newly linked library routine. At this point, everything appears as though the call had happened in the normal fashion.

As execution proceeds, further references to not-yet-loaded symbols extend the "frontier" of the program. Because invocations of the linker occur on subroutine calls and not on data references, the current frontier always includes a set of code segments and the data segments to which those code segments refer. Each linking operation brings in one new code segment, together with all of the additional data segments to which that code refers. If we were willing to intercept page faults, we could arrange to enter the linker on references to not-yet-loaded data. This approach would avoid loading data segments that are never really used, but the overhead of the faults might greatly increase execution time.

9.8 Summary and Concluding Remarks

In this chapter we focussed our attention on the back end of the compiler, and on *code generation*, *assembly*, and *linking* in particular.

Compiler back ends vary greatly in internal structure. We discussed one plausible structure, in which semantic analysis is followed by, in order, intermediate code generation, machine-independent code improvement, target code generation, and machine-specific code improvement (including register allocation and instruction scheduling). The semantic analyzer passes a syntax tree to the intermediate code generator, which in turn passes a *control flow graph* to the machine-independent code improver. Within the nodes of the control flow graph, we suggested that code be represented by instructions in a pseudo-assembly language with an unlimited number of *virtual registers*. In order to delay discussion of code improvement to Chapter 13, we also presented a simpler back-end structure in which code improvement is dropped, naive register allocation happens early, and intermediate and target code generation are merged into a single phase. This simpler structure provided the context for our discussion of code generation.

We also discussed intermediate forms (IFs). These can be categorized in terms of their *level*, or degree of machine independence. As examples we considered the high-level, tree-based Diana language used by most Ada compilers, and the medium-level Register Transfer Language of the Free Software Foundation GNU compilers. A well-defined IF facilitates the construction of *compiler families*, in which front ends for one or more languages can be paired with back ends for many machines.

Intermediate code generation is typically performed via ad hoc traversal of a syntax tree. Like semantic analysis, the process can be formalized in terms of attribute grammars. We presented part of a small example grammar and used it to generate code for the GCD program introduced in Chapter 1. We noted in passing that target code generation is often automated, in whole or in part, using a *code generator generator* that takes as input a formal description of the target machine and produces code that performs pattern matching on instruction sequences or trees.

In our discussion of assembly and linking we described the format of *relocatable* and *executable* object files, and discussed the notions of *name resolution* and *relocation*. We noted that while not all compilers include an explicit assembly phase, all compilation systems must make it possible to generate assembly code for debugging purposes, and must allow the programmer to write special-purpose routines in assembler. In compilers that use an assembler, the assembly phase is sometimes responsible for instruction scheduling and other low-level code improvement. The linker, for its part, supports separate compilation, by "gluing" together object files produced by multiple compilations. In many modern systems, significant portions of the linking task are delayed until load time or even run time, to allow programs to share the code segments of large, popular libraries. For many languages the linker must perform a certain amount of semantic checking, to guarantee type consistency. In more aggressive optimizing compilation systems (not discussed in this text), the linker may also perform interprocedural code improvement.

As noted in Section 1.5, the typical programming environment includes a host of additional tools, including debuggers, performance profilers, configuration and version managers, style checkers, preprocessors, pretty-printers, and perusal and cross-referencing utilities. Many of these tools, particularly in well-integrated environments, are directly supported by the compiler. Many make use, for example, of symbol-table information embedded in object files. Performance profilers often rely on special instrumentation code inserted by the compiler at subroutine calls, loop boundaries, and other key points in the code. Perusal, style-checking, and pretty-printing programs may share the compiler's scanner and parser. Configuration tools often rely on lists of inter-file dependences, again generated by the compiler, to tell when a change to one part of a large system may require that other parts be recompiled.

9.9 Review Questions

9.1 Explain what is meant by the "level" of an intermediate form (IF). What are the comparative advantages and disadvantages of high, medium, and low-level IFs?

9.2 What is the IF most commonly used in Ada compilers?

9.3 Name two advantages of a stack-based IF. Name one disadvantage.

9.4* Describe GNU RTL in general terms.

9.5 Explain the rationale for basing a family of compilers (several languages, several target machines) on a single IF.

9.6 Outline some of the major design alternatives for back-end compiler organization and structure.

9.7 Why might a compiler employ more than one IF?

9.8 What is a *code generator generator*? Why might it be useful?

9.9 What is a *basic block*?

9.10 What are *virtual registers*? What purpose do they serve?

9.11 What is the difference between *local* and *global* code improvement?

9.12 What is *register spilling*?

9.13 What are the distinguishing characteristics of a *relocatable* object file? An *executable* object file?

9.14 Why do operating systems typically *zero-fill* pages used for uninitialized data?

9.15 List four tasks commonly performed by an *assembler*.

9.16 Give three examples of *pseudoinstructions* and three examples of *directives* that an assembler might be likely to provide.

9.17 Why might a RISC assembler perform its own final pass of instruction scheduling?

9.18 Explain the distinction between *absolute* and *relocatable* words in an object file. Why is the notion of "relocatability" more complicated than it used to be?

9.19 What are the principal tasks of a *linker*?

9.20 How can a linker enforce type checking across compilation units?

9.21* Which of the tasks of the linker may be delayed until load time? What are the advantages and disadvantages of such *dynamic* linking?

9.22* What is *position-independent code*? What is it good for? What special precautions must a compiler follow in order to produce it?

9.10 Exercises

9.1 If you were writing a two-pass compiler, why might you choose a high-level IF as the link between the front end and the back end? Why might you choose a medium-level IF?

9.2 Investigate and describe the IF of the compiler you use most often. Can you instruct the compiler to dump it to a file which you can then inspect? Are there tools other than the back end of the compiler that operate on the IF (e.g., debuggers, code improvers, configuration managers, etc.)? Is the same IF used by compilers for other languages or machines?

9.3 Consider a language such as Ada or Modula-2, in which a module M can be divided into a specification (header) file and an implementation (body) file for the purpose of separate compilation (Section 10.2.1). Should M's specification itself be separately compiled, or should the compiler simply read it in the process of compiling *M*'s body and the bodies of other modules that use abstractions defined in *M*? If the specification is compiled, what should the output consist of?

9.4 Many research compilers (e.g., for SR [AO93], Cedar [SZBH86], Lynx [Sco91], and Modula-3 [Har92]) use C as their IF. C is well-documented and mostly machine-independent, and C compilers are much more widely available than alternative back ends. What are the disadvantages of generating C, and how might they be overcome?

9.5* Compare and contrast Diana with the notation we have been using for syntax tree attribute grammars.

9.6* If you have access to gcc, run it with various of the compile-time flags that cause it to dump its RTL intermediate code. Version 2.6 of the compiler supports fourteen such flags. All are of the form −d**X**, where **X** is one of j s L t f c S l g R J d k. In the order shown, these cause dumps of successively more processed RTL. Ask a local Unix guru to help you find and access the gcc.info files, which document RTL and the various compiler phases.

9.7 List as many ways as you can think of in which the back end of a just-in-time compiler might differ from that of a more conventional compiler. What design goals dictate the differences?

9.8 Suppose that *k* (the number of temporary registers) in Figure 9.8 is 4 (this is an artificially small number for modern machines). Give an example of an expression that will lead to register spilling under our naive register allocation algorithm.

9.9 Modify the attribute grammar of Figure 9.8 in such a way that it will generate the control flow graph of Figure 9.3 instead of the linear assembly code of Figure 9.9.

9.10 Add productions and attribute rules to the grammar of Figure 9.8 to handle Ada-style for loops (described in Section 6.5.1). Using your modified grammar, hand-translate the syntax tree of Figure 9.12 into pseudoassembly notation. Keep the index variable and the upper loop bound in registers.

9.11 One problem (of many) with the code we generated in Section 9.3 is that it computes at run time the value of expressions that could have been computed at compile time. Modify the grammar of Figure 9.8 to perform a simple form of *constant folding*: whenever both operands of an operator are compile-time constants, we should compute the value at compile time and then generate code that uses the value directly.

9.12 Modify the grammar of Figure 9.8 to generate jump code for Boolean expressions, as described in Section 6.4.1. You should assume short-circuit evaluation (Section 6.1.4).

9.13 Our GCD program did not employ subroutines. Extend the grammar of Figure 9.8 to handle procedures without parameters (feel free to adopt any

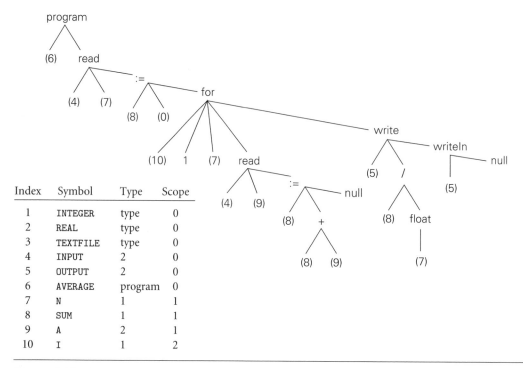

Index	Symbol	Type	Scope
1	INTEGER	type	0
2	REAL	type	0
3	TEXTFILE	type	0
4	INPUT	2	0
5	OUTPUT	2	0
6	AVERAGE	program	0
7	N	1	1
8	SUM	1	1
9	A	2	1
10	I	1	2

Figure 9.12 Syntax tree and symbol table for a program that computes the average of N real numbers. The children of the for node are the index variable, the lower bound, the upper bound, and the body.

reasonable conventions on the structure of the syntax tree). Be sure to generate appropriate prologue and epilogue code for each subroutine, and to save and restore any needed temporary registers.

9.14 The grammar of Figure 9.8 assumes that all variables are global. In the presence of subroutines, we would need to generate different code (with fp-relative displacement mode addressing) to access local variables and parameters. In a language with nested scopes we would need to dereference the static chain (or index into the display) to access objects that are neither local nor global. Suppose that we are compiling a language with nested subroutines, and are using a static chain. Modify the grammar of Figure 9.8 to generate code to access objects correctly, regardless of scope. You may find it useful to define a to_register subroutine that generates the code to load a given object. Be sure to consider both l-values and r-values, and parameters passed by both value and result.

9.15 Implement Figure 9.8 in your favorite programming language. Define appropriate data structures to represent a syntax tree; then generate code for some sample trees via ad hoc tree traversal.

9.16   Augment your solution to the previous exercise to handle various other language features. Several interesting options have been mentioned in earlier exercises. Others include functions, first-class subroutines, `case` statements, records and `with` statements, arrays (particularly those of dynamic size), and iterators.

9.17*   Find out how linking works under your favorite operating system. Can code be dynamically linked? Can (nonprivileged) users create shared libraries? How does the loader find the libraries that need to be linked to a program? If your compiler can be instructed to generate position-independent code, how does this code compare (in size and run-time efficiency) with the non-position-independent equivalent?

9.18   Find out what tools are available on your favorite system to inspect the content of object files (on a Unix system, use `nm`). Consider some program consisting of a modest number (three to six, say) of compilation units. Using the appropriate tool, list the imported and exported symbols in each compilation unit. Then link the files together. Draw an address map showing the locations at which the various code and data segments have been placed. Which instructions within the code segments have been changed by relocation?

9.19   If you have access to g++ (the Gnu C++ compiler), or to a C++ compiler based on AT&T's translator, investigate the encoding of type information in the names of external symbols. See if you can "reverse engineer" the algorithm used to generate the funny characters at the end of every name.

9.11   Bibliographic Notes

Standard compiler textbooks (e.g. those by Aho, Sethi, and Ullman [ASU86], Fischer and LeBlanc [FL88], or Appel [App97]) are an accessible source of information on back-end compiler technology, though the first two have grown a bit dated. More detailed information can be found in the text of Muchnick [Muc97]. Fraser and Hanson provide a wealth of detail on code generation and (simple) code improvement in their `lcc` compiler [FH95].

The Diana intermediate form is documented by Goos, Wulf, Evans, and Butler [GWEB83]. A simpler tree-based IF is described by Fraser and Hanson [FH95, chap. 5]. RTL is documented in a set of `texinfo` files distributed with `gcc` (available from *www.fsf.org/software*). Java byte code is documented by Lindholm and Yellin [LY97].

Ganapathi, Fischer, and Hennessy provide an early survey of automatic code generator generators [GFH82]. A later and more comprehensive survey is that of Henry and Damron [HD89]. The most widely used automatic code generation technique is based on LR parsing, and is due to Glanville and Graham [GG78].

Sources of information on assemblers, linkers, and software development tools include the texts of Beck [Bec97] and of Kernighan and Plauger [KP76].

Gingell et al. describe the implementation of shared libraries for the Sparc architecture and the SunOS variant of Unix [GLDW87]. Ho and Olsson describe a particularly ambitious dynamic linker for Unix [HO91]. Tichy presents a compilation system that avoids unnecessary recompilations by tracking dependences at a granularity finer than the source file [Tic86].

Data Abstraction and Object Orientation

In Chapter 3 we presented several stages in the development of data abstraction, with an emphasis on the scoping mechanisms that control the visibility of names. We began with global variables, whose lifetime spans program execution. We then added local variables, whose lifetime is limited to the execution of a single subroutine; nested scopes, which allow subroutines themselves to be local; and static variables, whose lifetime spans execution, but whose names are visible only within a single scope. These were followed by modules, which allow a collection of subroutines to share a set of static variables; module *types*, which allow the programmer to instantiate multiple instances of a given abstraction, and *classes*, which allow the programmer to define families of related abstractions.

Ordinary modules encourage a "manager" style of programming, in which a module exports an abstract type. Module types and classes allow the module itself to *be* the abstract type. The distinction becomes apparent in two ways: First, the explicit `create` and `destroy` routines typically exported from a manager module are replaced by creation and destruction of an instance of the module type. Second, invocation of a routine in a particular module instance replaces invocation of a general routine that expects a variable of the exported type as argument. Classes build on the module-as-type approach by adding mechanisms for *inheritance*, which allows new abstractions to be defined as refinements or extensions to existing ones, and *dynamic method binding*, which allows a new version of an abstraction to display newly refined behavior, even when used in a context that expects an earlier version. An instance of a class is known as an *object*; languages and programming techniques based on classes are said to be *object-oriented*.[1]

---

[1] In previous chapters we used the term "object" informally to refer to almost anything that can have a name. In this chapter we will use it only to refer to an instance of a class.

The stepwise evolution of data abstraction mechanisms presented in Chapter 3 is a useful way to organize ideas, but it does not completely reflect the historical development of language features. In particular, it would be inaccurate to suggest that object-oriented programming developed as an outgrowth of modules. Rather, all three of the fundamental concepts of object-oriented programming—encapsulation, inheritance, and dynamic method binding—have their roots in the Simula programming language, developed in the mid-1960s. In comparison to modern object-oriented languages, Simula was weak in the data hiding part of encapsulation, and it was in this area that Clu, Modula, Euclid, and related languages made important contributions in the 1970s. At the same time, the ideas of inheritance and dynamic method binding were adopted and refined in Smalltalk over the course of the 1970s. Smalltalk employs a distinctive "message-based" programming model, with dynamic typing and unusual terminology and syntax. The dynamic typing tends to make Smalltalk implementations relatively slow, and delays the reporting of errors. The language is also tightly integrated into a graphical programming environment, making it difficult to port to other systems. For these reasons, Smalltalk is less widely used than one might expect, given the influence it has had on subsequent developments. More recent object-oriented languages, including Eiffel, C++, Modula-3, Ada 95, and Java represent to a large extent a reintegration of the inheritance and dynamic method binding of Smalltalk with "mainstream" imperative syntax and semantics. Object orientation has also become important in functional languages; the leading notation is CLOS, the Common Lisp Object System [Kee89; Ste90, Chap. 28].

In Section 10.1 we provide an overview of object-oriented programming and of its three fundamental concepts. We consider encapsulation and data hiding in more detail in Section 10.2. We then consider object initialization and finalization in Section 10.3, and dynamic method binding in Section 10.4. In Section 10.5 we consider the subject of *multiple inheritance*, in which a class is defined in terms of more than one existing class. As we shall see, multiple inheritance introduces some particularly thorny semantic and implementation challenges. Finally, in Section 10.6, we revisit the definition of object orientation, considering the extent to which a language can or should model everything as an object. Most of our discussion will focus on Smalltalk, Eiffel, C++, and Java, though we shall have occasion to mention Simula, Modula-3, Ada 95, Oberon, and CLOS as well.

10.1 Object-Oriented Programming

With the development of ever-more complicated computer applications, data abstraction has become essential to software engineering. The abstraction provided by modules and module types has at least three important benefits:

1. It reduces *conceptual load* by minimizing the amount of detail that the programmer must think about at one time.

2. It provides *fault containment* by preventing the programmer from using a program component in inappropriate ways, and by limiting the portion of a program's text in which a given component can be used, thereby limiting the portion that must be considered when searching for the cause of a bug.

3. It provides a significant degree of *independence* among program components, making it easier to assign their construction to separate individuals, to modify their internal implementations without changing external code that uses them, or to install them in a library where they can be used by other programs.

Unfortunately, experience with modules and module types indicates that the reuse implied by the third of these points is difficult to achieve in practice. One often finds that a previously constructed module has almost, but not quite, the properties required by some new application. Perhaps one has a pre-existing queue abstraction, but would like to be able to insert and delete from either end, rather than being limited to first-in-first-out (FIFO) order. Perhaps one has a pre-existing dialog box abstraction for a graphical user interface, but without any mechanism to highlight a default response. Perhaps one has a package for symbolic math, but it assumes that all values are real numbers, rather than complex. In all these cases much of the advantage of abstraction will be lost if the programmer must copy the pre-existing code, figure out how it works inside, and modify it by hand, rather than using it "as-is." If it becomes necessary to change the abstraction at some point in the future (to fix a bug or implement an enhancement), the programmer will need to remember to fix all copies—a tedious and error-prone activity.

Object-oriented programming can be seen as an attempt to enhance opportunities for code reuse by making it easy to define new abstractions as *extensions* or *refinements* of existing abstractions. As a starting point for examples, consider a list of records. Figure 10.1 contains C++ code for the elements of such a list. The example employs a "module-as-type" style of abstraction: each element of a list is an object of class `list_node`. The class contains both *data members* (`prev`, `next`, `head_node`, and `val`) and *subroutine members* (`predecessor`, `successor`, `insert_before` and `remove`). Subroutine members are called *methods* in many object-oriented languages. The keyword `this` in C++ refers to the object of which the currently executing method is a member. In Smalltalk, the equivalent keyword is `self`; in Eiffel it is `current`.

Given the existence of the `list_node` class, we could define a list as follows:

```
class list {
    list_node header;
public:
    // no explicit constructor required;
    // implicit construction of 'header' suffices
    int empty () {
        return (header.singleton ());
    }
```

```
class list_err {                                  // exception
    public:
    char *description;
    list_err (char *s) {description = s;}
};

class list_node {
    list_node* prev;
    list_node* next;
    list_node* head_node;
public:
    int val;                              // the actual data in a node
    list_node () {                        // constructor
        prev = next = head_node = this;   // point to self
        val = 0;                          // default value
    }
    list_node* predecessor () {
        if (prev == this || prev == head_node) return 0;
        return prev;
    }
    list_node* successor () {
        if (next == this || next == head_node) return 0;
        return next;
    }
    int singleton () {
        return (prev == this);
    }
    void insert_before (list_node* new_node) {
        if (!new_node->singleton ())
            throw new list_err ("attempt to insert node already on list");
        prev->next = new_node;
        new_node->prev = prev;
        new_node->next = this;
        prev = new_node;
        new_node->head_node = head_node;
    }
    void remove () {
        if (singleton ())
            throw new list_err ("attempt to remove node not currently on list");
        prev->next = next;
        next->prev = prev;
        prev = next = head_node = this;   // point to self
    }
    ~list_node () {                       // destructor
        if (!singleton ())
            throw new list_err ("attempt to delete node still on list");
    }
};
```

Figure 10.1 A simple class for list nodes in C++. In this example we envision a list of integers.

```
    list_node* head () {
        return header.successor ();
    }
    void append (list_node *new_node) {
        header.insert_before (new_node);
    }
    ~list () {                      // destructor
        if (!header.singleton ())
            throw new list_err ("attempt to delete non-empty list");
    }
};
```

To create an empty list, one could then write

```
list* my_list_ptr = new list;
```

Records to be inserted into a list are created in much the same way:

```
list_node* elem_ptr = new list_node;
```

In C++, one can also simply declare an object of a given class:

```
list my_list;
list_node elem;
```

Our `list` class includes such an object (`header`) as a data member. When created with `new`, an object is allocated in the heap; when created via elaboration of a declaration it is allocated statically or on the stack, depending on lifetime. In either case, creation causes the invocation of programmer-specified initialization code. In C++, this code takes the form of a *constructor* method whose name is the same as that of the class itself. C++ also allows the programmer to specify a *destructor* method that will be invoked automatically when an object is destroyed, either by explicit programmer action or by return from the subroutine in which it was declared. The destructor's name is also the same as that of the class, but with a leading tilde (˜).

The `public` label within the list of members of `list_node` separates members required by the implementation of the abstraction from members available to users of the abstraction. In the terminology of Section 3.3.1, members that appear after the `public` label are exported from the class; members that appear before the label are not. The language also provides a `private` label, so the publicly visible portions of a class can be listed first if desired. Note that C++ classes are open scopes, as defined in Section 3.3.1; nothing needs to be explicitly imported.

As with packages in Ada or external (separately compiled) modules in Modula-2, some of the information about a class can be left out of the declaration, and provided in a separate file not visible to users of the abstraction. In our example, we could declare the public methods of `list_node` without providing their bodies:

```
class list_node {
    list_node* prev;
    list_node* next;
    list_node* head_node;
public:
    int val;
    list_node ();
    list_node* predecessor ();
    list_node* successor ();
    int singleton ();
    void insert_before (list_node* new_node);
    void remove ();
    ~list_node ();
};
```

This somewhat abbreviated class declaration might then be put in a `.h` "header" file, with function bodies relegated to a `.cc` "implementation" file. (Conventions for separate compilation in C were discussed in Section 3.6.2. The file name suffixes used here are those expected by the GNU g++ compiler.) Within the `.cc` file, the header of a method definition must identify the class to which it belongs by using a `::` *scope resolution* operator:

```
void list_node::insert_before (list_node* new_node) {
    if (!new_node->singleton ())
        throw new list_err ("attempt to insert node already on list");
    prev->next = new_node;
    new_node->prev = prev;
    new_node->next = this;
    prev = new_node;
    new_node->head_node = head_node;
}
```

Two rules govern the choice of what to put in the declaration of a class, rather than in separate definitions. First, the declaration must contain all the information that a programmer needs in order to use the abstraction correctly. Second, the declaration must contain all the information that the compiler needs in order to generate code. The second rule is generally broader: it tends to force information that is not required by the first rule into (the private part of) the interface, particularly in languages that use a value model of variables, instead of a reference model. If the compiler must generate code to allocate space (e.g., in stack frames) to hold a value of an object type, then it must know the size of the object; this is the rationale for including private data members in the class declaration. In addition, if the compiler is to expand any method calls in-line then it must have their code available. In-line expansion of the smallest, most common methods of an object-oriented program tends to be crucial for good performance.

Object-oriented programs tend to make many more subroutine calls than do ordinary imperative programs, and the subroutines tend to be shorter. Lots of things that would be accomplished by direct access to record fields in a von Neumann language tend to be hidden inside object methods in an object-oriented language. Many programmers in fact consider it bad style to declare public data members, because they give users of an abstraction direct access to the internal representation. Arguably, we should make the `val` field of `list_node` private, with `get_val` and `set_val` member functions to read and write it.

Suppose now that we already have a list abstraction, and would like a queue abstraction. We could define the queue from scratch, but much of the code would look the same as in Figure 10.1. In an object-oriented language we have a better alternative: we can *derive* the queue from the list, allowing it to *inherit* pre-existing data and subroutine members:

```
class queue : public list {                      // derive from list
public:
    // no specialized constructor or destructor required
    void enqueue (list_node* new_node) {
        append (new_node);
    }
    list_node* dequeue () {
        if (empty ())
            throw new list_err ("attempt to dequeue from empty queue");
        list_node* p = head ();
        p->remove ();
        return p;
    }
};
```

Here queue is said to be a *derived class* (also called a *child class* or *subclass*); list is said to be a *base class* (also called a *parent class* or *superclass*). The derived class automatically has all the data and subroutine members of the base class.[2] All the programmer needs to declare explicitly are members that a queue has but a list lacks: in this case, the enqueue and dequeue methods. We will see examples shortly in which derived classes have new data members as well.

By deriving new classes from old ones, the programmer can create arbitrarily deep *class hierarchies*, with additional functionality at every level of the tree. The standard library for Smalltalk has as many as seven levels of derivation (Figure 10.2): class FileStream is derived from ExternalStream, which is in turn derived, in order, from ReadWriteStream, WriteStream, Positional-Stream, Stream, and Object. (Unlike C++, Smalltalk has a single root superclass, Object, from which all other classes are derived. Java has a similar class, as does Eiffel; the latter refers to it as ANY.)

The astute reader may have noticed that our original list abstraction made the unfortunate assumption that the data in every item was to be an integer. This assumption really isn't necessary. Given an inheritance mechanism, we can create

---

2 Actually, users of a derived class in C++ can see the members of the base class only if the base class name is preceded with the keyword `public` in the first line of the derived class's declaration. We will discuss the visibility rules of C++ in more detail in Section 10.2.

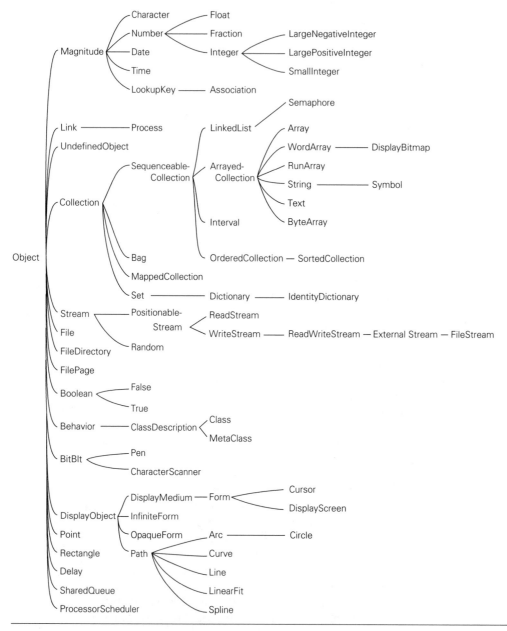

Figure 10.2 The standard class hierarchy of Smalltalk-80.

a general-purpose element base class that contains only the data and subroutine members needed to implement list operations:

```
class gp_list_node {
    gp_list_node* prev;
    gp_list_node* next;
    gp_list_node* head_node;
public:
    gp_list_node ();           // assume method bodies given separately
    gp_list_node* predecessor ();
    gp_list_node* successor ();
    int singleton ();
    void insert_before (gp_list_node* new_node);
    void remove ();
    ~gp_list_node ();
};
```

Now we can use this general-purpose class to derive lists and queues with specific types of data members:

```
class int_list_node : public gp_list_node {
public:
    int val;                    // the actual data in a node
    int_list_node () {
        val = 0;
    }
    int_list_node (int v) {
        val = v;
    }
};
```

Templates (generics) are commonly used to facilitate the construction of such type-specific classes; we will discuss this option further in Section 10.4.4.

  We have overloaded the constructor in int_list_node, providing two alternative implementations. One takes an argument, the other does not. Now the programmer can create int_list_nodes with or without specifying an initial value:

```
int_list_node element1;                        // val = 0
int_list_node *e_ptr = new int_list_node (13);  // val = 13
```

In C++, the compiler ensures that constructors for base classes are executed before those of derived classes. In our example, the constructor for gp_list_node will be executed first, followed by the constructor for int_list_node. We will discuss constructors further in Section 10.3.

  In addition to defining new data and subroutine members, a derived class can hide or replace members of base class(es). We will discuss data hiding in Section 10.2. To *replace* a method of a base class, a derived class simply redefines it. Suppose, for example, that we are creating an int_list_node class, but we want somewhat different semantics for the remove method. If written as in Figure 10.1, gp_list_node::remove will throw a list_err exception if the node to be removed is not currently on a list. If we want `int_list_node::remove` simply to return without doing anything in this situation we can declare it that way explicitly:

```
class int_list_node : public gp_list_node {
public:
...
    void remove () {
        if (!singleton ()) {
            prev->next = next;
            next->prev = prev;
            prev = next = head_node = this;
        }
    }
};
```

The disadvantage of this redefinition is that it pulls implementation details of `gp_list_node` into an `int_list_node` method, a potential violation of abstraction. (As a matter of fact, a C++ compiler will not accept the code above: as we shall see in Section 10.2, we would need to change the `gp_list_node` base class to make its `next` and `prev` members visible to derived classes.) A better approach is to leave the implementation details to the base class and simply catch the exception if it arises:

```
void int_list_node::remove () {
    try {
        gp_list_node::remove ();
    } catch (list_err) {
        ;   // do nothing
    }
}
```

This version of the code may be slightly slower than the previous one, depending on how `try` blocks are implemented, but it does a better job of maintaining abstraction. Note that the scope resolution operator (`::`) allows us to access the `remove` method of the base class explicitly, even though we have redefined it for `int_list_node`. Other object-oriented languages provide other means of obtaining this access. In Smalltalk and Java, members of the base class (superclass) can be accessed with the `super` keyword:

```
gp_list_node::remove ();    // C++
super.remove ();            // Java
super remove.              // Smalltalk
```

In Eiffel, the programmer can explicitly *rename* methods inherited from a base class, in order to make them accessible:

```
class int_list_node
inherit
    gp_list_node
        rename
            remove as old_remove
            ...      -- other renames
        end
```

Within methods of int_list_node, the remove method of gp_list_node can be invoked as old_remove. As we shall see in Section 10.5, C++ and Eiffel cannot use the keyword super, because it would be ambiguous in the presence of multiple inheritance.

In object-oriented programming, an abstraction that holds a collection of objects of some given class is often called a *container*. There are several different ways to build containers. In this section we have explored an approach in which objects are derived from a container element base class. The principal problem with this approach is that an object cannot be placed in a container unless its class is derived from the element class of the container. In order to put an *arbitrary* object into, say, a list, we can adopt an alternative approach, in which list nodes are separate objects containing *pointers* (or references) to the listed objects, rather than the data of the objects themselves. A third alternative is to make the list node a member (a subobject) of the listed object. In general, the design of consistent, intuitive, and useful class hierarchies is a complex and difficult art. Containers are only the tip of the iceberg.

10.2 Encapsulation and Inheritance

Encapsulation mechanisms enable the programmer to group data and the subroutines that operate on them together in one place, and to hide irrelevant details from the users of an abstraction. In the discussion above we have cast object-oriented programming as an extension of the "module-as-type" mechanisms of Simula and Euclid. It is also possible to cast object-oriented programming in a "module-as-manager" framework. In the first subsection below we consider the data-hiding mechanisms of modules in non-object-oriented languages. In the second subsection we consider the new data-hiding issues that arise when we add inheritance to modules to make classes. In the third subsection we briefly consider an alternative approach, in which inheritance is added to records, and (static) modules continue to provide data hiding.

10.2.1 Modules

Scope rules for data hiding were one of the principal innovations of Clu, Modula, Euclid, and other module-based languages of the 1970s. In Clu and Euclid, the declaration and definition (header and body) of a module always appear together. The header clearly states which of the module's names are to be exported. If a Euclid module *M* exports a type *T*, by default the remainder of the program can do nothing with objects of type *T* other than pass them to subroutines exported from *M*. *T* is said to be an *opaque* type. If desired, the Euclid programmer can explicitly grant code outside the module the ability to perform bit-wise assignment and/or equality tests on values of type *T*, or to access *T*'s fields (if a record), subscript it (if an array), or refer to its values by name (if an enumeration). In the following, for example, code outside module `Database` would be able to assign `tuple` variables to each other, and to access their `name` fields, but not to check them for equality or to access their other fields:

```
var Database : module
    exports (tuple with (:=, name))
    ...
    type tuple = record
        var name : packed array 1..80 of char
        ...
    end tuple
    ...
```

In Clu, a module (called a `cluster`) implements a single abstract type. Assignment and equality testing are permitted for that type, but because Clu uses a reference model for variables these operations copy or compare references to objects, not the objects themselves.

In Modula-2, programmers have the option of separating the header and body of a module. In Chapter 3 we looked only at so-called "internal" modules, in which the two parts appear together. In an "external" module (meant for separate compilation), the header appears in one source file and the body in another. Unfortunately, there is no way to divide the header into public and private parts; everything in it is public (i.e., exported). The only concession to data hiding is that a type may be made opaque by listing only its name in the header:

```
TYPE T;
```

In this case variables of type T can only be assigned, compared for equality, and passed to the module's subroutines. There is no way to disable assignment and comparison. Moreover, because the compiler cannot determine the size of an object (in the informal sense of the word) of type T by examining the module header alone, Modula-2 requires that all opaque types be pointers, which all have the same size and thus can be allocated statically or on the stack without knowledge of internal structure. (Some Modula-2 implementations permit additional opaque types, but only if they are implemented with the same number of bits as a pointer.)

Ada, which also allows the headers and bodies of modules (called `packages`) to be separated, eliminates the problems of Modula-2 by allowing the header of a package to be divided into public and private parts. A type can be exported opaquely by putting its definition in the private part of the header and simply naming it in the public part:

```
package foo is            -- header
    ...
    type T is private;
    ...
private          -- definitions below here are inaccessible to users
    ...
    type T is ...        -- full definition
    ...
end foo;
```

Variables of `private` types can be assigned, compared for equality, or passed to subroutines of the package. If desired, the Ada programmer can disable assignment and comparison with a more restrictive declaration:

```
type T is limited private;      -- replaces third line of example
```

Because they affect only the visibility of names, static, manager-style modules introduce no special code generation issues. Storage for variables and other data inside a module is managed in precisely the same way as storage for data immediately outside the module. If the module appears in a global scope, then its data can be allocated statically. If the module appears within a subroutine, then its data can be allocated on the stack, at known offsets, when the subroutine is called, and reclaimed when it returns.

Module types, as in Euclid, are somewhat more complicated: they allow a module to have an arbitrary number of *instances*. The obvious implementation then resembles that of a record. If all of the data in the module have a statically known size, then each individual datum can be assigned a static offset within the module's storage. If the size of some of the data is not known until run time, then the module's storage can be divided into fixed-size and variable-size portions, with a dope vector (descriptor) at the beginning of the fixed-size portion. Instances of the module can be allocated statically, on the stack, or in the heap, as appropriate. One additional complication arises for subroutines inside a module. How do they know which variables to use? We could, of course, replicate the code for each subroutine in each instance of the module, just as we replicate the data. This replication would be highly wasteful, however, as the copies would vary only in the details of address computations. A better technique is to create a single instance of each module subroutine, and to pass that instance, at run time, the address of the storage of the appropriate module instance. This address takes the form of an extra, hidden first parameter for every module subroutine. A Euclid call of the form

```
my_stack.push (x)
```

is translated as if it were really

```
push (my_stack, x)
```

When the header and body of a module appear in separate files, only the body needs to be compiled into runnable code. In a simple implementation, the compiler reads the header of module M when compiling the body of M, and also when compiling the body of any module that uses M. At the expense of implementation complexity, we can avoid the overhead of repeatedly scanning, parsing, and analyzing M's header by translating it into a symbol table, which we then access directly when compiling the bodies of M and its users. Most Ada implementations compile their module headers. All C and C++ implementations process module headers (.h files) via textual inclusion, as described in section 3.6.2. Modula-2 implementations vary: some work one way, some the other.

A change to a module body never requires us to recompile any of the module's users. A change to the private part of a module header may require us to recompile the module's users, but never requires us to change their code. A change to the public part of a header is a change to the module's interface: it will often require us to change the code of users.

It should be noted that while it is common to associate modules with compilation units (files that are separately compiled), the two need not necessarily go together. In Java, for example, each separately compiled program fragment specifies the module (called a *package*) to which it belongs. Each file belongs to a single package, but that package may be spread across several files. Only classes can be declared at the global level within a package; variables and subroutines (methods) are always declared within classes. Unless explicitly declared as `public`, a class is visible in all and only those compilation units that belong to the package. Standard C++ includes a `namespace` mechanism that provides similar functionality.

10.2.2 Classes

With the introduction of inheritance, object-oriented languages have needed to supplement the scope rules of module-based languages to cover additional issues. For example, should private members of a base class be visible to methods of a derived class? Should public members of a base class always be public members of a derived class (i.e., be visible to users of the derived class)? How much control should a base class exercise over the visibility of its members in derived classes?

We glossed over most of these questions in our examples in Section 10.1. For example, we might want to hide the `append` method of a queue, since it is superceded by `enqueue`. To effect this hiding in C++, the definition of class queue can specify that its base class is to be `private`:

```
class queue : private list {
public:
    using list::empty;
    using list::head;
    // but NOT using list::append
    void enqueue (gp_list_node* new_node);
    gp_list_node* dequeue ();
};
```

Here the appearance of `private` in the first line of the declaration indicates that public members of `list` will be visible to users of `queue` only if specifically made so by later parts of the declaration. We have made the `empty` and `head` methods visible by means of `using` declarations in `queue`'s public part.

In addition to the `public` and `private` labels, C++ allows members of a class to be designated `protected`. A protected member is visible only to methods of its own class or of classes derived from that class. In our examples, a protected member *M* of `list` would be accessible not only to methods of `list` itself, but also to methods of `queue`. Unlike public members, however, *M* would not be visible to arbitrary users of `list` or `queue` objects.

The `protected` keyword can also be used when specifying a base class:

```
class derived : protected base { ...
```

Here public members of the base class act like protected members of the derived class.

The basic philosophy behind the visibility rules of C++ can be summarized as follows:

- Any class can limit the visibility of its members. Public members are visible anywhere the class declaration is in scope. Private members are visible only inside the class's methods. Protected members are visible inside methods of the class or its descendants. (As an exception to the normal rules, a class can specify that certain other `friend` classes or subroutines should have access to its private members.)

- A derived class can restrict the visibility of members of a base class, but can never increase it. Private members of a base class are never visible in a derived class. Protected and public members of a public base class are protected or public, respectively, in a derived class. Protected and public members of a protected base class are protected members of a derived class. Protected and public members of a private base class are private members of a derived class.

- A derived class that limits the visibility of members of a base class by declaring that base class `protected` or `private` can restore the visibility of individual members of the base class by inserting a `using` declaration in the `protected` or `public` portion of the derived class declaration.

Other object-oriented languages take different approaches to visibility. Eiffel is more flexible than C++ in the patterns of visibility it can support, but it does not adhere to the first of the C++ principles above. Derived classes in Eiffel can both restrict and increase the visibility of members of base classes. Every method (called a `feature` in Eiffel) can specify its own *export status*. If the status is {NONE} then the member is effectively private (called *secret* in Eiffel). If the status is {ANY} then the member is effectively public (called *generally available* in Eiffel). In the general case the status can be an arbitrary list of class names, in which case the feature is said to be *selectively available* to those classes and their descendants only. Any feature inherited from a base class can be given a new status in a derived class.

Java follows C++ in the declaration of public, protected, and private members, but does not provide the protected and private designations for base classes; a derived class can neither increase *nor* restrict the visibility of members of a base class. (Of course, a derived class can always redefine a data or subroutine member with a method that generates a run-time error if used.) The protected keyword has a slightly different meaning in Java than it does in C++: a protected member of a Java class is visible not only within derived classes, but also within the entire package in which the class is declared.

In Smalltalk, the issue of member visibility never arises: the language allows code at run time to attempt to make a call to any method name in any object. If the object has a method of the given name (with the right number of parameters), then the invocation proceeds; otherwise a run-time error results. There is no way in Smalltalk to make a method available to some parts of a program but not to others.

10.2.3 Type Extensions

Smalltalk, Eiffel, C++, and Java were all designed from the outset as object-oriented languages, either starting from scratch or from an existing language without a strong encapsulation mechanism. They all support a module-as-type approach to abstraction, in which a single mechanism (the class) provides both encapsulation and inheritance. Several other languages, including Modula-3, Ada 95, Oberon, and CLOS, can be characterized as object-oriented extensions to languages in which modules already provide encapsulation. (Neither Modula-3 nor Oberon is strictly an extension to Modula-2, but both draw heavily on the syntax and semantics of their common predecessor.) Rather than alter the existing module mechanism, these languages provide inheritance and dynamic method binding through a mechanism for *extending* records. In Ada 95, for example, our list and queue abstractions could be defined as in Figure 10.3.

To control access to the structure of types, we hide them inside Ada packages. The procedures initialize, finalize, enqueue, and dequeue of gp_list .queue can convert their parameter self to a list_ptr, because queue is an extension of list. Package gp_list.queue is said to be a *child* of package gp_list because its name is prefixed with that of its parent. A child package in Ada 95 is similar to a derived class in Eiffel or C++, except that it is still a manager, not a type. Like Eiffel, but unlike C++, Ada 95 allows the body of a child package to see the private parts of the parent package.

All of the list and queue subroutines in Figure 10.3 take an explicit first parameter; Ada 95, Oberon, and CLOS do not use "object.method ()" notation. Modula-3 does use this notation, but only as syntactic sugar: a call to A.B (C, D) is interpreted as a call to B (A, C, D), where B is declared as a three-parameter subroutine. Arbitrary Ada code can pass an object of type queue to any routine

```
package gp_list is
    list_err : exception;
    type gp_list_node is tagged private;
        -- 'tagged' means extendible; 'private' means opaque
    type gp_list_node_ptr is access all gp_list_node;
        -- 'all' means that this can point at 'aliased' nonheap data
    procedure initialize (self : access gp_list_node);
    procedure finalize (self : access gp_list_node);
    function predecessor (self : access gp_list_node) return gp_list_node_ptr;
    function successor (self : access gp_list_node) return gp_list_node_ptr;
    function singleton (self : access gp_list_node) return boolean;
    procedure insert_before (self : access gp_list_node; new_node : gp_list_node_ptr);
    procedure remove (self : access gp_list_node);

    type list is tagged private;
    type list_ptr is access all list;
    procedure initialize (self : access list);
    procedure finalize (self : access list);
    function empty (self : access list) return boolean;
    function head (self : access list) return gp_list_node_ptr;
    procedure append (self : access list; new_node : gp_list_node_ptr);
private
    type gp_list_node is tagged record
        prev, next, head_node : gp_list_node_ptr;
    end record;
    type list is tagged record
        header : aliased gp_list_node;
        -- 'aliased' means that an 'all' pointer can refer to this
    end record;
end gp_list;
...
package body gp_list is
    -- definitions of subroutines
    ...
end gp_list;
...
package gp_list.queue is      -- 'child' of gp_list
    type queue is new list with private
        -- 'new' means it's a subtype; 'with' means it's an extension
    procedure initialize (self : access queue);
    procedure finalize (self : access queue);
    procedure enqueue (self : access queue; new_node : gp_list_node_ptr);
    function dequeue (self : access queue) return gp_list_node_ptr;
private
    type queue is new list with null record;
        -- no new data members
end gp_list.queue;
```

Figure 10.3 List and queue abstractions in Ada 95. The tagged types list and queue provide inheritance; the packages provide encapsulation. An int_list_node could be derived from gp_list_node in a similar manner. Declaring self to have type access XX (instead of XX_ptr) causes the compiler to recognize the subroutine as a method of the tagged type *(continued)*.

```
package body gp_list.queue is
    procedure initialize (self : access queue) is
    begin
        initialize (list_ptr (self));
    end initialize;

    procedure finalize (self : access queue) is
    begin
        finalize (list_ptr (self));
    end finalize;

    procedure enqueue (self : access queue; new_node : gp_list_node_ptr) is
    begin
        append (list_ptr (self), new_node);
    end enqueue;

    function dequeue (self : access queue) return gp_list_node_ptr is
    rtn : gp_list_node_ptr;
    begin
        if empty (list_ptr (self)) then
            raise list_err;
        end if;
        rtn := head (list_ptr (self));
        remove (rtn);
        return rtn;
    end dequeue;
end gp_list.queue;
```

Figure 10.3 (continued)

that expects a `list`; as in Java, there is no way for a derived type to hide the public members of a base type.

10.3 Initialization and Finalization

In Section 3.2 we defined the lifetime of an object to be the interval during which it occupies space and can thus hold data. Most object-oriented languages provide some sort of special mechanism to *initialize* an object automatically at the beginning of its lifetime. Following C++ terminology, we will call such a mechanism a *constructor*. It should be emphasized that a constructor does not allocate space; it initializes space that has already been allocated. A few languages provide a similar *destructor* mechanism to *finalize* an object automatically at the end of its lifetime. Several important issues arise:

choosing a constructor: An object-oriented language may permit a class to have zero, one, or many distinct constructors. In the latter case, different constructors may have different names, or it may be necessary to distinguish among them by number and types of arguments.

references and values: If variables are references, then every object must be created explicitly, and it is easy to ensure that an appropriate constructor is called. If variables are values, then object creation can happen implicitly as a result of elaboration. In this latter case, the language must either permit objects to begin their lifetime uninitialized, or it must provide a way to choose an appropriate constructor for every elaborated object.

execution order: When an object of a derived class is created in C++, the compiler guarantees that the constructors for any base classes will be executed, outermost first, before the constructor for the derived class. Moreover, if a class has members that are themselves objects of some class, then the constructors for the members will be called before the constructor for the object in which they are contained. These rules are a source of considerable syntactic and semantic complexity: when combined with multiple constructors, elaborated objects, and multiple inheritance they can sometimes induce a complicated sequence of nested constructor invocations, with overload resolution, before control even enters a given scope. Other languages have simpler rules.

garbage collection: Most object-oriented languages provide some sort of constructor mechanism. Destructors are comparatively rare. Their principal purpose is to facilitate manual storage reclamation in languages such as C++. If the language implementation collects garbage automatically, then the need for destructors is greatly reduced.

In the remainder of this section we consider these issues in more detail.

10.3.1 Choosing a Constructor

In Simula, the initialization code for a class takes the form of a begin...end block at the end of the class definition. The header of the class may include parameters; these are accessible to the initialization code, and must be specified in every call to new. If class B is derived from class A, then a call that creates a B object must specify parameters for both A and B. By default, the initialization code for A is called first, followed by the code for B. If desired, the code for A may specify that execution of the code for B should be *nested within* execution of the code for B:

```
CLASS A (I, J) INTEGER I, J;
...
BEGIN   COMMENT initialization code for A;
    initial;
    INNER;
    final;
END A;
...
```

```
A CLASS B (K) INTEGER K;
...
BEGIN    COMMENT initialization code for B;
    middle;
END B;
```

Here the keyword INNER indicates execution of the initialization code of the derived class, if any. To create an object of class A, the programmer writes myAobj :- NEW A (E1, E2), where E1 and E2 are actual parameter expressions matching I and J. (The :- operator in Simula indicates assignment of a reference, rather than a value.) NEW will return after executing the statements named initial and final above. To create an object of class B, the programmer writes myBobj :- NEW B (E1, E2, E3), where E1, E2, and E3 match I, J, and K, respectively. NEW will return after executing the statements named initial, middle, and final above, in that order.

The rationale for INNER is strongly connected to Simula's support for coroutines (described in Section 8.6). If the code for B contains a DETACH statement, then the portion of the "initialization" that follows the DETACH will execute in a separate coroutine, whose execution may interleave with that of B's creator. In other words, if B is a coroutine, then the statement named initial above will be executed before B begins its work, and the statement named final above will be executed after B has finished its work.

Smalltalk, Eiffel, C++, and Java all allow the programmer to specify more than one constructor for a given class. In C++ and Java, the constructors behave like overloaded subroutines: they must be distinguished by their numbers and types of arguments. In Smalltalk and Eiffel, different constructors can have different names; code that creates an object must name a constructor explicitly. In Eiffel one might say

```
class COMPLEX
creation
    new_cartesian, new_polar
feature {ANY}
    x, y : REAL;

    new_cartesian (x_val, y_val : REAL) is
    do
        x := x_val; y := y_val;
    end;

    new_polar (rho, theta : REAL) is
    do
        x := ro * cos (theta);
        y := ro * sin (theta)
    end;

    -- other public methods
```

```
feature {NONE}

    -- private methods

end -- class COMPLEX
...
a, b : COMPLEX;
...
!!b.new_cartesian (0, 1);
!!a.new_polar (pi/2, 1);
```

The !! operator is Eiffel's equivalent of `new`. Because class COMPLEX specified constructor ("creator") methods, the compiler will insist that every use of !! specify a constructor name and arguments. There is no straightforward analog of this code in C++; the fact that both constructors take two `real` arguments means that they could not be distinguished by overloading.

Smalltalk resembles Eiffel in the use of multiple named constructors, but it distinguishes more sharply between operations that pertain to an individual object and operations that pertain to a class of objects. Smalltalk also adopts an anthropomorphic programming model in which every operation is seen as being executed by some specific object in response to a request (a "message") from some other object. Since it makes little sense for an object O to create itself, O must be created by some other object (call it C) that represents O's class. Of course, because C is an object, it must itself belong to some class. The result of this reasoning is a system in which each class definition really introduces a *pair* of classes and a pair of objects to represent them.

Consider, for example, the standard class named Date. Corresponding to Date is a single object (call it D) that performs operations on behalf of the class. In particular, it is D that creates new objects of class Date. Because only objects execute operations (classes don't), we don't really need a name for D; we can simply use the name of the class it represents:

```
todaysDate <- Date today
```

This code causes D to execute the `today` constructor of class Date, and assigns a reference to the newly created object into a variable named todaysDate.

So what is the class of D? It clearly isn't Date, because D *represents* class Date. Smalltalk says that D is an object (in fact the only object) of the *metaclass* Date class. For technical reasons, it is also necessary for Date class to be represented by an object. To avoid an infinite regression, all objects that represent metaclasses are instances of a single class named Metaclass.

Modula-3 and Oberon provide no constructors at all: the programmer must initialize everything explicitly. Ada 95 supports constructors and destructors (called Initialize and Finalize routines) only for objects of types derived from the standard library type Controlled.

10.3.2 **References and Values**

Several object-oriented languages, including Simula, Smalltalk, and Java, use a programming model in which variables refer to objects. Other languages, including C++, Modula-3, Ada 95, and Oberon, allow a variable to have a value that *is* an object. Eiffel uses a reference model by default, but allows the programmer to specify that certain classes should be expanded, in which case variables of those classes will use a value model. The reference model is arguably more elegant, but generally requires that objects be allocated from the heap, and imposes (in the absence of compiler optimizations) an extra level of indirection on every access. The value model tends to be more efficient, but makes it difficult to control initialization.

With a reference model for variables every object is created explicitly, and it is easy to ensure that an appropriate constructor is called. With a value model for variables object creation can happen implicitly as a result of elaboration. In Modula-3, Ada 95, and Oberon, which don't really have constructors, elaborated objects begin life uninitialized and it is possible to accidentally attempt to use a variable before it has a value. In C++, the compiler ensures that an appropriate constructor is called for every elaborated object, but the rules it uses to identify constructors and their arguments can sometimes be confusing.

If a C++ variable of class `foo` is declared with no initial value, then the compiler will call `foo`'s zero-argument constructor (if no such constructor exists, but other constructors do, then the declaration is a static semantic error—a call to a nonexistent subroutine):

```
foo b;                  // calls foo::foo ()
```

If the programmer wants to call a different constructor, the declaration must specify constructor arguments to drive overload resolution:

```
foo b (10, 'x');        // calls foo::foo (int, char)
```

The most common argument list consists of a single object, of the same or different class:

```
foo a;
bar b;
...
foo c (a);              // calls foo::foo (foo&)
foo d (b);              // calls foo::foo (bar&)
```

Usually the programmer's intent is to declare a new object whose initial value is "the same" as that of the existing object. In this case it is more natural to write

```
foo a;                  // calls foo::foo ()
bar b;                  // calls bar::bar ()
...
foo c = a;              // calls foo::foo (foo&)
foo d = b;              // calls foo::foo (bar&)
```

In recognition of this intent, a single-argument constructor in C++ is called a *copy constructor*. It is important to realize here that the equals sign (=) in these declarations indicates initialization, not assignment. The effect is *not* the same as the similar code fragment

```
foo a, c, d;          // calls foo::foo () three times
bar b;                // calls bar::bar ()
...
c = a;                // calls foo::operator= (foo&)
d = b;                // calls foo::operator= (bar&)
```

Here c and d are initialized with the zero-argument constructor, and the later use of the equals sign indicates *assignment*, not initialization. The distinction is a common source of confusion in C++ programs. It arises from the combination of a value model of variables and an insistence that every elaborated object be initialized by a constructor. In CLOS, which requires objects to be passed to methods as explicit first parameters, object creation and initialization relies on overloaded versions of subroutines named `make-instance` and `initialize-instance`. Because CLOS employs a reference model uniformly, the issue of initializing elaborated objects does not arise.

In Eiffel, every variable is initialized to a default value. For built-in types (integer, floating-point, character, etc.), which are considered to be expanded, the default values are all zero. For references to objects, the default value is `nil`. For variables of expanded class types, the defaults are applied recursively to members. As noted above, new objects are created by invoking Eiffel's ! ! creation operator:

```
!!var.creator (args);
```

where var is a variable of some class type *T* and creator is a constructor for *T*. In the common case, var will be a reference, and the creation operator will allocate space for an object of class *T* and then call the object's constructor. This same syntax is permitted, however, when *T* is an expanded class type, in which case var will actually be an object, rather than a reference. In this case, the ! ! operator simply passes to the constructor the already-allocated object.

10.3.3 Execution Order

As we have seen, C++ insists that every object be initialized before it can be used. Moreover, if the object's class (call it *B*) is derived from some other class (call it *A*), C++ insists on calling an *A* constructor before calling a *B* constructor, so that the derived class is guaranteed never to see its inherited data members in an inconsistent state. When the programmer creates an object of class *B* (either via declaration or with a call to new), the creation operation specifies arguments for a *B* constructor. These arguments allow the C++ compiler to resolve overloading when multiple constructors exist. But where does the compiler obtain arguments for the *A* constructor? Simula's approach of adding them to the creation syntax is a clear violation of abstraction. The answer adopted in C++ is to allow the header of the constructor of a derived class to specify base class constructor arguments:

```
foo::foo ( foo_params ) :   bar ( bar_args ) {
    ...
```

Here `foo` is derived from `bar`. The list *foo_params* consists of formal parameters for this particular `foo` constructor. Between the parameter list and the opening brace of the subroutine definition is a "call" to a constructor for the base class `bar`. The arguments to the `bar` constructor can be arbitrarily complicated expressions involving the `foo` parameters. The compiler will arrange to execute the `bar` constructor before beginning execution of the `foo` constructor.

Similar syntax allows the C++ programmer to specify constructor arguments for class members that are themselves objects of some class:

```
class foo : bar {
    mem1_t member1;    // mem1_t and
    mem2_t member2;    // mem2_t are classes
    ...
}

foo::foo ( foo_params ) :   bar ( bar_args ), member1 ( mem1_args ),
        member2 ( mem2_args ) {
    ...
```

In Figure 10.1 we could have used this notation to initialize `prev`, `next`, `head_node`, and `val` in the constructor for `list_node`:

```
list_node () : prev (this), next (this), head_node (this), val (0) {
    // empty body -- nothing else to do
}
```

The significance of this alternative formulation is that it calls the copy constructors for the member objects, rather than calling the default (zero-argument) constructors, followed by `operator=`. For simple types such as pointers and integers there is no significant difference in the generated code. For complicated object-valued members, however, explicit constructors may differ from embedded assignments in both semantics and performance.

Like C++, Java insists that a constructor for a base class be called before the constructor for a derived class. The syntax is a bit simpler, however: the initial line of the code for the derived class constructor may consist of a "call" to the base class constructor:

```
super ( args );
```

As noted in Section 10.1, `super` is a Java keyword that refers to the base class of the class in whose code it appears. If the call to `super` is missing, the Java compiler automatically inserts a call to the base class's zero-argument constructor (in which case such a constructor must exist). Because Java uses a reference model uniformly for all objects, any class members that are themselves objects will actually be *references*, rather than "expanded" objects (to use the Eiffel term). Java simply initializes such members to nil. If the programmer wants something different, he or she must call new explicitly within the constructor of the surrounding class. Smalltalk and (in the common case) Eiffel adopt a similar approach. If an Eiffel class contains members of an expanded class type, that type is required to have a single constructor, with no arguments; the Eiffel compiler arranges to call this constructor when the surrounding object is created.

Smalltalk, Eiffel, and CLOS are all more lax than C++ regarding the initialization of base classes. The compiler or interpreter arranges to call the constructor (creator, initializer) for each newly created object automatically, but it does *not* arrange to call constructors for base classes automatically; all it does is initialize base class data members to default (0 or nil) values. If the derived class wants different behavior, its constructor(s) must call a constructor for the base class explicitly.

10.3.4 Garbage Collection

When a C++ object is destroyed, the destructor for the derived class is called first, followed by those of the base class(es), in reverse order of derivation. By far the most common use of destructors in C++ is manual storage reclamation. Suppose, for example, that we were to create a list or queue of character-string names:

```
class name_list_node : public gp_list_node {
    char *name;                  // pointer to the data in a node
public:
    name_list_node () {
        name = 0;                // empty string
    }
    name_list_node (char *n) {
        name = new char[strlen(n)];
        strcpy (name, n);   // copy argument into member
    }
    ~name_list_node () {
        if (name != 0) {
            delete name;    // reclaim space
        }
    }
};
```

The destructor in this class serves to reclaim space that was allocated in the heap by the constructor. In languages such as Simula, Smalltalk, Eiffel, CLOS, and Java, which provide automatic garbage collection, there is much less need for destructors. In fact, the entire idea of destruction is suspect in a garbage-collected language, because the programmer has little or no control over when an object is going to be destroyed. Java allows the programmer to declare a `finalize` method that will be called immediately before the garbage collector reclaims the space for an object, but the feature is not widely used.

10.4 Dynamic Method Binding

One of the principal consequences of inheritance/type extension is that a derived class *D* has all the members—data and subroutines—of its base class *C*. As long as *D* does not hide any of the publicly visible members of *C* (see Exercise 10.7), it makes sense to allow an object of class *D* to be used in any context that expects an object of class *C*: anything we might want to do to an object of class *C* we can also do to an object of class *D*. In Ada terminology, a derived class that does not hide any publicly visible members of its base class is a *subtype* of that base class.

The ability to use a derived class in a context that expects its base class is a form of polymorphism. If we imagine an administrative computing system for a university, we might derive classes `student` and `professor` from class `person`:

```
class person { ...
class student : public person { ...
class professor : public person { ...
```

Because both `student` and `professor` objects have all the properties of a `person` object, we should be able to use them in a `person` context:

```
student s;
professor p;
...
person *x = &s;
person *y = &p;
```

Moreover a subroutine such as

```
void person::print_mailing_label () { ...
```

would be polymorphic—capable of accepting arguments of multiple types:

```
s.print_mailing_label ();   // i.e. print_mailing_label (s)
p.print_mailing_label ();   // i.e. print_mailing_label (p)
```

As with other forms of polymorphism, we depend on the fact that `print_mailing_label` uses only those features of its formal parameter that all actual parameters will have in common.

But now suppose that we have redefined `print_mailing_label` in each of the two derived classes. We might, for example, want to encode certain information (student's year in school, professor's home department) in the corner of the label. Now we have multiple versions of our subroutine—`student::print_mailing_label` and `professor::print_mailing_label`, rather than the single, polymorphic `person::print_mailing_label`. Which version we will get depends on the object:

```
s.print_mailing_label ();    // student::print_mailing_label (s)
p.print_mailing_label ();    // professor::print_mailing_label (p)
```

But what about

```
x->print_mailing_label ();   // ??
y->print_mailing_label ();   // ??
```

Does the choice of the method to be called depend on the types of the *variables* x and y, or on the classes of the *objects* s and p to which those variables refer?

The first option (use the type of the reference) is known as *static method binding*. The second option (use the class of the object) is known as *dynamic method binding*. Dynamic method binding is central to object-oriented programming. Imagine, for example, that our administrative computing program has created a list of persons who have overdue library books. The list may contain both students and professors. If we traverse the list and print a mailing label for each person, dynamic method binding will ensure that the correct printing routine is called for each individual. In this situation the definitions in the derived classes are said to *override* the definition in the base class.

Unfortunately, as we shall see in Section 10.4.3, dynamic method binding imposes run-time overhead. While this overhead is generally modest, it is nonetheless a concern for small subroutines in performance-critical applications. Smalltalk and Modula-3 use dynamic method binding for all methods. Java and Eiffel use dynamic method binding by default, but allow individual methods to be labeled final (in Java) or frozen (in Eiffel), in which case they cannot be overridden by derived classes, and can therefore employ an optimized implementation. Simula, C++, and Ada 95 use static method binding by default, but allow the programmer to specify dynamic binding when desired. In these latter languages it is common terminology to distinguish between *overriding* a method that uses dynamic binding and (merely) *redefining* a method that uses static binding.

10.4.1 Virtual and Nonvirtual Methods

In Simula and C++, the programmer can specify that particular methods should be virtual. Calls to virtual methods are *dispatched* to the appropriate implementation at run time, based on the class of the object, rather than the type of the reference. In C++, the keyword virtual prefixes the subroutine declaration:[3]

```
class person {
public:
    virtual void print_mailing_label ();
    ...
```

---

3 C++ also uses the virtual keyword in certain circumstances to prefix the name of a base class in the header of the declaration of a derived class. This usage supports the very different purpose of *shared multiple inheritance*, which we will consider in Section 10.5.3.

In Simula, virtual methods are listed at the beginning of the class declaration:

```
CLASS Person;
    VIRTUAL: PROCEDURE PrintMailingLabel;
BEGIN
    ...
    PROCEDURE PrintMailingLabel...
        COMMENT body of subroutine
    ...
END Person;
```

Ada 95 adopts a different approach. Rather than associate dynamic dispatch with particular methods, the Ada 95 programmer associates dynamic dispatch with certain *references*. In our example, a formal parameter or an `access` variable (pointer) can be declared to be of the *class-wide* type `person'Class`, in which case all calls to all methods of that parameter or variable will be dispatched based on the class of the object to which it refers:

```
type person is tagged record ...
type student is new person with ...
type professor is new person with ...

procedure print_mailing_label (r : person) is ...
procedure print_mailing_label (s : student) is ...
procedure print_mailing_label (p : professor) is ...

procedure print_appropriate_label (r : person'Class) is
begin
    print_mailing_label (r);
    -- calls appropriate overloaded version, depending
    -- on type of r at run time
end print_appropriate_label;
```

The principal argument against static method binding—and thus in favor of dynamic binding based on the type of the referenced object—is that the static approach denies the derived class control over the consistency of its own state. Suppose, for example, that we are building an I/O library that contains a `text_file` class:

```
class text_file {
    char *name;
    long position;              // file pointer
public:
    void seek (long whence);    // virtual?
    ...
}
```

Now suppose we have a derived class `read_ahead_text_file`:

```
class read_ahead_text_file : public text_file {
    char *upcoming_characters;
public:
    void seek (long whence);    // redefinition
    ...
}
```

The code for `read_ahead_text_file::seek` will undoubtedly need to change the value of the cached `upcoming_characters`. If the method is not `virtual`, however, we cannot guarantee that this will happen: if we pass a `read_ahead_text_file` reference to a subroutine that expects a `text_file` reference as argument, and if that subroutine then calls `seek`, we'll get the version of `seek` in the base class.

10.4.2 Abstract Classes

In most object-oriented languages it is possible to omit the body of a virtual method in a base class. In C++ one does so by following the subroutine declaration with an "assignment" to zero:

```
class person {
    ...
public:
    virtual void print_mailing_label () = 0;
    ...
```

A bodyless virtual method is called an *abstract* method or, in C++, a *pure* virtual method. All virtual methods in Simula are abstract.

A class is said to be abstract if it has at least one abstract method. It is not possible to declare an object of an abstract class, because it would be missing at least one member. The only purpose of an abstract class is to serve as a base for other, *concrete* classes. A concrete class (or one of its intermediate ancestors) must provide a real definition for every abstract method it inherits. The existence of an abstract method in a base class provides a "hook" for dynamic method binding; it allows the programmer to write code that calls methods of (references to) objects of the base class, under the assumption that appropriate concrete methods will be invoked at run time. Classes that have no members other than abstract methods—no data members or method bodies—are called *interfaces* in Java. They support a restricted, "mix-in" form of multiple inheritance, which we will consider in Section 10.5.4.[4]

10.4.3 Member Lookup

With static method binding (e.g., as in Simula, C++, or Ada 95), the compiler can always tell which version of a method to call, based on the type of the variable being used. With dynamic method binding, however, the object referred to by

---

4 An abstract virtual method in Eiffel is called a *deferred feature*. (Recall that all features are virtual.) An abstract class is called a *deferred* class. A concrete class is called an *effective* class. An interface in the Java sense of the word is called a *fully deferred* class.

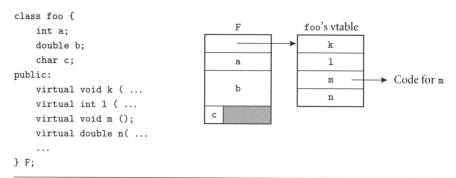

```
class foo {
    int a;
    double b;
    char c;
public:
    virtual void k ( ...
    virtual int l ( ...
    virtual void m ();
    virtual double n( ...
    ...
} F;
```

Figure 10.4 Implementation of virtual methods. The representation of object F begins with the address of the vtable for class foo. (All objects of this class will point to the same vtable.) The vtable itself consists of an array of addresses, one for the code of each virtual method of the class. The remainder of F consists of the representations of its data members.

a reference or pointer variable must contain sufficient information to allow the code generated by the compiler to find the right version of the method at run time. The most common implementation represents each object with a record whose first field contains the address of a *virtual method table* (*vtable*) for the object's class (see Figure 10.4). The vtable is an array whose *i*th entry indicates the address of the code for the object's *i*th virtual method. All objects of a given class share the same vtable.

Suppose that the `this` (`self`) pointer for methods is passed in register `r1`, that m is the third method of class `foo`, and that f is a pointer to an object of class `foo`. Then the code to call `f->m()` looks something like this:

```
r1 := f
r2 := *r1                 –– vtable address
r2 := *(r2 + (3−1) × 4)   –– assuming 4 = sizeof (address)
call *r2
```

On a typical RISC machine this calling sequence is two instructions (both of which access memory) longer than a call to a statically identified method. The extra overhead can be avoided whenever the compiler can deduce the type of the relevant object at compile time. The deduction is trivial for calls to methods of object-valued variables (as opposed to references and pointers).

If `bar` is derived from `foo`, we place its additional data members at the end of the "record" that represents it. We create a vtable for `bar` by copying the vtable for `foo`, replacing the entries of any virtual methods overridden by `bar`, and appending entries for any virtual methods declared in `bar` (Figure 10.5). If we have an object of class `bar` we can safely assign its address into a variable of type `foo*`:

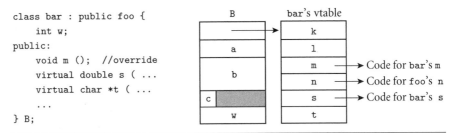

```
class bar : public foo {
    int w;
public:
    void m ();   //override
    virtual double s ( ...
    virtual char *t ( ...
    ...
} B;
```

Figure 10.5 Implementation of single inheritance. As in Figure 10.4, the representation of object B begins with the address of its class's vtable. The first four entries in the table represent the same members as they do for foo, except that one—m—has been over-ridden and now contains the address of the code for a different subroutine. Additional data members of bar follow the ones inherited from foo in the representation of B; additional virtual methods follow the ones inherited from foo in the vtable of class bar.

```
class foo { ...
class bar : public foo { ...
...
foo F;
bar B;
foo* q;
bar* s;
...
q = &B;      // ok; references through q will use prefixes
             // of B's data space and vtable
s = &F;      // static semantic error; F lacks the additional
             // data and vtable entries of a bar
```

In C++ (as in all the object-oriented languages we have considered, save Small-talk and CLOS), the compiler can verify the type correctness of this code stat-ically. It does not know what the class of the object referred to by q will be at run time, but it knows that it will either be foo or something derived (directly or indirectly) from foo, and this ensures that it will have all the members that may be accessed by foo-specific code.

Standard C++ allows "backwards" assignments by means of a dynamic_cast operator:

```
s = dynamic_cast<bar*> (q);
```

For backward compatibility C++ also supports traditional C-style casts of object pointers and references:

```
s = (bar*) q;    // permitted, but risky
```

With a C-style cast it is up to the programmer to ensure that the actual object involved is of an appropriate type: no dynamic semantic check is performed. Java employs the traditional cast notation, but performs the dynamic check. Eiffel has a *reverse assignment* operator, ?=, which assigns an object reference into a variable if and only if the type at run time is acceptable:

```
class foo ...
class bar inherit foo ...
...
f : foo;
b : bar;
...
f := b;      -- always ok
b ?= f;      -- reverse assignment: b gets f if f refers to a bar object
             -- at run time; otherwise b gets nil
```

Implementations of Eiffel, Java, and Standard C++ support dynamic checks on reverse assignment by including in each vtable the address of a run-time *type descriptor*. In C++, `dynamic_cast` is permitted only on pointers and references of polymorphic types, since objects of nonpolymorphic types do not have vtables.

In Smalltalk, variables are *untyped* references. A reference to any object may be assigned into any variable. Only when code actually attempts to invoke an operation (send a "message") at run time does the language implementation check to see whether the operation is supported by the object. The implementation is straightforward: data members of an object are never public; methods provide the only means of object interaction. The representation of an object begins with the address of a type descriptor. The type descriptor contains a dictionary that maps method names to code fragments. At run time, the Smalltalk interpreter performs a lookup operation in the dictionary to see if the method is supported. If not, it generates a "message not understood" error: the equivalent of a type clash error in Lisp. CLOS provides similar semantics, and invites similar implementations. The Smalltalk/CLOS approach is arguably more flexible than that of more statically typed languages, but it incurs significant run-time cost, and delays the reporting of errors.

In addition to imposing the overhead of indirection, virtual methods often preclude the in-line expansion of subroutines at compile time. The lack of in-line subroutines can be a serious performance problem when subroutines are small and frequently called. Like C, C++ attempts to avoid run-time overhead whenever possible: hence its use of static method binding as the default, and its heavy reliance on object-valued variables, for which even virtual methods can be dispatched at compile time.

On the other hand, under certain circumstances, it can be desirable to perform method lookup at run time even when the language permits compile-time lookup. In Java, for example, programs are usually distributed in a portable "byte code" format that is either interpreted or, in some implementations, compiled immediately before execution. The standard "virtual machine" interpreter for byte code looks methods up at run time. By doing so it avoids what is known as the *fragile base class* problem. Java implementations depend on the presence of a large standard library. This library is expected to evolve over time. Though the designers of the library will presumably be careful to maximize backward compatibility—seldom if ever deleting any members of a class—it is likely that users of old versions of the library will on occasion attempt to run code that was written with a new version of the library in mind. In such a situation it would be disastrous to rely on static assumptions about the representation of library classes: code that tries to use a newly added library feature could end up accessing memory beyond the end of the available representation. Run-time method lookup, by contrast, will produce a helpful "member not found in your version of the class" dynamic error message.

10.4.4 Related Concepts

Dynamic method binding in object-oriented languages is related to several concepts that we have considered at other points in this text, including polymorphism, generics, and first-class subroutines.

We have already noted that dynamic method binding introduces polymorphism into any code that expects a reference to an object of some base class foo. So long as objects of the derived class support the operations of the base class, the code will work equally well with references to objects of any class derived from foo. By declaring a reference parameter to be of class foo, for example, the programmer asserts that the subroutine uses only the "foo features" of the parameter, and will work on any object that provides those features.

One might be tempted to think that inheritance obviates the need for generics, but this is not the case. We can see an example in the gp_list_node class and its descendants of Section 10.1. By placing the structural aspects of an abstraction (in this case a list) in a base class, we make it easy to create type-specific lists: int_list_node, float_list_node, student_list_node, etc. Unfortunately, base class methods such as predecessor and successor return references of the base class type, which do not then support type-specific operations. To allow us to access the values stored in objects returned by the list-manipulation routines, we must perform an explicit type cast:

```
int_list_node_ptr q, r;
...
r = q->successor ();         // error: type clash
gp_list_node_ptr p = q->successor ();
cout << p.val;               // error: gp_list_nodes have no val
r = (int_list_node_ptr) q->successor ();
cout << r.val;               // ok
```

The cast on the fifth line here is both awkward and unsafe. We can't use a dynamic_cast operation because gp_list_node has no virtual members, and hence no vtable. We can confine the awkwardness to the definition of int_list_node by redefining member functions:

```
int_list_node* int_list_node::predecessor () {      // redefine
    return (int_list_node*) gp_list_node::predecessor ();
}
```

```
int_list_node* int_list_node::successor () {        // redefine
    return (int_list_node*) gp_list_node::successor ();
}
```

Unfortunately, redefining all of the appropriate arguments and return types of base class methods in every derived class is still a frustratingly tedious exercise, and the code is still unsafe: the compiler cannot verify type correctness. Generics get around both problems. In C++, we can write

```
template<class V>
class list_node {
    list_node<V>* prev;
    list_node<V>* next;
    list_node<V>* head_node;
public:
    V val;
    list_node<V>* predecessor () { ...
    list_node<V>* successor () { ...
    void insert_before (list_node<V>* new_node) { ...
    ...
};

template<class V>
class list {
    list_node<V> header;
public:
    list_node<V>* head () { ...
    void append (list_node<V> *new_node) { ...
    ...
};

typedef list_node<int> int_list_node;
typedef list<int> int_list;
...
int_list numbers;
int_list_node* first_int;
...
first_int = numbers->head ();
```

In a nutshell, generics exist for the purpose of abstracting over types, something that inheritance does not support. (NB: the type inference system of ML and related languages *does* suffice to abstract over types; ML does not require generics. On the other hand, while ML provides Euclid-like module types, it does not provide inheritance, and thus cannot be considered an object-oriented language.)

Eiffel has a generic facility similar to that of C++. As a convenient shorthand, it also allows the programmer to declare parameters and return values of methods to be of the same type as some "anchor" data member of the class. Then if a derived class redefines the anchor, the parameters and return values are automatically redefined as well, without the need to specify them explicitly:

```
class gp_list_node ...
...
class gp_list
feature {NONE}              -- private
    header : gp_list_node  -- to be redefined by derived classes
feature {ALL}              -- public
    head : like header is ...                 -- methods
    append (new_node : like header) is ...
    ...
end
...
class student_list_node inherit gp_list_node ...
...
class student_list
    inherit gp_list
    redefine header end
feature {NONE}
    header : student_list_node
    -- don't need to redefine head and append
end
```

The like mechanism does not eliminate the need for generics, but it makes it easier to define them, or to do without them in simple situations.

Because the dispatch of virtual methods is delayed until run time, dynamic method binding provides a mechanism similar to first-class subroutines (Sections 3.4 and 8.3.1). Code that looks like this in C++:

```
typedef void (*F_INT) (int);
    // F_INT is a type: pointer to function from int to void
void p (int a) {
    ...
}
void q (double b, F_INT f) {
    ...
    f (3);
    ...
}
q (3.14, &p);
```

can more-or-less be replaced by code that looks like this:

```
class foo {
public:
    virtual void f (int a) = 0;
};
void q (double b, foo& obj) {
    ...
    obj.f (3);
    ...
}
```

```
class bar : public foo {
public:
    virtual void f (int a) {
        ...
    }
} my_obj;
q (3.14, my_obj);
```

This latter, object-oriented version of the code has an important advantage over the pointer-to-subroutine version in C++: by adding data members to class `bar` (and object `my_obj`), we can provide method `f` with data on which to operate. In effect, the data members of an object with a virtual method behave like the referencing environment of a closure in a language with nested scopes (recall that C and C++ do not require closures, because they do not have nested scopes). In Ada 95, which has both nested scopes and classes (tagged types), the entries in vtables must themselves be closures, not just subroutine addresses.

In some cases, virtual methods and first-class subroutines can complement each other. Suppose, for example, that we are writing a discrete event simulation, as described in Section 8.6.4. We might like a general mechanism that allows us to schedule a call to an arbitrary subroutine, with an arbitrary set of parameters, to occur at some future point in time. If the subroutines we want to have called vary in their numbers and types of parameters, we won't be able to pass them to a general-purpose `schedule_at` routine. We can solve the problem with virtual methods, as shown in Figure 10.6. As we shall see in Section 12.2.3, this same technique is used in Modula-3 to encapsulate start-up arguments for newly created threads of control.

10.5* Multiple Inheritance

At times it can be useful for a derived class to inherit features from more than one base class. Suppose, for example, that we want our administrative computing system to keep all students of the same year (freshmen, sophomores, juniors, seniors, unmatriculated) on some list. It may then be desirable to derive class `student` from both `person` and `gp_list_node`. In C++ we can say

```
class student : public person, public gp_list_node { ...
```

Now an object of class `student` will have all the data and subroutine members of both a `person` and a `gp_list_node`. The declaration in Eiffel is analogous:

```
class student
inherit
    person;
    gp_list_node
feature
    ...
```

```
class fn_call {
public:
    virtual void trigger () = 0;
};
void schedule_at (fn_call& fc, time t) {
    ...
}
...
void foo (int a, double b, char c) {
    ...
}
class call_foo : public fn_call {
    int arg1;
    double arg2;
    char arg3;
    void (*ptr) (int, double, char);
public:
    call_foo (int a, double b, char c) :    // constructor
        arg1 (a), arg2 (b), arg3 (c) {
        // member initialization is all that is required
    }
    void trigger () {
        foo (arg1, arg2, arg3);
    }
};
...
call_foo cf (3, 3.14, 'x');               // declaration/constructor call
schedule_at (cf, now () + delay);
    // at some point in the future, the discrete event system
    // will call cf.trigger (), which will cause a call to
    // foo (3, 3.14, 'x')
```

Figure 10.6 Subroutine pointers and virtual methods. Class `call_foo` encapsulates a subroutine pointer and values to be passed to the subroutine. It exports a parameter-less subroutine that can be used to trigger the encapsulated call.

Multiple inheritance also appears in CLOS. Simula, Smalltalk, Modula-3, Ada 95, and Oberon have only single inheritance. Java provides a limited, "mix-in" form of multiple inheritance; we will discuss it further in Section 10.5.4.

To implement multiple inheritance, we must be able to generate both a "person view" and a "gp_list_node view" of a student object on demand, for example when assigning a reference to a student object into a person or gp_list_node variable. For one of the base classes (person, say) we can do the same thing we did with single inheritance: let the data members of that base class lie at the beginning of the representation of the derived class, and let the virtual methods of that base class lie at the beginning of the vtable. Then when we assign a reference to a student object into a person variable, code that manipulates the person variable will just use a prefix of the data members and the vtable.

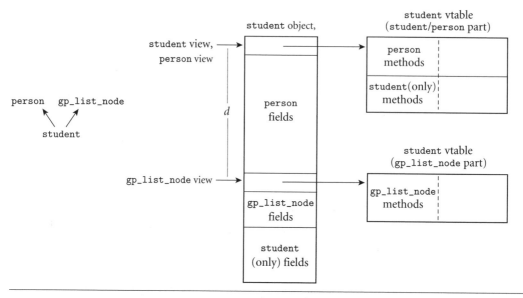

Figure 10.7 Implementation of (nonrepeated) multiple inheritance. The size d of the person portion of the object is a compile-time constant. We access the gp_list_node portion of the vtable by adding d to the address of a student object before indirecting. Likewise, we create a gp_list_node view of a student object by adding d to the object's address. As described in the text, each vtable entry consists of both a method address and a "this correction" value equal to the signed distance between the view through which the vtable was accessed and the view of the class in which the method was defined.

For the other base class (gp_list_node) things get more complicated: we can't put *both* base classes at the beginning of the derived class. One possible solution is shown in Figure 10.7. It is based loosely on the implementation described by Ellis and Stroustrup [ES90, Chap. 10]. Because the gp_list_node fields of a student follow the person fields, the assignment of a reference to a student object into a variable of type gp_list_node* requires that we adjust our "view" by adding the compile-time constant offset d.

The vtable for a student is broken into two parts. The first part lists the virtual methods of the derived class and the first base class (person). The second part lists the virtual methods of the second base class. (We have already introduced a method, print_mailing_label, defined in class person. We may similarly imagine that gp_list_node defines a virtual method debug_print that is supposed to dump a printable representation of the contents of the node to standard output.) Generalization to three or more base classes is straightforward; see Exercise 10.13.

Every data member of a student object has a compile-time-constant offset from the beginning of the object. Likewise, every virtual method has a compile-time-constant offset from the beginning of one of the parts of the vtable. The address of the person/student portion of the vtable is stored in the beginning of the object. The address of the gp_list_node portion of the vtable is stored at offset d. Note that both parts of the vtable are specific to class student. In particular, the gp_list_node part of the vtable is *not* shared by objects of class gp_list_node, because the contents of the tables will be different if student has overridden any of gp_list_node's virtual methods.

To call the virtual method print_mailing_label, originally defined in person, we can use a code sequence similar to the one shown in Section 10.4.3 for single inheritance. To call a virtual method originally defined in gp_list_node, we must first add the offset d to our object's address, in order to find the address of the gp_list_node portion of the vtable. Then we can index into this gp_list_node vtable to find the address of the appropriate method to call. But we are left with one final problem: what is the appropriate value of this to pass to the method?

As a concrete example, suppose that student does not override debug_print (even though it probably ought to). If our object is of class student, we should pass a gp_list_node view of it to debug_print: the address of the object, plus d. If, however, our object is of some class (transfer_student, perhaps) that does override debug_print, then we should pass a transfer_student view to debug_print. If we are accessing our object through a variable (a reference or a pointer) whose methods are dynamically bound, then we can't tell at compile time which one of these cases applies. Worse yet, we may not even know how to generate a transfer_student view if we have to: class transfer_student may not have been invented when this part of our code was compiled, so we certainly don't know how far into it the gp_list_node fields appear!

A common solution is for vtable entries to consist of a *pair* of fields. One is the address of the method's code; the other is a "this correction" value, to be added to the view through which we found the vtable. Returning to Figure 10.7, the "this correction" field of the vtable entry for debug_print would contain $-d$ if debug_print was overridden by student, and zero otherwise. In the gp_list_node part of the vtable for the (yet to be written) class transfer_student, the "this correction" field might contain some other value $-e$. In general, the "this correction" is the distance between the view of the class in which the method was *declared* (and through which we accessed the vtable) and the view of the class in which the method was *defined* (and which will therefore be expected by the subroutine's implementation).

If variable my_student contains a reference to (a student view of) some object at run time, and if debug_print is the third virtual method of gp_list_node, then the code to call my_student.debug_print would now look something like this:

```
r1 := my_student            -- student view of object
r1 := r1 + d                -- gp_list_node view of object
r2 := *r1                   -- address of appropriate vtable
r3 := *(r2 + (3−1) × 8)     -- method address
r2 := *(r2 + (3−1) × 8 + 4) -- this correction
r1 := r1 + r2               -- this
call *r3
```

Here we have assumed that both method addresses and `this` corrections are four bytes long. On a typical machine this code is three instructions (including one memory access) longer than the code required with single inheritance, and five instructions (including three memory access) longer than a call to a statically identified method. Unfortunately, the additional overhead stems from the mere existence of multiple inheritance in the language: we must incur it even in programs that turn out to use only single inheritance. Exercise 10.18 explores alternative implementations in which some of the information needed to call a virtual method is represented by executable code, rather than data structures.

10.5.1 Semantic Ambiguities

In addition to implementation complexities (only some of which we have discussed so far), multiple inheritance introduces potential semantic problems. Suppose that both `gp_list_node` and `person` define a `debug_print` method. If we have a variable s of type `student*` and we call s->`debug_print`, which version of the method should we get? In CLOS, we get the version from the base class that appeared first in the derived class's header. In Eiffel, we get a static semantic error if we try to define a derived class with such an ambiguity. In C++, we can define the derived class, but we get a static semantic error if we attempt to use a member whose name is ambiguous. In Eiffel we can use the feature renaming mechanism to get rid of naming conflicts when defining a derived class. In C++ we must redefine the ambiguous member explicitly:

```
void student::debug_print () {
    person::debug_print ();
    gp_list_node::debug_print ();
}
```

Here we have chosen to call the `debug_print` routines of both base classes, using the :: scope resolution operator to name them. We could of course have chosen to call just one, or to write our own code from scratch. We could even arrange for access to both routines by giving them new names:

```
void student::debug_print_person () {
    person::debug_print ();
}
void student::debug_print_list_node () {
    gp_list_node::debug_print ();
}
```

Things are a little messier if either or both of the identically named base class methods are virtual, and we want to override them in the derived class. Following Stroustrup [Str97, Sec. 25.6], we can solve the problem by interposing an "interface" class between each base class and the derived class:

```
class person_interface : public person {
    virtual void debug_print_person () = 0;
    void debug_print () {debug_print_person ();}
        // overrides person::debug_print
};
class list_node_interface : public gp_list_node {
    virtual void debug_print_list_node () = 0;
    void debug_print () {debug_print_list_node ();}
        // overrides gp_list_node::debug_print
};
class student : public person_interface, public list_node_interface {
public:
    void debug_print_person () { ...
    void debug_print_list_node () { ...
        ...
};
```

We leave it as an exercise (10.14) to show what happens if we assign a student object into a variable p of type person* and then call p->debug_print ().

A more serious ambiguity arises when a class *D* inherits from two base classes, *B* and *C*, both of which inherit from some common base class *A*. In this situation, should an object of class *D* contain one instance of the data members of class *A* or two? The answer would seem to be program-dependent. For example, suppose in our administrative computing system that we would like to keep all professors in the same department on a linked list. As with class student, we might want class professor to inherit from both person and gp_list_node:

```
class professor : public person, public gp_list_node { ...
```

Furthermore, suppose that professors occasionally take courses as nonmatriculated students. In this case we might want a new class that supports both sets of operations:

```
class student_prof : public student, public professor { ...
```

Class student_prof inherits from person and gp_list_node twice, through both student and professor. If we think about it, we probably want a student_prof to have *one* instance of the data members of class person—one name, one University ID number, one mailing address—and *two* instances of the data members of class gp_list_node—two predecessors and two successors, one set for linking into the list of nonmatriculated students and another for linking into the faculty list for some department:

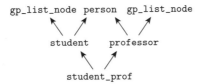

The gp_list_node case—separate copies from each branch of the inheritance tree—is known as *replicated inheritance*. The person case—a single copy from both branches of the tree—is known as *shared* inheritance. Both are forms of *repeated inheritance*. Replicated inheritance is the default in C++. Shared inheritance is the default in Eiffel. Shared inheritance can be obtained in C++ by specifying that a base class is virtual:

```
class student : public virtual person, public gp_list_node { ...
class professor : public virtual person, public gp_list_node { ...
```

In this case the members of class person are shared when inherited over multiple paths, while the members of class gp_list_node are replicated. Replicated inheritance of individual features can be obtained in Eiffel through the renaming mechanism described in Section 10.2.2:

```
class student inherit person; gp_list_node ...
class professor inherit person; gp_list_node ...

class student_prof
inherit
    student
        rename
            prev as prev_student,
            next as next_student
        end;
    professor
        rename
            prev as prev_prof,
            next as next_prof
        end
feature
    ...
end -- class student_prof
```

Features inherited with different final names are replicated; features inherited with the same final name are shared. Multiple inheritance in CLOS is always shared, unless the user interposes interface classes as shown above explicitly; there is no other renaming mechanism.

10.5.2 Replicated Inheritance

Replicated inheritance introduces no implementation problems beyond those described at the beginning of Section 10.5. As shown in Figure 10.8, an object (in this case of class D) that inherits a base class (A) over two different paths in the inheritance tree has two copies of A's data members in its representation, and a set of entries for the virtual methods of A in each of the parts of its vtable. Creation of a B view of a D object (e.g., when assigning a pointer to a D object into a B* variable) would not require the execution of any code. Creation of a

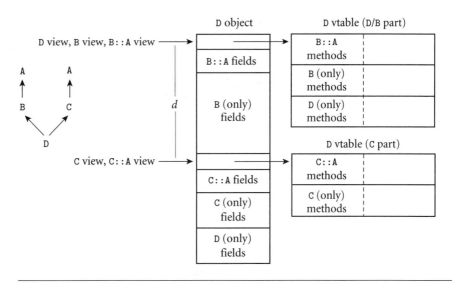

Figure 10.8 Implementation of replicated multiple inheritance. Each base class contains a complete copy of class A. As in Figure 10.7, the vtable for class D is split into two parts, one for each base class, and each vtable entry consists of a ⟨method address, this correction⟩ pair.

C view (e.g., when assigning into a C* variable) would require the addition of offset d.

Because of ambiguity, we cannot access A members of a D object by name. We can access them, however, if we assign a pointer to a D object into a B* or C* variable. Similarly, a pointer to a D object cannot be assigned into an A pointer directly: there would be no basis on which to choose the A for which to create a view. We can, however, perform the assignment through a B* or C* intermediary:

```
class A { ...
class B : public A { ...
class C : public A { ...
class D : public B, public C { ...
...
A* a;   B* b;   C* c;   D* d;
a = d;  // error; ambiguous
b = d;  // ok
c = d;  // ok
a = b;  // ok; a := d's B's A
a = c;  // ok; a := d's C's A
```

As described at the beginning of Section 10.5, vtable entries will need to consist of ⟨method address, this correction⟩ pairs.

10.5.3 **Shared Inheritance**

Shared inheritance introduces a new opportunity for ambiguity and additional implementation complexity. As in the previous section, assume that D inherits from B and C, both of which inherit from A. This time, however, assume that A is shared:

```
class A {
public:
    virtual void f ();
    ...
}
class B : public virtual A { ...
class C : public virtual A { ...
class D : public B, public C { ...
```

The new ambiguity arises if B or C overrides method f, declared in A: which version (if any) does D inherit? C++ defines a reference to f to be unambiguous (and therefore valid) if one of the possible definitions *dominates* the others, in the sense that its class is a descendant of the classes of all the other definitions. In our specific example, D can inherit an overridden version of f from either B or C. If both of them override it, however, any attempt to use f from within D's code will be a static semantic error. Eiffel provides comparatively elaborate mechanisms for controlling ambiguity. A class that inherits an overridden method over more than one path can specify which one it wants. Alternatively, through renaming, it can retain access to all versions.

To implement shared inheritance we must recognize that because a single instance of A is a part of both B and C, we cannot make the representations of both B and C contiguous in memory. In Figure 10.9, in fact, we have chosen to make neither B nor C contiguous. We insist, however, that the representation of every B, C, or D object (and every B, C, or D view of an object of a derived class) contain the address of the A part of the object at a compile-time constant offset from the beginning of the view. To access a data member of A, we first indirect through this address, and then apply the offset of the member within A. To call the nth virtual method declared in A, we execute the following code:

```
r1 := my_D_view              -- original view of object
r1 := *(r1 + 4)              -- A view
r2 := *r1                    -- address of A part of vtable
r3 := *(r2 + (n − 1) × 8)    -- method address
r2 := *(r2 + (n − 1) × 8 + 4) -- this correction
r1 := r1 + r2                -- this
call *r3
```

This code sequence is the same number of instructions in length as our sequence for nonvirtual base classes (Section 10.5, page 568), but involves one more memory access (to indirect through the A address). The code will work with any D

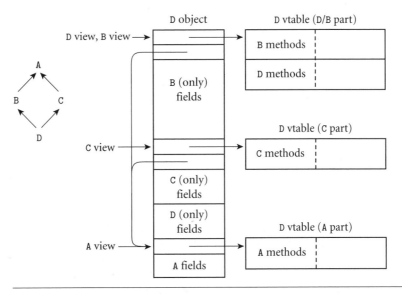

Figure 10.9 Implementation of shared multiple inheritance. Objects of class B, C, and D contain the address of their A components at a compile-time constant offset (in this case, immediately after the vtable address). As in Figures 10.7 and 10.8, this corrections for virtual methods in vtable entries are relative to the view of the class in which the method was declared (i.e., through which the vtable was accessed).

view of any object, including an object of a class derived from D, in which the D and A views might be more widely separated. The constant 4 in the second line assumes four-byte addresses, with the address of D's A part located immediately after D's initial vtable address. In an object with more than one virtual base class, the address of the part of the object corresponding to each such base would be found at a different offset from the beginning of the object.

The implementation strategy of Figure 10.9 works in C++ because we always know when a base class is `virtual` (shared). For data members and virtual methods of nonvirtual base classes, we continue to use the (cheaper) lookup algorithms of the previous two sections. In Eiffel, on the other hand, a feature that is inherited via replication at one level of the class hierarchy may be inherited via sharing later on. As a result, Eiffel requires a somewhat more elaborate implementation strategy (see Exercise 10.19).

We can avoid the extra level of indirection when accessing virtual methods of virtual base classes in C++ if we are willing to replicate portions of a class's vtable. We explore this option in Exercise 10.20.

10.5.4 Mix-In Inheritance

Before leaving the topic of multiple inheritance, we return briefly to the notion of a base class composed entirely of abstract methods, as mentioned in passing in

Section 10.4.2. Such a class is called an *interface* in Java. It has neither data members nor implementations of its methods.[5] It is therefore immune to most of the semantic ambiguities and implementation complexities of multiple inheritance.

Inheritance from one "real" base class and an arbitrary number of interfaces is known as *mix-in* inheritance—the virtual methods of the interface are "mixed into" the methods of the derived class. It may be stretching things a bit to speak of "inheriting" an interface, since the derived class must provide a definition for each of the interface's methods. Interfaces do, however, facilitate code reuse through polymorphism. If a formal parameter of a subroutine is declared to have an interface type, then any class that implements (inherits from) that interface can be passed as the corresponding actual parameter. The classes of objects that can legitimately be passed need not have a common class ancestor.

As an example, suppose that we have been given general-purpose Java code that will sort objects according to some textual field, display a graphic representation of an object within a web browser window (hiding and refreshing as appropriate), and store references to objects by name in a dictionary data structure. Each of these capabilities would be represented by an interface. If we have already developed some complicated class of objects `widget`, we can make use of the general-purpose code by mixing the appropriate interfaces into classes derived from `widget`, as shown in Figure 10.10.

As noted in Section 10.4.3, Java implementations usually look methods up by name at run time. In this case, the methods of an interface can simply be added to the method dictionary of any class that implements the interface. To implement mix-in inheritance without run-time method lookup, one simple approach is to augment the representation of objects of the class with the addresses of vtables for the implemented interfaces, as shown in Figure 10.11. Additional vtable pointers, like additional data members, are added to the end of the representation of objects of the base class to create the representation of the derived class. If interfaces and data members are added at several levels of the class hierarchy, then vtable pointers and data members may be interspersed at arbitrary offsets within objects.

10.6 Object-Oriented Programming Revisited

At the beginning of this chapter, we characterized object-oriented programming in terms of three fundamental concepts: encapsulation, inheritance, and dynamic method binding. Encapsulation allows the implementation details of an abstraction to be hidden behind a simple interface. Inheritance allows a new abstraction to be defined as an extension or refinement of some existing abstraction, obtaining some or all of its characteristics automatically. Dynamic method

---

5 Java actually does allow an interface to have data members, but such members are always constants; their values must be specified in the interface declaration.

```
public class widget { ...
}
interface sortable_object {
    String get_sort_name ();
    bool less_than (sortable_object o);
    // All methods of an interface are automatically public.
}
interface graphable_object {
    void display_at (Graphics g, int x, int y);
    // Graphics is a standard library class that provides a context
    // in which to render graphical objects.
}
interface storable_object {
    String get_stored_name ();
}
class named_widget extends widget implements sortable_object {
    public String name;
    public String get_sort_name () {return name;}
    public bool less_than (sortable_object o) {
        return (name.compareTo (o.get_sort_name ()) < 0);
        // compareTo is a method of the standard library class String.
    }
}
class augmented_widget extends named_widget
        implements graphable_object, storable_object {
    ...             // more data members
    public void display_at (Graphics g, int x, int y) {
        ...      // series of calls to methods of g
    }
    public String get_stored_name () {return name;}
}
...
class sorted_list {
    public void insert (sortable_object o) { ...
    public sortable_object first () { ...
    ...
}
class browser_window extends Frame {
    // Frame is the standard library class for windows.
    public void add_to_window (graphable_object o) { ...
    ...
}
class dictionary {
    public void insert (storable_object o) { ...
    public storable_object lookup (String name) { ...
    ...
}
```

Figure 10.10 Interface classes in Java. By implementing the sortable_object interface in named_widget and the graphable_object and storable_object interfaces in augmented_widget, we obtain the ability to pass objects of those classes to and from such routines as sorted_list.insert, browser_window.add_to_window, and dictionary.lookup.

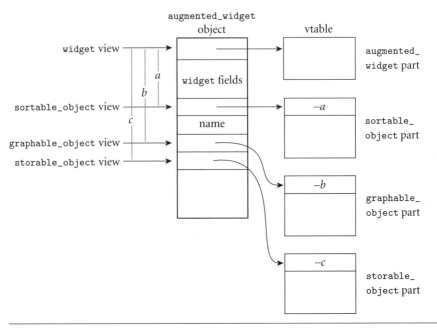

Figure 10.11 **Implementation of mix-in inheritance.** Objects of class `augmented_widget` contain four vtable addresses, one for the class itself (as in Figure 10.4), and three for the implemented interfaces. The view of the object that is passed to interface routines points directly at the relevant vtable pointer. The vtable then begins with a single `this` correction, used by all of its methods to regenerate a pointer to the object itself.

binding allows the new abstraction to display its new behavior even when used in a context that expects the old abstraction.

Different programming languages support these fundamental concepts to different degrees. In particular, languages differ in the extent to which they *require* the programmer to write in an object-oriented style. Some authors argue that a *truly* object-oriented language should make it difficult or impossible to write programs that are not object-oriented. From this purist point of view, an object-oriented language should present a *uniform object model* of computing, in which every data type is a class, every variable is a reference to an object, and every subroutine is an object method. Moreover, objects should be thought of in *anthropomorphic terms*: as active entities responsible for all computation.

Smalltalk comes close to this ideal. In fact, as described in the section below, even such control flow mechanisms as selection and iteration are modeled as method invocations in Smalltalk. On the other hand, Modula-3 and Ada 95 are probably best characterized as von Neumann languages that *permit* the programmer to write in an object-oriented style if desired.

So what about C++? It certainly has a wealth of features, including several (multiple inheritance, elaborate access control, strict initialization order, destructors, generics) that are useful in object-oriented programs and that are not found in Smalltalk. At the same time, it has a wealth of problematic wrinkles. Its simple types are not classes. It has subroutines outside of classes. It uses static method binding and replicated multiple inheritance by default, rather than the more costly `virtual` alternatives. Its unchecked C-style type casts provide a major loophole for type checking and access control. Its lack of garbage collection is a major obstacle to the creation of correct, self-contained abstractions. Probably most serious of all, C++ retains all of the low-level mechanisms of C, allowing the programmer to escape or subvert the object-oriented model of programming entirely. It has been suggested that the best C++ programmers are those who did *not* learn C first: they are not as tempted to write "C-style" programs in the newer language. On balance, it is probably safe to say that C++ is an object-oriented language in the same sense that Common Lisp is a functional language. With the possible exception of garbage collection, C++ provides all of the necessary tools, but it requires substantial discipline on the part of the programmer to use those tools "correctly."

10.6.1* The Object Model of Smalltalk

Smalltalk is to a large extent the canonical object-oriented language. The original version of Smalltalk was designed by Alan Kay as part of his doctoral work at the University of Utah in the late 1960s. It was then adopted by the Software Concepts Group at the Xerox Palo Alto Research Center (PARC), and went through five major revisions in the 1970s, culminating in the Smalltalk-80 language. We have mentioned several features of Smalltalk in previous sections. We focus here on Smalltalk's anthropomorphic programming model. A full introduction to the language is beyond the scope of this book.

Smalltalk is heavily integrated into its programming environment. In fact, unlike all of the other languages mentioned in this book, a Smalltalk program does not consist of a simple sequence of characters. Rather, Smalltalk programs are meant to be viewed within the *browser* of a Smalltalk implementation, where font changes and screen position can be used to differentiate between different parts of a given program unit. Together with the contemporary Interlisp and Pilot/Mesa projects at PARC, the Smalltalk group shares credit for developing the now ubiquitous concepts of bit-mapped screens, windows, menus, and mice.

Smalltalk uses an untyped reference model for all variables. Every variable refers to an object, but the class of the object need not be statically known. As described in Section 10.3.1 (and illustrated in Figure 10.2, page 536), every Smalltalk object is an instance of a class descended from a single base class named `Object`. All data is contained in objects. The most trivial of these are simple immutable objects such as `true` (of class `Boolean`) and 3 (of class `Integer`).

Operations are all conceptualized as *messages* sent to objects. The expression 3 + 4, for example, indicates sending a + message to the (immutable) object 3, with a reference to the object 4 as argument. In response to this message, the object 3 creates and returns a reference to the (immutable) object 7. Similarly, the expression a + b, where a and b are variables, indicates sending a + message to the object referred to by a, with the reference in b as argument. If a happens to refer to 3 and b refers to 4, the effect will be the same as it was in the case of the constants. As described in Section 6.1, multiargument messages have multi-word names. Each word ends with a colon; each argument follows a word. The expression

```
myBox displayOn: myScreen at: location
```

sends a `displayOn:at:` message to the object referred to by variable `myBox`, with the objects referred to by `myScreen` and `location` as arguments.

Even control flow in Smalltalk is conceptualized as messages. Consider the selection construct:

```
n < 0
    ifTrue: [abs <- n negated]
    ifFalse: [abs <- n]
```

This code begins by sending a < 0 message (a < message with 0 as argument) to the object referred to by n. In response to this message, the object referred to by n will return a reference to one of two immutable objects: `true` or `false`. This reference becomes the value of the n < 0 expression.

Smalltalk evaluates expressions left-to-right without precedence or associativity. The value of n < 0 therefore becomes the recipient of an `ifTrue:ifFalse:` message. This message has two arguments, each of which is a *block*. A block in Smalltalk is a fragment of code enclosed in brackets. It is an immutable object, with semantics roughly comparable to those of a lambda expression in Lisp. To execute a block we send it a `value` message.

When sent an `ifTrue:ifFalse:` message, the immutable object `true` sends a `value` message to its first argument (which had better be a block) and then returns the result. The object `false`, on the other hand, in response to the same message, sends a `value` message to its second argument (the block that followed `ifFalse:`). The left arrow (`<-`) in each block is the assignment operator. Assignment is not a message; it is a side effect of evaluation of the right-hand side. As in expression-based languages such Algol 68, the value of an assignment expression is the value of the right-hand side. The overall value of our selection expression will be the value of one of the blocks, namely a reference to n or to its additive inverse, whichever is nonnegative. For the sake of convenience, Boolean objects in Smalltalk also implement `ifTrue:`, `ifFalse:`, and `ifFalse:ifTrue:` methods.

Iteration is modeled in a similar fashion. For enumeration-controlled loops, class `Integer` implements `timesRepeat:` and `to:by:do:` methods:

```
pow <- 1.
10 timesRepeat:
    [pow <- pow * n]
```

```
sum <- 0.
1 to: 100 by: 2 do:
    [:i | sum <- sum + (a at: i)]
```

The first of these code fragments calculates n^{10}. In response to a `timesRepeat:` message, the integer k sends a `value` message to the argument (a block) k times. The second code fragment sums the odd-indexed elements of the array referred to by a. In response to a `to: by: do:` message, the integer k behaves as one might expect: it sends a `value:` message to its third argument (a block) $\lfloor (t - k + b)/b \rfloor$ times, where t is the first argument and b is the second argument. Note the colon at the end of `value:`. The plain `value` message is unary; the `value:` message has an argument; it is understood by blocks that have a (single) formal parameter. In our loop example, the integer 1 sends the messages `value: 1`, `value: 3`, `value: 5`, etc. to the block `[:i | sum <- sum + (a at: i)]`. The `:i |` at the beginning of the block is its formal parameter. The `at:` message is understood by arrays. For iteration with a step size of one, integers also provide a `to: do:` method.

Because it is an object, a block can be referred to by a variable:

```
b <- [n <- n + 1].          "b is now a closure"
c <- [:i | n <- n + i].     "so is c"
...
b value.                    "increment n by I"
c value:   3.               "increment n by 3"
```

A block with two parameters expects a `value: value:` message. A block with j parameters expects a message whose name consists of the word `value:` repeated j times. Comments in Smalltalk are double-quoted (strings are single-quoted).

For logically controlled loops, Smalltalk relies on the `whileTrue:` message, understood by blocks:

```
tail <- myList.
[tail next ~~ nil]
    whileTrue: [tail <- tail next]
```

This code sets `tail` to the final element of `myList`. The double-tilde (`~~`) operator means "does not refer to the same object as." The method `next` is assumed to return a reference to the element following its recipient. In response to a `whileTrue:` message, a block sends itself a `value` message. If the result of that message is a reference to `true`, the block sends a `value` message to the argument of the original message and repeats. Blocks also implement a `whileFalse:` method.

The blocks of Smalltalk allow the programmer to construct almost arbitrary control-flow constructs. Because of their simple syntax, Smalltalk blocks are even easier to manipulate than the lambda expressions of Lisp. In effect, a `to: by: do:` message turns iteration "inside out," making the body of the loop a simple message argument that can be executed (by sending it a `value` message) from within the body of the `to: by: do:` method. Smalltalk programmers can define similar methods for other container classes, obtaining all the power of iterators (Section 6.5.3) and much of the power of `call_with_current_continuation` (Section 8.5.4):

```
myTree inorderDo: [:node | whatever]
```

It is worth noting that the uniform object model of computation in Smalltalk does not necessarily imply a uniform implementation. Just as Clu implementations implement built-in immutable objects as values, despite their reference semantics (Section 6.1.2), a Smalltalk implementation is likely to use the usual machine instructions for computer arithmetic, rather than actually sending messages to integers. In a similar vein, the most common control flow constructs (`ifTrue: ifFalse:`, `to: by: do:`, `whileTrue:`, etc.) are likely to be recognized by a Smalltalk interpreter, and implemented with special, faster, code.

We end this section by observing that recursion works at least as well in Smalltalk as it does in other imperative languages. The following is a recursive implementation of Euclid's algorithm:

```
gcd: other                                   "other is a formal parameter"
    [self = other]
        ifTrue:   [↑self].                  "end condition"
    [self < other]
        ifTrue:   [↑self gcd: (other – self)]      "recurse"
        ifFalse:  [↑other gcd: (self – other)]     "recurse"
```

The up-arrow (↑) symbol is comparable to the `return` of C or Algol 68. The keyword `self` is comparable to `this` in C++. We have shown the code in mixed fonts, much as it would appear in a Smalltalk browser. The header of the method is identified by bold face type.

10.7 Summary and Concluding Remarks

This has been the last of our five core chapters on language design: names (Chapter 3), control flow (Chapter 6), types (Chapter 7), subroutines (Chapter 8), and objects (Chapter 10).

We began in Section 10.1 by identifying three fundamental concepts of object-oriented programming: encapsulation, inheritance, and dynamic method binding. We also introduced the terminology of classes, objects, and methods. We had already seen encapsulation in the modules of Chapter 3. Encapsulation allows the details of a complicated data abstraction to be hidden behind a comparatively simple interface. Inheritance extends the utility of encapsulation by making it easy for programmers to define new abstractions as refinements or extensions of existing abstractions. Inheritance provides a natural basis for polymorphic subroutines: if a subroutine expects an instance of a given class as argument, then an object of any class derived from the expected one can be used instead (assuming that it retains the entire existing interface). Dynamic method binding extends this form of polymorphism by arranging for a call to one of the parameter's methods to use the implementation associated with the class of the actual object at run time, rather than the implementation associated with the declared class of the parameter. We noted that some languages, including Modula-3 and Ada 95, support object orientation through a type extension mechanism, in which encapsulation is associated with modules, but inheritance and dynamic method binding are associated with a special form of record.

In later sections we covered object initialization and finalization, dynamic method binding, and multiple inheritance in some detail. In many cases we discovered tradeoffs between functionality on the one hand and simplicity and execution speed on the other. Treating variables as references, rather than values, often leads to simpler semantics, but requires extra indirection. Garbage collection, as previously noted in Section 7.7.3, dramatically eases the creation and maintenance of software, but imposes run-time costs. Dynamic method binding requires (in the general case) that methods be dispatched using vtables or some other lookup mechanism. Multiple inheritance, even when unused, requires the inclusion of `this` correction values in vtables. Shared multiple inheritance requires an extra level of indirection to find the data members of a virtual base class. Mix-in inheritance simplifies lookup in Java, but the fragile base class problem limits the extent to which implementations can rely on precomputed tables.

In several cases we saw time/space tradeoffs as well. In-line subroutines, as previously noted in Section 8.2.3, can dramatically improve the performance of code with many small subroutines, not only by eliminating the overhead of the subroutine calls themselves, but by allowing register allocation, common subexpression analysis, and other "global" code improvements to be applied across calls. At the same time, in-line expansion generally increases the size of object code. For virtual method dispatch, Exercise 10.18 explores replacing vtable components with executable code, again saving time at the expense of space (similar tradeoffs apply to the implementation of `case` statements in any imperative language). In classes with shared virtual inheritance, Exercise 10.20 explores replicating portions of the vtable in order to avoid one level of indirection.

Despite its lack of multiple inheritance, Smalltalk is widely regarded as the purest and most flexible of the object-oriented languages. Its lack of compile-time type checking, however, together with its "message-based" model of computation and its need for dynamic method lookup, render its implementations rather slow. C++, with its object-valued variables, default static binding, minimal dynamic checks, and high-quality compilers, is largely responsible for the growing popularity of object-oriented programming. Improvements in reliability, maintainability, and code reuse may or may not justify the high performance overhead of Smalltalk, or even the lower overhead of Eiffel. They almost certainly justify the relatively modest overhead of C++. With the ever-increasing size of software systems, the explosive growth of distributed computing on the Internet, and the development of highly portable object-oriented languages (Java) and binary object standards (ActiveX/OLE [Bro96], CORBA [Sie96]/JavaBeans [Sun97]), object-oriented programming will clearly play a major role in 21st century computing.

10.8 Review Questions

10.1 What are generally considered to be the three defining characteristics of object-oriented programming?

10.2 In what programming language of the 1960s does object orientation find its roots?

10.3 What is the purpose of the "private" part of an object interface? Why is it required?

10.4 What is a *container* class?

10.5 Explain the distinction between `private`, `protected`, and `public` class members in C++.

10.6 Explain the distinction between `private`, `protected`, and `public` base classes in C++.

10.7 What is meant by an *opaque* export from a module?

10.8 Explain why in-line subroutines are particularly important in object-oriented languages.

10.9 Describe the notion of *selective availability* in Eiffel.

10.10 Describe the key design difference between Smalltalk, Eiffel, and C++ on the one hand, and Oberon, Modula-3, and Ada 95 on the other.

10.11 What are *constructors* and *destructors*?

10.12 Why does C++ need destructors more than Eiffel does?

10.13 Why is object initialization simpler in a language with a reference model of variables (as opposed to a value model)?

10.14 Explain the difference between initialization and assignment in C++.

10.15 Explain the difference between static and dynamic method binding (i.e., between *virtual* and *nonvirtual* methods). Why does C++ use static method binding by default? Why do Smalltalk, Eiffel, and Java make *all* methods virtual?

10.16 Explain the connection between dynamic method binding and polymorphism.

10.17 What is a *pure* virtual function (a *deferred feature* in Eiffel)?

10.18 Describe how virtual functions can be used to achieve the effect of subroutine closures.

10.19 What is an *abstract* (*deferred*) *class*?

10.20 Explain why generics (templates) are still useful in C++ and Eiffel, despite the languages' already substantial support for polymorphism.

10.21 Explain the use of `like` in Eiffel.

10.22 What is a *vtable*? How is it used?

10.23 What is the *fragile base class* problem?

10.24* Explain the distinction between replicated and shared multiple inheritance. When is each desirable?

10.25* What is *mix-in* style inheritance?

10.26* Explain how even nonrepeated multiple inheritance introduces the need for multiple *views* of (the implementation of) an object, and for "`this` correction" fields in vtables.

10.27* Explain how shared multiple inheritance introduces the need for an additional level of indirection when accessing fields of certain parent classes.

10.28* Briefly describe some of the innovations of the Smalltalk programming language. Also describe some of its weaknesses.

10.9 Exercises

10.1 Some language designers argue that object orientation eliminates the need for nested subroutines. Do you agree? Why or why not?

10.2 Refer back to Exercise 6.23 (if you haven't tried to solve it, do so now). Given the ability to create an "iterator object" in a language such as C++, do you think that Clu or Icon-style iterators are still useful? Why or why not?

10.3 Design a class hierarchy to represent syntax trees for the CFG of Figure 4.5 (page 175). Provide a method in each class to return the value of a node. Provide constructors that play the role of the `make_leaf`, `make_un_op`, and `make_bin_op` subroutines.

10.4 Repeat the previous exercise, but using a variant record (union) type to represent syntax tree nodes. Repeat again using type extensions. Compare the three solutions in terms of clarity, abstraction, type safety, and extensibility.

10.5 Rewrite the list and queue classes of Section 10.1 in such a way that objects not derived from a container base class can still be inserted in a list or queue. You will probably want to include a pointer to data, rather than the data itself, in each node of a list/queue.

10.6 Use templates (generics) to abstract your solution to the previous question over the type of data in the list/queue.

10.7 In several object-oriented languages, including C++ and Eiffel, a derived class can hide members of the base class. In C++, for example, we can declare a base class to be `public`, `protected`, or `private`:

```
class B : public A { ...
    // public members of A are public members of B
    // protected members of A are protected members of B
...
class C : protected A { ...
    // public and protected members of A are protected members of C
...
class D : private A { ...
    // public and protected members of A are private members of D
```

In all cases, `private` members of A are inaccessible to methods of B, C, or D.

Consider the impact of `protected` and `private` base classes on dynamic method binding. Under what circumstances can a reference to an object of class B, C, or D be assigned into a variable of type A*?

10.8 What happens to the implementation of a class if we redefine a data member? For example, suppose we have:

```
class foo {
public:
    int a;
    char *b;
};
...
class bar : public foo {
public:
    float c;
    int b;
};
```

Does the representation of a `bar` object contain one b field or two? If two, are both accessible, or only one? Under what circumstances?

10.9 Discuss the relative merits of classes and type extensions. Which do you prefer? Why?

10.10 What do you think of C++ and Ada 95's decision to use static method binding, rather than dynamic, by default? Is the gain in implementation speed worth the loss in abstraction and reusability? Assuming that we sometimes want static binding, do you prefer the method-by-method approach of C++ or the variable-by-variable approach of Ada 95? Why?

10.11 If `foo` is an abstract class in a C++ program, why is it acceptable to declare variables of type `foo*`, but not of type `foo`?

10.12* Consider the Smalltalk implementation of Euclid's algorithm, presented at the end of Section 10.6.1. Trace the messages involved in evaluating 4 gcd: 6.

10.13 Suppose that class D inherits from classes A, B, and C, none of which share any common ancestor. Show how the data members and vtable(s) of D might be laid out in memory. Also show how to convert a reference to a D object into a reference to an A, B, or C object.

10.14 Consider the `person_interface` and `list_node_interface` classes described in Section 10.5.1 (page 569). If `student` is derived from `person_interface` and `list_node_interface`, explain what happens in the following method call:

```
student s;
person *p = &s;
...
p.debug_print ();
```

You may wish to use a diagram of the representation of a `student` object to illustrate the method lookups that occur and the views that are computed. You may assume the implementation described at the beginning of Section 10.5, without shared inheritance.

10.15* Given the inheritance tree on page 569, show a representation for objects of class `student_prof`. You may want to consult Figures 10.7, 10.8, and 10.9.

10.16* Given the memory layout of Figure 10.7 and the following declarations:

```
student& sr;
gp_list_node& nr;
```

show the code that must be generated for the assignment

```
nr = sr;
```

(Pitfall: be sure to consider `nil` pointers.)

10.17* Standard C++ provides a "pointer to member" mechanism for classes:

```
class C {
public:
    int a;
    int b;
} c;
int C::*pm = &C::a;
    // pm points to member a of an (arbitrary) C object
...
c->*pm = 3;     // assign 3 into c.a
```

Pointers to members are also permitted for subroutine members (methods), including virtual methods. How would you implement pointers to virtual methods in the presence of C++–style multiple inheritance?

10.18* As an alternative to using ⟨method address, this correction⟩ pairs in the vtable entries of a language with multiple inheritance, we could leave the entries as simple pointers, but make them point to code that updates this in-line, and then jumps to the beginning of the appropriate method. Show the sequence of instructions executed under this scheme. What factors will influence whether it runs faster or slower than the sequence shown in Section 10.5? Which scheme will use less space? (Remember to count both code and data structure size, and consider which instructions must be replicated at every call site.)

Pursuing the replacement of data structures with executable code even further, consider an implementation in which the vtable itself consists of executable code. Show what this code would look like and, again, discuss the implications for time and space overhead.

10.19* In Eiffel, shared inheritance is the default rather than the exception. Only renamed features are replicated. As a result, it is not possible to tell when looking at a class whether its members will be inherited replicated or shared by derived classes. Describe a uniform mechanism for looking up members inherited from base classes that will work whether they are replicated *or* shared. (Hint: Consider the use of dope vectors for records containing arrays of dynamic shape, as described in Section 7.4.3. For further details, consult the compiler text of Wilhelm and Maurer [WM95, Sec. 5.3].)

10.20* In Figure 10.9, consider calls to virtual methods declared in A, but called through a B, C, or D object view. We could avoid one level of indirection by appending a copy of the A part of the vtable to the D/B and C parts of the vtable (with suitably adjusted this corrections). Give calling sequences for this alternative implementation. In the worst case, how much larger may the vtable be for a class with n ancestors?

10.10 Bibliographic Notes

Appendix A contains bibliographic citations for the various languages discussed in this chapter, including Simula, Smalltalk, C++, Eiffel, Java, Modula-3, Ada 95, Oberon, and CLOS. Other object-oriented versions of Lisp include Loops [BS83a] and Flavors [Moo86]. Black et al. discuss the type system of Emerald [BHJ+87], a concurrent language with a polymorphic type system based on a notion of *conformance* that differs from class-based typing in interesting ways.

Ellis and Stroustrup [ES90] provide extensive discussion of both semantic and pragmatic issues for C++. Chapters 16 through 19 of Stroustrup's text on C++ [Str97] contain a good introduction to the design and implementation of container classes. Deutsch and Schiffman [DS84] describe techniques to implement Smalltalk efficiently. Borning and Ingalls [BI82] discuss multiple inheritance in an extension to Smalltalk-80. Dolby describes how an optimizing compiler can identify circumstances in which a nested object can be expanded (in the Eiffel sense) while retaining reference semantics [Dol97]. Driesen presents an alternative to vtables that requires whole-program analysis, but provides extremely efficient method dispatch, even in languages with dynamic typing and multiple inheritance [Dri93].

Component systems provide a standard for the specification of object interfaces, allowing code produced by arbitrary compilers for arbitrary languages to be joined together into a working program, often spanning a distributed collection of machines. CORBA [Sie96] is a component standard promulgated by the Object Management Group, a consortium of over 700 companies. ActiveX (DCOM) [Bro96] is a competing standard from Microsoft Corporation. OLE [Bro96] is a standard set of binary interfaces for ActiveX. JavaBeans [Sun97] is a CORBA-compliant binary standard for components written in Java.

Many of the seminal papers in object-oriented programming have appeared in the proceedings of the *ACM OOPSLA* conferences (Object-Oriented Programming Systems, Languages, and Applications), held annually since 1986, and published as special issues of *ACM SIGPLAN Notices*. Wegner [Weg90] enumerates the defining characteristics of object orientation. Meyer [Mey92, Sec. 21.10] explains the rationale for dynamic method binding.

Nonimperative Programming Models: Functional and Logic Languages

Previous chapters of this text have focused on imperative programming languages. In the current chapter we emphasize functional and logic languages instead. While imperative languages are far more widely used, "industrial strength" implementations exist for both functional and logic languages, and both models have commercially important applications. Lisp has traditionally been popular for the manipulation of symbolic data, particularly in the field of artificial intelligence. In recent years functional languages—statically typed ones in particular—have become increasingly popular for scientific and business applications as well. Logic languages are widely used for formal specifications and theorem proving and, less widely, for many other applications.

Of course, functional and logic languages have a great deal in common with their imperative cousins. Naming and scoping issues arise under every model. So do types, expressions, and the control-flow concepts of selection and recursion. All languages must be scanned, parsed, and analyzed semantically. In addition, functional languages make heavy use of subroutines—more so even than most von Neumann languages—and the notions of concurrency and nondeterminacy are as common in functional and logic languages as they are in the imperative case.

As noted in Chapter 1, the boundaries between language categories tend to be rather fuzzy. One can write in a largely functional style in many imperative languages, and many functional languages include imperative features (assignment and iteration). The most common logic language—Prolog—provides certain imperative features as well. Finally, it is easy to build a logic programming system in most functional programming languages.

Because of the overlap between imperative and functional concepts, we have had occasion several times in previous chapters to consider issues of particular importance to functional programming languages. Most such languages depend heavily on polymorphism (Sections 3.5 and 7.2.5). Most make heavy use of lists (Section 7.8). Several are dynamically scoped (Sections 3.3.2 and 3.3.4). All employ recursion (Section 6.6) for repetitive execution, with the result that program behavior and performance depend heavily on the evaluation rules for parameters (Section 6.6.2). All have a tendency to generate significant amounts of temporary data, which their implementations reclaim through garbage collection (Section 7.7.3).

We have had less occasion to remark on features of logic programming languages. Logic of course is used heavily in the design of digital circuits, and most programming languages provide a logical (Boolean) type and operators. Logic is also heavily used in the formal study of language semantics, specifically in *axiomatic* semantics.[1] It was only in the 1970s, however, that researchers began to employ the process of logical deduction as a general-purpose model of computing.

Our chapter begins in Section 11.1 with a brief introduction to the historical origins of the imperative, functional, and logic programming models. In the two major sections that follow, we look at functional and logic programming in turn. We consider several different functional languages, including Scheme, Common Lisp, ML, Miranda, Haskell, and Sisal, with a particular emphasis on Scheme. Among logic languages we consider only Prolog: it is by far the most widely used, and forms the basis of many of the others. We conclude each section with a discussion of theoretical foundations: *lambda calculus* for functional languages, *first-order predicate calculus* for logic languages. The formalism helps to clarify the notion of a "pure" functional or logic language, and illuminates the differences between the pure notation and its realization in more practical programming languages. As we shall see, the differences include both extensions (mostly for convenience) and limitations (for practicality of implementation).

11.1 Historical Origins

To understand the differences among programming models, it can be helpful to consider their theoretical roots, all of which predate the development of electronic computers. The imperative and functional models grew out of work undertaken by mathematicians Alan Turing, Alonzo Church, Stephen Kleene, Emil Post, and others in the 1930s. Working independently, these individuals developed several very different formalizations of the notion of an algorithm, or *effective procedure*, based on automata, symbolic manipulation, recursive function

---

[1] Axiomatic semantics models each statement or expression in the language as a *predicate transformer*—an inference rule that takes a set of conditions known to be true initially and derives a new set of conditions guaranteed to be true after the construct has been evaluated. The study of formal semantics is beyond the scope of this book.

definitions, and combinatorics. Over time, these various formalizations were shown to be equally powerful: anything that could be computed in one could be computed in the others. This result led Church to conjecture that *any* intuitively appealing model of computing would be equally powerful as well; this conjecture is known as *Church's thesis*.

Turing's model of computing was the *Turing machine*, an automaton reminiscent of a finite or pushdown automaton, but with the ability to access arbitrary cells of an unbounded storage "tape." The Turing machine computes in an imperative way, by changing the values in cells of its tape, just as a high-level imperative program computes by changing the values of variables. Church's model of computing is called the *lambda calculus*. It is based on the notion of parameterized expressions (with each parameter introduced by an occurrence of the letter λ—hence the notation's name). Lambda calculus was the inspiration for functional programming: one uses it to compute by substituting parameters into expressions, just as one computes in a high-level functional program by passing arguments to functions. The computing models of Kleene and Post are more abstract, and do not lend themselves directly to implementation as a programming language.

The goal of early work in computability was not to understand computers (aside from purely mechanical devices, computers did not exist) but rather to formalize the notion of an effective procedure. Over time, this work allowed mathematicians to formalize the distinction between a *constructive* proof (one that shows how to obtain a mathematical object with some desired property) and a *nonconstructive* proof (one that merely shows that such an object must exist, perhaps by contradiction, or counting arguments, or reduction to some other theorem whose proof is nonconstructive). In effect, a program can be seen as a constructive proof of the proposition that, given any appropriate inputs, there exist outputs that are related to the inputs in a particular, desired way. Euclid's algorithm, for example, can be thought of as a constructive proof of the proposition that every pair of nonnegative integers has a greatest common divisor.

Logic programming is also intimately tied to the notion of constructive proofs, but at a more abstract level. Rather than write a general constructive proof that works for all appropriate inputs, the logic programmer writes a set of *axioms* that allow the *computer* to discover a constructive proof for each particular set of inputs. Where the imperative programmer says

> To compute the gcd of a and b, check to see if a and b are equal. If so, print one of them and stop. Otherwise, replace the larger one by their difference and repeat.

and the functional programmer says

> The gcd of a and b is defined to be a when a and b are equal, and to be the gcd of c and d when a and b are unequal, where c is the smaller of

a and b, and d is their difference. To compute the gcd of a given pair of numbers, expand and simplify this definition until it terminates.

the logic programmer says

The proposition gcd (a, b, g) is true if (1) a, b, and g are all equal, or (2) there exist numbers c and d such that c is the minimum of a and b (i.e., min (a, b, c) is true), d is their difference (i.e., minus (a, b, d) is true), and gcd(c, d, g) is true. To compute the gcd of a given pair of numbers, search for a number g (and various numbers c and d) for which these two rules allow one to prove that gcd (a, b, g) is true.

11.2 Functional Programming

In a strict sense of the term, *functional programming* defines the outputs of a program as a mathematical function of the inputs, with no notion of internal state, and thus no side effects. Among the common functional programming languages, Miranda, Haskell, Sisal, and Backus's FP proposal [Bac78] are purely functional; Lisp/Scheme and ML include imperative features. To make functional programming practical, functional languages provide a number of features that are often missing in imperative languages. These include:

- First-class function values and higher-order functions
- Extensive polymorphism
- List types and operators
- Recursion
- Structured function returns
- Constructors (aggregates) for structured objects
- Garbage collection

In Section 3.4.2 we defined a first-class value to be one that can be passed as a parameter, returned from a subroutine, or (in a language with side effects) assigned into a variable. Under a strict interpretation of the term, first-class status also requires the ability to create (compute) new values at run time. In the case of subroutines, this notion of first-class status requires that we be able to create a subroutine whose behavior is determined dynamically. Subroutines are second-class values in most imperative languages, but first-class values (in the strict sense of the term) in all functional programming languages. A *higher-order function* takes a function as an argument, or returns a function as a result.

Polymorphism is important in functional languages because it allows a function to be used on as general a class of arguments as possible. As we have seen in Sections 7.1 and 7.2.5, Lisp and its dialects are dynamically typed, and thus inherently polymorphic, while ML, Miranda, Haskell, and their relatives obtain polymorphism through the mechanism of type inference. Lists are important in functional languages because they have a natural recursive definition, and are easily manipulated by operating on their first element and (recursively) the remainder of the list. Recursion is important because in the absence of side effects it provides the only means of doing anything repeatedly.

Several of the items in our list of functional language features (recursion, structured function returns, constructors, garbage collection) can be found in many but not all imperative languages. Fortran 77 has no recursion, nor does it allow structured types (i.e., arrays) to be returned from functions. Pascal and early versions of Modula-2 allow only simple and pointer types to be returned from functions. As we saw in Section 7.1.2, several imperative languages, including Ada, C, and Fortran 90, provide aggregate constructs that allow a structured value to be specified in-line. In most imperative languages, however, such constructs are lacking or incomplete. (It is extremely unusual, for example, to find one that can specify an [unnamed] functional value.) A pure functional language must provide completely general aggregates: it cannot build a structured object via assignment to subcomponents. Finally, though garbage collection is increasingly common in imperative languages, it is by no means universal, nor does it apply to objects allocated in the stack. Because of the desire to provide unlimited extent for first-class functions, functional languages tend to employ a (garbage-collected) heap for *all* dynamically allocated data (or at least for all data for which the compiler is unable to prove that stack allocation is safe).

Because Lisp was the original functional language, and is still the most widely used, several characteristics of Lisp are commonly, though inaccurately, described as though they pertained to functional programming in general. We will examine these characteristics (in the context of Scheme) in Section 11.2.1. They include:

- Homogeneity of programs and data: A program in Lisp is itself a list, and can be manipulated with the same mechanisms used to manipulate data.
- Self-definition: The operational semantics of Lisp can be defined elegantly in terms of an interpreter written in Lisp.
- Interaction with the user through a "read-eval-print" loop.

Many programmers—probably most—who have written significant amounts of software in both imperative and functional styles find the latter more aesthetically appealing. Moreover experience with a variety of large commercial projects [Wad98a] suggests that the absence of side effects makes functional programs significantly easier to write, debug, and maintain than are their imperative counterparts. When passed a given set of arguments, a pure function can always be counted on to return the same results. Issues of undocumented side effects, misordered updates, and dangling or (in most cases) uninitialized references simply don't occur. At the same time, most implementations of functional languages still fall short in terms of portability, richness of library packages, interfaces to other languages, and debugging and profiling tools. We will return to the tradeoffs between functional and imperative programming in Section 11.2.5.

11.2.1 A Review/Overview of Scheme

Most Scheme implementations employ an interpreter that runs a "read-eval-print" loop. The interpreter repeatedly reads an expression from standard input (generally typed by the user), evaluates that expression, and prints the resulting value. If the user types

```
(+ 3 4)
```

the interpreter will print

```
7
```

If the user types

```
7
```

the interpreter will also print

```
7
```

(The number 7 is already fully evaluated.) To save the programmer the need to type an entire program verbatim at the keyboard, most Scheme implementations provide a `load` function that reads (and evaluates) input from a file:

```
(load "my_Scheme_program")
```

As we noted in Section 6.1, Scheme (like all Lisp dialects) uses *Cambridge Polish* notation for expressions. Parentheses indicate a function application (or in some cases the use of a macro). The first expression inside the left parenthesis indicates the function; the remaining expressions are its arguments. Suppose the user types

```
((+ 3 4))
```

When it sees the inner set of parentheses, the interpreter will call the function +, passing 3 and 4 as arguments. Because of the outer set of parentheses, it will then attempt to call 7 as a zero-argument function—a run-time error:

```
eval: 7 is not a procedure
```

Unlike the situation in almost all other programming languages, extra parentheses change the semantics of Lisp/Scheme programs.

```
(+ 3 4)     ⇒  7
((+ 3 4))   ⇒  error
```

Here the ⇒ means "evaluates to." This symbol is not a part of the syntax of Scheme itself.

One can prevent the Scheme interpreter from evaluating a parenthesized expression by *quoting* it:

```
(quote (+ 3 4))  ⇒ (+ 3 4)
```

Here the result is a three-element list. More commonly, quoting is specified with a special shorthand notation consisting of a leading single quote mark:

```
'(+ 3 4) ⇒ (+ 3 4)
```

Though every expression has a type in Scheme, that type is generally not determined until run time. Most predefined functions check dynamically to make sure that their arguments are of appropriate types. The expression

```
(if (> a 0) (+ 2 3) (+ 2 "foo"))
```

will evaluate to 5 if a is positive, but will produce a run-time type clash error if a is negative or zero. User-defined functions can implement similar checks using predefined *type predicate* functions:

```
(boolean? x)    ; is x a Boolean?
(char? x)       ; is x a character?
(string? x)     ; is x a string?
(symbol? x)     ; is x a symbol?
(number? x)     ; is x a number?
(pair? x)       ; is x a (not necessarily proper) pair?
(list? x)       ; is x a (proper) list?
```

(This is not an exhaustive list.) A *symbol* in Scheme is comparable to what other languages call an identifier. The lexical rules for identifiers vary among Scheme implementations, but are in general much looser than they are in other languages. In particular, identifiers are permitted to contain a wide variety of punctuation marks:

```
(symbol? 'x$_%:&=*!) ⇒ #t
```

The symbol #t represents the Boolean value true. False is represented by #f. Note the use here of quote ('); the symbol begins with x.

To create a function in Scheme one evaluates a *lambda expression:*[2]

---

2 A word of caution for readers familiar with Common Lisp: A lambda expression in Scheme *evaluates to* a function. A lambda expression in Common Lisp *is* a function (or, more accurately, is automatically coerced to be a function, without evaluation). The distinction becomes important whenever lambda expressions are passed as parameters or returned from functions: they must be quoted in Common Lisp (with function or #') to prevent evaluation. Common Lisp also distinguishes between a symbol's *value* and its meaning as a function; Scheme does not: if a symbol represents a function, then the function is the symbol's value.

```
(lambda (x) (* x x)) ⇒ function
```

The first "argument" to `lambda` is a list of formal parameters for the function (in this case the single parameter x). The remaining "arguments" (again just one in this case) constitute the body of the function. As we will see in Section 11.2.2, Scheme differentiates between functions and so-called *special forms* (`lambda` among them), which resemble functions but have special evaluation rules. Strictly speaking, only functions have arguments, but we will also use the term informally to refer to the subexpressions that look like arguments in a special form.

A `lambda` expression does not give its function a name; this can be done using `let` or `define` (to be introduced in the next subsection). In this sense, a `lambda` expression is like the aggregates that we used in Section 7.1.2 to specify array or record values.

When a function is called, the language implementation restores the referencing environment that was in effect when the `lambda` expression was evaluated. It then augments this environment with bindings for the formal parameters and evaluates the expressions of the function body in order. The value of the last such expression becomes the value returned by the function:

```
((lambda (x) (* x x)) 3) ⇒ 9
```

Simple conditional expressions can be written using `if`:

```
(if (< 2 3) 4 5) ⇒ 4
(if #f 2 3)      ⇒ 3
```

In general, Scheme expressions are evaluated in applicative order, as described in Section 6.6.2. Special forms such as `lambda` and `if` are exceptions to this rule. The implementation of `if` checks to see whether the first argument evaluates to `#t`. If so, it returns the value of the second argument, without evaluating the third argument. Otherwise it returns the value of the third argument, without evaluating the second. We will return to the issue of evaluation order in Section 11.2.2.

Bindings

Names can be bound to values by introducing a nested scope:

```
(let ((a 3)
      (b 4)
      (square (lambda (x) (* x x)))
      (plus +))
  (sqrt (plus (square a) (square b)))) ⇒ 5.0
```

The special form `let` takes two arguments. The first of these is a list of pairs. In each pair, the first element is a name and the second is the value that the name is to represent within the second argument to let. The value of the construct as a whole is then the value of this second argument.

The scope of the bindings produced by let is let's second argument only:

```
(let ((a 3))
  (let ((a 4)
        (b a))
    (+ a b)))    ⇒ 7
```

Here b takes the value of the *outer* a. The "all at once" semantics for names in let precludes the definition of recursive functions. For these one employs letrec:

```
(letrec ((fact
          (lambda (n)
            (if (= n 1) 1
               (* n (fact (- n 1)))))))
        (fact 5))                        ⇒ 120
```

As noted in Section 3.3, Scheme is statically scoped. (Common Lisp is also statically scoped. Most other Lisp dialects are dynamically scoped.) While let and letrec allow the user to create nested scopes, they do not affect the meaning of global names (names known at the outermost level of the Scheme interpreter). For these Scheme provides a special form called define that has the side effect of creating a global binding for a name:

```
(define hypot
  (lambda (a b)
    (sqrt (+ (* a a) (* b b)))))
(hypot 3 4)                  ⇒ 5
```

Lists and Numbers

Like all Lisp dialects, Scheme provides a wealth of functions to manipulate lists. We saw many of these in Section 7.8; we do not repeat them all here. The three most important are car, which returns the head of a list, cdr ("coulder"), which returns the rest of the list (everything after the head), and cons, which joins a head to the rest of a list:

```
(car '(2 3 4))  ⇒ 2
(cdr '(2 3 4))  ⇒ (3 4)
(cons 2 '(3 4)) ⇒ (2 3 4)
```

Also useful is the null? predicate, which determines whether its argument is the empty list. Recall that the notation '(2 3 4) indicates a *proper* list, in which the final element is the empty list:

```
(cdr '(2))  ⇒ ()
(cons 2 3)  ⇒ (2 . 3)   ; an improper list
```

For fast access to arbitrary elements of a sequence, Scheme provides a `vector` type that is indexed by integers, like an array, and may have elements of heterogeneous types, like a record. Interested readers are referred to the Scheme manual [KCR98] for further information.

Scheme also provides a wealth of numeric and logical (Boolean) functions and special forms. The language manual describes a hierarchy of five numeric types: `integer`, `rational`, `real`, `complex`, and `number`. The last two levels are optional: implementations may choose not to provide any numbers that are not real. Most but not all implementations employ arbitrary-precision representations of both integers and rationals, with the later stored internally as (numerator, denominator) pairs.

Equality Testing and Searching

As described in Section 7.10, Scheme provides three different equality-testing functions. The `eq?` function tests whether its arguments refer to the same object; `eqv?` tests whether its arguments are provably semantically equivalent; `equal?` tests whether its arguments have the same recursive structure, with `eqv?` leaves.

To search for elements in lists, Scheme provides two sets of functions, each of which has variants corresponding to the three different forms of equality. The functions `memq`, `memv`, and `member` take an element and a list as argument, and return the longest suffix of the list (if any) beginning with the element:

```
(memq 'z '(x y z w))        ⇒ (z w)
(memq '(z) '(x y (z) w))    ⇒ #f
(member '(z) '(x y (z) w))  ⇒ ((z) w)
```

The `memq`, `memv`, and `member` functions perform their comparisons using `eq?`, `eqv?`, and `equal?`, respectively. They return `#f` if the desired element is not found. It turns out that Scheme's conditional expressions (e.g., `if`) treat anything other than `#f` as true.[3] One therefore often sees expressions of the form

```
(if (memq desired-element list-that-might-contain-it) ...
```

The functions `assq`, `assv`, and `assoc` search for values in *association lists* (otherwise known as *A-lists*). A-lists were introduced in Section 3.3.4 in the context of name lookup for languages with dynamic scoping (a picture can be found in Figure 3.15, page 138). An A-list is a dictionary implemented as a list of pairs. The first element of each pair is a key of some sort; the second element is information corresponding to that key. `Assq`, `assv`, and `assoc` take a key and an A-list as argument, and return the first pair in the list, if there is one, whose first element is `eq?`, `eqv?`, or `equal?`, respectively, to the key. If there is no matching pair, `#f` is returned.

---

3 One of the more confusing differences between Scheme and Common Lisp is that Common Lisp uses the empty list () for false, while most implementations of Scheme (including all that conform to the version 5 standard) treat it as true.

Control Flow and Assignment

We have already seen the special form if. It has a cousin named cond that resembles a more general if...elsif...else:

```
(cond
  ((< 3 2) 1)
  ((< 4 3) 2)
  (else 3))    ⇒ 3
```

The arguments to cond are pairs. They are considered in order from first to last. The value of the overall expression is the value of the second element of the first pair in which the first element evaluates to #t. If none of the first elements evaluates to #t, then the overall value is #f. The symbol else is permitted only as the first element of the last pair of the construct, where it serves as syntactic sugar for #t.

Recursion, of course, serves as the principal means of doing things repeatedly in Scheme. Many issues related to recursion were discussed in Section 6.6; we do not repeat that discussion here.

For programmers who wish to make use of side effects, Scheme provides assignment, sequencing and iteration constructs. Assignment employs the special form set! and the functions set-car! and set-cdr!:

```
(let ((x 2)
      (l '(a b)))
  (set! x 3)
  (set-car! l '(c d))
  (set-cdr! l '(e))
  ... x              ⇒ 3
  ... l              ⇒ ((c d) e)
```

The return values of the various varieties of set! are implementation-dependent.

Sequencing uses the special form begin:

```
(begin
  (display "hi ")
  (display "mom"))
```

Iteration uses the special form do and the function for-each:

```
(define iter-fib (lambda (n)
    ; print the first n+1 Fibonacci numbers
    (do ((i 0 (+ i 1))        ; initially 0, inc'ed in each iteration
         (a 0 b)              ; initially 0, set to b in each iteration
         (b 1 (+ a b)))       ; initially 1, set to sum of a and b
        ((= i n) b)            ; termination test and final value
      (display b)             ; body of loop
      (display " "))))         ; body of loop

(for-each (lambda (a b) (display (* a b)) (newline))
  '(2 4 6)
  '(3 5 7))
```

The first argument to do is a list of triples, each of which specifies a new variable, an initial value for that variable, and an expression to be evaluated and assigned (via set!) to that variable at the end of each iteration. The second argument to do is a pair that specifies the termination condition and the expression to be returned. At the end of each iteration all new values of loop variables (e.g., a and b) are computed using the current values. Only after all new values are computed are the assignments actually performed.

The function for-each takes as argument a function and a sequence of lists. There must be as many lists as the function takes arguments, and the lists must all be of the same length. For-each calls its function argument repeatedly, passing successive sets of arguments from the lists. In the example shown here, the unnamed function produced by the lambda expression will be called on the arguments 2 and 3, 4 and 5, and 6 and 7. The interpreter will print

```
6
20
42
()
```

The last line is the return value of for-each, assumed here to be the empty list. The language definition allows this value to be implementation-dependent; the construct is executed for its side effects.

Two other control-flow constructs have been mentioned in previous chapters. Delay and force (Section 6.6.2) permit the lazy evaluation of expressions. The call-with-current-continuation function (call/cc; Section 8.5.4) allows the current program counter and referencing environment to be saved in the form of a closure, and passed to a specified subroutine. We will discuss delay and force further in Section 11.2.2.

Programs as Lists

As should be clear by now, a program in Scheme takes the form of a list. In technical terms, we say that Lisp and Scheme are *homoiconic*: self-representing. A parenthesized string of symbols (in which parentheses are balanced) is called an *S-expression* regardless of whether we think of it as a program or as a list. In fact, a program *is* a list, and can be constructed, de-constructed, and otherwise manipulated with all the usual list functions.

Just as quote can be used to inhibit the evaluation of a list that appears as an argument in a function call, Scheme provides an eval function that can be used to evaluate a list that has been created as a data structure:

```
(define compose
  (lambda (f g)
    (lambda (x) (f (g x)))))
((compose car cdr) '(1 2 3))  ⇒ 2
```

```
(define compose2
  (lambda (f g)
    (eval (list 'lambda '(x) (list f (list g 'x)))
          (scheme-report-environment 5))))
((compose2 car cdr) '(1 2 3))                        ⇒ 2
```

In the first of these declarations, `compose` takes as arguments a pair of functions `f` and `g`. It returns as result a function that takes as parameter a value `x`, applies `g` to it, then applies `f`, and finally returns the result. In the second declaration, `compose2` performs the same function, but in a different way. The function `list` returns a list consisting of its (evaluated) arguments. In the body of `compose2`, this list is the *unevaluated* expression `(lambda (x) (f (g x)))`. When passed to `eval`, this list evaluates to the desired function. The second argument of `eval` specifies the referencing environment in which the expression is to be evaluated. In our example we have specified the environment defined by the Scheme version 5 report [KCR98].

The original description of Lisp [MAE+65] included a *self-definition* of the language: code for a Lisp interpreter, written in Lisp. Though Scheme differs in a number of ways from this early Lisp (most notably in its use of lexical scoping), such a *metacircular* interpreter can still be written easily [AS96, Chapter 4]. The code is based on the functions `eval` and `apply`. The first of these we have just seen. The second, `apply`, takes two arguments: a function and a list. It achieves the effect of calling the function, with the elements of the list as arguments.

The functions `eval` and `apply` can be defined as mutually recursive. When passed a number or a string, `eval` simply returns that number or string. When passed a symbol, it looks that symbol up in the specified environment and returns the value to which it is bound. When passed a list it checks to see whether the first element of the list is one of a small number of symbols that name so-called *primitive* special forms, built into the language implementation. For each of these special forms (`lambda`, `if`, `define`, `set!`, `quote`, etc.) `eval` provides a direct implementation. For other lists, `eval` calls itself recursively on each element and then calls `apply`, passing as arguments the value of the first element (which must be a function) and a list of the values of the remaining elements. Finally, `eval` returns what `apply` returned.

When passed a function f and a list of arguments l, `apply` inspects the internal representation of f to see whether it is primitive. If so it invokes the built-in implementation. Otherwise it retrieves (from the representation of f) the referencing environment in which f's lambda expression was originally evaluated. To this environment it adds the names of f's parameters, with values taken from l. Call this resulting environment e. Next `apply` retrieves the list of expressions that make up the body of f. It passes these expressions, together with e, one at a time to `eval`. Finally, `apply` returns what the `eval` of the last expression in the body of f returned.

As an example, consider the function `cadr`, defined as `(lambda (x) (car (cdr x)))`. Suppose that this function is represented internally as a three-element list C consisting of a surrounding referencing environment (an A-list, in this case the global one), a list of parameters (in this case the one-element list (x)), and a list of body expressions (in this case the one-element list ((car (cdr (x))))). Suppose also that p has been defined to be the list (a b). To evaluate the expression (cadr p), a Scheme interpreter written in Scheme would execute (eval '(cadr p) (scheme-report-environment 5)). When called, eval would begin its work by evaluating the car of its first argument, namely cadr, via a recursive call. This call would return the function c to which cadr is bound, represented internally as the three-element list C. Next eval would call itself recursively on p, returning the list (a b). Finally, eval would execute (apply c '(a b)) and return the result. Internally, apply would notice that c is represented by the list (E (x) (car (cdr (x)))), where E represents the global environment A-list. It would then execute (eval '(car (cdr (x))) (cons (cons 'x '(a b)) E)) and return the result. We do not trace the remainder of the recursion here. It terminates with primitive special forms in eval and primitive functions in apply. The latter include car, cdr, and cons.

The idea of self-definition—a Scheme interpreter written in Scheme—may seem a bit confusing unless one keeps in mind the distinction between the Scheme code that constitutes the interpreter and the Scheme code that the interpreter is interpreting. In particular, the interpreter is not running itself, though it could run a *copy* of itself. What we really mean by "self-definition" is that for all expressions E, we get the same result by evaluating E under the interpreter I that we get by evaluating E directly.

Suppose now that we wish to formalize the semantics of Scheme as some as-yet-unknown mathematical function $\mathcal{M}$ that takes a Scheme expression as an argument and returns the expression's value. (This value may be a number, a list, a function, or a member of any of a small number of other domains.) How might we go about this task? For certain simple strings of symbols we can define a value directly: strings of digits, for example, map onto the natural numbers. For more complex expressions, we note that

$$\forall E[\mathcal{M}(E) = (\mathcal{M}(I))(E)]$$

Put another way,

$$\mathcal{M}(I) = \mathcal{M}$$

Suppose now that we let $H(\mathcal{F}) = \mathcal{F}(I)$ where $\mathcal{F}$ can be any function that takes a Scheme expression as its argument. Clearly

$$H(\mathcal{M}) = \mathcal{M}$$

Our desired function $\mathcal{M}$ is said to be a *fixed point* of H. Because H is well defined (it simply applies its argument to I), we can use it to obtain a rigorous definition of $\mathcal{M}$. The tools to do so come from the field of denotational semantics, a subject beyond the scope of this book.[4]

---

4 Actually, H has an infinite number of fixed points. What we want (and what denotational semantics will give us) is called the *least* fixed point: the one that defines a value for as few strings of symbols as possible, while still producing the "correct" value for numbers and other simple strings.

```
(define simulate
  (lambda (dfa input)
(cons (car dfa)                        ; start state
      (if (null? input)
          (if (infinal? dfa) '(accept) '(reject))
        (simulate (move dfa (car input)) (cdr input))))))

(define infinal?
  (lambda (dfa)
(memq (car dfa) (caddr dfa))))

(define move
  (lambda (dfa symbol)
(let ((curstate (car dfa)) (trans (cadr dfa)) (finals (caddr dfa)))
  (list
   (if (eq? curstate 'error)
       'error
     (let ((pair (assoc (list curstate symbol) trans)))
       (if pair (cadr pair) 'error)))
   trans
   finals))))
```

Figure 11.1 **Scheme program to simulate the actions of a DFA.** The functions `cadr` and `caddr` are defined as `(lambda (x) (car (cdr x)))` and `(lambda (x) (car (cdr (cdr x))))`, respectively. Scheme provides a large collection of such abbreviations.

An Example

To conclude this section, we present a complete Scheme program to simulate the execution of a DFA (see Figure 11.1). We invoke the program by calling the function `simulate`, passing it a DFA description and an input string. The DFA description is a list of three items: the start state, the transition function, and a list of final states. The transition function is represented by a list of pairs. The first element of each pair is another pair, whose first element is a state and whose second element is an input symbol. If the current state and next input symbol match the first element of a pair, then the finite automaton enters the state given by the second element of the pair.

As it runs, the automaton accumulates as a list a trace of the states through which it has traveled, ending with the symbol `accept` or `reject`. For example, if we type

```
(simulate
 '(q0                                         ; start state
   (((q0 0) q2) ((q0 1) q1) ((q1 0) q3) ((q1 1) q0)  ; transition fn
    ((q2 0) q0) ((q2 1) q3) ((q3 0) q1) ((q3 1) q2))
   (q0))                                      ; final states
 '(0 1 1 0 1))                                ; input string
```

then the Scheme interpreter will print

```
(q0 q2 q3 q2 q0 q1 reject)
```

Careful examination of the DFA in this example will reveal that it accepts precisely those strings of zeros and ones in which each digit appears an even number of times. If we change the input string to 010010 the interpreter will print

```
(q0 q2 q3 q1 q3 q2 q0 accept)
```

11.2.2 Evaluation Order Revisited

In Section 6.6.2 we observed that the subcomponents of many expressions can be evaluated in more than one order. In particular, one is faced in a functional language with the question of whether or not to evaluate arguments before passing them to a function. Programmers accustomed to imperative languages usually expect what is called *applicative-order* evaluation, in which parameters are evaluated before they are passed. This is indeed the evaluation order employed in most cases by Scheme. The other extreme, in which parameters are always passed unevaluated, is called *normal-order* evaluation.

Suppose, for example, that we have defined the following function:

```
(define double (lambda (x) (+ x x)))
```

Evaluating the expression `(double (* 3 4))` in applicative order (as Scheme does), we have

```
    (double (* 3 4))
⇒   (double 12)
⇒   (+ 12 12)
⇒   24
```

Under normal-order evaluation we would have

```
    (double (* 3 4))
⇒   (+ (* 3 4) (* 3 4))
⇒   (+ 12 (* 3 4))
⇒   (+ 12 12)
⇒   24
```

Here we end up doing extra work: normal order causes us to evaluate `(* 3 4)` twice. In other cases, applicative-order evaluation can end up doing extra work. Suppose we have defined the following:

```
(define switch (lambda (x a b c)
    (cond ((< x 0) a)
          ((= x 0) b)
          ((> x 0) c))))
```

Evaluating the expression (switch -1 (+ 1 2) (+ 2 3) (+ 3 4)) in applicative order we have

```
    (switch -1 (+ 1 2) (+ 2 3) (+ 3 4))
⇒   (switch -1 3 (+ 2 3) (+ 3 4))
⇒   (switch -1 3 5 (+ 3 4))
⇒   (switch -1 3 5 7)
⇒   (cond   ((< -1 0) 3)
            ((= -1 0) 5)
            ((> -1 0) 7))
⇒   (cond   (#t 3)
            ((= -1 0) 5)
            ((> -1 0) 7))
⇒   3
```

Under normal-order evaluation we would have

```
    (switch -1 (+ 1 2) (+ 2 3) (+ 3 4))
⇒   (cond   ((< -1 0) (+ 1 2))
            ((= -1 0) (+ 2 3))
            ((> -1 0) (+ 3 4)))
⇒   (cond   (#t (+ 1 2))
            ((= -1 0) (+ 2 3))
            ((> -1 0) (+ 3 4)))
⇒   (+ 1 2)
⇒   3
```

Here normal-order evaluation avoids evaluating (+ 2 3) or (+ 3 4).

Under both evaluation orders we must provide exceptions to the rules in certain cases. Specifically, special forms such as cond must take *unevaluated* arguments, even under otherwise applicative-order evaluation, and arithmetic and logical functions such as + and < must actually yield values, even under otherwise normal-order evaluation, rather than passing their arguments on to something else.

In our overview of Scheme we have differentiated on several occasions between special forms and functions. Arguments to functions are always passed by sharing (Section 8.3.1), and are evaluated before they are passed (i.e., in applicative order). Arguments to special forms are passed unevaluated—in other words, by name. Each special form is free to choose internally when (and if) to evaluate its parameters. Cond, for example, takes a sequence of unevaluated pairs as arguments. It evaluates their cars internally, one at a time, stopping when it finds one that evaluates to #t.

Together, special forms and functions are known as *expression types* in Scheme. Some expression types are *primitive*, in the sense that they must be built into the language implementation. Others are *derived*; they can be defined in terms of primitive expression types. In an eval/apply based interpreter, primitive special forms are built into eval; primitive functions are recognized by apply. We have seen how the special form lambda can be used to create derived functions, which can be bound to names with `let`. Scheme provides an analogous special form, `syntax-rules`, that can be used to create derived special forms. These can then be bound to names with `let-syntax`. Derived special forms are known as *macro*s in Scheme, but they are only loosely related to the macros of other languages. In the terminology of this book, Scheme macros are functions whose arguments are passed by name instead of by sharing. They are immune to the problems discussed in Section 6.6.2, and may be implemented in any way that is consistent with their semantics. The macros of C and C++, by contrast, are a low-level mechanism for textual expansion.

Strictness and Lazy Evaluation

Evaluation order can have an effect not only on execution speed, but on program correctness as well. A program that encounters a dynamic semantic error or an infinite loop in an "unneeded" subexpression under applicative-order evaluation may terminate successfully under normal-order evaluation. A (side-effect-free) function is said to be *strict* if it requires all of its arguments to be defined, so that its result will not depend on evaluation order. A function is said to be *nonstrict* if it does not impose this requirement. A *language* is said to be strict if it requires all functions to be strict. A language is said to be nonstrict if it permits the definition of nonstrict functions. Expressions in a strict language can safely be evaluated in applicative order. Expressions in a nonstrict language cannot. ML and (with the exception of macros) Scheme are strict. Miranda and Haskell are nonstrict.

Lazy evaluation gives us the advantage of normal-order evaluation (not evaluating unneeded subexpressions) while running within a constant factor of the speed of applicative-order evaluation for expressions in which everything is needed. The trick is to tag every argument internally with a "memo" that indicates its value, if known. Any attempt to evaluate the argument sets the value in the memo as a side effect, or returns the value (without recalculating it) if it is already set. Lazy evaluation is particularly useful for "infinite" data structures, as described in Section 6.6.2. It can also be useful in programs that need to examine only a prefix of a potentially long list (see Exercise 11.8). Lazy evaluation is used for all arguments in Miranda and Haskell. It is available in Scheme through explicit use of `delay` and `force`. (Recall that the first of these is a special form that creates a (memo, closure) pair; the second is a function that returns the value in the memo, using the closure to calculate it first if necessary.) Where normal-order evaluation can be thought of as function evaluation using call by name parameters, lazy evaluation is sometimes said to employ "call by need."

The principal problem with lazy evaluation is its behavior in the presence of side effects. If an argument contains a reference to a variable that may be modified by an assignment, then the value of the argument will depend on whether it is evaluated before or after the assignment. Likewise, if the argument contains an assignment, values elsewhere in the program may depend on when evaluation occurs. These problems do not arise in Miranda or Haskell because they are purely functional: there are no side effects. Scheme leaves the problem up to the programmer, but requires that every use of a `delay`-ed expression be enclosed in `force`, making it relatively easy to identify the places where side effects are an issue. ML provides no mechanism for lazy evaluation. The same effect can be achieved with assignment and explicit functions (Exercise 11.10), but the code is rather awkward.

I/O: Streams and Monads

A major source of side effects can be found in traditional I/O, including the built-in functions `read` and `display` of Scheme: `read` will generally return a different value every time it is called, and multiple calls to `display`, though they never return a value, must occur in the proper order if the program is to be considered correct.

One way to avoid these side effects is to model input and output as *streams*: unbounded-length lists whose elements are generated lazily. We saw an example of a stream in Section 6.6.2, where we used Scheme's `delay` and `force` to implement a "list" of the natural numbers. Similar code in ML appears in Exercise 11.10.[5]

If we model input and output as streams, then a program takes the form

```
(define output (my_prog input))
```

When it needs an input value, function `my_prog` forces evaluation of the `car` of `input`, and passes the `cdr` on to the rest of the program. To drive execution, the language implementation repeatedly forces evaluation of the `car` of `output`, prints it, and repeats:

```
(define driver (lambda (s)
    (if (null? s) '()       ; nothing left
      (display (car s))
      (driver (cdr s)))))
(driver output)
```

To make things concrete, suppose we want to write a purely functional program that prompts the user for a sequence of numbers (one at a time!) and prints their squares. If Scheme employed lazy evaluation of `input` and `output` streams (it doesn't), then we could write:

```
(define squares (lambda (s)
  (cons "please enter a number\n"
       (let ((n (car s)))
         (if (eof-object? n) '()
           (cons (* n n) (cons #\newline (squares (cdr s)))))))))
(define output (squares input)))
```

---

5 Note that `delay` and `force` automatically *memoize* their stream, so that values are never computed more than once. Exercise 11.10 asks the reader to write a memoizing version of a nonmemoizing stream.

Prompts, inputs, and outputs (i.e., squares) would be interleaved naturally in time. In effect, lazy evaluation would *force* things to happen in the proper order: The `car` of `output` is the first prompt. The `cadr` of `output` is the first square, a value that requires evaluation of the `car` of `input`. The `caddr` of `output` is the second prompt. The `cadddr` of `output` is the second square, a value that requires evaluation of the `cadr` of `input`.

Streams formed the basis of the I/O system in early versions of Haskell. Unfortunately, while they successfully encapsulate the imperative nature of interaction at a terminal, they don't work very well for graphics or random access to files. More recent versions of Haskell employ a more general concept known as *monads*. In the context of the Haskell language, a monad is an abstract data type that supports a notion of sequencing. The values of the I/O monad are *actions* that the programmer can force to occur in a specified order.

Member functions of the Haskell I/O monad take actions as arguments or return actions as results. The `getChar` function, for example, returns an action which, when invoked, will read a character of input; `getChar` is said to be of type `IO Char`. The `putChar` function returns an action which, when invoked, will write a character of output; `putChar` is said to be of type `Char -> IO ()`. In general, the notation `IO t` denotes the type of an action which, when invoked, will return a result of type `t`.

The Haskell I/O monad distinguishes between the *definition* of an action and its *invocation*. Actions can be defined as components of arbitrarily complex data structures in purely functional code. But defining an action does *not* cause it to occur. For that we need the built-in operator `do`. (Do is actually syntactic sugar for a pair of more fundamental operators, `>>` and `>>=`; we ignore those operators here.) A trivial Haskell program might look like this:

```
main = do putStr "hi, mom\n"
```

When evaluated, `do` causes the invocation of the action returned by `putStr`. In general, `do` accepts a sequence of actions, separated by semicolons or newlines, which it invokes in order:

```
do  putStr "hi, "
    putStr "mom\n"
```

Because actions can be manipulated like ordinary values, we can compose them with arbitrary functions. The `putStr` function can be defined in terms of putChar:

```
putStr :: String -> IO ()    -- fn. from strings to null-typed actions
putStr s = sequence (map putChar s)
```

Strings in Haskell are simply lists of characters. The `map` function is assumed to take a function *f* and a list *l* as argument, and to return a list that contains the results of applying *f* to the elements of *l*:

```
map :: (a->b) -> [a] -> [b]
map f [] = []
map f (h:t) = f h : map f t    -- ':' is like cons in Scheme
```

Since `putChar` returns an action but does not invoke it, we must pass the result of `map` to a function that will invoke the actions in a list:

```
sequence :: [IO ()] -> IO ()
sequence [] = return ()
sequence (a:more) = do a; sequence more
```

Sequence accepts a list of (null-typed) actions as argument and returns a single action consisting of the sequential composition of the actions in the list. If `main` were to evaluate `sequence L`, the actions in L would occur.

In our examples `main` is allowed to use `do` because `main` is of type `IO ()`. Uses of `do` cannot occur in purely functional code. The typical Haskell program contains a small amount of high-level imperative code to sequence its I/O operations, while most of the program—both the computation of values and the determination of the order in which any nontrivial set of actions should occur— is purely functional. For a program whose I/O can be expressed in terms of streams, this top-level structure may consist of a single line:

```
main = interact my_program
```

The library function `interact` is of type `(String -> String) -> IO ()`. It takes as argument a function from strings to strings (in this case `my_program`). It calls this function, passing the contents of standard input as argument, and writes the result to standard output. Internally, `interact` uses the function `getContents`, which returns the program's input as a lazily-evaluated string: a stream. In a more sophisticated program, `main` may orchestrate much more complex I/O actions, including graphics and random access to files.

11.2.3 Higher-Order Functions

A function is said to be a *higher-order function* (also called a *functional form*) if it takes a function as an argument, or returns a function as a result. We have seen several examples already of higher-order functions: `call/cc` (page 472), `for-each` (page 600), `compose` (page 600), and `apply` (page 601). We also saw a Haskell version of the higher-order function map in Section 11.2.2. The Scheme version of `map` is slightly more general. Like `for-each`, it takes as argument a function and a *sequence* of lists. There must be as many lists as the function takes arguments, and the lists must all be of the same length. Map calls its function argument on corresponding sets of elements from the lists:

```
(map * '(2 4 6) '(3 5 7))   ⇒   (6 20 42)
```

Where `for-each` is executed for its side effects, and has an implementation-dependent return value, `map` is purely functional: it returns a list composed of the values returned by its function argument.

Programmers in Scheme (or in ML, Haskell, or other functional languages) can easily define other higher-order functions. Suppose, for example, that we want to be able to "fold" the elements of a list together, using an associative binary operator:

```
(define fold (lambda (f l i)
   (if (null? l) i    ; i is commonly the identity element for f
      (f (car l) (fold f (cdr l) i)))))
```

Now (fold + '(1 2 3 4 5) 0) gives us the sum of the first five natural numbers, and (fold * '(1 2 3 4 5) 1) gives us their product.

One of the most common uses of higher-order functions is to build new functions from existing ones:

```
(define total (lambda (l) (fold + l 0)))
(total '(1 2 3 4 5))                    ⇒ 15

(define total-all (lambda (l)
   (map total l)))
(total-all '((1 2 3 4 5)
            (2 4 6 8 10)
            (3 6 9 12 15)))             ⇒ (15 30 45)

(define make-double (lambda (f) (lambda (x) (f x x))))
(define twice (make-double +))
(define square (make-double *))
```

A common operation, named for logician Haskell Curry, is to replace a multi-argument function with a function that takes a single argument and returns a function that expects the remaining arguments:

```
(define curried-plus (lambda (a) (lambda (b) (+ a b))))
((curried-plus 3) 4)                    ⇒ 7
(define plus-3 (curried-plus 3))
(plus-3 4)                              ⇒ 7
```

Among other things, currying gives us the ability to pass a "partially applied" function to a higher-order function:

```
(map (curried-plus 3) '(1 2 3))         ⇒ (4 5 6)
```

It turns out that we can write a general-purpose function that "curries" its (binary) function argument:

```
(define curry (lambda (f) (lambda (a) (lambda (b) (f a b)))))
(((curry +) 3) 4)                       ⇒ 7
(define curried-plus (curry +))
```

ML, Miranda, and Haskell make it especially easy to define curried functions. Consider the following function in ML:

```
fun plus (a, b) : int = a + b;
==> val plus = fn : int * int -> int
```

Recall that the last line is printed by the ML interpreter, and indicates the inferred type of `plus`. The type declaration is required to disambiguate the overloaded + operator. Though one may think of `plus` as a function of two arguments, the ML definition says that all functions take a *single* argument. What we have declared is a function that takes a two-element *tuple* as argument. To call `plus`, we juxtapose its name and the tuple that is its argument:

```
plus (3, 4);
==> val it = 7 : int
```

The parentheses here are not part of the function call syntax; they delimit the tuple (3, 4). We can declare a single-argument function without parenthesizing its formal argument:

```
fun twice n : int = n + n;
==> val twice = fn : int -> int
twice 2;
==> val it = 4 : int
```

We can add parentheses in either the declaration or the call if we want, but because there is no comma inside, no tuple is implied:

```
fun double (n) : int = n + n;
twice (2);
==> val it = 4 : int
twice 2;
==> val it = 4 : int
double (2);
==> val it = 4 : int
double 2;
==> val it = 4 : int
```

Ordinary parentheses can be placed around any expression in ML.

Now consider the definition of a curried function:

```
fun curried_plus a = fn b : int => a + b;
==> val curried_plus = fn : int -> int -> int
```

Note the type of `curried_plus`: `int -> int -> int` groups implicitly as `int -> (int -> int)`. Where `plus` is a function mapping a pair (tuple) of integers to an integer, `curried_plus` is a function mapping an integer to a function that maps an integer to an integer.

```
curried_plus 3;
==> val it = fn : int -> int

plus 3;
==> Error: operator domain (int * int) and operand (int) don't agree
```

To make it easier to declare functions such as `curried_plus`, ML allows a sequence of operands in the formal parameter position of a function declaration:

```
fun curried_plus a b : int = a + b;
==> val curried_plus = fn : int -> int -> int
```

This form is simply shorthand for the declaration shown above; it does not declare a function of two arguments. Curried_plus has a single formal parameter, a. Its return value is a function with formal parameter b that in turn returns a + b.

Using tuple notation, our `fold` function might be declared as follows in ML:

```
fun fold (f, l, i) =
    case l of
        nil => i
      | h :: t => f (h, fold (f, t, i));
==> val fold = fn : ('a * 'b -> 'b) * 'a list * 'b -> 'b
```

The curried version would be declared as follows:

```
fun curried_fold f l i =
    case l of
        nil => i
      | h :: t => f (h, curried_fold f t i);
==> val fold = fn : ('a * 'b -> 'b) -> 'a list -> 'b -> 'b

curried_fold plus;
==> val it = fn : int list -> int -> int
curried_fold plus [1, 2, 3, 4, 5];
==> val it = fn : int -> int
curried_fold plus [1, 2, 3, 4, 5] 0;
==> val it = 15 : int
```

Note again the difference in the inferred types of the functions.

It is of course possible to define `curried_fold` by nesting occurrences of the explicit `fn` notation within the function's body. The shorthand notation, however, is substantially more intuitive and convenient. Note also that ML's syntax for function calls—juxtaposition of function and argument—makes the use of a curried function more intuitive and convenient than it is in Scheme:

```
curried_fold plus [1, 2, 3, 4, 5] 0;    (* ML *)
(((curried_fold +) '(1 2 3 4 5)) 0)     ; Scheme
```

11.2.4* Theoretical Foundations

Mathematical Functions

Mathematically, a function is a single-valued mapping: it associates every element in one set (the *domain*) with (at most) one element in another set (the *range*). In conventional notation, we indicate the domain and range by writing

$$\text{sqrt} : \mathcal{R} \longrightarrow \mathcal{R}$$

We can of course, have functions of more than one variable—that is, functions whose domains are Cartesian products:

$$\text{plus} : [\mathcal{R} \times \mathcal{R}] \longrightarrow \mathcal{R}$$

If a function provides a mapping for every element of the domain, the function is said to be *total*. Otherwise, it is said to be *partial*. Our *sqrt* function is partial: it does not provide a mapping for negative numbers. We could change our definition to make the domain of the function the nonnegative numbers, but such changes are often inconvenient, or even impossible: inconvenient because we would like all mathematical functions to operate on $\mathcal{R}$; impossible because we may not know which elements of the domain have mappings and which do not. Consider for example the function f that maps every natural number a to the smallest natural number b such that the digits of the decimal representation of a appear b digits to the right of the decimal point in the decimal expansion of π. Clearly $f(59) = 4$, because $\pi = 3.14159\ldots$. But what about $f(428945028)$, or in general $f(n)$ for arbitrary n? Absent results from number theory, it is not at all clear how to characterize the values at which f is defined. In such a case a partial function is essential.

It is often useful to characterize functions as sets; more precisely, as subsets of the Cartesian product of the domain and the range:

$$\text{sqrt} \subset [\mathcal{R} \times \mathcal{R}]$$

$$\text{plus} \subset [\mathcal{R} \times \mathcal{R} \times \mathcal{R}]$$

We can specify *which* subset using traditional set notation:

$$\text{sqrt} \equiv \left\{ (x, y) \in \mathcal{R} \times \mathcal{R} \mid y = x^2 \right\}$$

$$\text{plus} \equiv \left\{ (x, y, z) \in \mathcal{R} \times \mathcal{R} \times \mathcal{R} \mid z = x + y \right\}$$

Note that this sort of definition tells us what the value of a function like sqrt is, but it does *not* tell us how to compute it; more on this distinction below.

One of the nice things about the set-based characterization is that it makes it clear that a function is an ordinary mathematical object. We know that a function from A to B is a subset of $A \times B$. This means that it is an *element* of the *powerset* of $A \times B$—the set of all subsets of $A \times B$, denoted $2^{A \times B}$:

$$\text{sqrt} \in 2^{\mathcal{R} \times \mathcal{R}}$$

Similarly

$$\text{plus} \in 2^{\mathcal{R} \times \mathcal{R} \times \mathcal{R}}$$

Note the overloading of notation here. The powerset 2^A should not be confused with exponentiation, though it is true that for a finite set A the number of elements in the powerset of A is 2^n, where $n = |A|$, the cardinality of A.

Because functions are single-valued, we know that they constitute only *some* of the elements of $2^{A \times B}$. Specifically, they constitute all and only those sets of pairs in which the first component of each pair is unique. We call the set of such sets the *function space* of A into B, denoted $A \rightarrow B$. Note that $(A \rightarrow B) \subset 2^{A \times B}$. In our examples:

$$\mathsf{sqrt} \in [\mathcal{R} \rightarrow \mathcal{R}]$$

$$\mathsf{plus} \in [(\mathcal{R} \times \mathcal{R}) \rightarrow \mathcal{R}]$$

Now that functions are elements of sets, we can easily build higher-order functions:

$$\mathsf{compose} \equiv \{(f, g, h) \mid \forall x \in \mathcal{R}, \ h(x) = f(g(x))\}$$

What are the domain and range of compose? We know that f, g, and h are elements of $\mathcal{R} \rightarrow \mathcal{R}$. Thus

$$\mathsf{compose} \in [(\mathcal{R} \rightarrow \mathcal{R}) \times (\mathcal{R} \rightarrow \mathcal{R})] \rightarrow (\mathcal{R} \rightarrow \mathcal{R})$$

Note the similarity to the notation employed by the ML type inference system (Section 7.2.5).

Using the notion of "currying" from Section 11.2.3, we note that there is an alternative characterization for functions such as plus. Rather than a function from pairs of reals to reals, we can capture it as a function from reals to functions from reals to reals:

$$\mathsf{curried\_plus} \in \mathcal{R} \rightarrow (\mathcal{R} \rightarrow \mathcal{R})$$

We shall have more to say about currying below.

Lambda Calculus

As we suggested at the beginning of this chapter, and again in the subsection above, one of the limitations of the function-as-set notation is that it is *non-constructive*: it doesn't tell us how to *compute* the value of a function at a given point (i.e., on a given input). Church designed the lambda calculus to address this limitation. In its pure form, lambda calculus represents *everything* as a function. The natural numbers, for example, can be represented by a distinguished zero function (commonly the identity function) and a successor function. (One common formulation uses a select_second function that takes two arguments and returns the second of them. The successor function is then defined in such a way that the number *n* ends up being represented by a function which, when applied to select_second *n* times, returns the identity function [Mic89, Sec. 3.5]; [Sta95, Sec. 7.6]; see Exercise 11.19.) While of theoretical importance, this formulation of arithmetic is highly cumbersome. We will therefore take ordinary arithmetic as a given in the remainder of this section. (And of course all practical functional programming languages provide built-in support for both integer and floating-point arithmetic.)

A lambda expression can be defined recursively as (1) a *name*; (2) a lambda *abstraction* consisting of the letter λ, a name, a dot, and a lambda expression; (3) a function *application* consisting of two adjacent lambda expressions; or (4) a parenthesized lambda expression. To accommodate arithmetic, we will extend this definition to allow numeric literals.

When two expressions appear adjacent to one another, the first is interpreted as a function to be applied to the second:

$$\mathsf{sqrt}\ n$$

Most authors assume that application associates left-to-right (so $f\ A\ B$ is interpreted as $(f\ A)\ B$, rather than $f\ (A\ B)$), and that application has higher precedence than abstraction (so $\lambda x.A\ B$ is interpreted as $\lambda x.(A\ B)$, rather than $(\lambda x.A)\ B$). ML adopts these rules.

Parentheses are used as necessary to override default groupings. Specifically, if we distinguish between lambda expressions that are used as functions and those that are used as arguments, then the following unambiguous CFG can be used to generate lambda expressions with a minimal number of parentheses:

$$expr \rightarrow \mathsf{name}\ |\ number\ |\ \lambda\ \mathsf{name}\ .\ expr\ |\ func\ arg$$

$$func \rightarrow \mathsf{name}\ |\ (\ \lambda\ \mathsf{name}\ .\ expr\ )\ |\ func\ arg$$

$$arg \rightarrow \mathsf{name}\ |\ number\ |\ (\ \lambda\ \mathsf{name}\ .\ expr\ )\ |\ (\ func\ arg\ )$$

In words: we use parentheses to surround an abstraction that is used as either a function or an argument, and around an application that is used as an argument.

The letter λ introduces the lambda calculus equivalent of a formal parameter. The following lambda expression denotes a function that returns the square of its argument:

$$\lambda x.\mathsf{times}\ x\ x$$

The name (variable) introduced by a λ is said to be *bound* within the expression following the dot. In programming language terms, this expression is the variable's scope. A variable that is not bound is said to be *free*. As in a lexically scoped programming language, a free variable needs to be defined in some surrounding scope. Consider, for example, the expression $\lambda x.\lambda y.\mathsf{times}\ x\ y$. In the inner expression $(\lambda y.\mathsf{times}\ x\ y)$, y is bound but x is free. There are no restrictions on the use of a bound variable: it can play the role of a function, an argument, or both. Higher-order functions are therefore completely natural.

If we wish to refer to them later, we can give expressions names:

$$\mathsf{square} \equiv \lambda x.\mathsf{times}\ x\ x$$
$$\mathsf{identity} \equiv \lambda x.x$$
$$\mathsf{const7} \equiv \lambda x.7$$
$$\mathsf{hypot} \equiv \lambda x.\lambda y.\mathsf{sqrt}\ (\mathsf{plus}\ (\mathsf{square}\ x)\ (\mathsf{square}\ y))$$

Here $\equiv$ is a metasymbol meaning, roughly, "is an abbreviation for."

To compute with the lambda calculus, we need rules to evaluate expressions. It turns out that three rules suffice:

beta reduction: For any lambda abstraction $\lambda x.E$ and any expression M, we say

$$(\lambda x.E)\, M \to_\beta E[M\backslash x]$$

where $E[M\backslash x]$ denotes the expression E with all free occurrences of x replaced by M. Beta reduction is not permitted if any free variables in M would become bound in $E[M\backslash x]$.

alpha conversion: For any lambda abstraction $\lambda x.E$ and any variable y that has no free occurrences in E, we say

$$\lambda x.E \to_\alpha \lambda y.E[y\backslash x]$$

eta reduction: A rule to eliminate "surplus" lambda abstractions. For any lambda abstraction $\lambda x.E$, where E is of the form $F\,x$, and x has no free occurrences in F, we say

$$\lambda x.F\,x \to_\eta F$$

To accommodate arithmetic we will also allow an expression of the form op x y, where x and y are numeric literals and op is one of a small set of standard functions, to be replaced by its arithmetic value. This replacement is called *delta reduction*. In our examples we will need only the functions plus, minus, and times:

$$\text{plus}\ 2\ 3 \to_\delta 5$$
$$\text{minus}\ 5\ 2 \to_\delta 3$$
$$\text{times}\ 2\ 3 \to_\delta 6$$

Beta reduction resembles the use of call by name parameters (Section 8.3.1). Unlike Algol 60, however, the lambda calculus provides no way for an argument to carry its referencing environment with it; hence the requirement that an argument not move a variable into a scope in which its name has a different meaning. Alpha conversion serves to change names to make beta reduction possible. Eta reduction is comparatively less important. If square is defined as above, eta reduction allows us to say that

$$\lambda x.\text{square}\ x \to_\eta \text{square}$$

In English, square is a function that squares its argument; $\lambda x.\text{square}\ x$ is a function of x that squares x. The latter reminds us explicitly that it's a function (i.e., that it takes an argument), but the former is a little less messy-looking.

Through repeated application of beta reduction and alpha conversion (and possibly eta reduction), we can attempt to reduce a lambda expression to its simplest possible form—a form in which no further beta reductions are possible. An example can be found in Figure 11.2. In line (2) of this derivation we have to employ an alpha conversion because the argument that we need to substitute in for g contains a free variable (h) that is bound within g's scope. If we were to

$$(\lambda f.\lambda g.\lambda h.fg(h\,h))(\lambda x.\lambda y.x)h(\lambda x.x\,x)$$

$$\to_\beta \quad (\lambda g.\lambda h.(\lambda x.\lambda y.x)g(\underline{h\,h}))h(\lambda x.x\,x) \qquad (1)$$

$$\to_\alpha \quad (\lambda g.\lambda k.(\lambda x.\lambda y.x)g(k\,k))\underline{h}(\lambda x.x\,x) \qquad (2)$$

$$\to_\beta \quad (\lambda k.(\lambda x.\lambda y.x)h(k\,k))(\underline{\lambda x.x\,x}) \qquad (3)$$

$$\to_\beta \quad (\lambda x.\lambda y.x)\underline{h}((\lambda x.x\,x)\,(\lambda x.x\,x)) \qquad (4)$$

$$\to_\beta \quad (\lambda y.h)\underline{((\lambda x.x\,x)\,(\lambda x.x\,x))} \qquad (5)$$

$$\to_\beta \quad h \qquad (6)$$

Figure 11.2 Reduction of a lambda expression. The top line consists of a function applied to three arguments. The first argument is the "select first" function, which takes two arguments and returns the first. The second argument is the symbol h, which must either be a constant or a variable bound in some enclosing scope (not shown). The third argument is an "apply to self" function that takes one argument and applies it to itself. The particular series of reductions shown occurs in normal order. It terminates with a simplest (normal) form of simply h.

make the substitution of line (3) without first having renamed the bound h (as k), then the free h would have been *captured*, erroneously changing the meaning of the expression.

In line (5) of the derivation, we had a choice as to which subexpression to reduce. At that point the expression as a whole consisted of a function application in which the argument was itself a function application. We chose to substitute the main argument $((\lambda x.x\,x)\,(\lambda x.x\,x))$, unevaluated, into the body of the main lambda abstraction. This choice is known as *normal-order* reduction, and corresponds to normal-order evaluation of arguments in programming languages, as discussed in Sections 6.6.2 and 11.2.2. In general, whenever more than one beta reduction could be made, normal order chooses the one whose λ is leftmost in the overall expression. This strategy substitutes arguments into functions before reducing them. The principal alternative, *applicative-order* reduction, reduces both the function part and the argument part of every function application to the simplest possible form before substituting the latter into the former.

Church and Rosser showed in 1936 that simplest forms are unique: any series of reductions that terminates in a nonreducible expression will produce the same result. Not all reductions terminate however. In particular, there are expressions for which no series of reductions will terminate, and there are others in which normal-order reduction will terminate but applicative-order reduction will not. The example expression of Figure 11.2 leads to an infinite "computation" under applicative-order reduction. To see this, consider the expression at line (5). This line consists of the constant function $(\lambda y.h)$ applied to the argument $(\lambda x.x\,x)\,(\lambda x.x\,x)$. If we attempt to evaluate the argument before substituting it into the function, we run through the following steps:

$$(\lambda x.x\,x)\,(\lambda x.x\,x)$$
$$\rightarrow_\beta (\lambda x.x\,x)\,(\lambda x.x\,x)$$
$$\rightarrow_\beta (\lambda x.x\,x)\,(\lambda x.x\,x)$$
$$\rightarrow_\beta (\lambda x.x\,x)\,(\lambda x.x\,x)$$

$$\cdots$$

In addition to showing the uniqueness of simplest (normal) forms, Church and Rosser showed that if any evaluation order will terminate, normal order will. This pair of results is known as the *Church-Rosser theorem*.

Control Flow

We noted at the beginning of the previous subsection that arithmetic can be modeled in the lambda calculus using a distinguished zero function (commonly the identity) and a successor function. What about control flow constructs—selection and recursion in particular?

The select_first function, $\lambda x.\lambda y.x$, is commonly used to represent the Boolean value true. The select_second function, $\lambda x.\lambda y.y$, is commonly used to represent the Boolean value false. Let us denote these by T and F. The nice thing about these definitions is that they allow us to define an if function very easily:

$$\text{if} \equiv \lambda c.\lambda t.\lambda e.c\,t\,e$$

Consider:

$$\begin{aligned}
\text{if}\,T\,3\,4 \ &\equiv\ (\lambda c.\lambda t.\lambda e.c\,t\,e)\,(\lambda x.\lambda y.x)\,3\,4 \\
&\rightarrow_\beta^* (\lambda x.\lambda y.x)\,3\,4 \\
&\rightarrow_\beta^* 3
\end{aligned}$$

$$\begin{aligned}
\text{if}\,F\,3\,4 \ &\equiv\ (\lambda c.\lambda t.\lambda e.c\,t\,e)\,(\lambda x.\lambda y.y)\,3\,4 \\
&\rightarrow_\beta^* (\lambda x.\lambda y.y)\,3\,4 \\
&\rightarrow_\beta^* 4
\end{aligned}$$

Functions such as equal and greater_than can be defined to take numeric values as arguments, returning T or F.

Recursion is a little tricky. An equation such as

$$\text{gcd} \equiv \lambda a.\lambda b.(\text{if}\,(\text{equal}\,a\,b)\,a$$
$$(\text{if}\,(\text{greater\_than}\,a\,b)\,(\text{gcd}\,(\text{minus}\,a\,b)\,b)\,(\text{gcd}\,(\text{minus}\,b\,a)\,a)))$$

is not really a definition at all, because gcd appears on both sides. Our previous definitions (T, F, if) were simply shorthand: we could substitute them out to obtain a pure lambda expression. If we try that with gcd the "definition" just gets bigger, with new occurrences of the gcd name. To obtain a real definition, we first rewrite our equation using *beta abstraction* (the opposite of beta reduction):

$$\text{gcd} \equiv (\lambda g.\lambda a.\lambda b.(\text{if}(\text{equal } a \, b) \, a$$
$$(\text{if}(\text{greater\_than } a \, b) \, (g(\text{minus } a \, b) \, b) \, (g(\text{minus } b \, a) \, a)))) \, \text{gcd}$$

Now our equation has the form

$$\text{gcd} \equiv f \, \text{gcd}$$

where f is the perfectly well defined (nonrecursive) lambda expression

$$\lambda g.\lambda a.\lambda b.(\text{if}(\text{equal } a \, b) \, a$$
$$(\text{if}(\text{greater\_than } a \, b) \, (g \, (\text{minus } a \, b) \, b) \, (g \, (\text{minus } b \, a) \, a)))$$

Clearly gcd is a fixed point of f.

As it turns out, for any function f given by a lambda expression, we can find the least fixed point of f, if there is one, by applying the *fixed-point combinator*

$$\lambda h.(\lambda x.h(xx)) \, (\lambda x.h(xx))$$

commonly denoted **Y**. **Y** has the property that for any lambda expression f, if the normal-order evaluation of **Y**f terminates, then $f(\mathbf{Y}f)$ and **Y**f will reduce to the same simplest form (see Exercise 11.17). In the case of our gcd function, we have

$$\text{gcd} \equiv (\lambda h.(\lambda x.h(xx)) \, (\lambda x.h(xx)))$$
$$(\lambda g.\lambda a.\lambda b.(\text{if}(\text{equal } a \, b) \, a$$
$$(\text{if}(\text{greater\_than } a \, b) \, (g(\text{minus } a \, b) \, b) \, (g(\text{minus } b \, a) \, a))))$$

Figure 11.3 traces the evaluation of gcd 4 2. Given the existence of the **Y** combinator, most authors permit recursive "definitions" of functions, for convenience.

Structures

Just as we can use functions to build numbers and truth values, we can also use them to encapsulate values in structures. Using Scheme terminology for the sake of clarity, we can define simple list-processing functions as follows:

$$\text{cons} \equiv \lambda a.\lambda d.\lambda x.x \, a \, d$$
$$\text{car} \equiv \lambda l.l \, \text{select\_first}$$
$$\text{cdr} \equiv \lambda l.l \, \text{select\_second}$$
$$\text{nil} \equiv \lambda x.T$$
$$\text{null?} \equiv \lambda l.l(\lambda x.\lambda y.F)$$

$$\gcd 2\,4 \;\equiv\; \mathbf{Y}f\,2\,4$$

$$\equiv\; ((\lambda h.(\lambda x.h(x\,x))\,(\lambda x.h(x\,x)))f)\,2\,4$$

$$\rightarrow_\beta\; ((\lambda x.f(x\,x))\,(\lambda x.f(x\,x)))\,2\,4$$

$$\equiv\; (k\,k)\,2\,4,\;\text{ where } k \equiv \lambda x.f(x\,x)$$

$$\rightarrow_\beta\; (f(k\,k))\,2\,4$$

$$\equiv\; ((\lambda g.\lambda a.\lambda b.(\text{if}\,(=a\,b)\,a\,(\text{if}\,(>a\,b)\,(g(-a\,b)\,b)\,(g(-b\,a)\,a))))\,(k\,k))\,2\,4$$

$$\rightarrow_\beta\; (\lambda a.\lambda b.(\text{if}\,(=a\,b)\,a\,(\text{if}\,(>a\,b)\,((k\,k)(-a\,b)\,b)\,((k\,k)(-b\,a)\,a))))\,2\,4$$

$$\rightarrow_\beta^*\; \text{if}\,(=2\,4)\,2\,(\text{if}\,(>2\,4)\,((k\,k)\,(-2\,4)\,4)\,((k\,k)\,(-4\,2)\,2))$$

$$\equiv\; (\lambda c.\lambda t.\lambda e.c\,t\,e)\,(=2\,4)\,2\,(\text{if}\,(>2\,4)\,((k\,k)\,(-2\,4)\,4)\,((k\,k)\,(-4\,2)\,2))$$

$$\rightarrow_\beta^*\; (=2\,4)\,2\,(\text{if}\,(>2\,4)\,((k\,k)\,(-2\,4)\,4)\,((k\,k)\,(-4\,2)\,2))$$

$$\rightarrow_\delta\; F\,2\,(\text{if}\,(>2\,4)\,((k\,k)\,(-2\,4)\,4)\,((k\,k)\,(-4\,2)\,2))$$

$$\equiv\; (\lambda x.\lambda y.y)\,2\,(\text{if}\,(>2\,4)\,((k\,k)\,(-2\,4)\,4)\,((k\,k)\,(-4\,2)\,2))$$

$$\rightarrow_\beta^*\; \text{if}\,(>2\,4)\,((k\,k)\,(-2\,4)\,4)\,((k\,k)\,(-4\,2)\,2)$$

$$\rightarrow\; \ldots$$

$$\rightarrow\; (k\,k)\,(-4\,2)\,2$$

$$\equiv\; ((\lambda x.f(x\,x))k)\,(-4\,2)\,2$$

$$\rightarrow_\beta\; (f(k\,k))\,(-4\,2)\,2$$

$$\equiv\; ((\lambda g.\lambda a.\lambda b.(\text{if}\,(=a\,b)\,a\,(\text{if}\,(>a\,b)\,(g(-a\,b)\,b)\,(g(-b\,a)\,a))))\,(k\,k))\,(-4\,2)\,2$$

$$\rightarrow_\beta\; (\lambda a.\lambda b.(\text{if}\,(=a\,b)\,a\,(\text{if}\,(>a\,b)\,((k\,k)(-a\,b)\,b)\,((k\,k)(-b\,a)\,a))))\,(-4\,2)\,2$$

$$\rightarrow_\beta^*\; \text{if}\,(=(-4\,2)\,2)\,(-4\,2)\,(\text{if}\,(>(-4\,2)\,2)\,((k\,k)\,(-(-4\,2)\,2)\,2)\,((k\,k)\,(-2\,(-4\,2))\,(-4\,2)))$$

$$\equiv\; (\lambda c.\lambda t.\lambda e.c\,t\,e)$$

$$(=(-4\,2)\,2)\,(-4\,2)\,(\text{if}\,(>(-4\,2)\,2)\,((k\,k)\,(-(-4\,2)\,2)\,2)\,((k\,k)\,(-2\,(-4\,2))\,(-4\,2)))$$

$$\rightarrow_\beta^*\; (=(-4\,2)\,2)\,(-4\,2)\,(\text{if}\,(>(-4\,2)\,2)\,((k\,k)\,(-(-4\,2)\,2)\,2)\,((k\,k)\,(-2\,(-4\,2))\,(-4\,2)))$$

$$\rightarrow_\delta\; (=2\,2)\,(-4\,2)\,(\text{if}\,(>(-4\,2)\,2)\,((k\,k)\,(-(-4\,2)\,2)\,2)\,((k\,k)\,(-2\,(-4\,2))\,(-4\,2)))$$

$$\rightarrow_\delta\; T\,(-4\,2)\,(\text{if}\,(>(-4\,2)\,2)\,((k\,k)\,(-(-4\,2)\,2)\,2)\,((k\,k)\,(-2\,(-4\,2))\,(-4\,2)))$$

$$\equiv\; (\lambda x.\lambda y.x)\,(-4\,2)\,(\text{if}\,(>(-4\,2)\,2)\,((k\,k)\,(-(-4\,2)\,2)\,2)\,((k\,k)\,(-2\,(-4\,2))\,(-4\,2)))$$

$$\rightarrow_\beta^*\; (-4\,2)$$

$$\rightarrow_\delta\; 2$$

Figure 11.3 Evaluation of a recursive lambda expression. As explained in the body of the text, gcd is defined to be the fixed-point combinator **Y** applied to a beta abstraction f of the standard recursive definition for greatest common divisor. Specifically, **Y** is $\lambda h.(\lambda x.h(x\,x))\,(\lambda x.h(x\,x))$ and f is $\lambda g.\lambda a.\lambda b.(\text{if}\,(=a\,b)\,a\,(\text{if}\,(>a\,b)\,(g(-a\,b)\,b)\,(g(-b\,a)\,a)))$. For brevity we have used =, >, and − in place of equal, greater_than, and minus. We have performed the evaluation in normal order.

where select_first and select_second are the functions $\lambda x.\lambda y.x$ and $\lambda x.\lambda y.y$, respectively: functions we also use to represent true and false.

Using these definitions we can see that

$$
\begin{aligned}
\text{car(cons}\,A\,B) \;\equiv\; & (\lambda l.l\;\text{select\_first})\,(\text{cons}\,A\,B) \\
\rightarrow_\beta\; & (\text{cons}\,A\,B)\;\text{select\_first} \\
\equiv\; & ((\lambda a.\lambda d.\lambda x.x\,a\,d)\,A\,B)\;\text{select\_first} \\
\rightarrow_\beta^*\; & (\lambda x.x\,A\,B)\;\text{select\_first} \\
\rightarrow_\beta\; & \text{select\_first}\,A\,B \\
\equiv\; & (\lambda x.\lambda y.x)\,A\,B \\
\rightarrow_\beta^*\; & A
\end{aligned}
$$

$$
\begin{aligned}
\text{cdr(cons}\,A\,B) \;\equiv\; & (\lambda l.l\;\text{select\_second})\,(\text{cons}\,A\,B) \\
\rightarrow_\beta\; & (\text{cons}\,A\,B)\;\text{select\_second} \\
\equiv\; & ((\lambda a.\lambda d.\lambda x.x\,a\,d)\,A\,B)\;\text{select\_second} \\
\rightarrow_\beta^*\; & (\lambda x.x\,A\,B)\;\text{select\_second} \\
\rightarrow_\beta\; & \text{select\_second}\,A\,B \\
\equiv\; & (\lambda x.\lambda y.y)\,A\,B \\
\rightarrow_\beta^*\; & B
\end{aligned}
$$

$$
\begin{aligned}
\text{null?}\,\text{nil} \;\equiv\; & (\lambda l.l\,(\lambda x.\lambda y.\text{select\_second}))\,\text{nil} \\
\rightarrow_\beta\; & \text{nil}\,(\lambda x.\lambda y.\text{select\_second}) \\
\equiv\; & (\lambda x.\text{select\_first})\,(\lambda x.\lambda y.\text{select\_second}) \\
\rightarrow_\beta\; & \text{select\_first} \\
\equiv\; & T
\end{aligned}
$$

$$
\begin{aligned}
\text{null?}\,(\text{cons}\,A\,B) \;\equiv\; & (\lambda l.l\,(\lambda x.\lambda y.\text{select\_second}))\,(\text{cons}\,A\,B) \\
\rightarrow_\beta\; & (\text{cons}\,A\,B)\,(\lambda x.\lambda y.\text{select\_second}) \\
\equiv\; & ((\lambda a.\lambda d.\lambda x.x\,a\,d)\,A\,B)\,(\lambda x.\lambda y.\text{select\_second}) \\
\rightarrow_\beta^*\; & (\lambda x.x\,A\,B)\,(\lambda x.\lambda y.\text{select\_second}) \\
\rightarrow_\beta\; & (\lambda x.\lambda y.\text{select\_second})\,A\,B \\
\rightarrow_\beta^*\; & \text{select\_second} \\
\equiv\; & F
\end{aligned}
$$

Because every lambda abstraction has a single argument, lambda expressions are naturally curried. We generally obtain the effect of a multi-argument function by nesting lambda abstractions:

$$
\text{compose} \equiv \lambda f.\lambda g.\lambda x.f\,(g\,x)
$$

which groups as

$$\lambda f.(\lambda g.(\lambda x.(f\,(g\,x))))$$

We commonly think of compose as a function that takes two functions as arguments and returns a third function as its result. We could just as easily, however, think of compose as a function of three arguments: the f, g, and x above. The official story, or course, is that compose is a function of one argument that evaluates to a function of one argument that in turn evaluates to a function of one argument.

If desired, we can use our structure-building functions to define a noncurried version of compose whose (single) argument is a pair:

$$\text{paired\_compose} \equiv \lambda p.\lambda x.(\text{car}\,p)\,((\text{cdr}\,p)\,x)$$

If we consider the pairing of arguments as a general technique, we can write a curry function that reproduces the single-argument version, just as we did in Scheme in Section 11.2.3:

$$\text{curry} \equiv \lambda f.\lambda a.\lambda b.f\,(\text{cons}\,a\,b)$$

11.2.5 Functional Programming in Perspective

Side effect–free programming is a very appealing idea. As discussed in Sections 6.1.2 and 6.3, side effects can make programs both hard to read and hard to compile. By contrast, the lack of side effects makes expressions referentially transparent—independent of evaluation order. Programmers and compilers of a purely functional language can employ *equational reasoning*, in which the equivalence of two expressions at any point in time implies their equivalence at all times.

Unfortunately, there are common programming idioms in which the canonical side effect—assignment—plays a central role. Critics of functional programming often point to these idioms as evidence of the need for imperative language features. I/O is one example. We have seen (in Section 11.2.2) that sequential access to files can be modeled in a functional manner using streams. For graphics and random file access we have also seen that the monads of Haskell can cleanly isolate the invocation of actions from the bulk of the language, and allow the full power of equational reasoning to be applied to both the computation of values and the determination of the order in which I/O actions should occur.

Other commonly cited examples of "naturally imperative" idioms include:

initialization of complex structures: The heavy reliance on lists in Lisp, ML, and Haskell reflects the ease with which functions can build new lists out of the components of old lists. Other data structures—multidimensional arrays in particular—are much less easy to put together incrementally, particularly if the natural order in which to initialize the elements is not strictly row-major or column-major.

summarization: Many programs include code that scans a large data structure or a large amount of input data, counting the occurrences of various items or patterns. The natural way to keep track of the counts is with a dictionary data structure in which one repeatedly updates the count associated with the most recently noticed key.

in-place mutation: In programs with very large data sets, one must economize as much as possible on memory usage, to maximize the amount of data that will fit in memory or the cache. Sorting programs, for example, need to sort in place, rather than copying elements to a new array or list. Matrix-based scientific programs, likewise, need to update values in place.

These last three idioms are examples of what has been called the *trivial update problem*. If the use of a functional language forces the underlying implementation to create a new copy of the entire data structure every time one of its elements must change, then the result will be very inefficient. In imperative programs, the problem is avoided by allowing an existing structure to be modified in place.

One can argue that while the trivial update problem causes trouble in Lisp and its relatives, it does not reflect an inherent weakness of functional programming per se. What is required for a solution is a combination of convenient notation—to access arbitrary elements of a complex structure—and an implementation that is able to determine when the old version of the structure will never be used again, so it can be updated in place instead of being copied.

Sisal combines array types and iterative syntax with purely functional semantics. The iterative constructs are defined as syntactic sugar for tail recursive functions. When nested, these constructs can easily be used to initialize a multidimensional array. The semantics of the language say that each iteration of the loop returns a new copy of the entire array. The compiler can easily verify, however, that the old copy is never used after the return, and can therefore arrange to perform all updates in place. Similar optimizations could be performed in the absence of the imperative syntax, but require somewhat more complex analysis. Cann reports [Can92] that the Livermore Sisal compiler is able to eliminate 99–100% of all copy operations in standard numeric benchmarks.

Significant strides in both the theory and practice of functional programming have been made in recent years. Wadler [Wad98b] argues persuasively that the principal remaining obstacles to the widespread adoption of functional languages are social and commercial, not technical: most programmers have been trained in an imperative style; software libraries and development environments for functional programming are not yet as mature as are their imperative cousins. It seems likely that the coming decade will see a significant increase in the use of functional languages, pure functional languages in particular.

11.3 Logic Programming

Logic programming systems allow the programmer to state a collection of *axioms* from which theorems can be proven. The user of a logic program states a theorem, or *goal*, and the language implementation attempts to find a collection of axioms and inference steps (including choices of values for variables) that together imply the goal. Of the several existing logic languages, Prolog is by far the most widely used.

In almost all logic languages, axioms are written in a standard form known as a *Horn clause*. A Horn clause consists of a *head*,[6] or *consequent* term H, and a *body* consisting of terms B_i:

$$H \leftarrow B_1, B_2, \ldots, B_n$$

The semantics of this statement are that when the B_i are all true, we can deduce that H is true as well. When reading aloud, we say "H, if B_1, B_2, ..., and B_n." Horn clauses can be used to capture most, but not all, logical statements. (We will return to the issue of completeness in Section 11.3.2.)

In order to derive new statements, a logic programming system combines existing statements, cancelling like terms, through a process known as *resolution*. If we know that A and B imply C, for example, and that C implies D, we can deduce that A and B imply D:

$$\frac{C \leftarrow A, B \qquad D \leftarrow C}{D \leftarrow A, B}$$

In general, terms such as A, B, C, and D may consist not only of constants ("Rochester is rainy"), but also of *predicates* applied to *atoms* or to *variables*: rainy(Rochester), rainy(Seattle), rainy(X).

During resolution, free variables may acquire values through *unification* with expressions in matching terms, much as variables acquire types in ML (as discussed in Section 7.2.5):

$$\frac{\text{flowery}(X) \leftarrow \text{rainy}(X) \qquad \text{rainy(Rochester)}}{\text{flowery(Rochester)}}$$

In the following section we consider Prolog in more detail. We return to formal logic, and to its relationship to Prolog, in Section 11.3.2.

---

6 Note that the word 'head' is used for two different things in Prolog: the head of a Horn clause and the head of a list. The distinction between these is usually clear from context.

11.3.1 **Prolog**

Much as a Scheme interpreter evaluates functions in the context of a referencing environment in which other functions and constants have been defined, a Prolog interpreter runs in the context of a *database* of *clauses* (Horn clauses) that are assumed to be true. Each clause is composed of *terms*, which may be constants, variables, or *structures*. A constant is either an atom or a number. A structure can be thought of as either a logical predicate or a data structure.

Atoms in Prolog are similar to symbols in Lisp. Lexically, an atom looks like an identifier beginning with a lowercase letter, a sequence of "punctuation" characters, or a quoted character string:

```
foo        my_Const    +       'Hi, Mom'
```

Numbers resemble the integers and floating-point constants of other programming languages. A variable looks like an identifier beginning with an uppercase letter:

```
Foo        My_var      X
```

Variables can be *instantiated* to (i.e., can take on) arbitrary values at run time as a result of unification. The scope of every variable is limited to the clause in which it appears. There are no declarations. As in Lisp, type checking occurs only when a program attempts to use a value in a particular way at run time.

Structures consist of an atom called the *functor* and a list of arguments:

```
rainy(rochester)
teaches(scott, cs254)
bin_tree(foo, bin_tree(bar, glarch))
```

Prolog requires the opening parenthesis to come immediately after the functor, with no intervening space. Arguments can be arbitrary terms: constants, variables, or (nested) structures. Internally, a Prolog implementation can represent a structure using Lisp-like `cons` cells. Conceptually, the programmer may prefer to think of certain structures (e.g., `rainy`) as logical predicates.

The clauses in a Prolog database can be classified as *facts* or *rules*, each of which ends with a period. A fact is a Horn clause without a right-hand side. It looks like a single term (the implication symbol is implicit):

```
rainy(rochester).
```

A rule has a right-hand side:

```
snowy(X) :- rainy(X), cold(X).
```

The token `:-` is the implication symbol; the comma indicates "and." (`X` is snowy if `X` is rainy and `X` is cold.)

It is also possible to write a clause with an empty left-hand side. Such a clause is called a *query*, or a *goal*. Queries do not appear in Prolog programs. Rather, one builds a database of facts and rules and then initiates execution by giving the Prolog interpreter (or the compiled Prolog program) a query to be answered (i.e., a goal to be proven).

In most implementations of Prolog, queries are entered with a special ?- version of the implication symbol. If we were to type the following:

```
rainy(seattle).
rainy(rochester).
?- rainy(C).
```

the Prolog interpreter would respond with

```
C = seattle
```

Of course, `C = rochester` would also be a valid answer, but Prolog will find `seattle` first, because it comes first in the database. (Dependence on ordering is one of the ways in which Prolog departs from pure logic; we discuss this issue further below.) If we want to find all possible solutions, we can ask the interpreter to continue by typing a semicolon:

```
C = seattle;
C = rochester
```

If we type another semicolon, the interpreter will indicate that no further solutions are possible:

```
C = seattle;
C = rochester;
no
```

Similarly, given

```
rainy(seattle).
rainy(rochester).
cold(rochester).
snowy(X) :- rainy(X), cold(X).
```

the query

```
?- snowy(C).
```

will yield only one solution.

Resolution and Unification

The *resolution principle*, due to Robinson [Rob65], says that if C_1 and C_2 are Horn clauses and the head of C_1 matches one of the terms in the body of C_2, then we can replace the term in C_2 with the body of C_1. Consider the following example:

```
takes(jane_doe, his201).
takes(jane_doe, cs254).
takes(ajit_chandra, art302).
takes(ajit_chandra, cs254).
classmates(X, Y) :- takes(X, Z), takes(Y, Z).
```

Here if we let X be jane_doe and Z be cs254, we can replace the first term on the right-hand side of the last clause with the (empty) body of the second clause, yielding the new rule

```
classmates(jane_doe, Y) :- takes(Y, cs254).
```

In other words, Y is a classmate of jane_doe if Y takes cs254.

The pattern-matching process used to associate X with jane_doe and Z with cs254 is known as *unification*. Variables that are given values as a result of unification are said to be *instantiated*.

The unification rules for Prolog state that

- A constant unifies only with itself.
- Two structures unify if and only if they have the same functor and the same number of arguments, and the corresponding arguments unify recursively.
- A variable unifies with anything. If the other thing has a value, then the variable is instantiated. If the other thing is an uninstantiated variable, then the two variables are associated in such a way that if either is given a value later, that value will be shared by both.

Unification of structures in Prolog is very much akin to ML's unification of the types of formal and actual parameters. A formal parameter of type int * 'b list, for example, will unify with an actual parameter of type 'a * real list in ML by instantiating 'a to int and 'b to real.

Equality in Prolog is defined in terms of "unifiability." The goal =(A, B) succeeds if and only if A and B can be unified. For the sake of convenience, the goal may be written as A = B; the infix notation is simply syntactic sugar. In keeping with the rules above, we have

```
?- a = a.
yes                % constant unifies with itself
?- a = b.
no                 % but not with another constant
?- foo(a, b) = foo(a, b).
yes                % structures are recursively identical
?- X = a.
X = a;             % variable unifies with constant
no                 % only once
?- foo(a, b) = foo(X, b).
X = a;             % arguments must unify
no                 % only one possibility
```

It is possible for two variables to be unified without instantiating them. If we type

```
?- A = B.
```

the interpreter will respond

```
A = _123
B = _123
```

where _123 is an underscore followed by some arbitrary (implementation-dependent) integer that represents the (shared) location of A and B. In a similar vein, suppose we are given the following rules:

```
takes_lab(S) :- takes(S, C), has_lab(C).
has_lab(D) :- meets_in(D, R), is_lab(R).
```

(S takes a lab class if S takes C and C is a lab class. Moreover D is a lab class if D meets in room R and R is a lab.) An attempt to resolve these rules will unify the head of the second with the second term in the body of the first, causing C and D to be unified, even though neither is instantiated.

Lists

Like equality checking, list manipulation is a sufficiently common operation in Prolog to warrant its own notation. The construct [a, b, c] is syntactic sugar for the structure .(a, .(b, .(c, []))), where [] is the empty list and . is a built-in cons-like functor. This notation should be familiar to users of ML. Prolog adds an extra convenience, however: an optional vertical bar that delimits the "tail" of the list. Using this notation, [a, b, c] could be expressed as [a | [b, c]], [a, b | [c]], or [a, b, c | []]. The vertical-bar notation is particularly handy when the tail of the list is a variable:

```
member(X, [X|T]).
member(X, [H|T]) :- member(X, T).
```

```
sorted ([]).           % empty list is sorted
sorted ([X]).          % singleton is sorted
sorted([A, B | T]) :- A =< B, sorted ([B | T]).
    % compound list is sorted if first two elements are in order and
    % remainder of list (after first element) is sorted
```

Here =< is a built-in predicate that operates on numbers. Note that [a, b | c] is the *improper* list .(a, .(b, c)). The sequence of tokens [a | b, c] is syntactically invalid.

One of the interesting things about Prolog resolution is that it does not in general distinguish between "input" and "output" arguments (there are certain exceptions, such as the is predicate described in the following subsection). Thus given

```
append([], A, A).
append([H | T], A, [H | L]) :- append(T, A, L).
```

We can type

```
?- append([a, b, c], [d, e], L).
L = [a, b, c, d, e]
?- append(X, [d, e], [a, b, c, d, e]).
X = [a, b, c]
?- append([a, b, c], Y, [a, b, c, d, e]).
Y = [d, e]
```

This example highlights the difference between functions and predicates. The former have a clear notion of inputs (arguments) and outputs (results); the latter do not. In an imperative or functional language we apply functions to arguments to generate results. In a logic language we search for values for which a predicate is true.

Arithmetic

The usual arithmetic operators are available in Prolog, but they play the role of functors, not of functions. Thus +(2, 3), which may also be written 2 + 3, is a two-argument structure, not a function call. In particular, it will not unify with 5:

```
?- (2 + 3) = 5.
no
```

To handle arithmetic, Prolog provides a built-in functor, is, that unifies its first argument with the arithmetic value of its second argument:

```
?- is(X, 1+2).
X = 3
?- X is 1+2.
X = 3                % infix is also ok
?- 1+2 is 4-1.
no                   % first argument (1+2) is already instantiated
?- X is Y.
<error>              % second argument (Y) must already be instantiated
?- Y is 1+2, X is Y.
X = 3
Y = 3                % Y is instantiated by the time it is needed
```

Search/Execution Order

So how does Prolog go about answering a query (satisfying a goal)? What it needs is a sequence of resolution steps that will build the goal out of clauses in the database, or a proof that no such sequence exists. In the realm of formal logic, one can imagine two principal search strategies:

- Start with existing clauses and work forward, attempting to derive the goal. This strategy is known as *forward chaining*.
- Start with the goal and work backward, attempting to "unresolve" it into a set of pre-existing clauses. This strategy is known as *backward chaining*.

```
rainy(seattle).
rainy(rochester).
cold(rochester).
snowy(X) :- rainy(X), cold(X).
```

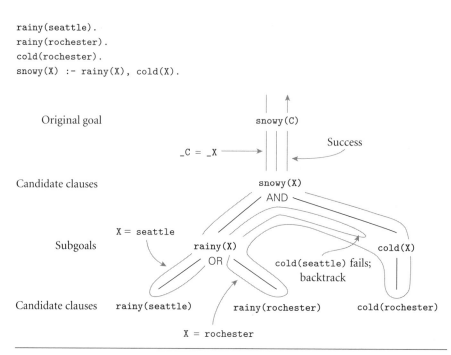

Figure 11.4 Backtracking search in Prolog. The tree of potential resolutions consists of alternating AND and OR levels. An AND level consists of subgoals from the right-hand side of a rule, all of which must be satisfied. An OR rule consists of alternative database clauses whose head will unify with the subgoal above; one of these must be satisfied. The notation $\_C = \_X$ is meant to indicate that while both C and X are uninstantiated, they have been associated with one another in such a way that if either receives a value in the future it will be shared by both.

If the number of existing rules is very large, but the number of facts is small, it is possible for forward chaining to discover a solution more quickly than backward chaining. In most circumstances, however, backward chaining turns out to be more efficient. Prolog is defined to use backward chaining.

Because resolution is associative and commutative (Exercise 11.23), a backward-chaining theorem prover can limit its search to sequences of resolutions in which terms on the right-hand side of a clause are unified with the heads of other clauses one by one in some particular order (e.g., left to right). The resulting search can be described in terms of a tree of subgoals, as shown in Figure 11.4. The Prolog interpreter (or program) explores this tree depth first, from left to right. It starts at the beginning of the database, searching for a rule *R* whose head can be unified with the top-level goal. It then considers the terms in the body of *R* as subgoals, and attempts to satisfy them, recursively, left to right. If at any point a subgoal fails (cannot be satisfied), the interpreter returns to the previous subgoal and attempts to satisfy it in a different way (i.e., to unify it with the head of a different clause).

The process of returning to previous goals is known as *backtracking*. It strongly resembles the control flow of generators in Icon (Section 6.5.3). Whenever a unification operation is "undone" in order to pursue a different path through the search tree, variables that were given values or associated with one another as a result of that unification are returned to their uninstantiated or unassociated state. In Figure 11.4, for example, the binding of X to seattle is broken when we backtrack to the rainy(X) subgoal. The effect is similar to the breaking of bindings between actual and formal parameters in an imperative programming language, except that Prolog couches the bindings in terms of unification rather than subroutine calls.

Space management for backtracking search in Prolog usually follows the single-stack implementation of iterators described in Section 8.6.3. The interpreter pushes a frame onto its stack every time it begins to pursue a new subgoal G. If G fails, the frame is popped from the stack and the interpreter begins to backtrack. If G succeeds, control returns to the "caller" (the parent in the search tree), but G's frame remains on the stack. Later subgoals will be given space *above* this dormant frame. If subsequent backtracking causes the interpreter to search for alternative ways of satisfying G, control will be able to resume where it last left off. Note that G will not fail unless all of its subgoals (and all of its siblings to the right in the search tree) have also failed, implying that there is nothing above G's frame in the stack. At the top level of the interpreter, a semicolon typed by the user is treated the same as failure of the most recently satisfied subgoal.

The fact that clauses are ordered, and that the interpreter considers them from first to last, means that the results of a Prolog program are deterministic and predictable. In fact, the combination of ordering and depth-first search means that the Prolog programmer must often consider the order to ensure that recursive programs will terminate. Suppose for example that we have a database describing a directed acyclic graph:

```
edge(a, b).   edge(b, c).   edge(c, d).
edge(d, e).   edge(b, e).   edge(d, f).
path(X, X).
path(X, Y) :- edge(Z, Y), path(X, Z).
```

The last two clauses tell us how to determine whether there is a path from node X to node Y. If we were to reverse the order of the terms on the right-hand side of the final clause, then the Prolog interpreter would search for a node Z that is reachable from X before checking to see whether there is an edge from Z to Y. The program would still work, but it would not be as efficient.

Now consider what would happen if in addition we were to reverse the order of the last two clauses:

```
path(X, Y) :- path(X, Z), edge(Z, Y).
path(X, X).
```

From a logical point of view, our database still defines the same relationships. A Prolog interpreter, however, will no longer be able to find answers. Even a

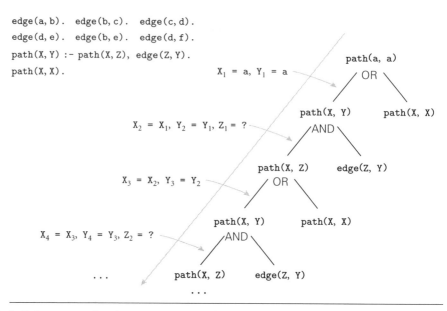

```
edge(a, b).  edge(b, c).  edge(c, d).
edge(d, e).  edge(b, e).  edge(d, f).
path(X, Y) :- path(X, Z), edge(Z, Y).
path(X, X).
```

Figure 11.5 Infinite regression in Prolog. In this figure even a simple query such as ?- path(a, a) will never terminate: the interpreter will never find the trivial branch.

simple query such as ?- path(a, a) will never terminate. To see why, consider Figure 11.5. The interpreter first unifies path(a, a) with the left-hand side of path(X, Y) :- path(X, Z), edge(Z, Y). It then considers the goals on the right-hand side, the first of which (path(X, Z)), unifies with the left-hand side of the very same rule, leading to an infinite regression. In effect, the Prolog interpreter gets lost in an infinite branch of the search tree, and never discovers finite branches to the right. We could avoid this problem by exploring the tree in breadth-first order, but that strategy was rejected by Prolog's designers because of its expense: it can require substantially more space, and does not lend itself to a stack-based implementation.

A Longer Example

In the previous section we saw how the order of clauses in the Prolog database, and the order of terms within a right-hand side, can affect both the efficiency of a Prolog program and its ability to terminate. Ordering also allows the Prolog programmer to indicate that certain resolutions are *preferred*, and should be considered before other, "fallback" options. Consider, for example, the problem of making a move in tic-tac-toe. (Tic-tac-toe is a game played on a 3 × 3 grid of squares. Two players, X and 0, take turns placing markers in empty squares. A player wins if he or she places three markers in a row, horizontally, vertically, or diagonally.)

Let us number the squares from 1 to 9 in row-major order. Further, let us use the Prolog fact x(n) to indicate that player X has placed a marker in square *n*, and o(m) to indicate that player O has placed a marker in square *m*. For simplicity, let us assume that the computer is player X, and that it is X's turn to move. We would like to be able to issue a query ?- move(A) that will cause the Prolog interpreter to choose a good square A for the computer to occupy next.

Clearly we need to be able to tell whether three given squares lie in a row. One way to express this is:

```
ordered_line(1, 2, 3).      ordered_line(4, 5, 6).
ordered_line(7, 8, 9).      ordered_line(1, 4, 7).
ordered_line(2, 5, 8).      ordered_line(3, 6, 9).
ordered_line(1, 5, 9).      ordered_line(3, 5, 7).
line(A, B, C) :- ordered_line(A, B, C).
line(A, B, C) :- ordered_line(A, C, B).
line(A, B, C) :- ordered_line(B, A, C).
line(A, B, C) :- ordered_line(B, C, A).
line(A, B, C) :- ordered_line(C, A, B).
line(A, B, C) :- ordered_line(C, B, A).
```

It is easy to prove that there is no winning strategy for tic-tac-toe: either player can force a draw. Let us assume, however, that our program is playing against a less-than-perfect opponent. Our task then is never to lose, and to maximize our chances of winning if our opponent makes a mistake. The following rules work well:

```
move(A) :- good(A), empty(A).

full(A) :- x(A).
full(A) :- o(A).
empty(A) :- not full(A).

% strategy:
good(A) :- win(A).          good(A) :- block_win(A).
good(A) :- split(A).        good(A) :- strong_build(A).
good(A) :- weak_build(A).
```

The initial rule indicates that we can satisfy the goal move(A) by choosing a good, empty square. The not is a built-in predicate that succeeds if its argument (a goal) cannot be proven; we discuss it further below. Square n is empty if we cannot prove it is full; that is, if neither x(n) nor o(n) is in the database.

The key to strategy lies in the ordering of the last five rules. Our first choice is to win:

```
win(A) :- x(B), x(C), line(A, B, C).
```

Our second choice is to prevent our opponent from winning:

```
block_win(A) :- o(B), o(C), line(A, B, C).
```

Our third choice is to create a "split"—a situation in which our opponent cannot prevent us from winning on the next move (see Figure 11.6):

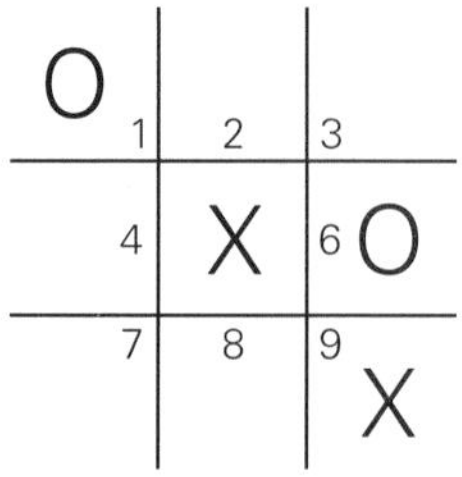

Figure 11.6 A "split" in tac-tac-toe. If X takes the bottom center square (square 8), no future move by O will be able to stop X from winning the game—O cannot block both the 2–5–8 line and the 7–8–9 line.

```
split(A) :- x(B), x(C), different(B, C),
    line(A, B, D), line(A, C, E), empty(D), empty(E).
same(A, A).
different(A, B) :- not same(A, B).
```

Here we have again relied on the built-in predicate not.

Our fourth choice is to build toward three in a row (i.e., to get two in a row) in such a way that the obvious blocking move won't allow our opponent to build toward three in a row:

```
strong_build(A) :- x(B), line(A, B, C), empty(C), not(risky(C)).
risky(C) :- o(D), line(C, D, E), empty(E).
```

Barring that, our fifth choice is to build toward three in a row in such a way that the obvious blocking move won't give our opponent a split:

```
weak_build(A) :- x(B), line(A, B, C), empty(C), not(double_risky(C)).
double_risky(C) :- o(D), o(E), different(D, E), line(C, D, F),
    line(C, E, G), empty(F), empty(G).
```

In case none of these goals can be satisfied, our final, default choice is to pick an unoccupied square, giving priority to the center, the corners, and the sides in that order:

```
good(5).    good(1).  good(3).  good(7).  good(9).
            good(2).  good(4).  good(6).  good(8).
```

Imperative Control Flow

We have seen that the ordering of clauses and of terms in Prolog is significant, with ramifications for efficiency, termination, and choice among alternatives. In addition to simple ordering, Prolog provides the programmer with several explicit control-flow features. The most important of these is known as the *cut*.

The cut is a zero-argument predicate written as an exclamation point: !. As a subgoal it always succeeds, but with a crucial side effect: it commits the interpreter to whatever choices have been made since unifying the parent goal with the left-hand side of the current rule, including the choice of that unification itself. For example, recall our definition of list membership:

```
member(X, [X|T]).
member(X, [H|T]) :- member(X, T).
```

If a given atom a appears in list L *n* times, then the goal ?- member(a, L) can succeed *n* times. These "extra" successes may not always be appropriate. They can lead to wasted computation, particularly for long lists, when member is followed by a goal that may fail:

```
prime_candidate(X) :- member(X, candidates), prime(X).
```

Suppose that prime(X) is expensive to compute. To determine whether a is a prime candidate, we first check to see whether it is a member of the candidates list, and then check to see whether it is prime. If prime(a) fails, Prolog will backtrack and attempt to satisfy member(a, candidates) again. If a is in the candidates list more than once, then the subgoal will succeed again, leading to reconsideration of the prime(a) subgoal, even though that subgoal is doomed to fail. We can save substantial time by cutting off all further searches for a after the first is found:

```
member(X, [X|T]) :- !.
member(X, [H|T]) :- member(X, T).
```

The cut on the right-hand side of the first rule says that if X is the head of L, we should not attempt to unify member(X, L) with the left-hand side of the second rule; the cut commits us to the first rule.

An alternative way of ensuring that member(X, L) succeeds no more than once is to embed a use of not in the second clause:

```
member(X, [X|T]).
member(X, [H|T]) :- not (X = H), member(X, T).
```

This code will display the same high-level behavior, but is slightly less efficient: now the interpreter will actually consider the second rule, abandoning it only after (re)unifying X with H and reversing the sense of the test.

It turns out that not is actually implemented by a combination of the cut and two other built-in predicates, call and fail:

```
not(P) :- call(P), !, fail.
not(P).
```

The call predicate takes a term as argument and attempts to satisfy it as a goal (terms are first-class values in Prolog). The fail predicate always fails.

In principle, it is possible to replace all uses of the cut with uses of not: to confine the cut to the implementation of not. Doing so often makes a program easier to read. As we have seen, however, it often makes it less efficient. In some cases, explicit use of the cut may actually make a program *easier* to read. Consider our tic-tac-toe example. If we type semicolons at the program, it will continue to generate a series of increasingly poor moves from the same location, even though we only want the first move. We can cut off consideration of the others by using the cut:

```
move(A) :- good(A), empty(A), !.
```

To achieve the same effect with not we would have to do more major surgery (Exercise 11.26).

In general, the cut can be used whenever we want the effect of if...then... else:

```
statement :- condition, !, then_part.
statement :- else_part.
```

The fail predicate can be used in conjunction with a "generator" to implement a loop. We have already seen how to effect a generator by driving a set of rules "backwards." Recall our definition of append:

```
append([], A, A).
append([H | T], A, [H | L]) :- append(T, A, L).
```

To enumerate the ways in which a list can be partitioned into pairs, we can follow a use of append with fail:

```
print_partitions(L) :- append(A, B, L),
                       write(A), write(' '), write(B), nl,
                       fail.
```

The nl predicate prints a newline character. The query print_partitions([a, b, c]) produces the following output:

```
[] [a, b, c]
[a] [b, c]
[a, b] [c]
[a, b, c] []
no
```

In some cases, we may have a generator that produces an unbounded sequence of values. The following, for example, generates all of the natural numbers:

```
natural(1).
natural(N) :- natural(M), N is M+1.
```

We can use this generator in conjunction with a "cut-fail" combination to iterate over the first *n* numbers:

```
my_loop(N) :- natural(I), I =< N,
              write(I), nl,          % loop body (nl prints a newline)
              I = N, !, fail.
```

So long as I is less than N, the equality predicate will fail and backtracking will pursue another alternative for natural. If I = N succeeds, however, then the cut will be executed, committing us to the current (final) choice of I, and terminating the loop.

This programming idiom—an unbounded generator with a test-cut-fail terminator—is known as *generate-and-test*. Like the iterative constructs of Scheme (pages 599–600), it is generally used in conjunction with side effects. One such side effect, clearly, is I/O. Another—modification of the database—is considered in the following subsection.

Prolog provides a variety of I/O features. In addition to `write` and `nl`, which print to the current output file, the `read` predicate can be used to read terms from the current input file. Individual characters are read and written with `get` and `put`. Input and output can be redirected to different files using `see` and `tell`. Finally, the built-in predicates `consult` and `reconsult` can be used to read database clauses from a file, so they don't have to be typed into the interpreter by hand.

The predicate `get` attempts to unify its argument with the next *printable* character of input, skipping over ASCII characters with codes below 32. In effect, it behaves as if it were implemented in terms of the simpler predicates `get0` and `repeat`:

```
get(X) :- repeat, get0(X), X > 32, !.
```

The `get0` predicate attempts to unify its argument with the single next character of input, regardless of value and, like `get`, cannot be resatisfied during backtracking. The `repeat` predicate, by contrast, can succeed an arbitrary number of times; it behaves as if it were implemented with the following pair of rules:

```
repeat.
repeat :- repeat.
```

Within the above definition of `get`, backtracking will return to `repeat` as often as needed to produce a printable character (one with ASCII code greater than 32). In general, `repeat` allows us to turn any predicate with side effects into a generator.

Database Manipulation

Clauses in Prolog are simply collections of terms, connected by the built-in functors `:-` and `,`, both of which can be written in infix form:

```
rainy(rochester).
rainy(seattle).              ≡  (rainy(rochester),
cold(rochester).                   (rainy(seattle),
snowy(X) :- rainy(X), cold(X).         (cold(rochester),
                                          :-(snowy(X), (rainy(X),
                                             cold(X))))))
```

The structural nature of clauses and database contents implies that Prolog, like Scheme, is *homoiconic*: it can represent itself. It can also modify itself. A running Prolog program can add clauses to its database with the built-in predicate `assert`, or remove them with `retract`:

```
?- rainy(X).
X = seattle;
X = rochester;
no
?- assert(rainy(syracuse)).
yes
?- rainy(X).
X = seattle;
X = rochester;
X = syracuse;
no
?- retract(rainy(rochester)).
yes
?- rainy(X).
X = seattle;
X = syracuse;
no
```

Figure 11.7 contains a complete Prolog program for tic-tac-toe. It uses `assert`, `retract`, the cut, `fail`, `repeat`, and `write` to play an entire game.

Individual terms can be created, or their contents extracted, using the built-in predicates `functor`, `arg`, and `=...` The goal `functor(T, F, N)` succeeds if and only if T is a term with functor F and number of arguments N:

```
?- functor(foo(a, b, c), foo, 3).
yes
?- functor(foo(a, b, c), F, N).
F = foo
N = 3
?- functor(T, foo, 3).
T = foo(_10, _37, _24)
```

The goal `arg(N, T, A)` succeeds if and only if its first two arguments (N and T) are instantiated, N is a natural number, T is a term, and A is the Nth argument of T:

```
?- arg(3, foo(a, b, c), A).
A = c
```

Using `functor` and `arg` together, we can create an arbitrary term:

```
?- functor(T, foo, 3), arg(1, T, a), arg(2, T, b), arg(3, T, c).
T = foo(a, b, c)
```

Alternatively, we can use the (infix) `=..` predicate, which "equates" a term with a list:

```
?- T =.. [foo, a, b, c].
T = foo(a, b, c)

?- foo(a, b, c) =.. [F, A1, A2, A3].
F = foo
A1 = a
A2 = b
A3 = c
```

```prolog
ordered_line(1, 2, 3).  ordered_line(4, 5, 6).  ordered_line(7, 8, 9).
ordered_line(1, 4, 7).  ordered_line(2, 5, 8).  ordered_line(3, 6, 9).
ordered_line(1, 5, 9).  ordered_line(3, 5, 7).
line(A, B, C) :- ordered_line(A, B, C).  line(A, B, C) :- ordered_line(A, C, B).
line(A, B, C) :- ordered_line(B, A, C).  line(A, B, C) :- ordered_line(B, C, A).
line(A, B, C) :- ordered_line(C, A, B).  line(A, B, C) :- ordered_line(C, B, A).

full(A) :- x(A).  full(A) :- o(A).  empty(A) :- not(full(A)).
% NB: empty must be called with an already-instantiated A.

same(A, A).  different(A, B) :- not(same(A, B)).

move(A) :- good(A), empty(A), !.

% strategy:
good(A) :- win(A).  good(A) :- block_win(A).  good(A) :- split(A).
good(A) :- strong_build(A).  good(A) :- weak_build(A).
good(5).  good(1).  good(3).  good(7).  good(9).  good(2).  good(4).  good(6).  good(8).

win(A) :- x(B), x(C), line(A, B, C).
block_win(A) :- o(B), o(C), line(A, B, C).
split(A) :- x(B), x(C), different(B, C), line(A, B, D), line(A, C, E), empty(D), empty(E).
strong_build(A) :- x(B), line(A, B, C), empty(C), not(risky(C)).
weak_build(A) :- x(B), line(A, B, C), empty(C), not(double_risky(C)).
risky(A) :- o(D), line(C, D, E), empty(E).
double_risky(C) :- o(D), o(E), different(D, E), line(C, D, F), line(C, E, G),
                   empty(F), empty(G).

all_full :- full(1), full(2), full(3), full(4), full(5),
            full(6), full(7), full(8), full(9).
done :- ordered_line(A, B, C), x(A), x(B), x(C), write('I won.'), nl.
done :- all_full, write('Draw.'), nl.

getmove :- repeat, write('Please enter a move: '), read(X), empty(X), assert(o(X)).
makemove :- move(X), !, assert(x(X)).
makemove :- all_full.

printsquare(N) :- o(N), write(' o ').
printsquare(N) :- x(N), write(' x ').
printsquare(N) :- empty(N), write('   ').
printboard :-
    printsquare(1), printsquare(2), printsquare(3), nl,
    printsquare(4), printsquare(5), printsquare(6), nl,
    printsquare(7), printsquare(8), printsquare(9), nl.
clear :- x(A), retract(x(A)), fail.
clear :- o(A), retract(o(A)), fail.

% main goal:
play :- not(clear), repeat, getmove, respond.
respond :- ordered_line(A, B, C), o(A), o(B), o(C), printboard, write('You won.'), nl.
    % shouldn't ever happen!
respond :- makemove, printboard, done.
```

Figure 11.7 Tic-tac-toe program in Prolog.

Note that

```
?- foo(a, b, c) = F(A1, A2, A3).
```

and

```
?- F(A1, A2, A3) = foo(a, b, c).
```

do not work: the term preceding a left parenthesis must be an atom, not a variable.

Using =.. and call, the programmer can arrange to pursue (attempt to satisfy) a goal created at run-time:

```
param_loop(L, H, F) :- natural(I), I >= L, I =< H,
                       G =.. [F, I], call(G),
                       I = H, !, fail.
```

The goal param_loop(5, 10, write) will produce the following output:

```
5678910
no
```

If we want the numbers on separate lines we can write

```
writeln(X) :- write(X), nl.
...
?- param_loop(5, 10, writeln).
```

Taken together, the predicates described above allow a Prolog program to create and decompose clauses, and to add and subtract them from the database. So far, however, the only mechanism we have for *perusing* the database (i.e., for determining its contents) is the built-in search mechanism. To allow programs to "reason" in more general ways, Prolog provides a clause predicate that attempts to match its two arguments against the head and body of some existing clause in the database:

```
?- clause(snowy(X), B).
X = _19
B = rainy(_19), cold(_19);
no
```

Here we have discovered (by entering a query and requesting further matches with a semicolon) that there is a single rule in the database whose head is a single-argument term with functor snowy. The body of that rule is the conjunction B = rainy(_19), cold(_19), where _19 is the (uninstantiated) argument of the head of the rule.

A clause with no body (a fact) matches the body true:

```
?- clause(rainy(rochester), true).
yes
```

Note that `clause` is quite different from call: it does not attempt to satisfy a goal, simply to match it against an existing clause:

```
?- clause(snowy(rochester)).
no
```

By perusing the database with `clause`, the Prolog programmer can write a meta-circular interpreter (i.e., an implementation of `call`, see Exercise 11.28), or an evaluator that uses a nonstandard search order (e.g., breadth-first or forward-chaining, see Exercise 11.29).

Various other built-in predicates can also be useful in constructing customized search strategies. The `var` predicate takes a single argument; it succeeds as a goal if and only if its argument is an uninstantiated variable. The `atom` and `integer` predicates succeed as goals if and only if their arguments are atoms and integers, respectively. The `name` predicate takes two arguments. It succeeds as a goal if and only if its first argument is an atom and its second is a list composed of the ASCII codes for the characters of that atom.

11.3.2* Theoretical Foundations

Predicate Calculus

In mathematical logic, a *predicate* is a function that maps constants (atoms) or variables to the values true and false. *Predicate calculus* provides a notation and inference rules for constructing and reasoning about *propositions (statements)* composed of predicate applications, *operators*, and the *quantifiers* $\forall$ and $\exists$.[7] Operators include and ($\wedge$), or ($\vee$), not ($\neg$), implication ($\rightarrow$), and equivalence ($\leftrightarrow$). Quantifiers are used to introduce bound variables in an appended proposition, much as λ introduces variables in the lambda calculus. The *universal* quantifier, $\forall$, indicates that the proposition is true for all values of the variable. The *existential* quantifier, $\exists$, indicates that the proposition is true for at least one value of the variable. Here are a few examples:

$$\forall C[\mathsf{rainy}(C) \wedge \mathsf{cold}(C) \rightarrow \mathsf{snowy}(C)]$$

(For all cities C, if C is rainy and C is cold, then C is snowy.)

$$\forall A, \forall B[(\exists C[\mathsf{takes}(A, C) \wedge \mathsf{takes}(B, C)]) \rightarrow \mathsf{classmates}(A, B)]$$

(For all students A and B, if there exists a class C such that A takes C and B takes C, then A and B are classmates.)

$$\forall N[(N > 2) \rightarrow \neg(\exists A, \exists B, \exists C[A^N + B^N = C^N])]$$

(Fermat's last theorem.)

---

7 Strictly speaking, what we are describing here is the *first-order* predicate calculus. There exist higher-order calculi in which predicates can be applied to predicates, not just to atoms and variables. Prolog allows the user to construct higher-order predicates using `call`; the formalization of such predicates is beyond the scope of this book.

One of the interesting characteristics of predicate calculus is that there are many ways to say the same thing. For example,

$$(P_1 \rightarrow P_2) \equiv (\neg P_1 \vee P_2)$$
$$(\neg \exists X[P(X)]) \equiv (\forall X[\neg P(X)])$$
$$\neg(P_1 \wedge P_2) \equiv (\neg P_1 \vee \neg P_2)$$

This flexibility of expression tends to be handy for human beings, but it can be a nuisance for automatic theorem proving. Propositions are much easier to manipulate algorithmically if they are placed in some sort of *normal form*. One popular candidate is known as *clausal form*. We consider this form below.

Clausal Form

As it turns out, clausal form is very closely related to the structure of Prolog programs: once we have a proposition in clausal form, it will be relatively easy to translate it into Prolog. We should note at the outset, however, that the translation is not perfect: there are aspects of predicate calculus that Prolog cannot capture, and there are aspects of Prolog (e.g., its imperative and database-manipulating features) that have no analogues in predicate calculus.

Clocksin and Mellish [CM94, chap. 10] describe a five-step procedure (based heavily on an article by Martin Davis [Dav63]) to translate an arbitrary first-order predicate proposition into clausal form. We trace that procedure here.

In the first step, we eliminate implication and equivalence operators. As a concrete example, the proposition

$$\forall A[\neg \mathsf{student}(A) \rightarrow (\neg \mathsf{dorm\_resident}(A) \wedge \neg \exists B[\mathsf{takes}(A, B) \wedge \mathsf{class}(B)])]$$

would become

$$\forall A[\mathsf{student}(A) \vee (\neg \mathsf{dorm\_resident}(A) \wedge \neg \exists B[\mathsf{takes}(A, B) \wedge \mathsf{class}(B)])]$$

In the second step, we move negation inward, so that the only negated items are individual terms (predicates applied to arguments):

$$\forall A[\mathsf{student}(A) \vee (\neg \mathsf{dorm\_resident}(A) \wedge \forall B[\neg(\mathsf{takes}(A, B) \wedge \mathsf{class}(B))])]$$
$$\equiv \forall A[\mathsf{student}(A) \vee (\neg \mathsf{dorm\_resident}(A) \wedge \forall B[\neg \mathsf{takes}(A, B) \vee \neg \mathsf{class}(B)])]$$

In the third step, we use a technique known as Skolemization (due to logician Thoralf Skolem) to eliminate existential quantifiers. Later in this section we will consider this technique further. Our example has no existential quantifiers at this stage, so we proceed.

In the fourth step, we move all universal quantifiers to the outside of the proposition (in the absence of naming conflicts, this does not change the proposition's meaning). We then adopt the convention that all variables are universally quantified, and drop the explicit quantifiers:

$$\mathsf{student}(A) \vee (\neg \mathsf{dorm\_resident}(A) \wedge (\neg \mathsf{takes}(A, B) \vee \neg \mathsf{class}(B)))$$

Finally, in the fifth step, we use the distributive, associative, and commutative rules of Boolean algebra to convert the proposition to *conjunctive normal form*, in which the operators $\wedge$ and $\vee$ are nested no more than two levels deep, with $\wedge$ on the outside and $\vee$ on the inside:

$$(\text{student}(A) \vee \neg\text{dorm\_resident}(A)) \wedge (\text{student}(A) \vee \neg\text{takes}(A, B) \vee \neg\text{class}(B))$$

Our proposition is now in clausal form. Specifically, it is in conjunctive normal form, with negation only of individual terms, with no existential quantifiers, and with implied universal quantifiers for all variables (i.e., for all names that are neither constants nor predicates). The clauses are the items at the outer level: the things that are and-ed together. To translate the proposition to Prolog, we convert each logical clause to a Prolog fact or rule. Within each clause, we use commutativity to move the negated terms to the right and the nonnegated terms to the left (our example is already in this form). We then note that we can recast the disjunctions as implications:

$$(\text{student}(A) \leftarrow \neg(\neg\text{dorm\_resident}(A)))$$
$$\wedge (\text{student}(A) \leftarrow \neg(\neg\text{takes}(A, B) \vee \neg\text{class}(B)))$$
$$\equiv (\text{student}(A) \leftarrow \text{dorm\_resident}(A))$$
$$\wedge (\text{student}(A) \leftarrow (\text{takes}(A, B) \wedge \text{class}(B)))$$

These are Horn clauses. The translation to Prolog is trivial:

```
student(A) :- dorm_resident(A).
student(A) :- takes(A, B), class(B).
```

Limitations

We claimed at the beginning of Section 11.3 that Horn clauses could be used to capture most, though not all, of first-order predicate calculus. So what is it missing? What can go wrong in the translation? The answer has to do with the number of nonnegated terms in each clause. If a clause has more than one, then if we attempt to cast it as an implication there will be a disjunction on the left-hand side of the $\leftarrow$ symbol, something that isn't allowed in a Horn clause. Similarly, if we end up with no nonnegated terms, then the result is a headless Horn clause, something that Prolog allows only as a query, not as an element of the database.

As an example of a disjunctive head, consider the statement "every living thing is an animal or a plant." In clausal form, we can capture this as

$$\text{animal}(X) \vee \text{plant}(X) \vee \neg\text{living}(X)$$

or equivalently

$$\text{animal}(X) \vee \text{plant}(X) \leftarrow \text{living}(X)$$

Because we are restricted to a single term on the left-hand side of a rule, the closest we can come to this in Prolog is

```
animal(X) :- living(X), not plant(X).
plant(X) :- living(X), not animal(X).
```

But this is not the same, because Prolog's not indicates inability to prove, not falsehood.

As an example of an empty head, consider Fermat's last theorem (page 641). Abstracting out the math, we might write

$$\forall N[\text{big}(N) \rightarrow \neg(\exists A, \exists B, \exists C[\text{works}(A, B, C, N)])]$$

which becomes the following in clausal form:

$$\neg \text{big}(N) \lor \neg \text{works}(A, B, C, N)$$

We can couch this as a Prolog query:

```
?- big(N), works(A, B, C, N).
```

(a query that will never terminate), but we cannot express it as a fact or a rule.

The careful reader may have noticed that facts are entered on the left-hand side of an (implied) Prolog :- sign:

```
rainy(rochester).
```

while queries are entered on the right:

```
?- rainy(rochester).
```

The former means

$$\text{rainy}(\text{rochester}) \leftarrow \text{true}$$

The latter means

$$\text{false} \leftarrow \text{rainy}(\text{rochester})$$

If we apply resolution to these two propositions, we end up with the contradiction

$$\text{false} \leftarrow \text{true}$$

This observation suggests a mechanism for automated theorem proving: if we are given a collection of axioms and we want to prove a theorem, we temporarily add the *negation* of the theorem to the database and then attempt, through a series of resolution operations, to obtain a contradiction.

Skolemization

In our earlier example of students and dorms, we were able to translate a proposition from predicate calculus into clausal form without worrying about existential quantifiers. But what about a statement like this one:

$$\exists X[\text{takes}(X, \text{cs254}) \land \text{class\_year}(X, 2)]$$

(There is at least one sophomore in cs254.) To get rid of the existential quantifier, we can introduce a *Skolem constant* x:

$$\text{takes}(\text{x}, \text{cs254}), \text{class\_year}(\text{x}, 2)$$

The mathematical justification for this change is based on something called the *axiom of choice*; intuitively, we say that if there exists an X that makes the statement true, then we can simply pick one, name it x, and proceed. (If there does not exist an X that makes the statement true, then we can choose some arbitrary x, and the statement will still be false.) It is worth noting that Skolem constants are not necessarily distinct; it is quite possible, for example, for x to name the same student as some other constant y that represents a sophomore in his201.

Sometimes we can replace an existentially quantified variable with an arbitrary constant x. Often, however, we are constrained by some surrounding universal quantifier. Consider the following example:

$$\forall X[\neg\text{dorm\_resident}(X) \lor \exists A[\text{campus\_address\_of}(X, A)]]$$

(Every dorm resident has a campus address.) To get rid of the existential quantifier, we must choose an address for X. Since we don't know who X is (this is a general statement about all dorm residents), we must choose an address that *depends on X*:

$$\forall X[\neg\text{dorm\_resident}(X) \lor \text{campus\_address\_of}(X, \text{f}(X))]$$

Here f is a *Skolem function*. If we used a simple Skolem constant instead, we'd be saying that there exists some single address shared by all dorm residents.

Whether Skolemization results in a clausal form that we can translate into Prolog depends on whether we need to know what the constant is. If we are using predicates `takes` and `class_year`, and we wish to assert as a fact that there is a sophomore in `cs254`, we can write:

```
takes(the_distinguished_sophomore_in_254, cs254).
class_year(the_distinguished_sophomore_in_254, 2).
```

Similarly, we can assert that every dorm resident has a campus address by writing:

```
campus_address_of(X, the_dorm_address_of(X)) :- dorm_resident(X).
```

Now we can search for classes with sophomores in them:

```
sophomore_class(C) :- takes(X, C), class_year(X, 2).
?- sophomore_class(C).
C = cs254
```

and we can search for people with campus addresses:

```
has_campus_address(X) :- campus_address_of(X, Y).
dorm_resident(li_ying).
?- has_campus_address(X).
X = li_ying
```

Unfortunately, we won't be able to identify a sophomore in `cs254` by name, nor will we be able to identify the address of `li_ying`.

11.3.3 Logic Programming in Perspective

In the abstract, logic programming is a very compelling idea: it suggests a model of computing in which we simply list the logical properties of an unknown value, and then the computer figures out how to find it (or tells us it doesn't exist). Unfortunately, the current state of the art falls quite a bit short of the vision, for both theoretical and practical reasons.

Parts of Logic Not Covered

As we have seen in Section 11.3.2, Horn clauses do not capture all of first-order predicate calculus. In particular, they cannot be used to express statements whose clausal form includes a disjunction with more than one nonnegated term. We can sometimes get around this problem in Prolog by using the not predicate, but the semantics are not the same (see the "closed world" subsection below).

Execution Order

While logic is inherently declarative, most logic languages explore the tree of possible resolutions in deterministic order. Prolog provides a variety of predicates, including the cut, fail, and repeat, to control that execution order (Section 11.3.1). It also provides predicates, including assert, retract, and call, to manipulate its database explicitly during execution.

In Section 11.3.1 (page 629), we saw that one must often consider execution order to ensure that a Prolog search will terminate. Even for searches that terminate, naive code can be *very* inefficient. Consider the problem of sorting. A natural declarative way to say that L2 is the sorted version of L1 is to say that L2 is a permutation of L1 and L2 is sorted:

```
declarative_sort(L1, L2) :- permutation(L1, L2), sorted(L2).
permutation([], []).
permutation(L, [H|T]) :- append(P, [H|S], L), append(P, S, W),
    permutation(W, T).
```

(The append and sorted predicates are defined on page 628.) Unfortunately, Prolog's default search strategy will take exponential time to sort a list based on these rules: it will generate permutations until it finds one that is sorted.

To obtain a more efficient sort, the Prolog programmer must adopt a less natural, "imperative" definition:

```
quicksort([], []).
quicksort([A|L1], L2) :- partition(A, L1, P1, S1),
    quicksort(P1, P2), quicksort(S1, S2), append(P2, [A|S2], L2).
partition(A, [], [], []).
partition(A, [H|T], [H|P], S) :- A >= H, partition(A, T, P, S).
partition(A, [H|T], P, [H|S]) :- A =< H, partition(A, T, P, S).
```

Even this sort is less efficient than one might hope in certain cases. When given an already-sorted list, for example, it takes quadratic time, instead of $O(n \log n)$.

A good heuristic for quicksort is to partition the list using the median of the first, middle, and last elements. Unfortunately, Prolog provides no easy way to access the middle and final elements of a list (it has no arrays).

As we saw in Chapter 10, it can be useful to distinguish between the *specification* of a program and its *implementation*. The specification says what the program is to do; the implementation says how it is to do it. Horn clauses provide an excellent notation for specifications. When augmented with search rules (as in Prolog) they allow implementations to be expressed in the same notation.

Some approaches to logic programming attempt to customize the run-time search strategy in a way that is likely to satisfy goals quickly. Darlington [Dar90], for example, describes a technique in which, when an intermediate goal G fails, we try to find alternative instantiations of the variables in G that will allow it to succeed, *before* backing up to previous goals and seeing whether the alternative instantiations will work in them as well. This "failure-directed search" seems to work well for certain classes of problems. Unfortunately, no general technique is known that will automatically discover the best algorithm (or even just a "good" one) for any given problem.

Negation and the "Closed World" Assumption

A collection of Horn clauses, such as the facts and rules of a Prolog database, constitutes a list of things assumed to be true. It does not include any things assumed to be false. This reliance on purely "positive" logic explains why Prolog's not predicate is different from logical negation. Unless the database is assumed to contain *everything* that is true (this is the *closed world assumption*), the goal not T can succeed simply because our current knowledge is insufficient to prove T. Moreover, negation in Prolog occurs *outside* any implicit existential quantifiers on the right-hand side of a rule. Thus

```
?- not takes(X, his201).
```

where X is uninstantiated, means

$$? \quad \neg \exists X[\mathsf{takes}(X, \mathsf{his201})]$$

rather than

$$? \quad \exists X[\neg \mathsf{takes}(X, \mathsf{his201})]$$

If our database indicates that jane_doe takes his201, then the goal takes(X, his201) can succeed, and not takes(X, his201) will fail:

```
?- not takes(X, his201).
no
```

If we had a way of putting the negation inside the quantifier, we might hope for an implementation that would respond

```
?- not takes(X, his201).
X = ajit_chandra
```

or even

```
?- not takes(X, his201).
X != jane_doe
```

A complete characterization of the values of X for which $\neg$takes(X, his201) is true would require a complete exploration of the resolution tree, something that Prolog does only when all goals fail, or when repeatedly prompted with semicolons. Mechanisms to incorporate some sort of "constructive negation" into logic programming are an active topic of research.

It is worth noting that the definition of not in terms of failure means that variable bindings are lost whenever not succeeds. For example

```
?- takes(X, his201).
X = jane_doe
?- not takes(X, his201).
no
?- not not takes(X, his201).
X = _395
```

When takes first succeeds, X is bound to jane_doe. When the inner not fails, the binding is broken. Then when the outer not succeeds, a new binding is created, to an uninstantiated value. Prolog provides no way to pull the binding of X out through the double negation.

11.4 Summary and Concluding Remarks

In this chapter we have focussed on nonimperative models of computing: specifically, on functional and logic languages. Where an imperative program computes principally through iteration and side effects (i.e., the modification of variables), a functional program computes principally through substitution of parameters into functions, and a logic program computes through the resolution of logical statements, driven by the ability to unify variables and terms.

For both functional and logic programming, we considered an example language, a collection of key issues, and an underlying formal model. Our functional language example was Scheme; our logic language example was Prolog. Our discussion of functional programming addressed first-class and higher-order functions, polymorphism, control flow and evaluation order, and support for list-based data. Our discussion of logic programming addressed clauses and terms, resolution and unification, search/execution order, list manipulation, and high-order predicates for inspection and modification of the database.

For imperative programming languages, the underlying formal model is often taken to be a Turing machine. For functional languages, the model is the lambda calculus. Both models evolved in the mathematical community as a means of formalizing the notion of an effective procedure, as used in constructive proofs. Logic programming is also related to proofs, but at a different level: where an imperative or functional program in some sense *is* a proof (of the ability to generate outputs from inputs), a logic program is a set of axioms from which the computer attempts to construct a proof.

Aside from hardware-imposed limits on arithmetic precision, disk and memory space, and so on, the full power of lambda calculus is available in languages such as Scheme, ML, and Haskell. Prolog, on the other hand, provides less than the full generality of resolution theorem proving, in the interests of time and space efficiency. Both functional and logic languages also tend to extend their formal counterparts with additional features, including assignment, I/O, imperative control flow, and higher-order functions and predicates for self-inspection and modification. We noted that both Scheme and Prolog are *homoiconic*: programs look like ordinary data structures, and can be created, modified, and executed on-the-fly. (A few other languages, notably Snobol, are also homoiconic.)

Lists feature prominently in most functional and logic programs, largely because they can easily be built incrementally, without the need to allocate and then modify state as separate operations. Many functional languages provide other structured data types as well. In Sisal, an emphasis on iterative syntax, tail recursive semantics, and high-performance compilers allows multidimensional array-based functional programs to achieve performance comparable to that of imperative programs.

As we stressed in Chapter 1, different models of computing are appealing in different ways. Imperative programs more closely mirror the underlying hardware, and can more easily be "tweaked" for high performance. Purely functional programs avoid the semantic complexity of side effects, and have proven particularly handy for the manipulation of symbolic (nonnumeric) data. Logic programs, with their highly declarative semantics and their emphasis on unification, are well-suited to problems that emphasize relationships and search. At the same time, their de-emphasis of control flow can lead to inefficiency. At the current state of the art, computers have surpassed people in their ability to deal with low-level details (e.g., of instruction scheduling), but people are still better at inventing good algorithms.

As we also stressed in Chapter 1, the borders between language classes are often very fuzzy. The backtracking search of Prolog strongly resembles the execution of generators in Icon. Unification in Prolog resembles (but is more powerful than) the pattern matching capabilities of ML and Haskell. (Unification is also used for type checking in ML and Haskell, but that is a *compile-time* activity.) Formal subroutines and garbage collection are available in many imperative languages, and recursion is available in most.

There is much to be said for programming in a purely functional or logic-based style. While most Scheme and Prolog programs make some use of imperative language features, those features tend to be responsible for a disproportionate share of program bugs. At the same time, there seem to be programming tasks—graphical I/O, for example—that are almost impossible to accomplish without side effects.

11.5 Review Questions

11.1 What mathematical formalism underlies functional programming? Logic programming?

11.2 Briefly describe the behavior of the Lisp/Scheme *read-eval-print* loop.

11.3 What is a *first-class* value?

11.4 What do we mean by the *extent* of a value?

11.5 What is the difference between eq?, eqv?, and equal? in Scheme?

11.6 Describe three ways in which Scheme programs can depart from a purely functional programming model.

11.7 What is an *association list*?

11.8 What does it mean for a language to be *homoiconic*?

11.9 What is an *S-expression*?

11.10 What is the difference between a function and a *special form* in Scheme?

11.11 What is the difference between *normal-order* and *applicative-order* evaluation? What is *lazy* evaluation?

11.12 What does it mean for a function to be *strict*?

11.13 What is *memoization*?

11.14 How can one accommodate I/O in a purely functional programming model?

11.15 What is a *higher-order* function (also known as a *functional form*)?

11.16 What is the difference between *partial* and *total* functions? Why is the difference important?

11.17 What is *currying*? What purpose does it serve in practical programs?

11.18* Define *beta reduction*, *alpha conversion*, and *eta reduction*.

11.19* What is *beta abstraction*?

11.20* State the *Church-Rosser theorem*.

11.21 What is the *trivial update problem* in functional programming?

11.22 What is a *Horn clause*?

11.23 Explain the difference between *facts*, *rules*, and *queries* in Prolog.

11.24 Briefly describe the process of *resolution* in logic programming.

11.25 What is a *unification*? Why is it important in logic programming?

11.26 Describe the difference between *forward chaining* and *backward chaining*.

11.27 Describe the Prolog search strategy. Discuss *backtracking* and the *instantiation* of variables.

11.28 Explain the purpose of the cut (!) in Prolog.

11.29 Describe three ways in which Prolog programs can depart from a pure logic programming model.

11.30 Describe the *generate-and-test* programming idiom.

11.31* Define the notion of *clausal form* in predicate calculus.

11.32* What is *Skolemization*? Explain the difference between Skolem constants and Skolem functions.

11.33 What sorts of logical statements cannot be captured in Horn clauses?

11.34 What is the *closed world assumption*? What problems does it cause for logic programming?

11.35 Summarize the arguments for and against side-effect-free programming.

11.36 Why do both functional and logic languages make such heavy use of lists?

11.6 Exercises

11.1 Is the `define` primitive of Scheme an imperative language feature? Why or why not?

11.2 It is possible to write programs in a purely functional subset of an imperative language such as C, but certain limitations of the language quickly become apparent. What features would need to be added to your favorite imperative language to make it genuinely useful as a functional language? (Hint: what does Scheme have that C lacks?)

11.3 Some authors characterize functional programming as one form of declarative programming. Others characterize functional programming as a separate computational model, co-equal with imperative and declarative programming. Which characterization do you prefer? Why?

11.4 Explain the connection between short-circuit Boolean expressions and normal-order evaluation. Why is cond a special form in Scheme, rather than a function?

11.5 Write a program in your favorite imperative language that has the same input and output as the Scheme program of Section 11.2.1 (DFA simulation). Can you make any general observations about the usefulness of Scheme for symbolic computation, based on your experience?

11.6 Suppose we wish to remove adjacent duplicate elements from a list (e.g., after sorting). The following Scheme function accomplishes this goal:

```
(define unique (lambda (L)
                (cond
                ((null? L) L)
                ((null? (cdr L)) L)
                ((eqv? (car L) (car (cdr L))) (unique (cdr L)))
                (else (cons (car L) (unique (cdr L))))))))
```

Write a similar function that uses the imperative features of Scheme to modify L "in place," rather than building a new list. Compare your function to the code above in terms of brevity, conceptual clarity, and speed.

11.7 Modify the Scheme program of Figure 11.1 to simulate an NFA (nondeterministic finite automaton), rather than a DFA. (The distinction between these automata is described in Section 2.3.) Since you cannot "guess" correctly in the face of a multi-valued transition function, you will need to use explicitly coded Prolog-style backtracking to search for an accepting series of moves (if there is one).

11.8 Consider the problem of determining whether two trees have the same *fringe*: the same set of leaves in the same order, regardless of internal structure. An obvious way to solve this problem is to write a function `flatten` that takes a tree as argument and returns an ordered list of its leaves. Then we can say

```
(define same-fringe (lambda (T1 T2)
    (equal (flatten T1) (flatten T2))))
```

Write a straightforward version of `flatten` in Scheme. How efficient is `same-fringe` when the trees differ in their first few leaves? How would your answer differ in a language such as Haskell, which uses lazy evaluation for all arguments? How hard is it to get Haskell's behavior in Scheme, using `delay` and `force`?

11.9 We have noted that lists in ML are homogeneous, while lists in Lisp/Scheme may contain elements of varying types. Discuss the advantages and disadvantages of homogeneity.

11.10 We can use encapsulation within functions to delay evaluation in ML:

```
datatype 'a delayed_list =
    pair of 'a * 'a delayed_list
    | promise of unit -> 'a * 'a delayed_list;
fun head (pair (h, r)) = h
    | head (promise (f)) = let val (a, b) = f() in a end;
fun rest (pair (h, r)) = r
    | rest (promise (f)) = let val (a, b) = f() in b end;
```

Now given

```
fun next_int (n) = (n, promise (fn () => next_int (n + 1)));
val naturals = promise (fn () => next_int (1));
```

we have

```
head (naturals)                    ⇒ 1
head (rest (naturals))             ⇒ 2
head (rest (rest (naturals)))      ⇒ 3
. . .
```

The delayed list `naturals` is effectively of unlimited length. It will be computed out only as far as actually needed. If a value is needed more than once, however, it will be recomputed every time. Show how to use pointers and assignment (Section 7.7.1, page 389) to memoize the values of a `delayed_list`, so that elements are computed only once.

11.11 At the end of Section 11.2.2 we showed how to implement interactive I/O in terms of the lazy evaluation of streams. Unfortunately, our code would not work as written, because Scheme uses applicative-order evaluation. We can make it work, however, with calls to `delay` and `force`.

Suppose we define `input` to be a function that returns an "istream"—a promise that when forced will yield a pair, the `cdr` of which is an istream:

```
(define input (lambda () (delay (cons (read) (input)))))
```

Now we can define the driver to expect an "ostream"—an empty list or a pair, the `cdr` of which is an ostream:

```
(define driver
  (lambda (s)
    (if (null? s) '()
      (display (car s))
      (driver (force (cdr s)))))))
```

Note the use of `force`.

Show how to write the function `squares` so that it takes an istream as argument and returns an ostream. You should then be able to type `(driver (squares (input)))` and see appropriate behavior.

11.12 Write new versions of `cons`, `car`, and `cdr` that operate on streams. Using them, rewrite the code of the previous exercise to eliminate the calls to `delay` and `force`. Note that the stream version of `cons` will need to avoid evaluating its second argument; you will need to learn how to define macros (derived special forms) in Scheme.

11.13 Write the standard quicksort algorithm in Scheme, without using any imperative language features. Be careful to avoid the trivial update problem; your code should run in expected time $n \log n$.

Rewrite your code using arrays (you will probably need to consult a Scheme manual for further information). Compare the running time and space requirements of your two sorts.

11.14 Write `insert` and `find` routines that manipulate binary search trees in Scheme (consult an algorithms text if you need more information). Explain why the trivial update problem does *not* impact the asymptotic performance of `insert`.

11.15 Write an ML version of the code in Figure 11.1 (page 603). Alternatively (or in addition), solve Exercises 11.7, 11.8, or 11.13 in ML.

11.16* In Figure 11.3 we evaluated our expression in normal order. Did we really have any choice? What would happen if we tried to use applicative order?

11.17* Prove that for any lambda expression f, if the normal-order evaluation of $\mathbf{Y}f$ terminates, where $\mathbf{Y}$ is the fixed-point combinator $\lambda h.(\lambda x.h(xx))$ $(\lambda x.h(xx))$, then $f(\mathbf{Y}f)$ and $\mathbf{Y}f$ will reduce to the same simplest form.

11.18* Given the definition of structures (lists) on page 619, what happens if we apply car or cdr to nil? How might you introduce the notion of "type error" into lambda calculus?

11.19* Let

$$\text{zero} \equiv \lambda x.x$$

$$\text{succ} \equiv \lambda n.(\lambda s.(s \text{ select\_second}) \, n)$$

where select_second $\equiv \lambda x.\lambda y.y$. Now let

$$\text{one} \equiv \text{succ zero}$$

$$\text{two} \equiv \text{succ one}$$

Show that

$$\text{one select\_second} = \text{zero}$$

$$\text{two select\_second select\_second} = \text{zero}$$

In general, show that

$$\text{succ}^n \text{ zero select\_second}^n = \text{zero}$$

Use this result to define a predecessor function pred. You may ignore the issue of the predecessor of zero.

Note that our definitions of T and F allow us to check whether a number is equal to zero:

$$\text{iszero} \equiv \lambda n.(n \text{ select\_first})$$

Using succ, pred, iszero, and if, show how to define plus and times recursively. These definitions could of course be made nonrecursive by means of beta abstraction and **Y**.

11.20 Write a Prolog version of the tree-enumerating Clu program of Figure 6.6 (page 289).

11.21 Restate the following Prolog rule using quantifiers:

```
sibling(X, Y) :- mother(M, X), mother(M, Y),
                 father(F, X), father(F, Y).
```

11.22 Write a gcd definition in Prolog. Does your definition work "backward" as well as forward? (Given integers d and n, can you use it to generate a sequence of integers m such that $\gcd(n, m) = d$?)

11.23 Show that resolution is commutative and associative. Specifically, if A, B, and C are Horn clauses, show that $(A \oplus B) = (B \oplus A)$ and that $((A \oplus B) \oplus C) = (A \oplus (B \oplus C))$, where $\oplus$ indicates resolution. Be sure to think about what happens to variables that are instantiated as a result of unification.

11.24 In the classmates example on page 627, the query ?- classmates (jane_doe, X) will succeed three times: twice with X = jane_doe, and once with X = ajit_chandra. Show how to modify the classmates(X, Y) rule so that a student is not considered a classmate of him or herself.

11.25 Modify the graph example on page 631 so that the goal path(X, Y), for arbitrary already-instantiated X and Y, will succeed no more than once, even if there are multiple paths from X to Y.

11.26 Using only not (no cuts), modify the tic-tac-toe example of Section 11.3.1 (page 632) so it will generate only one candidate move from a given board position. How does your solution compare to the cut-based one (page 636)?

11.27 Write Prolog rules to define a version of the member predicate that will generate all members of a list during backtracking, but without generating duplicates. Note that the cut and not based versions of Section 11.3.1 (page 635) will not suffice; when asked to look for an uninstantiated member, they find only the head of the list.

11.28 Use the clause predicate of Prolog to implement the call predicate (pretend that it isn't built-in). You needn't implement all of the built-in predicates of Prolog; in particular, you may ignore the various imperative control-flow mechanisms and database manipulators. Extend your code by making the database an explicit argument to call, effectively producing a meta-circular interpreter.

11.29 Use the clause predicate of Prolog to write a predicate call_bfs that attempts to satisfy goals breadth-first. (Hint: you will want to keep a queue of yet-to-be-pursued subgoals, each of which is represented by a stack that captures backtracking alternatives.)

11.30 Write a (list-based) *insertion sort* algorithm in Prolog. Here's what it looks like in C, using arrays:

```
void insertion_sort (int A[], int N)
{
    int i, j, t;
    for (i = 1; i < N; i++) {
        t = A[i];
        for (j = i; j > 0; j--) {
            if (t >= A[j-1]) break;
            A[j] = A[j-1];
        }
        A[j] = t;
    }
}
```

11.31 Quicksort works well for large lists, but has higher overhead than insertion sort for short lists. Write a sort algorithm in Prolog that uses quicksort initially, but switches to insertion sort (as defined in the previous exercise) for sublists of fifteen or fewer elements. (Hint: you can count the number of elements during the partition operation.)

11.32   Write a Prolog sorting routine that is guaranteed to take $O(n \log n)$ time in the worst case. (Hint: try *merge sort*; a description can be found in almost any algorithms or data structures text.)

11.33   Consider the following interaction with a Prolog interpreter:

```
?- Y = X, X = foo(X).
Y = foo(foo(foo(foo(foo(foo(foo(foo(foo(foo(
foo(foo(foo(foo(foo(foo(foo(foo(foo(foo(foo(
foo(foo(foo(foo(foo(foo(foo(foo(foo(foo(foo(
foo(foo(foo(foo(foo(foo(foo(foo(foo(foo(foo(
foo(foo(foo(foo(foo(foo(...
```

What is going on here? Why does the interpreter fall into an infinite loop? Can you think of any circumstances (presumably not requiring output) in which a structure such as this one would be useful? If not, can you suggest how a Prolog interpreter might implement checks to forbid its creation? How expensive would those checks be? Would the cost in your opinion be justified?

11.34*   Consider the following statement in predicate calculus:

$$\text{empty\_class}(C) \leftarrow \neg\exists X[\text{takes}(X, C)]$$

Translate this statement to clausal form. Can you translate the statement into Prolog? Does it make a difference whether you're allowed to use `not`? How about the following:

$$\text{takes\_everything}(X) \leftarrow \forall C[\text{takes}(X, C)]$$

Can this be expressed in Prolog?

11.35*   Consider the seemingly contradictory statement

$$\neg\text{foo}(X) \rightarrow \text{foo}(X)$$

Convert this statement to clausal form, and then translate into Prolog. Explain what will happen if you ask

```
?- foo(bar).
```

Now consider the straightforward translation, without the intermediate conversion to clausal form:

```
foo(X) :- not foo(X).
```

Now explain what will happen if you ask

```
?- foo(bar).
```

||.7 **Bibliographic Notes**

Lisp, the original functional programming language, dates from the work of McCarthy and his associates in the late 1950s. Bibliographic references for Lisp, Scheme, ML, Miranda, Haskell, and Sisal can be found in Appendix A. Historically important dialects of Lisp include Lisp 1.5 [MAE+65], MacLisp [Moo78] (no relation to the Apple Macintosh), and Interlisp [TM81].

The book by Abelson and Sussman [AS96], used for introductory programming classes at MIT and elsewhere, is a classic guide to fundamental programming concepts, and to functional programming in particular. Additional historical references can be found in the paper by Hudak [Hud89], which surveys the field from the point of view of Haskell, a pure functional language that draws ideas from ML, Miranda, and several other predecessors.

The lambda calculus was introduced by Church in 1941 [Chu41]. A classic reference is the text of Curry and Feys [CF58]. Barendregt's book [Bar84] is a standard modern reference. Michaelson [Mic89] provides an accessible introduction to the formalism, together with a clear explanation of its relationship to Lisp and ML. Stansifer [Sta95, Sec. 7.6] provides a good informal discussion and correctness proof for the fixed-point combinator **Y** (see Exercise 11.17).

John Backus, one of the original developers of Fortran, argued forcefully for a move to functional programming in his 1977 Turing Award lecture [Bac78]. His functional programming notation is known as FP. Peyton Jones [Pey87, Pey92] and Appel [App97, Chap. 15] discuss the implementation of functional languages. Wadler describes the use of monads [Wad97]. In other articles he relates experience with several "real-world" applications of functional programming [Wad98a], and discusses the remaining barriers to more widespread use of functional languages [Wad98b]. Practical information on lazy functional programming can be found in the frequently asked questions list of the `comp.lang.functional` newsgroup, available on-line at *www.cs.nott.ac.uk/Department/Staff/gmh/faq.html*. There are also newsgroups devoted to ML (*comp.lang.ml*) and Scheme (*comp.lang.scheme*).

Logic programming has its roots in automated theorem proving. Much of the theoretical groundwork was laid by Horn in the early 1950s [Hor51], and by Robinson in the early 1960s [Rob65]. The breakthrough for computing came in the early 1970s, when Colmeraurer and Roussel at the University of Aix–Marseille in France and Kowalski and his colleagues at the University of Edinburgh in Scotland developed the initial version of Prolog. Prolog was originally intended for research in natural language processing, but it soon became apparent that it could serve as a general-purpose language. Several versions of Prolog have since evolved. The one described here is the widely used Edinburgh dialect. The ISO standard [Int95a] is similar.

Several other logic languages have been developed, though none has yet to rival Prolog in popularity. The most widely used is probably OPS5 [BFKM86]. The more recent Gödel [HL94] includes modules, strong typing, a richer variety of logical operators, and enhanced control of execution order. Database query languages stemming from Datalog [Ull85][UW97, Secs. 4.2–4.4] are implemented using forward chaining. CLP (Constraint Logic Programming) and its variants are largely based on Prolog, but employ a more general constraint-satisfaction mechanism in place of unification [JM94]. Extensive on-line resources for logic programming can be found at *www.comlab.ox.ac.uk/archive/logic-prog.html*.

Concurrency

The bulk of this text has focused, implicitly, on *sequential* programs: programs with a single active execution context. As we saw in Chapter 6, sequentiality is fundamental to imperative programming. It also tends to be implicit in declarative programming, partly because practical functional and logic languages usually include some imperative features, and partly because people tend to develop imperative implementations and mental models of declarative programs (applicative order reduction, backward chaining with backtracking), even when language semantics do not require such a model.

By contrast, a program is said to be *concurrent* if it contains more than one active execution context—more than one "thread of control." Concurrency arises for at least three important reasons:

1. To capture the logical structure of a problem. Many programs, particularly servers and graphical applications, must keep track of more than one largely independent "task" at the same time. Often the simplest and most logical way to structure such a program is to represent each task with a separate thread of control. We touched on this "multi-threaded" structure when discussing coroutines (Section 8.6); we will return to it in Section 12.1.2.

2. To cope with independent physical devices. Some software is by necessity concurrent. An operating system may be interrupted by a device at almost any time. It needs one context to represent what it was doing before the interrupt, and another for the interrupt itself. Likewise a system for real-time control (e.g., of a factory, or even an automobile) is likely to include a large number of processors, each connected to a separate machine or device. Each processor has its own thread(s) of control, which must interact with the threads on other processors to accomplish the overall objectives of the system. Message-routing software for the Internet is in some sense a very large concurrent program, running on thousands of servers around the world.

3. To increase performance by running on more than one processor at once. Even when concurrency is not dictated by the structure of a program or the hardware on which it has to run, we can often increase performance by choosing to have more than one processor work on the problem simultaneously. On a large multiprocessor, the resulting parallel speedup can be very large.

Section 12.1 contains a brief overview of the history of concurrent programming. It highlights major advances in parallel hardware and applications, makes the case for multi-threaded programs (even on uniprocessors), and surveys the architectural features of modern multiprocessors. In Section 12.2 we survey the many ways in which parallelism may be expressed in an application. We introduce the message-passing and shared-memory approaches to communication and synchronization, and note that they can be implemented either in an explicitly concurrent programming language or in a library package intended for use with a conventional sequential language. Building on coroutines, we explain how a language or library can create and schedule threads. In the two remaining sections (12.3 and 12.4) we look at shared memory and message passing in detail. Most of the shared-memory section is devoted to synchronization.

12.1 Background and Motivation

Concurrency is not a new idea. Much of the theoretical groundwork for concurrent programming was laid in the 1960s, and Algol 68 includes concurrent programming features. Widespread interest in concurrency is a relatively recent phenomenon however; it stems in part from the availability of low-cost multiprocessors and in part from the proliferation of graphical, multimedia, and web-based applications, all of which are naturally represented by concurrent threads of control.

Concurrency is an issue at many levels of a typical computer system. At the digital logic level, almost everything happens in parallel: signals propagate down thousands of connections at once. At the next level up, the pipelining and superscalar features of modern processors are designed to exploit the *instruction-level* parallelism available in well-scheduled programs. In this chapter we will focus on medium to large scale concurrency, represented by constructs that are semantically visible to the programmer, and that can be exploited by machines with many processors. In Sections 12.1.3 and 12.3.4 we will also mention an intermediate level of parallelism available on special-purpose *vector* processors.

12.1.1 A Little History

The very first computers were single-user machines, used in *stand-alone* mode: people signed up for blocks of time, during which they enjoyed exclusive use of the hardware. Unfortunately, while single-user machines make good economic sense today, they constituted a terrible waste of resources in the late 1940s, when the cheapest computer cost millions of dollars. Rather than allow a machine to sit idle while the user examined output or pondered the source of a bug, computer centers quickly switched to a mode of operation in which users created *jobs* (sequences of programs and their input) off-line (e.g., on a keypunch machine) and then submitted them to an operator for execution. The operator would keep a *batch* of jobs constantly queued up for input on punch cards or magnetic tape. As its final operation, each program would transfer control back to a *resident monitor* program—a form of primitive operating system—which would immediately read the next program into memory for execution, from the current job or the next one, without operator intervention.

Unfortunately, this simple form of batch processing still left the processor idle much of the time, particularly on commercial applications, which tended to read a large number of data records from cards or tape, with comparatively little computation per record. To perform an I/O operation (to write results to a printer or magnetic tape, or to read a new program or input data into memory), the processor in a simple batch system would send a command to the I/O device and then *busy-wait* for completion, repeatedly testing a variable that the device would modify when done with its operation. Given a punch card device capable of reading four cards per second, a 40-kHz vacuum-tube computer would waste 10,000 instructions *per card* while waiting for input. If it performed fewer than 10,000 instructions of computation on average before reading another card, the processor would be idle more than half the time! To make use of the cycles lost to busy-waiting, researchers developed techniques to *overlap* I/O and computation. In particular, they developed *interrupt-driven I/O*, which eliminates the need to busy-wait, and *multiprogramming*, which allows more than one application program to reside in memory at once. Both of these innovations required new hardware support: the former to implement interrupts, the latter to implement memory protection, so that errors in one program could not corrupt the memory of another.

On a multiprogrammed batch system, the operating system keeps track of which programs are waiting for I/O to complete and which are currently *runnable*. To read or write a record, the currently running program transfers control to the operating system. The OS sends a command to the device to start the requested operation, and then transfers control immediately to a different program (assuming one is runnable). When the device completes its operation, it generates an interrupt, which causes the processor to transfer back into the operating system. The OS notes that the earlier program is runnable again. It then chooses a program from among those that are runnable and transfers back to it. The only time the processor is idle is when *all* of the programs that have been loaded into memory are waiting for I/O.

Interrupt-driven I/O introduced concurrency within the operating system. Because an interrupt can happen at an arbitrary time, including when control is already in the operating system, the interrupt handlers and the main bulk of the OS function as concurrent threads of control. If an interrupt occurs while the OS is modifying a data structure (e.g., the list of runnable programs) that may also be used by a handler, then it is possible for the handler to see that data

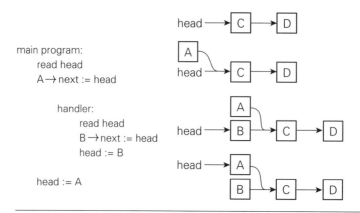

Figure 12.1 **Example of a race condition.** Here the currently running program attempts to insert a new element into the beginning of a list. In the middle of this operation, an interrupt occurs and the interrupt handler attempts to insert a different element into the list. In the absence of synchronization, one of the elements may be lost (unreachable from the head pointer).

structure in an inconsistent state (see Figure 12.1). This problem is an example of a *race condition*: the thread that corresponds to the main body of the OS and the thread that corresponds to the device are "racing" toward points in the code at which they touch some common object, and the behavior of the system depends on which thread gets there first. To ensure correct behavior, we must *synchronize* the actions of the threads: take explicit steps to control the order in which their actions occur. We discuss synchronization further in Section 12.3. It should be noted that not all race conditions are bad: sometimes any of the possible program outcomes are acceptable. The goal of synchronization is to resolve "bad" race conditions: those that might otherwise cause the program to produce incorrect results.

With increases in the size of physical memory, and with the development of virtual memory, it became possible to build systems with an almost arbitrary number of simultaneously loaded programs. Instead of submitting jobs off-line, users could now sit at a terminal and interact with the computer directly. To provide interactive response to keystrokes, however, the OS needed to implement *preemption*. Whereas a batch system switches from one program to another only when the first one blocks for I/O, a preemptive, *timesharing* system switches several times per second as a matter of course. These *context switches* prevent a compute-bound program from hogging the machine for seconds or minutes at a time, denying access to users at keyboards.

By the early 1970s, timesharing systems were relatively common. When augmented with mechanisms to allow data sharing or other forms of communication among currently runnable programs, they introduced concurrency in user-level applications. Shortly thereafter, the emergence of computer networks introduced true parallelism in the form of *distributed* systems: programs running on physically separate machines, and communicating with messages.

Most distributed systems reflect our second rationale for concurrency: they have to be concurrent in order to cope with multiple devices. A few reflect the third rationale: they are distributed in order to exploit the speedup available from multiple processors. Parallel speedup is more commonly pursued on single-chassis multiprocessors, with internal networks designed for very high bandwidth communication. Though multiprocessors have been around since the 1960s, they did not become commonplace until the 1980s.

12.1.2 The Case for Multithreaded Programs

Our first rationale for concurrency—to capture the logical structure of certain applications—has arisen several times in earlier chapters. In Section 7.9.1 we noted that interactive I/O must often interrupt the execution of the current program. In a video game, for example, we must handle keystrokes and mouse or joystick motions while continually updating the image on the screen. By far the most convenient way to structure such a program is to represent the input handlers as concurrent threads of control, which coexist with one or more threads responsible for updating the screen. In Section 8.6, we considered a screen saver program that used coroutines to interleave "sanity checks" on the file system with updates to a moving picture on the screen. We also considered discrete-event simulation, which uses coroutines to represent the active entities of some real-world system.

The semantics of discrete-event simulation require that events occur atomically at fixed points in time. Coroutines provide a natural implementation, because they execute one at a time. In our other examples, however—and indeed in most "naturally concurrent" programs—there is no need for coroutine semantics. By assigning concurrent tasks to threads instead of to coroutines, we acknowledge that those tasks can proceed in parallel if more than one processor is available. We also move responsibility for figuring out which thread should run when from the programmer to the language implementation.

The need for multithreaded programs has become particularly apparent in recent years with the development of web-based applications. In a browser such as Netscape Navigator or Internet Explorer (see Figure 12.2), there are typically many different threads simultaneously active, each of which is likely to communicate with a remote (and possibly very slow) server several times before completing its task. When the user clicks on a link, the browser creates a thread to request the specified document. For all but the tiniest pages, this thread will then receive a long series of message "packets." As these packets begin to arrive the thread must format them for presentation on the screen. The formatting task is akin to typesetting: the thread must access fonts, assemble words, and break the words into lines. For many special tags within the page, the formatting thread will spawn additional threads: one for each image, one for the background if any, one to format each table, possibly more to handle separate frames. Each spawned

```
procedure parse_page (address : url)
    contact server, request page contents
    parse_html_header
    while current_token in { "<p>", "<h1>", "<ul>", ...,
            "<background", "<image", "<table", "<frameset", ... }
        case current_token of
            "<p>"     :  break_paragraph
            "<h1>"    :  format_heading; match ("</h1>")
            "<ul>"    :  format_list; match ("</ul>")
            ...

            "<background" :
                        a : attributes := parse_attributes
                        fork render_background (a)
            "<image"  :  a : attributes := parse_attributes
                        fork render_image (a)
            "<table"  :  a : attributes := parse_attributes
                        scan forward for "</table>" token
                        token_stream s :=...    –– table contents
                        fork format_table (s, a)
            "<frameset" :
                        a : attributes := parse_attributes
                        parse_frame_list (a)
                        match ("</frameset>")

                ...

        ...

procedure parse_frame_list (a1 : attributes)
    while current_token in { "<frame", "<frameset", "<noframes>"}
        case current_token of
            "<frame"  :  a2 : attributes := parse_attributes
                        fork format_frame (a1, a2)

        ...
```

Figure 12.2 Thread-based code from a hypothetical Web browser. To first approximation, the parse_page subroutine is the root of a recursive-descent parser for HTML. In several cases, however, the actions associated with recognition of a construct (background, image, table, frameset) proceed concurrently with continued parsing of the page itself. In this example, concurrent threads are created with the fork operation. Other threads would be created automatically in response to keyboard and mouse events.

thread will communicate with the server to obtain the information it needs (e.g., the contents of an image) for its particular task. The user, meanwhile, can access items in menus to create new browser windows, edit bookmarks, change preferences, and so on, all in "parallel" with the rendering of page elements.

The use of many threads ensures that comparatively fast operations (e.g., display of text) do not wait for slow operations (e.g., display of large images). Whenever one thread *blocks* (waits for a message or I/O), the implementation automatically switches to a different thread. In a *preemptive* thread package, the implementation switches among threads at other times as well, to make sure that none of them hogs the CPU. Any reader who remembers the early, more sequential browsers will appreciate the difference that multithreading makes in perceived performance and responsiveness.

Without language or library support for threads, a browser must either adopt a more sequential structure, or centralize the handling of all delay-inducing events in a single *dispatch loop* (see Figure 12.3).[1] Data structures associated with the dispatch loop keep track of all the *tasks* the browser has yet to complete. The state of a task may be quite complicated. For the high-level task of rendering a page, the state must indicate which packets have been received and which are still outstanding. It must also identify the various subtasks of the page (images, tables, frames, etc.) so that we can find them all and reclaim their state if the user clicks on a "stop" button.

To guarantee good interactive response, we must make sure that no subaction of continue_task takes very long to execute. Clearly we must end the current action whenever we wait for a message. We must also end it whenever we read from a file, since disk operations are slow. Finally, if any task needs to compute for longer than about a tenth of a second (the typical human perceptual threshold), then we must divide the task into pieces, between which we save state and return to the top of the loop. These considerations imply that the condition at the top of the loop must cover the full range of asynchronous events, and that evaluations of the condition must be interleaved with continued execution of any tasks that were subdivided due to lengthy computation. (In practice we would probably need a more sophisticated mechanism than simple interleaving to ensure that neither input-driven nor compute-bound tasks hog more than their share of resources.)

The principal problem with a dispatch loop—beyond the complexity of subdividing tasks and saving state—is that it hides the algorithmic structure of the program. Every distinct task (retrieving a page, rendering an image, walking through nested menus) could be described elegantly with standard control-flow mechanisms, if not for the fact that we must return to the top of the dispatch loop at every delay-inducing operation. In effect, the dispatch loop turns the program "inside out," making the management of tasks explicit and the control flow within tasks implicit. A thread package turns the program "right-side out," making the management of tasks (threads) implicit and the control flow within threads explicit.

With the development of personal computers, much of the history of operating systems has repeated itself. Early PCs performed busy-wait I/O and ran one application at a time. With the development of Microsoft Windows and the

---

I We also saw a simpler example of such a loop in Section 8.6 (page 475).

```
type task_descriptor = record
     −− fields in lieu of thread-local variables, plus control-flow information
     . . .
ready_tasks : queue of task_descriptor
. . .
procedure dispatch
     loop
          −− try to do something input-driven
          if a new event E (message, keystroke, etc.) is available
               if an existing task T is waiting for E
                    continue_task (T, E)
               else if E can be handled quickly, do so
               else
                    allocate and initialize new task T
                    continue_task (T, E)
          −− now do something compute bound
               if ready_tasks is nonempty
                    continue_task (dequeue (ready_tasks), 'ok')

procedure continue_task (T : task, E : event)
     if T is rendering an image
          and E is a message containing the next block of data
               continue_image_render (T, E)
     else if T is formatting a page
          and E is a message containing the next block of data
               continue_page_parse (T, E)
     else if T is formatting a page
          and E is 'ok'        −− we're compute bound
               continue_page_parse (T, E)
     else if T is reading the bookmarks file
          and E is an I/O completion event
               continue_goto_page (T, E)
     else if T is formatting a frame
          and E is a push of the "stop" button
               deallocate T and all tasks dependent upon it
     else if E is the "edit preferences" menu item
          edit_preferences (T, E)
     else if T is already editing preferences
          and E is a newly typed keystroke
               edit_preferences (T, E)
     . . .
```

Figure 12.3 Dispatch loop from a hypothetical non-thread-based Web browser. The clauses in continue_task must cover all possible combinations of task state and triggering event. The code in each clause performs the next coherent unit of work for its task, returning when (1) it must wait for an event, (2) it has consumed a significant amount of compute time, or (3) the task is complete. Prior to returning, respectively, code (1) places the task in a dictionary (used by dispatch) that maps awaited events to the tasks that are waiting for them, (2) enqueues the task in ready_tasks, or (3) deallocates the task.

Multifinder version of the MacOS, PC vendors added the ability to hold more than one program in memory at once, and to switch between them on I/O. Because a PC is a single-user machine, however, the need for preemption was not felt as keenly as in multiuser systems. For a long time it was considered acceptable for the currently running program to hog the processor: after all, that program is what the (single) user wants to run. As PCs became more sophisticated, however, users began to demand concurrent execution of threads such as those in a browser, as well as "background" threads that update windows, check for e-mail, babysit slow printers, and so on. To some extent background computation can be accommodated by requiring every program to "voluntarily" yield control of the processor at well-defined "clean points" in the computation. This sort of "cooperative multiprogramming" was found in Windows 3.1 and MacOS version 7. Unfortunately, some programs do not yield as often as they should, and the inconsistent response of cooperatively multiprogrammed systems grew increasingly annoying to users. Windows 95 added preemption for 32-bit applications. Windows NT and MacOS X add preemption for all programs, running them in separate address spaces so bugs in one program don't damage another, or cause the machine to crash.

12.1.3 Multiprocessor Architecture

Single-chassis parallel computers can be grouped into two broad categories: those in which processors share access to common memory, and those in which they must communicate with messages. Some authors use the term *multicomputer* for message-passing machines, and reserve the term *multiprocessor* only for machines with shared memory. More commonly, *multiprocessor* is used for both classes, with the distinction being made by context or extra adjectives (e.g., *shared-memory multiprocessor*). The distinction between a multicomputer and a mere collection of computers on a network is that the former is more "tightly coupled," generally occupying a single cabinet or collection of cabinets, with fast, physically short interconnections and a common operating system. The distinction is sometimes a judgment call: one can buy fast, physically short interconnects for a collection of workstations, which are then administered as a multicomputer. One can also use a commercial multicomputer (with remote terminals) in place of a workstation network.

Small shared-memory multiprocessors are usually *symmetric*, in the sense that all memory is equally distant from all processors. Large shared-memory multiprocessors usually display a *distributed memory* architecture, in which each memory bank is physically adjacent to a particular processor or small group of processors. Any processor can access the memory of any other, but local memory is faster. The small machines are sometimes called SMPs, for "symmetric multiprocessor." Their large cousins are sometimes called NUMA machines, for "nonuniform memory access."

Since the late 1960s, the market for high-end supercomputers has been dominated by so-called *vector processors*, which provide special instructions capable of applying the same operation to every element of an array. Vector instructions are very easy to pipeline. They are useful in many scientific programs, particularly those in which the programmer has explicitly annotated loops whose iterations can execute concurrently (we will discuss such loops in Sections 12.2.3 and 12.3.4). Given current technological trends, however, it is widely believed that vector processors will be replaced in the next few years by machines built from general-purpose microprocessors. (At the same time, ideas from vector processors have made their way into the microprocessor world, for example in the form of the MMX extensions to the Pentium instruction set.)

From the point of view of a language or library implementor, the principal distinction between a message-based multicomputer and a shared-memory multiprocessor is that communication on the former requires the active participation of processors on both ends of the connection: one to send, the other to receive. On a shared-memory machine, a processor can read and write remote memory without the assistance of a remote processor. In most cases remote reads and writes use the same interface (i.e., load and store instructions) as local reads and writes. A few machines (e.g., the Cray T3E) support shared memory but require a processor to use special instruction sequences to access remote locations.

No matter what the communication model, every parallel computer requires some sort of interconnection network to tie its processors and memories together. Most small, symmetric machines are connected by a bus. A few are connected by a *crossbar* switch, in which every processor has a direct connection to every memory bank, forming a complete bipartite graph. Larger machines can be grouped into two camps: those with *indirect* and *direct* networks. An indirect network resembles a fishing net stretched around the outside of a cylinder (see Figure 12.4). The "knots" in the net are message-routing switches. A direct network has no internal switches: all connections run directly from one node to another. Both indirect and direct networks have many topological variants. Indirect networks are generally designed so that the distance from any node to any other is $O(\log P)$, where P is the total number of nodes. The distance between nodes in a direct network may be as large as $O(\sqrt{P})$. In practice, a hardware technique known as *wormhole routing* makes communication with distant nodes almost as fast as with neighbors.

In any machine built from modern microprocessors, performance depends critically on very fast (low latency) access to memory. To minimize delays, almost all machines depend on caches. On a message-passing machine, each processor caches its own memory. On a shared memory machine, however, caches introduce a serious problem: unless we do something special, a processor that has cached a particular memory location will not see changes that are made to that location by other processors. This problem—how to keep cached copies of a memory location consistent with one another—is known as the *coherence* problem (see Figure 12.5). On bus-based symmetric machines the problem is rel-

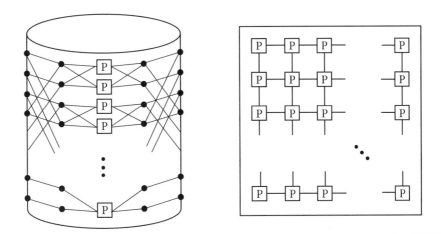

Figure 12.4 Multiprocessor network topology. In an *indirect* network (left), processing nodes are equally distant from one another. They communicate through a log-depth switching network. In a *direct* network (right), there are no switching nodes: each processing node sends messages through a small fixed number of neighbors.

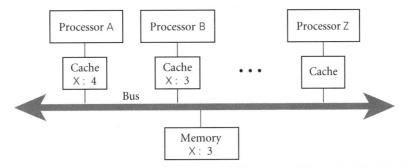

Figure 12.5 The cache coherence problem for shared-memory multiprocessors. Here processors A and B have both read variable X from memory. As a side effect, a copy of X has been created in the cache of each processor. If A now changes X to 4 and B reads X again, how do we ensure that the result is a 4 and not the still-cached 3? Similarly, if Z reads X into its cache, how do we ensure that it obtains the 4 from A's cache instead of the stale 3 from main memory?

atively easy to solve: the broadcast nature of the communication medium allows cache controllers to eavesdrop (*snoop*) on the memory traffic of other processors. When another processor writes a location that is contained in the local cache, the controller can either grab the new value off the bus or, more commonly, *invalidate* the affected cache line, forcing the processor to go back to memory (or to some other processor's cache) the next time the line is needed. Bus-based cache coherence algorithms are now a standard, built-in part of most commercial microprocessors. On large machines, the lack of a broadcast bus makes cache coherence a significantly more difficult problem; commercial implementations are available, but the subject remains an active topic of research.

As of 1999, small bus-based SMPs are available from dozens of manufacturers, with x86, MIPS, Alpha, PowerPC, Sparc, and PA/RISC processors. Larger, cache-coherent shared-memory multiprocessors are available from several manufacturers, including Convex, Sequent, and SGI. The Cray T3E is a large shared-memory multiprocessor *without* cache coherence; remote locations can be accessed directly, but are never cached. IBM's SP-2 is currently the leader among large, message-based multicomputers. The field is very much in flux: several large parallel machines and manufacturers have disappeared from the market in recent years; several more are scheduled to appear in the near future.

12.2 Concurrent Programming Fundamentals

We will use the word "concurrency" to characterize any program in which two or more execution contexts may be active at the same time. Under this definition, coroutines are not concurrent, because only one of them can be active at once. We will use the term "parallelism" to characterize concurrent programs in which execution is actually happening in more than one context at once. True parallelism thus requires parallel hardware. From a semantic point of view, there is no difference between true parallelism and the "quasiparallelism" of a preemptive concurrent system, which switches between execution contexts at unpredictable times: the same programming techniques apply in both situations.

Within a concurrent program, we will refer to an execution context as a *thread*. The threads of a given program are implemented on top of one or more *processes* provided by the operating system. OS designers often distinguish between a *heavyweight* process, which has its own address space, and a collection of *lightweight* processes, which may share an address space. Lightweight processes were added to most variants of Unix in the late 1980s and early 1990s, to accommodate the proliferation of shared-memory multiprocessors. Without lightweight processes, the threads of a concurrent program must run on top of more than one heavyweight process, and the language implementation must ensure that any data that is to be shared among threads is mapped into the address space of all the processes.

We will sometimes use the word *task* to refer to a well-defined unit of work that must be performed by some thread. In one common programming idiom, a collection of threads shares a common "bag of tasks": a list of work to be done. Each thread repeatedly removes a task from the bag, performs it, and goes back for another. Sometimes the work of a task entails adding new tasks to the bag.

Unfortunately, the vocabulary of concurrent programming is not consistent across languages or authors. Several languages call their threads processes. Ada calls them tasks. Several operating systems call lightweight processes threads. The Mach OS, from which OSF Unix is derived, calls the address space shared by lightweight processes a task. A few systems try to avoid ambiguity by coining new words, such as "actors" or "filaments." We will attempt to use the definitions of the preceding two paragraphs consistently, and to identify cases in which the terminology of particular languages or systems differs from this usage.

12.2.1 Communication and Synchronization

In any concurrent programming model, two of the most crucial issues to be addressed are *communication* and *synchronization*. Communication refers to any mechanism that allows one thread to obtain information produced by another. Communication mechanisms for imperative programs are generally based on either *shared memory* or *message passing*. In a shared-memory programming model, some or all of a program's variables are accessible to multiple threads. For a pair of threads to communicate, one of them writes a value to a variable and the other simply reads it. In a message-passing programming model, threads have no common state. For a pair of threads to communicate, one of them must perform an explicit `send` operation to transmit data to another.

Synchronization refers to any mechanism that allows the programmer to control the relative order in which operations occur in different threads. Synchronization is generally implicit in message-passing models: a message must be sent before it can be received. If a thread attempts to receive a message that has not yet been sent, it will wait for the sender to catch up. Synchronization is generally not implicit in shared-memory models: unless we do something special, a "receiving" thread could read the "old" value of a variable, before it has been written by the "sender." In both shared-memory and message-based programs, synchronization can be implemented either by *spinning* (also called *busy-waiting*) or by *blocking*. In busy-wait synchronization, a thread runs a loop in which it keeps re-evaluating some condition until that condition becomes true (e.g., until a message queue becomes nonempty or a shared variable attains a particular value)—presumably as a result of action in some other thread, running on some other processor. Note that busy-waiting makes no sense for synchronizing threads on a uniprocessor: we cannot expect a condition to become true while we are monopolizing a resource (the processor) required to make it true. (A thread on a uniprocessor may sometimes busy-wait for the completion of I/O, but that's a different situation: the I/O device runs in parallel with the processor.)

In blocking synchronization (also called *scheduler-based* synchronization), the waiting thread voluntarily relinquishes its processor to some other thread. Before doing so, it leaves a note in some data structure associated with the synchronization condition. A thread that makes the condition true at some point in the future will find the note and take action to make the blocked thread run again. We will consider synchronization again briefly in Section 12.2.4, and then more thoroughly in Section 12.3.

As noted in Section 12.1.3, the distinction between shared memory and message passing applies not only to languages and libraries but also to computer hardware. It is important to note that the model of communication and synchronization provided by the language or library need not necessarily agree with that of the underlying hardware. It is easy to implement message passing on top of shared-memory hardware. With a little more effort, one can also implement shared memory on top of message-passing hardware. Systems in this latter camp are sometimes referred to as *software distributed shared memory* (S-DSM).

12.2.2 Languages and Libraries

Concurrency can be provided to the programmer in the form of explicitly concurrent languages, compiler-supported extensions to traditional sequential languages, or library packages outside the language proper. The latter two alternatives are by far the most common: the vast majority of parallel programs currently in use are either annotated Fortran for vector machines or C/C++ code with library calls.

Most SMP vendors provide a parallel programming library based on shared memory and threads. Most Unix vendors are converging on the Posix *pthreads* standard [Ope96]. For message-passing hardware, efforts to provide a shared-memory programming model (i.e., via S-DSM) are still considered experimental: most of the library packages for multicomputers and networks provide a message-based programming model. Message-based packages can in turn be grouped into those that are intended primarily for communication among the processes of a single program and those that are intended primarily for communication across program boundaries. Packages in this latter camp usually implement one of the standard Internet protocols [PD96, chap. 6], and bear a strong resemblance to file-based I/O (Section 7.9).

The two most popular packages for message passing within a parallel program are PVM [Sun90, GBD$^+$94] and MPI [BDH$^+$95, SOHL$^+$95]. The two packages provide similar functionality in most respects—enough so that their developers are thinking about merging them [GKP96]. PVM is richer in the area of creating and managing processes on a heterogeneous distributed network, in which machines of different types may join and leave the computation during execution. MPI provides more control over how communication is implemented (to map it onto the primitives of particular high-performance multicomputers), and a richer set of communication primitives, especially for so-called *collective communication*: one-to-all, all-to-one, or all-to-all patterns of messages among a set of threads. Implementations of PVM and MPI are available for C, C++, and Fortran.

For communication based on requests from clients to servers, *remote procedure calls* (RPCs) provide an attractive interface to message passing. Rather than talk to a server directly, an RPC client calls a local *stub* procedure, which packages its parameters into a message, sends them to a server, and waits for a response, which it returns to the client in the form of result parameters. Several vendors provide tools that will generate stubs automatically from a formal description of the server interface. In the Unix world, Sun's RPC [Sri95] is the de facto standard. Several generalizations of RPC, most of them based on binary *components* (page 587), are currently competing for prominence for Internet-based computing.

In comparison to library packages, an explicitly concurrent programming language has the advantage of compiler support. It can make use of syntax other than subroutine calls, and can integrate communication and thread management more tightly with concepts such as type checking, scoping, and exceptions. At the same time, since most programs are sequential, it is difficult for a concurrent language to gain widespread acceptance, particularly if the concurrent features make the sequential case more difficult to understand. As noted in Section 12.1, Algol 68 included concurrent features, though they were never widely used. Concurrency also appears in more recent "mainstream" languages, including Ada, Modula-3, and Java. A little farther afield, but still commercially important, the Occam programming language, based on Hoare's Communicating Sequential Processes (CSP) notation, has an active user community. Occam was the language of choice for systems built from the INMOS transputer processor, widely used in Europe but recently discontinued. Andrews's SR language is widely used in teaching.

In the scientific community, expertise with vectorizing compilers has made its way into *parallelizing* compilers for multicomputers and multiprocessors, again exploiting annotations provided by the programmer. Several of the groups involved with this transition came together in the early 1990s to develop High Performance Fortran (HPF) [KLS$^+$94], a *data-parallel* dialect of Fortran 90. (A data-parallel program is one in which the principal source of parallelism is the application of common operations to the members of a very large data set. A *task-parallel* program is one in which much of the parallelism stems from performing *different* operations concurrently. A data-parallel language is one whose features are designed for data-parallel programs.)

12.2.3 Thread Creation Syntax

One could imagine a concurrent programming system in which a fixed collection of threads was created by the language implementation, but such a static form of concurrency is generally too restrictive. Most concurrent systems allow the programmer to create new threads at run time. Syntactic and semantic details vary considerably from one language or library to another. There are at least six common options: (1) co-begin, (2) parallel loops, (3) launch-at-elaboration, (4) `fork` (with optional `join`), (5) implicit receipt, and (6) early reply. The first two options delimit threads with special control-flow constructs. The others declare threads with syntax resembling (or identical to) subroutines.

The SR programming language provides all six options. Algol 68 and Occam use co-begin. Occam also uses parallel loops, as does HPF. Ada uses both launch-at-elaboration and `fork`. Modula-3 and Java use `fork/join`. Implicit receipt is the usual mechanism in RPC systems. The coroutine `detach` operation of Simula can be considered a form of early reply.

Co-Begin

In Algol 68 the behavior of a `begin...end` block depends on whether the internal expressions are separated by semicolons or commas. In the former case, we have the usual sequential semantics. In the latter case, we have either nondeterministic or concurrent semantics, depending on whether `begin` is preceded by the keyword `par`. The block

```
begin
    a := 3,
    b := 4
end
```

indicates that the assignments to a and b can occur in either order. The block

```
par begin
    a := 3,
    b := 4
end
```

indicates that they can occur in parallel. Of course, parallel execution makes little sense for such trivial operations as assignments; the `par begin` construct is usually used for more interesting operations:

```
par begin                  # concurrent #
    p (a, b, c),
    begin                  # sequential #
        d := q (e, f);
        r (d, g, h)
    end,
    s (i, j)
end
```

Here the executions of p and s can proceed in parallel with the sequential execution of the nested block (with the calls to q and r):

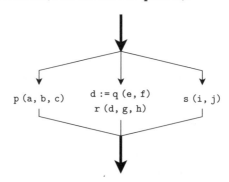

Several other concurrent languages provide a variant of `par begin`. In Occam, which uses indentation to delimit nested control constructs, one would write

```
par
  p (a, b, c)
  seq
    d := q (e, f)
    r (d, g, h)
  s (i, j)
```

In general, a control construct whose constituent statements are meant to be executed concurrently is known as `co-begin`. In an Algol 68 or Occam implementation, threads created by `co-begin` must share access to a common stack frame. To avoid this implementation complication, SR provides a variant of `co-begin` (delimited by `co...oc`) in which the constituent statements must all be procedure invocations.

Parallel loops

Several concurrent languages, including SR, Occam, and some dialects of Fortran, provide a loop whose iterations are to be executed concurrently. In SR one can say

```
co (i := 5 to 10) ->
    p (a, b, i)        # six instances of p, each with a different i
oc
```

In Occam:

```
par i = 5 for 6
  p (a, b, i)          # six instances of p, each with a different i
```

In SR it is the programmer's responsibility to make sure that concurrent execution is safe, in the sense that correctness will never depend on the outcome of race conditions. In the above example, access to global variables in the various instances of p would generally need to be synchronized, to make sure that those instances do not conflict with one another. In Occam, language rules prohibit conflicting accesses. The compiler checks to make sure that a variable that is written by one thread is neither read nor written by any concurrently active thread. In the code above, the Occam compiler would insist that all three parameters to p be passed by value (not result). Concurrently active threads in Occam communicate solely by sending messages.

Several parallel dialects of Fortran have provided parallel loops, with varying semantics. The `forall` loop adopted by HPF has since been incorporated into the 1995 revision of Fortran 90. Like the loops above, it indicates that iterations can proceed in parallel. To resolve race conditions, however, it imposes automatic, internal synchronization on the constituent statements of the loop, each of which must be an assignment statement or a nested `forall` loop. Specifically, all reads of variables in a given assignment statement, in all iterations, must occur before any write to the left-hand side, in any iteration. The writes of the left-hand side in turn must occur before any reads in the following assignment statement. In the following example, the first assignment in the loop will read $n - 1$ elements of B and $n - 1$ elements of C, and then update $n - 1$ elements of A. Subsequently, the second assignment statement will read all n elements of A and then update $n - 1$ of them.

```
forall (i=1:n-1)
    A(i) = B(i) + C(i)
    A(i+1) = A(i) + A(i+1)
end forall
```

Note in particular that all of the updates to A(i) in the first assignment statement occur before any of the reads in the second assignment statement. Moreover in the second assignment statement the update to A(i+1) is *not* seen by the read of A(i) in the "subsequent" iteration: the iterations occur in parallel and each reads the variables on its right-hand side before updating its left-hand side.

For loops that "iterate" over the elements of an array, the `forall` semantics are ideally suited for execution on a vector machine. With a little extra effort, they can also be adapted to a more conventional multiprocessor. In HPF, an extensive set of *data distribution* and *alignment* directives allows the programmer to scatter the elements of an array across the memory associated with a large number of processors. Within a `forall` loop, the computation in a given assignment statement is usually performed by the processor that "owns" the element on the assignment's left-hand side. In many cases an HPF or Fortran 95 compiler can prove that there are no dependences among certain (portions of) constituent statements of a `forall` loop, and can allow them to proceed without actually implementing synchronization.

Launch-At-Elaboration

In Ada and SR (and in many other languages), the code for a thread may be declared with syntax resembling that of a subroutine with no parameters. When the declaration is elaborated, a thread is created to execute the code. In Ada (which calls its threads `tasks`) we may write:

```
procedure P is
    task T is
        . . .
    end T;
begin -- P
    . . .
end P;
```

Task T has its own begin...end block, which it begins to execute as soon as control enters procedure P. If P is recursive, there may be many instances of T at the same time, all of which execute concurrently with each other and with whatever

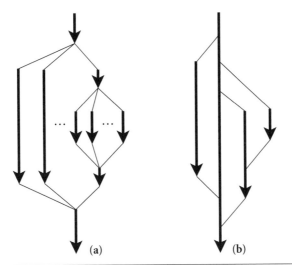

(a)   (b)

Figure 12.6 Lifetime of concurrent threads. With co-begin, parallel loops, or launch-at-elaboration (a), threads are always properly nested. With fork/join (b), more general patterns are possible.

task is executing (the current instance of) P. The main program behaves like an initial default task.

When control reaches the end of procedure P, it will wait for the appropriate instance of T (the one that was created at the beginning of this instance of P) to complete before returning. This rule ensures that the local variables of P (which are visible to T under the usual static scope rules) are never deallocated before T is done with them.

A launch-at-elaboration thread in SR is called a process.

Fork/Join

Co-begin, parallel loops, and launch-at-elaboration all lead to a concurrent control-flow pattern in which thread executions are properly nested (see Figure 12.6a). With parallel loops, each thread executes the same code, using different data; with co-begin and launch-at-elaboration, the code in different threads can be different. Put another way, parallel loops are generally data-parallel; co-begin and launch-at-elaboration are task-parallel.

The fork operation is more general: it makes the creation of threads an explicit, executable operation. The companion join operation allows a thread to wait for the completion of a previously forked thread. Because fork and join are not tied to nested constructs, they can lead to arbitrary patterns of concurrent control flow (Figure 12.6b).

In addition to providing launch-at-elaboration tasks, Ada allows the programmer to define task *types*:

```
task type T is
   ...
begin
   ...
end T;
```

The programmer may then declare variables of type `access T` (pointer to T), and may create new tasks via dynamic allocation:

```
pt : access T := new T;
```

The `new` operation is a `fork`: it creates a new thread and starts it executing. There is no explicit `join` operation in Ada, though parent and child tasks can always synchronize with one another explicitly if desired (e.g., immediately before the child completes its execution). In any scope in which a task type is declared, control will wait automatically at the end of the scope for all dynamically created tasks of that type to terminate. This convention avoids creating dangling references to local variables (Ada stack frames have limited extent).

Modula-3 provides both `fork` and `join`. The `fork` operation returns a reference of type `thread`; the `join` operation takes this reference as parameter:

```
t := Fork (c);
...
Join (t);
```

Each Modula-3 thread begins execution in a specified subroutine. The language designers could have chosen to make this subroutine the argument to `Fork`, but this choice would have forced all `Fork`ed subroutines to accept the same fixed set of parameters, in accordance with strong typing. To avoid this limitation, Modula-3 defines the parameter to `Fork` to be a "thread closure"[2] object (Modula-3 has object-oriented features). The object contains a reference to the thread's initial subroutine, together with any needed start-up arguments. The `Fork` operation calls the specified subroutine, passing a single argument: a reference to the thread closure object itself. The standard thread library defines a thread closure class with nothing in it except the subroutine reference. Programmers can define derived classes that contain additional fields, which the thread's subroutine can then access. There is no comparable mechanism to pass start-up arguments to a task in Ada; information that would be passed as thread closure fields in Modula-3 must be sent to the already-started task in Ada via messages or shared variables.

---

2 Thread closures should not be confused with the closures used for deep binding of subroutine referencing environments, as described in Section 3.4. Modula-3 uses closures in the traditional sense of the word when passing subroutines as parameters, but because its local objects have limited extent (again, see Section 3.4), it does not allow nested subroutines to be returned from functions or assigned into subroutine-valued variables. The subroutine reference in a thread "closure" is therefore guaranteed not to require a special referencing environment; it can be implemented as just a code address.

Threads may be created in SR by sending a message to a proc, which resembles a procedure with a separate forward declaration, called an op. One of the most distinctive characteristics of SR is a remarkably elegant integration of sequential and concurrent constructs, and of message passing and subroutine invocation. An SR procedure is actually defined as syntactic sugar for an op/proc pair that has been limited to call style forks, in which the parent thread waits for the child to complete before continuing execution. As in Ada, there is no explicit join operation in SR, though a parent and child can always synchronize with one another explicitly if desired.

In Java one obtains a thread by constructing an object of some class derived from a predefined class called Thread:

```
class image_renderer extends Thread {
    ...
    public void image_renderer ( args ) {
        -- constructor
    }
    public void run () {
        -- code to be run by the thread
    }
}
...
image_renderer rend = new image_renderer ( constructor_args );
```

Superficially, the use of new resembles the creation of dynamic tasks in Ada. In Java, however, the new thread does *not* begin execution when first created. To start it, the parent (or some other thread) must call the member function (method) named start, which is defined in Thread:

```
rend.start ();
```

Start makes the thread runnable, arranges for it to execute a member function named run, and returns to the caller. The programmer must define an appropriate run method in every class derived from Thread. The run method is meant to be called only by start; programmers should not call it directly, nor should they redefine start. There is also a join method:

```
rend.join ();     // wait for completion
```

Implicit Receipt

The mechanisms described in the last few paragraphs allow a program to create new threads at run time. In each case those threads run in the same address space as the existing threads. In RPC systems it is often desirable to create a new thread automatically in response to an incoming request from some *other* address space. Rather than have an existing thread execute a receive operation, a server can *bind* a communication channel (which may be called a link, socket, or connection) to a local thread body or subroutine. When a request comes in, a new thread springs into existence to handle it.

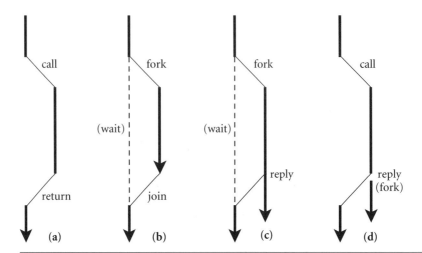

Figure 12.7 Threads, subroutine calls, and early reply. Conventionally, subroutine calls are conceptualized as using a single thread (a). Equivalent functionality can be achieved with separate threads (b). Early reply (c) allows a forked thread to continue execution after "returning" to the caller. To avoid creation of a callee thread in the common case, we can wait until the reply to do the fork (d).

In effect, the `bind` operation grants remote clients the ability to perform a `fork` within the server's address space. In SR the effect of `bind` is achieved by declaring a *capability* variable, initializing it with a reference to a procedure (an `op` for which there is a `proc`), and then sending it in a message to a thread in another address space. The receiving thread can then use that capability in a `send` or `call` operation, just as it would use the name of a local `op`. When it does so, the resulting message has the effect of performing a `fork` in the original address space. In RPC stub systems designed for use with ordinary sequential languages, the creation and management of threads to handle incoming calls is often less than completely automatic; we will consider the alternatives in Section 12.4.4.

Early Reply

The similarity of `fork` and implicit receipt in SR reflects an important duality in the nature of subroutines. We normally think of sequential subroutines in terms of a single thread which saves its current context (its program counter and registers), executes the subroutine, and returns to what it was doing before (Figure 12.7a). The effect is the same, however, if we have two threads: one that executes the caller and another that executes the callee (Figure 12.7b). The caller waits for the callee to *reply* before continuing execution. The call itself is a `fork`/`join` pair, or a `send` and `receive` on a communication channel that has been set up for implicit receipt on the callee's end.

The two ways of thinking about subroutine calls suggest two different implementations, but either can be used to implement the other. In general, a compiler will want to avoid creating a separate thread whenever possible, in order to save time. As noted in the subsection on `fork/join` above, SR uses the two-thread model of subroutine calls. Within a single address space, however, it implements them with the usual subroutine-call mechanism whenever possible. In a similar vein, the Hermes language [SBG+91], which models subroutines in terms of threads and message passing, is able to use the usual subroutine-call implementation in the common case.

If we think of subroutines in terms of separate threads for the caller and callee, there is actually no particular reason why the callee should have to complete execution before it allows the caller to proceed: all it really has to do is complete the portion of its work on which result parameters depend. *Early reply* is a mechanism that allows a callee to return those results to the caller without terminating. After an early reply, the caller and callee continue execution concurrently (Figure 12.7c).

If we think of subroutines in terms of a single thread for the caller and callee, then early reply can also be seen as a means of creating new threads. When the thread executing a subroutine performs an early reply, it splits itself into a pair of threads: one of these returns, the other continues execution in the callee (Figure 12.7d). In SR, any subroutine can execute an early reply operation:

```
reply
```

For calls within a single address space, the SR compiler waits until the `reply` before creating a new thread; a subroutine that returns without `reply`ing uses a single implementation thread for the caller and callee. Until the time of the `reply`, the stack frame of the subroutine belongs to the calling thread. To allow it to become the initial frame of a newly created thread, an SR implementation can employ a memory management scheme in which stack frames are allocated dynamically from the heap and linked together with pointers. Alternatively, the implementation can copy the current frame into the bottom of a newly allocated stack at the time of the reply. A fully general cactus stack (as described in Section 8.6.1) is not required in SR: every thread is created in its own subroutine, and subroutines do not nest. Early reply resembles the coroutine `detach` operation of Simula. It also appears in Lynx [Sco91].

Much of the motivation for early reply comes from applications in which the parent of a newly created thread needs to ensure that the thread has been initialized properly before it (the parent) continues execution. In a web browser, for example, the thread responsible for formatting a page will create a new child for each in-line image. The child will contact the appropriate server and begin to transfer data. The first thing the server will send is an indication of the image's size. The page-formatting thread (the parent of the image-rendering thread) needs to know this size in order to place text and other images properly on the page. Early reply allows the parent to create the child and then wait for it to reply with size information, at which point the parent and child can proceed in parallel. (We ignored this issue in Figure 12.2.)

In Java, a similar purpose is served by separating thread creation from invocation of the `start` method. In our browser example, a page-formatting thread that creates a child to render an image could call a `get_size` method of the child *before* it calls the child's `start` method. `Get_size` would make the initial contact with the server and return size information to the parent. Because `get_size` is a function member of the child, any data it initializes, including the size and connection-to-server information, will be stored in the thread's data members, where they will be available to the thread's `run` method.

12.2.4 Implementation of Threads

As we noted in Section 12.2, the threads of a concurrent program are usually implemented on top of one or more *processes* provided by the operating system. At one extreme, we could use a separate OS process for every thread; at the other extreme we could multiplex all of a program's threads on top of a single process. On a personal computer with a single address space and relatively inexpensive processes, the one-process-per-thread extreme is often acceptable. In a simple language on a uniprocessor, the all-threads-on-one-process extreme may be acceptable. Commonly, language implementations adopt an in-between approach, with a potentially large number of threads running on top of a smaller number of processes (see Figure 12.8).

The problem with putting every thread on a separate process is that processes (even "lightweight" ones) are simply too expensive in many operating systems. Because they are implemented in the kernel, performing any operation on them requires a system call. Because they are general-purpose, they provide features that most languages do not need, but have to pay for anyway. (Examples include separate address spaces, priorities, accounting information, and signal and I/O interfaces, all of which are beyond the scope of this book.) At the other extreme, there are two problems with putting all threads on top of a single process: first, it precludes parallel execution on a multiprocessor; second, if the currently running thread makes a system call that blocks (e.g., waiting for I/O), then none of the program's other threads can run, because the single process is suspended by the OS.

In the common two-level organization of concurrency (user-level threads on top of kernel-level processes), similar code appears at both levels of the system: the language run-time system implements threads on top of one or more processes in much the same way that the operating system implements processes on top of one or more physical processors. A multiprocessor operating system may attempt to ensure that processes belonging to the same application run on separate processors simultaneously, in order to minimize synchronization delays (this technique is called *coscheduling*, or *gang scheduling*). Alternatively, it may give an application exclusive use of some subset of the processors (this technique

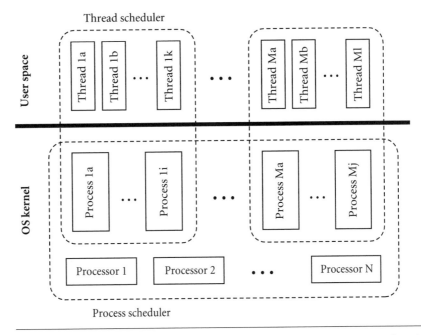

Figure 12.8 **Two-level implementation of threads.** A thread scheduler, implemented in a library or language run-time package, multiplexes threads on top of one or more kernel-level processes, just as the process scheduler, implemented in the operating system kernel, multiplexes processes on top of one or more physical processors.

is called *space sharing*, or *processor partitioning*). Such kernel-level issues are beyond the scope of this book; we concentrate here on user-level threads.

Typically, user-level threads are built on top of coroutines (Section 8.6). Recall that coroutines are a sequential control-flow mechanism, designed for implementation on top of a single OS process. The programmer can suspend the current coroutine and resume a specific alternative by calling the `transfer` operation. The argument to `transfer` is typically a pointer to the context block of the coroutine.

To turn coroutines into threads, we can proceed in a series of three steps. First, we hide the argument to `transfer` by implementing a *scheduler* that chooses which thread to run next when the current thread yields the processor. Second, we implement a *preemption* mechanism that suspends the current thread automatically on a regular basis, giving other threads a chance to run. Third, we allow the data structures that describe our collection of threads to be shared by more than one OS process, possibly on separate processors, so that threads can run on any of the processes.

Uniprocessor Scheduling

Figure 12.9 illustrates the data structures employed by a simple scheduler. At any

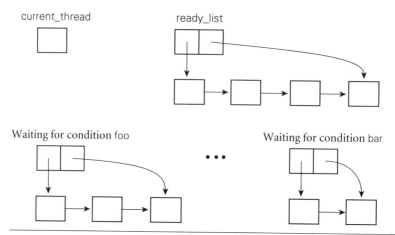

Figure 12.9 Data structures of a simple scheduler. A designated `current_thread` is running. Threads on the ready list are runnable. Other threads are blocked, waiting for various conditions to become true. If threads run on top of more than one OS-level process, each such process will have its own `current_thread` variable. If a thread makes a call into the operating system, its process may block in the kernel.

particular time, a thread is either *blocked* (i.e., for synchronization) or *runnable*. A runnable thread may actually be running on some processor or it may be awaiting its chance to do so. Context blocks for threads that are runnable but not currently running reside on a queue called the *ready list*. Context blocks for threads that are blocked for scheduler-based synchronization reside in data structures (usually queues) associated with the conditions for which they are waiting. To yield the processor to another thread, a running thread calls the scheduler:

```
procedure reschedule
    t : thread := dequeue (ready_list)
    transfer (t)
```

Before calling into the scheduler, a thread that wants to run again at some point in the future must place its own context block in some appropriate data structure. If it is blocking for the sake of fairness—to give some other thread a chance to run—then it enqueues its context block on the ready list:

```
procedure yield
    enqueue (ready_list, current_thread)
    reschedule
```

To block for synchronization, a thread adds itself to a queue associated with the awaited condition:

```
procedure sleep_on (ref Q : queue of thread)
    enqueue (Q, current_thread)
    reschedule
```

When a running thread performs an operation that makes a condition true, it removes one or more threads from the associated queue and enqueues them on the ready list.

Fairness becomes an issue whenever a thread may run for a significant amount of time while other threads are runnable. To give the illusion of concurrent activity, even on a uniprocessor, we need to make sure that each thread gets a frequent "slice" of the processor. With *cooperative multi-threading*, any long-running thread must yield the processor explicitly from time to time (e.g., at the tops of loops), to allow other threads to run. As noted in Section 12.1.2, this approach allows one improperly written thread to monopolize the system. Even with properly written threads, it leads to less than perfect fairness due to nonuniform times between `yields` in different threads.

Preemption

Ideally, we should like to multiplex the processor fairly and at a relatively fine grain (i.e., many times per second) *without* requiring that threads call `yield` explicitly. On many systems we can do this in the language implementation by using timer signals for *preemptive multithreading*. When switching between threads we ask the operating system (which has access to the hardware clock) to deliver a signal to the currently running process at a specified time in the future. The OS delivers the signal by saving the context (registers and `pc`) of the process at the top of the current stack and transferring control to a previously specified *handler* routine in the language run-time system. When called, the handler modifies the state of the currently running thread to make it appear that the thread had just executed a call to the standard `yield` routine. The handler then "returns" into `yield`, which transfers control to some other thread, as if the one that had been running had relinquished control of the process voluntarily.

Unfortunately, the fact that a signal may arrive at an arbitrary time introduces a race between voluntary calls to the scheduler and the automatic calls triggered by preemption. To illustrate the problem, suppose that a signal arrives when the currently running process has just enqueued the currently running thread onto the ready list in `yield`, and is about to call `reschedule`. When the signal handler "returns" into `yield`, the process will put the current thread into the ready list a second time. If at some point in the future the thread blocks for synchronization, its second entry in the ready list may cause it to run again immediately, when it should be waiting. Even worse problems can arise if a signal occurs in the middle of an `enqueue`, at a moment when the ready list is not even a properly structured queue. To resolve the race and avoid corruption of the ready list, thread packages commonly disable signal delivery during scheduler calls:

```
procedure yield
    disable_signals
    enqueue (ready_list, current_thread)
    reschedule
    reenable_signals
```

For this convention to work, *every* fragment of code that calls `reschedule` must disable signals prior to the call, and must re-enable them afterward. Because `reschedule` contains a call to `transfer`, signals may be disabled in one thread and re-enabled in another.

It turns out that the `sleep_on` routine must also assume that signals are disabled and enabled by the caller. To see why, suppose that a thread checks a condition, finds that it is false, and then calls `sleep_on` to suspend itself on a queue associated with the condition. Suppose further that a timer signal occurs immediately after checking the condition, but before the call to `sleep_on`. Finally, suppose that the thread is allowed to run after the signal makes the condition true. Since the first thread never got a chance to put itself on the condition queue, the second thread will not find it to make it runnable. When the first thread runs again, it will immediately suspend itself, and may never be awakened. To close this *timing window*—this internal in which a concurrent event may compromise program correctness—the caller must ensure that signals are disabled before checking the condition:

```
disable_signals
if not desired_condition
    sleep_on (condition_queue)
reenable_signals
```

On a uniprocessor, disabling signals allows the check and the sleep to occur as a single, *atomic* operation: they always appear to happen "all at once" from the point of view of other threads.

Multiprocessor Scheduling

A few concurrent languages (e.g., Distributed Processes [Bri78] and Lynx [Sco91]) are explicitly nonparallel: language semantics guarantee that only one thread will run in a given address space at a time, with switches among threads occurring only at well-defined points in the code. Most concurrent languages, however, permit threads to run in parallel. As we noted in Section 12.2, there is no difference from the programmer's point of view between true parallelism (on multiple processors) and the "quasiparallelism" of a system that switches between threads on timer interrupts: in both cases, threads must synchronize explicitly to cope with race conditions in the application program.

We can extend our preemptive thread package to run on top of more than one OS-provided process by arranging for the processes to share the ready list and related data structures (condition queues, etc.; note that each process must have a *separate* current_thread variable). If the processes run on different processors of a shared-memory multiprocessor, then more than one thread will be able to run at once. If the processes share a single processor, then the program will be able to make forward progress even when all but one of the processes are blocked in the operating system. Any thread that is runnable is placed in the ready list, where it becomes a candidate for execution by any of the application's processes. When a process calls reschedule, the queue-based ready list we have been using in our examples will give it the longest-waiting thread. The ready list of a more elaborate scheduler might give priority to interactive or time-critical threads, or to threads that last ran on the current processor, and may therefore still have data in the cache.

Just as preemption introduced a race between voluntary and automatic calls to scheduler operations, true or quasiparallelism introduces races between calls in separate OS processes. To resolve the races, we must implement additional synchronization to make scheduler operations in separate processes atomic. We will return to this subject in Section 12.3.2.

12.3 Shared Memory

As noted in Section 12.2.1, synchronization is the principal semantic challenge for shared-memory concurrent programs. One commonly sees two forms of synchronization: *mutual exclusion* and *condition synchronization*. Mutual exclusion ensures that only one thread is executing a *critical section* of code at a given point in time. Condition synchronization ensures that a given thread does not proceed until some specific condition holds (e.g., until a given variable has a given value). It is tempting to think of mutual exclusion as a form of condition synchronization (don't proceed until no other thread is in its critical section), but this sort of condition would require *consensus* among all extant threads, something that condition synchronization doesn't generally provide.

Our implementation of parallel threads, sketched at the end of Section 12.2.4, requires that *processes* (provided by the OS) use both mutual exclusion and condition synchronization to protect the ready list and related data structures. Mutual exclusion appears in the requirement that a process must never read or write the ready list while it is being modified by another process; condition synchronization appears in the requirement that a process in need of a thread to run must wait until the ready list is nonempty.

It is worth emphasizing that we do not in general want to overly synchronize programs. To do so would eliminate opportunities for parallelism, which we generally want to maximize in the interest of performance. The goal is to provide only as much synchronization as is necessary in order to eliminate "bad" race conditions: those that might otherwise cause the program to produce incorrect results.

In the first of the three subsections below we consider busy-wait synchronization mechanisms. In the second subsection we use busy-waiting among processes to implement a parallelism-safe thread scheduler. In the final subsection we use the scheduler to implement blocking synchronization for threads.

12.3.1 Busy-Wait Synchronization

Busy-wait condition synchronization is generally easy: if we can cast a condition in the form of "location X contains value Y," then a thread (or process) that needs to wait for the condition can simply read X in a loop, waiting for Y to appear. All that is required from the hardware is that individual load and store instructions be atomic. Providing this atomicity is not a trivial task (memory and/or busses must serialize concurrent accesses by processors and devices), but almost every computer ever made has done it.

Busy-wait mutual exclusion is harder. We consider it under Spin Locks below. We then consider a special form of condition synchronization, namely barriers. A barrier is meant to be executed by all of the threads in a program. It guarantees that no thread will continue past a given point in a program until all threads have reached that point. Like mutual exclusion (and unlike most condition synchronization), barriers require consensus among all extant threads. Barriers are fundamental to data-parallel computing. They can be implemented either with busy-waiting or with blocking; we consider the busy-wait version here.

Spin Locks

Dekker is generally credited with finding the first two-thread mutual exclusion algorithm that requires no atomic instructions other than load and store. Dijkstra [Dij65] published a version that works for n threads in 1965. Peterson [Pet81] published a much simpler two-thread algorithm in 1981. Building on Peterson's algorithm, one can construct a hierarchical n-thread lock, but it requires $O(n \log n)$ space and $O(\log n)$ time to get one thread into its critical Section [YA93]. Lamport [Lam87] published an n-thread algorithm in 1987 that takes $O(n)$ space and $O(1)$ time in the absence of competition for the lock. Unfortunately, it requires $O(n)$ time when multiple threads attempt to enter their critical section at once.

To achieve mutual exclusion in constant time, one needs a more powerful atomic instruction. Beginning in the 1960s, hardware designers began to equip their processors with instructions that read, modify, and write a memory location as a single atomic operation. The simplest read-modify-write instruction is known as `test_and_set`. It sets a Boolean variable to `true` and returns an indication of whether the variable was `false` previously. Given `test_and_set`, acquiring a spin lock is almost trivial:

```
type lock = Boolean := false;

procedure acquire_lock (ref L : lock)
    while not test_and_set (L)
        while L
            -- nothing -- spin
procedure release_lock (ref L : lock)
    L := false
```

Figure 12.10 A simple test-and-test_and_set lock. Waiting processes spin with ordinary read (load) instructions until the lock appears to be free, then use test_and_set to acquire it. The very first access is a test_and_set, for speed in the common (no competition) case.

```
while not test_and_set (L)
    -- nothing -- spin
```

In practice, embedding test_and_set in a loop tends to result in unacceptable amounts of bus traffic on a multiprocessor, as the cache coherence mechanism attempts to reconcile writes by multiple processors attempting to acquire the lock. This overdemand for hardware resources is known as *contention*, and is a major obstacle to good performance on large machines.

To reduce contention, the writers of synchronization libraries often employ a test-and-test_and_set lock, which spins with ordinary reads (satisfied by the cache) until it appears that the lock is free (see Figure 12.10). When a thread releases a lock there still tends to be a flurry of bus activity as waiting threads perform their test_and_sets, but at least this activity happens only at the boundaries of critical sections. On a large machine, bus or interconnect traffic can be further reduced by implementing a *backoff* strategy, in which a thread that is unsuccessful in attempting to acquire a lock waits for a while before trying again.

Many processors provide atomic instructions more powerful than test_and_set. Several can swap the contents of a register and a memory location atomically. A few can add a constant to a memory location atomically, returning the previous value. On the x86, most arithmetic instructions can be prefaced with a "lock" byte that causes them to update a memory location atomically. Recent versions of the MIPS, Alpha, and PowerPC architectures have converged on a pair of instructions called load_linked and store_conditional (LL/SC). The first of these instructions loads a memory location into a register and stores certain bookkeeping information into hidden processor registers. The second instruction stores the register back into the memory location, but only if the location has not been modified by any other processor since the load_linked was executed. In the time between the two instructions the processor is generally not allowed to touch memory, but it can perform an almost arbitrary computation in registers, allowing the LL/SC pair to function as a *universal* atomic primitive.

To add the value in register `r2` to memory location `foo`, atomically, one would execute the following instructions:

```
start:
    r1 := load_linked (foo)
    r1 := r1 + r2
    store_conditional (r1, foo)
    if failed goto start
```

If several processors execute this code simultaneously, one of them is guaranteed to succeed the first time around the loop. The others will fail and try again.

Using instructions such as `atomic_add` or LL/SC, one can build spin locks that are *fair*, in the sense that threads are guaranteed to acquire the lock in the order in which they first attempt to do so. One can also build locks that work well—with no contention—on arbitrarily large machines [MCS91]. Finally, one can use universal atomic primitives to build special-purpose concurrent data structures and algorithms that operate *without* locks, by modifying locations atomically in a carefully determined order. Lock-free concurrent algorithms are ideal for environments in which threads may pause (e.g., due to preemption) for arbitrary periods of time. In important special cases (e.g., parallel garbage collection [HM92] or queues [MS96]) lock-free algorithms can also be significantly faster than lock-based algorithms. Herlihy [Her91] and others have developed general-purpose techniques to turn sequential data structures into lock-free concurrent data structures, but these tend to be rather slow.

An important variant on mutual exclusion is the *reader–writer lock* [CHP71]. Reader–writer locks recognize that if several threads wish to *read* the same data structure, they can do so simultaneously without mutual interference. It is only when a thread wants to *write* the data structure that we need to prevent other threads from reading or writing simultaneously. Most busy-wait mutual exclusion locks can be extended to allow concurrent access by readers (see Exercise 12.8).

Barriers

Barriers are common in data-parallel numeric algorithms. In *finite element analysis*, for example, a physical object such as, say, a bridge may be modeled as an enormous collection of tiny metal fragments. Each fragment imparts forces to the fragments adjacent to it. Gravity exerts a downward force on all fragments. Abutments exert an upward force on the fragments that make up base plates. The wind exerts forces on surface fragments. To evaluate stress on the bridge as a whole (e.g., to assess its stability and resistance to failures), a finite element program might divide the metal fragments among a large collection of threads (probably one per physical processor). Beginning with the external forces, the program would then proceed through a sequence of iterations. In each iteration each thread would recompute the forces on its fragments based on the forces

```
shared count : integer := n
shared sense : Boolean := true
per-thread private local_sense : Boolean := true

procedure central_barrier
     local_sense := not local_sense
          –– each thread toggles its own sense
     if fetch_and_decrement (count) = 1
          –– last arriving thread
          count := n                    –– reinitialize for next iteration
          sense := local_sense          –– allow other threads to proceed
     else
          repeat
               –– spin
          until sense = local_sense
```

Figure 12.11 **A simple "sense-reversing" barrier.** Each thread has its own copy of local_sense. Threads share a single copy of count and sense.

found in the previous iteration. Between iterations, the threads would synchronize with a barrier. The program would halt when no thread found a significant change in any forces during the last iteration.

The simplest way to implement a busy-wait barrier is to use a globally shared counter, modified by an atomic `fetch_and_decrement` instruction (or equivalently by `fetch_and_add`, LL/SC, etc.). The counter begins at n, the number of threads in the program. As each thread reaches the barrier it decrements the counter. If it is not the last to arrive, the thread then spins on a Boolean flag. The final thread (the one that changes the counter from 1 to 0) flips the Boolean flag, allowing the other threads to proceed. To make it easy to reuse the barrier data structures in successive iterations (known as barrier *episodes*), threads wait for alternating values of the flag each time through. Code for this simple barrier appears in Figure 12.11.

Like a simple spin lock, the "sense-reversing" barrier can lead to unacceptable levels of contention on large machines. Moreover the serialization of access to the counter implies that the time to achieve an n-thread barrier is $O(n)$. It is possible to do better, but even the fastest software barriers require $O(\log n)$ time to synchronize n threads [MCS91]. Several large multiprocessors, including the Thinking Machines CM-5 and the Cray Research T3D and T3E have provided special hardware for near-constant-time busy-wait barriers.

12.3.2 **Scheduler Implementation**

To implement user-level threads, OS-level processes must synchronize access to the ready list and condition queues, generally by means of spinning. Code for a simple *reentrant* thread scheduler (one that can be "reentered" safely by a second process before the first one has returned) appears in Figure 12.12. As in the code in Section 12.2.4, we disable timer signals before entering scheduler code, to protect the ready list and condition queues from concurrent access by a process and its own signal handler.

Our code assumes a single "low-level" lock (`scheduler_lock`) that protects the entire scheduler. Before saving its context block on a queue (e.g., in `yield` or `sleep_on`), a thread must acquire the scheduler lock. It must then release the lock after returning from `reschedule`. Of course, because `reschedule` calls `transfer`, the lock will usually be acquired by one thread (the same one that disables timer signals) and released by another (the same one that reenables timer signals). The code for `yield` can implement synchronization itself, because its work is self-contained. The code for `sleep_on`, on the other hand, cannot, because a thread must generally check a condition and block if necessary as a single atomic operation:

```
disable_signals
acquire_lock (scheduler_lock)
if not desired_condition
    sleep_on (condition_queue)
release_lock (scheduler_lock)
reenable_signals
```

If the signal and lock operations were moved inside of `sleep_on`, the following race could arise: thread *A* checks the condition and finds it to be false; thread *B* makes the condition true, but finds the condition queue to be empty; thread *A* sleeps on the condition queue forever.

A spin lock will suffice for the "low-level" lock that protects the ready list and condition queues, so long as every process runs on a different processor. As we noted in Section 12.2.1, however, it makes little sense to spin for a condition that can only be made true by some other process using the processor on which we are spinning. If we know that we're running on a uniprocessor, then we don't need a lock on the scheduler (just the disabled signals). If we *might* be running on a uniprocessor, however, or on a multiprocessor with fewer processors than processes, then we must be prepared to give up the processor if unable to obtain a lock. The easiest way to do this is with a "spin-then-yield" lock, first suggested by Ousterhout [Ous82]. A simple example of such a lock appears in Figure 12.13. On a multiprogrammed machine, it might also be desirable to relinquish the processor inside `reschedule` when the ready list is empty: though no other process of the current application will be able to do anything, overall system

```
shared scheduler_lock : low_level_lock
shared ready_list : queue of thread
per-process private current_thread : thread

procedure reschedule
        −− assume that scheduler_lock is already held
        −− and that timer signals are disabled
        t : thread
        loop
            t := dequeue (ready_list)
            if t <> nil
                exit
            −− else wait for a thread to become runnable
            release_lock (scheduler_lock)
            −− window allows another thread to access ready_list
            −− (no point in reenabling signals;
            −− we're already trying to switch to a different thread)
            acquire_lock (scheduler_lock)
        transfer (t)
        −− caller must release scheduler_lock
        −− and reenable timer signals after we return

procedure yield
        disable_signals
        acquire_lock (scheduler_lock)
        enqueue (ready_list, current_thread)
        reschedule
        release_lock (scheduler_lock)
        reenable_signals

procedure sleep_on (ref Q : queue of thread)
        −− assume that caller has already disabled timer signals
        −− and acquired scheduler_lock, and will reverse
        −− these actions when we return
        enqueue (Q, current_thread)
        reschedule
```

Figure 12.12 Pseudocode for part of a simple reentrant (parallelism-safe) scheduler. Every process has its own copy of `current_thread`. There is a single shared `scheduler_lock` and a single `ready_list`. If processes have dedicated processors, then the `low_level_lock` can be an ordinary spin lock; otherwise it can be a "spin-then-yield" lock (Figure 12.13). The loop inside `reschedule` busy-waits until the ready list is nonempty. The code for `sleep_on` cannot disable timer signals and acquire the scheduler lock itself, because the caller needs to test a condition and then block as a single atomic operation.

```
type lock = Boolean := false;

procedure acquire_lock (ref L : lock)
    while not test_and_set (L)
        count := TIMEOUT
        while L
            count −:= 1
            if count = 0
                OS_yield          −− relinquish processor
                count := TIMEOUT

procedure release_lock (ref L : lock)
    L := false
```

Figure 12.13 A simple spin-then-yield lock, designed for execution on a multiprocessor that may be multiprogrammed (i.e., on which OS-level processes may be preempted). If unable to acquire the lock in a fixed, short amount of time, a process calls the OS scheduler to yield its processor. Hopefully the lock will be available the next time the process runs.

throughput may improve if we allow the operating system to give the processor to a process from another application.

On a large multiprocessor we might increase concurrency by employing a separate lock for each condition queue, and another for the ready list. We would have to be careful, however, to make sure it wasn't possible for one process to put a thread into a condition queue (or the ready list) and for another process to attempt to transfer into that thread before the first process had finished transferring out of it (see Exercise 12.9).

12.3.3 Scheduler-Based Synchronization

The problem with busy-wait synchronization is that it consumes processor cycles, cycles that are therefore unavailable for other computation. Busy-wait synchronization makes sense only if (1) one has nothing better to do with the current processor, or (2) the expected wait time is less than the time that would be required to switch contexts to some other thread and then switch back again. To ensure acceptable performance on a wide variety of systems, most concurrent programming languages employ scheduler-based synchronization mechanisms, which switch to a different thread when the one that was running blocks. In the remainder of this section we consider the three most common forms of scheduler-based synchronization: semaphores, monitors, and conditional critical regions.

In each case, scheduler-based synchronization mechanisms remove the waiting thread from the scheduler's ready list, returning it only when the awaited condition is true (or is likely to be true). By contrast, the spin-then-yield lock described in the previous subsection is still a busy-wait mechanism: the currently running process relinquishes the processor, but remains on the ready list. It will perform a `test_and_set` operation every time it gets a chance to run, until it finally succeeds. It is worth noting that busy-wait synchronization is generally "level-independent"—it can be thought of as synchronizing threads, processes, or processors, as desired. Scheduler-based synchronization is "level-*dependent*"—it is specific to threads when implemented in the language run-time system, or to processes when implemented in the operating system.

We will use a *bounded buffer* abstraction to illustrate the semantics of various scheduler-based synchronization mechanisms. A bounded buffer is a concurrent queue of limited size into which *producer* threads insert data, and from which *consumer* threads remove data. The buffer serves to even out fluctuations in the relative rates of progress of the two classes of threads, increasing system throughput. A correct implementation of a bounded buffer requires both mutual exclusion and condition synchronization: the former to ensure that no thread sees the buffer in an inconsistent state in the middle of some other thread's operation; the latter to force consumers to wait when the buffer is empty and producers to wait when the buffer is full.

Semaphores

Semaphores are the oldest of the scheduler-based synchronization mechanisms. They were described by Dijkstra in the mid-1960s [Dij68a], and appear in Algol 68. They are still heavily used today, both in library packages and in languages such as SR and Modula-3.

A semaphore is basically a counter with two associated operations, P and V.[3] A thread that calls P atomically decrements the counter and then waits until it is nonnegative. A thread that calls V atomically increments the counter and wakes up a waiting thread, if any. It is generally assumed that semaphores are fair, in the sense that threads complete P operations in the same order they start them. Implementations of P and V in terms of our scheduler operations appear in Figure 12.14.

A semaphore whose counter is initialized to one and for which P and V operations always occur in matched pairs is known as a *binary semaphore*. It serves as a scheduler-based mutual exclusion lock: the P operation acquires the lock; V releases it. More generally, a semaphore whose counter is initialized to k can be used to arbitrate access to k copies of some resource. The value of the counter at

---

3 P and V stand for the Dutch words *passeren* (to pass) and *vrijgeven* (to release). To keep them straight, speakers of English may wish to think of P as standing for "pause," since a thread will pause at a P operation if the semaphore count is negative. Algol 68 calls the P and V operations down and up, respectively.

```
type semaphore = record
        N : integer –– usually initialized to something nonnegative
        Q : queue of threads

procedure P (ref S : semaphore)
        disable_signals
        acquire_lock (scheduler_lock)
        S.N –:= 1
        if S.N < 0
                sleep_on (S.Q)
        release_lock (scheduler_lock)
        reenable_signals

procedure V (ref S : semaphore)
        disable_signals
        acquire_lock (scheduler_lock)
        S.N +:= 1
        if N <= 0
                –– at least one thread is waiting
                enqueue (ready_list, dequeue (S.Q))
        release_lock (scheduler_lock)
        reenable_signals
```

Figure 12.14 Semaphore operations, for use with the scheduler code of Figure 12.12.

any particular time is always k more than the difference between the number of P operations ($\#P$) and the number of V operations ($\#V$) that have occurred so far in the program. A P operation blocks the caller until $\#P \leq \#V + k$. Exercise 12.16 notes that binary semaphores can be used to implement general semaphores, so the two are of equal expressive power, if not of equal convenience.

Figure 12.15 shows a semaphore-based solution to the bounded buffer problem. It uses a binary semaphore for mutual exclusion, and two general (or *counting*) semaphores for condition synchronization. Exercise 12.12 considers the use of semaphores to construct an *n*-thread barrier.

Monitors

Though widely used, semaphores are also widely considered to be too "low-level" for well-structured, maintainable code. They suffer from two principal problems. First, because they are simply subroutine calls, it is easy to leave one out (e.g., on a control path with several nested `if` statements). Second, unless they are hidden inside an abstraction, uses of a given semaphore tend to get scattered throughout a program, making it difficult to track them down for purposes of software maintenance.

```
shared buf : array [1..SIZE] of bdata
shared next_full, next_empty : integer := 1, 1
shared mutex : semaphore := 1
shared empty_slots, full_slots : semaphore := SIZE, 0

procedure insert (d : bdata)
    P (empty_slots)
    P (mutex)
    buf[next_empty] := d
    next_empty := next_empty mod SIZE + 1
    V (mutex)
    V (full_slots)

function remove : bdata
    P (full_slots)
    P (mutex)
    d : bdata := buf[next_full]
    next_full := next_full mod SIZE + 1
    V (mutex)
    V (empty_slots)
    return d
```

Figure 12.15 Semaphore-based code for a bounded buffer. The `mutex` binary semaphore protects the data structure proper. The `full_slots` and `empty_slots` general semaphores ensure that no operation starts until it is safe to do so.

Monitors were suggested by Dijkstra [Dij72] as a solution to these problems. They were developed more thoroughly by Brinch Hansen [Bri73], and formalized by Hoare [Hoa74] in the early 1970s. They have been incorporated into at least a score of languages, of which Concurrent Pascal [Bri75], Modula (1) [Wir77b], and Mesa [LR80] have probably been the most influential.

A monitor is a module or object with operations, internal state, and a number of *condition variables*. Only one operation of a given monitor is allowed to be active at a given point in time. A thread that calls a busy monitor is automatically delayed until the monitor is free. On behalf of its calling thread, any operation may suspend itself by *wait*ing on a condition variable. An operation may also *signal* a condition variable, in which case one of the waiting threads is resumed, usually the one that waited first.

Because the operations (*entries*) of a monitor automatically exclude one another in time, the programmer is relieved of the responsibility of using P and V operations correctly. Moreover because the monitor is an abstraction, all operations on the encapsulated data, including synchronization, are collected together in one place. Hoare defined his monitors in terms of semaphores. Conversely, it is easy to define semaphores in terms of monitors (Exercise 12.15). Together, the two definitions prove that semaphores and monitors are equally powerful: each can express all forms of synchronization expressible with the other.

Hoare's definition of monitors employs one thread queue for every condition variable, plus two bookkeeping queues: the *entry queue* and the *urgent queue*. A thread that attempts to enter a busy monitor waits in the entry queue. When a thread executes a `signal` operation from within a monitor, and some other thread is waiting on the specified condition, then the `signaling` thread waits on the monitor's urgent queue and the first thread on the appropriate condition queue obtains control of the monitor. If no thread is waiting on the `signaled` condition, then the `signal` operation is a no-op. When a thread leaves a monitor, either by completing its operation or by `waiting` on a condition, it unblocks the first thread on the urgent queue or, if the urgent queue is empty, the first thread on the entry queue, if any.

Figure 12.16 shows a monitor-based solution to the bounded buffer problem. It is worth emphasizing that monitor condition variables are not the same as semaphores. Specifically, they have no "memory": if no thread is waiting on a condition at the time that a `signal` occurs, then the `signal` has no effect. Whereas a `V` operation on a semaphore increments the semaphore's counter, allowing some future `P` operation to succeed, an un-awaited `signal` on a condition variable is lost.

Correctness for monitors depends on the notion of a *monitor invariant*. The invariant is a predicate that captures the notion that "the state of the monitor is consistent." The invariant needs to be true initially, and at monitor exit. It also needs to be true at every `wait` statement and, in a Hoare monitor, at `signal` operations as well. For our bounded buffer example, a suitable invariant would assert that `full_slots` correctly indicates the number of items in the buffer, and that those items lie in slots numbered `next_full` through `next_empty - 1` (mod `SIZE`). Careful inspection of the code in Figure 12.16 reveals that the invariant does indeed hold initially, and that anytime we modify one of the variables mentioned in the invariant, we always modify the others accordingly before `waiting`, `signaling`, or returning from an entry.

The semantic details of monitors vary significantly from one language to the next. The two principal areas of variation are the semantics of the `signal` operation and the management of mutual exclusion when a thread `waits` inside a nested sequence of two or more monitor calls.

In general, one `signals` a condition variable when some condition on which a thread may be waiting has become true. If we want to guarantee that the condition is still true when the thread wakes up, then we need to switch to the thread as soon as the signal occurs—hence the need for the urgent queue, and the need to ensure the monitor invariant at `signal` operations. In practice, switching contexts on a `signal` tends to induce unnecessary scheduling overhead: a `signaling` thread seldom changes the condition associated with the `signal` during the remainder of its operation. To reduce the overhead, and to eliminate the need to ensure the monitor invariant, Mesa specifies that `signals` are only *hints*: the language run-time system moves some waiting thread to the ready list,

```
monitor bounded_buf
imports bdata, SIZE
exports insert, remove

    buf : array [1..SIZE] of data
    next_full, next_empty : integer := 1, 1
    full_slots : integer := 0
    full_slot, empty_slot : condition

    entry insert (d : bdata)
        if full_slots = SIZE
            wait (empty_slot)
        buf[next_empty] := d
        next_empty := next_empty mod SIZE + 1
        full_slots +:= 1
        signal (full_slot)

    entry remove : bdata
        if full_slots = 0
            wait (full_slot)
        d : bdata := buf[next_full]
        next_full := next_full mod SIZE + 1
        full_slots −:= 1
        signal (empty_slot)
        return d
```

Figure 12.16 Monitor-based code for a bounded buffer. Insert and remove are *entry* sub-routines: they require exclusive access to the monitor's data. Because conditions are memory-less, both insert and remove can safely end their operation by generating a signal.

but the signaler retains control of the monitor, and the waiter must recheck the condition when it awakes. In effect, the standard idiom

```
if not desired_condition
    wait (condition_variable)
```

in a Hoare monitor becomes

```
while not desired_condition
    wait (condition_variable)
```

in a Mesa monitor. Modula-3 takes a similar approach. An alternative appears in Concurrent Pascal, which specifies that a signal operation causes an immediate return from the monitor operation in which it appears. This rule keeps overhead low, and also preserves invariants, but precludes algorithms in which a thread does useful work in a monitor after `signaling` a condition.

In most monitor languages, a `wait` in a nested sequence of monitor operations will release mutual exclusion on the innermost monitor, but will leave the outer monitors locked. This situation can lead to *deadlock* if the only way for another thread to reach a corresponding `signal` operation is through the same outer monitor(s). In general, we use the term "deadlock" to describe any situation in which a collection of threads are all waiting for each other, and none of them can proceed. In this specific case, the thread that entered the outer monitor first is waiting for the second thread to execute a `signal` operation; the second thread, however, is waiting for the first to leave the monitor. Several monitor implementations for uniprocessors (including the original Modula implementation [Wir77a]) avoid the nested monitor problem by providing mutual exclusion across *all* operations of *all* monitors, releasing exclusion on all of them when a `wait` occurs.

Conditional Critical Regions

Conditional critical regions are another alternative to semaphores, proposed by Brinch Hansen at about the same time as monitors [Bri73]. A critical region is a syntactically delimited critical section in which code is permitted to access a *protected* variable. A *conditional* critical region also specifies a Boolean condition, which must be true before control will enter the region:

```
region protected_variable when Boolean_condition do

    . . .

end region
```

No thread can access a protected variable except within a `region` statement for that variable, and any thread that reaches a `region` statement waits until the condition is true and no other thread is currently in a region for the same variable. Regions can nest, though as with nested monitor calls, the programmer needs to worry about deadlock. Figure 12.17 uses conditional critical regions to implement a bounded buffer.

Conditional critical regions avoid the question of `signal` semantics, because they use explicit Boolean conditions instead of condition variables, and because conditions can only be awaited at the beginning of critical regions. At the same time, they introduce potentially significant inefficiency. In the general case, the code used to exit a conditional critical region must tentatively resume each waiting thread, allowing that thread to recheck its condition in its own referencing environment. Optimizations are possible in certain special cases (e.g., for conditions that depend only on global variables, or that consist of only a single Boolean variable), but in the worst case it may be necessary to perform context switches in and out of every waiting thread on every exit from a region.

Conditional critical regions appear in the concurrent language Edison [Bri81], and also seem to have influenced the synchronization mechanisms of Ada 95

```
buffer : record
    buf : array [1..SIZE] of data
    next_full, next_empty : integer := 1, 1
    full_slots : integer := 0

procedure insert (d : bdata)
    region buffer when full_slots < SIZE
        buf[next_empty] := d
        next_empty := next_empty mod SIZE + 1
        full_slots −:= 1

function remove : bdata
    region buffer when full_slots > 0
        d : bdata := buf[next_full]
        next_full := next_full mod SIZE + 1
        full_slots +:= 1
    return d
```

Figure 12.17 Conditional critical regions for a bounded buffer. Boolean conditions on the `region` statements eliminate the need for explicit condition variables.

and Java. Both of these latter languages might be said to blend the features of monitors and conditional critical regions, albeit in different ways.

The principal mechanism for synchronization in Ada, introduced in Ada 83, is based on message passing; we will describe it in Section 12.4. Ada 95 augments this mechanism with a notion of *protected object*. A protected object can have three types of member subroutines: functions, procedures, and *entries*. Functions can only read the data members of the object; procedures and entries can read and write them. An implicit reader–writer lock on the protected object ensures that potentially conflicting operations exclude one another in time: a procedure or entry obtains exclusive access to the object; a function can operate concurrently with other functions, but not with a procedure or entry.

Procedures and entries differ from one another in two important ways. First, an entry can have a Boolean expression *guard*, for which the calling task (thread) will wait before beginning execution (much as it would for the condition of a conditional critical region). Second, an entry supports three special forms of call: *timed* calls, which abort after waiting for a specified amount of time, *conditional* calls, which execute alternative code if the call cannot proceed immediately, and *asynchronous* calls, which begin executing alternative code immediately, but abort it if the call is able to proceed before the alternative completes.

In comparison to the conditions of conditional critical regions, the guards on entries of protected objects in Ada 95 admit a more efficient implementation, because they do not have to be evaluated in the context of the calling thread. Moreover, because all guards are gathered together in the definition of the protected object, the compiler can generate code to test them as a group as efficiently as possible, in a manner suggested by Kessels [Kes77]. Though an Ada task cannot wait on a condition in the middle of an entry (only at the beginning), it can *requeue* itself on another entry, achieving much the same effect.

In Java, every object accessible to more than one thread has an implicit mutual exclusion lock, acquired and released by means of `synchronized` statements:

```
synchronized (my_shared_obj) {
    ...     // critical section
}
```

All executions of `synchronized` statements that refer to the same shared object exclude one another in time. Synchronized statements that refer to different objects may proceed concurrently. As a form of syntactic sugar, a member function of a class may be prefixed with the `synchronized` keyword, in which case the body of the method is considered to have been surrounded by an implicit `synchronized (this)` statement. Invocations of nonsynchronized methods of a shared object—and direct accesses to public data members—can proceed concurrently with each other, or with `synchronized` statements or methods.

Within a `synchronized` statement or method, a thread can suspend itself by calling the predefined method `wait`. Wait has no arguments in Java: the language does not distinguish among the different reasons why threads may be suspended on a given object. As in Mesa, Java programs typically embed the use of `wait` within a condition-testing loop:

```
while (!condition) {
    wait ();
}
```

A thread that calls the `wait` method of an object releases the object's lock. With nested `synchronized` statements, however, or with nested calls to synchronized methods, the thread does *not* release locks on any other objects.

To resume a thread that is suspended on a given object, some other thread must execute the predefined method `notify` from within a `synchronized` statement or method that refers to the same object. Like `wait`, `notify` has no arguments. In response to a `notify` call, the language run-time system picks an arbitrary thread suspended on the object and makes it runnable. If there are no such threads then the `notify` is a no-op. In some situations, it may be appropriate to awaken *all* threads waiting in a given object. Java provides a built-in `notifyAll` method for this purpose.

It is important to realize when a `notify` occurs that the choice among waiting threads is arbitrary. If threads are waiting for more than one condition (i.e., if their `waits` are embedded in dissimilar loops), there is no guarantee that the "right" thread will awaken. To ensure that an appropriate thread does wake up, the programmer may choose to use `notifyAll` instead of `notify`. To ensure that only *one* thread continues, the first thread to discover that its condition has been satisfied must modify the state of the object in such a way that other awakened threads, when they get to run, will simply go back to sleep. Unfortunately, since all waiting threads will end up reevaluating their conditions every time one of them can run, this "solution" to the multiple-condition problem can be prohibitively expensive. In general, Java programmers tend to look for algorithms in which there are never threads waiting for more than one condition within a given object.

Java objects that use only `synchronized` methods (no other `synchronized` statements) closely resemble Mesa monitors in which there is a limit of one condition variable per monitor. By the same token, a `synchronized` statement in Java that begins with a `wait` in a loop resembles a conditional critical region in which the retesting of conditions has been made explicit. Because `notify` also is explicit, a Java program need not reevaluate conditions on every exit from a critical section—only those in which a `notify` occurs. It turns out to be possible (see Exercise 12.19) to solve completely general synchronization problems with conditional critical regions in which all threads wait for the same condition. If the programmer chooses, however—either with conditional critical regions or in Java—to have threads wait for more than one condition of the same object at the same time, then execution may cycle through an arbitrary number of threads before one of them finds that it is able to continue. The optimizations possible in Ada 95 do not generally apply: conditions must be evaluated in the context of the waiting thread.

Ada 95 code for a bounded buffer would closely resemble the pseudocode of Figure 12.17. Java code would use `wait`s within `while` loops in place of syntactically distinguished Boolean guards. Java code would also end each `insert` or `remove` operation with an explicit `notify`. We leave the details to Exercise 12.20.

12.3.4 Implicit Synchronization

In several shared-memory languages, the operations that threads can perform on shared data are restricted in such a way that synchronization can be implicit in the operations themselves, rather than appearing as separate, explicit operations. We have seen one example of implicit synchronization already: the `forall` loop of HPF and Fortran 95 (Section 12.2.3, page 675). Separate iterations of a `forall` loop proceed concurrently, semantically in lock-step with each other: each iteration reads all data used in its instance of the first assignment statement before any iteration updates its instance of the left-hand side. The left-hand side updates in turn occur before any iteration reads the data used in its instance of the second assignment statement, and so on. Compilation of `forall` loops for vector machines, while far from trivial, is more or less straightforward. On a more conventional multiprocessor, however, good performance usually depends on high-quality *dependence analysis*, which allows the compiler to identify situations in which statements within a loop do not in fact depend on one another, and can proceed without synchronization.

Dependence analysis plays a crucial role in other languages as well. In Section 6.6.1 we mentioned Sisal, a purely functional language with Pascal-like syntax (recall that iterative constructs in Sisal are syntactic sugar for tail recursion). Because Sisal is side-effect free, its constructs can be evaluated in any order, or concurrently, as long as no construct attempts to use a value that has yet to be computed. The Sisal implementation developed at Lawrence Livermore National Lab uses extensive compiler analysis to identify promising constructs for parallel execution. It also employs tags on data objects that indicate whether the object's value has been computed yet. When the compiler is unable to guarantee that a value will have been computed by the time it is needed at run time, the generated code uses tag bits for synchronization, spinning or blocking until they are properly set. Sisal's developers claim [Can92] that their language and compiler rival parallel Fortran in performance.

In a less ambitious vein, the Multilisp [Hal85, MKH91] dialect of Scheme allows the programmer to enclose any function evaluation in a special `future` construct:

```
(future (my-function my-args))
```

In a purely functional program, `future` is semantically neutral: program behavior will be exactly the same as if (`my-function my-args`) had appeared without the surrounding call. In the implementation, however, `future` arranges for the embedded function to be evaluated by a separate thread of control. The parent thread continues to execute until it actually tries to use the return value of `my-function`, at which point it waits for execution of the `future` to complete. If two or more arguments to a function are enclosed in `futures`, then evaluation of the arguments can proceed in parallel:

```
(parent-func (future (child-1 args-1)) (future (child-2 args-2)))
```

In a program that uses the imperative features of Scheme, the programmer must take care to make sure that concurrent execution of `futures` will not compromise program correctness. There are no additional synchronization mechanisms: `future` itself is Multilisp's only addition to Scheme.

Both Multilisp and Sisal employ the same basic idea: concurrent evaluation of functions in a side-effect-free language. Where the Sisal compiler attempts to find code fragments that can profitably be executed in parallel, the Multilisp programmer must identify them explicitly. In both languages, the synchronization required to delay a thread that attempts to use a yet-to-be-computed value is implicit. In some ways the `future` construct resembles the built-in `delay` and `force` of Scheme (Section 6.6.2). Where `future` supports concurrency, `delay` supports lazy evaluation: it defers evaluation of its embedded function until the return value is known to be needed. Any use of a `delayed` expression in Scheme must be surrounded by `force`. By contrast, synchronization on a `future` is implicit: there is no analog of `force`.

Several researchers have noted that the backtracking search of logic languages such as Prolog is also amenable to parallelization. Two strategies are possible.

The first is to pursue in parallel the subgoals found in the right-hand side of a rule. This strategy is known as *AND parallelism*. The fact that variables in logic, once initialized, are never subsequently modified ensures that parallel branches of an **AND** cannot interfere with one another. The second strategy is known as *OR parallelism*; it pursues alternative resolutions in parallel. Because they will generally employ different unifications, branches of an **OR** must use separate copies of their variables. In a search tree such as that of Figure 11.4 (page 630), **AND** parallelism and **OR** parallelism create new threads at alternating levels.

OR parallelism is *speculative*: since success is required on only one branch, work performed on other branches is in some sense wasted. **OR** parallelism works well, however, when a goal cannot be satisfied (in which case the entire tree must be searched), or when there is high variance in the amount of execution time required to satisfy a goal in different ways (in which case exploring several branches at once reduces the expected time to find the first solution). Both **AND** and **OR** parallelism are problematic in Prolog, because they fail to adhere to the deterministic search order required by language semantics.

Some of the ideas embodied in concurrent functional languages can be adapted to imperative languages as well. CC++ [Fos95], for example, is a concurrent extension to C++ in which synchronization is implicit in the use of *single-assignment* variables. To declare a single-assignment variable, the CC++ programmer prepends the keyword `synch` to an ordinary variable declaration. The value of a `synch` variable is initially undefined. A thread that attempts to read the variable will wait until it is assigned a value by some other thread. It is a run-time error for any thread to attempt to assign to a `synch` variable that already has a value.

In a similar vein, Linda [ACG86] is a set of concurrent programming mechanisms that can be embedded into almost any imperative language. It consists of a set of subroutines that manipulate a shared abstraction called the *tuple space*. The elements of tuple space resemble the tuples of ML (Section 7.2.5), except that they have single assignment semantics, and are accessed associatively by content, rather than by name. The `in` procedure adds a tuple to the tuple space. The `out` procedure extracts a tuple that matches a specified *pattern*, waiting if no such tuple currently exists. The `read` procedure is a nondestructive `out`. A special form of `in` forks a concurrent thread to calculate the value to be inserted, much like a `future` in Multilisp. All three subroutines can be supported as ordinary library calls, but performance is substantially better when using a specially designed compiler that generates optimized code for commonly occurring patterns of tuple space operations.

A few multiprocessors, including the Denelcor HEP [Jor85] and the Tera machine [ACC+90], provide special hardware support for single-assignment variables in the form of so-called *full–empty* bits. Each memory location contains a bit that indicates whether the variable in that location has been initialized. Any attempt to access an uninitialized variable stalls the current processor, causing it to switch contexts (in hardware) to another thread of control.

12.4 Message Passing

While shared-memory concurrent programming is common on small-scale multiprocessors, most concurrent programming on large multicomputers and networks is currently based on messages. In Sections 12.4.1 through 12.4.3 we consider three principal issues in message-based computing: naming, sending, and receiving. In Section 12.4.4 we look more closely at one particular combination of send and receive semantics, namely remote procedure call. Most of our examples will be drawn from the Ada, Occam, and SR programming languages, the Java network library, and the PVM and MPI library packages.

12.4.1 Naming Communication Partners

To send or receive a message, one must generally specify where to send it to, or where to receive it from: communication partners need names for (or references to) one another. Names may refer directly to a thread or process. Alternatively, they may refer to an *entry* or *port* of a module, or to some sort of *socket* or *channel* abstraction. We illustrate these options in Figure 12.18.

The first naming option—addressing messages to processes—appears in Hoare's original CSP proposal, and in PVM and MPI. Each PVM or MPI process has a unique `id` (an integer), and each `send` or `receive` operation specifies the `id` of the communication partner. MPI implementations are required to be reentrant; a process can safely be divided into multiple threads, each of which can send or receive messages on the process's behalf. PVM has hidden state variables that are not automatically synchronized, making threaded PVM programs problematic.

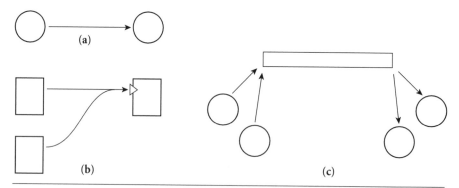

Figure 12.18 Three common schemes to name communication partners. In (a), processes name each other explicitly. In (b), senders name an *input port* of a receiver. The port may be called an *entry* or an *operation*. The receiver is typically a module with one or more threads inside. In (c), senders and receivers both name an independent *channel* abstraction, which may be called a *connection* or a *mailbox*.

The second naming option—addressing messages to ports—appears in Ada. An Ada *entry call* of the form `t.foo (args)` sends a message to the `entry` named `foo` in task (thread) `t` (`t` may be either a task name or the name of a variable whose value is a pointer to a task). As we saw in Section 12.2.3, an Ada task resembles a module; its entries resemble subroutine headers nested directly inside the task. A task receives a message that has been sent to one of its entries by executing an `accept` statement (to be discussed in Section 12.4.3). Every `entry` belongs to exactly one task; all messages sent to the same `entry` must be received by that one task.

The third naming option—addressing messages to channels—appears in Occam (though not in CSP). Channel declarations are supported with the built-in CHAN and CALL types:

```
CHAN OF BYTE stream :
CALL lookup (RESULT [36]BYTE name, VAL INT ssn) :
```

These declarations specify a one-directional channel named `stream` that carries messages of type BYTE and a two-directional channel named `lookup` that carries requests containing an integer named `ssn` and replies containing a 36-byte string named `name`. CALL channels are syntactic sugar for a pair of CHAN channels, one in each direction. To send a message on a CHAN channel, an Occam thread uses a special "exclamation point" operator:

```
stream ! 'x'
```

To send a message (and receive a reply) on a CALL channel, a thread uses syntax that resembles a subroutine call:

```
lookup (name, 123456789)
```

We noted in Section 12.2.3 ("parallel loops") that language rules in Occam prohibit concurrent threads from making conflicting accesses to the same variable. For channels, the basic rule is that exactly one thread may send to a channel, and exactly one may receive from it. (For CALL channels, exactly one thread may send requests, and exactly one may accept them and send replies). These rules are relaxed in Occam 3 to permit SHARED channels, which provide a mutual exclusion mechanism. Only one thread may accept requests over a SHARED CALL channel, but multiple threads may send them. In a similar vein, multiple threads may CLAIM a set of CHAN channels for exclusive use in a critical section, but only one thread may GRANT those channels; it serves as the other party for every message sent or received.

In SR and the Internet libraries of Java we see combinations of our naming options. An SR program executes on a collection of one or more *virtual machines*, each of which has a separate address space, and may be implemented on a separate node of a network. Within a virtual machine, messages are sent to (and received from) a channel-like abstraction called an op. Unlike an Occam channel, an SR op has no restrictions on the number or identity of sending and receiving threads: any thread that can see an op under the usual lexical scoping rules can send to it or receive from it. A receive operation must name its op explicitly; a send operation may do so also, or it may use a *capability* variable. A capability is like a pointer to an op, except that pointers work only within a given virtual machine, while capabilities work across the boundaries between them. Aside from start-up parameters and possibly I/O, capabilities provide the *only* means of communicating among separate virtual machines. At the outermost level, then, an SR program can be seen as having a port-like naming scheme: messages are sent (via capabilities) to ops of virtual machines, within which they may potentially be received by any local thread.

Java's standard java.net library provides two styles of message passing, corresponding to the UDP and TCP Internet protocols. UDP is the simpler of the two. It is a *datagram* protocol, meaning that each message is sent to its destination independently and unreliably. The network software will attempt to deliver it, but makes no guarantees. Moreover two messages sent to the same destination (assuming they both arrive) may arrive in either order. UDP messages use port-based naming (Figure 12.18b): each message is sent to a specific *Internet address* and *port number*.[4] The TCP protocol also uses port-based naming, but only for the purpose of establishing *connections* (Figure 12.18c), which it then uses for all subsequent communication. Connections deliver messages reliably and in order.

To send or receive UDP messages, a Java thread must create a *datagram socket*:

```
DatagramSocket my_socket = new DatagramSocket(port_id);
```

The parameter of the DatagramSocket constructor is optional; if it is not specified, the operating system will choose an available port. Typically servers specify a port and clients allow the OS to choose. To send a UDP message, a thread says

```
DatagramPacket my_msg = new DatagramPacket (buf, len, addr, port);
...  // initialize message
my_socket.send (my_msg);
```

The parameters to the DatagramPacket constructor specify an array of bytes buf, its length len, and the Internet address and port of the receiver.

For TCP communication, a server typically "listens" on a port to which clients send requests to establish a connection:

```
ServerSocket my_server_socket = new ServerSocket(port_id);
Socket client_connection = my_server_socket.accept();
```

---

4 Every machine on the Internet has its own unique address. As of 1999, addresses are 32-bit integers, usually printed as four period-separated fields (e.g., 192.5.54.209). Internet name servers translate symbolic names (e.g., gate.cs.rochester.edu) into numeric addresses. Port numbers are also integers, but are local to a given Internet address. Ports 1024 through 4999 are generally available for application programs; larger and smaller numbers are reserved for servers.

The `accept` operation blocks until the server receives a connection request from a client. Typically a server will immediately fork a new thread to communicate with the client; the parent thread loops back to wait for another connection with `accept`.

A client sends a connection request by passing the server's symbolic name and port number to the `Socket` constructor:

```
Socket server_connection = new Socket (host_name, port_id);
```

Once a connection has been created, a client and server in Java typically call member functions of the `Socket` class to create input and output `streams`, which support all of the standard Java mechanisms for text I/O (Section 7.9.3):

```
DataInputStream in =
    new DataInputStream(client_connection.getInputStream());
PrintStream out =
    new PrintStream(client_connection.getOutputStream());
// This is in the server; the client would make streams out
// of server_connection.
...
String s = in.readLine();
out.println ("Hi, Mom\n");
```

Among all the message-passing mechanisms we have considered, datagrams are the only one that does not provide some sort of *ordering* constraint. In general, most message-passing systems guarantee that messages sent over the same "communication path" arrive in order. When naming processes explicitly, a path links a single sender to a single receiver. All messages from that sender to that receiver arrive in the order sent. When naming ports, a path links an arbitrary number of senders to a single receiver (though as we saw in SR, if a receiver is a complex entity like a virtual machine, it may have many threads inside). Messages that arrive at a port in a given order will be seen by receivers in that order. Note, however, that while messages from the same sender will arrive at a port in order, messages from *different* senders may arrive in different orders.[5] When naming channels, a path links all the senders that can use the channel to all the receivers that can use it. A Java TCP connection has a single OS process at each end, but there may be many threads inside, each of which can use its process's end of the connection. An SR op can be used by any thread to which it is visible. In both cases, the channel functions as a queue: send (enqueue) and

---

5 Suppose, for example, that process A sends a message to port p of process B, and then sends a message to process C, while process C first receives the message from A and then sends its own message to port p of B. If messages are sent over a network with internal delays, and if A is allowed to send its message to C before its first message has reached port p, then it is possible for B to hear from C before it hears from A. This apparent reversal of ordering could easily happen on the Internet, for example, if the message from A to B traverses a satellite link, while the messages from A to C and from C to B use ocean-floor cables.

receive (dequeue) operations are ordered, so that everything is received in the order it was sent.

12.4.2 Sending

One of the most important issues to be addressed when designing a `send` operation is the extent to which it may block the caller: once a thread has initiated a `send` operation, when is it allowed to continue execution? Blocking can serve at least three purposes:

resource management: A sending thread should not modify outgoing data until the underlying system has copied the old values to a safe location. Most systems block the sender until a point at which it can safely modify its data, without danger of corrupting the outgoing message.

failure semantics: Particularly when communicating over a long-distance network, message passing is more error-prone than most other aspects of computing. Many systems block a sender until they are able to guarantee that the message will be delivered without error.

return parameters: In many cases a message constitutes a *request*, for which a *reply* is expected. Many systems block a sender until a reply has been received.

When deciding how long to block, we must consider synchronization semantics, buffering requirements, and the reporting of run-time errors.

Synchronization Semantics

On its way from a sender to a receiver, a message may pass through many intermediate steps, particularly if traversing the Internet. It first descends through several layers of software on the sender's machine, then through a potentially large number of intermediate machines, and finally up through several layers of software on the receiver's machine. We could imagine unblocking the sender after any of these steps, but most of the options would be indistinguishable in terms of user-level program behavior. If we assume for the moment that a message-passing system can always find buffer space to hold an outgoing message, then our three rationales for delay suggest three principal semantic options:

no-wait send: The sender does not block for more than a small, bounded period of time. The message-passing implementation copies the message to a safe location and takes responsibility for its delivery.

synchronization send: The sender waits until its message has been received.

remote-invocation send: The sender waits until it receives a reply.

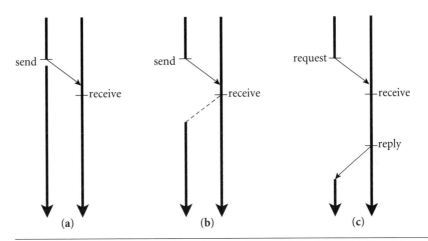

Figure 12.19 **Synchronization semantics for the** send **operation: no-wait** send **(a), synchro-nization** send **(b), and remote-invocation** send **(c).** In each diagram we have assumed that the original message arrives before the receiver executes its receive operation; this need not in general be the case.

These three alternatives are illustrated in Figure 12.19. No-wait send appears in SR and in the Java Internet library. Synchronization send appears in Occam. Remote-invocation send appears in SR, Occam, and Ada. PVM and MPI provide an implementation-oriented hybrid of no-wait send and synchronization send: a send operation blocks until the data in the outgoing message can safely be modified. In implementations that do their own internal buffering, this rule amounts to no-wait send. In other implementations, it amounts to synchronization send. PVM programs must be written to cope with the latter, more restrictive option. In MPI, the programmer has the option, if desired, to insist on no-wait send or synchronization send; performance may suffer on some systems if the request is different from the default.

Buffering

In practice, unfortunately, no message-passing system can provide a version of send that never waits (unless of course it simply throws some messages away). If we imagine a thread that sits in a loop sending messages to a thread that never receives them, we quickly see that unlimited amounts of buffer space would be required. At some point, any implementation must be prepared to block an overactive sender, to keep it from overwhelming the system. For any fixed amount of buffer space, it is possible to design a program that requires a larger amount of space to run correctly. Imagine, for example, that the message-passing system is able to buffer n messages on a given communication path. Now imagine a program in which A sends $n + 1$ messages to B, followed by one message to C. C then sends one message to B, on a different communication path. For its part, B insists on receiving the message from C before receiving the messages from A.

If *A* blocks after message *n*, implementation-dependent deadlock will result. The best that an implementation can do is to provide a sufficiently large amount of space that realistic applications are unlikely to find the limit to be a problem.

For synchronization `send` and remote-invocation `send`, buffer space is not generally a problem: the total amount of space required for messages is bounded by the number of threads, and there are already likely to be limits on how many threads a program can create. A thread that sends a reply message can always be permitted to proceed: we know that we shall be able to reuse the buffer space quickly, because the thread that sent the request is already waiting for the reply.

Error Reporting

In addition to limits on buffering, no-wait `send` suffers from the problem of error reporting. As long as the sender is blocked, errors that occur in attempting to deliver a message can be reflected back as exceptions, or as status information in result parameters or global variables. Once a sender has continued, there is no obvious way in which to report any problems that arise. For UDP, the solution is to state that messages are unreliable: if something goes wrong, the message is simply lost, silently. For TCP, the "solution" is to state that only "catastrophic" errors will cause a message to be lost, in which case the connection will become unusable and future calls will fail immediately. An even more drastic approach is taken in MPI: certain implementation-specific errors may be detected and handled at run time, but in general if a message cannot be delivered then the program as a whole is considered to have failed. PVM provides a *notification* mechanism that will send a message to a previously designated process in the event of a node or process failure. The designated process can then perform clean-up actions such as aborting any related, dependent processes, or starting new processes to pick up the work of those that failed.

Emulation of Alternatives

All three varieties of `send` can be emulated by the others. To obtain the effect of remote-invocation `send`, a thread can follow a no-wait `send` of a request with a `receive` of the reply. Similar code will allow us to emulate remote-invocation send using synchronization send. To obtain the effect of synchronization `send`, a thread can follow a no-wait `send` with a `receive` of an *acknowledgment* message, which the receiver will send immediately upon receipt of the original message. To obtain the effect of synchronization `send` using remote-invocation send, a thread that receives a request can simply reply immediately, with no return parameters.

To obtain the effect of no-wait `send` using synchronization `send` or remote-invocation `send`, we must interpose a buffer process (the message-passing analogue of our shared-memory bounded buffer) that replies immediately to

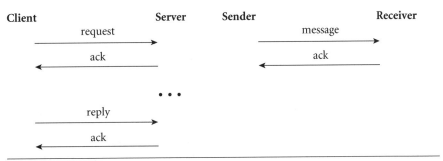

Figure 12.20 Acknowledgment messages. If the underlying message-passing system is unreliable, a language or library can provide reliability by waiting for *acknowledgment* messages, and resending if they don't appear within a reasonable amount of time. In the absence of piggy-backing, remote-invocation send (left) may require four underlying messages; synchronization send (right) may require two.

"senders" or "receivers" whenever possible. The space available in the buffer process makes explicit the resource limitations that are always present below the surface in implementations of no-wait send.

Unfortunately, user-level emulations of alternative send semantics are seldom as efficient as optimized implementations using the underlying primitives. Suppose for example that we wish to use remote-invocation send to emulate synchronization send. Suppose further that our implementation of remote-invocation send is built on top of network software that does not guarantee message delivery (we might perhaps have an implementation of Ada on top of UDP). In this situation the language run-time system is likely to employ hidden acknowledgment messages: after sending an (unreliable) request, the client's run-time system will wait for an acknowledgment from the server (Figure 12.20). If the acknowledgment does not appear within a bounded interval of time, then the run-time system will retransmit the request. After sending a reply, the server's run-time system will wait for an acknowledgment from the client. If a server thread can work for an arbitrary amount of time before sending a reply, then the run-time system will need to send separate acknowledgments for the request and the reply. If a programmer uses this implementation of remote-invocation send to emulate synchronization send, then the underlying network may end up transmitting a total of four messages (more if there are any transmission errors). By contrast, a "native" implementation of synchronization send would require only two underlying messages. In some cases the run-time system for remote-invocation send may be able to delay transmission of the first acknowledgment long enough to "piggy-back" it on the subsequent reply if there is one; in this case an emulation of synchronization send may transmit three underlying messages instead of only two. We consider the efficiency of emulations further in Exercises 12.26 and 12.29.

Syntax and Language Integration

In the emulation examples above, our hypothetical syntax assumed a library-based implementation of message passing. Because `send`, `receive`, `accept`, and so on are ordinary subroutines in such an implementation, they take a fixed, static number of parameters, two of which typically specify the location and size of the message to be sent. To send a message containing values held in more than one program variable, the programmer must explicitly *gather*, or *marshal*, those values into the fields of a record. On the receiving end, the programmer must *scatter* (*unmarshal*) the values back into program variables. By contrast, a concurrent programming language can provide message-passing operations whose "argument" lists can include an arbitrary number of values to be sent. Moreover, the compiler can arrange to perform type checking on those values, using techniques similar to those employed for subroutine linkage across compilation units (as described in Section 9.6.2). Finally, as we will see in Section 12.4.3, an explicitly concurrent language can employ non-procedure-call syntax, for example to couple a remote-invocation `accept` and `reply` in such a way that the `reply` doesn't have to explicitly identify the `accept` to which it corresponds.

12.4.3 Receiving

Probably the most important dimension on which to categorize mechanisms for receiving messages is the distinction between explicit `receive` operations and the *implicit* receipt described in Section 12.2.3 (page 679). Among the languages and systems we have been using as examples, only SR provides implicit receipt (some RPC systems also provide it, as we shall see in Section 12.4.4).

With implicit receipt, every message that arrives at a given port (or over a given channel) will create a new thread of control, subject to resource limitations (any implementation will have to stall incoming requests when the number of threads grows too large). With explicit receipt, a message must be queued until some already-existing thread indicates a willingness to receive it. At any given point in time there may be a potentially large number of messages waiting to be received. Most languages and libraries with explicit receipt allow a thread to exercise some sort of *selectivity* with respect to which messages it wants to consider.

In PVM and MPI, every message includes the `id` of the process that sent it, together with an integer *tag* specified by the sender. A `receive` operation specifies a desired sender `id` and message tag. Only matching messages will be received. In many cases receivers specify "wild cards" for the sender `id` and/or message tag, allowing any of a variety of messages to be received. Special versions of `receive` also allow a process to test (without blocking) to see if a message of a particular type is currently available (this operation is known as *polling*), or to "time out" and continue if a matching message cannot be received within a specified interval of time.

```
task buffer is
    entry insert (d : in bdata);
    entry remove (d : out bdata);
end buffer;

task body buffer is
    SIZE : constant integer := 10;
    subtype index is integer range 1..SIZE;
    buf : array (index) of bdata;
    next_empty, next_full : index := 1;
    full_slots : integer range 0..SIZE := 0;
begin
    loop
        select
          when full_slots < SIZE =>
            accept insert (d : in bdata) do
                buf(next_empty) := d;
            end;
            next_empty := next_empty mod SIZE + 1;
            full_slots := full_slots + 1;
        or
          when full_slots > 0 =>
            accept remove (d : out bdata) do
                d := buf(next_full);
            end;
            next_full := next_full mod SIZE + 1;
            full_slots := full_slots - 1;
        end select;
    end loop;
end buffer;
```

Figure 12.21 Bounded buffer in Ada, with an explicit manager task.

Because they are languages instead of library packages, Ada, Occam, and SR are able to use special, non-procedure-call syntax for selective message receipt. Moreover because messages are built into the naming and typing system, these languages are able to receive selectively on the basis of port/channel names and parameters, rather than the more primitive notion of tags. In all three languages, the selective `receive` construct is a special form of *guarded command*, as described in Section 6.7.

Figure 12.21 contains code for a bounded buffer in Ada 83. Here an active "manager" thread executes a `select` statement inside a loop. (Recall that it is also possible to write a bounded buffer in Ada using *protected objects*, without a manager thread, as described in Section 12.3.3.) The Ada `accept` statement receives the `in` and `in out` parameters (Section 8.3.1) of a remote invocation request. At the matching `end`, `accept` returns the `in out` and `out` parameters as a reply message. A client task would communicate with the bounded buffer using an *entry call*:

```
-- producer:                -- consumer:
buffer.insert (3);          buffer.remove (x);
```

The `select` statement in our buffer example has two arms. The first arm may be selected when the buffer is not full and there is an available `insert` request; the second arm may be selected when the buffer is not empty and there is an available `remove` request. Selection among arms is a two-step process: first the guards (`when` expressions) are evaluated, then for any that are true the subsequent `accept` statements are considered to see if a message is available. (The guard in front of an `accept` is optional; if missing it behaves like `when true =>`.) If both of the guards in our example are true (the buffer is partly full) and both kinds of messages are available, then either arm of the statement may be executed, at the discretion of the implementation. (For a discussion of issues of *fairness* in the choice among true guards, refer back to Section 6.7.)

Every `select` statement must have at least one arm beginning with `accept` (and optionally `when`). In addition, it may have three other types of arms:

```
when condition => delay how_long
      other_statements
...
or when condition => terminate
...
else ...
```

A `delay` arm may be selected if no other arm becomes selectable within *how_long* seconds. (Ada implementations are required to support delays as long as one day or as short as 20 ms.) A `terminate` arm may be selected only if all potential communication partners have already terminated or are likewise stuck in `select` statements with `terminate` arms. Selection of the arm causes the task that was executing the `select` statement to terminate. An `else` arm, if present, will be selected when none of the guards are true or when no `accept` statement can be executed immediately. A `select` statement with an `else` arm is not permitted to have any `delay` arms. In practice, one would probably want to include a `terminate` arm in the `select` statement of a manager-style bounded buffer.

Occam's equivalent of `select` is known as ALT. As in Ada, the choice among arms can be based both on Boolean conditions and on the availability of messages. (One minor difference: Occam semantics specify a one-step evaluation process; message availability is considered part of the guard.) The body of our bounded buffer example is shown below. Recall that Occam uses indentation to delimit control-flow constructs. Also note that Occam has no mod operator.

```
-- channel declarations:
CHAN OF BDATA producer, consumer :
CHAN OF BOOL request :

-- buffer manager:
...      -- (data declarations omitted)
```

```
WHILE TRUE
  ALT
    full_slots < SIZE & producer ? d
      SEQ
        buf[next_empty] := d
        IF
          next_empty = SIZE
            next_empty := 1
          next_empty < SIZE
            next_empty := next_empty + 1
        full_slots := full_slots + 1
    full_slots > 0 & request ? t
      SEQ
        consumer ! buf[next_full]
        IF
          next_full = SIZE
            next_full := 1
          next_full < SIZE
            next_full := next_full + 1
        full_slots := full_slots - 1
```

The question-mark operator (?) is Occam's `receive`; the exclamation-mark operator (!) is its `send`. As in Ada, an active manager thread must embed the `ALT` statement in a loop. As written here, the `ALT` statement has two guards. The first guard is true when `full_slots < SIZE` and a message is available on the channel named `producer`; the second guard is true when `full_slots > 0` and a message is available on the channel named `request`. Because we are using synchronization `send` in this example there is an asymmetry between the treatment of producers and consumers: the former need only send the manager data; the latter must send it a dummy argument and then wait for the manager to send the data back:

```
BDATA x :
```

```
-- producer:              -- consumer:
producer ! x              request ! TRUE
                          consumer ? x
```

The asymmetry could be removed by using remote invocation on `CALL` channels:

```
-- channel declarations:
CALL insert (VAL BDATA d) :
CALL remove (RESULT BDATA d) :

-- buffer manager:
WHILE TRUE
  ALT
    full_slots < SIZE & ACCEPT insert (VAL BDATA d)
      buf[next_empty] := d
      IF  -- increment next_empty, etc.
      ...
    full_slots > 0 & ACCEPT remove (RESULT BDATA d)
      d := buf[next_full]
      IF  -- increment next_full, etc.
      ...
```

Client code now looks like this:

```
-- producer:            -- consumer:
insert(x)               remove(x)
```

In the code of the buffer manager, the body of the ACCEPT is the single subsequent statement (the one that accesses buf). Updates to next_empty, next_full, and full_slots occur after replying to the client.

The effect of an Ada delay can be achieved in Occam by an ALT arm that "receives" from a *timer* pseudo-process:

```
clock ? AFTER quit_time
```

An arm can also be selected on the basis of a Boolean condition alone, without attempting to receive:

```
a > b & SKIP        -- do nothing
```

Occam's ALT has no equivalent of the Ada terminate, nor is there an else (a similar effect can be achieved with a very short delay).

In SR, selective receipt is again based on guarded commands:

```
resource buffer
  op insert (d : bdata)
  op remove () returns d : bdata
body buffer
  const SIZE := 10;
  var buf[0:SIZE-1] : bdata
  var full_slots := 0, next_empty := 0, next_full := 0
  process manager
    do true ->
      in insert (d) st full_slots < SIZE ->
          buf[next_empty] := d
          next_empty := next_empty % SIZE + 1
          full_slots++
      [] remove () returns d st full_slots > 0 ->
          d := buf[next_full]
          next_full := next_full % SIZE + 1
          full_slots--
      ni
    od
  end  # manager
end  # buffer
```

The st stands for "such that"; it introduces the Boolean half of a guard. Client code looks like this:

```
# producer:            # consumer:
call insert(x)         call remove(x)
```

If desired, an explicit reply to the client could be inserted between the access to buf and the updates of next_empty, next_full, and full_slots in each arm of the in.

In a significant departure from Ada and Occam, SR arranges for the parameters of a potential message to be in the scope of the `st` condition, allowing a receiver to "peek inside" a message before deciding whether to receive it:

```
in insert (d) st d % 2 = 1 ->        # only accept odd numbers
```

A receiver can also accept messages on a given port (i.e., of a given op) out-of-order, by specifying a *scheduling expression*:

```
in insert (d) st d % 2 = 1 by -d ->
   # only accept odd numbers, and pick the largest one first
```

Like an Ada `select`, an SR in statement can end with an `else` guard; this guard will be selected if no message is immediately available. There is no equivalent of `delay` or `terminate`.

12.4.4 Remote Procedure Call

Any of the three principal forms of `send` (no-wait, synchronization, remote-invocation) can be paired with either of the principal forms of `receive` (explicit or implicit). The combination of remote-invocation `send` with explicit receipt (e.g., as in Ada) is sometimes known as *rendezvous*. The combination of remote-invocation `send` with implicit receipt is usually known as *remote procedure call*. RPC is available in several concurrent languages (SR obviously among them), and is also supported on many systems by augmenting a sequential language with a *stub compiler*. The stub compiler is independent of the language's regular compiler. It accepts as input a formal description of the subroutines that are to be called remotely. The description is roughly equivalent to the subroutine headers and declarations of the types of all parameters. Based on this input the stub compiler generates source code for *client* and *server stubs*. A client stub for a given subroutine marshals request parameters and an indication of the desired operation into a message buffer, sends the message to the server, waits for a reply message, and unmarshals that message into result parameters. A server stub takes a message buffer as parameter, unmarshals request parameters, calls the appropriate local subroutine, marshals return parameters into a reply message, and sends that message back to the appropriate client. Invocation of a client stub is relatively straightforward. Invocation of server stubs is discussed in the subsection on "implementation."

Semantics

A principal goal of most RPC systems is to make the remote nature of calls as *transparent* as possible; that is, to make remote calls look as much like local calls as possible [BN84]. In a stub compiler system, a client stub should have the same interface as the remote procedure for which it acts as proxy; the programmer should usually be able to call the routine without knowing or caring whether it is local or remote.

Several issues make it difficult to achieve transparency in practice:

parameter modes: It is difficult to implement call-by-reference parameters across a network, since actual parameters will not be in the address space of the called routine. (Access to global variables is similarly difficult.)

performance: There is no escaping the fact that remote procedures may take a long time to return. In the face of network delays, one cannot use them casually.

failure semantics: Remote procedures are much more likely to fail than are local procedures. It is generally acceptable in the local case to assume that a called procedure will either run exactly once or else the entire program will fail. Such an assumption is overly restrictive in the remote case.

We can use value/result parameters in place of reference parameters so long as program correctness does not rely on the aliasing created by reference parameters. As noted in Section 8.3.1, Ada declares that a program is *erroneous* if it can tell the difference between pass-by-reference and pass-by-value/result implementations of in out parameters. If absolutely necessary, reference parameters and global variables can be implemented with message-passing thunks in a manner reminiscent of call-by-name parameters (Section 8.3.1), but only at very high cost. As noted in Section 7.10, a few languages and systems perform deep copies of linked data structures passed to remote routines.

Performance differences between local and remote calls can only be hidden by artificially slowing down the local case. Such an option is clearly unacceptable.

Exactly-once failure semantics can be provided by aborting the caller in the event of failure or, in highly reliable systems, by delaying the caller until the operating system or language run-time system is able to rebuild the failed computation using information previously dumped to disk. (Failure recovery techniques are beyond the scope of this text.) An attractive alternative is to accept "at-most-once" semantics with notification of failure. The implementation retransmits requests for remote invocations as necessary in an attempt to recover from lost messages. It guarantees that retransmissions will never cause an invocation to happen more than once, but it admits that in the presence of communication failures the invocation may not happen at all. If the programming language provides exceptions then the implementation can use them to make communication failures look just like any other kind of run-time error.

Implementation

At the level of the kernel interface, `receive` is an explicit operation on almost all operating systems. To make `receive` appear implicit to the application programmer, the code produced by an RPC stub compiler (or the run-time system of a language such as SR) must bridge this explicit-to-implicit gap. We describe

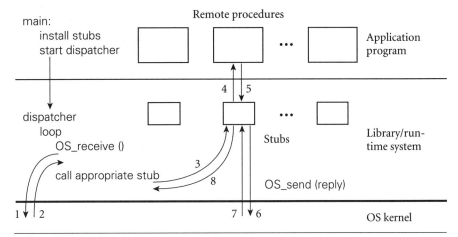

Figure 12.22 Implementation of a Remote Procedure Call server. Application code initializes the RPC system by installing stubs generated by the stub compiler (not shown). It then calls into the run-time system to enable incoming calls. Depending on details of the particular system in use, the dispatcher may use the main program's single process (in which case the call to start the dispatcher never returns), or it may create a pool of processes that handle incoming requests.

the implementation here in terms of stub compilers; in a concurrent language with implicit receipt the regular compiler does essentially the same work.

Figure 12.22 illustrates the layers of a typical RPC system. Code above the upper horizontal line is written by the application programmer. Code in the middle is a combination of library routines and code produced by the RPC stub generator. To initialize the RPC system, the application makes a pair of calls into the run-time system. The first provides the system with pointers to the stub routines produced by the stub compiler; the second starts a *message dispatcher*. What happens after this second call depends on whether the server is concurrent and, if so, whether its threads are implemented on top of one OS process or several.

In the simplest case—a single-threaded server on a single OS process—the dispatcher runs a loop that calls into the kernel to receive a message. When a message arrives, the dispatcher calls the appropriate RPC stub, which unmarshals request parameters and calls the appropriate application-level procedure. When that procedure returns, the stub marshals return parameters into a reply message, calls into the kernel to send the message back to the caller, and then returns to the dispatcher.

This simple organization works well so long as each remote request can be handled quickly, without ever needing to block. If remote requests must sometimes wait for user-level synchronization, then the server's process must manage a ready list of threads, as described in Section 12.2.4, but with the dispatcher integrated into the usual thread scheduler. When the current thread blocks (in application code), the scheduler/dispatcher will grab a new thread from the ready list. If the ready list is empty, the scheduler/dispatcher will call into the kernel to receive a message, fork a new thread to handle it, and then continue to execute runnable threads until the list is empty again.

In a multiprocess server, the call to start the dispatcher will generally ask the kernel to fork a "pool" of processes to service remote requests. Each of these processes will then perform the operations described in the previous paragraphs. In a language or library with a one-one correspondence between threads and processes, each process will repeatedly receive a message from the kernel and then call the appropriate stub. With a more general thread package, each process will run threads from the ready list until the list is empty, at which point it (the process) will call into the kernel for another message. So long as the number of runnable threads is greater than or equal to the number of processes, no new messages will be received. When the number of runnable threads drops below the number of processes, then the extra processes will call into the kernel, where they will block until requests arrive.

12.5 Summary and Concluding Remarks

Concurrency and parallelism have become ubiquitous in modern computer systems. It is probably safe to say that most computer research and development today involves concurrency in one form or another. High-end computer systems are almost always parallel, and multiprocessor PCs are becoming increasingly common. With the explosion in the mid-1990s of multimedia and Internet-based applications, multithreaded and message-passing programs have become central to day-to-day computing even on uniprocessors.

In this chapter we have provided an introduction to concurrent programming with an emphasis on programming language issues. We began with a quick synopsis of the history of concurrency, the motivation for multithreaded programs, and the architecture of modern multiprocessors. We then surveyed the fundamentals of concurrent software, including communication, synchronization, and the creation and management of threads. We distinguished between shared memory and message-passing models of communication and synchronization, and between language and library-based implementations of concurrency.

Our survey of thread creation and management described some six different constructs for creating threads: `co-begin`, parallel loops, launch-at-elaboration, `fork`/`join`, implicit receipt, and early reply. Of these `fork`/`join` is the most common; it is found in Ada, Java, Modula-3, SR, and library-based packages such as PVM and MPI. RPC systems usually use `fork`/`join` internally to implement implicit receipt. Regardless of thread creation mechanism, most concurrent programming systems implement their language or library-level threads on top of a collection of OS-level processes, which the operating system implements in a similar manner on top of a collection of hardware processors. We built our sample implementation in stages, beginning with coroutines on a uniprocessor, then adding a ready list and scheduler, then timers for preemption, and finally parallel scheduling on multiple processors.

Our section on shared memory focused primarily on synchronization. We distinguished between mutual exclusion and condition synchronization, and between busy-wait and scheduler-based implementations. Among busy-wait mechanisms we looked in particular at spin locks and barriers. Among scheduler-based mechanisms we looked at semaphores, monitors, and conditional critical regions. Of the three, semaphores are the simplest and most common. Monitors and conditional critical regions provide a better degree of encapsulation and abstraction, but are not amenable to implementation in a library. Conditional critical regions might be argued to provide the most pleasant programming model, but cannot in general be implemented as efficiently as monitors. We also considered the implicit synchronization found in the loops of High Performance Fortran, the functional constructs of Sisal, and the `future`-like constructs of Multilisp, Linda, and CC++.

Our section on message-passing examined four principal issues: how to name communication partners, how long to block when sending a message, whether to receive explicitly or implicitly, and how to select among messages that may be available for receipt simultaneously. We noted that any of the three principal `send` mechanisms (no-wait, synchronization, remote-invocation) can be paired with either of the principal `receive` mechanisms (explicit, implicit). Remote-invocation `send` with explicit receipt is sometimes known as *rendezvous*. Remote-invocation `send` with implicit receipt is generally known as *remote procedure call*.

As in previous chapters, we saw many cases in which language design and language implementation influence one another. Some mechanisms (cactus stacks, conditional critical regions, content-based message screening) are sufficiently complex that many language designers have chosen not to provide them. Other mechanisms (Ada-style parameter modes) have been developed specifically to facilitate an efficient implementation technique. And in still other cases (the semantics of no-wait send, blocking inside a monitor) implementation issues play a major role in some larger set of tradeoffs.

Despite the very large number of concurrent languages that have been designed to date, most concurrent programming continues to employ conventional sequential languages augmented with library packages. As of 1999, HPF and other concurrent languages for large-scale multicomputers have yet to seriously undermine the dominance of PVM and MPI. For smaller-scale shared-memory computing, programmers continue to rely on library packages in C and C++. At the very least, it would appear that a necessary (but not sufficient) condition for widespread acceptance of any concurrent language is that it be seen as an extension to some successful and popular sequential language, in which programmers have already made a substantial intellectual investment, and for which outstanding compilers are available. Among languages currently on the horizon, Java seems to be the most likely exception to this rule. Its suitability for network-based computing, its extreme portability across platforms, and the enthusiasm with which it has been embraced by the popular press appear to be establishing an enormous base of support in spite of initially poor compilers. For the relatively safe, on-demand construction of programs that span the Internet, Java currently has no serious competitor.

12.6 Review Questions

12.1 Explain the rationale for concurrency: why do people write concurrent programs?

12.2 Describe the evolution of computer operation from *stand-alone* mode to *batch processing*, to *multiprogramming* and *timesharing*.

12.3 Describe six different syntactic constructs commonly used to create new threads of control in a concurrent program.

12.4 Explain the difference between a thread and a coroutine.

12.5 What are the tradeoffs between language-based and library-based implementations of concurrency?

12.6 Name four explicitly concurrent programming languages.

12.7 What is *busy-waiting*? What is its principal alternative?

12.8 What is a *race condition*?

12.9 What is a *context switch*? What is *preemption*?

12.10 Explain the *coherence problem* in the context of multiprocessor caches.

12.11 Describe the *bag of tasks* programming model.

12.12 Explain the difference between *data parallelism* and *task parallelism*.

12.13 What is *coscheduling*? What is its purpose?

12.14 What is a *critical section*?

12.15 What does it mean for an operation to be *atomic*?

12.16 Explain the difference between *mutual exclusion* and *condition synchronization*.

12.17 Describe the behavior of a `test_and_set` instruction. Show how to use it to build a *spin lock*.

12.18 Describe the behavior of the `load_linked` and `store_conditional` instructions. What advantages do they offer in comparison to `test_and_set`?

12.19 Explain how a *reader–writer lock* differs from an "ordinary" lock.

12.20 What is a *barrier*? In what types of programs are barriers common?

12.21 What does it mean for code to be *reentrant*?

12.22 What is a *semaphore*? What operations does it support? How do *binary* and *general* semaphores differ?

12.23   What is a *monitor*? How do monitor *condition variables* differ from semaphores?

12.24   What is a *conditional critical region*? How does it differ from a monitor?

12.25   What is *deadlock*?

12.26   Describe the semantics of the HPF/Fortran 95 `forall` loop.

12.27   Explain the difference between **AND** *parallelism* and **OR** *parallelism* in Prolog.

12.28   What are *single-assignment variables*? In what languages do they appear?

12.29   What are *gather* and *scatter* operations in a message-passing program?

12.30   Describe three ways in which processes commonly name their communication partners.

12.31   What are the three principal synchronization options for the sender of a message? What are the tradeoffs among them?

12.32   Describe the tradeoffs between *explicit* and *implicit* message receipt.

12.33   What is a *remote procedure call* (RPC)? What is a *stub compiler*?

12.34   What are the obstacles to *transparency* in an RPC system?

12.35   What is a *rendezvous*? How does it differ from a remote procedure call?

12.36   What is an *early reply*?

12.7 Exercises

12.1   Give an example of a "benign" race condition: one whose outcome affects program behavior, but not correctness.

12.2   We have defined the *ready list* of a thread package to contain all threads that are runnable but not running, with a separate variable to identify the currently running thread. Could we just as easily have defined the ready list to contain *all* runnable threads, with the understanding that the one at the head of the list is running? (Hint: think about multiprocessors.)

12.3   Imagine you are writing the code to manage a hash table that will be shared among several concurrent threads. Assume that operations on the table need to be atomic. You could use a single mutual exclusion lock to protect the entire table, or you could devise a scheme with one lock per hash-table bucket. Which approach is likely to work better, under what circumstances? Why?

12.4   The typical spin lock holds only one bit of data, but requires a full word of storage, because only full words can be read, modified, and written atomically in hardware. Consider, however, the hash table of the previous exercise. If we choose to employ a separate lock for each bucket of the table, explain how to implement a "two-level" locking scheme that couples a conventional spin lock for the table as a whole with a *single bit* of locking information for each bucket. Explain why such a scheme might be desirable, particularly in a table with external chaining. (Hint: See the paper by Stumm et al. [UKGS94].)

12.5   Many of the most compute-intensive scientific applications are "dusty-deck" Fortran programs, generally very old and very complex. Years of effort may sometimes be required to rewrite a dusty-deck program to run on a parallel machine. An attractive alternative would be to develop a compiler that could "parallelize" old programs automatically. Explain why this is not an easy task.

12.6   The `load_linked` and `store_conditional` (LL/SC) instructions of Section 12.3.1 resemble an earlier universal atomic operation known as `compare-and-swap` (CAS). CAS was introduced by the IBM 370 architecture, and also appears in the 680x0 and SPARC V9 instruction sets. It takes three operands: the location to be modified, a value that the location is expected to contain, and a new value to be placed there if (and only if) the expected value is found. Like `store_conditional`, CAS returns an indication of whether it succeeded. The atomic add instruction sequence shown for `load_linked`/`store_conditional` on page 690 would be written as follows with CAS:

```
start:
    r1 := foo
    r3 := r1 + r2
    CAS (foo, r1, r3)
    if failed goto start
```

Discuss the relative advantages of LL/SC and CAS. Consider how they might be implemented on a cache-coherent multiprocessor. Are there situations in which one would work but the other would not? (Hints: consider algorithms in which a thread may need to touch more than one memory location. Also consider algorithms in which the contents of a memory location might be changed and then restored.)

12.7   On most machines, a SC instruction can fail for any of several reasons, including the occurrence of an interrupt in the time since the matching LL. What steps must a programmer take to make sure that algorithms work correctly in the face of such "spurious" SC failures?

12.8   Starting with the test-and-`test_and_set` lock of Figure 12.10, implement busy-wait code that will allow readers to access a data structure concurrently. Writers will still need to lock out both readers and other writers. You may use any reasonable atomic instruction(s) (e.g., LL/SC). Consider the issue of fairness. In particular, if there are *always* readers interested in accessing the data structure, your algorithm should ensure that writers are not locked out forever.

12.9 The mechanism used in Figure 12.12 (page 693) to make scheduler code reentrant employs a single OS-provided lock for all the scheduling data structures of the application. Among other things, this mechanism prevents threads on separate processors from performing P or V operations on unrelated semaphores, even when none of the operations needs to block. Can you devise another synchronization mechanism for scheduler-related operations that admits a higher degree of concurrency but that is still correct?

12.10 We have seen how the scheduler for a thread package that runs on top of more than one OS-provided process must both disable timer signals *and* acquire a spin lock to safeguard the integrity of the ready list and condition queues. To implement processes within the operating system, the kernel still uses spin locks, but with processors instead of processes, and hardware interrupts instead of signals. Unfortunately, the kernel cannot afford to disable interrupts for more than a small, bounded period of time, or devices may not work correctly. A straightforward adaptation of the code in Figure 12.12 will not suffice because it would attempt to acquire a spin lock (an unbounded operation) while interrupts were disabled. Similarly, the kernel cannot afford to acquire a spin lock and then disable interrupts because, if an interrupt occurs in-between these two operations, other processors may be forced to spin for a very long time. How would you solve this problem? (Hint: Look carefully at the loop in the middle of `reschedule`, and consider a hybrid technique that disables interrupts and acquires a spin lock as a single operation.)

12.11 To make spin locks useful on a multiprogrammed multiprocessor, one might want to ensure that no process is ever preempted in the middle of a critical section. That way it would always be safe to spin in user space, because the process holding the lock would be guaranteed to be running on some other processor, rather than preempted and possibly in need of the current processor. Explain why an operating system designer might not want to give user processes the ability to disable preemption arbitrarily. (Hint: Think about fairness and multiple users.) Can you suggest a way to get around the problem? (References to several possible solutions can be found in the paper by Kontothanassis, Wisniewski, and Scott [KWS97].)

12.12 Show how to use semaphores to construct an *n*-thread barrier.

12.13 Would it ever make sense to declare a semaphore with an initially negative count? Why or why not?

12.14 Without looking at Hoare's definition, show how to implement monitors with semaphores.

12.15 Using monitors, show how to implement semaphores. What is your monitor invariant?

12.16 Show how to use binary semaphores to implement general semaphores.

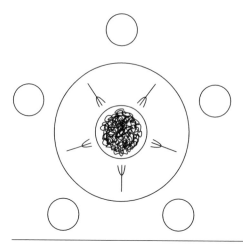

Figure 12.23 **The Dining Philosophers.** Hungry philosophers must contend for the forks to their left and right in order to eat.

12.17 Suppose that every monitor has a separate mutual exclusion lock, and that we want to release all locks when a thread `waits` in the innermost of a sequence of nested monitor calls. When the thread awakens it will need to reacquire the outer locks. In what order should it do so? (Hint: think about deadlock.) Can we guarantee that the awakened thread will be the next to run in the innermost monitor? (For further hints, see Wettstein [Wet78].)

12.18 In addition to the usual `signal` operation, Mesa and Modula-3 provide a `broadcast` operation that awakens *all* threads waiting on a given monitor condition variable. Show how the programmer can achieve a similar effect (awakening all threads) in a Hoare monitor. What is the advantage of the built-in `broadcast` operation?

12.19 Show how general semaphores can be implemented with conditional critical regions in which all threads wait for the same condition, thereby avoiding the overhead of unproductive wake-ups.

12.20 Write code for a bounded buffer using Java and/or the protected object mechanism of Ada 95.

12.21 The *dining philosophers problem* [Dij72] is a classic exercise in synchronization (Figure 12.23). Five philosophers sit around a circular table. In the center is a large communal plate of spaghetti. Each philosopher repeatedly thinks for a while and then eats for a while, at intervals of his or her own choosing. On the table between each pair of adjacent philosophers is a single fork. To eat, a philosopher requires both adjacent forks: the one on the left and the one on the right. Because they share a fork, adjacent philosophers cannot eat simultaneously.

Write a solution to the dining philosophers problem in which each philosopher is represented by a process and the forks are represented by shared data. Synchronize access to the forks using semaphores, monitors, or conditional critical regions. Try to maximize concurrency.

12.22 In the previous exercise you may have noticed that the dining philosophers are prone to deadlock. One has to worry about the possibility that all five of them will pick up their right-hand forks simultaneously, and then wait forever for their left-hand neighbors to finish eating.

Discuss as many strategies as you can think of to address the deadlock problem. Can you describe a solution in which it is provably impossible for any philosopher to go hungry forever? Can you describe a solution that is fair in a strong sense of the word (i.e., in which no one philosopher gets more chance to eat than some other over the long term)? For a particularly elegant solution, see the paper by Chandy and Misra [CM84].

12.23 In some concurrent programming systems, global variables are shared by all threads. In others, each newly created thread has a separate copy of the global variables, commonly initialized to the values of the globals of the creating thread. Under this private globals approach, shared data must be allocated from a special heap. In still other programming systems, the programmer can specify which global variables are to be private and which are to be shared.

Discuss the tradeoffs between private and shared global variables. Which would you prefer to have available, for which sorts of programs? How would you implement each? Are some options harder to implement than others? To what extent do your answers depend on the nature of processes provided by the operating system?

12.24 AND parallelism in logic languages is analogous to the parallel evaluation of arguments in a functional language (e.g., Multilisp). Does OR parallelism have a similar analog? (Hint: think about special forms [Section 11.2.2].) Can you suggest a way to obtain the effect of OR parallelism in Multilisp?

12.25 In Section 12.3.4 we claimed that both AND parallelism and OR parallelism were problematic in Prolog, because they failed to adhere to the deterministic search order required by language semantics. Elaborate on this claim. What specifically can go wrong?

12.26 Find out how message-passing is implemented in some locally available concurrent language or library. Does this system provide no-wait `send`, synchronization `send`, remote-invocation `send`, or some related hybrid? If you wanted to emulate the other options using the one available, how expensive would emulation be, in terms of low-level operations performed by the underlying system? How would this overhead compare to what could be achieved on the same underlying system by a language or library that provided an optimized implementation of the other varieties of `send`?

12.27 In Section 12.3.3 we cast monitors as a mechanism for synchronizing access to shared memory, and we described their implementation in terms of semaphores. It is also possible to think of a monitor as a module inhabited by a single process, which accepts request messages from other processes, performs appropriate operations, and replies. Give the details of a monitor implementation consistent with this conceptual model. Be sure to include condition variables. (Hint: See the discussion of early reply in Section 12.2.3, page 680.)

12.28 Show how shared memory can be used to implement message passing. Specifically, choose a set of message-passing operations (e.g. no-wait `send` and explicit message receipt) and show how to implement them in your favorite shared-memory notation.

12.29 When implementing reliable messages on top of unreliable messages, a sender can wait for an acknowledgment message, and retransmit if it doesn't receive it within a bounded period of time. But how does the receiver know that its acknowledgment has been received? Why doesn't the sender have to acknowledge the acknowledgment (and the receiver acknowledge the acknowledgment of the acknowledgment ...)? (For more information on the design of fast, reliable protocols, you might want to consult a text on computer networks [Tan96, PD96].)

12.30 An arm of an Occam `ALT` statement may include an *input guard*—a receive (?) operation—in which case the arm can be chosen only if a potential partner is trying to send a matching message. One could imagine allowing *output guards* as well: send (!) operations that would allow their arm to be chosen only if a potential partner were trying to receive a matching message. Neither Occam nor CSP (as originally defined) permits output guards. Can you guess why? Suppose you wished to provide them. How would the implementation work? (Hint: For ideas, see the articles of Bernstein [Ber80], Buckley and Silbershatz [BS83b], Bagrodia [Bag86], or Ramesh [Ram87].)

12.31 In Section 12.4.3 we described the semantics of a `terminate` arm on an Ada `select` statement: this arm may be selected if and only if all potential communication partners have terminated, or are likewise stuck in `select` statements with `terminate` arms. Occam and SR have no similar facility, though the original CSP proposal does. How would you implement `terminate` arms in Ada? Why do you suppose they were left out of Occam and SR? (Hint: For ideas, see the work of Apt and Francez [Fra80, AF84].)

12.8 Bibliographic Notes

Much of the early study of concurrency stems from a pair of articles by Dijkstra [Dij68a, Dij72]. Andrews and Schneider [AS83] provide an excellent survey of concurrent programming notations. A more recent book by Andrews [And91] extends this survey with extensive discussion of axiomatic semantics for concurrent programs and algorithmic paradigms for distributed computing. Holt et al. [HGLS78] is a useful reference for many of the classic problems in concurrency and synchronization. Anderson [ALL89] discusses thread package implementation details and their implications for performance. The July 1989 issue of *IEEE Software* and the September 1989 issue of *ACM Computing Surveys* contain survey articles and descriptions of many concurrent languages. References for monitors appear in Section 12.3.3.

Peterson's two-process synchronization algorithm appears in a remarkably elegant and readable two-page paper [Pet81]. Lamport's 1978 article on "Time, Clocks, and the Ordering of Events in a Distributed System" [Lam78] argued convincingly that the notion of global time cannot be well defined, and that distributed algorithms must therefore be based on causal *happens before* relationships among individual processes. Reader–writer locks are due to Courtois, Heymans, and Parnas [CHP71]. Mellor-Crummey and Scott [MCS91] survey the principal busy-wait synchronization algorithms and introduce locks and barriers that scale without contention to very large machines. The seminal paper on lock-free synchronization is that of Herlihy [Her91].

Concurrent logic languages are surveyed by Shapiro [Sha89], Tick [Tic91], and Ciancarini [Cia92]. Parallel Lisp dialects include Multilisp [Hal85, MKH91] (Section 12.3.4), Qlisp [GG89], and Spur Lisp [ZHL+89].

Remote procedure call received increasing attention in the wake of Nelson's doctoral research [Nel81, BN84]. Schroeder and Burrows [SB90] discuss the efficient implementation of RPC on a network of workstations. Bershad [BALL90] discusses its implementation across address spaces within a single machine.

Almasi and Gottlieb [AG94] describe the principal classes of parallel computers and the styles of algorithms and languages that work well on each. The leading texts on computer networks are by Tanenbaum [Tan96] and Peterson and Davie [PD96]. The recent text of Culler, Singh, and Gupta [CS98] contains a wealth of information on parallel programming and multiprocessor architecture. PVM [Sun90, GBD+94] and MPI [BDH+95, SOHL+95] are documented in a variety of articles and books. Sun RPC is documented in Internet RFC number 1831 [Sri95].

Software distributed shared memory (S-DSM) was originally proposed by Li as part of his doctoral research [LH89]. Stumm and Zhou [SZ90] and Nitzberg and Lo [NL91] provide early surveys of the field. The TreadMarks system from Rice University is widely considered the best of the more recent implementations [ACD+96].

Code Improvement 13

In Chapter 9 we discussed the generation, assembly, and linking of target code in the back end of a compiler. The techniques we presented led to correct but highly suboptimal code: there were many redundant computations, and inefficient use of the registers, multiple functional units, and cache of a modern microprocessor. This final chapter takes a look at *code improvement*: the phases of compilation devoted to generating *good* code. For the most part we will interpret "good" to mean *fast*. In a few cases we will also consider program transformations that decrease memory requirements. On occasion a real compiler may try to minimize power consumption, dollar cost of execution under a particular accounting system, or demand for some other resource; we will not consider these issues here.

There are several possible levels of "aggressiveness" in code improvement. In a very simple compiler, or in a "nonoptimizing" run of a more sophisticated compiler, we can use a *peephole optimizer* to peruse already-generated target code for obviously suboptimal sequences of adjacent instructions. At a slightly higher level, typical of the baseline behavior of production-quality compilers, we can generate near-optimal code for *basic blocks*. As described in Chapter 9, a basic block is a maximal-length sequence of instructions that will always execute in its entirety (assuming it executes at all). In the absence of delayed branches, each basic block in assembly language or machine code begins with the target of a branch or with the instruction after a conditional branch, and ends with a branch or with the instruction before the target of a branch. As a result, in the absence of hardware exceptions, control never enters a basic block except at the beginning, and never exits except at the end. Code improvement at the level of basic blocks is known as *local* optimization. It focuses on the elimination of redundant operations (e.g., unnecessary loads or common subexpression calculations), and on effective instruction scheduling and register allocation.

At higher levels of aggressiveness, production-quality compilers employ techniques that analyze entire subroutines for further speed improvements. These techniques are known as *global* optimization.[1] They include multi-basic-block versions of redundancy elimination, instruction scheduling, and register allocation, plus code modifications designed to improve the performance of loops. Both global redundancy elimination and loop improvement typically employ a *control flow graph* representation of the program, as described in section 9.1.1. Both employ a family of algorithms known as *data flow analysis* to trace the flow of information across the boundaries between basic blocks.

At the highest level of aggressiveness, many recent compilers perform various forms of *interprocedural* code improvement. Interprocedural improvement is difficult for two main reasons. First, because a subroutine may be called from many different places in a program, it is difficult to identify (or fabricate) conditions (available registers, common subexpressions, etc.) that hold at all call sites. Second, because many subroutines are separately compiled, an interprocedural code improver must generally subsume some of the work of the linker.

In the sections below we consider peephole, local, and global code improvement. We will not cover interprocedural improvement; interested readers are referred to other texts (see the bibliographic notes at the end of the chapter). Moreover, even for the subjects we cover, our intent will be more to "demystify" code improvement than to describe the process in detail. Much of the discussion (beginning in Section 13.3) will revolve around the successive refinement of code for a single subroutine. This extended example will allow us to illustrate the effect of several key forms of code improvement without dwelling on the details of how they are achieved. Entire books continue to be written on code improvement; it remains a very active research topic.

As in most texts, we will sometimes refer to code improvement as "optimization," though this term is really a misnomer: we will seldom have any guarantee that our techniques will lead to optimal code. As it turns out, even some of the relatively simple aspects of code improvement (minimization of register usage within a basic block, for example) can be shown to be NP-hard. True optimization is a realistic option only for small, special-purpose program fragments [Mas87]. Our discussion will focus on the improvement of code for imperative programs. Optimizations specific to functional or logic languages are beyond the scope of this book.

We begin in Section 13.1 with a more detailed consideration of the phases of code improvement. We then turn to peephole optimization in Section 13.2. It can be performed in the absence of other optimizations if desired, and the discussion introduces some useful terminology. In Sections 13.3 and 13.4 we consider local and global redundancy elimination. Sections 13.5 and 13.7 cover code improvement for loops. Section 13.6 covers instruction scheduling. Section 13.8 covers register allocation.

---

[1] The adjective 'global' is somewhat misleading in this context, since the improvements do not consider the program as a whole; 'intraprocedural' might be more accurate.

|3.| Phases of Code Improvement

As we noted in Chapter 9, the structure of the back end varies considerably from compiler to compiler. For simplicity of presentation we will continue to focus on the structure introduced in Section 9.1. In that section (as in Section 1.6) we characterized machine-independent and machine-specific code improvement as individual phases of compilation, separated by target code generation. We must now acknowledge that this was an oversimplification. In reality, code improvement is a substantially more complicated process, often comprising a very large number of phases.

In some cases optimizations depend on one another, and must be performed in a particular order. In other cases they are independent, and can be performed in any order. In still other cases it can be important to *repeat* an optimization, in order to recognize new opportunities for improvement that were not visible until some other optimization was applied.

We will concentrate in our discussion on the forms of code improvement that tend to achieve the largest increases in execution speed, and are most widely used. Compiler phases to implement these improvements are shown in Figure 13.1. Within this structure, the machine-independent part of the back end begins with intermediate code generation. This phase identifies fragments of the syntax tree that correspond to basic blocks. It then creates a control flow graph in which each node contains a linear sequence of three-address instructions for an idealized machine, typically one with an unlimited supply of *virtual registers*. The machine-specific part of the back end begins with target code generation. This phase strings the basic blocks together into a linear program, translating each block into the instruction set of the target machine and generating branch instructions that correspond to the arcs of the control flow graph.

Machine-independent code improvement in Figure 13.1 is shown as three separate phases. The first of these identifies and eliminates redundant loads, stores, and computations within each basic block. The second deals with similar redundancies across the boundaries between basic blocks (but within the bounds of a single subroutine). The third effects several improvements specific to loops; these are particularly important, since most programs spend most of their time in loops. In Sections 13.4, 13.5, and 13.7, we shall see that global redundancy elimination and loop improvement may actually be subdivided into several separate phases.

We have shown machine-specific code improvement as four separate phases. The first and third of these are essentially identical. As we noted in Section 5.6.2, register allocation and instruction scheduling tend to interfere with one another: the instruction schedules that do the best job of minimizing pipeline stalls tend to increase the demand for physical registers (commonly known as *register pressure*). A common strategy, assumed in our discussion, is to schedule instructions first, then allocate physical registers, then schedule instructions again. If it turns out that there aren't enough physical registers to go around, the register allocator

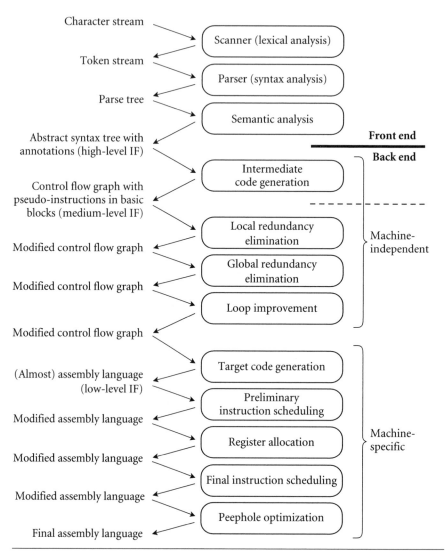

Figure 13.1 A more detailed view of the compiler structure originally presented in Figure 9.1 (page 493). Both machine-independent and machine-specific code improvement have been divided into multiple phases. As before, the dashed line shows a common "break point" for a two-pass compiler.

will generate additional load and store instructions to *spill* registers temporarily to memory. The second round of instruction scheduling attempts to fill any delays induced by the extra loads.

13.2 Peephole Optimization

In a simple compiler with no machine-independent code improvement, a code generator can simply walk the abstract syntax tree, producing naive code, either as output to a file or global list, or as annotations in the tree. As we saw in Chapters 1 and 9, however, the result is generally of very poor quality (contrast the code on page 1 with that of Figure 1.5). Among other things, every use of a variable as an r-value results in a load, and every assignment results in a store.

A relatively simple way to significantly improve the quality of naive code is to run a *peephole optimizer* over the target code. A peephole optimizer works by sliding a several-instruction window (a peephole) over the target code, looking for suboptimal patterns of instructions. The set of patterns to look for is heuristic; generally one creates patterns to match common suboptimal idioms produced by a particular front end, or to exploit special instructions available on a given machine. Here are a few examples:

Elimination of redundant loads and stores: The peephole optimizer can often recognize that the value produced by a load instruction is already available in a register. For example:

$r2 := r1 + 5$
$i := r2$ becomes
$r3 := i$
$r4 := r3 \times 3$

$r2 := r1 + 5$
$i := r2$
$r4 := r2 \times 3$

In a similar but less common vein, if there are two stores to the same location within the optimizer's peephole (with no possible intervening load from that location), then we can generally eliminate the first.

Constant folding: A naive code generator may produce code that performs calculations at run time that could actually be performed at compile time. A peephole optimizer can often recognize such code. For example:

$r2 := 3 \times 2$ becomes $r2 := 6$

Constant propagation: Sometimes we can tell that a variable will have a constant value at a particular point in a program. We can then replace occurrences of the variable with occurrences of the constant:

$r2 := 4$
$r3 := r1 + r2$ becomes
$r2 := \ldots$

$r2 := 4$
$r3 := r1 + 4$ and then
$r2 := \ldots$

$r3 := r1 + 4$
$r2 := \ldots$

The final assignment to r2 tells us that the previous value (the 4) in r2 was *dead*—it was never going to be needed. (By analogy, a value that may be needed in some future computation is said to be *live*.) Loads of dead values can be eliminated. Similarly,

$$
\begin{array}{l}
\text{r2} := 4 \\
\text{r3} := \text{r1} + \text{r2} \\
\text{r3} := *\text{r3}
\end{array}
\quad \text{becomes} \quad
\begin{array}{l}
\text{r3} := \text{r1} + 4 \\
\text{r3} := *\text{r3}
\end{array}
\quad \text{and then} \quad
\text{r3} := *(\text{r1}+4)
$$

(Assuming again that r2 is dead.)

Often constant folding will reveal an opportunity for constant propagation. Sometimes the reverse occurs:

$$
\begin{array}{l}
\text{r1} := 3 \\
\text{r2} := \text{r1} \times 2
\end{array}
\quad \text{becomes} \quad
\begin{array}{l}
\text{r1} := 3 \\
\text{r2} := 3 \times 2
\end{array}
\quad \text{and then} \quad
\begin{array}{l}
\text{r1} := 3 \\
\text{r2} := 6
\end{array}
$$

If the 3 in r1 is dead, then the initial load can also be eliminated.

Common subexpression elimination: When the same calculation occurs twice within the peephole of the optimizer, we can often eliminate the second calculation:

$$
\begin{array}{l}
\text{r2} := \text{r1} \times 5 \\
\text{r2} := \text{r2} + \text{r3} \\
\text{r3} := \text{r1} \times 5
\end{array}
\quad \text{becomes} \quad
\begin{array}{l}
\text{r4} := \text{r1} \times 5 \\
\text{r2} := \text{r4} + \text{r3} \\
\text{r3} := \text{r4}
\end{array}
$$

Often, as shown here, an extra register will be needed to hold the common value.

Copy propagation: Even when we cannot tell that the contents of register *b* will be constant, we may sometimes be able to tell that register *b* will contain the same value as register *a*. We can then replace uses of *b* with uses of *a*, so long as neither *a* nor *b* is modified:

$$
\begin{array}{l}
\text{r2} := \text{r1} \\
\text{r3} := \text{r1} + \text{r2} \\
\text{r2} := 5
\end{array}
\quad \text{becomes} \quad
\begin{array}{l}
\text{r2} := \text{r1} \\
\text{r3} := \text{r1} + \text{r1} \\
\text{r2} := 5
\end{array}
\quad \text{and then} \quad
\begin{array}{l}
\text{r3} := \text{r1} + \text{r1} \\
\text{r2} := 5
\end{array}
$$

Performed early in code improvement, copy propagation can serve to decrease register pressure. In a peephole optimizer it may allow us (as in this case, in which the copy of r1 in r2 is dead) to eliminate one or more instructions.

Strength reduction: Numeric identities can sometimes be used to replace a comparatively expensive instruction with a cheaper one. In particular, multiplication or division by powers of two can be replaced with adds or shifts:

$$
\text{r1} := \text{r2} \times 2 \quad \text{becomes} \quad \text{r1} := \text{r2} + \text{r2} \quad \text{or} \quad \text{r1} := \text{r2} << 1
$$

$$
\text{r1} := \text{r2} / 2 \quad \text{becomes} \quad \text{r1} := \text{r2} >> 1
$$

(This last replacement may not be correct when r2 is negative; see Exercise 13.1.) In a similar vein, algebraic identities allow us to perform simplifications such as the following:

$$
\text{r1} := \text{r2} \times 0 \quad \text{becomes} \quad \text{r1} := 0
$$

Elimination of useless instructions: Instructions such as the following can be dropped entirely:

r1 := r1 + 0
r1 := r1 × 1

Filling of load and branch delays: Several examples of delay-filling transformations appear in Section 5.6.1.

Exploitation of the instruction set: Particularly on CISC machines, sequences of simple instructions can often be replaced by a smaller number of more complex instructions. For example,

r1 := r1 & 0x0000FF00
r1 := r1 >> 8

can be replaced by an "extract byte" instruction. The sequence

r1 := r2 + 8
r3 := *r1

where r1 is dead at the end can be replaced by a single load of r3 using a base plus displacement addressing mode. Similarly,

r1 := *r2
r2 := r2 + 4

where *r2 is a four-byte quantity can be replaced by a single load with an auto-increment addressing mode. On many machines, a series of loads from consecutive locations can be replaced by a single, multiple-register load.

Because they use a small, fixed-size window, peephole optimizers tend to be very fast: they impose a small, constant amount of overhead per instruction. They are also relatively easy to write and, when used on naive code, can yield dramatic performance improvements. In many cases, it is easier to count on a peephole optimizer to fix suboptimal code than it is to generate better code in the first place.

It should be emphasized, however, that most of the forms of code improvement in the list above are not specific to peephole optimization. In fact, all but the last (exploitation of the instruction set) will appear in our discussion of more general forms of code improvement. The more general forms will do a better job, because they won't be limited to looking at a narrow window of instructions. In a compiler with good machine-specific and machine-independent code improvers, there may be no need for the peephole optimizer to eliminate redundancies or useless instructions, fold constants, perform strength reduction, or fill load and branch delays. In such a compiler the peephole optimizer serves mainly to exploit idiosyncracies of the target machine, and perhaps to clean up certain suboptimal code idioms that leak through the rest of the back end.

13.3 Redundancy Elimination in Basic Blocks

To implement local optimizations, the compiler must first identify the fragments of the syntax tree that correspond to basic blocks, as described in Section 9.1.1. Roughly speaking, these fragments consist of tree nodes that are adjacent according to in-order traversal, and contain no selection or iteration constructs. In Figure 9.8 (page 505) we presented an attribute grammar to generate linear (goto-containing) code for simple syntax trees. A similar grammar can be used to create a control flow graph (see Exercise 9.9).

A call to a user subroutine within a control flow graph could be treated as a pair of branches, defining a boundary between basic blocks, but as long as we know that the call will return we can simply treat it as an instruction with potentially wide-ranging side effects (i.e., as an instruction that may overwrite many registers and memory locations). As we noted in Section 8.2.3, the compiler may also choose to expand small subroutines in-line. In this case the behavior of the "call" is completely visible. If the called routine consists of a single basic block, it becomes a part of the calling block. If it consists of multiple blocks, its prologue and epilogue become part of the blocks before and after the call.

Throughout much of the remainder of this chapter we will trace the improvement of code for a single subroutine: specifically, one that calculates into an array the binomial coefficients $\binom{n}{m}$ for all $0 \leq m \leq n$. These are the elements of the nth row of Pascal's triangle. The mth element of the row indicates the number of distinct combinations of m items that may be chosen from among a collection of n items. In C, the code looks like this:

```
combinations (int n, int *A) {
    int i, t;
    A[0] = 1;
    A[n] = 1;
    t = 1;
    for (i = 1; i <= n/2; i++) {
        t = (t * (n+1-i)) / i;
        A[i] = t;
        A[n-i] = t;
    }
}
```

This code capitalizes on the fact that $\binom{n}{m} = \binom{n}{n-m}$ for all $0 \leq m \leq n$. One can prove (Exercise 13.2) that the use of integer arithmetic will not lead to round-off errors.

A syntax tree for our subroutine appears in Figure 13.2, with basic blocks identified. The corresponding control flow graph appears in Figure 13.3. To avoid artificial interference between instructions at this early stage of code improvement, we employ a medium-level intermediate form in which every calculated value is placed in a separate register. To emphasize that these are virtual registers (of which there is an unlimited supply), we name them v1, v2, ... We will use r1, r2, ... to represent physical registers in Section 13.8.

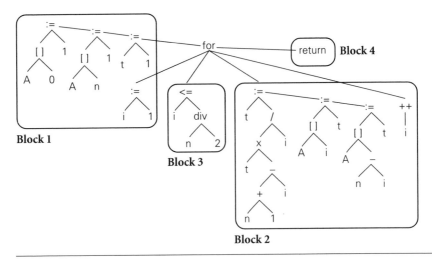

Figure 13.2 Syntax tree for the `combinations` **subroutine.** Portions of the tree corresponding to basic blocks have been circled.

The fact that no virtual register is assigned a value by more than one instruction in the original control flow graph is crucial to the success of our code improvement techniques. Informally, it says that every value that could eventually end up in a separate physical register will, at least at first, be placed in a separate virtual register. Of course if an assignment to a virtual register appears within a loop, then the register may take on a different value in every iteration. In addition, as we move through the various phases of code improvement we will relax our rules to allow a virtual register to be assigned a value in more than one place. The key point is that by employing a new virtual register whenever possible at the outset we maximize the degrees of freedom available to later phases of code improvement.

In the initial (entry) and final (exit) blocks, we have included code for the subroutine prologue and epilogue. We have assumed the MIPS calling conventions, described in Section 8.2.1. We have also assumed that the compiler has recognized that our subroutine is a leaf, and that it therefore has no need to save the return address (ra) or frame pointer (fp) registers. In all cases, references to n, A, i, and t in memory should be interpreted as performing the appropriate displacement addressing with respect to the stack pointer (sp) register. Though we assume that parameter values were passed in registers (physical registers r4 and r5 on the MIPS), our original (naive) code immediately saves these values to memory, so that references can be handled in the same way as they are for local variables. We make the saves by way of virtual registers so that they will be visible to the global value numbering algorithm described in Section 13.4.1. Eventually, after several stages of improvement, we will find that both the parameters and the local variables can be kept permanently in registers, eliminating the need for the various loads, stores, and copy operations.

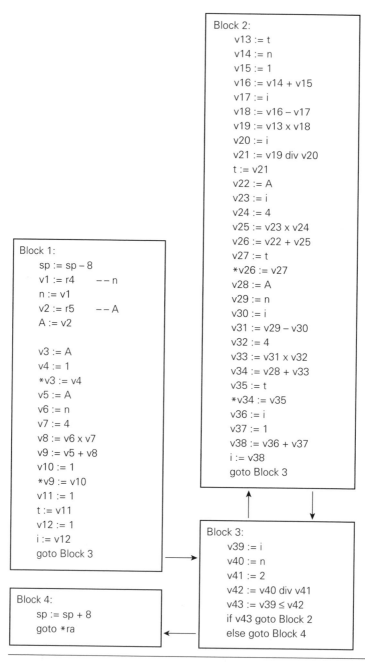

Figure 13.3 **Naive control flow graph for the** `combinations` **subroutine.** Note that reference parameter A contains the *address* of the array into which to write results; hence we write v3 := A instead of v3 := &A.

To improve the code within basic blocks, we need to minimize loads and stores, and to identify redundant calculations. One common way to accomplish these tasks is to translate the syntax tree for a basic block into an *expression DAG* (directed acyclic graph) in which redundant loads and computations are merged into individual nodes with multiple parents [ASU86, Sec. 9.8; FL88, Sec. 15.7]. Similar functionality can also be obtained without an explicitly graphical program representation, through a technique known as local *value numbering* [Muc97, Sec. 12.4]. We describe this technique below.

Value numbering assigns the same name (a "number") to any two or more symbolically equivalent computations ("values"), so that redundant instances will be recognizable by their common name. While performing local value numbering, we will also implement local constant folding, constant propagation, copy propagation, common subexpression elimination, strength reduction, and useless instruction elimination. (The distinctions among these optimizations will be clearer in the global case.)

We scan the instructions of a basic block in order, maintaining a dictionary to keep track of values that have already been loaded or computed. For a load instruction, $vi := x$, we consult the dictionary to see whether x is already in some register vj. If so, we simply add an entry to the dictionary indicating that uses of vi should be replaced by uses of vj. If x is not in the dictionary, we generate a load in the new version of the basic block, and add an entry to the dictionary indicating that x is available in vi. For a load of a constant into register vi, we check to see whether the constant is small enough to fit in the immediate operand of a compute instruction. If so, we add an entry to the dictionary indicating that uses of vi should be replaced by uses of the constant, but we generate no code: we'll embed the constant directly in the appropriate instructions when we come to them. If the constant is large, we consult the dictionary to see whether it has already been loaded (or computed) into some other register vj; if so, we note that uses of vi should be replaced by uses of vj. If the constant is large and not already available, then we generate instructions to load it into its register and then note its availability with an appropriate dictionary entry. In all cases, we create a dictionary entry for the target register of a load, indicating whether that register (1) should be used under its own name in subsequent instructions, (2) should be replaced by uses of some other register, or (3) should be replaced by some small immediate constant.

For a compute instruction, $vi := vj \; op \; vk$, we first consult the dictionary to see whether uses of vj or vk should be replaced by uses of some other registers or small constants vl and vm. If both operands are constants, then we can perform the operation at compile time, effecting constant folding. We then treat the constant as we did for loads above: keeping a note of its value if small, or of the register in which it resides if large. We also note opportunities to perform strength reduction or to eliminate useless instructions. If at least one of the operands is nonconstant (and the instruction is not useless), we consult the dictionary again to see whether the result of the (potentially modified) computation is already available in some register vn. This final lookup operation is keyed by a combination of the operator *op* and the operand registers or constants v*j* (or v*l*) and v*k* (or v*m*). If the lookup is successful, we add an entry to the dictionary indicating that uses of v*i* should be replaced by uses of v*n*. If the lookup is unsuccessful, we generate an appropriate instruction (e.g., v*i* := v*j* *op* v*k* or v*i* := v*l* *op* v*m*) in the new version of the basic block, and add a corresponding entry to the dictionary.

As we work our way through the basic block, the dictionary provides us with four kinds of information:

1. For each already-computed virtual register: whether it should be used under its own name, replaced by some other register, or replaced by an immediate constant.
2. For certain variables: what register holds the (current) value.
3. For certain large constants: what register holds the value.
4. For some (op, arg1, arg2) triples, where arg*i* can be a register name or a constant: what register already holds the result.

For a store instruction, x := v*i*, we remove any existing entry for x in the dictionary, and add an entry indicating that x is available in v*i*. We also note (in that entry) that the value of x in memory is stale. If x may be an alias for some other variable y, we must also remove any existing entry for y from the dictionary. (If we are *certain* that y is an alias for x, then we can add an entry indicating that the value of y is available in v*i*.) A similar precaution, ignored in the discussion above, applies to loads: if x may be an alias for y, and if there is an entry for y in the dictionary indicating that the value in memory is stale, then a load instruction v*i* := x must be preceded by a store to y. When we reach the end of the block, we traverse the dictionary, generating store instructions for all variables whose values in memory are stale. If any variables may be aliases for each other, we must take care to generate the stores in the order in which the values were produced. After generating the stores, we generate the branch (if any) that ends the block.

A naive approach to aliases is to assume that assignment to element *i* of an array may alter element *j*, for any *j*, that assignment through a pointer to an object of type *t* may alter any variable of that type, and that a call to a subroutine may alter any variable visible in the subroutine's scope (including at a minimum all globals). These assumptions are overly conservative, and can greatly limit the ability of a compiler to generate good code. More aggressive compilers perform extensive symbolic analysis of array subscripts in order to narrow the set of potential aliases for an array assignment. Similar analysis may be able to determine that particular array or record elements can be treated as un-aliased scalars, making them candidates for allocation to registers. Alias analysis for pointers is an active research topic (see the Bibliographic Notes at the end of the chapter).

In the process of local value numbering we automatically perform several important operations. We identify common subexpressions (none of which occur in our example), allowing us to compute them only once. We also implement constant folding and certain strength reductions. Finally, we perform local constant and copy propagation, and eliminate redundant loads and stores: our use of the dictionary to delay store instructions ensures that (in the absence of potential aliases) we never write a variable twice, or write and then read it again within the same basic block.

To increase the number of common subexpressions we can find, we may want to traverse the syntax tree prior to linearizing it, rearranging expressions into some sort of normal form. For commutative operations, for example, we can swap subtrees if necessary to put operands in lexicographic order. We can then recognize that a + b and b + a are common subexpressions. In some cases (e.g., in the context of array address calculations, or with explicit permission from the programmer), we may use associative or distributive rules to normalize expressions as well, though as we noted in Section 6.1.3 such changes can in general lead to arithmetic overflow or numerical instability. Unfortunately, straightforward normalization techniques will fail to recognize the redundancy in a + b + c and a + c; lexicographic ordering is simply a heuristic.

Figure 13.4 shows the control flow graph for our `combinations` subroutine after local redundancy elimination. We have eliminated 21 of the instructions in Figure 13.3, all of them loads of variables or constants. Thirteen of the eliminated instructions are in the body of the loop (Blocks 2 and 3) where improvements are particularly important. We have also performed strength reduction on the two instructions that multiply a register by the constant 4 and the one that divides a register by 2, replacing them by equivalent shifts.

13.4 Global Redundancy and Data Flow Analysis

In this section we will concentrate on the elimination of redundant loads and computations across the boundaries between basic blocks. We will translate the code of our basic blocks into *static single assignment* (SSA) form, which will allow us to perform global value numbering. Once value numbers have been assigned, we shall be able to perform global common subexpression elimination, constant propagation, and copy propagation. In a compiler both the translation to SSA form and the various global optimizations would be driven by data flow analysis. We will go into some of the details for global optimization (specifically, for the problems of identifying common subexpressions and useless store instructions) after a much more informal presentation of the translation to SSA form. We will also give data flow equations in Section 13.5 for the calculation of *reaching definitions*, used (among other things) to move invariant computations out of loops.

Global redundancy elimination can be structured in such a way that it catches local redundancies as well, eliminating the need for a separate local pass. The global algorithms are easier to implement and to explain, however, if we assume

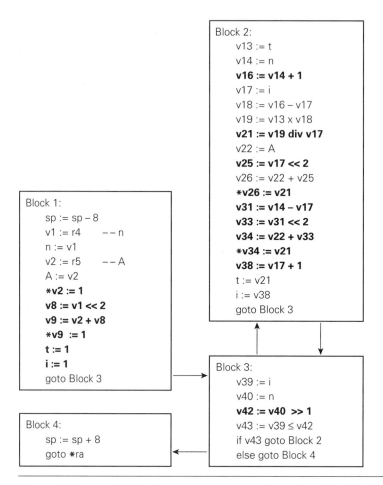

Figure 13.4 Control flow graph for the combinations **subroutine after local redundancy elimination and strength reduction.** Changes from Figure 13.3 are shown in boldface type.

that a local pass has already occurred. In particular, local redundancy elimination allows us to assume (in the absence of aliases, which we will ignore in our discussion) that no variable is read or written more than once in a basic block.

13.4.1 Static Single Assignment Form and Global Value Numbering

Value numbering, as introduced in Section 13.3, assigns a distinct name to every symbolically distinct value that is loaded or computed in a given body of code, allowing us to recognize when certain loads or computations are redundant. The first step in *global* value numbering is to distinguish among the values that may be written to a variable in different basic blocks. We accomplish this step using SSA form.

By convention, we assign subscripts to variable names: a different subscript for each distinct store instruction. We then assign matching subscripts to loads. If the instruction $v2 := x$ is guaranteed to read the value of x written by the instruction $x_3 := v1$, then we replace $v2 := x$ with $v2 := x_3$. If we cannot tell which version of x will be read, we use a hypothetical *selection function* ϕ to choose among the possible alternatives. In general, the calculation of SSA form (and of selection functions in particular) requires the use of data flow analysis. We will describe the concept of data flow in the context of global common subexpression elimination in Section 13.4.2. In the current section we will generate SSA code informally; data flow formulations can be found in the texts of Appel [App97, Sec. 19.1] and Muchnick [Muc97, Sec. 8.11].

In the `combinations` subroutine we assign the subscript 1 to the stores of t and i at the end of Block 1. We assign the subscript 2 to the stores of t and i at the end of Block 2. Thus at the end of Block 1 t_1 and i_1 are live; at the end of Block 2 t_2 and i_2 are live. What about Block 3? If control enters Block 3 from Block 1, then t_1 and i_1 will be live, but if control enters Block 3 from Block 2, then t_2 and i_2 will be live. We invent a function ϕ that returns its first argument if control enters Block 3 from Block 1, and its second argument if control enters Block 3 from Block 2. We then use this function to write new values t_3 and i_3. Since Block 3 does not modify either t or i, we know that t_3 and i_3 will be live at the end of the block. Morover, since control always enters Block 2 from Block 3, t_3 and i_3 will be live at the beginning of Block 2. The load of v13 in Block 2 is guaranteed to return t_3; the loads of v17 in Block 2 and of v39 in Block 3 are guaranteed to return i_3.

Fortunately, we won't actually have to generate code to compute ϕ at run time. Our goal with SSA is simply to assign names to loads in such a way that two expressions with the same name are guaranteed to represent the same value at run time. If two virtual registers are assigned the result of the same ϕ function, then their values will have been produced by (the same execution of) the same store instruction. Because ours is a simple subroutine, only one selection function is needed: it indicates whether control entered Block 3 from Block 1 or from Block 2. In a more complicated subroutine there could be additional selection functions, for other blocks with more than one predecessor.

SSA form for the `combinations` subroutine appears in Figure 13.5. With flow-dependent values determined by selection functions, we are now in a position to perform global value numbering. As in the local case, we peruse our code (in this case the entire subroutine) from beginning to end, keeping a dictionary that maps loaded and computed values to the names of virtual registers that contain them. Because our code is in SSA form, we never have to remove anything from the dictionary: no value is ever written by more than one instruction.

In Block 1 we simply add new entries to the dictionary; since local redundancies have been removed, the code is not affected. In Block 2, in the second

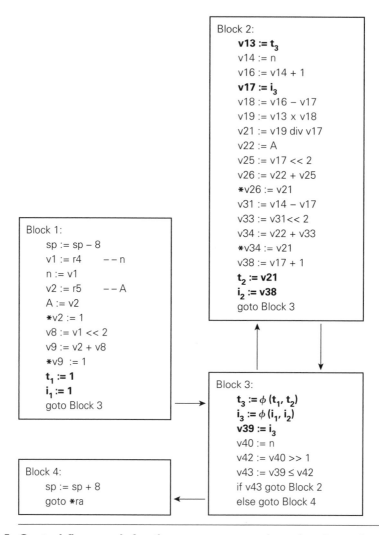

Figure 13.5 Control flow graph for the combinations **subroutine, in static single assignment (SSA) form.** Changes from Figure 13.4 are shown in boldface type.

instruction (v14 := n), we find that n is already in the dictionary, with virtual register v1. We therefore replace v14 with v1. We do *not* (yet) drop the load instruction; until we perform data-flow analysis, we won't know whether we can count on the load of v1 in Block 1 having already occurred. For now, we simply guarantee that whenever n is loaded we do it into virtual register v1. To accommodate the change, we must also change v14 to v1 in the third instruction. In a

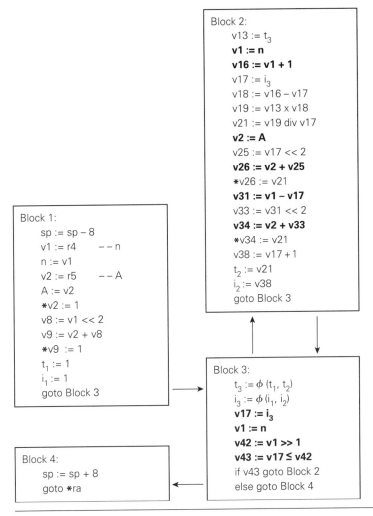

Figure 13.6 Control flow graph for the combinations **subroutine after global value numbering.** Changes from Figure 13.5 are shown in boldface type.

similar vein, we change v22 to v2 in the 8th, 10th, and 14th instructions.

In Block 3 we have more replacements. In the first instruction ($v39 := i_3$), we discover that the right-hand side was loaded into v17 in Block 2. We therefore replace v39 with v17, in both the first and fourth instructions. Similarly, we replace v40 with v1, in both the second and third instructions. There are no changes in Block 4.

The result of global value numbering on our combinations subroutine appears in Figure 13.6. In this case the only common values identified are variables loaded from memory. In a more complicated subroutine, we would also identify computations performed in more than one block. As with loads, we would change the second and subsequent computations so that all of them would place their results in the same virtual register. Static single assignment form is useful for a variety of code improvements. In our discussion here we use it only for global value numbering. We will drop it in later figures.

13.4.2 Global Common Subexpression Elimination

We have seen an informal example of data flow analysis in the construction of static single assignment form. We will now employ a more formal example for global common subexpression elimination. As a result of global value numbering, we know that any common subexpression will have been placed into the same virtual register wherever it is computed. We will therefore use virtual register names to represent expressions in the discussion below. The goal of global common subexpression elimination is to identify places in which an instruction that computes a value for a given virtual register can be eliminated, because the computation is certain to already have occurred on every control path leading to the instruction.

Many instances of data flow analysis can be cast in the following framework: (1) four sets for each basic block B, called In_B, Out_B, Gen_B, and $Kill_B$; (2) values for the *Gen* and *Kill* sets; (3) an equation relating the sets for any given block B; and (4) an equation relating the *Out* set of a given block to the *In* sets of its successors, or relating the *In* set of the block to the *Out* sets of its predecessors. The goal of the analysis is to find the smallest *In* and *Out* sets that satisfy the equations. These constitute a *least fixed point* for the equations, in a manner reminiscent of the self-definition of Lisp discussed in section 11.2.1. (We could fabricate additional solutions to the equations by adding extraneous information to the sets, but that would not be useful.)

In the case of global common subexpression elimination, In_B is the set of expressions (virtual registers) guaranteed to be available at the beginning of block B. These *available expressions* will all have been set by predecessor blocks. Out_B is the set of expressions guaranteed to be available at the end of B. $Kill_B$ is the set of expressions *killed* in B: invalidated by assignment to one of the variables used (directly or indirectly) to calculate the expression, and not subsequently recalculated in B. Gen_B is the set of expressions calculated in B and not subsequently killed in B. The data flow equations for available expression analysis are:[2]

$$Out_B = Gen_B \cup (In_B \smallsetminus Kill_B)$$

$$In_B = \bigcap_{\text{predecessors } C \text{ of } B} Out_C$$

---

2 Set notation here is standard: $\bigcup_i S_i$ indicates the union of all sets S_i; $\bigcap_i S_i$ indicates the intersection of all sets S_i; $A \smallsetminus B$, pronounced "A minus B" indicates the set of all elements found in A but not in B.

Available expression analysis is known as a *forward* data flow problem, because information flows forward across branches: the *In* set of a block depends on the *Out* sets of its predecessors. We shall see an example of a *backward* data flow problem later in this section.

We calculate the desired fixed point of our equations in an inductive (iterative) fashion, much as we computed FIRST and FOLLOW sets in Section 2.2.5. In our example program (ignoring assignments to sp), we have the following *Gen* and *Kill* sets:

$$
\begin{aligned}
Gen_1 &= \{v1, v2, v8, v9, n, A, t, i\} & Kill_1 &= \{v13, v17, v18, v19, v21, v31\} \\
Gen_2 &= \{v1, v2, v16, t, i\} & Kill_2 &= \{v13, v17, v18, v19, v21, v25, \\
& & & \quad v26, v31, v33, v34, v38, v43\} \\
Gen_3 &= \{v1, v17, v42, v43\} & Kill_3 &= \varnothing \\
Gen_4 &= \varnothing & Kill_4 &= \varnothing
\end{aligned}
$$

The *Kill* sets are not trivially visible from the code; they require that we know which variables and registers contributed to the values in each virtual register. This information can be gathered during local redundancy elimination (Exercise 13.10). Many of the virtual registers assigned values in a block do not appear in the *Gen* set, because they are killed by a store at the end of the block. In Block 2, for example, v13 and v17 are killed by the assignments to t and i, and these kill (transitively) v18, v19, v21, v25, v26, v31, v33, v34, and v38.

If we begin with $In_B = Out_B = \varnothing$ for all blocks B, one iteration of our data flow equations gives us $In_B = \varnothing$ and $Out_B = Gen_B$ for all B. (We could model the incoming parameters as members of In_1, but they are also covered by the assignments to v1 and v2.) If we then recalculate first the *In* sets and then the *Out* sets, a second iteration of the equations yields the following:

$$
\begin{aligned}
In_1 &= \varnothing & Out_1 &= \{v1, v2, v8, v9, n, A, t, i\} \\
In_2 &= \{v1, v17, v42, v43\} & Out_2 &= \{v1, v2, v16, v42, t, i\} \\
In_3 &= \{v1, v2, t, i\} & Out_3 &= \{v1, v2, v17, v42, v43, t, i\} \\
In_4 &= \{v1, v17, v42, v43\} & Out_4 &= \{v1, v17, v42, v43\}
\end{aligned}
$$

After one more iteration, we have

$$
\begin{aligned}
In_1 &= \varnothing & Out_1 &= \{v1, v2, v8, v9, n, A, t, i\} \\
In_2 &= \{v1, v2, v17, v42, v43, t, i\} & Out_2 &= \{v1, v2, v16, v42, t, i\} \\
In_3 &= \{v1, v2, t, i\} & Out_3 &= \{v1, v2, v17, v42, v43, t, i\} \\
In_4 &= \{v1, v2, v17, v42, v43\} & Out_4 &= \{v1, v2, v17, v42, v43\}
\end{aligned}
$$

At this point further iterations add no new information; we have reached the least fixed point. We can now exploit what we have learned. Whenever a virtual register is in the *In* set of a block, we can drop any assignment of that register in the block. In our example subroutine, we can drop the loads of v1, v2, and v17 in Block 2, and the load of v1 in Block 3. In addition, whenever a variable is in the *In* set of a block, we can replace a load of that variable with a register–register move on each of the potential paths into the block. In our example, we

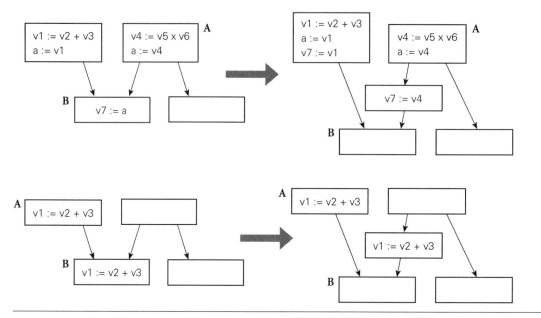

Figure 13.7 Splitting an edge of a control flow graph to eliminate a partially redundant load (top) or computation (bottom).

can replace the load of t in Block 2 and the load of i in Block 3 (the load of i in Block 2 has already been eliminated). To compensate, we must load v13 and v17 with the constant 1 at the end of Block 1, and move v21 into v13 and v38 into v17 at the end of Block 2. (The careful reader may note that v21 and v38 are not strictly necessary: if we computed new values directly into v13 and v17, we could eliminate the two register–register moves. This observation, while correct, need not be made at this time; it can wait until we perform induction variable optimizations and register allocation, to be described in Sections 13.5.2 and 13.8, respectively.)

If the block (call it A) in which a variable is written has more than one successor, only one of which (call it B) contains a redundant load, and if B has more than one predecessor, then we need to create a new block on the arc between A and B to hold the register–register move. This way the move will not be executed on code paths that don't need it. In a similar vein, if an expression is available from A but not from B's other predecessor, then we can move the load or computation of the expression back into the predecessor that lacks it or, if that predecessor has more than one successor, into a new block on the connecting arc. This move will eliminate a redundancy on the path through A. These "edge splitting" transformations are illustrated in Figure 13.7. In general, a load or computation is said to be *partially redundant* if it occurs more than once on some paths through the flow graph, but not on others. No edge splits are required in the `combinations` example.

Common subexpression elimination can have a complicated effect on register pressure. If we realize that the expression v10 + v20 has been calculated into, say, register v30 earlier in the program, and we exploit this knowledge to replace a later recalculation of the expression with a direct use of v30, then we may expand the span of instructions over which v30 is live. At the same time, if v10 and v20 are not used for other purposes in the intervening region of the program, we may *shrink* the range over which *they* are live. In a subroutine with a high level of register pressure, a good compiler may sometimes perform the inverse of common subexpression elimination (known as *forward substitution*) in order to eliminate the need to spill registers to memory.

Figure 13.8 shows the result of applying global common subexpression elimination to our example subroutine. Similar instances of data flow analysis can be used for constant propagation and copy propagation. We skip these analyses here; none of them yields improvements in our example. Instead, we turn our attention to *live variable analysis*, which is very important in our example, and in general in any subroutine in which global common subexpression analysis has eliminated load instructions.

Live variable analysis is the *backward* flow problem mentioned above. It determines which instructions produce values that will be needed in the future, allowing us to eliminate *dead* (useless) instructions. In our example we will concern ourselves only with values written to memory and with the elimination of dead stores. When applied to values in virtual registers as well, live variable analysis can help to identify other dead instructions. (None of these arise this early in the `combinations` example.)

For this instance of data flow analysis, In_B is the set of variables that are live at the beginning of block B. Out_B is the set of variables that are live at the end of the block. Gen_B is the set of variables read in B without first being written in B. $Kill_B$ is the set of variables written in B without having been read first. The data flow equations are:

$$In_B = Gen_B \cup (Out_B \smallsetminus Kill_B)$$
$$Out_B = \bigcup_{\text{successors } C \text{ of } B} In_C$$

In comparison to the equations for available expression analysis, the roles of *In* and *Out* have been reversed (that's why it's a backward problem), and the intersection operator in the second equation has been replaced by a union. Intersection ("all paths") problems require that information flow over *all* paths between blocks; union ("any path") problems require that it flow along *some* path. Further data flow examples appear in Exercises 13.8 and 13.9.

In our example program, we have:

$$
\begin{array}{llcllcl}
Gen_1 & = & \varnothing & \qquad & Kill_1 & = & \{n, A, t, i\} \\
Gen_2 & = & \varnothing & \qquad & Kill_2 & = & \{t, i\} \\
Gen_3 & = & \varnothing & \qquad & Kill_3 & = & \varnothing \\
Gen_4 & = & \varnothing & \qquad & Kill_4 & = & \varnothing
\end{array}
$$

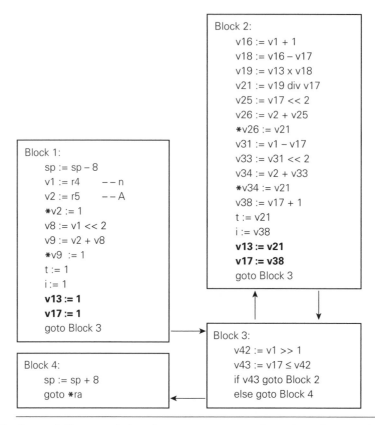

Figure 13.8 Control flow graph for the `combinations` **subroutine after performing global common subexpression elimination.** Note the absence of the many load instructions of Figure 13.6. Compensating register–register moves are shown in boldface type. Live variable analysis will allow us to drop the two pairs of instructions immediately before these moves, together with the stores of n and A (v1 and v2) in Block 1. It will also allow us to drop the changes to the stack pointer in the subroutine prologue and epilogue: we won't need space for local variables anymore.

We begin with $In_B = Out_B = \varnothing$ for all blocks B. (If our subroutine had written any nonlocal (e.g., global) variables, then these would have been initial members of Out_4.) One iteration of our data flow equations gives us $In_B = Gen_B$ and $Out_B = \varnothing$ for all blocks B. But since $Gen_B = \varnothing$ for all B, this is our fixed point! Common subexpression elimination has left us with a situation in which none of our parameters or local variables are live; all of the stores of t and i can be eliminated (see Figure 13.8). In addition, the fact that t and i can be kept entirely in registers means that we won't need to update the stack pointer in the subroutine prologue and epilogue: there won't be any stack frame.

Aliases must be treated in a conservative fashion in both common subexpression elimination and live variable analysis. If a store instruction might modify variable x, then for purposes of common subexpression elimination we must consider the store as killing any expression that depends on x. If a load instruction might access x, and x is not written earlier in the block containing the load, then x must be considered live at the beginning of the block. In our example we have assumed that the compiler is able to verify that, as a reference parameter, array A cannot alias either value parameter n or local variables t and i.

13.5 Loop Improvement I

Because programs tend to spend most of their time in loops, code improvements that improve the speed of loops are particularly important. In this section we consider two classes of loop improvements: those that move *invariant* computations out of the body of a loop and into its header, and those that reduce the amount of time spent maintaining *induction variables*. In Section 13.7 we will consider transformations that improve instruction scheduling by restructuring a loop body to include portions of more than one iteration of the original loop, and that manipulate multiply nested loops to improve cache performance or increase opportunities for parallelization.

13.5.1 Loop Invariants

A *loop invariant* is an instruction (i.e., a load or calculation) in a loop whose result is guaranteed to be the same in every iteration. Many loop invariants arise from addressing calculations for arrays. If a loop is executed n times and we are able to move an invariant instruction out of the body and into the header (saving its result in a register for use within the body), then we will eliminate $n - 1$ calculations from the program, a potentially significant savings.

In order to tell whether an instruction is invariant, we need to identify the bodies of loops, and we need to track the locations at which operand values are defined. The first task—identifying loops—is easy in a language such as Ada or Java, which relies exclusively on structured control flow: we simply save appropriate markers when linearizing the syntax tree. In a language with goto statements we may need to apply *control flow analysis* [ASU86, Sec. 10.4; App97, Sec. 18.1; Muc97, Chap. 7] to the control flow graph in order to identify loops.

Tracking the locations at which an operand may have been defined amounts to the problem of *reaching definitions*. Formally, we say an instruction that assigns a value v into a location (variable or register) l *reaches* a point p in the code if v may still be in l at p. Like the conversion to static single assignment form, considered informally in Section 13.4.1, the problem of reaching definitions can be structured as a set of forward, any-path data flow equations. We let Gen_B be the set of final assignments in block B (those that are not overwritten later in

B). For each assignment in *B* we also place in $Kill_B$ all *other* assignments (in any block) to the same location. Then we have

$$Out_B = Gen_B \cup (In_B \setminus Kill_B)$$

$$In_B = \bigcup_{\text{predecessors } C \text{ of } B} Out_C$$

Given In_B (the set of reaching definitions at the beginning of the block), we can determine the reaching definitions of all values used *within B* by a simple linear perusal of the code.

Given reaching definitions, we define an instruction to be a loop invariant if each of its operands (a) is a constant, (b) has reaching definitions that all lie outside the loop, or (c) has a single reaching definition, even if that definition is an instruction *d* located inside the loop, so long as *d* is itself a loop invariant. (If there is more than one reaching definition for a particular variable, then we cannot be sure of invariance unless we know that all definitions will assign the same value, something that most compilers do not attempt to infer.) As in previous analyses, we begin with the obvious cases and proceed inductively until we reach a fixed point.

In our `combinations` example, visual inspection of the code reveals two loop invariants: the assignment to v16 in Block 2 and the assignment to v42 in Block 3. Moving these invariants out of the loop (and dropping the dead stores and stack pointer updates of Figure 13.8) yields the code of Figure 13.9.

In the new version of the code v16 and v42 will be calculated even if the loop is executed zero times. In general this precalculation may not be a good idea. If an invariant calculation is expensive and the loop is not in fact executed, then we may have made the program slower. Worse, if an invariant calculation may produce a run-time error (divide by zero, for example), we may have made the program incorrect. A safe and efficient general solution is to insert an initial test for zero iterations *before* any invariant calculations; we consider this option in Exercise 13.5. In the specific case of the `combinations` subroutine our more naive transformation is both safe and (in the common case) efficient.

13.5.2 Induction Variables

An *induction variable* (or register) is one that takes on a simple progression of values in successive iterations of a loop. We will confine our attention here to arithmetic progressions; more elaborate examples appear in Exercises 13.11 and 13.12. Induction variables commonly appear as loop indices, subscript computations, or variables incremented or decremented explicitly within the body of the loop. Induction variables are important for two main reasons:

- They commonly provide opportunities for strength reduction, most notably by replacing multiplication with addition. For example, if i is a loop index

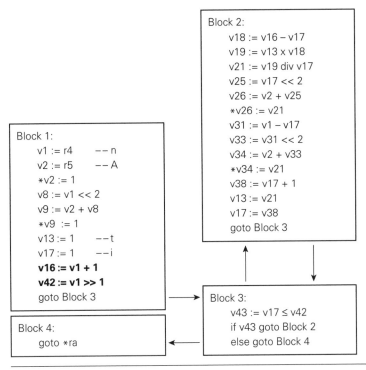

Figure 13.9 Control flow graph for the combinations **subroutine after moving the invariant calculations of** v16 **and** v42 **(shown in boldface type) out of the loop.** We have also dropped the dead stores of Figure 13.8, and have eliminated the stack space for t and i, which now reside entirely in registers.

variable, then expressions of the form t := k × i + c for i > a can be replaced by t_i := t_{i-1} + k, where t_a = k × a + c.

- They are commonly redundant: instead of keeping several induction variables in registers across all iterations of the loop, we can often keep a smaller number and calculate the remainder from those when needed (assuming the calculations are sufficiently inexpensive). The result is often a reduction in register pressure with no increase—and sometimes a decrease—in computation cost. In particular, after strength-reducing other induction variables, we can often eliminate the loop index variable itself, with an appropriate change to the end test (see Figure 13.10 for an example).

The algorithms required to identify, strength-reduce, and possibly eliminate induction variables are more-or-less straightforward, but fairly tedious [App97, Sec. 18.3; Muc97, Chap. 14]; we do not present the details here. Similar algorithms can be used to eliminate array and subrange bounds checks in many applications.

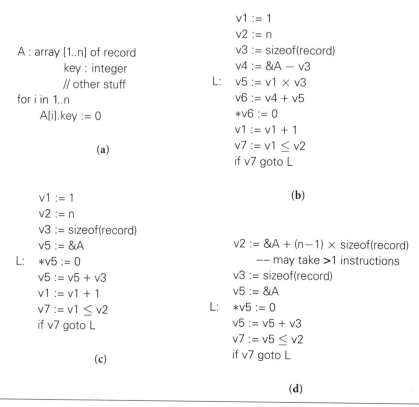

A : array [1..n] of record
    key : integer
    // other stuff
for i in 1..n
    A[i].key := 0

(a)

```
        v1 := 1
        v2 := n
        v3 := sizeof(record)
        v4 := &A − v3
L:      v5 := v1 × v3
        v6 := v4 + v5
        *v6 := 0
        v1 := v1 + 1
        v7 := v1 ≤ v2
        if v7 goto L
```

(b)

```
        v1 := 1
        v2 := n
        v3 := sizeof(record)
        v5 := &A
L:      *v5 := 0
        v5 := v5 + v3
        v1 := v1 + 1
        v7 := v1 ≤ v2
        if v7 goto L
```

(c)

```
        v2 := &A + (n−1) × sizeof(record)
            −− may take >1 instructions
        v3 := sizeof(record)
        v5 := &A
L:      *v5 := 0
        v5 := v5 + v3
        v7 := v5 ≤ v2
        if v7 goto L
```

(d)

Figure 13.10 **Code improvement of induction variables.** High-level pseudocode source is shown in (a). Target code prior to induction variable optimizations is shown in (b). In (c) we have performed strength reduction on v5, the array index, and eliminated v4, at which point v5 no longer depends on v1 (i). In (d) we have modified the end test to use v5 instead of v1, and have eliminated v1.

For our `combinations` example, the code resulting from induction variable optimizations appears in Figure 13.11. Two induction variables—the array pointers v26 and v34—have undergone strength reduction, eliminating the need for v25, v31, and v33. Similarly v18 has been made independent of v17, eiminating the need for v16. A fifth induction variable—v38—has been eliminated by replacing its single use (the right-hand side of a register–register move) with the addition that computed it. We assume that a repeat of local redundancy elimination in Block 1 has allowed the initialization of v34 to capitalize on the value known to reside in v9.

For presentation purposes, we have also calculated the division operation directly into v13, allowing us to eliminate v21 and its later assignment into v13. A real compiler would probably not make this change until the register allocation phase of compilation, when it would verify that the previous value in v13 is dead at the time of the division (v21 is not an induction variable; its progression of

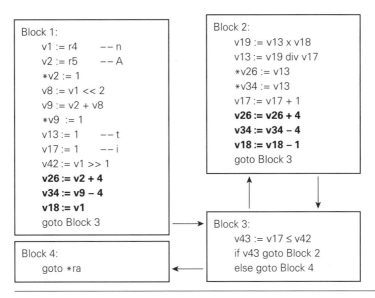

Figure 13.11 Control flow graph for the combinations **subroutine after optimizing induction variables.** Registers v26 and v34 have undergone strength reduction, allowing v25 and v21 to be eliminated. Registers v38 and v21 have been merged into v17 and v13.

values is not sufficiently simple). Making the change now eliminates the last redundant instruction in the block, and allows us to discuss instruction scheduling in comparative isolation from other issues.

13.6 Instruction Scheduling

In the example compiler stucture of Figure 13.1, the next phase after loop optimization is target code generation. As noted in Chapter 9, this phase linearizes the control flow graph and replaces the instructions of the medium-level intermediate form with target machine instructions. The replacements are often driven by an automatically generated pattern-matching algorithm. We will continue to employ our pseudoassembler "instruction set," so linearization will be the only change we see. Specifically, we will assume that the blocks of the program are concatenated in the order suggested by their names. Control will "fall through" from Block 2 to Block 3, and from Block 3 to Block 4 in the last iteration of the loop.

We will perform two rounds of instruction scheduling separated by register allocation. Given our use of pseudoassembler, we won't consider peephole optimization in any further detail. In Section 13.7, however, we will consider additional forms of code improvement for loops that could be applied *prior* to target code generation. We delay discussion of these because the need for them will be clearer after considering instruction scheduling.

On a pipelined machine, performance depends critically on the extent to which the compiler is able to keep the pipeline full. As explained in Section 5.6.1, delays may result when an instruction (1) needs a functional unit still in use by an earlier instruction, (2) needs data still being computed by an earlier instruction, or (3) cannot even be selected for execution until the outcome or target of a branch has been determined. In this section we consider cases (1) and (2), which can be addressed by reordering instructions within a basic block. A good solution to (3) requires branch prediction, generally with hardware assist. A compiler can solve the subproblem of filling branch delays in a more or less straightforward fashion [Muc97, Sec. 17.1.1].

If we examine the body of the loop in our `combinations` example, we find that the optimizations described thus far have transformed Block 2 from the 30 instruction sequence of Figure 13.3 into the eight instruction sequence of Figure 13.11 (not counting the final gotos). Unfortunately, on a pipelined machine without instruction reordering, this code is still distinctly suboptimal. In particular, the results of the second and third instructions are used immediately, but the results of multiplies and divides are commonly not available for several cycles. If we assume four-cycle delays, then our block will take sixteen cycles to execute.

To schedule instructions to make better use of the pipeline, we first arrange them into a directed acyclic graph (DAG), in which each node represents an instruction, and each arc represents a *dependence*,[3] as described in Section 5.6.1. Most arcs will represent *flow* dependences, in which one instruction uses a value produced by a previous instruction. A few will represent *anti*-dependences, in which a later instruction overwrites a value read by a previous instruction. In our example, these will correspond to updates of induction variables. If we were performing instruction scheduling after physical register allocation, then uses of the same register for independent values could increase the number of anti-dependences, and could also induce so-called *output* dependences, in which a later instruction overwrites a value written by a previous instruction. Anti- and output dependences can be hidden on an increasing number of machines by hardware register renaming.

Because common subexpression analysis has eliminated all of the loads and stores of i, n, and t in the `combinations` subroutine, and because there are no loads of elements of A (only stores), dependence analysis in our example will be dealing solely with values in registers. In general we would need to deal with values in memory as well, and to rely on alias analysis to determine when two

---

3 What we are discussing here is a *dependence DAG*. It is related to, but distinct from, the expression DAG mentioned in Section 13.3. In particular, the dependence DAG is constructed *after* the assignment of virtual registers to expressions, and its nodes represent instructions, rather than variables and operators.

Block 2:   Scheduled:

1. v19 := v13 x v18   v19 := v13 x v18
    —   v18 := v18 − 1
    —   —
    —   —
    —   —
2. v13 := v19 div v17   v13 := v19 div v17
    —   v17 := v17 + 1
    —   —
    —   —
    —   —
3. *v26 := v13   *v26 := v13
4. *v34 := v13   *v34 := v13
5. v17 := v17 + 1   v26 := v26 + 4
6. v26 := v26 + 4   v34 := v34 − 4
7. v34 := v34 − 4
8. v18 := v18 − 1
    –– fall through to Block 3
                                  (same)
Block 3:
    v43 := v17 ≤ v42
    if v43 goto Block 2
    –– else fall through to Block 4

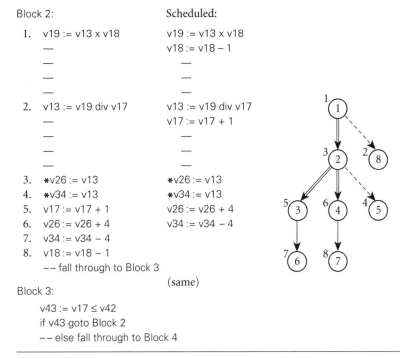

Figure 13.12 Dependence DAG for Block 2 of Figure 13.11, together with pseudocode for the entire loop, both before (left) and after (right) instruction scheduling. Circled numbers in the DAG correspond to instructions in the original version of the loop. Smaller adjacent numbers give the schedule order in the new loop. Solid arcs indicate flow dependences; dashed arcs indicate anti-dependences. Double arcs indicate pairs of instructions that must be separated by four additional instructions in order to avoid pipeline delays. Delays are shown explicitly in Block 2. Unless we modify the array indexing code (Exercise 13.19), only two instructions can be moved.

instructions might access the same location, and therefore share a dependence. If our target machine had condition codes (as described in Section 5.4), we would need to model these explicitly, tracking flow, anti-, and output dependences.

The dependence DAG for Block 2 of our combinations example appears in Figure 13.12. In this case the DAG turns out to be a tree. It was generated by examining the code from top to bottom, linking each instruction i to each subsequent instruction j such that j reads a register written by i (solid arcs) or writes a register read by i (dashed arcs). Any topological sort of the DAG (that is, any enumeration of the nodes in which each node appears before its children) will represent a correct schedule. Ideally we would like to choose a sort that minimizes overall delay. As with many aspects of code improvement, this task is NP-hard, so practical techniques rely upon heuristics.

To capture timing information, we define a function *latency (i, j)* that returns the number of cycles that must elapse between the scheduling of instructions i and j if j is to run after i in the same pipeline without stalling. (To maintain machine independence, this portion of the code improver must be driven by ta-bles of machine characteristics; those characteristics must not be "hard-coded.") Non-trivial latencies can result from data dependences or from conflicts for use of some physical resource, such as an incompletely pipelined functional unit. We will assume in our example that all units are fully pipelined, so all latencies are due to data dependences.

We now traverse the DAG from the roots down to the leaves. At each step we first determine the set of *candidate* nodes: those for which all parents have been scheduled. For each candidate i we then use the *latency* function with respect to already-scheduled nodes to determine the earliest time at which i could execute without stalling. We also precalculate the maximum over all paths from i to a leaf of the sums of the latencies on arcs; this gives us a lower bound on the time that will be required to finish the basic block after i has been scheduled. In our examples we will use the following three heuristics to choose among candidate nodes:

1. Favor nodes that can be started without stalling.

2. If there is a tie, favor nodes with the maximum delay to the end of the block.

3. If there is still a tie, favor the node that came first in the original source code (this strategy leads to more intuitive assembly language, which can be helpful in debugging).

Other possible scheduling heuristics include:

▪ Favor nodes that have a large number of children in the DAG (this increases flexibility for future iterations of the scheduling algorithm).

▪ Favor nodes that are the final use of a register (this reduces register pressure).

▪ If there are multiple pipelines, favor nodes that can use a pipeline that has not received an instruction recently.

If our target machine has multiple pipelines, then we must keep track for each instruction of the pipeline we think it will use, so we can distinguish between candidates that can start in the current cycle and those that cannot start until the next. (Imprecise machine models, cache misses, or other unpredictable delays may cause our guess to be wrong some of the time.)

Unfortunately, our example DAG leaves very little room for choice. The only possible improvements are to move Instruction 8 into one of the multiply or divide delay slots and Instruction 5 into one of the divide delay slots, reducing the total cycle count of Block 2 from 16 to 14. If we assume (1) that our target machine correctly predicts a backward branch at the bottom of the loop, and (2) that we can replicate the first instruction of Block 2 into a nullifying delay slot of the branch, then we incur no additional delays in Block 3 (except in the last iteration). The overall duration of the loop is therefore eighteen cycles per itera-tion before scheduling, 16 cycles per iteration after scheduling—an improvement of 11%. In Section 13.7 we will consider other versions of the block, in which rescheduling yields significantly faster code.

As noted near the end of Section 13.1, we shall probably want to repeat instruction scheduling after global code improvement and register allocation. If there are times when the number of virtual registers with useful values exceeds the number of physical registers on the target machine, then we shall need to generate code to *spill* some values to memory and load them back in again later. Rescheduling will be needed to handle any delays induced by the loads.

13.7* Loop Improvement II

As noted in Section 13.5, code improvements that improve the speed of loops are particularly important, because loops are where most programs spend most of their time. In this section we consider transformations that improve instruction scheduling by restructuring a loop body to include portions of more than one iteration of the original loop, and that manipulate multiply nested loops to improve cache performance or increase opportunities for parallelization.

13.7.1 Loop Unrolling and Software Pipelining

In Section 5.6.2 we were able to dramatically improve the performance of a dot-product loop by *unrolling* it: embedding two (in that case) iterations of the original loop in a single iteration of a new, longer loop, and allowing the scheduler to intermingle the instructions of the original iterations. If we apply this transformation to our `combinations` example we obtain the code of Figure 13.13. We have used separate names (here starting with the letter 't') for registers written in the initial half of the loop. This convention minimizes anti- and output dependences, giving us more latitude in scheduling. In an attempt to minimize loop overhead, we have also recognized that the array pointer induction variables (v26 and v34) need only be updated once in each iteration of the loop, provided that we use displacement addressing in the second set of store instructions. The new instructions added to the end of Block 1 cover the case in which n div 2, the number of iterations of the original loop, is not an even number.

Again assuming that the branch in Block 3 can be scheduled without delays, the total time for our unrolled loop (prior to scheduling) is 32 cycles, or 16 cycles per iteration of the original loop. After scheduling, this number is reduced to 12 cycles per iteration of the original loop. Unfortunately, eight cycles (four per original iteration) are still being lost to stalls. If we unroll the loop three times instead of two (see Exercise 13.20), we can bring the cost (with rescheduling) down to 11.3 cycles per original iteration, but this is not much of an improvement. The basic problem is illustrated in the top half of Figure 13.14. In the original version of the loop, the two store instructions cannot begin until after the divide delay. If we unroll the loop, then instructions of the internal iterations

```
Block 1:
    ...                 -- code from Block 1, figure 13.11
        v44 := v42 & 01
        if !v44 goto Block 3
        -- else fall through to Block 1a
Block 1a:
        *v26 := 1
        *v34 := 1
        v17 := 2
        v26 := v26 + 4
        v22 := v22 - 4
        v18 := v18 - 1
        goto Block 3
Block 2:                      Scheduled:
    1.  t19 := v13 × v18      t19 := v13 × v18
        —                     t18 := v18 - 1
        —                     t17 := v17 - 1
        —                     v18 := t18 - 1
        —                     —
    2.  t13 := v19 div v17    t13 := t19 div v17
        —                     v17 := t17 + 1
        —                     —
        —                     —
    3.  *v26 := t13           v19 := t13 × t18
    4.  *v34 := t13           *v26 := t13
    5.  t17 := v17 + 1        *v34 := t13
    6.  v26 := v26 + 8        v26 := v26 + 8
    7.  v34 := v34 - 8        v34 := v34 - 8
    8.  t18 := v18 - 1        v13 := v19 div t17
    9.  v19 := t13 × t18      —
        —                     —
        —                     —
        —                     *(v36+4) := v13
    10. v13 := t19 div t17    *(v34+4) := v13
        —
        —
        —
    11. *(v26 - 4) := v13
    12. *(v34 + 4) := v13
    13. v17 := t17 + 1
    14. v18 := t18 - 1
        -- fall through to Block 3
Block 3:                      (same)
        v43 := v17 ≤ v42
        if v43 goto Block 4
        -- else fall through to Block 4
```

Figure 13.13 Dependence DAG for Block 2 of the combinations **subroutine after unrolling two iterations of the body of the loop.** Also shown is linearized pseudocode for the entire loop, both before (left) and after (right) instruction scheduling. New instructions added to the end of Block 1 cover the case in which the number of iterations of the original loop is not a multiple of two.

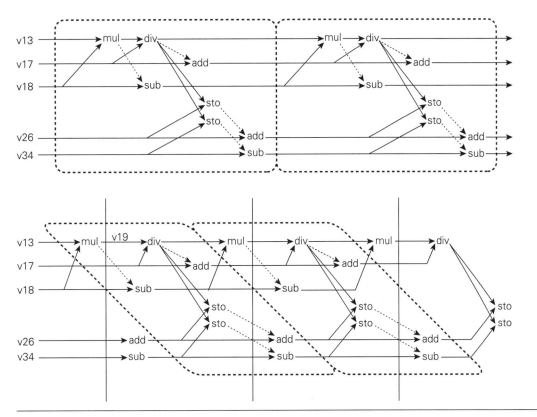

Figure 13.14 Software pipelining. The top diagram illustrates the execution of the original (non-pipelined) loop. In the bottom diagram, each iteration of the original loop has been spread across three iterations of the pipelined loop. Iterations of the original loop are enclosed in a dashed-line box; iterations of the pipelined loop are separated by solid vertical lines. In the bottom diagram we have also shown the code to prime the pipeline prior to the first iteration, and to flush it after the last.

can be intermingled, but six cycles of "shut down" cost (four delay slots and two stores) are still needed after the final divide.

A *software-pipelined* version of our `combinations` subroutine appears schematically in the bottom half of Figure 13.14, and as a control flow graph in Figure 13.15. The idea is to build a loop whose body comprises portions of several consecutive iterations of the original loop, with no internal start-up or shut-down cost. In our example, each iteration of the software-pipelined loop contributes to three separate iterations of the original loop. Within each new iteration (shown between vertical bars) nothing needs to wait for the divide to complete. To avoid delays, we have altered the code in several ways. First, because each iteration of the new loop contributes to several iterations of the original loop, we must ensure that there are enough iterations to run the new loop at least once (this is the purpose of the test in the new Block 1). Second, we have

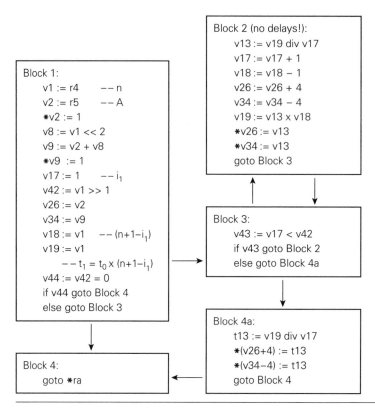

Figure 13.15 Control flow graph for the `combinations` **subroutine after software pipelining.** The additional code and test at the end of Block 1, the change to the test in Block 3 ($<$ instead of $\le$), and the new block (4a) make sure that there are enough iterations to accommodate the pipeline, prime it with the beginnings of the initial iteration, and flush the end of the final iteration. Suffixes on variable names in the comments in Block 1 refer to loop iterations: t_1 is the value of t in the first iteration of the loop; t_0 is a "zero-th" value used to prime the pipeline.

preceded and followed the loop with code to "prime" and "flush" the "pipeline": to execute the early portions of the first iteration and the final portions of the last few. As we did when unrolling the loop, we use a separate name (t13 in this case) for any register written in the new "pipeline flushing" code. Third, to minimize the amount of priming required we have initialized v26 and v34 one slot before their original positions, so that the first iteration of the pipelined loop can "update" them as part of a "-1th" original iteration. Finally, we have dropped the initialization of v13 in Block 1: our priming code has left that register dead at the end of the block. (Live variable analysis on virtual registers could have been used to discover this fact.)

Both the original and pipelined versions of the loop carry five nonconstant values across the boundary between iterations, but one of these has changed identity: whereas the origial loop carried the result of the divide around to the next multiply in register v13, the pipelined loop carries the result of the multiply forward to the divide in register v19. In more complicated loops it may be necessary to carry two or even three versions of a single register (corresponding to two or more iterations of the original loop) across the boundary between iterations of the pipelined loop. We must invent new virtual registers (similar to the new t13 and to the t registers in the unrolled version of the `combinations` example) to hold the extra values. In such a case software pipelining has the side effect of increasing register pressure.

Each of the instructions in the loop of the pipelined version of the `combinations` subroutine can proceed without delay. The total number of cycles per iteration has been reduced to ten. We can do even better if we combine loop unrolling and software pipelining. For example, by embedding two multiply–divide pairs in each iteration (drawn, with their accompanying instructions, from four iterations of the original loop, rather than just three), we can update the array pointers and check the termination condition half as often, for a net of only eight cycles per iteration of the original loop (see Exercise 13.21).

To summarize, loop unrolling serves to reduce loop overhead, and can also increase opportunities for instruction scheduling. Software pipelining does a better job of facilitating scheduling, but does not address loop overhead. A reasonable code improvement strategy is to unroll loops until the per-iteration overhead falls below some acceptable threshold of the total work, then employ software pipelining if necessary to eliminate scheduling delays.

13.7.2 Loop Reordering

The code improvement techniques that we have considered thus far have served two principal purposes: to eliminate redundant or unnecessary instructions, and to minimize stalls on a pipelined machine. Two other goals have become increasingly important in recent years. First, as improvements in processor speed have continued to outstrip improvements in memory latency, it has become increasingly important to minimize cache misses. Second, for parallel machines, it has become important to identify sections of code that can execute concurrently. As with other optimizations, the largest benefits come from changing the behavior of loops. We touch on some of the issues here; suggestions for further reading can be found at the end of the chapter.

Cache Optimizations

Probably the simplest example of cache optimization can be seen in code that traverses a multidimensional matrix (array):

```
for i := 1 to n
    for j := 1 to n
        A[i, j] := 0
```

If A is laid out in row-major order, and if each cache line contains m elements of A, then this code will suffer n^2/m cache misses. On the other hand, if A is laid out in column-major order, and if the cache is too small to hold n lines of A, then the code will suffer n^2 misses, fetching the entire array from memory m times. The difference can have an enormous impact on performance. A loop-reordering compiler can improve this code by *interchanging* the nested loops:

```
for j := 1 to n
    for i := 1 to n
        A[i, j] := 0
```

In more complicated examples, interchanging loops may improve locality of reference in one array, but worsen it in others. Consider this code to transpose a two-dimensional matrix:

```
for j := 1 to n
    for i := 1 to n
        A[i, j] := B[j, i]
```

If A and B are laid out the same way in memory, one of them will be accessed along cache lines, but the other will be accessed across them. In this case we may improve locality of reference by *tiling* or *blocking* the loops:

```
for it := 1 to n by b
    for jt := 1 to n by b
        for i := it to min (it + b − 1, n)
            for j := jt to min (jt + b − 1, n)
                A[i, j] := B[j, i]
```

Here the min calculations cover the possibility that b does not divide n evenly. They can be dropped if n is known to be a multiple of b. Alternatively, if we are willing to replicate the code inside the innermost loop, then we can generate different code for the final iteration of each loop (Exercise 13.24).

The new code iterates over $b \times b$ blocks of A and B, one in row-major order, the other in column-major order, as shown in Figure 13.16. If we choose b to be a multiple of m such that the cache can hold two $b \times b$ blocks of data simultaneously, then both A and B will suffer only one cache miss per m array elements, fetching everything from memory exactly once.[4] Tiling is useful in a

---

4 Although B is being written, not read, the hardware will fetch each line of B from memory on the first write to the line, so that the single modified element can be updated within the cache. The hardware has no way of knowing that the entire line will be modified before it is written back to memory.

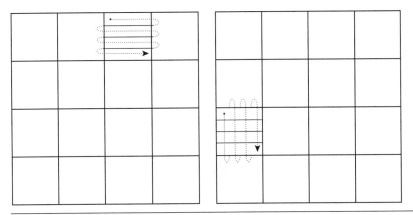

Figure 13.16 **Tiling (blocking) of a matrix operation.** As long as one tile of A and one tile of B can fit in the cache simultaneously, only one access in m will cause a cache miss (where m is the number of elements per cache line).

wide variety of algorithms on multidimensional arrays. Exercise 13.22 considers matrix multiplication.

Two other transformations that may sometimes improve cache locality are loop *distribution* (also called *fission* or *splitting*), and its inverse, loop *fusion* (also known as *jamming*). Distribution splits a single loop into multiple loops, each of which contains some fraction of the statements of the original loop. Fusion takes separate loops and combines them.

Consider, for example, the following code to reorganize a pair of arrays:

```
for i := 0 to n−1
    A[i] := B[M[i]];
    C[i] := D[M[i]];
```

Here M defines a mapping from locations in B or D to locations in A or C. If either B or D, but not both, can fit into the cache at once, then we may get faster code through distribution:

```
for i := 1 to n
    A[i] := B[M[i]];
for i := 1 to n
    C[i] := D[M[i]];
```

On the other hand, in the following code, separate loops may lead to *poorer* locality:

```
for i := 1 to n
    A[i] := A[i] + c
for i := 1 to n
    if A[i] < 0 then A[i] := 0
```

if A is too large to fit in the cache in its entirety, then these loops will fetch the entire array from memory twice. If we fuse them, however, we need only fetch A once:

```
for i := 1 to n
    A[i] := A[i] + c
    if A[i] < 0 then A[i] := 0
```

If two loops do not have identical bounds, it may still be possible to fuse them if we transform induction variables or *peel* some constant number of iterations off of one of the loops.

Loop distribution may serve to facilitate other transformations (e.g., loop interchange) by transforming an "imperfect" loop nest into a "perfect" one:

```
for i := 1 to n
    A[i] := A[i] + c
    for j := 1 to n
        B[i, j] := B[i, j] × A[i]
```

This nest is called imperfect because the outer loop contains more than just the inner loop. Distribution yields two outermost loops:

```
for i := 1 to n
    A[i] := A[i] + c
for i := 1 to n
    for j := 1 to n
        B[i, j] := B[i, j] × A[i]
```

The nested loops are now perfect, and can be interchanged if desired.

In keeping with our earlier discussions of loop optimizations, we note that loop distribution can reduce register pressure, while loop fusion can reduce loop overhead.

Loop Dependences

When reordering loops, we must be extremely careful to respect all data dependences. Of particular concern are so-called *loop-carried* dependences, which constrain the orders in which iterations can occur. Consider, for example, the following:

```
for i := 2 to n
    for j := 1 to n−1
        A[i, j] := A[i, j] − A[i−1, j+1]
```

Here the calculation of A[i, j] in iteration (i, j) depends on the value of A[i−1, j+1], which was calculated in iteration $(i-1, j+1)$. This dependence is often represented by a diagram of the *iteration space*:

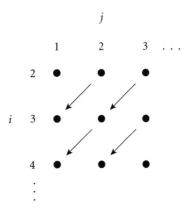

The i and j dimensions in this diagram represent loop indices, *not* array subscripts. The arcs represent the loop-carried flow dependence.

If we wish to interchange the i and j loops of this code (e.g., to improve cache locality), we find that we cannot do it, because of the dependence: we would end up trying to write A[i, j] before we had written A[i−1, j+1].

To analyze loop-carried dependences, high-performance optimizing compilers use symbolic mathematics to characterize the sets of index values that may cause the subscript expressions in different array references to evaluate to the same value. Compilers differ somewhat in the sophistication of this analysis. Most can handle linear combinations of loop indices. None, of course, can handle all expressions, since equivalence of general formulae is uncomputable. When unable to fully characterize subscripts, a compiler must conservatively assume the worst, and rule out transformations whose safety cannot be proven.

In many cases a loop with a fully characterized dependence that precludes a desired transformation can be modified in a way that eliminates the dependence.

In the most recent code above, for example, we can *reverse* the order of the j loop without violating the dependence:

```
for i := 2 to n
    for j := n−1 to 1 by −1
        A[i, j] := A[i, j] − A[i−1, j+1]
```

This change transforms the iteration space:

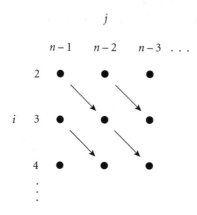

And now the loops can safely be interchanged:

```
for j := n−1 to 1 by −1
    for i := 2 to n
        A[i, j] := A[i, j] − A[i−1, j+1]
```

Another transformation that sometimes serves to eliminate a dependence is known as loop *skewing*. In essence, it reshapes a rectangular iteration space into a parallelogram, by adding the outer loop index to the inner one, and then subtracting from the appropriate subscripts:

```
for i := 2 to n
    for j := i+1 to i+n−1
        A[i, j−i] := A[i, j−i] − A[i−1, j+1−i]
```

A moment's consideration will reveal that this code accesses the exact same elements as before, in the exact same order. Its iteration space, however, looks like this:

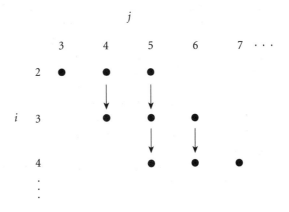

Now the loops can safely be interchanged. The transformation is complicated by the need to accommodate the sloping sides of the iteration space. To avoid using min and max functions, we can divide the space into two triangular sections, each of which has its own loop nest:

```
for j := 3 to n+1
    for i := 2 to j−1
        A[i, j−i] := A[i, j−i] − A[i−1, j+1−i]
for j := n+2 to 2×n−1
    for i := j−n+1 to n
        A[i, j−i] := A[i, j−i] − A[i−1, j+1−i]
```

Skewing has led to more complicated code than did reversal of the j loop, but it could be used in the presence of other dependences that would eliminate reversal as an option.

Several other loop transformations, including distribution, can also be used in certain cases to eliminate loop-carried dependences, allowing us to apply techniques that improve cache locality or (as discussed in the following subsection) enable us to execute code in parallel on a vector machine or a multiprocessor. Of course, no set of transformations can eliminate all dependences; some code simply can't be improved.

Parallelization

Loop iterations (at least in nonrecursive programs) constitute the principal source of operations that can execute in parallel. Ideally, one needs to find *independent*

loop iterations: ones with no loop-carried dependences. (In some cases, iterations can also profitably be executed in parallel even if they have dependences,
so long as they synchronize their operations appropriately.) In Sections 12.2.3
and 12.3.4 we considered loop constructs that allow the programmer to specify
parallel execution. Even in languages without such special constructs, a compiler
can often *parallelize* code by identifying—or creating—loops with as few loop-
carried dependences as possible. The transformations described in the previous
section are valuable tools in this endeavor.

Given a parallelizable loop, the compiler must consider several other issues in
order to ensure good performance. One of the most important of these is the
granularity of parallelism. For a very simple example, consider the problem of
"zero-ing out" a two-dimensional array, here indexed from 0 to $n-1$ and laid
out in row-major order:

```
for i := 0 to n−1
    for j := 0 to n−1
        A[i, j] := 0
```

On a machine containing several general-purpose processors, we would probably
parallelize the outer loop:

```
−− on processor pid:
for i := (n/p × pid) to (n/p ×(pid + 1) − 1)
    for j := 1 to n
        A[i, j] := 0
```

Here we have given each processor a band of rows to initialize. We have assumed
that processors are numbered from 0 to $p-1$, and that p divides n evenly.

The strategy on a vector machine is very different. Such a machine includes
a collection of v-element vector registers, and instructions to load, store, and
compute on vector data. The vector instructions are deeply pipelined, allowing
the machine to exploit a high degree of *fine-grain* parallelism. To satisfy the
hardware, the compiler needs to parallelize *inner* loops:

```
for i := 0 to n−1
    for j := 0 to n/v
        A[i, j:j+v−1] := 0        −− vector operation
```

Here the notation A[i, j:j+v−1] represents a v-element *slice* of A. The constant v
should be set to the length of a vector register (which we again assume divides n
evenly). The code transformation that extracts v-element operations from longer
loops is known as *strip mining*. It is essentially a one-dimensional form of tiling.

Other issues of importance in parallelizing compilers include *communication*
and *load balance*. Just as locality of reference reduces communication between

the cache and main memory on a uniprocessor, locality in parallel programs reduces communication among processors and between the processors and memory. Optimizations similar to those employed to reduce the number of cache misses on a uniprocessor can be used to reduce communication traffic on a multiprocessor.

Load balance refers to the division of labor among processors on a parallel machine. If we divide the work of a program among 16 processors, we shall obtain a speedup of close to 16 only if each processor takes the same amount of time to do its work. If we accidentally assign 5% of the work to each of 15 processors and 25% of the work to the sixteenth, we are likely to see a speedup of no more than four. For simple loops it is often possible to predict performance accurately enough to divide the work among processors at compile time. For more complex loops, in which different iterations perform different amounts of work or have different cache behavior, it is often better to generate *self-scheduled* code, which divides the work up at run time. In its simplest form, self-scheduling creates a "bag of tasks," as described in Section 12.2. Each task consists of a set of loop iterations. The number of such tasks is chosen to be significantly larger than the number of processors. When finished with a given task, a processor goes back to the bag to get another.

13.8 Register Allocation

In a simple compiler with no global optimizations, register allocation can be performed independently in every basic block. To avoid the obvious inefficiency of storing frequently accessed variables to memory at the end of many blocks, and reading them back in again in others, simple compilers usually apply a set of heuristics to identify such variables and allocate them to registers over the life of a subroutine. Obvious candidates for a dedicated register include loop indices, the implicit pointers of `with` statements in Pascal-family languages (Section 7.3.3), and scalar local variables and parameters.

It has been known since the early 1970s that register allocation is equivalent to the NP-hard problem of graph coloring. Following the work of Chaitin et al. [CAC+81] in the early 1980s, heuristic (nonoptimal) implementations of graph coloring have become a common approach to register allocation in aggressive optimizing compilers. We describe the basic idea here.

The first step is to identify virtual registers that *cannot* share a physical register, because they contain values that are live concurrently. To accomplish this step we use reaching definitions data-flow analysis (Section 13.5.1). For the software-pipelined version of our `combinations` subroutine (Figure 13.15, page 766), we can chart the *live ranges* of the virtual registers as shown in Figure 13.17. Note that the live range of v19 spans the backward branch at the end of Block 2; though typographically disconnected it is contiguous in time.

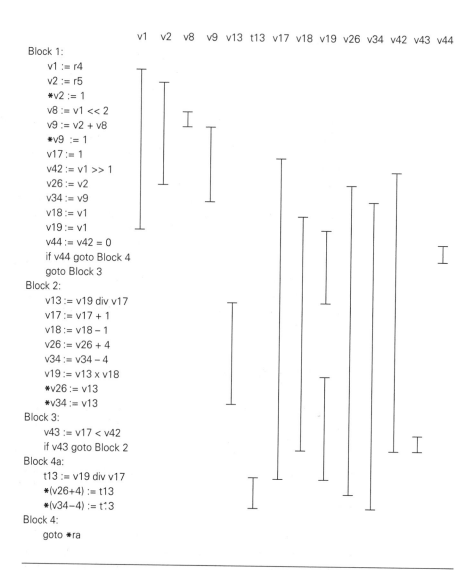

Figure 13.17 Live ranges for virtual registers in the software-pipelined version of the combinations **subroutine (Figure 13.15).**

Given these live ranges, we construct a *register interference graph*. The nodes of this graph represent virtual registers. Registers vi and vj are connected by an arc if they are simultaneously live. The interference graph corresponding to Figure 13.17 appears in Figure 13.18. The problem of mapping virtual registers onto the smallest possible number of physical registers now amounts to finding

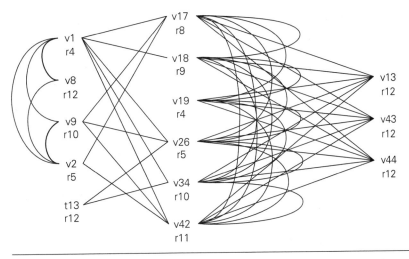

Figure 13.18 **Register interference graph for the software pipelined version of the** combinations **subroutine.** Using physical register names, we have indicated one of several possible seven-colorings.

a *minimal coloring* of this graph: an assignment of "colors" to nodes such that no arc connects two nodes of the same color.

In our example, we can find one of several optimal solutions by inspection. The six registers in the center of the figure constitute a clique (a completely connected subgraph); each must be mapped to a separate physical register. Moreover there are three cases—registers v1 and v19, v2 and v26, and v9 and v34—in which one register is copied into the other somewhere in the code, but the two are never simultaneously live. If we use a common physical register in each of these cases then we can eliminate the copy instructions. Registers v13, v43, and v44 are connected to every member of the clique, but not to each other; they can share a seventh physical register. Register v8 is connected to v1, v2, and v9, but not to anything else; we have arbitrarily chosen to have both it and t13 share with the three registers on the right.

Final code for the combinations subroutine appears in Figure 13.19. We have left v1/v19 and v2/v26 in r4 and r5, the registers in which their initial values were passed. Because our subroutine is a leaf, these registers are never needed for other arguments. Following MIPS conventions (Section 5.5.1), we have used registers r8 through r12 as additional temporary registers.

We have glossed over two important issues. First, on almost any real machine, physical registers are not uniform. Integer registers cannot be used for floating-point operations. Caller-saves registers should not be used for variables whose values are needed across subroutine calls. Registers that are overwritten by special instructions (e.g., byte search on a CISC machine) should not be used to hold values that are needed across such instructions. To handle constraints of this type, the register interference graph is usually extended to contain nodes

Block 1:
    *r5 := 1
    r12 := r4 << 2
    r10 := r5 + r12
    *r10 := 1
    r8 := 1
    r11 := r4 >> 1
    r9 := r4
    r12 := r11 = 0
    if r12 goto Block 4
    goto Block 3
Block 2:
    r12 := r4 div r8
    r8 := r8 + 1
    r9 := r9 − 1

    r5 := r5 + 4
    r10 := r10 − 4
    r4 := r12 × r9
    *r5 := r12
    *r10 := r12
Block 3:
    r12 := r8 < r11
    if r12 goto Block 2
Block 4a:
    r12 := r4 div r8
    *(r5+4) := r12
    *(r10−4) := r12
Block 4:
    goto *ra

Figure 13.19 Final code for the `combinations` **subroutine, after assigning physical registers and eliminating useless copy instructions.**

for both virtual and physical registers. Arcs are then drawn from each virtual register to the physical registers to which it should not be mapped. Each physical register is also connected to every other, to force them all to have separate colors. After coloring the resulting graph, we assign each virtual register to the physical register of the same color.

The second issue we've ignored is spilling. In many subroutines there will not be enough physical registers to go around. In this case it will not be possible to color the interference graph. Using a variety of heuristics (which we do not cover here), the compiler chooses virtual registers whose live ranges can be *split* into two or more subranges. Values that are live at the end of a subrange must be stored to memory. Values that are live at the beginning of a subrange must be loaded. It is easy to prove that with a sufficient number of range splits it is possible to color any graph, given at least three colors. The trick is to find a set of splits that keeps the spill cost low. Once register allocation is complete, as noted in Sections 13.1 and 13.6, we shall want to repeat instruction scheduling, in order to fill any newly created load delays.

13.9 Summary and Concluding Remarks

This chapter has addressed the subject of code improvement ("optimization"). We considered many of the most important optimization techniques, including peephole optimization; local and global (intra-subroutine) redundancy elimination (constant folding, constant propagation, copy propagation, common subexpression elimination); loop improvement (invariant hoisting, strength reduction or elimination of induction variables, unrolling and software pipelining, reordering for cache improvement or parallelization); instruction scheduling; and register allocation. Many others techniques, too numerous to mention, can be found in the literature or in production use.

To facilitate code improvement, we introduced several new data structures and program representations, including dependence DAGs (for instruction scheduling), static single-assignment (SSA) form (for many purposes, including global common subexpression elimination via value numbering), and the register interference graph (for physical register allocation). For many global optimizations we made use of data flow analysis. Specifically, we employed it to identify available expressions (for global common subexpression elimination), to identify live variables (to eliminate useless stores), and to calculate reaching definitions (to identify loop invariants; also useful for finding live ranges of virtual registers). We also noted that it can be used for global constant propagation, copy propagation, conversion to SSA form, and a host of other purposes.

An obvious question for both the writers and users of compilers is: among the many possible code improvement techniques, which produce the most "bang for the buck?" For modern RISC machines, instruction scheduling and register allocation are definitely on the list: basic-block level scheduling and elimination of redundant loads and stores are crucial in any production-quality compiler. Significant additional benefits accrue from some sort of global register allocation, if only to avoid repeated loads and stores of loop indices and other heavily used local variables and parameters. Beyond these basic techniques, which mainly amount to making good use of the hardware, the most significant benefits in von Neumann programs come from optimizing references to arrays, particularly within loops. Most production-quality compilers (1) perform at least enough common subexpression analysis to identify redundant address calculations for arrays, (2) hoist invariant calculations out of loops, and (3) perform strength reduction on induction variables, eliminating them if possible.

As we noted in the introduction to the chapter, code improvement remains an extremely active area of research. Much of this research addresses language features and computational models for which traditional optimization techniques have not been particularly effective. Examples include alias analysis for pointers in C, static resolution of virtual method calls in object-oriented languages (to permit inlining and interprocedural optimization), streamlined communication in message-passing languages, and a variety of issues for functional and logic languages. In some cases, new programming paradigms can change the goals of code improvement. For just-in-time compilation of Java programs, for example, the speed of the code improver may be as important as the speed of the code it produces. In other cases, new sources of information (e.g., feedback from run-time profiling) create new opportunities for improvement. Finally, advances in processor architecture (multiple pipelines, very wide instruction words, out-of-order execution, architecturally visible caches, speculative instructions) continue to create new challenges; processor design and compiler design are increasingly interrelated.

13.10 Review Questions

13.1 Describe several increasing levels of "aggressiveness" in code improvement.

13.2 What is a *control flow graph*? Why is it central to so many forms of global code improvement? How does it accommodate subroutine calls?

13.3 Give three examples of code improvements that must be performed in a particular order. Give two examples of code improvements that should probably be performed more than once (with other improvements inbetween).

13.4 What is *peephole optimization*? Describe at least four different ways in which a peephole optimizer might transform a program.

13.5 What is *constant folding*? *Constant propagation*? *Copy propagation*? *Strength reduction*?

13.6 What does it mean for a value in a register to be *live*?

13.7 What is *value numbering*? What is *static single assignment (SSA) form*? Why is SSA form needed for global value numbering, but not for local value numbering?

13.8 Give three distinct examples of *data flow analysis*. Explain the difference between *forward* and *backward* flow. Explain the difference between *all-paths* and *any-path* flow.

13.9 What is an *available expression*?

13.10 Describe at least three instances in which code improvement algorithms must consider the possibility of aliases.

13.11 What is a *loop invariant*? A *reaching definition*? An *induction variable*?

13.12 Describe the creation and use of a *dependence DAG*. Explain the distinction between *flow*, *anti-*, and *output* dependences.

13.13 What is *register pressure*? *Register spilling*?

13.14* What is the difference between *loop unrolling* and *software pipelining*? Explain why the latter may increase register pressure.

13.15* What is the purpose of *loop interchange*? *Loop tiling (blocking)*?

13.16* What are the potential benefits of *loop distribution*? *Loop fusion*? What is *loop peeling*?

13.17* What does it mean for loops to be *perfectly nested*? Why are perfect loop nests important?

13.18* What is a *loop-carried dependence*? Describe three loop transformations that may serve in some cases to eliminate such a dependence.

13.19* Describe the fundamental difference between the parallelization strategy for multiprocessors and the parallelization strategy for vector machines.

13.20 What is the *live range* of a register? Why might it not be a contiguous range of instructions?

13.21 What is a *register interference graph*? What is its significance? Why do production compilers depend on heuristics (rather than precise solutions) for register allocation?

13.22 List three reasons why it might not be possible to treat the physical registers of a microprocessor uniformly for purposes of register allocation.

13.11 Exercises

13.1 In Section 13.2 we suggested replacing the instruction r1 := r2 / 2 with the instruction r1 := r2 >> 1, and noted that the replacement may not be correct for negative numbers. Explain the problem. You will want to learn the difference between *logical* and *arithmetic* shift operations (see almost any assembly language manual). You will also want to consider the issue of rounding.

13.2 Prove that the division operation in the loop of the `combinations` subroutine (page 740) always produces a remainder of zero. Explain the need for the parentheses around the numerator.

13.3 Certain code improvements can sometimes be performed by the programmer, in the source-language program. Examples include introducing additional variables to hold common subexpressions (so that they need not be recomputed), moving invariant computations out of loops, and applying strength reduction to induction variables or to multiplications by powers of two. Describe several optimizations that cannot reasonably be performed by the programmer, and explain why some that could be performed by the programmer might best be left to the compiler.

13.4 In our initial translation of a syntax tree into medium-level intermediate code we assigned every loaded or computed value to a separate virtual register. The uniqueness of these registers is reminiscent of the *single-assignment variables* of section 12.3.4. The two ideas are *not* the same, however. Explain the difference.

13.5 In Section 6.5.1 (page 283) we suggested that the loop

```
// before
for (i = low; i <= high; i++) {
    // during
}
// after
```

be translated as

```
-- before
i := low
goto test
```

```
top:
      -- during
      index +:= 1
test:
      if i ≤ high goto top
      -- after
```

And indeed this is the translation we have used for the `combinations` subroutine. The following is an alternative translation:

```
      -- before
      i := low
      if i > high goto bottom
top:
      -- during
      index +:= 1
      if i ≤ high goto top
bottom:
      -- after
```

Explain why this translation might be preferable to the one we used. (Hints: consider the number of branches, the migration of loop invariants, and opportunities for delay slot filling.)

13.6 Beginning with the translation of the previous exercise, reapply the code improvements discussed in this chapter to the `combinations` subroutine.

13.7 Give an example in which the numbered heuristics listed on page 762 do not lead to an optimal code schedule.

13.8 Show that forward data flow analysis can be used to verify that a variable is assigned a value on every possible control path leading to a use of that variable (this is Java's notion of *definite assignment*, described in Section 6.1.2).

13.9 Show that *very busy* expressions (those that are guaranteed to be calculated on some future code path) can be detected via backward, all-paths data flow analysis. Suggest a space-saving code improvement for such expressions.

13.10 Explain how to gather information during local value numbering that will allow us to identify the sets of variables and registers that contributed to the value of each virtual register. (If the value of register vi depends on the value of register vj or of variable x, then during available expression analysis we say that $vi \in Kill_B$ if B contains an assignment to vj or x and does not contain a subsequent assignment to vi.)

13.11 Show how to strength-reduce the expression i^2 within a loop, where i is the loop index variable. You may assume that the loop step size is one.

13.12 Division is often much more expensive than addition and subtraction. Show how to replace expressions of the form i div c on the inside of a `for` loop with additions and/or subtractions, where i is the loop index variable and c is an integer constant. You may assume that the loop step size is one.

13.13 Consider the following high-level pseudocode:

```
read (n)
for i in 1..100
    B[i] := n × i
    if n > 0
        A[i] := B[i]
```

The condition n > 0 is loop-invariant. Can we move it out of the loop? If so, explain how. If not, explain why.

13.14 Should live variable analysis be performed before or after loop invariant elimination (or should it be done twice, before *and* after)? Justify your answer.

13.15 Starting with the naive gcd code of Figure 1.5 (page 23), show the result of local redundancy elimination (via value numbering) and instruction scheduling.

13.16 Continuing the previous exercise, draw the program's control flow graph and show the result of global value numbering. Next use data flow analysis to drive any appropriate global optimizations. Then draw and color the register conflict graph in order to perform global register allocation. Finally, perform a final pass of instruction scheduling. How does your code compare to the version shown on page 1?

13.17 Consider the following code:

```
v2 := *v1
v1 := v1 + 20
v3 := *v1
——
v4 := v2 + v3
```

Show how to shorten the time required for this code by moving the update of v1 forward into the delay slot of the second load. (Assume that v1 is still live at the end.) Describe the conditions that must hold for this type of transformation to be applied, and the alterations that must be made to individual instructions to maintain correctness.

13.18 Consider the following code:

```
v5 := v2 × v36

—

—

—

—

v6 := v5 + v1
v1 := v1 + 20
```

Show how to shorten the time required for this code by moving the up-date of v1 backward into a delay slot of the multiply. Describe the conditions that must hold for this type of transformation to be applied, and the alterations that must be made to individual instructions to maintain correctness.

13.19 In the spirit of the previous two exercises, show how to shorten the main loop of the `combinations` subroutine (prior to unrolling or pipelining) by moving the updates of v26 and v34 backward into delay slots. What percentage impact does this change make in the performance of the loop?

13.20* Using the code in Figures 13.11 and 13.13 as a guide, unroll the loop of the `combinations` subroutine three times. Construct a dependence DAG for the new Block 2. Finally, schedule the block. How many cycles does your code consume per iteration of the original (unrolled) loop? How does it compare to the software pipelined version of the loop (Figure 13.15)?

13.21* Write a version of the `combinations` subroutine whose loop is both un-rolled *and* software pipelined. In other words, build the loop body from the instructions between the leftmost and rightmost vertical bars of Figure 13.14, rather than from the instructions between adjacent bars. You should update the array pointers only once per iteration. How many cycles does your code consume per iteration of the original loop? How messy is the code to "prime" and "flush" the pipeline, and to check for sufficient numbers of iterations?

13.22* Consider the following code for matrix multiplication:

```
for (i = 0; i < n; i++) {
    for (j = 0; j < n; j++) {
        C[i][j] = 0;
    }
}
for (i = 0; i < n; i++) {
    for (j = 0; j < n; j++) {
        for (k = 0; k < n; k++) {
            C[i][j] += A[i][k] * B[k][j];
        }
    }
}
```

Describe the access patterns for matrices A, B, and C. If the matrices are large, how many times will each cache line be fetched from memory? Tile the inner two loops. Describe the effect on the number of cache misses.

13.23* Consider the following simple instance of Gaussian elimination:

```
for (i = 0; i < n-1; i++) {
    for (j = i+1; j < n; j++) {
        for (k = n-1; k >= i; k--) {
            A[j][k] -= A[i][k] * A[j][i] / A[i][i];
        }
    }
}
```

(Gaussian elimination serves to triangularize a matrix. It is a key step in the solution of systems of linear equations.) What are the loop invariants in this code? What are the loop-carried dependences? Discuss how to optimize the code. Be sure to consider locality-improving loop transformations.

13.24* Modify the tiled matrix transpose on page 768 to eliminate the min calculations in the bounds of the inner loops. Perform the same modification on your answer to Exercise 13.22.

13.25 Investigate the back-end structure of your favorite compiler. What levels of optimization are available? What techniques are employed at each level? What is the default level? Does the compiler generate assembly language or object code? What program transformations are performed by the assembler?

Find a disassembler (a debugger will work in a pinch). For several program fragments, instruct the compiler to produce assembly source and compare it to the output of the disassembler. How much has changed?

13.12 Bibliographic Notes

Standard compiler textbooks (e.g., those of Appel [App97]; Aho, Sethi, and Ullman [ASU86]; or Fischer and LeBlanc [FL88]) are an accessible source of information on back-end compiler technology. Much of the presentation here was inspired by the recent text of Muchnick [Muc97]: his *Advanced Compiler Design and Implementation* contains a wealth of detailed information and citations to related work. Much of the leading-edge compiler research appears in the annual *ACM Conference on Programming Language Design and Implementation*.

Throughout our study of code improvement, we concentrated our attention on the von Neumann family of languages. Analogous techniques for functional [App91; KKR+86; Pey87; Pey92; App97, Chap. 15]; object-oriented [AH95; GDDC97; App97, Chap. 14] and logic languages [DRSS96, FSS83, Zho96] are an active topic of research, but are beyond the scope of this book. A key challenge in functional languages is to identify repetitive patterns of calls (e.g., tail recursion), for which loop-like optimizations can be performed. A key challenge in object-oriented languages is to predict the targets of virtual subroutine calls statically, to permit in-lining and interprocedural code improvement. The dominant challenge in logic languages is to better direct the underlying process of goal-directed search.

Local value numbering is originally due to Cocke and Schwartz [CS69]; the global algorithm described here is based on that of Alpern, Wegman, and Zadeck [AWZ88]. Chaitin et al. [CAC+81] popularized the use of graph coloring for register allocation. Cytron et al. [CFR+91] describe the generation and use of static single-assignment form. Instruction scheduling from basic-block dependence DAGs is described by Gibbons and Muchnick [GM86]. Massalin provides a delightful discussion of circumstances under which it may be desirable (and possible) to generate a truly *optimal* program [Mas87].

Sources of information on loop transformations and parallelization include the text of Wolfe [Wol96] and the excellent survey of Bacon, Graham, and Sharp [BGS94]. Banerjee provides a detailed discussion of loop dependence analysis [Ban97]. Rau and Fisher discuss fine-grain *instruction-level* parallelism, of the sort exploitable by vector, wide-instruction-word, or superscalar processors [RF93]. Alias analysis for pointers is an active topic of research [CBC93, Deu94, HHN94, LRZ93, DMM98].

In recent years, several research groups have considered the analysis of programs for which source code is unavailable (e.g., because those programs were purchased from a third party in binary form). General-purpose binary instrumentation tools [LS95, SE94, RVL+97] can be used to profile or trace programs, or to emulate alternative memory architectures [SFL+94, SG96]. More aggressive tools can translate object files from one machine architecture to another (e.g., to run x86 binaries on another vendor's hardware [SCK+93, HH97]). While it is provably impossible to recover all high-level semantic information from examination of low-level code, recent advances suggest that the level of information available is often surprisingly rich.

Appendix A

Programming Languages Mentioned

This appendix provides brief descriptions, bibliographic references, and (in many cases) URLs for on-line information concerning each of the principal programming languages mentioned in this book. The URLs are accurate as of early 1999, though they are subject to change as people move files around. Check the URL (*www.cs.rochester.edu/u/scott/pragmatics/A.html*) for the most current appendix material. A similar but longer appendix may be found in the text by Finkel [Fin96, pp. 423 ff]. Some additional URLs can be found in the bibliographic references.

For many languages XXX, there exists an Internet newsgroup *comp.lang.XXX*. Many of these newsgroups host frequently-asked-question (FAQ) lists. Bill Kinnersley maintains an extremely useful index of on-line materials for hundreds of programming languages at *cuiwww.unige.ch/langlist*. Other resources include the Yahoo language sub-index (*www.yahoo.com/Computers_and_Internet /Programming_Languages/*), the WWW Virtual Library page on computer languages (*src.doc.ic.ac.uk/bySubject/Computing/Languages.html*), and the HyperNews languages list (*www.hypernews.org/HyperNews/get/computing /lang-list.html*).

Figure A.1 shows the genealogy of some of the more influential or widely used programming languages. The date for each language indicates the approximate time at which its features became widely known. Arrows indicate principal influences on design. Many influences, of course, cannot be shown in a single figure.

Ada: Originally intended to be the standard language for all software commissioned by the U.S. Department of Defense [Ame83]. Prototypes designed by teams at several sites; final '83 language developed by a team at Honeywell's Systems and Research Center in Minneapolis and Alsys Corp. in France, led by Jean Ichbiah. A very large language, descended largely from Pascal. Design rationale articulated in a remarkably clear companion document [IBFW91]. Ada 95 [Int95b] is a revision developed under government contract by a team at Intermetrics, Inc. It fixes several subtle problems in the earlier language, and adds objects, shared-memory synchronization, and several other features. Freely available implementation distributed by Ada Core Technologies (*www.gnat.com*) under terms of the Free Software Foundation's GNU public license.

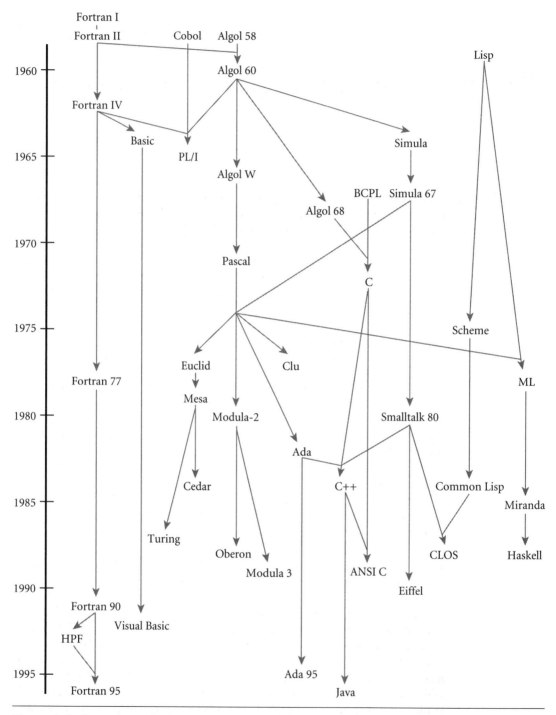

Figure A.1 Genealogy of selected programming languages. Dates are approximate.

Algol 60: The original block-structured language. The original definition by Naur et al. [NBB⁺63] is considered a landmark of clarity and conciseness. It includes the original use of Backus-Naur Form (BNF).

Algol 68: A large and relatively complex successor to Algol 60, designed by a committee led by A. van Wijngaarden. Includes (among other things) structures and unions, expression-based syntax, reference parameters, a reference model of variables, and concurrency. The official definition [vMP⁺75] uses unconventional terminology and is very difficult to read; other sources [Pag76, Lv77] are more accessible.

Algol W: A smaller, simpler alternative to Algol 68, proposed by Niklaus Wirth and C. A. R. Hoare [WH66, Sit72]. The precursor to Pascal. Introduced the case statement.

APL: Designed by Kenneth Iverson in the late 1950s and early 1960s, primarily for the manipulation of numeric arrays. Functional. Extremely concise. Powerful set of operators. Employs an extended character set. Intended for interactive use. Original syntax [Ive62] was nonlinear; implementations generally use a revised syntax due to a team at IBM [IBM87]. Extensive on-line resources available at *www.acm.org/sigapl*.

Basic: Simple imperative language, originally intended for interactive use. Original version developed by John Kemeny and Thomas Kurtz of Dartmouth College in the early 1960s. Dozens of dialects exist. Microsoft's Visual Basic [Mic91], which bears little resemblance to the original, is the most widely used today. Minimal subset defined by ANSI standard [Ame78b].

C: One of the most successful imperative languages. Originally defined by Brian Kernighan and Dennis Ritchie of Bell Labs as part of the development of Unix [KR78]. Concise syntax. Unusual declaration syntax. Intended for systems programming. Weak type checking. No dynamic semantic checks. Standardized by ANSI/ISO in 1990 [Ame90]. Extensions for international character sets adopted in 1994. More extensive changes under consideration by an ISO working group as of this writing [Int98a]. Freely available implementation (gcc) distributed for many platforms by the Free Software Foundation (*www.fsf.org/software/gcc/*).

C++: The most successful of several object-oriented successors to C. Designed by Bjarne Stroustrup of Bell Labs. Includes (among other things) generalized reference types, both static and dynamic method binding, extensive facilities for overloading and coercion, and multiple inheritance. No automatic garbage collection. Useful references include Stroustrup's text [Str97] and the reference manual of Ellis and Stroustrup [ES90]. Recently standardized by the ISO [Int98b]. Freely available implementation included in the gcc distribution (see C).

Cedar: See Mesa and Cedar.

CLOS: The Common Lisp Object System [Kee89; Ste90, Chap. 28]. A set of object-oriented extensions to Common Lisp, now incorporated into the ANSI standard language (see Common Lisp). The leading notation for object-oriented functional programming.

Clu: Developed by Barbara Liskov and associates at MIT in the late 1970s [LG86]. Designed to provide an unusually powerful set of features for data abstraction [LSAS77]. Also includes iterators and exception handling. Freely available implementations for most Unix platforms at *ftp://ftp.lcs.mit.edu/pub/pclu*.

Cobol: Originally developed by the U.S. Department of Defense in the late 1950s and early 1960s by a team led by Grace Murray Hopper [Uni60]. Long the most widely used programming language in the world. Standardized by ANSI in 1968; revised in 1974 and 1985 [Ame85]. Intended principally for business data processing. Introduced the concept of structures. Elaborate I/O facilities.

Common Lisp: The standard modern Lisp (see also Lisp). A large language. Includes (among other things) static scoping, an extensive type system, exception handling, and object-oriented features (see CLOS). For years the standard reference was the book by Guy Steele, Jr. [Ste90]. More recently the language has been standardized by ANSI [Ame96]. An abridged hypertext version of the standard is available on-line at *www.harlequin.com/education/books/HyperSpec*.

CSP: See Occam.

Eiffel: An object-oriented language developed by Bertrand Meyer and associates at the Société des Outils du Logiciel à Paris [Mey92]. Includes (among other things) multiple inheritance, automatic garbage collection, and powerful mechanisms for renaming of data members and methods in derived classes. Extensive on-line resources available at *www.eiffel.com*.

Euclid: Imperative language developed by Butler Lampson and associates at the Xerox Palo Alto Research Center in the mid-1970s [LHL+77]. Designed to eliminate many of the sources of common programming errors in Pascal, and to facilitate formal verification of programs. Has closed scopes and module types.

Fortran: The original high-level imperative language. Developed in the mid-1950s by John Backus and associates at IBM. The most important versions are Fortran I, Fortran II, Fortran IV, Fortran 77, and Fortran 90. The latter two are documented in a pair of ANSI standards [Ame78a, Ame92]. Fortran 90 [MR96] (updated in 1995) is a major revision to the language, adding (among other things) recursion, pointers, new control constructs, and a wealth of array operations. As of 1999, Fortran 77 is still more widely used. Freely available implementation (g77) distributed by the Free Software Foundation (*www.fsf.org/software/*).

Haskell: The leading purely functional language. Descended from Miranda. Designed by a committee of researchers beginning in 1987. Includes curried functions, higher-order functions, nonstrict semantics, static polymorphic typing, pattern matching, list comprehensions, modules, monadic I/O, and layout (indentation)-based syntactic grouping. Haskell 98 [PHA+99] is the most recent as of this writing; design of Haskell 2 is under way. On-line resources available at *haskel.org/.*

Icon: The successor to Snobol. Developed by Ralph Griswold (Snobol's principal designer) at the University of Arizona [GG97]. Adopts more conventional control-flow constructs, but with powerful iteration and search facilities based on pattern-matching and backtracking. Implementations, documentation, and other resources available at *www.cs.arizona.edu/icon/.*

Java: Object-oriented language based largely on a subset of C++. Developed by James Gosling and associates at Sun Microsystems in the early 1990s [AG98, GJS96]. Intended for the construction of highly portable, architecture-neutral programs. Defined in conjunction with an intermediate *byte code* format intended for execution on a Java *virtual machine* [LY97]. Includes (among other things) a reference model of (class-typed) variables, mix-in inheritance, threads, and extensive predefined libraries for graphics, communication, and other activities. Heavily used for transmission of program fragments (*applets*) over the Internet. Implementations, documentation, news, advertising, and numerous other resources available at *www.sun.com/java.*

Linda: A set of language extensions intended to add concurrency to conventional programming languages. Developed by David Gelernter for his doctoral research at SUNY Stony Brook in the early 1980s and later refined by Gelernter and his student, Nicholas Carriero, at Yale University. Based on the notion of a distributed, associative *tuple space.* On-line information at *www.cs.yale.edu/HTML/YALE/CS/Linda/linda.html.* Commercial implementations available from *www.sca.com/site/products/linda.html.*

Lisp: The original functional language [McC60]. Developed by John McCarthy in the late 1950s as a realization of Church's lambda calculus. Many dialects exist. The two most common today are Common Lisp and Scheme (see separate entries). Historically important dialects include Lisp 1.5 [MAE+65], MacLisp [Moo78], and Interlisp [TM81].

Mesa and Cedar: Mesa [LR80] is a successor to Euclid developed in the 1970s at Xerox's Palo Alto Research Center by a team led by Butler Lampson. Includes monitor-based concurrency. Along with Interlisp and Smalltalk, one of three companion projects that pioneered the use of personal workstations, with bitmapped displays, mice, and a graphical user interface. Cedar [SZBH86] is a successor to Mesa with (among other things) complete type safety, exceptions, and automatic garbage collection.

Miranda: Purely functional language designed by David Turner in the mid-1980s [Tur86]. Resembles ML in several respects; has type inference and automatic currying. Unlike ML, provides list comprehensions (Section 7.8), and uses lazy evaluation for all arguments. Uses indentation and line breaks for syntactic grouping. Commercial implementations available from Research Software Ltd. of Canterbury, England.

ML: Functional language with "Pascal-like" syntax. Originally designed in the mid- to late 1970s by Robin Milner and associates at the University of Edinburgh as the meta-language (hence the name) for a program verification system. Pioneered aggressive compile-time type inference and polymorphism. Has a few imperative features. Several dialects exist; the most widely used is Standard ML [MTHM97]. Stansifer's book [Sta92] is an accessible introduction. Standard ML of New Jersey, a project of Princeton University and Bell Labs, has produced freely available implementations for many platforms; see *cm.bell-labs.com/cm/cs/what/smlnj/*.

Modula and Modula-2: The immediate successors to Pascal, developed by Niklaus Wirth. The original Modula [Wir77b] was an explicitly concurrent monitor-based language. It is sometimes called Modula (1) to distinguish it from its successors. The more commercially important Modula-2 [Wir85b] was originally designed with coroutines (Section 8.6), but no real concurrency. Both languages provide mechanisms for module-as-manager style data abstractions. Modula-2 was standardized by the ISO in 1996 [Int96]. A freely available implementation for x86 Linux (and moderately priced implementations for several other Unix variants) is available from the University of Karlsruhe, Germany at *ftp://i44ftp.info.uni-karlsruhe.de/pub/mocka*.

Modula-3: A major extension to Modula-2 developed by Luca Cardelli, Jim Donahue, Mick Jordan, Bill Kalsow, and Greg Nelson at the Digital Systems Research Center and the Olivetti Research Center in the late 1980s [Har92]. Intended to provide a level of support for large, reliable, and maintainable systems comparable to that of Ada, but in a simpler and more elegant form. Extensive online resources, including pointers to both free and commercial implementations, available at *www.research.compaq.com/src/modula-3/html/*.

Oberon: A deliberately minimal language designed by Niklaus Wirth [Wir88b, RW92]. Essentially a subset of Modula-2 [Wir88a], augmented with a mechanism for type extension (Section 10.2.3) [Wir88c]. Implementations, documentation, and other resources available at *www.oberon.ethz.ch/*.

Occam: A concurrent language [JG88] based on CSP [Hoa78], Hoare's notation for message-based communication using guarded commands and synchronization send. The language of choice for systems built from INMOS Corporation's *transputer* processors, widely used in Europe. Uses indentation and line breaks for syntactic grouping. Extensive on-line resources, including pointers to several free implementations, available at *www.hensa.ac.uk/parallel/occam/index.html*.

Pascal: Designed by Niklaus Wirth in the late 1960s [Wir71], largely in reaction to Algol 68, which was widely perceived as bloated. Heavily used in the 1970s and 1980s, particularly for teaching. Introduced subrange and enumeration types. Unified structures and unions. For many years the standard reference was Wirth's book with Kathleen Jensen [JW91]; more recently, the language has been standardized by the ISO and ANSI [Int90]. Freely available implementation distributed by the Free Software Foundation (*agnes.dida.physik.uni-essen .de/~gnu-pascal*).

Perl: A "scripting" language, designed primarily to automate operations on text files [WS91]. Borrows features from C, `sed` and `awk` [AKW78] (two other scripting languages), and various Unix *shell* (command interpreter) languages. Extensive on-line resources available at *www.perl.com*.

PL/I: A large, general-purpose language designed in the mid-1960s as a successor to Fortran, Cobol, and Algol [Bee70]. Never managed to displace its predecessors; kept alive largely through IBM corporate influence.

Postscript: A stack-based language for the description of graphics and print operations [Ado86, Ado90]. Developed and marketed by Adobe Systems, Inc. Based in part on the Forth programming language [Bro87]. Generated by many word processors and drawing programs. Most professional-quality printers contain a Postscript interpreter.

Prolog: The most widely used logic programming language. Developed in the early 1970s by Alain Colmerauer and Philippe Roussel of the University of Aix–Marseille in France and Robert Kowalski and associates at the University of Edinburgh in Scotland. Many dialects exist. Partially standardized in 1995 [Int95a]. Numerous implementations, both free and commercial, are available. The AI group at CMU maintains a large Prolog repository at *www.cs.cmu.edu/afs/cs .cmu.edu/project/ai-repository/ai/lang/prolog/0.html*; additional information can be found at *www.comlab.ox.ac.uk/archive/logic-prog.html#Prolog*.

Scheme: A small, elegant dialect of Lisp (see also Lisp) developed in the mid-1970s by Guy Steele and Gerald Sussman [KCR98]. Standardized by the IEEE and ANSI. Has static scoping and true first-class functions [Ins91]. Widely used for teaching. The book by Abelson and Sussman [AS96], used for introductory programming classes at MIT and elsewhere, is a classic guide to fundamental programming concepts, and to functional programming in particular. The AI group at CMU maintains a large Scheme repository at *www.cs.cmu.edu/afs /cs.cmu.edu/project/ai-repository/ai/lang/scheme/0.html*. Another repository can be found at *www.cs.indiana.edu/scheme-repository/*.

Simula: Designed at the Norwegian Computing Centre, Oslo, in the mid-1960s by Ole-Johan Dahl, Bjørn Myhrhaug, and Kristen Nygaard [BDMN73, ND78]. Extends Algol 60 with *classes* and *coroutines*. The name of the language reflects its suitability for discrete-event simulation (Section 8.6.4). Free Simula-to-C translator available at *ftp://ftp.inria.fr/lang/simula/*.

Sisal: A functional language with "imperative-style" syntax. Developed by James McGraw and associates at Lawrence Livermore National Laboratory in the early to mid-1980s [MSA+85, FCO90, Can92]. Intended primarily for high-performance scientific computing, with automatic parallelization. A descendant of the dataflow language Val [McG82]. Implementations, documentation, and other resources available at *www.llnl.gov/sisal/*.

Smalltalk: The quintessential object-oriented language. Developed by Alan Kay, Adele Goldberg, Dan Ingalls, and associates at the Xerox Palo Alto Research Center throughout the 1970s, culminating in the Smalltalk-80 language [GR89]. Anthropomorphic programming model based on "messages" between active objects. The Smalltalk group at the University of Illinois maintains a variety of resources at *st-www.cs.uiuc.edu/*. Commercial Smalltalk implementations are available from several sources. Little Smalltalk, a line-oriented Smalltalk subset developed by Timothy Budd, is available for many platforms free of charge at *ftp://ftp.cs.orst.edu/pub/budd/little/ReadMe.html*.

Snobol: Developed by Ralph Griswold and associates at Bell Labs in the 1960s [GPP71]. The principal version is SNOBOL4. Intended primarily for processing character strings. Includes an extremely rich set of string-manipulating primitives and a novel control-flow mechanism based on the notions of *success* and *failure*. Implementations, documentation, and other resources available at *ftp://ftp.cs.arizona.edu/snobol/*.

SR: Concurrent programming language developed by Greg Andrews and colleagues at the University of Arizona in the 1980s [AO93]. Integrates not only sequential and concurrent programming but also shared memory, semaphores, message passing, remote procedures, and rendezvous into a single conceptual framework and simple syntax. Implementations, documentation, and other resources available at *ftp://ftp.cs.arizona.edu/sr/*.

Turing: Derived from Euclid by Richard Holt and associates at the University of Toronto in the early 1980s [HMRC88]. Originally intended as a pedagogical language, but can be used for a wide range of applications. Turing Plus and Object-Oriented Turing are more recent descendants, also developed by Holt's group. Documentation and implementations available at *www.holtsoft.com/turing/home.html*.

Language Design and Language Implementation

Throughout this text we have had occasion to remark on the many connections between language design and language implementation. This appendix lists many such connections, with pointers to sections of the text in which they are discussed.

Language features that many designers now believe were mistakes, at least in part because of implementation difficulties:

- by-name parameters in Algol 60: Section 8.3.1 (Call By Name)
- dangling `else` in Pascal: Sections 2.2.5 (Writing an LL(1) Grammar), 2.4, and 6.4; Exercise 2.22
- dot-dot token of Pascal: Section 2.2.1
- labels as parameters: Section 8.3.1 (Label Parameters)
- lexical complexity in Fortran: Sections 2.2.1 and 2.4
- nonlocal `goto`s: Sections 6.2 and 8.5.4
- `ON` conditions in PL/I: Section 8.5
- real bounds on `do` loops in Fortran 77: Section 6.5.1
- separate compilation mechanisms in (early) C: Section 3.6.2

Potentially useful features omitted from some languages because of concern that they might be too difficult or slow to implement:

- array slice operations: Section 7.4.1 (Slices and Array Operations)
- closures, first-class subroutines, and unlimited extent: Sections 3.4.1, 3.4.2, 7.7.3, 8.2, 8.2.2, 8.3.1 (Closures as Parameters), 8.3.3, 8.5.4, 8.6, 10.4.4, and 12.3.3 (Fork/Join); Exercise 8.6
- comparing records with holes for equality: Section 7.3.2
- conditional critical regions: Section 12.3.3 (Conditional Critical Regions)

- continuations: Sections 6.2, 6.8, and 8.5.4
- coroutines: Section 8.6
- dynamic arrays and variable-length strings: Sections 7.4.2 and 7.5
- early reply: Section 12.2.3 (Early Reply)
- exception handling: Sections 8.5 and 8.5.4
- garbage collection: Sections 7.7, 7.7.3, 7.11, 10.3.4, 10.6, and 11.2; Exercise 7.24
- higher-order functions: Section 11.2.3
- iterators: Sections 6.5.3, 8.6.3, and 6.8
- lazy evaluation: Sections 6.6.2 and 11.2.2
- multiple inheritance: Section 10.5
- nested comments: Section 2.2
- nondeterminacy (with fairness): Sections 6.7, 6.8, and 12.4.3
- recursion in Fortran: Section 3.2
- side-effect freedom: Sections 6.1.2, 6.3, 6.6, 6.8, 11.2.2, and 12.3.4
- type checked separate compilation: Section 9.6.2
- type inference by unification: 7.2.5
- type-checked I/O: Section 7.9.3
- homoiconography: Sections 7.8, 11.2.1 (Programs as Lists), and 11.3.1 (Database Manipulation)

Language limitations adopted at least in part out of concern for implementation complexity or cost:

- column-major order for arrays in Fortran: Section 7.4.3
- dynamic scope (to allow the use of an A-list): Sections 3.3.2 and 3.3.4
- fixed size for opaque exports in Modula-2: Section 10.2.1
- in `reverse`, `downto`, and constant step for `for` loops: Sections 6.5.1 (Empty Bounds) and 6.8
- lack of nested threads (to avoid cactus stacks): Sections 8.6.1 and 12.2.3 (Early Reply)
- lack of ranges in `case` statement labels: Sections 6.4.2 and 6.8
- limit on nesting level of subroutines (for displays): Section 8.1
- limited character sets: Sections 7.4.1 and 7.4.1 (Slices and Array Operations)
- limited length of identifiers: Section 2.1.1
- limited length of lines: Section 2.1.1
- limits on the size and member types of sets: Section 7.6
- mix-in inheritance (as in Java): Section 10.5.4
- nonvirtual member functions in C: Section 10.4.1

- prohibition against forward references: Sections 3.3.3 and 3.6.1
- restricted bodies for co...oc statements in SR: Sections 12.2.3 (Co-Begin) and 12.2.3 (Early Reply)

Language features introduced at least in part to facilitate efficient or elegant implementations:

- access all and aliased types in Ada 95: Sections 7.7 and 7.7.2; Exercises 7.22 and 7.23
- Ada parameter modes (to cover rendezvous): Sections 8.3.1 (Parameter Modes in Ada) and 12.4.4 (Semantics)
- case statements: Section 6.4.2
- decimal arithmetic: Section 7.1.2
- explicit deletion of dynamic objects in Pascal, C, and others: Section 7.7 (see also garbage collection above)
- imperative features in functional languages: Sections 6.3, 7.7.1 (Value Model), and 11.2.1 (Control Flow and Assignment)
- inline keyword for subroutines in C++: Sections 6.6.2, 6.8, and 8.2.3
- local scope for for loop index: Sections 6.5.1 (Access to the Index Outside the Loop) and 6.8
- mixed integer sizes in C (and to some extent subranges in Pascal): Sections 7.1.2 and 7.1.2 (Subrange Types)
- packed types: Section 7.3.2
- parameter modes (two reasons, e.g., to pass by reference): Section 8.3.1 (Variations on Value and Reference Parameters)
- pointer arithmetic in C: Sections 5.6.2 (The Impact of Subroutine Calls), 6.1.2 (Combination Assignment Operators), and 7.7.1 (Pointers and Arrays in C)
- private parts of a module specification: Sections 3.3.1 (Modules) and 10.1; Exercise 3.8
- pseudoenumeration (for) loop in C: Section 6.5.2
- short-circuit Boolean evaluation: Sections 6.1.4, 6.4.1, and 6.8
- variant parts at end of record; allocation of constrained records in Pascal and Ada: Sections 7.3.4 and 7.3.4 (Variants in Ada)
- the cut, assert, fail, etc., in Prolog: Sections 11.3.1 (Imperative Control Flow) and 11.3.1 (Database Manipulation)
- with statements: Section 7.3.3

Tradeoffs in which implementation plays a significant role:

- blocking semantics in monitors: Section 12.3.3 (Monitors)

Cases in which ease or difficulty of implementation significantly affected the success of a language:

- Smalltalk (with respect to quality of environment): Sections 1.5 and 10.6.1

Cases in which a machine architecture makes reasonable features unreasonably expensive:

- recursion in Fortran on the IBM 704: Section 3.2
- threads on a Sparc: Section 5.6.2 (The Impact of Subroutine Calls)
- shared memory on a multicomputer or network: Section 12.2.1

Miscellany:

- choosing to count with doubles: Exercise 5.4
- etymology of `car` and `cdr` in Lisp: Section 7.8
- C porting bugs: Exercise 7.4

Bibliography

[ACC+90] Robert Alverson, David Callahan, Daniel Cummings, Brian Koblenz, Allan Porterfield, and Burton Smith. The Tera computer system. In *Proceedings of the 1990 International Conference on Supercomputing*, pp. 1–6, Amsterdam, The Netherlands, June 1990. ACM Press, New York, NY. In *ACM Computer Architecture News*, 18(3), September 1990.

[ACD+96] Cristiana Amza, Alan L. Cox, Sandhya Dwarkadas, Pete Keleher, Honghui Lu, Ramakrishnan Rajamony, Weimin Yu, and Willy Zwaenepoel. TreadMarks: Shared memory computing on networks of workstations. *IEEE Computer*, 29(2):18–28, February 1996.

[ACG86] Shakil Ahuja, Nicholas Carriero, and David Gelernter. Linda and friends. *IEEE Computer*, 19(8):26–34, August 1986.

[Ado86] Adobe Systems, Inc. *PostScript Language Tutorial and Cookbook*. Addison-Wesley, Reading, MA, 1986.

[Ado90] Adobe Systems, Inc. *PostScript Language Reference Manual*. Addison-Wesley, Reading, MA, second edition, 1990.

[AF84] Krzysztof R. Apt and Nissim Francez. Modeling the distributed termination convention of CSP. *ACM Transactions on Programming Languages and Systems*, 6(3):370–379, July 1984.

[AG94] George S. Almasi and Allan Gottlieb. *Highly Parallel Computing*. Benjamin/Cummings, Redwood City, CA, second edition, 1994.

[AG98] Ken Arnold and James Gosling. *The Java Programming Language*. The Java Series. Addison-Wesley, Reading, MA, second edition, 1998.

[AH95] Ole Agesen and Urs Hölzle. Type feedback v. concrete type inference: A comparison of optimization techniques for object-oriented languages. In *OOPSLA '95 Conference Proceedings: Object-Oriented Programming Systems, Languages, and Applications*, pp. 91–107, Austin, TX, October 1995. In *ACM SIGPLAN Notices*, 30(10), October 1995.

[AKW78] Alfred V. Aho, Brian W. Kernighan, and Peter J. Weinberger. *AWK: A Pattern Scanning and Processing Language.* Bell Telephone Labs, Murray Hill, NJ, second edition, September 1978.

[ALL89] Thomas E. Anderson, Edward D. Lazowska, and Henry M. Levy. The performance implications of thread management alternatives for shared-memory multiprocessors. *IEEE Transactions on Computers*, 38(12):1631–1644, December 1989.

[Ame78a] American National Standards Institute, New York. *Programming Language FORTRAN*, 1978. ANSI X3.9-1978.

[Ame78b] American National Standards Institute, New York. *Programming Language Minimal BASIC*, 1978. ANSI X3.60-1978.

[Ame83] American National Standards Institute, New York. *Reference Manual for the Ada Programming Language*, January 1983. ANSI/MIL 1815 A-1983.

[Ame85] American National Standards Institute, New York. *Programming Language COBOL*, 1985. ANSI X3.23-1985. (Supercedes earlier ANSI standards from 1968 and 1974.)

[Ame90] American National Standards Institute, New York. *Programming Language C*, 1990. ANSI/ISO 9899-1990 (Revision and redesignation of ANSI X3.159-1989.)

[Ame92] American National Standards Institute, New York. *Programming Language, FORTRAN—Extended*, 1992. ANSI X3.198-1992. Also ISO 1539-1991 (E).

[Ame96] American National Standards Institute, New York. *Programming Language—Common Lisp*, 1996. ANSI X3.226:1994.

[And91] Gregory R. Andrews. *Concurrent Programming: Principles and Practice.* Benjamin/Cummings, Redwood City, CA, 1991.

[AO93] Gregory R. Andrews and Ronald A. Olsson. *The SR Programming Language: Concurrency in Practice.* Benjamin/Cummings, Redwood City, CA, 1993.

[App91] Andrew W. Appel. *Compiling with Continuations.* Cambridge University Press, Cambridge, England, 1991.

[App97] Andrew W. Appel. *Modern Compiler Implementation.* Cambridge University Press, Cambridge, England, 1997. Text available in ML, Java, and C versions. C version specialized by Maia Ginsburg.

[AS83] Gregory R. Andrews and Fred B. Schneider. Concepts and notations for concurrent programming. *ACM Computing Surveys*, 15(1):3–43, March 1983.

[AS96] Harold Abelson and Gerald Jay Sussman, with Julie Sussman. *Structure and Interpretation of Computer Programs.* MIT Press, Cambridge, MA, second edition, 1996. Supplementary resources available at *mitpress.mit.edu/sicp/.*

[Ass93] Association for Computing Machinery, New York, NY. *Proceedings of the Second ACM SIGPLAN History of Programming Languages Conference*, Cambridge, MA, April 1993. In *ACM SIGPLAN Notices*, 28(3), March 1993.

[ASU86] Alfred V. Aho, Ravi Sethi, and Jeffrey D. Ullman. *Compilers: Principles, Techniques, and Tools*. Addison-Wesley, Reading, MA, 1986.

[AU72] Alfred V. Aho and Jeffrey D. Ullman. *The Theory of Parsing, Translation and Compiling*. Prentice Hall Series in Automatic Computation. Prentice Hall, Englewood Cliffs, NJ, 1972. Two-volume set.

[AWZ88] Bowen Alpern, Mark N. Wegman, and F. Kenneth Zadeck. Detecting equality of variables in programs. In *Conference Record of the Fifteenth ACM Symposium on Principles of Programming Languages*, pp. 1–11, San Diego, CA, January 1988.

[Bac78] John W. Backus. Can programming be liberated from the von Neumann style? A functional style and its algebra of programs. *Communications of the ACM*, 21(8):613–641, August 1978. The 1977 Turing Award lecture.

[Bag86] Rajive L. Bagrodia. A distributed algorithm to implement the generalized alternative command of CSP. In *Proceedings of the Sixth International Conference on Distributed Computing Systems*, pp. 422–427, Cambridge, MA, May 1986. IEEE Computer Society Press, Washington, DC.

[BALL90] Brian N. Bershad, Thomas E. Anderson, Edward D. Lazowska, and Henry M. Levy. Lightweight remote procedure call. *ACM Transactions on Computer Systems*, 8(1):37–55, February 1990.

[Ban97] Utpal Banerjee. *Dependence Analysis*, volume 3 of *Loop Transformations for Restructuring Compilers*. Kluwer Academic Publishers, Boston, MA, 1997.

[Bar84] Hendrik Pieter Barendregt. *The Lambda Calculus: Its Syntax and Semantics*, volume 103 of *Studies in Logic and the Foundations of Mathematics*. North-Holland, Amsterdam, The Netherlands, revised edition, 1984.

[BC93] Peter Bumbulis and Donald D. Cowan. RE2C: A more versatile scanner generator. *ACM Letters on Programming Languages and Systems*, 2(1–4):70–84, March–December 1993.

[BDH+95] Jehoshua Bruck, Danny Dolev, Ching-Tien Ho, Marcel-Catalin Rosu, and Ray Strong. Efficient message passing interface (MPI) for parallel computing on clusters of workstations. In *Proceedings of the Seventh Annual ACM Symposium on Parallel Algorithms and Architectures*, pp. 64–73, Santa Barbara, CA, July 1995.

[BDMN73] Graham M. Birtwistle, Ole-Johan Dahl, Bjørn Myhrhaug, and Kristen Nygaard. *SIMULA Begin*. Auerback Publishers, Inc., Philadelphia, PA, 1973.

[Bec97] Leland L. Beck. *System Software: An Introduction to Systems Programming*. Addison-Wesley, Reading, MA, third edition, 1997.

[Bee70] David Beech. A structural view of PL/I. *ACM Computing Surveys*, 2(1):33–64, March 1970.

[Ben86] John L. Bentley. *Programming Pearls*. Addison-Wesley, Reading, MA, 1986.

[Ber80] Arthur J. Bernstein. Output guards and nondeterminism in 'Communicating Sequential Processes'. *ACM Transactions on Programming Languages and Systems*, 2(2):234–238, April 1980.

[BFKM86] Lee Brownston, Robert Farrell, Elaine Kant, and Nancy Martin. *Programming Expert Systems in OPS5: An Introduction to Rule-Based Programming*. Addison-Wesley Series in Artificial Intelligence. Addison Wesley, Reading, MA, 1986.

[BGS94] David F. Bacon, Susan L. Graham, and Oliver J. Sharp. Compiler transformations for high-performance computing. *ACM Computing Surveys*, 26(4):345–420, December 1994.

[BHJ+87] Andrew Black, Norman Hutchinson, Eric Jul, Henry Levy, and Lawrence Carter. Distribution and abstract types in Emerald. *IEEE Transactions on Software Engineering*, SE–13(1):65–76, January 1987.

[BHPS61] Yehoshua Bar-Hillel, Micha A. Perles, and Eliahu Shamir. On formal properties of simple phrase structure grammars. *Zeitschrift für Phonetik, Sprachwissenschaft und Kommunikationsforschung*, 14:143–172, 1961.

[BI82] Alan H. Borning and Daniel H. H. Ingalls. Multiple inheritance in Smalltalk-80. In *AAAI-82: The National Conference on Artificial Intelligence*, pp. 234–237, Pittsburgh, PA, August 1982. American Association for Artificial Intelligence.

[BN84] Andrew D. Birrell and Bruce J. Nelson. Implementing remote procedure calls. *ACM Transactions on Computer Systems*, 2(1):39–59, February 1984.

[Bri73] Per Brinch Hansen. *Operating System Principles*. Prentice Hall, Englewood Cliffs, NJ, 1973.

[Bri75] Per Brinch Hansen. The programming language Concurrent Pascal. *IEEE Transactions on Software Engineering*, SE–1(2):199–207, June 1975.

[Bri78] Per Brinch Hansen. Distributed processes: A concurrent programming concept. *Communications of the ACM*, 21(11):934–941, November 1978.

[Bri81] Per Brinch Hansen. The design of Edison. *Software—Practice and Experience*, 11(4):363–396, April 1981.

[Bro87] Leo Brodie. *Starting FORTH: An Introduction to the FORTH Language and Operating System for Beginners and Professionals*. Prentice Hall Software Series. Prentice Hall, Englewood Cliffs, NJ, second edition, 1987.

[Bro96] Kraig Brockschmidt. How OLE and COM solve the problems of component software design. *Microsoft Systems Journal*, 11(5):63–82, May 1996.

[BS83a] Daniel G. Bobrow and Mark J. Stefik. The LOOPS manual. Technical report, Xerox Palo Alto Research Center, Palo Alto, CA, 1983.

[BS83b] G. N. Buckley and A. Silbershatz. An effective implementation for the generalized input-output construct of CSP. *ACM Transactions on Programming Languages and Systems*, 5(2):223–235, April 1983.

[BW88] Hans-Juergen Boehm and Mark Weiser. Garbage collection in an uncooperative environment. *Software—Practice and Experience*, 18(9):807–820, September 1988.

[CAC+81] Gregory Chaitin, Marc Auslander, Ashok Chandra, John Cocke, Martin Hopkins, and Peter Markstein. Register allocation via coloring. *Computer Languages*, 6(1):47–57, 1981.

[Cai82] R. Cailliau. How to avoid getting SCHLONKED by Pascal. *ACM SIGPLAN Notices*, 17(12):31–40, December 1982.

[Can92] David Cann. Retire Fortran? A debate rekindled. *Communications of the ACM*, 35(8):81–89, August 1992.

[CBC93] Jong-Deok Choi, Michael Burke, and Paul Carini. Efficient flow-sensitive interprodecural computation of pointer-induced aliases and side effects. In *Conference Record of the 20th ACM Symposium on Principles of Programming Languages*, pp. 232–245, Charleston, SC, January 1993. ACM Press, New York.

[Cer89] Paul Ceruzzi. *Beyond the Limits—Flight Enters the Computer Age*. MIT Press, Cambridge, MA, 1989.

[CF58] Haskell B. Curry and Robert Feys, with two sections by William Craig. *Combinatory Logic*. Volume 1 of Studies in Logic and the Foundations of Mathematics. North-Holland, Amsterdam, The Netherlands, 1958.

[CFR+91] Ronald Cytron, Jeanne Ferrante, Barry K. Rosen, Mark N. Wegman, and F. Kenneth Zadeck. Efficiently computing static single assignment form and the control dependence graph. *ACM Transactions on Programming Languages and Systems*, 13(4):451–490, October 1991.

[Cho56] Noam Chomsky. Three models for the description of language. *IRE Transactions on Information Theory*, IT-2(3):113–124, September 1956.

[Cho62] Noam Chomsky. Context-free grammars and pushdown storage. In *Quarterly Progress Report No. 65*, pp. 187–194. MIT Research Laboratory for Electronics, Cambridge, MA, 1962.

[CHP71] P. J. Courtois, F. Heymans, and David L. Parnas. Concurrent control with 'readers' and 'writers'. *Communications of the ACM*, 14(10):667–668, October 1971.

[Chu41] Alonzo Church. *The Calculi of Lambda-Conversion*. Annals of Mathematical Studies #6. Princeton University Press, Princeton, NJ, 1941.

[Cia92] Paolo Ciancarini. Parallel programming with logic languages: A survey. *Computer Languages*, 17(4):213–239, October 1992.

[CL83] Robert P. Cook and Thomas J. LeBlanc. A symbol table abstraction to implement languages with explicit scope control. *IEEE Transactions on Software Engineering*, SE–9(1):8–12, January 1983.

[Cle86] J. Craig Cleaveland. *An Introduction to Data Types*. Addison-Wesley, Reading, MA, 1986.

[CLFL94] Jeffrey S. Chase, Henry M. Levy, Michael J. Feeley, and Edward D. La-zowska. Sharing and protection in a single-address-space operating system. *ACM Transactions on Computer Systems*, 12(4):271–307, November 1994.

[CM84] K. Mani Chandy and Jayadev Misra. The drinking philosophers problem. *ACM Transactions on Programming Languages and Systems*, 6(4):632–646, October 1984.

[CM94] William F. Clocksin and Christopher S. Mellish. *Programming in Prolog*. Springer-Verlag, Berlin, West Germany, fourth edition, 1994.

[Coh81] Jacques Cohen. Garbage collection of linked data structures. *ACM Computing Surveys*, 13(3):341–367, September 1981.

[Con63] Melvin E. Conway. Design of a separable transition-diagram compiler. *Communications of the ACM*, 6(7):396–408, July 1963.

[Cou84] B. Courcelle. Attribute grammars: Definitions, analysis of dependencies, proof methods. In *Methods and Tools for Compiler Construction: An Advanced Course*, Bernard Lorho, editor, pp. 81–102. Cambridge University Press, Cambridge, England, 1984.

[CS69] John Cocke and Jacob T. Schwartz. Programming languages and their compilers: Preliminary notes. Technical report, Courant Institute of Mathematical Sciences, New York University, New York, 1969.

[CS98] David E. Culler and Jaswinder Pal Singh, with Anoop Gupta. *Parallel Computer Architecture: A Hardware/Software Approach*. Morgan Kaufmann, San Francisco, 1998.

[CW85] Luca Cardelli and Peter Wegner. On understanding types, data abstraction, and polymorphism. *ACM Computing Surveys*, 17(4):471–522, December 1985.

[Dar90] Jared L. Darlington. Search direction by goal failure in goal-oriented programming. *ACM Transactions on Programming Languages and Systems*, 12(2):224–252, April 1990.

[Dav63] Martin Davis. Eliminating the irrelevant from mechanical proofs. In *Proceedings of a Symposium in Applied Mathematics*, volume 15, pp. 15–30. American Mathematical Society, Providence, RI, 1963.

[DB76] L. Peter Deutsch and Daniel G. Bobrow. An efficient incremental automatic garbage collector. *Communications of the ACM*, 19(9):522–526, September 1976.

[DDH72] Ole-Johan Dahl, Edsger W. Dijkstra, and Charles Antony Richard Hoare. *Structured Programming*. A.P.I.C. Studies in Data Processing #8. Academic Press, New York, 1972.

[DeR69] Franklin L. DeRemer. *Practical Translators for LR(k) Languages*. Ph. D. dissertation, Massachusetts Institute of Technology, 1969.

[DeR71] Franklin L. DeRemer. Simple LR(k) grammars. *Communications of the ACM*, 14(7):453–460, July 1971.

[Deu94] Alain Deutsch. Interprocedural may-alias analysis for pointers: Beyond k-limiting. In *Proceedings of the SIGPLAN '94 Conference on Programming Language Design and Implementation*, pp. 230–241, Orlando, FL, June 1994. In *ACM SIGPLAN Notices*, 29(6), June 1994.

[Dij60] Edsger W. Dijkstra. Recursive programming. *Numerische Mathematik*, 2:312–318, 1960. Reprinted as pp. 221–228 of Rosen [1967].

[Dij65] Edsger W. Dijkstra. Solution of a problem in concurrent programming control. *Communications of the ACM*, 8(9):569, September 1965.

[Dij68a] Edsger W. Dijkstra. Co-operating sequential processes. In *Programming Languages*, F. Genuys, editor, pp. 43–112. Academic Press, London, England, 1968.

[Dij68b] Edsger W. Dijkstra. Go To statement considered harmful. *Communications of the ACM*, 11(3):147–148, March 1968.

[Dij72] Edsger W. Dijkstra. Hierarchical ordering of sequential processes. In *Operating Systems Techniques*, Charles Antony Richard Hoare and Ronald H. Perrott, editors. A.P.I.C. Studies in Data Processing #9, pp. 72–93. Academic Press, London, England, 1972. Also *Acta Informatica*, 1(8):115–138, 1971.

[Dij75] Edsger W. Dijkstra. Guarded commands, nondeterminacy, and formal derivation of programs. *Communications of the ACM*, 18(8):453–457, August 1975.

[Dij76] Edsger W. Dijkstra. *A Discipline of Programming*. Prentice Hall Series in Automatic Computation. Prentice Hall, Englewood Cliffs, NJ, 1976.

[Dij82] Edsger W. Dijkstra. How do we tell truths that might hurt? *ACM SIGPLAN Notices*, 17(5):13–15, May 1982.

[Dio78] Bernard A. Dion. *Locally Least-Cost Error Correctors for Context-Free and Context-Sensitive Parsers*. Ph. D. dissertation, University of Wisconsin–Madison, 1978. Computer Sciences Technical Report #344.

[DMM98] Amer Diwan, Kathryn S. McKinley, and J. Eliot B. Moss. Type-based alias analysis. In *Proceedings of the SIGPLAN '98 Conference on Programming Language Design and Implementation*, pp. 106–117, Montreal, Quebec, Canada, June 1998. In *ACM SIGPLAN Notices*, 33(5), May 1998.

[Dol97] Julian Dolby. Automatic inline allocation of objects. In *Proceedings of the SIGPLAN '97 Conference on Programming Language Design and Implementation*, pp. 7–17, Las Vegas, NV, June 1997. In *ACM SIGPLAN Notices*, 32(5), May 1997.

[Dri93] Karel Driesen. Selector table indexing and sparse arrays. In *OOPSLA '93 Conference Proceedings: Object-Oriented Programming Systems, Languages, and Applications*, pp. 259–270, Washington, DC, September 1993. In *ACM SIGPLAN Notices*, 28(10), October 1993.

[DRSS96] Steven Dawson, C. R. Ramakrishnan, Steven Skiena, and Terrence Swift. Principles and practice of unification factoring. *ACM Transactions on Programming Languages and Systems*, 18(5):528–563, September 1996.

[DS84] L. Peter Deutsch and Alan M. Schiffman. Efficient implementation of the Smalltalk-80 system. In *Conference Record of the Eleventh Annual ACM Symposium on Principles of Programming Languages*, pp. 297–302, Salt Lake City, UT, January 1984.

[Dya95] Lev J. Dyadkin. Multibox parsers: No more handwritten lexical analyzers. *IEEE Software*, 12(5):61–67, September 1995.

[Ear70] Jay Earley. An efficient context-free parsing algorithm. *Communications of the ACM*, 13(2):94–102, February 1970.

[Eng84] Joost Engelfriet. Attribute grammars: Attribute evaluation methods. In *Methods and Tools for Compiler Construction: An Advanced Course*, Bernard Lorho, editor, pp. 103–138. Cambridge University Press, Cambridge, England, 1984.

[ES90] Margaret A. Ellis and Bjarne Stroustrup. *The Annotated C++ Reference Manual*. Addison-Wesley, Reading, MA, 1990.

[Eve63] R. James Evey. Application of pushdown store machines. In *Proceedings of the 1963 Fall Joint Computer Conference*, pp. 215–227, Las Vegas, NV, November 1963. AFIPS Press, Montvale, NJ.

[FCO90] John T. Feo, David Cann, and Rod R. Oldehoeft. A report on the Sisal language project. *Journal of Parallel and Distributed Computing*, 10(4):349–365, December 1990.

[FG84] Alan R. Feuer, and Narain Gehani, editors. *Comparing and Assessing Programming Languages: Ada, C, Pascal*. Prentice Hall Software Series. Prentice Hall, Englewood Cliffs, NJ, 1984.

[FH95] Christopher W. Fraser and David R. Hanson. *A Retargetable C Compiler: Design and Implementation*. Benjamin/Cummings, Redwood City, CA, 1995.

[Fin96] Raphael A. Finkel. *Advanced Programming Language Design*. Addison-Wesley, Menlo Park, CA, 1996.

[FL80] Charles N. Fischer and Richard J. LeBlanc, Jr. Implementation of runtime diagnostics in Pascal. *IEEE Transactions on Software Engineering*, SE–6(4):313–319, July 1980.

[FL88] Charles N. Fischer and Richard J. LeBlanc, Jr. *Crafting a Compiler*. Benjamin/Cummings, Menlo Park, CA, 1988.

[Fle76] A. C. Fleck. On the impossibility of content exchange through the by-name parameter transmission technique. *ACM SIGPLAN Notices*, 11(11):38–41, November 1976.

[FMQ80] Charles N. Fischer, Donn R. Milton, and Sam B. Quiring. Efficient LL(1) error correction and recovery using only insertions. *Acta Informatica*, 13(2):141–54, February 1980.

[Fos95] Ian Foster. Compositional C++. In *Debugging and Building Parallel Programs*, Chapter 5, pp. 167–204. Addison-Wesley, Reading, MA, 1995. Available in hypertext at *www.mcs.anl.gov/dbpp/text/node51.html*.

[Fra80] Nissim Francez. Distributed termination. *ACM Transactions on Programming Languages and Systems*, 2(1):42–55, January 1980.

[FSS83] Stefan M. Freudenberger, Jacob T. Schwartz, and Micha Sharir. Experience with the SETL optimizer. *ACM Transactions on Programming Languages and Systems*, 5(1):26–45, January 1983.

[FWH92] Daniel P. Friedman, Mitchell Wand, and Christopher T. Haynes. *Essentials of Programming Languages*. MIT Press and McGraw-Hill, Cambridge, MA and New York, 1992.

[FY69] Robert R. Fenichel and Jerome C. Yochelson. A Lisp garbage collector for virtual memory computer systems. *Communications of the ACM*, 12(11):611–612, November 1969.

[Gar70] Martin Gardner. The fantastic combinations of John Conway's new solitaire game 'Life'. *Scientific American*, 223(4):120–123, October 1970.

[Gar89] James Gardner. *From C to C: An Introduction to ANSI Standard C, with Reference Manual*. Harcourt Brace Jovanovich, San Diego, CA, 1989.

[GBD+94] Al Geist, Adam Beguelin, Jack Dongarra, Weicheng Jiang, Robert Manchek, and Vaidyalingam S. Sunderam. *PVM: Parallel Virtual Machine: A Users' Guide and Tutorial for Networked Parallel Computing*. Scientific and Engineering Computation series. MIT Press, Cambridge, MA, 1994. Available in hypertext at *www.netlib.org/pvm3/book/pvm-book.html*.

[GDDC97] David Grove, Greg DeFouw, Jeffrey Dean, and Craig Chambers. Call graph construction in object-oriented languages. In *OOPSLA '97 Conference Proceedings: Object-Oriented Programming Systems, Languages, and Applications*, pp. 108–124, Atlanta, GA, October 1997. In *ACM SIGPLAN Notices*, 32(10), October 1997.

[GFH82] Mahadevan Ganapathi, Charles N. Fischer, and John L. Hennessy. Retargetable compiler code generation. *ACM Computing Surveys*, 14(4):573–592, December 1982.

[GG78] R. Steven Glanville and Susan L. Graham. A new method for compiler code generation. In *Conference Record of the Fifth Annual ACM Symposium on Principles of Programming Languages*, pp. 231–240, Tucson, AZ, January 1978.

[GG89] Ron Goldman and Richard P. Gabriel. Qlisp: Parallel processing in Lisp. *IEEE Software*, 6(4):51–59, July 1989.

[GG97] Ralph E. Griswold and Madge T. Griswold. *The Icon Programming Language*. Peer-to-Peer Communications, San Jose, CA, third edition, 1997. Previous editions published by Prentice Hall.

[GJS96] James Gosling, Bill Joy, and Guy L. Steele Jr. *The Java Language Specification*. The Java Series. Addison-Wesley, Reading, MA, edition 1.0, 1996. Available in hypertext at *java.sun.com/docs/books/jls/html/index.html*.

[GKP96] George Al Geist, J. A. Kohl, and P. M. Papadopoulos. PVM and MPI: a comparison of features. *Calculateurs Paralleles*, 8(2), 1996.

[GLDW87] Robert A. Gingell, Meng Lee, Xuong T. Dang, and Mary S. Weeks. Shared libraries in SunOS. In *Proceedings of the 1987 Summer USENIX Conference*, pp. 131–145, Phoenix, AZ, June 1987.

[GM86] Phillip B. Gibbons and Steven S. Muchnick. Efficient instruction scheduling for a pipelined architecture. In *Proceedings of the SIGPLAN '86 Symposium on Compiler Construction*, pp. 11–16, Palo Alto, CA, July 1986. In *ACM SIGPLAN Notices*, 21(7), July 1986.

[Gol84] Adele Goldberg. *Smalltalk-80: The Interactive Programming Environment*. Addison-Wesley Series in Computer Science. Addison-Wesley, Reading, MA, 1984.

[Gol96] David Goldberg. Computer arithmetic. In *Computer Architecture: A Quantitative Approach*, by John L. Hennessy and David A. Patterson, pp. A1–A77. Morgan Kaufmann, San Francisco, second edition, 1996.

[Goo75] John B. Goodenough. Exception handling: Issues and a proposed notation. *Communications of the ACM*, 18(12):683–696, December 1975.

[Gor79] Michael J. C. Gordon. *The Denotational Description of Programming Languages: An Introduction*. Springer-Verlag, New York, NY, 1979.

[GPP71] Ralph E. Griswold, J. F. Poage, and I. P. Polonsky. *The Snobol4 Programming Language*. Prentice Hall, Englewood Cliffs, NJ, second edition, 1971.

[GR62] Seymour Ginsburg and H. Gordon Rice. Two families of languages related to ALGOL. *Journal of the ACM*, 9(3):350–371, 1962.

[GR89] Adele Goldberg and David Robson. *Smalltalk-80: The Language*. Addison-Wesley Series in Computer Science. Addison-Wesley, Reading, MA, 1989.

[Gri81] David Gries. *The Science of Programming*. Texts and Monographs in Computer Science. Springer-Verlag, New York, NY, 1981.

[GSB+93] William E. Garrett, Michael L. Scott, Ricardo Bianchini, Leonidas I. Kontothanassis, R. Andrew McCallum, Jeffrey A. Thomas, Robert Wisniewski, and Steve Luk. Linking shared segments. In *Proceedings of the USENIX Winter '93 Technical Conference*, pp. 13–27, San Diego, CA, January 1993.

[GTW78] J. A. Goguen, J. W. Thatcher, and E. G. Wagner. An initial algebra approach to the specification, correctness, and implementation of abstract data types. In *Current Trends in Programming Methodology*, Raymond T. Yeh, editor. Volume 4, pp. 80–149. Prentice Hall, Englewood Cliffs, NJ, 1978.

[Gut77] John Guttag. Abstract data types and the development of data structures. *Communications of the ACM*, 20(6):396–404, June 1977.

[GWEB83] Gerhard Goos, William A. Wulf, Arthur Evans, Jr., and Kenneth J. Butler, editors. *DIANA: An Intermediate Language for Ada*. Volume 161 of Lecture Notes in Computer Science. Springer-Verlag, Berlin, West Germany, 1983.

[Hal85] Robert H. Halstead, Jr. Multilisp: A language for concurrent symbolic computation. *ACM Transactions on Programming Languages and Systems*, 7(4):501–538, October 1985.

[Han81] David R. Hanson. Is block structure necessary? *Software—Practice and Experience*, 11(8):853–866, August 1981.

[Har92] Samuel P. Harbison. *Modula-3*. Prentice Hall, Englewood Cliffs, NJ, 1992.

[HD68] E. A. Hauck and B. A. Dent. Burroughs' B6500/B7500 stack mechanism. In *Proceedings of the AFIPS Spring Joint Computer Conference*, volume 32, pp. 245–251, 1968. Reprinted as pp. 244–250 of Siewiorek, Bell, and Newell [1982].

[HD89] Robert R. Henry and Peter C. Damron. Algorithms for table-driven code generators using tree-pattern matching. Technical Report 89-02-03, Computer Science Department, University of Washington, Seattle, WA, February 1989.

[Her91] Maurice P. Herlihy. Wait-free synchronization. *ACM Transactions on Programming Languages and Systems*, 13(1):124–149, January 1991.

[HGLS78] Richard C. Holt, G. Scott Graham, Edward D. Lazowska, and Mark A. Scott. *Structured Concurrent Programming with Operating Systems Applications*. Addison-Wesley Series in Computer Science. Addison-Wesley, Reading, MA, 1978.

[HH97] Raymond J. Hookway and Mark A. Herdeg. DIGITAL FX!32: Combining emulation and binary translation. *DIGITAL Technical Journal*, 9(1):3–12, 1997.

[HHN94] Joseph Hummel, Laurie J. Hendren, and Alexandru Nicolau. A general data dependence test for dynamic, pointer-based data structures. In *Proceedings of the SIGPLAN '94 Conference on Programming Language Design and Implementation*, pp. 218–229, Orlando, FL, June 1994. In *ACM SIGPLAN Notices*, 29(6), June 1994.

[HJBG81] John L. Hennessy, Norman Jouppi, Forest Baskett, and John Gill. MIPS: A VLSI processor architecture. In *Proceedings of the CMU Conference on VLSI Systems and Computations*, pp. 337–346. Computer Science Press, Rockville, MD, October 1981.

[HL94] Patricia M. Hill and John W. Lloyd. *The Gödel Programming Language*. Logic Programming Series. MIT Press, Cambridge, MA, 1994.

[HM92] Maurice P. Herlihy and J. Elliot B. Moss. Lock-free garbage collection for multiprocessors. *IEEE Transactions on Parallel and Distributed Systems*, 3(3):304–311, May 1992.

[HMRC88] Richard C. Holt, Philip A. Matthews, J. Alan Rosselet, and James R. Cordy. *The Turing Programming Language: Design and Definition*. Prentice Hall, Englewood Cliffs, NJ, 1988.

[HO91] W. Wilson Ho and Ronald A. Olsson. An approach to genuine dynamic linking. *Software—Practice and Experience*, 21(4):375–390, April 1991.

[Hoa69] Charles Antony Richard Hoare. An axiomatic basis of computer programming. *Communications of the ACM*, 12(10):576–580+, October 1969.

[Hoa74] Charles Antony Richard Hoare. Monitors: An operating system structuring concept. *Communications of the ACM*, 17(10):549–557, October 1974.

[Hoa75] Charles Antony Richard Hoare. Recursive data structures. *International Journal of Computer and Information Sciences*, 4(2):105–132, June 1975.

[Hoa78] Charles Antony Richard Hoare. Communicating Sequential Processes. *Communications of the ACM*, 21(8):666–677, August 1978.

[Hoa81] Charles Antony Richard Hoare. The emperor's old clothes. *Communications of the ACM*, 24(2):75–83, February 1981. The 1980 Turing Award lecture.

[Hoa89] Charles Antony Richard Hoare. Hints on programming language design. In *Essays in Computing Science*, Cliff B. Jones, editor, pp. 193–216. Prentice Hall, New York, NY, 1989. Based on a keynote address presented at the *First ACM Symposium on Principles of Programming Languages*, Boston, MA, October, 1973.

[Hor51] Alfred Horn. On sentences which are true of direct unions of algebras. *Journal of Symbolic Logic*, 16(1):14–21, March 1951.

[Hor87] Ellis Horowitz. *Programming Languages: A Grand Tour*. Computer Software Engineering Series. Computer Science Press, Rockville, MD, third edition, 1987.

[HP96] John L. Hennessy and David A. Patterson. *Computer Architecture: A Quantitative Approach*. Morgan Kaufmann, San Francisco, second edition, 1996.

[HU79] John E. Hopcroft and Jeffrey D. Ullman. *Introduction to Automata Theory, Languages, and Computation*. Addison-Wesley Series in Computer Science. Addison-Wesley, Reading, MA, 1979.

[Hud89] Paul Hudak. Conception, evolution, and application of functional programming languages. *ACM Computing Surveys*, 21(3):359–411, September 1989.

[IBFW91] Jean Ichbiah, John G. P. Barnes, Robert J. Firth, and Mike Woodger. *Rationale for the Design of the Ada Programming Language*. Ada Companion Series. Cambridge University Press, Cambridge, England, 1991.

[IBM87] IBM Corporation. *APL2 Programming: Language Reference*, 1987. SH20-9227.

[IEE87] IEEE Standards Committee. IEEE standard for binary floating-point arithmetic. *ACM SIGPLAN Notices*, 22(2):9–25, February 1987. Standard adopted by IEEE, March 1985; by ANSI, July 1985.

[Ing61] Peter Z. Ingerman. Thunks: A way of compiling procedure statements with some comments on procedure declarations. *Communications of the ACM*, 4(1):55–58, January 1961.

[Ins91] Institute of Electrical and Electronics Engineers, New York, NY. *IEEE/ANSI Standard for the Scheme Programming Language*, 1991. IEEE 1178-1990.

[Int90] International Organization for Standardization, Geneva, Switzerland. *Information Technology—Programming Languages—Pascal*, 1990. ISO/IEC 7185:1990 (revision and redesignation of ANSI/IEEE 770X).

[Int95a] International Organization for Standardization, Geneva, Switzerland. *Information Technology—Programming Languages—Prolog—Part 1: General Core*, 1995. ISO/IEC 13211-1:1995.

[Int95b] International Organization for Standardization, Geneva, Switzerland. *Information Technology—Programming Languagess—Ada*, 1995. ISO/IEC 8652:1995 (E). Available in hypertext at *www.adahome.com/rm95/*.

[Int96] International Organization for Standardization, Geneva, Switzerland. *Information Technology—Programming Languages—Part 1: Modula-2, Base Language*, 1996. ISO/IEC 10514-1:1996.

[Int98a] International Organization for Standardization, Geneva, Switzerland. *Programming Language—C*, August 1998. WG14/N843 Committee Draft revision of ISO 9899-1990. Available at *wwwold.dkuug.dk/jtc1/sc22/open/n2794/*.

[Int98b] International Organization for Standardization, Geneva, Switzerland. *Programming Languages—C++*, 1998. ISO/IEC 14882:1998.

[Ive62] Kenneth E. Iverson. *A Programming Language*. John Wiley & Sons, New York, 1962.

[JG88] Geraint Jones and Michael Goldsmith. *Programming in occam2*. Prentice Hall International Series in Computer Science. Prentice Hall, Englewood Cliffs, NJ, second edition, 1988.

[JM94] Joxan Jaffar and Michael J. Maher. Constraint logic programming: A survey. *Journal of Logic Programming*, 20:503–581, May–July 1994.

[Joh75] S. C. Johnson. Yacc—Yet another compiler compiler. Technical Report 32, Computing Science, AT&T Bell Laboratories, Murray Hill, NJ, 1975.

[JOR75] Mehdi Jazayeri, William F. Ogden, and William C. Rounds. The intrinsically exponential complexity of the circularity problem for attribute grammars. *Communications of the ACM*, 18(12):697–706, December 1975.

[Jor85] Harry F. Jordan. HEP architecture, programming and performance. In *Parallel MIMD Computation: The HEP Supercomputer and its Applications*, Janusz S. Kowalik, editor, pp. 1–40. MIT Press, Cambridge, MA, 1985.

[JPAR68] Walter L. Johnson, James H. Porter, Stephanie I. Ackley, and Douglas T. Ross. Automatic generation of efficient lexical processors using finite state techniques. *Communications of the ACM*, 11(12):805–813, December 1968.

[JW91] Kathleen Jensen and Niklaus Wirth. *Pascal User Manual and Report: ISO Pascal Standard*. Springer-Verlag, New York, fourth edition, 1991. Revised by Andrew B. Mickel and James F. Miner.

[Kas65] T. Kasami. An efficient recognition and syntax analysis algorithm for context-free languages. Technical Report AFCRL–65–758, Air Force Cambridge Research Laboratory, Bedford, MA, 1965.

[KCR98] Richard Kelsey, William Clinger, and Jonathan Rees, editors. Revised report on the algorithmic language Scheme. *ACM SIGPLAN Notices*, 33(9):26–76, September 1998. With H. Abelson, N. I. Adams IV, D. H. Bartley, G. Brooks, R. K. Dybvig, D. P. Friedman, R. Halstead, C. Hanson, C. T. Haynes, E. Kohlbecker, D. Oxley, K. M. Pitman, G. J. Rozas, G. L. Steele Jr., G. J. Sussman, and M. Wand. Available as *ftp://ftp.cs.indiana.edu/pub/scheme-repository/doc/standards/r5rs-html.tar.gz*.

[Kee89] Sonya E. Keene. *Object-Oriented Programming in Common Lisp: A Programmer's Guide to CLOS*. Addison-Wesley, Reading, MA, 1989. Contributions by Dan Gerson.

[Ker81] Brian W. Kernighan. Why Pascal is not my favorite programming language. Technical Report 100, Computing Science, AT&T Bell Laboratories, Murray Hill, NJ, 1981. Reprinted as pp. 170–186 of Feuer and Gehani [1984].

[Kes77] J. L. W. Kessels. An alternative to event queues for synchronization in monitors. *Communications of the ACM*, 20(7):500–503, July 1977.

[KKR+86] David Kranz, Richard Kelsey, Jonathan Rees, Paul Hudak, James Philbin, and Norman Adams. ORBIT: An optimizing compiler for Scheme. In *Proceedings of the SIGPLAN '86 Symposium on Compiler Construction*, pp. 219–233, Palo Alto, CA, June 1986. In *ACM SIGPLAN Notices*, 21(7), July 1986.

[Kle56] Stephen C. Kleene. Representation of events in nerve nets and finite automata. In *Automata Studies*, number 34 in Annals of Mathematical Studies, Claude E. Shannon and John McCarthy, editors, pp. 3–41. Princeton University Press, Princeton, NJ, 1956.

[KLS+94] Charles H. Koelbel, David B. Loveman, Robert S. Schreiber, Guy L. Steele Jr., and Mary E. Zosel. *The High Performance Fortran Handbook*. Scientific and Engineering Computation Series. MIT Press, Cambridge, MA, 1994.

[Knu65] Donald E. Knuth. On the translation of languages from left to right. *Information and Control*, 8(6):607–639, December 1965.

[Knu68] Donald E. Knuth. Semantics of context-free languages. *Mathematical Systems Theory*, 2(2):127–145, June 1968. Correction appears in Volume 5, pp. 95–96.

[Knu84] Donald E. Knuth. Literate programming. *The Computer Journal*, 27(2):97–111, May 1984.

[KP76] Brian W. Kernighan and Phillip J. Plauger. *Software Tools*. Addison-Wesley, Reading, MA, 1976.

[KP78] Brian W. Kernighan and Phillip J. Plauger. *The Elements of Programming Style*. McGraw-Hill, New York, NY, second edition, 1978.

[Kr73] Jaroslav Král. The equivalence of modes and the equivalence of finite automata. *ALGOL Bulletin*, 35:34–35, March 1973.

[KR78] Brian W. Kernighan and Dennis M. Ritchie. *The C Programming Language*. Prentice Hall Software Series. Prentice Hall, Englewood Cliffs, NJ, 1978.

[KWS97] Leonidas I. Kontothanassis, Robert Wisniewski, and Michael L. Scott. Scheduler-conscious synchronization. *ACM Transactions on Computer Systems*, 15(1):3–40, February 1997.

[Lam78] Leslie Lamport. Time, clocks, and the ordering of events in a distributed system. *Communications of the ACM*, 21(7):558–565, July 1978.

[Lam87] Leslie Lamport. A fast mutual exclusion algorithm. *ACM Transactions on Computer Systems*, 5(1):1–11, February 1987.

[Les75] Michael E. Lesk. Lex—A lexical analyzer generator. Technical Report 39, Computing Science, AT&T Bell Laboratories, Murray Hill, NJ, 1975.

[LG86] Barbara Liskov and John Guttag. *Abstraction and Specification in Program Development*. MIT Electrical Engineering and Computer Science Series. MIT Press, Cambridge, MA, 1986.

[LH89] Kai Li and Paul Hudak. Memory coherence in shared virtual memory systems. *ACM Transactions on Computer Systems*, 7(4):321–359, November 1989.

[LHL+77] Butler W. Lampson, J. J. Horning, R. L. London, J. G. Mitchell, and G. J. Popek. Report on the programming language Euclid. *ACM SIGPLAN Notices*, 12(2):1–79, February 1977.

[Lom75] David B. Lomet. Scheme for invalidating references to freed storage. *IBM Journal of Research and Development*, 19(1):26–35, January 1975.

[Lom85] David B. Lomet. Making pointers safe in system programming languages. *IEEE Transactions on Software Engineering*, SE–11(1):87–96, January 1985.

[Lou93] Kenneth C. Louden. *Programming Languages: Principles and Practice*. PWS-KENT Series in Computer Science. PWS Publishing Company, Boston, 1993.

[LP80] D. C. Luckam and W. Polak. Ada exception handling: An axiomatic approach. *ACM Transactions on Programming Languages and Systems*, 2(2):225–233, April 1980.

[LR80] Butler W. Lampson and David D. Redell. Experience with processes and monitors in Mesa. *Communications of the ACM*, 23(2):105–117, February 1980.

[LRS74] Philip M. Lewis II, Daniel J. Rosenkrantz, and Richard E. Stearns. Attributed translations. *Journal of Computer and System Sciences*, 9(3):279–307, December 1974.

[LRZ93] William Landi, Barbara G. Ryder, and Sean Zhang. Interprocedural modification side effect analysis with pointer aliasing. In *Proceedings of the SIGPLAN '93 Conference on Programming Language Design and Implementation*, pp. 56–67, Albuquerque, NM, June 1993. In *ACM SIGPLAN Notices*, 28(6), June 1993.

[LS68] Philip M. Lewis II and Richard E. Stearns. Syntax-directed transduction. *Journal of the ACM*, 15(3):465–488, July 1968.

[LS79] Barbara Liskov and Alan Snyder. Exception handling in CLU. *IEEE Transactions on Software Engineering*, SE–5(6):546–558, November 1979.

[LS83] Barbara Liskov and Robert Scheifler. Guardians and actions: Linguistic support for robust, distributed programs. *ACM Transactions on Programming Languages and Systems*, 5(3):381–404, July 1983.

[LS95] James R. Larus and Eric Schnarr. EEL: Machine-independent executable editing. In *Proceedings of the SIGPLAN '95 Conference on Programming Language Design and Implementation*, pp. 291–300, La Jolla, CA, June 1995. In *ACM SIGPLAN Notices*, 30(6), June 1995.

[LSAS77] Barbara Liskov, Alan Snyder, Russel Atkinson, and J. Craig Schaffert. Abstraction mechanisms in CLU. *Communications of the ACM*, 20(8):564–576, August 1977.

[Lv77] C. H. Lindsey and S. G. van der Meulen. *Informal Introduction to ALGOL 68*. North-Holland, Amsterdam, The Netherlands, revised edition, 1977.

[LY97] Tim Lindholm and Frank Yellin. *The Java Virtual Machine Specification*. The Java Series. Addison-Wesley, Reading, MA, 1997.

[Mac77] M. Donald MacLaren. Exception handling in PL/I. In *Proceedings of an ACM Conference on Language Design for Reliable Software*, David B. Wortman, editor, pp. 101–104, Raleigh, NC, 1977. In *ACM SIGPLAN Notices*, 12(3), March 1977.

[MAE+65] John McCarthy, Paul W. Abrahams, Daniel J. Edwards, Timothy P. Hart, and Michael I. Levin. *LISP 1.5 Programmer's Manual*. MIT Press, Cambridge, MA, second edition, 1965.

[Mai90] Harry G. Mairson. Deciding ML typability is complete for deterministic exponential time. In *Conference Record of the Seventeenth Annual ACM Symposium on Principles of Programming Languages*, pp. 382–401, San Francisco, January 1990.

[Mas87] Henry Massalin. Superoptimizer: A look at the smallest program. In *Proceedings of the Second International Conference on Architectural Support for Program-*

ming Languages and Operating Systems, pp. 122–126, Palo Alto, CA, October 1987. In *ACM SIGPLAN Notices*, 22(10), October 1987.

[McC60] John McCarthy. Recursive functions of symbolic expressions and their computation by machine, Part I. *Communications of the ACM*, 3(4):184–195, April 1960.

[McG82] James R. McGraw. The VAL language: Description and analysis. *ACM Transactions on Programming Languages and Systems*, 4(1):44–82, January 1982.

[MCS91] John M. Mellor-Crummey and Michael L. Scott. Algorithms for scalable synchronization on shared-memory multiprocessors. *ACM Transactions on Computer Systems*, 9(1):21–65, February 1991.

[Mey92] Bertrand Meyer. *Eiffel: The Language*. Prentice Hall Object-Oriented Series. Prentice Hall, New York, 1992.

[Mic89] Greg Michaelson. *An Introduction to Functional Programming through Lambda Calculus*. International Computer Science Series. Addison-Wesley, Wokingham, England, 1989.

[Mic91] Microsoft Corporation, Redmond, WA. *Microsoft Visual Basic Language Reference*, 1991. Document DB20664-0491.

[MKH91] Eric Mohr, David A. Kranz, and Robert H. Halstead, Jr. Lazy task creation: A technique for increasing the granularity of parallel programs. *IEEE Transactions on Parallel and Distributed Systems*, 2(3):264–280, July 1991.

[MLB76] Michael Marcotty, Henry F. Ledgard, and Gregor V. Bochmann. A sampler of formal definitions. *ACM Computing Surveys*, 8(2):191–276, June 1976.

[Moo78] David A. Moon. *MacLisp Reference Manual*. MIT Artificial Intelligence Laboratory, 1978.

[Moo86] David A. Moon. Object-oriented programming with Flavors. In *OOPSLA '86 Conference Proceedings: Object-Oriented Programming Systems, Languages, and Applications*, pp. 1–8, Portland, OR, September 1986. In *ACM SIGPLAN Notices*, 21(11), November 1986.

[MOSS96] Stephan Murer, Stephen Omohundro, David Stoutamire, and Clemens Szyperski. Iteration abstraction in Sather. *ACM Transactions on Programming Languages and Systems*, 18(1):1–15, January 1996.

[MR96] Michael Metcalf and John Reid. *Fortran 90/95 Explained*. Oxford University Press, London, England, 1996.

[MS96] Maged M. Michael and Michael L. Scott. Simple, fast, and practical nonblocking and blocking concurrent queue algorithms. In *Proceedings of the Fifteenth Annual ACM Symposium on Principles of Distributed Computing*, pp. 267–275, Philadelphia, PA, May 1996.

[MSA+85] James R. McGraw, S. K. Skedzielewski, S. J. Allan, Rod R. Oldehoeft, J. Glauert, C. Kirkham, W. Noyce, and R. Thomas. SISAL: *Streams and Iteration in a Single Assignment Language: Reference Manual Version 1.2.* Lawrence Livermore National Laboratory, Livermore, CA, March 1985. Manual M-146, Revision 1.

[MTHM97] Robin Milner, Mads Tofte, Robert Harper, and David MacQueen. *The Definition of Standard ML—Revised.* MIT Press, Cambridge, MA, 1997.

[Muc97] Steven S. Muchnick. *Advanced Compiler Design and Implementation.* Morgan Kaufmann, San Francisco, 1997.

[MYD95] Bruce J. McKenzie, Corey Yeatman, and Lorraine De Vere. Error repair in shift-reduce parsers. *ACM Transactions on Programming Languages and Systems,* 17(4):672–689, July 1995.

[NBB+63] Peter Naur (ed.), J. W. Backus, F. L. Bauer, J. Green, C. Katz, J. McCarthy, A. J. Perlis, H. Rutishauser, K. Samelson, B. Vauquois, J. H. Wegstein, A. van Wijngaarden, and M. Woodger. Revised report on the algorithmic language ALGOL 60. *Communications of the ACM,* 6(1):1–23, January 1963. Original version appeared in the May 1960 issue.

[ND78] Kristen Nygaard and Ole-Johan Dahl. The development of the Simula languages. In *Proceedings of the ACM SIGPLAN History of Programming Languages Conference,* ACM Monograph Series, 1981, Richard L. Wexelblat, editor, pp. 439–493, Los Angeles, CA, June 1978. Academic Press, New York, NY. In *ACM SIGPLAN Notices,* 13(8), August 1978.

[Nel81] Bruce J. Nelson. *Remote Procedure Call.* Ph. D. dissertation, Carnegie-Mellon University, 1981. School of Computer Science Technical Report CMU-CS-81-119.

[NL91] Bill Nitzberg and Virginia Lo. Distributed shared memory: A survey of issues and algorithms. *IEEE Computer,* 24(8):52–60, August 1991.

[Ope96] Open Software Foundation. *OSF DCE Application Development Reference, Release 1.1.* OSF DCE Series. Prentice Hall, Upper Saddle River, NJ, 1996.

[Ous82] John K. Ousterhout. Scheduling techniques for concurrent systems. In *Proceedings of the Third International Conference on Distributed Computing Systems,* pp. 22–30, Miami/Ft. Lauderdale, FL, October 1982. IEEE Computer Society Press, Silver Spring, MD.

[Pag76] Frank G. Pagan. *A Practical Guide to Algol 68.* Wiley Series in Computing. John Wiley & Sons, London, England, 1976.

[Par72] David L. Parnas. On the criteria to be used in decomposing systems into modules. *Communications of the ACM,* 15(12):1053–1058, December 1972.

[Pat85] David A. Patterson. Reduced instruction set computers. *Communications of the ACM,* 28(1):8–21, January 1985.

[PD80] David A. Patterson and David R. Ditzel. The case for the reduced instruction set computer. *Computer Architecture News*, 8(6):25–33, October 1980.

[PD96] Larry L. Peterson and Bruce S. Davie. *Computer Networks: A Systems Approach*. Morgan Kaufmann, San Francisco, 1996.

[Pet81] Gary L. Peterson. Myths about the mutual exclusion problem. *Information Processing Letters*, 12(3):115–116, June 1981.

[Pey87] Simon L. Peyton Jones. *The Implementation of Functional Programming Languages*. Prentice Hall, Englewood Cliffs, NJ, 1987.

[Pey92] Simon L. Peyton Jones. Implementing lazy functional languages on stock hardware: The Spinless Tagless G-machine. *Journal of Functional Programming*, 2(2):127–202, 1992.

[PH98] David A. Patterson and John L. Hennessy. *Computer Organization and Design: The Hardware-Software Interface*. Morgan Kaufmann, San Francisco, second edition, 1998.

[PHA+99] Simon L. Peyton Jones (ed.), John Hughes (ed.), Lennart Augustsson, Dave Barton, Brian Boutel, Warren Burton, Joseph Fasel, Kevin Hammond, Ralf Hinze, Paul Hudak, Thomas Johnsson, Mark Jones, John Launchbury, Erik Meijer, John Peterson, Alastair Reid, Colin Runciman, and Philip Wadler. *Haskell 98: A Non-strict, Purely Functional Language*, February 1999. Available in hypertext at *haskell.systemsz.cs.yale.edu/onlinereport*.

[Rad82] George Radin. The 801 minicomputer. In *Proceedings of the First International Symposium on Architectural Support for Programming Languages and Operating Systems*, pp. 39–47, Palo Alto, CA, March 1982. In *ACM SIGPLAN Notices*, 17(4), April 1982.

[Ram87] S. Ramesh. A new efficient implementation of CSP with output guards. In *Proceedings of the Seventh International Conference on Distributed Computing Systems*, pp. 266–273, Berlin, West Germany, September 1987. IEEE Computer Society Press, Washington, DC.

[RF93] B. Ramakrishna Rau and Joseph A. Fisher. Instruction-level parallel processing: History, overview, and perspective. *Journal of Supercomputing*, 7(1/2):9–50, May 1993.

[Rob65] J. Alan Robinson. A machine-oriented logic based on the resolution principle. *Journal of the ACM*, 12(1):23–41, January 1965.

[RR64] Brian Randell and Lawford J. Russell, editors. *ALGOL 60 Implementation: The Translation and Use of ALGOL 60 Programs on a Computer*. A.P.I.C. Studies in Data Processing #5. Academic Press, New York, 1964.

[RS59] Michael O. Rabin and Dana S. Scott. Finite automata and their decision problems. *IBM Journal of Research and Development*, 3(2):114–125, 1959.

[RS70] Daniel J. Rosenkrantz and Richard E. Stearns. Properties of deterministic top-down grammars. *Information and Control*, 17(3):226–256, October 1970.

[Rub87] Frank Rubin. 'GOTO considered harmful' considered harmful. *Communications of the ACM*, 30(3):195–196, March 1987. Further correspondence appears in Volume 30, Numbers 6, 7, 8, 11, and 12.

[Rut67] Heinz Rutishauser. *Description of ALGOL 60*. Springer-Verlag, New York, NY, 1967.

[RVL+97] Ted Romer, Geoff Voelker, Dennis Lee, Alec Wolman, Wayne Wong, Hank Levy, and Brian Bershad. Instrumentation and optimization of Win32/Intel executables using Etch. In *Proceedings of the USENIX Windows NT Workshop*, pp. 1–8, Seattle, WA, August 1997.

[RW92] Martin Reiser and Niklaus Wirth. *Programming in Oberon—Steps Beyond Pascal and Modula*. Addison-Wesley, Reading, MA, 1992.

[SB90] Michael Schroeder and Michael Burrows. Performance of Firefly RPC. *ACM Transactions on Computer Systems*, 8(1):1–17, February 1990.

[SBG+91] Robert E. Strom, David F. Bacon, Arthur P. Goldberg, Andy Lowry, Daniel M. Yellin, and Shaula Alexander Yemini. *Hermes: A Language for Distributed Computing*. Prentice Hall Series in Innovative Technology. Prentice Hall, Englewood Cliffs, NJ, 1991.

[SBN82] Daniel P. Siewiorek, C. Gordon Bell, and Allen Newell. *Computer Structures: Principles and Examples*. McGraw-Hill Computer Science Series. McGraw-Hill, New York, NY, 1982.

[SCK+93] Richard L. Sites, Anton Chernoff, Matthew B. Kirk, Maurice P. Marks, and Scott G. Robinson. Binary translation. *Communications of the ACM*, 36(2):69–81, February 1993.

[Sco91] Michael L. Scott. The Lynx distributed programming language: Motivation, design, and experience. *Computer Languages*, 16(3/4):209–233, 1991.

[SDB84] Mayer D. Schwartz, Norman M. Delisle, and Vimal S. Begwani. Incremental compilation in Magpie. In *Proceedings of the SIGPLAN '84 Symposium on Compiler Construction*, pp. 122–131, Montreal, Quebec, Canada, June 1984. In *ACM SIGPLAN Notices*, 19(6), June 1984.

[SE94] Amitabh Srivastava and Alan Eustace. ATOM: A system for building customized program analysis tools. In *Proceedings of the SIGPLAN '94 Conference on Programming Language Design and Implementation*, pp. 196–205, Orlando, FL, June 1994. In *ACM SIGPLAN Notices*, 29(6), June 1994.

[Seb99] Robert W. Sebesta. *Concepts of Programming Languages*. Addison-Wesley, Reading, MA, fourth edition, 1999.

[Set96] Ravi Sethi. *Programming Languages: Concepts and Constructs.* Addison-Wesley, Reading, MA, second edition, 1996.

[SF80] Marvin H. Solomon and Raphael A. Finkel. A note on enumerating binary trees. *Journal of the ACM*, 27(1):3–5, January 1980.

[SF88] Michael L. Scott and Raphael A. Finkel. A simple mechanism for type security across compilation units. *IEEE Transactions on Software Engineering*, SE–14(8):1238–1239, August 1988.

[SFL+94] Ioannis Schoinas, Babak Falsafi, Alvin R. Lebeck, Steven K. Reinhardt, James R. Larus, and David A. Wood. Fine-grain access control for distributed shared memory. In *Proceedings of the Sixth International Conference on Architectural Support for Programming Languages and Operating Systems*, pp. 297–306, San Jose, CA, October 1994. In *ACM SIGPLAN Notices*, 29(11), November 1994.

[SG96] Daniel J. Scales and Kourosh Gharachorloo. Shasta: A low overhead, software-only approach for supporting fine-grain shared memory. In *Proceedings of the Seventh International Conference on Architectural Support for Programming Languages and Operating Systems*, pp. 174–185, Cambridge, MA, October 1996. In *ACM SIGPLAN Notices*, 31(9), September 1996.

[SH92] A. S. M. Sajeev and A. John Hurst. Programming persistence in χ. *IEEE Computer*, 25(9):57–66, September 1992.

[Sha89] Ehud Shapiro. The family of concurrent logic programming languages. *ACM Computing Surveys*, 21(3):412–510, September 1989. Correction appears in Volume 21, Number 4.

[Sie96] Jon Siegel. *CORBA Fundamentals and Programming.* John Wiley & Sons, New York, 1996.

[Sip97] Michael Sipser. *Introduction to the Theory of Computation.* PWS Publishing Company, Boston, 1997.

[Sit72] Richard L. Sites. Algol W reference manual. Technical Report STAN-CS-71-230, Computer Science Department, Stanford University, Stanford, CA, February 1972.

[SOHL+95] Marc Snir, Steve Otto, Steven Huss-Lederman, David Walker, and Jack Dongarra. *MPI: The Complete Reference.* Scientific and Engineering Computation series. MIT Press, Cambridge, MA, 1995. Available in hypertext at *www.netlib.org/utk/papers/mpi-book/mpi-book.html*.

[Sri95] Raj Srinivasan. RPC: Remote procedure call protocol specification version 2. Internet Request for Comments #1831, August 1995. Available as *www.cis.ohio-state.edu/htbin/rfc/rfc1831.html*.

[SS71] Dana S. Scott and Christopher Strachey. Toward a mathematical semantics for computer language. In *Proceedings, Symposium on Computers and Automata*, Jerome Fox, editor, pp. 19–46. Polytechnic Institute of Brooklyn Press, New York, 1971.

[SS89] Richard Snodgrass and Karen P. Shannon. *The Interface Description Language: Definition and Use.* Computer Science Press, Rockville, MD, 1989.

[Sta92] Ryan D. Stansifer. *ML Primer.* Prentice Hall, Englewood Cliffs, NJ, 1992.

[Sta95] Ryan D. Stansifer. *The Study of Programming Languages.* Prentice Hall, Englewood Cliffs, NJ, 1995.

[Sta00] William Stallings. *Computer Organization and Architecture: Designing for Performance.* Prentice Hall, Upper Saddle River, NJ, fifth edition, 2000.

[Ste90] Guy L. Steele Jr. *Common Lisp—The Language.* Digital Press, Bedford, MA, second edition, 1990. Available in hypertext at *www-cgi.cs.cmu.edu/afs/cs.cmu.edu/ project/ai-repository/ai/html/cltl/clm/clm.html.*

[Sto77] Joseph E. Stoy. *Denotational Semantics: The Scott-Strachey Approach to Programming Language Semantics.* Volume 1 of MIT Press Series in Computer Science. MIT Press, Cambridge, MA, 1977.

[Str91] Bjarne Stroustrup. *The C++ Programming Language.* Addison-Wesley, Reading, MA, second edition, 1991.

[Str97] Bjarne Stroustrup. *The C++ Programming Language.* Addison-Wesley, Reading, MA, third edition, 1997.

[Sun90] Vaidyalingam S. Sunderam. PVM: A framework for parallel distributed computing. *Concurrency—Practice and Experience,* 2(4):315–339, December 1990.

[Sun97] Sun Microsystems, Mountain View, CA. *JavaBeans,* July 1997. Available at *www.java.sun.com/beans.*

[SW67] H. Schorr and W. M. Waite. An efficient machine-independent procedure for garbage collection in various list structures. *Communications of the ACM,* 10(8):501–506, August 1967.

[SW94] James E. Smith and Shlomo Weiss. PowerPC 601 and Alpha 21064: A tale of two RISCs. *IEEE Computer,* 27(6):46–58, June 1994.

[SZ90] Michael Stumm and Songnian Zhou. Algorithms implementing distributed shared memory. *IEEE Computer,* 23(5):54–64, May 1990.

[SZBH86] Daniel C. Swinehart, Polle T. Zellweger, Richard J. Beach, and Robert B. Hagmann. A structural view of the Cedar programming environment. *ACM Transactions on Programming Languages and Systems,* 8(4):419–490, October 1986.

[Tan78] Andrew S. Tanenbaum. A comparison of Pascal and ALGOL 68. *The Computer Journal,* 21(4):316–323, November 1978.

[Tan96] Andrew S. Tanenbaum. *Computer Networks.* Prentice Hall, Upper Saddle River, NJ, third edition, 1996.

[Tan99] Andrew S. Tanenbaum, with James R. Goodman. *Structured Computer Organization.* Prentice Hall, Upper Saddle River, NJ, fourth edition, 1999.

[Tic86] Walter F. Tichy. Smart recompilation. *ACM Transactions on Programming Languages and Systems*, 8(3):273–291, July 1986.

[Tic91] Evan Tick. *Parallel Logic Programming.* Logic Programming Series. MIT Press, Cambridge, MA, 1991.

[TM81] Warren Teitelman and Larry Masinter. The Interlisp programming environment. *IEEE Computer*, 14(4):25–33, April 1981.

[TR81] Timothy Titelbaum and Thomas Reps. The Cornell Program Synthesizer: A syntax-directed programming environment. *Communications of the ACM*, 24(9):563–573, September 1981.

[Tur86] David A. Turner. An overview of Miranda. *ACM SIGPLAN Notices*, 21(12):158–166, December 1986.

[UKGS94] Ronald C. Unrau, Orran Krieger, Benjamin Gamsa, and Michael Stumm. Experiences with locking in a NUMA multiprocessor operating system kernel. In *Proceedings of the First USENIX Symposium on Operating Systems Design and Implementation*, pp. 139–152, Monterey, CA, November 1994.

[Ull85] Jeffrey D. Ullman. Implementation of logical query languages for databases. *ACM Transactions on Database Systems*, 10(3):289–321, September 1985.

[Uni60] United States Department of Defense. *COBOL, Initial Specifications for a Common Business Oriented Language*, 1960. Revised in 1961 and again in 1962.

[UW97] Jeffrey D. Ullman and Jennifer Widom. *A First Course in Database Systems.* Prentice Hall, Upper Saddle River, NJ, 1997.

[VF82] Thomas R. Virgilio and Raphael A. Finkel. Binding strategies and scope rules are independent. *Computer Languages*, 7(2):61–67, 1982.

[VF94] Jack E. Veenstra and Robert J. Fowler. Mint: A front end for efficient simulation of shared-memory multiprocessors. In *Proceedings of the Second International Workshop on Modeling, Analysis and Simulation of Computer and Telecommunication Systems (MASCOTS '94)*, pp. 201–207, Durham, NC, January 1994. IEEE Computer Society Press, Los Alamitos, CA.

[vMP+75] A. van Wijngaarden, B. J. Mailloux, J. E. L. Peck, C. H. A. Koster, M. Sintzoff, C. H. Lindsey, L. G. L T. Meertens, and R. G. Fisker. Revised report on the algorithmic language ALGOL 68. *Acta Informatica*, 5(1–3):1–236, 1975. Also *ACM SIGPLAN Notices*, 12(5):1–70, May 1977.

[Wad97] Philip Wadler. How to declare an imperative. *ACM Computing Surveys*, 29(3):240–263, September 1997.

[Wad98a] Philip Wadler. An angry half-dozen. *ACM SIGPLAN Notices*, 33(2):25–30, February 1998. NB: table of contents on cover of issue is incorrect.

[Wad98b] Philip Wadler. Why no one uses functional languages. *ACM SIGPLAN Notices*, 33(8):23–27, August 1998.

[Wat77] David Anthony Watt. The parsing problem for affix grammars. *Acta Informatica*, 8(1):1–20, 1977.

[Web89] Fred Webb. Fortran story—The real scoop. Submitted to *alt.folklore .computers*, 1989. Quoted by Mark Brader in the ACM *RISKS* on-line forum, volume 9, issue 54, December 12, 1989.

[Weg90] Peter Wegner. Concepts and paradigms of object-oriented programming. *OOPS Messenger*, 1(1):7–87, August 1990. Expanded version of the keynote address from *OOPSLA '89*.

[Wet78] Horst Wettstein. The problem of nested monitor calls revisited. *ACM Operating Systems Review*, 12(1):19–23, January 1978.

[Wex78] Richard L. Wexelblat, editor. *Proceedings of the ACM SIGPLAN History of Programming Languages Conference*, ACM Monograph Series, 1981, Los Angeles, CA, June 1978. Academic Press, New York. In *ACM SIGPLAN Notices*, 13(8), August 1978.

[WH66] Niklaus Wirth and Charles Antony Richard Hoare. A contribution to the development of ALGOL. *Communications of the ACM*, 9(6):413–431, June 1966.

[Wil9x] Paul R. Wilson. Uniprocessor garbage collection techniques. *ACM Computing Surveys*, to appear. Shorter version presented at the *International Workshop on Memory Management*, St. Malo, France, September 1992. Volume 637 of Lecture Notes in Computer Science, Springer-Verlag, Berlin, Germany, 1992. Available at *ftp://ftp.cs.utexas.edu/pub/garbage/bigsurv.ps*.

[Wir71] Niklaus Wirth. The programming language Pascal. *Acta Informatica*, 1(1):35–63, 1971.

[Wir76] Niklaus Wirth. *Algorithms + Data Structures = Programs*. Prentice Hall Series in Automatic Computation. Prentice Hall, Englewood Cliffs, NJ, 1976.

[Wir77a] Niklaus Wirth. Design and implementation of Modula. *Software—Practice and Experience*, 7(1):67–84, January–February 1977.

[Wir77b] Niklaus Wirth. Modula: A language for modular multiprogramming. *Software—Practice and Experience*, 7(1):3–35, January–February 1977.

[Wir80] Niklaus Wirth. The module: A system structuring facility in high-level programming languages. In *Language Design and Programming Methodology*, Jeffrey M. Tobias, editor. Volume 79 of Lecture Notes in Computer Science, pp. 1–24. Springer-Verlag, Berlin, West Germany, 1980. Proceedings of a symposium held at Sydney, Australia, September 1979.

[Wir85a] Niklaus Wirth. From programming language design to computer construction. *Communications of the ACM*, 28(2):159–164, February 1985. The 1984 Turing Award lecture.

[Wir85b] Niklaus Wirth. *Programming in Modula-2*. Texts and Monographs in Computer Science. Springer-Verlag, New York, third, corrected edition, 1985.

[Wir88a] Niklaus Wirth. From Modula to Oberon. *Software—Practice and Experience*, 18(7):661–670, July 1988.

[Wir88b] Niklaus Wirth. The programming language Oberon. *Software—Practice and Experience*, 18(7):671–690, July 1988.

[Wir88c] Niklaus Wirth. Type extensions. *ACM Transactions on Programming Languages and Systems*, 10(2):204–214, April 1988. Relevant correspondence appears in Volume 13, Number 4.

[WJ93] Paul R. Wilson and Mark S. Johnstone. Real-time non-copying garbage collection. In *OOPSLA '93 Workshop on Memory Management and Gargage Collection*, Washington, DC, September 1993.

[WM95] Reinhard Wilhelm and Dieter Maurer. *Compiler Design*. Addison-Wesley, Wokingham, England, 1995. Translated from the German by Stephen S. Wilson.

[WMWM87] Janet H. Walker, David A. Moon, Daniel L. Weinreb, and Mike McMahon. The Symbolics Genera programming environment. *IEEE Software*, 4(6):36–45, November 1987.

[Wol96] Michael Wolfe. *High Performance Compilers for Parallel Computing*. Addison-Wesley, Redwood City, CA, 1996.

[WRH71] William A. Wulf, Donald B. Russel, and A. Nico Habermann. Bliss: A language for systems programming. *Communications of the ACM*, 14(12):780–790, December 1971.

[WS91] Larry Wall and Randal L. Schwartz. *Programming Perl*. O'Reilly and Associates, Sebastopol, CA, 1991.

[WSH77] J. Welsh, M. J. Sneeringer, and C. A. R. Hoare. Ambiguities and insecurities in Pascal. *Software—Practice and Experience*, 7(6):685–696, November–December 1977.

[YA93] Jae-Heon Yang and James H. Anderson. Fast, scalable synchronization with minimal hardware support (extended abstract). In *Proceedings of the Twelfth Annual ACM Symposium on Principles of Distributed Computing*, pp. 171–182, Ithaca, NY, August 1993.

[You67] Daniel H. Younger. Recognition and parsing of context-free languages in time n^3. *Information and Control*, 10(2):189–208, February 1967.

[ZHL+89] Benjamin G. Zorn, Kimson Ho, James Larus, Luigi Semenzato, and Paul Hilfinger. Multiprocessing extensions in Spur Lisp. *IEEE Software*, 6(4):41–49, July 1989.

[Zho96] Neng-Fa Zhou. Parameter passing and control stack management in Prolog implementation revisited. *ACM Transactions on Programming Languages and Systems*, 18(6):752–779, November 1996.

Index

**Computer Science and Engineering Textbooks
from Morgan Kaufmann Publishers**

Artificial Intelligence

Genetic Programming: An Introduction
  Wolfgang Banzhaf, Peter Nordin, Robert E. Keller, and Frank D. Francone
Essentials of Artificial Intelligence
  Matt Ginsberg
Readings in Agents
  Edited by Michael N. Huhns and Munindar P. Singh
Case-Based Reasoning
  Janet Kolodner
Genetic Programming III: Darwinian Invention and Problem Solving
  John R. Koza, Forrest H. Bennett III, David Andre, and Martin A. Keane
Elements of Machine Learning
  Pat Langley
Readings in Intelligent User Interfaces
  Mark T. Maybury and Wolfgang Wahlster
Probabilistic Reasoning in Intelligent Systems: Networks of Plausible Inference
  Judea Pearl
Artificial Intelligence: An Introduction
  Nils J. Nilsson
Introduction to Knowledge Systems
  Mark Stefik

Computer Architecture

The Student's Guide to VHDL
  Peter J. Ashenden
Parallel Computer Architecture: A Hardware/Software Approach
  David E. Culler and Jaswinder Pal Singh with Anoop Gupta
Computer Architecture: A Quantitative Approach 2ed.
  John L. Hennessy and David A. Patterson
Readings in Computer Architecture
  Edited by Mark D. Hill, Norman P. Jouppi, and Gurindar S. Sohi
Introduction to Parallel Algorithms and Architectures: Arrays, Trees & Hypercubes
  F. Thomson Leighton
Advanced Compiler Design & Implementation
  Steven S. Muchnick
Parallel Programming with MPI
  Peter S. Pacheco
Computer Organization & Design: The Hardware/Software Interface 2ed.
  David A. Patterson and John L. Hennessy

Database
Distributed Algorithms
  Nancy A. Lynch
Readings in Database Systems 3ed.
  Edited by Michael Stonebraker and Joseph M. Hellerstein
Principles of Multimedia Database Systems
  V. S. Subrahmanian
Principles of Database Query Processing for Advanced Applications
  Clement T. Yu and Weiyi Meng
Advanced Database Systems
  Carlo Zaniolo, Stefano Ceri, Christos Faloutsos, Richard T. Snodgrass, V. S. Subrahmanian, and Roberto Zicari

Human-Computer Interaction and Computer Graphics
Readings in Human-Computer Interaction: Toward the Year 2000 2ed.
  Edited by Ronald M. Baecker, Jonathan Grudin, William Buxton, and Saul Greenberg
Readings in Information Visualization: Using Vision to Think
  Edited by Stuart K. Card, Jock Mackinlay, and Ben Shneiderman

Multimedia Information & Systems
Readings in Information Retrieval
  Edited by Karen Sparck Jones and Peter Willett

Networking
Understanding Networked Applications: A First Course
  David G. Messerschmitt
Computer Networks: A Systems Approach 2ed.
  Larry L. Peterson and Bruce S. Davie
Optical Networks: A Practical Perspective
  Rajiv Ramaswami and Kumar N. Sivarajan
High-Performance Communication Networks 2ed.
  Jean Walrand and Pravin Varaiya

Theory
Fundamentals of the Theory of Computation: Principles and Practice
  Raymond Greenlaw and H. James Hoover

Forthcoming
Database: Principles, Programming, Performance 2ed.
  Patrick E. O'Neil
Introduction to Data Compression 2ed.
  Khalid Sayood
Interactive Programming in Java
  Lynn Andrea Stein
Computers as Components: Principles of Embedded Computing System Design
  Wayne Wolf